Introduction to Computer Science with C++

REVISED PRINTING

Introduction to Computer Science with C++

Kenneth A. Lambert
WASHINGTON & LEE UNIVERSITY

Douglas W. Nance
CENTRAL MICHIGAN UNIVERSITY

Thomas L. Naps
LAWRENCE UNIVERSITY

PWS PUBLISHING COMPANY
I(T)P *An International Thomson Publishing Company*
Boston • Albany • Bonn • Cincinnati • Detroit • London • Madrid
Melbourne • Mexico City • New York • Pacific Grove • Paris
San Francisco • Singapore • Tokyo • Toronto • Washington

To Sara, Jason, Caleb, and Catherine

◆ ◆ ◆ ◆ ◆ ◆ ◆ ◆ ◆ ◆ ◆ ◆ ◆ ◆

To Keith

◆ ◆ ◆ ◆ ◆ ◆ ◆ ◆ ◆ ◆ ◆ ◆ ◆ ◆

In memory of the Goulds, beloved Grandparents

◆ ◆ ◆ ◆ ◆ ◆ ◆ ◆ ◆ ◆ ◆ ◆ ◆ ◆

PWS PUBLISHING COMPANY
20 Park Plaza, Boston, MA 02116-4324

Reprinted in 1997 by PWS Publishing Company, a division of International Thomson Publishing Inc. Original copyright © 1996 by West Publishing Company.

Sponsoring Editor: *David Dietz*
Marketing Manager: *Nathan Wilbur*
Production Manager: *Elise S. Kaiser*
Manufacturing Buyer: *Andrew Christensen*
Compositor: *Carlisle Communications*
Interior Designer: *Johnston Design Office*
Cover Image: *Pamela J. Vermeer*
Copyeditor: *Lorretta Palagi*

   This book is printed on recycled, acid-free paper.

Printed and bound in the United States of America by West Publishing Company.
97 98 99 00 — 10 9 8 7 6 5 4 3

Library of Congress Cataloging-in-Publication Data

Lambert, Kenneth (Kenneth A.)
   Introduction to computer science with C++/Kenneth
A. Lambert, Douglas W. Nance, Thomas L. Naps.
     p.   cm.
   Includes bibliographical references and index.
   ISBN (revised printing) 0-534-95204-6
    1. Computer science.   2. C++ (Computer program language)
I. Nance, Douglas W.   II. Title.
QA76.L26   1996   95-43868
005.13'3—dc20   CIP

For more information, contact:
PWS Publishing Company
20 Park Plaza
Boston, MA 02116

International Thomson Publishing Europe
Berkshire House 168-173
High Holborn
London WC1V 7AA
England

Thomas Nelson Australia
102 Dodds Street
South Melbourne, 3205
Victoria, Australia

Nelson Canada
1120 Birchmont Road
Scarborough, Ontario
Canada M1K 5G4

International Thomson Editores
Campos Eliseos 385, Piso 7
Col. Polanco
11560 Mexico D.F., Mexico

International Thomson Publishing GmbH
Königswinterer Strasse 418
53227 Bonn, Germany

International Thomson Publishing Asia
221 Henderson Road
#05-10 Henderson Building
Singapore 0315

International Thomson Publishing Japan
Hirakawacho Kyowa Building, 31
2-2-1 Hirakawacho
Chiyoda-ku, Tokyo 102
Japan

Table of Contents

CHAPTER 17◆   Binary Trees, General Trees, and Graphs   718

Preface

In many introductory science and math courses one textbook is used over two or three semesters. This spiral approach allows, at each stage of the course sequence, and integration of recurring themes as well as a gradual increase in the complexity and abstraction of the concepts presented. Although a student's introductory experience in computer science has matured into a two-semester sequence (typically labeled CS1 and CS2 following the guidelines of the ACM's Curriculum Committee), we still find a dearth of texts designed to span such a sequence. Too often we find that CS1 is taught using a text that does not go much beyond learning to write programs in a particular language. Then, in the CS2 course, students are asked to switch gears and adapt to a much more rigorous style of presentation. A related problem has arisen concerning students' knowledge of a programming language when they begin the CS2 course. This was not a major problem when CS1 and CS2 used Pascal, because most instructors could assume that most students had covered most of the language in CS1. However, the enormous size of C++ has made it possible to cover widely varying subsets of the language in the CS1 course, so students may come to CS2 with widely different competencies in the language.

Our goal in developing *Introduction to Computer Science with* C++ was to provide a text that viewed CS1 and CS2 as a unified whole. In particular, this text was designed with the following objectives in mind:

1. To provide students with a fundamental understanding of how to solve problems in C++. Such knowledge of C++ is viewed as one of the foundational blocks that allows students to explore the ideas and techniques of computer science.

2. To present C++ in a context that emphasizes a structured, top-down approach to problem solving. Students should realize that computer science is primarily problem solving, not programming.

3. To demonstrate the application of software engineering principles in design, coding, and testing of large programs.

4. To introduce students to the essential data structures such as linked lists, stacks, queues, trees, and (to a lesser extent) graphs. This introduction emphasizes the specification of each structure as an abstract data type before discussing implementations and applications of that structure.

5. To make students aware of the importance of object-oriented methods in developing software, particularly in the design and implementation of abstract data types.

6. To provide a systematic approach to the study of algorithms, an approach that focuses first on understanding the action of the algorithm and then on analyzing the algorithm from a space/time perspective. In particular, searching, sorting, and recursive algorithms are covered in detail.

7. To give students an overview of what lies ahead in computer science.

Overview and Organization

Chapters 1-10 constitute the core of a CS1 course. The material in Chapters 1 through 6 covers the basics of problem solving and algorithm development, using the standard control structures of expression evaluation, sequencing, selection, iteration, and procedural abstraction. This material is presented at a deliberate pace. If students in the class have already had some programming experience, these chapters may be covered rapidly. However, students must be able to solve problems with top-down design and stepwise refinement. If this is overlooked, they will have difficulty designing solutions to more complex problems later.

Subprograms are presented fairly early in the text. User-defined functions with input and output parameters are presented in Chapter 4 before either selection statements (Chapter 5) or iteration statements (Chapter 6). This facilitates good problem solving habits in that a completely modular approach can be emphasized early in the course.

We have made a large effort to acknowledge the increasing importance of object-oriented methods in the computer science community. In the first 6 chapters, this effort takes the form of allusions to and brief discussions of object-oriented design when appropriate. However, we have deliberately avoided presenting the object-oriented features of C++ in the first 6 chapters. We believe that students can best learn the fundamentals of algorithm development if they are provided with a simple model of computation and a small subset of C++ syntax. The object-oriented model of computation and the object-oriented features of C++ are neither simple nor small; they are best introduced only when needed, primarily to develop data structures in the second half of a first course in computer science and to continue this development in the second course in computer science.

The material in Chapters 7 through 10 covers the use of basic data structures such as strings, records, files, and arrays. Careful attention is paid to the specification and implementation of all data structures as abstract data types. The focus in this part of the text shifts from the procedural approach used in developing algorithms to an object-oriented approach used in developing abstract data types.

Chapter 7 provides a transition from a procedural approach to an object-oriented approach. We specify an abstract data type for strings, and then present the two different approaches as possible implementations. The first uses a C++ type definition and standard string library functions. The second develops a C++ class definition. We discuss the trade-offs in the use of the two approaches, and then use the string class to develop other data structures in the remainder of the text.

Chapter 8 explores object-oriented design in more depth, using examples from data processing (a bank account management system) and mathematics (rational numbers). Appropriate examples of some useful features of object-oriented design, such as operator overloading, inheritance, and software reuse, are discussed and developed in these examples. We introduce a standard method of discussing user requirements, specifying attributes and behavior, and declaring and implementing a class and then we use this method in the remaining chapters.

Chapter 9 introduces file stream processing. The focus of this chapter is the use of file stream operations, primarily in conjunction with numeric, character, and string data. Because of its simple approach, this chapter could be used earlier or later in the first course if desired.

Chapter 10 discusses array operations in detail. We develop three important classes using arrays—a safe array class with range checking, an ordered collection class, and a sorted collection class.

Chapters 11 through 19 contain material for what might typically be called a CS2 course. Chapters 11 through 13 collectively present more detailed treatment of the software engineering principles that were introduced in earlier chapters. Chapter 11 introduces big-O analysis as the essential tool used by the computer scientist in evaluating alternative strategies from a time/space perspective. Simple sorting and searching algorithms are used as examples for the application of big-O analysis. By reviewing some of the algorithms already presented in Chapter 10, we allow the student to concentrate on the intricacies of big-O analysis without having to worry about unraveling new and complex algorithms.

Chapter 12 continues and amplifies the formalism used to present abstract data types introduced in Chapters 7 and 8. This formalism consists of specifying the ADT's attributes and operations as a set of language-independent preconditions and postconditions before moving to a C++ class declaration as an interface for the ADT. Rules for using and implementing ADTs are developed. One-key tables and two-key tables are presented as examples of ADTs. Because these ADTs lend themselves naturally to the use of keys and elements of different data types, the notions of generic ADTs and parameterized types can be introduced in this chapter and can be implemented with C++ class templates. Because students have studied big-O analysis in the preceding chapter, they are well equipped to compare and contrast the efficiencies of various implementations of these ADTs. These two ADTs and the use of class templates recur in the remainder of the text as we explore more advanced techniques for implementing other ADTs.

Chapter 13 pulls together and expands on the software engineering issues that have been introduced in earlier chapters. The first three sections present a detailed treatment of the analysis, design, implementation, testing, maintenance, and obsolescence stages of the software system life cycle. The last two sections of the chapter discuss two topics of rising prominence, formal verification and object-oriented software engineering.

Chapters 14 through 17 cover the use of essential data structures and recursion in advanced problem solving techniques. Each data structure is first defined as an abstract data type and then declared as a C++ class. Various implementations are discussed and compared using the big-O terminology of Chapter 11. This provides a convincing demonstration of the utility of big-O analysis. Chapter 14, devoted to dynamic memory management, pointers, and linked lists, discusses how linked lists might be used as an alternative implementation of the ADTs that were introduced in Chapters 10 and 12. Chapter 15 covers stacks and queues, discussing parsing and simulation as applications of these ADTs. Chapter 16 explores recursion in depth. A graduated series of examples is presented, culminating with the use of trial-and-error backtracking as a problem-solving technique. Chapter 17 provides examples of the utility of recursion by using it as the primary technique for processing data in binary trees, general trees, and graphs. The importance of binary search trees as an alternative way of representing keyed tables is also discussed, with comparisons drawn to the array and linked list implementations previously covered in Chapters 12 and 14. The material on general trees, graphs, and networks in the final two sections of Chapter 17 can be omitted without affecting a student's understanding of the chapters that follow.

The background in software engineering and data structures found in Chapters 11 through 17 prepares the student for the more complex sorting and searching algorithms of Chapters 18 and 19. In Chapter 18, sorting methods that break the $O(n^2)$ barrier are investigated. These methods include the shell sort, quick sort, heap sort, and merge sort. Chapter 19 scrutinizes search techniques such as hashing, indexing, indexed sequential search, B-trees, and tries.

Throughout the text, we have attempted to explain and develop concepts carefully. These are illustrated by frequent examples and diagrams. New concepts are then used in complete programs to show how they aid in solving problems. We place an early and consistent emphasis on good writing habits and neat, readable documentation. We frequently offer communication and style tips where appropriate.

Features

This text has a number of noteworthy pedagogical features.

- *Chapter outlines:* Lists of the important topics covered are given at the beginning of each chapter.
- *Objectives:* Each section starts with a concise list of topics and learning objectives in each section.
- *Communication and style tips:* These are suggestions for programming style that are intended to enhance readability. The ACM has recently encouraged the development of communication skills to enhance the portability of programs.
- *Exercises:* Short-answer questions appear at the end of each section that are intended to build analytical skills.
- *Programming problems and projects:* Starting with Chapter 2, lengthy lists of suggestions for complete programs and projects are given at the end of each chapter. These cover different problem areas in computer science, such as data processing and mathematics. Some problems and projects run from chapter to chapter, providing students with a sense of problem solving as a cumulative enterprise that often requires programming in the large. Several assignments focus explicitly on improving students' communication skills in refining designs and writing documentation.
- *Module specifications:* Specifications are given for many program modules.
- *Structure charts:* We provide charts that reflect modular development and include the use of data flow arrows to emphasize transmission of data to and/or from each module. These charts set the stage for understanding the use of value and reference parameters when functions are introduced.
- *Notes of interest:* These are tidbits of information intended to create awareness of and interest in various aspects of computer science, including its historical context. Special attention is paid to issues of computer ethics and security.
- *Suggestions for test programs:* Ideas included in the exercises are intended to encourage students to use the computer to determine answers to questions and to see how to implement concepts in short programs.
- *Focus on program design:* With the exception of Chapters 1 and 2, a complete program is listed at the end of the chapter that illustrates utilization of the concepts developed within the chapter. This section includes the complete development of a project, from user requirements to specifications to pseudocode design to implementation and testing.
- *Running, testing, and debugging hints:* These hints will be useful to students as they work on the programming problems at the end of each chapter.

- *Reading references:* When appropriate, pointers are given to excellent sources for further reading on topics introduced in the text.
- New terms are italicized when introduced.

In the back of the book there is a complete glossary, as well as appendixes on reserved words, useful library functions, syntax diagrams, character sets, and a random number generator. The final section of the book provides answers to selected exercises.

This book covers only that portion of C++ necessary for the first two courses in computer science. Students wanting to learn more about the language are referred to the excellent sources given in Appendix 1.

◆ Ancillaries

It is our belief that a broad-based teaching support package is essential for an introductory course using C++. Thus, the following ancillary materials are available from West Publishing Company;

1. Laboratory manual: In keeping with our intent to provide a modern approach and to meet the growing need for laboratory experience as put forth by the new ACM curriculum guidelines, there is a laboratory manual closely tied to the text's pedagogy. The manual provides two kinds of exercises. Each lab experience begins with a few exercises relating to a small set of new concepts, such as the use of reference parameters with functions. The lab experience then uses these new concepts to extend several cumulative, semester-long programming projects. Students thus use the lab experience to build their competence incrementally, and to get a sense of how various concepts play a role in programming in the large. The example programs in the lab experiences are written in platform-independent C++.
2. Program disk: To give students direct access to programs from the text, a disk containing most of these programs is bundled with the book. The disk is in DOS format, but the programs are written in platform-independent C++, which can be run immediately on most implementations.
3. Instructor's manual: This manual contains the following for each chapter:
   a. Outline
   b. Teaching test questions
   c. Chapter test questions
   d. Answers to test questions.
4. Transparency masters: More than 100 transparency masters are available to adopters of the text. The set of masters includes figures, tables, and selected other material from the text.
5. Computerized test bank: Adopters of this edition will receive a computerized test-generation system. This provides a test bank system that allows adopters to edit, add, or delete test questions.

Each program segment in the text and in the lab manual has been compiled and run. Hence, original versions were all working. Unfortunately, the publication process does allow errors in code to occur after a program has been run. Every effort has been made to produce an error-free text, although this cannot be guaranteed with certainty. We assume full responsibility for all errors and omissions. If you detect any, please be tolerant and notify us or West Publishing Company so they can be corrected in subsequent printings and editions.

◆ Acknowledgments

We would like to take this opportunity to thank those who in some way contributed to the completion of this text. Several reviewers contributed significant constructive comments during various phases of manuscript development. They include:

Pam Vermeer and Tom Whaley of Washington and Lee University offered many helpful suggestions on making the minefield of C++ safer for first-year students.

Six other people deserve special mention because, without their expertise, this book would not exist:

Lorretta Palagi, copyeditor. Lorretta has a wonderful sense of where to apply Occam's razor to a sentence or paragraph, and made many useful suggestions for improving not only style, but content as well.

Peter Krall, production editor. Peter has done a great job of coordinating work on several texts simultaneously. He keeps things running smoothly, and it is a pleasure working with him.

Ellen Stanton, promotion manager. Ellen worked hard to highlight the features of the text that will make it known to the computer science community, and has done a fine job.

Betsy Friedman, developmental editor. Betsy lined up great reviewers and provided them with all of the relevant questions. She then digested the reviews into analyses that focused our attention immediately on the improvements that needed to be made at each phase of the development process.

Halee Dinsey, developmental editor. Halee assisted in putting together several of the ancillary materials.

Jerry Westby, executive editor. Jerry initiated our collaboration on this project. His insight into what makes a book useful is uncanny. We are grateful for his high standards, and for pushing us to make needed changes one more time during the revision process. It is a privilege to work with an editor who is right at the top of his field.

Kenneth A. Lambert
December, 1995

Computer Science, Computer Architecture, and Computer Languages

A jet airplane crash-lands near a large American city. Though the plane catches fire on impact, all of the passengers and crew members miraculously survive. Investigators find no clues from the crew or the flight recorders that point to the cause of the crash. However, using reports of observers on the ground about the behavior of the plane, they construct a computer simulation of the plane's behavior in the air. From this simulation, they hypothesize that a flaw in the plane's rudder might have caused it to go into a tailspin. They examine the parts of the rudder found at the crash site, and confirm their hypothesis. The results of their investigation will be used to correct the flaw in the rudders of several hundred airplanes.

The investigators who constructed this simulation solved a problem by designing a program and running it on a computer. They may not have been trained as computer scientists, but they used techniques that have come to be associated with this exciting new field.

This chapter provides a quick introduction to computer science, computer architecture, and computer languages. Section 1.1 provides a preview of the study of computer science. Section 1.2 examines the structure and parts of a computer and introduces the idea of computer software. Section 1.3 analyzes how computer languages are used to make a computer run.

As you read this chapter, do not be overly concerned about the introduction and early use of technical terminology. All terms will be subsequently developed. A good approach to an introductory chapter like this is to reread it periodically. This will help you maintain a good perspective on how new concepts and techniques fit in the broader picture of using computers. Finally, remember that learning a language that will make a computer work can be exciting; being able to control such a machine can lead to quite a sense of accomplishment.

1.1 Computer Science: A Preview

Computer science is a very young discipline. Electronic computers were initially developed in the 1940s. Those who worked with computers in the 1940s and 1950s often did so by teaching themselves about computers; most schools did not offer any instruction in computer science at that time. However, as these early pioneers in computers learned more about the machines they were using, a collection of principles began to evolve into the discipline we now call computer science. Because it emerged from the efforts of people using computers in a variety of disciplines, the influence of these disciplines can often be seen in computer science. With that in mind, in the next sections we will briefly describe what computer science is.

Computer Science as Computer Literacy

In the 1990s, computer-literate people know how to use a variety of computer software to make their professional and domestic lives more productive and easier. This software includes, for instance, word processors for writing and data management systems for storing every conceivable form of information (from address lists to recipes).

The computer-literate person who wants to acquire an understanding of computer science is in much the same position as the driver of a car who wants to learn how to change its spark plugs. For the driver, this curiosity can lead to a study of how automobile engines function generally. For the literate user of computer software, this curiosity can lead from the software's instruction manual to designing and writing a program with that software, and then to a deep understanding of a computer as a general-purpose problem-solving tool. The computer-literate person will come to understand that the collection of problems that computer science encompasses and the techniques used to solve those problems are the real substance of this rapidly expanding discipline.

Computer Science as Mathematics and Logic

The problem-solving emphasis of computer science borrows heavily from the areas of mathematics and logic. Faced with a problem, computer scientists must first formulate a solution. This method of solution, or *algorithm* as it is often called in computer science, must be thoroughly understood before the computer scientists make any attempt to implement the solution on the computer. Thus, at the early stages of problem solution, computer scientists work solely with their minds and do not rely on the machine (except, perhaps, as a word processor for making notes).

Once the solution is understood, computer scientists must then state the solution to this problem in a formal language called a *programming language.* This parallels the fashion in which mathematicians or logicians must develop a proof or argument in the formal language of mathematics. This formal solution as stated in a programming language must then be evaluated in terms of its correctness, style, and efficiency. Part of this evaluation process involves entering the formally stated algorithm as a programmed series of steps for the computer to follow.

Another part of the evaluation process is distinctly separate from a consideration of whether or not the computer produces the "right answer" when the program is executed. Indeed, one of the main areas of emphasis throughout this book is in developing well-designed solutions to problems and in recognizing the difference between such solutions and ones that work, but are not elegant. True computer scientists seek not just solutions to problems, but the best possible solutions.

Computer Science as Science

Perhaps nothing is as intrinsic to the scientific method as the formulation of hypotheses to explain phenomena and the careful testing of these hypotheses to prove them right or wrong. This same process plays an integral role in the way computer scientists work.

When confronted with a problem, such as a long list of names that needs to be arranged in alphabetical order, computer scientists formulate a hypothesis in the form of an algorithm that they believe will effectively solve the problem. Using mathematical techniques, they can make predictions about how such a proposed algorithm will solve the problem. But because the problems facing computer scientists arise from the world of real applications, predictive techniques relying solely on mathematical theory are not sufficient to prove an algorithm correct. Ultimately, computer scientists must implement their solutions on computers and test them in the complex situations that originally gave rise to the problems. Only after such thorough testing can the hypothetical solutions be declared right or wrong.

Moreover, just as many scientific principles are not 100% right or wrong, the hypothetical solutions posed by computer scientists are often subject to limitations. An understanding of those limitations—of when the method is appropriate and when it is not—is a crucial part of the knowledge that computer scientists must have. This is analogous to the way in which any scientist must be aware of the particular limitations of a scientific theory in explaining a given set of phenomena.

Do not forget the experimental nature of computer science as you study this book. You must participate in computer science to truly learn it. Although a good book can help, *you* must solve the problems, implement those solutions on the computer, and then test the results. View each of the problems you are assigned as an experiment for which you are to propose a solution, and then verify the correctness of your solution by testing it on the computer. If the solution does not work exactly as you hypothesized, do not become discouraged. Instead, ask yourself why it did not work; by doing so you will acquire a deeper understanding of the problem and your solution. In this sense, the computer represents the experimental tool of the computer scientist. Do not be afraid to use it for exploration.

Computer Science as Engineering

Whatever the area of specialization, an engineer must neatly combine a firm grasp of scientific principles with implementation techniques. Without knowledge of the principles, the engineer's ability to design creative models for a problem's solution is severely limited. Such model-building is crucial to the engineering design process. The ultimate design of a bridge, for instance, is the result of an engineer considering many possible models of the bridge and then selecting the best one. The transformation of abstract ideas into models of a problem's solution is thus central to the engineering design process. The ability to generate a variety of models that can be explored is the hallmark of creative engineering.

Similarly, the computer scientist is a model-builder. Faced with a problem, the computer scientist must construct models for its solution. Such models take the form of an information structure to hold the data pertinent to the problem and the algorithmic method to manipulate that information structure to actually solve the problem. Just as an engineer must have an in-depth understanding of scientific principles to build a model, so must a computer scientist. With these principles, the computer scientist can conceive of models that are elegant, efficient, and appropriate to the problem at hand.

An understanding of principles alone is not sufficient for either the engineer or the computer scientist. Experience with the actual implementation of hypothetical

A NOTE OF INTEREST

Ethics and Computer Science

Ethical issues in computer science are rapidly gaining public attention. As evidence, consider the following article from the *Washington Post.*

Should law-enforcement agencies be allowed to use computers to help them determine whether a person ought to be jailed or allowed out on bond? Should the military let computers decide when and on whom nuclear weapons should be used?

While theft and computer viruses have not gone away as industry problems, a group of 30 computer engineers and ethicists who gathered in Washington recently agreed that questions about the proper use of computers is taking center stage. At issue is to what degree computers should be allowed to make significant decisions that human beings normally make.

Already, judges are consulting computers, which have been programmed to predict how certain personality types will behave. Judges are basing their decisions more on what the computer tells them than on their own analysis of the arrested person's history. Computers are helping doctors decide treatments for patients. They played a major role in the July 1988 shooting of the Iranian jetliner by the USS *Vincennes,* and they are the backbone of this country's Strategic Defense Initiative ("Star Wars").

Representatives from universities, IBM Corp., the Brookings Institution, and several Washington theological seminaries [recently discussed] what they could do to build a conscience in the computer field.

The computer industry has been marked by "creativity and drive for improvement and advancement," not by ethicalconcerns, said Robert Melford, chairman of the computing-ethics subcommittee of the Institute of Electrical and Electronics Engineers.

Computer professionals, Melford said, often spend much of their time in solitude, separated from the people affected by their programs who could provide valuable feedback.

Unlike hospitals, computer companies and most organized computer users have no staff ethicists or ethics committees to ponder the consequences of what they do. Few businesses have written policies about the proper way to govern computers. But there is evidence that technical schools, at least, are beginning to work an ethical component into their curricula. [For example, in recent years,] all computer engineering majors at Polytechnic University in Brooklyn [have been required to take a course in ethics.] The Massachusetts Institute of Technology is considering mandating five years of study instead of the current four to include work in ethics.

Affirmation that such questions should be addressed by computer scientists is contained in the 1991 curriculum guidelines of the Association for Computing Machinery, Inc. These guidelines state that "Undergraduates should also develop an understanding of the historical, social, and ethical context of the discipline and the profession."

You will see further Notes of Interest on this area of critical concern later in this book.

models is also necessary. Without such experience, you can have only very limited intuition about what is feasible and how a large-scale project should be organized to reach a successful conclusion. Ultimately, computers are used to solve problems in the real world. In the real world, you will need to design programs that come in on time, that are within (if not under) the budget, and that solve all aspects of the original problem. The experience you acquire in designing problem solutions and then implementing them is vital to your being a complete computer scientist. Hence, remember that you cannot actually study computer science without actively doing it. To merely read about computer science techniques will leave you with an unrealistic perspective of what is possible.

Computer Science as Communication

As the discipline of computer science continues to evolve, communication is assuming a more significant role in the undergraduate curriculum. The Association for Computing Machinery, Inc., curriculum guidelines for 1991 state, ". . . undergraduate programs should prepare students to . . . define a problem clearly;

. . . document that solution; . . . and to communicate that solution to colleagues, professionals in other fields, and the general public" (p. 7).

It is no longer sufficient to be content with a program that runs correctly. Extra attention should be devoted to the communication aspects associated with such a program. For instance, you might be asked to submit a written proposal prior to designing a solution, or to document a program carefully and completely as it is being designed, or to write a follow-up report after a program has been completed. These are some ways in which communication can be emphasized as an integral part of computer science. Several opportunities will be provided in the exercises and problem lists of this text for you to focus on the communication aspects associated with computer science.

Computer Science as an Interdisciplinary Field

The problems solved by computer scientists come from a variety of disciplines—mathematics, physics, chemistry, biology, geology, economics, business, engineering, linguistics, and psychology, to name but a few. As a computer scientist working on a problem in one of these areas, you must be a quasi-expert in that discipline as well as in computer science. For instance, you cannot write a program to manage the checking account system of a bank unless you thoroughly understand how banks work and how that bank runs its checking accounts. As a minimum, you must be literate enough in other disciplines to converse with the people for whom you are writing programs and to learn precisely what it is they want the computer to do for them. Because such people may be naive about the computer and its capabilities, you will have to possess considerable communication skills as well as a knowledge of that other discipline.

Are you beginning to think that a computer scientist must be knowledgeable about much more than just the computer? If so, you are correct. Too often, computer scientists are viewed as technicians, tucked away in their own little worlds and not thinking or caring about anything other than computers. Nothing could be further from the truth. The successful computer scientist must be able to communicate, to learn new ideas quickly, and to adapt to ever-changing conditions. Computer science is emerging from its early dark ages into a mature field, one that we hope you will find rewarding and exciting. In studying computer science, you will develop many talents; this text can get you started on the road to that development process.

1.2 Computer Architecture

OBJECTIVES

- to understand the historical development of computers
- to know what constitutes computer hardware
- to know what constitutes computer software

This section is intended to provide you with a brief overview of what computers are and how they are used. Although there are various sizes, makes, and models of computers, you will see that they all operate in basically the same straightforward manner. Whether you work on a personal computer that costs a few hundred dollars or on a mainframe that costs in the millions, the principles of making the machine work are essentially the same.

Modern Computers

The search for aids to perform calculations is almost as old as number systems. Early devices included the abacus, Napier's bones, the slide rule, and mechanical adding machines. More recently, calculators have changed the nature of personal computing as a result of their availability, low cost, and high speed. The development of computers over time is highlighted in Figure 1.1. For more

◆ FIGURE 1.1

Development of computers

Era	Early Computing Devices		Mechanical Computers	Electro-mechanical Computers
Year	1000 B.C.	A.D. 1614 1650	1900	1945
Development	Abacus	Napier's bones	Adding machine Slide rule Difference engine Analytic engine	Cogged wheels Instruction register Operation code Address Plug board Harvard Mark I Tabulating machine

complete information, see *People and Computers, Partners in Problem Solving* by John F. Vinsonhaler, Christian C. Wagner, and Castelle G. Gentry, West Publishing Company, 1989.

The last few decades have seen the most significant change in computing machines in the world's history as a result of improvements that have led to modern computers. As recently as the 1960s, a computer required several rooms because of its size. However, the advent of silicon chips has reduced the size and increased the availability of computers so that parents are able to purchase personal computers as presents for their children. These smaller computers are also more powerful than the early behemoths.

What is a computer? According to *Webster's New World Dictionary of the American Language* (2nd College Edition), a computer is "an electronic machine which, by means of stored instructions and information, performs rapid, often complex calculations or compiles, correlates, and selects data." Basically, a computer can be thought of as a machine that manipulates information in the form of numbers and characters. This information is referred to as *data*. What makes computers remarkable is the extreme speed and precision with which they can store, retrieve, and manipulate data.

Several types of computers currently are available. An oversimplification is to categorize computers as mainframes, minicomputers, or microcomputers. In this grouping, *mainframe* computers are the large machines used by major companies, government agencies, and universities. They have the capability of being used by as many as 100 or more people at the same time and can cost millions of dollars. *Minicomputers,* in a sense, are smaller versions of large computers. They can be used by several people at once but have less storage capacity and cost far less. *Microcomputers* are frequently referred to as personal computers. They have limited storage capacity (in a relative sense), are generally used by one person at a time, and can be purchased for as little as a few hundred dollars.

◆ FIGURE 1.1
Continued

Noncommercial Electronic Computers	Batch Processing	Time-Sharing Systems	Personal Computers
1945 1950	1965	1975	Present
First-generation computers Vacuum tubes Machine language programming ENIAC	Second-generation computers Transistors Magnetic core memory Assemblers Compilers UNIVAC I IBM 704	Third-generation computers Integrated circuit technology Operating system software Teleprocessing	Fourth-generation computers Fifth-generation computers (supercomputers) Microprocessors Workstations

As you begin your work with computers, you will hear people talking about *hardware* and *software*. Hardware refers to the actual machine and its support devices. Software refers to programs that make the machine do something. Many software packages exist for today's computers. They include word processing, database programs, spreadsheets, games, operating systems, and compilers. You can (and will!) learn to create your own software. In fact, that is what this book is all about.

A *program* can be thought of as a set of instructions that tells the machine what to do. When you have written a program, the computer will behave exactly as you have instructed it. It will do no more or no less than what is contained in your specific instructions. For example, the following listing is a C++ program that allows three scores to be entered from a keyboard, computes their average, and then prints the result:

```cpp
// Program file: average.cpp
// This program reads three scores and displays their average.

#include <iostream.h>
#include <iomanip.h>

int main ()

{
    int score1, score2, score3;
    float average;
    cout << "Enter the first score and press <Enter>: " ;
    cin >> score1;
    cout << "Enter the second score and press <Enter>: " ;
```

```
        cin >> score2;
        cout << "Enter the third score and press <Enter>: " ;
        cin >> score3;
        average = float(score1 + score2 + score3) / 3;
        cout << fixed << showpoint << setprecision(2);
        cout << "The average score is " << average << endl;
        return 0;
}
```

Do not be concerned about specific parts of this program. It is intended only to illustrate the idea of a set of instructions. Very soon, you will be able to write significantly more sophisticated programs.

Learning to write programs requires two skills.

1. You need to be able to use specific terminology and punctuation that can be understood by the machine; that is, you need to learn a programming language.
2. You need to be able to develop a plan for solving a particular problem. This plan—or algorithm—is a sequence of steps that, when followed, will lead to a solution of the problem.

Initially, you may think that learning a language is the more difficult task because your problems will have relatively easy solutions. Nothing could be further from the truth! **The single most important thing you can do as a student of computer science is to develop the skill to solve problems.** Once you have this skill, you can learn to write programs in several different languages.

Computer Hardware

Let's take another look at the question: What is a computer? Our previous answer indicated it is a machine. Although there are several forms, names, and brands of computers, each consists of a *main unit* that is subsequently connected to peripheral devices. The main unit of a computer consists of a *central processing unit (CPU)* and *main (primary) memory.* The CPU is the "brain" of the computer. It contains an *arithmetic/logic unit (ALU),* which is capable of performing arithmetic operations and evaluating expressions to see if they are true or false, and the *control unit,* which controls the action of the remaining components so your program can be followed step by step, or *executed.*

Main memory can be thought of as mailboxes in a post office. It is a sequence of locations where information representing instructions, numbers, characters, and so on can be stored. Main memory is usable while the computer is turned on. It is where the program being executed is stored along with data it is manipulating.

As you develop a greater appreciation of how the computer works, you might wonder: How are data stored in memory? Each memory location has an address and is capable of holding a sequence of *binary digits* (0 or 1), which are commonly referred to as *bits.* Instructions, symbols, letters, numbers, and so on are translated into an appropriate pattern of binary digits and then stored in various memory locations. These are retrieved, used, and changed according to instructions in your program. In fact, the program itself is similarly translated and stored in part of main memory. Main memory can be envisioned as in Figure 1.2, and the main unit can be envisioned as in Figure 1.3.

◆ FIGURE 1.2
Main memory

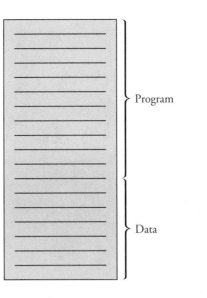

Program

Data

◆ FIGURE 1.3
Main unit

Peripherals can be divided into three categories: *input devices, output devices,* and *secondary (auxiliary) memory devices.* Input devices are necessary to give information to a computer. Programs are entered through an input device and then program statements are translated and stored as previously indicated. One input device (a typical keyboard) is shown in Figure 1.4.

Output devices are necessary to show the results of a program. These are normally in the form of a screen, line printer, impact printer, or laser printer (Figure 1.5). Input and output devices are frequently referred to as *I/O devices.*

Secondary (auxiliary) memory devices are used if additional memory is needed. On small computers, these secondary memory devices could be floppy disks or hard disks (Figure 1.6), CD-ROM disks, or magnetic tapes. Programs and data waiting to be executed are kept "waiting in the wings" in secondary memory.

Communication between components of a computer is frequently organized around a group of wires called a *bus*. The relationship between a bus and various computer components can be envisioned as in Figure 1.7. A photograph of a bus

◆ **FIGURE 1.4**
Keyboard

◆ **FIGURE 1.5**
(a) Screen, (b) line printer (mainframe), (c) impact printer (microcomputer), and (d) laser printer

(a)

(b)

(c)

(d)

◆ FIGURE 1.6
(a) Disk drive and (b) microcomputer with hard disk

(a)   (b)

◆ FIGURE 1.7
Illustration of a bus

is shown in Figure 1.8. What appear to be lines between the slots are actually wires imprinted on the underlying board. Boards with wires connected to peripheral devices can be inserted into the slots.

Computer Software

As previously stated, software refers to programs that make the machine do something. Software consists of two kinds of programs: *system software* and *applications software.*

System software includes what is often called the *operating system.* (For instance, the ubiquitous DOS stands for Disk Operating System.) The operating system for a computer is a large program and is usually supplied with a computer. This program allows the user to communicate with the hardware. More specifically, an operating system might control computer access (via passwords), allocate peripheral resources (perhaps with a printer queue), schedule shared resources (for CPU use), or control execution of other programs.

◆ **FIGURE 1.8**
Bus

Applications software consists of programs designed for a specific use. Examples of applications software include programs for word processing, text editing, simulating spreadsheets, playing games, designing machinery, and figuring payrolls. Most computer users work with applications software and have little need to learn a computer language; the programs they require have already been written to accomplish their tasks.

1.3 Computer Languages

What is a computer language? All data transmission, manipulation, storage, and retrieval is actually done by the machine using electrical pulses representing sequences of binary digits. If eight-digit binary codes are used, there are 256 numbered instructions from 00000000 to 11111111. Instructions for adding two numbers would consist of a sequence of these eight-digit codes.

Instructions written in this form are referred to as *machine language*. It is possible to write an entire program in machine language. However, this is very time consuming and difficult to read and understand.

Therefore, the next level of computer language allows words and symbols to be used in an unsophisticated manner to accomplish simple tasks. For example, the machine code for adding two integers might be

0100001100111010001111010100000100101011101000010

This is replaced by

```
LOAD A
ADD B
STORE C
```

This causes the number in **A** to be added to the number in **B** and the result to be stored for later use in **C**. This computer language is an *assembly language,* which is generally referred to as a *low-level language.* What actually happens is that words and symbols are translated into appropriate binary digits and the machine uses the translated form.

Although assembly language is an improvement on machine language for readability and program development, it is still a bit cumbersome. Consequently,

A NOTE OF INTEREST

Why Learn C++?

C++ is a superset of C, which is a programming language developed at AT&T Bell Laboratories by Dennis Ritchie in 1972. Ritchie originally intended C to be used to write the UNIX operating system and to write tools to be used with that system. Over the years, however, C has achieved widespread popularity for writing various systems' programs in industry, and is now the language of choice in most graduate schools of computer science. According to Richard P. Gabriel ("The end of history and the last programming language," *Journal of Object-Oriented Programming,* July–August 1993), C and C++ are among the few programming languages that are not either dead or moribund. There are several reasons for this. C is available on a wide range of computers and requires minimal computer resources to design, implement, and run programs. C represents a simple machine model, one that closely corresponds to the structure of actual computers. This property supports the development of very efficient programs. C is also similar to several different popular programming languages, like Pascal, FORTRAN, and assembly language. Finally, C requires almost no mathematical sophistication to learn.

Critics claim that C is a dangerous language in three respects. First, C encourages professional programmers to write large systems that lack structure and are difficult to read and maintain. Second, C encourages beginning programmers to learn bad habits, such as writing small programs that lack structure and are difficult to read and

maintain. Third, C lacks many of the fail-safe features of modern programming languages, such as thorough compile-time type checking.

Responding to this challenge, Bjarne Stroustrup, also of AT&T Bell Laboratories, developed C++ in the 1980s. C++ incorporates all of the desirable and undesirable features of C enumerated above. However, some additional features, if used properly, make C++ a safer language and support the design and implementation of well-structured, easily maintained programs for both beginners and professionals. For example, C++ has strong support for data types and type checking, and also features that support the discipline of *object-oriented programming.* Object-oriented programming is a method of developing and maintaining large software systems that we will introduce and discuss in later chapters in this text.

Critics claim that C++ introduces its own costs: The language is enormous, the machine model that it represents is more complex than that of C, and programmers must have more mathematical sophistication to make use of its improved features. However, if Gabriel is right, students will do well to learn this language, because it will be used in industry for many years to come.

Our approach in this text will be to focus on those features of C++ that support the design and implementation of well-structured programs that are easy to read and maintain. C++ is a powerful tool that should be wielded carefully.

many *high-level languages* have been developed; these include Pascal, PL/I, FORTRAN, BASIC, COBOL, C, Ada, Modula-2, Logo, and others. These languages simplify even further the terminology and symbolism necessary for directing the machine to perform various manipulations of data. For example, in these languages, the task of adding two integers would be written as

```
C := A + B;          (Pascal, Modula-2, Ada)
C = A + B;           (PL/I, C++)
C = A + B            FORTRAN, BASIC
ADD A, B GIVING C    (COBOL)
MAKE "C :A + :B      (Logo)
```

A high-level language makes it easier to read, write, and understand a program. This book develops the concepts, symbolism, and terminology necessary for using C++ as a programming language for solving problems. After you have become proficient in using C++, you should find it relatively easy to learn the nuances of other high-level languages.

For a moment, let's consider how an instruction such as

```
C = A + B;
```

gets translated into machine code. The actual bit pattern for this code varies according to the machine and software version, but it could be as previously indicated. In order for the translation to happen, a special program called a *compiler* "reads" the high-level instructions and translates them into machine code. This compiled version is then run using some appropriate data, and the results are presented through some form of output device. The special programs that activate the compiler, run the machine-code version, and cause output to be printed are examples of system programs (software). The written program is a *source program,* and the machine-code version generated by the compiler is an *object program* (also referred to as *object code*).

As you will soon see, the compiler does more than just translate instructions into machine code. It also detects certain errors in your source program and prints appropriate messages. For example, if you write the instruction

```
C = (A + B;
```

in which a parenthesis is missing, when the compiler attempts to translate this line into machine code, it will detect that ")" is needed to close the parenthetical expression. It will then give you an error message such as

```
Error: ')' expected
```

You will then need to correct the error (and any others) and recompile your source program before running it with the data.

You are now ready to begin a detailed study of C++. You will undoubtedly spend much time and encounter some frustration during the course of your work. We hope your efforts result in an exciting and rewarding learning experience. Good luck.

SUMMARY

Key Terms

algorithm
applications software
arithmetic/logic unit (ALU)
assembly language
binary digits
bits
bus
central processing unit (CPU)
comments
compiler
control unit
data executable statement

executed
hardware
high-level language
input device
I/O devices
low-level language
machine language
main (primary) memory
main unit
mainframe
microcomputer minicomputer
object code

object program
operating system
output device
program
programming language
secondary (auxiliary) memory
   devices
software
source program
syntax
system software

2 Problem Solving Fundamentals: Data Types and Output

Chapter 1 presented an overview of computers and computer languages. We are now ready to examine problems that computers can solve. First we need to know how to solve a problem and then we need to learn how to use a programming language to implement our solution on the computer. Section 2.1 lays the foundation for what many consider to be the most important aspect of entry-level courses in computer science—program development. The problem-solving theme in this section is continued throughout the text.

Before looking at problem solving and writing programs for the computer, we should consider some psychological aspects of working in computer science. Studying computer science can cause a significant amount of frustration for these reasons:

1. Planning is a critical issue. First, you must plan to develop instructions to solve your problem and then you should plan to translate those instructions into code before you sit down at the keyboard. You should not attempt to type in code "off the top of your head."

2. Time is a major problem. You cannot expect to complete a programming assignment by staying up late the night before it is due. You must begin early and expect to make several revisions before your final version is ready.

3. Successful problem solving and programming require extreme precision. Generally, concepts in computer science are not difficult; however, implementation of these concepts allows no room for error. For example, one misplaced word in a 1000-line program could prevent the program from working.

In other words, you must be prepared to plan well, start early, be patient, handle frustration, and work hard to succeed in software development. If you cannot do this, you will probably not enjoy software development nor be successful at it.

2.1 Program Development— Top-Down Design

The key to writing a successful program is planning. Good programs do not just happen; they are the result of careful design and patience. Just as an artist commissioned to paint a portrait would not start out by shading in the lips and eyes, a good computer programmer would not attack a problem by immediately trying to write code for a program to solve the problem. Writing a program is like writing an essay: An overall theme is envisioned, an outline of major ideas is developed, each major idea is subdivided into several parts, and each part is developed using individual sentences.

Six Steps to Good Programming Habits

In developing a program to solve a problem, six steps should be followed: analyze the problem, develop an algorithm, document the program, write code for the program, run the program, and test the results. These steps will help develop good problem-solving habits and, in turn, solve programming problems correctly. A brief discussion of each of these steps follows:

Step 1: Analyze the Problem. This is not a trivial task. Before you can do anything, you must know exactly what it is you are to do. You must be able to formulate a clear and precise statement of what is to be done. You should understand completely what data are available and what may be assumed. You should also know exactly what output is desired and the form it should take. When analyzing a complex problem, it helps to divide the problem into subproblems whose solutions can be developed and tested independently before they are combined into a complete solution.

Step 2: Develop an Algorithm. An algorithm is a finite sequence of effective statements that, when applied to the problem, will solve it. An *effective statement* is a clear, unambiguous instruction that can be carried out. Each algorithm you develop should have a specific beginning; by the completion of one step, the next step should be uniquely determined; and have an ending that is reached in a reasonable amount of time.

Step 3: Document the Program. It is very important to completely document a program. The writer knows how the program works; if others are to modify it, they must know the logic used. Moreover, users will need to know the details of how to use the program effectively. Documentation can come directly out of steps 1 and 2 before you write any code.

Step 4: Write Code for the Program. When the algorithm correctly solves the problem, you can think about translating your algorithm into a high-level language. An effective algorithm will significantly reduce the time you need to complete this step.

Step 5: Run the Program. After writing the code, you are ready to run the program. This means that, using an editor, you type the program code into the computer, compile the program, and run the program. At compile time, you may discover syntax errors, which are mistakes in the way you have formed sentences in the program. Once these errors have been corrected, you may discover other errors at run time. Some of these mistakes may be as simple as an attempt to divide by zero. Other errors, called logic errors, may be more subtle and cause the program to produce mysterious results. They may require a reevaluation of all or parts of your algorithm. The probability of having to make some corrections or changes is quite high.

Step 6: Test the Results. After your program has run, you need to be sure that the results are correct, that they are in a form you like, and that your program produces the correct solution in all cases. To be sure the results are correct, you must look at them and compare them with what you expect. In the case of a program that uses arithmetic operations, this means checking some results with pencil and paper. With complex programs, you will need to test the program thoroughly by running it many times using data that you have carefully selected. Often you will need to make revisions by returning to one of the previous steps.

You should bear in mind that programs of any significant size (more than 100 lines of code) are never constructed all at once. The six steps just described are used to build programs incrementally. That is, a program is created out of small pieces that are designed, coded, tested, and documented to solve small problems. These pieces are then glued together to solve the problem set for the overall program.

Developing Algorithms

Algorithms for solving a problem can be developed by stating the problem and then subdividing the problem into major subtasks. Each subtask can then be subdivided into smaller tasks. This process is repeated until each remaining task is one that is easily solved. This process is known as *top-down design,* and each successive subdivision is referred to as a *stepwise refinement.* Tasks identified at each stage of this process are called *modules.* The relationship between modules can be shown graphically in a *structure chart* (see Figure 2.1).

To illustrate developing an algorithm, we will use the problem of updating a checkbook after a transaction has been made. A first-level refinement is shown in Figure 2.2. An arrow pointing into a module means information is needed before the task can be performed. An arrow pointing out of a module means the module task has been completed and information required for subsequent work is available. Each of these modules could be further refined as shown in Figure 2.3. Finally, one of the last modules could be refined as shown in Figure 2.4. The complete top-down design could then be envisioned as illustrated in Figure 2.5. Notice that each remaining task can be accomplished in a very direct manner.

As a further aid to understanding how data are transmitted, we will list *module specifications* for each main (first-level) module. Each module specification includes a description of inputs or data received, outputs or information returned, and the task performed by the module. In cases where there are no inputs or outputs, none are specified.

For the checkbook-balancing problem, complete module specifications are as follows:

Module: Get information
Task: Have the user enter information from the keyboard.
Outputs: starting balance, transaction type, transaction amount

Module: Perform computations
Task: If transaction is a deposit, add it to the starting balance; otherwise, subtract it.
Inputs: starting balance, transaction type, transaction amount
Output: ending balance

Module: Display results

◆ FIGURE 2.1
Structure chart illustrating top-down design

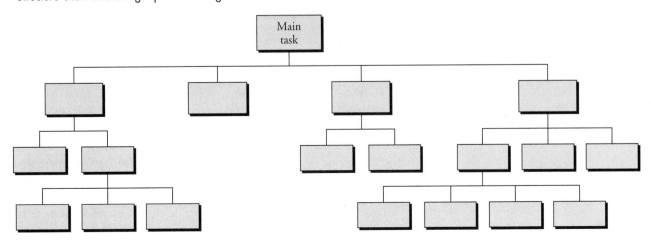

◆ **FIGURE 2.2**
First-level refinement

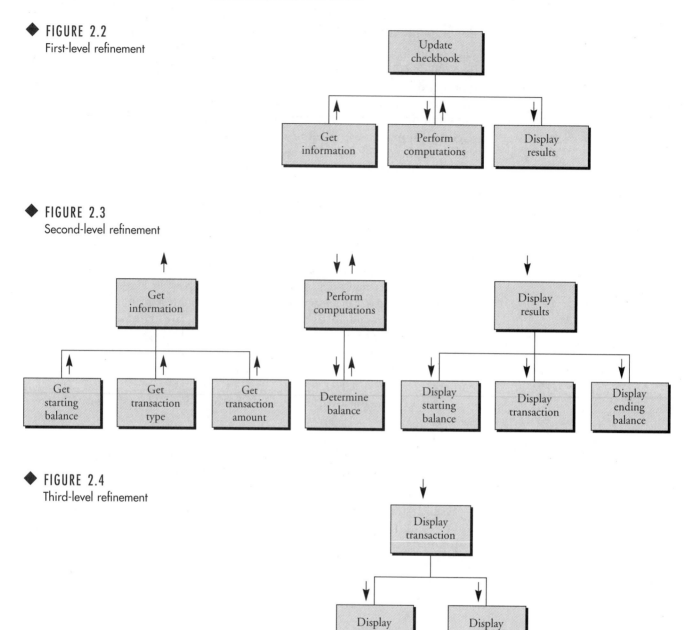

◆ **FIGURE 2.3**
Second-level refinement

◆ **FIGURE 2.4**
Third-level refinement

Task: Display results in a readable form.

Inputs: starting balance, transaction type, transaction amount, ending balance

At least two comments should be made about top-down design. First, different people can (and probably will) have different designs for the solution of a problem. However, each good design will have well-defined modules with functional subtasks. Second, the graphic method just used helps to formulate general logic for solving a problem but is somewhat awkward for translating to code. Thus, we will use a stylized, half-English, half-code method called *pseudocode* to illustrate stepwise refinement in such a design. Pseudocode is written in English, but the sentence structure and indentations will suggest C++ code. Major tasks will be

◆ FIGURE 2.5

Structure chart for top-down design

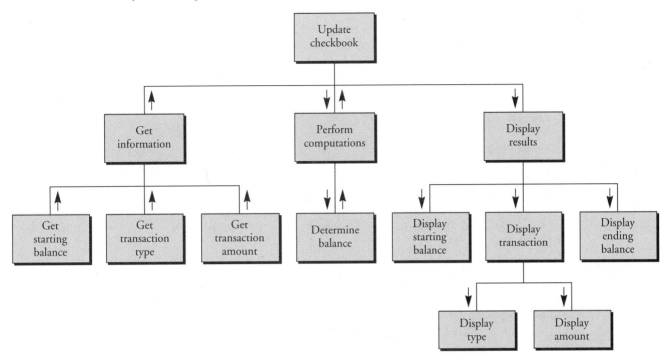

numbered with whole numbers and subtasks with decimal numbers. After you become used to the pseudocode notation, the numbering of lines will be omitted. First-level pseudocode for the checkbook-balancing problem is

1. Get information
2. Perform computations
3. Display results

A second-level pseudocode development produces

1. Get information
    1.1 get starting balance
    1.2 get transaction type
    1.3 get transaction amount
2. Perform computations
    2.1 if deposit then
            add to balance
        else
            subtract from balance
3. Display results
    3.1 display starting balance
    3.2 display transaction
    3.3 display ending balance

Finally, step 3.2 of the pseudocode is subdivided as previously indicated into

3.2 display transaction
    3.2.1 display transaction type
    3.2.2 display transaction amount

Two final comments are in order. First, each module developed should be tested with data for that module. Once you are sure each module does what you want, the whole program should work when the modules are used together. Second, the process of dividing a task into subtasks is especially suitable for writing programs in C++. As you will see, the language supports development of subprograms for specific subtasks.

A C++ program for the checkbook-balancing problem follows:

```cpp
// Program file: chbook.cpp
// This program updates a checkbook.

#include <iostream.h>
#include <iomanip.h>

int main ()
{
        float starting_balance, ending_balance, trans_amount;
        char trans_type;

// Module for getting the data.

        cout << "Enter the starting balance and press <Enter>: " ;
        cin >> starting_balance;
        cout << "Enter the transaction type (D) deposit or (W) withdrawal " ;
        cout << "and press <Enter>: " ;
        cin >> trans_type;
        cout << "Enter the transaction amount and press <Enter>: " ;
        cin >> trans_amount;

// Module for performing computations.

        if (trans_type == 'D')
                ending_balance = starting_balance + trans_amount;
        else
                ending_balance = starting_balance - trans_amount;

// Module for displaying results.

        cout << fixed << showpoint << setprecision(2);
        cout << endl;
        cout << "Starting balance   $" << setw(8) << starting_balance << endl ;
        cout << "Transaction      $" << setw(8) << trans_amount << setw(2)
             << trans_type << endl ;
        cout << setw(33) << "---------" << endl ;
        cout << "Ending balance    $" << setw(8) << ending_balance << endl ;

        return 0;
}
```

(modules marked: 1, 2, 3)

Notice how sections of the program correspond to module specifications. Sample runs of the program produce this output:

```
Enter the starting balance and press <Enter>: 235.16
Enter the transaction type (D) deposit or (W) withdrawal and press <Enter>: D
Enter the transaction amount and press <Enter>: 75.00
```

```
Starting Balance          $   235.16

Transaction               $    75.00 D

                              --------

Ending Balance            $   310.16

Enter the starting balance and press <Enter>: 310.16
Enter the transaction type (D) deposit or (W) withdrawal and press <Enter>: W
Enter the transaction amount and press <Enter>: 65.75

Starting Balance          $   310.16

Transaction               $    65.75 W
                              --------

Ending Balance            $   244.41
```

You probably would not use the power of a computer for something as simple as this program. You could just press a few calculator keys instead. However, as you will see, the language supports development of subprograms for specific subtasks. You will, for example, soon be able to enhance this program to check for overdrafts, save the new balance for later use, and repeat the process for several transactions. Learning to think in terms of modular development now will aid you not just in creating algorithms to solve problems, but in writing programs to solve problems.

Software Engineering

The phrase *software engineering* is used roughly to refer to the process of developing and maintaining very large software systems. Before becoming engrossed in the specifics of solving problems and writing relatively small programs, it is instructive to consider the broader picture faced by those who develop software for "real-world" use.

It is not unusual for software systems to be programs that, if written in this size type, would require between 100 and 150 pages of text. These systems must be reliable, economical, and subject to use by a diverse audience. Because of these requirements, software developers must be aware of and practice certain techniques.

As you might imagine, such large programs are not the work of a single individual but are developed by teams of programmers. Issues such as communication, writing style, and technique become as important as the development of algorithms to solve particular parts of the problem. Management, coordination, and design are major considerations that need resolution very early in the process. Although you will not face these larger organizational issues in this course, you will see how some of what you learn has implications for larger design issues.

Software engineering has been so titled because techniques and principles from the more established engineering disciplines are used to guide the large-scale development required in major software. To illustrate, consider the problems faced by an engineer who is to design and supervise construction of a bridge. This analysis was presented by Alfred Spector and David Gifford in an article entitled "A Computer Science Perspective on Bridge Design" published in *Communications of the ACM* (April 1986).

A NOTE OF INTEREST

Software Verification

Sitting 70 kilometers east of Toronto on the shore of Lake Ontario, the Darlington Nuclear Generating Station looks much like any other large nuclear power plant of the Canadian variety. But behind its ordinary exterior lies an unusual design feature.

Darlington is the first Canadian nuclear station to use computers to operate the two emergency shutdown systems that safeguard each of its four reactors. In both shutdown systems, a computer program replaces an array of electrically operated mechanical devices—switches and relays—designed to respond to sensors that are monitoring conditions critical to a reactor's safe operation, such as water levels in boilers.

Darlington's four reactors supply enough electricity to serve a city of 2 million people. Its Toronto-based builder, Ontario Hydro, opted for sophisticated software rather than old-fashioned hardware in the belief that a computer-operated shutdown system would be more economical, flexible, reliable, and safe than one under mechanical control.

This new approach, however, turned out to have unanticipated costs. To satisfy regulators that the shutdown software would function as advertised, Ontario Hydro engineers had to go through a frustrating but essential checking process that required nearly three years of extra effort. "There are lots of examples where software has gone wrong with serious consequences," says engineer Glenn H. Archinoff of Ontario Hydro. "If you want a shutdown system to work when you need it, you have to have a high level of assurance."

The Darlington experience demonstrates the tremendous effort involved in establishing the correctness of even relatively short and straightforward computer programs. The 10,000 "lines" of instructions, or code, required for each shutdown system pale in comparison with the 100,000 lines that constitute a typical word-processing program or the millions of lines needed to operate a long-distance telephone network or a space shuttle.

Engineers designing a bridge view it first as a hierarchy of substructures. This decomposition process continues on the substructures themselves until a level of very fundamental objects (such as beams and plates) ultimately is reached. This decomposition technique is similar to the stepwise refinement technique used by software designers, who break a complex problem down into a hierarchy of subproblems each of which ultimately can be solved by a relatively simple algorithm.

Engineers build conceptual models before actually constructing a bridge. This model-building allows them to evaluate various design alternatives in a way which eventually leads to the best possible design for the application being considered. This process is analogous to the way in which a skilled software designer builds models of a software system using structure charts and first-level pseudocode descriptions of modules. The designer then studies these conceptual models and eventually chooses the most elegant and efficient model for the application.

By the fashion in which engineers initially break down the bridge design, they insure that different aspects of the design can be addressed by different subordinate groups of design engineers working in a relatively independent fashion. This is similar to the goal of a software designer who oversees a program development team. The design of the software system must insure that individual components may be developed simultaneously by separate groups whose work will not have harmful side effects when the components are finally pulled together.

This overview is presented to give you a better perspective on how developments in this text are part of a greater whole. As you progress through your study of C++, you will see specific illustrations of how concepts and techniques can be viewed as part of the software engineering process.

Software System Life Cycle

Software engineering is the process by which large software systems are produced. As you might imagine, these systems need to be maintained and modified; ultimately, they are replaced with other systems. This entire process parallels that of an organism. That is, there is a development, maintenance, and subsequent demise. Thus, this process is referred to as the *software system life cycle*. Specifically, a system life cycle can be viewed in the following phases:

1. Analysis
2. Design
3. Coding
4. Testing/verification
5. Maintenance
6. Obsolescence.

It probably comes as a surprise that computer scientists view this process as having a phase that precedes the design phase. However, it is extremely critical that a problem be completely understood before any attempt is made to design a solution. The analysis phase is complicated by the fact that potential users may not supply enough information when describing their intended use of a system. Analysis requires careful attention to items such as exact form of input, exact form of output, how data entry errors (there will be some) should be handled, how large the databases will become, how much training in the use of the system will be provided, and what possible modifications might be required as the intended audience increases/decreases. Clearly, the analysis phase requires an experienced communicator.

The design phase is what much of this book is about. This is where the solution is developed using a modular approach. Attention must be paid to techniques that include communication, algorithm development, writing style, teamwork, and so on. The key product of this phase is a detailed specification of the intended software product.

Coding closely follows design. Unfortunately, many beginning students want to write code too quickly. This can be a painful lesson if you have to scrap several days' worth of work because your original design was not sufficient. You are encouraged to make sure your designs are complete before writing any code. In the real world, teams of designers work long hours before programmers ever get a chance to start writing code.

The testing phase of a large system is a significant undertaking. Early testing is done on individual modules to get them running properly. Larger data sets must then be run on the entire program to make sure the modules interact properly with the main program. When the system appears ready to the designers, it is usually field tested by selected users. Each of these testing levels is likely to require changes in the design and coding of the system.

Finally, the system is released to the public and the maintenance phase begins. This phase lasts throughout the remainder of the program's useful life. During this phase, we are concerned with repairing problems that arise after the system has been put into use. These problems are not necessarily bugs introduced during the coding phases. More often they are the result of user needs that change over time. For instance, annual changes in the tax laws necessitate changes in even the best payroll programs. Or problems may arise as a result of misinterpretation of user needs during the early analysis phase. Whatever the reason, we must expect that a program will have to undergo numerous changes during its lifetime. During the maintenance phase, the time spent documenting the original program will be repaid many times over. One of the worst tasks imaginable in software development is to be asked to maintain an undocumented program. Undocumented code can quickly become virtually unintelligible, even to the program's original author. Indeed, one of the measures of a good program is how well it stands up to the maintenance phase.

Of course, no matter how good a program is it will eventually become obsolete. At that time, the system life cycle starts all over again with the development of a new system to replace the obsolete one. Hence, the system life cycle is never ending, being itself part of a larger repetitive pattern that continues to evolve with changing user needs and more powerful technology.

Object-Oriented Design

During the last few years, a methodology has emerged that promises to make the task of maintaining large software systems easier. According to this method, large software systems should be constructed from smaller software components called objects. Software objects are a bit like building blocks, in that they can be pulled out of a box and put together in different ways to construct different applications. Objects can also be customized, that is, they can be adapted if they do not quite fit the task at hand. It is claimed that the use of software objects results in several benefits:

1. Because software objects can represent the behavior of the "real" objects that a software system is created to model, the differences between the analysis, design, and coding phases of the software life cycle tend to collapse.
2. Instead of changing existing code or writing new code, software maintenance involves plugging objects into a system or unplugging them from a system.
3. Systems can be more easily developed in increments, starting with a rough prototype whose detailed functions are eventually filled in until they are complete.

Although object-oriented design holds much promise for the development of solutions to complex problems, it is not necessarily the easiest and most straightforward way to learn to solve problems with a computer. In particular, the need for objects will not become apparent until we begin to define and use our own data structures for solving problems in Chapters 7 and 8. After we have explored some other typical problem-solving techniques, we will introduce object-oriented problem solving and programming with C++ in Chapters 7 through 11.

EXERCISES 2.1

1. Which of the following can be considered effective statements; that is, considered to be clear, unambiguous instructions that can be carried out? For each statement, explain why it is effective or why it is not.
   a. Pay the cashier $9.15.
   b. Water the plants a day before they die.
   c. Determine all positive prime numbers less than 1,000,000.

      d. Choose X to be the smallest positive fraction.

      e. Invest your money in a stock that will increase in value.

2. What additional information must be obtained in order to understand each of the following problems?

      a. Find the largest number of a set of numbers.

      b. Alphabetize a list of names.

      c. Compute charges for a telephone bill.

3. Outline the main tasks for solving each of the following problems.

      a. Write a good term paper.

      b. Take a vacation.

      c. Choose a college.

      d. Get a summer job.

      e. Compute the semester average for a student in a computer science course and print all pertinent data.

4. Refine the main tasks in each part of Exercise 3 into a sufficient number of levels so that the problem can be solved in a well-defined manner.

5. Use pseudocode to write a solution for each of the following problems. Indicate each stage of your development.

      a. Compute the wages for two employees of a company. The input information will consist of the hourly wage and the number of hours worked in one week. The output should contain a list of all deductions, gross pay, and net pay. For this problem, assume deductions are made for federal withholding taxes, state withholding taxes, social security, and union dues.

      b. Compute the average test score for five students in a class. Input for this problem will consist of five scores. Output should include each score and the average of these scores.

6. Develop an algorithm to find the total, average, and largest number in a given list of 25 numbers.

7. Develop an algorithm to find the greatest common divisor (GCD) of two positive integers.

8. Develop an algorithm for solving the following system of equations:

$$ax + by = c$$
$$dx + ey = f$$

9. Draw a structure chart and write module specifications for each of the following exercises.

      a. Exercise 5a.

      b. Exercise 5b.

      c. Exercise 6.

10. Discuss how the top-down design principles of software engineering are similar to the design problems faced by a construction engineer for a building. Be sure to include anticipated work with all subcontractors.

11. Using the construction analogy of Exercise 10, give an example of some specific communication required between electricians and the masons who finish the interior walls. Discuss why this information flow should be coordinated by a construction engineer.

12. State the phases of the software system life cycle.

13. Contact some company or major user of a software system to see what kinds of modifications might be required in a system after it has been released to the public. (Your own computer center might be sufficient.)

2.2 Writing Programs

Words in C++

Consider the following complete C++ program.

```cpp
// Program file: reswords.cpp
// This program illustrates the use of reserved words.

#include <iostream.h>
#include <iomanip.h>

const int LOOP_LIMIT = 10;
const char SKIP = ' ';

int main ()
{

        int j, number, sum;
        float average;

        sum = 0;
        for (j = 1; j <= LOOP_LIMIT; ++j)
        {
                cout << "Enter a number and press <Enter>: ";
                cin >> number;
                sum = sum + number;
        }
        average = sum / LOOP_LIMIT;
        cout << fixed << showpoint << setprecision(2);
        cout << endl;
        cout << setw(10) << SKIP << "The average is"
                << setw(8) << average
                << endl;
        cout << endl;
        cout << setw(10) << SKIP << "The number of scores is"
                << setw(3)
                << LOOP_LIMIT << endl;
        return 0;

}
```

This program—and most programming languages—requires the use of words when writing code. In C++, words that have a predefined meaning that cannot be changed are called *reserved words*. Some other predefined words (*library identifiers*) can have their meanings changed if the programmer has strong reasons for doing so. Other words (*programmer-supplied identifiers*) must be created according to a well-defined set of rules, but can have any meaning, subject to those rules.

C++ is case sensitive. This means that the word **while** will have a different meaning to the compiler than the word **While**, even though the two words might appear to mean the same thing to a human being. All reserved words and all library identifiers in C++ must be typed in lowercase letters only. Identifiers that you create for your own purposes may be typed in any case you like, as long as you remember that the same words written in different cases will mean different things.

Reserved Words

In C++, reserved words are predefined and cannot be used in a program for anything other than the purpose for which they are reserved. Some examples are **for**, **if**, **while**, **do**, **switch**, and **int**. As you continue in C++, you will learn where and how these words are used. The C++ reserved words are listed in Table 2.1.

Library Identifiers

A second set of predefined words, library identifiers, can have their meanings changed by the programmer. For example, if you could develop a better algorithm for the trigonometric function **sin**, you could then substitute it in the program. However, these words should not be used for anything other than their intended use. This list will vary somewhat from compiler to compiler, so you should obtain a list of library identifiers used in your local implementation of C++. Some library identifiers are listed in Table 2.2 and in Appendix 2. The term *keywords* is used to refer to both reserved words and library identifiers in subsequent discussions.

Syntax

Syntax refers to the rules governing construction of valid statements. This includes the order in which words and statements occur, together with appropriate punctuation. We use two methods of expressing syntax rules in this book. In the body of the text, the form of most new expressions in the language will be written using an angle bracket notation. In this notation, words that appear directly in the expression, such as **if** and **==**, will be written as is. Other components of the expression requiring further definition, such as type names or parameter lists, will be described by enclosing a term, like **type name** or **parameter list** within angle brackets (< and >). Thus, the rule for function call expressions looks like this:

<function name> (<actual parameter list>)

◇ **TABLE 2.1**
Reserved words

asm	continue	float	new	signed	try
auto	default	for	operator	sizeof	typedef
break	delete	friend	private	static	union
case	do	goto	protected	struct	unsigned
catch	double	if	public	switch	virtual
char	else	inline	register	template	void
class	enum	int	return	this	volatile
const	extern	long	short	throw	while

◇ **TABLE 2.2**
Some library identifiers

cin
cout
fixed
pow
setprecision
setw
showpoint
sin
sqrt

A NOTE OF INTEREST

Program Libraries

When the computer scientist John Backus developed the programming language FORTRAN in 1954, he decided to place the code for frequently used mathematical functions in compiled libraries. Programmers writing applications in FORTRAN had merely to link their own programs with the libraries to use these functions. Soon they began to construct and share libraries of their own functions. The practice of borrowing software tools "off the shelf" from libraries became a standard way of constructing large software systems quickly and safely. A library enhanced program safety, in that its tools were already debugged or shown to work correctly. A library enhanced system maintenance, in that changes to the importing application or to the exporting library could be made independently. Finally, a library enhanced the portability of a software system from one hardware installation to another, in that low-level, machine-dependent tasks could be packaged in the library and thereby insulated from the rest of the system.

One of the reasons C++ is so popular is that there are so many program libraries that enhance the safety, maintenance, and portability of systems written in the language.

◇ **TABLE 2.3**
Valid and invalid identifiers

Identifier	Valid	If Invalid, Reason
Sum	Yes	
X+Y	No	+ is not allowed
Average	Yes	
Text1	Yes	
1stNum	No	Must start with a letter or _
X30	Yes	
K mart	No	Spaces are not allowed
ThisIsaLongOne	Yes	

This rule means that a function call expression is a function name, followed by a left paren, followed by a list of actual parameters if the function expects any, followed by a right paren.

Another method of expressing a syntax rule uses a diagram. A list of syntax diagrams covering the portion of C++ used in this text appears in Appendix 3.

Identifiers

Reserved words and library identifiers are restricted in their use. Most C++ programs require programmer-supplied identifiers; the more complicated the program, the more identifiers are needed. **A valid identifier must start with a letter of the alphabet or an underscore (_) and must consist of only letters, digits, and underscores.** A syntax diagram for forming identifiers appears in Appendix 3.

Table 2.3 gives some valid and invalid identifiers along with the reasons for those that are invalid. A valid identifier can be of any length. However, some versions of C++ recognize only the first part of a long identifier, for example, the first 8 or the first 10 characters. Therefore, identifiers such as **MathTestScore1** and **MathTestScore2** might be the same identifier to a computer and could not be used as different identifiers in a program. Thus, you should learn what restrictions are imposed by your compiler.

The most common use of identifiers is to name the variables to be used in a program. Other uses for identifiers include symbolic constants, new data types, and subprogram names, all of which are discussed later. Even though single-letter identifiers are permitted, you should always use descriptive names for identifiers because, you'll see, descriptive names are easier to follow in a program.

Basic Program Components

A large, well-structured C++ program normally consists of many small *modules* whose text appears in different files. A small, simple program like many of those used in this text appears in a single file. For now, a simple program in C++ consists of five components: an optional set of *preprocessor directives,* an optional *constant and type definition section,* a *main program heading,* an optional *declaration section,* and a *statement section.* These five components are illustrated in the program shown in Figure 2.6.

Figure 2.7 illustrates the program components of the sample program that started this section; appropriate program parts are indicated.

The preprocessor directives are usually the first part of any C++ program. Preprocessor directives are preceded by the symbol **#**. One of them, **#include**, should be used if you wish to use certain library identifiers in your program. **#include** directs the preprocessor to include the contents of the designated library file with your source program for compilation. **#include** should be followed by the name of a library file. For now, the name of the library file should be enclosed in angle brackets. In later chapters of this text, we will see some library file names enclosed in double quotes.

The constant and type definition section contains the definitions of symbolic constants and names of data types used in the rest of the program.

Constants name values that cannot change in a program. The form for defining a constant is

```
const <type identifier> <identifier> = <value>;
```

An example of a constant definition is

```
const int LOOP_LIMIT = 10;
```

◆ **FIGURE 2.6**

Components of a simple C++ program

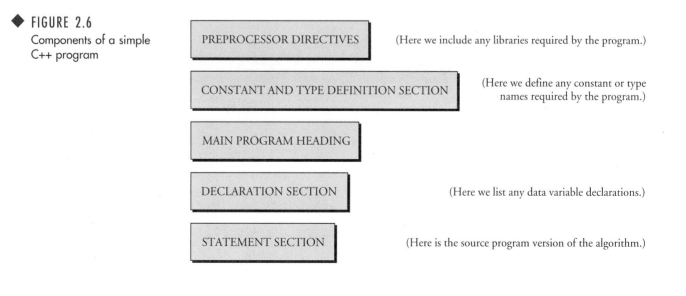

PREPROCESSOR DIRECTIVES   (Here we include any libraries required by the program.)

CONSTANT AND TYPE DEFINITION SECTION   (Here we define any constant or type names required by the program.)

MAIN PROGRAM HEADING

DECLARATION SECTION   (Here we list any data variable declarations.)

STATEMENT SECTION   (Here is the source program version of the algorithm.)

◆ FIGURE 2.7

Components of example program

```
// Program file: reswords.cpp
// This program illustrates the use of reserved words.
```

Preprocessor directives ⟶
```
#include <iostream.h>
#include <iomanip.h>
```

Constant definition section ⟶
```
const int LOOP_LIMIT = 10;
const char SKIP = ' ';
```

Main program heading ⟶
```
int main ()
{
```

Declaration section ⟶
```
    int j, number, sum;
    float average;
```

Statement section ⟶
```
    sum = 0;
    for (j = 1; j <= LOOP_LIMIT; ++j)
    {
        cout << "Enter a number and press <Enter>:";
        cin >> number;
        sum = sum + number;
    }
    average = sum / LOOP_LIMIT;
    cout << fixed << showpoint << setprecision(2);
    cout << endl;
    cout << setw(10) << SKIP << "The average is"
        << setw(8)
        << average << endl;
    cout << endl;
    cout << setw(10) << SKIP << "The number of scores is"
        << setw(3)
        << LOOP_LIMIT << endl;
    return 0;
}
```

If a constant is used that has not been declared, an error will occur when the program is compiled. Values of constant identifiers cannot be changed during program execution.

If a value is of type **char**, it must be enclosed in single quotation marks (apostrophes).

Any number of constants can be defined in this section. A typical constant definition portion of the declaration section could be

```
const char SKIP = ' ';
const int CLASS_SIZE = 35;
const int SPEED_LIMIT = 65;
const float CM_TO_INCHES = 0.3937;
```

We will discuss the mechanism for defining new data types in Chapters 5 and 7.

The main program heading is required in any C++ program. It consists of the word **int**, followed by the word **main**, followed by a set of parentheses. The program heading indicates the starting point of execution at run time.

The remainder of the program is sometimes referred to as the *main block*. A main block must begin with a left curly brace (`{`) and end with a right curly brace (`}`). The major parts of a main block are a declaration section and a statement section. The declaration section is used to declare (name) variables that are necessary to the program. If a variable is used that has not been declared, an error will occur when the program is compiled. For now, we assume all data used in a C++ program must be one of three *simple types:* **int**, **float**, or **char**. Types **int**, **float**, and **char** are discussed in Section 2.3.

Variables name values that can change in a program. The form required for declaring variables is somewhat different from that used for defining constants. One form simply omits the reserved word **const**:

```
<type identifier> <identifier> = <value>;
```

```
int sum = 0;
char ch = 'a';
```

When you need to declare more than one variable of the same type, it is convenient to list the variable names after the type on one line.

```
int length, width, area;
```

In general, it is considered good, defensive programming practice to provide variables with initial values when they are declared. Failure to do so can be the cause of mysterious program errors at execution time.

The fifth basic component of a simple C++ program is the statement section. This section contains the statements that cause the computer to do something.

Writing Code in C++

We are now ready to examine the use of the statement section of a program. In C++, a basic unit of grammar is an *executable statement,* which consists of library identifiers, programmer-defined identifiers, reserved words, numbers, and/or characters together with appropriate punctuation.

One of the main rules for writing code in C++ is that a semicolon almost always terminates executable statements. For example, if the expression

```
cout << setw(20) << "The results are" << setw(8) << sum << "and" << setw(6)
     << aver
```

is to be used in a program, it will not be treated as a statement unless it is followed by a semicolon. Thus, it should be

```
cout << setw(20) << "The results are" << setw(8) << sum << "and" << setw(6)
     << aver;
```

There is one typical instance where a semicolon is not needed. Occasionally, you will wish to enclose a series of statements within curly braces, so that they can be treated as a statement unit (the main program block is a good example). In this case, a semicolon is not needed after the right curly brace. You can visualize the statement section as shown in Figure 2.8.

FIGURE 2.8
Executable section

```
                                            ⎡ {
                                            |     <statement 1>
                                            |     <statement 2>
                                            |         .
              Executable  ────────▶         |         .
              section                       |         .
                                            |     <statement n – 1>
                                            |     <statement n>
                                            ⎣ }
```

C++ does not require each statement to be on a separate line. Actually, you could write a program as one long line (which may wrap around to fit the screen) if you wish; however, it would be difficult to read. Compare, for example, the readability of the following two programs.

```
// program file: format.cpp
// This program illustrates the use of formatting.
#include <iostream.h> #include <iomanip.h> const int AGE = 26; int main () { int
j, sum; sum = 0; for (j = 1; j <= 10; ++j) {sum = sum + j;} cout << setw(28) << "My
name is George" << endl; cout << setw(27) << "My age is " << AGE << endl; cout <<
endl; cout << setw(28) << "The sum is " << sum << endl; return 0;}
```

```
// Program file: format.cpp
// This program illustrates the use of formatting.

#include <iostream.h>
#include <iomanip.h>

const int AGE = 26;

int main ()
{
      int j, sum;

      sum = 0;
      for (j = 1; j <= 10; ++j)
      {
            sum = sum + j;
      }
      cout << setw(28) << "My name is George" << endl;
      cout << setw(27) << "My age is " << AGE << endl;
      cout << endl;
      cout << setw(28) << "The sum is " << sum << endl;
      return 0;
}
```

You are not expected to know exactly what the statements mean at this point, but it should be obvious that the second program is much more readable than the first. In addition, it is easier to change if corrections are necessary. Note, however, that these programs would be executed similarly because C++ ignores extra spaces and line boundaries.

We will discuss many kinds of statements in the following chapters. In every program in this text, you will see the statement

```
return 0;
```

at the end. When it occurs in the main program, this statement tells the computer that the program is finished running.

Formatting Conventions for Identifiers

You will have noticed by now that in our examples, constant identifiers have been written in uppercase letters, and all other identifiers, including variable and function names, have been written in lowercase letters. We believe that this convention helps the reader to pick out the constant names from the other names, when no other cues are available from the context. In addition, underscores are used to make multiword identifiers, like **monthly_pay**, more readable.

Program Comments

Programming languages typically include some provision for putting *comments* in a program. These comments are nonexecutable and are used to document and explain various parts of the program. In C++, progammers commonly use an *end-of-line comment*. An end-of-line comment begins with two slash characters (//) and runs for just one line. For multiline comments, we just place the slash characters at the beginning of each line.

EXERCISES 2.2

1. List the rules for forming valid identifiers.
2. Which of the following are valid identifiers? Give an explanation for those that are invalid.
   a. **7Up**
   b. **Payroll**
   c. **Room222**
   d. **Name List**
   e. **A**
   f. **A1**
   g. **1A**
   h. **Time&Place**
   i. **const**
   j. **X*Y**
   k. **ListOfEmployees**
   l. **Lima,Ohio**
3. Which of the following are valid program headings? Give an explanation for those that are invalid.
   a. **int main()**
   b. **PROGRAM GettingBetter (output);**
   c. **main(input, output)**
   d. **MAIN();**
4. Name the five main sections of a simple C++ program.
5. Write constant definition statements for the following.
   a. your gender
   b. your age
   c. pi

6. Find all errors in the following definitions and declarations.

a. `const char ch 'a';`
   `float salary;`

b. `int const;`

c. `int 32;`

d. `area int;`

e. `char int;`

7. Discuss the significance of a semicolon in writing C++ statements. Include an explanation of when semicolons are not required in a program.

2.3 Data Types and Output

OBJECTIVES

- to understand and be able to use the data types **int**, **float**, and **char**
- to understand the difference between the floating-point form and the fixed-point form of decimal numbers
- to understand the syntax for and use of output statements
- to be able to format output

Type int

C++ requires that all variables used in a program be given a *data type*. Since numbers in some form will be used in computer programs, we will first look at numbers of type **int**. Values of this type are used to represent integers or whole numbers. Some rules that must be observed when using integers follow:

1. Plus (+) signs do not have to be written before a positive integer, though they may be.

2. Minus (–) signs must be written when using a negative number.

3. Decimal points cannot be used when writing integers. Although 14 and 14.0 have the same value, 14.0 is not of type **int**.

4. Commas cannot be used when writing integers; hence, 271,362 is not allowed; it must be written as 271362.

5. Leading zeros should be avoided. If you use leading zeros, the compiler will interpret the number as an octal (base 8) number.

There is a limit on the largest and the smallest integer constants. The way you determine this limit is discussed in Chapter 3. Different machines have different values for these constants; you should check your C++ implementation to see what they are. Operations with integers and integer variables are examined in Chapter 3.

C++ also supports the data types **short int** and **long int**, which represent, respectively, a smaller and a larger range of integer values than **int**. Adding the prefix **unsigned** to any of these types means that you wish to represent nonnegative integers only. For example, the declaration

    unsigned short int x, y;

reserves memory for representing two relatively small nonnegative integers.

Type float

Values of type **float** are used to represent real numbers. Plus (+) and minus (–) signs for data of type **float** are treated exactly as with integers. When working with real numbers, however, trailing zeros are ignored. As with integers, leading zeros should be avoided. Thus, +23.45, 23.45, and 23.450 have the same value, but 023.45 may be interpreted by some C++ compilers as an octal number followed by a decimal point, which is a syntax error.

All real numbers seen thus far have been in *fixed-point* form. The computer will also accept real numbers in *floating-point* or exponential form. Floating-point form is an equivalent method for writing numbers in scientific notation to accommodate numbers that may have very large or very small values. The difference is that, instead of writing the base decimal times some power of 10, the base decimal is followed by E and the appropriate power of 10. For example, 231.6 in scientific notation would be 2.316×10^2 and in floating-point form would be 2.316E2. Table 2.4 sets forth several fixed-point decimal numbers with the equivalent scientific notation and floating-point form. Floating-point form for real numbers does not require exactly one digit on the left of the decimal point. In fact, it can be used with no decimal points written. To illustrate, 4.16E1, 41.6, 416.0E–1, and 416E–1 have the same value and all are permissible. However, it is not a good habit to use floating-point form for decimal numbers unless exactly one nonzero digit appears on the left of the decimal. In most other cases, fixed-point form is preferable.

In addition to **float**, C++ supports the types **double** and **long double**. The latter two data types support increasingly precise representation of real numbers, at the cost of more computer memory. Also, **double** is the data type of any numeric literal that is expressed in fixed-point notation in a program. However, to avoid confusion, we will use the term "real number" or **float** to characterize fixed-point numeric literals in this text.

When using real numbers in a program, you may use either fixed-point or floating-point form. But the computer prints out real numbers in floating-point form unless you specify otherwise. Formatting of output is discussed later in this section.

Type char

Another data type available in C++ is **char**, which is used to represent character data. In standard C++, data of type **char** can be only a single character (which could be a blank space). These characters come from an available character set that differs somewhat from computer to computer, but always includes the letters of the alphabet (uppercase and lowercase); the digits 0, 1 , 2, 3, 4, 5, 6, 7, 8, and 9; and special symbols such as #, &, !, +, –, *, /, and so on. A common character set is given in Appendix 4.

Character constants of type **char** must be enclosed in single quotation marks when used in a program. Otherwise, they are treated as variables and subsequent use may cause a compilation error. Thus, to use the letter A as a constant, you would type **'A'**. The use of digits and standard operation symbols as characters is also permitted; for example, **'7'** would be considered a character, but 7 is an integer.

Several nonprintable characters, such as the backspace, the horizontal tab, the newline, and the bell, are represented by using the backslash (\) in an escape sequence. For example, to use the backspace character, one would type **'\b'** in a C++ program.

Strings

Strings are used in programs to represent textual information, such as the names of people and companies.

◇ **TABLE 2.4**
Forms for equivalent
numbers

Fixed-point	Scientific Notation	Floating-point
46.345	4.6345×10^1	4.6345E1
59214.3	5.92143×10^4	5.92143E4
0.00042	4.2×10^{-4}	4.2E–4
36000000000.0	3.6×10^{10}	3.6E10
0.000000005	5.0×10^{-9}	5.0E–9
–341000.0	-3.41×10^5	–3.41E5

In C++, a string constant must be enclosed in double quotation marks. The following are examples of strings:

1. `"Hello world!"`
2. `"125"`
3. `""`
4. `"\n"`
5. `"\t"`
6. `"the word \"hello\""`

Note the difference between the second string, "125", and the integer value 125. They are different data types in C++. The third string, " ", is the empty string, because it contains no characters.

The fourth string contains a backslash (\) or escape character. This character tells the compiler to treat the following character, `'n'`, not as a literal character, but as a special code that represents a special character, in this case, a newline character. Thus, the string `"\n"` really contains just one character, the newline character. The fifth string represents a horizontal tab character. The last string uses two backslash characters to wrap double quotes around the word "hello". Note that when you wish the double quotes to appear literally in a string, they must be escaped with the backslash character. In general, to mention any special character in a string, including the backslash character itself, you prefix it with a backslash character. Consult your local implementation for a list of these special characters.

Students with experience in BASIC usually expect the equivalent of a string variable for storing names and other textual information. String variables are discussed in Chapter 7.

Output

The goal of most programs is to output something. What gets printed (either on paper, on a screen, or in a file) is referred to as output. The simplest way to produce screen output in C++ is to direct a value to the *standard output stream*. This stream is made available to a program by including the C++ library file **iostream.h**:

```
#include <iostream.h>
```

The name of this stream is **cout**, and the operator used to direct output to this stream is **<<**. Output values are usually character strings, numbers, numerical expressions, or variable names. The general form of an output statement is

`cout << expression 1 << expression 2 << . . . << expression n;`

You can think of **cout** as the name of an intelligent agent. This agent receives a message from you that you wish to display a value on the terminal screen and it then performs the desired action. The agent may also understand messages to format the output in a special way. We will discuss the methods for creating our own intelligent agents when we introduce object-oriented programming in Chapters 7 through 11.

Normally, the output statement causes subsequent output to be on the same line. If you wish subsequent output to begin on the next line, you must direct an end-of-line character to the standard output stream. When output is to a monitor, the following two lines each cause the cursor to move to the next line for the next I/O operation:

```
cout << '\n';

cout << endl;
```

The following are examples of single-line and multiline output:

```
cout << "This is a test. ";

cout << "How many lines are printed?" << endl;
```

causes the output

```
This is a test. How many lines are printed?
```

whereas,

```
cout << "This is a test." << endl;

cout << "How many lines are printed?" << endl;
```

causes the output

```
This is a test.
How many lines are printed?
```

Character strings can be printed by enclosing the string in double quotation marks. Numerical data can be printed by typing the desired number or numbers. Thus,

```
cout << 100;
```

produces

```
100
```

EXAMPLE 2.1

Let's write a complete C++ program to print the address
1403 South Drive
Apartment 3B
Pittsburgh, PA 15238
A complete program to print this is

```
// Program file: printaddr.cpp
// This program prints an address

#include <iostream.h>

int main()
{
        cout << "1403 South Drive" << endl;

        cout << "Apartment 3B" << '\n';

        cout << "Pittsburgh, PA 15238" << "\n";

        return 0;
}
```

Note the different ways of instructing the computer to output a newline to the terminal screen.

Formatting Integers

Output of integers can be controlled by *formatting*. First, you must include the library file **iomanip.h** to have access to the formatting functions:

```
#include <iomanip.h>
```

Second, you specify the field width for the next output directive by calling the **setw** function with the size of the number of columns to be filled. Then, on the next output directive, the value of an integer, identifier, or integer expression will be printed on the right side of the specified field. Thus,

```
cout << setw(10) << 100 << setw(10) << 50 << setw(10) << 25 ;
```

produces

```
-------100--------50--------25
```

where each "-" indicates a blank.

Some illustrations for formatting integer output are

Program Statement	Output
`cout << setw(6) << 123;`	`---123`
`cout <<15 << setw(5) << 10;`	`15---10`
`cout << setw(7) << -263 << setw(3)`	
`     << 21;`	`----263-21`
`cout << setw(6) << +5062;`	`--5062`
`cout << setw(3) << 65221;`	`65221`

The output of end of lines at the beginning and end of the executable section will separate desired output from other messages or directions. Thus, the previous program for printing an address could have been

```
int main()
{
        cout << endl << endl;

        cout << "1403 South Drive" << endl;

        cout << "Apartment 3B" << endl;

        cout << "Pittsburgh, PA, 15238" << endl;

        return 0;
}
```

Formatting Real Numbers

Output of real numbers can also be controlled by formatting. First, you must include the **iomanip.h** library to have access to the formatting functions. As with integers, you use **setw** to specify the total field width of each real number. However, if you wish real numbers to be displayed in decimal form, you must specify a fixed-point format with the number of positions to the right of the decimal. The following output statement does this for a desired precision of two places to the right of the decimal:

```
cout << fixed << showpoint << setprecision(2);
```

Then,

```
cout << setw(8) << 736.23;
```

produces

```
--736.23
```

The functions **fixed** and **showpoint** instruct the output stream to display real numbers in fixed-point format using a decimal point. The function **setprecision** specifies the number of digits to the right of the decimal point to be displayed. A precision of 2 will remain in effect for all subsequent outputs of real numbers, until the programmer specifies a change with another **setprecision** function.

Formatting real numbers causes the following to happen:

1. The decimal point uses one position in the specified field width.
2. Trailing zeros are printed to the specified number of positions to the right of the decimal.
3. Leading plus (+) signs are omitted.
4. Leading minus (–) signs are printed and use one position of the specified field.
5. Digits appearing to the right of the decimal have been rounded rather than truncated.

As with integers, if a field width is specified that is too small, most versions of C++ will default to the minimum width required to present all digits to the left of the decimal as well as the specified digits to the right of the decimal. Real numbers in floating-point form can also be used in a formatted output statement. The following table illustrates how output using data of type **float** can be formatted.

Program Statement	Output
`cout << setprecision(3) << setw(10)` `<< 765.432;`	`---765.432`
`cout << setprecision(2) << setw(10)` `<< 023.14;`	`-----23.14`
`cout << setprecision(2) << setw(10)` `<< 65.50`	`-----65.50`
`cout << setprecision(2) << setw(10)` `<< +341.2;`	`----341.20`
`cout << setprecision(2) << setw(10)` `<< -341.2;`	`----341.20`
`cout << setprecision(2) << setw(10)` `<< 16.458;`	`-----16.46`
`cout << setprecision(4) << setw(10)` `<< 0.00456;`	`----0.0046`
`cout << setprecision(2) << setw(6)` `<< 136.51;`	`136.51`

Formatting Strings

Strings and string constants can be formatted by using **setw** to specify field width. The string will be right justified in the field. Unlike real numbers, strings are truncated when necessary. Thus,

```
cout << "field" << setw(10) << "width" << setw(15) <<
"check" << endl;
```

would produce

```
field-----width----------check
```

and

```
cout << setw(4) << "check" << endl;
```

would produce

```
chec
```

Test Programs

Programmers should develop the habit of using *test programs* to improve their knowledge and programming skills. Test programs should be relatively short and written to provide an answer to a specific question. Test programs allow you to play with the computer. You can answer "What if . . . " questions by adopting a "try it and see" attitude. This is an excellent way to become comfortable with your computer and the programming language you are using.

EXERCISES 2.3

1. Which of the following are valid **int** constants? Explain why the others are invalid.

   a. 521   e. +65
   b. -32.0   f. 6521492183
   c. 5,621   g. -0
   d. +00784

2. Which of the following are valid **float** constants? Explain why the others are invalid.

   a. 26.3   f. 43E2
   b. +181.0   g. -0.2E-3
   c. -.14   h. 43,162.3E5
   d. 492.   i. -176.52E+1
   e. +017.400   j. 1.43000E+2

3. Change the following fixed-point decimals to floating-point decimals with exactly one nonzero digit to the left of the decimal.

   a. 173.0
   b. 743927000000.0
   c. -0.000000023
   d. +014.768
   e. -5.2

4. Change the following floating-point decimals to fixed-point decimals.

   a. `-1.0046E+3`

   b. `4.2E-8`

   c. `9.020E10`

   d. `-4.615230E3`

   e. `-8.02E-3`

5. Indicate the data type for each of the following:

   a. `-720`

   b. `-720.0`

   c. `150E3`

   d. `150`

   e. `"150"`

   f. `"23.4E2"`

   g. `23.4E-2`

6. Write and run test programs for each of the following:

   a. Examine the output for a decimal number without field width specified; for example,

```
cout << 2.31;
```

   b. Try to print a message without using quotation marks for a character string; for example,

```
cout << Hello;
```

7. For each of the following, write a program that would produce the indicated output.

```
a. Score                 b. Price

86                          $19.94
82                          $100.00
79                          $58.95
```

where "S" is in column 10.   where "P" is in column 50.

8. Assume the hourly wages of five students are 3.65, 4.10, 2.89, 5.00, and 4.50. Write a program that produces the following output, where the "E" of Employee is in column 20.

```
Employee    Hourly Wage

1            $   3.65
2            $   4.10
3            $   2.89
4            $   5.00
5            $   4.50
```

9. What is the output from the following segment of code on your printer or terminal?

```
cout << "My test average is" << 87.5;
cout << setw(20) << "My test average is"
     << setw(10) << 87.5;
cout << setw(25) << "My test average is"
     << setprecision(2) << setw(10) << 87.5;
cout << setw(25) << "My test average is"
     << setprecision(2) << setw(6) << 87.5;
```

10. Write a program that produces the following output. Start Student in column 20 and Test in column 40.

```
Student Name                         Test Score

Adams, Mike                             73

Conley, Theresa                         86

Samson, Ron                             92

O'Malley, Colleen                       81
```

11. The Great Lakes Shipping Company is going to use a computer program to generate billing statements for their customers. The heading of each bill is to be

```
     GREAT LAKES SHIPPING COMPANY
     SAULT STE. MARIE, MICHIGAN
```

```
Thank you for doing business with our company. The information listed below
was used to determine your total cargo fee. We hope you were satisfied with
our service.
```

```
CARGO       TONNAGE         RATE/TON        TOTAL DUE
```

Write a complete C++ program that produces this heading.

12. What output is produced by each of the following statements or sequence of statements when executed by the computer?

```cpp
a. cout << 1234 << setw(8) << 1234 << setw(6) << 1234;
b. cout << setw(4) <<12 << setw(4) << -21 << setw(4)
        << 120;
c. cout << "FIGURE AREA PERIMETER";
   cout << "";
   cout << endl;
   cout << "SQUARE" << setw(5) << 16 << setw(12) <<16;
   cout << endl;
   cout << "RECT " << setw(5) << 24 << setw(12) << 20;
```

13. Write a complete program that produces the following table:

```
WIDTH        LENGTH        AREA
4            2             8

21           5             105
```

14. What output is produced when each of the following is executed?

```cpp
a. cout << setprecision(2) << setw(15) << 2.134;
b. cout << setprecision(2) << setw(5) << 423.73;
c. cout << setprecision(3) << setw(8) << -42.1;
d. cout << setprecision(2) << setw(2) << -4.21E3;
e. cout << 10.25;
f. cout << 1.25 << setprecision(2) << setw(6)
        << 1.25 << setprecision(1)
        << setw(2) << 1.25;
```

15. Write a complete program that produces the following output:

Hourly Wage	Hours Worked	Total
5.0	20.0	100.00
7.50	15.25	114.375

16. What type of data would be used to print each of the following?

   a. your age

   b. your grade-point average

   c. your name

   d. a test score

   e. the average test score

   f. your grade

SUMMARY

Key Terms

comments	keyword	standard identifier
constant definition	module	standard simple type
data type	module specifications	statement section
declaration section	object-oriented design	stepwise refinement
executable statement	program heading	string
fixed point	pseudocode	string constant
floating point	reserved words	structure chart
formatting	software engineering	top-down design
identifier	software system life cycle	variable declaration

Keywords

int	**long**	**char**
float	**unsigned**	**const**
short	**double**	

Key Concepts

◆ Six steps in problem solving include the following: analyze the problem, develop an algorithm, document the program, write code for the program, run the program, and test the results against answers manually computed with paper and pencil.

◆ Top-down design is a process of dividing tasks into subtasks until each subtask can be readily accomplished.

◆ Stepwise refinement refers to refinements of tasks into subtasks.

◆ A structure chart is a graphic representation of the relationship between modules.

◆ Software engineering is the process of developing and maintaining large software systems.

◆ The software system life cycle consists of the following phases: analysis, design, coding, testing/verification, maintenance, and obsolescence.

◆ Valid identifiers must begin with a letter or underscore and they can contain only letters, digits, and underscores.

◆ The five components of a simple C++ program are preprocessor directives, constant and type definitions, program heading, declaration section, and executable statement section.

◆ Semicolons are used to terminate most executable statements.

◆ Extra spaces and blank lines are ignored in C++.

◆ Output is generated by using **cout** and **<<**.

◆ Strings are formatted using the function **setw** with a positive integer that specifies the total field width, for example,

```
cout << setw(30) << "This is a string";
```

◆ The following table summarizes the use of the data types **int**, **float**, and **char**.

Data Type	Permissible Data	Formatting
int	Numeric	**setw**(an integer); for example `cout << setw(6) << 25;`

float	Numeric	**fixed**, **showpoint**, **setprecision**(an integer), and **setw**(an integer);
		for example
		`cout << showpoint`
		`        << setprecision(2)`
		`        << setw(8) << 1234.5;`

char	Character	**setw**(an integer); for example `cout << setw(6) << 'A';`

PROGRAMMING PROBLEMS AND PROJECTS

1. Write and run a short program to print your initials in block letters. Your output could look like

```
JJJJJ               A              CCC
   J              A A            C     C
   J             A   A           C
   J            AAAAAAA          C
J  J           A       A          C     C
 JJJ          A         A          CCC
```

2. Design a simple picture and print it using output statements. If you plan the picture using a sheet of graph paper, keeping track of spacing will be easier.

3. Write and run a program to print your mailing address.

4. Our lady of Mercy Hospital prints billing statements for patients when they are ready to leave the hospital. Write a program that prints a heading for each statement as follows:

```
////////////////////////////////////////////////
/                                                /
/                                                /
/            Our Lady of Mercy Hospital          /
/                                                /
/                                                /
/                                                /
/                                                /
/                  1306 Central City             /
/                                                /
/                                                /
/               Phone (416) 333-5555             /
/                                                /
/                                                /
/                                                /
/                                                /
////////////////////////////////////////////////
```

5. Your computer science instructor wants course and program information included as part of every assignment. Write a program that can be used to print this information. Sample output should look like this:

```
*****************************************
*                                       *
*        Author:        Mary Smith      *
*        Course:        CPS-150          *
*        Assignment:    Program #3      *
*                                       *
*        Due Date:      September 18    *
*        Instructor:    Mr. Samson      *
*                                       *
*****************************************
```

6. As part of a programming project that will compute and print grades for each student in your class, you have been asked to write a program that produces a heading for each student report. The columns in which the various headings should be are as follows:

the border for the class name starts in column 30

Student Name starts in column 20

Test Average starts in column 40

Grade starts in column 55.

Write a program to print the heading as follows:

```
                             ************************
                             *                      *
                             *  CPS 150     C++      *
                             *                      *
                             ************************

             Student Name    Test Average    Grade
```

3 More Problem Solving Fundamentals: Calculation and Input

You have probably used a pocket calculator. Pocket calculators provide a set of built-in arithmetic functions. Many pocket calculators also provide built-in constants, such as PI, and users can program them to perform a series of functions that share data with variables. In this chapter we will discuss all of these concepts, including arithmetic operations, using data in a program, obtaining input, and using constants and variables. We will also discuss the use of functions to perform standard operations such as finding a square root or raising a number to a given power.

3.1 Arithmetic in C++

OBJECTIVES

- to understand what an expression is in C++

- to be able to evaluate arithmetic expressions using data of type **int**

- to be able to evaluate arithmetic expressions using data of type **float**

- to understand the order of operations for evaluating expressions

- to be able to identify mixed-mode expressions

- to be able to distinguish between valid and invalid mixed-mode expressions

- to be able to evaluate mixed-mode expressions

Basic Operations for Integers

Integer arithmetic in C++ allows the operations of addition, subtraction, multiplication, division, and modulus to be performed. The notation for these operations is shown on Table 3.1.

In a standard integer division problem, there is a quotient and a remainder. In C++, the slash (/) produces the quotient and **%** produces the remainder when the first operand is positive. For example, in the problem 17 divided by 3, **17 / 3** produces 5, and **17 % 3** produces 2. Avoid using / 0 (zero) and % 0 (zero). Division by zero will cause a run-time error. Several integer expressions and their values are shown in Table 3.2. Notice that when 3 is multiplied by –2, the expression is written as **3 * (–2)** rather than **3 * –2**. The parentheses make the expression more readable, but are not required.

Order of Operations for Integers

Expressions involving more than one operation are frequently used when writing programs. When this happens, it is important to know the order in which these operations are performed. The priorities for these are as follows:

1. All expressions within a set of parentheses are evaluated first. If there are parentheses within parentheses (the parentheses are nested), the innermost expressions are evaluated first.

◇ **TABLE 3.1**
Integer arithmetic operations

Symbol	Operation	Example	Value
+	Addition	3 + 5	8
–	Subtraction	43 – 25	18
*	Multiplication	4 * 7	28
/	Division	9 / 2	4
%	Modulus	9 % 2	1

◇ **TABLE 3.2**
Values of integer expressions

Expression	Value
–3 + 2	–1
2 – 3	–1
–3 * 2	–6
3 * (–2)	–6
–3 * (–2)	6
17 / 3	5
17 % 3	2
17 / (–3)	–5
–17 / 3	–5
–17 % 7	–3
–17 / (–3)	5

◇ **TABLE 3.3**
Integer arithmetic priority

Expression or Operation	Priority
( )	1. Evaluate from inside out.
*, %, /	2. Evaluate from left to right.
+, –	3. Evaluate from left to right.

2. The operations *, %, and / are evaluated next in order from left to right.
3. The operations + and – are evaluated last from left to right.

These operations are the operations of algebra and are summarized in Table 3.3.

To illustrate how expressions are evaluated, consider the values of the expressions listed in Table 3.4. As expressions get more elaborate, it can be helpful to list partial evaluations in a manner similar to the order in which the computer performs the evaluations. For example, suppose the expression

$$(3 - 4) + 18 / 5 + 2$$

is to be evaluated. If we consider the order in which subexpressions are evaluated, we get

```
(3 - 4) + 18 / 5 + 2
   ↓
  -1    + 18 / 5 + 2
              ↓
  -1    +     3   + 2
   ↓
          2         + 2
                ↓
                4
```

◇ **TABLE 3.4**
Priority of operations

Expression	Value
3 - 4 * 5	-17
3 - (4 * 5)	-17
(3 - 4) * 5	-5
3 * 4 - 5	7
3 * (4 - 5)	-3
17 - 10 - 3	4
17 - (10 - 3)	10
(17 - 10) - 3	4
-42 + 50 % 17	-26

Using Modulus and Division

Modulus and division can be used when it is necessary to perform conversions within arithmetic operations. For example, consider the problem of adding two weights given in units of pounds and ounces. This problem can be solved by converting both weights to ounces, adding the ounces, and then converting the total ounces to pounds and ounces. The conversion from ounces to pounds can be accomplished by using modulus and division. If the total number of ounces is 243, then **243 / 16** yields the number of pounds (15), and **243 % 16** yields the number of ounces (3).

Representation of Integers

Computer representation of integers is different from what we see when we work with integers. Integers are stored in *binary notation,* and the operations performed on them are those of *binary arithmetic.* Thus, the integer 19, which can be written as

$$19 = 16 + 0 + 0 + 2 + 1$$
$$= 1 * 2^4 + 0 * 2^3 + 0 * 2^2 + 1 * 2^1 + 1 * 2^0$$

is stored as 1 0 0 1 1. This binary number is actually stored in a *word* in memory, which consists of several individual locations called bits, as mentioned in Chapter 1. The number of bits used to store an integer is machine dependent. If you use a 16-bit machine, then 19 is

19

In this representation, the leftmost bit is reserved for the sign of the integer (1 meaning negative, 0 meaning positive).

We can make two observations regarding the storage and mechanics of the operations on integers. First, integers produce exact answers; numbers are stored exactly (up to the limits of the machine). Second, a maximum and a minimum number can be represented. In a 16-bit machine, these numbers are

where the leftmost 0 represents a positive number equaling 32,767, and

where the leftmost 1 represents a negative number equaling -32,768.

To find out what the minimum and maximum integer values for your particular system are, you can use the C++ library constants discussed in Section 3.4.

If a program contains an integer operation that produces a number outside of your machine's range, this is referred to as *integer overflow,* which means that the number is too large or too small to be stored. Ideally, an error message would be printed when such a situation arises. However, many systems merely store an unpredictable value and continue with the program. In Section 5.3, we will discuss how to protect a program against this problem.

Basic Operations for Real Numbers

The operations of addition, subtraction, and multiplication are the same for data of type **float** as for integers. Additionally, real division is now permitted. Modulus is restricted to data of type **int**. The symbol for division of data of type **float** is the slash (/). The *real arithmetic operations* are shown on Table 3.5.

◇ **TABLE 3.5**
Real arithmetic operations

Symbol	Operation	Example	Value
+	Addition	**4.2 + 19.36**	23.56
–	Subtraction	**19.36 – 4.2**	15.16
*	Multiplication	**3.1 * 2.0**	6.2
/	Division	**54.6 / 2.0**	27.3

Division is given the same priority as multiplication when arithmetic expressions are evaluated by the computer. The rules for order of operation are the same as those for evaluating integer arithmetic expressions. A summary of these operations is shown in Table 3.6. Some example calculations using data of type **float** are shown on Table 3.7.

◇ **TABLE 3.6**
Real arithmetic priority

Expression or Operation	Priority
( )	1. Evaluate from inside out.
*, /	2. Evaluate from left to right.
+, –	3. Evaluate from left to right.

◇ **TABLE 3.7**
Type float calculations

Expression	Value
–1.0 + 3.5 + 2.0	4.5
–1.0 + 3.5 * 2.0	6.0
2.0 * (1.2 – 4.3)	–6.2
2.0 * 1.2 – 4.3	–1.9
–12.6 / 3.0 + 3.0	–1.2
–12.6 / (3.0 + 3.0)	–2.1

As expressions get a bit more complicated, it is again helpful to write out the expression and evaluate it step by step. For example,

```
18.2 + (-4.3) * (10.1 + (72.3 / 3.0 - 4.5))
                                    ↓
18.2 + (-4.3) * (10.1 +   (24.1     - 4.5))
                                      ↓
18.2 + (-4.3) * (10.1 +             19.6)
                                 ↓
18.2 + (-4.3) *           29.7
                       ↓
18.2 +              -127.71
          ↓
       -109.51
```

Representation of Real Numbers

As with integers, real numbers are stored and operations are performed using binary notation. Unlike integers, however, the storage and representation of real numbers frequently produce answers that are not exact. For example, an operation such as

1 / 3.0

produces the repeating decimal .3333. . . . At some point, this decimal must be truncated or rounded so that it can be stored. Such conversions produce *round-off errors.*

Now let us consider some errors that occur when working with real numbers. A value very close to zero may be stored as 0. Thus, you may think you are working with

$1.23 * 10^{-20}$ = .00000000000000000000123

but, in fact, this value may have been stored as a zero. This condition is referred to as *underflow.* Generally, this would not be a problem because replacing numbers very close to zero with 0 does not affect the accuracy of most answers. However, sometimes this replacement can make a difference; therefore, you should be aware of the limitations of the system on which you are working.

Because operations with real numbers are not stored exactly, errors referred to as *representational errors* can be introduced. To illustrate, suppose we are using a machine that only yields three digits of accuracy (most machines exhibit much greater accuracy) and we want to add the three numbers 45.6, -45.5, and .215. The order in which we add these numbers makes a difference in the result we obtain. For example, -45.5 + 45.6 yields .1. Then, .1 + .215 yields .315. Thus, we have

(-45.5 + 45.6) + .215 = .315

However, if we consider 45.6 + .215 first, then the arithmetic result is 45.815. Since our hypothetical computer only yields three digits of accuracy, this result will be stored as 45.8. Then, -45.5 + 45.8 yields .3. Thus, we have

-45.5 + (45.6 + .215) = .3

This operation produces a representational error.

Another form of representational error occurs when numbers of substantially different size are used in an operation. For example, consider the expression 2 + .0005. We would expect this value to be 2.0005, but stored to only three digits of accuracy, the result would be 2.00. In effect, the smaller of the two numbers disappears or is cancelled from the expression. This form of error is called a *cancellation error.*

Although representational and cancellation errors cannot be avoided, their effects can be minimized. Operations should be grouped in such a way that numbers of approximately the same magnitude are used together before the resulting operand is used with another number. For example, all very small numbers should be summed before adding them to a large number.

Attempting to store very large real numbers can result in *real overflow.* In principle, real numbers are stored with locations reserved for the exponents. An oversimplified illustration using base 10 digits is

$$\boxed{1\;\;2\;\;3\;\;+\;\;0\;\;8}$$

for the number $123 * 10^8$. Different computers place different limits on the size of the exponent that can be stored. An attempt to use numbers outside the defined range causes overflow in much the same way that integer overflow occurs, with results that depend on the particular run-time system.

Mixed-Mode Expressions

Arithmetic expressions using data of two or more types are called *mixed-mode expressions.* In a mixed-mode expression involving both **int** and **float** data types, the value will be of type **float**. When formatting output of mixed-mode expressions, always format for real numbers. *Note:* Avoid using % with mixed-mode expressions. The way in which C++ deals with mixed-mode expressions in general is fairly complex and is discussed in detail in Section 3.6. You may wish to avoid using mixed-mode expressions until you read that section.

EXERCISES 3.1

1. Find the value of each of the following expressions:
   a. `17 - 3 * 2`
   b. `-15 * 3 - 4`
   c. `123 % 5`
   d. `123 / 5`
   e. `5 * 123 / 5 - 123 % 5`
   f. `-21 * 3 * (-1)`
   g. `14 * (3 - 18 / 4) - 50`
   h. `100 - (4 * (3 - 2)) * (-2)`
   i. `-56 % 3`
   j. `14 * 8 % 5 - 23 / (-4)`
2. Find the value of each of the following expressions:
   a. `3.21 - - 5.02 - 6.1`
   b. `6.0 / 2.0 * 3.0`
   c. `6.0 / (2.0 + 3.0)`
   d. `-20.5 * (2.1 + 2.0)`
   e. `-2.0 * ((56.8 / 4.0 + 0.8) + 5.0)`
   f. `1.04E2 * 0.02E3`
   g. `800.0E-2 / 4.0 - 15.3`

3. Which of the following are valid expressions? For those that are valid, indicate whether they are of type **int** or **float**.

    a. 18 - (5 * 2)
    b. (18 - 5) * 2
    c. 18 - 5 * 2.0
    d. 25 * (14 % 7.0)
    e. 1.4E3 * 5
    f. 28 / 7
    g. 28.0 / 4
    h. 10.5 + 14 / 3
    i. 24 / 6 / 3
    j. 24 / (6 / 3)

4. Evaluate each of the valid expressions in Exercise 3.

5. What is the output produced by the following program?

```
#include <iostream.h>
#include <iomanip.h>

int main()
{
    cout << showpoint << fixed << setprecision(3);
    cout << endl << "Expression Value" << endl;
    cout << "----------------" << endl << endl;
    cout << " 10 / 5" << setw(12) << 10/5 << endl;
    cout << " 2.0+7*(-1)" << 2.0 + 7 * (-1) << endl << endl;
    return 0;
}
```

OBJECTIVES

- to understand the utilization of memory for storing data
- to distinguish between the name of a memory location and the value stored in a memory location
- to be able to use variables in assignment statements, expressions, and output statements

Memory Locations

It is frequently necessary to store values for later use. This is done by putting the value into a *memory location* and using a symbolic name to refer to this location. If the contents of the location are to be changed during a program, the symbolic name is referred to as a *variable;* if the contents are not to be changed, it is referred to as a *constant.*

A graphic way to think about memory locations is to envision them as boxes; each box is named and a value is stored inside. For example, suppose a program is written to add a sequence of numbers. If we name the memory location to be used **sum**, initially we have

which depicts a memory location that has been reserved and can be accessed by a reference to **sum**. If we then add the integers 10, 20 , and 30 and store them in **sum**, we have

It is important to distinguish between the name of a memory location (**sum**) and the value or contents of a memory location (**60**). The name does not change during

a program, but the contents can be changed as often as necessary. (Contents of memory locations that are referred to by constants cannot be changed.) If **30** were added to the contents in the previous example, the new value stored in **sum** could be depicted as

```
 90
```
sum

Those symbolic names representing memory locations whose values will be changing must be declared before they are used (as indicated in Section 2.4); for example,

```
int sum;
```

Those that represent memory locations whose values will not be changing must also be defined before they are used.

Assignment Statements

Now we will examine how the contents of variables are manipulated. When variables are declared in a C++ program, they contain values. However, a programmer does not know what these values are. Henceforth, we shall denote these system-supplied values with a question mark (?). The programmer may put a value into a memory location with an *assignment statement* in the form of

```
<variable name> = <value>;
```

or

```
<variable name> = <expression>;
```

where **<variable name>** is the name of the memory location. For example, if **sum** has an unknown value, then

    sum = 30;

changes

| ? | to | 30 |
sum   **sum**

Some important rules follow concerning assignment statements:

1. The assignment is always made from right to left (←).
2. Constants cannot be on the left side of the assignment symbol.
3. The expression can be a constant, a constant expression, a variable that has previously been assigned a value, or a combination of variables and constants.
4. Normally, values on the right side of the assignment symbol are not changed by the assignment.
5. The variable and expression must be of compatible data types.
6. Only one value can be stored in a variable at a time, so the previous value of a variable is thrown away.

One common error that beginners make is trying to assign from left to right.

Repeated assignments can be made. For example, if **sum** is an integer variable, the statements

    sum = 50;

    sum = 70;

    sum = 100;

produce first 50, then 70, and finally 100 as shown.

| 5̶0̶ 7̶0̶ 100 |
sum

In this sense, memory is destructible in that it retains only the last value assigned.

C++ variables are symbolic addresses that can hold values. When a variable is declared, the type of values it will store must be specified *(declared)*. Storing a value of the wrong type in a variable leads to a program error. This means that data types must be compatible when using assignment statements. For now, consider all of the basic data types—**char**, **int**, and **float**—as compatible with each other. This means that assignments of values to variables are allowed for any possible combination of these types on both sides of an assignment statement. Type compatibility and type conversion are discussed in Section 3.6.

Assignments of character constants to a character variable require that the constant be enclosed in single quotation marks. For example, if **letter** is of type **char** and you want to store the letter C in **letter**, use the assignment statement

    letter = 'C';

This could be pictured as

```
┌───────┐
│   C   │
└───────┘
 letter
```

Furthermore, only one character can be assigned or stored in a character variable at a time.

Expressions

Actual use of variables in a program is usually more elaborate than what we have just seen. Variables may be used in any manner that does not violate their type declarations. This includes both arithmetic operations and assignment statements. For example, if **score1**, **score2**, **score3**, and **average** are **float** variables,

```
score1 = 72.3;

score2 = 89.4;

score3 = 95.6;

average = (score1 + score2 + score3) / 3.0;
```

is a valid fragment of code.

Now consider the problem of accumulating a total. Assuming **new_score** and **total** are integer variables, the following code is valid:

```
total = 0;
new_score = 5;
total = total + new_score;
new_score = 7;
total = total + new_score;
```

As this code is executed, the values of memory locations for **total** and **new_score** could be depicted as

	total	new_score
`total = 0;`	`0`	`?`
`new_score = 5;`	`0`	`5`
`total = total + new_score;`	`5`	`5`
`new_score = 7;`	`5`	`7`
`total = total + new_score;`	`12`	`7`

Output

Variables and variable expressions can be used when creating output. When used in an output statement, they perform the same function as a constant. For example, if the assignment statement

```
age = 5;
```

has been made, these two statements

```
cout << 5;
cout << age;
```

produce the same output. If **age1**, **age2**, **age3**, and **sum** are integer variables and the assignments

```
age1 = 21;
age2 = 30;
age3 = 12;
sum = age1 + age2 + age3;
```

are made, then

```
cout << "The sum is" << 21 + 30 + 12;
cout << "The sum is" << age1 + age2 + age3;
cout << "The sum is" << sum;
```

all produce the same output.

Formatting variables and variable expressions in output statements follows the same rules that were presented in Chapter 2 for formatting constants. The statements needed to write the sum of the problem we just saw in a field width of four are

```
cout << "The sum is" << setw(4) << 21 + 30 + 12;
cout << "The sum is" << setw(4) << age1 + age2 + age3;
cout << "The sum is" << setw(4) << sum;
```

EXAMPLE 3.1

Suppose you want a program to print data about the cost of three textbooks and the average price of the books. The variable declaration section could include:

```
float math_text, bio_text, comp_sci_text, total, average;
```

A portion of the program could be

```
math_text = 23.95;

bio_text = 27.50;

comp_sci_text = 19.95;

total = math_text + bio_text + comp_sci_text;

average = total / 3;
```

The output could be created by

```
cout << setprecision(2) << endl;
cout << "Text                Price" << endl;
cout << "----                -----" << endl;
cout << endl;
cout << "Math" << setw(18) << math_text << endl;
cout << "Biology" << setw(15) << bio_text << endl;
cout << "CompSci" << setw(15) << comp_sci_text << endl;
cout << endl;
```

```
cout << "Total" << setw(17) << total << endl;
cout << endl;
cout << "The average price is" << setw(7) << average << endl;
```

The output would be

```
Text                 Price
----                 -----

Math                 23.95

Biology              27.50

CompSci              19.95

Total                71.40

The average price is    23.80
```

Software Engineering

The communication aspect of software engineering can be simplified by judicious choices of meaningful identifiers. Systems programmers must be aware that over time many others will need to read and analyze the code. Some extra time spent thinking about and using descriptive identifiers provides great timesavings during the testing and maintenance phases. Code that is written using descriptive identifiers is referred to as *self-documenting code.*

EXERCISES 3.2

1. Assume the variable declaration section of a program is

```
int age, IQ;
float income;
```

Indicate which of the following are valid assignment statements. If a statement is invalid, give the reason why.

```
a. age = 21;
b. IQ = age + 100;
c. IQ = 120.5;
d. age + IQ = 150;
e. income = 22000;
f. income = 100 * (age + IQ);
g. age = IQ / 3;
h. IQ = 3 * age;
```

2. Write and run a test program to illustrate what happens when values of one data type are assigned to variables of another type.

3. Suppose **a**, **b**, and **temp** have been declared as integer variables. Indicate the contents of **a** and **b** at the end of each sequence of statements.

```
a. a = 5;          b. a = 31;
   b = -2;            b = 26;
   a = a + b;         temp = a;
   b = b - a;         a = b;
                      b = temp;
```

```
c. a = 0;                          d. a = -8;
   b = 7;                             b = 3;
   a = a + b % 2 * (-3);              temp = a + b;
   b = b + 4 * a;                     a = 3 * b;
                                      b = a;
                                      temp = temp + a + b;
```

4. Suppose **x** and **y** are real variables and the assignments

```
x = 121.3;
y = 98.6;
```

have been made. What output statements would cause the following output?

a. The value of x is   121.3
b. The sum of x and y is   219.9
c. x =   121.3
**   y =   98.6**
**   -------**
**   Total =   219.9**

5. Assume the variable declaration section of a program is

```
int age, height;
float weight;
char gender;
```

What output would be created by the following program fragment?

```
age = 23;
height = 73;
weight = 186.5;
gender = 'M';
cout << setprecision(1);
cout << "Gender" << setw(10) << gender << endl;
cout << "Age" << setw(14) << age << endl;
cout << "Height" << setw(11) << height << " inches" << endl;
cout << "Weight" << setw(14) << weight << " lbs" << endl;
```

6. Write a complete program that allows you to add five integers and then print
   a. The integers.
   b. Their sum.
   c. Their average.

7. Assume **ch** and **age** have been appropriately declared. What output is produced by the following?

```
ch = 'M';
age = 21;
cout  << setw(40) <<   "*****************************" << endl;
cout << setw(11) << "*" << setw(29) << "*" << endl;
cout << setw(11) << "*"<< setw(7) << "Name" << setw(9) << "Age";
cout << setw(6) << "Gender" << setw(4) << "*" << endl;
cout << setw(11) << "*" setw(7) << "____" << setw(9) << "___" << setw(9)
     << "___" << setw(4) << "*" << endl;
cout << endl;
cout << setw(11) << "*" << setw(8) << "Jones" << setw(8) << age << setw(9) << ch
     << setw(4) << "*" << endl;
```

```
cout << endl;
cout << setw(11) << "*" << setw(29) << "*" << endl;
cout << setw(40)   << "*****************************"   <<   endl;
```

8. Assume the variable declaration section of a program is

```
int weight1, weight2;
float average_weight;
```

and the following assignment statements have been made:

```
weight1 = 165;
weight2 = 174;
average_weight = (weight1 + weight2) / 2;
```

a. What output would be produced by the following section of code?

```
cout << "Weight" << endl;
cout << "_____" endl;
cout << endl;
cout << weight1 << endl;
cout << weight2 << endl;
cout << endl;
cout << "The average weight is" << (weight1 + weight2) / 2 << endl;
```

b. Write a segment of code to produce the following output (use **average_weight**).

```
             weight
             ------
              165
              174
              ---
Total         339
```
The average weight is 169.5 pounds.

9. Assume the variable declaration section of a program is **char letter;** and the following assignment has been made: **letter = 'A';** . What output is produced from the following segment of code?

```
cout << setw(40) << "This reviews string formatting" << endl;
cout << "When a letter" << letter << "is used" << endl;
cout << setw(14) << "Oops!" << setw(20) << "I forgot to format." << endl;
cout << setw(22) << "When a letter" << setw(2) << letter << setw(9) << "is used"
     << endl;
cout << setw(38) << "it is a string of length one." << endl;
```

3.3 ▸ Input

- to be able to use the standard input stream and its operator to get data for a program
- to be able to design a program that supports interactive input of data

Earlier, "running a program" was subdivided into the three general categories of getting the data, manipulating it appropriately, and printing the results. Our work thus far has centered on creating output and manipulating data. We are now going to focus on how to get data for a program.

Input Statements

Data for a program are usually obtained from an input device, which can be a keyboard or disk. When such data are obtained from the keyboard, the standard input stream, **cin**, normally is associated with one of these input devices.

The standard input stream, **cin**, is used in a similar way to the standard output stream, **cout**. **cin** behaves like an intelligent agent that knows how to take input from the keyboard and pass it back to a program. To make **cin** available to a program, you must include the C++ library file **iostream.h**:

```
#include <iostream.h>
```

To obtain input from the standard input stream, you direct it into a variable with the operator >> (note that the arrows point in the opposite direction from the output operator, <<). For example, assume that **length** is a variable of type **int**. Then the following statement takes input from the keyboard and stores it in **length**:

```
cin >> length;
```

When an input statement is used to get data, the value of the data item is stored in the indicated memory location. Data read into a program must match the type of variable specified. To illustrate, if a variable declaration section includes

```
int age;
float wage;
```

and the data items are

```
21          5.25
```

then

```
cin >> age >> wage;
```

results in

```
  21          5.25
 age          wage
```

Interactive Input

Interactive input refers to entering values from the keyboard while the program is running. An input statement causes the program to halt and wait for data items to be typed. For example, if you want to enter three scores at some point in a program, you can use

```
cin >> score1 >> score2 >> score3;
```

as program statements. At this point, you must enter at least three integers, separated by at least one blank space, and press <Enter>. The remaining part of the program is then executed. To illustrate, the following program reads in three integers and prints the integers and their average as output.

```
// Program file: input.cpp
// This program illustrates the use of input statements.

#include <iostream.h>
#include <iomanip.h>

const char SKIP = ' ';

int main ()
{
```

```
int score1, score2, score3;
float average;

cin >> score1 >> score2 >> score3;
average = float(score1 + score2 + score3) / 3;
cout << endl;
cout << setw(10) << SKIP << "The numbers are" << setw(4)
     << score1 << setw(4) << score2 << setw(4) << score3
     << endl;
cout << endl;
cout << setprecision(2);
cout << setw(10) << SKIP << "Their average is" << setw(8)
     << average << endl;
return 0;

}
```

When the program runs, if you type in

89 90 91

and press <Enter>, output is

The numbers are 89 90 91

Their average is   90.00

Interactive programs should have a prompting message to the user so the user knows what to do when the program pauses for input. For example, the problem in the previous example can be modified by the line

```
cout >> "Please enter 3 scores separated by spaces, ";
cout >> "and then press <Enter>. ";
```

before the line

```
cin >> score1 >> score2 >> score3;
```

The screen will display the message

Please enter 3 scores separated by spaces and then press <Enter>.

when the program is run. Another method for getting the three inputs mentioned above is to prompt the user for each one on a separate line. Clearly stated screen messages to the person running a program are what make a program *user-friendly*.

EXAMPLE 3.2

Pythagorean triples are sets of three integers that satisfy the Pythagorean theorem. That is, integers *a, b,* and *c* such that $a^2 + b^2 = c^2$. The integers 3, 4, and 5 make up such a triple because $3^2 + 4^2 = 5^2$. Formulas for generating Pythagorean triples are $a = m^2 - n^2$, $b = 2mn$, and $c = m^2 + n^2$ where *m* and *n* are positive integers such that $m > n$. The following interactive program allows the user to enter values for *m* and *n* and then have the Pythagorean triple printed:

```
// Program file: triples.cpp
// This program illustrates Pythagorean triples.
```

```cpp
#include <iostream.h>
#include <iomanip.h>

int main ()
{

    int m, n, a, b, c;

    cout << "Enter a positive integer and press <Enter>. ";
    cin >> n;
    cout << "Enter a positive integer greater than " << n << endl;
    cout << "and press <Enter>. ";
    cin >> m;
    a = (m * m) - (n * n);
    b = 2 * m * n;
    c = (m * m) + (n * n);
    cout << endl;
    cout << "For m = " << m << " and n = " << n << endl;
    cout << "the Pythagorean triple is ";
    cout << setw(5) << a << setw(5) << b << setw(5) << c << endl;
    return 0;

}
```

Sample runs of this program (using data 1,2 and 2,5) produce the following:

```
Enter a positive integer and press <Enter>. 1
Enter a positive integer greater than 1 and press <Enter>. 2

For M = 2 and N = 1 the Pythagorean triple is 3 4 5

Enter a positive integer and press <Enter>. 2
Enter a positive integer greater than 2 and press <Enter>. 5

For M = 5 and N = 2 the Pythagorean triple is 21 20 29
```

Reading Numeric Data

Reading numeric data into a program is reasonably straightforward. At least one character of whitespace must be used to separate numbers. Whitespace characters are typed by hitting the space bar, the Tab key, or the Enter key.

Character Sets

Before we look at reading character data, we need to examine the way in which character data are stored. In the **char** data type, each character is associated with an integer. Thus, the sequence of characters is associated with a sequence of integers. The particular sequence used by a machine for this purpose is referred to as the *collating sequence* for that *character set*. The principal sequence currently in use is the American Standard Code for Information Interchange (ASCII).

Each collating sequence contains an ordering of the characters in a character set and is listed in Appendix 4. For programs in this text, we use the ASCII code. As shown in Table 3.8, 52 of these characters are letters, 10 are digits, and the rest are special characters.

◇ TABLE 3.8
ASCII ordering of a
character set

Ordinal	Character	Ordinal	Character	Ordinal	Character
32	ƀ	64	@	96	'
33	!	65	A	97	a
34	"	66	B	98	b
35	#	67	C	99	c
36	$	68	D	100	d
37	%	69	E	101	e
38	&	70	F	102	f
39	'	71	G	103	g
40	(	72	H	104	h
41	)	73	I	105	i
42	*	74	J	106	j
43	+	75	K	107	k
44	,	76	L	108	l
45	–	77	M	109	m
46	.	78	N	110	n
47	/	79	O	111	o
48	0	80	P	112	p
49	1	81	Q	113	q
50	2	82	R	114	r
51	3	83	S	115	s
52	4	84	T	116	t
53	5	85	U	117	u
54	6	86	V	118	v
55	7	87	W	119	w
56	8	88	X	120	x
57	9	89	Y	121	y
58	:	90	Z	122	z
59	;	91	[	123	{
60	<	92	\	124		
61	=	93	]	125	}
62	>	94	^	126	~
63	?	95	—		

Note: Codes 00–31 and 127 are nonprintable control characters.

Reading Character Data

Reading characters from the standard input stream using >> is much the same as reading numeric data. If you want to read in a student's initials followed by three test scores, the following code will do that:

```
char first_initial, middle_initial, last_initial;
int score1, score2, score3;

cin >> first_initial >> middle_initial >> last_initial >> score1
    >> score2 >> score3;
```

When program execution is halted, you would type in something like

```
J D K 89 90 91
```

and press <Enter>.

Debugging Output Statements

A frequently used technique for debugging programs is to insert an output statement to print the values of variables. Once you have determined that the desired values are obtained, you can delete the output statements. For example, if your program segment is to read in three scores and three initials, you could write

```
cin >> score1 >> score2 >> score3;
cout << score1 << " " << score2 << " " << score3;
// for debugging
cin >> first_initial >> middle_initial >> last_initial;
cout << first_initial << " " << middle_initial << " " last_initial;
// for debugging
```

These debugging lines might be left in until the program has been sufficiently tested for input.

EXERCISES 3.3

1. Discuss the difference between **cin** and **cout**.
2. Assume a variable declaration section is

```
int num1, num2;

float num3;

char ch;
```

and you wish to enter the data

```
15   65.3   -20
```

Explain what results from each statement. Also indicate what values are assigned to appropriate variables.

a. `cin >> num1 >> num3 >> num2;`

b. `cin >> num1 >> num2 >> num3;`

c. `cin >> num1 >> num2 >> ch >> num3;`

d. `cin >> num2 >> num3 >> ch >> num2;`

e. `cin >> num2 >> num3 >> ch >> ch >> num2;`

f. `cin >> num3 >> num2;`

g. `cin >> num1 >> num3;`

h. `cin >> num1 >> ch >> num3;`

3. Write a program statement to be used to print a message to the screen directing the user to enter data in the form used for Exercise 2. Write an appropriate program statement (or statements) to produce a screen message and write an appropriate input statement for each of the following.
   a. Desired input is number of hours worked and hourly pay rate.
   b. Desired input is three positive integers followed by –999.
   c. Desired input is price of an automobile and the state sales tax rate.
   d. Desired input is the game statistics for one basketball player (check with a coach to see what must be entered).
   e. Desired input is a student's initials, age, height, weight, and gender.

4. Assume variables are declared as in Exercise 2. If an input statement is

```
cin >> num1 >> num2 >> ch >> num3;
```

   indicate which lines of the following data do not result in an error message. For those that do not, indicate the values of the variables. For those that produce an error, explain what the error is.
   a. `83 95 100`
   b. `83 95.0 100`
   c. `83-72 93.5`
   d. `83-72 93.5`
   e. `83.5`
   f. `70 73-80.5`
   g. `91 92 93 94`
   h. `-76-81-16.5`

5. Why is it a good idea to print values of variables that have been read into a program?

6. Write a complete program that will read your initials and five test scores. Your program should then compute your test average and print all information in a reasonable form with suitable messages.

3.4 Using Constants

The word *constant* has several interpretations. In this section, we distinguish between a symbolic constant, like PI, and a literal constant, like 3.14. Symbolic constants are defined by giving them the values of literal constants. Recall that a C++ program consists of preprocessor directives, an optional constant and type definition section, a program heading, an optional variable declaration section, and an executable section. We will now examine uses for constants defined in the constant subsection.

Rationale for Uses

There are many reasons to use constants in a program. If a number is to be used frequently, the programmer may wish to give it a descriptive name in the constant definition subsection and then use the descriptive name in the executable section, thus making the program easier to read. For example, if a program included a segment that computed a person's state income tax, and the state tax rate was 6.25% of taxable income, the constant section might include:

```
const float STATE_TAX_RATE = 0.0625;
```

This defines both the value and type for **STATE_TAX_RATE**. In the executable portion of the program, the statement

```
state_tax = income * STATE_TAX_RATE;
```

computes the state tax owed. Or suppose you wanted a program to compute areas of circles. Depending on the accuracy you desire, you could define π as

```
const float PI = 3.14159;
```

You could then have a statement in the executable section such as

```
area = PI * radius * radius;
```

where **area** and **radius** are appropriately declared variables.

Perhaps the most important use of constants is for values that are currently fixed but subject to change for subsequent updates of the program. If these are defined in the constant section, they can be used throughout the program. If the value changes later, only one change need be made to keep the program current. This prevents the need to locate all uses of a constant in a program. Some examples might be

```
const float MINIMUM_WAGE = 4.25;
const int SPEED_LIMIT = 65;
const float PRICE = 0.75;
const float STATE_TAX_RATE = 0.0625;
```

Software Engineering

The appropriate use of constants is consistent with principles of software engineering. Communication between teams of programmers is enhanced when program constants have been agreed on. Each team should have a list of these constants for use as they work on their part of the system.

The maintenance phase of the software system life cycle is also aided by use of defined constants. Clearly, a large payroll system is dependent on being able to perform computations that include deductions for federal tax, state tax, FICA, Medicare, health insurance, retirement options, and so on. If appropriate constants are defined for these deductions, system changes are easily made as necessary. For example, the current salary limit for deducting FICA taxes is $53,400. Since this amount changes regularly, one could define

```
const float FICA_LIMIT = 53400.00;
```

Program maintenance is then simplified by changing the value of this constant as the law changes.

Library Constants

Some constants are provided in C++ libraries. For example, it is often necessary to determine the range of integer values allowed by a particular computer system, or

A NOTE OF INTEREST

Defined Constants and Space Shuttle Computing

An excellent illustration of the utilization of defined constants in a program was given by J. F. ("Jack") Clemons, former manager of avionics flight software development and verification for the space shuttle on-board computers. In an interview with David Gifford, editor for *Communications of the ACM*, Clemons was asked: "Have you tried to restructure the software so that it can be changed easily?"

His response was, "By changing certain data constants, we can change relatively large portions of the software on a mission-to-mission basis. For example, we've designed the software so that characteristics like atmospheric conditions on launch day or different lift-off weights can be loaded as initial constants into the code. This is important when there are postponements or last-minute payload changes that invalidate the original inputs."

◇ **TABLE 3.9**
Library constants for maximum numeric values

Library Constant	Meaning
`INT_MAX`	The maximum allowable positive integer value
`INT_MIN`	The maximum allowable negative integer value
`FLT_MAX`	The maximum allowable positive float value
`FLT_MIN`	The maximum allowable negative float value
`FLT_DIG`	The maximum number of digits of precision

the range of real number values, or the number of digits of precision supported by the system. The C++ library files **limits.h** and **float.h** define constants for each of these important values for your particular system. When you include these files at the beginning of your source program, each of the constants appearing in Table 3.9 will be available for use.

Formatting Constants

Formatting symbolic constants is identical to formatting real and integer values as discussed in Section 2.3.

◆ **3.5 Library Functions**

OBJECTIVES

- to understand the reasons for having library functions
- to be able to use library functions in a program
- to be able to use appropriate data types for the arguments of library functions

Some standard operations required by programmers are squaring numbers and finding square roots of numbers. Because these operations are so basic, C++ provides *library functions* for them. Different versions of C++ and other programming languages have differing library functions available, so you should always check which functions can be used. Appendix 2 sets forth many of those available in most versions of C++.

A function can be used in a program if it appears in the following form:

```
<function name>(<argument list>)
```

where the *argument* is a value or variable with an assigned value. When a function appears in this manner, it is said to be *called* or *invoked*. A function is invoked by using it in a program statement. After the function performs its work, it may *return a value*. If, for example, you want to raise 3 to the fourth power, you include the **math.h** library and then

```
cout << pow(3, 4) << endl;
```

produces the desired result and returns it as a value to the caller.

Many functions operate on numbers, starting with a given number and returning some associated value. Table 3.10 shows five math library functions, each with its argument type, data type of return, and an explanation of the value returned. A more complete list of library functions can be found in Appendix 2.

Several examples of specific function expressions together with the value returned by each expression are depicted in Table 3.11.

◇ TABLE 3.10
Some math library functions

Function Declaration	Action of Function
`double fmod(double x, double y);`	Returns floating-point remainder of **x** / **y**
`double log(double x);`	Returns natural logarithm of **x**
`double pow(double x, double y);`	Returns **x** raised to power of **y**
`double sqrt(double x);`	Returns square root of **x**
`double cos(double x);`	Returns cosine of **x**

◇ TABLE 3.11
Values of function expressions

Expression	Value
`pow(2, 4)`	16
`pow(2.0, 4)`	16.0
`pow(-3, 2)`	9
`sqrt(25.0)`	5.0
`sqrt(25)`	5
`sqrt(0.0)`	0.0
`sqrt(-2.0)`	Not permissible

Using Functions

When a function is invoked, it produces a value in much the same way that 3 + 3 produces 6. Thus, use of a function should be treated similarly to use of constants or values of an expression. Typical uses are in assignment statements,

```
x = sqrt(16.0);
```

output statements,

```
cout << setw(20) << pow(2, 5);
```

or arithmetic expressions

```
hypotenuse = sqrt(pow(base, 2) + pow(height, 2));
```

Arguments of functions can be expressions, variables, or constants.

3.6 Type Compatibility and Type Conversion

We mentioned in Section 3.2 that the operands of arithmetic expressions and assignment statements must be of compatible data types. For example, we saw that we could not only add an integer to an integer, but also add an integer to a real number. In the latter case, the run-time system performs an *implicit type conversion* of the integer operand before performing the addition, and then returns a real number as the sum. This kind of type conversion is also referred to as *type promotion,* in that the value of a less inclusive type, **int**, is elevated to a value of a more inclusive type, **float**.

Implicit type conversion also occurs when an integer value is assigned to a variable of type **float**. In this case, a copy of the integer value is placed in the real number's storage location, and then promoted by adding to it a fractional part of zero. For example, assuming that **real_number** is of type **float**, the following two lines of code would produce an output of 3.00:

```
real_number = 3;
cout << fixed << setprecision(2) << showpoint
    << real_number << endl;
```

Conversely, when you assign a real number to a variable of type **int**, the system drops or truncates a copy of the real number's value before placing it in the integer's storage location. Thus, the following two lines of code would display the value 5, assuming that **whole_number** is an **int**:

```
whole_number = 5.76;
cout << whole_number << endl;
```

The Character Set Once Again

It turns out that characters and integers are also compatible types in C++. This means that character values can be assigned to integer variables, integer values can be assigned to character variables, and integers can be added to characters. Moreover, each of these operations involves an implicit type conversion. To make sense of this apparently strange phenomenon, we must consider the character set once more.

Ordering a character set requires association of an integer with each character. Data types ordered in some association with the integers are known as *ordinal data types.* Each integer is the ordinal of its associated value. Character sets are considered to be an ordinal data type, as shown in Table 3.8. In each case, the ordinal of the character appears to the left of the character. Using ASCII, as shown in Table 3.8, the ordinal of a capital a (A) is 65, the ordinal of the character representing the Arabic number one (1) is 49, the ordinal of a blank (b) is 32, and the ordinal of a lowercase a (a) is 97.

Once we realize that characters are really represented as integers in a computer, we can begin to see how we can perform mixed-mode operations on these two data types. When a character value is assigned to an integer variable, the run-time system copies the character's ordinal into the integer's storage location. Thus, assuming an ASCII representation and our **whole_number** variable of type **int**, the following two lines of code would display the number 65:

```
whole_number = 'A';
cout << whole_number << endl;
```

Conversely, assuming that letter is of type **char**, the following two lines of code would display the letter A:

```
letter = 65;
cout << letter << endl;
```

When arithmetic operations are performed on characters (either two character values or one character and one integer), each character value is first promoted to a more inclusive type, namely, an integer. Then the system performs the operation, and the result returned is an integer. For example, the following two lines of code would display the value 66:

```
whole_number = 'A' + 1;
cout << whole_number << endl;
```

It turns out that since the decimal digits are in the collating sequence from 0 to 9 in the character set, the integer value of a given digit can be computed quite easily with *character arithmetic*. For example, assuming that **digit** is of type **int**, the following two lines of code compute and display the integer value of the digit 5:

```
digit = '5' - '0';
cout << digit << endl;
```

In the next example, we show how to use character arithmetic to convert an uppercase letter to lowercase.

EXAMPLE 3.3

To show how character arithmetic can be used to convert an uppercase letter to lowercase, let us assume that our task is to convert the letter **'H'** into the letter **'h'**. We first subtract **'A'** from **'H'** to obtain

```
'H' - 'A'
```

which is

```
72 - 65 = 7
```

We now add **'a'** to get

```
'H' - 'A' + 'a'
```

which yields

```
72 - 65 + 97 = 104
```

This is the ordinal of **'h'**. It can be converted to the letter by assigning it to a variable of type **char**. Thus,

```
letter = 'H' - 'A' + 'a';
```

places the letter **'h'** in the variable **letter**, where **letter** is of type **char**.

In general, the following is sufficient for converting from uppercase to lowercase, where the two names are of type **char**:

```
lower_case = upper_case - 'A' + 'a';
```

Note that if you always use the same ASCII ordering,

```
-'A' + 'a'
```

could be replaced by the constant 32. If you choose to do this, 32 should be given a name. A typical definition is

```
const int UPPER_TO_LOWER_SHIFT = 32;
```

You would then write the lowercase conversion as

```
lower_case = upper_case + UPPER_TO_LOWER_SHIFT;
```

Type Casts

Occasionally, we would like to force the conversion of a value from one type to another without resorting to an assignment statement. For example, the expression **whole_number % real_number** will generate an error, because the modulus operator is not defined on real numbers. We would like to convert the real number to an integer within the expression, rather than complicate matters by declaring an extra integer variable, assigning the real number to it, and then using the integer variable.

C++ provides a set of operators called *type casts* for performing *explicit type conversions* of this sort. You can think of a type cast as a function, whose name is the name of the type to which you wish to convert a value. The argument of this function is the value to be converted, and the value returned by the function is the converted value. For example, the following line of code uses the type cast for integers to display the integer value 3:

```
cout << int(3.14) << endl;
```

Our method of converting an uppercase letter to lowercase can make good use of the type cast for characters:

```
cout << char(upper_case - UPPER_TO_LOWER_SHIFT) << endl;
```

The form of a type cast that we will use in this text is

```
<type name> ( <expression> )
```

where **<type>** is the name of the target type and **<expression>** evaluates to a type of value that the cast is capable of converting. This form may not be recognized by some C++ compilers. In those cases, a more standard, but less readable form to use is

```
(<type name>) <expression>
```

EXERCISES 3.6

1. Find the value of each of the following expressions.
   a. **sqrt(15.51)**
   b. **pow(-14.2, 3)**
   c. **4 * 11 % sqrt(16)**
   d. **pow(17 / 5 * 2, 2)**
   e. **-5.0 + sqrt(5 * 5 - 4 * 6) / 2.0**

2. Write a test program that illustrates what happens when an inappropriate argument is used with a function. Be sure to include something like **sqrt(-1)**.

3. Two standard algebraic problems come from the Pythagorean theorem and the quadratic formula. Assume variables *a*, *b*, and *c* have been declared in a program. Write C++ expressions that allow you to evaluate the following.

   a. The length of the hypotenuse of a right triangle: $\sqrt{a^2+b^2}$
   b. both solutions to the quadratic formula:

   $$\frac{-b \pm \sqrt{b^2-4ac}}{2a}$$

4. Indicate whether the following are valid or invalid expressions. Find the value of those that are valid; explain why the others are invalid.

  a. `-6 % (sqrt(16))`
  b. `8 / sqrt(65)`
  c. `sqrt(63 % (2))`
  d. `-sqrt(pow(3, 2) - 7)`
  e. `sqrt(16 / (-3))`
  f. `sqrt(pow(-4, 2))`

5. Using ASCII, find the values of each of the following expressions.

  a. `13 + 4 % 3`
  b. `'E'`
  c. `'E' + 1`
  d. `5`
  e. `'5'`
  f. `'+'`
  g. `40`

6. Assume the variable declaration section of a program is

  `float x; int a; char ch;`

  What output is produced by each of the following program fragments?

  a. `x = -4.3;`
    `cout << setprecision(2) << setw(6) << x << int(x)`
        `<< endl;`
  b. `x = -4.3;`
    `a = x;`
    `cout << a << int('a');`
  c. `ch = char(76);`
    `cout << setw(5) << ch << setw(5) << char(ch - 1);`

7. Write a complete program to print each uppercase letter of the alphabet and its ordinal in the collating sequence used by your machine's version of C++.

8. Using ASCII, show how each of the following conversions can be made.

  a. A lowercase letter converted into its uppercase equivalent.
  b. A digit entered as a **char** value into its indicated numeric value.

Writing styles and suggestions are gathered for quick reference in the following style tip summary. These tips are intended to stimulate rather than terminate your imagination.

COMMUNICATION AND STYLE TIPS

1. Use descriptive identifiers. Words—sum, score, average—are easier to understand than letters—a, b, c or x, y, z.
2. Use the constant definition section to define an appropriately named blank and use it to control line spacing for output. Thus, you could have

```
const char SKIP = ' ';
const char INDENT = ' ';
```

and then output statements could be

```
cout << setw(20) << SKIP << message
     << setw(10) << SKIP << message;
```

or

```
cout << setw(20) << INDENT << message
     << setw(10) << SKIP << message;
```

3. Output of a column of reals should have decimal points in a line.

```
  14.32
 181.50
  93.63
```

4. Output can be made more attractive by using columns, left and right margins, underlining, and blank lines.
5. Extra output statements at the beginning and end of the executable section will separate desired output from other messages.

```
cout << endl;
      .
      .
      .
```

(program body here)

```
cout << endl;
```

FOCUS ON PROGRAM DESIGN

Complete programs are used to illustrate concepts developed throughout the text. In each case, a typical problem is stated. A solution is developed in pseudocode and illustrated with a structure chart. Module specifications are written for appropriate modules. Now, on to the problem for this chapter.

Write a complete program to find the unit price for a pizza. Input for the program consists of the price and size of the pizza. Size is the diameter of the pizza ordered. Output consists of the price per square inch. A first-level development is

1. Get the data
2. Perform the computations
3. Print the results

A structure chart for this problem is given in Figure 3.1. Module specifications for the main modules are

Module: Get data
Task: Gets cost and size of pizza from the user at the keyboard.
Outputs: cost and size

◆ FIGURE 3.1
Structure chart for the pizza
problem

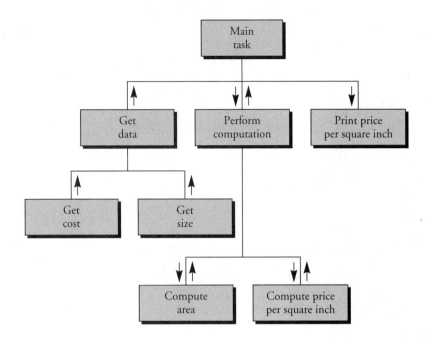

Module: Compute price per square inch
Task: Compute the price per square inch of pizza.
Input: cost and size of pizza
Output: price per square inch

Module: Print results
Task: Print the price per square inch.
Input: price per square inch

A further refinement of the pseudocode produces

1. Get the data
   1.1 get price
   1.2 get size
2. Perform the computations
   2.1 compute area
   2.2 calculate unit price

Step 3 of the pseudocode, "Print the results," only requires printing the price per square inch, so no further development is required. A complete program for this follows:

```
// Program file: pizza.cpp

#include <iostream.h>
#include <iomanip.h>
#include <math.h>

const float PI = 3.14;

int main ()
{

        float size, radius, cost, area, price_per_square_inch;

        // This module gets the data.
```

```
cout << "Enter the pizza price and press <Enter>. ";
cin >> cost;                                                    } 1
cout << "Enter the pizza size and press <Enter>. ";
cin >> size;

// This module computes the unit price.

radius = size / 2;
area = PI * pow(radius, 2);                                     } 2
price_per_square_inch = cost / area;

// This module prints the results.

cout << setprecision(2) << endl;
cout << "The price per square inch is $" << setw(4)
     << price_per_square_inch << endl;                          } 3
return 0;
}
```

A sample run of this program yields

```
Enter the pizza price and press <Enter>. 10.50
Enter the pizza size and press <Enter>. 16
The price per square inch is $0.05
```

SUMMARY

Key Terms

argument
assignment statement
batch input
binary arithmetic
binary notation
cancellation error
character set
collating sequence
constant
input

integer arithmetic operations:
  +, –, *, /, %
integer overflow
interactive input
invoke (call)
library (built-in) constant
library (built-in) function
memory location
mixed-mode expression
ordinal data type
overflow

prompt
real arithmetic operations:
  +, –, *, /
real overflow
representational error
self-documenting code
underflow
user-friendly
variable
word

Key Concepts

◆ Operations and priorities for data of type **int** and **float** are summarized as follows:

Data Type	Operations	Priority
int	***, %, /**	1. Evaluate in order from left to right.
	+, –	2. Evaluate in order from left to right.
float	***, /**	1. Evaluate in order from left to right.
	+, –	2. Evaluate in order from left to right.

◆ Mixed-mode expressions involving **int** and **float** values return values of type **float**.

- Priority for order of operations on mixed-mode expressions is
  1. *, /: in order from left to right.
  2. +, –: in order from left to right.
- Overflow is caused by a value too large for computing on a particular machine.
- Underflow is caused by a value too small (close to zero) for computing. These numbers are automatically replaced by zero.
- A memory location can have a name that can be used to refer to the contents of the location.
- The name of a memory location is different from the contents of the memory location.
- Self-documenting code is code that is written using descriptive identifiers.
- Assignment statements are used to assign values to memory locations, for example

  sum = 30 + 60;

- Variables and variable expressions can be used in output statements.
- **cin** is used to get data; the correct form is

  cin >> variable1 >> variable 2 . . . >> variable *n;*

- **cin >> <variable>;** causes a value to be transferred to the variable location.
- Interactive input expects data items to be entered from the keyboard at appropriate times during execution of the program.
- Data types for variables in an input statement should match data items read as input.
- Appropriate uses for constants in the declaration section include frequently used numbers; current values subject to change over time, for example, **(MINIMUM_WAGE = 4.25)**.
- Five math library functions available in C++ are **pow**, **sqrt**, **sin**, **cos**, and **tan**.
- Functions can be used in assignment statements, for example,

  x = sqrt(16.0);

  in output statements

  cout << pow(-8, 2);

  and in arithmetic expressions

  x = sqrt(3.78) + pow(5, 5);

- Type casts can be used to convert one type of value to another type, for example **int(3.14)**.

PROGRAMMING PROBLEMS AND PROJECTS

Write a complete C++ program for each of the following problems. Each program should use one or more input statements to obtain the necessary values. Each input statement should be preceded by an appropriate prompting message.

1. Susan purchases a computer for $985. The sales tax on the purchase is 5.5%. Compute and print the total purchase price.

2. Find and print the area and perimeter of a rectangle that is 4.5 feet long and 2.3 feet wide. Print both rounded to the nearest tenth of a foot.

3. Compute and print the number of minutes in a year.

4. Light travels as $3 * 10^8$ meters per second. Compute and print the distance a light beam would travel in one year. (This is called a light year.)

5. The 1927 New York Yankees won 110 games and lost 44. Compute their winning percentage and print it rounded to three decimal places.

6. A 10-kilogram object is traveling at 12 meters per second. Compute and print its momentum (momentum is mass times velocity).

7. Convert 98.0 degrees Fahrenheit to degrees Celsius.

8. Given a positive number, print its square and square root.

9. The Golden Sales Company pays its salespeople $0.27 for each item they sell. Given the number of items sold by a salesperson, print the amount of pay due.

10. Given the length and width of a rectangle, print its area and perimeter.

11. The kinetic energy of a moving object is given by the formula $KE=(1/2)mv^2$. Given the mass *(m)* and the speed *(v)* of an object, find its kinetic energy.

12. Dr. Lisa Thompson wants a program to enable her to balance her checkbook. She wishes to enter a beginning balance, five letters for an abbreviation for the recipient of the check, and the amount of the check. Given this information, write a program that will find the new balance in her checkbook.

13. A supermarket wants to install a computerized weighing system in its produce department. Input to this system will consist of a single-letter identifier for the type of produce, the weight of the produce purchase (in pounds), and the cost per pound of the produce. A typical input screen would be

Enter each of the following:

```
Description <Enter> A
Weight <Enter> 2.0
Price/lb. <Enter> 1.98
```

Print a label showing the input information along with the total cost of the purchase. The label should appear as follows:

```
%%%%%%%%%%%%%%%%%%%%%%%%%%%%%%%%%%%%%%%%%%%%

              Penny Spender Supermarket
                  Produce Department

     ITEM         WEIGHT        COST/lb        COST

     A            2.0 lb        $1.98         $3.96

                      Thank you!

%%%%%%%%%%%%%%%%%%%%%%%%%%%%%%%%%%%%%%%%%%%%
```

14. The New Wave Computer Company sells its product, the NW-PC, for $675. In addition, they sell memory expansion cards for $69.95, disk drives for $198.50, and software for $34.98 each. Given the number of memory cards, disk drives, and software packages desired by a customer purchasing an NW-PC, print out a bill of sale that appears as follows:

```
***************************
      New Wave Computers

           ITEM              COST
  1 NW-PC                   $675.00
  2 Memory card              139.90
  1 Disk drive               198.50
  4 Software                 139.92


           TOTAL       $1153.32
```

15. Write a test program that allows you to see the characters contained within the character set of your computer. Given a positive integer, you can use the **char** type cast to determine the corresponding character. On most computers, only integers less than 256 are valid for this. Also, remember that most character sets contain some unprintable characters such as ASCII values less than 32. Print your output in the form:

Character number nnn is x.

16. Mr. Vigneault, a coach at Shepherd High School, is working on a program that can be used to assist cross-country runners in analyzing their times. As part of the program, a coach enters elapsed times for each runner given in units of minutes, seconds, and hundredths. In a 5000-meter (5K) race, elapsed times are entered at the one-mile and two-mile marks. These elapsed times are then used to compute "splits" for each part of the race; that is, how long did it take a runner to run each of the three race segments. Write a complete program that will accept as input three times given in units of minutes, seconds, and hundredths and then produce output that includes the split for each segment. Typical input would be

Runner number		**234**
Mile times:	**1**	**5:34.22**
	2	**11:21.67**
Finish time:		**17:46.85**

Typical output would be

Runner number	**234**
Split one	**5:34.22**
Split two	**5:47.45**
Split three	**6:25.18**
Finish time	**17:46.85**

17. Many (but not all) instructors in beginning computer science courses encourage their students to use meaningful identifiers in writing code. It is natural to wonder to what extent this practice is followed outside the educational world. Investigate this issue by contacting several programmers who work for nearby companies. Prepare a complete written report of your conversations for distribution to class members. Include charts that summarize your findings.

4 Subprograms: Functions for Problem Solving

Recall from Section 2.3 the process of solving a problem by stepwise refinement of tasks into subtasks. This top-down design method is especially suitable for writing C++ programs to solve problems using *subprograms.*

The concept of a subprogram is not difficult to understand. It is a program within a program and is provided by most programming languages. Each subprogram should complete some task, the nature of which can range from simple to complex. You could have a subprogram that prints only a line of data, or you could rewrite an entire program as a subprogram. To extend the metaphor of the programmable pocket calculator introduced in Chapter 3, we create a subprogram by giving a name to a sequence of program statements. We then specify the data that this sequence will take as inputs and return as outputs. Next, we store this name with the built-in functions in the calculator. Finally, we use the name as if it were a built-in function wherever it is appropriate in any program.

4.1 Program Design

OBJECTIVES

- to understand the concepts of modularity and bottom-up testing
- to be aware of the use of structured programming

Modularity

We have previously discussed and illustrated the process of solving a problem by top-down design. Using this method, we divide the main task into major subtasks, and then continue to divide the subtasks (stepwise refinement) into smaller subtasks until all subtasks can be easily performed. Once an algorithm for solving a problem has been developed using top-down design, the programmer then writes code to translate the general solution into a C++ program.

As you have seen, code written to perform one well-defined subtask can be referred to as a *module.* One should be able to design, code, and test each module in a program independently from the rest of the program. In this sense, a module is a subprogram containing all definitions and declarations needed to perform the indicated subtask. Everything required for the subtask (but not needed in other parts of the program) can be created in the subprogram. Consequently, the definitions and declarations have meaning only when the module is being used.

At the lowest level in a programming language like C++, a module is a single function. However, one can also think, at a higher level in a design, of a module as consisting of several functions and related data. One important kind of higher level module of this sort is known as an *abstract data type*. The design and construction of abstract data type modules are discussed in some detail in Chapters 7 through 11. You have already been using some standard abstract data type modules whenever you have used the operations on integers, real numbers, and characters in your C++ programs.

A program that has been created using modules to perform various tasks is said to possess *modularity*. In general, modular programs are easier to test, debug, and correct than programs that are not modular because each independent module can be tested by running it from a test driver. Then, once the modules are running correctly, they can become part of a longer program. This independent testing of modules is referred to as *bottom-up testing*. A modular program is also easier to maintain than a nonmodular program, because we can replace one module without modifying the other modules at all. For example, a new version of the C++ compiler might provide faster operations for floating-point arithmetic in the module that defines these operations. All you would have to do to maintain your system is to recompile your program.

Structured Programming and Design

Structured programming is the process of developing a program where emphasis is placed on the flow of control between independent modules. *Structured design* is the process of organizing communication between modules. Connections between these modules are specified in parameter lists and are usually controlled by the main program. Structured programming and design are especially suitable to large programs being worked on by teams. By carefully designing the modules and specifying what information is to be received by and returned from the module, a team of programmers can independently develop a module and then connect it to the complete program.

The remainder of this chapter is devoted to seeing how subprograms can be written to accomplish specific tasks. Subprograms in C++ are called *functions*. We discussed library functions in Section 3.5. We will now learn how to write our own functions.

4.2   User-Defined Functions

User-defined functions resemble the library functions **sqrt** and **pow** that were introduced in Section 3.5. To review briefly, note the following concepts when using these functions:

1. An argument is required for each; thus, **sqrt(y)** and **pow(2, 5)** are appropriate.
2. Functions can be used in expressions; for example,

   ```
   x = sqrt(y) + sqrt(z);
   ```
3. Functions can be used in output statements; for example,

   ```
   cout << setw(8) << setprecision(2) << sqrt(3);
   ```

Need for User-Defined Functions

It is relatively easy to envision the need for functions that are not on the list of library functions available in C++. For example, if you must frequently cube numbers, it would be convenient to have a function named **cube** that would allow you to make an assignment such as

A NOTE OF INTEREST

Structured Programming

From 1950 to the early 1970s programs were designed and written on a linear basis. Programs written and designed on such a basis can be called unstructured programs. These programs consist of long linear sequences of statements. Control flows from each statement in the sequence to the next statement, unless it is transferred by means of a **GOTO** statement. Structured programming, on the other hand, organizes a program around separate semi-independent modules that are linked by a single sequence of simple commands, including structured control statements for selection and iteration (see Chapters 5 and 6).

In 1964, mathematicians Corrado Bohm and Guiseppe Jacopini proved that any program logic, regardless of complexity, can be expressed by using the control structures of sequencing, selection, and iteration. This result is termed the *structure theorem*. This theorem, combined with the efforts of Edger W. Dijkstra, led to a significant move toward structured programming and away from the use of **GOTO** statements.

In fact, in a letter to the editor of *Communications of the ACM* (Volume 11, March 1968), Dijkstra stated that the **GOTO** statement "should be abolished from all 'higher level' programming languages. . . . [The **GOTO** statement] is just too primitive; it is too much an invitation to make a mess of one's program."

Structured programming concepts were applied to a large-scale data processing application for the first time in IBM Corporation's "New York Times Project," which ran from 1969 to 1971. Using these techniques, programmers posted productivity figures from four to six times higher than those of the average programmer. In addition, the error rate was a phenomenally low 0.0004 per line of coding.

```
x = cube(y);
```

Other examples from mathematics include computing a factorial ($n!$), computing a discriminant ($b^2 - 4ac$), and finding roots of a quadratic equation:

$$\frac{-b \pm \sqrt{b^2 - 4ac}}{2a}$$

In business, a motel might like to have available a function to determine a customer's bill given the number in the party, the length of stay, and any telephone charges. Similarly, a hospital might need a function to compute the room charge for a patient given the type of room (private, ward, and so on) and various other options, including telephone (yes or no) and television (yes or no). Functions such as these are not library functions. However, in C++, we can create *user-defined functions* to perform these tasks. The following diagram illustrates the components of a simple C++ program that has one user-defined function:

```cpp
#include <iostream.h>

// Function: cube
// Computes the cube of an integer
//
// Input: an integer value
// Output: an integer representing the cube of the input

int cube (int x);

int main()
{
```

```
        int number;

        cout << "enter a number followed by <Enter>."
        cin >> number;
        cout << "The cube of"<< number <<"is"<< cube(number) << endl;
        return 0;
}


int cube(int x);
{
        return x * x * x;
}
```

Function Declarations

In the previous two chapters of this text, you learned how to import library functions from library files with the **#include** directive, and then how to invoke or call these functions in your application program. An important point to remember is that you do not know anything about how these functions are written or *implemented*. All you know is the *declaration* of a function. A function's declaration consists of its name, the number and kind of arguments it expects when you invoke it, and the type of value, if any, that it returns when its job is done. A function's declaration gives you all the information you need to know in order to use the function, and no more. For example, the declaration of the library function **pow** might be written as follows:

```
    double pow(double base, double exponent);
```

The first word in this expression, **double**, tells us the type of value returned by the function. The second word, **pow**, is the name of the function. The words enclosed in the parentheses and separated by commas denote the types of arguments expected when the function is invoked, that is, two arguments of type **double**. Note that the names used for these arguments, **base** and **exponent**, also serve to document the role that they play in the function.

The general form for a function declaration is

<return type> <function name> (<list of argument specifiers>);

to which the following comments apply:

1. **<function name>** is any valid identifier.
2. The function name should be descriptive.
3. **<return type>** declares the data type for the function name. This indicates what type of value, if any, will be returned to the caller.

It is good programming practice to supply with a declaration some comments that describe the inputs or data received by the function (its *arguments*) and the output or information returned (its *value* or *result*). In addition, we might specify any assumptions about the function's arguments that must be satisfied so that the function can perform its task correctly. For example, the function **sqrt** assumes that its argument is not just any double, but a nonnegative double. Therefore, we supply a comment about the function's arguments and value:

```
// Function: sqrt
// Compute the square root of a double-precision floating-point number
//
// Input: a nonnegative double-precision floating-point number
// Output: a nonnegative double-precision floating-point number
// representing the square root of the data received

double sqrt(double x);
```

Note that we have given the reader no information about *how* the function performs its task. Nonetheless, the reader has enough information to invoke or use the function. This is the kind of function declaration and comment that we will use in examples of user-defined functions throughout this text. Hereafter, when we say declaration, we mean a C++ function declaration and any supporting comments. Writing out all of your function declarations in this way will encourage you to think in terms of the uses of your functions before you become immersed in their implementation details.

Declaring Functions in a Program

Before you can use functions that you write yourself, you must provide declarations for them. All function declarations, if there are any, should appear in the region of your source program file between the global data declarations and the main program heading:

```
preprocessor directives

global data declarations

function declaration 1
    .
    .
    .
function declaration n

int main()
{
        main program data declarations

        statements

}

function implementation 1
    .
    .
    .
function implementation n
```

Implementing Functions in a Program

After you have decided how your functions will be used and what their declarations will be, and even after you have written a main program that will call them, you can then turn to the job of implementing or writing them. A function *implementation* describes in detail how the function performs its task. Simply put, a function implementation is a complete, brief program that produces some effects if certain assumptions about the arguments to the function are satisfied. For example, let's assume that the data value **x** is a number. Then the following expression produces the square of the number:

```
x * x
```

We can use this expression to implement a function **sqr(x)**, where **x** is any number, as follows:

```
double sqr(double x)
{
     return x * x;
}
```

You will note that the first line of the implementation, called the *function heading,* looks almost like a function declaration. The only difference is that the semicolon following the right parenthesis is omitted. The rest of the implementation after the heading is a little program block. Like the main program block, this block contains optional data declarations and at least one executable statement. The single statement in our example says that the block will return (as the value of the function) the result of multiplying **x** (the argument of the function) by itself. The form for a function implementation is

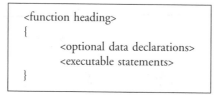

Function Headings

A function heading in a C++ program must match up with a corresponding function declaration. A return type and a function name must be the same in a heading as they are in a declaration, and the types of the arguments must match and be in the same positions. In addition, each type in the argument list of a function heading must be followed by an argument name, usually called a *formal parameter.* The formal parameter list must match the number of the arguments (usually called *actual parameters*) used when the function is called. Thus, if you are writing a function to compute the area of a rectangle and you want to call the function from the main program by

```
rect_area = area(width, length);
```

the function implementation might have

```
int area (int w, int l)
```

as a heading. The two formal parameters, **w** and **l**, correspond to the actual parameters, **width** and **length**. In general, you should make sure the formal parameter list and actual parameter list match up as indicated;

```
(int w, int l) (width, length)
```

A function to compute the cube of an integer could use the following as a heading:

```
int cube(int x)
```

The general form for a function heading is

> <return type> <function name> (<list of formal parameters>)

Using this general form, we note the following:

1. <function name> is any valid identifier.

a. The function name should be descriptive.

b. If it is expected, some value should be returned in the executable section of the function.

2. <return type> declares the data type for the function name. This indicates what type of value will be returned to the caller, if expected.

3. The list of formal parameters consists of a series of pairs of names, where the first name in the pair is the name of a data type, and the second name in the pair is the name of a formal parameter. The pairs in the list must be separated by commas.

Hereafter in this chapter, when we say *heading,* we mean a C++ function heading.

The formal parameters in a function heading must also match the types of the arguments used when the function is called. The compiler uses the same type checking rules for matching the types of formal and actual parameters as it does for matching the operands of an assignment statement. When an actual parameter passed to a function is not exactly the same type as the formal parameter in its position, the compiler checks to see whether or not the actual parameter's type can be converted by an implicit type cast to the type of the formal parameter. For example, an integer value passed to a function that expects a **float** would be converted to a float before being processed in the function. Conversely, a **float** that is passed to a function expecting an **int** would be implicitly truncated to an **int**.

Data and Executable Statements in a Function Implementation

As in the main program, a function does not have to have a declaration section, but when there is one, only constants and variables needed in the function should be declared. Further, the section is usually not very elaborate because the purpose of a function is normally a small, single task.

The executable statement section of a function's implementation has the same form as the executable statement section of the main program. Remember that at least one statement, of the form **return <expression>**, should return the value of the function if a returned value is expected.

We will now illustrate user-defined functions with several examples.

EXAMPLE 4.1

Implement a function to compute the cube of an integer. First, consider what a typical call to this function from the main program will look like:

```
a = cube(5);
```

Then decide what the assumptions about the arguments are, what the effects of the function will be, and write down a function declaration:

```
// Function: cube
// Computes the cube of an integer
//
// Input: an integer value
// Output: an integer representing the cube of the input

int cube (int x);
```

Because the actual parameter from the caller will be of **int** type, we have as an implementation

```
int cube (int x)
{
        return x * x * x;
}
```

EXAMPLE 4.2

Let us write a function to perform the task of computing unit cost for pizza. Data sent to the function are size and cost. The function returns the unit cost. Formal parameters are cost and size. Using the function name **price_per_square_inch**, the function could be invoked in a main program as follows:

```
unit_cost = price_per_square_inch(cost, price);
```

Therefore, we write the declaration

```
// Function: price_per_square_inch
// Computes the price per square inch of pizza
//
// Input: two positive real numbers representing the cost in dollars and
// cents and the diameter in inches of a pizza
// Output: a real number representing the price, in dollars and cents, per
// square inch of pizza

float price_per_square_inch(float cost, float size);
```

The implementation then is

```
float price_per_square_inch(float cost, float size)
{
        float radius, area;

        radius = size / 2.0;
        area = PI * sqr(radius);
        return cost / area;
}
```

You should note that this function has some *locally declared data.* The variable **radius** is declared within the local block of the function, because it is needed only for computing the area of a pizza. In general, data that are not needed elsewhere in a program should be declared locally within functions. You should also note that there are two important, unstated assumptions made by this implementation: first, the constant **PI** must be defined; and second, the function **sqr** must be declared. These names can be defined or declared in the area above the main program. The function **sqr** must then also be implemented, along with the function **price_per_square_inch**, after the main program.

EXAMPLE 4.3

We want to implement a function that converts digits to integer values. Our version of the function, called **char_to_int**, has the following declaration:

```
// Function: char_to_int
// Computes the integer value of a digit
//
// Input: a digit
// Output: the integer value represented by the digit

int char_to_int(char ch);
```

The implementation uses the method we developed in Chapter 3:

```
int char_to_int(char ch)
{
        return ch - '0';
}
```

Use in a Program

Now that you have seen several examples of user-defined functions, let us consider their use in a program. Once they are written, they can be used in the same manner as library functions. This usually means in one of the following forms.

1. *Assignment statements:*

```
a = 5;

b = cube(a);
```

2. *Arithmetic expressions:*

```
a = 5;

a = 3 * cube(a) + 2;
```

3. *Output statements:*

```
a = 5;
cout << setw(17) << cube(a) << endl;
```

Using Stubs

As programs get longer and incorporate more subprograms, a technique frequently used to get the program running is *stub programming*. A stub program is a no-frills, simple version of what will be a final program. It does not contain details of output and full algorithm development. It does contain declarations and rough implementations of each subprogram. When the stub version runs, you know your logic is correct and values are appropriately being passed to and from subprograms. Then you can fill in the necessary details to get a complete program.

Using Drivers

The main program is sometimes referred to as the *main driver*. When subprograms are used in a program, this driver can be modified to check subprograms in a sequential fashion. For example, you can start with a main driver that gets some input data:

```
// Program file: driver.cpp

#include<iostream.h>

int main()
{
        int data;

        cout << "Enter an integer:";
        cin >> data;
        return 0;
}
```

You can think of this driver as a "function factory" for building and testing functions. First, you add a function declaration, and then add a rough implementation of the function that simply returns a value, usually, the value of one of the arguments of the function. You test this function stub by placing a call to the function, with an input value, inside of an output statement in the main driver. If you were building the **sqr** function, your next version of the program would look like this:

```
// Program file: driver.cpp

#include <iostream.h>

// Function: sqr
// Computes the square of a number
//
// Input: a double-precision floating-point number
// Output: a double-precision floating-point number representing the square
// of the input

double sqr(double x);

int main()
{
     int data;

     cout << "Enter an integer:";
     cin >> data;
     cout << "The square is " << sqr(data) << endl;
     return 0;
}

double sqr(double x)
{
     return x;
}
```

Once you are sure that a subprogram is running and that data are being transmitted properly to it, you can proceed to fill in the rest of the details of its implementation. In the case of the **sqr** function, you merely substitute **x * x** for **x** in the **return** statement, and test the driver again. As you complete the implementation, you can be more confident that the function will return the values expected.

Functions Without Returned Values

Some functions require data to do their work, but return no values to their callers. For example, displaying several values with their labels to the terminal screen is such a task. This function might be called as follows:

```
display_results(result1, result2, result3);
```

The implementation of this function would probably send the parameter values and the appropriate string labels to the standard output stream. Note that the function call appears all by itself in a complete C++ statement. That is, a value is not assigned to a variable or passed on as intermediate value within a more complex expression. Functions of this sort are called *void functions,* in that they return no values. The example function is declared as follows:

```
void display_results(int result1, int result2,
    int result3);
```

The reserved word **void** indicates that the function is not meant to return a value. When a void function is implemented, it need not end with a return statement:

```
void display_results(int result1, int result2, int result3)
{
    cout << "The first result is " << result1 << endl;
    cout << "The second result is " << result2 << endl;
    cout << "The third result is " << result3 << endl;
}
```

The declarations of **void** functions have the following form:

```
void <function name> ( <list of argument specifiers> );
```

Functions Without Parameters

Occasionally, a function is needed to do some work without receiving any data from the caller. It may or may not return a value as well. An example of such a function is one whose task is that of displaying a chunk of text as a header for a table of output data. One might invoke this function as follows:

```
display_header();
```

This function takes no data from parameters, and returns no value to the caller. Its sole purpose is to display some text on the terminal screen. Its declaration is

```
void display_header();
```

Its implementation might display a header for a table of names and grades:

```
void display_header()
{
    cout << "GRADES FOR COMPUTER SCIENCE 110" << endl;
    cout << endl;
    cout << "Student Name            Grade" << endl;
    cout << "------------            -----" << endl;
}
```

Another example of this kind of function would display a sign-on or greeting at the start of a program.

An example of a function that takes no parameters, but still returns a result to the caller, would be a function that controls interactive input. The function prompts the user for input, reads the input value, and then returns it to the caller. The function might be used as follows:

```
data = get_data();
```

Note that since this function returns a value, the value should be used by the caller. In this example, the value is stored in a variable with an assignment statement. A declaration for the function is

```
int get_data();
```

Its implementation would prompt the user for an integer value, read it in from the standard input stream, and then return it as the value of the function. Because a place is needed to store the value during input, we declare a local variable for this purpose within the function:

```
int get_data()
{
        int number;

        cout << "Enter an integer value, followed by "
             << "<Enter>.";
        cin >> number;
        return number;
}
```

EXERCISES 4.2

1. Indicate which of the following are valid function declarations. Explain what is wrong with those that are invalid.
   a. `round_tenth (double x);`
   b. `double make_change (X, Y);`
   c. `int max (int x, int y, int z);`
   d. `char sign (double x);`

2 Find all errors in each of the following functions.

   a.
   ```
   int average (int n1, int n2);
   {
       return N1 + N2 / 2;
   }
   ```
   b.
   ```
   int total (int n1, int n2)
   {
       int sum;
       return 0;
       sum = n1 + n2;
   }
   ```

3. Write a function for each of the following.
   a. Round a real number to the nearest tenth.
   b. Round a real number to the nearest hundredth.

   c. Convert degrees Fahrenheit to degrees Celsius.

   d. Compute the charge for cars at a parking lot; the rate is 75 cents per hour or fraction thereof.

4. Write a program that uses the function you wrote for Exercise 3d to print a ticket for a customer who parks in the parking lot. Assume the input is in minutes.

5. Use the functions **sqr** and **cube** to write a program to print a chart of the integers 1 to 5 together with their squares and cubes. Output from this program should be

Number	Number Squared	Number Cubed
------	-------------	-----------
1	1	1
2	4	8
3	9	27
4	16	64
5	25	125

6. Write a program that contains a function that allows the user to enter a base (a) and exponent (x) and then have the program print the value of a^x.

4.3 Parameters

Value Parameters

We have seen that parameters are used so that data values can be transmitted, or passed, from the caller to a function. If values are to be passed *only* from the caller to a function, the parameters are called *value parameters*. The following program demonstrates the use of value parameters:

```cpp
// Program file: area.cpp

#include <iostream.h>

// Function: area
// Computes the area of a rectangle
//
// Inputs: two integers representing the length and the
// width of the rectangle
// Outputs: an integer representing the area of the
// rectangle

int area(int length, int width);

int main()
{
        int this_length, this_width;

        cout << "Enter the length: ";
        cin >> this_length;
```

```
        cout << "Enter the width: ";
        cin >> this_width;
        cout << "The area is "
             << area(this_length, this_width) << endl;
        return 0;
}


int area(int length, int width)
{
        return length * width;
}
```

In this program, the formal parameters **length** and **width** are used for one-way transmission of values to the function **area.** When the function is called, the values of the actual parameters, **this_length** and **this_width**, are copied into separate memory locations for the formal parameters **length** and **width**. The fact that there are separate memory locations for the formal and actual parameters guarantees that any changes to the formal parameters will leave the actual parameters unchanged.

Suppose that the user enters 8 for **this_length** and 7 for **this_width**. The state of the machine is now

| 8 |

this_length

| 7 |

this_width

Note that the only memory locations visible to the program are those for the variables **this_length** and **this_width**. The function is then called to compute the area. The system *allocates* memory locations for the formal parameters **length** and **width**. These names and their memory locations now become visible to the block of statements within the function. The system then places copies of the values 8 and 7 into the memory locations for **length** and **width**. This is why value parameters are said to be *passed by value*. The state of the machine is now

| 8 |

this_length

| 7 |

this_width

| 8 |

length

| 7 |

width

When the function returns from its call, the system *deallocates* the memory locations for **length** and **width**. Also, because the function is no longer active, its formal parameters are no longer visible to the program. The values of **this_length** and **this_width**, which are still visible, have not changed. A value parameter always indicates a *local copy* of the value transmitted to the function.

Reference Parameters

You will frequently want a function to return more than one value to a caller. A good example of a task that calls for more than one value to be returned is the interaction with the user for two input values in the program that computes the area of a rectangle. The C++ code for this task reads integer values from the keyboard into two variables:

```
cout << "Enter the length: ";
cin >> this_length;
cout << "Enter the width: ";
cin >> this_width;
```

We could document this task as follows:

```
// Prompts the user for two input integers representing the length and
// width of a rectangle
```

We can represent information to be returned with *reference parameters* in the parameter list of a C++ function. In a function declaration, reference parameters are declared by using the symbol **&** before the appropriate formal parameters. The form of a reference parameter declaration in a function declaration is

> <type name> &<formal parameter name>

The C++ declaration for a function **get_data** to perform this task can be added to the documentation:

```
// Function: get_data
// Prompts the user for two input integers representing the length and width
// of a rectangle
//
// Outputs: two integers representing the length and width of a rectangle

void get_data(int &length, int &width);
```

Note that the parameter and type names look the same as they would in declarations of functions that would use the parameters to receive data. However, in this function they will be used to return information to the caller, as is indicated by the **&** symbols.

The form of a reference parameter declaration in the heading of a function implementation is

> <type name> &<formal parameter name>

Our `get_data` function can now be implemented as follows:

```
void get_data(int &length, int &width)
{
    cout << "Enter the length: ";
    cin >> length;
    cout << "Enter the width: ";
    cin >> width;
}
```

When reference parameters are declared, values appear to be sent from the function to the caller. Actually, when reference parameters are used, values are not transmitted at all. Reference parameters in the function heading are merely *aliases* for actual variables used by the caller. Thus, variables are said to be *passed by reference* rather than by value. When reference parameters are used, any change of values in the function produces a corresponding change of values in the caller's block.

The notion of aliasing can be seen during a run of the program where the user enters the values 8 and 7 as inputs. Just before the function **get_data** returns, the state of the machine is as follows:

```
┌─────┐
│  8  │
└─────┘
this_length
length

┌─────┐
│  7  │
└─────┘
this_width
width
```

Note that there are only two memory locations for data in the program thus far. However, each location has two different names associated with it, which means that an assignment to either of the two names, say, **this_width** or **width**, will change the value stored in the corresponding memory location.

Technically, **length** and **width** do not exist as variables. They contain pointers to the same memory locations as **this_length** and **this_width**, respectively. Thus, a statement in the function such as

```
length = 5;
```

causes the memory location reserved for **length** to receive the value 5. That is, it causes the net action

```
this_length = 5;
```

Thus, constants cannot be used when calling a function with reference parameters. For example,

```
get_data(8, 7);
```

produces an error because 8 and 7 are passed in the positions of reference parameters.

An error would also occur if we tried to pass the value of an expression in the position of a reference parameter. For example, the following call would generate an error for the second parameter:

```
get_data(this_length, this_width + 1);
```

In general, the only legitimate actual parameter to pass by reference is a variable or the name of another function's parameter. The reason for this is that only names of this sort can refer to memory locations capable of being aliased by a reference parameter.

The next example also shows a useful function that requires reference parameters.

EXAMPLE 4.4

Many problems call for a function that will exchange the values of data in two variables. For any two variables **a** and **b**, the effect of calling the function **swap(a, b)** will be to replace the value of **a** with the value of **b**, and to replace the value of **b** with the value of **a**. Clearly, a function that returns a single value cannot accomplish this task. We will assume that the values to be swapped are real numbers. Two parameters will be used both to receive data from the caller and to return information as well. Thus, the function's declaration can be written as follows:

```
// Function: swap
// Exchanges the values of the two input variables
//
// Inputs: two real numbers
// Outputs: the two real numbers in reversed order

void swap(float &a, float &b);
```

The function's implementation will use a temporary variable to save one of the input values during the exchange:

```
void swap(float &a, float &b)
{
    float temp;

    temp = a;
    a = b;
    b = temp;
}
```

Note that this function itself returns no value to the caller. This is not unusual for functions that have reference parameters.

COMMUNICATION AND STYLE TIPS

It is considered good programming practice to design a function to be as *general* as possible. General functions solve a *class* of problems rather than a particular problem. For example, functions to get the length and to get the width solve particular problems, whereas a function to get any integer value solves both of these particular problems, as well as others. You should strive to make your functions as general as those you find in the C++ libraries. Designing general functions from scratch is not an easy thing to do. Frequently, you will not spot the need for a general function until you have written several more specialized functions that reveal a common or redundant pattern of code. When that happens, you can take two steps to design a more general function. First, write a single function that contains the common pattern of code that you see in the more specialized functions. Second, add parameters that will allow the callers of the new function to use it for their more specialized purposes.

A NOTE OF INTEREST

The History of Parameter Passing

The use of parameters to communicate information among subprograms is almost as old as the use of subprograms. As soon as subprograms became available in high-level programming languages, programmers realized that subprograms would be virtually useless without parameters. The inclusion of parameters in programming languages allowed programmers to design better code in two respects. First, the use of parameters made code more readable. The parameters of a subprogram module gave it a manifest interface for receiving information from and sending it to other modules. Second, the use of parameters made subprograms more general. Before parameters became available, each subprogram's operations were restricted to a particular problem involving particular data. The addition of parameters allowed programmers to generalize their solutions to manipulate whole classes of data.

The design of different parameter passing mechanisms has been an important chapter in the history of programming languages. Each major step in this process has reflected both the vision of computer scientists about what they consider important in a programming context and the limitations of the available hardware and software technology.

When the use of parameters first appeared in the mid 1950s in the programming language FORTRAN, the focus of programmers was on efficiency. FORTRAN was used primarily to perform mathematical and scientific computations (the acronym stands for **FOR**mula **TRAN**slation language). This kind of application demanded a high processing speed and large amounts of memory. But early processors were slow, and memory was expensive. With these resources at a premium, John Backus, the designer of FORTRAN, decided that all parameters in the language would be passed by reference. Pass by reference is less expensive than pass by value, because no extra memory needs to be allocated for a local copy of the actual parameter, and no extra processing time is needed to copy it. Because FORTRAN subprograms always manipulated the actual arguments passed to them by reference, the subprograms ran very quickly even when large data structures were passed. The use of a single-parameter passing mode also made the language easy to learn and the compiler for it easy to write.

Needless to say, the early FORTRAN programs were not safe. Programmers discovered this to be true especially for large programs that passed many parameters among subprograms. Unintended side effects were numerous. Because of the way that constant symbols were represented, even constants could be changed if they were passed as parameters to FORTRAN subprograms!

After a few years of experience with FORTRAN, John McCarthy, a mathematician at the Massachusetts Institute of Technology, designed LISP. LISP, short for **LIS**t **P**rocessing

Language, was intended for processing lists of symbols and was based on a theory of computation known as the recursive lambda calculus. According to this theory, programs should consist of functions that receive zero or more arguments and return a single value. In the process, these functions should not change the arguments themselves. To enforce this requirement, McCarthy designed a pass by value mechanism for parameters. In cases where an actual argument was a simple data type, like a number, functions worked on a local copy of the actual argument, so that no side effects were possible. Efficiency was not important, because LISP was a highly interactive and interpreted language. Thus, the time taken to allocate the extra memory for a formal parameter and copy the value of the actual parameter to it was insignificant when compared to the time taken to interpret LISP expressions generally. In cases where an actual argument was a structured data type, such as a string or a list of numbers, a copy of a pointer to the argument was passed for reasons of efficiency. The parameter passing mechanism of LISP thus reflected concerns of both safety and efficiency.

The primary teaching language in computer science for the last 20 years until recently has been Pascal. Named after the French mathematician, Pascal was designed by Niklaus Wirth. Pascal has two parameter passing modes. Pass by value worked like pass by value in LISP. However, Wirth extended pass by value to structured data values as well, making this mode expensive to use at run time. Pass by reference worked as in FORTRAN, except that constants and expressions were disallowed as actual reference parameters. Pascal also allows subprograms to be passed as parameters. This is an important development in our story, in that subprograms can be generalized still further by being parameterized for more specific subprograms. The following example of a general summation function in Pascal illustrates this point:

```
function sum(low, high : integer;
function f(x : integer) : integer) :
integer;
    var
        i, accum : integer;
    begin
    accum := 0;
    for i := low to high do
        accum := accum + f(i);
    sum := accum;
    end;

begin
writeln(sum(1, 10, square));
end.
```

continued

EXERCISES 4.3

1. Find the errors in the following function declarations.

a.
```
// Function: get_data
// Prompts user for two integer input values
//
// Outputs: two integers

void get_data(int length, int width);
```

b.
```
// Function: area
// Computes the area of a rectangle
//
// Inputs: two integers representing the length and
// the width of the rectangle
// Outputs: an integer representing the area of the
// rectangle

int area(int length, int &width);
```

c.
```
// Function: circle_attributes
// Computes the diameter and area of a circle
//
// Input: a real number representing the radius of the
// circle
// Outputs: two real numbers representing the diameter
// and area of the circle

void circle_attributes(float &radius,
        float &diameter, float &area);
```

2. Write and test a function **int_divide** that receives two integer values and two integer variables from the caller. When the function completes execution, the values in these variables should be the quotient and the remainder produced by dividing the second value by the first value. Be sure to name your parameters descriptively so as to aid the reader of the function.

4.4 Functions as Subprograms

Functions can be used as subprograms for a number of purposes. Two significant uses are to facilitate the top-down design philosophy of problem solving and to avoid having to write repeated segments of code.

Functions facilitate problem solving. Recall the Focus on Program Design problem in Chapter 3. In that problem, you were asked to compute the unit cost for a pizza. The main modules were

1. Get the data
2. Perform the computations
3. Print the results

A function can be written for each of these tasks and the program can then call each function as needed. Thus, the statement portion of the program would have the form

```
data = get_data();
results = perform_computations(data);
print_results(results);
```

This makes it easy to see and understand the main tasks of the program.

Once you develop the ability to write and use subprograms, you will usually write programs by writing the main program first. Your main program should be written so it can be easily read by a nonprogrammer but still contain enough structure to enable a programmer to know what to do if asked to write code for the tasks. In this sense, it is not necessary for a person reading the main program to understand *how* a subprogram accomplishes its task; it need only be apparent *what* the subprogram does.

When you design subprograms, you should also consider the problem of data flow. The most difficult aspect of learning to use subprograms is handling transmission of data. Recall from the structure charts shown earlier that arrows were used to indicate whether data were received by and/or sent from a module. Also, each module specification indicated if data were received by that module and if information was sent from it. Since a subprogram will be written to accomplish the task of each module, we must be able to transmit data as indicated. Once you have developed this ability, using functions becomes routine.

Using Subprograms

Use of subprograms facilitates writing programs for problems whose solutions have been developed using top-down design. A function can be written for each main task.

How complex should a function be? In general, functions should be relatively short and perform a specific task. Some programmers prefer to limit functions to no more than one full screen of text. If longer than a page or screen, the task might need to be subdivided into smaller functions.

Cohesive Subprograms

The cohesion of a subprogram is the degree to which the subprogram performs a single task. A subprogram that is developed in such a way is called a *cohesive subprogram.* As you use subprograms to implement a design based on modular development, you should always try to write cohesive subprograms.

The property of cohesion is not well defined. Subtask complexity varies in the minds of different programmers. In general, if the task is unclear, the corresponding subprogram will not be cohesive. When this happens, you should subdivide the task until a subsequent development allows cohesive subprograms.

To illustrate briefly the concept of cohesion, consider the first-level design of a problem to compute grades for a class. Step 3 of this design could be

3. Process grades for each student

Clearly, this is not a well-defined task. Thus, if you were to write a subprogram for this task, the subprogram would not be cohesive. Consider the subsequent development:

3. Process grades for each student
    while not end of input
    3.1 get a line of data
    3.2 compute average
    3.3 compute letter grade
    3.4 print data
    3.5 compute totals

Here we see that functions to accomplish subtasks 3.1, 3.2, 3.3, and 3.4 would be cohesive because each subtask consists of a single task. The final subtask, compute totals, may or may not result in a cohesive subprogram. More information is needed before you can decide what is to be done at this step.

Functional Abstraction

The purpose of using functions is to simplify reasoning. During the design stage, as a problem is subdivided into tasks, the problem solver (you) should have to consider only what a function is to do and not be concerned about details of the function. Instead, the function name and comments at the beginning of the function should be sufficient to inform the user as to what the function does. Developing functions in this manner is referred to as *functional abstraction* (this notion is also called *procedural abstraction,* because some languages support subprograms known as *procedures* that are similar to functions).

Functional abstraction is the first step in designing and writing a function. The list of parameters and comments about the action of the function should precede development of the body of the function. This forces clarity of thought and aids design. Use of this method might cause you to discover that your design is not sufficient to solve the task and a redesign is necessary. Therefore, you could reduce design errors and save time when writing code.

Functional abstraction becomes especially important when teams work on a project. Each member of the writing team should be able to understand the purpose and use of functions written by other team members without having to analyze the body of each function. This is analogous to the situation in which you use a predefined function without really understanding how the function works.

Functional abstraction is perhaps best formalized in terms of preconditions and postconditions. A *precondition* is a comment that states precisely what is true before a certain action is taken. A *postcondition* states what is true after the action has been taken. Carefully written preconditions and postconditions used with functions enhance the concept of functional abstraction. (Additional uses of preconditions and postconditions are discussed in Sections 5.6 and 6.5.)

In summary, functional abstraction means that, when writing or using functions, you should think of them as single, clearly understood units, of which each accomplishes a specific task.

Information Hiding

Information hiding can be thought of as the process of hiding the implementation details of a subprogram. This is just what we do when we use a top-down design to solve a problem. We decide which tasks and subtasks are necessary to solve a problem without worrying about how the specific subtasks will be accomplished. In the sense of software engineering, information hiding is what allows teams to work on a large system: It is only necessary to know what another team is doing, not how they are doing it.

A NOTE OF INTEREST

Computer Ethics: Hacking and Other Intrusions

A famous sequence of computer intrusions has been detailed by Clifford Stoll. The prime intruder came to Stoll's attention in August 1986, when an intruder attempted to penetrate a computer at Lawrence Berkeley Laboratory (LBL). Instead of denying the intruder access, management at LBL went along with Stoll's recommendation that they attempt to unmask the intruder, even though the risk was substantial because the intruder had gained system-manager privileges.

The intruder, Markus H., a member of a small group of West Germans, was unusually persistent, but no computer wizard. He made use of known deficiencies in the half-dozen or so operating systems, including UNIX, VMS, VM-TSO, and EMBOS, with which he was familiar, but he did not invent any new modes of entry. He penetrated 30 of the 450 computers then on the network system at LBL.

After Markus H. was successfully traced, efforts were instituted to make LBL's computers less vulnerable. To ensure high security, it would have been necessary to change all passwords overnight and recertify each user. This and other demanding measures were deemed impractical. Instead, deletion of all expired passwords was instituted; shared accounts were eliminated; monitoring of incoming traffic was extended, with alarms set in key places; and education of users was attempted.

The episode was summed up by Stoll as a powerful learning experience for those involved in the detection process and for all those concerned about computer security. That the intruder was caught at all is testimony to the ability of a large number of concerned professionals to keep the tracing effort secret.

In a later incident, an intruder left the following embarrassing message in a computer file assigned to Clifford Stoll: "The cuckoo has egg on his face." The reference was to Stoll's book, *The Cuckoo's Egg,* which tracked the intrusions of the West German hacker just described. The embarrassment was heightened by the fact that the computer, owned by Harvard University with which astronomer Stoll is now associated, was on the Internet network. The intruder, or intruders, who goes by the name of Dave, also attempted to break into dozens of other computers on the same network—and succeeded.

The *nom de guerre* of "Dave" was used by one or more of three Australians recently arrested by the federal police down under. The three, who at the time of their arrest were respectively 18, 20, and 21 years of age, successfully penetrated computers in both Australia and the United States.

The three Australians went beyond browsing to damage data in computers in their own nation and the United States. At the time they began their intrusions in 1988 (when the youngest was only 16), there was no law in Australia under which they could be prosecuted. It was not until legislation making such intrusions prosecutable was passed that the police began to take action.

Interface and Documentation

Independent subprograms need to communicate with the main program and other subprograms. A formal statement of how such communication occurs is called the *interface* of the subprogram. This usually consists of comments at the beginning of a subprogram and includes all the documentation the reader will need to use the subprogram. We have seen examples of subprogram interfaces in the function declarations and headings that have appeared in this chapter.

Software Engineering

Perhaps the greatest difference between beginning students in computer science and "real-world" programmers is how they perceive the need for documentation. Typically, beginning students want to make a program run; they view anything that delays this process as an impediment. Thus, some students consider using descriptive identifiers, writing variable dictionaries, describing a problem as part of program documentation, and using appropriate comments throughout a program as a nuisance. In contrast, system designers and programmers who write code for a living often spend up to 50% of their time and effort on documentation. There are at least three reasons for this difference in perspective.

First, real programmers work on large, complex systems with highly developed logical paths. Without proper documentation, even the person who developed an algorithm will have difficulty following its logic six months later. Second, communication among teams is required as systems are developed. Complete, clear statements about what the problems are and how they are being solved are essential. Third, programmers know they can develop algorithms and write the necessary code. They are trained so that problems of searching, sorting, and file manipulation are routine. Knowing that they can solve a problem thus allows them to devote more time and energy to documenting how the solution has been achieved.

We close this section with a revision of the program from Chapter 3 that found the unit cost for a pizza. The original program was designed using module specifications, but implemented in C++ as a long sequence of statements in the main program section. The revision will implement each module of the design as a C++ function to be called from the main program section. The structure chart is shown in Figure 4.1. The module specifications are

Module: Get data
Task: Gets cost and size of pizza from the user at the keyboard.
Outputs: cost and size

Module: Compute price per square inch
Task: Compute the price per square inch of pizza.
Input: Cost and size of pizza
Output: price per square inch

Module: Print results
Task: Print the price per square inch.
Input: price per square inch

◆ FIGURE 4.1
Structure chart for the pizza problem

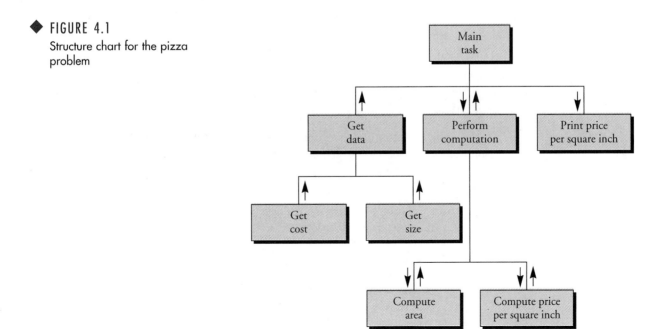

The module for getting the data receives no data, but returns two data values to the caller. The C++ function declaration specifies a function named **get_data** and two reference parameters, **cost** and **size**, in which the input data are returned to the caller:

```
// Function: get_data
// Gets cost and size of pizza from the user
// at the keyboard
//
// Outputs: The cost and size

void get_data(float &cost, int &size);
```

The C++ function implementation prompts the user for the cost and then for the size of the pizza, and returns the two input values in the reference parameters:

```
void get_data(float &cost, int &size)
{
    cout << "Enter the pizza price and press"
        << "<Enter>. ";
    cin >> cost;
    cout << "Enter the pizza size and press"
        <<"<Enter>. ";
    cin >> size;
}
```

We next write a function for performing the desired computations. This function receives the cost and size and then returns the price per square inch. Thus, cost and size are parameters and the price per square inch is the returned value of the function. If we name the function **price_per_square_inch**, we can write its declaration as follows:

```
// Function: compute price per square inch
// Compute the price per square inch of pizza
//
// Input: cost and size of pizza
// Output: price per square inch

float price_per_square_inch(float cost, int size);
```

The implementation of this function also requires variables **radius** and **area** to be declared in the data declaration section of the function. Assuming **PI** has been defined as a constant and **sqr** has been defined as a function, the function's implementation is

```
float price_per_square_inch(float pizza_cost,
    int pizza_size)
{
    float radius, area;
    radius = pizza_size / 2;
    area = PI * sqr(radius);
    return pizza_cost / area;
}
```

A function to print the results receives the unit cost. A declaration for the function is

```
// Function: print results
// Print the price per square inch
//
// Input: price per square inch

void print_results(float price_per_sq_inch);
```

The function's implementation is:

```
void print_results(float price_per_sq_inch)
{
        cout << fixed << showpoint << setprecision(2) << endl;
        cout << "The price per square inch is $";
        cout << setw(6) << price_per_sq_inch << endl;
}
```

The complete program for this problem is as follows:

```
// Program file: pizza.cpp

#include <iostream.h>
#include <iomanip.h>

const float PI = 3.14159;

// Function: get_data
// Gets cost and size of pizza from the user at the keyboard
//
// Outputs: The cost and size

void get_data(float &cost, int &size);

// Function: compute price per square inch
// Compute the price per square inch of pizza
//
// Input: cost and size of pizza
// Output: price per square inch

float price_per_square_inch(float cost, int size);

// Function: print results
// Print the price per square inch
//
// Input: price per square inch

void print_results(float price_per_sq_inch);

// Function: sqr
// Computes the square of a number
//
// Input: a real number
// Output: a real number representing the square of the input
```

```cpp
float sqr(float x);

int main()
{
    int size;
    float cost, price;

    get_data(cost, size);
    price = price_per_square_inch(cost, size);
    print_results(price);
    return 0;
}


void get_data(float &cost, int &size)
{
    cout << "Enter the pizza price and press <Enter>. ";
    cin >> cost;
    cout << "Enter the pizza size and press <Enter>. ";
    cin >> size;
}


float price_per_square_inch(float cost, int size)
{
    float radius, area;
    radius = size / 2;
    area = PI * sqr(radius);
    return cost / area;
}


void print_results(float price_per_sq_inch)
{
    cout << fixed << showpoint << setprecision(2)
        << endl;
    cout << "The price per square inch is $";
    cout << setw(6) << price_per_sq_inch << endl;
}

float sqr(float x)
{
    return x * x;
}
```

1 (for get_data function)

2 (for price_per_square_inch function)

3 (for print_results function)

Note the way in which the use of subprograms has simplified the structure of the main program, as compared with the original version in Chapter 3.

```
get_data (cost, size);
```

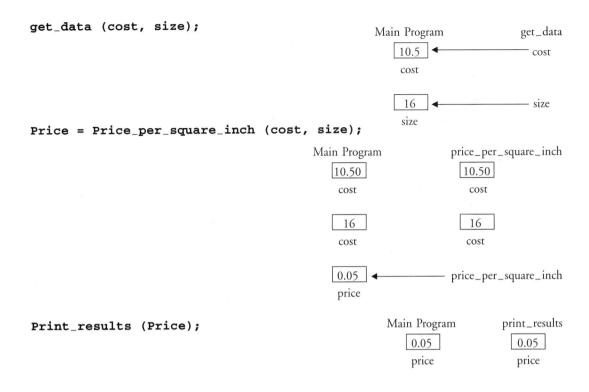

```
Price = Price_per_square_inch (cost, size);
```

```
Print_results (Price);
```

Sample runs of this program produce the following output:

```
Enter the pizza price and press <Enter>. 10.50
Enter the pizza size and press <Enter>. 16

The price per square inch is $ 0.05

Enter the pizza price and press <Enter>. 8.75
Enter the pizza size and press <Enter>. 14

The price per square inch is $ 0.06
```

EXERCISES 4.4

1. Draw a structure chart for a program that prompts the user for an integer, computes its square root, and displays this result with an informative label on the terminal screen. Your chart should contain three modules: one for getting the data, one for computing the result, and one for printing the result. Be sure to label the data flow between the modules with arrows.

2. Construct a main program module in C++, and add to it the declarations of three functions that will carry out the tasks of the modules from the previous exercise.

3. Implement and test each of the functions from Exercise 2. You will have to declare at least one integer variable to pass the data from module to module.

4.5 Scope of Identifiers

Global and Local Identifiers

Identifiers used to declare variables in the declaration section of a program can be used throughout the entire program. For purposes of this section, we will think of the global text of the program file as a *block* and the main program and each subprogram as a *subblock* for the main program or subprogram. Each subblock may contain a parameter list, a local declaration section, and the body of the block. A program file block can be envisioned as shown in Figure 4.2. Furthermore, if **X1** is a variable in the main program block, we will indicate this as shown in Figure 4.3, where an area in memory has been set aside for **X1**. When a program contains a subprogram, a separate memory area within the memory area for the program is set aside for the subprogram to use while it executes. Thus, if the program file contains a function named **subprog1**, we can envision this as shown in Figure 4.4. If **subprog1** contains the variable **X2**, we have the program shown in Figure 4.5. This could be indicated in the program by

```
const float PI = 3.14;

float subprog1 (float x2);

int main;
{
        float x1;

        subprog1(x1);
        .
        .
        .
```

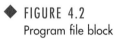

◆ **FIGURE 4.2**
Program file block

◆ **FIGURE 4.3**
Variable location in main block

The *scope of an identifier* refers to the area of the program text in which it can be used. When subprograms are used, each identifier is available to the block in which it is declared and any nested blocks. Identifiers are not available outside their blocks.

Identifiers that are declared before the main block are called *global identifiers;* identifiers that are restricted to use within the main block or a subblock are called *local identifiers.* Constant **PI** in Figure 4.5 can be used throughout the main program and in the function **subprog1**; therefore it is a global identifier. Variable **X1** can be used in the main program but not in the function **subprog1**; it is a local identifier. Variable **X2** can only be used within the function where it is declared; it is a local identifier. Any attempt to reference **X2** outside the function will result in an error. Lastly, function **subprog1** can be used either in the main program block, within another function's block, or within its own block. This last use is a recursive one, which we will discuss in Chapter 12.

◆ FIGURE 4.4
Illustration of a subblock

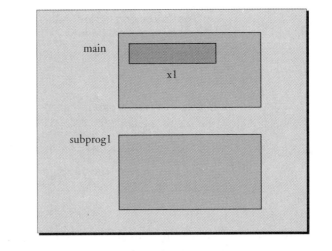

◆ FIGURE 4.5
Variable location within a subblock

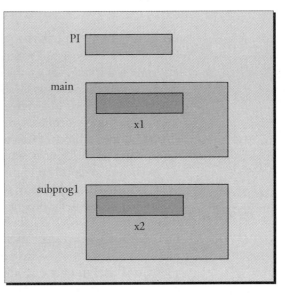

As a matter of C++ syntax, function names must be declared as global identifiers. Constant, variable, and type names can be declared either globally or locally. However, as a matter of good programming style, constant and type names are usually declared globally, and variable names are declared locally.

Let us now examine an illustration of local and global identifiers. Consider the program and function declaration

```
const int A = 10;

subprog(int a1);

int main()
{
      int x, y;
      .
      .
}

int subprog (int a1)
{
      float x;
      .
      .
```

Blocks for this program can be envisioned as shown in Figure 4.6. Because **A** is global, the statement

```
cout << A << a1 << x << endl;
```

could be used in the function **subprog** although **A** has not been specifically declared there. However,

```
cout << A << a1 << x << endl;
```

could not be used in the main program because **a1** and **x** are local to the function **subprog**.

Using Global Identifiers

In general, it is not good practice to refer to global variables within functions. A *side effect* is a change in a nonlocal variable that is the result of some action taken in a program. The use of locally defined variables in functions and in the main program block helps to avoid unexpected side effects and protects your programs. In addition, locally defined variables facilitate debugging and top-down design and enhance the portability of functions. This is especially important if different people are working on different functions for a program.

The use of global constants is different. Because the values cannot be changed by a function, it is preferred that constants be defined in the data declaration section before the main program block and then be used whenever needed by any subprogram. This is especially important if the constant is subject to change over time, for example, **STATE_TAX_RATE**. When a change is necessary, one change in the main program is all that is needed to make all subprograms current. If a constant is used in only one function, some programmers prefer to have it defined near the point of use. Thus, they would define it in the subprogram in which it is used.

◆ FIGURE 4.6
Scope of identifiers

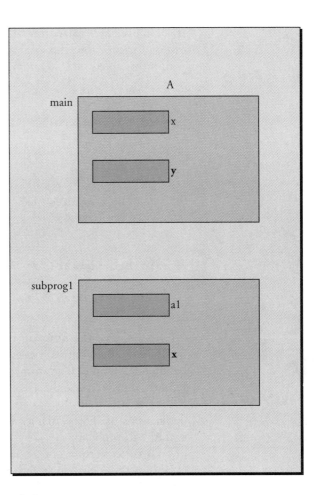

Side Effects and Parameters

Unintentional side effects are frequently caused by the misuse of reference parameters. Since any change in a reference parameter causes a change in the corresponding actual parameter in the calling program or function, you should use reference parameters only when your intent is to produce such changes. In all other cases, use value parameters. For example, the following program would produce a syntax error, because a function attempts to access a variable declared in the main block:

```
void bad_square();

int main()
{
        int main_data = 2;

        bad_square();
        return 0;

}

void bad_square();
{
        main_data = main_data * main_data;
}
```

If we move the declaration of **main_data** outside of the main block, we can extend its scope into the local block of the function, unless the name is redeclared within the function as a parameter or local variable:

```
int main_data = 2;

void bad_square();

int main()
{

       bad_square();
       return 0;
}

void bad_square();
{
       main_data = main_data * main_data;
}
```

We have named the function **bad_square** to indicate that the assignment that occurs in the function is bad programming practice, even though the result might be intended by the programmer. Not only does the use of this function result in a serious side effect, but there is no indication in the function's declaration or in the function's call that the function will modify the global variable. Keeping the declarations of these variables inside the main program block will help to guard against this problem.

A better version of this program moves the declaration of the global variable back into the main block and passes the variable as a reference parameter to the function:

```
void better_square(int &x);

int main()
{
       int main_data = 2;

       better_square(main_data);
       return 0;
}

void better_square(int &x)
{
     x = x * x;
}
```

The function **better_square** improves on **bad_square** in two respects. First, the function now has a *manifest interface*. A function has a manifest interface if we can see, just from looking at the function's declaration and the function's call, exactly what data the function is manipulating, and that it will be subject to change within the function. In other words, we are given clear notice that a side effect will occur in the function, and a clear indication of what that side effect will be. Second, the function can be used to take the square of any variable passed to it as an actual parameter. We have indicated this by using **x** to name the formal parameter of the function. Thus, **better_square** is more general than **bad_square**, which could take the square of just one variable.

While **better_square** is an improvement on **bad_square**, we can write a still better version of this function:

```
int best_square(int x);

int main()
{
    int main_data = 2;

    main_data = best_square(main_data);
    return 0;
}

int best_square(int x)
{
    return x * x;
}
```

This version of the function is the best one for two reasons. First, it has a manifest interface. The caller knows exactly what data will be used by the function. Second, the function produces no side effects. The caller passes the function a value to be squared, and the square of this value is returned to the caller. In particular, if the caller passes a variable to this function, the caller can be sure that the function will not change the variable. If the caller wants to set a variable to the value returned by the function, then this assignment must be explicitly done by the caller after the function returns its value.

All three versions of the function in this example are technically correct, in that they accomplish the task intended by the programmer. However, as the example demonstrates, whenever possible, it is best to write functions that have manifest interfaces and that produce no side effects.

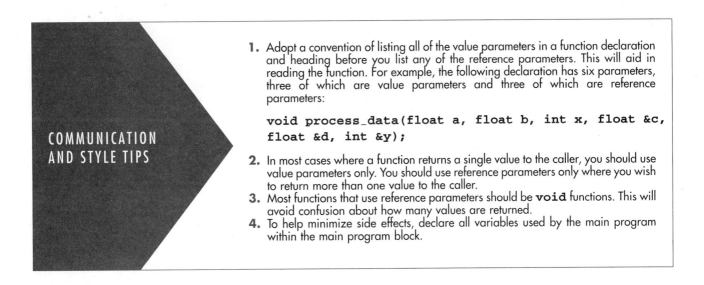

COMMUNICATION
AND STYLE TIPS

1. Adopt a convention of listing all of the value parameters in a function declaration and heading before you list any of the reference parameters. This will aid in reading the function. For example, the following declaration has six parameters, three of which are value parameters and three of which are reference parameters:

```
void process_data(float a, float b, int x, float &c,
float &d, int &y);
```

2. In most cases where a function returns a single value to the caller, you should use value parameters only. You should use reference parameters only where you wish to return more than one value to the caller.
3. Most functions that use reference parameters should be **void** functions. This will avoid confusion about how many values are returned.
4. To help minimize side effects, declare all variables used by the main program within the main program block.

A NOTE OF INTEREST

John Backus

You have read about John Backus, the inventor of FOR-TRAN, in a note of interest on program libraries in Chapter 2 and we also mentioned him earlier in this chapter. Backus has had a long and distinguished career as a computer scientist with IBM. During the late 1950s, he sat on a committee that developed ALGOL, the first *block-structured* programming language. The block structure of ALGOL represented a significant advance over FORTRAN. A block in ALGOL is a set of related data declarations and executable statements. The data declared in a block are visible only within it. This greatly enhances program security, readability, and maintenance. Most modern programming languages developed after ALGOL, including C++, have been block structured.

In 1977, Backus was given the Turing Award for his contributions to computer science at the annual meeting of the Association for Computing machinery. Each recipient of this annual award presents a lecture. Backus discussed a new discipline in his talk called *function-oriented programming*. This style of programming was developed to address concerns about the reliability and maintainability of large software systems. One of the principal causes of errors in large programs is the presence of side effects and unintentional modifications of variables. These modifications can occur anywhere in a program with assignment statements whose targets are global variables. Backus proposed that function-oriented programming could eliminate side effects by eliminating the assignment statement and keeping global variables to a minimum. Function-oriented programs consist of sets of function declarations and *function applications*. A function application simply evaluates the arguments to a function, applies the function to these values, and returns a result to the caller. No assignment statements to global variables are allowed within a function. No side effects occur.

The philosophy of function-oriented programming has motivated the design of function-oriented languages. These languages do not allow the programmer to perform assignments to global variables within functions. Though C++ allows programmers to declare and use functions, the language does not forbid this kind of side effect. However, by exercising some discipline, C++ programmers can still emulate a function-oriented style to prevent side effects from occurring in their programs.

Names of Identifiers

Because separate areas in memory are set aside when subprograms are used, it is possible to have identifiers with the same name in both the main program and a subprogram. Thus

```
int main()
{
        int age;
        .
        .
}


int subprog (int age)
```

can be envisioned as shown in Figure 4.7. When the same name is used in this manner, any reference to this name results in action being taken as locally as possible. Thus, the assignment statement

```
age = 20;
```

made in the function **subprog** assigns 20 to **age** in the function but not in the main program (see Figure 4.8).

Now that you know you can use the same name for an identifier in a subprogram and the main program, the question is "Should you?" There are two schools of thought regarding this issue. If you use the same name in the functions, it facilitates matching parameter lists and independent development of functions.

◆ FIGURE 4.7
Relation of identifiers

◆ FIGURE 4.7
Relation of identifiers

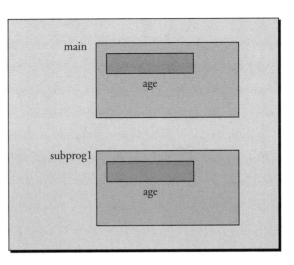

◆ FIGURE 4.8
Assigning values in subprograms

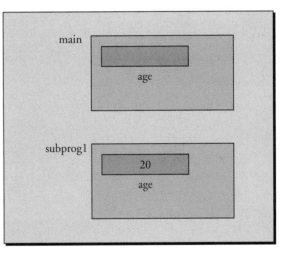

However, this practice can be confusing when you first start working with subprograms. Thus, some instructors prefer using different, but related, identifiers. For example,

```
display_data (score1, score2);
```

in the main program could have a function heading of

```
void display_data (int sc1, int sc2);
```

In this case, the use of **sc1** and **sc2** is obvious. Although this may facilitate better understanding in early work with subprograms, it is less conducive to portability and independent development of functions. Both styles are used in this text.

Multiple Functions

More than one function can be used in a program. When this occurs, all of the previous uses and restrictions of identifiers apply to each function. Blocks for

◆ FIGURE 4.9

FUNCTION A

FUNCTION B

FUNCTION C

◆ FIGURE 4.10
Identifiers in multiple subprograms

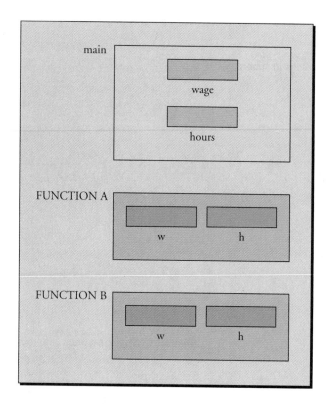

multiple functions can be depicted as shown in Figure 4.9. Identifiers in the main program can be accessed by each function. However, local identifiers in the functions cannot be accessed outside their blocks.

When a program contains several functions, they can be called from the main part of the program in any order.

The same names for identifiers can be used in different functions. Thus, if the main program uses variables **wage** and **hours**, and both of these are used as arguments in calls to different functions, you have the situation shown in Figure 4.10.

Using the same names for identifiers in different functions makes it easier to keep track of the relationship between variables in the main program and their associated parameters in each subprogram.

EXERCISES 4.5

1. Explain the difference between local and global identifiers.
2. State the advantages of using local identifiers.
3. Discuss some appropriate uses for global identifiers. List several constants that would be appropriate global definitions.
4. What is meant by the scope of an identifier?
5. Write a test program that will enable you to see
   a. what happens when an attempt is made to access an identifier outside of its scope; and
   b. how the values change as a result of assignments in the subprogram and the main program when the same identifier is used in the main program and a subprogram.
6. Review the following program:

```
int main()
{
        int a, b;
        float x;
        char ch;
        .
        .
}
int sub1(int a1)
{
        int b1;
        .
        .
        }


int sub2(int a1, int b1)
{
        float x1;
        char ch1;
        .
        .
}
```

   a. List all global variables.
   b. List all local variables.
   c. Indicate the scope of each identifier.

7. Provide a schematic representation of the program and all subprograms and variables in Exercise 6.
8. Using the program with variables and subprograms as depicted in Figure 4.11, state the scope of each identifier.

◆ FIGURE 4.11

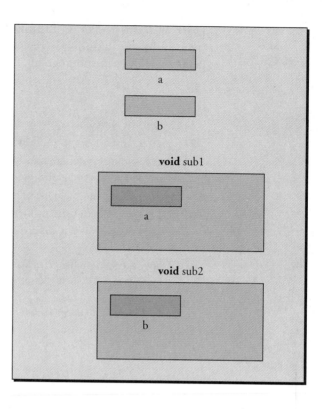

9. What is the output from the following program?

```
#include <iostream.h>

void sub1 (int a);

int main()
{
    int a;
    a = 10;

    cout << a << endl;
    sub1 (a);
    cout << a << endl;
    return 0;
}

void sub1 (int a)
{
    a = 20;
    cout << a << endl;
}
```

10. Write appropriate headings and declaration sections for the program and subprograms illustrated in Figure 4.12.

◆ FIGURE 4.12

11. Find all errors in the following program.

```
int main()
{
        float x, y;
        x = 10;
        y = 2 * x;
        cout << x << y << endl;
        sub1(x);
        cout << x1 << x << y << endl;
        return 0;
}

void sub1 (int x1)
{
        cout << x1 << x << y << endl;
}
```

12. Discuss the advantages and disadvantages of using the same names for identifiers in a subprogram and the main program.

To encourage people to shop downtown, the Downtown Businesses Association partially subsidizes parking. They have established the E-Z Parking parking lot where customers are charged $0.75 for each full hour of parking. There is no charge for part of an hour. Thus, if someone has used the lot for less than an hour, there would be no charge.

The E-Z Parking parking lot is open from 9:00 A.M. until 11:00 P.M. When a vehicle enters, the driver is given a ticket with the entry time printed in military style. Thus, if a car entered the lot at 9:30 A.M., the ticket would read 930. If a vehicle entered at 1:20 P.M., the ticket would read 1320. When the vehicle leaves, the driver presents the ticket to the attendant and the amount due is computed.

Let us now develop a solution and write a program to assist the attendant. Input consists of a starting and ending time. Output should be a statement to the customer indicating the input information, the total amount due, a heading, and a closing message. Sample output for the data 1050 (10:50 A.M.) and 1500 (3:00 P.M.) is

```
Please enter the time in and press <Enter>. 1050
Please enter the time out and press <Enter>. 1500


            E - Z Parking


   Time in: 1050 Time out: 1500


 Amount due      $ 3.00


Thank you for using E - Z Parking


          BUCKLE UP
       and DRIVE SAFELY
```

A first-level development for this problem is

1. Get the data
2. Compute amount
3. Print results

A structure chart for this problem is given in Figure 4.13. (Recall, an arrow pointing into a module indicates data are being received, whereas an arrow pointing out indicates data are being sent from the module.) Module specifications for the three main modules are

Module: Get data
Task: Prompts user for and inputs entry time and exit time.
Outputs: integers representing entry time and exit time

Module: Compute amount
Task: Computes the amount due in dollars and cents.
Inputs: integers representing entry time and exit time
Output: a real number representing the amount due

Module: Print results
Task: prints heading, entry and exit times, amount due, and closing message.
Inputs: integers representing entry time and exit time and a real number representing the amount due

◆ FIGURE 4.13
Structure chart for the parking lot program

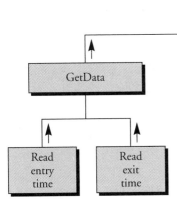

By examining the module specifications, we see that **get_data** needs two parameters, **compute_amount** needs two parameters, and **print_results** needs three parameters.

A second-level pseudocode development is

1. Get the data
   1.1 prompt user for time entered
   1.2 read time entered
   1.1 prompt user for time exited
   1.4 read time exited
2. Compute amount
   2.1 compute number of hours
   2.2 compute amount due
3. Print results
   3.1 print a heading
   3.2 print amount due
   3.3 print a closing message

A complete program for this is

```
// This program prints statements for customers of the E-Z
// Parking lot.  Interactive input consists of entry
// time and exit time from the lot. Output consists of a
// customer statement. Emphasis is placed on using
// functions to develop the program.

// Program file: parking.cpp

#include <iostream.h>
#include <iomanip.h>

const float HOURLY_RATE = 0.75;
const char INDENT =' ';
```

```
// Function: get_data
// Prompts user for and inputs entry time and exit time

// Outputs: integers representing entry time and exit time

void get_data (int 8entry_time, int 8exit_time);

// Function: compute_amount
// Computes the amount due in dollars and cents
//
// Inputs: integers representing entry time and exit time
// Output: a real number representing the amount due

float compute_amount (int entry_time, int exit_time);

// Function: print_results
// Prints heading, entry and exit times, amount due, and closing message
//
// Inputs: integers representing entry time and exit time and a real number
// representing the amount due

void print_results (int entry_time, int exit_time, float amount_due);

// Function: print_heading
// Print a heading for the ticket

void print_heading();

// Function: print_message
// Print a closing message for the ticket

void print_message();

int main()
{
    int entry_time;     // Time of entry into parking lot
    int exit_time;      // Time of exit from parking lot
    float amount_due;   // Cost of parking in lot

    get_data (entry_time, exit_time);
    amount_due = compute_amount(entry_time, exit_time);
    print_results (entry_time, exit_time, amount_due);
    return 0;
}

void get_data(int &entry_time int &exit_time)
{
    cout << "Please enter the time in 24 hour notation and press <Enter>. ";
    cin >> entry_time;
    cout << "Please enter the time out and press <Enter>. ";
    cin >> exit_time;
}
```

```
float compute_amount (int entry_time, int exit_time)
{
      int number_of_hours;

      number_of_hours = (exit_time - entry_time) / 100;
      return number_of_hours * HOURLY_RATE;
}
```
> 2

```
void print_heading()
{
      cout << endl;
      cout << setw(11) << INDENT << "E - Z Parking" << endl;
      cout << setw(11) << INDENT << "-------------------" << endl;
      cout << endl;
}

void print_message()
{
      cout << endl;
      cout << setw(1) << INDENT << "Thank you for using E - Z Parking" << endl;
      cout << endl;
      cout << setw(13) << INDENT << "BUCKLE UP";
      cout << setw(16) << INDENT << "and";
      cout << setw(11) << INDENT << "DRIVE SAFELY";
      cout << endl;
}

void print_results (int entry_time, int exit_time, float amount_due)
{
      print_heading();
      cout << fixed << showpoint << setprecision(2);
      cout << setw(4) << INDENT << "Time in: " << setw(6) << entry_time
         << endl;
      cout << setw(4) << INDENT << "Time out:" << setw(6) << exit_time
         << endl;
      cout << endl;
      cout << setw(4) << INDENT << "Amount due $"
         << setw(6) << amount_due << endl;
      print_message();
}
```
> 3

A sample run using the data 930 as entry time and 1320 as exit time produces

```
Please enter the time in and press <Enter>. 930
Please enter the time out and press <Enter>. 1320

               E - Z Parking

     Time in: 0930 Time out: 1320

     Amount due     $  2.25

Thank you for using E - Z Parking

          BUCKLE UP
        and DRIVE SAFELY
```

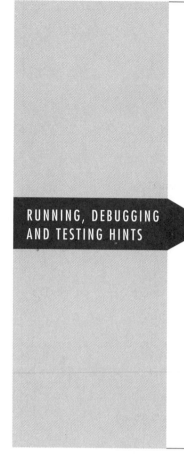

RUNNING, DEBUGGING AND TESTING HINTS

1. Each subprogram can be tested separately to see if it is producing the desired result. This is accomplished by a main program that calls and tests only the subprogram in question.
2. You can use related or identical variable names in the parameter lists. For example,

   ```
   float compute (int n1, int n2);
   ```

   or

   ```
   float compute (int number1, int number2);
   ```

   could be called by

   ```
   compute (number1, number2);
   ```

3. Be sure the type, order, and purpose of actual parameters and formal parameters agree. You can do this by listing them one below the other. For example,

   ```
   void display_data (char init1, char init2, int sc);
   ```

   could be called by

   ```
   display_data ('a', 'b', 9);
   ```

4. Be sure that you really need to use a reference parameter in a function before you declare it. If a function returns only one value to the caller, use no reference parameters.
5. If a function does not seem to return a value to the caller as expected, perhaps a parameter has not been declared as a reference parameter. Check the function's heading and declaration to be sure that the symbol **&** is associated with the desired output parameter.

SUMMARY

Key Terms

actual parameter	local copy	reference parameter
address	local identifier	scope of an identifier
alias	main driver	side effect
block	manifest interface	structured design
bottom-up testing	modularity	structured programming
cohesive subprogram	pass by reference	stub programming
formal parameter	pass by value	subblock
functional abstraction	postcondition	subprogram
global identifier	precondition	user-defined function
information hiding	procedural abstraction	value parameter
interface		

Keywords

return **void**

Key Concepts

◆ A subprogram is a program within a program; functions are subprograms.
◆ Subprograms can be utilized to perform specific tasks in a program. Functions are often used to initialize variables, get data, print headings (no parameters needed), perform computations, and print data.

◆ The general form for a function declaration is

> <type identifier> <name> (<parameter list>);

◆ A typical parameter list is

void display_data (int n1, int n2, float x, float y);

◆ A formal parameter is one listed in the subprogram heading; it is like a blank waiting to receive a value from the calling program.

formal parameters

void arithmetic (char sym, int n1, int n2);

◆ An actual parameter is a variable listed in the subprogram call in the calling program.

actual parameters

arithmetic (symbol, num1, num2);

◆ The formal parameter list in the subprogram heading must match the number and types of actual parameters used in the main program when the subprogram is called.

void arithmetic (char sym, int n1, int n2);
arithmetic (symbol, num1, num2);

◆ The type of an actual parameter being passed to a function must be compatible with the type of the formal parameter in its position in a function heading; implicit type conversions are made whenever possible.

◆ If the symbol **&** appears in a formal parameter declaration, then the formal parameter is a reference parameter; otherwise, the formal parameter is a value parameter.

◆ For value parameters, a copy of the actual parameter's value is passed to a function when it is called.

◆ Pass by value is safe; the value of the actual parameter does not change during the call of the function.

◆ For reference parameters, the address of the actual parameter is passed to the function when it is called.

◆ Pass by reference is not safe; it should be used with caution and only when side effects are intended.

◆ Global identifiers can be used by the main program and all subprograms.

◆ Local identifiers are available only to the main program block or the subprogram block in which they are declared.

◆ Each identifier is available to the block in which it is declared.

◆ Identifiers are not available outside their blocks.

◆ The scope of an identifier refers to the area of text in which the identifier is available.

◆ Understanding the scope of identifiers is aided by graphic illustration of blocks in a program; thus, the following program can be visualized as shown

◆ FIGURE 4.14

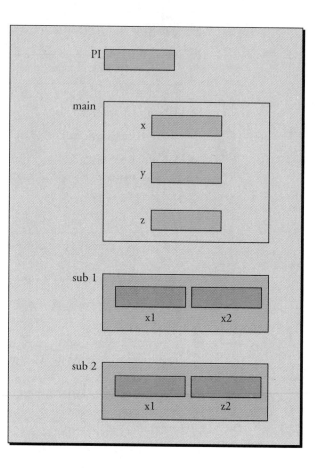

in Figure 4.14. A user-defined function is a subprogram that performs a specific task.

```
const float PI = 3.14;

float sub1(float);
float sub2(float);

int main()
{
    float x, y, z;

    .
    .
    .
}

float sub1(float x1)
{
    float x2;
    .
    .
    .
}
```

```
float sub2(float x1)
{
    float z2;
        .
        .
        .

}
```

◆ The form for a user-defined function is

<type identifier> <function name> (<parameter list>)
{
        <data declarations>
        <executable statements>
}

PROGRAMMING PROBLEMS AND PROJECTS

The following programming problems will be run on a very limited set of data. In later chapters, as you build your programming skills, you will run these problems with larger databases and subprograms for various parts. Problems marked with a box to the left of the number are referred to and used repeatedly; carefully choose the ones on which to work and then develop them completely. *Be sure to package coherent tasks in functions wherever possible.*

1. Write a program to get the coefficients of a quadratic equation

$$ax^2 + bx + c = 0$$

from the keyboard and then print the value of the discriminant $b^2 - 4ac$. A sample display for getting input is

Enter coefficients a, b, and c for the quadratic equation

$ax^2 + bx + c = 0$
a = ?
b = ?
c = ?

Run this program at least three times using test data that result in $b^2 - 4ac = 0$, $b^2 - 4ac > 0$, and $b^2 - 4ac < 0$.

2. Write a program to compute the cost for carpeting a room. Input should consist of the room length, room width, and carpet price per square yard. Use constants for the pad charge and installation charge. Include a heading as part of the output. A typical input screen would be:

What is the room length in feet? <Enter> ?
What is the room width in feet? <Enter> ?
What is the carpet price/square yard? <Enter> ?

Output for a sample run of this program (without a heading) could be

Dimensions of the room (in feet) are 17 × 22.
The area to be carpeted is 41.6 square yards.
The carpet price is $11.95 per yard.

Room dimensions	17 x 22
Carpet required	41.6 square yards
Carpet price/yard	$11.95
Pad price/yard	$2.95
Installation cost/yard	$ .95
Total cost/yard	$15.85
Total cost	$659.36

3. Williamson's Paint and Papering store wants a computer program to help them determine how much paint is needed to paint a room. Assuming a room is to have four walls and the ceiling painted, input for the program should be the length, width, and height of the room. Use a constant for the wall height (usually eight feet). One gallon of paint should cover 250 square feet. Cost of paint for the walls and ceiling should be entered by the user. Output should be the amount and cost for each kind of paint, and the total cost.

4. The Fairfield College faculty recently signed a three-year contract that included salary increments of 7, 6, and 5% respectively, for the next three years. Write a program that allows a user to enter the current salary and then prints the compounded salary for each of the next three years.

5. Several instructors use various weights (percentage of the final grade) for test scores. Write a program that allows the user to enter three test scores and the weight for each score. Output should consist of the input data, the weighted score for each test, and the total score (sum of the weighted scores).

6. The Roll-Em Lanes bowling team would like to have a computer program to print the team results for one series of games. The team consists of four members whose names are Weber, Fazio, Martin, and Patterson. Each person on the team bowls three games during the series; thus, the input will contain three lines, each with four integer scores. Your output should include all input data, individual series totals, game average for each member, team series, and team average. Sample output is

NAME	GAME 1	GAME 2	GAME 3	TOTAL	AVERAGE
Weber	212	220	190	622	207.3
Fazio	195	235	210	640	213.3
Martin	178	190	206	574	191.3
Patterson	195	215	210	620	206.7

Team Total: 2456

Team Average: 818.7

7. The Natural Pine Furniture Company has recently hired you to help them convert their antiquated payroll system to a computer-based model. They know you are still learning, so all they want right now is a program that will print a one-week payroll report for three employees. You should use the constant definition section for the following:

a. Federal withholding tax rate, 18%

b. State withholding tax rate, 4.5%

c. Hospitalization, $25.65

d. Union dues, $7.85

Each line of input will contain the employee's initials, the number of hours worked, and the employee's hourly rate. Your output should include a report for each employee and a summary report for the company files. A sample employee form follows:

```
Employee:                        JIM
Hours Worked:                  40.00
Hourly Rate:                    9.75
Total Wages:                  390.00

     Deductions:
     Federal Withholding       70.20
     State Withholding         17.55
     Hospitalization           26.65
     Union Dues                 7.85
     Total Deductions         122.25

     Net Pay                 $267.75
```

Output for a summary report could be

```
        Natural Pine Furniture Company

                 Weekly Summary

    Gross Wages:

    Deductions:
            Federal Withholding
            State Withholding
            Hospitalization
            Union Dues
                    Total Deductions

    Net Wages
```

8. The Child-Growth Encyclopedia Company wants a computer program that will print a monthly sales chart. Products produced by the company, prices, and sales commissions for each are

a. Basic encyclopedia, $325.00; 22%

b. Child educational supplement, $127.50; 15%

c. Annual update book, $18.95; 20%

Monthly sales data for one region consist of a two-letter region identifier (such as MI) and three integers, representing the number of units sold for each product listed above. A typical input screen would be:

```
What is your sales region? MI
How many Basic Encyclopedia were sold? 150
How many Child Supplements were sold? 120
How many Annual Updates were sold? 105
```

Write a program that will get the monthly sales data for two sales regions and produce the desired company chart. The prices may vary from month to month and should be defined in the constant definition section. The commissions are not subject to change. Typical output could be:

MONTHLY SALES CHART

		Basic Encyclopedia	Child Supplement	Annual Update
	Region			
Units sold	MI	150	120	105
(by region)	TX	225	200	150
Total units sold:		375	320	255
Price/unit		$325.00	$127.50	$18.95
Gross Sales:		$121,875.00	$40,800.00	$4,832.25
Commission rate		22%	15%	20%
Commissions paid:		$26,812.50	$6,120.00	$966.45

9. The Village Variety Store is having its annual Christmas sale. They would like you to write a program to produce a daily report for the store. Each item sold is identified by a code consisting of one letter followed by one digit. Your report should include data for three items. Each of the three lines of data will include item code, number of items sold, original item price, and reduction percentage. Your report should include a chart with the input data, sale price per item, and total amount of sales per item. You should also print a daily summary. Sample input is

```
A1 13  5.95 15
A2 24  7.95 20
A3 80  3.95 50
```

Typical output form could be:

Item Code	# Sold	Original Price	Reductions	Sale Price	Income
A1	13	$5.95	15%	$5.06	$65.78

Daily Summary

Gross Income:

10. The Holiday-Out Motel Company, Inc., wants a program that will print a statement for each overnight customer. Each line of input will contain room number (integer), number of nights (integer), room rate (real), telephone charges (real), and restaurant charges (real). You should use the constant definition section for the date and current tax rate. Each customer statement should include all input data, the date, tax rate and amount, total due, appropriate heading, and appropriate closing message. Test your program by running it for two customers. The tax rate applies only to the room cost. A typical input screen is

```
Room number? 135
Room rate? 39.95
Number of nights? 3
Telephone charges? 3.75
Meals? 57.50
```

A customer statement form is

```
        Holiday-Out Motel Company, Inc.

Date:              XX-XX-XX
Room #             135
Room Rate:         $39.95
Number of Nights: 3
Room Cost:         $119.85
Tax: XXX%          4.79
     Subtotal:     $124.64

Telephone:         3.75
Meals:             57.50

    TOTAL DUE     $185.89


    Thank you for staying at Holiday-Out
              Drive safely
            Please come again
```

11. As a part-time job this semester, you are working for the Family Budget Assistance Center. Your boss has asked you to write and execute a program that will analyze data for a family. Input for each family will consist of

```
Family ID number (int)
Number in family (int)
Income (float)
Total debts (float)
```

Your program should output the following:

a. An appropriate header.

b. The family's identification number, number in family, income, and total debts.

c. Predicted family living expenses ($3000 times the number in family).

d. The monthly payment necessary to pay off the debt in one year.

e. The amount the family should save [the family size times 2% of the income minus debt—Fafam_Size * 0.02 * (income – debt)] .

f. Your service fee (0.5% of the income).

Run your program for the following two families:

Identification Number	Size	Income	Debt
51		18,000.00	4800.00
4		26,000.00	3200.00

Output for the first family could be:

```
        Family Budget Assistance Center
                March 1989
            Telephone: (800)555-1234

Identification number        51
Family size                  4
Annual income                $ 18000.00
Total debt                   $ 2000.00
Expected living expenses     $ 12000.00
Monthly payment              $ 166.67
Savings                      $ 1280.00
Service fee                  $ 90.00
```

12. The Caswell Catering and Convention Service has asked you to write a computer program to produce customers' bills. The program should read in the following data.

a. The number of adults to be served.

b. The number of children to be served.

c. The cost per adult meal.

d. The cost per child's meal (60% of the cost of the adult's meal).

e. The cost for dessert (same for adults and children).

f. The room fee (no room fee if catered at the person's home).

g. A percentage for tip and tax (not applied to the room fee).

h. Any deposit should be deducted from the bill.

Write a program and test it using data sets 2, 3, and 4 from the following table:

Set	Child Count	Adult Count	Adult Cost	Dessert Cost	Room Cost	Tip/Tax Rate	Deposit
1	7	23	12.75	1.00	45.00	18%	50.00
2	3	54	13.50	1.25	65.00	19%	40.00
3	15	24	12.00	0.00	45.00	18%	75.00
4	2	71	11.15	1.50	0.00	6%	0.00

Note that data set 1 was used to produce the following sample output.

```
     Caswell Catering and Convention Service
                    Final Bill

Number of adults: 23
Number of children: 7
Cost per adult without dessert:      $    12.75
Cost per child without dessert:      $     7.65
Cost per dessert:                    $     1.00
Room fee:                            $    45.00
Tip and tax rate:                          0.18

Total cost for adult meals:          $   293.25
Total cost for child meals:          $    53.55
Total cost for dessert:              $    30.00
Total food cost:                     $   376.80
```

```
Plus tip and tax:                      $     67.82
Plus room fee:                         $     45.00
Less deposit:                          $     50.00

Balance due:                           $    439.62
```

13. The Maripot Carpet Store has asked you to write a computer program to calculate the amount a customer should be charged. The president of the company has given you the following information to help in writing the program.

   a. The carpet charge is equal to the number of square yards purchased times the carpet cost per square yard.

   b. The labor cost is equal to the number of square yards purchased times the labor cost per square yard. A fixed fee for floor preparation is added to some customers' bills.

   c. Large-volume customers are given a percentage discount but the discount applies only to the carpet charge, not the labor costs.

   d. All customers are charged 4% sales tax on the carpet; there is no sales tax on the labor cost.

Write the program and test it for customers 2, 3, and 4.

Customer	Sq. yds.	Cost per sq. yd.	Labor per sq. yd.	Prep. Cost	Discount
1	17	18.50	3.50	38.50	0.02
2	40	24.95	2.95	0.00	0.14
3	23	16.80	3.25	57.95	0.00
4	26	21.25	0.00	80.00	0.00

Note that the data for customer 1 were used to produce the following sample output.

```
Square yards purchased:                      17
    Cost per square yard:      $     18.50
   Labor per square yard:      $      3.50
  Floor preparation cost:      $     38.50
         Cost for carpet:      $    314.50
          Cost for labor:      $     98.00
      Discount on carpet:      $      6.29
           Tax on carpet:      $     12.33
      Charge to customer:      $    418.54
```

14. The manager of the Croswell Carpet Store has asked you to write a program to print customers' bill. The manager has given you the following information.

The store expresses the length and width of a room in terms of feet and tenths of a foot. For example, the length might be reported as 16.7 feet.

The amount of carpet purchased is expressed as square yards. It is found by dividing the area of the room (in square feet) by nine.

The store does not sell a fraction of a square yard. Thus, square yards must always be rounded up.

The carpet charge is equal to the number of square yards purchased times the carpet cost per square yard. Sales tax equal to 4% of the carpet cost must be added to the bill.

All customers are sold a carpet pad at $2.25 per square yard. Sales tax equal to 4% of the pad cost must be added to the bill.

The labor cost is equal to the number of square yards purchased times $2.40, which is the labor cost per square yard. No tax is charged on labor.

Large-volume customers may be given a discount. The discount may apply only to the carpet cost (before sales tax is added), only to the pad cost (before sales tax is added), only to the labor cost, or to any combination of the three charges.

Each customer is identified by a five-digit number and that number should appear on the bill. The sample output follows:

```
       Croswell Carpet Store
              Invoice

Customer number:              26817

             Carpet :        574.20
                Pad :         81.00
              Labor :         86.40

           Subtotal :        741.60
      Less discount :         65.52

           Subtotal :        676.08
           Plus tax :         23.59
              Total :        699.67
```

Write the program and test it for the following three customers.

a. Mr. Wilson (customer 81429) ordered carpet for his family room, which measures 25 feet long and 18 feet wide. The carpet sells for $12.95 per square yard and the manager agreed to give him a discount of 8% on the carpet and 6% on the labor.

b. Mr. and Mrs. Adams (customer 04246) ordered carpet for their bedroom, which measures 16.5 by 15.4 feet. The carpet sells for $18.90 per square yard and the manager granted a discount of 12% on everything.

c. Ms. Logan (customer 39050) ordered carpet that cost $8.95 per square yard for her daughter's bedroom. The room measures 13.1 by 12.5 feet. No discounts were given.

15. Each week Abduhl's Flying Carpets pays its salespeople a base salary plus a bonus for each carpet they sell. In addition, they pay a commission of 10% of the total sales made by each salesperson. Write a program to compute a salesperson's salary for the month by inputting Base, Bonus, Quantity, and Sales, and making the necessary calculations. Use the following test data:

Salesperson	Base	Bonus	Quantity	Commission	Sales
1	250.00	15.00	20	10%	1543.69
2	280.00	19.50	36	10%	2375.90

The commission figure is 10%. Be sure you can change this easily if necessary. Sample output follows:

```
        Salesperson :           1
               Base :         250.00
              Bonus :          15.00
           Quantity :          20
        Total Bonus :         300.00
         Commission :          10%
              Sales :        1543.69
   Total Commission :         154.37
                Pay :         704.37
```

16. "Think Metric" is the preferred way of having members of a nonmetric society become familiar with the metric system. Unfortunately, during the transition, many people are forced to rely on converting from their present system to the metric system. Develop a solution and write a program to help people convert their height and weight from inches and pounds to centimeters and kilograms. The program should take keyboard input of a person's height (in feet and inches) and weight (rounded to the nearest pound). Output should consist of the height and weight in metric units.

17. Discuss the issue of documenting subprograms with instructors of computer science, upper-level students majoring in computer science, and some of your classmates. Prepare a report for the class on this issue. Your report should contain information about different forms of documentation, the perceived need for documentation by various groups, the significance of documenting data transmission, and so forth. If possible, use specific examples to illustrate good documentation of subprograms versus poor documentation of subprograms.

18. Reread the material in Section 4.4 concerning functional abstraction. Then, from Problems 5, 7, 8, and 11, select one that you have not yet worked. Develop a structure chart and write module specifications for each module required for the problem you have chosen. Also, write a main driver for your program and write complete documentation for each subprogram including comments about all parameters.

CHAPTER 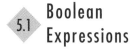 **5** Selection Statements

The previous chapters set the stage for using computers to solve problems. You have seen how programs in C++ can be used to get data, perform computations, and print results. You should be able to write complete, short programs, so it is now time to examine other aspects of problem solving.

Let us review the metaphor of the programmable pocket calculator that we have been using in the last two chapters. Our calculator allows us to solve some simple and complex problems by using built-in functions or by creating and using functions of our own. However, the calculator is limited in that it can only take input, calculate results, and display them as output. We would like the calculator to be more flexible, to be able to respond in different ways to different inputs or changes in its environment.

A major feature of a full-fledged computer, as opposed to our calculator, is the ability to make decisions. For example, a condition is examined and a decision is made as to which program statement is executed next. Statements that permit a computer to make decisions are called *selection statements*. Selection statements are examples of *control structures* because they allow the programmer to control the flow of execution of program statements.

5.1 Boolean Expressions

Before looking at decision making, we need to examine the logical constructs in C++, which include a new data type called *Boolean*. This data type allows you to represent something as true or false. Although this sounds relatively simple (and it is), this is a very significant feature of computers.

Defining Boolean Constants and a Boolean Data Type

Thus far we have used only the three data types **int**, **float**, and **char**. In any C++ program, the value 0 means *false,* and any other value means *true*. Instead of having to remember these associations, it would be convenient to use the names **TRUE** and **FALSE** to denote the boolean constants, as well as to use the name **boolean** when we wish to refer to the data type itself. For example, we might like to declare a variable **b** of type **boolean**, and assign it an initial value of **TRUE**:

```
boolean b = TRUE;
```

So that C++ programs can use these names properly, we define the constants **FALSE** and **TRUE** to have the values 0 and 1, respectively:

```
const int FALSE = 0;
const int TRUE = 1;
```

To create a new type name for declaring variables, function parameters, and function returns of these values, we use a C++ *type definition:*

```
typedef int boolean;
```

typedef is a reserved word in C++. The general form of a type definition is

typedef <data type> <new type name>;

where data type is any C++ data type. All our **typedef** example does is to create a synonym, **boolean**, for a built-in type name, **int**.

Some systems may have already defined the words **TRUE** and **FALSE** for system use. In that case, you can override these definitions by using the preprocessor directive **#undef**, as follows:

```
#undef FALSE
#undef TRUE

const int FALSE = 0;
const int TRUE = 1;
```

If we define the new names above the main program, Boolean variables can be declared anywhere in the program and manipulated according to the scope rules:

```
#undef FALSE
#undef TRUE

const int FALSE = 0;
const int TRUE = 1;

typedef int boolean;

int main()
{
     boolean a, b;

     a = FALSE;
     b = TRUE;
        .
        .
        .
```

As with other data types, if two variables are of type **boolean**, the value of one variable can be assigned to another variable as

```
b = TRUE;
a = b;
```

and can be envisioned as

TRUE

a

TRUE

b

Saving a New Type Definition in a Library File

The Boolean values **TRUE** and **FALSE** and the type name **boolean** will be mentioned in many applications. Entering the same five lines of code by hand to define these names in every new source program will be an annoying task. Instead, we can place the definitions in a library file to be included at the top of every program that uses them. The file is named **boolean.h** and contains these definitions:

```
// Library file: boolean.h

// Defines Boolean constants and a type name for any application.

#undef FALSE
#undef TRUE

const int FALSE = 0;
const int TRUE = 1;

typedef int boolean;
```

This file can then be included in any source program by means of the following line of code:

```
#include "boolean.h"
```

Note the use of double quotes to enclose the file name rather than angle brackets. In general, names of programmer-defined libraries will appear this way when they are included in example programs in this text. Names of standard libraries will continue to appear in angle brackets.

Placing the definitions of a new type in a library file is another example of information hiding. Programmers who use the **boolean.h** library need not be concerned with the representation of Boolean values as integers, any more than they have already been concerned with the representation of integers as bit patterns. All that we need to know about Boolean values, aside from their names, is how they can be used to make decisions in programs.

Relational Operators and Simple Boolean Expressions

In arithmetic, integers and reals can be compared for the relationships of equality, inequality, less than, and greater than. C++ also provides for the comparison of numbers or values of variables. The operators used for comparison are called *relational operators* and there are six of them. Their arithmetic notation, C++ notation, and meaning are given in Table 5.1. Note that the equality operator in C++ is **==**, not **=**. As you know, **=** means assignment in C++. The equality operator

◇ TABLE 5.1
Relational operators

Arithmetic Operation	Relational Operator	Meaning
=	==	Is equal to
<	<	Is less than
>	>	Is greater than
≤	<=	Is less than or equal to
≥	>=	Is greater than or equal to
≠	!=	Is not equal to

◇ **TABLE 5.2**
Values of simple Boolean expressions

Simple Boolean Expression	Boolean Value
7 == 7	TRUE
-3.0 == 0.0	FALSE
4.2 > 3.7	TRUE
-18 < -15	TRUE
13 < 0.013	FALSE
-17.32 != -17.32	FALSE
a == b	TRUE

does not change the values of its operands, whereas the assignment operator does. Be careful not to confuse them.

When two numbers or variable values are compared using a single relational operator, the expression is referred to as a *simple Boolean expression*. Each simple Boolean expression has the Boolean value **TRUE** or **FALSE** according to the arithmetic validity of the expression. In general, data of most of the built-in types can be compared. For example, when a character value is compared to an integer, the ASCII value of the character is used. When comparing reals, however, the computer representation of a real number might not be the exact real number intended.

Table 5.2 sets forth several Boolean expressions and their respective Boolean values, assuming the assignment statements **a = 3** and **b = 3** have been made.

Arithmetic expressions can also be used in simple Boolean expressions. Thus,

```
4 < (3 + 2)
```

has the value **TRUE**. When the computer evaluates this expression, the parentheses dictate that **(3 + 2)** is evaluated first and then the relational operator. Sequentially, this becomes

```
4 < (3 + 2)
4 < 5
TRUE
```

What if the parentheses had not been used? Could the expression be evaluated? This type of expression necessitates a priority level for the relational operators and the arithmetic operators. A summary for the priority of these operations follows:

Expression	Priority
( )	1
*, /, %	2
+, -	3
==, <, >, <=, >=, !=	4

Thus, we see that the relational operators are evaluated last. As with arithmetic operators, these are evaluated in order from left to right. Thus, the expression

```
4 < 3 + 2
```

could be evaluated without parentheses and would have the same Boolean value.

The following example illustrates the evaluation of a somewhat more complex Boolean expression.

EXAMPLE 5.1

Indicate the successive steps in the evaluation of the following Boolean expression:

```
10 % 4 * 3 - 8 <= 18 + 30 / 4 - 20
```

The steps in this evaluation are

```
10 % 4 * 3 - 8 <= 18 + 30 / 4 - 20
  ↓
2 * 3 - 8 <= 18 + 30 / 4 - 20
  ↓
6 - 8 <= 18 + 30 / 4 - 20
  ↓
- 2 <= 18 + 30 / 4 - 20
              ↓
- 2 <= 18 + 7 - 20
          ↓
- 2 <= 25 - 20
        ↓
- 2 <= 5
  ↓
TRUE
```

As shown here, even though parentheses are not required when using arithmetic expressions with relational operators, it is usually a good idea to use them to enhance the readability of the expression and to avoid using an incorrect expression.

Boolean Functions

Suppose we wish to have a function called **even** that takes an integer as an argument and returns the value **TRUE** if the integer is even and **FALSE** otherwise. We compare the remainder of dividing the argument by 2 to 0. We then return this result:

```
boolean even(int x)
{
      return x % 2 == 0;
}
```

Logical Operators and Compound Boolean Expressions

Boolean values can also be generated by using *logical operators* with simple Boolean expressions. The logical operators used by C++ are **&&** (meaning *and*), **||** (meaning *or*), and **!** (meaning *not*). Operators **&&** and **||** are used to connect two Boolean expressions, and **!** is used to negate the Boolean value of an expression; hence, it is sometimes referred to as *negation*. When one of these connectives or negation is used to generate Boolean values, the complete expression is referred to as a *compound Boolean expression*.

If **&&** is used to join two simple Boolean expressions, the resulting compound expression is true only when both simple expressions are true. If **||** is used, the result is true if either or both of the expressions are true. This is summarized as follows:

Expression 1 (E1)	Expression 2 (E2)	E1 && E2	E1 || E2
TRUE	TRUE	TRUE	TRUE
TRUE	FALSE	FALSE	TRUE
FALSE	TRUE	FALSE	TRUE
FALSE	FALSE	FALSE	FALSE

As previously indicated, ! merely produces the logical complement of an expression as follows:

Expression (E)	! E
TRUE	FALSE
FALSE	TRUE

Illustrations of the Boolean values generated using logical operators are given in Table 5.3.

Complex Boolean expressions can be generated by using several logical operators in an expression. The priority for evaluating these operators is

Operator	Priority
!	1
&&	2
||	3

When complex expressions are being evaluated, the logical operators, arithmetic expressions, and relational operators are evaluated during successive passes through the expression. The priority list is now as follows:

Expression or Operation	Priority
( )	Evaluate from inside out
!	Evaluate from left to right
*, /, %	Evaluate from left to right
+, -	Evaluate from left to right
<, <=, >, >=, ==, !=	Evaluate from left to right
&&	Evaluate from left to right
||	Evaluate from left to right

◇ TABLE 5.3
Values of compound
Boolean expressions

Expression	Boolean Value
(4.2 >= 5.0) && (8 == (3 + 5))	FALSE
(4.2 >= 5.0) || (8 == (3 + 5))	TRUE
(-2 < 0) && (18 >= 10)	TRUE
(-2 < 0) || (18 >= 0)	FALSE
(3 > 5) && (14.1 == 0.0)	FALSE
(3 > 5) || (14.1 == 0.0)	FALSE
! (18 == (10 + 8))	FALSE
! (- 4 > 0)	TRUE

As a matter of style, it is useful to parenthesize any comparison that is used as an operand for a logical operator. The following examples illustrate evaluation of some complex Boolean expressions.

EXAMPLE 5.2

```
(3 < 5) || (21 < 18) && (-81 > 0)
(3 < 5) || FALSE && (-81 > 0)   (parentheses first, then &&)
(3 < 5) || FALSE && TRUE
(3 < 5) || FALSE
TRUE || FALSE
TRUE
```

EXAMPLE 5.3

```
! ((-5.0 == -6.2) || ((7 < 3) && (6 == (3 + 3))))
        ↓                    ↓               ↓
! (     FALSE     || ( FALSE  &&    (6 == 6)))
                                        ↓
! (     FALSE     || ( FALSE  &&      TRUE))
                                        ↓
! (     FALSE     ||           FALSE)
                        ↓
!               FALSE
        ↓
      TRUE
```

Short-Circuit Evaluation of Boolean Expressions

Whenever two Boolean expressions are separated by a logical operator in C++, either **&&** or **||**, the run-time system uses *short-circuit evaluation.* The rules for this kind of evaluation are as follows:

1. In compound Boolean expressions connected by **||**, stop and return **TRUE** at the first Boolean expression that returns **TRUE**. Evaluate the next Boolean expression only if the current one returns **FALSE**. This rule captures the notion that a disjunction is **TRUE** only if at least one of the disjuncts is **TRUE**, and **FALSE** only if all of the disjuncts are **FALSE**.

2. In compound Boolean expressions connected by **&&**, stop and return **FALSE** at the first Boolean expression that returns **FALSE**. Evaluate the next Boolean expression only if the current one returns **TRUE**. This rule captures the notion that a conjunction is **FALSE** only if at least one of the conjuncts is **FALSE**, and **TRUE** only if all of the conjuncts are **TRUE**.

Short-circuit evaluation can enhance the efficiency of programs. For example, C++ actually evaluates the expression in Example 5.2 in three lines rather than six:

```
(3 < 5) || (21 < 18) && (-81 > 0)
                ↓
(3 < 5) || FALSE
    ↓
TRUE
```

Short-circuit evaluation can also be used to make some simple decisions. For example, one might guard against division by zero as follows:

```
(y != 0) && (x / y == 2)
```

Note that if **y** equals zero, the second expression, which divides a number by **y**, will not be evaluated in C++.

EXERCISES 5.1

1. Assume the variable declaration section of a program is

```
boolean flag1, flag2;
```

What output is produced by the following segment of code?

```
flag1 = TRUE;
flag2 = FALSE;
cout << flag1 << " " << TRUE << " " << flag2 << endl;
flag1 = flag2;
cout << flag2 << endl;
```

2. Assume the variable declaration section of a program is

```
char ch;
boolean flag;
```

For each of the following assignment statements indicate whether it is valid or invalid.
   a. `flag = "true";`
   b. `flag = T;`
   c. `flag = TRUE;`
   d. `ch = flag;`
   e. `ch = true;`
   f. `ch = 'T';`

3. Evaluate each of the following expressions.
   a. `(3 < 7) && (2 < 0) || (6 == 3 + 3)`
   b. `((3 < 7) && (2 < 0)) || (6 == 3 + 3)`
   c. `(3 < 7) && ((2 < 0) || (6 == 3 + 3))`
   d. `! ((-4.2 < 3.0) && (10 < 20))`
   e. `(! (-4.2 < 3.0)) || (! (10 < 20))`

4. For each of the following simple Boolean expressions, indicate whether it is **TRUE**, **FALSE**, or invalid.
   a. `-3.01 <= -3.001`
   b. `-3.0 == -3`
   c. `25 - 10 < 3 * 5`
   d. `42 % 5 < 42 / 5`
   e. `-5 * (3 + 2) >= 2 * (-10)`
   f. `10 / 5 < 1 + 1`
   g. `3 + 8 % 5 == 6 - 12 % 2`

5. For each of the following expressions, indicate whether it is valid or invalid. Evaluate those that are valid.
   a. `3 < 4 || 5 < 6`
   b. `! 3.0 == 6 / 2`
   c. `! (TRUE || FALSE)`
   d. `! TRUE || FALSE`
   e. `! TRUE || ! FALSE`
   f. `! (18 < 25) && || (-3 < 0)`
   g. `8 * 3 < 20 + 10`

A NOTE OF INTEREST

George Boole

George Boole was born in 1815 in Lincoln, England. Boole was the son of a small shopkeeper and his family belonged to the lowest social class. In an attempt to rise above his station, Boole spent his early years teaching himself Latin and Greek. During this period, he also received elementary instruction in mathematics from his father.

At the age of 16, Boole worked as a teacher in an elementary school. He used most of his wages to help support his parents. At the age of 20 (after a brief, unsuccessful attempt to study for the clergy), he opened his own school. As part of his preparation for running his school, he had to learn more mathematics. This activity led to the development of some of the most significant mathematics of the nineteenth century.

Boole's major contributions were in the field of logic. An indication of his genius is given by the fact that his early work included the discovery of invariants. The mathematical significance of this is perhaps best explained by noting that the theory of relativity developed by Albert Einstein would not have been possible without the previous work on invariants.

Boole's first published contribution was *The Mathematical Analysis of Logic,* which appeared in 1848 while he was still working as an elementary teacher and the sole support for his parents. In 1849, he was appointed professor of mathematics at Queen's College in Cork, Ireland. The relative freedom from financial worry and time constraints the college appointment provided allowed him to pursue his work in mathematics. His masterpiece, *An Investigation of the Laws of Thought, on which Are Founded the Mathematical Theories of Logic and Probabilities,* was published in 1854. Boole was then 39, relatively old for such original work. According to Bertrand Russell, pure mathematics was discovered by Boole in this work.

The brilliance of Boole's work laid the foundation for what is currently studied as formal logic. The data type Boolean is named in honor of Boole because of his contribution to the development of logic as part of mathematics. Boole died in 1864. His early death resulted from pneumonia contracted by keeping a lecture engagement when he was soaked to the skin.

6. Assume the variable declaration section of a program is

```
int int1, int2;
float fl1, fl2;
boolean flag1, flag2;
and the values of the variables are
```

0	8	-15.2	-20.0	FALSE	TRUE
int1	int2	fl1	fl2	flag1	flag2

Evaluate each of the following expressions:

a. `(int1 <= int2) || ! (fl2 == fl1)`
b. `! (flag1) || ! (flag2)`
c. `! (flag1 && flag2)`
d. `((fl1-fl2) < 100/int2) && ((int1 < 1) && ! (flag2))`
e. `! ((int2 - 16 / 2) == int1) && flag1`

7. DeMorgan's Laws state the following:

a. `! (A || B)` is equivalent to `(! A) && (! B)`
b. `! (A && B)` is equivalent to `(! A) || (! B)`

Write a test program that demonstrates the validity of each of these equivalent statements.

if
5.2 Statements

- to learn the syntax of the **if** statement
- to understand the flow of control when using an **if** statement
- to be able to use an **if** statement in a program
- to understand why compound statements are needed
- to be able to use correct syntax in writing a compound statement
- to be able to design programs using **if** statements

The first decision-making statement we will examine is the **if** statement. An **if** statement is used to make a program do something only when certain conditions are used. The form and syntax for an **if** statement are

```
if (<Boolean expression>)
    <statement>
```

where **statement** represents any C++ statement. Note that the parentheses enclosing the Boolean expression are required.

The Boolean expression can be any valid expression that is either true or false at the time of evaluation. If it is **TRUE**, the statement following the Boolean expression is executed. If it is **FALSE**, control is transferred to the first program statement following the complete **if** statement. In general, code would have the form

```
<statement 1>
if (<Boolean expression>)
    <statement 2>
<statement 3>
```

as illustrated in Figure 5.1.

As a further illustration of how an **if** statement works, consider the program fragment

```
sum = 0.0;
cin >> num;
if (num > 0.0)
    sum = sum + num;
cout << fixed << showpoint << setprecision(2) << setw(10) << sum << endl;
```

◆ FIGURE 5.1
if flow diagram

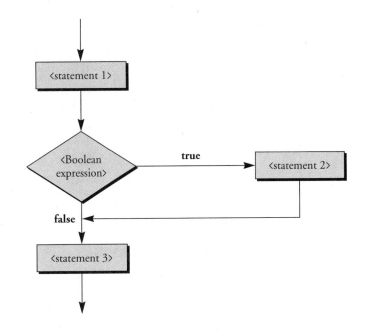

If the value read is 75.85, prior to execution of the **if** statement, the contents of **num** and **sum** are

75.85		0.0
num		**sum**

The Boolean expression **num > 0.0** is now evaluated and, since it is **TRUE**, the statement

```
sum = sum + num;
```

is executed and we have

75.85		75.85
num		**sum**

The next program statement is executed and produces the output

```
75.85
```

However, if the value read is –25.5, the variable values are

-25.5		0.0
num		**sum**

The Boolean expression **num > 0.0** is **FALSE** and control is transferred to the line

```
cout << fixed << showpoint << setprecision(2) << setw(10) << sum << endl;
```

Thus, the output is

```
0.00
```

Now, let's suppose you want a program in which one objective is to count the number of zeros in the input. Assuming suitable initialization and declaration, a program fragment for this task could be

```
cin >> num;
if (num == 0)
    zero_count = zero_count + 1;
```

One writing style for using an **if** statement calls for indenting the program statement to be executed if the Boolean expression is **TRUE**. This, of course, is not required. The following code

```
if (num == 0)
    zero_count = zero_count + 1;
```

could be written

```
if (num == 0) zero_count = zero_count + 1;
```

However, the indenting style for simple **if** statements is consistent with the style used with more elaborate conditional statements.

Compound Statements

The last concept needed before looking further at selection in C++ is that of a *compound statement*. In a C++ program, simple statements end with a semicolon. Thus,

```
cin >> a >> b;
a = 3 * b;
cout << b;
```

are three simple statements.

In some instances, it is necessary to perform several simple statements when some condition is true. For example, you may want the program to do certain things if a condition is true. In this situation, several simple statements that can be written as a single compound statement would be helpful. In general, there are several C++ constructs that require compound statements. A compound statement is created by using the symbols **{** and **}** at the beginning and end, respectively, of a sequence of simple statements. Correct syntax for a compound statement is

```
{
        <statement 1>
        <statement 2>
             .
             .
             .
        <statement n >
}
```

Simple statements within a compound statement end with semicolons. The end of the compound statement is not followed by a semicolon.

When a compound statement is executed within a program, the entire segment of code between **{** and **}** is treated as a single action. This is referred to as a *statement block*. It is important that you develop a consistent, acceptable writing style for writing compound statements. What you use will vary according to your instructor's wishes and your personal preferences. Examples in this text will align each statement within the compound statement with the enclosing symbols. Thus,

```
{
        cin >> a >> b;
        a = 3 * b;
        cout << b;
}
```

is a compound statement in a program; what it does is easily identified.

Using Compound Statements

As you might expect, compound statements can be (and frequently are) used as part of an **if** statement. The form and syntax for this are

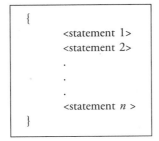

```
if (<Boolean expression>)
{
        <statement 1>
           .
           .
           .
        <statement n>
}
```

Program control is exactly as before depending on the value of the Boolean expression. For example, suppose you are writing a function to keep track of and compute fees for vehicles in a parking lot where separate records are kept for senior citizens. A segment of code in the procedure could be

```
if (customer == 'S')
{
    senior_count = senior_count + 1;
    amount_due = senior_citizen_rate;
}
```

if Statements with Functions

The next example designs a program to solve a problem using an **if** statement with function.

Let us write a program that reads two integers and prints them in the order of larger first, smaller second. The first-level pseudocode solution is

1. Read numbers
2. Determine the larger
3. Print results

◆ FIGURE 5.2
Structure Chart for Ordering
Two Numbers

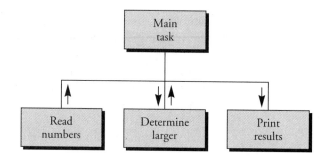

A structure chart for this is given in Figure 5.2. Reading the numbers and printing the results require no further discussion of their design or implementation. Our strategy for determining the larger of the two numbers will be to maintain three variables, **min**, **max,** and **temp**. Step 2 assumes that the numbers have been read in to variables **min** and **max**. We will compare the values, and if **min** is greater than **max**, we will use the variable **temp** to help swap the values of **min** and **max**. Thus, step 2 will have the effect of placing the larger value in **max** and the smaller value in **min**. The pseudocode for step 2 is

```
if min > max
    assign min to temp
    assign max to min
    assign temp to max
```

This algorithm translates to the following C++ function:

```
// Function: determine_larger
// Enforces the ordering relation min <= max between two integer variables
//
// Inputs: two integer variables in random order
// Outputs: min will contain the smaller of the two inputs, and max the larger
```

```
void determine_larger(int &min, int &max)
{
      int temp;

      if (min > max)
      {
            temp = min;
            min = max;
            max = temp;
      }
}
```

A complete program for this follows:

```
// Program file: minmax.cpp

#include <iostream.h>
#include <iomanip.h>

const char SKIP = ' ';

// Function: get_data
// Prompts for and obtains two integers from user
//
// Outputs: two integers

void get_data(int &first, int &second);

// Function: determine_larger
// Enforces the ordering relation min <= max between two integer variables
//
// Inputs: two integer variables in random order
// Outputs: min will contain the smaller of the two inputs, and max the larger

void determine_larger(int &min, int &max);

// Function: print_results
// Displays results on screen
//
// Inputs: two integers, the smaller in min, the larger in max

void print_results(int min, int max);

int main()
{
      int min, max;

      get_data(min, max);
      determine_larger(min, max);
      print_results(min, max);
      return 0;
}
```

```
void get_data(int &first, int &second)
{
     cout << "Enter the first number and press <Enter>."
     cin >> min;
     cout << "Enter the second number and press <Enter>."
     cin >> max;
}
```
} 1

```
void determine_larger(int &min, int &max)
{
     int temp;
     if (min > max)
     {
          temp = min;
          min = max;
          max = temp;
     }
}
```
} 2

```
void print_results(int min, int max)
{
     cout << setw(19) << SKIP << "Larger number" << setw(15)
          << "Smaller number" << endl;
     cout << setw(19) << SKIP << "--------------"
          << setw(15) << "--------------" << endl;
     cout << endl;
     cout << set(26) << min << setw(15) << max << endl;
}
```
} 3

Sample runs of this program produce

```
Enter the first number and press <Enter>. 35
Enter the second number and press <Enter>. 115


                         Larger number          Smaller number
                         -------------          --------------

                            115                     35


Enter the first number and press <Enter>. 85
Enter the second number and press <Enter>. 26


                         Larger number          Smaller number
                         -------------          --------------

                             85                     26
```

Note that two runs of this program are required to test the logic of the **if** statement.

EXERCISES 5.2

1. What is the output from each of the following program fragments? Assume the following assignment statements precede each fragment:

```
a = 10;
b = 5;
```

```
a. if (a <= b)
        b = a;
   cout << a << endl << b << endl;
b. if (a <= b)
   {
        b = a;
        cout << a << endl << b << endl;
   }
c. if (a < b)
        temp = a;
   a = b;
   b = temp;
   cout << a << endl << b endl;
d. if (a < b)
   {
        temp = a;
        a = b;
        b = temp;
   }
   cout << a << endl << b << endl;
e. if ((a < b) || (b - a < 0))
   {
        a = a + b;
        b = b - 1;
        cout << a << endl << b << endl;
   }
   cout << a << endl << b << endl;
f. if ((a < b) && (b - a < 0))
   {
        a = a + b;
        b = b - 1;
        cout << a << endl << b << endl;
   }
   cout << a << endl << b << endl;
```

2. Write a test program to illustrate what happens when a semicolon is inadvertently inserted after a Boolean expression in an **if** statement. For example,

```
if (a > 0);
        sum = sum + a;
```

3. Find and explain the errors in each of the following program fragments. Assume all variables have been suitably declared.

```
a. if (a == 10)
        cout << a << endl;
b. x = 7;
   if (3 < x < 10)
   {
        x = x + 1;
        cout << x << endl;
   }
```

```
c. count = 0;
   sum = 0;
   a = 50;
   if (a > 0)
        count = count + 1;
   sum = sum + a;
d. cin >> ch;
   if (ch = 'a' || 'b')
        cout << ch << endl;
```

4. What is the output from each of the following program fragments? Assume all variables have been suitably declared.

```
a. j = 18;
   if (j % 5 == 0)
        cout << j << endl;
b. a = 5;
   b = 90;
   b = b / a - 5;
   if (b > a)
        b = a * 30;
   cout << a << endl << b << endl;
```

5. Can a simple statement be written using a { . . . } block? Write a short program that allows you to verify your answer.

6. Discuss the differences in the following programs. Predict the output for each program using sample values for **num**.

```
a. int main()
   {
        int num;
        cout << "Enter an integer and press <Enter>.";
        cin >> num;
        if (num > 0)
             cout << endl;
        cout << setw(22) << "The number is" << setw(6)
             << num << endl;
        cout << endl;
        cout << setw(30) << "The number squared is"
             << setw(6) << num * num << endl;
        cout << setw(28) << "The number cubed is"
             << setw(6) << num * num * num << endl;
        cout << endl;
        return 0;
   }
b. int main()
   {
        int num;
        cout << "Enter an integer and press <Enter>. ";
        cin >> num;
        if (num > 0)
        {
             cout << endl;
             cout << setw(22) << "The number is"
                  << setw(6) << num << endl;
             cout << endl;
```

```
        cout << setw(30) << "The number squared is"
             << setw(6) << num * num << endl;
        cout << setw(28) << "The number cubed is"
             << setw(6) << num * num * num << endl;
        cout << endl;
    }
    return 0;
}
```

7. Discuss writing style and readability of compound statements.

8. Find all errors in the following compound statements.

a.
```
{
    cin >> a
    cout << a << endl
}
```

b.
```
{
    sum = sum + num
};
```

c.
```
{
    cin >> size1 >> size2;
    cout << setw(8) << size1 << setw(8) << size2
         << endl
}
```

d.
```
{
    cin << age << weight;
    total_age = total_age + age;
    total_weight = total_weight + weight;
    cout << setw(8) << age << weight << endl;
```

9. Write a single compound statement that will do the following:

  a. Read three integers from the keyboard.
  b. Add them to a previous total.
  c. Print the numbers on one line.
  d. Skip a line (output).
  e. Print the new total.

10. Write a program fragment that reads three reals, counts the number of positive reals, and accumulates the sum of positive reals.

11. Write a program fragment that reads three characters and then prints them only if the letters have been read in alphabetical order (for example, print "boy" but do not print "dog").

12. Given two integers, **A** and **B**, **A** is a divisor of **B** if **B % A = 0**. Write a complete program that reads two positive integers **A** and **B** and then, if **A** is a divisor of **B**,

  a. Print **A**.
  b. Print **B**.
  c. Print the result of **B** divided by **A**.
  For example, the output could be

```
A is 14

B is 42

B divided by A is 3
```

5.3 if . . . else Statements

Form and Syntax

The previous section discussed the one-way selection statement **if**. The second selection statement we will examine is the two-way selection statement **if . . . else**. Correct form and syntax for **if . . . else** are

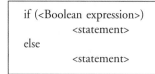

```
if (<Boolean expression>)
        <statement>
else
        <statement>
```

Flow of control when using an **if . . . else** statement is as follows:

1. The Boolean expression is evaluated.
2. If the Boolean expression is **TRUE**, the statement following the expression is executed and control is transferred to the first program statement following the complete **if . . . else** statement.
3. If the Boolean expression is **FALSE**, the statement following **else** is executed and control is transferred to the first program statement following the **if . . . else** statement.

A flow diagram is given in Figure 5.3.

A few points follow that you should remember concerning **if . . . else** statements:

1. The Boolean expression can be any valid expression having a value of **TRUE** or **FALSE** at the time it is evaluated.
2. The complete **if . . . else** statement is one program statement and is separated from other complete statements by a semicolon whenever appropriate.
3. Writing style should include indenting within the **else** option in a manner consistent with indenting in the **if** option.

◆ FIGURE 5.3
if . . . else flow diagram

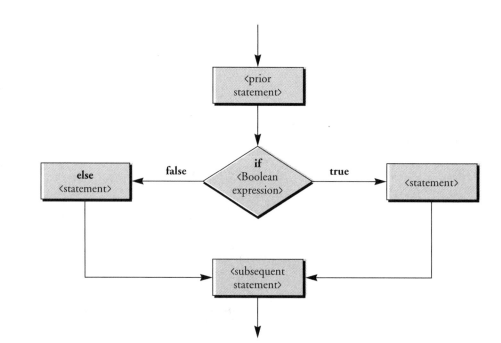

Artificial Intelligence

Artificial intelligence (AI) research seeks to understand the principles of human intelligence and apply those principles to the creation of smarter computer programs. The original goal of AI research was to create programs with humanlike intelligence and capabilities, yet after many years of research, little progress has been made toward this goal.

In recent years, however, AI researchers have pursued much more modest goals with much greater success. Programs based on AI techniques are playing increasingly important roles in such down-to-earth areas as medicine, education, recreation, business, and industry. Such programs come nowhere near achieving human levels of intelligence, but they often have capabilities that are not easily achieved with non-AI programs.

The main principles of AI can be summarized as follows:

Search: A method whereby the computer solves a problem by searching through all logically possible solutions.

Rules: Knowledge about what actions to take in particular circumstances is stored as rules; each rule has the form **if** situation **then** action or conclusion.

Reasoning: Programs can use reasoning to draw conclusions from the facts and rules available to the program.

Planning: The control program plans the actions that must be taken to accomplish a particular goal, then modifies the plan if unexpected obstacles are encountered; this is most widely used in robot control.

Pattern recognition: Important for rule-based systems, the **if** part of a rule specifies a particular pattern of facts; the rule is to be applied when that pattern is recognized in the facts known to the program.

Knowledge bases: Storage of the facts and rules that govern the operation of an AI program.

EXAMPLE 5.5

Let us write a program fragment to keep separate counts of negative and nonnegative numbers entered as data. Assuming all variables have been suitably declared and initialized, an **if . . . else** statement could be used as follows:

```
cout << "Please enter a number and press <Enter>.";
cin >> num;
if (num < 0)
        neg_count = neg_count + 1;
else
        non_neg_count = non_neg_count + 1;
```

Using Compound Statements

Program statements in both the **if** option and the **else** option can be compound statements. When using compound statements in these options, you should use a consistent, readable indenting style; remember to use **{ . . . }** for each compound statement; and do not put a semicolon before **else**.

EXAMPLE 5.6

Suppose you want a program to read a number, count it as negative or nonnegative, and print it in either a column of nonnegative numbers or a column of negative numbers. Assuming all variables have been suitably declared and initialized, the fragment might be

```
cout << "Please enter a number and press <Enter>.";
cin >> num;
if (num < 0)
{
     neg_count = neg_count + 1;
     cout << setw(15) << num << endl;
}                                                  // end of if option
else
{
     non_neg_count = non_neg_count + 1;
     cout << setw(30) << num << endl;
}                                                  // end of else option
```

We next consider an example of a program fragment that requires the use of compound statements within an **if . . . else** statement.

EXAMPLE 5.7

We want to write a function that computes gross wages for an employee of the Florida OJ Canning Company. Input includes hours worked and the hourly rate. Overtime (more than 40 hours) pay is computed as time-and-a-half. A function would be

```
const float WEEKLY_HOURS = 40.0;
const float TIME_AND_A_HALF = 1.5;

float compute_wages (float hours, float pay_rate)
{
     float overtime;
     if (hours <= WEEKLY_HOURS )
          return hours * pay_rate;
     else
     {
          overtime = TIME_AND_A_HALF *
               (hours - WEEKLY_HOURS ) * pay_rate;
          return WEEKLY_HOURS * pay_rate + overtime;
     }
}
```

Robust Programs

If a program is completely protected against all possible crashes from bad data and unexpected values, it is said to be *robust*. The preceding examples have all assumed that desired data would be accurately entered from the keyboard. In actual practice, this is seldom the case. The **if . . . else** statements can be used to guard against bad data entries. For example, if a program is designed to use positive numbers, you could guard against negatives and zero by

```
cout << "Enter a positive number and press <Enter>. ";
cin >> number;
if (number <= 0)
     cout << "You entered a nonpositive number." << endl;
```

```
else
          .
          . (code for expected action here)
          .
```

This program protection can be used anywhere in a program. For example, if you are finding square roots of numbers, you could avoid a program crash by using this code:

```
if (num < 0)
        cout << "The number " << num << " is negative"
               << endl;
    else
          .
          . (rest of action here)
          .
```

In actual practice, students need to balance robustness against amount of code and efficiency. An overemphasis on making a program robust can detract from time spent learning new programming concepts. You should discuss this with your instructor and decide what is best for your situation. Generally, there should be an agreement between the programmer and the customer regarding the level of robustness required. For most programs and examples in this text, it is assumed that valid data are entered when requested.

EXAMPLE 5.8

Callers of functions that take input would like to be signaled that it is within a given lower and upper bound. For example, a function that inputs the age of an employee might check to see that the integer value entered by the user is greater than 17 and less than 70 (assuming these are conventional age limits for employable persons). In this example, the function would return **TRUE** if the age is greater than 17 and also less than 70, or **FALSE** otherwise. The caller of the function takes care of prompting the user for information, and of error recovery, such as an error message and a loop for more input. The function, named **get_valid_data**, is passed the values of the lower and the upper bounds, and variables for the data and a Boolean flag indicating a valid input value. One might invoke the function as follows:

```
boolean age_ok;
int age;

cout << "Enter the employee's age: ";
get_valid_data(17, 70, age, age_ok);
if (! age_ok)
    cout << "Age must be greater than 17 and less than 100" << endl;
else
    <process the age, etc.>
```

A declaration of the function is therefore

```
// Function: get_valid_data
// Takes an input integer from the user and checks it for validity
```

```
//
// Inputs: two integers representing the lower and upper bounds of valid input
// Outputs: an integer representing the input and a Boolean value representing
// its validity

void get_valid_data(int low, int high, int &data, boolean &data_ok);
```

The function does not prompt the user, but simply reads data. The function then compares the data to the limits. If the data are within the limits, the flag is set to **TRUE**; if not, the flag is set to **FALSE**.

```
void get_valid_data(int low, int high, int &data, boolean &data_ok)
{
    cin >> data;
    if ((data > low) && (data < high))
        data_ok = TRUE;
    else
        data_ok = FALSE;
}
```

Guarding Against Overflow

As we discussed in Chapter 3, integer overflow occurs when the absolute value of an integer exceeds a maximum, and real overflow occurs when a value is obtained that is too large to be stored in a memory location. Both of these values vary according to the compiler being used. The maximum value of an integer is named by the constant **INT_MAX**, and the maximum value of a real number is named by the constant **FLT_MAX**. Both constants become available to a C++ program by including the library files **limits.h** and **float. h.**

One method that is used to guard against integer overflow is based on the principle of checking a number against some function of **INT_MAX**. Thus, if you want to multiply a number by 10, you would first compare it to **INT_MAX / 10**. A typical segment of code could be

```
if (num > INT_MAX / 10)
    (overflow message)
else
{
    num = num * 10;
    (rest of action)
}
```

We can now use this same idea with a Boolean-valued function. For example, consider the function

```
boolean near_overflow (int num)
{
        return num > INT_MAX / 10;
}
```

This could be used in the following manner:

```
if (num > near_overflow(num))
    (overflow message)
```

```
else
{
     num = num * 10;
     (rest of action)
}
```

EXERCISES 5.3

1. What output is produced from each of the following program fragments? Assume all variables have been suitably declared.

   a.
   ```
   a = -14;
   b = 0;
   if (a < b)
        cout << a << endl;
   else
        cout << a * b << endl;
   ```

   b.
   ```
   a = 50;
   b = 25;
   count = 0;
   sum = 0;
   if (a == b)
        cout << a << b << endl;
   else
   {
        count = count + 1;
        sum = sum + a + b;
        cout << a << b << endl;
   }
   cout << count << sum << endl;
   ```

   c.
   ```
   temp = 0;
   a = 10;
   b = 5;
   f (a > b)
        cout << a << b << endl;
   else
        temp = a;
   a = b;
   b = temp;
   cout << a << b << endl;
   ```

2. Find all errors in the following program fragments.

   a.
   ```
   if (ch < '.')
        char_count = char_count + 1;
   cout << ch << endl;
   else
        period_count = period_count + 1;
   ```

   b.
   ```
   if (age < 20)
   {
        young_count = young_count + 1;
        young_age = young_age + age;
   };
   else
   {
   ```

```
                         old_count = old_count + 1;
                         old_age = old_age + age;
                   };
             c. if (age < 20)
                   {
                         young_count = young_count + 1;
                         young_age = young_age + age
                   }
                   else
                         old_count = old_count + 1;
                   old_age = old_age + age;
```

3. Write a program to balance your checkbook. Your program should get an entry from the keyboard, keep track of the number of deposits and checks, and keep a running balance. The data consist of a character, D (deposit) or C (check), followed by an amount.

 5.4

Nested and Extended if Statements

OBJECTIVES

- to learn the syntax of nested **if** statements
- to know when to use nested **if** statements
- to be able to use extended **if** statements
- to be able to trace the logic of nested **if** statements
- to develop a consistent writing style when using nested **if** statements

Multiway Selection

Sections 5.2 and 5.3 examined one-way (**if**) and two-way (**if . . . else**) selection. Because each of these is a single C++ statement, either can be used as part of a selection statement to achieve multiple selection. In this case, the multiple selection statement is referred to as a *nested if statement.* These nested statements can be any combination of **if** or **if . . . else** statements.

To illustrate, let us write a program fragment to issue interim progress reports for students in a class. If a student's score is below 50, the student is failing. If the score is between 50 and 69 inclusive, the progress is unsatisfactory. If the score is 70 or above, the progress is satisfactory. The first decision to be made is based on whether the score is below 50 or not; the design is

```
if score >= 50

        .
        .  (progress report here)
        .

    else
        cout << setw(34)
            << "You are currently failing." << endl;
```

We now use a nested **if . . . else** statement for the progress report for students who are not failing. The complete fragment is

```
if score >= 50
    if score >= 69
        cout << setw(38) << "Your progress is satisfactory." << endl;
    else
        cout << setw(40) << "Your progress is unsatisfactory." << endl;
else
    cout << setw(34) << "You are currently failing." << endl;
```

One particular instance of nesting selection statements requires special development. When additional **if . . . else** statements are used in the **else** option, we call this an *extended if statement* and use the following form:

```
if (<condition 1>)
        .
        . (action 1 here)
        .
else if (<condition 2>)
        .
        . (action 2 here)
        .
else if (<condition 3>)
        .
        . (action 3 here)
        .
else
        .
        . (action 4 here)
        .
```

Using this form, we could redesign the previous fragment that printed progress reports as follows:

```
if (score > 69)
      cout << setw(38) << "Your progress is satisfactory." << endl;
else if (score > 50)
      cout << setw(40) << "Your progress is unsatisfactory." << endl;
else
      cout << setw(34) << "You are currently failing." << endl;
```

If you trace through both fragments with scores of 40, 60, and 80, you will see they produce identical output.

Another method of writing the nested fragment is to use sequential selection statements as follows:

```
if (score > 69)
    cout << setw(38) << "Your progress is "
         << "satisfactory." << endl;
if ((score <= 69) && (score >= 50))
    cout << setw(40) << "Your progress is "
         << "unsatisfactory." << endl;
if (score < 50)
    cout << setw(34) << "You are currently failing."
         << endl;
```

However, there are two reasons why this is not considered good programming practice. First, this is less efficient because the condition of each **if** statement is evaluated each time through the program. Second, only one of the three conditions can be true; they are said to be *mutually exclusive*. In general, mutually exclusive conditions are most accurately represented with nested **if . . . else** statements. You should generally avoid using sequential **if** statements if a nested statement can be used.

Tracing the flow of logic through nested or extended **if** statements can be tedious. However, it is essential that you develop this ability. For practice, let us trace through the following example.

EXAMPLE 5.9

Consider the nested statement

```
if (a > 0)
    if (a % 2 == 0)
            sum1 = sum1 + a;
    else
            sum2 = sum2 + a;
else if (a == 0)
    cout << setw(18) << "a is zero" << endl;
else
    neg_sum = neg_sum + a;
cout << setw(17) << "All done" << endl;
```

We will trace through this statement and discover what action is taken when **a** is assigned 20, 15, 0, and -30, respectively. For **a = 20**, the expression **a > 0** is **TRUE**, hence

```
a % 2 == 0
```

is evaluated. This is **TRUE** so

```
sum1 = sum1 + a;
```

is executed and control is transferred to

```
cout << setw(17) << "All done" << endl;
```

For **a = 15, a > 0** is **TRUE** and

```
a % 2 == 0
```

is evaluated. This is **FALSE**, so

```
sum2 = sum2 + a;
```

is executed and control is again transferred out of the nested statement to

```
cout << setw(17) << "All done" << endl;
```

For **a = 0, a > 0** is **FALSE**, thus

```
a == 0
```

is evaluated. Since this is **TRUE**, the statement

```
cout << setw(18) << "a is zero" << endl;
```

is executed and control is transferred to

```
cout << setw(17) << "All done" << endl;
```

Finally, for **a = -30, a > 0** is **FALSE**, thus

```
a == 0
```

is evaluated. This is **FALSE**, so

```
neg_sum = neg_sum + a;
```

is executed and control is transferred to

```
cout << setw(17) << "All done" << endl;
```

Note that this example traces through all possibilities involved in the nested statement. This is essential to guarantee your statement is properly constructed.

Designing solutions to problems that require multiway selection can be difficult. A few guidelines can help. If a decision has two courses of action and one is complex and the other is fairly simple, nest the complex part in the **if** option and the simple part in the **else** option. This method is frequently used to check for bad data. An example of the program design for this could be:

```
        .
        . (get the data)
        .

if (data_ok)
        .
        . (complex action here)
        .
else (message about bad data)
```

This method could also be used to guard against dividing by zero in computation. For instance, we could have

```
divisor = <value>;
if (divisor != 0)
        .
        . (proceed with action)
        .
else
        cout << "division by zero" << endl;
```

When there are several courses of action that can be considered sequentially, an extended **if . . . else** should be used. To illustrate, consider the program fragment of Example 5.10.

EXAMPLE 5.10

Let us write a program fragment that allows you to assign letter grades based on students' semester averages. Grades are to be assigned according to the following scale:

$100 >= X >= 90$	A
$90 > X >= 80$	B
$80 > X >= 70$	C
$70 > X >= 55$	D
$55 > X$	E

Extended **if** statements can be used to accomplish this as follows:

```
if (average >= 90)
        grade = 'A';
else if (average >= 80)
        grade = 'B';
else if (average >= 70)
        grade = 'C';
else if (average >= 55)
        grade = 'D';
else
        grade = 'F';
```

Because any average of more than 100 or less than zero would be a sign of some data or program error, this example could be protected with a statement as follows:

```
if ((average <= 100) && (average >= 0))
        .
        . (compute letter grade)
        .
else
        cout << setw(38) << "There is an error. Average "
             << "is" << setw(8) << average << endl;
```

Protecting parts of a program in this manner will help you avoid unexpected results or program crashes. It also allows you to identify the source of an error.

Form and Syntax

The rule for matching **else** in nested selection statements is:

*When an **else** is encountered, it is matched with the most recent **if** that has not yet been matched.*

The matching of **if**s with **else**s is a common source of errors. When designing programs, you should be very careful to match them correctly. For example, consider the following situation, which can lead to an error:

```
if (<condition 1>)
        .
        . (action 1)
        .
else
        .
        . (action 2)
        .
```

where action 1 consists of an **if** statement. Specifically, suppose you want a fragment of code to read a list of positive integers and print those that are perfect squares. A method of protecting against negative integers and zero could be:

```
cin >> num;
if (num > 0)
        .
        . (action 1 here)
        .
else
        cout << num << " is not positive." << endl;
```

If we now develop action 1 so that it prints only those positive integers that are perfect squares, it is

```
if (sqrt(num) == int(sqrt(num)))
    cout << num << endl;
```

Nesting this selection statement in our design, we have

```
cin >> num;
if (num > 0)
    if (sqrt(num) == int(sqrt(num))
        cout << num << endl;
    else
        cout << num << " is not positive." << endl;
```

If you now use this segment with input of 20 for **num**, the output is

```
20 is not positive.
```

Thus, this fragment is not correct to solve the problem. The indenting is consistent with our intent, but the actual execution of the fragment treated the code as

```
cin >> num;
if (num > 0)
    if (sqrt(num) == int(sqrt(num)))
        cout << num << endl;
    else
        cout << num << " is not positive." << endl;
```

because the **else** is matched with the most recent **if**. This problem can be resolved by redesigning the fragment as follows:

```
cin >> num;
if (num <= 0)
    cout << num << " is not positive." << endl;
else if (sqrt(num) == int(sqrt(num)))
    cout << num << endl;
```

COMMUNICATION AND STYLE TIPS

It is very important to use a consistent, readable writing style when using nested or extended **if** statements. The style used here for nested **if** statements is to indent each nested statement a single tab stop. Also, each **else** of an **if . . . else** statement is in the same column as the **if** of that statement. This allows you to see at a glance where the **else**s match with the **if**s. For example,

```
if
    if
    else
else
```

An extended **if** statement has all the **else**s on the same indenting level as the first **if**. This reinforces the concept of extended **if**. For example,

```
if
else if
else if
else
```

We conclude this section with an example that uses nested **if** statements.

EXAMPLE 5.11

Write a program that computes the gross pay for an employee of the Clean Products Corporation of America. The corporation produces three products: A, B, and C. Supervisors earn a commission of 7% of sales and representatives earn 5%. Bonuses of $100 are paid to supervisors whose commission exceeds $300 and to representatives whose commission exceeds $200. Input is in the form

```
S 18 15 10
```

where the first position contains an **S** or **R** for supervisor or representative, respectively. The next three integers include the number of units of each of the products sold. Because product prices may vary over time, the constant definition section will be used to indicate the current prices. The constants for this problem will be

```
const float SUPER_RATE = 0.07;
const float REP_RATE = 0.05;
const float A_PRICE = 13.95;
const float B_PRICE = 17.95;
const float C_PRICE = 29.95;
```

A first-level pseudocode development for this problem is

1. Get the data
2. Compute commission and bonus
3. Print heading
4. Print results

The structure chart for this is given in Figure 5.4. Module specifications for each of the main modules follow:

Module: Get the data
Task: Read input data from the keyboard.
Outputs: employee classification and sales of products A, B, and C

Module: Compute commission and bonus
Task: if a supervisor

        compute total commission
        compute bonus

    else

        compute total commission
        compute bonus

◆ FIGURE 5.4
Structure chart for Example 5.11

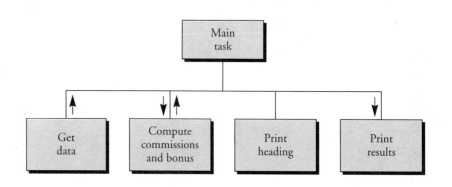

Inputs: classification, a_sales, b_sales, c_sales
Outputs: a_commission, b_commission, c_commission, total_commission, bonus

Module: Print heading
Task: Print a heading for the report.

Module: Print results
Task: Print the employee's report.
Inputs: classification
                 a_sales
                 b_sales
                 c_sales
                 a_commission
                 b_commission
                 c_commission
                 total_commission
                 bonus

Modules for Get data, Print heading, and Print results are similar to those previously developed. The module Compute the commission and bonus requires some development. Step 2 of the pseudocode becomes

2. Compute commission and bonus
   2.1 if employee is supervisor
             compute supervisor's earnings
        else
             compute representative's earnings

where "compute supervisor's earnings" is refined to

   2.1.1 compute commission from sales of A
   2.1.2 compute commission from sales of B
   2.1.3 compute commission from sales of C
   2.1.4 compute total commission
   2.1.5 compute supervisor's bonus
          2.1.5.1 if total commission > 300
                         bonus is 100.00
                   else
                         bonus is 0.00

A similar development follows for computing a representative's earnings. Step 3 will be an appropriate function to print a heading. Step 4 will contain whatever you feel is appropriate for output. It should include at least the number of sales, amount of sales, commissions, bonuses, and total compensation.

The main program for this problem is

```
int main()
{
        int a_sales, b_sales, c_sales;          // Sales of Products A, B, C
        float a_comm, b_comm, c_comm;           // Commission on sales of A, B, C
        float bonus;                            // Bonus, if earned
        float total_commission;                 // Commission on all products
        char classification;                    // S-Supervisor or R-Representative
```

```
        get_data(classification, a_sales, b_sales, c_sales);
        compute_commission_and_bonus(classification, a_sales,
              b_sales, c_sales, a_comm, b_comm,
              c_comm, total_commission, bonus);
        print_heading(classification);
        print_results(classification, a_sales, b_sales, c_sales, a_comm, b_comm,
              c_comm, total_commission, bonus);
        return 0;
}
```

A complete program for this is

```
// This program computes gross pay for an employee. Note the use of constants
// and selection.

// Program file: sales.cpp

#include <iostream.h>
#include <iomanip.h>

const float SUPER_RATE = 0.07;
const float REP_RATE = 0.05;
const float A_PRICE = 13.95;
const float B_PRICE = 17.95;
const float C_PRICE = 29.95;
const char SKIP = ' ';

// Function: get_data
// gets input data from the user
//
// Outputs: Outputs: employee classification and sales of products A, B, and C

void get_data(char &classification, int &a_sales, int &b_sales, int &c_sales);

// Function: compute_commission_and_bonus
// If a supervisor
//            compute total commission
//            compute bonus
//      else
//            compute total commission
//            compute bonus
// Inputs: classification, a_sales, b_sales, c_sales
// Outputs: a_commission, b_commission, c_commission,
// total_commission, bonus

void compute_commission_and_bonus(char classification, int a_sales,
        int b_sales, int c_sales, float &a_commission, float& b_commission,
        float &c_commission, float &total_commission, float &bonus);

void print_heading(char classification);
```

```cpp
// Function: print_results
// Prints employee's report
//
// Inputs:     classification
//             a_sales
//             b_sales
//             c_sales
//             a_commission
//             b_commission
//             c_commission
//             total_commission
//             bonus

void print_results(char classification, int a_sales, int b_sales, int c_sales,
     float a_comm, float b_comm, float c_comm, float total_commission,
     float bonus);

// Function: print_heading
// Print heading for results
//
// Input: classification

void print_heading(char classification);

int main()
{
     int a_sales, b_sales, c_sales;          // Sales of Products A, B, C
     float a_comm, b_comm, c_comm;           // Commission on sales of A, B, C
     float bonus;                            // Bonus, if earned
     float total_commission;                 // Commission on all products
     char classification;                    // S-Supervisor or R-Representative

     get_data(classification, a_sales, b_sales, c_sales);
     compute_commission_and_bonus(classification, a_sales,
          b_sales, c_sales, a_comm, b_comm,
          c_comm, total_commission, bonus);
     print_heading(classification);
     print_results(classification, a_sales, b_sales, c_sales, a_comm, b_comm,
          c_comm, total_commission, bonus);
     return 0;
}

void get_data(char &classification, int &a_sales, int &b_sales, int &c_sales)
{
     cout << "Enter S or R for classification.";
     cin >> classification;
     cout << "Enter a_sales, b_sales, c_sales.";
     cin >> a_sales >> b_sales >>c_sales;
}
```
1

```
void compute_commission_and_bonus(char classification, int a_sales,
      int b_sales, int c_sales, float &a_commission, float& b_commission,
      float &c_commission, float &total_commission, float &bonus)
{
      if (classification == 'S')              // Supervisor
      {
            a_commission = a_sales * A_PRICE * SUPER_RATE;
            b_commission = b_sales * B_PRICE * SUPER_RATE;
            c_commission = c_sales * C_PRICE * SUPER_RATE;
            total_commission = a_commission + b_commission + c_commission;
            if (total_commission > 300.0)
                  bonus = 100.0;
            else
                  bonus = 0.0 ;
      }
      else                                    // Representative
      {
            a_commission = a_sales * A_PRICE * REP_RATE;
            b_commission = b_sales * B_PRICE * REP_RATE;
            c_commission = c_sales * C_PRICE * REP_RATE;
            total_commission = a_commission + b_commission + c_commission;
            if (total_commission > 200.0)
                  bonus = 100.0;
            else
                  bonus = 0.0;
      }
}


void print_heading(char classification)
{
      cout << endl;
      cout << setw(10) << SKIP << "Clean Products Corporation of America"
            << endl;
      cout <<  setw(10)  <<  SKIP <<  "------------------------------"
            << endl;
      cout << endl;
      cout << setw(10) << SKIP << "Sales Report for" << setw(10)
            << "June" << endl;
      cout << endl;
      cout << setw(10) << SKIP << "classification"<< endl;
      if (classification == 'S')
            cout << setw(12) << SKIP << "Supervisor"<< endl;
      else
            cout << setw(12) << SKIP << "Representative"<< endl;
      cout << endl;
      cout << setw(12) << SKIP << "Product      Sales      Commission" << endl;
      cout << setw(12) << SKIP << "-----        ----       ---------" << endl;
      cout << endl;
}
```

2

3

```
void print_results(char classification, int a_sales, int b_sales, int c_sales,
      float a_comm, float b_comm, float c_comm, float total_commission,
      float bonus)

{
      cout << fixed << showpoint << setprecision(2);
      cout << setw(15) << SKIP << "A" << setw(13) << a_sales << setw(14)
           << a_comm << endl;
      cout << setw(15) << SKIP << "B" << setw(13) << b_sales << setw(14)
           << b_comm << endl;
      cout << setw(15) << SKIP << "C" << setw(13) << c_sales << setw(14)
           << c_comm << endl;
      cout << endl;
      cout << setw(31) << "Subtotal"<< setw(3) << "$" << setw(9)
           << total_commission << endl;
      cout << endl;
      cout << setw(31) << "Your bonus is:" << setw(3) << "$" << setw(9)
           << bonus << endl;
      cout << setw(43) << "------" << endl;
      cout << endl;
      cout << setw(31) << "Total Due" << setw(3) << "$" << setw(9)
           << total_commission + bonus << endl;
}
```

A sample run produces the following output:

```
Enter R or S for classification. S
Enter a_sales, b_sales, c_sales 1100 990 510


          Clean Products Corporation of America

          Sales Report for        June

          classification          Supervisor

          Product     Sales       Commission
          -------     -----       ----------

          A           1100        1074.15

          B           990         1243.93

          C           510         1069.21

                      Subtotal    $3387.30

                      Your bonus is:   $100.00

                      Total Due   $3487.30
```

Program Testing

In actual practice, a great deal of time is spent testing programs in an attempt to make them run properly when they are installed for some specific purpose. Formal program verification is discussed in Section 5.6 and is developed more fully in subsequent course work. However, examining the issue of which data are minimally necessary for program testing is appropriate when working with selection statements.

As you might expect, test data should include information that tests every logical branch in a program. Whenever a program contains an **if . . . else** statement of the form

```
if (<condition>)
        (action 1 here)
else
        (action 2 here)
```

the test data should guarantee that both the **if** and the **else** options are executed.

Nesting and use of extended **if** statements require a bit more care when selecting test data. In general, a single **if . . . else** statement requires at least two data items for testing. If an **if . . . else** statement is nested within the **if** option, at least two more data items are required to test the nested selection statement.

For purposes of illustration, let us reexamine the module Compute Commission and Bonus from Example 5.11. This module contains the logic

```
if (classification == 'S')
        .
        .
        .

        if (total_commission  >  300.00)
                .
                .
                .

        else
                .
                .
                .

else
        .
        .
        .

    if (total_commission  > 200.00)
            .
            .
            .

    else
            .
            .
            .
```

To see what data should minimally be used to test this function, consider the following table:

Classification	Total Commission
S	400.00
S	250.00
R	250.00
R	150.00

It is a good idea to also include boundary conditions in the test data. Thus, the previous table could also have listed 300.00 as the total commission for **S** and 200.00 as the total commission for **R**.

In summary, you should always make sure every logical branch is executed when running the program with test data.

EXERCISES 5.4

1. Consider the program fragment

```
if (x >= 0.0)
     if x < 1000.00
     {
         y = 2 * x;
         if (x <= 500)
              x = x / 10;
     }
     else
         y = 3 * x;
else
     y = abs(x);
```

Indicate the values of **x** and **y** after this fragment is executed for each of the following initial values of **x**.

a. x = 381.5;

b. x = -21.0;

c. x = 600.0;

d. x = 3000.0;

2. Write and run a test program that illustrates the checking of all branches of nested **if . . . else** statements.

3. Rewrite each of the following fragments using nested or extended **if** statements without compound conditions.

```
a. if ((ch == 'M') && (sum > 1000))
       x = x + 1;
   if ((ch == 'M') && (sum <= 1000))
       x = x + 2;
   if ((ch == 'F') && (sum > 1000))
       x = x + 3;
   if ((ch == 'F') && (sum <= 1000))
       x = x + 5;
b. cin >> num;
   if ((num > 0) && (num <= 10000))
   {
       count = count + 1;
```

```
        sum = sum + num;
    }
    else
        cout << setw(27) << "Value out of range" << endl;
c. if ((a > 0) && (b > 0))
        cout << setw(22) << "Both positive" << endl;
    else
        cout << setw(22) << "Some negative" << endl;
d. if (((a > 0) && (b > 0)) || (c > 0))
        cout << setw(19) << "Option one" << endl;
    else
        cout <<setw(19) << "Option two" << endl;
```

4. Consider each of the following program fragments.

```
a.    if (a < 0)
          if (b < 0)
                a = b;
          else
                a = b + 10;
      cout << a << b << endl;
b.    if (a < 0)
      {
          if (b < 0)
                a = b;
      }
      else
          a = b + 10;
      cout << a << b << endl;
c. if (a == 0)
          a = b + 10;
   else if (b < 0)
          a = b;
      cout << a << b << endl;
d. if (a >= 0)
          a = b + 10;
   if (b < 0)
          a = b;
      cout << a << b << endl;
```

Indicate the output of each fragment for each of the following assignment statements.

```
i. a = -5;
   b = 5;
ii. a = -5;
    b = -3;
iii. a = 10;
     b = 8;
iv. a = 10;
    b = -4;
```

5. Look back to Example 5.10, in which we assigned grades to students, and rewrite the grade assignment fragment using a different nesting. Could you rewrite it without using any nesting? Should you?

6. Many nationally based tests report scores and indicate in which quartile the score lies. Assuming the following quartile designation,

Score	Quartile
100–75	1
74–50	2
49–25	3
24–0	4

write a program to read a score from the keyboard and report in which quartile the score lies.

7. What are the values of **a**, **b**, and **c** after the following program fragment is executed?

```
a = -8; b = 21;
c = a + b;
if (a > b)
{
     a = b;
     c = a * b;
}
else if (a < 0)
{
     a = abs(a);
     b = b - a;
     c = a * b;
}
else
     c = 0;
```

8. Create minimal sets of test data for each part of Exercise 4 and for Exercise 7. Explain why each piece of test data has been included.

9. Discuss a technique that could be used as a debugging aid to guarantee that all possible logical paths of a program have been used.

5.5 switch Statements

OBJECTIVES

- to learn the syntax of the **switch** statement

- to understand how **switch** statements can be used as an alternate method for multiway selection

- to be able to use **switch** statements in designing programs

Thus far, this chapter has examined one-way selection, two-way selection, and multiway selection. Section 5.4 illustrated how multiple selection can be achieved using nested and extended **if** statements. Because multiple selection can sometimes be difficult to follow, C++ provides an alternative method of handling this concept, the **switch** statement.

Form and Syntax

C++ **switch** statements are often used when several options depend on the value of a single variable or expression. The general structure for a **switch** statement follows:

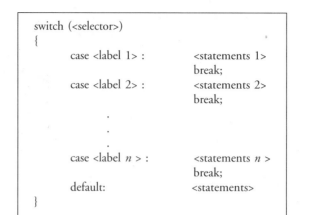

```
switch (<selector>)
{
        case <label 1> :           <statements 1>
                                   break;
        case <label 2> :           <statements 2>
                                   break;
                   .
                   .
                   .
        case <label n > :          <statements n >
                                   break;
        default:                   <statements>
}
```

◆ FIGURE 5.5
The **switch** statement flow diagram

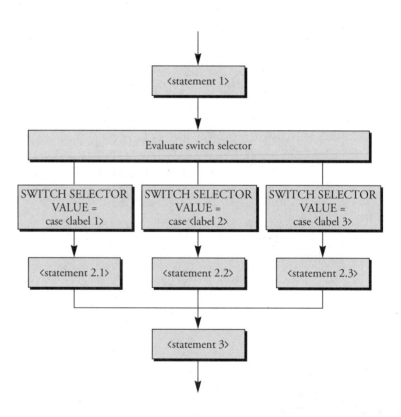

This structure is shown graphically in Figure 5.5. The words **switch, case, break**, and **default** are reserved. The selector can be any variable or expression whose value is any data type we have studied previously except for **float** (only ordinal data types can be used). Values of the selector constitute the labels. Thus, if **age** is an integer variable whose values might be 18, 19, and 20, we could have

```
switch (age)
{
        case 18 :          <statement 1>
                           break;
        case 19 :          <statement 2>
                           break;
```

```
            case 20 :        <statement 3>
                             break;
            default:         <default statement>
      }
```

When this program statement is executed, the value of **age** will determine to which statement control is transferred. More specifically, the program fragment

```
age = 19;
switch (age)
{
    case 18 :     cout << "I just became a legal voter." << endl;
                  break;
    case 19 :     cout << "This is my second year to vote." << endl;
                  break;
    case 20 :     cout << "I am almost twenty-one." << endl;
                  break;
    default:      if (age > 20)
                      cout << "I have all of the privileges of adulthood."
                              << endl;
                  else
                      cout << "I have no privileges at all." << endl;

}
```

produces the output

This is my second year to vote.

Before considering more examples, several comments are in order. The flow of logic within a **switch** statement is as follows:

1. The value of the selector is determined.
2. The first instance of value is found among the labels.
3. The statements following this value are executed.
4. **break** statements are optional. If a **break** statement occurs within these statements, then control is transferred to the first program statement following the entire **switch** statement; otherwise, execution continues. In general, you should end every case with a **break** statement.

The selector can have a value of any type previously studied except **float**. Only ordinal data types may be used.

Several cases may be associated with an alternative action. For example, if **<statement 1>** should be run when **age** has the integer value of 10 or 100, the **switch** statement could appear as

```
switch (age)
{
    case 10:
    case 100 :     <statement 1>
                    break;
    case 19 :      <statement 2>
                    break;
    case 20 :      <statement 3>
                    break;
    default :      <default statement>
}
```

Writing style for a **switch** statement should be consistent with your previously developed style. The lines containing options should be indented. Thus, a typical **switch** statement is

COMMUNICATION AND STYLE TIPS

```
switch (score)
{
        case 10:
        case 9:
        case 8:         cout << "Excellent" << endl;
                        break;
        case 7:
        case 6:
        case 5 :        cout << "Fair" << endl;
                        break;
        case 4:
        case 3:
        case 2:
        case 1:
        case 0:         cout << "Failing" << endl;
                        break;
        default:        cout << "Error in switch "
                             << "statement" << score
                             << endl;

}
```

All possible values of the **switch** selector do not have to be listed. However, if a value that is not listed is used, subtle logic errors can occur. Consequently, it is preferable to use a *default option*. If certain values require no action, the program will finish executing the **switch** statement by running the default as the last option; for example,

```
switch (age)
{
      case 10:
      case 100 :    <statement 1>
                    break;
      case 19 :     <statement 2>
                    break;
      case 20 :     <statement 3>
                    break;
      default:      cout << "There is no case for " << age << endl;
}
```

Like the **break** statement, the **default** statement is optional.

At this stage, we will consider several examples that illustrate various uses of **switch** statements. Because our purpose is for illustration, the examples are somewhat contrived. Later examples will serve to illustrate how these statements are used in solving problems.

EXAMPLE 5.12

The selector can have a value of type **char**, and the ordinal of the character determines the option. Thus, the label list must contain the appropriate characters in single quotation marks. If **grade** has values **'A'**, **'B'**, **'C'**, **'D'**, or **'F'**, a **switch** statement could be

```
switch (grade)
{
        case 'A' :       points = 4.0;
                         break;
        case 'B' :       points = 3.0;
                         break;
        case 'C' :       points = 2.0;
                         break;
        case 'D' :       points = 1.0;
                         break;
        case 'F' :       points = 0.0;
}
```

EXAMPLE 5.13

Let us rewrite the following program fragment using a **switch** statement

```
if ((score == 10) || (score == 9))
        grade = 'A'
else if ((score == 8) || (score == 7))
        grade = 'B'
else if ((score == 6) || (score == 5))
        grade = 'C'
else
        grade = 'F';
```

If we assume **score** is an integer variable with values 0, 1, 2, . . . , 10, we could use a **switch** statement as follows:

```
switch (score)
{
        case 10:
        case 9:         grade = 'A';
                        break;
        case 8:
        case 7:         grade = 'B';
                        break;
        case 6:
        case 5:         grade = 'C';
                        break;
        case 4:
        case 3:
        case 2:
        case 1:
        case 0 : grade = 'F';
}
```

A NOTE OF INTEREST

A Software Glitch

The software glitch that disrupted AT&T's long-distance telephone service for nine hours in January 1990 dramatically demonstrates what can go wrong even in the most reliable and scrupulously tested systems. Of the roughly 100 million telephone calls placed with AT&T during that period, only about half got through. The breakdown cost the company more than $60 million in lost revenues and caused considerable inconvenience and irritation for telephone-dependent customers.

The trouble began at a "switch"—one of 114 interconnected, computer-operated electronic switching systems scattered across the United States. These sophisticated systems, each a maze of electronic equipment housed in a large room, form the backbone of the AT&T long-distance telephone network.

When a local exchange delivers a telephone call to the network, it arrives at one of these switching centers, which can handle up to 700,000 calls an hour. The switch immediately springs into action. It scans a list of 14 different routes it can use to complete the call, and at the same time hands off the telephone number to a parallel, signaling network, invisible to any caller. This private data network allows computers to scout the possible routes and to determine whether the switch at the other end can deliver the call to the local company it serves.

If the answer is no, the call is stopped at the original switch to keep it from tying up a line, and the caller gets a busy signal. If the answer is yes, a signaling-network computer makes a reservation at the destination switch and orders the original switch to pass along the waiting call—after that switch makes a final check to ensure that the chosen line is functioning properly. The whole process of passing a call down the network takes 4 to 6 seconds. Because the switches must keep in constant touch with the signaling network and its computers, each switch has a computer program that handles all the necessary communications between the switch and the signaling network.

AT&T's first indication that something might be amiss appeared on a giant video display at the company's network control center in Bedminster, New Jersey. At 2:25 p.m. on Monday, January 15, 1990, network managers saw an alarming increase in the number of red warning signals appearing on many of the 75 video screens showing the status of various parts of AT&T's worldwide network. The warnings signaled a serious collapse in the network's ability to complete calls within the United States.

To bring the network back up to speed, AT&T engineers first tried a number of standard procedures that had worked in the past. This time, the methods failed. The engineers realized they had a problem they'd never seen before. Nonetheless, within a few hours, they managed to stabilize the network by temporarily cutting back on the number of messages moving through the signaling network. They cleared the last defective link at 11:30 that night.

Meanwhile, a team of more than 100 telephone technicians tried frantically to track down the fault. Because the problem involved the signaling network and seemed to bounce from one switch to another, they zeroed in on the software that permitted each switch to communicate with the signaling-network computers.

The day after the slowdown, AT&T personnel removed the apparently faulty software from each switch, temporarily replacing it with an earlier version of the communications program. A close examination of the flawed software turned up a single error in one line of the program. Just one month earlier, network technicians had changed the software to speed the processing of certain messages, and the change had inadvertently introduced a flaw into the system. From that finding, AT&T could reconstruct what had happened.

Use in Problems

The **switch** statements should not be used for relational tests involving large ranges of values. For example, if one wanted to examine a range from 0 to 100 to determine test scores, nested selection would be better than a **switch** statement. We close this section with some examples that illustrate how **switch** statements can be used in solving problems.

EXAMPLE 5.14

Suppose you are writing a program for a gasoline station owner who sells four grades of gasoline: regular, premium, unleaded, and super unleaded. Your program reads a character (R, P, U, S) that designates which kind of gasoline was purchased and then takes subsequent action. The outline for this fragment is

```
cin >> gas_type;
switch (gas_type)
{
        case 'R' :      <action for regular>;
                        break;
        case 'P' :      <action for premium>;
                        break;
        case 'U' :      <action for unleaded>;
                        break;
        case 'S' :      <action for super unleaded>;
                        break;
}
```

Equivalent of Extended if statements

As previously indicated, **switch** statements can sometimes (ordinal data types) be used instead of extended **if** statements when multiple selection is required for solving a problem. The following example illustrates this use.

EXAMPLE 5.15

An alternative method of assigning letter grades based on integer scores between 0 and 100 inclusive is to divide the score by 10 and assign grades according to some scale. This idea could be used in conjunction with a **switch** statement as follows:

```
new_score = score / 10;
switch (new_score)
{
        case 10:
        case 9:         grade = 'A';
                        break;
        case 8:         grade = 'B';
                        break;
        case 7:         grade = 'C';
                        break;
        case 6:
        case 5:         grade = 'D';
                        break;
        case 4:
        case 3:
        case 2:
        case 1:
        case 0:         grade = 'F';
}
```

EXERCISES 5.5

1. Discuss the need for program protection when using a **switch** statement.

2. Show how the following **switch** statement could be protected against unexpected values.

```
switch (age / 10)
{
        case 10:
        case 9:
        case 8:
        case 7:     cout << setw(40) << "These are retirement years" << endl;
                    break;

        case 6:
        case 5:
        case 4:     cout << setw(40) << "These are middle age years" << endl;
                    break;

        case 3:
        case 2:     cout << setw(40) << "These are mobile years" << endl;
                    break;

        case 1:     cout << setw(40) << "These are school years" << endl;
}
```

3. Find all errors in the following statements.

```
a. switch (a)
   case 1        :
                         break;
   case 2        :      a = 2 * a
                        break;
   case 3        ;      a = 3 * a;
                        break;
   case 4; 5; 6 :       a = 4 * a;
   }
b. switch (num)
   {
        case 5      num = num + 5;
                    break;
        case 6:
        case 7:     ; num = num + 6;
                    break;
        case 7, 8, 9, 10 : num = num + 10;
   }
c. switch (age)
   {
        15, 16, 17 : y_count = y_count + 1;
                     cout << age << y_count << endl;
        case 18:
        case 19:
        case 20:    m_count = m_count + 1;
        case 21:    cout << age endl;
   }
```

```
d. switch (ch)
   {
        a :      points =      4.0;
                 break;
        b :      points =      3.0;
                 break;
        c :      points =      2.0;
                 break;
        d :      points =      1.0;
                 break;
        e :      points =      0.0
   }
e. switch (score)
   {
        case 5 :      grade = 'A';
                      break;
        case 4 :      grade = 'B';
                      break;
        case 3 :      grade = 'C';
                      break;
        case 2 :
        case 1:,
        case 0:       grade = 'E';
   }
f. switch (num / 10)
   {
        case 1 :      num = num + 1;
                      break;
        case 2 :      num = num + 2;
                      break;
        case 3 :      num = num + 3;
   }
```

4. What is the output from each of the following program fragments?

```
a. a = 5;
   power = 3;
   switch (power)
   {
        case 0:       b = 1;
                      break;
        case 1:       b = a;
                      break;
        case 2:       b = a * a;
                      break;
        case 3:       b = a * a * a;
   }
   cout << a << power << b << endl;
```

```
b. gas_type = 'S';
   cout << "You have purchased ";
   switch (gas_type)
   {
       case 'R':        cout << "Regular";
                        break;
       case 'P':        cout << "Premium";
                        break;
       case 'U':        cout << "Unleaded";
                        break;
       case 'S':        cout << "Super Unleaded";
   }
   cout << "gasoline" << endl;
c. a = 6;
   b = -3;
   switch (a)
   {
       case 10:
       case 9:
       case 8:           switch b
                         {
                             case -3:
                             case -4:
                             case -5:     a = a * b;
                                          break;
                             case 0:
                             case -1:
                             case -2:     a = a + b;
                         }
                         break;
       case 7:
       case 6:
       case 5:           switch (b)
                         {
                             case -5:
                             case -4:     a = a * b;
                                          break;
                             case -3:
                             case -2:     a = a + b;
                                          break;
                             case -1:
                             case 0:      a = a - b;
                         }
   }
   cout << a << b << endl;
d. symbol = '-';
   a = 5;
   b = 10;
   switch (symbol)
   {
       case '+' :       num = a + b;
       case '-' :       num = a - b;
```

```
        case '*' :        num = a * b;
    }
    cout << a << b << num << endl;
```

5. Rewrite each of the following program fragments using a **switch** statement.

a.
```
if (power = 1)
    num = a;
if (power = 2)
        num = a * a;
if (power = 3)
    num = a * a * a;
```

b. Assume **score** is an integer between 0 and 10.

```
if (score > 9)
        grade = 'A'
else if (score > 8)
        grade = 'B'
else if (score > 7)
        grade = 'C'
else if (score > 5)
        grade = 'D'
else
        grade = 'E';
```

c. Assume measurement is either **'M'** or **'N'**.

```
if (measurement == 'M')
{
    cout << setw(37) << "This is a metric measurement." << endl;
    cout << setw(42) << "It will be converted to nonmetric." << endl;
    length = num * CM_TO_INCHES;
}
else
{
    cout << setw(40) << " This is a nonmetric measurement. << endl;
    cout << setw(39) << "It will be converted to metric." << endl;
    length = num * INCHES_TO_CM;
}
```

6. Show how a **switch** statement can be used in a program to compute college tuition fees. Assume there are different fee rates for each of undergraduates (U), graduates (G), non-U.S. students (F), and special students (S).

7. Use nested **switch** statements to design a program fragment to compute postage for domestic (noninternational) mail. The design should provide for four weight categories for both letters and packages. Each can be sent first, second, third, or fourth class.

5.6 Assertions

OBJECTIVES

- to know how to use assertions as preconditions
- to know how to use assertions as postconditions

An *assertion* is a statement about what we expect to be true at the point in the program where the assertion is placed. For example, if you wish to compute a test average by dividing the **sum_of_scores** by **number_of_students**, you could state your intent that **number_of_students** is not equal to zero with a comment:

```
// assert that (number_of_students != 0)
class_average = sum_of_scores/ number_of_students;
```

Assertions are usually Boolean-valued expressions and typically concern program action. In the preceding example, the assertion that appears in a comment would remind the programmer that a certain condition must be true before an action is taken. Modern programming languages such as C++ provide a way of executing an assertion at run time. The computer verifies that the assertion is true, and if it is false, the computer halts program execution with an error message. To use this kind of feature in C++, you must include the **assert.h** library file:

```
#include <assert.h>
```

Then you can state your assertion by calling the function **assert** with the Boolean expression as a parameter. The previous example might now look like this:

```
assert(number_of_students != 0);
class_average = sum_of_scores / number_of_students;
```

At execution time, this program would halt with an error message before an attempt to divide by zero.

Assertions frequently come in pairs: one preceding program action and one following the action. In this format, the first assertion is a precondition and the second is a postcondition. To illustrate preconditions and postconditions, consider the following segment of code:

```
if (num1 < num2)
{
    temp = num1;
    num1 = num2;
    num2 = temp;
}
```

The intent of this code is to have **num1** be greater than or equal to **num2**. If we intend for both **num1** and **num2** to be positive, we can write

```
assert((num1 >= 0) && (num2 >= 0));               // Precondition
if (num1 < num2)
{
    temp = num1;
    num1 = num2;
    num2 = temp;
}
assert((num1 >= num2) && (num2 >= 0));             // Postcondition
```

As a second example, consider a **switch** statement used to assign grades based on quiz scores.

```
switch (score)
{
    case 10:      grade = 'A';
                  break;
    case 9:
    case 8:       grade = 'B';
                  break;
```

```
                    case 7:
                    case 6:        grade = 'C';
                                   break;

                    case 5:
                    case 4:        grade = 'D';
                                   break;

                    case 3:
                    case 2:
                    case 1:
                    case 0:        grade = 'E';
              }
```

Assertions can be used as preconditions and postconditions in the following manner.

```
assert((score >= 0) && (score <= 10));                  // Precondition
switch (score)
{
      case 10:      grade = 'A';
                    break;

      case 9:
      case 8:       grade = 'B';
                    break;

      case 7:
      case 6:       grade = 'C';
                    break;

      case 5:
      case 4:       grade = 'D';
                    break;

      case 3:
      case 2:
      case 1:
      case 0:       grade = 'E';
}
assert((((score = 10) && (grade = 'A')) ||              // Postcondition
          ((score = 9) && (grade = 'B')) ||
          ((score = 8) && (grade = 'B')) ||
          ((score = 7) && (grade = 'C')) ||
          ((score = 6) && (grade = 'C')) ||
          ((score = 5) && (grade = 'D')) ||
          ((score = 4) && (grade = 'D')) ||
          (((score >= 0) && (score <= 3)) && (grade = 'E'))));
```

Assertions can be used in *program proofs*. Simply put, a program proof is an analysis of a program that attempts to verify the correctness of program results. A detailed study of program proofs is beyond the scope of this text. If, however, you use assertions as preconditions and postconditions now, you will better understand them in subsequent courses. They are especially useful for making a program safer, even if you cannot be sure that their use will guarantee that the program is correct. If you do choose to use assertions in this manner, be aware that the postcondition of one action is the precondition of the next action.

FOCUS ON PROGRAM DESIGN

The Gas-N-Clean Service Station sells gasoline and has a car wash. Fees for the car wash are $1.25 with a gasoline purchase of $10.00 or more and $3.00 otherwise. Three kinds of gasoline are available: regular at $1.149, unleaded at $1.199, and super unleaded at $ 1.289 per gallon. Write a program that prints a statement for a customer. Input consists of number of gallons purchased, kind of gasoline purchased (R, U, S, or, for no purchase, N), and car wash desired (Y or N). Use the constant definition section for gasoline prices. Your output should include appropriate messages. Sample output for these data is

```
Enter number of gallons and press <Enter>. 9.7
Enter gas type (R, U, S, or N) and press <Enter>. R
Enter Y or N for car wash and press <Enter>. Y


            ***********************************
            *                                 *
            *     Gas-N-Clean Service Station  *
            *                                 *
            *          July 25, 1995          *
            *                                 *
            ***********************************

            Amount of gasoline purchased        9.700 Gallons

            Price per gallon            $       1.149

            Total gasoline cost         $      11.15

            Car wash cost               $       1.25

            Total due                   $      12.40

                    Thank you for stopping

                    Please come again

                Remember to buckle up and drive safely
```

A first-level pseudocode development is

1. Get data
2. Compute charges
3. Print results

A structure chart for this problem is given in Figure 5.6. Module specifications for the main modules follow:

Module: Get the data
Task: Get information interactively from the keyboard.
Outputs: number of gallons purchased, type of gasoline, a choice as to whether or not a car wash is desired

Module: Compute the charges
Task: Compute the gas cost, wash cost, and total cost.
Inputs: number of gallons, gas type, wash option
Outputs: gas cost, wash cost, total cost

◆ FIGURE 5.6
Structure chart for the Gas-
N-Clean Service Station
problem

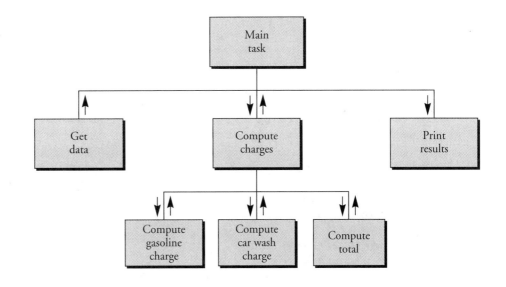

Module: Print the results
Task: Print the results.
Inputs: number of gallons purchased, type of gasoline, gas cost, wash cost, total
cost

Further refinement of the pseudocode produces

1. Get data
   1.1 read number of gallons
   1.2 read kind of gas purchased
   1.3 read car wash option
2. Compute charges
   2.1 compute gasoline charge
   2.2 compute car wash charge
   2.3 compute total
3. Print results
   3.1 print heading
   3.2 print information in transaction
   3.3 print closing message

Module 2 consists of three subtasks. A refined pseudocode development of this step
is

2. Compute charges
   2.1 compute gasoline charge
       2.1.1 switch gas_type
                   'R'
                   'U'
                   'S'
                   'N'
   2.2 compute car wash charge
       2.2.1 if wash_option is yes
                   compute charge
               else
                   charge is 0.0

2.3 compute total
2.3.1 Total is gas_cost plus wash_cost

A C++ program for this problem follows.

```cpp
// This program is used to compute the amount due from a
// customer of the Gas-N-Clean Service Station. Constants
// are used for gasoline prices. Note the use of nested
// selection to compute cost of the car wash.

//Program file: gas.cpp

#include <iostream.h>
#include <iomanip.h>

const char SKIP = ' ';
const float REGULAR_PRICE = 1.149;
const float UNLEADED_PRICE = 1.199;
const float SUPER_UNLEADED_PRICE = 1.289;

// Function: print_heading
// Prints a signon message for program

void print_heading();

// Function: get_data
// Get information interactively from the keyboard.
// Outputs: number of gallons purchased, type of gasoline,
// a choice as to whether or not a car wash is desired

void get_data(float &num_gallons, char &gas_type, char &wash_option);

// Function : compute_charges
// Computes the gas cost, wash cost, and total cost
// Inputs: number of gallons, gas type, wash option
// Outputs: gas cost, wash cost, total cost

void compute_charges(int num_gallons, char gas_type, char wash_option,
        float &gas_cost, float &wash_cost, float &total_cost);

// Function: print_message
// Prints a signoff message for program

void print_message();

// Function: print_results
// Print the results
//
// Inputs: number of gallons purchased, type of gasoline, gas cost, wash option,
// wash cost, total cost

void print_results (float num_gallons, char gas_type, char wash_option,
        float gas_cost, float wash_cost, float total_cost);
```

```
int main()
{
     char gas_type;                  //      Type of gasoline purchased (R,U,S,N)
     char wash_option;               //      Character designating option (Y,N)
     float num_gallons;              //      Number of gallons purchased
     float gas_cost;                 //      Computed cost for gasoline
     float wash_cost;                //      Car wash cost
     float total_cost;               //      Total amount due

     get_data(num_gallons, gas_type, wash_option);
     compute_charges(num_gallons, gas_type, wash_option, gas_cost, wash_cost,
          total_cost);
     print_results (num_gallons, gas_type, wash_option, gas_cost, wash_cost,
          total_cost);
     return 0;
}


void print_heading()
{
     cout << endl;
     cout << setw(20) << SKIP << "****************************************"
          << endl;
     cout << setw(20) << SKIP << "*                                      *"
          << endl;
     cout << setw(20) << SKIP << "*     Gas-N-Clean Service Station      *"
          << endl;
     cout << setw(20) << SKIP << "*                                      *"
          << endl;
     cout << setw(20) << SKIP << "*" << setw(12) << SKIP << "July 25, 1992"
          << setw(12) << SKIP << " *" << endl;
     cout << setw(20) << SKIP << "*                                      *"
          << endl;
     cout << setw(20) << SKIP << "****************************************"
          << endl;
     cout << endl;
}


void get_data(float &num_gallons, char &gas_type, char &wash_option)
{
     cout << "Enter number of gallons and press <Enter>. ";
     cin >> num_gallons;
     cout << "Enter gas type (R, U, S, or N) and press <Enter>. ";
     cin >> gas_type;
     cout << "Enter Y or N for car wash and press <Enter>. ";
     cin >> wash_option;
}


void compute_charges(int num_gallons, char gas_type, char wash_option,
     float &gas_cost, float &wash_cost, float &total_cost)
{
     switch (gas_type)
```

```
    {
        case 'R':            gas_cost = num_gallons * REGULAR_PRICE;
                             break;
        case 'U':            gas_cost = num_gallons * UNLEADED_PRICE;
                             break;
        case 'S':            gas_cost = num_gallons * SUPER_UNLEADED_PRICE;
                             break;
        case 'N':            gas_cost = 0.0;
    }
    // Compute car wash cost
    if (wash_option == 'Y')
        if (gas_cost >= 10.0)
                wash_cost = 1.25;
        else
                wash_cost = 3.0;
    else
        wash_cost = 0.0;
    total_cost = gas_cost + wash_cost;
}


void print_message()
{
    cout << endl;
    cout << setw(28) << SKIP << "Thank you for stopping" << endl;
    cout << endl;
    cout << setw(30) << SKIP << "Please come again" << endl;
    cout << endl;
    cout << setw(20) << SKIP << "Remember to buckle up and drive safely"
        << endl;
    cout << endl;
}


void print_results (float num_gallons, char gas_type, char wash_option,
float gas_cost, float wash_cost, float total_cost)
{
    print_heading();
    cout << fixed << showpoint;
    cout << setw(10) << SKIP << "Amount of gasoline purchased"
        << setw(12) << SKIP << setw(6) << setprecision(3) << num_gallons
        << " Gallons" << endl;
    cout << setw(10) << SKIP << "Price per gallon" << setw(22)
        << SKIP << "$";
    switch (gas_type)
    {
        case 'R':       cout << setw(7) << REGULAR_PRICE << endl;
                        break;
        case 'U':       cout << setw(7) << UNLEADED_PRICE << endl;
                        break;
        case 'S':       cout << setw(7) << SUPER_UNLEADED_PRICE << endl;
                        break;
        case 'N':       cout << setw(7) << 0.0 << endl;
    }
```

```
        cout << setw(10) << SKIP << "Total gasoline cost"
             << setw(19) << SKIP << "$"
             << setw(6) << setprecision(2) << gas_cost << endl;
    if (wash_cost > 0)
            cout << setw(10) << SKIP << "Car wash cost"
                    << setw(25) << SKIP << "$" << setw(6) << wash_cost << endl;
    cout << setw(48) << SKIP << "-------" << endl;
    cout << setw(25) << SKIP << "Total due"
             << setw(14) << SKIP << "$" << setw(6) << total_cost << endl;
    print_message();
}
```

RUNNING, DEBUGGING AND TESTING HINTS

1. `if . . . else` is a single statement in C++.
2. A misplaced semicolon used with an `if` statement can be a problem. For example,

   Incorrect

   ```
   if (a > 0) ;
       cout << a << endl;
   ```

   Correct

   ```
   if (a > 0)
       cout << a << endl;
   ```

3. Be careful with compound statements as options in an `if . . . else` statement. They must be in a `{ . . . }` block, and a trailing `}` must not be followed by a semicolon.

   Incorrect

   ```
   if (a >= 0)
       cout << a << endl;
       a = a + 10;
   else
       cout << a << " is negative" << endl;
   ```

   Correct

   ```
   if (a >= 0)
   {
       cout << a << endl;
       a = a + 10;
   }
   else
       cout << a << " is negative" << endl;
   ```

4. Your test data should include values that will check both options of an `if . . . else` statement.

(continued)

5. The `if . . . else` statement can be used to check for other program errors. In particular,

   a. Check for bad data by

```
cin >> <data>;
if (<bad data>)
```
       •
       • (error message)
       •
```
else
```
       •
       • (proceed with program)
       •

   b. Check for reasonable computed values by

```
if (<unreasonable values>)
```
       •
       • (error message)
       •
```
else
```
       •
       • (proceed with program)
       •

For example, if you were computing a student's test average, you could have

```
if (test_average > 100) || (test_average < 0)
```
       •
       • (error message)
       •
```
else
```
       •
       • (proceed with program)
       •

6. Be careful with Boolean expressions. You should always keep expressions reasonably simple, use parentheses, and minimize use of `!`.

7. Be careful to properly match `else`s with `if`s in nested `if . . . else` statements. Indenting levels for writing code are very helpful.

```
if (<condition 1>)
    if (<condition 2>)
```
       •
       • (action here)
       •

(continued)

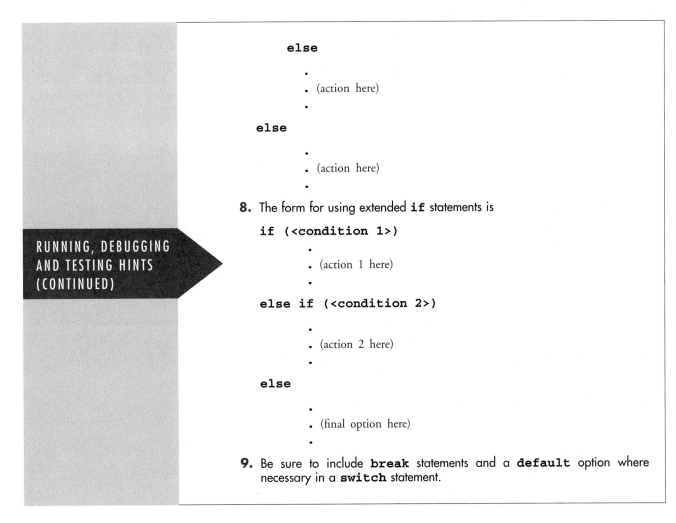

RUNNING, DEBUGGING AND TESTING HINTS (CONTINUED)

```
          else

             .
             . (action here)
             .

      else

             .
             . (action here)
             .
```

8. The form for using extended **if** statements is

```
if (<condition 1>)

             .
             . (action 1 here)
             .
else if (<condition 2>)

             .
             . (action 2 here)
             .
else

             .
             . (final option here)
             .
```

9. Be sure to include **break** statements and a **default** option where necessary in a **switch** statement.

SUMMARY

Key Terms

{ ... } block
compound Boolean expression
compound statement
control structure
extended **if** statement

logical operators: **&&, ||, !**
negation
nested **if** statement
short-circuit evaluation
relational operator

robust
selection statement
simple Boolean expression
type definition

Key Terms (optional)

assertion

program proof

Keywords

break
case
default

if
else

switch
typedef

Key Concepts

◆ Boolean constants have the values **1 = TRUE** and **0 = FALSE**. To make these values obvious in programs, one can define them as symbolic constants. Because some C++ compilers use the symbols **TRUE** and **FALSE** for other purposes, one can "undefine" them with the preprocessor directive **#undef** before reusing them, as follows:

```
#undef TRUE
#undef FALSE
const int TRUE = 1;
const int FALSE = 0;
```

◆ Data types can be given more descriptive names by using a **typedef**. For example, a data type for Boolean variables can be defined with

```
typedef int boolean;
```

and variables can then be declared with

```
boolean done = FALSE;
```

◆ Frequently used data definitions, such as those for the **boolean** type, can be placed in a program library and included in application programs. For example, the library file **boolean.h** can be included with

```
#include "boolean.h"
```

◆ Relational operators are **==, >, <, >=, <=, !=**.
◆ Logical operators **&&, ||**, and **!** are used as operators on Boolean expressions.
◆ Boolean expressions will be interpreted during execution as having the values 1 (meaning true) or 0 (meaning false).
◆ A complete priority listing of arithmetic operators, relational operators, and logical operators is

Expression or Operation	Priority
( )	Evaluate from inside out
!	Evaluate from left to right
*, /, %	Evaluate from left to right
+, -	Evaluate from left to right
<, <=, >, >=, ==, !=	Evaluate from left to right
&&	Evaluate from left to right
||	Evaluate from left to right

◆ The values of compound Boolean expressions connected by **||** or **&&** are computed by using short-circuit evaluation.
◆ A selection statement is a program statement that transfers control to various branches of the program.
◆ A compound statement is sometimes referred to as a **{ . . . }** block; when it is executed, the entire segment of code between the **{** and **}** is treated like a single statement.
◆ **if ... else** is a two-way selection statement.
◆ If the Boolean expression in an **if ... else** statement is **TRUE**, the command following **if** is executed; if the expression is **FALSE**, the command following **else** is executed.

◆ Multiple selections can be achieved by using decision statements within decision statements; this is termed multiway selection.
◆ An extended **if** statement is a statement of the form

```
if (<condition 1>)

        •
        •  (action 1 here)
        •

else if (<condition 2>)

        •
        •  (action 2 here)
        •

else if (<condition 3>)

        •
        •  (action 3 here)
        •

else

        •
        •  (action 4 here)
        •
```

◆ Program protection can be achieved by using selection statements to guard against unexpected results.
◆ The **switch** statements can sometimes be used as alternatives to multiple selection.
◆ **default**, a reserved word in C++, can be used to handle values not listed in the **switch** statement.

PROGRAMMING PROBLEMS AND PROJECTS

The first 13 problems listed here are relatively short, but to complete them you must use concepts presented in this chapter.

Some of the remaining programming problems are used as the basis for writing programs for subsequent chapters as well as for this chapter. In this chapter, each program is run on a very limited set of data. Material in later chapters permits us to run the programs on larger databases. The problems marked by a color square are referred to and used repeatedly, so carefully choose which ones you work on and then develop them completely.

1. A three-minute telephone call to Scio, New York, costs $1.15. Each additional minute costs $0.26. Given the total length of a call in minutes and calculate and print the cost.

2. When you first learned to divide, you expressed answers using a quotient and a remainder rather than a fraction or decimal quotient. For example, if you divided 7 by 2, your answer would have been given as 3 r. 1. Given two integers, divide the larger by the smaller and print the answer in this form. Do not assume that the numbers are entered in any order.

3. Revise Problem 2 so that, if there is no remainder, you print only the quotient without a remainder or the letter r.

4. Given the coordinates of two points on a graph, find and print the slope of a line passing through them. Remember that the slope of a line can be undefined.

5. Dr. Lae Z. Programmer wishes to computerize his grading system. He gives five tests, then averages only the four highest scores. An average of 90 or better earns a grade of A; 80—89, a grade of B; and so on. Write a program that accepts five test scores and prints the average and grade according to this method.

6. Given the lengths of three sides of a triangle, print whether the triangle is scalene, isosceles, or equilateral.

7. Given the lengths of three sides of a triangle, determine whether or not the triangle is a right triangle using the Pythagorean theorem. Do not assume that the sides are entered in any order.

8. Given three integers, print only the largest.

9. The island nation of Babbage charges its citizens an income tax each year. The tax rate is based on the following table:

Income Tax	Tax Rate
$ 0–5,000	0
5,001–10,000	3%
10,001–20,000	5.5%
20,001–40,000	10.8%
Over $40,000	23.7%

Write a program that, when given a person's income, prints the tax owed rounded to the nearest dollar.

10. Many states base the cost of car registration on the weight of the vehicle. Suppose the fees are as follows:

Weight	Cost
Up to 1500 pounds	$23.75
1501 to 2500 pounds	27.95
2501 to 3000 pounds	30.25
Over 3000 pounds	37.00

Given the weight of a car, find and print the cost of registration.

11. The Mapes Railroad Corporation pays an annual bonus as a part of its profit sharing plan. This year all employees who have been with the company for 10 years or more will receive a bonus of 12% of their annual salary, and those who have worked at Mapes from 5 through 9 years receive a bonus of 5.75%. Those who have been with the company for less than 5 years receive no bonus.

Given the initials of an employee, the employee's annual salary, and the number of years employed with the company, find and print the bonus. All bonuses are rounded to the nearest dollar. Output should be in the following form.

```
        MAPES RAILROAD CORP.

Employee xxx
Years of service nn
Bonus earned: $ yyyy
```

12. A substance floats in water if its density (mass/volume) is less than 1 g/cm^3. It sinks if it is 1 or more. Given the mass and volume of an object and calculate and print whether it will sink or float.

13. Mr. Arthur Einstein, your high school physics teacher, wants a program for English-to-metric conversions. You are given a letter indicating whether the measurement is in pounds (P), feet (F), or miles (M). Such measures are to be converted to newtons, meters, and kilometers, respectively. (There are 4.9 newtons in a pound, 3.28 feet in a meter, and 1.61 kilometers in a mile.) Given an appropriate identifying letter and the size of the measurement, convert it to metric units. Print the answer in the following form:

`3.0 miles = 4.83 kilometers.`

14. The Caswell Catering and Convention Service (Chapter 4, Problem 12) has decided to revise its billing practices and is in need of a new program to prepare bills. The changes Caswell wishes to make follow.

   a. For adults, the deluxe meals will cost $15.80 per person and the standard meals will cost $11.75 per person, dessert included. Children's meals will cost 60 percent of adult meals. Everyone within a given party must be served the same meal type.

   b. There are five banquet halls. Room A rents for $55.00, room B rents for $75.00, room C rents for $85.00, room D rents for $100.00 , and room E rents for $130.00. The Caswells are considering increasing the room fees in about six months and this should be taken into account.

   c. A surcharge, currently 7%, is added to the total bill if the catering is to be done on a weekend (Friday, Saturday, or Sunday).

   d. All customers will be charged the same rate for tip and tax, currently 18%. It is applied only to the cost of food.

   e. To induce customers to pay promptly, a discount is offered if payment is made within 10 days. This discount depends on the amount of the total bill. If the bill is less than $100.00, the discount is 0.5%; if the bill is at least $100.00 but less than $200.00, the discount is 1.5%; if the bill is at least $200.00 but less than $400.00, the discount is 3%; if the bill is at least $400.00 but less than $800.00, the discount is 4%; and, if the bill is at least $800.00, the discount is 5%.

   Test your program on each of the following three customers.

   Customer A: This customer is using room C on Tuesday night. The party includes 80 adults and 6 children. The standard meal is being served. The customer paid a $60.00 deposit. *Customer B:* This customer is using room A on Saturday night. Deluxe meals are being served to 15 adults. A deposit of $50.00 was paid. *Customer C:* This customer is using room D on Sunday afternoon. The party includes 30 children and 2 adults, all of whom are served the standard meal.

   Output should be in the same form as that for Problem 12, Chapter 4.

15. State University charges $90.00 for each semester hour of credit, $200.00 per semester for a regular room, $250.00 per semester for an air-conditioned room, and $400.00 per semester for food. All students are charged a $30.00 matriculation fee. Graduating students must also pay a $35.00 diploma fee. Write a program to compute the fees that must be paid by a student. Your program should include an appropriate warning message if a student is taking more than 21 credit hours or fewer than 12 credit hours. A typical line of data for one student would include room type (R or A), student number (in four digits), credit hours, and graduation status (T or F).

16. Write a program to determine the day of the week a person was born given his or her birth date. Following are the steps you should use to find the day of the week corresponding to any date in this century.

a. Divide the last two digits of the birth year by 4. Put the quotient (ignoring the remainder) in **total**. For example, if the person was born in 1983, divide 83 by 4 and store 20 in **total**.

b. Add the last two digits of the birth year to **total**.

c. Add the last two digits of the birth date to **total**.

d. Using the following table, find the "month number" and add it to **total**.

January = 1

February = 4

March = 4

April = 0

May = 2

June = 5

July = 0

August = 3

September = 6

October = 1

November = 4

December = 6

e. If the year is a leap year and if the month you are working with is either January or February, then subtract 1 from the **total**.

f. Find the remainder when **total** is divided by 7. Look up the remainder in the following table to determine the day of the week the person was born. Note that you should not use this procedure if the person's year of birth is earlier than 1900.

1 = Sunday

2 = Monday

3 = Tuesday

4 = Wednesday

5 = Thursday

6 = Friday

0 = Saturday

Typical input is

5-15 78

where the first entry (5-15) represents the birth date (May 15) and the second entry (78) represents the birth year. An appropriate error message should be printed if a person's year of birth is before 1900.

17. Community Hospital needs a program to compute and print a statement for each patient. Charges for each day are as follows:

a. room charges: private room, $125.00; semiprivate room, $95.00; or ward, $75.00

b. telephone charge: $1.75

c. television charge: $3.50

Write a program to get a line of data from the keyboard, compute the patient's bill, and print an appropriate statement. Typical input is

5PNY

where **5** indicates the number of days spent in the hospital, **P** represents the room type (**P, S**, or **W**), **N** represents the telephone option (**Y** or **N**), and **Y** represents the television option (**Y** or **N**). A statement for the data given follows.

```
Community Hospital

Patient Billing Statement

Number of days in hospital: 5 Type of room: Private

Room charge                      $ 625.00

Telephone charge                 $   0.00

Television charge                $  17.50

     TOTAL DUE          $642.50
```

18. Write a program that converts degrees Fahrenheit to degrees Celsius and degrees Celsius to degrees Fahrenheit. In the input the temperature is followed by a designator (F or C) indicating whether the given temperature is Fahrenheit or Celsius.

19. The city of Mt. Pleasant bills its residents for sewage, water, and sanitation every three months. The sewer and water charge is figured according to how much water is used by the resident. The scale is

Amount (gallons)	Rate (per gallon)
Less than 1000	$0.03
1000 to 1999	$30 + $0.02 for each gallon over 1000
2000 or more	$50 + $0.015 for each gallon over 2000

The sanitation charge is $7.50 per month.

Write a program to read the number of months for which a resident is being billed (1, 2, or 3) and how much water was used; then print a statement with appropriate charges and messages. Use the constant definition section for all rates and include an error check for incorrect number of months. Typical input is

3 2175

20. Al Derrick, owner of the Lucky Wildcat Well Corporation, wants a program to help him decide whether or not a well is making money. Data for a well will consist of one or two lines. The first line contains a single character (D for a dry well, O for oil found, and G for gas found) followed by a real number for the cost of the well. If an "O" or "G" is detected, the cost will be followed by an integer indicating the volume of oil or gas found. In this case, there will also be a second line containing an "N" or "S" indicating whether or not sulfur is present. If there is sulfur, the "S" will be followed by the percentage of sulfur present in the oil or gas. Unit prices are $5.50 for oil and $2.20 for gas. These should be defined as constants. Your program should compute the total revenue for a well (reduce output for sulfur present) and print all pertinent information with an appropriate message to Mr. Derrick. A gusher is defined as a well with profit in excess of $50,000. Typical input is

G 8000.00 20000 S 0.15

21. The Mathematical Association of America hosts an annual summer meeting. Each state sends one official delegate to the section officer's meeting at this summer session. The national organization reimburses the official state delegates according to the following scale:

Round-trip Mileage	Rate
Up to 500 miles	15 cents per mile
501 to 1000 miles	$75.00 plus 12 cents for each mile over 500
1001 to 1500 miles	$135.00 plus 10 cents for each mile over 1000
1501 to 2000 miles	$185.00 plus 8 cents for each mile over 1500
2001 to 3000 miles	$225.00 plus 6 cents for each mile over
3001 or more miles	$285.00 plus 5 cents for each mile over 3000

Write a program that will accept as input the number of round-trip miles for a delegate and compute the amount of reimbursement.

22. Dr. Lae Z. Programmer (Problem 5) wants you to write a program to compute and print the grade for a student in his class. The grade is based on three examinations (worth a possible 100 points each), five quizzes (10 points each), and a 200-point final examination. Your output should include all scores, the percentage grade, and the letter grade. The grading scale is

90 <= average	<= 100	A
80 <= average	< 90	B
70 <= average	< 80	C
60 <= average	< 70	D
0 <= average	< 60	E
Typical input is		

```
80 93 85 (examination scores)
9 10 8 7 10 (quiz scores)
175 (final examination)
```

23. Dr. Lae Z. Programmer now wants you to modify Problem 22 by adding a check for bad data. Any time an unexpected score occurs, you are to print an appropriate error message and terminate the program.

24. A quadratic equation is one of the form

$$ax^2 + bx + c = 0$$

where $a \neq 0$. Real number solutions to this equation are given by

$$x = \frac{-b \pm \sqrt{b^2 - 4ac}}{2a}$$

where the quantity $(b^2 - 4ac)$ is referred to as the discriminant of the equation. Write a program to read three integers as the respective coefficients (a, b, and c), compute the discriminant, and print the solutions. Use the following rules:

a. discriminant = 0 -> single root.

b. discriminant < 0 -> no real number solution.

c. discriminant > 0 -> two distinct real solutions.

25. Write a program that gets as input the lengths of three sides of a triangle. Output should first identify the triangle as scalene, isosceles, or equilateral. The program should use the Pythagorean theorem to determine whether or not scalene or isosceles triangles are right triangles. An appropriate message should be part of the output.

26. The sign on the attendant's booth at the Pentagon parking lot is

PENTAGON VISITOR PARKING	
Cars:	
First 2 hours	Free
Next 3 hours	0.50/hour
Next 10 hours	0.25/hour
Trucks:	
First 1 hour	Free
Next 2 hours	1.00/hour
Next 12 hours	0.75/hour
Senior Citizens:	No charge

Write a program that will accept as input a one-character designator (C, T, or S) followed by the number of minutes a vehicle has been in the lot. The program should then compute the appropriate charge and print a ticket for the customer. Any part of an hour is to be counted as a full hour.

27. Milt Walker, the chief of advertising for the Isabella Potato Industry, wants you to write a program to compute an itemized bill and total cost of his "This Spud's for You!" ad campaign. The standard black-and-white full-page ads have base prices as follows:

Drillers' News (code N) $ 400

Playperson (code P) $2000

Outdoors (code O) $ 900

Independent News (code I) $1200

Each ad is allowed 15 lines of print with a rate of $20.00 for each line in excess of 15 lines. Each ad is either black and white (code B) and subject to the base prices, or is in color (code C) and subject to the following rates: Three color (code T), 40% increase over base; full color (code F), 60% increase over base.

   Write a program to input Milt's choice of magazine (N, P, O, or I), the number of lines of print (integer), and either black and white (B) or color (C) with a choice of three colors (T) or full color (F). Output should include an appropriate title, all the information and costs used to compute the price of an ad, the total price of the ad, and finally the total price of all ads.

28. Write a program that will add, subtract, multiply, and divide fractions. Input will consist of a single line representing a fraction arithmetic problem as follows: integer/integer operation integer/integer. For example, a line of input might be

`2/3 + 1/2`

Your program should do the following:

a. Check for division by zero.

b. Check for proper operation symbols.

c. Print the problem in its original form.

d. Print the answer.

e. Print all fractions in horizontal form.

   Your answer need not be in lowest terms. For the sample input

`2/3 + 1/2`

sample output is

```
2     1     7
-- + -- = --
3     2     6
```

29. Write an interactive program that permits the user to print various recipes. Write a procedure for each recipe. After the user enters a one-letter identifier for the desired recipe, a **switch** statement should be used to call the appropriate function. Part of the code could be

```
cin >> selection;
switch (selection)
{
        case 'J':       jambalaya;
                        break;
        case 'S':       spaghetti;
                        break;
        case 'T': tacos;
}
```

30. The force of gravity is different for each of the nine planets in our solar system. For example, on Mercury it is only 0.38 times as strong as on Earth. Thus, if you weigh 100 pounds (on Earth), you would weigh only 38 pounds on Mercury. Write an interactive program that allows you to enter your Earth weight and your choice of planet to which you would like your weight converted. Output should be your weight on the desired planet together with the planet name. The screen message for input should include a menu for planet choice. Use a **switch** statement in the program for computation and output. The relative forces of gravity are

Earth   1.00

Jupiter   2.65

Mars   0.39

Mercury   0.38

Neptune   1.23

Pluto   0.05

Saturn   1.17

Uranus   1.05

Venus   0.78

31. Cramer's Rule is a method for solving a system of linear equations. If you have two equations with variables x and y written as

$ax + by = c$
$dx + ey = f$

then the solution for x and y can be given as

$$x = \frac{\begin{vmatrix} c & b \\ f & e \end{vmatrix}}{\begin{vmatrix} a & b \\ d & e \end{vmatrix}}$$

$$y = \frac{\begin{vmatrix} a & c \\ d & f \end{vmatrix}}{\begin{vmatrix} a & b \\ d & e \end{vmatrix}}$$

Using this notation,

$$\begin{vmatrix} a & b \\ d & e \end{vmatrix}$$

is the determinant of the matrix

$$\begin{bmatrix} a & b \\ d & e \end{bmatrix}$$

and is equal to *ae - bd*.

Write a complete program that will solve a system of two equations using Cramer's rule. Input will be all coefficients and constants in the system. Output will be the solution to the system. Typical output is

For the system of equations

$x + 2y = 5$

$2x - y = 0$

we have the solution

$x = 1$

$y = 2$

Use an **if . . . else** statement to guard against division by zero.

32. Contact a programmer and discuss the concept of robustness in a program. Prepare a report of your conversation for class. Your report should include a list of specific instances of how programmers make programs robust.

33. Conduct an unscientific survey of at least two people from each of the following groups: students in upper-level computer science courses, instructors of computer science, and programmers working in industry. Your survey should attempt to ascertain the importance of and use of robustness at each level. Discuss the similarities and differences of your findings with those of other class members.

34. Selecting appropriate test data for a program that uses nested selection is a nontrivial task. Create diagrams that allow you to trace the flow of logic when nested selection is used. Use your diagrams to draw conclusions about minimal test data required to test all branches of a program that uses nested selection to various levels.

6 Repetition Statements

The previous chapter on selection introduced you to a control structure that takes advantage of a computer's ability to make choices. A second major control structure takes advantage of a computer's ability to repeat the same task many times. The control structures for selection and repetition allow us to specify any algorithm we need to solve a problem with a computer.

This chapter examines the different methods C++ permits for performing a process repeatedly. For example, as yet we cannot conveniently write a program that solves the simple problem of adding the integers from 1 to 100 or processing the grades of 30 students in a class. By the end of this chapter, you will be able to solve these problems three different ways. The three forms of repetition (loops) are

```
1. for <a definite number of times> <do an action>
2. while <condition is true> <do an action>
3. do <action> while <condition is true>
```

Each of these three loops contains the basic constructs necessary for repetition: a variable is assigned some value, the variable value changes at some point in the loop, and repetition continues until the value reaches some predetermined value. When the predetermined value (or **boolean** condition) is reached, repetition is terminated and program control moves to the next executable statement.

Pretest and Post-test Loops

A loop that uses a condition to control whether or not the body of the loop is executed before going through the loop is a *pretest* or *entrance-controlled loop*. The testing condition is the *pretest condition*. If the condition is **TRUE**, the body of the loop is executed. If the condition is **FALSE**, the program skips to the first line of code following the loop. The **for** loop and the **while** loop are pretest loops.

A loop that examines a Boolean expression after the loop body is executed is a *post-test* or *exit-controlled loop*. This is the **do . . . while** loop.

Fixed Repetition Versus Variable Condition Loops

Fixed repetition (iterated) loops are used when it can be determined in advance how often a segment of code needs to be repeated. For instance, you might know that you need a predetermined number of repetitions of a segment of code for a program that adds the integers from 1 to 100 or for a program that uses a fixed

6.1 Classifying Loops

number of data lines, for example, game statistics for a team of 12 basketball players. The number of repetitions need not be constant. For example, a user might enter information during execution of a program that would determine how often a segment should be repeated. In this chapter, we will introduce a class of **for** loops that are fixed repetition loops.

Variable condition loops are needed to solve problems for which conditions change within the body of the loop. These conditions involve sentinel values, Boolean flags, arithmetic expressions or end-of-line and end-of-file markers (see Chapter 9). A variable condition loop provides more power than a fixed repetition loop. The **while** and **do . . . while** loops are variable condition loops.

6.2 ▸ The for Loop

OBJECTIVES

- to understand how the loop control variable is used in a loop
- to understand the flow of control when using a fixed repetition loop in a program
- to be able to use a **for** loop in a program
- to be able to use a **for** loop that counts down in a program

The **for** loop is a pretest loop. Although one can write variable condition **for** loops in C++, we will discuss only fixed repetition **for** loops. The typical form of a **for** loop is

```
for ( <initialization expression>; <termination condition>; <update expression> )
        <statement>
```

In the following example, a **for** loop displays all of the numbers between 1 and 10:

```
for (i = 1; i <= 10; i = i + 1)
        cout << i << endl;
```

A **for** loop is considered to be a single executable statement. The information contained within the parentheses is referred to as the heading of the loop. The actions performed in the loop are referred to as the body of the loop. The heading of a **for** loop consists of three parts:

1. *Initialization expression:* In fixed repetition **for** loops, this part sets a *control variable* to an initial value. This variable will control the number of times that the body of the loop is executed.
2. *Termination condition:* This part normally consists of a comparison of the control variable to a value. The body of the loop will execute while this condition is **TRUE**.
3. *Update expression:* This part normally consists of a statement that makes the value of the control variable approach the value specified in the termination condition. In **for** loops that count up, this part increments the control variable by some value; in **for** loops that count down, this part decrements the control variable by some value.

The internal logic of a **for** loop that counts up is as follows:

1. The *control variable* is assigned an initial value in the initialization expression.
2. The termination condition is evaluated.
3. If the termination condition is **TRUE** then
   (a) the body of the loop is executed and
   (b) the update expression is evaluated.
4. If the termination condition is **FALSE** then
   control of the program is transferred to the first statement following the loop.

As you can see, a **for** loop proceeds by *counting up* from a *lower bound* to an *upper bound.* A flow diagram for this example is given in Figure 6.1.

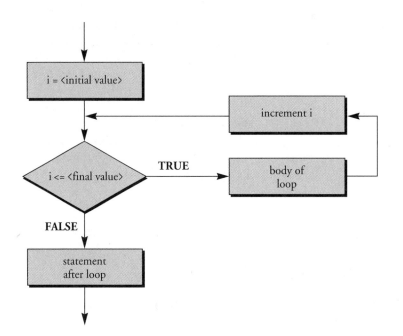

We have discussed only a typical form of the **for** loop, one that counts up. We will see variations on this form, such as **for** loops that count from an upper bound down to a lower bound, or count by some factor other than one, in later sections of this chapter.

The Increment and Decrement Operators

C++ has a pair of operators that increment or decrement variables. These operators are very concise and handy to use in loops. The increment operator, **++**, precedes a variable in a complete C++ statement. For example, the statement

```
++x;
```

would increment (add one to) the variable **x**. It has the same effect as the assignment statement

```
x = x + 1;
```

Thus, the example **for** statement could be rewritten more concisely as

```
for (i = 1; i <= 10; ++i)
        cout << i << endl;
```

The decrement operator, **--**, precedes a variable in a complete C++ statement. The operator has the effect of subtracting one from the variable and storing the result in it.

Accumulators

The problem of adding the integers from 1 to 100 needs only one statement in the body of the loop. This problem can be solved by code that constructs an *accumulator*. An accumulator merely sums values of some variable. In the following code, the loop control variable, **lcv**, successively assumes the values 1, 2, 3, . . . , 100.

```
sum = 0;

for (lcv = 1; lcv <= 100; ++lcv)

        sum = sum + lcv;
```

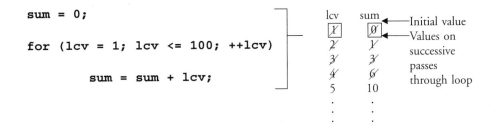

This program segment contains an example of graphic documentation. Throughout the text, these insets will be used to help illustrate what the code is actually doing. The insets are not part of the program; they merely show what some specific code is trying to accomplish.

To see how **sum** accumulates these values, let us trace through the code for several values of **lcv**. Initially, **sum** is set to zero by

```
sum = 0;
```

When **lcv** is assigned the value 1,

```
sum = sum + lcv;
```

produces

1	Ø 1
lcv	**sum**

For **lcv = 2**, we get

2	1̸ 3
lcv	**sum**

lcv = 3 yields

3	3̸ 6
lcv	**sum**

Note that **sum** has been assigned a value equal to 1 + 2 + 3. The final value for **lcv** is 100. Once this value has been added to **sum**, the value of **sum** will be 5050, which is the sum of 1 + 2 + 3 + ... + 100. Accumulators are frequently used in loops. The general form for this use is

```
accumulator = 0;
for (lcv = <initial value>; lcv <= <final value>; ++lcv)
        accumulator = accumulator + lcv;
```

Scope of a Loop Control Variable

In general, the loop control variable of a **for** loop must be declared before it is used in the loop. In accordance with the scope rules of C++, the scope of this variable will be the program block within which it is declared. However, on many occasions, a loop control variable will only be used within a loop. In these cases, using a variable whose scope extends beyond a loop opens the program to serious side effects. To minimize these, the loop control variable can be declared when it is initialized within the loop. The visibility of the variable will be restricted to the body of the loop and to the area of the program text below the loop but within the block where the loop appears. For example, the following loop performs the equivalent task of our first example, but its loop control variable cannot be accessed above the body of the loop:

```
// References to i are not allowed here
// (i has not been declared yet).

for (int i = 1; i <= 10; ++i)
        cout << i << endl;

// References to i are allowed here.
// Its value will be 11 when the loop is done.
```

In general, it is safe programming practice to restrict the scope of variables to only those areas of a program in which it is necessary to access them.

Some comments concerning the syntax and form of **for** loops are now necessary:

1. The loop control variable must be declared as a variable. We will usually declare this variable as part of the loop heading.
2. The loop control variable can be any valid identifier.
3. The loop control variable can be used within the loop just as any other variable except that the value of the variable should not be changed by the statements in the body of the loop.
4. The initial and final values can be constants or variable expressions with appropriate values.
5. The loop will be repeated for each value of the loop control variable in the range indicated by the initial and final values.

At this point you might try writing some test programs to see what happens if you do not follow these rules. Then consider the following examples, which illustrate the features of **for** loops.

EXAMPLE 6.1

Write a segment of code to list the integers from 1 to 10 together with their squares and cubes. This can be done by

```
for (int j = 1; j <= 10; ++j)
    cout << j << setw(10) << j * j << setw(8) << j * j * j << endl;
```

This segment produces

1	1	1
2	4	8
3	9	27
4	16	64
5	25	125
6	36	216
7	49	343
8	64	512
9	81	729
10	100	1000

EXAMPLE 6.2	Write a **for** loop to produce the following design:

```
       **
      *  *
     *    *
    *      *
   *        *
```

Assuming the first asterisk is in column 20, the following loop will produce the desired result. Note carefully how the output is formatted.

```
for (int j = 1; j <= 5; ++j)
    cout << setw(21 - j) << '*' << setw(2 * j - 1) << '*' << endl;
```

EXAMPLE 6.3	When computing compound interest, it is necessary to evaluate the quantity $(1 + r)^n$ where r is the interest rate for one time period and n is the number of time periods. A **for** loop can be used to perform this computation. If we declare a variable **base,** this can be solved by

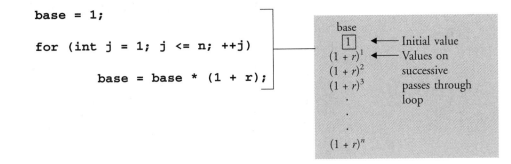

```
base = 1;

for (int j = 1; j <= n; ++j)

    base = base * (1 + r);
```

base
$\boxed{1}$ ◄—— Initial value
$(1 + r)^1$ ◄—— Values on
$(1 + r)^2$ successive
$(1 + r)^3$ passes through
.   loop
.
.
$(1 + r)^n$

for Loops that Count Down

A second kind of pretest, fixed repetition loop is a **for** loop that counts down. This loop does exactly what you expect; it is identical to a **for** loop that counts up, except the loop control variable is decreased by one instead of increased by one each time through the loop. This is referred to as a *decrement*. The test is loop control value >= final value. The loop terminates when the loop control value is less than the final value. The decrement operator is used to adjust the loop control variable on each pass through the loop. Proper form and syntax for a loop of this type are the same as that of **for** loops that count up; however, the contents of the statements within the loop heading will be the opposite of those for loops that count up:

1. The initialization part sets the control variable to an upper bound rather than a lower bound.
2. The termination part consists of a comparison to see whether the control variable is greater than or equal to a value that is the lower bound of the loop.
3. The update part decrements rather than increments the control variable by some value.

We will now consider an example of a **for** loop that counts down.

<table>
<tr><td>EXAMPLE 6.4</td></tr>
</table>

Illustrate the control values of a **for** loop that counts down by writing the control value during each pass through the loop. The segment of code for this could be

```
for (int k = 20; k >= 15; --k)
        cout << "K =" << setw(4) << k << endl;
```

and the output is

```
K =      20
K =      19
K =      18
K =      17
K =      16
K =      15
```

Loops that Count by Factors Other than One

Thus far, we have examined **for** loops that count up or count down. They do this by incrementing or decrementing a loop control variable by one. There are some occasions when we would like to count by a factor of two or more. One example is the problem of adding all of the even numbers between a lower and an upper bound. For this problem, the loop should count up or down by twos. The following example solves this problem for the numbers 2 through 10 by incrementing the loop control variable by two in an assignment expression:

```
sum = 0;
for (int j = 2; j <= 10; j = j + 2)
        sum = sum + j;
cout << sum << endl;
```

Writing Style for Loops

As you can see, writing style is an important consideration when writing code using loops. There are three features to consider. First, the body of the loop should be indented. Compare the following two pieces of code:

```
for (int j = 1; j <= 10; ++j)
{
        cin >> num >> amt;
        total1 = total1 + amt;
        total2 = total2 + num;
        cout << "The number is" << setw(6) << num << endl;
}
cout << "The total amount is" << fixed << showpoint << setw(8) << setprecision(2)
     << total1 << endl;
average = total2 / 10.0;
```

```
for (int j = 1; j <= 10; ++j)
{
cin >> num >> amt;
total1 = total1 + amt;
total2 = total2 + num;
cout << "The number is" << setw(6) << num << endl;
}
cout << "The total amount is" << fixed << showpoint << setw(8) << setprecision(2)
     << total1 << endl;
average = total2 / 10.0;
```

The indenting in the first segment makes it easier to determine what is contained in the body of the loop than it is in the second segment, without any indenting.

Second, blank lines can be used before and after a loop for better readability. Compare the following:

```
cin >> x >> y;
cout << fixed << showpoint;
cout << setw(6) << setprecision(2) << x << setw(6) << y << endl;
cout << endl;

for  (int j = -3; j <= 5; ++j)
        cout << setw(3) << j << setw(5) << '*' << endl;

sum = sum + x;
cout << setw(10) << setprecision(2) << sum << endl;

cin >> x >> y;
cout << fixed << showpoint;
cout << setw(6) << setprecision(2) << x << setw(6) << y << endl;
cout << endl;
for  (int j = -3; j <= 5; ++j)
        cout << setw(3) << j << setw(5) << '*' << endl;
sum = sum + x;
cout << setw(10) << setprecision(2) << sum << endl;
```

Again, the first segment is a bit more clear because it emphasizes that the entire loop is a single executable statement and makes it easy to locate the loop.

Third, comments used within loops make them more readable. In particular, a comment could accompany the end of a compound statement that is the body of a loop. The general form for this is

```
// Get a test score
for (int j = 1; j <= 50; ++j)
{
      .
    . (body of the loop)
      .
} // end of for loop
```

We close this section with an example that uses a **for** loop to solve a problem.

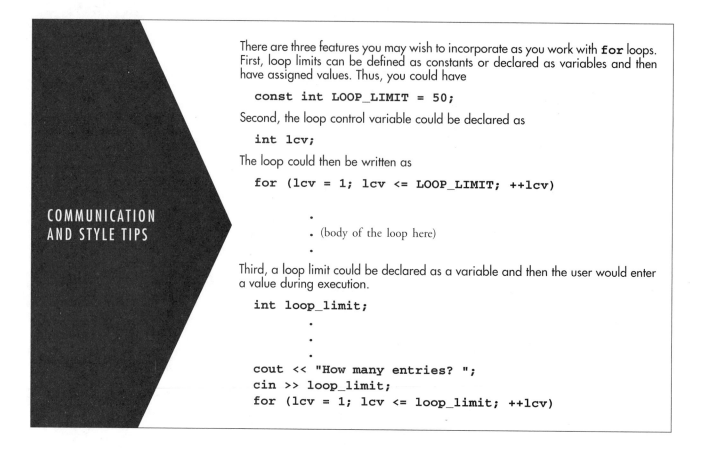

COMMUNICATION AND STYLE TIPS

There are three features you may wish to incorporate as you work with **for** loops. First, loop limits can be defined as constants or declared as variables and then have assigned values. Thus, you could have

```
const int LOOP_LIMIT = 50;
```

Second, the loop control variable could be declared as

```
int lcv;
```

The loop could then be written as

```
for (lcv = 1; lcv <= LOOP_LIMIT; ++lcv)

        .
        .  (body of the loop here)
        .
```

Third, a loop limit could be declared as a variable and then the user would enter a value during execution.

```
int loop_limit;
        .
        .
        .
cout << "How many entries? ";
cin >> loop_limit;
for (lcv = 1; lcv <= loop_limit; ++lcv)
```

EXAMPLE 6.5

Suppose you have been asked to write a segment of code to compute the test average for each of 30 students in a class and the overall class average. Data for each student consist of the student's initials and four test scores.

A first-level pseudocode development is

1. Print a heading
2. Initialize total
3. Process data for each of 30 students
4. Compute class average
5. Print a summary

A **for** loop could be used to implement step 3. The step could first be refined to

3. Process data for each of 30 students
   3.1 get data for a student
   3.2 compute average
   3.3 add to total
   3.4 print student data

The code for this step is

```
for (int lcv = 1; lcv <= CLASS_SIZE; ++lcv)
{
        cout << "Enter three initials and press <Enter>. ";
        cin >> init1 >> init2 >> init3;
        cout << "Enter four test scores and press <Enter>. ";
```

```
cin >> score1 >> score2 >> score3 >> score4;
average = (score1 + score2 + score3 + score4) / 4.0;
total = total + average;
cout << endl;
cout << setw(4) << init1 << init2 << init3;
cout << setw(6) <<score1 << setw(6) << score2
     << setw(6) << score3 << setw(6) <<score4;
cout << setprecision(2) << setw(10) << average
     << endl;

}
```

EXERCISES 6.2

1. What is the output from each of the following segments of code?
   a. for (k = 3; k <= 8; ++k)
         cout << setw(k) << '*' << endl;
   b. for (j = 1; j <= 10; ++j)
         cout << stew(4) << j << ":" << setw(5)
             << (10-J) << endl;
   c.   a = 2;
     for (j = (3 * 2 - 4); j <= 10 * a; ++j)
         cout << stew(4) << j << endl;
   d. for (j = 50; j >= 30; --j)
         cout << setw(5) << (51 - j) << endl;

2. Write a test program for each of the following.
   a. Illustrate what happens when the loop control variable is assigned a value inside the loop.
   b. Demonstrate how an accumulator works. For this test program, sum the integers from 1 to 10. Your output should show each partial sum as it is assigned to the accumulator.

3. Write segments of code using a loop that counts up and a loop that counts down to produce the following designs. Start each design in column 2.

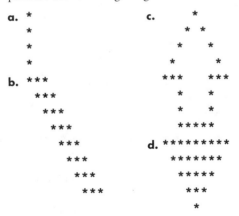

4. Which of the following segments of code do you think accomplishes its intended task? For those that do not, what changes would you suggest?

   a. for (k = 1; k <= 5; ++k);
       cout << k << endl;
   b. sum = 0;
     for (j = 1; j <= 10; ++j)
        cin >>a;

```
            sum = sum + a;
            cout << setw(15) << sum << endl;
   c.       sum = 0;
         for (j = -3; j <= 3; ++j)
              sum = sum + j;
   d. a = 0;
      for (k = 1; k <= 10; ++k)
      {
           a = a + k;
           cout << setw(5) << k << setw(5) << a << setw(5)
                << (a + k) << endl;
      }
      cout << setw(5) << k << setw(5) << a << setw(5)
           << (a + k) << endl;
```

5. Produce each of the following outputs using a loop that counts up and a loop that counts down.

   a. 1 2 3 4 5
   b. *
         *
            *
               *
                  *

6. Rewrite the following segment of code using a loop that counts down to produce the same result.

```
sum = 0;
for (k = 1; k <= 4; ++k)
{
        cout << setw(21 + k) << endl;
        sum = sum + k;
}
```

7. Rewrite the following segment of code using a loop that counts up to produce the same result.

```
for (j = 10; j >= 2; --j)
        cout << setw(j) << j << endl;
```

8. Write a complete program that produces a table showing the temperature equivalents in degrees Fahrenheit and degrees Celsius. Let the user enter the starting and ending values. Use the formula

```
cels_temp = 5.0/9.0 (faren_temp - 32.0)
```

9. Write a complete program to produce a chart consisting of the multiples of 5 from –50 to 50 together with the squares and cubes of these numbers. Use a function to print a suitable heading and user-defined functions for square and cube.

10. The formula $A = P(1 + R)^N$ can be used to compute the amount due (A) when a principal (P) has been borrowed at a monthly rate (R) for a period of N months. Write a complete program that will read in the principal, annual interest rate (divide by 12 for monthly rate), and number of months and then produce a chart that shows how much will be due at the end of each month.

A NOTE OF INTEREST

Charles Babbage

The first person to propose the concept of the modern computer was Charles Babbage (1791–1871), a man truly ahead of his time. Babbage was a professor of mathematics at Cambridge University, as well as an inventor. As a mathematician, he realized the time-consuming and boring nature of constructing mathematical tables (squares, logarithms, sines, cosines, and so on). Because the calculators developed by Pascal and Leibniz could not provide the calculations required for these more complex tables, Babbage proposed the idea of building a machine that could compute the various properties of numbers, accurate to 20 digits.

With a grant from the British government, he designed and partially built a simple model of the difference engine. However, the lack of technology in the 1800s prevented him from making a working model. Discouraged by his inability to materialize his ideas, Babbage imagined a better version, which would be a general-purpose, problem-solving machine—the analytical engine.

The similarities between the analytical engine and the modern computer are amazing. Babbage's analytical engine, which was intended to be a steam-powered device, had four components:

1. A "mill" that manipulated and computed the data
2. A "store" that held the data

3. An "operator" of the system that carried out instructions
4. A separate device that entered data and received processed information via punched cards.

After spending many years sketching variations and improvements for this new model, Babbage received some assistance in 1842 from Ada Augusta Byron (see the next Note of Interest).

6.3 while Loops

In Section 6.2, we studied **for** loops in which the body of the loop is repeated a fixed number of times. For some problems, this kind of loop is inappropriate, because a segment of code may need to be repeated an unknown number of times. The condition controlling the loop must be variable rather than constant. C++ provides two repetition statements that are especially well suited to handle variable control conditions, one with a pretest condition and one with a post-test condition.

A useful pretest loop with variable conditions in C++ is the **while** loop. The condition controlling the loop is a Boolean expression written between parentheses. Correct form and syntax for such a loop are

```
while ( <Boolean expression> )
       <statement>
```

Note that the parentheses enclosing the Boolean expression are required. The flow diagram for a **while** loop is given in Figure 6.2. Program control, when using a **while** loop, is in order as follows:

1. The loop condition is examined.
2. If the loop condition is **TRUE**, the entire body of the loop is executed before another check is made.
3. If the loop condition is **FALSE**, control is transferred to the first statement following the loop. For example,

```
a = 1;
while (a < 0)
{
       num = 5;
       cout << num << endl;
       a = a + 10
}
cout << a << endl;
```

produces the single line of output

```
1
```

Before analyzing the components of the **while** statement, we should consider a short example.

◆ FIGURE 6.2

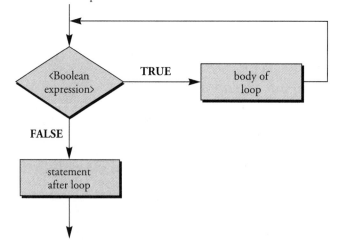

EXAMPLE 6.6   This example prints some powers of two.

```
power2 = 1;

while (power2 < 100)

{

        cout << power2 << endl;

        power2 = power2 * 2;

}
```

The output from this segment of code is

```
    1
    2
    4
    8
   16
   32
   64
```

With this example in mind, let us examine the general form for using a **while** loop.

1. The condition can be any expression that has a Boolean value. Standard examples include relational operators and Boolean variables; thus, each of the following would be appropriate.

```
while (j < 10)
while (a < b)
while (! done)
```

2. The Boolean expression must have a value prior to entering the loop.

3. The body of the loop can be a simple statement or a compound statement.

4. Provision must be made for appropriately changing the loop control condition in the body of the loop. If no such changes are made, the following could happen:

a. If the loop condition is **TRUE** and no changes are made, a condition called an *infinite loop* is caused. For example,

```
a = 1;
while (a > 0)
{
        num = 5;
        cout<< num << endl;
}
cout << a << endl;
```

The condition **a > 0** is **TRUE**, the body is executed, and the condition is retested. However, because the condition is not changed within the loop body, it will always be **TRUE** and will cause an infinite loop. It will not produce a compilation error but, when you run the program, the output will be a column of fives.

b. If the loop condition is **TRUE** and changes are made, but the condition never becomes **FALSE**, you again have an infinite loop. An example of this is

```
power3 = 1;
while (power3 != 100)
{
        cout << power3 << endl;
        power3 = power3 * 3
}
```

Since the variable **power3** never is assigned the value 100, the condition **power3 != 100** is always **TRUE**. At run time, the computer will continue to multiply **power3** by 3 until an integer overflow error occurs.

Sentinel Values

The Boolean expression of a variable control loop is frequently controlled by a *sentinel value*. For example, a program might require the user to enter numeric data. When there are no more data, the user will be instructed to enter a special (sentinel) value. This then signifies the end of the process. Example 6.7 illustrates the use of such a sentinel.

EXAMPLE 6.7

Here we write a segment of code that allows the user to enter a set of test scores and then print the average score.

```
num_scores = 0;
sum = 0;
cout << "Enter a score and press <Enter>, -999 to quit. ";
cin >> score;
while (score != -999)
{
        num_scores = num_scores + 1;
        sum = sum + score;
        cout << "Enter a score and press <Enter>, -999 to quit. ";
        cin >> score;
}
if (num_scores > 0)
{
        average = sum / float(num_scores);
        cout << endl;
        cout << "The average of" << setw(4) << num_scores << " scores is"
            << fixed << showpoint << setw(6) setprecision(2) << average << endl;
}
else
        cout << "No scores were entered" << endl;
```

Writing Style

Writing style for **while** loops should be similar to that adopted for **for** loops; that is, indenting, skipped lines, and comments should all be used to enhance readability.

Using Counters

Because **while** loops can be repeated a variable number of times, it is a common practice to count the number of times the loop body is executed. This is accomplished by declaring an appropriately named integer variable, initializing it to zero before the loop, and then incrementing it by one each time through the loop. For example, if you use **count** for your variable name, Example 6.6 (in which we printed some powers of two) could be modified to

```
count = 0;
power2 = 1;

while (power2 < 100)
{
        cout << power2 << endl;
        power2 = power2 * 2;
        count = count + 1;
}

cout << "There are" << setw(4) << count << " powers of 2 less than 100." << endl;
```

The output from this segment of code is

```
        1
        2
        4
        8
       16
       32
       64

There are 7 powers of 2 less than 100.
```

Although the process is tedious, it is instructive to trace the values of variables through a loop where a *counter* is used. Therefore, let us consider the segment of code we have just seen. Before the loop is entered, we have

    count power2

The loop control is **power2 < 100 (1 < 100)**. Since this is **TRUE**, the loop body is executed and the new values become

    count power2

Prior to each successive time through the loop, the condition **power2 < 100** is checked. Thus, the loop produces the following sequence of values:

count	power2
1	2
2	4
3	8
4	16
5	32
6	64
7	128

Although **power2** is 128, the remainder of the loop is executed before checking the loop condition. Once a loop is entered, it is executed completely before the loop control condition is reexamined. Because **128 < 100** is **FALSE**, control is transferred to the statement following the loop.

Compound Conditions

All previous examples and illustrations of **while** loops have used simple Boolean expressions. However, because any Boolean expression can be used as a loop control condition, compound Boolean expressions can also be used. For example,

```
cin >> a >> b;
while ((a > 0) && (b > 0))
{
        cout << a << b << endl;
        a = a - 5;
        b = b - 3;
}
```

will go through the body of the loop only when the boolean expression **(a > 0) && (b > 0)** is **TRUE**. Thus, if the values of **a** and **b** obtained from the keyboard are

    17   8

the output from this segment of code is

    17   8

    12   5

    7   2

Compound Boolean expressions can be as complex as you wish to make them. However, if several conditions are involved, the program can become difficult to read and debug; therefore, you may wish to redesign your solution to avoid this problem.

EXERCISES 6.3

1. Compare and contrast **for** loops with **while** loops.
2. Write a test program that illustrates what happens when you have an infinite loop.
3. What is the output from each of the following segments of code?

```
a. k = 1;
   while (k <= 10)
   {
        cout << k << endl;
        k = k + 1;
   }
b. a = 1;
   while (17 % a < 5)
   {
        cout << a << 17 % a << endl;
        a = a + 1;
   }
c. a = 2;
   b = 50;
   while (a < b)
        a = a * 3;
   cout << a << b << endl;
d. count = 0;
   sum = 0;
   while (count < 5)
   {
        count = count + 1;
        sum = sum + count;
        cout << "The partial sum is" << setw(4) << sum
             << endl;
   }
   cout << "The count is" << setw(4) << count << endl;
e. x = 3.0;
   y = 2.0;
   while (x * y < 100)
        x = x * y;
   cout << setprecision(2) << setw(10) << x setw(10)
        << y < endl;
```

4. Indicate which of the following are infinite loops and explain why they are infinite.

```
a. j = 1;
   while (j < 10)
        cout << j;
        j = j + 1;
b. a = 2;
   while (a < 20)
   {
        cout << a << endl;
        a = a * 2;
   }
c. a = 2;
   while (a <> 20)
   {
        cout << a << endl;
        a = a * 2;
   }
```

A NOTE OF INTEREST

Ada Augusta Byron

Ada Augusta Byron, Countess of Lovelace (1815–1852), became interested in Charles Babbage's efforts when she was translating a paper on the analytical engine from French to English. Upon meeting Babbage, she began the task of writing an original paper. Through the process, she documented Babbage's ideas and made it possible to understand Babbage's original intentions. Over time, she became a full collaborator on the project, correcting some errors and suggesting the use of the binary system of storage rather than the decimal.

Lady Lovelace's most important contribution was her concept of a loop. She observed that a repetition of a sequence of instructions often was necessary to perform a single calculation. Thus, she discovered that by using a single set of cards and a conditional jump facility, the calculation could be performed with a fraction of the effort. This idea has earned her the distinction of being the first programmer. In honor of her role as the first computer programmer, the U.S. Department of Defense named its computer language Ada.

```
d. b = 15;
   while (b / 3 == 5)
   {
        cout << b << b / 5 << endl;
        b = b - 1;
   }
```

5. Write a **while** loop for each of the following tasks.

   a. Print a positive real number, **num**, and then print successive values where each value is 0.5 less than the previous value. The list should continue as long as values to be printed are positive.

   b. Print a list of squares of positive integers as long as the difference between consecutive squares is less than 50.

6. Write a segment of code that reads a positive integer and prints a list of powers of the integer that are less than 10,000.

6.4 do . . . while Loops

OBJECTIVES

- to understand that a **do...while** loop is a post-test loop

- to understand the flow of control using a **do...while** loop

- to be able to use a **do...while** loop in a program

- to be able to use **do...while** loops with multiple conditions

The previous two sections discussed two kinds of repetition. We looked at fixed repetition using **for** loops and variable repetition using **while** loops. C++ provides a second form of variable repetition, a **do . . . while** loop, which is a *post-test* or *exit-controlled loop*. The basic form and syntax for a **do . . . while** loop are

```
do
{
        <statement>
} while (<Boolean expression>);
```

A flow diagram for a **do . . . while** loop is given in Figure 6.3. Prior to examining this form, let us consider the following fragment of code:

◆ FIGURE 6.3

do . . . while ⟨Boolean expression⟩

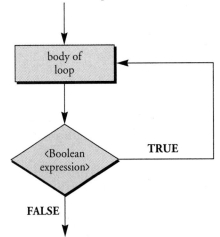

```
count = 0;
do
{
        count = count + 1;
        cout << count << endl;
} while (count < 5);
cout << setw(10) << "All done" << endl;
```

The output for this fragment is

```
1
2
3
4
5
All done
```

With this example in mind, the following comments concerning the use of a **do
. . . while** loop are in order.

1. The Boolean expression must have a value before it is used at the end of the loop.
2. The loop must be entered at least once because the Boolean expression is not evaluated until after the loop body has been executed.
3. When the Boolean expression is evaluated, if it is **TRUE**, control is transferred back to the top of the loop; if it is **FALSE**, control is transferred to the next program statement.
4. Provision must be made for changing values inside the loop so that the Boolean expression used to control the loop will eventually be **FALSE**. If this is not done, you will have an infinite loop, as shown here:

```
j = 0;
do
{
   j = j + 2;
   cout << j << endl;
} while (j != 5);
```

5. Writing style for using **do . . . while** loops should be consistent with your style for other loop structures.

There is one important difference between **while** and **do . . . while** loops. A **do . . . while** loop must be executed at least once, but a **while** loop can be skipped if the initial value of the Boolean expression is **FALSE**. Because of this, **do . . . while** loops are generally used less frequently than **while** loops.

<table>
<tr><td>

EXAMPLE 6.8

</td><td>

An early method of approximating square roots was the Newton-Raphson method. This method consisted of starting with an approximation and then getting successively better approximations until the desired degree of accuracy was achieved.

Writing code for this method, each **new_guess** is defined to be

</td></tr>
</table>

```
new_guess = 1.0/2.0 * (old_guess + number / old_guess)
```

Thus, if the number entered was 34 and the first approximation was 5, the second approximation would be

```
1/2 * (5 + 34 / 5)   (5.9)
```

and the third approximation would be

```
1/2 * (5.9 + 34 / 5.9)   (5.83135593)
```

Let's see how a **do . . . while** loop can be used to obtain successively better approximations until a desired degree of accuracy is reached. Assume **number** contains the number whose square root we wish to approximate, **old_guess** contains a first approximation, and **DESIRED_ACCURACY** is a defined constant. A loop used in the solution of this problem is

```
cout << setprecision(8) << setw(12) << new_guess << endl;
do
{
     old_guess = new_guess;
     new_guess = 1/2 * (old_guess + number / old_guess);
     cout << setw(12) << new_guess << endl;
} while (abs(new_guess - old_guess) >= DESIRED_ACCURACY);
```

If **DESIRED_ACCURACY** is 0.0001, **number is 34**, and **new_guess** is originally 5, the output from this segment is

```
5.00000000

5.90000000

5.83135593

5.83095191

5.83095189
```

<table>
<tr><td>

EXAMPLE 6.9

</td><td>

Interactive programming frequently requires the use of a menu to give the user a choice of options. For example, suppose you want a menu like this one:

</td></tr>
</table>

```
Which of the following recipes do you wish to see?

    (T)acos
    (J)ambalaya
    (G)umbo
    (Q)uit

Enter the first letter and press <Enter>.
```

This screen message could be written as a function **menu** and the main program could use a **do . . . while** loop as follows:

```
do
{
        menu();
        cin >> selection;
        switch (selection)
        {
                case 'T' :      tacos();
                                break;
                case 'J' :      jambalaya();
                                break;
                case 'G' :      gumbo();
                                break;
                case 'Q' :      goodbye_message();
        }
} while (selection != 'Q');
```

where **tacos**, **jambalaya**, **gumbo**, and **goodbye_message** are each separate functions with appropriate messages.

Compound Conditions

The Boolean expression used with a **do . . . while** loop can be as complex as you choose to make it. However, as with **while** loops, if the expression gets too complicated, you might enhance program readability and design by redesigning the algorithm to use simpler expressions.

Choosing the Correct Loop

"Which type of loop should I use?" is a question often faced by programmers. A partial answer is easy. If a loop is to be repeated a predetermined number of times during execution, a **for** loop is preferable. If the number of repetitions is not known, one of the variable control loops is preferable.

The more difficult part of the answer is deciding which variable control loop is appropriate. Simply stated, if a control check is needed before the loop is executed, use a **while** loop. If the check is needed at the end of the loop, use a **do . . . while** loop. Remember, however, that a **do . . . while** loop must always be executed at least once. Therefore, if there is a possibility that the loop will never be executed, a **while** loop must be used. For example, when reading data (especially from files, see Chapter 9), if there is a possibility of no data, a **while** loop must be used with a prompting input statement or other control check prior to the loop. Thus, you could have

```
        cout << "Enter a score, -999 to quit. ";
        cin << score;
        while (score != -999)
        {
            .

            . (process data)

            .

            cout << "Enter a score, -999 to quit. ";
            cin << score;
        }
```

In the event either variable control loop can be used, the problem itself might help with the decision. Does the process need to be repeated until something happens, or does the process continue as long as (while) some condition is true? If either of these is apparent, use the code that most accurately reflects the solution to the problem.

Data Validation

Variable condition loops can be used to make programs more robust. In particular, suppose you are writing an interactive program that expects positive integers to be entered from the keyboard, with a sentinel value of -999 to be entered when you wish to quit. You can guard against bad data by using the following:

```
do
{
        cout << "Enter a positive integer; <-999> to quit. ";
        cin >> num;
} while ((num > 0) && (num != -999));
```

This process of examining data prior to its use in a program is referred to as *data validation*, and loops are useful for such validation. A second example of using a loop for this purpose follows.

EXAMPLE 6.10

One problem associated with interactive programs is guarding against typing errors. This example illustrates how a **do . . . while** loop can be used to avoid having something entered other than the anticipated responses. Specifically, suppose users of an interactive program are asked to indicate whether or not they wish to continue by entering either a **Y** or **N**. The screen message could be

    Do you wish to continue? <Y or N>

You wish to allow any of **Y, y, N**, or **n** to be used as an appropriate response. Any other entry is considered an error. This can be accomplished by the following:

```
do
{
        cout << "Do you wish to continue? <Y or N> ";
        cin >> response;
        good_response = (response == 'Y') || (response == 'y') ||
        (response == 'N') || (response == 'n');
} while (! good_response);
```

Any response other than those permitted as good data (**Y, y, N, n**) results in **good_response** being **FALSE** and the loop being executed again.

EXERCISES 6.4

1. Explain the difference between a pretest loop and a post-test loop.

2. Indicate what the output will be from each of the following code fragments.

   a.
   ```
   a = 0;
   b = 10;
   do
   {
        a = a + 1;
        b = b - 1;
        cout << a << b << endl;
   } while (a <= b);
   ```

   b.
   ```
   power = 1;
   do
   {
        power = power * 2;
        cout << power << endl;
   } while (power <= 100);
   ```

   c.
   ```
   j = 1;
   do
   {
        cout << j << endl;
        j = j + 1;
   } while (j <= 10);
   ```

   d.
   ```
   a = 1;
   do
   {
        cout << a << 17 % a << endl;
        a = a + 1;
   } while (17 % a != 5);
   ```

3. Indicate which of the following are infinite loops and explain why.

   a.
   ```
   j = 1;
   do
   {
        cout << j << endl;
   } while (j <= 10);
   j = j + 1;
   ```

   b.
   ```
   a = 2;
   do
   {
        cout << a << endl;
        a = a * 2;
   } while (a <= 20);
   ```

   c.
   ```
   a = 2;
   do
   {
        cout << a << endl;
        a = a * 2;
   } while (a != 20);
   ```

```
    d. b = 15;
       do
       {
           cout << b << b / 5 << endl;
           b = b - 1;
       } while (b / 3 >= 5);
```

4. Write a **do . . . while** loop for each of the following tasks.

    a. Print a positive real number, **num**, and then print successive values where each value is 0.5 less than the previous value. The list should continue as long as values to be printed are positive.

    b. Print a list of squares of positive integers as long as the difference between consecutive squares is less than 50.

5. Discuss whether or not a priming read is needed before a **do . . . while** loop that is used to get data.

6. Give an example of a situation that would require a predetermined number of repetitions.

7. In mathematics and science, many applications require a certain level or degree of accuracy obtained by successive approximations. Explain how the process of reaching the desired level of accuracy would relate to loops in C++.

8. Write a program that utilizes the algorithm for approximating a square root as shown in Example 6.8. Let the defined accuracy be 0.0001. Input should consist of a number whose square root is desired. Your program should guard against bad data entries (negatives and zero). Output should include a list of approximations and a check of your final approximation.

9. Compare and contrast the three repetition structures previously discussed in this chapter.

6.5 Loop Verification

OBJECTIVES

- to understand how input assertions and output assertions can be used to verify loops

- to understand how loop invariants and loop variants can be used to verify loops

Loop verification is the process of guaranteeing that a loop performs its intended task. Such verification is part of program testing and correctness to which we referred in Chapter 5.

Some work has been done on constructing formal proofs to determine if loops are "correct." We now examine a modified version of loop verification; a complete treatment of the issue will be the topic of subsequent course work.

Preconditions and Postconditions with Loops

Preconditions and postconditions can be used with loops. Loop preconditions are referred to as *input assertions*. They state what can be expected to be true before the loop is entered. Loop postconditions are referred to as *output assertions*. They state what can be expected to be true when the loop is exited.

To illustrate input and output assertions, we consider the mathematical problem of summing the proper divisors of a positive integer. For example, we have these integers:

Integer	Proper Divisors	Sum
6	1, 2, 3	6
9	1, 3	4
12	1, 2, 3, 4, 6	16

As part of a program that will have a positive integer as input, and as output, will have a determination of whether the integer is perfect (sum = integer), abundant (sum > integer), or deficient (sum < integer), it is necessary to sum the divisors. The following loop performs this task:

```
divisor_sum = 0;
for (trial_divisor = 1; trial_divisor <= num / 2; ++trial_divisor)
        if (num % trial_divisor == 0)
            divisor_sum = divisor_sum + trial_divisor;
```

An input assertion for this loop is

Precondition: 1. num is a positive integer.
                      2. divisor_sum = 0.

An output assertion is

Postcondition: divisor_sum is the sum of all proper divisors of num.

When these are placed with the previous code, we have

```
divisor_sum = 0;
assert((num > 0) && (divisor_sum > 0));
for (trial_divisor = 1; trial_divisor <= num / 2; ++trial_divisor)
        if (num % trial_divisor == 0) then
                divisor_sum = divisor_sum + trial_divisor;
// Postcondition: divisor_sum is the sum of all proper divisors of num.
```

Note that we pass the precondition to the **assert** function of C++, so that the run-time system actually establishes the truth of that assertion. However, we cannot do this with the postcondition, because the sum of all the proper divisors of a number is just what we are computing in the **for** loop!

Invariant and Variant Assertions

A *loop invariant* is an assertion that expresses a relationship between variables that remains constant throughout all iterations of the loop. In other words, it is a statement that is true both before the loop is entered and after each pass through the loop. An invariant assertion for the preceding code segment could be

divisor_sum is the sum of proper divisors of num that are less than or equal to trial_divisor.

A *loop variant* is an assertion whose truth changes between the first and final execution of the loop. The loop variant expression should be stated in such a way that it guarantees the loop is exited. Thus, it contains some statement about the loop variable being incremented (or decremented) during execution of the loop. In the preceding code, we could have

trial_divisor is incremented by 1 each time through the loop. It eventually exceeds the value num / 2, at which point the loop is exited.

Variant and invariant assertions usually occur in pairs.

We now use four kinds of assertions—input, output, variant, and invariant—to produce the formally verified loop that follows:

```
divisor_sum = 0;

// Precondition:    1. Num is a positive integer.          (input assertion)
//                  2. divisor_sum = 0.
```

```
assert((num > 0) && (divisor_sum == 0));

for (trial_divisor = 1; trial_divisor <= num / 2; ++trial_divisor)

// trial_divisor is incremented by 1 each time          (variant  assertion)
// through the loop. It eventually exceeds the
// value (num / 2), at which point the loop is exited.

    if (num % trial_divisor == 0)
            divisor_sum = divisor_sum + trial_divisor;

// divisor_sum is the sum of proper divisors of          (invariant  assertion)
// num that are less than or equal to trial_divisor.

// Postcondition: divisor_sum is the sum of              (output  assertion)
// all proper divisors of num.
```

In general, code that is presented in this text does not include formal verification of the loops. This issue is similar to that of robustness. In an introductory course, a decision must be made on the trade-off between learning new concepts and writing robust programs with formal verification of loops. We encourage the practice, but space and time considerations make it inconvenient to include such documentation at this level. We close this discussion with another example illustrating loop verification.

EXAMPLE 6.11   Consider the problem of finding the greatest common divisor (**gcd**) of two positive integers. To illustrate, we have this information:

num1	num2	gcd(num 1, num2)
8	12	4
20	10	10
15	32	1
70	40	10

A segment of code to produce the **gcd** of two positive integers after they have been ordered as **small**, **large**, is

```
trial_gcd = small;
gcd_found = FALSE;
while (! gcd_found)
    if ((large % trial_gcd == 0) && (small % trial_gcd == 0))
    {
            gcd = trial_gcd;
            gcd_found = TRUE;
    }
    else
            trial_gcd = trial_gcd - 1;
```

Using assertions as previously indicated, this code would appear as

```
trial_gcd = small;
gcd_found = FALSE;

// Precondition:      1. small <= large
//                    2. trial_gcd (small) is the first candidate for gcd
//                    3. gcd_found is FALSE

assert((small <= large) && (small == trial_gcd) && ! gcd_found);

while (! gcd_found)

// trial_gcd assumes integer values ranging from small
// to 1. It is decremented by 1 each time through the
// loop. When trial_gcd divides both small and large,
// the loop is exited. Exit is guaranteed since 1
// divides both small and large.

        if ((large % trial_gcd == 0) && (small % trial_gcd == 0))

// When trial_gcd divides both large and small, then gcd is assigned that value.

        {

                assert((large % trial_gcd == 0) && (small % trial_gcd == 0));

                gcd = trial_gcd;
                gcd_found = TRUE;
        }
        else
                trial_gcd = trial_gcd - 1;

// Postcondition: gcd is the greatest common divisor of small and large.
```

EXERCISES 6.5

1. Write appropriate input assertions and output assertions for each of the following loops.

```
a. cin >> score;
   while (score != -999)
   {
           num_scores = num_scores + 1;
           sum = sum + score;
   cout << "Enter a score; -999 to quit. ";
   cin >> score;
   }
b. count = 0;
   power2 = 1;
   while (power2 < 100)
   {
           cout << power2 << endl;
           power2 = power2 * 2;
           count = count + 1;
   }
```

c. (From Example 6.8)

```
do
{
    old_guess = new_guess;
    new_guess = 1/2 * (old_guess + number / old_guess);
    cout << setprecision(8) << setw(10) << new_guess << endl;
} while (abs(new_guess - old_guess) < DESIRED_ACCURACY);
```

2. Write appropriate loop invariant and loop variant assertions for each of the loops in Exercise 1.

3. Consider the following loop. The user enters a number, **guess**, and the computer then displays a message indicating whether the guess is correct, too high, or too low. Add appropriate input assertions, output assertions, loop invariant assertions, and loop variant assertions to the following code.

```
correct = FALSE;
count = 0;
while ((count < MAX_TRIES) && (! correct))
{
        count = count + 1;
        cout << "Enter choice number " << count << endl;
        cin >> guess;
        if (guess == choice)
        {
                correct = TRUE;
                cout << "Congratulations!" << endl;
        }
        else if (guess < choice)
                cout << "Your guess is too low" << end;
        else
                cout << "Your guess is too high" << endl;
}
```

6.6 Nested Loops

OBJECTIVES

- to be able to use nested loops
- to understand the flow of control when using nested loops
- to be able to employ a consistent writing style when using nested loops

In this chapter, we have examined three loop structures. Each of them has been discussed with respect to syntax, semantics, form, writing style, and use in programs. But remember that each loop is treated as a single C++ statement. In this sense, it is possible to have a loop as one of the statements in the body of another loop. When this happens, the loops are said to be *nested*.

Loops can be nested to any depth; that is; a loop can be within a loop within a loop, and so on. Also, any of the three types of loops can be nested within any loop. However, a programmer should be careful not to design a program with nesting that is too complex. If program logic becomes too difficult to follow, you might be better off redesigning the program, perhaps by splitting off the inner logic into a separate subprogram.

Flow of Control

As a first example of using a loop within a loop, consider

```
for (k = 1; k <= 5; ++k)
        for (j = 1; j <= 3; ++j)
                cout << (k + j) << endl;
```

When this fragment is executed, the following happens:

1. Variable **k** is assigned a value.
2. For each value of **k**, the following loop is executed.

```
for (j = 1; j <= 3; ++j)
    cout << (k + j) << endl;
```

Thus, for **k = 1**, the "inside" or nested loop produces the output

```
2
3
4
```

At this point, **k = 2** and the next portion of the output produced by the nested loop is

```
3
4
5
```

The complete output from these nested loops is

```
2
3 from k = 1
4

3
4 from k = 2
5

4
5 from k = 3
6

5
6 from k = 4
7

6
7 from k = 5
8
```

As you can see, for each value assigned to the index of the outside loop, the inside loop is executed completely. Suppose you want the output to be printed in the form of a chart as follows:

2	3	4
3	4	5
4	5	6
5	6	7
6	7	8

The pseudocode design to produce this output is

    1. for (k = 1; k <= 5; ++k)
           produce a line

A refinement of this is

    1. for (k = 1; k <= 5; ++k)
       1.1 print on one line
       1.2 advance the printer

The C++ code for this development becomes

```
for (k = 1; k <= 5; ++k)
{
    for (j = 1; j <= 3; ++j)              // print on one line
        cout << setw(4) << (k + j);
    cout << endl;                         // advance the printer
}
```

Our next example shows how nested loops can be used to produce a design.

EXAMPLE 6.12

Use nested **for** loops to produce the following output:

```
*
**
***
****
*****
```

The left asterisks are in column 10. The first-level pseudocode to solve this problem could be

    1. for (k = 1; k <= 5; ++k)
           produce a line

A refinement of this could be

    1. for (k = 1; k <= 5; ++k)
       1.1 print on one line
       1.2 advance the printer

Step 1.1 is not yet sufficiently refined, so our next level could be

    1. for (k = 1; k <= 5; ++k)
       1.1 print on one line
          1.1.1 put a blank in column 9
          1.1.2 print k asterisks
       1.2 advance the printer

We can now write a program fragment to produce the desired output as follows:

```
for (k = 1; k <= 5; ++k)
{
    cout << setw(9) << ' ';
    for (j = 1; j <= k; ++j)
        cout << '*';
    cout << endl;
}
```

A significant feature has been added to this program fragment. Note that the upper bound for the inner loop is the loop control variable of the outer loop.

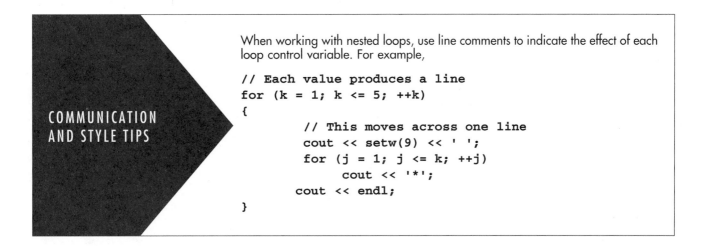

COMMUNICATION AND STYLE TIPS

When working with nested loops, use line comments to indicate the effect of each loop control variable. For example,

```
// Each value produces a line
for (k = 1; k <= 5; ++k)
{
        // This moves across one line
        cout << setw(9) << ' ';
        for (j = 1; j <= k; ++j)
            cout << '*';
        cout << endl;
}
```

Thus far, nested loops have been used only with **for** loops, but any of the loop structures can be used in nesting. Our next example illustrates a **do . . . while** loop nested within a **while** loop.

EXAMPLE 6.13   Trace the flow of control and indicate the output for the following program fragment:

```
a = 10;
b = 0;
while (a > b)
{
        cout << setw(5) << a << endl;
        do
        {
            cout << setw(5) << a << setw(5) << b << setw(5) << (a + b) << endl;
            a = a - 2;
        } while (a > 6);
        b = b + 2;
}
cout << endl;
cout << setw(20) << "All done" << endl;
```

The assignment statements produce

10		0
a		b

and **a > b** is **TRUE**; thus, the **while** loop is entered. The first time through this loop the **do . . . while** loop is used. Output for the first pass is

```
   10
   10    0   10
```

and the values for **a** and **b** are

```
   8          0
   a          b
```

The Boolean expression **a > 6** is **TRUE** and the **do . . . while** loop is executed again to produce the next line of output:

```
   8        0        8
```

and the values for **a** and **b** become

```
   6          0
   a          b
```

At this point, **a > 6** is **FALSE** and control transfers to the line of code

```
b = b + 2;
```

Thus, the variable values are

```
   6          2
   a          b
```

and the Boolean expression **a > b** is **TRUE**. This means the **while** loop will be repeated. The output for the second time through this loop is

```
   6
   6        2        8
```

and the values for the variables are

```
   4          4
   a          b
```

Now **a > b** is **FALSE** and control is transferred to the line following the **while** loop. Output for the complete fragment is

```
   10
   10       0        10
   8        0        8
   6
   6        2        8
```

All done

This example is a bit contrived and tracing the flow of control somewhat tedious. However, it is important for you to be able to follow the logic involved in using nested loops.

Writing Style

As usual, you should be aware of the significance of using a consistent, readable style of writing when using nested loops. There are at least three features you should consider.

1. *Indenting:* Each loop should have its own level of indenting. This makes it easier to identify the body of the loop. If the loop body consists of a compound statement, the { and } should start in the same column. Using our previous indenting style, a typical nesting might be

```
for (k= 1; k <= 10; ++k)
{
        while (a > 0)
        {
                do
                {
                        .


                        .


                        .

                } while (<condition>);    // end of do . . . while loop
                <statement>
        }                                  // end of while loop
        <statement>
}                                          // end of for loop
```

If the body of a loop becomes very long, it is sometimes difficult to match the { with the proper }. In this case, you should either redesign the program (for example, write a separate subprogram) or be especially careful.

2. *Using comments:* Comments can precede a loop and explain what the loop will do, or they can be used with statements inside the loop to explain what the statement does. They should be used to indicate the end of a loop where the loop body is a compound statement.

3. *Skipping lines:* This is an effective way of isolating loops within a program and making nested loops easier to identify.

A note of caution is in order with respect to writing style. Program documentation is important; however, excessive use of comments and skipped lines can detract from readability. You should develop a happy medium.

Statement Execution in Nested Loops

Using nested loops can significantly increase the number of times statements get executed in a program. To illustrate, suppose a program contains a **do . . . while** loop that gets executed six times before it is exited, as illustrated here:

```
         ┌─ do
         │   .
6 times  │   .  (action here)
         │   .
         └─ while (<condition 1);
```

If one of the statements inside this loop is another loop, the inner loop will be executed six times. Suppose this inner loop is repeated five times whenever it is entered. This means each statement within the inner loop will be executed 6 × 5 = 30 times when the program is run. This is illustrated by

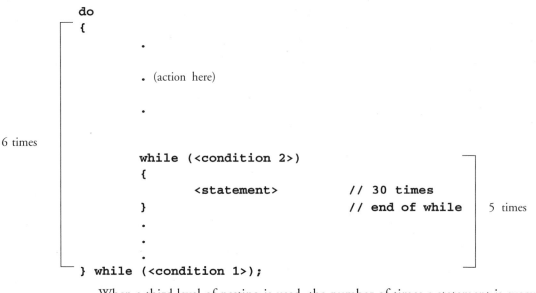

```
                        do
                        {
                                  .
                                  . (action here)
                                  .

6 times
                                  while (<condition 2>)
                                  {
                                          <statement>              // 30 times
                                  }                                // end of while      5 times
                                  .
                                  .
                                  .
                        } while (<condition 1>);
```

When a third level of nesting is used, the number of times a statement is executed can be determined by the product of three factors, $n_1 * n_2 * n_3$, where n_1 represents the number of repetitions of the outside loop, n_2 represents the number of repetitions for the first level of nesting, and n_3 represents the number of repetitions for the innermost loop.

We close this section with an example of a program that uses nested loops to print a multiplication table.

EXAMPLE 6.14 This example presents a complete program whose output is the multiplication table from 1×1 to 10×10. A suitable heading is part of the output.

```cpp
// Program file: multab.cpp

#include <iostream.h>
#include <iomanip.h>

const char INDENT = ' ';

// Function: print_heading
// Print a heading for multiplication table

void print_heading();

// Function: print_table
// Print multiplication table

void print_table();

int main()
{
    print_heading();
    print_table();
    return 0;
}
```

```
void print_heading()
{
    cout << endl;
    cout <<   setw(17) << INDENT << "Multiplication Table" << endl;
    cout <<   setw(17) << INDENT << "--------------------" << endl;
    cout <<   setw(10) << INDENT << "(  Generated by nested for loops   )"
            << endl;
    cout << endl;
}


void print_table()
{
    int row, column;

    //Print the column heads
    cout  << setw(10) << INDENT << "          1  2  3  4  5  6  7  8  9 10"
        << endl;
    cout  << setw(10) << INDENT << "---!-------------------------------"
        << endl;
    // Now start the loop
    for (row = 1; row <= 10; ++row)
    {
        // print one row
        cout << setw(12) << row << " !";
        for (column = 1; column <= 10; ++column)
            cout << setw(3) << (row * column);
        cout << endl;
    } // end of each row
    cout << endl;
}
```

The output from this program is

```
          Multiplication Table
          --------------------

      (  Generated by nested for loops  )


              1     2     3     4     5     6     7     8     9    10
     ---!-----------------------------------------------------------
       1 !    1     2     3     4     5     6     7     8     9    10
       2 !    2     4     6     8    10    12    14    16    18    20
       3 !    3     6     9    12    15    18    21    24    27    30
       4 !    4     8    12    16    20    24    28    32    36    40
       5 !    5    10    15    20    25    30    35    40    45    50
       6 !    6    12    18    24    30    36    42    48    54    60
       7 !    7    14    21    28    35    42    49    56    63    70
       8 !    8    16    24    32    40    48    56    64    72    80
       9 !    9    18    27    36    45    54    63    72    81    90
      10 !   10    20    30    40    50    60    70    80    90   100
```

A NOTE OF INTEREST

A Digital Matter of Life and Death

The radiation-therapy machine, a Therac 25 linear accelerator, was designed to send a penetrating X ray or electron beam deep into a cancer patient's body to destroy embedded tumors without injuring skin tissue. But in three separate instances in 1985 and 1986, the machine failed. Instead of delivering a safe level of radiation, the Therac 25 administered a dose that was more than 100 times larger than the typical treatment dose. Two patients died and a third was severely burned.

The malfunction was caused by an error in the computer program controlling the machine. It was a subtle error that no one had picked up during the extensive testing the machine had undergone. The error surfaced only when a technician happened to use a specific, unusual combination of keystrokes to instruct the machine.

The Therac incidents and other cases of medical device failures caused by computer errors have focused attention on the increasingly important role played by computers in medical applications. Computers or machines with built-in microprocessors perform functions that range from keeping track of patients to diagnosing ailments and providing treatments.

"The impact of computers on medical care and the medical community is the most significant factor that we have to face," says Frank E. Samuel Jr., president of the Health Industry Manufacturers Association (HIMA), based in Washington, D.C. "Health care will change more dramatically in the next 10 years because of software-driven products than for any other single cause." Samuel made his remarks at a recent HIMA-sponsored conference on the regulation of medical software.

At the same time, reports of medical devices with computer-related problems are appearing more and more frequently. In 1985, the Food and Drug Administration (FDA) reported that recalls of medical devices because of computer faults had roughly doubled over the previous five years. Since then, the number of such complaints has risen further.

The FDA, in its mandated role as guardian of public health and safety, is now preparing to regulate the software component of medical devices. The agency's effort has already raised questions about what kinds of products, software, and information systems should be regulated.

EXERCISES 6.6

1. Write a program fragment that uses nested loops to produce each of the following designs.

```
a. *****        b.      *        c. ***
    ****              ***           ***
    ***              *****          ***
    **              *******         ***
    *               *****         ******
                     ***          ******
                      *           ******
```

2. What is the output from each of the following code fragments?

```
a. for (k = 2; k <= 6; ++k)
   {
           for (j = 5; j <= 10; ++j)
                cout << (k + j);
           cout << endl;
   }
b. for k = 2; k <= 6; ++k)
   {
           for (j = 5; j <= 10; ++j)
                cout << (k + j);
           cout << endl;
   }
```

```
c. sum = 0;
   a = 7;
   while (a < 10)
   {
            for (k = a; k <= 10; ++k)
                    sum = sum + k;
            a = a + 1;
   }
   cout << sum << endl;
d.    sum = 0;
   for (k = 1; k <= 10; ++k)
            for (j = (10 * k - 9); j <= (10 * k); ++j)
                    sum = sum + J;
   cout << sum << endl;
```

3. What output is produced from the following segment of code?

```
a = 4;
b = 7;
do
{
        num = a;
        while (num <= b)
        {
                for (k = a; k <= b; ++k)
                        cout << setw(4) << num;
                cout << endl;
                num = num + 1;
        } // end of while
        cout << endl;
        a = a + 1;
}
while (a != b); // end of do...while loop
```

4. Write a program fragment that uses nested loops to produce the following output.

2	4	6	8	10
3	6	9	12	15
4	8	12	16	20
5	10	15	20	25

6.7 Repetition and Selection

OBJECTIVES

- to be able to use a selection statement within the body of a loop
- to be able to use a loop within an option of a selection statement

Selection Within Repetition (Loops)

In Chapter 5 we discussed the use of selection statements. In this chapter we have discussed the use of three different types of loops. It is now time to see how they are used together. We will first examine selection statements contained within the body of a loop.

EXAMPLE 6.15

Write a program fragment that computes gross wages for employees of the Florida OJ Canning Company. The data consist of three initials, the total hours worked, and the hourly rate; for example,

JHA 44.5 12.75

Overtime (more than 40 hours) is computed as time-and-a-half. The output should include all input data and a column of gross wages.

A first-level pseudocode development for this program is

1. while more_employees
    1.1 process one employee
    1.2 print results

This could be refined to

1. while more_employees
    1.1 process one employee
        1.1.1 get data
        1.1.2 compute wage
    1.2 print results

Step 1.1.2 can be refined to

1.1.2 compute wage
    1.1.2.1 if hours <= 40.0
            compute regular time
        else
            compute time-and-a-half

and the final algorithm for the fragment is

1. while more_employees
    1.1 process one employee
        1.1.1 get data
        1.1.2 compute wage
            1.1.2.1 if hours <= 40.0
                    compute regular time
                else
                    compute time-and-a-half
    1.2 print results

The code for this fragment follows:

```
cout << fixed << showpoint;
cout << "Any employees? <Y> or <N> ";
cin >> choice;
more_employees = (choice == 'Y') || (choice == 'y');
while (more_employees)
{
        cout << endl;
        cout << "Enter initials, hours, and payrate. ";
        cin >> init1 << init2 << init3 << hours << pay_rate;
        if (hours <= 40.0)
                total_wage = hours * pay_rate;
        else
```

```
                {
                        overtime = 1.5 * (hours - 40.0) * pay_rate;
                        total_wage = 40 * pay_rate + overtime;
                }
                cout << endl;
                cout << setw(5) << init1 << init2 << init3;
                cout << setprecision(2) << setw(10) << hours << setw(10) << pay_rate;
                cout << setw(10) << '$' << setw(7) << total_wage;
                cout << endl;
                cout << "Any more employees? <Y> or <N> ";
                cin >> choice;
                more_employees = (choice == 'Y') || (choice == 'y');
        }
```

Repetition (Loops) Within Selection

The next example illustrates the use of a loop within an **if** statement.

EXAMPLE 6.16

Write a program fragment that allows you to read an integer from the keyboard. If the integer is between 0 and 50, you are to print a chart containing all positive integers less than the integer, their squares, and their cubes. Thus, if 4 is read, the chart is

1	1	1
2	4	8
3	9	27

The design for this problem has a first-level pseudocode development of

1. input num
2. if (num > 0) && (num < 50)
   2.1 print the chart

Step 2.1 can be refined to

2.1 print the chart
    2.1.1 for (k = 1; k <= (num - 1); ++k)
        2.1.1.1 print each line

We can now write the code for this fragment as follows:

```
cin >> num;
if ((num > 0) && (num < 50))
        for (k = 1; k <= num - 1; ++k)
                cout << k << (k * k) << (k * k * k << endl;
```

EXERCISES 6.7

1. Find and explain the errors in each of the following program fragments. Assume all variables have been suitably declared.

a. a = 25;
  flag = TRUE;

```
        while (flag == TRUE)
            if (a >= 100)
            {
                    cout << a << endl;
                    flag = FALSE;
            }
    b. for (k = 1; k <= 10; ++k)
            cout << k << (k * k) << endl;
        if (k % 3 == 0)
        {
            cout << k;
            cout << " is a multiple of three" << endl;
        }
```

2. What is the output from each of the following program fragments? Assume all variables have been suitably declared.

```
    a. for (k = 1; k <= 100; ++k)
            if (k % 5 == 0)
                    cout << k << endl;
    b. j = 20;
       if (j % 5 == 0)
            for (k = 1: k <= 100; ++k)
                    cout << k << endl;
    c. a = 5;
       b = 90;
       do
       {
           b = b / a - 5;
           if (b > a)
                    b = a + 30;
       } while (b >= 0);
       cout << a << b << endl;
    d. count = 0;
       for (k = -5; k <= 5; ++k)
           if (k % 3 == 0)
           {
                    cout << "k = " << setw(4) << k<< " output ";
                    while (count < 10)
                    {
                            count = count + 1;
                            cout << setw(4) << count << endl;
                    }
                    count = 0;
                    cout << endl;
           }
    e. a = 5;
       b = 2;
       if (a < b)
            for (k = a; k <= b; ++k)
                    cout << k << endl;
       else
            for (k = a; k >= b; --k)
                    cout << k << endl;
```

```
f. for (k = -5; k <= 5; ++k)
   {
       cout << "k = " << setw(4) << k " output ";
       a = k;
       if (k < 0)
               // k = -5, -4, -3, -2, -1
               do
               {
                       cout << setw(5) << (-2 * a) <<
endl;
                       a = a + 1;
               } while (a > 0);
       else // K = 0, 1, 2, 3, 4, 5
               while (a % 2 == 0)
               {
                       cout << a << endl;
                       a = a + 1;
               }
       cout << endl;
   }
```

3. Write a program fragment that reads reals from the keyboard, counts the number of positive reals, and accumulates their sum.

4. Given two integers, **a** and **b**, **a** is a divisor of **b** if **b % a = 0**. Write a complete program that reads a positive integer **b** and then prints all the positive divisors of **b**.

FOCUS ON PROGRAM DESIGN

This program illustrates the combined use of repetition and selection statements. This is the problem statement: Write a program that allows positive integers to be entered from the keyboard and, for each such entry, list all primes less than or equal to the number. The program should include a check for bad data and use of a sentinel value to terminate the process. Typical output for the integer 17 is

```
Enter a positive integer; <-999> to quit. 17

         The number is 17. The prime numbers less than or equal
         to 17 are:

                              2
                              3
                              5
                              7
                             11
                             13
                             17


Enter a positive integer; <-999> to quit. -999
```

For purposes of this program, note the mathematical property that a number **k** is prime if it has no divisors (other than 1) less than its square root. For example, because 37 is not divisible by 2, 3, or 5, it is prime. Thus, when we check for divisors, it is only necessary to check up to **sqrt(k)**. Also note that 1 is not prime by definition.

A first-level pseudocode development for this problem is

1. Get a number
   while more_data
        2. Examine the number
        3. Get a number

A structure chart for this problem is shown in Figure 6.4. The module specifications for the main modules are

Module: Get a number
Task: Get an entry from the keyboard.
Output: a number

Module: Examine the number
Task:
if the number is 1
    Print a message
else
    Print a heading.
    Print list of all primes less than or equal to the integer read
Input: The integer read

◆ FIGURE 6.4

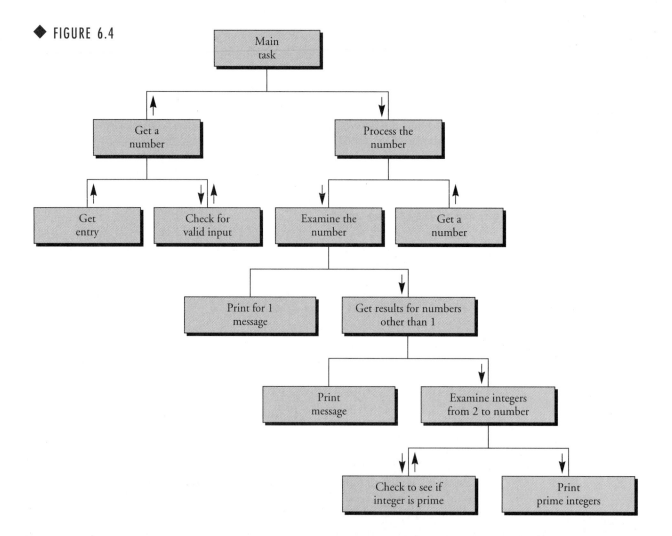

A second-level development is

    1. Get a number
       1.1 Get entry from the keyboard
      while more_data
          2. Examine the number
         if number is 1
            2.1 print a message for 1
         else
            list the primes
            2.2 print a message
            2.3 check for primes less than or equal to number
         3. Get a number
            3.1 Get entry from the keyboard
            3.2 Check for valid entry

Step 2.3 can be refined to
         2.3 check for primes less than or equal to number
       for (k = 2; k <= number; ++k)
            2.3.1 check to see if k is prime
            2.3.2 if k is prime
               print k in list of primes

Instead of maintaining **more_data** as a simple Boolean flag, we will write a function that takes the number as a parameter, determines whether or not the number is the sentinel value, and returns **TRUE** or **FALSE** depending on what it finds. The pseudocode for this function is

    Make sure it is a valid entry or the sentinel value for terminating the process. If it is the sentinel value, return FALSE; otherwise, return TRUE.

Thus, the complete pseudocode development is

    1. Get a number
       1.1 Get entry from the keyboard

      while more_data

          2. Examine the number
         if number is 1
            2.1 print a message for 1
         else
            list the primes
            2.2 print a message
            2.3 check for primes less than or equal to number
          for (k = 2; k <= number; ++k)
              2.3.1 check to see if k is prime
              2.3.2 if k is prime
                 print k in list of primes
         3. Get a number
            3.1 Get entry from the keyboard
            3.2 Check for valid entry

With this pseudocode development, the main program would be

```
                                  num = get_a_number();
                                  while (more_data(num))
                                  {
                                       examine_the_number(num);
                                       num = get_a_number(num);
                                  }
```

The complete program for this problem follows:

```cpp
// Program file: primes.cpp

#include <iostream.h>
#include <iomanip.h>
#include <math.h>
#include "boolean.h"

const char SKIP = ' ';

int get_a_number();

// Function: print_one_message
// Print a message for 1

void print_one_message();

// Function: print_message
// Print a heading for the output
//
// Input: the integer read

void print_message(int number);

// Function: list_all_primes
// Print list of all primes less than or equal to the integer read
//
// Input: the integer read

void list_all_primes(int number);

// Function: list_all_primes
// If integer read is one,
// then print a message for one
// else
// Print list of all primes less than or equal to the integer read
// /
// Input: the integer read

void examine_the_number(int number);

// Function: more_data
// Determines whether number = -999 (the sentinel for end of input)
// Input: the integer read
// Output: TRUE, if the input is not the sentinel, FALSE otherwise
```

```
boolean more_data(int number);

int main()
{
      int number;

      number = get_a_number ();
      while (more_data(number))
      {
            examine_the_number (number);
            number = get_a_number ();
      }
       return 0;
}

int get_a_number()
{
      int number;
      boolean done;

      do
      {
            cout << endl;
            cout << "Enter a positive integer; <-999> to quit.";
            cin >> number;
            done = (number == -999) || (number >= 0);
      } while (! done);      // assumes valid data
      return number;
}

void print_one_message()
{
      cout << endl;
      cout << setw(10) << SKIP << "------------------------------" << endl;
      cout << endl;
      cout << setw(20) << SKIP << "1 is not prime by definition." << endl;
}

void print_message(int number)
{
      cout << endl;
      cout << setw(10) << SKIP << "------------------------------" << endl;
      cout << endl;
      cout << setw(20) << SKIP << "The number is " << number
            << " The prime numbers" << endl;
      cout << setw(20) << SKIP << "less than or equal to "<< number
            << " are:" << endl;
      cout << endl;
}

void list_all_primes(int number)
{
```

1

```
        boolean prime;
        int candidate, divisor;
        float limit_for_check;

        for (candidate = 2; candidate <= number; ++candidate)
        {
                prime = TRUE;
                divisor = 2;
                limit_for_check = sqrt(candidate);
                while ((divisor <= limit_for_check) && prime)
                        if (candidate % divisor == 0)
                                prime = FALSE;                 // Candidate has a divisor
                        else
                                divisor = divisor + 1;
                if (prime)                                     //Print list of primes
                        cout << setw(35) << candidate << endl;
        }
}


void examine_the_number(int number)
{
        if (number == 1)
                print_one_message();
        else
        {
                print_message(number);
                list_all_primes (number);
        }
}


boolean more_data(int number)
{
        return number != -999;
}
```

Sample runs of this program produce this output:

```
    Enter a positive integer; <-999> to quit. 10

                                    --------------------------------------------
                                    The number is 10. The prime numbers
                                    less than or equal to 10 are:

                                                 2
                                                 3
                                                 5
                                                 7


    Enter a positive integer; <-999> to quit. 17

                                    --------------------------------------------
```

```
        The number is 17. The prime numbers less than or equal
        to 17 are:

                            2
                            3
                            5
                            7
                           11
                           13
                           17

Enter a positive integer; <-999> to quit. 1

             1 is not prime by definition.

Enter a positive integer; <-999> to quit. 25

        ------------------------------------------------
        The number is 25. The prime numbers less than or equal
        to 25 are:

                            2
                            3
                            5
                            7
                           11
                           13
                           17
                           19
                           23

Enter a positive integer; <-999> to quit. -3
Enter a positive integer; <-999> to quit. 2

        ------------------------------------------------
        The number is 2. The prime numbers less than or equal
        to 2 are:

                            2

Enter a positive integer; <-999> to quit. -999
```

More efficient algorithms than what we used here do exist. However, the purpose of this program was to see how loops can be used to solve a problem.

RUNNING, DEBUGGING AND TESTING HINTS

1. Most errors involving loops are not compilation errors. Thus, you will not be able to detect most errors until you try to run the program.
2. An error that will not be detected by the compiler is an infinite loop. The fragment

```
b = 10;
while (b > 0)
{
    cin >> a;
    cout << a << endl;
}
```

will loop forever, because **b** never becomes zero inside the loop.
3. Carefully check entry conditions for each loop.
4. Carefully check exit conditions for each loop. Make sure the loop is exited (not infinite) and that you have the correct number of repetitions.
5. Loop entry, execution, and exit can be checked by
   a. pencil and paper check on initial and final values
   b. count of the number of repetitions
   c. use of debugging output statements:
      i. Boolean condition prior to loop,
      ii. variables inside loop,
      iii. values of the counter in loop,
      iv. Boolean values inside the loop, and
      v. values after loop is exited.

SUMMARY

Key Terms

accumulator	input assertion	post-test (exit-controlled) loop
counter	loop invariant	pretest condition
data validation	loop variant	pretest (entrance-controlled) loop
decrement	loop verification	
fixed repetition (iterated) loop	nested loop	sentinel value
infinite loop	output assertion	variable condition loop

Keywords

do   **for**   **while**

Key Concepts

◆ The following table provides a comparison summary of the three repetition structures discussed in this chapter.

Traits of Loops	**for** Loop	**while** Loop	**do . . . while** Loop
Pretest loop	Yes	Yes	No
Post-test loop	No	No	Yes
{ . . . } for compound statements	Required	Required	Required
Repetition	Fixed/variable	Variable	Variable

◆ A fixed repetition loop is to be used when you know exactly how many times something is to be repeated.

◆ The basic form of a **for** loop is

```
for (j = 1; j <= 5; ++j)
    <statement>
```

◆ A **while** loop is a pretest loop that can have a variable loop control; a typical loop is

```
score = 0;
sum = 0;
more_data = TRUE;
while (more_data)
{
    sum = sum + score;
    cout << "Enter a score; -999 to quit. ";
    cin >> score;
    more_data = (score != -999);
}
```

◆ A counter is a variable whose purpose is to indicate how often the body of a loop is executed.
◆ An accumulator is a variable whose purpose is to sum values.
◆ An infinite **while** loop is caused by having a **TRUE** loop control condition that is never changed to **FALSE**.
◆ A post-test loop has a Boolean condition checked after the loop body has been completed.
◆ A **do . . . while** loop is a post-test loop; a typical loop is

```
do
{
    cout << "Enter a positive integer; <-999> to quit . ";
    cin >> num;
} while ((num > 0) && (num != -999));
```

◆ **do . . . while** and **while** are variable control loops; **for** is usually a fixed control loop.
◆ **while** and **for** are pretest loops; **do . . . while** is a post-test loop.
◆ Any one of these loops can be nested within any other of the loops.
◆ Indenting each loop is important for program readability.
◆ Several levels of nesting make the logic of a program difficult to follow.
◆ Loops and conditionals are frequently used together. Careful program design will facilitate writing code in which these concepts are integrated; typical forms are

```
while (<condition1>) do
{
    .
    .
    .

    if (<condition2>)
        .
        .
        .
```

```
        else
            .
            .
            .

    } // end of while
```

◆ and

```
    if <condition>
    {
        .

        .

        .

        for (j = <value1>; j <= <valueN>; ++j)
        {
            .

            .

            .

        } // end of for loop . . .
    } // end of if...else
        .

        .

        .
```

1. The Caswell Catering and Convention Service (Problem 12, Chapter 4, and Problem 14, Chapter 5) wants you to upgrade their program so they can use it for all of their customers.

2. Modify your program for a service station owner (Focus on Program Design, Chapter 5) so that it can be used for an unknown number of customers. Your output should include the number of customers and all other pertinent items in a daily summary.

3. Modify the Community Hospital program (Problem 17, Chapter 5) so that it can be run for all patients leaving the hospital in one day. Include appropriate bad data checks and daily summary items.

4. The greatest common divisor (gcd) of two integers a and b is a positive integer c such that c divides a, c divides b, and for any other common divisor d of a and b, d is less than or equal to c. (For example, the gcd of 18 and 45 is 9.) One method of finding the gcd of two positive integers (a, b) is to begin with the smaller (a) and see if it is a divisor of the larger (b). If it is, then the smaller is the gcd. If not, find the next largest divisor of a and see if it is a divisor of b. Continue this process until you find a divisor of both a and b. This is the gcd of a and b.

Write an interactive program that will accept two positive integers as input and then print out their gcd. Enhance your output by printing all divisors of *a* that do not divide *b*. A sample run could produce

Enter two positive integers. 42 72

The divisors of 42 that do not divide 72 are:

```
        42
        21
        14
         7
```

The gcd of 42 and 72 is 6.

5. The least common multiple (LCM) of two positive integers *a* and *b* is a positive integer *c* such that *c* is a multiple of both *a* and *b* and for any other multiple *m* of *a* and *b*, *c* is a divisor of *m*. (For example, the LCM of 12 and 8 is 24.) Write a program that allows the user to enter two positive integers and then print the LCM. The program should guard against bad data and should allow the user the option of "trying another pair" or quitting.

6. A perfect number is a positive integer such that the sum of the proper divisors equals the number. Thus, 28 = 1 + 2 + 4 + 7 + 14 is a perfect number. If the sum of the divisors is less than the number, it is deficient. If the sum exceeds the number, it is abundant.

   a. Write a program that allows the user to enter a positive integer and then displays the result indicating whether the number entered is perfect, deficient, or abundant.

   b. Write another program that allows the user to enter a positive integer *N* and then displays all perfect numbers less than or equal to *N*.

   Your programs should guard against bad data and should allow the user the option of entering another integer or quitting.

7. In these days of increased awareness of automobile mileage, more motorists are computing their miles per gallon (mpg) than ever before. Write a program that will perform these computations for a traveler. Data for the program will be entered as indicated by the following table:

Odometer Reading	Gallons of Fuel Purchased
18828 (start)	—
19240	9.7
19616	10.2
19944	8.8
20329	10.1
20769 (finish)	10.3

The program should compute the mpg for each tank and the cumulative mpg each time the tank is filled. Your output should produce a chart with the following headings:

Odometer (begin)	Odometer (end)	Fuel (tank)	Miles (tank)	Fuel (trip)	Miles (trip)	Mpg (tank)	Mpg (trip)

8. Parkside's Other Triangle is generated from two positive integers, one for the size and one for the seed. For example,

Size 6, Seed 1	Size 5, Seed 3
1 2 4 7 2 7	3 4 6 9 4
3 5 8 3 8	5 7 1 5
6 9 4 9	8 2 6
1 5 1	3 7
6 2	8
3	

The size gives the number of columns. Seed specifies the starting value for column 1. Column n contains n values. The successive values are obtained by adding 1 to the previous value. When 9 is reached, the next value becomes 1.

Write a program that reads pairs of positive integers and produces Parkside's Other Triangle for each pair. The check for bad data should include checking for seeds between 1 and 9 inclusive.

9. Modify the sewage, water, and sanitation problem (Problem 19, Chapter 5) so that it can be used with data containing appropriate information for all residents of the community.

10. Modify the program for the Lucky Wildcat Well Corporation (Problem 20, Chapter 5) so that it can be run with data containing information about all of Al Derrick's wells.

11. Modify the program concerning the Mathematical Association of America (Problem 21, Chapter 5). There will be 50 official state delegates attending the next summer national meeting. The new data file will contain the two-letter state abbreviation for each delegate. Output should include one column with the state abbreviation and another with the amount reimbursed.

12. In Fibonacci's sequence, *0, 1, 1, 2, 3, 5, 8, 13, . . .* the first two terms are 0 and 1 and each successive term is formed by adding the previous two terms. Write a program that will read positive integers and then print the number of terms indicated by each integer read. Be sure to test your program with data that includes the integers 1 and 2.

13. Dr. Lae Z. Programmer is at it again. Now that you have written a program to compute the grade for one student in his class (Problems 5, 22, and 23, Chapter 5), he wants you to modify this program so it can be used for the entire class. He will help you by making the first entry be a positive integer representing the number of students in the class. Your new version should compute an overall class average and the number of students receiving each letter grade.

14. Modify the Pentagon parking lot problem (Problem 26, Chapter 5) so that it can be used for all customers in one day. In the new program, time should be entered in military style as a four-digit integer. The lot opens at 0600 (6:00 a.m.) and closes at 2200 (10:00 p.m.). Your program should include appropriate summary information.

15. The Natural Pine Furniture Company (Problem 7, Chapter 4) now wants you to refine your program so that it will print a one-week pay report for each employee. You do not know how many employees there are, but you do know that all information for each employee is on a separate line. Each line of input will contain the employee's initials, the number of hours worked, and the hourly rate. You are to use the constant definition section for the following:

Federal withholding tax rate	18%
State withholding tax rate	4.5%
Hospitalization	$25.65
Union dues	$ 7.85

Your output should include a report for each employee and a summary report for the company files.

16. Orlando Tree Service, Incorporated, offers the following services and rates to its customers:

  a. Tree removal $500 per tree

  b. Tree trimming $80 per hour

  c. Stump grinding $25 plus $2 per inch for each stump whose diameter exceeds ten inches. The $2 charge is only for the diameter inches in excess of ten.

Write a complete program to allow the manager, Mr. Sorwind, to provide an estimate when he bids on a job. Your output should include a listing of each separate charge and a total. A 10% discount is given for any job whose total exceeds $1000. Typical data for one customer are

```
R 7
T 6.5
G 8    8    10    12    14    15    15    20    25
```

where **R**, **T**, and **G** are codes for removal, trimming, and grinding, respectively. The integer following **G** represents the number of stumps to be ground. The next line of integers represents the diameters of stumps to be ground.

17. A standard science experiment is to drop a ball and see how high it bounces. Once the "bounciness" of the ball has been determined, the ratio gives a bounciness index. For example, if a ball dropped from a height of 10 feet bounces 6 feet high, the index is 0.6 and the total distance traveled by the ball is 16 feet after one bounce. If the ball were to continue bouncing, the distance after two bounces would be 10 ft + 6 ft + 6 ft + 3.6 ft = 25.6 ft. Note that distance traveled for each successive bounce is the distance to the floor plus 0.6 of that distance as the ball comes back up.

    Write a program that lets the user enter the initial height of the ball and the number of times the ball is allowed to continue bouncing. Output should be the total distance traveled by the ball. At some point in this process, the distance traveled by the ball becomes negligible. Use the constant section to define a "negligible" distance (for example, 0.00001 inches). Terminate the computing when the distance becomes negligible. When this stage is reached, include the number of bounces as part of the output.

18. Write a program that prints a calendar for one month. Input consists of an integer specifying the first day of the month (1 = Sunday) and an integer specifying how many days are in a month.

19. An amortization table shows the rate at which a loan is paid off. It contains monthly entries showing the interest paid that month, the principal paid, and the remaining balance. Given the amount of money borrowed (the principal), the annual interest rate, and the amount the person wishes to repay each month, print an amortization table. (Be certain that the payment desired is larger than the first month's interest.) Your table should stop when the loan is paid off, and should be printed with the following heads.

MONTH NUMBER   INTEREST PAID   PRINCIPAL PAID   BALANCE

20. Computers work in the binary system, which is based on powers of 2. Write a program that prints out the first 15 powers of 2 beginning with 2 to the zero power. Print your output in headed columns.

21. Print a list of the positive integers less than 500 that are divisible by either 5 or 7. When the list is complete, print a count of the number of integers found.

22. Write a program that reads in 20 real numbers, then prints the average of the positive numbers and the average of the negative numbers.

23. In 1626, the Dutch settlers purchased Manhattan Island from the Indians. According to legend, the purchase price was $24. Suppose that the Indians had invested this amount at 3% annual interest compounded quarterly. If the money had earned interest from the start of 1626 to the end of last year, how much money would the Indians have in the bank today? (*Hint:* Use nested loops for the compounding.)

24. Write a program to print the sum of the odd integers from 1 to 99.

25. The theory of relativity holds that as an object moves, it gets smaller. The new length of the object can be determined from the formula:

$$NewLength = Original\ Length * \sqrt{(1 - B^2)}$$

where B^2 is the percentage of the speed of light at which the object is moving, entered in decimal form. Given the length of an object, print its new length for speeds ranging from 0 to 99% of the speed of light. Print the output in the following columns:

Percent of Light   Speed   Length
----------------   -----   ------

26. Mr. Christian uses a 90%, 80%, 70%, 60% grading scale on his tests. Given a list of test scores, print out the number of A's, B's, C's, D's, and F's on the test. Terminate the list of scores with a sentinel value.

27. The mathematician Gottfried Leibniz determined a formula for estimating the value of pi (π):

$$\pi/4 = 1 - 1/3 + 1/5 - 1/7 + 1/9 - 1/11 + \ldots$$

Evaluate the first 200 terms of this formula and print its approximation of π.

28. In a biology experiment, Carey finds that a sample of an organism doubles in population every 12 hours. If she starts with 1000 organisms, in how many hours will she have 1 million?

29. C++ does has a function that permits raising a number to a power. We can easily write a program to perform this function, however. Given an integer to represent the base number and a positive integer to represent the power desired, write a program that prints the number raised to that power.

30. Mr. Thomas has negotiated a salary schedule for his new job. He will be paid one cent ($0.01) the first day, with the daily rate doubling each day. Write a program that will find his total earnings for 30 days. Print your results in a table set up as follows:

Day Number	Daily Salary	Total Earned
1	.01	.01
2	.02	.03
3	.	.
.	.	.
.	.	.
30		

31. Write a program to print the perimeter and area of rectangles using all combinations of lengths and widths running from 1 foot to 10 feet in increments of 1 foot. Print the output in headed columns.

32. Teachers in most school districts are paid on a salary schedule that provides a salary based on their number of years of teaching experience. Suppose that a beginning teacher in the Babbage School District is paid $19,000 the first year. For each year of experience after this up to 12 years, a 4% increase over the preceding value is received. Write a program that prints a salary schedule for teachers in this district. The output should appear as follows:

Years Experience	Salary
0	$19,000
1	$19,760
2	$20,550
3	$21,372
.	.
.	.
.	.
12	

(Actually, most teacher's salary schedules are more complex than this. As an additional problem, you might like to find out how the salary schedule is determined in your school district and write a program to print the salary schedule.)

33. The Euclidean algorithm can be used to find the greatest common divisor (gcd) of two positive integers (n_1, n_2). For example, suppose $n_1 = 72$ and $n_2 = 42$; you can use this algorithm in the following manner:
(1) Divide the larger by the smaller:

$72 = 42 * 1 + 30$

(2) Divide the divisor (42) by the remainder (30):

$42 = 30 * 1 + 12$

(3) Repeat this process until you get a remainder of zero:

$$30 = 12 * 2 + 6 \qquad 12 = 6 * 2 + 0$$

The last nonzero remainder is the gcd of n_1 and n_2.

Write a program that lets the user enter two integers and then prints each step in the process of using the Euclidean Algorithm to find their gcd.

34. Cramer's Rule for solving a system of equations was given in Problem 31, Chapter 5. Add an enhancement to your program by using a loop to guarantee that the coefficients and constants entered by the user are precisely those that were intended.

35. Gaussian Elimination is another method used to solve systems of equations. To illustrate, if the system is

$$x - 2y = 1$$
$$2x + y = 7$$

Gaussian Elimination would start with the augmented matrix

$$\begin{bmatrix} 1 & -2 & 1 \\ 2 & 1 & 7 \end{bmatrix}$$

and proceed to produce the identity matrix on the left side

$$\begin{bmatrix} 1 & 0 & 3 \\ 0 & 1 & 1 \end{bmatrix}$$

At this stage, the solution to the system is seen to be $x = 3$ and $y = 1$.

Write a program in which the user enters coefficients for a system of two equations containing two variables. The program should then solve the system and display the answer. Your program should include the following:

a. A check for bad data

b. A solvable system check

c. A display of partial results as the matrix operations are performed.

36. A Pythagorean triple consists of three integers A, B, and C such that $A^2 + B^2 = C^2$. For example, 3 , 4, 5 is such a triple because $3^2 + 4^2 = 5^2$. These triples can be generated by positive integers m, n, $(m > n)$ where $a = m^2 - n^2$, $b = 2mn$, and $c = m^2 + n^2$. These triples will be primitive (no common factors) if m and n have no common factors and are not both odd. Write a program that allows the user to enter a value for m and then prints all possible primitive Pythagorean triples such that $m > n$. Use one function to find the greatest common factor of m and n, another to see if m and n are both odd, and another to guard against overflow. For the input value of $m = 5$, typical output would be

m	n	a	b	c	a^2	b^2	c^2
2	1	3	4	5	9	16	25
3	2	5	12	13	25	144	169
4	1	15	8	17	225	64	289
4	3	7	24	25	49	576	625
5	2	21	20	29	441	400	841
5	4	9	40	41	81	1600	1681

37. This chapter's Focus on Program Design problem determined whether or not an integer was prime by checking for divisors less than or equal to the square root of the number. The check started with 2 and incremented trial divisors by 1 each time as seen by the code

```
prime = TRUE;
divisor = 2;
limit_for_check = sqrt(candidate);
while ((divisor <= limit_for_check) && prime)
    if (candidate % divisor == 0)
        prime = FALSE;
    else
        divisor = divisor + 1;
```

Other methods can be used to determine whether or not an integer N is prime. For example, you may

a. check divisors from 2 to N - 1 incrementing by 1.

b. check divisors from 2 to $(N - 1)/2$ incrementing by 1.

c. check divisor 2, 3, 5, . . . $(N - 1)/2$ incrementing by 2.

d. check divisor 2, 3, 5, . . . sqrt(N) incrementing by 2.

Write a program that allows the user to choose between these options in order to compare relative efficiency of different algorithms. Use a function for each option.

38. The prime factorization of a positive integer is the positive integer written as the product of primes. For example, the prime factorization of 72 is

$$72 = 2 * 3 * 3 * 4$$

Write a program that allows the user to enter a positive integer and then displays the prime factorization of the integer. A minimal main program could be

```
num = get_a_number ();
if (number_is_prime(num))
    cout << num<< " is prime" << endl;
else
    print_factorization(num);
```

Enhancements to this program could include an error trap for bad dta and a loop for repeated trials.

39. As you might expect, instructors of computer science do not agree on whether a **do . . . while** loop or a **while** loop is the preferred variable control loop in C++. Interview several computer science instructors at your institution to determine what preference (if any) they have regarding these two forms of repetition. Prepare a class report based on your interviews. Include advantages and disadvantages of each form of repetition.

40. Examine the repetition constructs of at least five other programming languages. Prepare a report that compares and contrasts repetition in each of the languages. Be sure to include information such as which languages provide for both fixed and variable repetition and which languages have more than one kind of variable repetition. Which language appears to have the most desirable form of repetition? Include your rationale for this decision in your report.

41. Examine some old computer science texts and talk to some computer science instructors who worked with the early languages to see how repetition was achieved in the "early days." Prepare a brief chronological chart for class display that depicts the various stages in developing repetition.

CHAPTER 7 Strings

Thus far in this text, you have been designing algorithms to solve problems, and coding your solutions in C++ using the major control structures of sequencing, selection, iteration, and functional abstraction. In this chapter, we begin a shift in focus that will guide us through the rest of the text. We consider how to solve problems by structuring the data of a program appropriately, using strings as our first example.

We have been using strings in C++ programs for the purpose of displaying messages to the user. However, many problems require that we be able to take strings as input from the user and analyze them. For example, names, words, phrases, and sentences are frequently used as part of some information that must be analyzed. Word processing programs would be very difficult to design and implement without high-level algorithms and data structures for string processing.

We began this chapter by examining how to represent a string as a data type. We will show how to declare string variables that can be input and output with the standard operators. Then we will study some standard C++ library functions for processing string variables, and write some functions of our own for analyzing them. Finally, we will use strings to explore the design and implementation of new data types with C++ *classes*.

7.1 Thinking of Strings as an Abstract Data Type

Data Abstraction

When designing the solution to a problem initially we are not concerned about the specifics of how data will be manipulated. These are implementation details that can (and should) be dealt with at a fairly low level in a modular development. The properties of a data structure, however, are part of the design at a fairly high level.

The separation between the conceptual definition of a data structure and its eventual implementation is called *data abstraction.* This process of deferring details to the lowest possible level parallels the method of designing algorithms; that is, design first and do implementation details last.

Abstract Data Types

Two abstraction concepts have been previously discussed: functional or procedural abstraction and data abstraction. A third form of abstraction arises from the use of data types. In Chapter 4, we mentioned that one kind of module in a program consists of a set of operations and related data. We referred to a module of this kind as an *abstract data type,* and pointed out that such modules already exist in programming languages for standard data types such as **int, float**, and **char**. We now provide a more formal definition of an abstract data type:

> An abstract data type (ADT) consists of a set of values, a defined set of properties of these values, and a set of operations for processing the values.

Note that the definition of an ADT makes no mention of how it is implemented, or even of the uses to which it may be put in a program. We have not been overly concerned about the implementation details of any of the standard abstract data types in C++. Indeed, we have barely been aware of them at all. In this and the following chapters, you will learn how to construct new data types that both solve interesting problems and behave in a similar way—so as not to distract users with detail. Your growth as a computer scientist will be enhanced if you develop a perspective of abstract data types and use this perspective in the design of problem solutions.

The String ADT

Strings are used to represent textual information. Strings themselves have an internal structure consisting of a sequence of character values. To keep our discussion of strings simple for the moment, we will ignore how strings are represented in the memory of computers and how their component parts are manipulated. We will focus only on the operations it would be useful to have on whole strings, and defer the details of their implementation until later sections. Some of the most useful operations on strings follow:

1. The input of string data from the keyboard into a string variable
2. The output of string data from a string variable to the terminal screen
3. Copying of data from one string variable to another
4. Testing two strings for the relationships less than, greater than, or equality.

Programmers who use these operations are called *clients* of the string type. Clients would like to view the string operations abstractly. That is, the only information about these operations available to clients should be the declarations of C++ functions and their supporting comments. If the required functions are already available in a standard C++ library, clients can simply use these. If they are not available, other programmers, called *servers,* will have to write them and make them available to clients as a new library. The main point here is that clients who use strings should know as little about their internal representation as clients who use standard data types such as **int** and **char**. For example, a client of strings should be able to write the following code, which displays the numerically greater of two integer values and the alphabetically greater of two string values:

```
int x, y;
string name1, name2;

cout << "Enter two integers, separated by a space: ";
cin >> x >> y;
if (x > y)
        cout << x << endl;
else
        cout << y << endl;
cout << "Enter two names, separated by a space: ";
```

```
cin >> name1 >> name2;
if (string_greater(name1, name2))
        cout << name1 << endl;
else
        cout << name2 << endl;
```

Note that the client declares string variables in the same way as integer variables, simply by using a type name and a list of variable names. Note also that the use of the operations does not reveal how they are implemented or how the data are represented. In the following sections, we will play the roles of clients who use the abstract string data type and servers who implement it, though in large software projects, clients and servers are seldom the same individuals.

Before we can play the role of clients who declare and use string variables, we must play the role of servers who define a data type to represent strings. We begin by presenting a fairly formal specification of the operations provided by the string ADT. The inputs, outputs, and any other assumptions about the data or the effects of the operations are described in terms of preconditions and postconditions, as introduced in Chapter 5:

Input operation	
Preconditions:	The parameter is a string variable in an unpredictable state.
Postconditions:	String variable contains a string value input from the keyboard.
Output operation	
Preconditions:	The parameter is a string variable, appropriately initialized.
Postconditions:	The value of the variable is displayed on the screen.
Copy operation	
Preconditions:	The first parameter is a string variable in an unpredictable state. The second parameter is a string literal, or a string variable appropriately initialized. The number of characters stored in the second parameter does not exceed the maximum physical size of the first parameter.
Postconditions:	The value of the second parameter is copied into the first parameter.
Length operation	
Preconditions:	The parameter is a string variable, appropriately initialized.
Postconditions:	The number of characters currently in the string is returned.
Equality operation	
Preconditions:	The two parameters are string variables appropriately initialized.
Postconditions:	The Boolean value TRUE is returned if the strings are equal, and FALSE is returned otherwise.
Less than operation	
Preconditions:	The two parameters are string variables appropriately initialized.
Postconditions:	The Boolean value TRUE is returned if the first string is less than the second string, and FALSE is returned otherwise.
Greater than operation	
Preconditions:	The two parameters are string variables appropriately initialized.
Postconditions:	The Boolean value TRUE is returned if the first string is greater than the second string, and false is returned otherwise.

Implementing the String ADT

Perhaps the quickest and easiest way to implement a string ADT is to do so in a way that is compatible with the way that strings are implemented and used by two important C++ libraries, the **string.h** library and the **iostream.h** library. This strategy, called *software reuse,* gives clients immediate access to many high-level operations for string processing, including input and output operations.

We represent a string as an *array of characters.* This representation is compatible with the one used in the standard libraries. For now, the only thing we need to know is that an array of characters is a sequence of memory locations capable of storing many characters. The size or number of memory locations available in any array is specified by an integer constant in the type definition. Here is an example of code that uses an integer constant and an array type to define a new string type name:

```
const int MAX_STRING_SIZE = 11;
typedef char string[MAX_STRING_SIZE];
```

The form of the type definition that uses an array is

```
typedef <element type> <new type name>[integer constant];
```

You have already seen **typedef** used to create a synonym, **boolean**, for a predefined type, **int**, in Chapter 5. The present example specifies that **char** is the type of data stored in each memory location in an array, **string** is the name of the type, and **MAX_STRING_SIZE** is the number of memory locations available in any string variable for storing characters.

Declaring String Variables

When a string type name is available, we can play the role of clients by using the type name to declare string variables. Our example of code can be extended with the declaration of two variables:

```
const int MAX_STRING_SIZE = 11;
typedef char string[MAX_STRING_SIZE];
string first_name, last_name;
```

Several comments are in order at this point:

1. When the computer encounters the variable declarations, it reserves memory for two arrays that can store 11 characters each.
2. The computer places a special character called the *null character,* represented by '\0' in C++, in the first memory cell in each array. The rest of the data in the two arrays is unpredictable.
3. The null character is used by several standard C++ string library functions as a sentinel value to detect the end of the character data actually in a string variable at any given time. Library functions that insert characters into string variables will move the null character to the appropriate position to indicate the new end of the string. The null character is not counted as part of the string data, and programmers normally need not concern themselves with processing it. However, its presence in all strings implies that the size of the

◆ FIGURE 7.1
Memory allocated for two
new string variables

```
first_name   \0 |   |   |   |   |   |   |   |   |   |   |
              0   1   2   3   4   5   6   7   8   9   10
last_name    \0 |   |   |   |   |   |   |   |   |   |   |
```

arrays used to represent the strings must always be one greater than the maximum number of characters stored in the arrays. Thus, in our example,
MAX_STRING_SIZE is 11, but the array will represent strings of up to 10
characters in length.

The state of the two string variables in this example is illustrated in Figure 7.1.
Note that each memory cell in the arrays is labeled with a number, ranging from 0
to 10, and that the null character is stored at position 0. We will demonstrate
shortly how to use these numbers to access individual characters within strings.

Input and Output of String Variables

If we use the standard input and output streams, **cin** and **cout**, the input and
output of string variables become very easy. To input a string from the keyboard
into a string variable, we use the name of the string variable in an input statement.
For example, assuming that string variables are declared as above, the statements

```
cout << "Enter the first name: ";
cin >> first_name;
cout << "Enter the last name: ";
cin >> last_name
```

will prompt the user to enter two names at the keyboard. The computer handles
string input at the keyboard in the same way it handles numeric input. Leading and
trailing whitespace characters are ignored. The string data are entered into a string
variable when a carriage return is encountered or the next string data appear on a
line.

The following statement would input two strings separated by whitespace
characters, without prompting the user:

```
cin >> first_name >> last_name;
```

Suppose the user entered the names "Mary" and "Lopez" at the keyboard. The state
of the two string variables would be as shown in Figure 7.2. Note that the
computer has moved the null character to the right of the input data in each string.

◆ FIGURE 7.2
String variables after input
of string values

```
first_name   M | a | r | y | \0 |   |   |   |   |   |   |
              0   1   2   3   4   5   6   7   8   9   10
last_name    L | o | p | e | z | \0 |   |   |   |   |   |
```

Once string variables have been modified with input statements, their
contents can be displayed on the terminal screen with output statements. For
example, the following statement displays the full name just entered:

```
cout << "The full name is " << first_name << " "
     << last_name << endl;
```

The computer displays all of the characters in the arrays, up to but not including the null character. The format of string data for output is handled in the same way as numeric data. A string can be aligned in a desired column by using **setw** to specify a field width:

```
cout << setw(40) << first_name << " " << last_name
     << endl;
```

EXAMPLE 7.1   This example is a C++ program that prompts for the user's name and age and responds with a message.

```
// Program file: strio.cpp

#include <iostream.h>

const int MAX_STRING_SIZE = 11;
typedef char string[MAX_STRING_SIZE]

int main()
{
     string first_name, last_name;
     int age;

     cout << "Enter your first name: ";
     cin >> first_name;
     cout << "Enter your last name: ";
     cin >> last_name;
     cout << "Enter your age: ";
     cin >> age;
     cout << first_name << " " << last_name << ", you're only " << age
          << " years old?" << endl;
     return 0;
}
```

A run of this program with sample input produces

```
Enter your first name: John
Enter your last name: Barleycorn
Enter your age: 43
John Barleycorn, you're only 43 years old?
```

Assignment to String Variables

One common way to initialize a string variable is to assign a value to it when it is declared. The form for this declaration is

<string type name> <variable name> = <string value>;

where **\<string value\>** is a *string literal* or sequence of characters enclosed in double quotes. For example, the declarations

```
const int MAX_STRING_SIZE = 11;
typedef char string[MAX_STRING_SIZE];
string first_name = "John";
string last_name = "Barleycorn";
```

would not only reserve memory for two strings, but initialize them with string values as well. The state of the two string variables is shown in Figure 7.3. Two comments are in order at this point.

◆ **FIGURE 7.3**

String variables after initialization

first_name	J	o	h	n	\0						
	0	1	2	3	4	5	6	7	8	9	10
last_name	B	a	r	l	e	y	c	o	r	n	\0

1. Because C++ does no *range bound error* checking with arrays, you should be careful to use string literals whose lengths are less than the size of the target string variables. *The length of a string literal should be at most one character less than the size of the target string variable.*

2. *A declaration is the only place where you can assign a string variable a value.* All other attempts to assign values to string variables will cause errors in most C++ implementations. You might think that this restriction would prohibit common operations such as copying a string value from one variable into another, but we will demonstrate an easy way to do this in a moment.

Using Standard String Library Functions

Once we have initialized string variables, it would be useful to be able to copy their contents to other string variables or to compare two strings for their lexicographic order. The use of the built-in assignment and comparison operations with string variables is not supported in most C++ implementations. However, there are several functions in the standard **string.h** library that cover our needs for assignment and comparison fairly well.

The first of these functions, **strcpy**, has the form

> strcpy(\<destination string variable\>, \<source string\>)

This function will copy the source string, including its null character, into the destination string variable. In effect, the function performs the assignment

> \<destination string variable\> = \<source string\>

which is normally disallowed in many implementations of C++. The source string or second parameter to **strcpy** can be either a string variable or a string literal. The first parameter or destination string variable is modified as a result of the operation. Once again, care should be taken that the length of the source string is less than the maximum size of the destination string variable.

EXAMPLE 7.2
This example is a C++ program that uses a temporary string variable to exchange the values of two other string variables. Note the use of the assignment operator to initialize the string variables in the declaration, and the use of **strcpy** to perform the same operation in the statements.

```
// Program file: strswap.cpp

#include <iostream.h>
#include <string.h>

const int MAX_STRING_SIZE = 21;
typedef char string[MAX_STRING_SIZE];

int main()
{
        string first_name = "John";
        string last_name = "Doe";
        string temp;

        cout << first_name << " " << last_name << endl;
        strcpy(temp, first_name);
        strcpy(first_name, last_name);
        strcpy(last_name, temp);
        cout << first_name << " " << last_name << endl;
        return 0;

}
```

The output of this program would be

```
John Doe
Doe John
```

Another operation that is frequently used with strings is comparison. Each string has some lexicographic relationship to any other string, as defined by the collating sequence of characters within the strings. For example, the strings "hi", "there", and "Jane" are in the lexicographic relationship "Jane" < "hi"< "there" (note that 'J' precedes 'h' as an ASCII value). However, we cannot use the operator < in a program to demonstrate this relationship. Instead, we can use the standard string library function **strcmp**. This function has the form

> strcmp(<left string>, <right string>)

where the left string is a variable or literal that would appear to the left of a comparison operator, and the right string is a variable or literal that would appear to the right of a comparison operator. Neither the left string nor the right string is modified. The function has the following behavior:

1. It returns an integer less than 0 if the left string is less than the right string.
2. It returns 0 if the left string is equal to the right string.
3. It returns an integer greater than 0 if the left string is greater than the right string.
4. It returns an integer less than 0 if the left string is a substring of the right string, beginning with the first character in each string.

EXAMPLE 7.3   The following C++ program compares two input strings and displays a message about their lexicographic relationship:

```cpp
// Program file: strcomp.cpp

#include <iostream.h>
#include <string.h>

const int MAX_STRING_SIZE = 21;
typedef char string[MAX_STRING_SIZE];

int main()
{
      string name1, name2;
      int order;
      char sign;

      cout << "Enter the first name: ";
      cin >> name1;
      cout << "Enter the second name: ";
      cin >> name2;
      order = strcmp(name1, name2);
      if (order < 0)
            sign = '<';
      else if (order > 0)
            sign = '>';
      else
            sign = '=';
      cout << name1 << " " << sign << " " << name2 << endl;
      return 0;
}
```

Here are several sample runs of this program:

```
Enter the first name: Mary
Enter the second name: Mary
Mary = Mary

Enter the first name: Jane
Enter the second name: Bill
Jane > Bill

Enter the first name: Jane
Enter the second name: Marks
Jane < Marks

Enter the first name: William
Enter the second name: Williams
William < Williams
```

Another useful string library function, **strcat**, *concatenates* one string to the end of another string. This function is used to build larger strings out of smaller ones. Its form is

> strcat(<first string>, <second string>);

where the first string is a string variable and the second string is either a variable or a literal. **strcat** places the characters in the second string at the end of the characters in the first string, and returns the result in the first string. Note that the first string is modified, but the second string is not.

The last string library function that we will introduce is **strlen**. Its form is

> strlen(<string>)

This function takes a string variable or literal as a parameter, and returns the number of characters currently in the string. Recall that a declaration of a string variable merely reserves space in computer memory for holding string data. Until the string is initialized with data, its length is actually zero. After the string is initialized, its length can range up to one less than the size of the array that represents the string. The following piece of C++ code will output zero immediately after the string variable is declared, and then output its new length after the user initializes it:

```
const int MAX_STRING_SIZE = 21;
typedef char string[MAX_STRING_SIZE];
string name;

cout << strlen(name) << endl;
cout << "Enter your name: ";
cin >> name;
cout << strlen(name) << endl;
```

A sample run of this code would produce

```
0
Enter your name: Beatrice
8
```

EXAMPLE 7.4   This example is a C++ program that checks for a possible range bound error before it concatenates one string to another one.

```
// Program file: strcheck.cpp

#include <iostream.h>
#include <string.h>

const int MAX_STRING_SIZE = 21;
typedef char string[MAX_STRING_SIZE];

int main()
{
    string first_name1, last_name

    cout << "Enter the first name: ";
    cin >> first_name
    cout << "Enter the second name: ";
```

```
cin >> last_name2;
if (strlen(first_name1) + strlen(last_name) >= MAX_STRING_SIZE)
        cout << "ERROR: not enough memory to concatenate names.";
else
{
        strcat(first_name, last_name);
        cout << first_name;
}
cout << endl;
return 0;
}
```

Note that the test for the error computes the sum of the lengths of the two input strings. This will be the length of the string that results from the concatenation. The length of this new string must be at most one less than the size of the array representing it.

Accessing Characters Within String Variables

Because we represent string variables as arrays of characters, we can access individual characters at different positions in a string by using an operation called *array indexing*. An *index* is an integer value used to specify a memory location in an array. In C++, the index of the first memory location in an array is 0, the index of the second is 1, and so on, until the index of the last memory location in the array, which is always the size of the array minus 1. Array indexing is used both to get the value of data stored in a memory location and to store data there as well. For example, the following code stores the character 'a' in the first position in a string, and then outputs the value at that position:

```
const int MAX_STRING_SIZE = 21;
typedef char string[MAX_STRING_SIZE];
string name;

name[0] = 'a';
cout << name[0] << endl;
```

The general form of an array indexing operation is

<array variable>[<integer value>]

The integer value can be an integer literal, an integer variable, a symbolic integer constant, or any other expression that returns an integer value. There are two important points to make about array indexing with strings:

1. If MAX_STRING_SIZE is the size of the array, then a reference of the form

`<string variable>[MAX_STRING_SIZE]`

is a range bound error and could cause the program to behave mysteriously at run time. With array indexing, `<string variable>[MAX_STRING_SIZE - 1]` indicates the position of the last data location in the array, and `<string variable>[0]` indicates the first data location.

2. The null character normally will be found one index position beyond the last character of the string currently stored in an array. Thus, if `strlen(<string variable>)` is the number of characters in the string, the reference

```
<string variable>[strlen(<string variable>)]
```

will be to the array cell containing the null character.

Much string processing at the character level consists of traversing the array of characters with a loop. The general form of a loop that visits every character in a string should be

```
int length = strlen(string_variable);

for (int index = 0; index < length; ++index)
        do something with string_variable[index];
```

Note that the first character visited in the array is at position 0, whereas the last character visited is at position `length - 1`. If the string's length is 0, then the body of the loop is not entered and no characters are visited at all. Note also that we compute the length of the string before the loop is started. If we computed the string's length in the heading of the loop, the program might be very inefficient.

EXAMPLE 7.5   Suppose a user wishes to count the number of instances of a given character in a string. The user enters the string and the character at the keyboard, and the program displays a count of the number of instances of the character in the string. The following C++ program would solve this problem:

```
// Program file: charcnt.cpp

#include <iostream.h>
#include <string.h>

const int MAX_STRING_SIZE = 21;
typedef char string[MAX_STRING_SIZE];

int main()
{
    string word;
    char ch;
    int count, length;

    cout << "Enter the word: ";
    cin >> word;
    cout << "Enter the character to be counted: ";
    cin >> ch;
    length = strlen(word);
    count = 0;
    for (int j = 0; j < length; ++j)
            if (word[j] == ch)
                    ++count;
```

```
        cout << "There are " << count << " " << ch << "s in "
            << word << endl;
        return 0;
}
```

A sample run of this program would produce

```
Enter the word: macadamia
Enter the character to be counted: a
There are 4 a's in macadamia
```

EXERCISES 7.1

1. Indicate which of the following string comparisons are TRUE or FALSE using the full ASCII character set.
   a. "Mathematics" less than "CompScience"
   b. "Jefferson" less than "Jeffersonian"
   c. "Smith Karen" less than "Smithsonian"
   d. "Tom" greater than "apple"
   e. "#45" less than or equal to "$45"
   f. "Hoof in mouth" less than "Foot in door"
   g. "453012" greater than "200000"

2. Write a test program that allows you to examine the following Boolean expressions.
   a. "William Joe" < "Williams Bo"
   b. "James" > "Jameson"

3. Assume the following declarations.

```
typedef char string20[20];
typedef char string10[10];
string20 a = "There are 19 chars.";
string20 b = "Only 14 chars.";
string10 c = "8 chars.";
```

   a. Indicate whether the following are valid or invalid.
   ```
     i. a = b;
    ii. c = a + b;
   iii. strcpy(b, a);
    iv. strcpy(c, b);
     v. strcat(b, c);
    vi. for (int j = 0; j < 20; ++j)
          c[j] = a[j] + b[j];
   vii. for (int j = 0; j < 20; ++j)
          if (j <= 10)
              a[j] = c[j];
          else
              b[j] = c[j];
   ```
   b. Write a segment of code that will make the string **c** consist of the strings **a** and **b** where the lesser (alphabetically) of **a** and **b** is the first part of **c**.

4. Assume string variable **word** of size 100 has been declared and data have been read into it from the keyboard. Write a segment of the code to count the number of occurrences of the letter 'M' in the string **word**.

7.2 Defining String Functions

Now that we are armed with a high-level representation of string variables and some high-level standard C++ operations, we can focus on building some useful string processing functions of our own. First of all, it would be useful to create string comparison functions that correspond more closely to the standard C++ comparison operators <, =, and >. The string library function **strcmp** returns one of three possible integer values, depending on which of these relationships is true. For example, we would like a function with a more specific name, **string_equal**, that returns a Boolean value and can be used in the context of Boolean expressions in **if** statements and loops. We will design and implement **string_equal**, and leave the development of other string comparison functions as exercises.

The declaration of **string_equal** is

```
// Function: string_equal
// Tests two strings to see if they are equal
//
// Inputs: two strings
// Output: Boolean value TRUE, if the strings are equal,
// FALSE otherwise

boolean string_equal(string str1, string str2);
```

The implementation simply checks the result of calling the **strcmp** function with the two parameters:

```
boolean string_equal(string str1, string str2)
{
        return strcmp(str1, str2) == 0;
}
```

Many string processing operations test individual characters for certain properties or modify the characters in some way. For example, it would be useful to determine whether a string contains only digits, or to convert the letters in a string to uppercase. For this reason, C++ provides a standard library of character processing functions, **ctype.h**. The forms of two typical character functions, **isdigit** and **toupper**, are

```
isdigit(<character value>)
```

```
toupper(<character value>)
```

isdigit tests the character parameter to determine whether it is a digit. If it is, the function returns a nonzero value. If it is not, the function returns zero. Several other functions exist that perform tests of this sort in the **ctype.h** library. All of them are prefixed with **is**. **toupper** tests the character parameter to determine whether it is a lowercase letter. If it is, the function returns the corresponding uppercase letter. If it is not, the function returns the original character parameter. None of the functions in the **ctype.h** library modifies its parameters.

Functions for processing strings as input parameters are defined like any other functions in C++. You decide on an appropriate name to describe the task, and then specify the input for the function. Let's write a function that tests a string to see whether it can represent an integer. This function would be useful for detecting errors in numeric input from the keyboard. The function takes a string as a parameter, and returns a Boolean value. This value will be TRUE if all of the characters in the string are digits, or FALSE otherwise. The declaration of the function is:

```
// Function: is_integer
// Tests for a valid decimal representation of an integer
//
// Input: a string
// Output: a Boolean value (TRUE if valid, FALSE otherwise)

boolean is_integer(string str);
```

The implementation examines each character in the string, until a character is not a digit or the last character is reached. We use a **while** loop to terminate execution when the first nondigit is found:

```
boolean is_integer(string str)
{
      boolean no_bad_digits = TRUE;
      int i, length;

      i = 0;
      length = strlen(str);
      while (no_bad_digits && (i < length))
            if (! isdigit(str[i]))
                    no_bad_digits = FALSE;
            else
                    ++i;
      return no_bad_digits;
}
```

EXAMPLE 7.6   This example is a C++ program that checks an input string to see whether it is a valid representation of an integer:

```
// Program file: intcheck.cpp

#include <iostream.h>
#include <string.h>
#include <ctype.h>

#include "boolean.h"

const int MAX_STRING_SIZE = 21;
typedef char string[MAX_STRING_SIZE];

// Function: is_integer
// Tests for a valid representation of an integer
//
// Input: a string
// Output: a Boolean value (TRUE if valid, FALSE otherwise)

boolean is_integer(string str);
```

```
int main()
{
    string number;

    cout << "Enter an integer: ";
    cin >> number;
    if (is_integer(number))
        cout << "A valid representation";
    else
        cout << "Not a valid representation";
    cout << endl;
    return 0;
}


boolean is_integer(string str)
{
    boolean no_bad_digits = TRUE;
    int i, length;

    i = 0;
    length = strlen(str);
    while (no_bad_digits && (i < length))
        if (! isdigit(str[i]))
            no_bad_digits = FALSE;
        else
            ++i;
    return no_bad_digits;
}
```

Here are several sample runs of this program:

```
Enter an integer: 3214
A valid representation

Enter an integer: 3,214
Not a valid representation

Enter an integer: 3.214
Not a valid representation
```

Now that we have a function to check that a string is a valid representation of an integer, it is useful to write a function that converts a valid representation to the corresponding integer value. The declaration of this function, which will accept a string representation of an integer as a parameter and return the corresponding integer, is

```
// Function: to_integer
// Converts a string representation to an integer
//
// Input: a string representing an integer in digits
// Output: the corresponding integer value

int to_integer(string str);
```

The implementation of the function assumes that the string parameter represents an integer. Therefore, it uses a **for** loop to visit each character in the string. The algorithm for converting a string of digits to an integer value is not difficult. Each digit in the string represents a power of ten. As the loop visits each digit from left to right in the string, it multiplies a running total by 10 and adds the integer value represented by the digit to the total. The running total is initially zero. Here is the algorithm:

```
Set total to 0
For each digit from the leftmost to the rightmost do
        Set total to 10 * total
        + the integer value represented by the digit
```

As you saw in Chapter 3, the integer value represented by a digit is obtained by subtracting '0' from the digit. The implementation of **to_integer** is

```cpp
int to_integer(string str)
{
        int length, total;

        length = strlen(str);
        total = 0;
        for (int j = 0; j < length; ++j)
                total = 10 * total + str[j] - '0';
        return total;
}
```

EXAMPLE 7.7

This example is a C++ program that accepts only valid integer input from the keyboard before using it in computation.

```cpp
// Program file: toint.cpp

#include <iostream.h>
#include <string.h>
#include <ctype.h>

#include "boolean.h"

const int MAX_STRING_SIZE = 21;
typedef char string[MAX_STRING_SIZE];

// Function: is_integer
// Tests for a valid decimal representation of an integer
//
// Input: a string
// Output: a Boolean value (TRUE if valid, FALSE otherwise)

boolean is_integer(string str);

// Function: to_integer
// Converts a string representation to an integer
//
// Input: a string representing an integer in digits
// Output: the corresponding integer value
```

```
int to_integer(string str);

int main()
{
      string number;

      cout << "Enter an integer: ";
      cin >> number;
      if (is_integer(number))
            cout << "The integer is " << to_integer(number);
      else
            cout << "Not a valid representation";
      cout << endl;
      return 0;
}


boolean is_integer(string str)
{
      boolean no_bad_digits = TRUE;
      int i, length;

      i = 0;
      length = strlen(str);
      while (no_bad_digits && (i < length))
            if (! isdigit(str[i]))
                  no_bad_digits = FALSE;
            else
                  ++i;
      return no_bad_digits;
}


int to_integer(string str)
{
      int length, total;

      length = strlen(str);
      total = 0;
      for (int j = 0; j < length; ++j)
            total = 10 * total + str[j] - '0';
      return total;
}
```

Here are several sample runs of this program:

```
Enter an integer: 3214
3214

Enter an integer: 3,214
Not a valid representation

Enter an integer: 3.214
Not a valid representation
```

Our final example of a programmer-defined string function is one that modifies its parameter. This function converts the letters in its string parameter to uppercase. This function will be useful for handling case sensitivity in searching and sorting problems in Chapter 10. In C++, the contents of array parameters can be modified even though they are not declared as reference parameters. The reason for this is that the address of the actual array parameter is passed to the function, even when the & symbol is not included in the declaration. In fact, you should be careful to omit the & symbol from a declaration in any case of array parameters. The declaration of our **make_uppercase** function for strings is

```
// Function: make_uppercase
// Converts the letters in a string to uppercase
//
// Input: a string
// Output: the input string with the letters converted to uppercase

void make_uppercase(string str);
```

The implementation uses a **for** loop to visit every character in the string. It passes each character to the **toupper** function mentioned previously. The result is stored back into the string:

```
void make_uppercase(string str)
{
        int length = strlen(str);

        for (int j = 0; j < length; ++j)
                str[j] = toupper(str[j]);
}
```

Building a Library of String Functions

As we begin to write more programs that use string variables, it becomes tedious to type out or even copy the associated data type definitions and function implementations for each new program. It would be convenient to package all of this code in a separate file and have the system bring it into any application that uses it automatically. We can accomplish this by building our own library to be included by any program that needs to use strings. Put another way, we would like to separate the roles of clients and server for the string type by confining the server to the task of writing the string library, and clients to the task of using the library. We introduced the concept of a programmer-defined library in Chapter 5, where we placed the definitions of Boolean constants and a type name in such a file.

Our new library will contain the constant and type definitions for the string type. It will also contain the string processing functions developed so far in this chapter. The code is written in two files that are separate from the client program files. We will call these files **strlib.h** and **strlib.cpp**. **strlib.h** is called a *header file*. A header file contains the definitions of constants and types and the function declarations that are available to clients. The contents of our header file will have the form

```
#ifndef <file identifier>
<constant and type definitions>
<function declarations>
#define <file identifier>
#endif
```

Note the use of the preprocessor directives **#ifndef, #define**, and **#endif**. These directives are used to prevent the preprocessor from including a library file more than once in an application at compile time. Thus far in this text, we have not had to worry about this possibility, because only one client, the main program application, has been including files. However, the string library file will now include the **boolean.h** file, and a main program application may do so as well. The new directives work to prevent multiple inclusions from occurring as follows:

1. The first directive, **#ifndef**, asks if a file identifier has been defined. If it has, that means that the library file has already been preprocessed, so the preprocessor skips the current inclusion by jumping to **#endif** at the end of the file.

2. If the file identifier has not been defined, the preprocessor will reach the **#define** directive after preprocessing the library file. This directive then makes visible a global file identifier, so that the next inclusion after this one will behave as in step 1.

For example, the **boolean.h** header file should be rewritten so that multiple inclusions will be avoided:

```
// Library header file: boolean.h

#ifndef BOOLEAN_H

const int TRUE = 1;
const int FALSE = 0;

typedef int boolean;

#define BOOLEAN_H
#endif
```

Note that the file identifier, **BOOLEAN_H**, is not likely to be used by an application or another library file.

An example header file for the library with the functions we have developed so far in this chapter is

```
// Library header file: strlib.h

#ifndef STRINGLIB_H

#include "boolean.h"

const int MAX_STRING_SIZE = 21;
typedef char string[MAX_STRING_SIZE];

// Function: string_equal
// Tests two strings to see if they are equal
//
```

```
// Inputs: two strings
// Output: Boolean value TRUE, if the strings are equal, FALSE otherwise

boolean string_equal(string str1, string str2);

// Function: is_integer
// Tests for a valid representation of an integer
//
// Input: a string
// Output: a Boolean value (TRUE if valid, FALSE otherwise)

boolean is_integer(string str);

// Function: to_integer
// Converts a string representation to an integer
//
// Input: a string representing an integer in digits
// Output: the corresponding integer value

int to_integer(string str);

// Function: make_uppercase
// Converts the letters in a string to uppercase
//
// Input: a string
// Output: the input string with the letters converted to uppercase

void make_uppercase(string str);

#define STRINGLIB_H
#endif
```

The other library file for the string type, **strlib.cpp**, is called an *implementation file*. This file contains the implementations of the functions for the library, as well as preprocessor directives to include any other libraries required for the implementation:

```
// Library implementation file: strlib.cpp

#include <string.h>
#include <ctype.h>
#include "strlib.h"

// Function implementations

boolean string_equal(string str1, string str2)
{
        return strcmp(str1, str2) == 0;
}

boolean is_integer(string str)
{
```

```
                     boolean no_bad_digits = TRUE;
                     int i, length;

                     i = 0;
                     length = strlen(str);
                     while (no_bad_digits && (i < length))
                             if (! isdigit(str[i]))
                                     no_bad_digits = FALSE;
                             else
                                     ++i;
                     return no_bad_digits;
          }

          int to_integer(string str)
          {
                     int length, total;

                     length = strlen(str);
                     total = 0;
                     for (int j = 0; j < length; ++j)
                             total = 10 * total + str[j] - '0';
                     return total;
          }

          void make_uppercase(string str)
          {
                     int length = strlen(str);

                     for (int j = 0; j < length; ++j)
                             str[j] = toupper(str[j]);
          }
```

Note that the new library includes the two standard C++ library header files **string.h** and **ctype.h**. The header file for our own library, **strlib.h**, is also included, so that the implementation has access to the data and function declarations.

The code in the library can now be tested. All we need is a small main program to serve as a driver for our library. For example, the following program might test the library we have written thus far:

```
// Program file: testlib.cpp

#include <iostream.h>

#include "boolean.h"
#include "strlib.h"

int main()
{
      string word1, word2, number;

      cout << "Testing strlib functions." << endl << endl;
      cout << "Testing string_equal." << endl;
```

```
        cout << "Enter two different words several times, "
             << "and then two identical words." << endl << endl;
        do
        {
                cout << "Enter the first word: ";
                cin >> word1;
                cout << "Enter the second word: ";
                cin >> word2;
        } while (! string_equal(word1, word2));
        cout << "Testing make_uppercase." << endl;
        make_uppercase(word1);
        cout << word1 << endl;
        cout << "Testing is_integer." << endl;
        cout << "Enter several bad representations of integers," << endl;
        cout << "and then a good one." << endl << endl;
        do
        {
                cout << "Enter an integer: ";
                cin >> number;
                cout << "The integer is " << number << endl;
        } while (! is_integer(number));
        cout << "Testing to_integer." << endl;
        cout << "Enter several good representations of integers," << endl;
        cout << "and then a bad one." << endl << endl;
        cout << "Enter an integer: ";
        cin >> number;
        while (is_integer(number))
        {
                cout << "The integer is " << to_integer(number) << endl;
                cout << "Enter an integer: ";
                cin >> number;
        }
        cout << "Testing completed." << endl;
        return 0;
}
```

A sample run of this program would be

```
Testing strlib functions.

Testing string_equal.
Enter two different words several times,
and then two identical words.

Enter the first word: Mark
Enter the second word: Mary
Enter the first word: Janice
Enter the second word: Mary
Enter the first word: Mary
Enter the second word: Mary
Testing make_uppercase.
MARY
Testing is_integer.
Enter several bad representations of integers, and then a good one.
```

```
Enter an integer: 34.5
The integer is 34.5
Enter an integer: 67.4
The integer is 67.4
Enter an integer: 21
The integer is 21
Testing to_integer.
Enter several good representations of integers, and then a bad one.
Enter an integer: 16
The integer is 16
Enter an integer: 1034
The integer is 1034
Enter an integer: 4.6
Testing completed.
```

This little driver program tests the tools provided by our library. If there are syntax errors in the library file, the preprocessor will detect them before the file is included. The library file can be easily built and tested incrementally. A more complete version of our library is left as an exercise. Another library implementation, using a C++ class definition, is developed in Section 7.3.

EXERCISES 7.2

1. Add the other two string comparison functions, **string_less** and **string_greater**, to the library **strlib.cpp**.

2. Write separate string comparison functions for equal to, less than, and greater than that are not case sensitive.

3. Write a function **make_lowercase** that changes the uppercase letters in its string parameter to lowercase letters.

4. Write a character processing function, **isvowel**, that tests a character to determine whether or not it is a vowel. Use the function in a program to count the number of vowels in an input string.

5. Write a function **remove_punctuation** with one string parameter. The function should modify its parameter by removing the punctuation mark ('.', ',', '?', '!', ':', or ';') at the end of the string, if there is one.

6. Write a function **capitalize** with one string parameter. The function should modify its parameter by capitalizing its first letter and making all of the other letters lowercase.

7. Write a function **string_swap** that exchanges the values of two string variables.

8. Clients of our abstract string type would like to examine individual characters in strings, without having to perform array indexing. Write a function **nth_char** that takes two parameters, a string and the position of a desired character, and returns the character at the specified position in the string. Specify in the declaration that the position parameter must range from one to the length of the string, inclusive.

9. Write a function **append_char**. This function takes a string and a character as parameters. If there is room for the character in the string, the function places it after the last character (be sure to move the null character over, as well). If there is no room for the character in the string, the function does nothing.

10. The constant definition for the maximum length of all strings is located in the **strlib.h** file. This means that all applications that include this file will be restricted to the use of strings of this maximum size. Explain how you could place this definition in some other part of the system so that different applications could specify their own maximum sizes of strings.

A NOTE OF INTEREST

Why Computer Scientists Number Things from Zero to *N* – 1

In Chapter 1, we mentioned that C++ incorporates features of high-level programming languages that make programs easy to read, modify, and maintain, and features of low-level programming languages that give programmers control over the structure and behavior of real computers. The numbering of array indices from zero rather than one is one of the low-level features of the language that calls for further comment.

An array index is numbered from zero in C++ because of the way in which the individual array cells are represented and accessed in the computer's memory. You can think of the computer's memory as a huge stack of cells or little boxes. Each cell has an address, which allows the computer to locate it and either fetch data from it or store data in it. Now, suppose that five of these cells have to be allocated for a new array variable in a program. The computer locates the next available contiguous block of five cells, and copies the address of the first cell into a sixth cell. This address will be the *base address* of the entire array. Suppose this base address is 276 in our example, and a programmer wishes to store data in the second cell of the array. The address of the second cell, or 277, can be computed by taking the base address of the array, or 276, from the sixth cell and adding 1 to it. The address of the third cell can be obtained by adding 2 to the base address, the address of the fourth cell by adding 3, and so on. In general, the address of the Nth cell in an array can be computed by adding $N - 1$ to the base address. The value $N - 1$ is called the *offset* of the Nth cell from the base address. The offset of the first cell in any array is zero, and the offset of the last cell is $N - 1$, where N is the total number of cells in the array.

There is also a more important reason why an array index is numbered from zero. The address of the first cell in the entire memory of a computer typically is zero. The address of the last cell in memory is then $N - 1$, where N is

the total number of cells in memory. You might think that computer scientists are a weird bunch, having set up computer systems so that their internal components are numbered in a way that is consistently off by one from the way that ordinary folks would number them. However, there is a very good reason to number things from zero to $N - 1$ in computers. Each address must itself be capable of being stored in a memory cell in the computer. As you know, a memory cell can store a number of finite size. The size of the number represented depends on the number of bits available in the memory cell. In general, numbers ranging from zero to $2^N - 1$ can be stored in a memory cell containing N bits. For example, numbers ranging from zero to 255 and representing the ASCII character set can be stored in eight-bit memory cells.

Most computer scientists agree that it would be better to number an array index from one to N in a high-level programming language. This notation would be more intuitive and agree with common sense. Some languages, like Pascal, allow the programmer to specify the lowest and highest index values when an array type is defined, and a Pascal programmer typically will define an index from one to N. The compiler then takes care of translating a reference like `a[1]` to the underlying machine address `a[0]`.

You might then ask why the designers of C++ still made array indexing a low-level feature of the language. The reason is that programmers can then manipulate arrays not just with standard indexing, but with *pointer arithmetic*. Assume the reference `a[1]` in C++ adds 1 to the base address of the array `a`. Then the reference `a` by itself is to the base address of the array. Therefore, the reference `*(a + 1)` locates the same array cell in memory as the reference `a[1]`. Needless to say, pointer arithmetic is an even lower level feature of C++ than regular indexing, and is not recommended for novices!

7.3   Recasting the String Type as a Class

Abstract Data Types and Data Security

Viewed as an abstract data type, the string type developed in the preceding sections consists of a set of high-level operations, such as copying, input, output, comparisons, and concatenation. Viewed as a C++ implementation, the string type consists of a **typedef** and several C++ function definitions. Some of these definitions are provided in the C++ library **string.h**, while we have created the others in a library **strlib.h**. Though this implementation of the string ADT is quite useful, it is not ideal. The primary problem is that the data in the implementation are not secure. There are too many ways in which client modules can access the data and cause side effects. For example, the length of a given string should change only as a result of running string processing functions with it, typically with code like

```
string greeting;              // Length of the
                              // string is 0 here.

strcpy(greeting, "Hi");       // Length of the
                              // string is 2 here.

strcat(greeting, " There!");  // Length of the
                              // string is 9 here.
```

Given the scope rules of C++, nothing prevents the user of this module from removing the null character, `'\0'`, which marks the end of the data in the string, from its current position in the array. The following line of code does just that:

```
greeting[strlen(greeting)] = ' ';   // Substitute ' ' for
                                     // '\0' in string.
```

Because the null character has been overwritten in the array, the length of the string is now undefined. Many of the string processing functions will no longer operate as expected with this string.

Errors due to side effects in large software systems are usually more subtle than this one. But the problem is quite general. What we would like to do is to develop a way of writing a software module that restricts the access that users have to the module's data to just those operations or functions provided by the module. Program comments, warnings, and self-imposed restraint are not enough: These restrictions must be imposed by the compiler of the programming language. In other words, statements such as the last one should be prohibited outside of the module that implements the data structure.

Data Encapsulation and Classes

An ADT should give clients just a *logical view* of the data, in terms of the operations on it, so that clients need not be concerned with the details of how the data are *represented*. For example, a string ADT might have operations for assignment, output, input, and comparisons. Ideally, the user of a string should not be able to access its component parts except by invoking these operations. If this is the case, the data are said to be *encapsulated*. Clearly, if we can encapsulate the data within modules, then we can control the kind of communication among modules that causes errors in large software systems, and we will be less likely to disturb other modules during the maintenance of a given module.

C++ allows programmers to define ADTs as *classes*. By defining an ADT as a class, we can restrict the access that clients have to the data of any objects or *instances* of that class. An instance of a class or an object is like an intelligent agent that takes a request for a service from a client and processes its own internal data to carry out the request.

We now show how to define and implement strings as a class. Since this is your first opportunity to define and implement a C++ class, do not expect to master all of the details right away. We will develop other ADTs as classes in later chapters, and we will use the string class developed here in the rest of the text.

Declaring a String Class

At a minimum, the string class should provide clients with the following operations:

1. Create string objects and name them with variables.
2. Input data into a string object.
3. Output a string object.
4. Copy the contents of a string object to another string object.
5. Compare two string objects for the standard relationships of equality, etc.
6. Examine the current length of a string object.
7. Examine the character at a given position in a string object.
8. Append a character to the end of a string object.

As in Section 1, these operations should be specified more formally, in terms of their preconditions and postconditions. For example, the **append** operation should assume that the current length of the string is less than the maximum number of characters that can be stored in a string. The ADT can enforce conditions, where necessary, by invoking the C++ **assert** function introduced in Chapter 5. The development of these specifications is left as an exercise.

A description of an individual class in C++ consists of two parts, a *declaration section* and an *implementation section,* which are usually placed in separate files. This arrangement resembles the one we used in Section 7.2 for constructing a new library. The first file for our string class, called **strlib.h**, contains the declaration section of the class. Its text appears as follows:

```
// Class declaration file: strlib.h

#ifndef STRLIB_H

#include <iostream.h>

#include "boolean.h"

// Declaration section

const int MAX_STRING_SIZE = 21;

class string
{

    public:

    // Class constructors

    string();
    string(const char str[MAX_STRING_SIZE]);
    string(const string &str);

    // Member functions

    int length();
    char nth_char(int n);
```

```
        void append_char(char ch);
        boolean operator == (const string &str);
        boolean operator < (const string &str);
        boolean operator > (const string &str);
        boolean operator <= (const string &str);
        boolean operator >= (const string &str);
        boolean operator != (const string &str);
        string& operator = (const char str[MAX_STRING_SIZE]);
        string& operator = (const string &str);
        friend istream& operator >> (istream &is, string &str);
        friend ostream& operator << (ostream &os, const string &str);

    private:

    // Data members

    char data[MAX_STRING_SIZE];

};


#define STRLIB_H
#endif
```

The general form for writing a simple class declaration section in C++ is

```
<preprocessor directives>
<constant definitions>
class <class name>
{
        public:
        <public data declarations>
        <public function declarations>
        private:
        <private data declarations>
        <private function declarations>
};
```

Several items call for further comment:

1. The data and the functions belonging to a class are called its *members*. The data are sometimes called *data members*, and the functions are sometimes called *member functions*.
2. *Public* members can be used directly by the client of the class. They should be restricted to the minimum necessary to serve a client.
3. *Private* members cannot be used directly by a client. Private member functions may be invoked indirectly by invoking public member functions, and private member data may be accessed indirectly by invoking public member functions.
4. The declarations of the member functions look exactly like the declarations of other functions in C++.
5. A semicolon must follow the right curly brace at the end of the declaration part of the class.

6. Note that the single data member declared in the string class declaration, **data**, is an array of characters. This is just the representation that we used in Section 7.1, but now the array and its components will not be directly accessible to clients.

Implementing a String Class

For the implementation of the string class, we will borrow some ideas about representing the character data in a string from the array implementation in Section 7.1. By doing this, our new implementation can continue to draw on and benefit from the string operations provided by the C++ library **string.h**.

The string class implementation section will have the form

```
// Class implementation file: strlib.cpp
// Implementation section
#include <string.h>
#include <ctype.h>
#include <assert.h>
#include "strlib.h"
<function implementation 1>
.

.
<function implementation n>
```

The headings of the function implementations must have the form

```
<return type> <class name>::<function name> (<optional parameter list>)
```

This form enables the compiler to resolve conflicts with the names of other, globally defined functions. Otherwise, data declarations and function implementations have the same syntax as those you have already seen in C++.

Creating Instances of a String Class with Class Constructors

Instances of a class, or objects, can be created in C++ in several ways. We can declare one or more instances as variables. If no *class constructors* are provided in the class declaration, the computer creates the named instances and leaves their data members in an unpredictable state, just as with ordinary C++ variable declarations. To guarantee that new instances of a class always have their data members initialized, you should specify class constructors for that purpose.

Default Class Constructors

Our string class declaration specifies three class constructors. The first constructor, **string()**, is run when a program declares string variables as in the following code:

```
string first_name, last_name;
```

This kind of class constructor is called a *default class constructor*. It should provide a reasonable initial value for an object when the client does not specify one. In this case, clients want the two strings that are to be initialized to be empty. Thus, the implementation of the default constructor function should set the first character in the array data member to the null character:

```
string::string()
{
        data[0] = '\0';
}
```

Note that the implementer references the array data member, **data**, for the string object even though it is not visible as a parameter. The use of the prefix **string**:: in a function heading allows the data and other member functions of the string class to be visible in the function implementation. Note also that the class constructor has no return type.

Class Constructors for Specifying Initial Values

The second constructor, **string(const char str[MAX_STRING_SIZE])**, is run when clients wish to declare a string variable with an initial string value, as in the code

```
string name("John Doe");
```

In this example, the client appears to pass a string literal as a parameter to the variable **name**. What really happens is that the computer runs the second constructor function. This function expects a *constant parameter,* which represents the parameter passing mode of string literals in C++. The implementation of this constructor invokes the **strcpy** function to copy the string literal into the data member for the new string object:

```
string::string(const char str[MAX_STRING_SIZE])
{
        strcpy(data, str);
}
```

Copy Constructors

The third constructor is called the *copy constructor* for the string class. The computer runs this function automatically whenever a string object is passed by value as a parameter to a function. Recall that when C++ passes data by value in a parameter, the data value is copied to a temporary memory location for the use of the function. If a class does not specify its own copy constructor, the computer performs what is known as a *shallow copy* of the object when it is passed by value. In a shallow copy, not all of the object's data members are necessarily copied into temporary memory locations.

To guarantee a complete copy in all situations, we define a copy constructor that takes another string object as a parameter:

```
string::string(const string &str)
{
        strcpy(data, str.data);
}
```

The parameter, a string object, is passed by *constant reference.* This mode of passing parameters combines the efficiency of pass by reference with the safety of pass by value. Though the address of the actual parameter will be passed when the function is called, the compiler will not permit the data in the parameter to be modified. The data member of the new string object, called the *receiver object,* is the first parameter to **strcpy**. The data member of the string object to be copied, called the *parameter object,* is accessed by the expression **str.data**. In general, any of the data members of a parameter like this one can be accessed within a member function in the class implementation by using the form

.<data member name>

Processing Instances of a String Class

Once a string object has been created and initialized, clients can process it by using any public member function. For example, the following code appends the character 's' to a string initialized as "rose":

```
string flower("rose");

flower.append_char('s');
```

Note that the dot notation is used again with an object. In this case, we run a member function by prefixing the object's name and a dot to it. The general form for this operation, called *sending a message to an object,* is

<object name>.<public member function name>(<parameter list>);

The **append_char** member function first uses **assert** to verify that its preconditions are TRUE. Then it adds the character parameter and the null character to the end of the object receiving the message:

```
void string::append_char(char ch)
{
        int length = strlen(data);

        assert(length < MAX_STRING_SIZE - 1);
        data[length] = ch;
        data[length + 1] = '\0';
}
```

Note that unlike the constructor functions, the **append_char** function specifies a return type, **void**, in its implementation. In general, the headings of the function implementations must match up with the declarations in the class declaration module. The implementation of the **length** and **nth_char** member functions is left as an exercise.

String Operators, Polymorphism, and Overloading

Many of the built-in operators in C++ are *polymorphic.* The term *polymorphic* means "many structures." For example, +, ==, and >> are polymorphic for integers and real numbers. This means that the same operators designate the same general operations (arithmetic, comparions, input/output), even though the actual operations performed may vary with the type or structure of the operands (think of the difference between scanning input characters and converting them to an integer and doing the same thing for a real number, even though the symbol >> is used for both).

C++ allows a programmer to reuse any built-in operator (or function name, also) to designate an operation on new data types. This process is called *overloading an operation.* For example, rather than use the named function

```
string_equal(str1, str2)
```

clients can use

```
str1 == str2
```

We begin by specifying the declaration of the member function to be overloaded:

```
boolean operator == (const string &str);
```

Note that **operator** is a reserved word in C++. The receiver object will be the left operand of the comparison, and the parameter object will serve as the right operand. The general form for specifying operators is

```
<return type> operator <standard operator symbol> (<parameter list>);
```

The implementation is written by placing a similar form in the function heading:

```
boolean string::operator == (const string &str)
{
        return strcmp(data, str.data) == 0;
}
```

Note that the implementation makes use of the **strcmp** function introduced in Section 7.1.

The operators <=, >=, <, >, and != can all be used to designate and implement the other comparison functions specified in the class declaration module. These functions will have roughly the same form as the one we have developed here, and the implementations are left as exercises.

The string class declaration module specifies two different member functions for assignment:

```
string& operator = (const string &str);
string& operator = (const char str[MAX_STRING_SIZE]);
```

The first one allows assignments of one string variable to another, whereas the second one allows assignments of string literals to string variables. The assignment operator in C++ should normally return an *l-value.* An l-value is an object that can be the target of an assignment operation in C++. In the case of simple assignment statements such as **a = b**;, the l-value returned by the operation is not used. However, in the case of a *cascade* of assignments, such as **(a = b) = c**;, the expression **(a = b)** must return an l-value that can serve as the target of the value **c**. In this case, the l-value returned should be **a**.

For this mechanism to work correctly, the return type of an assignment operator should be a reference to the class of the target object. The return type for our assignment operator for strings is therefore specified as **string&**. The implementations of each assignment operation are similar, but not exactly the same:

```
string& string::operator = (const string &str)
{
        strcpy(data, str.data);
        return *this;
}

string& string::operator = (const char str[MAX_STRING_SIZE])
{
        strcpy(data, str);
        return *this;
}
```

The effect of the first line of code in each implementation should be obvious to you by now. In the first case, we access the parameter object's data member to copy the source string to the receiver string. In the second case, we copy the parameter, a string literal, directly. The effect of the second line of code is to return the receiver object. The reserved word **this** always refers to the address of the receiver object. To gain access within the return statement to the object itself, we apply the *dereference operator* (*) to **this**. The receiver object will be returned as an l-value because the return type is specified as a reference to a class.

Friends of a Class

The other operators that we wish to reuse for the string class are <<, the inserter for output streams, and >>, the extractor for input streams. Instead of code like

```
word.input();
word.output();
cout << endl;
```

we would like to see code like this:

```
cin >> word;
cout << word << endl;
```

Reusing these operators will cause us to extend the definitions in the built-in stream classes in C++. First, we must locate the classes where the operators are already defined. The inserter belongs to the **ostream** class, and the extractor belongs to the **istream** class. These two classes define, respectively, the abstract behavior of all output streams and all input streams in C++. The class **ofstream** (for output files) inherits behavior from **ostream**, the class **ifstream** (for input files) inherits behavior from **istream**, and the class **iostream** (for keyboard and screen) inherits behavior from both **ostream** and **istream**. The class hierarchy diagram in Figure 7.4 depicts the relationships among the stream classes. Some careful changes will allow us to use these operators for both interactive and file

◆ FIGURE 7.4
Class hierarchy diagram of some stream classes

input and output of our string objects. Operations on file streams are discussed in detail in Chapter 9.

There should be files for the **ostream** and **istream** classes somewhere in your C++ implementation. We could add our new definitions of the operators to these files, but that would not be a good design tactic. Modifying a standard C++ library file reduces the portability of a software system, in that these modifications will also have to be made to the corresponding library on any other computer system. Instead, C++ provides a means of overloading an operator from a client class (the stream class, in this case) from within a server's (the string class's) module. This is known as *becoming a friend of a class*. To accomplish this, we prefix the declaration of a member function in the server class with the reserved word **friend**. For example, to reuse the inserter operator of the **ostream** class we write the following declaration:

```
friend ostream& operator << (ostream &os, const string &str);
```

The are two things to note about this declaration.

1. The expression **ostream&** means "address of a stream." This is the type of object returned by the stream operators. Its purpose is to serve as a receiver or l-value for the next message sent in a cascade of messages in a statement, such as

```
cout << "Hi" << " there!" << endl;.
```

2. An output stream and a string are passed as parameters to the operator.

The implementation of our extractor accesses the data in the string parameter's array representation and sends it to the output stream parameter:

```
ostream& operator << (ostream &os, const string &str)
{
        os << str.data;
        return os;
}
```

Note that the built-in function designated by the inserter (output an array of characters) is used to implement a new function designated by the inserter (output a string object). One benefit of using << in our implementation is that we do not need to learn anything new about output streams in order to add a new class of objects to those that can be output. Moreover, the use of << allows this behavior to be valid for either output file streams (see Chapter 9) or the standard output stream (the screen).

The extractor operator receives similar treatment. We first declare an extractor that is a friend for the **istream** class:

```
friend istream& operator >> (istream &is, string &str);
```

The implementation of our extractor uses >> to read characters from the stream into the string parameter's array representation.

```
istream& operator >> (istream &is, string &str)
{
        is >> str.data;
        return is;
}
```

In general, when a particular member function of a server class (like our string class) is qualified as a **friend** for a client class (the stream classes in our example), the data and member functions of the server class become accessible to the client class within the implementation of the member function in question.

EXAMPLE 7.8

The following program uses the string class that we have just developed to place two input strings in alphabetical order and output them.

```
// Program file: alphabet.cpp

#include <iostream.h>

#include "boolean.h"

#include "strlib.h"

int main()
{
        string word1, word2, temp;

        cout << "Enter the first word: ";
        cin >> word1;
        cout << "Enter the second word: ";
        cin >> word2;
        if (word1 > word2)
        {
                temp = word1;
                word1 = word2;
                word2 = temp;
        }
        cout << word1 << " " << word2 << endl;
        return 0;
}
```

Classes Versus typedefs

We are now in a position to assess the alternatives of representing a string type with a **typedef** or as a class. First, we summarize the benefits of using **typedef**:

1. We can define a new string type and the associated high-level operations quickly, using techniques we already understand well.
2. Because the representation of a string type as an array is compatible with the representation used in standard C++ stream and string libraries, many high-level operations are already available for our new type.

There is only one apparent cost of using **typedef** to define a string type. The representation of a string is globally defined. Therefore, the representation is unprotected from indiscriminate use by clients.

The most apparent benefit of defining a string type as a class is that the representation is protected. The access of clients to data is limited to operations specified by the string class. The cost of using classes is having to learn some new syntax.

A NOTE OF INTEREST

Pure and Hybrid Object-Oriented Languages

It is possible to classify programming languages in terms of the degree to which they possess object-oriented features. Older languages like FORTRAN, C, and standard Pascal have no object-oriented features at all. None of them supports classes, user-defined polymorphic operators, data encapsulation, or message passing.

Smalltalk and Eiffel purport to be object-oriented languages in a "pure" sense. In these languages, every data type is a class. All data values, including classes themselves, are objects. All subprograms and operators can be overloaded. Data can be fully encapsulated. Every operation on data comes about as a result of a message being sent to an object.

A third class of languages is a hybrid of object-oriented languages and older languages. Many of these are the older languages themselves, with object-oriented features grafted on. For example, C++ is an extension of C. Most current implementations of Pascal have object-oriented extensions. CLOS, or Common LISP Object System, is an object-oriented extension that comes with almost every Common LISP package.

The difference between hybrid languages and the pure object-oriented languages is that it is possible to write programs in a hybrid language that omit the object-oriented features entirely. For example, one could write a large program, or even a large software system consisting of many library modules, in C++ that would be indistinguishable from a C program. This possibility has led to a debate in the computer science community concerning the desirability of hybrid languages.

Proponents of the pure object-oriented languages argue that the object-oriented approach has superceded more traditional styles of programming. Therefore, one should use a language that enforces the superior approach, rather than a language that allows drift or slippage into inferior

approaches. Moreover, proponents claim that the pure languages are better vehicles for training new computer scientists, because they enforce object-oriented thinking from the very beginning.

Proponents of the hybrid languages offer several counters to these points. First, it is not clear that object orientation is the best or most natural way to approach all problems. For example, problems in numerical analysis may find more natural solutions in terms of systems of functions, calling for a function-oriented approach. The notion of sending a message to a number to add one to itself seems somewhat silly from this perspective. A hybrid language offers object orientation as one possible approach, among others, that can be chosen when it is the most natural alternative.

Second, although object orientation might be the best possible approach to the design and maintenance of large software systems, smaller programs might be more easily designed and written using traditional techniques of structured programming.

Finally, a pure object-oriented language may not be the best vehicle for teaching programming. Beginning programmers start with simple problems, but pure object-oriented languages do not rest on a simple model of computation. Beginning programmers need to learn about the structure and behavior of real computers, about concepts such as memory, the distinction between an address and a data value, branching, and subprogram calls. Pure object-oriented languages tend to insulate a programmer from these features of real machines.

We suggest that you study and try out several of these languages, if they are available, and make your own judgments about the relative virtues of pure object-oriented and hybrid programming languages.

This assessment applies to the choice of **typedef** or class for representing any abstract data type. In general, the benefit of security achieved with encapsulation in classes far outweighs the cost of learning the new syntax. A hidden benefit, which does not appear in our discussion of the string class, is that once a class has been developed, it can be very quickly specialized to create new abstract data types. We will see examples of this power in later chapters.

EXERCISES 7.3

1. Write complete formal specifications for the string class operations listed at the beginning of this section.

2. Implement all the string operations specified by the class declaration, and test the string class with the program from Example 7.8.

3. Describe the difference between the references to **data** and **str.data** in operations like **strcpy(data, str.data)** in the string class implementation.

4. Try to access the data member **data** of a string object in a C++ program, and explain what happens.

5. One could reimplement the auxiliary string processing functions discussed in Section 7.2 either as top-level C++ functions [for example, **is_integer(<string object>)**] or as string member functions [for example, **<string object>.is_integer()**]. Try each of these alternatives in a C++ program, and discuss the advantages and disadvantages of each version.

FOCUS ON PROGRAM DESIGN

Good writing style traditionally has emphasized short to medium-length words and sentences. An important part of text evaluation is obtaining statistics on word and sentence length. This kind of computation is now a standard tool provided with word processing packages. Let us design a small text analysis system that works on individual sentences entered at the keyboard. The program will proceed interactively as follows:

1. The user is prompted for a sentence, which is a series of words ending with a word that is terminated by a period ('.').
2. The system computes and displays statistics about the number of words in the sentence and the average length of a word. It also displays the longest word in the sentence.
3. The user is asked whether another input is desired with a yes/no prompt. If the answer is 'Y', the program repeats steps 1 and 2, and if 'N', the program terminates.

The top-level module runs a simple query driver loop:

> **Module:** Main program
> Do
>> Prompt for a sentence
>> Analyze a sentence
>> Query for further input
> While query does not equal 'N'

Here is a C++ main program that represents this main program module:

```
int main()
{
    char query;
    do
    {
        cout << "Enter a sentence [terminating with a period ('.')]: ";
        analyze_sentence();
        cout << "Run once more? [Y/N]: ";
        cin >> query;
    } while ((query == 'Y') || (query == 'y'));
    return 0;
}
```

The module to analyze a sentence is responsible for taking input from the keyboard computing the statistics, and displaying them. This process can be described by a loop that reads individual words from the keyboard, until a word terminated by a period is entered:

Module: Analyze a sentence
Task: Read words from keyboard and update statistics, until word ending with '.' is reached

Initialize the data
Do
Input a word
Update the statistics
While the word does not end with '.'
Display the statistics

The statistics will consist of the number of words, the total number of characters in the words, the average length of a word, and the longest word in the sentence. Therefore, this module will need two integer variables and two string variables to maintain the data. The integer data are locally declared, initialized to 0, and simply passed to the other modules for further processing:

```
void analyze_sentence()
{
        string word, longest_word;
        int word_count, char_count;

        word_count = 0;
        char_count = 0;
        do
        {
                cin >> word;
                update_statistics(word, longest_word, word_count, char_count);
        } while (word.nth_char(word, word.length()) != '.');
        display_statistics(longest_word, word_count, char_count);
}
```

The module for updating the statistics is responsible for increasing the count of characters and words, and changing the value of the longest word if necessary.

Module: Update statistics
Task: Adjust character count and word count and adjust longest word if necessary
Inputs: The current input word, the longest word so far, word count, character count

If the length of current input word > length of longest word so far then
        Set longest word so far to current input word
Increment the word count by one
Increment the character count by the length of the input word

Updating statistics compares the length of the current input word to the length of the longest word seen so far. If the new word is longer, it becomes the longest word.

```
void update_statistics(string word, string &longest_word, int &word_count,
    int &char_count)
{
    int length = word.length();

    if (length > longest_word.length())
        longest_word = word;
    ++word_count;
    char_count = char_count + length;
}
```

The display of statistics module computes the average length of a word as a function of the word count and the character count. Then it displays the labeled statistics on the terminal screen:

```
void display_statistics(string longest_word, int word_count, int char_count)
{
    cout << endl << "Number of words: " << word_count << endl;
    cout << "Number of characters: " << char_count << endl;
    cout << "Average length of a word: " << char_count / word_count << endl;
    cout << "Longest word: " << longest_word << endl << endl;
}
```

Our program will use the string class library developed in this chapter. The main C++ program is

```
// Program file: stats.cpp

#include <iostream.h>

#include "boolean.h"

#include "strlib.h"

// <function declarations>

void main()
{
    char query;
    do
    {
        cout << "Enter a sentence [terminating with a period ('.')]: ";
        analyze_sentence();
        cout << "Run once more? [Y/N]: ";
        cin >> query;
    } while ((query == 'Y') || (query == 'y'));
}

// <function implementations>
```

RUNNING, DEBUGGING AND TESTING HINTS

1. When defining a string type as an array of characters, always leave room for the null character in the array. The maximum size of an array should therefore be one greater than the number of characters allowed in a string.
2. Make sure that there is room in a string variable for storing character data. For example, the lengths of the two string parameters should be examined before they are passed to the **strcat** function. If the sum of their lengths is less than the maximum size of the string type, then the function can be run safely.
3. When using array indexing to access characters in a string, be careful to avoid range bound errors. In general, a safe array index value is an integer ranging from 0 to one less than the size of the array.
4. Do not use the & symbol when defining string parameters (implemented as arrays) for a function. Array parameters are automatically passed by reference anyway.
5. Be sure to account for case sensitivity when designing string processing programs. For example, the string "Jane" is not the same as the string "jane". Use a case conversion function if case sensitivity should be disabled.
6. Try to run potentially expensive functions, like **strlen**, outside of loops.

SUMMARY

Key Terms

array indexing	constant reference	member function
array of characters	copy constructor	null character
cascade	data member	overloading
class	encapsulation	polymorphism
class constructor	friend of a class	range bound error
class declaration section	header file	receiver object
class implementation section	implementation file	server
client	index	software reuse
concatenate	instance	stream class hierarchy
constant parameter	l-value	string literal

Key Words

class	**private**	**this**
friend	**public**	

Key Concepts

◆ Data abstraction is the process of separating a conceptual definition of a data structure from its implementation details.
◆ An abstract data type (ADT) consists of a class of objects, a defined set of properties for the objects, and a set of operations for processing the objects.
◆ Strings can be treated as abstract data by defining a string type with **type-def**, as follows:

```
const int MAX_STRING_SIZE = 21;
typedef char string[MAX_STRING_SIZE];
```

◆ Variables and function parameters can then be declared by using the string type, as follows:

```
string last_name, first_name;

boolean string_equal(string str1, string str2);
```

◆ A number of high-level operations on strings are already available in the C++ libraries **string.h** and **iostream.h**. Software should be reused in this way wherever possible.

◆ The standard input and output operators, << and >>, can be used for interactive input and output of strings. Where **word** is a string variable, the statements

```
cin >> word;
cout << word << endl;
```

would take input of a string from the keyboard and echo it on the terminal screen.

◆ The library function **strcpy** can be used to assign or copy the contents of a string to a string variable. The library function **strlen** returns the number of characters currently in a string variable. Where **word** is a string variable, the statements

```
strcpy(word, "Hello");
cout << strlen(word) << endl;
```

would display 5 on the terminal screen.

◆ The null character (**'\0'**) normally marks the end of the characters currently stored in a string variable. The standard library functions make use of this sentinel character.

◆ If strings are represented as arrays of characters, we can use array indexing to access individual characters at selected positions in the strings. Where **str1** and **str2** are strings defined in this way, the assignment

```
str2[0] = str1[0]
```

copies the character at the first position in **str1** to the first position in **str2**.

◆ The loop

```
for (int index = 0; index <= strlen(str1); ++index)
    str2[index] = str1[index];
```

would copy all of the characters, including the null character, in **str1** to **str2**.

◆ Where **word** is a string variable, the loop

```
for (int index = 0; index <strlen(word); ++index)
    cout << word[index];
```

would display all of the characters in the string variable before the null

◆ Libraries for abstract data types can be created by specifying a header file and an implementation file.

◆ Multiple inclusions of a library file can be avoided by using the **#ifndef**, **#define**, and **#endif** preprocessor directives in the library header file, as follows:

```
#ifndef <file identifier>

<constant and type definitions>

<function declarations>

#define <file identifier>
#endif
```

◆ A class declaration specifies the public and private data and function members for a class of objects.

◆ A class implementation provides the implementations of the member functions for a class of objects.

◆ Polymorphic operators have the same general meaning, but can be used with data of different types or classes.

◆ A polymorphic operator can be reused by declaring a member function as an **operator**.

◆ A polymorphic operator an also be reused by declaring a function member to be a **friend** of the class in which the operator is defined.

PROGRAMMING PROBLEMS AND PROJECTS

1. Write and test a function, **robust_read_int**, that handles the problem of bad digits in integer input from the keyboard. The function should read the data as a string and test it for bad digits. If all of the digits are valid, the function converts the string representation to an integer value and returns it. Otherwise, the function displays an error message, prompts for new input, and repeats the process until a valid integer is successfully entered. The function should use string library functions wherever possible.

2. Add a parameter to **robust_read_int** from Problem 1 that serves as the prompt to the user for new input. Test the function with prompts from several different applications, such as "Enter the person's age:" or "Enter the number of computers sold:".

3. Write and test a function, **robust_read_float**, that performs the same kind of error handling as **robust_read_int** (Problems 1 and 2), but detects bad digits in real numbers. The function should return a **float** value (remember that C++ allows integers to be assigned to **float** variables).

4. Write and test a program that determines whether or not input strings are palindromes. A palindrome is a string that reads the same forward or backward. Run the program on palidromes such as "TOT" and "MADAMIMADAM", and on strings that are not palindromes, such as "STRING".

5. Write a program that counts the number of times a given word appears in a sentence. The inputs from the keyboard are a given word, and then a sentence, which is a series of words ending in a word that ends with a period ('.'). The program should not be case sensitive.

6. Write a Boolean function, **proper_name**, that tests a string to see whether or not it is a proper name. A proper name begins with an uppercase letter.

7. Write a function, **make_adverb**, that takes a string variable as a parameter. The function assumes that the string represents an adjective. The function should change the string to an adverb by concatenating the string "ly" with it.

8. Write a function, **make_plural**, that takes a string as a parameter. The function assumes that the string represents a noun. If the string ends in 's', the function

changes it to the plural form by adding 'es' to it; otherwise, the function constructs the plural form by simply adding 's'.

9. Write a function, **strip_punctuation**, that removes a trailing punctuation mark from a string if one exists.

10. Write a function, **our_copy**, that performs the same operation as **strcpy** (but does not use **strcpy!**).

11. Write a function, **search_char**, that takes a string variable and a character value as parameters. The function returns an integer value. This value should be -1 if the character parameter does not occur anywhere in the string. Otherwise, this value should be the position (counting from 0) of the first instance of the character in the string.

12. Write a function, **position_copy**, that takes a string variable and two integer values, **low** and **high**, as input parameters. The function returns a string variable as an output parameter. This output string parameter should contain the portion of the input string that lies between the two integer inputs. You can assume that the user of the function will pass two integer values that are in the relationship

    0 <= low <= high < length of string.

13. Write a function, **substring**, that takes two string variables as input parameters. If the second string parameter is a substring within the first string parameter, the function returns as its value an integer denoting the starting position of the first occurrence of the substring in the other string. Otherwise, the function returns -1, to indicate that there were no occurrences of the substring in the other string.

Building Structured Data with Classes and Objects

The first seven chapters of this text have acquainted you with a wide range of tools and techniques for programming and problem solving in C++. The first set of tools is the fundamental operations of arithmetic, assignment, input, and output. The second set of tools consists of the control structures of selection and looping. The third set of tools represents the abstraction mechanisms of functions and data structures and the techniques of structured programming and modular design. You now have the means to design, implement, and test correct, efficient, readable, and maintainable programs that solve interesting problems.

Nevertheless, through the study and development of large and complex software systems over the years, computer scientists have come to the conclusion that the techniques and tools that we have discussed are far from adequate for dealing with the challenges of building these systems. In this chapter, we will discuss how a relatively new method of software development, called *object-oriented programming,* can be added to our arsenal of tools and techniques for problem solving. We begin with a discussion of the basic ideas of this philosophy. Then we introduce some simple examples in C++ that illustrate some of these ideas. Finally, we develop some typical data structures using object-oriented methods.

8.1 The Philosophy of Object-Oriented Programming

OBJECTIVES

- to understand the problems associated with software maintenance
- to understand the way in which reuse of software enhances software maintenance
- to become familiar with some basic terms of object-oriented programming

The Problem of Software Maintenance

Perhaps the most serious problem posed by a large software system is that of *maintaining* it over a period of years. After the initial release of a commercial system, users send complaints about errors and requests for additional features or functions to the developers almost immediately. Before a new version with corrections and additional features or functions can be released, the developers must search through the system to fix the errors and add or remove features or functions. They must do so in such a way as not to disturb other parts of the system that are already working correctly. Moreover, the developers must divide up the maintenance tasks so that they can work independently and efficiently. Finally, some of the developers who maintain the software may not have been on the original development team. All of these factors add time and cost to the maintenance of large software systems.

The tools and techniques of structured programming and modular design go part of the way toward easing the software maintenance task. For example, if an error occurs in a particular function of a system, a programmer might locate the error in a C++ function within a particular library file and be able to fix the problem by changing a single line of code within the function. If an error occurs while the system is using a particular data structure such as a linked list, a programmer might find and correct the problem in the C++ library file where the list processing functions are implemented.

In Chapter 7, we saw that another kind of error, a side effect, is more difficult to track down. Many side effects are caused by allowing clients too much access to the implementation of a module. We also saw that implementing a module as a class in C++ helps to control this kind of side effect by encapsulating or denying clients direct access to the data.

Reuse of Software

Another major factor that adds to the cost of software maintenance is the need to rewrite entire modules to add features or functions to a system. For example, suppose that a module already exists in a bank management system for processing checking accounts. Savings accounts resemble checking accounts to a certain extent, as do the functions for processing each kind of account. However, using conventional structured programming techniques, developers must add a completely new module with a different set of data type definitions and functions for savings accounts. Much of this code will not only be redundant, but may also contain errors.

Developers should be able to *reuse* existing software modules to build new ones. In the example of savings and checking accounts, a developer could write a module for handling the structure and behavior that all accounts have in common. Other developers could then *specialize* this module, with extra data or functions, for more specific kinds of accounts. By reusing software, developers can eliminate the redundancy and many of the errors that occur with more conventional methods. As we will see shortly, object-oriented programming provides a way of reusing software in this manner.

Basic Ideas and Terminology of Object-Oriented Programming

We need to become acquainted with some of the basic ideas and terminology of object-oriented programming before we look at some examples. According to this perspective, an *object* is a collection of *attributes* and *behavior*. The attributes of an object are defined by the data values that are stored in it. For example, the attributes of a student object might be a name ("John Doe"), a class (SOPHO-MORE), and a grade point average (3.56). The behavior of an object is defined by the set of *messages* to which it responds. For example, we might send a message to a list object requesting its current length. It would respond by returning its length as a value. Or we might send a message to a list to remove its first element. It would respond by deleting its first element, decrementing its own length, and returning the deleted element as a value. One or more parameters may also be sent with a message to an object. For example, a new element might be sent with a message to insert it into a list object. The list would respond by inserting the element into its proper place and incrementing its own length. If an object does not respond to a message sent to it, the system will halt with an error, preferably at compile time.

We can think of an object as a *server*, to which a user makes requests as a *client*. None of the data belonging to a server is accessible to a client, unless the client invokes a server-defined request to use or modify that data. In other words, the data belonging to an object is fully encapsulated. Figure 8.1 illustrates these concepts.

Each object is an instance of a class that defines its data and behavior. The user of an object obtains its services by creating an instance of its class and then

◆ **FIGURE 8.1**

Anatomy of objects as clients and servers

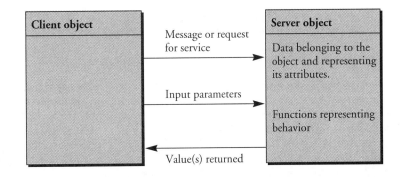

sending messages to this instance. The implementer of an object defines its services or behavior by defining the class to which the object belongs. An object that passes a message to another object is called the *sender* of the message; the object that receives the message is called the *receiver*.

The common behavior of several classes may be generalized by defining a *base class*. Each of the original, more specific classes can retain its own distinctive behavior as a *derived class*. Behavior can be added to a derived class to specialize it further, even if this behavior redefines the behavior already defined in the base class. The process of adding derived classes therefore allows developers to reuse existing software very easily.

As we saw in Chapter 7, the common behavior of several classes is also expressed by means of overloading the operations that define similar behavior. The operators that designate these operations are said to be *polymorphic,* or to have many forms. A polymorphic operator, such as <, really has one general meaning when used by clients: determine whether two objects are related by less than. But it can have more than one specific meaning when implemented by different server classes, such as integers and strings, which carry out different operations on different data representations to determine the relation.

The following sections illustrate the use of these ideas to develop reusable software modules in C++.

8.2 A Bank Account Class

Our first example of the design of a class comes from the domain of finance and data processing.

User Requirements

Consider the problem of managing bank accounts. Banks offer several different kinds of accounts, such as checking, checking with interest, passbook savings, and CD accounts, among others. Security is absolutely essential. We do not want Smith's deposit going into Jones's account, unless it is a joint account. Therefore, we would like to represent different but related classes of bank accounts, and do so in a way that protects the data belonging to each instance of an account.

We can start by thinking of an abstract class called **account**. This class will define the data that belong to any account object, and the behavior that any account object should exhibit. The data might be just a balance, represented by a **float**. The behavior might be expressed by messages to

1. Deposit an amount.
2. Withdraw an amount.
3. Look up the balance.

A NOTE OF INTEREST

The Origins of the Object-Oriented Philosophy

We saw in an earlier note of interest that a philosophy can serve as the underpinning of a new approach to problem solving and software design. Such was the case with function-oriented programming. This approach was the direct result of efforts of two computer scientists, John McCarthy and John Backus, to bring a certain formal theory of computation, the recursive lambda calculus, to bear on the design of complex software systems. The object-oriented approach to problem solving and software design has a different kind of origin. In this case, there is no single theory of computation we can point to as the model for the approach. Object orientation in languages, programming style, and thinking has evolved over time and is the result of diverse sources and trends that eventually converged on a single body of ideas. However, there is one computer scientist in whose vision these sources and trends

have been brought together. This scientist, Alan Kay, recounts the history of the development of the object-oriented philosophy in "The Early History of Smalltalk," *ACM SIGPLAN Notices*, Volume 28, No. 3, March, 1993. Some of the important sources in the development of the object-oriented approach were

Ivan Sutherland's work on an interactive graphical programming environment called *Sketchpad*.

The development of Simula, a language for representing classes of objects.

Kay's work on Smalltalk, the first complete environment for object-oriented software development.

The work of Douglas Engelbart, Daniel Ingalls, Kay, and others at Xerox on WIMP (window, icon, mouse, pull-down menu) user interfaces.

The first two messages would each take one **float** parameter representing the amount, and the object would return a **float** representing the updated balance. The third message would take no parameters, and the object would return a **float** representing the current balance of the account.

In addition to this behavior, clients should be able to create new account objects, either by specifying an initial value for the balance or by assuming that the object will initialize its own balance to 0.00. Clients should also be able to assign a bank account object to a bank account variable, and to pass a bank account parameter by value to a C++ function.

Specifying the Operations

A formal specification of the bank account operations follows:

Create operation (default value)
Preconditions: The account object is in an unpredictable state.
Postconditions: **balance** is set 0.00 in the account object.

Create operation (initial value specified)
Preconditions: The account object is in an unpredictable state, and the parameter **new_balance** is a real number representing the initial amount to be deposited into the account.
Postconditions: **balance** is set to **new_balance** in the account object.

Deposit operation
Preconditions: The receiver object is appropriately initialized, and **amount** is the amount (a real number) to be deposited.
Postconditions: **balance** is increased by **amount**, and its value is returned to the sender.

Withdraw operation
Preconditions: The receiver object is appropriately initialized, and **amount** is the amount (a real number) to be withdrawn.

Postconditions:	If there are sufficient funds, **balance** is decreased by **amount**, and its value is returned to the sender; otherwise, -1 is returned to the sender.
Get balance operation	
Preconditions:	The receiver object is appropriately initialized.
Postconditions:	**balance** is returned to the sender.
Assignment operation	
Preconditions:	The receiver and parameter objects are appropriately initialized.
Postconditions:	The attributes of the parameter object have been copied into the receiver object, and a reference to the receiver is returned.

Declaring the Class

Now that we are aware of the requirements and specifications of an abstract account class, we can implement it in C++. As we saw in Chapter 7, a description of an individual class in C++ usually consists of two parts, a declaration section and an implementation section, that are placed in separate files. The first file for our account class, named **account.h**, contains the declaration section of the class. Its text appears as follows:

```
// Class declaration file: account.h

#ifndef ACCOUNT_H

// Declaration section

class account
{

        public:

        // Class constructors

        account();
        account(float initial_balance);
        account(const account &a);

        // Member functions

        float deposit(float amount);
        float withdraw(float amount);
        float get_balance();
        account& operator = (const account &a);

        private:

        // Data members

        float balance;

};

#define ACCOUNT_H
#endif
```

Note that the copy constructor, which is the third class constructor declared here, was not included in the formal specifications. For every new class introduced in this text, we will assume that clients desire to have a copy constructor, and one will appear in each class declaration.

Implementing the Class

The second file, containing the implementation section of the class, is named `account.cpp`:

```cpp
// Class implementation file: account.cpp

#include "account.h"

// Implementation section

account::account()
{
        balance = 0.00;
}

account::account(float initial_balance)
{
        balance = initial_balance;
}

account::account(const account &a)
{
        balance = a.balance;
}

float account::deposit(float amount)
{
        balance = balance + amount;
        return balance;
}

float account::withdraw(float amount)
{
        if (amount > balance)
                return -1;
        else
        {
                balance = balance - amount;
                return balance;
        }
}

float account::get_balance()
{
        return balance;
}
```

```
account& account::operator = (const account &a)
{
        balance = a.balance;
        return *this;
}
```

EXAMPLE 8.1   The following program illustrates the use of the account class that we have just defined.

```
// Program file: bankdriv.cpp

#include <iostream.h>
#include <iomanip.h>

#include "account.h"

int main()
{
      account judy(50.00);                    // Set up two accounts and a dummy target
      account jim(100.00);
      account target;

      cout << fixed << showpoint << setprecision(2);
      cout << "Judy's balance = $"
           << judy.get_balance() << endl;                // Look up balances
      cout << "Jim's balance = $" << jim.get_balance() << endl;
      cout << "Depositing $20.00 to Jim, new balance = $" // A deposit
           << jim.deposit(20.00) << endl;
      cout << "Result of overdraft from Judy ($51.00) = " // An attempted overdraft
           << judy.withdraw(51.00) << endl;
      target = judy;                          // Copy to dummy target
      cout << "Target's balance = $" << target.get_balance() << endl;
      return 0;
}
```

The output that this program produces is

```
Judy's balance = $50.00
Jim's balance = $100.00
Depositing $20.00 to Jim, new balance = $120.00
Result of overdraft from Judy ($51.00) = -1.00
Target's balance = $50.00
```

Using the Class with Functions

There are many occasions for which we might want to include a class in a program and process its instances by means of functions. For example, consider the problem of interacting with the user for the input of the amount to withdraw from a bank account. We may already have an application that contains a set of user interface functions created for this purpose. Suppose that this program has represented accounts as real numbers, and we now wish to use our account class. The function for interacting with a user for a withdrawal might have looked like this:

```
typedef float account;
 .
 .
 .
void make_withdrawal(account &this_account)
{
        float amount;

        cout << "Enter the amount to withdraw: ";
        cin << amount;
        if ((amount > this_account) || (amount < 0))
                cout << "Sorry, insufficient funds." << endl;
        else
        {
                this_account = this_account - amount;
                cout << "Thank you. Your new balance is " << this_account << endl;
        }
}
```

Our new version can reuse this function by passing an account object as the parameter, and using member functions to perform the appropriate tasks:

```
void make_withdrawal(account &this_account)
{
        float amount;

        cout << "Enter the amount to withdraw: ";
        cin << amount;
        if ((amount > this_account.get_balance()) || (amount < 0))
                cout << "Sorry, insufficient funds." << endl;
        else
        {
                this_account.withdraw(amount);
                cout << "Thank you. Your new balance is "
                        << this_account.get_balance() << endl;
        }
}
```

An alternative to this approach is to make this function a member of the account class. Then it could be invoked as

```
this_account.make_withdrawal();
```

There are two problems with this second approach:

1. It makes more work for the developer, who must write new code for the account class rather than reuse existing code in the user interface module.
2. It makes application-specific components, such as the messages to the user in a particular context, part of a general class definition. This makes the account class less general and application independent than it should be.

As you can see, the processing of classes and their instances integrates very easily with the more conventional style of programming in C++. This feature enables developers to introduce objects and the object-oriented style into an existing software system without redesigning and rewriting the entire system.

Each of these exercises asks you to add attributes or behavior to the bank account class we have just discussed.

1. Add a data member for representing an account user's name, using the string class developed in Chapter 7. Add behavior so that each account is given a user's name when it is created.

2. Add a data member for representing a password, using the string class developed in Chapter 7. Add behavior so that each account is given a password when it is created.

3. Update the member function **get_balance**, **deposit**, and **withdraw** so that each takes a user name and password as parameters. Perform the expected operations only if the name and password sent by the client match the name and password data members of the account. Otherwise, do nothing.

4. Add a data member to maintain a record of the number of times a user has failed to enter the correct name and password. It should be set to zero when the account is created and whenever the user successfully makes a deposit, withdrawal, or balance check. It should be incremented whenever these operations are unsuccessful.

5. Add a **private** member function that is run when the number of failed transactions becomes greater than 3. It should print a message that the user's ATM card is being confiscated.

8.3 A Rational Number Class

OBJECTIVES

- to be able to design a numeric class whose use and behavior are compatible with the use and behavior of built-in numeric data types

- to understand the use of overloaded operations in designing a numeric class with conventional behavior

- to be able to use overloaded operations to implement mixed-mode operations on new classes and built-in data types

Our next example of the design of a class comes from pure mathematics, a different domain than that of finance and data processing. C++ has standard data types for representing real numbers and integers, but not rational numbers. In this section, we develop a new class, called **rational**, that allows applications to use rational numbers in much the same way as the other kinds of numbers are used.

User Requirements

A rational number has two attributes, a numerator and a denominator, both of which are integer values. One constructor operation for rational numbers should therefore take two integer parameters representing these attributes. For example, one might create the rational numbers 1/2 and 5/6 as follows:

```
rational one_half(1, 2);
rational five_sixths(5, 6);
```

The state of the objects representing these two numbers is depicted in Figure 8.2.
Because rational numbers are expressed in the form

$$\frac{numerator}{denominator}$$

definitions of the form

```
rational <name>(<integer>, 0);
```

should not be allowed. Therefore, a precondition of the class constructor is that the denominator can be any integer other than zero.

Clients should be able to perform some standard arithmetic operations on rational numbers and output the resulting values. For example, the following statement would output the sum of the two example numbers just defined to the screen:

```
cout << one_half + five_sixths << endl;
```

The output of this statement would be

4/3

Note that the sum of the two numbers is expressed in lowest terms.

◆ FIGURE 8.2

The state of two rational number objects

	one_half		five_sixths
numerator	1	numerator	5
denominator	2	denominator	6

Keyboard input of rational numbers would allow users to work with rational numbers interactively. To make the scanning of the input simple, we might require a definite format, such as

<integer>/<integer><enter key>

Assignment of one rational number to another should also be provided, in the form

<rational number variable> = <rational number object>

where **<rational number object>** is the value returned by an expression.

Finally, users of rational numbers would like to compare them for the standard relationships of equality, less than, and greater than. The following code is an example of the use of the equality operator with two rational numbers:

```
rational one_half(1, 2);
rational number;

cout << "Enter a rational number: ";
cin >> number;
if (number == one_half)
.
.
.
```

Note that we have provided a second class constructor that takes no initial values for the numerator and the denominator. This constructor is used to create rational number objects that will be targets of subsequent input or assignment operations. These numbers can be given a default initial value of 1/1.

Specifying the Operations

Now that the clients' requirements have been discussed, we can present a formal specification of the desired operations for rational numbers:

Create operation (default value)
Preconditions: The rational number is in an unpredictable state.
Postconditions: **numerator** is set to 1, and **denominator** is set to 1.

Create operation (initial value specified)

Preconditions: The rational number is in an unpredictable state, **new_numer** is an integer value, and **new_denom** is an integer value other than zero.

Postconditions: **new_numer/new_denom** is first reduced to lowest terms. Then **numerator** is set to **new_numer**, and **denominator** is set to **new_denom**.

Addition operation

Preconditions: Receiver and parameter objects are rational numbers appropriately initialized.

Postconditions: A rational number representing the sum of the two rational numbers is returned.

Subtraction operation

Preconditions: Receiver and parameter objects are rational numbers appropriately initialized.

Postconditions: A rational number representing the difference of the two rational numbers is returned.

Multiplication operation

Preconditions: Receiver and parameter objects are rational numbers appropriately initialized.

Postconditions: A rational number representing the product of the two rational numbers is returned.

Division operation

Preconditions: Receiver and parameter objects are rational numbers appropriately initialized, and the denominator of the parameter object does not equal zero.

Postconditions: A rational number representing the division of the two rational numbers is returned.

Equality operation

Preconditions: Receiver and parameter objects are rational numbers appropriately initialized.

Postconditions: The Boolean value TRUE is returned if the two rational numbers are equal, and FALSE is returned otherwise.

Assignment operation

Preconditions: Receiver and parameter objects are rational numbers appropriately initialized.

Postconditions: **numerator** and **denominator** of the parameter object are copied into the receiver object.

Input operation

Preconditions: The receiver is an **istream** object appropriately initialized, and the parameters are a rational number object appropriately initialized and an **istream** object appropriately initialized. The form of input to the stream should be

`<integer>/<integer> <enter key>`

Postconditions: The numerator and the denominator in the rational number parameter are modified by the input values, and the istream object is returned.

Output operation

Preconditions: The receiver is an **ostream** object appropriately initialized, and the parameters are a rational number object appropriately initialized and an **ostream** object appropriately initialized.

Postconditions: The rational number parameter is written to the stream in the form `<numerator>/<denominator>`.

Note that the specifications state that a rational number will not be created if the denominator is a zero, and that any new rational number will be reduced to lowest terms when it is created.

The class declaration module for rational numbers can now be presented:

```cpp
// Class declaration file: rational.h

#ifndef RATIONAL_H

// Declaration section

#include <iostream.h>

#include "boolean.h"

class rational
{

public:

// Class constructors

rational();
rational(int new_numer, int new_denom);
rational(const rational &r);

// Member functions

rational operator + (rational r);
rational operator - (rational r);
rational operator * (rational r);
rational operator / (rational r);
boolean operator == (rational r);
rational& operator = (rational r);
friend istream& operator >> (istream &is, rational &r);
friend ostream& operator << (ostream &os, rational r);

private:

// Data members

int numerator, denominator;

// Member function

void reduce();

};

#define RATIONAL_H
#endif
```

There are several things to note about this class declaration:

1. A third class constructor, the copy constructor, has been included so that rational numbers may be passed by value as parameters to functions.

2. Rational numbers are passed by value, rather than by constant reference, to the member functions. Recall that we used the constant reference mode for string parameters in Chapter 7, for reasons of efficiency. Because passing a rational number by value requires copying only two integer values, this mode can be used here.

3. The input and output operators of the stream classes are specified as friends, as they were in Chapter 7.

4. The class declaration declares **reduce** as a **private** member function. This function will be run by the class implementation whenever a rational number object must be reduced to lowest terms.

Implementing the Class

The class implementation for rational numbers appears in the **rational.cpp** file. We present the portion of the file that defines the three class constructors below:

```
// Class implementation file: rational.cpp

#include <assert.h>

#include "rational.h"
#include "gcd.h"

// Implementation section

rational::rational()
{
        numerator = 1;
        denominator = 1;
}

rational::rational(int new_numer, int new_denom)
{
        assert(new_denom != 0);
        numerator = new_numer;
        denominator = new_denom;
        reduce();
}

rational::rational(const rational &r)
{
        numerator = r.numerator;
        denominator = r.denominator;
}
```

Only the second constructor calls for comment. A precondition of the operation is that the **new_denom** parameter must not be a zero. Therefore, the implementation verifies this condition with the C++ **assert** function. A postcondition of the operation is that the new rational number has been reduced to lowest terms. To achieve this result, we compute the greatest common divisor of the two parameters, and then reduce them by dividing by this factor. Here is the implementation of the **reduce** function:

```
void rational::reduce()
{
        int common_divisor = gcd(numerator, denominator);
        numerator = numerator / common_divisor;
        denominator = denominator / common_divisor;
}
```

The implementation of the **gcd** function, which was used in an example in Section 6.5, appears in the library file **gcd.cpp**, and is left as an exercise.

The development of the arithmetic operations for rational numbers depends on our knowledge of the rules of rational number arithmetic. These rules are specified by the following relations:

$$\frac{n_1}{d_1} + \frac{n_2}{d_2} = \frac{n_1 d_2 + n_2 d_1}{d_1 d_2}$$

$$\frac{n_1}{d_1} - \frac{n_2}{d_2} = \frac{n_1 d_2 - n_2 d_1}{d_1 d_2}$$

$$\frac{n_1}{d_1} \times \frac{n_2}{d_2} = \frac{n_1 n_2}{d_1 d_2}$$

$$\frac{n_1/d_1}{n_2/d_2} = \frac{n_1 d_2}{d_1 n_2}$$

We present the implementation of the addition operation, and leave the others as exercises:

```
rational rational::operator + (rational r)
{
        int numer = numerator * r.denominator + r.numerator * denominator;
        int denom = denominator * r.denominator;
        rational sum(numer, denom);
        return sum;
}
```

The first two lines of code in this implementation use the rule for addition to compute the numerator and the denominator of the sum. The third line uses these values to construct a new rational number expressed in lowest terms. The last line returns the new rational number to the caller of the function.

The output operation writes a rational number to an output stream in the form **<numerator>/<denominator>**:

```
ostream& operator << (ostream &os, rational r)
{
        os << r.numerator << "/" << r.denominator;
        return os;
}
```

Note that we have been careful to write the data to the output stream in exactly the same form as it might appear for reading from an input stream. This technique will become important when we start processing file streams in Chapter 9.

The input operation expects data in the input stream to have the form `<integer>/<integer>`. Therefore, the implementation uses **assert** to enforce the use of this format:

```
istream& operator >> (istream &is, rational &r)
{
        char division_symbol;
        is >> r.numerator >> division_symbol >> r.denominator;
        assert(division_symbol == '/');
        assert(r.denominator != 0);
        r.reduce();
        return is;
}
```

Note that the implementation also verifies that the denominator from the input stream is not a zero, and reduces the rational number to lowest terms.

The implementations of the assignment and equality operations are left as exercises.

EXAMPLE 8.2   This example is a program that prompts the user for three rational numbers and outputs the result of an expression of the form **r1 + r2 * r3**.

```
// Program file: ratdriv.cpp

#include <iostream.h>

#include "rational.h"

int main()
{
        rational r1, r2, r3;
        cout << "Enter the first number (<integer>/<integer>): ";
        cin >> r1;
        cout << "Enter the second number (<integer>/<integer>): ";
        cin >> r2;
        cout << "Enter the third number (<integer>/<integer>): ";
        cin >> r3;
        cout << "The result of r1 + r2 * r3 is " << r1 + r2 * r3 << endl;
        return 0;
}
```

An example run of this program might produce the output

```
Enter the first number (<integer>/<integer>): 1/2
Enter the second number (<integer>/<integer>): 1/2
Enter the third number (<integer>/<integer>): 1/2
The result of r1 + r2 * r3 is 3/4
```

Note that the output is **3/4** rather than **3/2**. This means that the standard operator precedence of multiplication over addition is also enforced for rational numbers.

Mixed-Mode Operations

In Chapter 3, you were introduced to the notion of a mixed-mode operation. This kind of operation has two operands of different types, and performs a type conversion operation before computing a result value. For example, the addition operation promotes an integer operand to a real number before adding it to a real number operand. The result returned is then a real number.

When a rational number class is added to a software system, clients might be provided with a similar capability to perform mixed-mode operations on rational numbers and other kinds of numbers. For example, where the operands are an integer and a rational number, the integer would first be promoted to a rational number, and then rational number arithmetic would be performed. Where the operands are a real number and a rational number, the rational number would first be promoted to a real number, and then real number arithmetic would be performed. The following code and its output when executed illustrate some mixed-mode operations:

```
rational one_half(1, 2);
cout << fixed << showpoint;
cout << "Rational + integer =" << one_half + 2 << endl;
cout << "Rational + real =" << one_half + 3.4 << endl;

Rational + integer = 5/2
Rational + real = 3.9
```

Table 8.1 illustrates some operand and return types for addition.

We can provide mixed-mode operations for arithmetic with rational numbers by overloading. Let's consider just the case of addition, and leave the other operations for exercises. For the cases where the first operand is a rational number, we add public member functions to the class declaration module of the rational number class:

```
rational operator + (int operand);
float operator + (float operand);
```

Each of these operations adds a number (an **int** or a **float**) to the receiver object, a rational.

To add an **int** to a rational number, we must promote the **int** to a rational number. We use the **int** parameter to create a new rational number object, and then add it (using the rational number operation named '+') to the receiver:

```
rational rational::operator + (int operand)
{
        rational new_operand(operand, 1);
        return *this + new_operand;
}
```

◇ **TABLE 8.1**

Types of data for mixed-mode addition

Operand 1 Type	Operand 2 Type	Result Type
int	rational	rational
rational	int	rational
float	rational	float
rational	float	float

To add a **float** to a rational number, we must promote the rational number to a **float**. We cast the receiver's numerator as a float, divide the result by its denominator, and then add the result (using the real number operation '+') to the **float** parameter:

```
float rational::operator + (float operand)
{
        return float(numerator) / denominator + operand;
}
```

The other two addition operations expect a rational number as the second operand. In these cases, the rational number is not the receiver object. Therefore, they must be declared outside of the class declaration, at the global level:

```
rational operator + (int left_operand, rational right_operand);
float operator + (float left_operand, rational right_operand);
```

Note that both operands now appear as formal parameters within the parameter lists of the declarations. The implementation of the first operation is

```
rational operator + (int left_operand, rational right_operand)
{
        rational new_operand(left_operand, 1);
        return new_operand + right_operand;
}
```

The implementation of the last addition operation requires that the rational number parameter be promoted to a **float** before it is added to the **float** parameter. However, because the code is no longer within the scope of the class declaration (we can't use the prefix **rational::** in the function heading), we do not have access to the numerator and denominator of the rational number. To solve this problem and preserve information hiding, we declare a new member function, **make_float**, that promotes its object to a **float**. Its implementation is left as an exercise, but we use it here to implement the last addition operation:

```
float operator + (float left_operand, rational right_operand)
{
        return left_operand + right_operand.make_float();
}
```

EXERCISES 8.3

1. Complete the implementation of the rational number class, including the mixed-mode operations and the **make_float** type cast, and test it with a simple driver program. (*Hint:* Two rational numbers are equal if and only if $n_1d_2 = n_2d_1$.)

2. What is the total number of mixed-mode operations (+, −, *, /) for the three data types **int**, **float**, and **rational**?

3. State a general formula for the total number of mixed-mode operations, where M is the number of operators and N is the number of data types.

4. The implementation of rational numbers presented in this section always reduces a rational number to lowest terms when it is created. Another method would be to wait until an output operation to express a rational number in lowest terms. Assess the costs and benefits of these two strategies. (Be sure to take into account the speed of evaluating complex arithmetic operations and the possibility of integer overflow.)

5. Rational numbers such as 9/1 should be output as whole numbers, and used as whole numbers in arithmetic and comparison operations. Write a member function,

whole_number, that returns a Boolean value and a type cast, **make_int**, that can be used in conjunction to convert such numbers to integers.

8.4 Derived Classes and Inheritance

One of the advantages of using classes and objects in a program is that they can be reused to develop new features. Consider the bank account example of Section 8.2. We defined a class to represent the kind of data and behavior that any account might possess, such as depositing into or withdrawing from a balance. Many more specialized kinds of bank accounts exist that have both this general sort of data and behavior and also other, more specific data and behavior. For example, a savings account will need data and operations to compute the interest on the balance. A timed savings account will not allow withdrawals before a certain date from the time of the deposit.

Instead of reinventing the wheel and defining a whole new class for each of these types of bank accounts, we can make each new kind of account a derived class of our abstract account class. Each class derived from **account** then *inherits* all of the common, more abstract data and behavior from the account class. To each derived class we need only add the data and behavior necessary to define it as a special class of account.

C++ provides support for defining derived classes. A derived class declaration is quite similar to a top-level class declaration. For example, here is a declaration of a **savings_account** class, with specific data and behavior for representing the computation of interest:

```
// Class declaration file: savings.h

#ifndef SAVINGS_H

#include "account.h"

// Declaration section

class savings_account : public account
{
        public:

        // Class constructors

        savings_account(float initial_balance);

        // Member functions

        float get_interest();
        void compute_interest(float rate);

        private:

        // Data members

        float interest;

};

#define SAVINGS_H
#endif
```

The only difference in form between a derived class declaration and a top-level class declaration lies in the text immediately following the reserved word **class**. As before, we have the name of the new class. Then we see a colon (":"), followed by an *access specifier,* followed by the name of the class from which the new class is being derived. The form for this is

class <new derived class name> : <access specifier> <parent class name>

The access specifier in this example is the reserved word **public**. This means that the public members of the base class are also public in the derived class. If this specifier were the reserved word **private**, then the public members of the base class would become private members in the derived class. Figure 8.3 is a class hierarchy diagram showing the relationship between the account class and the savings account class. Note that the member functions **deposit**, **withdraw**, and **get_balance** are not declared in the savings account class. They are declared in the base class, **account**, but are still considered public members of the savings account class by inheritance.

The implementation file of the savings account class is

```
// Class implementation file: savings.cpp

// Implementation section

#include "savings.h"

savings_account::savings_account(float initial_balance)
        : account(initial_balance)
{
        interest = 0.00;
}

float savings_account::get_interest()
{
        return interest;
}

void savings_account::compute_interest(float rate)
{
        interest = get_balance() * rate;
}
```

◆ FIGURE 8.3
The account and savings account classes

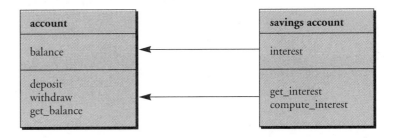

The class constructor for **savings_account** must first run the constructor for the base class, **account**, so that the data members belonging to the base class can be initialized. This is done by placing an expression of the form

```
: <base class constructor name> (<list of actual parameters>)
```

immediately after the heading of the constructor for the derived class. After this step, the data member **interest** belonging to the derived class is initialized.

Within the implementation of the member function **compute_interest**, we cannot refer directly to the savings account's balance. The reason for this is that access to private data members cannot be inherited from a base class. Therefore, we must access the savings account's balance indirectly, by invoking the base class public member function **get_balance**. As you might suppose, lack of direct access to the data members of a base class can make the use of derived classes and reuse inconvenient. We will see a way to remedy this problem shortly.

The following lines of code create and use a new instance of our savings account class:

```
savings_account my_account(50.00);
my_account.withdraw(20.00);
my_account.compute_interest(.025);
cout << fixed << showpoint << setprecision(2);
cout << "Balance = $" << my_account.get_balance() << endl;
cout << "Interest = $" << my_account.get_interest() << endl;
```

The first line declares a new savings account called **my_account**. The computer runs the class constructor for savings accounts. This in turn runs the class constructor in the base class, which gives **my_account** an initial balance of 50.00. The constructor in the derived class then sets the interest to a default value of 0.00.

The second line sends a message to **my_account** to withdraw 20.00. Since this member function is also not defined for savings accounts, the computer locates and runs the function as defined in the base class.

The third line sends a message to **my_account** to compute the interest, with a rate of .025. Since a member function is defined for this message directly in the **savings_account** class, this function is invoked.

The last two lines of code send messages to **my_account** for the values of the balance and interest so they can be displayed to the user. The request for the balance has the effect of invoking a member function of the base class, whereas the request for the interest has the effect of invoking a member function of the derived class.

The rule that the computer uses for deciding which member function to run when a message is sent to an object is fairly simple. If a member function corresponding to the message exists in the defining class, then it is run. Otherwise, the computer searches for a member function in the base class, if one exists. This search continues until a member function is found in the next most immediate ancestor class, if one exists. If no member function is found, a syntax error occurs. The same search process occurs for **public** data member references as well.

As you can see, derived classes and inheritance provide powerful techniques for reusing software and eliminating redundant code.

EXAMPLE 8.3   The following driver program tests the savings account class that we have just
implemented:

```
// Program file: bankdriv.cpp

#include <iostream.h>
#include <iomanip.h>
#include "savings.h"

int main()
{
    savings_account smith(0.00), jones(45.00);

    cout << fixed << showpoint << setprecision(2);
    cout << "Smith's balance = $" << smith.get_balance() << endl;
    cout << "Jones's balance = $" << jones.get_balance() << endl;
    smith.deposit(50.00);
    cout << "Smith's balance = $" << smith.get_balance() << endl;
    cout << "Jones's balance = $" << jones.get_balance() << endl;
    smith.withdraw(20.00);
    cout << "Smith's balance = $" << smith.get_balance() << endl;
    cout << "Jones's balance = $" << jones.get_balance() << endl;
    smith.compute_interest(.025);
    cout << "Smith's interest = $" << smith.get_interest() << endl;
    return 0;
}
```

The program produces the output

```
Smith's balance = $0.00
Jones's balance = $45.00
Smith's balance = $50.00
Jones's balance = $45.00
Smith's balance = $30.00
Jones's balance = $45.00
Smith's interest = $0.75
```

Inheritance and Protected Members

In the previous section, we mentioned that **private** data members of a base class
cannot be directly referenced from a derived class. For example, the savings account
class must invoke a **public** member function of the account class, such as
get_balance(), to access the value of the private data member **balance**. This
kind of encapsulation is too restrictive. A derived class ought to be able to access
frequently used and modified data members of a base class directly. A less restrictive
type of encapsulation can be obtained by using the access specifier **protected** for
certain data and member functions. A data or function member of a class is
considered *protected* if it is visible to a derived class, but not visible to any other part
of a program. Thus, **protected** members behave like **public** members for
derived classes, but like **private** members for any other classes or modules in a
software system.

The following code updates the account class by making the balance a **protected** data member rather than a **private** one:

```
// Class declaration file: account.h

#ifndef ACCOUNT_H

// Declaration section

class account
{

        public:

        // Class constructors

        account(float initial_balance);
        account(const account &a);

        // Member functions

        float deposit(float amount);
        float withdraw(float amount);
        float get_balance();

        protected:

        // Data members

        float balance;

};

#define ACCOUNT_H
#endif
```

We have replaced the reserved word **private** in the previous version with the reserved word **protected**. The implementation section of this module is the same as before.

Once we have made this change in the account class declaration, we can refer to the data member **balance** in the savings account class declaration. For example, the member function **compute_interest** can be changed so that the balance is referenced directly:

```
void savings_account::compute_interest(float rate)
    {
    interest = balance * rate;
    }
```

EXERCISES 8.4

1. Where would you define the data and behavior for representing passwords in savings accounts? Which access mode should a password have within the class hierarchy?

2. Add members to the savings account class given in this section for maintaining a current interest rate.

3. A checking account is a special version of an account that requires data and behavior for maintaining the number of checks written. Write a derived class of account called **checking_account** that captures this information.

4. Draw a diagram showing the hierarchy of classes used in a system that manages checking and savings accounts.

5. Some checking accounts bear interest. Propose a strategy for reusing the existing classes in a bank management system to support checking accounts with interest. Draw a diagram of the new class hierarchy.

6. Unlike the other kinds of accounts, timed savings accounts may not permit access via a password. Explain how you would fit timed savings accounts into a bank management system as a new class, in such a way that the use of a password for these accounts would be disallowed. Draw a diagram of the new class hierarchy.

FOCUS ON PROGRAM DESIGN

Thus far in this text, the end-of-chapter focus section has stated a problem, written out the top-level design of a solution as an algorithm, refined the design if necessary, and presented a complete program to solve the problem. In more recent chapters, we have had to focus more on the design of the appropriate data structures for solving a problem as well. Now that we are using object-oriented techniques, our focus must shift somewhat further away from top-down design and refinement of algorithms. In this section, we present part of a complete program, and leave the rest for the programming problems and projects. In fact, it would be in the object-oriented spirit if this project and those to follow were divided up among students who form a team of programmers.

We begin as usual with a problem statement. But now we immediately consider how the behavior of certain classes of objects can help to solve the problem. If these classes have already been written, we can use them right away. If they do not quite fit the problem at hand, perhaps we can reuse them by creating a derived class for the desired behavior. Some algorithm and data structure design will still be necessary at the level of implementing a new class, but in general, there will be less work to do because there is less code to write. Rather than thinking in terms of data structures and algorithms, we can think in terms of clients and servers, many of which already exist and simply need to be hooked together in the appropriate way.

Consider the problem of simulating an automated teller machine (ATM). An ATM is a server that allows users to enter a name (on the card) and password to gain access to different kinds of bank accounts. The user can then select among various functions, each of which may request other inputs. A successful transaction results in output to the user, and may result in a change to an account. An unsuccessful transaction (using a bad password, for example) may lead to other outputs.

The ATM relies on other servers for support. Three of these are an **iostream** class, a string class, and an account class. The role of the ATM is to serve as an interface handler that controls the communication between a user and his or her account. Put another way, you can think of an ATM class as both a model for an ATM machine and as an "application class" that drives the simulation.

To design an object-oriented system to solve this problem, we first take an inventory of existing classes to see how they can capture the desired behavior. Let's assume that we have an account class at our disposal. The account class has been extended to support user names and passwords.

Now that we know what we have, we can think about what we have to develop. The ATM can be represented as a new class. It will use, as servers, the **iostream** class, the string class, and the account class. It will maintain the following data members:

1. Master name and password (used to start up or shut down the system)
2. Current account (the account currently being processed).

The ATM will serve users in two different modes:

1. *Master user mode:* This mode allows an authorized bank employee to start up the machine in customer mode, to perform service functions such as entering a new account, and to shut the machine down.
2. *Customer mode:* This mode allows an authorized customer to access an account to perform transactions.

Let's look at the abstract behavior that the ATM provides for each mode.

1. Master mode
   1.1 enter a new account
   1.2 start customer mode
   1.3 shut machine down
2. Customer mode
   2.1 get name and password
   2.2 if they belong to master mode then
   2.3 run master mode
   2.4 else if they belong to an account then
   2.5 perform a transaction on the account
   2.6 else handle user error

Many of the numbered items in both modes describe messages to which an ATM object can respond. Master mode really is a menu-driven command interpreter. Let's develop code for the algorithm. First, when the message **master_mode** is sent to an ATM object, a member function should enter a command loop. The loop should display the master mode menu and wait for the user to enter the number of a command. When this occurs, the ATM runs the corresponding member function. After the function returns, the loop is entered once more. The following code might be an implementation of the **master_mode** member function:

```
void ATM::master_mode()
{
    int command;

    do
```

```
                    {
                            print_master_menu();
                            command = get_command(1, 3);
                            switch (command)
                            {
                                    case 1:     enter_account();
                                                break;
                                    case 2:     customer_mode();
                                                break;
                                    case 3:     shut_down();
                            }
                    } while (command != 3);
            }
```

Note that the manager launches customer mode by entering command 2, and shuts the machine down by entering command 3.

The member function **customer_mode** is

```
void ATM::customer_mode()
{
      string name, password;
      boolean master_on = FALSE;

      do
      {
            cout << "Enter your name: ";
            cin >> name;
            cout << "Enter your password: ";
            cin >> password;
            if (master_account(name, password))
                    master_on = TRUE;
            else if (customer_account(name, password))
                    perform_transaction();
            else
                    cout << "Sorry, you entered an incorrect name or password."
                            << endl;
      } while (! master_on);
}
```

master_account is a member function that returns TRUE if the name and password match those of an authorized employee, and FALSE otherwise. The loop terminates when an authorized employee enters a name and password for master mode.

perform_transaction displays a menu of transaction options to the user, takes a command number, and performs the corresponding command:

```
void ATM::perform_transaction()
{
      int command;

      print_transaction_menu();
      command = get_command(1, 3);
      switch (command)
```

```
        {
                case 1:          get_balance();
                                 break;
                case 2:          make_deposit();
                                 break;
                case 3:          make_withdrawal();
        }
}
```

As you can see, the ATM class that we have developed thus far is a large body of code, broken down into many small member functions (the use of classes does not free developers entirely from top-down design and algorithm development!). Most of these can be declared **private**, for the internal use of the ATM class only. A single member function, **master_mode**, can be declared **public**. This function can be invoked from a main program in C++, right after an ATM instance is declared. It would run master mode and wait for commands. The main program would be

```
// Program file: atmdriv.cpp

#include <iostream.h>

#include "atm.h"

int main()
{
        string name, password;

        cout << "Enter your name: ";
        cin >> name;
        cout << "Enter your password: ";
        cin >> password;
        ATM teller(name, password);
        teller.master_mode();
        return 0;
}
```

Here is the header file for the ATM class:

```
// Class declaration file: atm.h

#ifndef ATM_H

#include "boolean.h"
#include "account.h"

// Declaration section

class ATM
{

        public:

        // Class constructors
```

```
            ATM(string n, string p);

            // Member functions

            void master_mode();

            private:

            // Data members
            // Used to start up or shut
            // down the system

            string master_name, master_password;

            // The account currently being processed

            account current_account;

            // Member functions

            void customer_mode();
            boolean master_account(string n, string p);
            boolean customer_account(string n, string p);
            void perform_transaction();
            void get_balance();
            void make_deposit();
            void make_withdrawal();
            int get_command(int low, int high);
            void enter_account();
            void shut_down();
            void print_transaction_menu();
            void print_master_menu();

      };


      #define ATM_H
      #endif
```

The complete implementation file is left as an exercise.

RUNNING, DEBUGGING AND TESTING HINTS

1. Before you write a definition of a new class, write out a description of the data members and abstract behavior that the class should exhibit.
2. Write a simple driver program to test each member function of a class.

SUMMARY

Key Terms

access specifier

attribute

base class

behavior

class hierarchy

derived class

inheritance

protected member

receiver

sender

Keywords

protected

Key Concepts

◆ A class defines the abstract behavior and attributes belonging to an object.

◆ Objects provide services by responding to the messages sent by clients.

◆ Objects can be used to model or simulate objects in the real world, such as bank accounts, or computational objects, such as rational numbers.

◆ Classes can reuse data and behavior by inheriting them from a base class.

◆ Derived classes can specialize inherited behavior by extending it or overriding it.

◆ Data and behavior can be hidden from all users by declaring them **private** within a class.

◆ Data and behavior can be made available to all users by declaring them **public** within a class.

◆ Data and behavior can be made available to derived classes but hidden from all other users by declaring them **protected** within a class.

SUGGESTION FOR FURTHER READING

Booch, Grady, *Object-Oriented Analysis and Design,* 2nd ed., Redwood City, CA: Benjamin/Cummings, 1994.

Coad, Peter, and Yourdon, Edward, *Object-Oriented Analysis,* 2nd ed., Englewood Cliffs, NJ: Yourdon Press, 1991.

Jacobson, I., Christerson, M., Jonsoon, P., and Overgaard, G., *Object-Oriented Software Engineering,* Reading, MA: Addison-Wesley, 1992.

Rumbaugh, J., *et al., Object-Oriented Modeling and Design,* Englewood Cliffs, NJ: Prentice Hall, 1991.

Wirfs-Brock, R., Wilkerson, B., and Wiener, L. *Designing Object-Oriented Software,* Englewood Cliffs, NJ: Prentice Hall, 1990.

PROGRAMMING PROBLEMS AND PROJECTS

1. Implement and extend the ATM class to handle user errors by confiscating a card after three unsuccessful attempts to gain access to an account.

2. Write a program to be used by the registrar of a university. The program should get information from the keyboard and the data for each student should include student name, student number, classification (1 for freshman, 2 for sophomore, 3 for junior, 4 for senior, or 7 for special student), hours completed, hours taking, and grade-point average. You should design a class to represent a student as an abstract data type. This class should use the string class developed in Chapter 7.

3. Robert Day, basketball coach at Indiana College, wants you to write a program to help him analyze information about his basketball team. He wants a data structure for each player containing the player's name, position played, high school graduated from, height, scoring average, rebounding average, grade-point average, and seasons

of eligibility remaining. You should design a class to represent a player as an abstract data type.

4. Complex numbers are numbers of the form $a + bi$ where a and b are real and i represents **sqrt(-1)**. Complex number arithmetic is defined by

Sum $(a + bi) + (c + di) = (a + c) + (b + d)i$

Difference $(a + bi) - (c + di) = (a - c) + (b - d)i$

Product $(a + bi)(c + di) = (ac - bd) + (ad + bc)i$

Quotient $(a + bi)/(c + di) = \dfrac{ac + bd}{c^2 + d^2} + \dfrac{(bc - a\,d)i}{c^2 + d^2}$

Write a program that will perform these calculations on two complex numbers. Each line of data consists of a single character designator (S, D, P, or Q) followed by four reals representing two complex numbers. For example, $(2 + 3i) + (5 - 2i)$ is represented by

```
S2 3 5 - 2
```

An instance of a class should be used for each complex number. The arithmetic operators should be overloaded to carry out the operations. Input and output should be in the form $a + bi$ (overload the input and output operators as well).

5. The Readmore Public Library wants a program to keep track of the books checked out. Information for each book should be kept in an object and the data members should include the author's name, a nonfiction designator (Boolean), the title, the library catalog number, and the copyright date. Each customer can check out at most ten books. Develop an abstract data type for representing a book as a C++ class. There should be public member functions for returning each attribute of a book, and input and output operations for initializing and printing them as well.

6. Modify Problem 5 so that a daily printout is available that contains a summary of the day's transactions at the Readmore Public Library. You will need an object for each customer containing the customer's name and library card number. Be sure to make provision for books that are returned.

7. Write a program that uses objects to analyze poker hands. Each hand consists of five objects (cards). Each object should have one data member for the suit and one for the value. Rankings for the hands from high to low are

    straight flush
    four of a kind
    full house
    flush
    straight
    three of a kind
    two pair
    one pair
    none of the above

Your program should read data for five cards from the keyboard, evaluate the hand, and print out the hand together with a message indicating its value.

8. Problem 7 can be modified in several ways. A first modification is to compare two different hands using only the ranking indicated. A second (more difficult) modification is to also compare hands that have the same ranking. For example, a pair of 8s is better than a pair of 7s. Extend Problem 7 to incorporate some of these modifications.

9. The University Biology Department has a Conservation Club that works with the state Department of Natural Resources. Their project for the semester is to help capture and tag migratory birds. You have been asked to write a computer program to help them store information. In general, the program must have information for each bird tagged entered interactively in an object for subsequent use. For each bird tagged, you need a data member for the tag number, tagging site, sex, bird type, date, and name of the DNR officer doing the tagging. After all data have been entered, the program should print the contents of the object.

10. Mrs. Crown, your computer science instructor, wants to keep track of the maintenance record of her computers and has turned to you for help. She wants to keep track of the type of machine, its serial number (up to ten characters), the year of purchase, and a Boolean variable indicating whether the machine is under service contract. Write a program that permits the entry of this information and prints a record for a machine.

11. Write a program to read data containing the name, address, telephone number, and class of friends into an object and print its contents.

12. The Falcon Manufacturing Company wishes to keep computerized structures of its telephone-order customers. They want the name, street address, city, state, and zip code for each customer. They include either a "T" if the customer is a business, or an "F" if the customer is an individual. A 30-character description of each business is also included. An individual's credit limit is in the structure.

    Write a program to read the information for the customer from the keyboard and print the information on the screen.

13. Visit your local registrar and discuss how structures of students are processed. Discover what data are kept for each student, how the data are entered, and what the data members for each student are. Have the registrar explain what operations are used with a student's data. Specifically, how is information added to or deleted from a student's record? What kinds of lists must the registrar produce for those within the system who need information about students?

    Prepare a written report of your visit for the class. Be sure to include a graphic that shows how a student's record can be envisioned.

14. Select an unworked problem from the previously listed programming problems for this chapter. Construct a structure chart and write all documentary information necessary for this problem. Do not write code. When finished, have a classmate read your documentation to see if precisely what is to be done is clear.

9 Files

Having now completed eight chapters, you've made significant steps in the process of learning to use a programming language for the purpose of solving problems. Thus far, however, it has been impossible to work with large amounts of data. To write programs that solve problems using large databases, it is necessary to be able to store, retrieve, and manage the data. Consider the relatively simple problem of using a computer to compute and print water bills for a community of 30,000 customers. If the data needed consist of a customer name, address, and amount of water used, you can imagine that entering this information interactively every billing period would involve an enormous amount of time. In addition to saving that time, it is often desirable to save information between runs of a program for later use. For example, in large software systems, the information output by one program might be the input of another program.

To avoid these problems, we can store data in some secondary storage device, usually magnetic tapes or disks. Data can be created by one program, stored on these devices, and then accessed by other programs when necessary. It is also possible to modify and save this information for other runs of the same program or for running another program using these same data. In this chapter, we look at storage and retrieval of data in another data structure called a *file*.

9.1 Streams and Stream Processing

OBJECTIVES

- to understand the use of streams in obtaining input and output data
- to understand how streams are used to access data in files
- to be able to use loops with file streams

Before you can work with files, you need to become acquainted with the notion of a *stream*. You can think of a stream as a channel or conduit on which data are passed from senders to receivers. Data can be sent out on a stream; in which case, we are using an *output stream*. Or data can be received from a stream; in which case, we are using an *input stream*. Streams are connected to *devices*. For example, at program startup, the standard input stream, named by **cin**, is connected to the keyboard device, and the standard output stream, named by **cout**, is connected to the terminal screen. Thus, you can think of the keyboard as the *source* from which data are received from an input stream, and of the terminal screen as the *destination* to which data are sent on an output stream.

The essential characteristic of stream processing is that data elements must be sent to or received from a stream one at a time or in *serial* fashion. For example, if we have a collection of data elements to be printed on the terminal screen, they must be written one after the other, not all at once. When you think about the use of streams for interactive input and output, this restriction makes sense. For output, each character sent to the output stream must wait its turn to be displayed on a terminal screen. For input, the receiver in the program must wait for each character typed at the keyboard.

We can think of a stream as an abstract data type. Stream processing requires at least five abstract operations. First, the stream must be *opened* for use. If the stream has been opened for input, an operation is needed to *get* the next data item from the stream. In addition, an operation is needed to detect the *end of an input stream,* or the condition that there are no more data to be received from the stream. If the stream has been opened for output, an operation is needed to *put* the next data item into the stream. Finally, when the program is finished using a stream, an operation is necessary to *close* it.

The Standard Input and Output Streams

You are already familiar with the use of the standard input and output streams in C++. Let's take a look at how they work in more detail. These streams and the operations we perform on them become available to a program by including the **iostream.h** library. In the case of the standard input stream, a programmer obtains access to the variable **cin**, which names the stream, and the operator **>>**, which is used to receive or get the next data item from the stream. In the case of the standard output stream, a programmer obtains access to the variable **cout**, which names the stream, and the operator **<<**, which is used to send or put the next data item to the stream. The operations that open and close these streams are run automatically by the system when the program begins and finishes execution. Opening the streams simply connects each stream to its respective device, the keyboard or the terminal screen. Closing the streams disconnects them. The standard input and output streams and the devices to which they are connected are depicted in Figure 9.1.

File Streams

Files are data structures that are stored on a *disk device.* To work with a file, you must connect a stream to the file on a disk. The kind of stream used to receive input from a file is called an *input file stream.* The kind of stream used to send output to a file is called an *output file stream.* Input and output file streams and the devices to which they are connected are depicted in Figure 9.2. To create a file stream, you must first include the C++ library file **fstream.h.** After doing so, two new classes, **ofstream** (output file stream) and **ifstream** (input file stream), become available to a program.

◆ FIGURE 9.1
The standard input and output streams and their devices

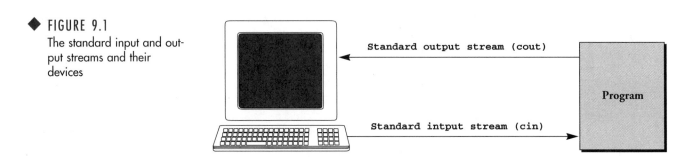

Standard output stream (cout)

Standard intput stream (cin)

Program

◆ FIGURE 9.2

Input and output file streams
and a disk device

Output File Streams

You can declare and open an output file stream as in the following example:

```
#include <fstream.h>
  .
  .
  .
ofstream out_file;
  .
  .
  .
out_file.open("myfile");
```

Syntactically, the second line of code is a C++ variable declaration. The class name, **ofstream**, appears on the left, followed by the variable name, **out_file**. The third line of code tells the system to connect the output file stream to a file on disk named **"myfile"**. The syntax of this statement is that used for expressing calls of member functions with objects introduced in Chapters 7 and 8. It consists of the name of the file stream, followed by a period ("."), followed by a call to the **open** function with a string parameter. When this statement is executed, the following steps take place:

1. If a file named **"myfile"** exists on disk, it is opened for output and connected to the output stream **out_file**. If any data are in the file when it is opened, the data are erased from the file.

2. Otherwise, a file named **"myfile"** does not exist on disk. A new file with that name is created, opened for output, and connected to the output stream **out_file**.

The general form for creating an output file stream is

```
ofstream <stream variable name>;
<stream variable name>.open(<file name>);
```

The stream variable name can be any legitimate C++ identifier. The file name must be a string that is consistent with the way files can be named on your particular implementation. You should consult your local system manual for the rules governing the naming of files.

When a program is finished using a file stream, it should be closed. Most computer systems close any data files when a program terminates execution. However, the **close** function can be run with the file stream to do this under program control. If **out_file** is an output file stream, the following statement will close the stream:

```
out_file.close();
```

Note that the name of the file does not appear as a parameter to this function, as it does with **open**.

Detecting Errors Opening and Closing Files

Occasionally, an error occurs when a program attempts to open or close a stream on a file. For example, a disk may be full and no more room exists for new data when a new file is requested. To detect these errors, C++ provides a fail function, **fail()**, for use with streams. The following code shows how to detect and respond to these errors in opening and closing an output file stream:

```
#include <fstream.h>
#include <assert.h>
.
.
.
ofstream out_file;
.
.
.
out_file.open("myfile");
assert(! out_file.fail());
        <send data to file>
out_file.close();
assert(! out_file.fail());
```

Using Output File Streams

Once a file stream has been opened for output, all of the operations for terminal screen output that you are familiar with can be used for file output. For example, assuming that the variable **out_file** names an output file stream, the following statement will write a line of text to the file:

```
out_file << "This is a test." << endl;
```

Note that this statement has exactly the same format as a statement to write the same data to the terminal screen using the standard output stream:

```
cout << "This is a test." << endl;
```

The output of integers and real numbers works the same way:

```
out_file << "The number ten is " << 10 << " or " << 10.0
        << endl;
```

If the C++ library for formatting output, **iomanip.h**, is included, you will be able to use familiar formatting commands with file output:

```
#include <iomanip.h>
.
.
.
out_file << setprecision(4);
out_file << setw(10) << 3.1416 << endl;
```

There are two important points to note here about output streams.

1. The operations on output streams are *abstract*. It does not matter whether the destination of the output is a file on disk or the terminal screen. All we need to know is the name of the stream and the form of the statement to send data to the stream. Moreover, the results of sending data to output streams are similar, even when the destinations are different devices. The data saved in a disk file should "look the same" as the data displayed on a terminal screen. You can verify that this is the case by running our sample statements, and then examining the contents of your test file with a local text editor.

2. Programs that use output stream processing are *portable*. They can be written on one hardware system, transported to another hardware system, and then recompiled and run on the latter system without changes to the code. This will be true even though the representation of files on a disk and data on a terminal screen tend to vary greatly from system to system. If we had to make changes to a program every time we wanted to move it to a new hardware system, we would have an enormous maintenance headache. The use of conventional output streams insulates a program from these machine dependencies in areas where they are most likely to occur.

Loops with Output File Streams

Most of the examples of sending data to an output file stream that we have seen thus far are unrealistic, in that only one or two data values are written. Programs typically output large amounts of data to files. One typical form of data processing with files takes input data from the user at the keyboard, processes the data, and writes the results to a file. A pseudocode algorithm for this process is

```
Open the output file
Read data from the keyboard
While data do not equal a sentinel value do
        Process the data
        Write the result to the file, followed by a carriage return
        Read data from the keyboard
Close the output file
```

Note that each data value will be followed by a carriage return in the file. It is essential that a carriage return or a space character be used to separate the data values in the file. This will allow the data values to be recognized and read from the file subsequently.

EXAMPLE 9.1   The following program uses a **while** loop to read integers from the keyboard and write them to a file until a sentinel is encountered.

```
// Program file: kbdfile.cpp

#include <iostream.h>
#include <fstream.h>

const int SENTINEL = -999;
```

```
int main()
{
    int data;
    ofstream out_file;

    out_file.open("myfile");
    cout << "Enter an integer (-999 to end input): ";
    cin >> data;
    while (data != SENTINEL)
    {
        out_file << data << " ";
        cout << "Enter an integer (-999 to end input): ";
        cin >> data;
    }
    out_file.close();
    return 0;
}
```

Input File Streams

You can create an input file stream as in the following example:

```
#include <fstream.h>
   .
   .
   .
ifstream in_file;
   .
   .
   .
in_file.open("myfile");
```

Syntactically, the first line of code is a C++ variable declaration. The class name, **ifstream**, appears on the left, followed by the variable name, **in_file**. The third line of code tells the system to connect the input file stream to a file on disk named **"myfile"**. The syntax of this statement is the same as that for output streams. When this statement is executed, the following steps take place:

1. If a file named **"myfile"** exists on disk, it is opened for input and connected to the input stream **in_file**.

2. Otherwise, a file named **"myfile"** does not exist on disk. On some implementations of C++, a new file with that name is created, opened for input, and connected to the input stream **in_file**.

The general form for creating an input file stream is

ifstream <stream variable name>;
<stream variable name>.open(<file name>);

The stream variable name can be any legitimate C++ identifier. The file name must be a string that is consistent with the way files can be named on your particular system.

Using Input File Streams

We have seen that programs can use the standard operator **<<**, called an *inserter,* to send data to the terminal screen or to an output file. Programs can also use the standard operator **>>**, called an *extractor,* to receive data from the keyboard or from an input file.

Let us review what happens when a program gets data from the keyboard or standard input stream.

1. The user types one or more characters at the keyboard, followed by a blank space or by a carriage return.
2. The computer converts the characters to the data value that the characters represent. What the characters represent depends on the type of variable used for input. For example, the characters '1', '0', and '4' will be converted to the integer value 104 if the program's input statement is receiving the input data for an integer variable. Or the same characters will be placed into a string value "104" if the input statement is using a string variable.
3. The computer stores the data value from step 2 in the variable following the **>>** operator.

The success of an input operation from the keyboard thus depends on two things: the format of the data typed by the user, and the data type of the variable appearing in the input statement. For example, the code

```
int int_var;
float float_var;
string string_var;


cin >> int_var >> float_var >> string_var;
```

will run successfully, if the user types a string of digits, followed by one or more whitespace characters, followed by a string of digits that may or may not contain a decimal point, followed by one or more whitespace characters, followed by a string of characters, followed by optional whitespace characters, and ending with a carriage return.

There are two important things to note about the standard input stream. First, at the source or keyboard, the data are individual characters. At the receiving end, however, these data are implicitly converted to a type that the program can use, such as integers, real numbers, or strings.

Once we are aware of these two conditions, we can proceed to use an input file stream in the same way as we use the keyboard. For example, assuming that the file **"myfile"** contains a line of characters representing an integer, a real number, and a string, the following program will successfully read these data from the file and display it on the terminal screen:

```
// Program file: filescr.cpp


#include <iostream.h>
#include <fstream.h>
#include <assert.h>
#include "strlib.h"
```

```
int main()
{
      int int_var;
      float float_var;
      string string_var;
      ifstream in_file;
      in_file.open("myfile");
      assert(! in_file.fail());
      in_file >> int_var >> float_var >> string_var;
      cout << int_var << float_var << string_var << endl;
      in_file.close();
      assert(! in_file.fail());
      return 0;
}
```

COMMUNICATION AND STYLE TIPS

The use of the << and >> operators in programs that process files enhances program maintenance. Because these operators work with integers, real numbers, and strings, client programmers do not have to change the code of the input and output operations when the data type of the elements in the file is changed. In general, servers should use the standard operators to define input and output operations for new classes, as was illustrated with strings in Chapter 7 and rational numbers in Chapter 8.

Loops with Input File Streams

The contents of an input file are almost never as precisely determined as those you just saw in the last example. Usually, all we know is the general format of a file and the type of data used to receive the input. The number of these data values that are stored in the file is *indefinite*. There may be 2, 20, or 20,000 of them. Processing input file data will consist of reading each data value from the file stream, processing it, and halting when there are no more data to be read from the stream.

C++ provides a special function, **eof()**, that returns nonzero (meaning TRUE) when there are no more data to be read from an input file stream, and zero (meaning FALSE) otherwise. The general form for using this function is

```
<input file stream>.eof()
```

If we assume that **data** is the variable into which each data element of a file will be read, **in_file** is the input file stream, and **process_data(data)** is the specification of a function that processes the data, then the following code can serve as a model of input file processing in many C++ programs:

```
in_file >> data;
while (! in_file.eof())
{
      process(data);
      in_file >> data;
}
```

There are several important points to make about this model:

1. An attempt to read an initial datum from the file stream must be made *before* the **eof** function is executed. If the file contains no data initially, then **eof** will return TRUE after this initial input operation. This operation is sometimes called a *priming input statement.*
2. Placing the **eof** condition at the beginning of a **while** loop guards against processing data after the program has reached the end of the file stream.
3. Placing the next extraction operation at the bottom of the loop allows the loop to advance through the file to the end of the input data.
4. When this model is used, remember that **eof** is TRUE when an attempt to read a value is made and there are no remaining values in the file.

EXAMPLE 9.2

The following program reads integers from an input file and displays them in a column on the terminal screen. The program assumes that the integers in the file are separated by one or more whitespace characters.

```
// Program file: intfile.cpp

#include <iostream.h>
#include <fstream.h>

int main()
{
    int data;
    ifstream in_file;
    in_file.open("myfile");
    in_file >> data;
    while (! in_file.eof())
    {
        cout << data << endl;
        in_file >> data;
    }
    in_file.close();
    return 0;
}
```

COMMUNICATION AND STYLE TIPS

1. Always test for the end-of-file condition before processing data read from an input file stream. This means:
  a. Use a priming input statement before the loop.
  b. Use an input statement at the bottom of the loop.
2. Use a **while** loop for getting data from an input file stream. (A **for** loop is desirable only when you know the exact number of data items in the file.)

Career Opportunities in Computer Science

The list "Fastest Growing Occupations, 1990–2005," published by the Bureau of Labor Statistics, includes computer programmers and computer system analysts. During this time period, the number of these jobs is expected to increase by 78.9%. If this job grouping is broadened to include all computer and data processing professionals, 24,000 workers joined the employment rolls between December 1991 and December 1992. Employment grew 4% in this area, compared to 0.5.% for total nonagricultural employment (*Forecasts: Cahners Economics*). Employment of computer professionals is expected to grow much faster than the average of all occupations through the year 2005 (*Occupational Outlook Handbook*).

In 1992, a total of 751 employers were surveyed to determine which academic disciplines were of greatest interest to employers. Of these, 60% mentioned computer science.

The relative ranking of the disciplines has remained very stable since 1980 when they were first compiled. The same three disciplines—computer science, electrical engineering, and mechanical engineering—have been on the top of the list, sought after by about two-thirds of the responding companies. (Peterson, *Job Opportunities*).

Unemployment among computer specialists is traditionally exceptionally low, and almost all who enter the workforce find jobs. In 1990, the median annual income was about $38,700 for a systems analyst and about $34,000 for a computer programmer (*Occupational Outlook Handbook*).

All able students—particularly women and minorities, who have been traditionally underrepresented in the sciences—are encouraged to consider computer science as a career.

EXERCISES 9.1

1. Assume that an input file stream, **in_file**, has been opened on a file containing two integers, and that **number** is an integer variable. Describe what happens when each of the following pieces of code is run:

   a.
   ```
   in_file >> number;
   cout << number << endl;
   in_file >> number;
   cout << number << endl;
   in_file >> number;
   cout << number << endl;
   ```
   b.
   ```
   in_file >> number;
   while (! in_file.eof())
   {
       cout << number << endl;
       in_file >> number;
   }
   ```
   c.
   ```
   while (! in_file.eof())
   {
       in_file >> number;
       cout << number << endl;
   }
   ```

2. Write and test a program that allows you to input your name, address, and age from the keyboard (define a string type and variables for the first two inputs). Then save this information in an output file. Be sure to place separators, either spaces or carriage returns, between the data values in the file. Examine the file with a text editor to make sure that the data have been saved.

3. Write and test a program to input the data from the output file of Exercise 2 and display it on the terminal screen.

4. Extend the program of Exercise 1 so that you can input many names, addresses, and ages from the keyboard and then save them in a file (halt keyboard input when name is "done").

5. Extend the program of Exercise 2 so that it reads all of the names, addresses, and ages from a file and displays them on the terminal screen.

6. Write a program that copies integers from an input file to an output file. You should assume that the data in the input file are separated by spaces or carriage returns. Test the program with files containing zero, one, and ten data values. You can create test files with a text editor.

7. Extend the program of Exercise 6 so that it echoes the input data to the terminal screen as they are processed.

9.2 Using Functions with Files

OBJECTIVES

- to be able to design functions for use with file streams
- to be able to use file streams in conjunction with strings
- to understand the use of buffered input of data from file streams into strings

Now that you know how to create and use file streams, we will examine how to write functions that package some useful file handling operations. Consider the problem of opening a file. This process is seldom as simple as we have seen in our examples so far, where we have assumed that the only file being processed is named **"myfile"**. In many cases, the user will be asked for the name of the desired file to be opened for input or output. This task involves prompting the user for the file name, reading the name into a string variable (as defined in Chapter 7), and passing the variable on to the **open** operation for the file stream. In addition, we might also check for a successful opening of the stream. We can hide these details in a pair of functions, **open_input_file** and **open_output_file**, that can be called in any application as follows:

```
open_input_file(in_file);
open_output_file(out_file);
```

in_file and **out_file** have been declared as input and output file streams, respectively.

Each function opens a stream on the file whose name the user specifies. The file stream is returned as a reference parameter. The declaration of **open_input-_file** is

```
// Function: open_input_file
// Prompts user for a file name and opens
// input stream on the file
//
// Outputs: an input file stream

void open_input_file(ifstream &in_file);
```

The implementation of **open_input_file** is

```
void open_input_file(ifstream &in_file)
{
        char in_file_name[80];

        cout << "Enter the input file name: ";
        cin >> in_file_name;
        in_file.open(in_file_name);
        assert(! in_file.fail());
}
```

Note that the file stream is passed as a *reference parameter*. You should never try to pass a stream as a value parameter. This may be a syntax error in some implementations of C++. **open_output_file** has a similar declaration and implementation.

Another useful function copies the contents of a file of integers to another file. The function assumes that the two files have been successfully opened, one for input and one for output. Its declaration declares just the file stream parameters:

```
// Function: copy_integers
// Copies integers from one file to another
//
// Inputs: an opened input file wherein integers are separated by spaces
// and an opened output file
// Output: an output file containing the contents of the input file

void copy_integers(ifstream &in_file, ofstream & outfile);
```

The implementation uses our standard **while** loop structure for input file processing:

```
void copy_integers(ifstream &in_file, ofstream &out_file)
{
      int data;

      in_file >> data;
      while (! in_file.eof())
      {
            out_file << data << " ";
            in_file >> data;
      }
}
```

EXAMPLE 9.3

The following program uses the functions developed above to copy integers from an input file to an output file.

```
// Program file: intfile.cpp

#include <iostream.h>
#include <fstream.h>
#include <assert.h>

int main()
{
      ifstream in_file;
      ofstream out_file;

      open_input_file(in_file);
      open_output_file(out_file);
      copy_integers(in_file, out_file);
      in_file.close();
      out_file.close();
      return 0;
}
```

Note that the **copy_integers** function assumes that the application will be opening and closing its files. File processing functions can be more general if they are not responsible for these details.

Files and Strings

File and string processing form the backbone of many word processing and database applications. In the following examples, we will use the string class developed in Section 7.3. Consider the problem of searching for a given word in a file. The user inputs the desired word and file name from the keyboard. The program searches for the first instance of the word in the file. If the word is found, the program displays the position of the word in the file and asks the user whether a search for the next instance is desired. If the word is not found, the program terminates with a message. An algorithm describing the top-level process is

```
Set position to 0
Open input file
Get word from user
Do
            Search file for next instance of word
            If word is found then
                        Display position of word in file
                        Ask user whether another search is desired
            Else
                        Display message that word was not found
While word was found and another search is desired
Close input file
```

The main loop can be controlled by two Boolean flags, **word_found** and **another_search**. The process of searching a file for the next instance of a given word can be handled by a function, **search_for_word**. The function has four parameters: an opened input file stream, the desired word, the **word_found** flag, and the position of the word in the file. We can use the **open_input_file** function developed earlier in the chapter to open the file and detect an error. We can now translate the main algorithm to a main program in C++:

```cpp
int main()
{
    string desired_word;
    boolean word_found, another_search;
    char query;
    ifstream in_file;
    int position = 0;

    open_input_file(in_file);
    cout << "Enter the word you would like to find: ";
    cin >> desired_word;
    do
    {
        search_for_word(in_file, desired_word, position, word_found);
        if (word_found)
        {
```

```
                              cout << "The word is at position " << position << endl;
                              cout << "Search for the next instance?[Y/N] ";
                              cin >> query;
                              another_search = (query == 'Y') || (query == 'y');
                    }
              else
                              cout << "The word was not found." << endl;
    } while (word_found && another_search);
    in_file.close();
    return 0;
}
```

The declaration of the function that performs the search is

```
// Function: search_for_word
// Searches for the next instance of a given word in a file
//
// Inputs: an opened input file stream, a word, and a position
// Outputs: the file stream and a Boolean flag that will be TRUE
// if the next instance of the word was found, or FALSE otherwise.
// If the word was found, its position in the file will be returned.
// If the word was not found, the file stream will be at its end

void search_for_word(ifstream &in_file, string desired_word,
      int &position, boolean &word_found);
```

On each call, the function advances through the file stream, until the next instance of the desired word is found or the end-of-file condition is reached. The function increments the position parameter after reading each word. If the function finds the word in the file, it sets the flag to TRUE and returns the word's position; otherwise, it sets the flag to FALSE. An algorithm describing the search process is

> Read a word from the file
> Increment the position
> While not end of file and the input word does not equal the desired word do
> > Read a word from the file
> > Increment the position
> Set word_found to not end of file

Note that the loop stops when we hit the end of file (there are no more words to consider) or when we have found the next instance of the desired word. The loop describes a standard process called *sequential search*. In a sequential search, we begin at the first available data item, examine it, and continue until a match is found or we run out of items to consider. If the search terminates with no more items to consider, then we have not found a match, as the assignment to the flag at the end of the algorithm indicates. The translation of the algorithm into the C++ function is

```
void search_for_word(ifstream &in_file, string desired_word,
      int &position, boolean &word_found)
{
      string input_word;

      in_file >> input_word;
      ++position;
      while (! in_file.eof() && (input_word != desired_word))
```

```
        {
            in_file >> input_word;
            ++position;
        }
        word_found = ! in_file.eof();
}
```

Note that the end-of-file condition is tested before the strings are compared in the **while** loop condition. The order of these two subexpressions within the Boolean expression is critical. If the end-of-file condition is TRUE, the next subexpression will be skipped over, and the Boolean expression will return FALSE. This kind of process, known as short-circuit evaluation, was introduced in Chapter 5 and guards against errors such as comparing two strings when the data for one are not defined. In our example, if the two strings were compared before the end of file was tested and end of file happened to be TRUE, the program might produce mysterious and erroneous results.

The complete C++ program for searching for a word in a file is left as an exercise.

Buffered File Input

We frequently wish to take account of the line-by-line format of text in file processing. For example, we might want to count the number of lines in a file or copy the contents of one file to another with the same format. Unfortunately, the techniques we have seen thus far are inadequate for this purpose. The standard **>>** operator for file input treats the end-of-line character in a file as a separator between words, not lines.

C++ provides an **istream** function, **getline**, that will allow us to input lines of text from files. The form of a call to **getline** for reading a line of text is

> <input stream>.getline(<character array variable>, <maximum length>);

getline reads characters from the input stream and stores them in the character array variable, until the number of characters read is one less than the maximum length specified or the end-of-line character is reached in the stream. The end-of-line character is not stored in the variable. However, the null character is stored in the variable. Therefore, the client must be careful to pass to **getline** a character array whose size is greater than or equal to the **<maximum length>** parameter.

For example, suppose we declared a character array variable called **line**, whose maximum possible size is 81, and we wished to read a line of text from a file stream called **in_file** into the variable. The following code declares the variable, inputs the text, and places the null character in the appropriate position in the character array:

```
    char line[81];
    in_file.getline(line, 81);
```

The maximum number of characters that can be read is one less than the size of the array. This will allow room for the null character to be placed at the end of the array if the line of text is 80 characters.

getline supports a process called *buffered file input*. This process utilizes a block of computer memory called a *buffer*, into which the data from a file are placed for transmission to a program. The main advantage of buffered file input is efficiency: because the system reserves a block of memory of definite size for input data, the process can run very quickly. The main disadvantage is that some data may not be read, if the data extend beyond the size of the buffer. Therefore, when we use **getline** for file processing, we must be careful to assume that the length of a line in a text file does not exceed the maximum size of a variable that we use to receive the input.

EXAMPLE 9.4

In this example, we copy the contents of one text file to another, maintaining the line-by-line format. We assume that the maximum length of a line of text in the source file is 100 characters, or **MAX_STRING_SIZE - 1**.

```
// Program file: buffcopy.cpp

#include <iostream.h>
#include <fstream.h>
#include <assert.h>

const int MAX_STRING_SIZE = 101;

// Function: open_input_file
// Prompts user for a file name and opens input stream on the file
//
// Outputs: an input file stream

void open_input_file(ifstream &in_file);

// Function: open_output_file
// Prompts user for a file name and opens output stream on the file
//

// Outputs: an output file stream

void open_output_file(ofstream &out_file);

// Function: copy_file
// Copies contents of one text file to another
//
// Inputs: opened input and output file streams

void copy_file(ifstream &in_file, ofstream &out_file);

int main()
{
    ifstream in_file;
    ofstream out_file;

    open_input_file(in_file);
    open_output_file(out_file);
    copy_file(in_file, out_file);
    in_file.close();
    out_file.close();
    return 0;
}
```

```
void open_input_file(ifstream &in_file)
{
        char in_file_name[MAX_STRING_SIZE];
        cout << "Enter the input file name: ";
        cin >> in_file_name;
        in_file.open(in_file_name);
        assert(! in_file.fail());
}

void open_output_file(ofstream &out_file)
{
        char out_file_name[MAX_STRING_SIZE];

        cout << "Enter the output file name: ";
        cin >> out_file_name;
        out_file.open(out_file_name);
        assert(! out_file.fail());
}

void copy_file(ifstream &in_file, ofstream &out_file)
{
        char line[MAX_STRING_SIZE];

        while (! in_file.eof())
        {
                in_file.getline(line, MAX_STRING_SIZE);
                out_file << line << endl;
        }
}
```

EXERCISES 9.2

1. Write a function that counts and displays on the screen the number of words in an input file. The program assumes that words in the file are separated by blank spaces or carriage returns. Test the program with files containing no words, one word, and several words.

2. Write a function that determines what the longest word in a file is. The function should display the longest word and its length on the terminal screen.

3. Write a function that finds and displays the average length of the words in a file.

4. Write a function that prompts the user for a word from the keyboard. Write a second function that counts the number of times that this word appears in a file. The program that uses this function should display the word count on the terminal screen.

5. The **getline** function works with the standard input stream, **cin**, as well as with input file streams. Write a program that takes string input from the keyboard with **getline**.

6. The **getline** function expects a string parameter that has been defined as a character array. Show how you can overload the **getline** function so that clients can use it with an instance of the string class developed in Chapter 7.

7. The use of the **open** function with a character array parameter causes the same problem as the **getline** function (Exercise 6). Show how you can overload this function, for both input file streams and output file streams, so that clients can pass an instance of the string class to it instead.

A NOTE OF INTEREST

Computer Ethics: Viruses

Tiny programs that deliberately cause mischief are epidemic among computers and are causing nervousness among those who monitor them.

Written by misguided or immature programmers, the "computer viruses" are placed on computer systems by piggybacking them on legitimate programs and messages. There, they may be passed along or instructed to wait until a prearranged moment to burst forth and destroy data.

At NASA Headquarters in Washington, several hundred computers had to be resuscitated after being infected. NASA officials have taken extra precautions and reminded their machines' users to follow routine computer hygiene: Don't trust foreign data or strange machines.

Viruses have the eerie ability to perch disguised among legitimate data just as biological viruses hide among genes in human cells, then spring out unexpectedly, multiplying and causing damage. Experts say that even when they try to study viruses in controlled conditions, the programs can get out of control and erase everything in a computer. The viruses can be virtually impossible to stop if their creators are determined enough.

"The only way to protect everybody against them is to do something much worse than the viruses: Stop talking to one another with computers," says William H. Murray, an information-security specialist at Ernst and Whinney financial consultants in Hartford, Connecticut.

Hundreds of programs and files have been destroyed by the viruses, and thousands of hours of repair or prevention time have been logged. Programmers have quickly produced antidote programs with such titles as Vaccine, Flu Shot, Data Physician, and Syringe.

Experts say known damage is minimal compared with the huge, destructive potential. They express the hope that the attacks will persuade computer users to minimize access to programming and data.

Viruses are the newest of evolving methods of computer mayhem. One type of virus is the Trojan Horse: It looks and acts like a normal program but contains hidden commands that eventually take effect, ordering mischief. The "time bomb" explodes at a set time; the "logic bomb" goes off when the computer arrives at a certain result during normal computation. The "salami attack" executes barely noticeable small acts, such as shaving a penny from thousands of accounts.

A virus typically is written as perhaps only a few hundred characters in a program containing tens of thousands of characters. When the computer reads legitimate instructions, it encounters the virus, which instructs the computer to suspend normal operations for a fraction of a second. During that time, the virus instructs the computer to check for other copies of itself and, if none is found, to make and hide copies. Instruction to commit damage may be included.

Is Your Machine at Risk?

1. Computer viruses are actually miniature computer programs. Most were written by immature programmers intent on destroying information in computers for fun.
2. Those who write virus programs often conceal them on floppy disks that are inserted in the computer.
3. An immature programmer makes the disk available to others, saying it contains a useful program or game. These programs can be lent to others or put onto computerized "bulletin boards" where anyone can copy them for personal use.
4. A computer receiving the programs will "read" the disk and the tiny virus program at the same time. The virus may then order the computer to do a number of things:

   - Tell it to read the virus and follow instructions.
   - Tell it to make a copy of the virus and place it on any disk inserted in the machine today.
   - Tell it to check the computer's clock, and on a certain date destroy all information that tells where data are stored on any disk: If an operator has no way of retrieving information, it is destroyed.
   - Tell it not to list the virus programs when the computer is asked for an index of programs.

5. In this way, the computer will copy the virus onto many disks—perhaps all or nearly all the disks used in the infected machine. The virus may also be passed over the telephone, when one computer sends or receives data from another.
6. Ultimately hundreds or thousands of people may have infected disks and potential time bombs in their systems.

9.3 Character Input and Output

Many problems call for the input and output of individual characters with file streams. Consider the problems of counting the total number of characters in a file and counting the total number of lines of text in a file. If these data include individual space or carriage return characters, we cannot rely on formatting conventions and the use of the **>>** operator for input. Recall that the **>>** operator treats space or carriage return characters as separators between data values in an input stream. Therefore, the **>>** operator cannot be used to input whitespace characters as data values in their own right. C++ provides two lower level operators, **get** and **put**, for handling character-level operations on streams.

Character Output with **put**

Character output with **put** is not much different than character output with **<<**. Assuming that **name** is a character array and **out_file** is an output file stream, the following two loops will have exactly the same effect on the file:

```
for (int j = 0; j < strlen(name); j ++)
    out_file << name[j];

for (int j = 0; j < strlen(name); j ++)
    out_file.put(name[j]);
```

The form of a statement that uses **put** is

```
<output file stream>.put(<character value>);
```

put is called as a function with a character value as its parameter. The function call is associated with the output stream by placing a period (".") between the name of the stream and the name of the function.

In general, **put** is defined such that it can work with any output stream. The loop

```
for (int j = 0; j < strlen(name); j ++)
    cout.put(name[j]);
```

will print the contents of the string on the terminal screen.

Character Input with **get**

Character input with **get** works in much the same way as character input with **>>**. One difference is that blank space and carriage return characters will be treated as character values in their own right. The form of a statement that uses **get** is

```
<input stream>.get(<character variable>);
```

The following statement would get the first character in a file and place it in the character variable **ch**:

```
in_file.get(ch);
```

Detecting the End of File at the Character Level

A special character value is reserved to mark the end of a file of characters. In the case of an empty file, this character is the only character present in the file. It is important to detect this character during input, so that further input is not attempted. It turns out that after the end-of-file character has been read with **get**, the **eof** function will return TRUE. Otherwise, it will return FALSE.

<file stream>.eof() can be used to control a **while** loop for processing an entire stream of characters. A standard form of a loop for processing character-level input from a file stream is

```
<input stream name>.get(<character variable>);
while (! <input stream name>.eof())
     process_data(<character variable>);
     <input stream name>.get(<character variable>);
```

Note the order of the operations in this process. We get a character first, since there will be at least one character in the file. Then the condition in the **while** loop protects the program from attempting to get or process any more characters when the end-of-file condition becomes TRUE. The first step in the body of the loop is to process the character just read (either the initial one or the one from the previous pass through the loop). The second step in the loop is to get the next character, which eventually will be the end-of-file character.

The next three examples illustrate algorithms for counting the number of characters in a file, counting the number of lines in a file, and copying the contents of one file to another file.

EXAMPLE 9.5

```
// This program counts and displays the number of characters in a file.
// We don't count the end-of-file character as one of these.

// Program file: charcnt.cpp

#include <iostream.h>
#include <fstream.h>

int main()
{
     ifstream in_file;
     char ch;
     int count;

     in_file.open("myfile");
     count = 0;
     in_file.get(ch);
     while (! in_file.eof())
     {
          ++count ;
          in_file.get(ch);
     }
     cout << "The total number of characters in myfile is " << count << endl;
     in_file.close();
     return 0;
}
```

EXAMPLE 9.6   To count the number of lines of text in a file, we can count the number of instances of the carriage return character denoted by '**\n**' in C++.

```cpp
// This program counts and displays the number of lines in a file.

// Program file: linecnt.cpp

#include <iostream.h>
#include <fstream.h>

int main()
{
      ifstream in_file;
      char ch;
      int count;

      in_file.open("myfile");
      count = 0;
      in_file.get(ch);
      while (! in_file.eof())
      {
            if (ch == '\n')
                  ++count;
            in_file.get(ch);
      }
      in_file.close();
      cout << "The total number of lines in myfile is " << count << endl;
      return 0;

}
```

EXAMPLE 9.7
```cpp
// This program copies the contents of one file to
another file.

// Program file: copyfile.cpp

#include <iostream.h>
#include <fstream.h>

int main()
{
      ifstream in_file;
      ofstream out_file;
      char ch;

      in_file.open("myfile");
      out_file.open("newfile");
      in_file.get(ch);
      while (! in_file.eof())
      {
            out_file.put(ch);
            in_file.get(ch);
```

```
    }
    in_file.close();
    out_file.close();
    return 0;
}
```

The last example calls for some comment. We copy every character from the input file to the output file, except for the input file's end-of-file character. This might lead you to think that the output file has no end-of-file character. However, the computer takes care of appending an end-of-file character to an output file whenever it is closed. Therefore, we were right to ignore the input file's end-of-file character. If we had copied it to the output file, this file would have contained two end-of-file characters, and would not have reflected the contents of the input file accurately.

EXERCISES 9.3

1. Assume that an input file stream, **in_file**, has been opened on a file, and that **ch** is a character variable. Describe what happens when each of the following pieces of code is run:

   a.
   ```
   in_file.get(ch);
   cout.put(ch);
   in_file.get(ch);
   cout.put(ch);
   in_file.get(ch);
   cout.put(ch);
   ```
   b.
   ```
   in_file.get(ch);
   while (! in_file.eof())
   {
       cout.put(ch);
       in_file.get(ch);
   }
   ```
   c.
   ```
   while (! in_file.eof())
   {
       in_file.get(ch);
       cout.put(ch);
   }
   ```

2. Write a program that deletes all blanks from a file. Your program should save the revised file for later use. (*Hint:* Copy the contents of the input file to another file, omitting the blanks.)

3. Write a program using a **switch** statement to scramble a file by replacing all blanks with an asterisk (*), and interchanging all A's with U's and E's with I's. Your program should print out the scrambled file and save it for subsequent use.

4. Write a program to update a file by numbering the lines consecutively as 1, 2, 3, ... The input file should not be modified.

5. Write a program to count the number of uppercase characters in a file.

6. Write a program to count the number of words in a text file. Assume that each word is followed by a blank or a period. The program should use **get** rather than **>>** to receive the input from the file.

7. Write a program to find the longest word in a file. Output should include the word and its length. The program should use **get** rather than **>>** to receive the input from the file.

8. Write a program to compute the average length of words in a file. The program should use **get** rather than **>>** to receive the input from the file.

9. Write a program that performs a search-and-replace operation on a file. The program will prompt the user for the word to search for and the word to use as a replacement. The program should replace all of the instances of the target word with the replacement word.

FOCUS ON PROGRAM DESIGN

The summary program for this chapter analyzes sentences in a file of text. It builds on the summary program in Chapter 7, in which we analyzed single sentences entered from the keyboard. That program displayed statistics about the number of characters and words in the sentence, and printed the longest word in the sentence as well. We used strings to represent words and string functions to handle the tasks of input, output, comparison, and determining word length.

The current program will prompt the user for a file name and open the file. If no error occurs, the program will compute and display statistics for

1. The total number of sentences in the file
2. The total number of words in the file
3. The average length of a sentence in the file
4. The length of the longest sentence in the file.

The program will recognize several kinds of sentences: those ending in a period ('.'), a question mark ('?'), and an exclamation point ('!'). Normally, a word ending with one of these characters will be treated as the last word in a sentence. As a special case, if one of these characters does not end the last word in the file, then that word is also treated as the last word in a sentence.

After the statistics are displayed, the program will ask the user if the analysis of another file is desired. If the answer is "Yes," the program will repeat the process; otherwise, the program will terminate execution.

A reasonable top-level module is

```
Do
        Open input file
        If there was no error opening the file then
                Initialize data
                Analyze sentences in file
                Close input file
                Display statistics
        Else
                Display error message
        Query user for another analysis
While answer to query = "Yes"
```

Before we can examine the submodules within this module, we must make explicit the data that are transmitted among them. The modules for opening and closing a file, and for analyzing sentences in the file, require a file stream. The modules for initializing data, analyzing sentences, and displaying statistics all require three integers, which represent the total number of sentences, the total number of words, and the length of the longest sentence. The average sentence length of a sentence can be computed locally in the display statistics module as a function of the other data. This data flow is shown in the structure chart in Figure 9.3.

◆ FIGURE 9.3

A structure chart for analyzing sentences

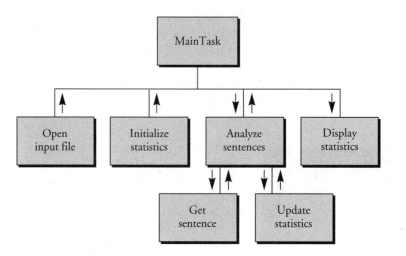

The main module translates to the following C++ main program:

```
int main()
{
    char query;
    ifstream in_file;
    int word_count, sentence_count, longest_sentence_length;

    do
    {
        open_input_file(in_file);
        initialize_data(word_count, sentence_count, longest_sentence_length);
        analyze_sentences(in_file, word_count, sentence_count,
            longest_sentence_length);
        in_file.close();
        display_statistics(word_count, sentence_count, longest_sentence_length);
        cout << "Analyze another file?[Y/N] ";
        cin >> query;
    } while ((query == 'Y') || (query == 'y'));
    return 0;
}
```

The module to initialize the data sets all of the integers to 0.

Module: Initialize data
Task: Sets all integers to 0
Outputs: integers representing the total number of sentences, the total number
of words, and the length of the longest sentence

Set sentence count to 0
Set word count to 0
Set longest sentence length to 0

The C++ implementation is

```
void initialize_data(int &word_count, int &sentence_count,
        int &longest_sentence_length)
```

```
        {
                word_count = 0;
                sentence_count = 0;
                longest_sentence_length = 0;
        }
```

The module to analyze sentences must repeatedly invoke a process we developed in the program in Chapter 7 to analyze a single sentence. The difference here is that we read a sentence from a file and return just a word count. This value is then passed with the other data to a submodule that updates the statistics. The subprocesses are structured within a standard input file process.

Module: Analyze sentences
Task: Read sentences from a file and compute statistics
Inputs: a file stream and integers representing the total number of sentences, the total number of words, and the length of the longest sentence
Outputs: the integers updated

>   Do
>   Get a word count on an input sentence
>   If the word count > 0 then
>   Update statistics
>   While not end of file

Note that a sentence may have a word count of zero. This occurs only in the special case where the input file is empty. The C++ implementation maintains the word count of the current input sentence as a local variable, **current_count**:

```
void analyze_sentences(ifstream &in_file, int &word_count, int &sentence_count,
      int &longest_sentence_length)
{
      int current_count;

      do
      {
              get_sentence(in_file, current_count);
              if (current_count > 0)
                      update_statistics(current_count, word_count, sentence_count,
                              longest_sentence_length);
      } while (! in_file.eof());

}
```

The module to display statistics computes the average length of a sentence and displays the four integer values with descriptive labels. Here is the C++ implementation:

```
  void display_statistics(int word_count, int sentence_count,
        int longest_sentence_length)
  {
      cout << endl << "Statistics for the current file. " << endl << endl;
      cout << "The number of words is " << word_count << "." << endl;
      cout << "The number of sentences is " << sentence_count << "." << endl;
      cout << "The average length of a sentence is "
              << word_count / sentence_count << "." << endl;
      cout << "The longest sentence had " << longest_sentence_length
              << " words." << endl << endl;
  }
```

The get sentence module reads words from the file and maintains a count of them. This is an iterative process with two possible termination conditions: either the end of file has been reached, or the last input word contains a sentence termination character ('.', '?', or '!') at the end.

Module: Get sentence
Task: Reads words from a sentence and maintains a count of words
Input: an input file stream
Output: the count of words in the sentence; 0 words means no sentence at all

> Set count to 0
> Read a word from the file
> If not end of file then
> > Increment count by one
> > While not end of file and word not at end of sentence do
> > > Read a word from the file
> > > Increment count by one

The initial test for an end of file guards against the case where the file is empty. The C++ implementation is

```cpp
void get_sentence(ifstream &in_file, int &count)
{
        string word;

        count = 0;
        in_file >> word;
        if (! in_file.eof())
        {
                ++count;
                while (! in_file.eof() && ! end_of_sentence(word))
                {
                        in_file >> word;
                        ++count;
                }
        }
}
```

The update statistics module increments the word count and the sentence count and adjusts the length of the longest sentence if necessary.

Module: Update statistics
Task: Increments word and sentence counts and adjusts length of longest sentence if necessary
Inputs: integers representing the number of words in the current sentence, the total number of sentences, the total number of words, and the length of the longest sentence
Outputs: the last three input integers updated

> Increment the word count by the number of words in the current sentence
> Increment the sentence count by one
> If number of words in the current sentence > length of the longest sentence then

Set length of the longest sentence to number of words in the current sentence

The C++ implementation is

```
void update_statistics(int current_count, int &word_count,
      int &sentence_count,
      int &longest_sentence_length)
{
      word_count = word_count + current_count;
      ++sentence_count;
      if (current_count > longest_sentence_length)
            longest_sentence_length = current_count;
}
```

At the lowest level of our design, the end-of-sentence module tests a word to see whether it marks the end of a sentence.

Module: End of sentence
Task: Determine whether a word marks the end of a sentence
Input: a word
Output: TRUE, if the word ends with '.', '?', or '!'; FALSE otherwise

Here is the C++ implementation of the module:

```
boolean end_of_sentence(string word)
{
      char last_ch = word.nth_char(word.length());

      return(last_ch == '.') || (last_ch == '?') || (last_ch == '!');
}
```

RUNNING, DEBUGGING AND TESTING HINTS

1. **>>** treats an end-of-line marker and a blank space as input separators.
2. **get** treats an end-of-line marker and a blank space as character data.
3. Always test for the end-of-file condition after getting a character from an input file. If the condition is TRUE, do not attempt to process the most recently read character or to read more characters from the file.

SUMMARY

Key Terms

buffer	input file stream	source device
destination device	output file stream	stream
end of input stream	serial processing	

Key Concepts

◆ Files can be used to store data between runs of a program.
◆ Access to file stream operations can be obtained by

```
#include <fstream.h>.
```

◆ An input file stream can be declared by

```
ifstream <stream name>;.
```

◆ An output file stream can be declared by

```
ofstream <stream name>;.
```

◆ File streams must be opened before they can be written to or read from.
◆ A file stream can be opened by

```
<stream name>.open(<file name>);.
```

◆ A file stream can be closed by

```
<stream name>.close();.
```

◆ An error in connecting a stream to a file can be detected by

```
<stream name>.fail();.
```

◆ For input data of most types, reading from a file stream can be accomplished by

```
<input file stream name> >> <variable name> . . .
                         >> <variable name>;.
```

◆ For output data of most types, writing to a file stream can be accomplished by

```
<output file stream name> << <expression> . . .
                          << <expression>;.
```

◆ When reading data from a file stream with >>, the absence of more data in an input stream can be detected by reading a datum and then running

```
<input stream name>.eof().
```

This condition will be TRUE if there is no more data to be read, and FALSE otherwise.
◆ When reading character-level input, the absence of more data in an input stream can be detected by reading a character and then running

```
<input stream name>.eof().
```

◆ A line of text can be read from an input stream by using the buffered input function getline, as follows:

```
<input stream name>.getline(<character array variable>,
<maximum length>);.
```

◆ Character data can be read from an input stream by

```
<input stream name>.get(<character variable>);.
```

◆ Character data can be written to an output stream by

```
<output stream name>.put(<character value>);.
```

◆ A file exists outside the program block in secondary storage.

PROGRAMMING
PROBLEMS
AND PROJECTS

1. Write a program to print the contents of a text file omitting any occurrences of the letter "e" from the output.
2. A text file contains a list of integers in order from lowest to highest. Write a program to read and print the text file with all duplications eliminated.
3. Mr. John Napier, professor at Lancaster Community College, wants a program to compute grade-point averages. Each line of a text file contains three initials followed

by an unknown number of letter grades. These grades are A, B, C, D, or E. Write a program that reads the file and prints a list of the students' initials and their grade-point averages. (Assume an A is 4 points, a B is 3 points, and so on.) Print an asterisk next to any grade-point average that is greater than 3.75.

4. An amortization table (Problem 19, Chapter 6) shows the rate at which a loan is paid off. It contains monthly entries showing the interest paid that month, the principal paid, and the remaining balance. Given the amount of money borrowed (the principal), the annual interest rate, and the amount the person wishes to repay each month, print an amortization table. (The payment desired must be larger than the first month's interest.) Your table should stop when the loan is paid off, and should be printed with the following heads:

MONTH NUMBER   INTEREST PAID   PRINCIPAL PAID   BALANCE

Create an enumerated data type for the month number. Limit this to require that the loan be paid back within 60 months.

5. Mr. Christian (Problem 26, Chapter 6) uses a 90%, 80%, 70%, 60% grading scale on his tests. Given a list of test scores, print the number of A's, B's, C's, D's, and E's on the test. Terminate the list of scores with a sentinel value.

6. Write a program to print the perimeter and area of rectangles using all combinations of lengths and widths running from 1 foot to 10 feet in increments of 1 foot. Print the output in headed columns.

7. Using a team of three or four students, contact businesses and offices that use computers for data storage. Find exactly how they enter, store, and retrieve data. Discuss with them methods by which they use their databases and how large the databases are. Discuss what they like and dislike about data entry and retrieval. Ask if they have suggestions for modifying any aspect of working with their databases. Prepare a report for class that summarizes your team's findings.

8. Write a program that can be used as a text analyzer. Your program should be capable of reading an input file and keeping track of the frequency of occurrence of each letter of the alphabet. There should also be a count of all characters (including blanks) encountered that are not in the alphabet. Your output should be the data file printed line-by-line followed by a histogram reflecting the frequency of occurrence of each letter in the alphabet. For example, the following histogram indicates five occurrences of a, two of b, and three of c.

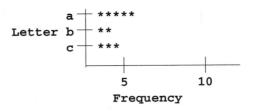

9. The Third Interdenominational Church has on file a list of all of its benefactors (a maximum of 20 names, each up to 30 characters) along with an unknown number of amounts that each has donated to the church. You have been asked to write a program that does the following:

a. Print the name of each donor and the amount (in descending order) of any donations given by each.

b. Print the total amounts in ascending order.

c. Print the grand total of all donations.

d. Print the largest single amount donated and the name of the benefactor who made this donation.

10. Read in a list of 50 integers from the data file **numberlist**. Place the even numbers into an output file called **even**, the odd numbers into an output file called **odd**, and the negatives into an output file called **negative**. Print all three files after all numbers have been read.

11. Ms. Alicia Citizen, your school's student government advisor, has come to you for help. She wants a program to total votes for the next student government election. Fifteen candidates will be in the election with five positions to be filled. Each person can vote for up to five candidates. The five highest vote getters will be the winners.

A data file called **votelist** contains a list of candidates (by candidate number) voted for by each student. Any line of the file may contain up to five numbers, but if it contains more than five numbers, it is discarded as a void ballot. Write a program to read the file and print a list of the total votes received by each candidate. Also, print the five highest vote getters in order from highest to lowest vote totals.

12. The data file **instructorlist** contains a list of the instructors in your school along with the room number to which each is assigned. Write a program that, given the name of the instructor, does a linear search to find and print the room to which the instructor is assigned.

13. Update the ATM management program from Chapter 8 to store new bank accounts in a file. The **<<** and **>>** operations should be used to define output and input operations for an account, and each new account entered from the keyboard in master mode should be stored at the end of the output file.

14. Add a member function to the ATM class of Problem 13 that displays the contents of a file of bank accounts on the screen. The function should be added to the master mode menu.

C H A P T E R ❖ 10 Arrays

Thus far in this text, we have been able to store large amounts of data in files, but we have been unable to manipulate it in a convenient way. For example, we can write a program that allows the user to enter a long list of bank accounts interactively and save the list in a file. However, the file structure does not efficiently support functions to process the accounts in the list, such as searching for an account, updating information in it, or computing statistics on all of the accounts in the list. Other objects are difficult to represent at all with the data structures at our disposal. Consider the example of representing a student whose attributes are a name and a list of ten quiz grades. Representing these attributes as eleven separate named data members in a class definition is unwieldy.

Fortunately, C++ provides a structured data type called an *array* to facilitate solving problems that require working with large amounts of data. The use of arrays permits us to set aside a group of memory locations that we can then manipulate as a single entity or that gives us direct access to any component. We already used arrays in Chapter 7 to develop strings. Other standard applications for arrays include creating tabular output (tables), alphabetizing a list of names, analyzing a list of test scores, and keeping an inventory.

In this chapter, we discuss the use of the array as a general data structuring mechanism. Then we develop two classes, the ordered collection and the sorted collection, that make array processing safe and convenient.

❖ 10.1 Arrays

Basic Idea and Notation

As previously mentioned, many instances arise in which several variables of the same data type are required. Let us at this point work with a list of five integers: 18, 17, 21, 18, and 19. Prior to this chapter, we would have declared five variables—**A**, **B**, **C**, **D**, and **E**—and assigned them appropriate values, or read them from the keyboard. This would have produced five values in memory, each accessed by a separate identifier.

18	17	21	18	19
A	B	C	D	E

If the list was very long, this would be an inefficient way to work with these data; an alternative is to use an array. In C++, we declare a variable as an array variable using either of the following methods:

1. `int list[5];`
2. `typedef int list_type[5];`
   `list_type list;`

With either of these declarations, we now have five integer variables with which to work. They are denoted by

list[0]   list[1]   list[2]   list[3]   list[4]

and each is referred to as a *component* (or *element*) *of the array*. A good way to visualize these variables is to assume that memory locations are aligned in a column on top of each other and the name of the column is **list**. If we then assign the five values of our list to these five variables, we have the following in memory:

list

18	list [0]
17	list [1]
21	list [2]
18	list [3]
19	list [4]

The components of an array are referred to by their relative position in the array. This relative position is called the *index* or *subscript* of the component. In the array of our five values, the component **list[2]** has an index of 2 and a value of 21. Note that an array index is always numbered from zero rather than one. The index of the last component in an array is always $N - 1$, where N is the number of elements in the array.

For the sake of convenience, you may choose to depict an array by listing only the index beside its appropriate component. Thus, **list** could be shown as

list   0
1
2
3
4

If you choose this method, remember that the array elements are referenced by the array name and the index, for example, **list[2]** for the third component. Whichever method you use, it is important to remember that each array component is a variable and can be treated exactly like any other declared variable of that base type in the program.

Declaring an Array

An earlier declaration of an array was

```
int list[5];
```

Let us now examine this declaration more closely. Several comments are in order.

1. The key word **int** indicates the data type for the components. This can, of course, be another data type such as **char**, as we have seen in our definition of a string type.
2. **[5]** is the syntax that indicates the array consists of five memory locations accessed by specifying each of the numbers, 0, 1, 2, 3, and 4. We frequently say the array is of length five. The information inside the brackets must be an integer constant or an expression whose value can be computed at compile time. This value must lie in the range from 1 to an upper bound defined for the particular system on which you are running your programs. (You can look this value up in the manual for your system.) The integer constant can be expressed either literally (**[5]**) or as a named constant (**[MAX_LIST_SIZE]**). The latter form is preferred for better program maintenance.
3. **list**, the name of the variable, can be any valid identifier. As always, it is good practice to use descriptive names to enhance readability.

The form for declaring an array variable is

```
<component type> <variable name> [ <integer value> ] ;
```

where **<component type>** is any predefined or user-defined data type and **<variable name>** is any valid identifier.

The following example illustrates another declaration of an array variable.

EXAMPLE 10.1   Suppose you want to create a list of 10 integer variables for the hours worked by 10 employees as follows:

Employee Number	Hours Worked
0	35
1	40
2	20
3	38
4	25
5	40
6	25
7	40
8	20
9	45

Declare an array that has 10 components of type **int** and show how it can be visualized. A descriptive name for the variable could be **hours**. There are 10 items, so we will define a constant, **MAX_LIST_SIZE = 10**, and use **[MAX_LIST_SIZE]** in the array variable declaration. Because the data consist of integers, the component type will be **int**. An appropriate definition and subsequent declaration could be

```
const int MAX_LIST_SIZE = 10;
int hours[MAX_LIST_SIZE];
```

At this stage, the components can be visualized as

hours

	hours[0]
	hours[1]
	hours[2]
	hours[3]
	hours[4]
	hours[5]
	hours[6]
	hours[7]
	hours[8]
	hours[9]

After making appropriate assignment statements, **hours** can be visualized as

hours

35	hours[0]
40	hours[1]
20	hours[2]
38	hours[3]
25	hours[4]
40	hours[5]
25	hours[6]
40	hours[7]
20	hours[8]
45	hours[9]

Other Element Types

The previous two arrays used element types that were integers. The following examples illustrate some array definitions with other element types.

EXAMPLE 10.2

Declare an array that allows you to store the hourly price for a share of IBM stock. A descriptive name could be **stock_prices**. A price is quoted at each hour from 9:00 A.M. to 3:00 P.M., so we will use **MAX_LIST_SIZE = 7** in the declaration section. Because the data consist of real numbers, the data type must be **float**. A possible declaration could be

```
const int MAX_LIST_SIZE = 7;
float stock_prices[MAX_LIST_SIZE];
```

This would then allow us to store the 9:00 A.M. price in **stock_prices[0]**, the 1:00 P.M. price in **stock_prices[4]**, and so on.

EXAMPLE 10.3

The declaration

```
const int MAX_LIST_SIZE = 6;
char alphas[MAX_LIST_SIZE];
```

will reserve six character components.

EXAMPLE 10.4

The declaration

```
#include "boolean.h"
const int MAX_LIST_SIZE = 4;
boolean flags[MAX_LIST_SIZE];
```

will produce an array whose components are Boolean values.

It is important to note that in each example, the array components will have no predictable values assigned until the program specifically makes some kind of assignment. Declaring an array does not assign values to any of the components.

COMMUNICATION AND STYLE TIPS

The use of descriptive constants is not essential for creating arrays. However, programs that use this method are much easier to maintain than those that use declarations such as **int list[20];**. You will appreciate the use of symbolic constants and array type names better when you learn how to process arrays with loops and functions in the following sections of this chapter.

Assignment Statements

Suppose we have declared an array

```
constant int MAX = 5;
int a[MAX];
```

and we want to put the values 1, 4, 9, 16, and 25 into the respective components. We can accomplish this with the assignment statements

```
a[0] = 1;
a[1] = 4;
a[2] = 9;
a[3] = 16;
a[4] = 25;
```

If variables **b** and **c** of type **int** are declared in the program, then the following are also appropriate assignment statements.

```
a[3] = b;
c = a[2];
a[2] = a[4];
```

If you want to interchange values of two components (for example, exchange **a[2]** with **a[3]**), you could use a third integer variable:

```
b = a[2];
a[2] = a[3];
a[3] = b;
```

This exchange is frequently used in sorting algorithms, so let us examine it more closely. Assume **b** contains no previously assigned value, and **a[2]** and **a[3]** contain 4 and 9, respectively.

	4	a[2]
b	9	a[3]

The assignment statement **b = a[2];** produces

	4	a[2]
4	9	a[3]
b		

The assignment statement **a[2] = a[3];** produces

	9	a[2]
4	9	a[3]
b		

and finally the assignment statement **a[3] = b;** produces

	9	a[2]
4	4	a[3]
b		

in which the original values of **a[2]** and **a[3]** have been interchanged.

Arithmetic

Components of an array can also be used in any appropriate arithmetic operation. For example, suppose **a** is the following array of integers

a

1	a[0]
4	a[1]
9	a[2]
16	a[3]
25	a[4]

and that the values of the components of the array are to be added. This could be accomplished by the statement

```
sum = a[0] + a[1] + a[2] + a[3] + a[4];
```

Each of the following would also be a valid use of an array component:

```
b = 3 * a[1];
c = a[4] % 3;
d = a[1] * a[4];
```

For the array **a** given earlier, these assignment statements produce

55	12	1	100
sum	b	c	d

Some invalid assignment statements and the reasons they are invalid follow:

```
a[6] = 7;
```

This statement will compile and run. However, because 6 is not a valid subscript for the array, the program may behave strangely.

```
a[2.0] = 3;
```

The statement will not compile, because a subscript of type **float** is not allowed.

Reading and Writing

Because array components are names for variables, they can be used in input and output statements. For example, if **scores** is an array of five integers and you want to input the scores 65, 43, 98, 75, and 83 from the keyboard, you could use the code

```
cin >> scores[0] >> scores[1] >> scores[2] >> scores[3]
    >> scores[4];
```

This would produce the array

scores

65	scores[0]
43	scores[1]
98	scores[2]
75	scores[3]
83	scores[4]

If you want to print the scores above 80, you could use the code

```
cout << setw(10) << scores[2] << setw(10) << scores[4] << endl;
```

to produce

```
        98              83
```

It is important to note that you cannot input or output values into or from an entire array by a reference to the array name. Statements such as **cout << a;** are legitimate, but will display the address of the array rather than its contents.

Out-of-Range Array References

You have seen that an array in C++ has index values in the range $0 \ldots N - 1$, where N is the number of cells for storing data in the array. For example, the data declarations

```
const MAX_LIST_SIZE = 5;
int week_days[MAX_LIST_SIZE];
```

cause the system to allocate five cells of memory for an array whose index ranges from 0 to 4. The index values used in array references should also range from 0 to 4. If a programmer uses an index value outside of this range, a *range bound error* is said to occur. If the offending index is a variable, as in

```
int i = 5;
week_days[i] = 10;
```

the error will occur at run time, though the computer will not halt program execution with an error message that this error has occurred.

Even if the offending index is a constant, as in

```
week_days[5] = 10;
```

the error will not be caught at compile time. *C++ does not do range bound error checking.* This means that the program will compile and execute, and the reference will be to some other area of memory than the cells allocated for the array. In the case of an assignment to that location, a serious side effect will occur and may cause the program to behave in very mysterious ways.

Range bound errors in C++ programs are most often caused by failure to remember that the upper bound on the array index is $N - 1$, where N is the number of cells in the array. One way to avoid range bound errors with arrays is to be careful always to use an index that satisfies the condition $0 <= \text{index} < N$, where N is the integer constant used to define the array type. You may wish to use the C++ assertion facility to place this precondition on array references in spots in a program where range bound errors are likely to occur.

In Section 10.5, we will develop an array class that supports range bound checking.

EXERCISES 10.1

1. Using descriptive names, define an array type and declare subsequent variables for each of the following:
   a. A list of 35 test scores
   b. The prices of 20 automobiles
   c. The answers to 50 true or false questions
   d. A list of letter grades for the classes you are taking this semester

2. Write a test program in which you declare an array of three components, read values into each component, sum the components, and print the sum and value of each component.

3. Assume the array **list** is declared as

```
int list[100];
```

   and that all other variables have been appropriately declared. Label the following as valid or invalid. Include an explanation for any that are invalid.
   a. `cin >> list[3];`
   b. `a = list[3] + list[4];`
   c. `cout << list;`
   d. `list[10] = 3.2;`
   e. `max = list[50];`
   f. `average = (list[0] + list[8]) / 2;`
   g. `cout << list[25, 50, 75];`
   h. `cout << list[10] + list[25];`
   i. `for (j = 0; j < 100; ++j)`
          `cin >> list;`
   j. `list[36] = list[100];`
   k. `list_type[47] = 92;`
   l. `list[40] = list[41] / 2;`

4. Change each of the following so that a **typedef** is used to define the array type.
   a. `char letter_list[26];`
   b. `char company_name[30];`
   c. `float score_list[30];`

5. Consider the array declared by

```
int waist_sizes[5]
```

   a. Sketch how the array should be envisioned in memory.
   b. After assignments

```
waist_sizes[0] = 34;
waist_sizes[1] = 36;
waist_sizes[2] = 32;
waist_sizes[3] = 2 * 15;
waist_sizes[4] = (waist_sizes[0] + waist_sizes[2]) / 2;
```

have been made, sketch the array and indicate the contents of each component.

6. Let the array money be declared by

```
float money[3];
```

Let **temp, x**, and **y** be **float** variables and assume **money** has the following values:

money
19.26	money[0]
10.04	money[1]
17.32	money[2]

Assuming **money** contains the values indicated before each segment is executed, indicate what the array would contain after each section of code.

```
a. temp = 173.21;
   x = temp + money[1];
   money[0] = x;
b. if (money[1] < money[0])
   {
        temp = money[2];
        money[1] = money[1];
        money[0] = temp;
   }
c. money[2] = 20.0 - money[2];
```

7. Let the array **list** be declared by

```
float list[10];
```

Write a program segment to initialize all components of **list** to 0.0.

A NOTE OF INTEREST

Monolithic Idea: Invention of the Integrated Circuit

One of the most significant breakthroughs in the history of technology occurred in the late 1950s. Prior to 1958, computer circuitry was limited because transistors, diodes, resistors, and capacitors were separate units that had to be wired together and soldered by hand. Although designers could design intricate computer supercircuits using 500,000 transistors, they were almost impossible to build because of the extensive handwork involved. For example, a circuit with 100,000 components could require more than 1,000,000 soldered connections. It was virtually impossible to assemble that many components without human error. Thus, the electronics industry was faced with an apparently insurmountable limit.

About this time, Jack St. Clair Kilby developed what has come to be known as the Monolithic Idea. He decided you could put the components of an entire circuit in a monolithic block of silicon. The idea, together with Robert Noyce's work on interconnecting circuits, allowed electronics engineers to overcome the obstacle presented by separate components. Kilby and Noyce's work resulted in the integrated circuit, the most important new product in the history of electronics. For their efforts, both men were awarded the National Medal of Science.

10.2 Using Arrays

OBJECTIVES

- to be able to use loops to input data into an array
- to be able to use loops to output data from an array
- to be able to assign array values by component assignment

Loops for Input and Output

One advantage of using arrays is the small amount of code needed when **for** loops are used to manipulate array components. For example, suppose a list of 100 scores is to be used in a program. If an array is declared by

```
const int MAX_LIST_SIZE = 100;
int scores[MAX_LIST_SIZE];
```

the values can be read into the array using a **for** loop as follows:

```
for (j = 0; j < MAX_LIST_SIZE ; ++j)
{
    cout << "Enter a score: ";
    cin >> scores[j];
}
```

Note that the control variable is initialized to zero, and that the comparison in the termination condition is a simple less than operator (<). The reason for this is that the index positions in the array have been defined to range from 0 to 99, inclusive. Note also that the size of the array, **MAX_LIST_SIZE**, is used both in the array variable declaration and in the **for** loop. If we want to change the size of the array, we need only change the value 100 in the constant definition, and not in the array variable declaration or in the loop. As always, the use of symbolic constants greatly enhances program maintenance. Note finally that a statement such as **cin >> score** will not have the desired effect. You may only read data elements into individual components of the array.

Loops can be similarly used to produce output of array components. For example, if the array of test scores just given is to be printed in a column,

```
for (j = 0; j < MAX_LIST_SIZE; ++j)
    cout << scores[j] << endl;
```

will accomplish this. If the components of **scores** contain the values

scores	
78	scores[0]
93	scores[1]
.	.
.	.
82	scores[99]

the loop for writing produces

```
78
93
.
.
.
82
```

Note that you cannot cause the array components to be printed by a statement such as **cout << scores**. You must refer to the individual components.

Loops for output are seldom this simple. Usually we are required to format the output in some manner. For example, suppose the array **scores** is as declared earlier and we wish to print 10 scores to a line, each with a field width of five spaces. The following segment of code would accomplish this.

```
for (j = 0; j < MAX_LIST_SIZE; ++j)
{
    cout << setw(5) << scores[j];
    if (j % 10 == 0)
        cout << endl;
}
```

Loops for Assigning

Loops can also be used to assign values to array components. In certain instances, you might wish to have an array contain values that are not read from the keyboard. The following examples show how loops can be used to solve such instances.

EXAMPLE 10.5

Recall array **a** in Section 10.1 in which we made the following assignments:

```
a[0] = 1;
a[1] = 4;
a[2] = 9;
a[3] = 16;
a[4] = 25;
```

These assignments could have been made with the loop

```
for (j = 0; j < 4; ++j)
    a[j] = (j + 1) * (j + 1);
```

EXAMPLE 10.6

Suppose an array is needed whose components contain the letters of the alphabet in order from A to Z. Assuming you are using the ASCII character set, the desired array could be declared by

```
const int MAX_LIST_SIZE = 26;
char alphabet[MAX_LIST_SIZE];
```

The array alphabet could then be assigned the desired characters by the statement

```
for (j = 0; j < MAX_LIST_SIZE; ++j)
    alphabet[j] = char(j + 'A');
```

If **j = 0;** we have

```
alphabet[0] = char('A');
```

Thus,

```
alphabet[0] = 'A';
```

Similarly, for **j = 1;** we have

```
alphabet[1] = char(1 + 'A');
```

Eventually we obtain

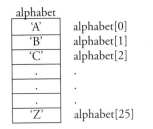

alphabet
'A'	alphabet[0]
'B'	alphabet[1]
'C'	alphabet[2]
.	.
.	.
.	.
'Z'	alphabet[25]

Assignment of values from components of one array to corresponding components of another array is a frequently encountered problem. For example, suppose the arrays **a** and **b** are declared as

```
const int MAX_LIST_SIZE = 50;
float a[MAX_LIST_SIZE];
float b[MAX_LIST_SIZE];
```

If **b** has been assigned values and you want to put the contents of **b** into **a** component by component, you must use the loop

```
for (j = 0; j < MAX_LIST_SIZE; ++j)
    a[j] = b[j];
```

Now suppose you tried a shortcut, by assigning one whole array variable to another:

```
a = b;
```

This assignment does *not* cause 50 assignments to be made at the component level. In some implementations of C++, the assignment will cause the name **a** to be an alias for the array **b**. The reason for this is that references to array variables are really references to the addresses of the arrays. In other implementations of C++, the assignment is a syntax error. It would be a good practice to write a function that copies components from one array to another and use it in your various programs.

Processing with Loops

Loops are especially suitable for reading, writing, and assigning array components, and they can be used in conjunction with arrays to process data. The following examples illustrate additional uses of loops for processing data contained in array variables.

EXAMPLE 10.7   Recall the problem earlier in this section in which we read 100 test scores into an array. Assume the scores have been read and you now wish to find the average score and the largest score. Assume variables **sum, max**, and **average** have been appropriately declared. The following segment will compute the average.

```
sum = 0;
for (j = 0; j < MAX_LIST_SIZE; ++j)
    sum = sum + scores[j];
average = sum / MAX_LIST_SIZE;
```

sum

| 235 |
| 310 |

For example, on the fourth time through the **for** loop, **sum** would accumulate from 235 to 310.

scores

0	80
1	65
2	90
j = 3	75
.	.
.	.
97	93
98	86
99	79

The maximum score can be found by using the following segment of code:

```
max = scores[0];
for (j = 1; j < MAX_LIST_SIZE; ++ j)
    if (scores[j] > max)
        max = scores [j];
```

max

| 80 |
| 90 |

scores

0	80
1	65
2	90
j = 3	75

. .

97	93
98	86
99	79

For example, when **j** is 2, **max** would be updated from 80 to 90.

EXAMPLE 10.8

Write a segment of code to find the smallest value of array **a** and the index of the smallest value. Assume the variables have been declared as

```
const int MAX_LIST_SIZE = 100;
float a[MAX_LIST_SIZE];
float min;
int index;
```

and the values have been read into components of **a**. The following code will solve the problem:

```
index = 0;
for (j = 1; j < MAX_LIST_SIZE; ++ j)
    if (a[j] < a [index])
        index = j;
```

index

| 0̸ |
| 1̸ |
| 3 |

a

0	80
1	65
2	90
j = 3	62

. .

97	93
98	86
99	79

For this data, when **j** is 3, **index** would be updated from 1 to 3.

A standard problem encountered when working with arrays is that of not knowing exactly how many components of an array will be needed. In C++, the standard array data type has a fixed size. Thus, you must decide some upper limit for the length of the array. A standard procedure is to declare a reasonable limit, keeping two points in mind.

1. The length must be sufficient to store all the data.
2. The amount of storage space must not be excessive; do not set aside excessive amounts of space that will not be used.

EXERCISES 10.2

1. Assume the following array declarations:

```
typedef int num_list_type[5];
typedef boolean answer_list_type[10];
typedef char name_list_type[20];

num_list_type list, scores;
answer_list_type answers;
name_list_type initials;
```

Indicate the contents of the arrays after each segment of code.

a.
```
for (j = 0; j < 5; ++j)
    list[j] = j / 3;
```
b.
```
for (j = 1; j < 6; ++j)
{
    list[j - 1] = j + 3;
    scores[j - 1] = list[j - 1] / 3;
}
```
c.
```
for (j = 0; j < 10; ++j)
    if (j % 2 == 0)
        answers[j] = TRUE;
    else
        answers[j] = FALSE;
```
d.
```
for (j = 0; j < 20; ++j)
    initials[j] = char(j + 64);
```

2. Write a test program to illustrate what happens when you try to use an index that is not in the defined range for an array; for example, try to use the loop

```
for (j = 0; j < 10; ++j)
    cin >> a[j];
```

when **a** has been declared as **int a[5];**

3. Let the array **best** be declared by

```
int best[30];
```

and assume that test scores have been read into **best**. What does the following section of code do?

```
count = 0;
for (j = 0; j < 30; ++j);
    if (best[j] > 90)
        ++count;
```

4. Declare an array and write a segment of code to do the following:

a. Read 20 integer test scores into the array.

b. Count the number of scores greater than or equal to 55.

5. Declare an array using a **typedef** and write a section of code to read a name of 20 characters from a line of input.

6. Let the array **list** be declared by **int list[7];** and assume the components have values of

list

-2	list[0]
3	list[1]
0	list[2]
-8	list[3]
20	list[4]
14	list[5]
-121	list[6]

Show what the array components would be after the following program segment is executed:

```
for (j = 0; j < 7; ++j)
    if (list[j] < 0)
        list[j] = 0;
```

7. Assume array **a** is declared as

```
float a[100];
```

Write a segment of code that uses a loop to initialize all components to zero.

8. Let the array **n** be declared as **char n[21];** and assume the array components have been assigned the values

J	O	H	N		S	M	I	T	H
n[0]	n[1]	n[2]	n[3]	n[4]	n[5]	n[6]	n[7]	n[8]	n[9]

What output is produced by the following?

a.
```
for (j= 0; j < 10; ++j)
    cout << n[j];
cout << endl;
```
b.
```
for (j= 0; j < 5; ++j)
    cout << n[j];
cout << ", ";
for (j= 0; j < 4; ++j)
    cout << n[j];
cout << endl;
```
c.
```
for (j = 9; j >= 0; --j)
    cout << n[j];
```

9. Assume an array has been declared as

```
int test_scores[50];
```

Write a segment of code to print a suitable heading (assume this is a list of test scores) and then output a numbered list of the array components.

Array Parameters and Functions

OBJECTIVES

- to be able to use functions to process arrays
- to be able to pass arrays as parameters to functions
- to understand the difference between array parameters and parameters of other data types

Functions can be used with array parameters to maintain a structured design. Consider the problem of computing the mean of a list of test scores. We can represent the list of scores as an array that can be passed to several functions for processing. A first-level pseudocode development of a solution to this problem is as follows:

1. Get the scores **(function get_data)**
2. Compute the average **(function calc_mean)**
3. Print a header **(function print_header)**
4. Print the results **(function print_results)**

The functions **get_data**, **calc_mean**, and **print_results** all take an array parameter and an integer parameter representing the number of data elements currently stored in the array. Here are the declarations of these functions:

```
// Function: get_data
// Gets list of scores from the user at the keyboard
// until a sentinel is entered
//
// Inputs: length, representing the maximum physical size
// of the list
// Outputs: an array of integers representing the list
// and length, representing
// its logical size
```

```
void get_data(int list[ ], int &length);


// Function: calc_mean
// Computes the mean of the scores in the list
//
// Inputs: an array of integers and its length
// Output: a real number representing the mean of the
// integers in the array


float calc_mean(int list[ ], int length);


// Function: print_results
// Displays the scores and the mean score
//
// Inputs: an array of integers and the mean on the
// screen


void print_results(int list[ ], int length, float ave);
```

There are several things to note about these declarations:

1. None of the arrays appears to be passed by reference to the functions, but they all are. Recall from our discussion of character arrays in Section 7.2 that the address of an actual parameter of an array is always passed to a function. In the case of actual parameters that are array variables, the corresponding formal parameters in the function will serve as aliases for the variables. Therefore, changes to the array cells referenced by a formal array parameter will also be changes to the array cells referenced by the actual parameter.

2. The maximum size of each array does not appear to be specified in the formal parameter declarations, where we see a pair of empty square brackets (**[ ]**). Because the arrays are all passed by reference, the computer does not have to know how large the actual array will be when a function is called. Leaving the physical size of the array unspecified in the formal parameter declaration will allow a function to be called with arrays of different physical sizes, as long as the element type (in this case, **int**), is the same.

3. The **length** parameter for **get_data** represents the *physical size* of the array parameter when the function is called, and it represents the *logical size,* or number of data elements input, when the function returns.

4. Though the form **<element type> <parameter name> [ ]** is most commonly used to declare array parameters, other forms may specify the physical size of the array or may precede the array parameter name with an array type name.

The implementation of **get_data** is

```
void get_data(int list[ ], int &length)
{
    int data, logical_length;

    logical_length = 0;
    cout << "Enter an integer (" << INPUT_SENTINEL
        << " to end input): ";
    cin >> data;
    while ((logical_length < length) && ! end_of_input(data))
```

```
    {
        list[logical_length] = data;
        ++logical_length;
        cout << "Enter an integer (" << INPUT_SENTINEL
            << " to end input): ";
        cin >> data;
    }
    length = logical_length;
}
```

Using two different lists and their lengths, **get_data** could be called by

```
const int MAX1 = 10;
const int MAX2 = 20;

int list1[MAX1];
int list2[MAX2];

int length1 = MAX1;
int length2 = MAX2;

get_data(list1, length1);
get_data(list2, length2);
```

The average score in a list could be computed by the function **calc_mean**:

```
float calc_mean (int list[ ], int length)
{
    int sum = 0;

    for (int j = 0; j < length; ++j)
        sum = sum + list[j];
    return float(sum) / length;
}
```

A function to print a heading would be written in a manner similar to that we have used previously. If we want the output to be

```
Test Scores
-----------
    99
    98
    97
    96
    95


The average score on this test was 97.00.
```

the function for the heading could be

```
void print_header()
{
    cout << endl;
    cout << "Test Scores" << endl;
    cout << "-----------" << endl;
    cout << endl;
}
```

A function to print the results could be

```
void print_results (int list[ ], int length, float ave)
{
    for (int j = 0; j < length; ++j)
        cout << setw(5) << list[j] << endl;
    cout << endl << fixed << showpoint << setprecision(2);
    cout << "The average score on this test was"
        << setw(6) << ave << endl;
}
```

This function could be called by

```
    print_results(scores, length, ave);
```

where **ave** is found by

```
    ave = calc_mean(scores, length);
```

The important thing to remember about array parameters is that they are treated very differently than parameters of other data types in C++. For reasons of efficiency, the address of a C++ array variable (which is actually identified by the array name and also is the address of the first data value in the array) is always passed to a function expecting an array parameter. The following rules of thumb will help in designing functions for processing arrays:

1. Never use the **&** symbol when specifying a formal array parameter in a function declaration or heading.

2. Specify a constant array formal parameter, of the form **const <element type> <parameter name> [ ]**, when you want to guarantee that no changes will be made to the array variable being passed to a function.

The special nature of array parameters in C++ can be a source of confusion for beginning programmers. In Section 10.5, we develop a new array class that allows array parameters to be treated like parameters of other data types in C++.

EXERCISES 10.3

1. Assume the following declarations have been made in a program.

```
typedef int row_type[10];
typedef float column_type[30];
typedef char string20_type[21];

row_type list1, list2;
column_type aray;
string20_type name1, name2;
int a[10];
int b[10];
```

Indicate which of the following are valid function declarations. Write an appropriate line of code that will use each valid declaration. Include an explanation for those that are invalid.

a. void new_list (row_type x, column_type y);

b. void new_list (row_type &x, column_type &y);

c. void new_list (int x[ ]);

d. void new_list (row_type &x, row_type &y);

e. void new_list (row_type &row_type);

f. void word_week (int days[7]);

g. void surname (name x);

    h. `void surnames (string20_type x, string20_type y);`

    i. `void get_data (int x, name &y);`

    j. `void table (row_type &x, row_type &y);`

2. When possible, use the declarations of Exercise 1 to write function declarations so that each of the following statements in the main program is an appropriate call to a function. Explain any inappropriate calls.

    a. `old_list (list1, aray);`

    b. `change_list (list1, name1, b);`

    c. `scores (a, b);`

    d. `surname (string20_type);`

3. Write an appropriate function declaration and a line of code to call the function for each of the following.

    a. A function to input 20 test scores into an array.

    b. A function to count the number of occurrences of the letter 'A' in an array of 50 characters.

    c. A function to input integer test scores from the keyboard, count the number of scores, count the number of scores greater than or equal to 90, and save this information for later use.

4. Assume the following declarations have been made:

```
typedef int column_type[10];
column_type list1, list2;
```

Indicate the contents of each array after the call to the corresponding function.

    a.
```
void sample (column_type &list1, column_type list2)
{
    for (int j = 0; j < 10; ++j)
    {
        list1[j] = j *j;
        list2[j] = list1[j] % 2;
    }
}

for (int k = 0; k < 10; ++k)
{
    list1[k] = 0;
    list2[k] = 0;
}
sample (list1, list2);
```

    b. Replace the function call with

```
sample (list2, list1);
```

    c. Replace the function call with consecutive calls

```
sample (list1, list2);
sample (list2, list1);
```

5. Write a function to examine an array of integers and then return the maximum value, minimum value, and number of negative values to the main program.

6. Discuss some of the implementation details you would need in order to read a list of names into an array.

OBJECTIVES

- to be able to sort an array using a selection sort
- to be able to search an array using a sequential search

Sorting an Array

Arrays often need to be sorted in either ascending or descending order. We will consider here one of the easier methods for doing this, the *selection sort*, and examine another method, the *quick sort*, in Chapter 12.

Suppose we have an array **a** of five integers that we wish to sort from smallest to largest. The values currently in **a** are as depicted on the left; we wish to end up with values as on the right.

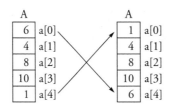

The basic idea of a selection sort is

For each index position *I*
1. Find the smallest data value in the array from positions *I* through length – 1, where length is the number of data values stored.
2. Exchange the smallest value with the value at position *I*.

The first pass through the loop produces

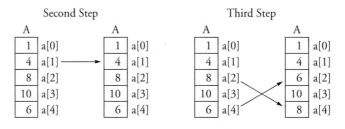

The second, third, and fourth passes produce

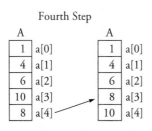

Notice that in the second pass, since the second smallest number was already in place, we need not exchange anything. Before writing the algorithm for this sorting procedure, note the following:

1. If the array is of length *n,* we need *n* – 1 steps.
2. We must be able to find the smallest number.
3. We need to exchange appropriate array components.

When the code is written for this sort, note that strict inequality (<) rather than weak inequality (<=) is used when looking for the smallest remaining value. The algorithm to sort by selection is

For each j from 0 to n - 1 do
      Find the smallest value among a[j], a[j + 1], . . . a[n - 1]
            and store the index of the smallest value in index
      Exchange the values of a[j] and a[index], if necessary

In Section 10.2, Example 10.8, we saw a segment of code required to find the smallest value of array **a.** With suitable changes, we will incorporate this in the segment of code as a function, **find_minimum**, for the selection sort. We will also develop a function, **swap**, that exchanges the elements in an array when necessary.

Using these two functions, the implementation of a **sort** function is

```
void sort(int a[ ], int length)
{
    int min_index = 0;

    for (int j = 0; j < length - 1; ++j)
    {
        min_index = find_minimum(a, j, length);
        if (min_index != j)
            swap(a[j], a[min_index]);
    }
}
```

The function for finding the minimum value in an array takes three parameters: the array, the position to start the search, and the length or logical size of the array. The function returns the index position of the minimum element in the array. Its implementation uses a **for** loop:

```
int find_minimum(int a[ ], int first, int length)
{
    int min_index = first;

    for (int k = first + 1; k < length; ++k)
        if (a[k] < a[min_index])
            min_index = k;
    return min_index;
}
```

The **swap** function exchanges the values of two integer variables:

```
void swap(int &x, int &y)
{
    int temp = x;
    x = y;
    y = temp;
}
```

Let us now trace this sort for the five integers in the array we sorted at the beginning of this section.

```
     a
    ┌────┐
    │  6 │  a[0]
    ├────┤
    │  4 │  a[1]
    ├────┤
    │  8 │  a[2]
    ├────┤
    │ 10 │  a[3]
    ├────┤
    │  1 │  a[4]
    └────┘
```

For **j = 0, min_index = 0** (in **find_minimum**), and this produces

```
    ┌──────────┐
    │    0     │
    └──────────┘
    min_index
```

For the loop (in **find_minimum**) **for (k = 1; k < 5; ++k)**, we get successive assignments

k	min_index
1	1
2	1
3	1
4	4

The statements (in **swap**)

```
temp = a[j];
a[j] = a[min_index];
a[min_index] = temp;
```

produce the partially sorted array:

```
     a
    ┌────┐
    │  1 │  a[0]
    ├────┤
    │  4 │  a[1]
    ├────┤
    │  8 │  a[2]
    ├────┤
    │ 10 │  a[3]
    ├────┤
    │  6 │  a[4]
    └────┘
```

EXAMPLE 10.9

This example accomplishes these tasks:

1. Inputs real numbers from the keyboard.
2. Prints the numbers in a column of width six with two places to the right of the decimal.
3. Sorts the array from low to high.
4. Prints the sorted array using the same output format.

An expanded pseudocode development for this is

1. Print greeting (**function print_greeting**)
2. Get data (**function get_data**)
3. Output list of data (**function print_list**)
4. Sort list (**function sort_list**)
5. Output sorted list (**function print_list**)

```
// Program file: sort.cpp

// This program illustrates the use of a sorting algorithm
// with an array of reals. Output includes data in both an
// unsorted and a sorted list. The data are formatted and
// numbered to enhance readability.

#include <iostream.h>
#include <iomanip.h>
#include "boolean.h"

const char SKIP = ' ';
const int MAX_LIST_SIZE = 5;
const float INPUT_SENTINEL = -999.0;

// Function: print_greeting
// Displays sign-on message about purpose of the program

void print_greeting();

// Function: get_data
// Reads data from keyboard into list
//
// Inputs: length represents physical size of list
// Outputs: a list of real numbers and its length, representing logical size of
// list

void get_data(float list[ ], int &length);

// Function: print_list
// Prints contents of list to terminal screen
//
// Inputs: a list of real numbers and its length

void print_list(float list[ ], int length);

// Function: sort_list
// Sorts contents of list into ascending order
//
// Inputs: a list of real numbers and its length
// Output: a sorted list of real numbers

void sort_list(float list[ ], int length);

// Function: end_of_input
// Informs caller whether or not input data is end-of-input sentinel
//
// Input: a real number
// Output: TRUE, if number is end of input sentinel, FALSE otherwise

// Function: find_minimum
// Finds position of minimum element in list between first and length
//
```

```cpp
// Inputs: a list, the first position, and the length
// Output: the index position of the minimum element in the list

int find_minimum(float list[ ], int first, int length);

// Function: swap
// Exchanges two real numbers
//
// Inputs: two real number variables
// Outputs: the two variables, with their values exchanged

void swap(float &x, float &y);

boolean end_of_input(float data);

int main()
{
      int length = MAX_LIST_SIZE;
      float list[MAX_LIST_SIZE];

      print_greeting();
      get_data(list, length);
      cout << setw(10) << SKIP << "The original list is as follows:'' << endl;
      cout << endl;
      print_list(list, length);
      sort_list(list, length);
      cout << setw(10) << SKIP << "The sorted list is as follows:" << endl;
      cout << endl;
      print_list(list, length);
      return 0;
}

void print_greeting()
{
cout << setprecision(2) << fixed << showpoint;
cout << endl;
cout << setw(10) << SKIP << "This sample program does the following:"
      << endl;
cout << endl;
cout << setw(12) << SKIP << "1 Gets reals from the keyboard." << endl;
cout << setw(12) << SKIP << "2 Prints the data." << endl;
cout << setw(12) << SKIP << "3 Sorts the data from low to high." << endl;
cout << setw(12) << SKIP << "4 Prints a sorted list of the data."
      << endl;
cout << endl;
}

void get_data(float list[ ], int &length)
{
      int logical_length = 0;
      float data;

      cout << "Enter a real number (-999 to stop input): ";
      cin >> data;
```

```
        while((logical_length < length) && ! end_of_input(data))
        {
              list[logical_length] = data;
              ++logical_length;
              cout << "Enter a real number (-999 to stop input): ";
              cin >> data;
        }
        if (! end_of_input(data) && (logical_length == length))
              cout << "There is more data." << endl;
        length = logical_length;
}

void print_list(float list[ ], int length)
{
        cout << endl;
        for (int j = 0; j < length; ++j)
              cout << setw(12) << SKIP << '<' << j + 1 << '>' << setw(6)
                    << list[j]
                    << endl;
}

void sort_list(float list[ ], int length)
{
        int min_index = 0;

        for (int j = 0; j < length - 1; ++j)
        {
              min_index = find_minimum(list, j, length);
              if (min_index != j)
                    swap(list[j], list[min_index]);
        }
}

int find_minimum(float list[ ], int first, int length)
{
        int min_index = first;

        for (int j = first + 1; j < length; ++ j)
              if (list[j] < list[min_index])
                    min_index = j;
        return min_index;
}

void swap(float &x, float &y)
{
        float temp = x;
        x = y;
        y = temp;
}

boolean end_of_input(float data)
{
        return data == INPUT_SENTINEL;
}
```

The output for this program is

```
This sample program does the following:

   1 Gets reals from the keyboard.
   2 Prints the data.
   3 Sorts the data from low to high.
   4 Prints a sorted list of the data.

The original data are as follows:

      <1>      34.56

      <2>      78.21

      <3>      23.30

      <4>      89.90

      <5>      45.00

The sorted list is as follows:

      <1>      23.30

      <2>      34.56

      <3>      45.00

      <4>      78.21

      <5>      89.90
```

Searching an Array

The need to search an array for a value is a common problem. For example, you might wish to replace a test score for a student, delete a name from a directory or mailing list, or upgrade the pay scale for certain employees. These and other problems require you to be able to examine elements in some list until the desired value is located. When it is found, some action is taken. In this section, we assume all lists are nonempty.

The searching algorithm we examine is the most common method, a *sequential (linear) search.* This process is accomplished by examining the first element in some list and then proceeding to examine the elements in the order they appear until a match is found. Variations of this basic process include searching a sorted list for the first occurrence of a value, searching a sorted list for all occurrences of a value, and searching an unsorted list for the first occurrence of a value. We will look at another method, the *binary search,* in Chapter 12.

To illustrate a sequential search, suppose you have an array **a** of integers and you want to find the first occurrence of some particular value (**num**). As you search the array, if the desired value is located, you want to print its position. If the value is not in the array, an appropriate message should be printed. The code for such a search follows:

```
index = 0;
while ((index < length) && (num != a[index]))
        ++index;
```

A reasonable message for output is

```
if (index == length)
        cout << num << " is not in the list." << endl;
else
        cout << num << " is in position" << setw(5)
                << index << endl;
```

Let's now consider some variations of this problem. Our code works for both a sorted and an unsorted list. However, if we are searching a sorted list, the algorithm can be improved. For example, if the array components are sorted from low to high, we need to continue the search only until the value in an array component exceeds the value of **num**. At that point, there is no need to examine the remaining components. The only change required in the loop for searching is to replace **num != a[index]** with **num > a[index]**. Thus, we have

```
index = 0;
while ((index < length) && (num > a[index]))
        ++index;
```

A relatively easy modification of the sequential search is to examine a list for all occurrences of some value. When searching an array, you would generally print the positions and values when a match is found. To illustrate, if **a** is an array of integers and **num** has an integer value, we can search **a** for the number of occurrences of **num** by

```
count = 0;
for (index = 0; index < length; ++index)
    if (num == a[index])
    {
            ++count;
            cout << num << " is in position" << setw(5)
                    << index<< endl;
    }
```

This code works for an unsorted list. A modification of the code for working with a sorted list is included as an exercise.

EXERCISES 10.4

1. Assume the array **column** is to be sorted from low to high using the selection sort.

column

–20
10
0
10
8
30
–2

a. Sketch the contents of the array after each of the first two passes.

b. How many exchanges are made during the sort?

2. Write a test program that prints the partially sorted arrays after each pass during a selection sort.

A NOTE OF INTEREST

Too Few Women in the Computer Science Pipeline?

Studies show that women in computer science programs in U.S. universities terminate their training earlier than men do. Between 1983 and 1986 (the latest year for which we have such figures) the percentage of bachelor's degrees in computer science awarded to women was in the range of 36 to 37% and the percentage of master's degrees was in the range of 28 to 30%. During the same time span, the percentage of doctoral degrees awarded to women was in the range of only 10 to 12%, and it has remained at that level, with the exception of a slight increase in 1989. If we look at the people who are training the future computer scientists, we may find a clue as to why this discrepancy exists. Women currently hold only 6.5% of the faculty positions in the computer science and computer engineering departments in the 158 PhD-granting institutions included in the 1988–1989 Taulbee Survey. In fact, a third of these departments have no female faculty members at all. This pattern of decreasing representation is often described as pipeline shrinkage: as women move along the academic pipeline, their percentages continue to shrink.

The ACM Committee on the Status of Women has made a number of recommendations to promote change, including the following:

Ensure equal access to computers for young girls and boys and develop educational software appealing to both.
Establish programs (such as science fairs, scouting programs, and conferences in which women speak about their careers in science and engineering) to encourage high school girls to continue with math and science.

Develop programs to pair undergraduate women with women graduate students or faculty members who serve as role models, providing encouragement and advice.
Provide women with opportunities for successful professional experiences (such as involvement in research projects) beginning as early as the undergraduate years.
Establish programs that make women computer scientists visible to undergraduates and graduate students. Women can be invited to campuses to give talks or to serve as visiting faculty members (as, for example, in the National Science Foundation's Visiting Professorships for Women).
Encourage men and women to serve as mentors for young women in the field.
Maintain lists of qualified women computer scientists to increase the participation of women in influential positions such as program committees, editorial boards, and policy boards.
Establish more reentry programs that enable women who have stopped their scientific training prematurely to retrain as computer scientists.
Increase awareness of, and sensitivity to, subtle discrimination and its effects.
Develop and enforce safety procedures on campus. Provide safe access at all hours to public terminal areas, well-lit routes from offices to parking lots, and services to escort those walking on campus after dark.
Provide affordable, quality childcare.

3. Change the code for the selection sort so it sorts an array from high to low.

4. Write a complete program that does the following:
   a. Read 10 reals into an array from the keyboard.
   b. If the first real is positive, sort the array from high to low; if it is negative, sort the array from low to high.
   c. Print a numbered column containing the sorted reals with the format of 10 columns of field width and two decimal places of precision.

5. Modify the selection sort by including a counter that counts the number of assignments of array elements made during a sort.

6. Using the modification in Exercise 5, sort lists of differing lengths that contain randomly generated numbers. Display the results of how many assignments were made for each sort on a graph. Use lists whose lengths are multiples of 10.

7. Suppose you have an array of student names and an array of these students' test scores. How would the array of names be affected if you sorted the test scores from high to low?

A Safe Array Class

10.5

OBJECTIVES

- to understand why standard arrays are not safe
- to be able to design and implement a new array class that performs run-time range checking

User Requirements

The C++ array is a useful data structure, but some features can cause inconvenience for clients or, even worse, errors in clients' programs. Perhaps the most serious problem is the absence of built-in range checking, either at compile time or at run time. Recall that references to data locations within an array must be specified by an index value that is within the range from zero (the first location) to **MAX_ARRAY_SIZE - 1** (the last location), where **MAX_ARRAY_SIZE** is the number of locations specified by the array variable declaration. Because range errors go undetected, they may cause undesirable behavior such as logic errors (unexpected output) or system crashes (side effects on the underlying operating system). Clearly, an array would be safer if it detected range errors and halted program execution with a message, rather than cause logic errors or crashes.

Other features of arrays are inconvenient. For example, a client ought to be able to copy the contents of one whole array to another by means of a simple assignment statement (**a = b**), though this is prohibited in most implementations of C++. A client might also wish to compare two arrays for equality, which would mean the equality of the data elements at each position in the two arrays.

We can solve many of these problems by defining a new class in C++ to represent arrays. The class will assume that all arrays have the same maximum physical size, and they all contain the same type of data elements. Each of these attributes will be defined by client applications before the array class is defined. Clients are expected to define the constant **MAX_ARRAY_SIZE** and the type name **element** for these purposes, and to place them in the header file **element.h**. For example, a client might provide information for an array class capable of holding 50 integers as follows:

```
// Library header file: element.h

#ifndef ELEMENT_H

const int MAX_ARRAY_SIZE = 50;
typedef int element;

#define ELEMENT_H
#endif
```

The use of instances of the safe array class should be consistent with the use of standard C++ arrays. In particular, the use of the subscript notation for referencing data elements within an array should be supported. For example, the following code would declare and initialize an array of 50 integers to zero:

```
array a;

for (int j = 0; j < MAX_ARRAY_SIZE; ++j)
    a[j] = 0;
```

Specifying the Operations

A formal specification of the operations for the safe array class follows:

Create operation	
Preconditions:	The array is in an unpredictable state.
Postconditions:	Memory is reserved for an array object capable of storing **MAX_ARRAY_SIZE** data elements.

Subscript operation

Preconditions: The receiver is an array object, appropriately initialized.
The index parameter is an integer value in the range
`0 <= index < MAX_ARRAY_SIZE`.

Postconditions: The location of the data element, which can be used either to reference or to store a value, is returned.

Assignment operation

Preconditions: The receiver is an array object in an unpredictable state.
The parameter is an array object, appropriately initialized.

Postconditions: The contents of the parameter object are copied into the receiver object.

Equality operation

Preconditions: The receiver is an array object, appropriately initialized.
The parameter is an array object, appropriately initialized.
Objects in the arrays can be compared using a standard equality operation.

Postconditions: Returns TRUE if each pair of objects in the two arrays are equal, and FALSE otherwise.

Declaring the Class

The four operations specified for the safe array class are creation, subscripting, assignment, and testing for equality. To maintain consistency with the conventional uses of arrays, we will use the standard operators for subscripting, assignment, and equality in the class declaration, and provide overloaded operations for them in the class implementation.

```
// Class declaration file: array.h

#ifndef ARRAY_H

// Declaration section

// We assume that the type element and
// the constant MAX_ARRAY_SIZE have been defined by the
// application in element.h

#include "boolean.h"
#include "element.h"

class array
{

    public:

    // Class constructors

    array();
    array(const array &a);

    // Member functions
```

```
        element& operator [ ] (int index);
        array& operator = (const array &a);
        boolean operator == (const array &a);

        private:

        // Data members

        element data[MAX_ARRAY_SIZE];

};

#define ARRAY_H
#endif
```

Note that the data member for a safe array object is represented as an unsafe array. The implementation will detect any range errors that might occur before accessing data elements in this unsafe array.

Implementing the Class

The first member functions to be implemented are the creation operation and the the copy constructor. The creation operation initializes no data members, and therefore runs no statements of its own:

```
array::array()
{
}
```

The copy constructor iterates through the elements in the data member of the safe array parameter, copying the value of each into the corresponding location in the data member of the receiver object:

```
array::array(const array &a)
{
    for (int j = 0; j < MAX_ARRAY_SIZE; ++j)
        data[j] = a.data[j];
}
```

The assignment operation requires a similar process of copying data elements from the array parameter to the receiver object. In this case, a reference to the receiver is returned:

```
array& array::operator = (const array &a)
{
    for (int j = 0; j < MAX_ARRAY_SIZE; ++j)
        data[j] = a.data[j];
    return *this;
}
```

Note that both of these operations assume that an assignment operation exists for the element objects. Remember that complex objects (like bank accounts, strings, and safe arrays) should implement their own assignment operations, so that all of their data members are accurately copied.

The equality operation can be implemented as a simple search for two elements that are not equal. As soon as the search finds such a pair, the process stops and returns FALSE. Otherwise, if the search reaches the end of the arrays, it returns TRUE:

```
boolean array::operator == (const array &a)
{
      boolean equal = TRUE;
      int j = 0;

      while ((j < MAX_ARRAY_SIZE) && equal)
            if (data[j] != a.data[j])
                  equal = FALSE;
            else
                  ++j;
      return equal;
}
```

The subscript operation provides the primary benefit of a safe array class: run-time range checking. The implementation uses **assert** to enforce the preconditions governing the index value. If the value of the index parameter is out of range, the program will halt with an error message. Otherwise, the operation returns a reference to the data element at the specified index position in the data member:

```
element& array::operator [ ] (int index)
{
      assert((index >= 0) && (index < MAX_ARRAY_SIZE));
      return data[index];
}
```

EXAMPLE 10.10   The following program is a driver for testing most of the safe array class operations.

```
// Program file: araydriv.cpp

#include <iostream.h>

#include "array.h"

int main()
{
      array a, b;
      int i;

      for (i = 0; i < MAX_ARRAY_SIZE; ++i)             // Test subscripts
            a[i] = i;

      cout<< "Values in array a are: " << endl;
      for (i = 0; i < MAX_ARRAY_SIZE; ++i)
            cout << a[i] << " ";
      cout << endl;

      b = a;                                           // Test assignment
```

```
        cout<< "Values in array b are: " << endl;
        for (i = 0; i < MAX_ARRAY_SIZE; ++i)
              cout << b[i] << " ";
        cout << endl;

        if (b == a)                              // Test comparison
              cout << "They're equal" << endl;
        else
              cout << "They're not equal" << endl;

        cout << a[MAX_ARRAY_SIZE] << endl;       // Test range error check
        return 0;
}
```

When run with **MAX_ARRAY_SIZE = 10**, the program produces the following output (the error message generated by **assert** may vary on different implementations):

```
Values in array a are:
0 1 2 3 4 5 6 7 8 9
Values in array b are:
0 1 2 3 4 5 6 7 8 9
They're equal
Assertion failed: (index >= 0) && (index < MAX_ARRAY_SIZE), file array.cpp,
line
 39
(press <return> to exit)
```

EXERCISES 10.5

1. Write and test a program that runs the following code with safe arrays and explain what happens:

   ```
   array a;
   for (int i = 0; i <= MAX_ARRAY_SIZE; ++i)
         a[i] = i;
   ```

2. Discuss the limitations imposed by the use of the **element** type to define the safe array class.

3. Discuss the limitations imposed by the use of the constant **MAX_ARRAY_SIZE** to define the safe array class.

4. Discuss the feasibility of using safe and unsafe arrays in the same application, in order to overcome the limitations of the safe array class.

5. The assignment and equality operations for safe arrays reference every memory location in the arrays. Discuss any problems that might arise from these references. For example, predict what happens when you run the following pieces of code:

   a. ```
      array a;
      for (int i = 0; i < MAX_ARRAY_SIZE; ++i)
            cout << a[i] << endl;
      ```

   b. ```
      array a, b;
      a = b;
      ```

   c. ```
      array a, b;
      for (int i = 0; i < MAX_ARRAY_SIZE; ++i)
            a[i] = i;
      ```
      ```

```
if (a == b)
        cout << "They're the same" << endl;
else
        cout << "They're not the same" << endl;
```

10.6 An Ordered Collection Class

OBJECTIVES

- to understand the difference between the physical size of an array and its logical size
- to be able to design and implement a new class that prohibits references to uninitialized data elements in an array

User Requirements

In almost any application that uses an array, the client must distinguish between the *physical size* of the array (the maximum number of memory locations available for data elements) and the *logical size* of the array (the number of data elements currently stored in the array). Failure to do this can cause errors when clients attempt to access data locations in an array where no data values have yet been stored. For example, an array **list** might be declared to have a maximum number of five integer elements, and three integers might be currently stored in positions 0 through 2. This situation is depicted in Figure 10.1. The data at index positions 3 and 4 are still be unpredictable, so the references **list[3]** and **list[4]** for these values may cause errors.

Clients can keep track of the logical array within a physical array in two ways:

1. The first method stores a special sentinel value at the index position immediately following the last data element currently in the array. As you saw in Chapter 7, this method is used by C++ to recognize the boundary of a string value (the null character) within an array of characters. The cost of this method is that one location in the array must be given up to store the sentinel value. Moreover, some data elements, such as bank account objects, might not be easily represented as sentinel values.

2. The second method omits a sentinel value, but maintains a separate integer variable as a counter of the number of data elements currently stored in the array. We have seen this method used in many examples in this chapter, where a variable **length** maintains this value. When a new array is declared or reinitialized, **length** is set to zero, to reflect the fact that there are no data elements stored in the array. **length** is then passed with the array variable to any function that processes the array. Any subscript reference to a data element in an array, either for looking up or for storing a value, should use an index that satisfies the condition **0 <= index < length**. The costs of this method are that a separate variable must be maintained for the length or logical size of the array, and extra operations must be provided for adding or removing data elements.

We can use the second method to develop a new class or ADT called an *ordered collection*. An ordered collection provides subscript access to just those data locations where elements have been stored. It does this by maintaining its own logical size as an attribute. A client can request the logical size of an ordered collection, determine whether subscripting is allowed, and, if so, what the legitimate range of an index should be. Finally, a set of operations for adding or

◆ **FIGURE 10.1**

The logical size of an array may be different from its physical size removing data elements is provided by the ordered collection class. A piece of code that illustrates the use of ordered collections of integers follows:

```
ordered_collection list1, list2;
int i, length;

// length should be 0
cout << "Length of list1 = " << list1.length() << end;

// Store data elements in
// 1/2 of the physical array
for (i = 0; i < MAX_ARRAY_SIZE / 2; ++i)
        list1.add_last(i);

// Print the logical array
for (i = 0; i < list1.length(); ++i)
        cout << i << " " << list[i] << endl;

// Copy one logical array to another
list2 = list1;

// Compare logical arrays
if (list1 == list2)
        cout << "They're equal" << endl;
else
        cout << "They're not equal" << endl;

// Remove and print each value
// and the length of the logical
// array after each removal
length = list1.length();
for (i = 0; i < length; ++i)
        cout << "Value = " << list1.remove_first()
                << "Length = " << list1.length() << endl;

// Halt with error: no data exists!
cout << list1[0] << endl;
```

As you can see, an ordered collection class allows clients to work with logical arrays in a manner that preserves the use of conventional array operations such as subscripting, assignment, and comparison. The difference is that the use of ordered collections is safer than the use of arrays, because references to unitialized data elements are not allowed.

Specifying the Operations

The formal specification of the operations for an ordered collection follows:

Create operation	
Preconditions:	The ordered collection is in an unpredictable state.
Postconditions:	Memory is reserved for an ordered collection object capable of storing **MAX_ARRAY_SIZE** data elements, and **length** is set to 0.

Length operation

Preconditions: The receiver is an ordered collection object, appropriately initialized.

Postconditions: The value of **length** is returned.

Subscript operation

Preconditions: The receiver is an ordered collection object, appropriately initialized, **length** must be greater than 0, and the **index** parameter is an integer value in the range **0 <= index < length**.

Postconditions: The location of the data element, which can be used either to reference or to store a value, is returned.

Assignment operation

Preconditions: The receiver is an ordered collection object in an unpredictable state. The parameter is an ordered collection object, appropriately initialized.

Postconditions: The contents of the parameter object, from position 0 to position **length − 1**, are copied into the receiver object, and the receiver's length is set to the parameter's length.

Equality operation

Preconditions: The receiver is an ordered collection object, appropriately initialized. The parameter is an ordered collection object, appropriately initialized. Objects in the ordered collection can be compared using a standard equality operation.

Postconditions: Returns TRUE if the two collections are the same length and each pair of objects in the two collections is equal, and FALSE otherwise.

Add last operation

Preconditions: The receiver is an ordered collection object, appropriately initialized. The parameter is an **element** object, and **length < MAX_ARRAY_SIZE**.

Postconditions: **length** is incremented by one, and the parameter element is placed in the last position in the ordered collection.

Remove last operation

Preconditions: The receiver is an ordered collection object, appropriately initialized, and **length > 0**.

Postconditions: **length** is decremented by one, and the last data element in the ordered collection is returned.

Add first operation

Preconditions: The receiver is an ordered collection object, appropriately initialized, the parameter is an **element** object, and **length < MAX_ARRAY_SIZE**.

Postconditions: **length** is incremented by one, the data elements in the ordered collection are shifted up by one index position, and the parameter element is placed in the first position in the ordered collection.

Remove first operation

Preconditions: The receiver is an ordered collection object, appropriately initialized, and **length > 0**.

Postconditions: **length** is decremented by one, the data elements in the ordered collection that come after the first element are shifted down by one index position, and the first element in the ordered collection is returned.

> **Remove operation**
>
> Preconditions: The receiver is an ordered collection object, appropriately
>   initialized, the parameter is the data element to be removed, the
>   parameter must equal an element currently in the list, and
>   **length** is greater than zero.
>
> Postconditions: **length** is decremented by one, and the data elements in the
>   ordered collection that come after the parameter element are
>   shifted down by one index position.

Declaring the Class

The class declaration module for the ordered collection class is

```
// Class declaration file: ordercol.h

#ifndef ORDERCOL_H

// Declaration section

// We assume that the type element and
// the constant MAX_ARRAY_SIZE have been defined by the
// application in element.h

#include "boolean.h"
#include "element.h"

class ordered_collection
{

    public:

    // Class constructors

    ordered_collection();
    ordered_collection(const ordered_collection &oc);

    // Member functions

    int length();
    element& operator [ ] (int index);
    ordered_collection& operator = (const ordered_collection &oc);
    boolean operator == (const ordered_collection &oc);
    void add_last(element e);
    element remove_last();
    void add_first(element e);
    element remove_first();
    void remove(element e);

    protected:
```

```
// Data members

element data[MAX_ARRAY_SIZE];
int c_length;

};

#define ORDERCOL_H
#endif
```

Note that the data member for storing the data elements is represented in the same way as the data member of a safe array. We name the data member for representing the length **c_length**, to avoid name conflicts with the member function **length.** We also declare the data members to be **protected,** so that any derived classes of **ordered_collection** will have direct access to them.

Implementing the Class

Many of the operations on an ordered collection resemble those on a safe array, except that the **c_length** data member is updated and used as a limit rather than **MAX_ARRAY_SIZE**. Instead of doing nothing, the first class constructor sets **c_length** to zero to indicate an ordered collection with no data elements:

```
ordered_collection::ordered_collection()
{
      c_length = 0;
}
```

The copy constructor iterates through the elements in the data members of the two ordered collections, but uses the length of the parameter collection as an upper bound:

```
ordered_collection::ordered_collection(const ordered_collection &oc)
{
    for (int j = 0; j < oc.c_length; ++j)
        data[j] = oc.data[j];
    c_length = oc.c_length;
}
```

The implementations of the assignment and equality operations are similar, and are left as exercises. The subscript operation enforces the precondition that the index parameter is greater than or equal to zero and less than **c_length** :

```
element& ordered_collection::operator [ ] (int index)
{
      assert((index >= 0) && (index < c_length));
      return data[index];
}
```

The **add_last** operation enforces the precondition that **c_length** is less than **MAX_ARRAY_SIZE**, so there will be room in the array to store the data element:

```
void ordered_collection::add_last(element e)
{
      assert(c_length < MAX_ARRAY_SIZE);
      data[c_length] = e;
      ++c_length;
}
```

Note the order of the statements in this implementation. The value of **c_length** will always be one greater than the index position of the last data element currently in the ordered collection. Therefore, the expression **data[c_length]** refers to the next available location for new data, where **c_length < MAX_ARRAY_SIZE**. We are careful to store the new data element there, and increment **c_length** afterwards.

The **remove_last** operation enforces the precondition that **c_length** is greater than zero. It then decrements **c_length** by one and returns the data element that was at the end of the ordered collection:

```
element ordered_collection::remove_last()
{
    assert(c_length > 0);
    --c_length;
    element removed_item = data[c_length];
    return removed_item;
}
```

Note that the order of the statements for modifying **c_length** and accessing the data element is the inverse of the order of the statements in the implementation of **add_last**. Whenever **c_length** is decremented, it can be used to access the data value that used to be at the end of the ordered collection.

The three remaining operations—**add_first, remove_first**, and **remove**—may involve substantial movement of data elements within the array representing the ordered collection. For example, when we remove the first data element, all of the data to the right of this position must be shifted one position to the left. Before this can be done, the data element in the first position must be saved in a temporary location. Starting with position zero, a **for** loop copies the data element in the next location into the position immediately to the left. This process continues until the element at position **c_length - 1** has been copied. Finally, **c_length** is decremented:

```
element ordered_collection::remove_first()
{
    assert(c_length > 0);
    element removed_item = data[0];
    for (int i = 0; i < c_length -1; ++i)
        data[i] = data[i + 1];
    --c_length;
    return removed_item;
}
```

The implementations of the **remove_first** and **remove** operations are left as exercises.

EXAMPLE 10.11

This example program inputs a series of bank account objects, as discussed in Chapter 8, from a file into an ordered collection. It then displays the contents of each account on the screen. The program assumes that the **element** type has been defined as **account**, that the standard stream operations have been overloaded for account objects, and that the file **myfile** contains the accounts. The program will display a message if there is not enough room in the ordered collection for all of the accounts in the file.

```cpp
// Program file: bankfile.cpp

#include <iostream.h>
#include <fstream.h>
#include "account.h"
#include "ordercol.h"

int main()
{
    ifstream in_file;
    ordered_collection accounts;
    account new_account;

    in_file.open("myfile");
    in_file >> new_account;
    while (! in_file.eof() && (accounts.length() < MAX_ARRAY_SIZE))
    {
        accounts.add_last(new_account);
        in_file >> new_account;
    }
    if (! in_file.eof() && (accounts.length() == MAX_ARRAY_SIZE))
        cout << "Some accounts could not be input into the list. " << endl;
    in_file.close();
    for (int i = 0; i < accounts.length(); ++i)
        cout << accounts[i] << endl;
    return 0;
}
```

EXERCISES 10.6

1. Discuss the difference between the physical size of an array and its logical size.

2. Clients complain that halting the program with an error message is too severe a price to pay for attempting to remove a data element from an empty ordered collection. They argue that a Boolean flag could be returned, indicating the success or failure of the operation, instead. Discuss the relative merits of these two approaches.

3. Someone has proposed using an ordered collection rather than an array to implement a string class. She claims that the new implementation will not have to waste a storage location on the null character. Discuss the merits of this proposal.

4. Implement the remaining operations for the ordered collection class, and test it with the sample code presented earlier in this section.

5. Add an operation to the ordered collection class to search the collection for a given element. If the element is found, its index position in the ordered collection should be returned. Otherwise, -1 should be returned. You should use the sequential search algorithm developed in Section 10.4.

6. Add an operation to the ordered collection class to sort the data elements in the collection. You should use the selection sort algorithm developed in Section 10.4.

7. Add an operation to input data elements from an input stream into an ordered collection. You should use the **friend** designation with the **>>** operator of the **istream** class, as we did for strings in Chapter 7. Be sure that this operation has the same functionality as the process described in example 10.11.

8. Add an operation for output of ordered collections, similar to the one for input in Exercise 7.

10.7 A Sorted Collection Class

User Requirements

Many applications demand that data values be kept in sorted order. For example, dictionaries and telephone books are two kinds of collections of data values that must be maintained in alphabetical order. One could use the ordered collection class to represent these kinds of data, as long as a sort operation is provided to alphabetize the data after additions of data to the collection. However, the sort operation can be very expensive to use with large collections. Clearly, an ordered collection that could maintain its contents in sorted form without resorting to a sort operation would be very desirable for these applications.

We can design a new class, called a *sorted collection,* that fulfills these requirements. The new class has many of the characteristics of an ordered collection, such as a length and subscripting to look up a data element's value. However, to keep its data elements sorted, a sorted collection prohibits insertions at arbitrary positions in the collection. The sorted collection permits only one insertion operation, and that one operation always puts a data element in its proper place in the collection.

Specifying the Operations

Because a sorted collection has so many of the attributes and behaviors of an ordered collection, it will be convenient to specify it as a derived class of an ordered collection. The situation here is similar to that of the savings account class discussed in Chapter 8. We assume that all of the operations on ordered collections can be used on sorted collections, except for adding a data element to the beginning or the end of the collection, and for subscripting for the target of an assignment statement. We add an operation called **add** for insertions that enforces a sorted order in the collection:

Create operation
Preconditions: The sorted collection is in an unpredictable state.
Postconditions: Memory is reserved for a sorted collection object capable of storing **MAX_ARRAY_SIZE** data elements, and **length** is set to 0.

Length operation
Preconditions: The receiver is a sorted collection object, appropriately initialized.
Postconditions: The value of **length** is returned.

Subscript operation
Preconditions: The receiver is a sorted collection object, appropriately initialized, **length** must be greater than 0, and the **index** parameter is an integer value in the range **0 <= index < length**.
Postconditions: The data element is returned for use as a value only.

Assignment operation
Preconditions: The receiver is a sorted collection object in an unpredictable state. The parameter is a sorted collection object, appropriately initialized.
Postconditions: The contents of the parameter object, from position 0 to position **length - 1**, are copied into the receiver object, and the receiver's length is set to the parameter's length.

Equality operation

Preconditions: The receiver is a sorted collection object, appropriately initialized. The parameter is a sorted collection object, appropriately initialized. Objects in the sorted collection can be compared using a standard equality operation.

Postconditions: Returns TRUE if the two collections are the same length and each pair of objects in the two collections is equal, and FALSE otherwise.

Add operation

Preconditions: The receiver is a sorted collection object, appropriately initialized, the parameter is an **element** object, and **length < MAX_ARRAY_SIZE.**

Postconditions: **length** is incremented by one, and the parameter element is placed in its proper position in the sorted collection.

Remove last operation

Preconditions: The receiver is a sorted collection object, appropriately initialized, and **length > 0**.

Postconditions: **length** is decremented by one, and the last data element in the sorted collection is returned.

Remove first operation

Preconditions: The receiver is a sorted collection object, appropriately initialized, and **length > 0**.

Postconditions: **length** is decremented by one, the data elements in the sorted collection that come after the first element are shifted down by one index position, and the first element in the sorted collection is returned.

Remove operation

Preconditions: The receiver is an sorted collection object, appropriately initialized. The parameter is the data element to be removed, the parameter must equal an element currently in the list, and **length > 0**.

Postconditions: **length** is decremented by one, and the data elements in the ordered collection that come after the parameter element are shifted down by one index position.

Declaring the Class

The class declaration module for the sorted collection class is

```
// Class declaration file: sortcol.h

#ifndef SORTCOL_H

// Declaration section

// We assume that the type element and
// the constant MAX_ARRAY_SIZE have been defined by the
// application in element.h

#include "element.h"
#include "ordercol.h"

class sorted_collection : protected ordered_collection
{
```

```
public:

    // Class constructors

    sorted_collection();
    sorted_collection(const sorted_collection &sc);

    // Member functions

    // These five are inherited from
    // the base class
    ordered_collection::length;
    ordered_collection::operator ==;
    ordered_collection::remove_first;
    ordered_collection::remove_last;
    ordered_collection::remove;

    // These three are
    // implemented here.
    sorted_collection& operator = (const sorted_collection &sc);
    const element& operator [ ] (int index);
    void add(element e);

    // Data members defined in base class

};


#define SORTCOL_H
#endif
```

There are several things to note about this class declaration:

1. The sorted collection class inherits attributes and behavior from the ordered collection class in **protected** mode. This means that **public** and **protected** data and member functions from the ordered collection or base class will be available for the implementation of the sorted collection class, unless they are redefined by the sorted collection class. If inheritance were specified in **public** mode, all of the **public** members of the ordered collection class, such as **add_first**, would also be available to other clients as well. A derived class should be declared in **protected** mode whenever we wish to deny other clients access to some of the public members of the base class.

2. Other clients are given access to five member functions of the base class by listing them in the following form in the **public** section:

   <class name>::<member name>;

   This kind of declaration is called an *access adjustment*. In general, an access adjustment broadens the scope of access no wider than the mode of access specified by the base class.

3. The remaining three member function declarations specify operations to be implemented by the sorted collection class. Note that the assignment and the subscript operations are not inherited from the base class. In the case of the assignment, we must return the address of an object of a specific class (sorted collection, in this case). In the case of the subscript, we prohibit the use of the returned element as an l-value by specifying the return type as a constant reference.

Implementing the Class

The class constructors for the sorted collection simply invoke the corresponding constructors in the base class:

```
sorted_collection::sorted_collection()
      : ordered_collection()
{
}


sorted_collection::sorted_collection(const sorted_collection &sc)
      : ordered_collection(sc)
{
}
```

The new operation to add a data element by putting it in its proper place calls for some development. The operation faces three possiblities:

1. The collection is empty. The new data element goes at the beginning.
2. The new data element is greater than the last element in the collection. The new data element goes at the end.
3. The new data element is less than or equal to some data element in the middle of the collection. We search for this place, shift the data elements over to the right from there, and put the new data element in that place.

The implementation reflects these alternatives as follows:

```
void sorted_collection::add(element e)
{
      int place = 0;

      assert(c_length < MAX_ARRAY_SIZE);
      if ((c_length == 0) || (e > data[c_length - 1]))
            data[c_length] = e;
      else
      {
            while (e > data[place])
                  ++place;
            for (int index = c_length; index > place ; --index)
                  data[index] = data[index - 1];
            data[place] = e;
      }
      ++c_length;
}
```

The implementations of the assignment and subscript operations are left as exercises.

1. Implement the assignment and subscript operations for sorted collections.

2. Design and test a program that attempts to use the subscript operator to assign a value to a position in a sorted collection. Explain the error that occurs.

3. Explain why the subscript operator for ordered collections cannot be used for sorted collections. What effect will this have on clients of sorted collections?

4. Draw a class hierarchy diagram that describes the relationships among the array data type, the safe array class, the ordered collection class, and the sorted collection class.

5. Design and implement a class constructor for sorted collections that takes an ordered collection as a parameter. The constructor should add the data from the ordered collection to the sorted collection.

6. Design and implement a member function called **merge** for sorted collections. **merge** takes a sorted collection as a parameter. A precondition is that the sum of the lengths of the receiver and parameter collections must be less than or equal to **MAX_ARRAY_SIZE**. **merge** should add the data elements of the parameter collection to the receiver collection.

 ## 10.8 Multidimensional Arrays

OBJECTIVES

- to understand the need for representing the data for some problems as a two-dimensional grid

- to be able to represent this data structure as a two-dimensional array

- to be able to declare a two-dimensional array

- to be able to manipulate the components of a two-dimensional array

- to be able to use two-dimensional arrays with functions

The arrays that we have been using thus far are *one dimensional,* in that we locate each data element in the array by specifying a single index position. However, some data structures are more naturally modeled by representing the data in the form of a rectangular grid in which each element is located by specifying a row and column. For example, consider the problem of representing a *bitmap* for a monochrome computer screen. The bitmap consists of a set of Boolean values representing the state of the dots or pixels on the screen. TRUE means "on" or the pixel is white; FALSE means "off" or the pixel is black. Each pixel or bit also has a position, specified by counting down and to the right from the upper left corner of the screen, starting with position <0, 0>, where the first coordinate is the row position and the second coordinate is the column position, to the lower right corner, whose position represents the upper bounds (-1) of the rows and columns (see Figure 10.2).

```
<0,0>




                                                    <639,449>
```

◆ FIGURE 10.2
Positions of pixels in upper left corner and lower right corner of screen

A two-dimensional array
representing a bitmap

	0	1	2	3	4	5
0	0	0	0	0	0	0
1	0	0	0	0	0	0
2	1	1	1	1	1	1
3	0	0	0	0	0	0
4	0	0	0	0	0	0

We can conveniently represent a bitmap as a two-dimensional array of Boolean values. You can think of the array as a rectangular grid of data cells, formatted into rows and columns. Figure 10.3 depicts a two-dimensional array of five rows and six columns (representing quite a small bitmap!). As you might expect with C++, the rows are numbered from zero to $R - 1$, where R is the number of rows, and the columns are numbered from zero to $C - 1$, where C is the number of columns. Note that the data elements in row 2 have been set to TRUE (1 in C++), while all of the other data elements have been set to FALSE (0 in C++). Thus, this would be a bitmap representation of a horizontal line displayed in the middle of a screen or window.

The type for a bitmap can be specified with a **typedef**:

```
const MAX_ROW_SIZE = 5;
const MAX_COL_SIZE = 6;

typedef boolean bitmap[MAX_ROW_SIZE] [MAX_COL_SIZE];
```

The form for defining a two-dimensional array type is

typedef <element type> <type name>[<integer constant>] [<integer constant>];

Note two things about this definition:

1. It resembles a definition of a one-dimensional array type, except that the sizes of the two dimensions are specified by the integer constants enclosed in the square brackets.
2. The first set of brackets always encloses the number of rows in an array, whereas the second set of brackets always encloses the number of columns in an array.

Alternatively, a two-dimensional array variable could be declared with the following form:

<element type> <variable name>[<integer constant>] [<integer constant>];

Two-dimensional array variables can be listed in declarations just like one-dimensional arrays:

```
bitmap screen1, screen2;
```

References to individual data elements within a two-dimensional array use two index values. For example, the following statement would assign the value TRUE to the cell in row 3, column 1, of the array **screen1:**

```
screen1[3] [1] = TRUE;
```

Two-dimensional array indexing in C++ always has the form

<array variable>[<integer value of row>] [<integer value of column>]

Now suppose that we wish to initialize the bitmap **screen1** so that all of its bits are off (set to FALSE). In general, processing a two-dimensional array requires the use of nested loops. In this particular case, we wish to visit every cell in the array and set it to FALSE. Therefore, we use a nested **for** loop:

```
for (int row = 0; row < MAX_ROW_SIZE; ++row)        // move through each row
    for (int col = 0; col < MAX_COL_SIZE; ++col)    // move through each col
        screen1[row][col] = FALSE;
```

Note that the inner loop visits all of the columns in one row before the outer loop moves to the next row. This is called processing the array in *row-major order*. An alternative method, using *column-major order*, could be specified as

```
for (int col = 0; col < MAX_COL_SIZE; ++row)        // move through each col
    for (int row = 0; row < MAX_ROW_SIZE; ++col)    // move through each row
        screen1[row][col] = FALSE;
```

Searching a two-dimensional array for a given value requires the use of a nested **while** loop. This is left as an exercise.

Two-dimensional arrays are passed as parameters to functions in the same way as other arrays. For example, we could package the code for initializing a bitmap in a function **clear_bitmap**:

```
void clear_bitmap(bitmap map)
{
for (int row = 0; row < MAX_ROW_SIZE; ++row)
    for (int col = 0; col < MAX_COL_SIZE; ++col)
        map[row][col] = FALSE;
}
```

COMMUNICATION AND STYLE TIPS

1. Use descriptive identifiers when working with two-dimensional arrays. For example, **row** and **col** are appropriate identifiers for index variables, and **MAX_ROW_SIZE** and **MAX_COL_SIZE** are useful identifiers for specifying the upper bounds of an array type.
2. Remember that C++ does not report range bound errors with any arrays, so use care when indexing.

EXERCISES 10.8

1. Define a C++ type for representing bitmaps of 300 rows and 400 columns.
2. Define a C++ type for representing two-dimensional arrays of integers that have 20 rows and 10 columns.
3. Write a C++ function that searches the arrays defined in Exercise 2 for a given integer value. The function should return the row and column positions if the value is found, as well as the Boolean value TRUE. If the value is not found, the function should return FALSE.
4. Assume that a bitmap has the same number of rows and columns, and that **clear_bitmap** has been run to initialize all of the bits. Write a C++ function that

sets the bits to FALSE on a diagonal running from the upper left corner of the bit-map to the lower right corner.

5. Discuss the design of a safe bitmap class.

As you saw in Chapter 7, much of word processing involves the use of strings to represent words or sentences. Many applications must maintain tables or dictionaries that are keyed by words that are associated with other information, like salaries or phone numbers. We will examine how to set up a table that allows an application to count the frequencies of all of the words in a file. The application will use the sorted collection class developed in Section 10.7.

The input to the program will be a text file. The output will be two columns of data. In the first column will be an alphabetical listing of the words in the file. In the second column will be integers representing the frequency of each word in the file.

To solve this problem, the program will need two classes of objects: one for representing a word and its frequency, and the other for representing a table of such objects. We can define a new class, called **entry**, to represent a word and its frequency. Because the words must appear in alphabetical order when displayed, the table of entries can be represented as a sorted collection.

An entry class will have two attributes: a string representing a word and an integer representing the word's frequency. The operation to create an entry will take a new word as a parameter, and set its frequency to 1. The class will support operations to increment the frequency and to return the values of the word and its frequency.

The sorted collection class is the same as that developed in Section 10.7, with the addition of a search function. You developed a search function for ordered collections in Exercise 5 of Section 10.6. That function should be modified so that its parameter is a string rather than a data element. The implementation of the function should compare the string with the data element. This means that the entry class should provide comparison operations that take strings as parameters as well as entries as parameters. Comparisons of entries are still needed for the **add** and **remove** operations.

The completion of these two classes is left as an exercise. We now describe the design of the program. The general idea is to enter a loop that reads words from a file. As each word is input, the program searches the collection for an entry for that word. If no entry is found, the program creates one with the word and adds it to the collection. If an entry is found, the program indexes into the collection with the value returned by the search function, and sends the increment message to the entry for the word. When this process is completed, the program loops through the collection, displaying the word and frequency of each entry in an appropriate format. Therefore, we have two top-level program modules:

1. Enter the data from the file into the table.
2. Display the data from the table to the screen.

The main program block would be

```
int main()
{
    sorted_collection table;

    get_data(table);
    print_results(table);
    return 0;
}
```

The **get_data** function prompts the user for a file name, opens it for input, runs the loop described earlier, and closes the file:

```cpp
void get_data(sorted_collection &table)
{
        ifstream in_file;
        string word;
        char fname[10];
        int index;
        entry old_entry;

        cout << "Enter the file name: ";
        cin >> fname;
        in_file.open(fname);
        in_file >> word;
        while (! in_file.eof())
        {
                index = table.search(word);
                if (index == -1)
                {
                        entry new_entry(word);
                        table.add(new_entry);
                }
                else
                {
                        old_entry = table[index];
                        old_entry.increment();
                        table.remove(old_entry);
                        table.add(old_entry);
                }
                in_file >> word;
        }
        in_file.close();
}
```

The **print_results** function displays a header and then loops through the table, displaying the word and the frequency of each entry on a line:

```cpp
void print_results(sorted_collection &table)
{
        entry next_entry;

        cout << setw(25) << "Word" << setw(5) << "Frequency" << endl;
        for (int i = 0; i < table.length(); ++i)
        {
                next_entry = table[i];
                cout << setw(25) << next_entry.word()
                        << setw(5) << next_entry.frequency() << endl;
        }
}
```

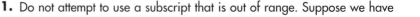

1. Do not attempt to use a subscript that is out of range. Suppose we have

```
int list[6];
```

An inadvertent reference such as

```
for (int j = 0; j <= 6; ++j)
cout << list[j];
```

may produce mysterious results at run time.

2. Comparing array components to each other can lead to errors in using subscripts. Two common misuses are shown.

   a. Attempting to compare `a[j]` to `a[j + 1]`. If this does not stop at `a[length - 2]`, then `j + 1` will be out of range.

   b. Attempting to compare `a[j - 1]` to `a[j]`. This presents the same problem at the beginning of an array. Remember, `j - 1` should have a value that is not less than zero.

3. Using a safe array class that supports run-time range checking will help to catch the errors described in tips 1 and 2.

4. Make sure the array index is correctly initialized, and that the termination condition evaluates all of the relevant subconditions. For example,

```
length = 0;
in_file >> data;
while ((length < MAX_ARRAY_SIZE) && ! in_file.eof())
{
    a[length] = data;
    ++length;
    in_file >> data
}
```

The first value is stored in `a[0]`, `a[length]` will not be referenced when `length == MAX_ARRAY_SIZE`, and `length` will indicate the number of data elements read when the loop is finished.

5. Make sure that all array elements that are referenced for their values have been initialized. Avoid using loops with **MAX_ARRAY_SIZE** as an upper bound, unless you are initializing an array. Use an integer variable to maintain the logical size of the array. Better still, use an ordered collection class to guarantee that references to unitialized data in an array will be caught at run time.

RUNNING, DEBUGGING AND TESTING HINTS

SUMMARY

Key Terms

access adjustment	logical size	selection sort
bitmap	one-dimensional array	sequential (linear) search
column-major order	ordered collection	sorted collection
component (element) of an array	physical size	two-dimensional array
index (subscript)	row-major order	

Key Concepts

♦ An array is a structured variable; a declaration of a single variable reserves several memory locations for data elements.

◆ It is good practice to use a symbolic constant to declare the size of array variables; for example,

```
const int MAX_ARRAY_SIZE = 10;
int list1[MAX_ARRAY_SIZE];
float list2[MAX_ARRAY_SIZE];
```

◆ Arrays can be visualized as lists; thus, the preceding arrays could be envisioned as

◆ Each component of an array is a variable of the declared type and can be used in the same way as any other variable of that type.

◆ Loops can be used to read data into arrays; for example,

```
length = 0;
in_file >> data;
while ((length < MAX_ARRAY_SIZE) && ! in_file.eof())
{
        a[length] = data;
        ++length;
        in_file >> data
}
```

◆ Loops can be used to print data from arrays; for example, if **scores** is an array of 20 test scores, the scores can be printed by

```
for (int j = 0; j < 20; ++j)
        cout << scores[j] << endl;
```

◆ Manipulating components of an array is generally accomplished by using the index as a loop variable; for example, assuming the preceding **scores** array, to find the smallest value in the array we can use

```
small = scores[0];
for (int j = 1; j < 20; ++j)
        if (scores[j] < small)
                small = scores[j];
```

◆ A selection sort is one method of sorting elements in an array from high to low or low to high. This sort repeatedly finds the minimum element in the unsorted portion of the array and exchanges it with the first element in that portion.

◆ C++ array parameters are always passed by reference, and should not be declared as reference parameters.

◆ A sequential search of a list consists of examining the first item in a list and then proceeding through the list in sequence until the desired value is found or the end of the list is reached.

◆ The physical size of an array is the total number of memory locations available for storing data elements in it.

◆ The logical size of an array is the number of data elements currently stored in it; this size may differ from the array's physical size.

◆ An ordered collection enables clients to work with just the logical size of an array of data elements.

◆ A sorted collection enables clients to work with an array of data elements whose alphabetical ordering is maintained automatically.

◆ Two-dimensional arrays may be specified by declaring a variable that has upper bounds on two indices:

```
boolean bitmap[20] [10];
```

◆ References to cells in two-dimensional arrays specify the index of the row first and the index of the column second:

```
bitmap[row] [col] = FALSE;
```

PROGRAMMING PROBLEMS AND PROJECTS

1. Using the ordered collection class developed in Section 10.6 and the sorted collection class developed in Section 10.7, write a program to read an unknown number of integer test scores from the keyboard (assume at most 150 scores). Print the original list of scores, the scores sorted from low to high, the scores sorted from high to low, the highest score, the lowest score, and the average score.

2. Write a program to help you balance your checkbook. The input consists of the beginning balance and then a sequence of transactions, each followed by a transaction code. Deposits are followed by a "D" and withdrawals are followed by a "W." The output should consist of a list of transactions, a running balance, an ending balance, the number of withdrawals, and the number of deposits. Include an appropriate message for overdrawn accounts. Your program should represent the attributes and behavior of a transaction as a class.

3. One of the problems faced by designers of word processors is that of printing text without separating a word at the end of a line. Write a program to read several lines of text as input. Then print the message with each line starting in column 10 and no line exceeding column 70. No word should be separated at the end of a line.

4. Your local state university has to raise funds for an art center. As a first step, they are going to approach five previously identified donors and ask for additional donations. Because the donors wish to remain anonymous, only the respective totals of their previous donations are available for input. After they are contacted, the additional donations are listed at the end of input in the same order as the first 5 entries. Write a computer program to read the first 20 entries into one data structure and the second 5 entries into a second data structure. Compute the previous total donations and the new donations for the art center. Print the following:

   a. The list of previous donations
   b. The list of new donations
   c. An unsorted list of total donations
   d. A sorted list of total donations
   e. Total donations before the fund drive
   f. Total donations for the art center
   g. The maximum donation for the art center

Be sure to choose the appropriate data structures from the safe array class, the ordered collection class, or the sorted collection class, as developed in Sections 10.5, 10.6, and 10.7, respectively.

5. Read in a list of 10 integers from the keyboard. Place the even numbers into a collection called **even**, the odd numbers into a collection called **odd**, and the negatives into a collection called **negative**. Print all three collections after all numbers have been read.

6. Read in 10 real numbers. Print the average of the numbers followed by all the numbers that are greater than the average.

7. Read in the names of five candidates in a class election and the number of votes received by each. Print the list of candidates, the number of votes they received, and the percentage of the total votes they received sorted into order from the winner to the person with the fewest votes. You may assume that all names are 20 characters in length.

8. In many sports events, contestants are rated by judges with an average score being determined by discarding the highest and lowest scores and averaging the remaining scores. Write a program in which eight scores are entered, computing the average score for the contestant.

9. Given a list of 20 test scores (integers), print the score that is nearest to the average.

10. The Game of Nim is played with three piles of stones. There are three stones in the first pile, five stones in the second, and eight stones in the third. Two players alternate taking as many stones as they like from any one pile. Play continues until someone is forced to take the last stone. The person taking the last stone loses. Write a program that permits two people to play the game of Nim using an array to keep track of the number of stones in each pile.

11. There is an effective strategy that can virtually guarantee victory in the game of Nim. Devise a strategy and modify the program in Problem 10 so that the computer plays against a person. Your program should be virtually unbeatable if the proper strategy is developed.

12. The median of a set of numbers is the value in the middle of the set if the set is arranged in order. The mode is the number listed most often. Given a list of 21 numbers, print the median and mode of the list.

13. The standard deviation is a statistic frequently used in education measurement. Write a program that, given a list of test scores, will find and print the standard deviation of the numbers. The standard deviation formula can be found in most statistics books.

14. Revise Problem 13 so that after the standard deviation is printed, you can print a list of test scores that are more than one standard deviation below the average and a list of the scores more than one standard deviation above the average.

15. The z-score is defined as the mean score earned on a test divided by the standard deviation. Given input data containing an unknown number of test scores (maximum of 100), print a list showing each test score (from highest to lowest) and the corresponding z-score.

16. Salespeople for the Wellsville Wholesale Company earn a commission based on their sales. The commission rates are as follows:

Sales	Commission (%)
$0 — 1000	3
1001 — 5000	4.5
5001 — 10000	5.25
Over 10000	6

In addition, any salesperson who sells above the average of all salespeople receives a $50 bonus, and the top salesperson receives an additional $75 bonus.

Given the names and amounts sold by each of 10 salespeople, write a program that prints a table showing the salesperson's name, the amount sold, the commission rate, and the total amount earned. The average sales should also be printed.

17. Write a language translation program that permits the entry of a word in English, with the corresponding word of another language being printed. The dictionary words can be stored in parallel collections, with the English array being sorted into alphabetical order prior to the first entry of a word. Your program should first sort the dictionary of words.

18. Elementary and middle school students are often given the task of converting numbers from one base to another. For example, 19 in base 10 is 103 in base 4 ($1 \times 4^2 + 0 \times 4^1 + 3 \times 4^0$). Conversely, 123 in base 4 is 27 in base 10. Write an interactive program that allows the user to choose from the following:

<1>	Convert from base 10 to base A
<2>	Convert from base A to base 10
<3>	Quit

If option 1 or 2 is chosen, the user should then enter the intended base and the number to be converted. A sample run of the program would produce this output:

This program allows you to convert between bases. Which of the following would you like?

```
        <1>        Convert from base 10 to base A
        <2>        Convert from base A to base 10
        <3>        Quit
```

Enter your choice and press <Enter>. 1

Enter the number in base 10 and press <Enter>. 237

Enter the new base and press <Enter>. 4

The number 237 in base 4 is: 3231

Press <Enter> to continue

This program allows you to convert between bases. Which of the following would you like?

```
        <1>        Convert from base 10 to base A
        <2>        Convert from base A to base 10
        <3>        Quit
```

Enter your choice and press <Enter>. 2

What number would you like to have converted? 2332

Converting to base 10, we get:

```
2 * 1 = 2
3 * 4 = 12
3 * 16 = 48
2 * 64 = 128

The base 10 value is 190

Press <Enter> to continue

This program allows you to convert between bases. Which
of the following would you like?
        <1>     Convert from base 10 to base A
        <2>     Convert from base A to base 10
        <3>     Quit

Enter your choice and press <Enter>. 3
```

19. One of the principles underlying the concept of data abstraction is that implementation details of data structures should be deferred to the lowest possible level. To illustrate, consider the high-level design to which we referred in a previous discussion of data abstraction. Our program required you to work with a list of names and an associated list of numbers (student names and test scores). The following first-level design was suggested:

1. GetNames (function here);

2. GetScores (function here);

3. SortByName (function here);

4. PrintNamesAndScores (function here);

5. SortByScore (function here);

Write complete documentation for each of these modules, including a description of all parameters and data structures required.

Present your documentation to the class. Ask if your classmates have questions about the number or type of parameters, the data structures required, and/or the main tasks to be performed by each module.

20. Contact programmers at your university and/or some businesses and discuss with them the use of lists as a data type. Ask what kinds of programming problems require the use of a list, how the programmers handle data entry (list length), and what operations they perform on the list (search, sort, and so on). Give an oral report of your findings to the class.

21. Select a programming problem from this chapter that you have not yet worked on. Construct a structure chart and write all documentary information necessary for the problem you have chosen. Do not write code. When you are finished, have a classmate read your documentation to see if precisely what is to be done is clear.

22. Consult your local implementation of C++ to see if it supports graphics operations, such as drawing and erasing points on the screen. If your system allows this, write a program that uses the data structure and functions developed in Section 10.8 to represent and draw a diagonal line on the screen.

11 Algorithm Analysis: Space and Time Considerations

Nothing puzzles me more than time and space.
Charles Lamb, 1775–1834

In this chapter, we introduce a technique for analyzing the efficiency of algorithms. We can then use this technique, known as *big-O analysis,* to categorize algorithms with respect to the length of time and the amount of storage they require for their execution with data sets of different sizes. In Sections 11.2 and 11.3, we will use big-O analysis to examine the time efficiency of some simple sorting algorithms. In Section 11.4, we will use big-O analysis to describe the interplay between the time and storage requirements of an algorithm. In Section 11.5, we will analyze the time efficiency of simple *search algorithms.* Finally, in the Focus on Program Design section, we will discuss a scheme for developing programs to measure empirically the efficiency of an algorithm.

11.1 Designing Programs: A Look Back and a Look Ahead

OBJECTIVES

- to develop a perspective on the study of computer science beyond the learning of a particular programming language, such as C++

- to be able to identify criteria by which complex software is evaluated

This chapter marks an important step in your exploration of computer science. Up to this point, it has been difficult to divorce your study of computer science from the learning of C++. You have developed problem-solving skills, but the problems we have encountered have been very focused. That is, the problems were chosen specifically to illustrate a particular feature of C++. This is the way that problem-solving skills must be developed: Start with small problems and work toward large ones.

By now you know many of the features of the C++ programming language. You are ready to direct your attention toward larger, more complex problems that require you to integrate many of the particular skills you have developed. Now our attention will be directed more toward issues of software design and less toward describing C++. If we need a particular feature of C++ that has not yet been discussed, we will introduce it when appropriate. But our primary objective is to study more complex problems and the software design issues that arise out of them. From here on, we view C++ primarily as the vehicle to implement, test, and experiment with our solutions to problems. The techniques of software design we are about to explore will enable us to write programs that have the following characteristics:

- *Large:* Actually our programs could properly be called systems since they typically involve numerous modules that interact to solve one complex problem.
- *Reliable:* The measure of the reliability of a system is that it can anticipate and handle all types of exceptional circumstances.
- *Flexible:* The system should be easily modified to handle circumstances that may change in the future.
- *Expandable and reusable:* If the system is successful, it will frequently spawn new computing needs. We should be able to incorporate solutions to these new needs into the original system with relative ease.
- *Efficient:* The system should make optimal use of time and space resources.
- *Structured:* The system should be divided into compact modules, each of which is responsible for a specific, well-defined task.
- *User-friendly:* The system should be clearly documented so that it is easy to use. Internal documentation helps programmers maintain the software, and external documentation helps users use it.

In designing software to meet these criteria, one of the key skills you must develop is the ability to choose the appropriate tools for the job. You should not have to rediscover algorithms and techniques for information storage and retrieval each time you write a new program. As a computer scientist, you must have a detailed knowledge of algorithms and data storage techniques at your fingertips and be able to apply this knowledge when designing software to solve a variety of problems. You should be able to look into your storehouse of algorithms and data storage strategies, choose the most appropriate methods, and then tailor them to the application at hand.

As you expand your knowledge of computer science, you will find that a given problem frequently lends itself to more than one method of solution. Hence, in addition to knowing the individual principles, you must also be able to evaluate them comparatively. This comparative evaluation must be conducted in as systematic and quantitative a fashion as possible. That is, you must be able to justify your choice of a method by presenting cogent arguments based on facts and figures pertinent to the problem. Given this perspective on computer science, we must turn our attention to a twofold task:

1. Stocking our algorithmic toolbox with methods that have become standards in computer science.
2. Developing criteria for knowing which tool to choose in a particular situation.

To begin this task, we reach back to the sorting and searching algorithms we first saw in Chapter 10. We also consider some new techniques for sorting and searching. We then evaluate these techniques for their efficiency in terms of execution time and use of space (memory) resources. To conduct such a time/space analysis, we introduce what has come to be known as big-O notation. In effect, big-O notation is the mathematical measuring stick by which computer scientists quantitatively evaluate algorithms. It allows us to place algorithms into categories based on their efficiency. Such categorization helps us determine whether or not a proposed solution is practical in terms of the real-world requirements and constraints dictated by the problem.

11.2 Simple Sorting Algorithms

Our discussion in this section will use an array of objects that we want to sort in ascending order according to a given attribute for each object. The attribute on which the sort is based is known as the key attribute. For instance, we may wish to arrange a list of student objects in alphabetical order according to student last name or a list of inventory objects in order according to product identification numbers. To provide a suitable setting for our upcoming discussion of the sorting problem, we will make the following assumptions:

1. The objects being sorted are of type **element**. **element** is a synonym for whatever class of object we wish to place in an array.

2. If necessary, the **element** class overloads the standard C++ operators **==**, **>**, and **<** that are used by the sort algorithms. Operator **=** is used for copying elements, while **>** and **<** compare two elements with respect to the key attribute.

For example, the following declarations would provide a setting for sorting a simple array of integers:

```
const int MAX_LIST_SIZE = 100;
typedef int element;
typedef element list_type[MAX_LIST_SIZE];
```

We wish to write a sort function that meets the following specifications:

```
// Function: sort
// Sorts a list of elements into ascending order
//
// Inputs: a list of elements in random order and its
// current length
// Output: the list of elements arranged in ascending
// order

void sort(list_type list, int n);
```

Two aspects of these declarations are worth noting. First, the fashion in which we have made our constant and type definitions allows this function to sort an array of any size and base type provided that the definitions are appropriately altered. This method of declaration represents an attempt to make the C++ function abstract: It embodies an algorithm that can sort a variety of data types.

Second, the measure of an algorithm's run-time efficiency is in direct proportion to the number of elementary machine operations that must be performed as the algorithm is executed. With sorting algorithms, these elementary machine operations compare and interchange two data items. Depending on the amount of data in the element type in the preceding declarations, it is entirely possible that interchanging two data items could be considerably more costly in machine time than comparing two items. Why? An interchange of large data items will generate a loop that moves a significant number of bytes at the machine language level.

Our analysis of run-time efficiency should take this into account. It may well be more important to minimize data interchanges at the expense of comparisons. This complication did not enter into our earlier discussion of sorting because, at that stage, we were concerned with sorting arrays of simple, unstructured data items only.

Bubble Sort

The *bubble sort* represents an alternative to the selection sort algorithm discussed in Section 10.4. Given a list of data objects stored in an array, a bubble sort causes a pass through the array to compare adjacent pairs of keys. Whenever two keys are out of order with respect to each other, the associated objects are interchanged. The effect of such a pass through a list of names is traced in Figure 11.1, where a "snapshot" of the array after each comparison is given. Notice that after such a pass, we are assured that the list will have the name that comes last in alphabetical order in the final array position. That is, the last name will "sink" to the bottom of the array, and preceding names will gradually "percolate" to the top.

If one pass through an array of n objects can guarantee that the object with the key that comes last in order is in the appropriate position, then slicing off the last element and passing through the remaining $n - 1$ entries using the same logic will guarantee that the object with the key second to last in order is in its appropriate position. Repeating the process for a total of $n - 1$ passes eventually

◆ **FIGURE 11.1**
Trace of bubble sort on an array with four names

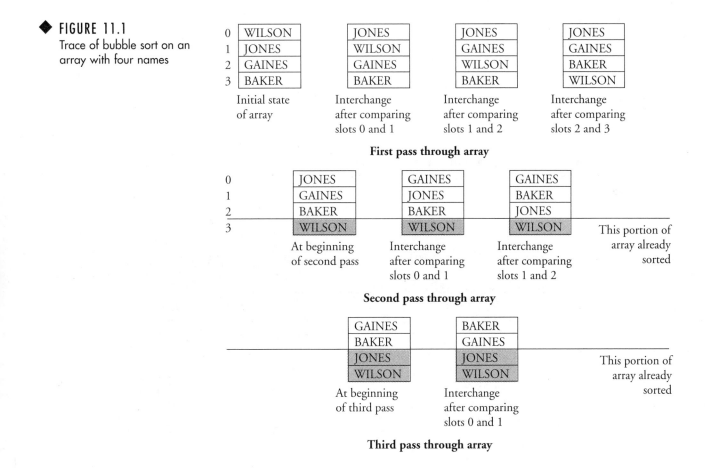

ensures that all objects are in their appropriate positions. In general, on the kth pass through the array, $n - k$ comparisons of pairs must be made.

Thus, the bubble sort algorithm involves a nested loop structure. The outer loop controls the number of (successively smaller) passes through the array. The inner loop controls the pairs of adjacent entries being compared.

If we ever make a complete pass through the inner loop without having to make an interchange, we can declare the array sorted and avoid all future passes through the array. A top-level pseudocode development of the algorithm is

1. Initialize counter k to zero
2. Initialize Boolean exchange_made to TRUE
3. While (k < n – 1) and exchange_made
    3.1. Set exchange_made to FALSE
    3.2. Increment counter k
    3.3. For each j from 0 to n – k
        3.3.1. If entry in jth slot > entry in(j + 1)st slot
        3.3.1.1. Exchange these entries
        3.3.1.2. Set exchange_made to TRUE

The complete C++ function to implement this algorithm for an array of objects follows. The function assumes the existence of appropriate data declarations.

```
void bubble_sort(list_type list, int n)
{

    int j, k;
    boolean exchange_made = TRUE;
    element temp;

    k = 0;

    // Make up to n - 1 passes through array, exit
    // early if no exchanges are made on previous pass

    while ((k < n - 1) && exchange_made)
    {

        exchange_made = FALSE;
        ++k;
        // Number of comparisons on kth pass
        for (j = 0; j < n - k; ++j)
            if (list[j] > list[j + 1])
            {
                // Exchange must be made
                temp = list[j];
                list[j] = list[j + 1];
                list[j + 1] = temp;
                exchange_made = TRUE;
            }
    }
}
```

| EXAMPLE 11.1 | Trace the action of the function **bubble_sort** if **n** is 5 and the array **list** initially contains |

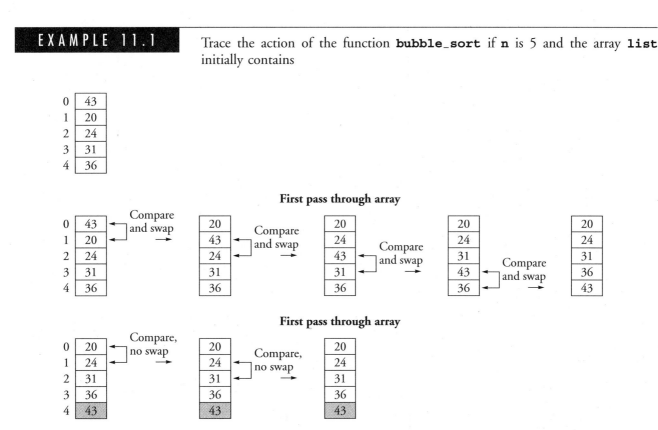

exchange_made remained false throughout the inner loop, so the algorithm is done.

In the next section we analyze in detail the run-time efficiency of the bubble sort. But we should first consider two other sorting algorithms to which the efficiency of bubble sort may be compared: *selection sort* and *insertion sort*.

Selection Sort Revisited

Since its introduction in Chapter 10, we have used the selection sort algorithm to sort arrays of elements. Now let's compare it to the bubble sort algorithm.

The strategy of the bubble sort is to place the (current) largest array value in the (current) last array slot, then seal off that slot from future consideration, and repeat the process. The selection sort algorithm has a similar plan, but it attempts to avoid the multitude of interchanges of adjacent entries. To do this, on the kth pass through the array, it determines the position of the smallest entry among

```
list[k], list[k + 1], ..., list[n]
```

Then this smallest entry is swapped with the kth entry, **k** is incremented by 1, and the process is repeated. Figure 11.2 illustrates how this algorithm works on repeated passes through an array with six entries. Asterisks are used to indicate the successively smallest (alphabetically) entries as they are being correctly located in the array.

As we see next, the C++ function for selection sort uses, as its inner loop, a simple algorithm to find the minimum entry and store its position in the variable

FIGURE 11.2

Trace of selection sort logic

Original order of Keys	k = 0	k = 1	k = 2	k = 3	k = 4
DAVE	ARON*	ARON*	ARON*	ARON*	ARON*
TOM	TOM	BEV*	BEV*	BEV*	BEV*
PAM	PAM	PAM	DAVE*	DAVE*	DAVE*
ARON	DAVE	DAVE	PAM	PAM*	PAM*
BEV	BEV	TOM	TOM	TOM	SAM*
SAM	SAM	SAM	SAM	SAM	TOM*

min_position. This inner loop avoids the potentially frequent interchange of array elements that is necessary in the inner loop of **bubble_sort**.

```
void selection_sort(list_type list, int n)
{

    int index;
    element temp;

    // Make n - 1 passes through successively smaller segments

    for (int j = 0; j < n - 1; ++j)
    {

        index = j;
        // Find index of the smallest element
        for (int k = j + 1; k < n; ++k)
            if (list[k] < list[index])
                index = k;
        if (index != j)
        {
            // Exchange must be made
            temp = list[index];
            list[index] = list[j];
            list[j] = temp;
        }
    }
}
```

Example 11.2 indicates that the selection sort algorithm swaps no data values until exiting the inner loop. This apparently reduces the number of data interchanges and makes the selection sort more efficient than the bubble sort. Is this a significant improvement? Or have other subtle inefficiencies been introduced to offset this apparent gain? These are difficult questions to answer unless we have a better grasp of how to measure program efficiency. We'll explore efficiency in the next section; but first, let's look at one more sorting algorithm for comparison purposes.

EXAMPLE 11.2   Trace the action of the function `selection_sort` if **n** is 5 and the array **list** initially contains

Insertion Sort

Although it reduces the number of data interchanges, the selection sort apparently will not allow an effective—and automatic—loop exit if the array becomes ordered during an early pass. In this regard, bubble sort is more efficient than selection sort for an array that is nearly ordered from the beginning. However, even with just one entry out of order, bubble sort's early loop exit can fail to reduce the number of comparisons that are made.

The insertion sort attempts to take greater advantage of an array's partial ordering. The goal is that on the kth pass through, the kth element among

```
list[0], list[1], ..., list[k]
```

should be inserted into its rightful place among the first k entries in the array. Thus, after the kth pass (k starting at 1), the first k elements of the array should be in sorted order. This is analogous to the fashion in which many people pick up playing cards and arrange them in order in their hands. Holding the first ($k - 1$) cards in order, a person will pick up the kth card and compare it with cards already held until its appropriate spot is found. The following steps will achieve this logic:

1. For each k from 1 to n - 1 { k index of array element to insert }
    1.1 Set item_to_insert to list[k]
    1.2 Set j to k – 1 (j starts at j – 1 and is decremented until insertion position is found)
    1.3 While (insertion position not found) and (not beginning of array)
        1.3.1 If item_to_insert < list[j]
            1.3.1.1 Move list[j] to index position j + 1
            1.3.1.2 Decrement j by 1
        1.3.2 Else
            1.3.2.1 The insertion position has been found
    1.4 item_to_insert should be positioned at index j + 1

In effect, for each pass, the index **j** begins at the ($k - 1$)st element and moves that element to position $j + 1$ until we find the insertion point for what was originally the kth element.

◆ FIGURE 11.3

Trace of repeated passes from insertion sort

Original order of Keys	First pass $k = 1$	Second pass $k = 2$	Third pass $k = 3$	Fourth pass $k = 4$	Fifth pass $k = 5$
PAM	PAM	DAVE	ARON	ARON	ARON
SAM	SAM*	PAM	DAVE	DAVE	BEV
DAVE	DAVE	SAM*	PAM	PAM	DAVE
ARON	ARON	ARON	SAM*	SAM	PAM
TOM	TOM	TOM	TOM	TOM*	SAM
BEV	BEV	BEV	BEV	BEV	TOM*

Insertion sort for each value of **k** is traced in Figure 11.3. In each column of this diagram the data items are sorted in alphabetical order relative to each other above the item with the asterisk; below this item the data are not affected.

To implement the insertion sort algorithm in C++ we have the following code:

```
void insertion_sort(list_type list, int n)
{
    int j, k;
    element item_to_insert;
    boolean still_looking;

    // On the kth pass, insert item k into its correct position among
    // the first k entries in array.

    for (k = 1; k < n; ++k)
    {
    // Walk backwards through list, looking for slot to insert list[k]
        item_to_insert = list[k];
        j = k - 1;
        still_looking = TRUE;
        while ((j >= 0) && still_looking )
                if (item_to_insert < list[j])
                {
                    list[j + 1] = list[j];
                    --j;
                }
                else
                    still_looking = FALSE;
    // Upon leaving loop, j + 1 is the index
    // where item_to_insert belongs
    list[j + 1] = item_to_insert;
    }
}
```

Array at beginning of the
kth stage

0	1	2	$\cdots$	k - 1	k			
			$\cdots$					

Sorted

Unsorted

kth element inserted in its rightful place
among first k entries on kth pass

EXAMPLE 11.3

Trace the action of the function **insertion_sort** if **n** is 5 and the array **list** initially contains

EXERCISES 11.2

1. Which of the sorting methods studied in this section allows a possible early exit from its inner loop? What is the potential advantage of using this early exit?

2. Which of the sorting methods studied in this section allows a possible early exit from its outer loop? What is the potential advantage of using this early exit?

3. Which of the sorting methods studied in this section does not allow for the possibility of an early exit from its inner or outer loops? What potential advantage does this method have over the other two methods that were presented?

4. Suppose that, initially, an array contains seven integer entries arranged in the following order:

```
0  43
1  40
2  18
3  24
4  39
5  60
6  12
```

Trace the order of the array entries after each successive pass of the bubble sort.

5. Repeat Exercise 4 for the selection sort.

6. Repeat Exercise 4 for the insertion sort.

7. Consider the following sort algorithm. Which of the methods studied in this section does this new algorithm most closely resemble? In what ways is it different from that method? Trace the action of this new sort algorithm on the array from Exercise 4.

```
void sort(list_type list, int n)
{
        int j, k;
        boolean exchange_made = TRUE;
        element temp;

        k = 0;
        while ((k < n - 1) && exchange_made)
        {
                exchange_made = FALSE;
                ++k;
                for (j = n - 1; j > k + 1; -j)
                    if (list[j] < list[j - 1])
                    {
                            temp = list[j];
                            list[j] = list[j - 1];
                            list[j - 1] = temp;
                            exchange_made = TRUE;
                    }
        }
}
```

8. Consider the following sort algorithm. Which of the methods studied in this section does this new algorithm most closely resemble? In what ways is it different from that method? Trace the action of this new sort algorithm on the array from Exercise 4.

```
void sort(list_type list, int n)
{
        int j, k, position;
        element temp;

        for (k = 0; k < n - 1; ++k)
        {
```

```
                        position = 0;
                        for (j = 1; j < n - k + 1; ++j)
                                if (list[j] > list[position])
                                        position = j;
                        temp = list[n - k + 1];
                        list[n - k + 1] = list[position];
                        list[position] = temp;

                }

        }
```

9. Consider the following sort algorithm. Which of the methods studied in this section does this new algorithm most closely resemble? In what ways is it different from that method? Trace the action of this new sort algorithm on the array from Exercise 4.

```
void sort(list_type list, int n)
{
        int j, k;
        boolean done;
        element temp;

        for (k = n - 1; k > 0; --k)
        {
                j = k;
                done = FALSE;
                while ((j <= n - 1) && ! done)
                        if (list[j] > list[j + 1])
                        {
                                temp = list[j];
                                list[j] = list[j - 1];
                                list[j - 1] = temp;
                                ++j;
                        }
                        else
                                done = TRUE;
        }
}
```

10. Devise sample data sets to demonstrate the *best case* and *worst case* behavior of the bubble sort, insertion sort, and selection sort. That is, for each sorting algorithm, construct data sets that illustrate the minimum and maximum number of comparisons required for that particular algorithm.

11. Construct a data set in which just one value is out of order and yet the Boolean test of the **exchange_made** variable never allows an early exit from the outer loop of bubble sort. How does the insertion sort perform on this same data set? Better, worse, or the same? Explain why.

12. Modify the sorting algorithms of this section so that they receive an additional argument indicating whether the sort should be in ascending or descending order.

13. The inner loop of an insertion sort can be modified merely to find the appropriate position for the kth array entry instead of actually shifting items to make room for this entry. The shifting of items and placement of the original kth entry can then be achieved in a separate loop. Write a new insertion sort function that implements this modification. Intuitively, is your new version more or less efficient than the old version? Why?

14. Modify all of the sorting algorithms presented in this chapter to include counters for the number of comparisons and data interchanges that are made. Then run those sorting algorithms on a variety of data sets, maintaining a chart of the counters for each algorithm. Prepare a written statement to summarize your conclusions about the relative efficiencies of the algorithms.

11.3 Which Sort Is Best? A Big-O Analysis

OBJECTIVES

- to understand the formal definition of big-O notation
- to be able to use big-O notation to classify the time efficiency of algorithms involving nonrecursive, iterative control constructs
- to see the relationship between an algorithm's big-O classification and its expected run time on a computer
- to recognize often-used big-O categories
- to apply big-O notation in analyzing the time efficiencies of the bubble sort, selection sort, and insertion sort algorithms

Computers do their work in terms of certain fundamental operations: comparing two numbers, moving the contents of one memory word to another, and so on. It should come as no surprise to you that a simple instruction in a high-level language such as C++ may be translated (via a compiler) into many of these fundamental machine-level instructions. On most modern computers the speeds of these fundamental operations are measured in microseconds—that is, millionths of a second—although some larger supercomputers are beginning to break the nanosecond (billionth of a second) barrier. Let's assume, for the sake of argument, that we are working with a hypothetical computer that requires one microsecond to perform one of its fundamental operations.

With execution speeds of this kind, it makes little sense to analyze the efficiency of those portions of a program that perform only initializations and final reporting of summary results. The key to analyzing a function's efficiency is to scrutinize its loops and, even more importantly, its nested loops. Consider the following two examples of nested loops intended to sum each of the rows of an $N \times N$ two-dimensional array matrix, storing the row sums in the one-dimensional array **rows** and the overall total in **grand_total**.

EXAMPLE 11.4

```
grand_total:= 0;
for (k = 0; k< n - 1; ++k)
{
        rows[k] = 0;
        for (j = 0; j < n - 1; ++j)
        {
                rows[k] = rows[k] + matrix[k,j];
                grand_total = grand_total+ matrix[k,j];
        }
}
```

EXAMPLE 11.5

```
grand_total = 0;
for (k = 0; k < n - 1; ++k)
{
        rows[k] = 0;
        for (j = 0; j < n - 1; ++j)
                rows[k] = rows[k] + matrix[k,j];
        grand_total = grand_total+ rows[k];
}
```

If we analyze the number of addition operations required by these two examples, it should be immediately obvious that Example 11.5 is better in this respect. Because

Example 11.4 incorporates the accumulating of **grand_total** into its inner loop, it requires $2N^2$ additions. That is, the additions **rows[k] + matrix[k, j]** and **grand_total + matrix[k, j]** are each executed N^2 times, for a total of $2N^2$. Example 11.5, on the other hand, accumulates **grand_total** after the inner loop; hence it requires only $N^2 + N$ additions, which is less than $2N^2$ for any N after 1. Example 11.5 is seemingly guaranteed to execute faster than Example 11.4 for any nontrivial value of N.

But note that "faster" here may not have much significance in the real world of computing. Assuming that our hypothetical computer allows us to declare an array that is 1000 by 1000. Example 11.4 would require two seconds to perform its additions; Example 11.5 would require just over one second. On a larger 100,000 by 100,000 array, Example 11.4 would crunch numbers for slightly under six hours and Example 11.5 would take about three hours.

Although Example 11.5 is certainly better from an aesthetic perspective, it is not good enough to be appreciably different from a user's perspective. That is, in situations where one version will respond within seconds, so will the other. Conversely, when one is annoyingly slow, the other will be also. In terms of the *order of magnitude* of run time involved, these versions should not be considered significantly different. For the 1000 by 1000 array, both versions would be fast enough to allow their use in an interactive environment. For the 100,000 by 100,000 array, both versions would dictate an overnight run in batch mode since an interactive user is no more willing to wait three hours than six hours for a response.

Thus, because of the phenomenal execution speeds and very large amounts of available memory on modern computers, proportionally small differences between algorithms often have little practical impact. Such considerations have led computer scientists to devise a method of algorithm classification that makes more precise the notion of order of magnitude as it applies to time and space considerations. This method of classification, typically referred to as *big-O notation* (in reference to "on the *o*rder of"), hinges on the following definition:

> **Big-O notation:** Suppose there exists a function $f(n)$ defined on the nonnegative integers such that the number of operations required by an algorithm for an input of size n is less than some constant C times $f(n)$ for all but finitely many n. That is, the number of operations is *proportional* to $f(n)$ for all large values of n. Such an algorithm is said to be an $O[f(n)]$ algorithm relative to the number of operations it requires to execute. Similarly, we could classify an algorithm as $O[f(n)]$ relative to the number of memory locations it requires to execute.

Figure 11.4 provides a graphical aid to understanding this formal definition of big-O notation. In general, we expect an algorithm's run time to increase as it manipulates an increasing number of data items, that is, as n increases. This increasing run time is depicted by the somewhat irregular, wavy curve in Figure 11.4. Now compare the wavy curve representing actual run time to the smoother curve of $C^*f(n)$. Note that, for some small values of n, the actual number of operations for the algorithm may exceed $C^*f(n)$. However, the graph indicates that there is a point on the horizontal axis beyond which $C^*f(n)$ is always greater than the number of operations required for n data items. This is precisely the criterion that defines an algorithm's being $O[f(n)]$.

To say that an algorithm is $O[f(n)]$ thus indicates that the function $f(n)$ may be useful in characterizing how the algorithm is performing for large n. For such n,

◆ FIGURE 11.4
Graphical representation of
$O(f(n))$

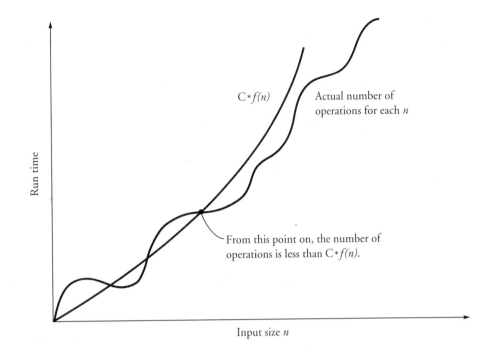

we are assured that the operations required by the algorithm will be bounded by a constant times $f(n)$. The phrasing "for all large values of n" in the definition highlights the fact that there is little difference in the choice of an algorithm if n is reasonably small. For example, almost any sorting algorithm would sort 100 integers instantly.

We should also note that a given algorithm may be $O[f(n)]$ for many different functions f. As Figure 11.5 depicts, any algorithm that is $O(n^2)$ will also be $O(n^3)$.

Our main interest in classifying an algorithm with big-O notation is to find a relatively simple function $f(n)$ such that $C*f(n)$ parallels the number of operations as closely as possible. Hence, saying that an algorithm is $O(n^2)$ is considered a better characterization of its efficiency than saying it is $O(n^3)$.

The importance of the constant C, known as the constant of proportionality, lies in comparing algorithms that share the same function $f(n)$; it makes almost no difference in the comparison of algorithms for which $f(n)$ is of different magnitude. It is therefore appropriate to say that the function $f(n)$ dominates the run-time performance of an algorithm and characterizes it in its big-O analysis. The following example should help clarify this situation.

Consider two algorithms L_1 and L_2 with run-times equal to $2n^2$ and n^2, respectively. The constants of proportionality of L_1 and L_2 are 2 and 1, respectively. The dominating function $f(n)$ for both of these algorithms is n^2, but L_2 runs twice as fast as L_1 for a data set of n values. The different sizes of the two constants of proportionality indicate that L_2 is faster than L_1. Now suppose that the function $f(n)$ for L_2 is n^3. Then, even though its constant of proportionality is half of what it is for L_1, L_2 will be frustratingly slower than L_1 for large n. This latter comparison is shown in Figure 11.6.

EXAMPLE 11.6   Use big-O analysis to characterize the two code segments from Examples 11.4 and 11.5, respectively.

◆ **FIGURE 11.5**
Any algorithm that is $O(n^2)$ is also $O(n^3)$

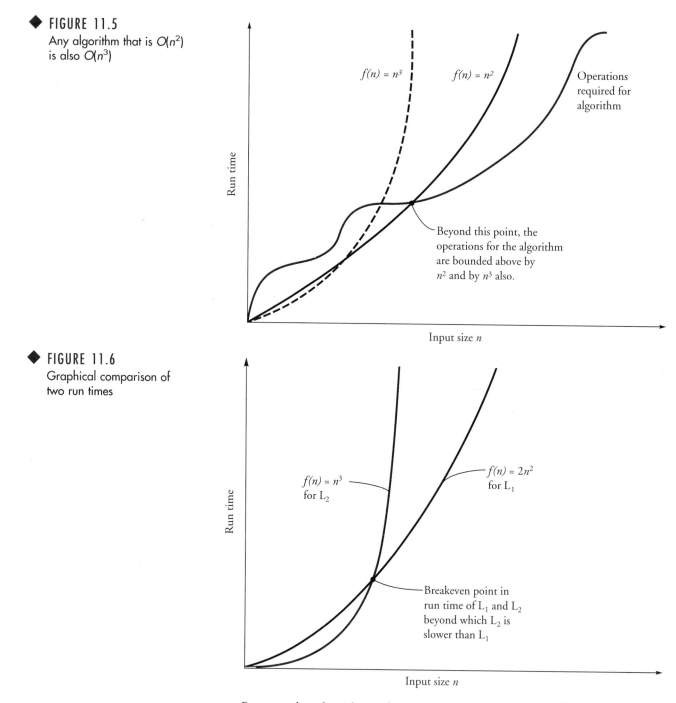

$f(n) = n^3$ $f(n) = n^2$ Operations required for algorithm

Beyond this point, the operations for the algorithm are bounded above by n^2 and by n^3 also.

Run time

Input size n

◆ **FIGURE 11.6**
Graphical comparison of two run times

$f(n) = n^3$ for L_2 $f(n) = 2n^2$ for L_1

Breakeven point in run time of L_1 and L_2 beyond which L_2 is slower than L_1

Run time

Input size n

Because the algorithm of Example 11.4 performs $2N^2$ additions, it is characterized as $O(N^2)$ with 2 as a constant of proportionality. We previously determined that the code of Example 11.5 performs $N^2 + N$ additions. However, $N^2 + N <= 1.1N^2$ for any $N >= 10$. Hence, we can characterize Example 11.5 as an $O(N^2)$ algorithm using 1.1 as a constant of proportionality. These two characterizations demonstrate that, although Example 11.5 is almost twice as fast as Example 11.4, they are in the same big-O category. Coupled with our earlier analysis of these two examples, this is an indication that algorithms in the same big-O category may be expected to have the same orders of magnitude in their run times.

How well does the big-O notation provide a way of classifying algorithms from a real-world perspective? To answer this question, consider Table 11.1. This table presents some typical $f(n)$ functions we will use to classify algorithms and their order of magnitude run times for inputs of various sizes on a hypothetical computer. From this table, we can see that an $O(n^2)$ algorithm will take hours to execute for an input of size 10^5. How many hours is dependent on the constant of proportionality in the definition of the big-O notation.

Regardless of the value of this constant of proportionality, a categorization of an algorithm as an $O(n^2)$ algorithm has thus achieved a very practical goal. We now know that, for an input of size 10^5, we cannot expect an immediate response for such an algorithm. Moreover, we also know that, for a reasonably small constant of proportionality, we have an algorithm for which submission as an overnight job would not be impractical. That is, unlike an $O(n^3)$ algorithm, we could expect the computer to finish executing our algorithm in a time frame that would be acceptable if it could be scheduled to not interfere with other uses of the machine. On the other hand, an $O(n^3)$ algorithm applied to a data set of this size would be completely impractical.

How does one determine the function $f(n)$ that categorizes a particular algorithm? We give an overview of that process here and illustrate it by doing actual analyses for our three sorting algorithms. It is generally the case that, by analyzing the loop structure of an algorithm, we can estimate the number of run-time operations (or amount of memory units) required by the algorithm as a sum of several terms, each dependent on n, the number of items being processed by the algorithm. That is, typically we are able to express the number of run-time operations (or amount of memory) as a sum of the form

$$f_1(n) + f_2(n) + \ldots + f_k(n)$$

Moreover, it is also typical for us to identify one of the terms in this expression as the *dominant term*. A dominant term is one that, for bigger values of n, becomes so large that it allows us to ignore all the other terms from a big-O perspective. For instance, suppose that we had an expression involving two terms such as

$$n^2 + 50n$$

Here, the n^2 term dominates the $50n$ term since, for $n >= 50$, we have

$$n^2 + 50n <= n^2 + n^2 = 2n^2$$

Thus, $n^2 + 50n$ would lead to an $O(n^2)$ categorization because of the dominance of the n^2 term.

◇ **TABLE 11.1**
Some typical $f(n)$ functions and associated run times

Assuming proportionality constant $K = 1$ and one operation per microsecond, approximate run times for input of size			
$f(n)$	10^3	10^5	10^6
$log_2 n$	0.000010 seconds	0.000017 seconds	0.000020 seconds
n	0.001 seconds	0.1 seconds	1 second
$n\, log_2 n$	0.01 seconds	1.7 seconds	20 seconds
n^2	1 second	3 hours	12 days
n^3	17 minutes	32 centuries	3×10^4 centuries
2^n	10^{285} centuries	10^{10^4} years	10^{10^5} years

In general, the problem of big-O categorization reduces to finding the dominant term in an expression representing the number of operations or amount of memory required by an algorithm.

EXAMPLE 11.7

Use big-O notation to analyze the time efficiency of the following fragment of C++ code.

```
for (k = 1; k <= n / 2; ++k)
{
    .
    .
    .
    for (j = 1; j <= n * n; ++j)
    {
        .
        .
        .
    }
}
```

Since these loops are nested, the number of times statements within the innermost loop are executed is the product of the number of repetitions of the two individual loops. Hence the efficiency is $n^3/2$, or $O(n^3)$ in big-O terms, with a constant of proportionality equal to 1/2.

Note that the important principle illustrated by this example is that, for two loops with $O[f_1(n)]$ and $O[f_2(n)]$ efficiencies, the efficiency of the nesting of these two loops (in any order) is $O[f_1(n) * f_2(n)]$.

EXAMPLE 11.8

Use big-O notation to analyze the time efficiency of the following fragment of C++ code.

```
for (k = 1; k <= n / 2; ++k)
{
    .
    .
    .
}
for (j = 1; j <= n * n; ++j)
{
    .
    .
    .
}
```

Since one loop follows the other, the number of operations executed by both of them is the sum of the individual loop efficiencies. Hence the efficiency is $n/2 + n^2$, or $O(n^2)$ in big-O terms.

The important principle illustrated by Example 11.8 is that, for two loops with $O[f_1(n)]$ and $O[f_2(n)]$ efficiencies, the efficiency of the sequencing of these two loops (in any order) is $O[f_D(n)]$ where $f_D(n)$ is the dominant of the functions $f_1(n)$ and $f_2(n)$.

<hr>

EXAMPLE 11.9

Use big-O notation to analyze the time efficiency of the following fragment of C++ code.

```
k = n;
while (k > 1)
{
        .
        .
        .
        k = k / 2;
}
```

Since the loop control variable is cut in half each time through the loop, the number of times that statements inside the loop will be executed is $\log_2 n$. Note that the halving of a loop is central to the binary search algorithm, which will be explored further in Section 11.5. The principle emerging from Example 11.9 is that an algorithm that halves the data remaining to be processed on each iteration of a loop will be an $O(\log_2 n)$ algorithm.

<hr>

Table 11.2, which lists frequently occurring dominant terms, will prove helpful in our future big-O analyses of algorithms.

It is worthwhile to characterize briefly some of the classes of algorithms that arise due to the dominant terms listed in Table 11.2. Algorithms whose efficiency is dominated by a $\log_a n$ term [and hence are categorized as $O(\log_a n)$] are often called *logarithmic algorithms*. Because $\log_a n$ will increase much more slowly than n itself, logarithmic algorithms are generally very efficient. Algorithms whose efficiency can be expressed in terms of a polynomial of the form

$$a_m n^m + a_{m-1} n^{m-1} + \ldots + a_2 n^2 + a_1 n + a_0$$

are called *polynomial algorithms*. Since the highest power of n will dominate such a polynomial, such algorithms are $O(n^m)$. The only polynomial algorithms we will discuss in this book have $m = 1, 2,$ or 3, and they are called *linear, quadratic,* or *cubic algorithms,* respectively.

Algorithms with efficiency dominated by a term of the form a^n are called *exponential algorithms*. Exponential algorithms are of more theoretical rather than

◇ **TABLE 11.2**

Common dominant terms in expressions for algorithmic efficiency, based on the variable n

n dominates $\log_a n$, a is often 2
$n \log_a n$ dominates n, a is often 2
n^2 dominates $n \log_a n$
n^m dominates n^k when $m > k$
a^n dominates n^m for any $a > 1$ and $m \geq 0$

practical interest because they cannot reasonably be run on typical computers for moderate values of *n*.

Big-O Analysis of Bubble Sort

We are now ready to carry out some real comparisons between the three sorting methods we have discussed so far—bubble, insertion, and selection. To do so, we must determine functions $f(n)$ that allow us to make statements like "Sorting algorithm X requires $O[f(n)]$ comparisons." If it turns out that all three sorts share the same $f(n)$ function, then we can conclude that the differences between them are not approaching an order of magnitude scale. Rather, they would be more subtle distinctions, which would not appear as dramatic run-time differences.

We also realize that the key to doing a big-O analysis is to focus our attention on the loops in the algorithm. We do that first for the bubble sort. Recall the loop structure of the bubble sort.

```
k = 0;
exchange_made = TRUE;
while ((k < n - 1) && exchange_made)
{
        exchange_made = FALSE;
        ++k;
        for (j = 0; j < n - k; ++j)
            if (list[j] > list[j + 1])
            {
                    temp = list[j];
                    list[j] = list[j + 1];
                    list[j + 1] = temp;
                    exchange_made = TRUE;
            }
}
```

Inner Loop

Outer Loop

Assume that we have a worst case possible for bubble sort, in which the **exchange_made** variable is always set to TRUE so that an early exit is never made from the outer loop. If we then consider the comparison at the top of the inner loop, we note that it will be executed first $n - 1$ times, then $n - 2$ times, and so on down to one time for the final execution of the inner loop. Hence, the number of comparisons will be the sum of the sequence of numbers:

$(n - 1) (n - 2)$

.
.
.

1

A formula from algebra will show this sum to be

$n(n - 1) / 2$

Thus we conclude that the bubble sort is an $O(n^2)$ algorithm in those situations for which the **exchange_made** test does not allow an early loop exit.

A NOTE OF INTEREST

Artificial Intelligence and the Complexity of Algorithms

Perhaps no area of computer science demands as much in terms of efficient algorithms as does *artificial intelligence* (AI). Those engaged in research in this field are concerned with writing programs that have the computer mimic intelligent human behavior in limited domains such as natural language understanding, theorem proving, and game playing. Why is efficiency so important in such programs? Typically the strategy behind such a system is to have the computer search an enormous number of possibilities for the solution to the problem it is given. These possibilities comprise what is typically called the *state space* for the problem. For instance, for a computer program that plays a game such as checkers or chess, the state space would be a suitable representation of all game board configurations that could eventually be generated from the current state of the game. The computer's goal is to search through the state space, looking for a state in which it would win the game. The state space determined by the initial configuration of a chess game has been computed to be about 10^{120} different possible moves. The time required for a computer to examine each of these different moves, assuming it could examine one every microsecond, would be 10^{95} years. Even for a simpler game such as checkers, the time

required for a computer to search all states in the game would require 10^{23} years.

The reason for these extraordinarily large and impractical time frames is that a "brute force" strategy of searching all states in such AI applications leads to exponential algorithms. To avoid exponential algorithms, researchers in artificial intelligence have attempted to follow the lead of human reasoning. That is, the human mind seems able to eliminate many of the possibilities in a search space without ever examining them. Similarly AI programmers attempt to weed out large sections of the state space to be searched using what are known as *heuristics*. Heuristics are rules of thumb that enable one to rule out a vast number of possible states by doing some relatively simple computations. For instance, in checkers or chess, a heuristic might involve a mathematical formula that attached a positive or negative weight to a particular state of the game. Those states for which the heuristic value indicates a probable lack of success in future searching are simply eliminated from the state space. Since a heuristic is the computational equivalent of an educated guess, it runs the risk of making an error. However, it is often viewed as a worthwhile risk if it can enhance the efficiency of the search algorithm to a category that is no longer exponential.

Big-O Analysis of Insertion Sort

Recall that the loop structure of the insertion sort is given by

```
for (k = 1; k < n; ++k)
{
        item_to_insert = list[k];
        j := k - 1;
        still_looking = TRUE;
        while ((j >= 0) && still_looking )
                if (item_to_insert < list[j])
                {
                        list[j + 1] = list[j];
                        --j;
                }
                else
                        still_looking = FALSE;
        list[j + 1] = item_to_insert;
}
```

Inner Loop

Outer Loop

Here, if the inner loop is never short-circuited by **still_looking**, the comparison appearing as its first statement will be executed once for the first execution of the outer loop, then twice, and so on, reaching $n - 1$ executions on the final pass.

We have a situation virtually identical to our preliminary analysis of the bubble sort. That is, the number of comparisons can be bounded by $n^2/2$ and the algorithm is therefore $O(n^2)$. Of course, with the insertion sort, the hope is that setting the Boolean variable **still_looking** in the **else** clause can reduce the number of comparisons made by the inner loop. However, it is clear that we can concoct many data sets for which this will have little or no effect. So, as with bubble sort, we are forced to conclude that insertion sort cannot guarantee better than $O(n^2)$ comparisons.

Big-O Analysis of Selection Sort

The loop structure of this algorithm was given by

```
for (int j = 0; j < length - 1; ++j)
{
    index = j;
    for (int k = j + 1; k < length; ++k)
        if (list[k] < list[index])
            index = k;
    if (index != j)
    {
        temp = list[index];
        list[index] = list[j];
        list[j] = temp;
    }
}
```

Inner Loop

Outer Loop

A little investigation uncovers a familiar pattern to the nested loops of the selection sort. Observe that the first time the inner loop is executed, the comparison in the **if** statement will be made $n - 1$ times. Then it will be made $n - 2$ times, $n - 3$ times, etc., and, finally, just one time. This is precisely the way the **if** statement in the bubble sort was executed in repeated passes. Thus, like the bubble and insertion sorts, the selection sort is an $O(n^2)$ algorithm in terms of number of comparisons. The area in which the selection sort potentially offers better efficiency is that the number of interchanges of data in array locations is guaranteed to be $O(n)$ because the swap in selection sort occurs in the outer loop. In both of the other sorts, the swap occurs in the inner loop but is subject to a conditional test. This means that, in their worst cases, both of the other algorithms require $O(n^2)$ swaps as well as $O(n^2)$ comparisons.

Despite the fact that selection sort will usually fare better in the number of data interchanges required to sort an array, it has a drawback not found in the other two. It is apparently impossible to short-circuit the nested loop in selection sort when it is given a list in nearly sorted order. So, for such data sets, the selection sort may be an order of magnitude worse than the other two. This is initially rather disheartening news. It seems as if it is impossible to declare any of the sorts a decisive winner. Indeed, our big-O analyses indicate that there is little to choose from the bubble, insertion, and selection algorithms.

The fact that we were able to reach such a conclusion systematically, however, is significant. It reveals the value of a big-O analysis. After all, even knowledge of a negative variety can be valuable in choosing appropriate algorithms under certain circumstances. For instance, if a particular application usually involved adding a small amount of data at the end of an already sorted list and then resorting, we now know we should avoid a selection sort. Moreover, when we study more powerful sorting techniques in the next section (and again in Chapter 18), we will see that it is indeed possible to break the $O(n^2)$ barrier limiting each of our three methods.

1. Do a big-O analysis for those statements inside each of the following nested loop constructs.

a.
```
for (k = 1; k <= n; ++k)
     for (j = 6; j <= m; ++j)
        .
        .
        .
```

b.
```
for (k = 1; k <= n; ++k)
  {
        j := n;
        while (j > 0)
        {
              .
              .
              .
           j = j / 2;
        }
  }
```

c.
```
k = 1;
do
  {
        j = 1;
        do
        {
              .
              .
              .
           j = 2 * j;
        } while j <= n;
        ++k;
  } while k <= n;
```

2. Suppose we have an algorithm that requires precisely

$$6 * \log_2 n + 34 * n^2 + 12$$

operations for an input of n data items. Indicate which of the following are valid big-O classifications of the algorithm.

a. $O(n^3)$

b. $O(n^2)$

c. $O(n)$

d. $O(n^2 * \log_2 n)$

e. $O(n * \log_2 n)$

f. $O(\log_2 n)$

g. $O(1)$

Of those that you have indicated are valid, which is the best big-O classification? Why?

3. A certain algorithm always requires 32 operations, regardless of the amount of data input. Provide a big-O classification of the algorithm that reflects the efficiency of the algorithm as accurately as possible.

4. An algorithm has an efficiency $O[n^2 \sin(n)]$. Is it any better than $O(n^2)$ for a large integer n?

5. Suppose that each of the following expressions represents the number of logical operations in an algorithm as a function of n, the size of the list being manipulated. For each expression, determine the dominant term and then classify the algorithm in big-O terms.

a. $n^3 + n^2\log_2 n + n^3\log_2 n$

b. $n + 4n^2 + 4^n$

c. $48n^4 + 16n^2 + \log_8 n + 2^n$

6. Consider the following nested loop construct. Categorize its efficiency in terms of the variable n using big-O notation. Finally, suppose the statements indicated by the ellipses required four main memory accesses (each requiring one microsecond) and two disk file accesses (each requiring one millisecond). Express in milliseconds the amount of time this construct would require to execute if n were 1000.

```
x = 1;
do
{
        y = n;
        while (y > 0)
        {
                .
                .
                .
                --y;
        }
        x = x + x;
} while x < n * n;
```

7. Look back at the data set you constructed for Exercise 11 in Section 11.2. Evaluate the performance of insertion sort on that data set in terms of a big-O analysis.

8. You and a friend are engaged in an argument. She claims that a certain algorithm is $O(n^2 * \log_2 n)$ in its efficiency. You claim that it is $O(n^2)$. Consider and answer the following questions.

a. Are there circumstances under which both of you could be correct? If so, explain them.

b. Are there circumstances under which both of you could be wrong? If so, explain them.

c. Are there circumstances under which she could be right and you could be wrong? If so, explain them.

d. Are there circumstances under which she could be wrong and you could be right? If so, explain them.

9. You and your friend are engaged in another argument. She claims that a certain algorithm is $O(n^2 + \log_2 n)$ in efficiency. You claim that it is $O(n^2)$. Consider and answer the following questions.

a. Are there circumstances under which both of you could be correct? If so, explain them.

b. Are there circumstances under which both of you could be wrong? If so, explain them.

c. Are there circumstances under which she could be right and you could be wrong? If so, explain them.

d. Are there circumstances under which she could be wrong and you could be right? If so, explain them.

10. Is an $O(n^2)$ algorithm also an $O(n^3)$ algorithm? Justify your answer in a carefully written paragraph.

11.4 The Time/Space Trade-off: Pointer Sort and Radix Sort

OBJECTIVES

- to understand the concept of a pointer
- to understand the difference between physically sorting and logically sorting
- to be able to apply pointers when logically sorting an array without interchanging data items
- to understand what is meant by the time/space trade-off
- to understand the radix sort algorithm and be able to trace its action on appropriate data sets
- to analyze the time and space efficiency of the radix sort algorithm
- to understand why the radix sort algorithm is not as generally applicable as other sorting algorithms we have studied

Early in our discussion of efficiency considerations, we noted that true run-time efficiency was best measured in fundamental machine operations and that one instruction in a high-level language may actually translate into many such primitive operations. To illustrate this, suppose that the data being sorted by one of our algorithms are records, each of which requires 100 bytes of internal storage. Then, depending on your computer, it is entirely conceivable that one comparison or assignment statement in a high-level language could generate a machine language loop with 100 repetitions of such fundamental operations: one for each of the bytes that must be swapped. Those seemingly innocent portions of code, which swap two records using a temporary storage location, actually lead to the movement of 300 bytes inside the machine.

The first question we address in this section is whether, in such a situation, we can replace this large-scale internal transfer of entire records with the much swifter operation of swapping two integers. Although the solution we discuss does not achieve an order of magnitude speed increase in the big-O sense, it nonetheless reduces the number of actual machine-level swaps by a factor proportional to the record length involved, a factor that could produce a noticeable improvement in the function's run time.

Bubble Sort Implemented with Pointers

So far our algorithms to sort data have implicitly assumed that the data are to be *physically sorted,* that is, the data are to be arranged in order within the array being sorted. Hence, the data in the first index of our list array are the data that come first in order according to the key field; the data in the second index, second in order; and so on. However, if we are only interested in processing the data of a list in order by key field, is it really necessary that the data be arranged in physically ordered fashion in computer memory? No. It is possible to step logically through the data in order by key without physically arranging it that way in memory. To do so, we must use another array of *pointers.*

> **Pointer:** A pointer is a memory location in which we store the location of a data item as opposed to the data item itself. In the case of an array, a pointer is the index position of a data item in the array.

Pointers can keep track of the *logical order* of the data without requiring it to be physically moved. At the end of our sorting routine, **pointer[0]** tells us the location of the data that should come first in our alphabetical listing; **pointer[1]** contains the location of the data that should come second; and so on. The sorting algorithm itself uses the logic of the bubble sort to interchange pointers instead of interchanging actual data. The actual data never move; they remain precisely where

◆ **FIGURE 11.7**

"Before" (left) and "After" (right) snapshots of pointer sort

	Key field of **list**		**pointer**
0	MAXWELL		0
1	BUCKNER		1
2	LANIER		2
3	AARON		3

Snapshot of **list** and **pointer** immediately after initialization

	Key field of **list**		**pointer**
	MAXWELL		3
	BUCKNER		1
	LANIER		2
	AARON		0

Snapshot of **list** and **pointer** returned by **pointer_bubble_sort**

they were stored on initial input. Instead of the expensive, time-consuming swapping of potentially large records, we are able to swap integer pointers quickly.

A C++ function to implement this *pointer sort* technique follows. In addition to the declarations we have already been using in this chapter, this function assumes an external declaration of the form

```
typedef int pointer_array[MAX_LIST_SIZE];
```

Besides the **list** array, the function receives an array **pointer** of type **pointer_array**. The function initializes the pointer array to the state pictured in the "Before" snapshot of Figure 11.7. Then, via repeated swaps of integer pointers, the array is returned as shown in the "After" snapshot. As the figure indicates, the **list** array itself is never altered.

```
void pointer_bubble_sort(list_type list, pointer_array pointer, int n)
{
        int j, k, temp;
        boolean exchange_made = TRUE;

        // Initialize pointer array

        for (k = 0; k < n; ++k)
                pointer[k] = k;

        k = 0;

        // Make up to n - 1 passes through array, exit early if no exchanges are made
        // on previous pass

        while ((k < n - 1) && exchange_made)
        {
            exchange_made = FALSE;
            ++k;
            for (j = 0; j < n - k; ++j)
                if (list[pointer[j]] > list[pointer[j + 1]])// Compare via pointers
                {
                        temp = pointer[j]; // Swap pointers
                        pointer[j] = pointer[j + 1];
                        pointer[j + 1] = temp;
                        exchange_made = TRUE;
                }
        }
}
```

EXAMPLE 11.10

Given the physically ordered list of Figure 11.7, trace the action of function **pointer_bubble_sort** on the array of pointers during each pass through the algorithm.

First pass

Second pass

Third pass

EXAMPLE 11.11

Suppose that **pointer_bubble_sort** was invoked from a main program or another function via the call

```
pointer_bubble_sort (student_list, pointer,
    number_of_students);
```

where **number_of_students**, **student_list**, and **pointer** are of appropriate types. If the logical order established by the pointer array is alphabetical by student name, explain how a report that listed students alphabetically could be printed after this invocation. Assume the existence of a function **print_heading** to print column headings for the report and a function **print_student** to receive an individual student object and print it in formatted form as one detail line of the report.

After the call to **pointer_bubble_sort**, **pointer[0]** contains the position of the object that is first in alphabetical order, **pointer[1]** contains the position of the object that is second, and so on. Hence the following loop will step through all of the entries in the desired order:

```
print_heading();
for (k = 0; k < number_of_students; ++k)
        print_student(student_list[pointer[k]]);
```

Efficiency Analysis for Sorts Implemented with Pointers. The pointer technique illustrated here for the bubble sort may also be used with the insertion and selection algorithms. In any of these cases, the mere introduction of the pointer strategy will not reduce the big-O categorization of the sort. However, in cases where the data items being sorted use enough internal storage to slow down swapping times substantially, the pointer sort can attain a considerable savings in run time.

Is this run-time savings achieved without any sacrifice? An old saying that has been passed down by computer people since the days of the early vacuum tube machines is "You get nothing for nothing." We have not escaped the consequences of that adage by using pointers to increase run-time efficiency. The pointers store *data about data;* this requires additional memory. If your application is not approaching the limits of memory, this cost may not be crucial. In certain situations, however, it could be the last straw for a program running short of memory. Thus, the pointer sort is essentially a trade-off; by using more memory, we get a program that runs faster.

This *time/space trade-off* continually recurs in the analysis of computer algorithms. Many sophisticated techniques to increase speed will need to store substantial data about data to do so. Those algorithms that solve a problem in a fashion that saves space *and* decreases run time are indeed worthy of special praise. We will be sure to note them.

Finally, the notion of a pointer, as defined and introduced here, plays an important role in our study of data structures beginning in Chapter 14. The time you spend exploring the details of the pointer sort technique will prove very valuable in your understanding of this topic in the future.

Radix Sort

The *radix sort* algorithm is also called the *bin sort,* a name derived from its origin as a technique used on (now obsolete) machines called card sorters. These machines would sort a deck of keypunched cards by shuffling the cards into small bins, then collecting the cards from the bins into a newly arranged deck, and repeating this shuffling–collection process until the deck was magically sorted. There was, as we shall see, a very clever algorithm behind this rapid shuffling.

For integer data, the repeated passes of a radix sort focus first on the ones digit of each number, then on the tens digit, the hundreds digit, and so on until the highest order digit of the largest number is reached. For string data, the first pass hinges on the rightmost character in each string with successive passes always shifting their attention one character position to the left. To illustrate the algorithm, we will trace it on the following list of nine integers:

```
459 254 472 534 649 239 432 654 477
```

On each pass through this data, radix sort will arrange it into ten sublists (bins)—one sublist for each of the digits 0 through 9. Hence, on the first pass, all the numbers with a ones digit equal to zero are grouped in one sublist, all those with a ones digit equal to one are grouped in another sublist, and so on. The resulting sublists follow:

Digit	Sublist		
0			
1			
2	472	432	
3			
4	254	534	654
5			
6			
7	477		
8			
9	459	649	239

The sublists are then collected into one large list with the numbers in the sublist for 0 coming first, then those in the sublist for 1, and so on up to the sublist for 9. Hence we would have a newly arranged list:

472 432 254 534 654 477 459 649 239

This new list is again partitioned into sublists, this time keying on the tens digit. The result is shown below:

Digit	Sublist		
0			
1			
2			
3	432	534	239
4	649		
5	654	254	459
6			
7	472	477	
8			
9			

Note that in each sublist the data are arranged in order relative to their last two digits. The sublists would now be collected into a new master list:

432 534 239 649 654 254 459 472 477

Now, focusing on the hundreds digit, the master list would be classified into ten sublists one more time. These final sublists are shown below. When the sublists are collected from this final partitioning, the data are arranged in ascending order.

Digit	Sublist			
0				
1				
2	239	254		
3				
4	432	459	472	477
5	534			
6	649	654		
7				
8				
9				

A pseudocode statement of the radix sort algorithm follows.

1. Begin with the current digit as the ones digit
2. while there is still a digit on which to classify data
    2.1 for each number in the master list
        2.1.1 add that number to appropriate sublist, keying on current digit
    2.2 for each sublist (from 0 through 9)
        2.2.1 append that sublist to a newly arranged master list
    2.3 Advance the current digit one place to the left

If the radix sort is being applied to character strings instead of integers, this algorithm would have to proceed from the rightmost character to the leftmost character instead of from the ones digit to the highest order digit.

Efficiency of Radix Sort. An analysis of the loop structure in the preceding pseudocode for radix sort indicates that, for each pass through the outer **while** loop, $O(n)$ operations must be performed. These $O(n)$ operations consist of the arithmetic necessary to isolate a particular digit within a number, appending that number to the proper sublist, and then collecting it again into a new master list. Since the outer **while** loop will only be executed C times—where C is the number of digits (or characters) in the integer (or string)—the radix sort is an $O(n)$ sorting algorithm.

Although the radix sort is significantly faster than the other $O(n^2)$ algorithms we have studied in this chapter, there are again trade-off factors to consider. It is potentially much less space efficient than the other sorting algorithms we have studied. This is due to the need for storing sublists for each of the possible digits in the number or characters in the string. Using arrays to store the sublists and without any prior knowledge about the distribution of the data, we would be forced to allocate an additional $10n$ storage locations when sorting an array of n integers and $27n$ storage locations when sorting n strings of letters and blanks. We shall alleviate this memory crunch somewhat when we study linked lists in Chapter 14, but even then the radix sort will remain a space-inefficient algorithm compared to other sorting algorithms. Other criteria negating the very good time efficiency of the radix sort are its inflexibility for data of varying size and the fact that, although $O(n)$ in time, its constant of proportionality in this regard is often large enough to make it less time efficient than the more sophisticated sorting algorithms we will study in Chapter 18.

EXAMPLE 11.12   Assume the existence of the following declarations and function to perform a radix sort on an array of four-digit numbers.

```
int const MAX_LIST_SIZE = 100;

typedef int list_type[MAX_LIST_SIZE];
typedef list_type bin_structure_type[10];
typedef int bin_counter_type[10];

// Function: digit
// Computes the kth digit in number
//
```

```
// Inputs: integers number and k
// Output: the kth digit in number

int digit(int number, int k);

// Function: initialize_counters
// Initializes all counters to zero
void initialize_counters(bin_counter_type bin_counters);

// Function: add_to_bin
// Insert number in bin_structure indicated by place
//
// Inputs: a bin_structure, a bin_counter a number and a place
// Outputs: a bin_structure and a bin_counter

void add_to_bin(bin_structure_type bins,
      bin_counter_type bin_counters, int number, int place);

void collect_bins(list_type list, bin_structure_type bins,
      bin_counter_type bin_counters);
```

Then the C++ code for this radix sort would be

```
void radix_sort(list_type list, int n)
{
    int j, k;
    bin_structure_type bins;
    bin_counter_type bin_counters;

    initialize_counters(bin_counters);

    // For k loop controls digit used to classify data.
    for (k = 1; k <= 4; ++k)
    {
        // For j loop iterates through all numbers, putting them into
        // bin determined by kth digit.
        for (j = 0; j < n; ++j)
            add_to_bin(bins, bin_counters, list[j], digit(list[j], k));
        collect_bins(list, bins, bin_counters);
        initialize_counters(bin_counters);
    }
}
```

EXERCISES 11.4

1. Suppose that you are given the following list of keys:

0	9438
1	3216
2	416
3	9021
4	1142
5	3316
6	94

Show what the contents of the pointer array would be after each pass through the outer loop of function **pointer_bubble_sort** discussed in this section.

2. Consider again the data set given in Exercise 1. How many passes would be made through the outer loop of the radix sort algorithm for these data? Trace the contents of the array after each of these passes.

3. Consider the following list of strings:

0	CHOCOLATE
1	VANILLA
2	CARAMEL
3	PEACH
4	STRAWBERRY
5	CHERRY

How many passes would be made through the outer loop of the radix sort algorithm for these data? Trace the contents of the list after each of these passes.

4. Explain the difference between physical and logical ordering.

5. Cite an application in which the mere logical ordering of data, as achieved by the pointer sort technique, would not be sufficient; that is, give an application in which physical ordering of data is required.

6. What is the time/space trade-off? Define and discuss various contexts in which it may arise.

7. When the bubble sort was modified with an array of pointers, did it improve its $O(n^2)$ run-time efficiency in a significant sense? Under what circumstances would you call the improvement in efficiency significant? Provide your answer to this question in a short essay in which you define "significant" and then explain why the circumstance you describe would lead to a significant improvement.

8. The bubble, insertion, and selection sort algorithms are all $O(n)$ in their space requirements. That is, each algorithm requires memory proportional to n to sort the items in an array of n items. From a big-O perspective, what are the space requirements of these algorithms when the pointer sort technique is incorporated into their logic?

9. Would you expect the pointer strategy to have the *least* effect on the run-time efficiency of the bubble, selection, or insertion sort? Provide a rationale for your answer in a short essay.

10. Suppose you have 1000 objects to be sorted. Would the run-time efficiency of the pointer sort increase significantly if the 1000 objects were broken into four groups, each group sorted, and then merged together as one large sorted array as compared to sorting the initial unsegmented array? Why or why not?

11. Incorporate the pointer sort technique into the selection sort algorithm.

12. Incorporate the pointer sort technique into the insertion sort algorithm.

13. Write the assumed and any other necessary functions in the version of **radix_sort** given in Example 11.12.

14. Write a radix sort function to sort an arbitrary array of integers. Analyze the space efficiency of your function.

15. Write a radix sort function to sort an array of strings. Analyze the space efficiency of your function. Be sure to state carefully the assumptions you make about strings in performing your analysis of space efficiency.

16. Describe the complications in implementing the radix sort algorithm for an array of real numbers. Discuss a strategy that could be used to overcome these complications.

A NOTE OF INTEREST

Computer Graphics, Visualization, and Virtual Reality

In *computer graphics*, the efficiency of algorithms and the speed of the processing hardware are of vital importance. Recent hardware developments now enable scientists to transform numeric data into computer images approaching the quality of photographs in their realism. The essential principle behind such graphics is to develop a numerical model of a physical phenomenon and then, via sophisticated mathematical algorithms, transform the model into a picture on the screen of a high-resolution graphics workstation. With faster computers and algorithms, more considerations of physical laws can be built into such models. The result of being able to incorporate more such laws is to produce images that appear very realistic.

The computational cost of such photorealism remains steep, however, progress is being made. Each year the Association of Computing Machinery's Special Interest Group on Computer Graphics (ACM SIGGRAPH) sponsors an art show at their annual meeting. The best of the digital imagery displayed at these shows is typically highlighted in the July issue of *Communications of the ACM*. For example, "Digital Image—Digital Cinema" [*Communications of the ACM*, 33, No. 7 (July 1990):30–39] and "Art & Design & Computer Graphics Technology" [*Communications of the ACM*, 34, No. 7 (July 1991):30–39] present full-color portfolios that demonstrate the degree to which the computer is influencing art and graphic design.

Who knows? Might we someday achieve the situation described by Robert Heinlein in his science-fiction novel *The Moon Is a Harsh Mistress*. In this story the president of the United States, Adam Selene, appears only on television, never in person. Why? Because he is not a human being, but solely the product of computer-generated graphic images. Such animation may soon be possible as faster hardware merges with the more efficient rendering algorithms that experts in computer graphics are now developing. Such techniques are giving rise to a new area of research known as virtual reality, in which the computer is used to view ideas without having to build a physical model.

Though it's unlikely that virtual reality will create a simulated president such as Adam Selene, it is already having a dramatic effect in design-intensive fields such as architecture. Donald Greenberg of Cornell University described such virtual reality systems in "Computers and Architecture" [*Scientific American*, 264, No. 8 (February 1991)]. According to Greenberg, "advanced modeling and rendering algorithms allow designers and clients to walk visually through buildings long before construction . . . seeing results of their design decisions immediately and revising them interactively."

Simple Search Algorithms

Many programs extensively employ algorithms that find a particular data item in a large collection of such items. Such algorithms, typically called *search algorithms*, are given the value of a key field that identifies the item being sought; they then return either all of the data associated with that particular key or a flag indicating that it could not be found. You saw a search algorithm in Section 10.4 when we described some operations that were frequently required in processing arrays. We now explore search algorithms and subject them to an efficiency analysis using the big-O notation we have developed.

The search operation will look for an object in a list that is associated with a target key value. Thus, rather than comparing two objects of type element, the search algorithm will have to compare a key value and an object of type element. We will assume that the element type has overloaded the standard operators for comparing a key value and an object of the element type. The general setup for the search algorithms we discuss in this chapter is given by the following skeletal declarations:

```
int const MAX_LIST_SIZE = 100;
typedef int element;
typedef element list_type[MAX_LIST_SIZE];

// Function: search
// Find the object associated with the target key
// value
//
// Inputs: a list of objects, its length, and a
// target key value
// Outputs: if the target key is found, Boolean
// value TRUE and the object
// associated with the target key; otherwise,
// Boolean FALSE

boolean search(list_type list, int n,
       key_type target, element &object,);
```

Figure 11.8 graphically portrays this setup.

◆ **FIGURE 11.8**

General setup for search algorithm

Search

Relative Position	Key	OtherData
0	adams jr	112 N. 6TH ST
1	baker ml	318 S. 8TH AVE
.	.	.
.	.	.
50	miller gk	912 W. 13TH AVE
51	neville ac	884 E. 60TH ST
.	.	.
.	.	.
End of list		

Target
| miller gk |

To be returned
↓   InfoWanted

Sequential Search Algorithm

The task of a computer scientist working with search algorithms may be compared to that of a librarian. Just as the librarian must devise a method of storing books on shelves in a fashion that allows patrons to easily find the books they want, so must a computer scientist devise methods of organizing large collections of electronic data so that records within that data can always be quickly found. Imagine the plight of the librarian who just throws books on shelves as they are unpacked from shipping boxes, without any consideration toward organizing the chaos! Unless the library had an artificially small collection, it would take patrons an impractical length of time to find their reading material. Because of the lack of any organizational order imposed on the books, the only search strategy available would be to pull books from the shelves in some arbitrary sequence until the desired book was found.

As a programmer given a completely unordered set of data, this is the same strategy you would have to follow. The logic of such a *sequential search* strategy is extremely simple and appears in the following function **sequential_search**.

```
boolean sequential_search(list_type list, int n,
    key_type target, element &object)
{
    int k = 0;
    boolean found = FALSE;
    while ((k < n) && ! found)
        if (list[k] == target)
            found = TRUE;
        else
            ++k;
    if (found)
        object = list[k];
    return found;
}
```

Efficiency of Sequential Search. Unfortunately, the simplicity of the sequential search is offset by its inefficiency as a search strategy. Obviously, the average number of probes into the list before the target key is found will be $n/2$, where n is the number of records in the list. For unsuccessful invocations of the function, all n records must be checked before we can conclude failure. Thus, in terms of a big-O classification, the method is clearly $O(n)$. This may not seem bad when compared to the $O(n^2)$ efficiency of our sorting methods, but searching is conceptually a much simpler operation than sorting: It should be significantly faster. Moreover, though $O(n)$ may seem fast enough at microsecond speeds, there are many applications where an $O(n)$ time factor can be unacceptably slow.

For instance, when a compiler processes your source program in C++, it must continually search a list of identifiers that have been previously declared. (This list is typically called a *symbol table.*) Hence, in such an application, the search operation merely represents the inner loop within a much more complex outer loop that is repeating until it reaches the end of your source file: an inner loop that, repeated at $O(n)$ speeds, would make your compiler intolerably slow.

Another situation in which $O(n)$ is not good enough for searching occurs when the list being searched is stored in a *disk file* instead of a main memory array. Now, because accessing data on disk is a much slower operation than accessing data in main memory, each probe into the list might conceivably require approximately one millisecond (one-thousandth of a second) instead of a microsecond. Searching such a list of one million records at $O(n)$ speed would hence require one thousand seconds instead of just one second, which is too long to wait for one record and is certain to generate angry users. We conclude that, although the sequential search may be fast enough for small and infrequently accessed lists stored in main memory, we need something that is better by an order of magnitude for many practical applications.

Binary Search Algorithm

By paying what may initially seem like a small price, we can dramatically increase the efficiency of our search effort using a *binary search* algorithm.

1. The list of objects with keys must be maintained in physically sorted order unless we are willing to use an additional list of pointers similar to that used in the **pointer_bubble_sort** algorithm. (See the exercises at the end of this section.)

2. The number of objects in the list must be maintained in a separate variable.

3. We must be able to access randomly, by relative position, objects in the list. This is the type of access you have in C++ arrays.

For instance, suppose that the list of integer keys appearing in Figure 11.9 has the access facility of the third point just cited and that we wish to locate the randomly accessible data associated with the target key 1649. The strategy of the binary search is to begin the search in the middle of the list. In the case of Figure 11.9, this would mean beginning the search with the key found at position 4. Since the target we are seeking is greater than the key found at position 4, we are able to conclude that the key we want will be found among positions 5 through 9—if at all.

We will split those positions that remain viable candidates for finding the target by accessing the middle position:

$$(5 + 9) / 2 = 7$$

Since the key at position 7 is greater than **target**, we are able to conclude that the key being sought will be found in positions 5 or 6—if it is to be found at all. Notice that, after only two accesses into the list, our list of remaining viable candidates for a match has shrunk to 2. (Compare this figure to a sequential search after two accesses into the same list.) We now split the distance between positions 5 and 6, arriving (by integer arithmetic) at position 5. Here we find the key being sought after a mere three probes into the list.

Crucial to the entire binary search algorithm are two pointers, **low** and **high**, to the bottom and top, respectively, of the current list of viable candidates. We must repeatedly compute the middle index of that portion of the list between **low** and **high** and compare the data at that middle index to the target using the following logic.

```
If list[middle] equals the target
        Search is done
        Target has been found in list
Else if list[middle] < target
        Low must be set to middle + 1
Else
        High must be set to middle - 1
```

Should these pointers ever merge, that is, if **high** were to equal to **low**, we would conclude that the target does not appear in the list. The entire algorithm is formalized in the following C++ function:

◆ FIGURE 11.9

Physically ordered random access list of keys for binary search

Position	Key
0	1119
1	1203
2	1212
3	1519
4	1604
5	1649
6	1821
7	2312
8	2409
9	3612

Number of Records $n = 10$
target = 1649

```
boolean binary_search(list_type list, int n, key_type target, element &object)
{
        int low, middle, high;
        boolean found = FALSE;

        low = 0;
        high = n - 1;
        while ((low = high) && ! found)
        {
                middle = (low + high) / 2;
                if (list[middle] == target)
                        found = TRUE;
                else if (list[middle] < target)
                        low = middle + 1;
                else
                        high = middle - 1;
        }
        if (found)
            object = list[middle];
        return found;
}
```

EXAMPLE 11.13   Trace the action of function **binary_search** as it locates the record associated with target 1519 in the array of Figure 11.9.

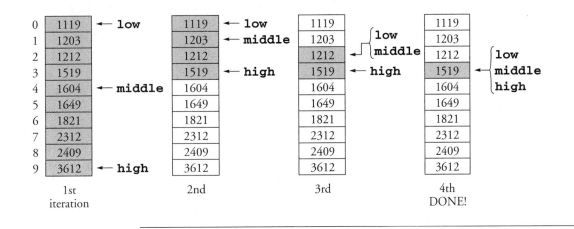

EXAMPLE 11.14   Trace the action of function **binary_search** as it reports that target 2392 cannot be found in the array of Figure 11.9.

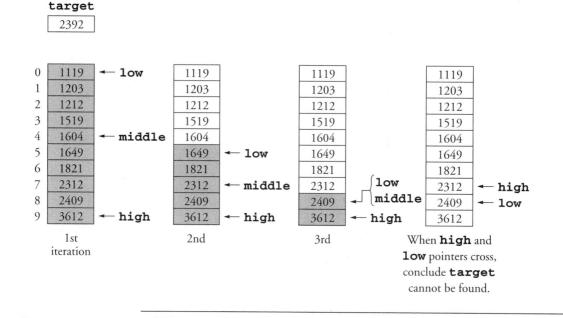

Efficiency of Binary Search. As indicated by the shaded portions of the lists in the preceding examples, the binary search continually halves the size of the list that must still be searched. This continual halving is critical to the effectiveness of the algorithm. When applied to the list of keys in Figure 11.9, the method in the worst case would require four different accesses. For an ordered list of 50,000 keys, the worst case efficiency is a mere 16 different accesses. (In case you do not believe this dramatic increase in efficiency as the list gets larger, try plugging 50,000 into a hand-held calculator and count how many times you must halve the displayed number to reduce it to 1.) The same list of 1,000,000 records stored on disk that would require approximately 1000 seconds to search sequentially will result in a virtually instantaneous response with the binary search strategy.

More formally, for a list of n items, the maximum number of times we would cut the list in half before finding the target item or declaring the search unsuccessful is

$$(\log_2 n) + 1$$

Thus, the binary search is the first $O(\log_2 n)$ algorithm we have studied (see Example 11.10). In terms of the categorizations discussed in Section 11.3, it is a logarithmic algorithm. Expressions involving a $\log_2 n$ factor will arise frequently as we analyze other algorithms. They are extremely fast when compared to $O(n)$ algorithms, particularly for large values of n.

The drawback of the binary search lies not in any consideration of its processing speed but rather in a reexamination of the price that must be paid for being able to use it. For a volatile list (that is, one undergoing frequent additions and deletions), the requirement of maintaining the list in physical order can be quite costly. For large lists, it makes the operations of adding and deleting records so inefficient that the very fast search speed is all but negated. We will analyze this problem of list maintenance in more detail in future chapters.

Key-to-Address Transformations

A search technique so simple that it is often overlooked presents itself in certain situations where a record's key value can be transformed conveniently into a position within a list by applying a function to the key value. For instance, suppose that a school assigns its students five-digit identification numbers in which the first two digits indicate the student's year of matriculation and the last three digits are simply assigned in a sequential fashion among students matriculating in a given year. Hence the fourteenth student admitted in the class of 1992 would have the identification number

$$\underbrace{9\ 2}_{\text{year of matriculation}} \qquad\qquad \underbrace{0\ 1\ 4}_{\text{sequence number within that year}}$$

In such a situation, student records could be stored in a two-dimensional table in which rows were indexed by year of matriculation and columns indexed by sequence number within a given year. Then the integer arithmetic operations

```
key / 1000
```

and

```
key % 1000
```

would yield a given student's row and column index, respectively. The address of a student's record could therefore be obtained from the student's identification number using a mere two operations.

In such situations, the search efficiency to locate a student's record is O(1) in its big-O classification. The apparent restriction that must apply for this technique to work is that the transformation applied to a key to yield an address cannot yield the same address for two different students. As we shall see in Chapter 19, even this restriction can be relaxed somewhat if slightly more sophisticated search techniques are employed. Another drawback of the key-to-address transformation technique is its potentially inefficient use of space. You will perform such a space analysis for this strategy in this section's exercises.

EXERCISES 11.5

1. Suppose that an array contains key values

   18 40 46 50 52 58 63 70 77 90

   in index locations 0 through 9. Trace the index values for the **low**, **high**, and **middle** pointers in the binary search algorithm if the **target** 43 is being sought. Repeat for **target** values 40 and 90.

2. In Exercise 10 of Section 11.2 we defined the notions of best case and worst case behavior of an algorithm. Devise sample data sets to demonstrate the best case and worst case behavior of the binary search algorithm.

3. What is a compiler symbol table? Explain why a sequential search applied to such a table is not a practical strategy.

4. Explain the difference in run-time efficiency considerations for a program that manipulates data in a main memory array versus one that accesses data stored in a disk file.

5. How many times would the **while** loop in function **binary_search** be executed if $n = 1,000,000$?

6. Consider the following modified version of the binary search algorithm. (Modifications are indicated by a comment highlighted by asterisks.) Will this new version of the binary search algorithm work correctly for all data? If not, specify a situation in which this version will fail.

```
boolean binary_search(list_type list, int n, key_type target, element &object)
{
     int low, middle, high;
     boolean found = FALSE;

     low = 0;
     high = n;
     while ((low < high) && ! found)
     {
         middle = (low + high) / 2;
         if (list[middle] = target)
             found = TRUE;
         else if (list[middle] < target)
             low = middle;          // *** Modification here ***
         else
             high = middle;         // *** Modification here ***
     }
     if (found)
         object = list[middle];
     return found;
}
```

7. Consider the following modified version of the binary search algorithm. (Modifications are indicated by a comment highlighted by asterisks.) Will this new version of the binary search algorithm work correctly for all data? If not, specify a situation in which this version will fail.

```
boolean binary_search(list_type list, int n, key_type target, element &object)
{
     int low, middle, high;
     boolean found = FALSE;

     low = 0;
     high = n;
     do                               // *** Use do. . .while instead of while ***
     {
         middle = (low + high) / 2;
         if (list[middle] = target)
             found = TRUE;
         else if (list[middle] < target)
             low = middle + 1;
         else
             high = middle - 1;
     } while ((low < high) && ! found); // *** Loop exit condition
     if (found)
         object = list[middle];
     return found;
}
```

8. Consider the example of a key-to-address transformation for student identification numbers given in this section. Discuss the space efficiency of this strategy. On what factor is the space efficiency dependent?

9. Devise a key-to-address transformation to locate records in a data structure for employees of the East Publishing Company. Departments in the company are identified by a one-letter code A–Z. An employee's payroll identification number consists of a department code followed by another one-letter code representing the employee's pay rate classification, and a two-digit number assigned in sequential fashion to employees within a given department. Hence, the identification number DX40 is assigned to the 40th employee in department D; the X indicates the employee's pay rate category.

10. The requirement for the binary search that the data in an array be physically ordered can actually be circumvented by keeping track of the logical order of the data via a pointer array analogous to that used in the pointer sort. Rewrite the binary search algorithm under such an assumption. Explain why it might be advantageous to use this technique.

11. Implement the following modification to the sequential search algorithm. Temporarily insert the key for which you are searching at the end of the list. Search sequentially until you find this key; then examine the position where you found it to determine whether or not the search was successful. Note that this strategy requires your knowing the number of items in the list rather than a sentinel value stored at the end of the list. Comment on the run-time efficiency of this new strategy versus the sequential search algorithm discussed in this chapter.

12. Modify the insertion sort algorithm of Section 11.2 so that it finds the insertion point for the next array entry using an appropriate modification of the halving strategy employed by the binary search algorithm. Once this insertion point is determined, other array entries must be moved accordingly to make room for the entry being inserted. After completing this modified version of the insertion sort, perform a big-O analysis of its efficiency.

13. Imagine that you have been hired to write an information retrieval program for a company or organization. You must interview people within the organization to determine exactly what their information retrieval needs are. Construct questions that you could ask in such an interview to enable you to determine which search strategy would be most appropriate for the program you must write. Then, in an essay explain how answers to these questions would dictate your choice of search strategy.

FOCUS ON PROGRAM DESIGN

Rather than present a complete program as we have done in previous Focus on Program Design sections, we will use this chapter's Focus section to examine how we can augment a program to help us analyze its own efficiency. This technique, known as *profiling,* consists of inserting counters that accumulate the total number of times that certain critical operations are performed as an algorithm executes.

To illustrate the technique, we return to the program developed in the Focus on Program Design section for Chapter 6. Recall that the central **list_all_primes** function of this program determined all primes less than or equal to a specified positive integer called **number**. Portions of this original program are presented here, along with new additions (indicated by shading) that illustrate the profiling technique.

Before discussing these additions, however, we will turn our attention to trying to analyze the time efficiency of the **list_all_primes** function. The nested loop structure of this function is given by the following schematic:

```
for each candidate from 2 to number
   .                                              ┐
   .                                              │
   .                                              │
   while            Inner while                   │  Outer for loop
   .                loop executed                 │  executed
   .                candidate – 2 or              │  number – 1 times
                    fewer times                   ┘
```

Certainly the schematic indicates that we are safe in saying that function **list_all_primes** is $O(\textbf{number}^2)$ in its time efficiency. However, the early exit condition from the inner loop will be reached quite often. This leads us to believe that the algorithm may actually be substantially faster than $O(\textbf{number}^2)$.

Unfortunately, determining how much faster it is than $O(\textbf{number}^2)$ by using a purely mathematical analysis may be impossible or at least require a knowledge of mathematical number theory beyond our present means. We propose instead to use the computer to help us analyze the algorithm from an empirical perspective. An examination of the shaded code in the partial listing given here indicates that profiling the **list_all_primes** algorithm is achieved by:

1. Declaring a global Boolean constant that is set to TRUE to "turn on" profiling. All executable statements related to profiling are conditionally qualified by

   if PROFILE . . .

   Thus, to turn off profiling in the program, you would merely set this constant to FALSE.
2. A global variable **profiled_operations** is initialized to zero upon entry to **list_all_primes** and then increased by 1 each time an addition or % operation is performed.
3. A **profile_report** function is called conditionally by the main program to report a comparison between N^2 and the actual number of operations performed during execution of the algorithm.

We should justify the use of globally declared data within the function **list_all_primes**. The alternative would be to add extra parameters to the formal parameter list of **list_all_primes**—parameters that are concerned with profiling instead of the actual algorithm implemented by **list_all_primes**. That is, the profiling data items are completely extraneous to the logic of the function; they are there only to measure empirically the performance of the algorithm. As such, adding them to the formal parameter list would make the interface to the function considerably more confusing than necessary.

We emphasize that the use of global data is an exceptional circumstance, occurring in specialized contexts such as profiling. In general, the maxim that functions should only use locally declared data remains true.

A complete program listing follows. The results of sample runs are discussed after the listing.

```cpp
// Program file: primes.cpp
#include <iostream.h>
#include <iomanip.h>
#include <math.h>
#include "boolean.h"
```

```
const char SKIP = ' ';

// Global data for profiling only
const boolean PROFILE = TRUE;
int profiled_operations;

int get_a_number();

// Function: print_one_message
// Print a message for 1

void print_one_message();

// Function: print_message
// Print a heading for the output
//
// Input: the integer read

void print_message(int number);

// Function: list_all_primes
// Print list of all primes less than or equal to the integer read
//
// Input: the integer read

void list_all_primes(int number);

// Function: list_all_primes
// If integer read is one,
// then print a message for one
// else
// Print list of all primes less than or equal to the integer read
//
// Input: the integer read

void examine_the_number(int number);

// Function: more_data
// Determines whether number = -999 (the sentinel for end of input)
// Input: the integer read
// Output: TRUE, if the input is not the sentinel, FALSE otherwise

boolean more_data(int number);

// Function: profile_report
// Report a comparison of number of profiled operations to O(number^2)
//
// Inputs: the number being profiled and a global count of operations
void profile_report(int number);

int main()
{
      int number;
```

```
        number = get_a_number ();
        while (more_data(number))
        {
                examine_the_number (number);
                number = get_a_number ();
        }
        return 0;
}


int get_a_number()
{
        int number;
        boolean done;


        do
        {
                cout << endl;
                cout << "Enter a positive integer; <-999> to quit.";
                cin >> number;
                done = (number == -999) || (number >= 0);
        } while (! done); // assumes valid data
        return number;
}


void print_one_message()
{
        cout << endl;
        cout << setw(10) << SKIP
                << "--------------------------"
                << endl;
        cout << endl;
        cout << setw(20) << SKIP << "1 is not prime by definition." << endl;
}


void print_message(int number)
{
        cout << endl;
        cout << setw(10) << SKIP
                << "--------------------------"
                << endl;
        cout << endl;
        cout << setw(20) << SKIP << "The number is " << number << ". "
                << " The prime numbers" << endl;
        cout << setw(20) << SKIP << "less than or equal to "<< number
                << " are:" << endl;
        cout << endl;
}
void list_all_primes(int number)
{
```

```
        boolean prime;
        int candidate, divisor;
        float limit_for_check;

        if (PROFILE)
            profiled_operations = 0;
        for (candidate = 2; candidate <= number; ++candidate)
        {
            prime = TRUE;
            divisor = 2;
            limit_for_check = sqrt(candidate);
            while ((divisor <= limit_for_check) && prime)
            {
                    if (candidate % divisor == 0)
                            prime = FALSE; // Candidate has a divisor
                    else
                            ++divisor;
                    if (PROFILE)
                            ++profiled_operations;
            }
            if (prime)                              //Print in list of primes
                cout << setw(35) << candidate << endl;
        }
}
void examine_the_number(int number)
{
        if (number == 1)
                print_one_message();
        else
        {
                print_message(number);
                list_all_primes (number);
                profile_report (number)
        }
}


boolean more_data(int number)
{
        return number != -999;
}


void profile_report(int number)
{
    cout << endl;
    cout << "    For N: " << setw(3) << number << endl;
    cout << endl;
    cout << "    Number of profiled operations: "
         << profiled_operations << endl;
    cout << "    Compare to O(number^2): "
         << number * number << endl;
    cout << endl;
}
```

Here are a few sample runs, with profiling output only.

```
Enter a positive integer, <-999> to quit. 17
                .
              . (primes listed here)
                .
    For N: 17
    Number of profiled operations: 55
    Compare to O(N^2): 289
Enter a positive integer, <-999> to quit. 45
                .
              . (primes listed here)
                .
    For N: 45
    Number of profiled operations: 296
    Compare to O(N^2): 2025
Enter a positive integer, <-999> to quit. 100
                .
              . (primes listed here)
                .
    For N: 100
    Number of profiled operations: 1133
    Compare to O(N^2): 10000
Enter a positive integer, <-999> to quit. 150
                .
              . (primes listed here)
                .
    For N: 150
    Number of profiled operations: 2414
    Compare to O(N^2): 22500
Enter a positive integer, <-999> to quit. -999
```

What have we learned from the runs of this profiled program? The observed number of operations that are reported by the program offer empirical evidence that we are well within the bounds of an $O(N^2)$ algorithm. They indicate that we can perhaps even place the algorithm into a more efficient big-O category. What category? This could be explored by fine-tuning the **profile_report** function to compare the actual number of performed operations with n^r for values of r less than 2 or with $n * \log_2 n$.

At the time we introduced the **list_all_primes** algorithm in Chapter 6, we commented that it was not necessarily the best way to perform this task. We can now suggest a number of ways to improve the algorithm and evaluate the efficiency of each succeeding version of the algorithm by a combination of formal big-O analysis and empirical profiling. Our series of refinements is illustrative of a process that can often be applied to the first version of an algorithm. That is, reflection on how a given algorithm works can often lead to a new algorithm, which achieves the same end in a much more efficient manner.

Observation 1 The greatest divisor of a number, other than itself, cannot exceed one-half of the number.

Observation 2 Divisors of a number come in pairs. For instance, 36 is divided evenly by 4 since 4 * 9 = 36. Here the divisor 4 is paired with the divisor 9. The search for divisors in the inner loop of our algorithm need not consider the larger value in such a divisor pair. Why? Because it cannot find such a larger divisor without first finding the smaller value in the divisor pair.

Observation 3 The Greek mathematician Eratosthenes devised a "sieve" technique for finding all prime numbers between 2 and **num**. The *sieve of Eratosthenes* can be viewed as a Boolean array indexed from 2 to **num** and initialized to TRUE in all of its locations. Successive array indices are

Multiples of 2 greater than 2 are set to FALSE.
Multiples of 3 greater than 3 are set to FALSE.
Multiples of 4 can be ignored. Why?
Multiples of 5 greater than 5 are set to FALSE.
Multiples of 6 can be ignored. Why?
Multiples of 7 greater than 7 are set to FALSE.

and so on. The prime numbers are those array indices where a true value remains.

You will be asked to continue exploration of such prime number algorithms in the problems. Profiling can be a valuable aid in such exploration. It provides statistical evidence of an algorithm's performance in cases where pure mathematical analysis may be inconclusive.

RUNNING, DEBUGGING AND TESTING HINTS

1. When profiling an algorithm, use a Boolean constant that can be set to TRUE or FALSE to turn profiling on or off, respectively.
2. When using integer counters in profiling a program, be careful that the number of operations executed by the algorithm does not overflow the capacity of integer storage. Most C++ implementations offer additional integer data types that can accommodate values too large for standard integers. Consult local system reference materials to find out what your version of C++ may offer in this regard.

SUMMARY

Key Terms

artificial intelligence
best case
big-O analysis
big-O notation
bin sort
binary search
bubble sort
compiler symbol table
computer graphics
cubic algorithm
data about data
disk file
dominant term

exponential algorithm
heuristics
insertion sort
linear algorithm
logarithmic algorithm
logical order
$\log_2 n$ search algorithm
order of magnitude
permutation
physically sorted
pointer sort
pointers
polynomial algorithm

profile
proportional
quadratic algorithm
radix sort
search algorithm
selection sort
sequential search
sieve of Eratosthenes
state space
symbol table
time/space trade-off
worst case

Key Concepts

◆ An integral part of designing efficient software is the selection of appropriate algorithms to perform the task at hand.

◆ Two of the criteria used in selecting algorithms for a given task are time and space efficiency. An algorithm's time efficiency determines how long it requires to run. An algorithm's space efficiency is a measure of how much primary and secondary memory it consumes.

◆ Three simple sorting algorithms are the bubble sort, insertion sort, and selection sort. The latter minimizes the number of data interchanges that must be made at the expense of not being more efficient for data that are already partially ordered.

◆ Pointer sort and radix sort are techniques to enhance the time efficiency of a sort at the expense of increased space requirements.

◆ Three simple search algorithms are the sequential search, binary search, and key-to-address transformation technique.

◆ Profiling is an empirical technique that can be used to measure an algorithm's efficiency when a big-O analysis is inconclusive.

◆ Big-O analyses of sort and search algorithms discussed in this chapter are summarized in the following table:

Algorithms	Time Efficiency	Additional Comments
Bubble sort	$O(n^2)$ comparisons and interchanges in worst case	Can be faster if input data already almost sorted.
Insertion sort	$O(n^2)$ comparisons and interchanges in worst case	Also can be faster if input data already almost sorted.
Selection sort	$O(n^2)$ comparisons, $O(n)$ interchanges in worst case	Not significantly faster if input data already almost sorted.
Pointer sort	Reflects number of comparisons of method on which it is layered	Though number of interchanges not reduced, amount of data swapped for each interchange is potentially less. Drawback is the additional memory required for pointers.
Radix sort	$O(n)$ comparisons and interchanges	Limited in the types of data on which it works, though $O(n)$ may have a large constant of proportionality, which can make the $O(n)$ rating a misleading one. For arrays, it has a large space requirement for storing sublists.
Sequential search	$O(n)$ probes into list in worst case	Most inefficient of search algorithms we will study, but still appropriate for small lists stored in main memory.
Binary search	$O(\log_2 n)$ probes in worst case	Drawbacks are that we must continually maintain a count of number of records in list and that the list must be maintained in sorted order.
Key-to-address transformation	$O(1)$ list probes	Not applicable for many types of keys. Potential space inefficiencies.

1. Incorporate each of the observations cited in the Focus on Program Design section into the **list_all_primes** algorithm. For each successive modification to the algorithm, run a series of tests in which you use profiling to measure the efficiency of the resulting algorithm. Write up the results of your experimentation, addressing these issues:

a. Which technique produces the fastest runs?

b. Does any technique appear to be an order of magnitude better in its time efficiency? Cite results from profiling to back up your claims in this regard.

c. What trade-offs are involved in using these techniques to achieve a faster run time?

2. Suppose that you know the keys in a list are arranged in increasing order. How could the sequential search algorithm presented in this chapter be improved with this knowledge? Rewrite the C++ function to incorporate this improvement and then test your new function in a complete program.

3. Rewrite the binary search algorithm presented in this chapter with a splitting strategy other than halving. One possibility would be to use an interpolation strategy that would examine the target's distance from the current **low** and **high** pointers. This is more analogous to the way in which we look up names in a phone book. That is, for a name beginning with *S,* we do not open the phone book to the middle page but rather to a point approximately two-thirds of the way from the beginning of the book. Test run your program against a pure binary search and, through tracing the performance of each algorithm, determine whether there is any significant difference between the two techniques.

4. Repeat Problem 3, but change your algorithm so that, after the initial interpolative guess as to the location of the target, data locations are examined sequentially in an appropriate direction until the key is found or until it can be determined that the key is not in the list.

5. Consider a list of records for students at a university. The list includes fields for student name, credits taken, credits earned, and total grade points. Write a program that, based on a user's request, will sort the list of records in ascending or descending order keying on one of the four fields within the record. For instance, the user might specify that the sort should proceed in descending order according to credits earned. As much as possible, try to refrain from having to write a separate sort function for each particular ordering and field. Experiment by developing different functions based on each of the five sorting strategies discussed in this chapter.

6. Consider the same list of records as in Problem 5. Now write a function to sort the records in descending order by credits earned. Records having the same number of credits earned should be arranged in descending order by total grade points. Those with the same number of credits earned and total grade points should be arranged alphabetically by name. Incorporate this function into the complete program that you wrote for Problem 5. Experiment by developing different functions based on each of the five sorting strategies discussed in this chapter.

7. Rewrite the pointer sort with the pointer array as a local variable instead of as a global variable. How would this affect a higher level function that calls on the pointer sort? Illustrate by calling your new version of the pointer sort from a sample main program.

8. Merge the segmenting strategy described in Exercise 10 from Section 11.4 with the insertion sort, bubble sort, and selection sort algorithms. Empirically test how this affects the run time of the sort on a file of 1000 records. Does altering the number of segments affect the run time?

9. Implement the binary search algorithm for a disk file containing approximately 1000 records of the structure described in Problem 5.

10. Design a complete program to load information into the data base for employees of East Publishing Company described in Exercise 9 of Section 11.5. Then repeatedly call on a search function to retrieve the information associated with a given employee's identification key.

11. A *permutation* of the integers from 1 to N is an arrangement of these integers in which no repetition occurs. For example,

3 1 4 5 2

and

5 3 2 4 1

are two permutations of the integers from 1 to 5. Write a function to load an array indexed from $0 \ldots N - 1$ with a randomly generated permutation of the integers from 0 to $N - 1$. (If your version of C++ does not have a random number generator, see Appendix 5, in which an algorithm for generating random numbers in standard C++ is discussed.) This function should be an $O(n)$ algorithm. Once you have written this function, use it to load an array repeatedly, which is then passed to a sorting algorithm such as bubble, selection, or insertion sort. Add profiling counters to the sort algorithm to keep track of the number of comparisons and data interchanges performed by the algorithm. Average these profiling counters over repeated invocations of the sort function and describe how these averages fit into the big-O analyses that were done in this chapter. Do you observe any discrepancies between your averages and the predictions of the big-O analyses? If so, attempt to explain them. For any or all of Problems 12 through 16, design a program to answer the question posed. Then analyze the time efficiency of your program by using an appropriate combination of big-O analysis and profiling. Run your program to try to see the relationship between big-O classification and actual run time as measured by a clock. Finally, for each program you implement, attempt to refine its run-time efficiency by making observations similar to those described in the Focus on Program Design section of this chapter.

12. In the first century A.D. the numbers were separated into "abundant" (such as 12, whose divisors have a sum greater than 12), "deficient" (such as 9, whose divisors have a sum less than 9), and "perfect" (such as 6, whose divisors add up to 6). In all cases, you do not include the number itself. For example, the only numbers that divide evenly into 6 are 1, 2, 3, and 6, and 6 = 1 + 2 + 3. Write a program to list all numbers between 2 and N and classify each as abundant, deficient, or perfect and keep track of the numbers in each class.

13. In the first century A.D., Nicomachus wrote a book entitled *Introduction Arithmetica*. In it, the question "How can the cubes be represented in terms of the natural numbers?" was answered by the statement that "Cubical numbers are always equal to the sum of successive odd numbers and can be represented this way." For example,

$$1^3 = 1 = 1$$
$$2^3 = 8 = 3 + 5$$
$$3^3 = 27 = 7 + 9 + 11$$
$$4^3 = 64 = 13 + 15 + 17 + 19$$

Write a program to find the successive odd numbers whose sum equals k^3 for k having the values from 1 to N.

14. A conjecture, first made by the mathematician Goldbach, whose proof has defied all attempts, is that "every even number larger than two can be written as the sum of two prime numbers." For example,

$$4 = 2 + 26 = 3 + 38 = 3 + 5$$
$$10 = 3 + 7100 = 89 + 11$$

Write a program that determines for every even integer N with $2 <= N$ two prime numbers P and Q such that $N = P + Q$.

15. A pair of numbers M and N are called "friendly" (or they are referred to as an "amicable pair") if the sum of all the divisors of M (excluding M) is equal to the number N and the sum of all the divisors of the number N (excluding N) is equal to M ($M \neq N$). For example, the numbers 220 and 284 are an amicable pair because the only numbers that divide evenly into 220 (1, 2, 4, 5, 10, 11, 20, 22, 44, 55, and 110) add up to 284, and the only numbers that divide evenly into 284 (1, 2, 4, 71, and 142) add up to 220. Write a program to find at least one other pair of amicable numbers. Be prepared to let your program search for some time.

16. A consequence of a famous theorem (of the mathematician Fermat) is the fact that

$$2^{(P-1)} \% P = 1$$

for every odd prime number P. An odd positive integer K satisfying

$$2^{(K-1)} \% K = 1$$

is called a pseudoprime. Write a program to determine a table of pseudoprimes and primes between 2 and N. How many pseudoprimes occur that are not prime numbers?

17. The importance of communication skills in "selling" a program to those who will eventually use it should not be underestimated. Keeping this in mind, write a user's guide for the program you developed in Problem 5. You should assume that the user is able to log onto (or boot) the system, but beyond that has no other knowledge of how to run this or any other program. Remember that unless the user's guide is very, very clear *and* very, very concise, it will probably be thrown in a file drawer—and your program never used.

18. (For the mathematically inclined) consider the claim that exponential algorithms will, *in general,* become practical on parallel processing machines. Provide a carefully constructed argument in which you show that adding more processors to a machine can never result in an exponential algorithm becoming practical for a wide variety of data sets. Your argument should explain the relationship between the number of processors used and the size of the data set that can be accommodated in reasonable time by the exponential algorithm. In essay form, justify the claim that the only real mathematical answer to solving a problem with an exponential algorithm in reasonable time is to discover a nonexponential algorithm that solves the same problem.

19. One of the drawbacks to the bubble sort algorithm is that a data set with just one item out of order can lead to worst-case performance for the algorithm. First, explain how this can happen. Because of this phenomenon, a variation on the bubble sort called a *shaker sort* will, on alternative passes through the array, put the largest entry into the last index and then the smallest entry into the first index. Explain how this idea can eliminate the worst case performance of bubble sort on an array with just one item out of order. Then implement the shaker sort algorithm. Profile the number of comparisons and data interchanges in both the shaker sort and the bubble sort for a variety of data sets. Keep track of the empirical results you obtain from profiling these two algorithms. Finally, in a written report, compare the performance of these two algorithms based on your empirical data. Be sure that your report addresses situations in which the shaker sort will actually perform worse than the plain bubble sort.

12 Data: From Abstraction to Implementation

Our life is frittered away by detail . . . Simplify, simplify.
Henry David Thoreau,
1817–1862

In the first six chapters of this book, we discussed the control structures typically used in developing algorithms. We introduced techniques to describe such control structures before we wrote them in C++. For instance, we have used pseudocode to depict iterative and decisional considerations involved in algorithms. We've used modular structure charts to model the stepwise refinement process that subdivides a complex problem into smaller, more manageable problems.

In Chapters 7 through 10, we discussed some typical data structures used in conjunction with algorithms to solve problems. Some of these, such as files and arrays, are built in to C++. Other data structures, such as lists and strings, must be constructed by the programmer. In Chapters 7 and 8, we introduced the C++ class as the primary means of building new data structures. Classes allow programmers to implement systems that have been specified using object-oriented design. We have presented object-oriented design in an informal, highly pragmatic way. We now wish to consider the problem of designing and implementing data structures from a more abstract, conceptual perspective.

In Section 12.1, we discuss the importance of building abstract models of data and draw analogies to the model building often done by engineers. In Section 12.2, we show how a C++ class can be used to bridge the gap between an object-oriented design of an abstract data type and its implementation. We use a one-key table as an example. We introduce the notion of a *generic type* in Section 12.3, by showing how one can parameterize a one-key table for its component types using a C++ *class template*. In Section 12.4, we use the generic one-key table ADT to implement a two-key table ADT. Each of these abstract data types is presented first as a conceptual object, equipped with formal properties and operations; various implementations of these abstractions are also discussed and evaluated. As we pursue our study of data structures in later chapters, the two abstract data types introduced in this chapter will continue to appear in applications.

12.1 The Computer Scientist as a Builder of Models

Recall the goals we set for ourselves in Section 11.1: designing software systems that are large, reliable, flexible, expandable, and efficient. Clearly, these are nontrivial. How can we have a reasonable chance of attaining them? The evolution of the answer to this question is an indication of how far the young discipline of computer science has progressed. In the late 1950s and early 1960s, there was a widely held belief that designing effective software systems was something akin to an occult art. That is, those who succeeded in designing such systems did so for a variety of mysterious reasons that could not be discerned. Their success, as opposed to the high percentage of software designers who failed, was somewhat mystical—similar to the spark of unfathomable inspiration that separates a great painter from a doodler.

Object-Oriented Software Engineering

This view of successful software designers began to change in the latter part of the 1960s. As we saw in Chapter 2, their methodology is typical of an engineer's approach to problem solving. What characterizes this engineering approach? To answer the question, consider the various phases involved in the successful development of a complex structure such as a bridge. First, the engineer gets together with the (often nontechnical) people who want the bridge built to learn about the function of the bridge: Is it to be part of a heavily traveled urban freeway or a one-lane country road? From such meetings, the engineer develops a conceptual picture of the bridge. This picture exists as an abstract entity in the engineer's mind and perhaps in very rough form as an initial drawing. At this stage the engineer is working with ideas and ignoring most physical construction details; that is, the engineer is working with *abstractions.*

As an object-oriented model, the bridge consists of a set of attributes and behaviors, specifying the relationships among its component parts and to its environment and potential users.

The next steps allow the engineer to come successively closer to the tangible implementation of the bridge as a physical structure. A miniature prototype of the bridge will be built. The prototype will consist of only a few attributes that allow the engineer to study the behavior of the bridge. This model will allow the engineer to come face-to-face with many potential construction problems. It also provides a way to check whether the bridge will serve the needs specified by those who originally wanted the bridge built. This prototype will be followed by the development of detailed plans in blueprint form. Again this represents a step away from the purely abstract view of the bridge toward its actual implementation. These blueprints provide the essential details to the contractor who will eventually build the bridge. This contractor completes the entire process by implementing the engineer's plans in the physical structure of the bridge. One can think of object-oriented design as the building of successively more refined and detailed prototypes, each of which fills in more of the attributes and behavior specified in a model.

As we review the engineering approach, two important points should be made.

1. The entire process that culminates in the building of the bridge is a series of refinements from an abstract view of the bridge to its very tangible implementation. This process parallels very closely the phases in the development of a successful software system, beginning with a purely conceptual view of the problem to be solved and culminating with the implementation of a solution to that problem in (C++) program code.
2. This engineering approach truly places the emphasis on design issues. The design process is a very creative endeavor. Typically, during the design process, engineers will want to try various combinations of possible options and will

frequently change their minds about many significant aspects of the overall design. The time for such experimentation is when the design exists only in abstract form, that is, when such creative considerations are possible—even encouraged—because of the openness of the conceptual model. As the model draws nearer to actual implementation, a myriad of details specific to the chosen implementation make similar "what-if" reasoning expensive and often impossible for all practical purposes.

As early software developers analyzed frequent programming failures, they looked to the already established field of engineering for a paradigm. The engineering methodology of successively refining abstract models toward an eventual implementation made sense as an approach to developing programs also. A system designer who moves too quickly into the detailed coding phase of a programming project is analogous to an engineer who allows construction of a bridge to begin before adequate planning has been done. Both are heading for final results that are inelegant and riddled with serious flaws. However, because of the more rigorous design methodology embedded for years in their profession, engineers did not find themselves in this predicament as often as did programmers.

The solution seemed obvious: Attempt to embed a similarly rigorous methodology into the discipline of computer science. Hence software engineering has developed into an important area of study within computer science. It represents an attempt to apply the structured methods of engineering to software development. At the same time, it fosters creativity by freeing the system designer from the details of program code and allowing work at a higher level of abstraction. Its goal is to assure that software is produced in a way that is cost effective and reliable enough to deserve the increasing trust we are placing in it. We will follow its dictates as we begin our excursion into more advanced programming methodology.

When an object-oriented programming language is available, object-oriented modeling and design help software engineers realize an abstract model directly in an implementation. The attributes and behavior of an abstract class can be implemented directly in the form of classes in an object-oriented programming language like C++. This has two major consequences for the software development process:

1. Prototypes can be developed very rapidly when there is little or no gap between design and implementation.
2. Many design errors still cannot be detected prior to implementation. In an object-oriented implementation, these errors are much easier to locate and correct.

We will examine many examples of this process in the remaining chapters of this book.

EXERCISES 12.1

1. What are the characteristics of the software engineering approach to system development?
2. From a software design perspective, explain why it is less costly to consider changes in design when the system is being modeled abstractly instead of when it is being implemented. Be sure to specify what factors enter into your consideration of the term *costly*.
3. You are working on a large software project as part of a development team. Another member of the team maintains that doing a conceptual design for the software will

only result in getting a late start in writing C++ code and will make the project fall behind schedule. Write a tactful memorandum to this team member in which you provide a convincing argument against the team member's position.

12.2 The One-Key Table Abstract Data Type

OBJECTIVES

- to understand what is involved in defining an abstract data type (ADT)

- to understand what is meant by data abstraction

- to see how ADTs facilitate conceptual model building

- to understand what is meant by the implementation of an ADT

- to formally define and be able to use the one-key table ADT

- to compare and contrast several implementations of the one-key table ADT

- to see the motivation for two guidelines that govern the definition and implementation of all ADTs: the ADT use rule and the ADT implementation rule

- to recognize the shortcomings of each of these implementations and recognize the need for more sophisticated implementations to be studied in future chapters.

In Chapter 11, we approached sorting and searching from the perspective of manipulating an array of objects, each of which had a designated key field. So many data processing activities organize information by key fields that it would seem worth our while to view a collection of such objects from an abstract perspective. Doing so may allow us to bring the power of abstraction to bear in a variety of applications. The best way to clarify the conceptual, model-building approach is to provide an example.

EXAMPLE 12.1

We have been storing a person's age in a database. Each year, we must increment the person's age by one. We also wish to add information about the person's height and weight, and remove any information about the person's waistline. The database (called person) is represented so that we can add, retrieve, or remove information (all integer values) by specifying keys (all string values). The following pseudocode algorithm describes our task:

1. Retrieve the value at the "age" key from person.
2. Add one to this value.
3. Store the sum at the "age" key in person.
4. Store the person's height at the "height" key in person.
5. Store the person's weight at the "weight" key in person.
6. Remove the value at the "waistline" key in person.

The states of a sample table before and after this process are depicted in Figure 12.1.

The high-level solution presented in Example 12.1 is totally independent of considerations regarding how the one-key tables will be represented in C++. Such considerations are details of the eventual implementation of one-key tables and must be completely avoided at this early stage of design. To consider them now would place severe restrictions on the design endeavor.

Instead, the high-level pseudocode takes the perspective that one-key tables are abstract entities that are manipulated by abstract operations such as *retrieve* and *store*. As we begin to refine this pseudocode, it is necessary to pin down exactly what we mean by these abstractions. That is, we must define the notion of a one-key table precisely enough to ensure that our pseudocode algorithm is unambiguous. Yet, our definition must be entirely conceptual: It must be free from

◆ FIGURE 12.1
States of a one-key table before and after operations

specifics about how a one-key table will be implemented in a programming language. Such a definition will allow us to refine our algorithm without worrying about details of how a one-key table will eventually be represented.

To define a one-key table, or any other data type, at such a conceptual level is to define it as an abstract data type (ADT).

Abstract data type (ADT): An ADT is a collection of data objects that share a defined set of properties and operations for processing the objects.

In providing a definition for an ADT such as a one-key table, we must specify both the properties and operations shared by all one-key tables. Typically the properties are specified by describing the individual elements composing an object *and* the relationships among those individual elements. The operations may be specified using preconditions and postconditions. Similar to the way in which we defined a loop precondition in Section 6.5, a precondition for an ADT operation must indicate what can be expected to be true before the operation is performed. A postcondition indicates what can be expected to be true after the operation is performed.

Toward that end, we introduce the following definition of the one-key table ADT:

One-key table: A one-key table is a collection of objects, each of which belongs to the same class. Each object in the collection is associated with a unique key value. The set of all key values must have a well-defined ordering in the sense that, for two different key values *a* and *b*, we can determine whether $a < b$ or $a > b$. Clearly, data values such as integers, real numbers, symbols of an enumerated type, and strings meet this ordering criterion. Some examples of one-key tables are shown in Figure 12.2. Note that the objects stored in the tables are of relatively simple types; objects with a more complex internal structure may be stored in one-key tables as well.

◆ FIGURE 12.2

Some typical one-key tables

person		salaries		lineup		class_rank	
key	value	key	value	key	value	key	value
age	44	ortiz	55000.00	C	Berra	1	Steinmetz
height	70	smith	45000.00	CF	Mantle	2	O'Leary
weight	150	vaselli	62000.00	SS	Kubek	3	Rakowski

The operations for a one-key table follow.

Create operation
Preconditions: Receiver is an arbitrary one-key table in an unpredictable state.
Postconditions: Receiver is initialized to an empty table.
Empty operation
Precondition: Receiver is a one-key table.
Postcondition: If receiver contains no objects, the Boolean value TRUE is
                 returned; otherwise, the Boolean value FALSE is returned.

Length operation

Precondition: Receiver is a one-key table.
Postcondition: The number of objects currently in the table is returned.

Store operation

Preconditions: Receiver is a one-key table. **target** is a key value. **item** is an object to be inserted in receiver. If target is not a key already in the table, there is memory available to store **item**.

Postconditions: If an object is already associated with **target** in receiver, it is replaced by **item**. Otherwise, receiver has **item** inserted and associated with **target**.

Remove operation

Preconditions: Receiver is a one-key table. **target** is a key value associated with an object to be removed from the table.

Postconditions: If the object with the **target** key can be found in the table, it is removed, **item** contains the object associated with **target**, and the operation returns TRUE. Otherwise, the operation returns FALSE, **item**'s contents are undefined, and the table is left unchanged.

Retrieve operation

Preconditions: Receiver is a one-key table, and **target** is a key value to be found in the table.

Postconditions: If the **target** can be found in the table, then **item** contains the object associated with **target** and the operation returns TRUE. Otherwise, the operation returns FALSE, and **item**'s contents are undefined. In either case, the one-key table is left unchanged.

Several comments are now in order.

1. The term *receiver* refers to the object or the instance of the ADT being operated on.

2. Some of the operations, such as **length**, **empty**, and **retrieve**, merely reveal information about the internal state of the object. Other operations, such as **store** and **remove**, change information in the internal state of the object.

3. Note that a one-key table is described from a completely conceptual perspective: There is no hint of a realization of one-key tables in a particular programming language.

4. The **create** operation will be a standard operation for every ADT we discuss. It represents an initialization process which any object must undergo before it can be successfully acted on by other operations. We have tried to emphasize this point in the definition of the ADT by frequently mentioning the need for a "previously created" one-key table in the precondition for an operation. In future ADT definitions we shall frequently leave this unsaid. Remember that the assumption is that no object is ever acted on by any operation until it has been created.

The effect of each operation is highlighted in Figure 12.3 for a one-key table in which the key is a string representing a name and the object is a real number representing a grade point average.

FIGURE 12.3

The effects of the operations on a one-key table

Store 3.45 at key "Smith, Jane" ——————→ Smith, Jane | 3.45 |

Run the empty operation ——————→ FALSE

Store 2.86 at key "Woods, Bob" ——————→ Smith, Jane | 3.45 |
Woods, Bob | 2.86 |

Run the length operation ——————→ 2

Retrieve the value at key "Woods, Bob" —→ 2.86

Store 3.25 at key "Smith, Jane" ——————→ Smith, Jane | 3.25 |
Woods, Bob | 2.86 |

Remove the value at key "Woods, Bob" —→ Smith, Jane | 3.25 |

FIGURE 12.4

Hierarchy of levels of abstraction for implementing a one-key table

> Abstract model: one-key table

> Implementation of model as a C++
> data structure and C++ functions

> Implementation of C++ data structure as a series of memory
> cells and machine language instructions

The separation of an ADT's specification from declarations and instructions that implement the data type in a particular language is called *data abstraction*. It turns out that some abstract data types will have very easy implementations in C++. The C++ implementations of other abstract data types will be much less direct. At early stages of problem analysis, we don't want the considerations of a programming language to influence our solution to the problem. Such considerations should come later, after we have accurately described the problem.

An abstract data type may be viewed as a formal description of data elements and relationships that are envisioned by the software engineer; it is thus a conceptual model. Ultimately, however, this model will be implemented in an appropriate computer language via declarations for the elements and relationships and instructions (often in the form of function calls) for the operations. At an even deeper level, the implementation of the abstract data type in a computer language is translated by the compiler into a physical, electronic representation on a particular computer. This hierarchy of levels of abstraction is illustrated in Figure 12.4.

A C++ Interface for the One-Key Table ADT

The first step in moving toward an implementation of an ADT in an object-oriented language such as C++ is to restate the operations that act on ADT objects as declarations of public member functions in a class declaration module. We shall call such a collection of function declarations the C++ *interface for an ADT*. A class declaration module that specifies the interface for the one-key table ADT is

```
// Class declaration file: onetable.h

#ifndef ONE_TABLE_H

#include "boolean.h"
#include "element.h"
#include "assoc.h"

// Declaration section

// We assume that constant MAX_TABLE_SIZE
// and types boolean, element, association, and key_type
// are already defined.

class one_key_table
{

    public:

    // Class constructors

    one_key_table();
    one_key_table(const one_key_table &table);

    // Member functions

    int length();
    boolean empty();
    void store(const key_type &target, const element &item);
    boolean retrieve(const key_type &target, element &item);
    boolean remove(const key_type &target, element &item);
    one_key_table& operator = (const one_key_table &table);

    protected:

    // Data members

    int table_length;
    association data[MAX_TABLE_SIZE];

};

#define ONE_TABLE_H
#endif
```

You should be familiar with class declaration modules from our discussion of them in Chapters 7 and 8. Note several things about this module:

1. There is a declaration of a second class constructor, the copy constructor. This constructor does not appear in the abstract definition of the ADT, but is necessary for the C++ implementation. The computer uses this operation whenever an instance of a one-key table is passed as a value parameter to a function or is returned as a function's value.

2. The assignment operator is overloaded, so that a one-key table object can be assigned to a variable.

3. The remaining public member functions exactly reflect the operations that we listed in the conceptual definition given earlier. This should be true in general for any ADT that we implement as a C++ class.

4. The key and element types are abstract, in that we do not really have to know what they are from the perspective of the one-key table class.

5. The protected data members in the class declaration section also provide a clue as to how we will be representing a one-key table in C++. We will maintain the current length of a table in a data member called **table_length**. We will use an array, called **data**, of *association* objects to store the data in the table. The association class, declared in the header file **assoc.h**, must therefore be included before the declaration of the one-key table class.

6. The use of the association class to implement a one-key table class is completely hidden from users of the one-key table. They have awareness only of using keys, elements, and one-key tables.

The following example presents a short driver module that would use the one-key table class just declared. We assume that the header file **element.h** has defined the **element** type as an **int** and the **key_type** as a **string**.

EXAMPLE 12.2

```
// Program file: tabdriv.cpp

#include <iostream.h>
#include "strlib.h"
#include "element.h"
#include "onetable.h"

int main()
{
    one_key_table john;                    // Create table

    element item;                          // Auxiliary variable

    john.store("weight", 150);
    john.store("height", 72);
    john.store("age", 40);                 // Store some data

    if (john.retrieve("age", item))        // Retrieve the data
        cout << "Age = " << item << endl;
    else
        cout << "Failure" << endl;
    if (john.retrieve("height", item))     // Retrieve the data
        cout << "Height = " << item << endl;
```

```
    else
        cout << "Failure" << endl;
    if (john.retrieve("weight", item))      // Retrieve the data
        cout << "Weight = " << item << endl;
    return 0;

}
```

Implementations of the One-Key Table ADT

We will consider two implementations of a one-key table in this section; each will have major shortcomings from an efficiency perspective. In future chapters, we will explore more sophisticated implementations that can improve these inefficiencies. Before we examine the implementations, let us discuss the association ADT. Briefly, an association consists of two attributes, a key and a value. The only purpose of an association is to help us organize the data in a one-key table. We specify the interface for the association ADT as follows.

Create operation	
Preconditions:	Receiver is an association in an unpredictable state. **key** is a key value. **item** is the object to be associated with **key**.
Postcondition:	Receiver is initialized to associate **item** with **key**.
Get key operation	
Preconditions:	Receiver is an association.
Postconditions:	**key** is returned.
Get value operation	
Preconditions:	Receiver is an association.
Postconditions:	**value** is returned.
Set value operation	
Preconditions:	Receiver is an association. **item** is an object to be inserted.
Postconditions:	**item** replaces the object currently in the association.

The C++ class declaration module for association is

```
// Class declaration file: assoc.h

#ifndef ASSOC_H

#include "element.h"

// Declaration section

// We assume that types element and key_type are already
// defined.

class association
{
        public:

        // Class constructors

        association();
        association(const association &a);
        association(const key_type &key,
            const element &item);
```

```
// Member functions

key_type get_key();
element get_value();
void set_value(const element &item);
association& operator = (const association &a);


private:

// Data members

key_type the_key;
element the_value;
};


#define ASSOC_H
#endif
```

Implementation 1: Physically Ordered Array with Binary Search The strategy of this implementation is to maintain the array of associations in physical order by key. For example, the association at **data[0]** will have the smallest key, while the association at **data[table_length - 1]** will have the largest key.

EXAMPLE 12.3

This ordering will support a binary search during the **retrieve** operation. The code for this is modeled after the algorithm we analyzed in Chapter 11:

```
boolean one_key_table::retrieve(const key_type &target,
    element &item)
{
    int first, last, middle;
    key_type key;
    boolean success = FALSE;

    first = 0;
    last = table_length - 1;
    while ((first = last) && ! success)
    {
        middle = (first + last) / 2;
        key = data[middle].get_key();
        if (key == target)
            success = TRUE;
        else if (key > target)
            last = middle - 1;
        else
            first = middle + 1;
    }
    if (success)
        item = data[middle].get_value();
    return success;
}
```

◆ **FIGURE 12.5**

Storing an item at a new
key in a one-key table

Step 1: assert(table_length < MAX_TABLE_SIZE) ;

Step 2: search for key greater than or equal to key to be stored

Step 3–4: keys not equal and room exists, so shift data to the right.

Step 5: insert new association into appropriate slot and increment table_length

To store an object in the table in this implementation, we must do the following:

1. Search for the first association in the array that has a key greater than or equal to that of the item we are adding.
2. If the association's key is equal to our target key, just replace the item in that association with our new item and quit.
3. Otherwise, examine the current length of the table to ensure that there is room to add a new association. In this implementation, use the C++ **assert** function to halt program execution if there is no memory available. Otherwise, beginning with the current association, move all associations down one slot in the array.
4. Finally, create and insert a new association into the array slot that has been vacated and increase by 1 the length of the table.

These actions are highlighted in Figure 12.5. Carefully study Figure 12.5 in conjunction with examining the code in Example 12.4.

EXAMPLE 12.4

Write complete C++ code for the **store** operation. This operation must maintain a correspondence between the physical order of the associations in the array and the logical order of the keys in the associations.

```
void one_key_table::store(const key_type &target, const element &item)
{
        int probe = 0;
        boolean found = FALSE;
        key_type key;

        while ((probe < table_length) && ! found)          // Search for position
        {
                key = data[probe].get_key();
                if (key >= target)
                        found = TRUE;
                else
                        ++probe;
        }
        if (found && (key == target))                      // Key already in table
                data[probe].set_value(item);
        else
        {
                assert(table_length < MAX_TABLE_SIZE); // Room available?
                for (int i = table_length; i > probe; --i) // Yes, move them over
                        data[i] = data[i - 1];
                association a(target, item);
                data[probe] = a;
                ++table_length;
        }
}
```

As you can see, the excellent efficiency of retrievals with this implementation is paid for by potentially expensive insertions and removals. The **create**, **remove**, **empty**, and **length** operations are left as exercises.

Implementation 2: Unordered Array with Sequential Search Our second implementation attempts to eliminate the inefficiency involved in moving a potentially large number of objects each time a **store** is performed. The encapsulation of the one-key table ADT still includes an array of associations and a counter. However, now when an association is added, it is merely added after the last item currently stored in the array. Figure 12.6 illustrates this

◆ FIGURE 12.6

A more efficient store operation

Physical order of keys in array does not correspond to logical order in table.

Therefore, new data are always added to the right of the last data in the table.

strategy. As you can see, the increase in efficiency of the **store** operation is being bargained for a decrease in efficiency for retrievals. The **retrieve** operation would now require a sequential search. The details of this implementation are left for you as exercises.

These trade-offs in efficiency for various operations are what make the one-key table ADT a particularly interesting one to study. We will return to it often in future chapters.

Observations on ADTs and Their Implementations

We can now make some observations about the relationship between ADTs and their various implementations. These observations represent general conclusions that may be applied to all of the ADTs we will study. Here, we illustrate them with the one-key table ADT and its two implementations.

First, high-level logic, such as that presented in Example 12.1, cannot distinguish between different implementations of an ADT. We should be able to plug any implementation of an ADT into high-level logic without changing that logic. This shielding of high-level logic from any implementation details is summarized in the following two rules:

> **ADT use rule:** Algorithms that use an abstract data type should only access variables of that ADT through the operations provided in the ADT definition.

> **ADT implementation rule:** An implementation of an abstract data type must provide an interface that is entirely consistent with the operations specified in the ADT's definition.

If users and implementors of ADTs comply fully with these rules, all high-level logic will be plug-compatible with all possible implementations of an ADT. The implementation is said to exhibit *information hiding:* It hides information from higher level logic. This is the ideal. In some situations, the syntax of C++ will force us into compromising the ideal. We will be careful to point those situations out and hold such compromises to a minimum.

Second, if high-level logic cannot tell the difference between two implementations, then why would we ever want more than one implementation of an ADT? Part of the answer lies in the different time and space efficiencies that various implementations provide. For instance, applications that perform frequent retrievals from a one-key table would benefit from the choice of the implementation in which the physical order of the associations in the array mirrors the logical order of the keys in the associations.

Another aspect of the answer to this question is the limitations that an implementation may impose as it attempts to model an abstraction. For instance, an array implementation of the one-key table ADT imposes a maximum length limitation. When we study linked lists in Chapter 14, we will be able to provide an implementation of the one-key table ADT that does not have this maximum length restriction.

The availability of different implementations of an ADT—all compatible from their outward interface—gives rise to some very exciting prospects for the software design endeavor we have been describing in this chapter. At a high level, we design complex software by constructing a model that operates only on abstract data types. Once we have a high-level model with which we are satisfied, we can plug in the best implementation of the ADT for our particular application.

A NOTE OF INTEREST

Association Lists and Dictionaries

The idea of associating data objects with key values in tables probably received its first expression in a programming language when LISP was developed more than 30 years ago. LISP, an acronym for List Processing Language, was designed to process lists of symbolic information in AI applications. These applications frequently need to associate information with a symbol. For example, a natural language processing application will have to maintain a dictionary of terms in a language. The keys for a dictionary would be symbols representing the words, and the values would be definitions or other information associated with the words. Every dialect of LISP recognizes a particular kind of list called an *association list*. An association list is a list consisting of key/value pairs. Once an association list has been defined, a LISP programmer can look up the value associated with a given key by using the LISP function **assoc**.

The object-oriented language Smalltalk, which is also used in many symbol processing applications, comes with a built-in hierarchy of collection classes. One subclass of the Smalltalk collection class is called a *dictionary class*. The dictionary class is similar to the association list in LISP. One difference is that the implementation of a dictionary in Smalltalk is geared toward very efficient retrievals, whereas a LISP association list supports only a linear search method.

Our one-key table ADT borrows much from these ideas in LISP and Smalltalk. In particular, the order of the data in the conceptual table is not specified for the user of the table, but it may be important for the efficiency of the implementation. One major difference is that we allow any key values that can be ordered, whereas LISP and Smalltalk usually allow only strings or symbols as keys. Another major difference is that all of the data values in our one-key table must be of the same type; LISP and Smalltalk allow objects of different types to be stored in the same association list or dictionary.

If formalized big-O analysis is inconclusive about which is the best implementation, it is relatively painless to experiment with several implementations. Different implementations can be plugged in, we can empirically profile their performance, and then choose the best. With the ADT approach, all this experimentation can be done without any modification of the high-level model.

EXERCISES 12.2

1. Complete the implementation of the one-key table by developing code for the **create**, **length**, **empty**, and **remove** operations. Be sure to obey the ADT implementation rule.

2. Provide a big-O efficiency analysis of the two different implementations of the store operation. You should consider both the number of comparisons and data interchanges in this analysis.

3. Consider the second implementation of the **store** operation. Is there a way to take advantage of the fact that the array is sorted when looking for the target key's appropriate position? If so, write an improved version of the function and provide a big-O analysis.

4. Provide a big-O efficiency analysis of the **remove** operation. You should consider both the number of comparisons and data interchanges in this analysis.

5. Is there a way to improve the efficiency of the **remove** operation for the second implementation? If so, write a new version and provide a big-O analysis.

6. Some applications may need to process all of the objects currently in a one-key table. For example, one might wish to output all of the objects in the order of their keys. It would be useful to provide two new operations, called **keys** and **values**. **keys** returns a sorted array of the keys currently in the table, and **values** returns an unsorted array of the objects currently in the table. First specify these as ADT operations with preconditions and postconditions, and then write the C++ code for them.

7. Describe the differences between the one-key table ADT and the ordered collection and sorted collection abstract data types discussed in Chapter 10.

12.3 ◆ The One-Key Table as a Generic Type

The one-key table is a fairly flexible ADT. Objects of any type can be stored in a table, as long as the objects are all of the same type. Objects may be associated with keys of any type, as long as the keys are capable of being ordered. We have used the type names **element** and **key_type** to indicate this generality, both in the abstract specification of the ADT and in the C++ implementations of the one-key table. In fact, both **element** and **key_type** are also ADTs, so we have a good example of how three different ADTs (including **association**) can be used to construct a new ADT.

Nevertheless, our one-key table ADT has a serious limitation. We have said that **element** and **key_type** can be any types we wish, but all tables in an individual application must have the same **element** type and the same **key_type**. The reason for this is that there can be only one definition of **element** and one definition of **key_type** in an application. This means that clients who wish to use a table of integers keyed by strings and a table of strings keyed by integers cannot use our ADT. A client may object that a table is a table, no matter what the key type and element type are. The client is right: if the table, key, and element types are truly abstract, then they should not interact in this restrictive way.

A similar problem arises in the case of algorithms. If an algorithm for computing the square root of a number only functioned for one particular number, users would object that the algorithm should work for any number in the problem domain. We write an algorithm to solve a general class of problem instances, and typically represent the algorithm as a function and the class of problem instances as a formal parameter to the function.

In the case of data types, we would like to generalize ADTs to accommodate a class of different component types. When an ADT is defined, its component types would be specified as formal parameters. When an object of that type is created, the application would fill in the formal type parameters with the particular component types desired. In the case of the one-key table, an application could use several different key and element types, and still be using the same ADT for one-key tables. This kind of ADT is known as a generic type.

Class Templates

Not all programming languages support the definition of generic types. In C++, a class template is used to represent generic ADTs. In the case of one-key tables, a C++ class template allows the pseudocode

> Create a table of integers keyed by strings
> Create a table of real numbers keyed by strings
> Create a table of persons keyed by strings
> Create a table of strings keyed by integers

to be represented in C++ as

```
one_key table<string, int> ints_by_strings;
one_key table<string, float> floats_by_strings;
one_key table<string, person> persons_by_strings;
one_key table<int, string> strings_by_ints;
```

in one application, where the identifiers listed in angle brackets are the names of types or classes in C++. These statements would create new, empty tables capable of storing elements of the specified types at keys of the specified types. Once they are created, each of these tables is manipulated by using the standard operations described in our ADT definition.

We will first consider how to define a class template to allow users to specify the element type of a one-key table, and then show how to extend the definition to support the parameterization of key types. We start with the class declaration module of the one-key table from Section 12.2, and replace every instance of the type name **element** with the shorter notation **E**. **E** will serve as the formal parameter name for the element type. For example, the member function declaration

```
void store(const key_type &target, const element &item);
```

becomes

```
void store(const key_type &target, const E &item);
```

Because associations contain elements, the association class must also be generalized to take the element type as a parameter. We pass the type parameter **E** to the association class when we define the data member for the array, using the notation <E>, as follows:

```
association<E> data[MAX_TABLE_SIZE];
```

Finally, we specify that **E** is a type parameter for a one-key table class template by changing the heading of the class declaration to be

```
template <class E> class one_key_table
```

The rest of the code for the data members and declarations of member functions remains the same:

```
// Class declaration file: onetable.h

#ifndef ONE_TABLE_H

#include "boolean.h"
#include "element.h"
#include "assoc.h"

// Declaration section

// Generic class for element type E.

// We assume that constant MAX_TABLE_SIZE
// and the key type are already defined in element.h.

template <class E> class one_key_table
{

    public:

    // Class constructors

    one_key_table();
    one_key_table(const one_key_table<E> &table);

    // Member functions
```

```
                        int length();
                        boolean empty();
                        void store(const key_type &target, const E &item);
                        boolean retrieve(const key_type &target, E &item);
                        boolean remove(const key_type &target, E &item);
                        one_key_table<E>& operator = (const one_key_table<E> &table);

                        protected:

                        // Data members

                        int table_length;
                        association<E> data[MAX_TABLE_SIZE];

                };

                #define ONE_TABLE_H
                #endif
```

Before we can use the new template class, we must make changes in the class implementation module for the one-key table and in the modules that implement the association ADT. For example, the implementation of the **store** function would now be

```
template <class E>
void one_key_table<E>::store(const key_type &target, const E &item)
{
        int probe = 0;
        boolean found = FALSE;
        key_type key;

        while ((probe < table_length) && ! found)          // Search for position
        {
                key = data[probe].get_key();
                if (key >= target)
                        found = TRUE;
                else
                        ++probe;
        }
        if (found && (key == target))                      // Key already in table
                data[probe].set_value(item);
        else
        {
                assert(table_length < MAX_TABLE_SIZE);     // Room available?
                for (int i = table_length; i > probe; --i) // Yes, move them over
                        data[i] = data[i - 1];
                association<E> a(target, item);
                data[probe] = a;
                ++table_length;
        }
}
```

Note four things about the changes that have been made to this function:

1. The notation **template <class E>** appears above the function heading. The same prefix should appear above the function heading of every member function in the implementation module.
2. The notation **<E>** appears after the class name in the function heading. This notation should also be the same in the heading of every member function.
3. The symbol **E** appears where the element type is specified in the formal parameter list in the function heading. Here we are using the template parameter to refer to the type of a formal parameter to the function.
4. The notation **<E>** appears once more, when a new association is created. Here, we are passing a template parameter to another type.

If the use of **E** and **<E>** in the preceding example still seems confusing, here is a rule of thumb for distinguishing them: We use the angle bracket notation when we wish to specify an object as a parameter of a type; we omit the angle brackets when we wish to refer to a type directly (as the type of a variable or parameter of a function).

The remaining changes to the one-key table class are left as exercises. The following example is a driver program that tests the revised classes. We assume that the key type is defined as **string**.

EXAMPLE 12.5

```cpp
// Program file: testgen1.cpp

#include <iostream.h>
#include <iomanip.h>
#include "boolean.h"
#include "strlib.h"
#include "onetable.h"

int main()
{
    one_key_table<int> ints;              // Create tables
    one_key_table<string> strings;
    one_key_table<float> floats;

    int i; // Auxiliary variables
    float f;
    string s;

    ints.store("age", 40);                // Store some data
    strings.store("hair color", "brown");
    floats.store("salary", 50540.00);

    if (ints.retrieve("age", i))          // Retrieve the data
        cout << "Age = " << i << endl;
    if (floats.retrieve("salary", f))
        cout << fixed << setprecision(2) << showpoint
             << "Salary = " << f << endl;
```

```
        if (strings.retrieve("hair color", s))
                cout << "Hair color = " << s << endl;
    return 0;
}
```

To remove the remaining restriction that all tables in an application have the same key type, we can extend the template class by adding a formal parameter for the key type. As before, we start by replacing each instance of the word **key_type** in the current class declaration module by a shortened form, in this case, **K**. Because the association class uses the key type, we pass **K** as a parameter to **association** in the data member declaration, as follows:

```
    association<K, E> data[MAX_TABLE_SIZE];
```

Finally, we change the heading of the class declaration to be

```
    template <class K, class E> class one_key_table
```

Once again, the rest of the code for the data structures and function declarations remains the same:

```
// Class declaration file: onetable.h

#ifndef ONE_TABLE_H

#include "boolean.h"
#include "element.h"
#include "assoc.h"

// Declaration section

// Generic class for key type K and element type E.

// We assume that constant MAX_TABLE_SIZE is already defined.

template <class K, class E> class one_key_table
{

    public:

    // Class constructors

    one_key_table();
    one_key_table(const one_key_table<K, E> &table);

    // Member functions

    int length();
    boolean empty();

    void store(const K &target, const E &item);
    boolean retrieve(const K &target, E &item);
    boolean remove(const K &target, E &item);
    one_key_table<K, E>& operator =
        (const one_key_table<K, E> &table);
```

```
protected:

    // Data members

    int table_length;
    association<K, E> data[MAX_TABLE_SIZE];

};


#define ONE_TABLE_H
#endif
```

The implementation of the default class constructor specifies a list of two type parameters for the class template above the function heading:

```
template<class K, class E>
one_key_table<K, E>::one_key_table()
{
    table_length = 0;
}
```

When the rest of the class implementation module for the one-key table and the modules for the association class have been suitably modified, we can run the test driver in the next example.

EXAMPLE 12.6

```
// Program file: testgen2.cpp

#include <iostream.h>
#include "strlib.h"
#include "onetable.h"

int main()
{
    one_key_table<string, int> ints_by_strings;       // Create tables
    one_key_table<int, string> strings_by_ints;

    int i_element; // Auxiliary variables
    string s_element;

    ints_by_strings.store("age", 40);                 // Store some data
    strings_by_ints.store(911, "emergency");

    if (ints_by_strings.retrieve("age", i_element))    // Retrieve the data
        cout << "Age = " << i_element << endl;
    if (strings_by_ints.retrieve(911, s_element))
        cout << "911 = " << s_element << endl;
    return 0;
}
```

The process of recognizing the need for generalizing a type is a bit like the process of spotting patterns of instructions that can be generalized as functions. In the case of functions, we see a general pattern that is shared by several chunks of code. We place this pattern in a function block, and parameterize the function for whatever variations occur in the original patterns. In the case of data types, we have a general pattern in a class definition that would have to be repeated in new class definitions if we were to use other component types (tables of integers, tables of strings, etc.). We preserve this pattern in a generic type, and parameterize the type for the component types that might vary for different applications of the type. We now formalize these ideas in another principle for the design of abstract data types:

> **ADT Generality Rule:** An abstract data type should not be limited by the types of its components. Wherever possible, users should be able to specify the component types of a generic abstract data type.

Generic types provide an extremely powerful way of modeling data, and C++ class templates are an excellent way of representing generic types in a programming language. Many of the abstract data types that we discuss in the following chapters are good candidates for generalization. Therefore, we will make frequent use of class templates in our implementations.

EXERCISES 12.3

1. Complete the implementation of the one-key table ADT that is parameterized for the element type only.
2. Complete the implementation of the one-key table ADT that is parameterized for the element type and the key type.
3. Generalize the ordered collection class from Chapter 10 so that one application can create lists of several different element types.
4. Generalize the sorted collection class from Chapter 10 so that one application can create sorted lists of different element types.
5. Use a generic sorted collection class to implement the **keys** member function described in Exercise 6 of Section 12.2.
6. Use a generic ordered collection class to implement the **values** member function described in Exercise 6 of Section 12.2.

12.4 The Two-Key Table Abstract Data Type

Consider the problem of maintaining statistics for a baseball league. The statistics might be printed in a newspaper as follows:

	AB	HITS	2B	3B	HR	AVE
Alomar	521	192	25	6	29	.369
Brett	493	180	16	3	41	.365
Canseco	451	160	30	1	50	.354
Dribble	590	205	41	10	20	.347
Hubble	501	167	21	2	17	.333
Marachino	485	156	32	4	24	.321
Noguchi	562	180	24	2	32	.320
Perez	499	159	21	4	21	.318
Sokoloski	480	149	16	10	15	.310
Tanenbaum	490	150	14	0	23	.306

A database for storing this information should be organized so that we could quickly obtain answers to queries such as "How many hits does Alomar have?" One way to conceptualize this organization is to imagine a table in which the desired data object is retrieved by specifying two keys, the name of the player and the category of the statistic. In the case of our example query, the answer might be obtained by running the abstract operation

```
retrieve the data at keys "Alomar" and "HITS"
```

This manner of conceptualizing and using a database is so common that we will develop a new abstract data type, the two-key table, that can be used by any application. As with the one-key table, we first specify the attributes and behavior of the two-key table conceptually. Then we choose an implementation in C++. Finally, we do a big-O analysis of the behavior of our implementation and discuss the trade-offs of alternative implementations.

Two-key table: A two-key table is a collection of objects, each of which belongs to the same class. Each object in the collection is associated with two key values, called *key1* and *key2*. Each key1 value, called a *primary key*, is unique. Each key2 value, called a *secondary key*, may be used with more than one primary key, but must indicate a unique data element when associated with a primary key. The set of all key1 values must have a well-defined ordering in the sense that, for two different key1 values *a* and *b*, we can determine whether $a < b$ or $a > b$. The same property holds for the set of all key2 values.

The operations for a two-key table follow.

Create operation
Preconditions: Receiver is an arbitrary two-key table in an unpredictable state.
Postconditions: Receiver is initialized to an empty table.

Empty operation
Precondition: Receiver is a two-key table.
Postcondition: If receiver contains no objects, the Boolean value TRUE is returned; otherwise, the Boolean value FALSE is returned.

Store operation
Preconditions: Receiver is a two-key table. **key1** is the key1 value. **key2** is the key2 value. **item** is an object to be inserted in **receiver.** If **key1** and **key2** do not specify an item already in the table, there is memory available to store **item.**
Postconditions: If an object is already associated with **key1** and **key2** in the table, it is replaced by **item.** Otherwise, the table has **item** inserted and associated with the key1 and key2 values.

Remove operation
Preconditions: Receiver is a two-key table. **key1** and **key2** are the key values associated with an object to be removed from the table.
Postconditions: If the object with the key values **key2** and **key2** can be found in the table, it is removed from the table, **item** contains the object associated with the key values **key2** and **key2**, and the operation returns TRUE. Otherwise, the operation returns FALSE, **item**'s contents are undefined, and the table is left unchanged.

<table>
<tr><td>Retrieve operation</td><td></td></tr>
<tr><td>Preconditions:</td><td>Receiver is a two-key table. key1 and key2 are the key values associated with an object to be found in the table.</td></tr>
<tr><td>Postconditions:</td><td>If the pairing of key1 and key2 can be found in table, then item contains the object associated with key1 and key2 and the operation returns TRUE. Otherwise, the operation returns FALSE, and item's contents are undefined. In either case, the table is left unchanged.</td></tr>
</table>

As you can see from these definitions, a two-key table is really an extension of a one-key table with an extra key. Note that we do not specify a **length** operation, however, because a two-key table is not a linear data structure.

A Class Template for the Two-Key Table Abstract Data Type

In the spirit of our policy of making ADTs as general and flexible as possible, we will represent our conceptual definition of the two-key table ADT as a C++ class template. This will allow an application to specify the type of each key and the item type when a two-key table is created. For example, the table of baseball statistics discussed earlier could be declared as

```
two_key_table<string, string, int> statistics;
```

where the last parameter is the type of data to be stored in the table, and the other parameters are the types of keys (first and second, respectively).

The C++ class declaration module for a two-key table class template is

```
// Class declaration file: twotable.h

#ifndef TWO_TABLE_H

#include "boolean.h"

// Declaration section

// Generic class for key1 type K1, key2 type K2, and element type E.

template <class K1, class K2, class E> class two_key_table
{

    public:

    // Class constructors

    two_key_table();
    two_key_table(const two_key_table<K1, K2, E> &table);

    // Member functions

    boolean empty();
    void store(const K1 &key1, const K2 &key2, const E &item);
    boolean retrieve(const K1 &key1, const K2 &key2, E &item);
```

```
    boolean remove(const K1 &key1, const K2 &key2, E &item);
    two_key_table<K1, K2, E>& operator = (const two_key_table<K1, K2, E> &table);

protected:

// Data members

// To go here when we consider alternative implementations

};


#define TWO_TABLE_H
#endif
```

Note that the interface to the class template, the function declarations, and component type parameters, exactly mirrors our conceptual definition.

A Two-Dimensional Array Implementation

Since a two-key table is a two-dimensional data structure at the conceptual level, we might try to represent it as a two-dimensional array in C++. After all, we represented a one-key table as a one-dimensional array. Each row of the array would represent a **key1**, while each column would represent a **key2**. We could then choose between a direct mapping of keys to index positions along each dimension of the array (supporting efficient retrievals) or a random mapping (supporting efficient insertions).

Because there are now two keys to map to two index positions in the array, the association class must be extended to represent the association of a value with two keys. We do this by defining a derived class of association, **two_key_association**, that contains the extra key. This approach has the effect of preserving the original association class for the use of one-key tables:

```
// Class declaration file: twoassoc.h

#ifndef TWO_ASSOC_H

// Declaration section

template <class K1, class K2, class E> class two_key_association : public
    association
{
    public:

    // Class constructors

    two_key_association();
    two_key_association(const two_key_association<K1, K2, E> &a);
    two_key_association(const K1 &key1, const K2 &key2,
        const E &new_item);

    // Member functions
```

```
      K2 get_key2();
      two_key_association<K1, K2, E>& operator =
            (const two_key_association<K1, K2, E> &a);

      private:

      // Data members
      K2 the_key2;

};


#define TWO_ASSOC_H
#endif
```

Two other questions must be answered before we can write the definitions of the data members for the two-key table. First, what will be the maximum size of a two-key table? The answer to this question for one-key tables was specified by a constant, **MAX_TABLE_SIZE**, used to define the maximum size of the array representing the table, and defined in the header file **element.h**. For a two-dimensional array, we will need two constants, **MAX_ROW_SIZE** and **MAX_COL_SIZE**, to define the maximum sizes of the two dimensions. Application modules will again specify these values, with the understanding that **MAX_ROW_SIZE** represents the maximum number of possible **key1** values in a two-key table, and **MAX_COL_SIZE** represents the maximum number of possible **key2** values.

Second, how will we maintain the current number of objects stored in a two-key table? A one-key table used an integer data member, **table_length**, representing the next available location in the array for storing data. The situation in a two-dimensional array is more complicated. We need to know both the position of the next available row (for a new **key1**) and the next available column in each row (for a new **key2**). Therefore, we will define two data members, an integer variable and an array of integers, to represent these attributes.

The data members for the two-dimensional array can now be added to the class declaration module of the two-key table:

```
// Data members

two_key_association<K1, K2, E> data[MAX_ROW_SIZE][MAX_COL_SIZE];
int row_length;
int col_lengths[MAX_ROW_SIZE];
```

The next example shows how we would implement the **store** operation, assuming that we simply pick the next available row and column for a new object at **key1** and **key2.**

EXAMPLE 12.7

Write the implementation of the member function that stores an object in a two-key table. We assume that if the **key1** is new, we enter at a new row, and if **key2** is new, we enter at a new column.

```
template <class K1, class K2, class E>
void two_key_table<K1, K2, E>::store(const K1 &key1, const K2 &key2, const E &item)
{
     int row, col;
     boolean found = FALSE;
     key_type row_key, col_key;

     row = 0;
     col = 0;
     while ((row < row_length) && ! found)          // Search key1 in rows
     {
          data[row][col].get_key(row_key);
          if (key1 == row_key)
               found = TRUE;
          else
               ++row;
     }
     if (found)                                      // key1 already in table
     {
          found = FALSE;                             // Search for key2 in column
           while ((col < column_lengths[row]) && ! found)
          {
               col_key = data[row][col].get_key2();
               if (key2 == col_key)
                    found = TRUE;
               else
                    ++col;
          }
          if (found)                                 // key2 also already in table
               data[row][col].set_value(item);
          else
          {
               assert(column_lengths[row] < MAX_COL_SIZE);   // Room available
               two_key_association<E><K1><K2> a(key1, key2, item);  // for column?
               data[row][col] = a;                   // Add a new key2
               ++column_lengths[row];
          }
     }
     else
     {
          assert(row_length < MAX_ROW_SIZE);   // Room available for row?
          association a<K1, K2, E>(target, item);
          data[row][0] = a;                    // Add a new key1
          column_lengths[row] = 1;
          ++row_length;
     }
}
```

By now, you will probably have surmised that there are some serious drawbacks to this implementation. The most obvious one is the length and complexity of the **store** operation presented above. With so many alternative cases to consider and data to maintain, this code will be very difficult to read, understand, and get correct. Moreover, the **retrieve** and **remove** operations will be almost as complicated.

As far as efficiency is concerned, the current implementation introduces a new data structure, the array for maintaining the current lengths of the columns, that results in a linear growth of memory for the maximum number of secondary keys that an application needs in a table. The current version also forces us to add a data member to the association class to represent a second key. The only advantage is that binary searches for a target object might be very fast, assuming that one can get the code correct!

The choice of this implementation seems so unreasonable that we will not even leave its completion as an exercise, but rather look for a simpler one.

Using One-Key Tables to Implement Two-Key Tables

Another way to think of a two-key table is as a one-key table. Each key in this table will represent a **key1** in the two-key table. At each of these keys, we store another one-key table. Each key in each of these tables will represent a **key2** in the two-key table. Thus, the data elements stored at the keys in the nested one-key tables will be the data elements stored in the two-key table.

The advantage of this representation is that it allows us to use higher level components to construct our two-key table ADT. This will allow us to use higher level operations as well. For example, the operation for retrieving a data element at **key1** and **key2** in a two-key table can now be conceptualized as follows:

1. Retrieve the element at key1 of the top-level one-key table
2. If the retrieval is successful then
3. From this element (also a one-key table), retrieve the element at key2

The advantage of this implementation over the two-dimensional array implementation is that in this one, the code for the search operations has already been written, so we just invoke them by name. In the two-dimensional array implementation, we are forced to reinvent the wheel by rewriting this code.

Here is a class declaration module for a two-key table that uses one-key tables to support high-level implementations of two-key operations:

```
// Class declaration file: twotable.h

#ifndef TWO_TABLE_H

#include "boolean.h"
#include "onetable.h"

template <class K1, class K2, class E> class two_key_table
{

    public:

    // Class constructors

    two_key_table();

    two_key_table(const two_key_table<K1, K2, E> &table);
```

```
// Member functions

boolean empty();
void store(const K1 &key1, const K2 &key2, const E &item);
boolean retrieve(const K1 &key1, const K2 &key2, E &item);
boolean remove(const K1 &key1, const K2 &key2, E &item);
two_key_table<K1, K2, E>& operator = (const two_key_table<K1, K2, E> &table);

protected:

// Data members

one_key_table<K1, one_key_table<K2, E>> data;

};


#define TWO_TABLE_H
#endif
```

The interface of the two-key table class stays the same, but the new implementation has just one data member. This is a one-key table whose key type is **K1** and whose element type is another one-key table. The key type of this second one-key table is **K2** and its element type is **E**. Carefully examine the line of code that defines this data member, especially the ordering of the angle brackets, so that you understand how the type parameters are passed to set up the data structure.

The next example shows how we can take advantage of the new data member definitions to implement the **retrieve** operation for two-key tables.

EXAMPLE 12.8   Write the implementation of the **retrieve** operation for the two-key table class specified in the class declaration module given earlier.

```
template <class K1, class K2, class E>
boolean two_key_table<K1, K2, E>::retrieve(const K1 &key1, const K2 &key2, E &item)
{
      one_key_table<K2, E> table;

      if (data.retrieve(key1, table))          // Retrieve nested table
            return table.retrieve(key2, item);   // Retrieve data item
      else
            return FALSE;
}
```

After working through the code for the two-dimensional array implementation, this code must seem almost magically simple. However, this code represents a straightforward use of the one-key tables in the new data representation. Using the data member **data**, we attempt to retrieve a table at **key1**. If we are successful, we use this table to attempt to retrieve an item at **key2**. If we are successful here, the item is returned and the function returns TRUE. If either of the retrievals fails, the function returns FALSE.

Not only is this version easy to read, understand, and get correct, but we no longer need to consider the alternatives of linear search or binary search to implement a retrieval. These considerations have been resolved at a lower level, during the implementation of the one-key table. The next example shows how to implement a **store** operation for this version. Be sure to compare it to the other version in Example 12.7.

EXAMPLE 12.9

Write the implementation of the **store** operation for the one-key table implementation of the two-key table ADT.

```
template <class K1, class K2, class E>
void two_key_table<K1, K2, E>::store (const K1 &key1, const K2 &key2, const E &item)
{
        one_key_table<K2, E> table;

        data.retrieve(key1, table);     // Access nested table, if any
        table.store(key2, item);        // Store data in table
        data.store(key1, table);        // Place nested table in top-level table
}
```

Comparing the Two Implementations

Our intuition in choosing a two-dimensional array implementation for a two-key table seemed natural: One can think of each structure as consisting of a grid in which a data item is located by specifying a row and column. Moreover, since we were able to map a key in a one-key table to an index position in a one-dimensional array, it seemed logical to try to map two keys to the two indices of a two-dimensional array. However, when we turned to the actual data structures and algorithms for implementing this version, we quickly became lost in a welter of complexity. We found it necessary to introduce complex auxiliary data structures, like an array of column lengths and a two-key association class, and to write pages of code for each individual operation.

By reconceiving a two-key table as a one-key table whose data items are other one-key tables, we were able to simplify both the data structures used in the implementation and the code used in the operations. The one-key table ADT handles most of the work of representing the data and implementing the operations. We no longer have to think about using auxiliary ADTs such as the association, much less about subclassing it to represent a second key. We no longer have to decide between an implementation that supports binary search (fast retrievals) or linear search (fast insertions).

On the other hand, the one-key table implementation gives us less control over the way that a two-key table behaves than we might wish. If a client of the two-key table desires fast retrievals and the one-key table implements a linear search, the client is stuck with that. Moreover, clients can no longer specify separate maximum row and column sizes for two-key tables. This last factor can lead to a serious inefficiency in the use of memory, where storage would be allocated for rows or columns in the table that are not really needed by the application. We will see a way to remedy this last problem in later chapters.

The contrast between the two implementations can be viewed as a contrast between a *layered system* and an *unlayered system*. The one-key table implementation places a layer of high-level types and operations between the two-key table ADT and the underlying C++ data structures and operations. The two-dimensional array implementation represents the two-key table ADT directly in terms of the underlying C++ data structures and operations. Layered systems are generally easy to design and maintain; unlayered systems may be more efficient but are usually much more difficult to design and maintain.

These considerations lead us to formulate one more principle for the design of abstract data types:

> **ADT layering rule:** Existing abstract data types should be used to implement new abstract data types, unless direct control over the underlying data structures and operations of the programming language is a critical factor. A well-designed implementation consists of layers of ADTs.

EXERCISES 12.4

1. Complete the one-key table implementation of the two-key table ADT.

2. Write a program that uses a two-key table to store and retrieve the baseball statistics described earlier in this section. Explain how you handle the data in the last column, which appear to be real numbers rather than integers.

3. A data item is located in a three-key table by specifying three keys. Write an abstract definition and an appropriate C++ class declaration module for this ADT. Remember to adhere to the ADT reuse and layering rules.

FOCUS ON PROGRAM DESIGN

Suppose that you are computer operations manager for Wing-and-a-Prayer Airlines. In that role, you receive the following important memorandum:

```
                    MEMORANDUM
              Wing-and-a-Prayer Airlines

     TO: Computer Operations Manager
   FROM: Vice President in Charge of Scheduling
   DATE: August 28, 1995
     RE: Matching flights and pilots

As you know, we presently have 1500 flights (with
identification numbers 3000 to 4499) and employ 1400
pilots (with identification numbers 1000-2399) to fly
them. However, because of factors such as type of
airplane, amount of pilot experience, pilot geographic
locations, and FAA regulations, each of our pilots
qualifies to fly on only a relatively small percentage of
flights. To help our schedulers, we frequently need to
answer questions such as the following:

1. Given a flight, what are the identification numbers of
   the pilots qualified to fly it?
2. Given a pilot number, what are the flight numbers that
   pilot is qualified to fly?
3. Given a flight number and a pilot number, do we have a
   match? In other words, is the specified pilot
   qualified for the particular flight?

Right now our schedulers attempt to answer such questions
by time-consuming manual methods. I'm sure that you can
easily computerize this task for them. Thanks in advance
for your help in this matter.
```

◆ FIGURE 12.7
Flight/pilot data base for
Wing-and-a-Prayer Airlines

	Flight Number					
Pilot Number	3000	3001	3002	...	4498	4499
1000	TRUE	FALSE	FALSE	...	TRUE	FALSE
1001	FALSE	FALSE	FALSE	...	TRUE	TRUE
1002	TRUE	TRUE	FALSE	...	FALSE	FALSE
.	.	.	.	...	.	.
.	.	.	.	...	.	.
2398	FALSE	TRUE	FALSE	...	FALSE	FALSE
2399	FALSE	FALSE	TRUE	...	FALSE	TRUE

Faced with this charge, one abstract conceptualization you might consider is that of the table pictured in Figure 12.7. Here a TRUE entry in a particular row and column indicates the pilot is qualified for the corresponding flight; FALSE indicates the pilot is not qualified. Given the two-dimensional table of Figure 12.7 as a model of the pilot/flight data for Wing-and-a-Prayer, we choose a two-key table ADT to represent the data. The first key will be the pilot number, and the second key will be the flight number, both represented as integers. The data will be Boolean values.

We define the following constants in **element.h** to represent the dimensions of the table:

```
const MIN_PILOT = 1000;
const MAX_PILOT = 2399;
const MIN_FLIGHT = 3000;
const MAX_FLIGHT = 4999;


const MAX_TABLE_SIZE = MAX_FLIGHT - MIN_FLIGHT + 1;
```

We begin the design of the algorithms by writing the pseudocode for the top-level query loop:

1. Initialize all of the items in the table to FALSE
2. Load the table by reading pairs of numbers representing a pilot and a flight for which the pilot is qualified. Assign TRUE to these locations.
3. Do
   3.1 Read a Query
   3.2 If Query is a flight number then
      3.2.1 Travel along corresponding column, writing out number of each qualified pilot
   3.3 Else if Query is a pilot number
      3.3.1 Travel along corresponding row, writing out each flight for which the pilot is qualified
   3.4 Else if Query is flight and pilot number
      3.4.1 Access information at that row and column
      3.4.2 If TRUE
         Write ('QUALIFIED') Else
         Write ('NOT QUALIFIED')
While the user wishes to continue with queries

The first two steps set up the two-key table with data values. The third step handles the interaction with the users of the system. Each of these steps can be implemented as a C++ function that passes the table as a parameter. Assuming function names **init_table**, **get_data**, and **take_queries** for these steps, we have a main program

```
#include <iostream.h>
#include "boolean.h"
#include "element.h"
#include "twotable.h"

int main()

{
        two_key_table<int, int, boolean> is_qualified;

        init_table(is_qualified);
        get_data(is_qualified);
        take_queries(is_qualified);
        return 0;
}
```

The process of associating the initial value FALSE with each pair of pilots and flights in the table can be described by a nested loop. The outer loop runs through consecutive pilot numbers from 1000 to 2399. The inner loop runs through consecutive flight numbers from 3000 to 4999. On each pass through the inner loop, we invoke the **store** operation with the two loop control variables to insert the value FALSE into the appropriate place in the table:

```
void init_table(two_key_table<int, int, boolean> &table)
{
      boolean can_fly = FALSE;

      for (int pilot = MIN_PILOT; pilot <= MAX_PILOT; ++pilot)
            for (int flight = MIN_FLIGHT; flight <= MAX_FLIGHT; ++flight)
                  table.store(pilot, flight, can_fly);

}
```

Setting the flags of the pilots who are qualified for certain flights is a process of prompting the user for the relevant pilot/flight pairs. The function uses two auxiliary functions, **get_integer** and **more_input_desired**. **get_integer** prints a message and recovers from any input errors. **more_input_desired** returns the Boolean result of asking the user whether to continue the process.

```
void get_data(two_key_table<int, int, boolean> &table)
{
      int pilot, flight;
      boolean can_fly = TRUE;

      do
      {
            cout << "Enter pilot number from " << MIN_PILOT << " to "
                 << MAX_PILOT << ": ";
```

```
            pilot = get_integer(MIN_PILOT, MAX_PILOT);
            cout << "Enter flight number from " << MIN_FLIGHT << " to "
                << MAX_FLIGHT << ": ";
            flight = get_integer(MIN_FLIGHT, MAX_FLIGHT);
            table.store(pilot, flight, can_fly);
        } while (more_input_desired());
    }
```

Alternatively, we could qualify every third pilot automatically for every fourth flight, just so we would have some test data to run:

```
void get_data(two_key_table<int, int, boolean> &table)
{
    boolean can_fly = TRUE;
    for (int pilot = MIN_PILOT; pilot <= MAX_PILOT; ++pilot)
        if (pilot % 3 == 0)
            for (int flight = MIN_FLIGHT; flight <= MAX_FLIGHT;
                ++flight)
            if (flight % 4 == 0)
                table.store(pilot, flight, can_fly);
}
```

The main query loop displays a menu of four commands: display all of the flights for a given pilot, display all of the pilots for a given flight, answer yes or no for a given pilot/flight pair, and quit the program. Depending on the user's choice, the system runs any of three different functions to carry out the commands.

```
void take_queries(two_key_table<int, int, boolean> &table)
{
    char query;
    do
    {
        display_menu();
        query = get_char('1', '4');
        switch (query)
        {
            case '1':   find_flights(table);
                        break;
            case '2':   find_pilots(table);
                        break;
            case '3':   find_pilot_and_flight(table);
                        break;
            default:    cout << "Program terminated." << endl;
        }
    } while (query != '4');
}
```

To find all of the flights for which a given pilot is qualified, we get the pilot number from the user and run a retrieval on each flight number in the table. The successful retrievals lead to output:

```
void find_flights(two_key_table<int, int, boolean> &table)
{
    int pilot;
```

```
        cout << "Enter a pilot number, from " << MIN_PILOT << " to "
            << MAX_PILOT << ": ";
        pilot = get_integer(MIN_PILOT, MAX_PILOT);
        cout << "Eligible flights." << endl;
        for (int flight = MIN_FLIGHT; flight <= MAX_FLIGHT; ++flight)
                if (table.retrieve(pilot, flight, can_fly) && can_fly)
                        cout << flight << endl;
}
```

Note that the Boolean value of **retrieve** specifies whether or not there is an entry in the table at a given pilot and flight, whereas the Boolean value **can_fly** specifies the information stored at these keys.

To find all of the pilots who are qualified for a given flight, we get the flight number from the user and run a retrieval on each pilot number in the table. The successful retrievals lead to output:

```
void find_pilots(two_key_table<int, int, boolean> &table)
{
        int flight;

        cout << "Enter a flight number, from " << MIN_FLIGHT << " to "
            << MAX_FLIGHT << ": ";
        flight = get_integer(MIN_FLIGHT , MAX_FLIGHT );
        cout << "Eligible pilots." << endl;
        for (int pilot = MIN_PILOT; pilot <= MAX_PILOT; ++pilot)
                if (table.retrieve(pilot, flight, can_fly) && can_fly)
                        cout << pilot << endl;
}
```

To find whether or not a given pilot is eligible for a given flight, we get both values from the user and run one retrieval:

```
void find_pilot_and_flight(two_key_table<int, int, boolean> &table)
{
        int pilot, flight;
        boolean can_fly;

        cout << "Enter a pilot number, from " << MIN_PILOT << " to "
            << MAX_PILOT << ": ";
        pilot = get_integer(MIN_PILOT, MAX_PILOT);
        cout << "Enter a flight number, from " << MIN_FLIGHT << " to "
            << MAX_FLIGHT << ": ";
        flight = get_integer(MIN_FLIGHT, MAX_FLIGHT);
        if (table.retrieve(pilot, flight, can_fly) && can_fly)
                cout << "The pilot is eligible for this flight" << endl;
        else
                cout << "The pilot is not eligible for this flight" << endl;
}
```

The auxiliary functions **more_input_desired**, **display_menu**, **get_integer**, and **get_char** are

```cpp
void display_menu()
{
        cout << "1 Find the flights for a given pilot" << endl;
        cout << "2 Find the pilots for a given flight" << endl;
        cout << "3 Find whether or not a given pilot is qualified for a given
               << "flight"
               << endl;
        cout << "4 Terminate program" << endl;
        cout << endl << "Enter a number: ";
}


int get_integer(int min, int max)
{
        int data;
        cin >> data;
        while ((data < min) || (data > max))
        {
                cout << "Error: number must be >= " << min << " and <= "
                     << max << endl;
                cout << "Try again: ";
                cin >> data;
        }
        return data;
}


char get_char(char min, char max)
{
        char data;

        cin >> data
        while ((data < min) || (data > max))
        {
                cout << "Error: character must be >= " << min << " and <= "
                     << max << endl;
                cout << "Try again: ";
                cin >> data;
        }
        return data;
}


boolean more_input_desired()

{
        char query;

cout << "Do you wish to continue? [Y/N] " ;
        cin >> query;
        return (query == 'Y') || (query == 'y');
}
```

1. When accessing an ADT, be sure that you only use those operations specified in the ADT definition. This is the ADT use rule. For instance, it would be wrong to access an object in a one-key table by referring to its array index. This would be assuming that the implementor of the ADT is storing data in an array. Such an assumption is not warranted according to the definition of this ADT.

2. When writing the implementation of an ADT, be sure that the functions you develop obey the interface established by the ADT's definition. This is the ADT implementation rule. For instance, if you, as implementor, need a counter to keep track of the number of objects in a one-key table, don't add the counter as an extra parameter in function calls. Instead, encapsulate it as a private or protected data member of the implementation.

3. When providing the implementation of an ADT, be sure that each individual operation is thoroughly tested and debugged before it is used by higher level logic. Then if errors occur when higher level modules execute, you can be assured that these errors are the result of the algorithms that use the ADT and are not in the implementation of the ADT.

4. The importance of the `create` operation for an ADT should not be underestimated. From the implementor's perspective, here is where crucial initializations occur that will ensure the smooth functioning of other operations. From the perspective of the user of the ADT, you must be sure to call the create operation for each instance of a variable of that type. Failing to do so will usually lead to very bizarre program behavior.

SUMMARY

Key Terms

abstract data type	data abstraction	primary key
abstraction	implementation	secondary key
ADT generality rule	information hiding	two-dimensional array
ADT implementation rule	interface for an ADT	implementation
ADT layering rule	one-key table	two-key table
ADT use rule	physically ordered array	unordered array
	implementation	implementation

Key Concepts

◆ Computer scientists engage in a modeling process as they develop software to satisfy users' needs. In this respect, the way in which a computer scientist works parallels the engineering profession. Consequently, this systematic approach toward the development of successful software is often called software engineering.

◆ Abstract data types are defined apart from considerations of their implementation in a particular programming language. A complete definition for an abstract data type must include a description of the individual elements, the relationship between these individual elements, and the operations that can be performed on them. These operations are conveniently specified as function and function declarations.

◆ The ADT use rule, the ADT implementation rule, the ADT generality rule, and the ADT layering rule are guidelines governing the relationship between implementations of an ADT and higher level algorithms using that implementation.

◆ We must often determine which of a variety of implementations is best in terms of time and space efficiency for a particular application.

◆ The one-key table is an ADT characterized by operations that store, retrieve, or remove data. All of these operations are performed relative to a particular key value.

◆ A physically ordered array with binary search and an unordered array with pointer sort are two ways of implementing a one-key table.

◆ The two-key table is an ADT characterized by operations that store, retrieve, or remove data. All of these operations are performed relative to two particular key values.

◆ A two-dimensional array and a one-key table of one-key tables are two ways of implementing a two-key table.

PROGRAMMING
PROBLEMS
AND PROJECTS

Many of the problems in this chapter require that you write the implementation for an ADT and then use that ADT in a program. It is often interesting to work on such a problem with a classmate. One of you provides the implementation of the ADT; the other writes the higher level algorithm that uses the ADT. If you both obey the ADT use implementation rules, you should be able to work independently of each other and develop an elegant solution to the problem.

In other problems you are asked to write an ADT definition as part of your answer to the problem. Your definition should be presented first in formal precondition and postcondition form and then translated into an appropriate C++ interface. Be sure you are not ambiguous in your presentation of the definition and interface. This aspect of these problems will serve to test the precision with which you write and document.

1. Complete the program in the Focus on Program Design section and test it.

2. Write a small-scale text editor system by loading lines of text from a file into an array of strings.

   a. Allow the user of your program to modify appropriately the text in this array of strings. These modifications should be performed by accessing the strings in the array only through string ADT operations.

   b. Once the text has been modified, write the array of strings out to a new text file.

   c. Test your text editor by using it to create and then modify a modest C++ program, which you then provide as input to your compiler.

3. Write a simple database manager for a bank that uses a one-key table class to store bank accounts of the kind discussed in Chapter 8.

4. If you are familiar with the notion of a set from your previous work in mathematics, formalize the definition of a set as an abstract data type. Be sure to minimally include the following operations in your definition:

   Given a value *V* and a set *S*, determine whether or not *V* is in *S*.

   Given two sets *S*1 and *S*2, determine whether or not *S*1 is equal to *S*2. Given two sets *S*1 and *S*2, determine whether or not *S*1 is a subset of *S*2.

   Given a value *V* and a set *S*, add the value *V* to the set *S*.

   Given a value *V* and a set *S*, remove the value *V* from the set *S*.

   Given two sets *S*1 and *S*2, return their set intersection.

   Given two sets *S*1 and *S*2, return their set difference.

   Given two sets *S*1 and *S*2, return their union.

5. Invented by mathematician John H. Conway (*Scientific American,* October 1970, p. 120), The Game of Life models the growth and changes in a complex collection of living organisms. The model can be interpreted as applying to a collection of micro-organisms, an ecologically closed system of animals or plants, or an urban development. Start with a checkerboard of size $N \times N$ on which "markers" are to be placed. Each location that is not on a border has eight neighbors. The markers are born, survive, or die during a "generation" according to the following rules:

Survival: Markers with two or three neighboring markers survive to the next generation.

Death: Markers with four or more neighbors die from overcrowding and are removed for the next generation. Markers with zero or one neighbors die from isolation and are removed for the next generation.

Birth: Each empty location that has exactly three markers in the eight neighboring locations is a birth location. A marker is placed in the location for the next generation.

For example, on a 6×6 space the following pattern

would look as follows in the next generation:

Certain patterns are stable; for example,

Other patterns repeat a sequence:

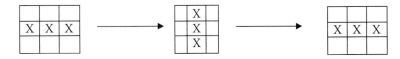

Because, conceptually, two $N \times N$ matrices are required to implement The Game of Life, it is clear that memory limitations could easily become a problem for a large N. After initializing the first generation, print it. Then calculate the next generation in another array and print this too. Repeat for a specified number of generations. Your output should be an "X" for live cells and a blank otherwise.

Develop the high-level logic of your program by employing the fundamental assign/retrieve operations for matrices.

6. The radix sort algorithm, presented in Section 11.4, uses the notion of bins: data repositories that contain numbers or strings in a particular category as the algorithm progresses. Formalize the concept of a bin for the radix sort algorithm by providing an ADT definition for it. Then provide an implementation for your bin ADT and use the operations provided by the bin ADT to write a high-level version of the radix sort.

7. The definition of the one-key table ADT in Section 12.4 specifies that each object in the list must have a unique key value, that is, a key value shared by no other value in the list. Consider a variation on this ADT in which we allow multiple records to share the same key value (for example, several people may have identical names). Call this ADT a one-key table with duplicate keys.

a. Provide a complete definition for this ADT. Be very precise about what happens for each of the **store**, **remove**, and **retrieve** operations. Do you need to add any new operations because of the possibility of duplicate keys?

b. Translate your definition from part **a** into a C++ interface for a one-key table with duplicate keys.

c. Develop an implementation for this ADT. Discuss in a written statement any limitations of your implementation relative to the definition and interface of parts **a** and **b.**

d. Test your implementation by plugging it into a program like that of this chapter's Focus on Program Design section. In a program such as this one, how can you distinguish between employees who have the same name?

CHAPTER ◆ 13 Software Engineering and the System Life Cycle

I believe in Michelangelo, Velazquez, and Rembrandt; in the might of design.
George Bernard Shaw
(1856–1950)

In Chapter 12 and in earlier chapters, we discussed a philosophy of software design called software engineering. This philosophy emphasizes an evolutionary progression from the building of a conceptual model of the system to the eventual implementation of that model in a programming language such as C++. At the heart of this progression lies the abstract data type as a means of conceptualizing the data needs of the system before considering how those needs are to be implemented.

In Chapter 11, we described some relatively simple algorithms to perform operations on arrays and illustrated how to evaluate such algorithms using big-O notation. The purpose of this description was twofold. First, as software designers, we need to be aware of the variety of algorithms available to perform a particular task such as sorting or searching. Chapter 11 began to equip us with this knowledge in a systematic, organized fashion. Second, along with an understanding of various algorithms, we must be able to evaluate and select the best of all possible algorithms for a particular application. Big-O analysis provides us with a guide for such evaluation and selection.

It is now time to put the methods described in the preceding chapters into the context of large-scale systems development. In so doing, we will describe a series of phases known as the software system life cycle. As we walk through these phases, we hope you begin to appreciate the enormous complexity involved in the development of successful software systems. It is not uncommon for a problem that appears to be simple to spawn a variety of complications. Handling such complications in a graceful and efficient fashion is an essential ingredient to succeeding in computer science.

In Section 13.1, we examine the initial analysis phase of the system life cycle. This phase is followed by the design and implementation phases, as described in Section 13.2. Section 13.3 treats the testing, maintenance, and obsolescence stages.

Sections 13.4 and 13.5 provide a brief glimpse of some future directions in software engineering. In Section 13.4, we discuss formal verification as an alternative to testing. In Section 13.5, we investigate a design paradigm called *object-oriented design*.

13.1 The Analysis Phase of the System Life Cycle

OBJECTIVES

- to understand what is done during the analysis phase of systems development
- to be able to define the responsibilities of a systems analyst
- to gain additional familiarity with the use of data flow diagrams as a tool for modeling user needs
- to recognize the importance of oral and written communication skills in the analysis phase

It has been said that the only simple problems in computing are those defined in textbooks. Perhaps a key to the truth of this statement is its use of the word *defined*. Once a problem has been specifically defined, the most difficult obstacle to solving that problem may well have been surmounted. In the analysis phase you must define in detail the problem that you are charged with solving.

It is important to remember that in trying to provide such a definition, you are typically working with a problem originally posed by someone other than yourself. We have tried to emphasize this fact in the preceding chapter by introducing problems in the form of memoranda from computer users. This is done to emphasize that programs are written not for computer scientists but for computer users, users who often know virtually nothing about the computer other than a vague (and often inaccurate) notion that it can magically take care of all of their record-keeping and computational needs. Bridging the gap between potentially naive users and the computer-oriented people who eventually are responsible for implementing the software system constitutes the first phase of the system life cycle.

Though many people are aware that *systems analysts* work with computers in some way, few know specifically what a systems analyst does. More than anything else, the systems analyst is responsible for the *analysis* phase of the system life cycle. A systems analyst talks to the users who initally request the system to learn exactly what these users need. This is done not only by talking to users, but also by studying in detail what these users do. For instance, a systems analyst working for a bank on an automated teller system would have to become an expert on the various duties and responsibilities of a teller. Having learned what the automated system is supposed to do, the systems analyst must then develop formal specifications describing the system and its requirements. The technical people who design and code the software will work from these specifications.

Using Data Flow Diagrams

A *data flow diagram* is a graphic specification technique often used by systems analysts to provide a clear picture of a user's requirements. On the surface, a data flow diagram could be viewed as a collection of circular "bubbles" joined by strings. (In fact, data flow diagrams are sometimes referred to as bubble diagrams.) The strings connecting the bubbles are officially called data flows and are named in a way that reflects the information they carry. The circular bubbles represent processes that transform incoming data flows into outgoing data flows, which may in turn be acted on by another process.

Figure 13.1 depicts a portion of a data flow diagram that describes how a payroll department might operate. Rectangular boxes in a data flow diagram indicate initial sources and final destinations of data flows. In Figure 13.1, the EMPLOYEE is both an initial source (of hours worked and ID number) and a final destination (of a formatted paycheck). Parallel lines highlight a database that must be accessed to do the required processing. For instance, in Figure 13.1, the hourly rate must be retrieved from the EMPLOYEE INFORMATION FILE by the COMPUTE PAY process.

◆ FIGURE 13.1
Data flow diagram for payroll department

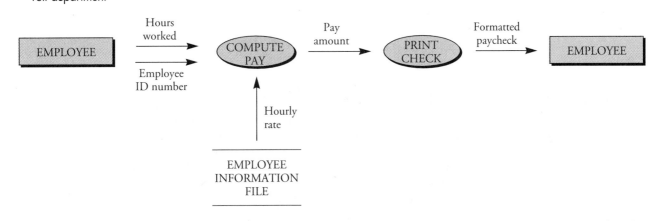

| EXAMPLE 13.1 | You receive the following memorandum from the registrar at the University of Hard Knocks. In it she requests you to automate the university's record-keeping on its students. Provide a data flow diagram to depict the information processing done by the registrar. |

MEMORANDUM
University of Hard Knocks

TO: Director of Data Processing
FROM: Head Registrar
DATE: July 29, 1995
RE: Automation of record-keeping on students

As you know, we presently maintain our student records by manual methods. We believe the time has come to computerize this operation and request that you do so for us.

Here is what we need. Each student's record consists of his or her name, the number of credits that student has taken, the number of credits earned, and the total grade points for that student. We maintain these records by a student's last name. Of course, at numerous times, we must add new students to our records and remove those who have graduated or withdrawn from school. Students often come into our office and request to see their current record, so we must be able to find that information quickly. At the end of each semester we print a grade report for each student. This report consists of the four items cited plus the student's GPA. At the end of the year, the Dean of Students requests two lists of graduating seniors. One of these lists is to be printed in alphabetical order by student name. The other is printed in order by student grade point average.

Certainly the situation described in this memo is an oversimplification of any real college registrar's office. However, even this relatively unsophisticated situation can offer us some interesting food for thought. For one thing, the memo demonstrates the fact that your first contact with a user requesting the system will often leave gaps in your knowledge about the system that is actually needed. The head registrar's memo leaves unanswered the following questions:

1. What is the university's definition of grade points?
2. When grade reports are printed for each student, is it important that they be printed in any particular order?
3. Since grade reports are printed at the end of each semester, do you need some means of updating a student's record at the end of a semester?
4. What is the method used to compute a student's GPA?
5. What separates seniors who graduate from those seniors who don't graduate?
6. Is the list printed in order by student GPA arranged from best student to worst student or vice versa?

You would have to communicate those questions to the registrar before the specifics of the system could be modeled in a data flow diagram. Suppose that you do that and receive the following reply.

MEMORANDUM
University of Hard Knocks

    TO: Director of Data Processing
  FROM: Head Registrar
  DATE: August 2, 1995
    RE: Responses to your questions

Question 1: Four grade points are assigned for a
one-credit A grade, three for a B, two for a C, one for a
D, and zero for an F. Courses worth more than one credit
have their corresponding grade points multiplied
accordingly.

Question 2: Grade reports should be printed in
alphabetical order by student last name.

Question 3: At the end of each semester, faculty members
turn in grades for each class they teach. We use the
grades on these class rosters to update a student's
academic information before printing a grade report.

Question 4: GPA is computed as the quotient of total
grade points divided by credits taken.

Question 5: A graduating senior must have earned at least
120 credits.

Question 6: The list is to be printed from best student
to worst student.

◆ FIGURE 13.2

Data flow diagram of information to be processed in registrar's system

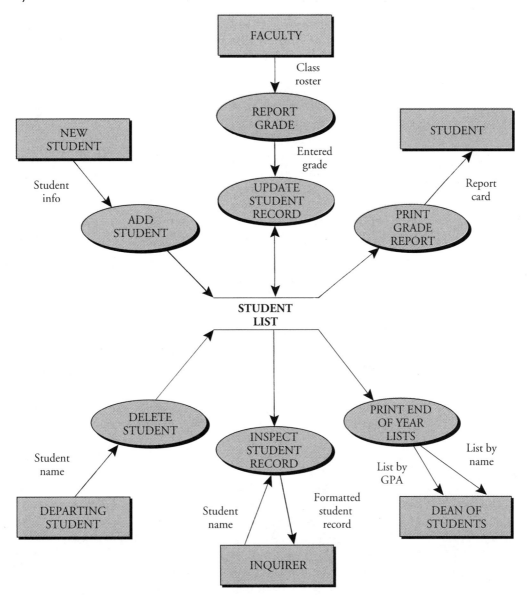

This sort of dialogue with the registrar allows you, a systems analyst, to generate the data flow diagram in Figure 13.2. In this figure, the process Print Grade Report transforms a student academic record into an appropriately formatted report card. Similarly, the process Update Student Record transforms newly reported grades for a student into an appropriately updated student record in the Student List database.

Perfecting the Model

The role of the data flow diagram in the various phases of modeling that occur in the development of a system is to provide an initial overview of the fashion in which a user processes information. Data flow diagrams for a system would be developed before any decisions are made regarding the modular structure and abstract data types on which the eventual program will be based. In this sense, they represent the first step in the progression of structured techniques used to ensure that a software system adequately meets the needs of its end users.

For more complex systems, data flow diagrams such as that appearing in Figure 13.2 may have to be refined into a collection of more detailed subordinate diagrams. Additionally, the systems analyst may have to provide written specifications for each process represented in the diagram. A more detailed discussion of these aspects of the analysis phase may be found in *Modern Structured Analysis* by Edward Yourdon (Englewood Cliffs, N.J.: Prentice-Hall, 1989).

The systems analyst serves as a liaison and translator between the users and the implementors of the system. Depending on the size and structure of the organization, the systems analyst may or may not become involved in the design and coding of the system. Typically, such involvement will occur in smaller organizations where the analyst may wear many hats, but not in larger organizations where staff sizes allow for a greater degree of specialization.

Because an exact assessment of the end user's needs is vital for the most satisfactory design of the system, the systems analyst must have excellent interpersonal communication skills as well as a strong computer background.

It is beyond the scope of this text to present any detailed treatment of systems analysis strategies. Instead, we will occasionally present specifications for programs in the form of memoranda from hypothetical users. These memoranda will serve as realistic reminders of the role of the user in the software development process. Yet they will be simplistic enough to avoid the massive headaches often connected with the analysis phase of a project. Instead, we will concentrate on the next phases of the software system life cycle.

EXERCISES 13.1

1. Consider the memorandum from Wing-and-a-Prayer's vice president in charge of scheduling (see the Focus on Program Design of Chapter 12). Draw a data flow diagram to model the information processing that it describes.

2. Draw a data flow diagram to model the information processing activities that you do each month to maintain your checking account at a local bank.

3. BugFree Incorporated sells software for personal computers. Most orders that BugFree receives come from subscribers to computer magazines who respond to BugFree's advertisement by filling out forms in the ads and then mailing them to the company. BugFree also uses a toll-free phone number to accept orders, answer inquiries, and handle payments and cancellations of orders. Software ordered from BugFree is either sent directly to the customer or to local computer stores, which then distribute the product to the customer. This rapidly expanding business must keep records on its customers, product inventory, and billing information. Draw a data flow diagram to depict the flow of information at BugFree.

4. For this task, you'll work with another student. Each of you should develop a memorandum to specify what you view as the information-processing needs of an administrative office at your school (or any other office environment with which you may be familiar). Your memorandum should provide information similar to that provided by the registrar at the University of Hard Knocks (see Example 13.1). Exchange your

memoranda and draw a data flow diagram to model the activity described in the other person's memo. Then get together with the other person to resolve any questions you might have and to critique the accuracy and completeness of the other's data flow diagram.

5. Consider the following memorandum from the registrar at the renowned American Basket Weaving University—one of the main competitors of the University of Hard Knocks.

```
                        MEMORANDUM
            American Basket Weaving University

   TO: Director of Data Processing
 FROM: Head Registrar
 DATE: July 29, 1996
   RE: Automation of record-keeping on students

Records for students at our school consist of a
university identification number, a last name, a first
name, a middle initial, a Social Security number, a list
of courses the student has taken along with the grade
received in each course, and a list of extracurricular
activities in which the student has indicated an
interest. A university identification number for a
student consists of a six-digit number; the first two
digits represent the year a student entered the
university. The remaining four digits are simply assigned
on a sequential basis as students are admitted to the
school. For instance, the student with ID number 930023
is the 23rd student admitted in the class that entered
A.B.W.U. in 1993.

Given this database, we frequently need to work with it
in the following ways:
■ Find and display all data for a particular student, as
  identified by university ID number.
■ Add and delete student records from the database.
■ Print records for all students in Social Security
  number order, starting with the most recent class and
  working backwards.
■ Add, change, or delete the information on a course for
  a particular student. For instance, change the grade
  received by student 930023 in CompSci2 from C to B.
■ Find all students with an extracurricular interest that
  matches a particular target interest. Students'
  extracurricular interests are viewed as arbitrarily
  long strings. These strings are entered into our
  records directly from information provided by students
  on their registration forms. For instance, a given
  student may have indicated PLAYING BASKETBALL and GOING
  TO PLAYS as her two interests. We would want to be able
  to find this student (as well as students who indicated
  an interest such as WATCHING BASKETBALL or SHOOTING
  BASKETBALLS) if we were to search our database for
  students who had an interest matching BASKETBALL.
```

Develop a data flow diagram to model the information processing that occurs in the registrar's office at A.B.W.U.

6. Write an essay in which you defend or attack the following position: To prepare for a career as a systems analyst, it is more important to develop interpersonal communication skills than it is to acquire a mass of technical knowledge about specific computer systems.

13.2 The Design and Implementation Phases of the System Life Cycle

Given specifications for the user's requirements, the next phase in the system's development is the construction of a relatively detailed design plan. This will guide future work on the implementation of the system. Note that, during the design phase, emphasis switches from understanding and specifying user needs to specifying how we will develop a software system to meet those needs. As such, we begin to consider, from a technical perspective, the data structures that will be needed to process information in the system. This processing of information must be achieved in a fashion consistent with the data flow diagrams and other documents produced during the analysis phase.

Design

The key feature of a design plan is that it must effectively divide the overall problem into a collection of smaller, more manageable problems. Each of these smaller units will be handled by a separate program module in the implementation phase. These modules should be tested, verified, and debugged individually before being integrated into the entire system.

We can draw certain analogies between this modular structuring of a program and the boss–worker relationships that typically exist in any large corporation. Just as any effective boss must be able to delegate responsibilities, program modules that control the major logical decisions in a software system must be able to rely on lower level modules to perform subordinate tasks reliably.

Modular structure charts, which we have been using throughout this text, represent one of the most important graphic tools used by software designers to reflect the relationships between the modules comprising the entire software system. Given a comprehensive data flow diagram from the analysis phase, the software designer can transform this into an initial structure chart by roughly equating each process in the data flow diagram with a module in the structure chart (see Figure 13.3). This initial structure chart can then be refined into a more detailed design by establishing hierarchical relationships between modules and by adding lower level modules.

◆ **Figure 13.3**
Modular structure chart for three-module system

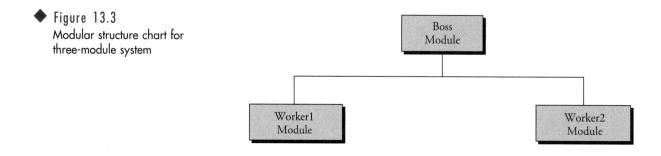

What distinguishes a good modular structure from a poor one? To answer this question we may again draw some apt comparisons between software structure and corporate boss–worker relationships. First, we note that such a structure should be developed in a *top-down* fashion. The overriding principle of top-down design is that we make decisions about the responsibilities of top-level bosses before deciding what the lower level workers are to do. If such decisions are made in a way that progresses downward on a level-by-level basis in the structure chart, we find that boss modules truly will control the major logic of a program, just as corporate bosses should be in control of the most important aspects of their company's policy.

To proceed in an opposite, bottom-up fashion is to court organizational disaster. That is, if we decide what worker modules are to do before considering the responsibilities of boss modules, we frequently run into situations where a boss module is forced into some very clumsy program logic. By proceeding bottom-up, we are not able to see the full range of subordinate tasks that a boss may require. The end result is that the boss will have to take care of minor details—a situation comparable to a corporate executive's having to momentarily leave his or her desk to go out on the assembly line and fasten a bolt that everyone else had forgotten. Such distraction can only result in the boss's doing a poorer job in more important areas of responsibility.

A second criterion to be used in judging the modular structure of a system is the degree to which individual modules are *functionally cohesive*. That is, each module should focus on achieving one particular predefined task without having unexpected side effects on the performance of other modules in the same system. For instance, a module responsible for formatting an output line in a report should not also be updating a field within a customer's record. This could potentially cause great confusion for the module whose assigned task was to guarantee updating of the entire customer record. Thus, as a system designer, you must ensure that you break down the system into its component modules following the "natural" lines of decomposition. The case studies presented in our Focus on Program Design sections will help you develop a feel for what such natural lines are. This talent will be further honed as you take more advanced courses in software engineering.

A third criterion used to evaluate the modular structure of a system is the way in which the modules within the system interact with each other. This interface between a pair of modules is often referred to as *coupling*. In drawing modular structure charts, we have used unlabeled arrows to indicate whether a given module receives data from its calling module, returns information to its calling module, or both. These data flow arrows have thus given some sense of the coupling between two modules.

Ideally, a given module in a system works independently of the others. Yet we can never attain this ideal because modules must interact with each other in any meaningful system. Hence the goal is to hold this interaction to a minimum. That is, there should be no more coupling between modules than necessary to allow them to perform their respective tasks within the framework of the overall system.

Consider the following example of a situation in which an excess of coupling could exist between two modules. Suppose we have a module to update a customer record for a business. One of the tasks subordinate to updating this record is to read new transactions in which the customer has taken part and to update the balance owed field within the customer record. Schematically, the relationship between these two modules is given in Figure 13.4.

◆ FIGURE 13.4

Portion of modular structure
chart for coupling example

The coupling question that arises from this figure is: How do the data flow arrows between the modules Update Customer Record and Update Balance Owed eventually resolve themselves as parameters? One possibility would be for Update Customer Record to pass the entire customer record to Update Balance Owed as a reference parameter. A second possibility is for Update Customer Record merely to pass the balance owed field within the customer record to Update Balance Owed. From a data coupling perspective, the second alternative is much better. In the first alternative, more coupling than necessary exists between the modules because Update Balance Owed is given access to more than it requires to do its specific task. A careless error in Update Balance Owed could inadvertently alter another field such as an address or name within the customer record. Hence, the Update Balance Owed module could have erroneous side effects that might corrupt the entire system. The second alternative, on the other hand, completely eliminates the chance of this happening by simply not allowing Update Balance Owed to access fields it does not specifically need. Thus, minimizing coupling has guarded the system against any inadvertent side effects of a low-level module.

Having generated a structure chart in which modules are functionally cohesive and minimally coupled, the designer must then describe the general data structures to be manipulated by the system and the logic to be followed by each module. In an ideal world, the former could be done simply by specifying the abstract data types that the system will need. This ideal situation occurred in the Focus on Program Design section of Chapter 12. There we had a flight scheduling application for which the two-key table ADT provided a perfect fit.

In more complex situations, an ADT may provide only a starting point in describing the data structures required by the system. For example, we may need the operations provided by a one-key table ADT plus a few more operations that are not included in the ADT's definition. This situation occurs in the registrar's system we analyzed in Example 13.1. This application requires everything offered by a one-key table ADT plus the ability to traverse the table in decreasing GPA order as well as alphabetically by name.

Fortunately, because we have designed our ADT as a class to be used in an object-oriented system, we can easily add new features by means of derived classes and inheritance, as we have seen in Chapters 8 and 10.

Because applications frequently require variations on off-the-shelf ADTs, it is not inappropriate for the designer to give some indication of how such variations might be accomplished. This is illustrated in the following example.

EXAMPLE 13.2   Design a modular structure chart along with the data structures for the registrar's system analyzed in Example 13.1.

As a designer presented with a data flow diagram from the analysis phase (Figure 13.2), your task is to transform it into an appropriate modular structure chart for the system. To a certain extent, the processes specified in the data flow diagram have already provided an initial breakdown of the problem facing the registrar. This initial breakdown can be represented in what is frequently called a first-cut (or first-level) structure chart, an early, relatively rough modular structure for a system. It's called "first-cut" because we intend to modify and expand on its structure as we go through a stepwise refinement of the system's design.

The first-cut structure chart for the registrar's system is presented in Figure 13.5. Transforming this first-cut structure chart into a final modular structure that completely specifies the system's design will require careful consideration of such issues as the user interface presented by our program and the implementation of data structures needed by the system. First, we want our top-level program to interact with users through a menu of choices. We want the user to be able to select a particular operation; the program should then dispatch processing to the appropriate subordinate module. Hence, we will need a Get Selection module that is assigned the task of handling this interface between the user and the menu of choices. Second, we must begin to consider the pertinent data structures, their implementation, and the subordinate modules necessary to access these data structures.

◆ **FIGURE 13.5**

First-cut structure chart for registrar's system

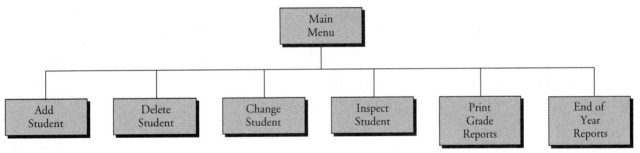

For the registrar's system, the crucial data structure is the one-key table of student records. As we have already indicated, the one-key table used in this system must be extended to allow for traversing in name and in GPA order. In this design of the registrar's system, we will use a derived class of the one-key table called a traversal table. A traversal table inherits the behavior of a one-key table for storing and fast retrievals on a student key name. It extends this behavior to support traversals of the data in the table according to a specified attribute of the data.

Therefore, we will need the new subclass and new modules to produce formatted lists in name order and GPA order. With these considerations taken into account, a refined structure chart emerges. This final structure chart (Figure 13.6) now provides us with a detailed blueprint of the system's design.

After determining the modular structure chart and major data structures for a system, the final step in the design process is to develop specifications for each module in the system. A variety of techniques are available for doing this; our preference is to follow the three-step approach we have used consistently throughout the text:

1. *Specify the task to be performed by the module.* This should be a brief description of what the module does, with minimal reference to how it does it or who is using it.

2. *Specify the input data for the module.* This serves to specify the preconditions for the module; that is, what we know to be true upon entry to the module.

3. *Specify the output data for the module.* This serves to specify the postconditions for the module; that is, what we know to be true upon leaving the module.

◆ **FIGURE 13.6**
Modular structure for registrar's system

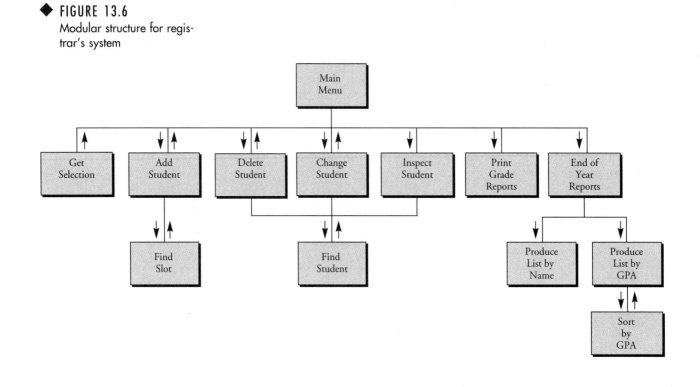

EXAMPLE 13.3

Provide a modular specification for the Add Student module in the design of the registrar's system from Example 13.2.

Because that design specified a physically ordered array as an implementation technique for the student list, our modular specification should take this into account.

> **Module:** Add Student
> **Task:** Adds student record to table of students
> **Inputs:** A table of students
> **Output:** A table of students with length increased by 1

| **EXAMPLE 13.4** | Provide a modular logic specification for the Find Student module in the design of the registrar's system from Example 13.2. |

Module: Find Student
Task: Attempts to locate record for student in table of students
Inputs: Table of students and target name
Outputs: A Boolean value TRUE if found, and the record for the student, or the Boolean value FALSE if not found

In summary, the design phase of the system life cycle includes developing specifications for

1. The modular structure of the program
2. The major data structures to be used by the program
3. The logic needed by individual modules.

The system designer thus produces a set of documents that is then used by programmers who begin the actual coding of the system in an appropriate computer language. As we shall see, an effective design will facilitate this coding effort and will lead to a rather natural way of testing and verifying the correctness of the software that is written.

Implementation

In the implementation phase, you must churn out the code in C++ (or another appropriate language) necessary to put into effect the blueprint developed in the design phase. Although the terminology "churn out" may seem a bit degrading considering the amount of effort that must go into the writing of a program, we use it to stress the importance of the design phase. Given an appropriate set of formal specifications from the design phase, coding the programs really can be an easy task. The completeness of the design phase is the key to determining how easy coding is. Time spent in the design phase will be more than repaid by time gained in coding. This point cannot be overemphasized! The most common mistake made by most beginning programmers is jumping almost immediately into the *coding phase,* thereby digging themselves into holes they could have avoided by more thorough consideration of design issues.

A side issue of the coding phase is *documentation,* the insertion of explanatory remarks into your program so that it makes sense when read by someone else (or by yourself at some time in the distant future). Few computer scientists like to write documentation. However, that does not eliminate the absolute need to write it.

In the real world, programs are worked on by teams of programmers, not just one individual. In such an environment, you must explain to other people who will have to work with it what your code is doing. Moreover, should your code have to undergo revisions in the future (often termed *program maintenance*), your documentation will be vitally important. Without it, those programmers doing the revisions could waste days or even weeks trying to decipher logic that the passage of time has made cryptic. Computer lore is filled with horror stories of programmers who were assigned the unenviable task of maintaining poorly documented code. Edward Yourdon has presented this problem by saying,

Virtually every major organization that began computerizing 20 years ago is now faced with 20-year-old systems whose implementation is a mystery, and, far worse, whose user requirements are a mystery. The only solution to this crisis in the future is to maintain accurate, up-to-date documentation for as long as the system itself survives [*Modern Structured Analysis* (Englewood Cliffs, N.J.: Prentice-Hall, 1989), p. 448].

At a minimum, each module you write should include documentation stating its general purpose, identifying all parameters and major local variables, and clarifying any obscure code segments. So, get into the habit of documenting all functions via the "Function; Inputs; Outputs" style that we have been using throughout the text. When combined with other written specifications from the analysis and design phases, well-documented code will help ensure that your software system has a long and productive lifetime.

EXERCISES 13.2

1. What is meant by the term *functionally cohesive* in reference to modular structure charts?

2. What is meant by the term *coupling* in reference to modular structure charts?

3. Explain why the following portion of a modular structure chart for a payroll system is not functionally cohesive. Correct the modular structure to make it more functionally cohesive.

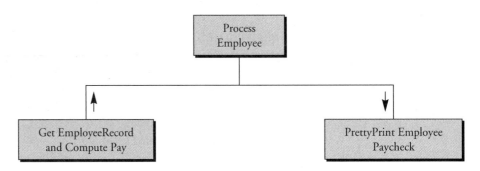

4. Suppose that we have a search module that receives a customer identification key and then searches for that customer's record in a table of records, returning it to the calling module. Suppose also that this search module prints a **"CANNOT FIND CUSTOMER"** message if the record associated with this key cannot be located. From the perspective of functional cohesion, why is the printing of this message a poor strategy?

5. Explain why using global variables is a poor strategy from a data coupling perspective.

6. Suppose that a student record at the University of Hard Knocks contains information about the student's grades in courses the student has taken and about the tuition that the student owes the university. Why should a module that computes a student's grade point average not be passed the entire student record as a parameter?

7. Data flow diagrams and modular structure charts are graphic modeling tools related to the development cycle of a software system. Discuss the similarities and differences between these two tools.

8. In Exercise 6 of Section 13.1 you analyzed a system requested by the registrar at American Basket Weaving University. Now follow up this analysis by doing a design for the system. Include a complete set of module specifications in your design.

13.3 Testing, Maintenance, and Obsolescence Phases of the System Life Cycle

OBJECTIVES

- to realize that we must develop well-conceived strategies for testing software if we are to ensure its reliability

- to understand the differences between modular, system, and acceptance testing

- to understand the difference between white box and black box testing

- to know what is meant by the robustness of a module

- to be able to use the finite state machine paradigm as a means of guarding against invalid input

- to gain insight into developing test cases for modules

- to realize the importance of being able to maintain a software system over its lifetime of use

A program's usefulness is ultimately demonstrated in the final three phases—testing, maintenance, and obsolescence—of the system life cycle.

Testing

An endeavor far more creative than coding and documentation is the testing that must be coordinated with a system's implementation. This chapter's Notes of Interest will attest to the importance of software reliability; it has become a moral and ethical issue as well as a technical one. Given this importance, how do we systematically verify the correctness of the software we develop?

First, we must realize that the testing and verification phase is a critical and full-fledged phase of the system life cycle. As such, time must be allocated for it. A common mistake made by beginning programmers is to assume the correctness of their program after one or two successful test runs. Though you should feel confident that your software will be error-free if it has been carefully designed, even well-designed systems must be thoroughly tested and verified before being released to users.

As an example, consider the following statistics, which summarize the percentages of total project time (not including maintenance) devoted to testing in several computerized systems developed for Air Force space missions.

Mission	Percent
SAGE	47
NAVAL TACTICAL DATA SYSTEM	50
GEMINI	47
SATURN V	49

[See R. W. Jensen and C. C. Tonies, *Software Engineering* (Englewood Cliffs, N.J.: Prentice-Hall, 1979), p. 330.] Such statistics are amazingly consistent across a wide variety of large system development projects. "In examining conventionally scheduled projects," Frederick P. Brooks "found few that allowed one-half of the projected schedule for testing, but that most did indeed spend half of the actual schedule for that purpose. Many of these were on schedule until and except in system testing" [*The Mythical Man-Month* (Reading, Mass.: Addison-Wesley, 1982)].

The general rule of thumb is that the *testing phase* of a large project can (and should) consume roughly half of the time scheduled for the project. Of course, assignments in a programming course may not be of the same magnitude as an Air Force space mission, but the message is clear. If you fail to schedule a considerable amount of time to verify the correctness of your program, your users (or instructor) will inevitably find bugs in it.

How exactly does one verify the correctness of a large program? One way is to construct formal mathematical proofs of your algorithm's correctness. Though progress is being made in applying this type of formal mathematical approach (see Section 13.4), the complex problems of most real-world systems do not allow this method to be used efficiently. Consequently, the most often employed method of verifying a program's correctness is to test it thoroughly.

Modular Testing. If testing is important enough to take 50% of your time, it must clearly require more than a haphazard approach. Hence, we counsel against strategies such as creating your test data "on the fly" or creating test data by random techniques. Testing must be planned to be convincing. The plan that we shall briefly describe here begins with *modular testing*. Modular testing is the natural outgrowth of the principles of modular design.

The key to modular testing is to test each individual module as it is developed. Do not wait until the entire system has been coded to begin your testing. Thus, testing on the modular level involves the following steps:

1. Develop short *driver modules* that artificially call the modules you have written and report the values returned by these modules.
2. Develop short *stub modules* that (again, artificially) are called by the modules you have written. Such stubs should report the intermediate values they are sent and return appropriate values so that the module being tested can continue execution.
3. Design *test cases* that exercise all the logical possibilities the module may encounter. Be aware that such test cases consist of more than just strategically chosen input data. Each set of input data must also include its expected result (sometimes called the *test oracle*) if it is truly to convince anyone of the module's correctness.

We have already discussed techniques for writing drivers and stubs in Chapter 4. It is the third point about testing on the modular level to which we must turn our attention.

In designing test cases, programmers begin to mix methods of science and art. Every mathematician knows that we can never actually prove anything by testing examples (that is, input data). So, how can we verify a module's correctness by merely concocting examples? One proposed answer is to classify input data according to possible testing conditions. Hence, a finite set of well-chosen equivalence classes of test cases can be sufficient to cover an infinite number of possible inputs. Deciding what such equivalence classes should be is the point at which the process becomes more of an art than a science.

EXAMPLE 13.5

To illustrate these principles, consider the fee structure at the E-Z Park parking lot. Parking fees for vehicles are based on the following rules:

The module is given two data items: a character, which may be 'C' or 'T' indicating whether the vehicle is a car or truck; and an integer number indicating the number of hours the vehicle spent in the parking lot. Cars are charged $1.00 for each of the first three hours they are in the lot and $0.50 for each hour after that. Trucks are charged $2.00 for each of the first four hours they are in the lot and $0.75 per hour thereafter.

After computing the appropriate charge, a new module (**compute_parking_fee**) is to call on another new module (**pretty_print_ticket**), which appropriately formats a parking fee ticket showing the vehicle type, hours parked, and resulting fee. The **compute_parking_fee** module is given here:

```
// Function: compute_parking_fee
//
// Task: computes charge for parking and calls pretty_print_ticket to output ticket
// Inputs: vehicle type in vehicle category and time spent in hours

void compute_parking_fee (char vehicle_category, int hours)
{
        float charge;

        switch (vehicle_category)
        {
            case 'C':    if (hours <= 3)
                                charge = hours;
                         else
                                charge = 3 + (hours - 3) * .5;
                         break;
            case 'T':    if (hours <= 4)
                                charge = hours * 2;
                         else
                                charge = 8 + (hours - 4) * .75;
        }
        pretty_print_ticket(vehicle_category, hours, charge);
}
```

An appropriate driver main program would simply allow us to repeatedly send data to the **compute_parking_fee** module to check its behavior in a variety of situations. An appropriate stub for the call to **pretty_print_ticket** would merely inform us that we reached this subordinate module and print the values received so that we could be sure they had been transmitted correctly. At this stage, the stub need not concern itself with detailed, formatted output; we are at the moment interested only in testing **compute_parking_fee**.

In testing this module, we can begin by identifying the following six *equivalence classes:*

1. A car in the lot less than three hours
2. A car in the lot exactly three hours
3. A car in the lot more than three hours
4. A truck in the lot less than four hours
5. A truck in the lot exactly four hours
6. A truck in the lot more than four hours.

Choosing one test case for each equivalence class, we arrive at the following set of test cases.

Vehicle Category	Hours	Expected Results
'C'	2	Charge = 2.00
'C'	3	Charge = 3.00
'C'	5	Charge = 4.00
'T'	3	Charge = 6.00
'T'	4	Charge = 8.00
'T'	8	Charge = 11.00

The test cases for exactly three hours for a car and exactly four hours for a truck are particularly important since they represent *boundary conditions* at which a carelessly constructed conditional check could easily produce a wrong result.

This parking lot example, though illustrative of the method we wish to employ, is artificially simple. The next example presents a more complex testing situation.

EXAMPLE 13.6

Consider developing a strategy to test the sorting algorithms we discussed in Chapter 11. Recall that each of these algorithms—bubble sort, insertion sort, and selection sort—received an array of physical size **MAX_LIST_SIZE** and an integer **n** to indicate the logical size of the array, that is, the number of items currently stored in the array.

Our criterion for choosing equivalence classes of test data for such a sorting algorithm is based on two factors:

1. The size of *n,* the number of items to be sorted
2. The ordering of the original data.

The following table presents a partitioning of test data into equivalence classes for this example.

Size of *n*	Order of Original Data	Expected Results
n = 1	Not applicable	Array to be arranged in
n = 2	Ascending	ascending order
n = 2	Descending	for all cases.
n midsize and even	Descending	
n midsize and even	Ascending	
n midsize and even	Randomized	
n midsize and odd	Ascending	
n midsize and odd	Descending	
n midsize and odd	Randomized	
n = physical array size	Ascending	
n = physical array size	Descending	
n = physical array size	Randomized	

The module should be run for a minimum of 12 cases, one for each of the classes dictated by our table. Ideally, a few subcases should be run for each of the randomized cases. We cannot overemphasize the importance of testing seemingly trivial cases such as **n = 1** and **n = 2**. These lower boundary conditions are typical examples of data that may cause an otherwise perfectly functioning loop to be incorrectly skipped. Similarly, it is important to test the upper boundary condition in which **n** reaches the physical array size.

Testing for Robustness. Yet another issue in modular testing is the question of how a module will react when it receives invalid data. For instance, in our current version of the **compute_parking_fee** module in Example 13.5, there is a potentially disastrous side effect that occurs when the module receives a vehicle type other than 'C' or 'T' . (What is it?)

Similar reasoning dictates that the sort test data of Example 13.6 should perhaps contain test cases for **n = 0** and **n** greater than the physical array size even though such cases should not arise in normal use of the sort module. A *robust* module is one that guards against harmful side effects when it receives invalid or unexpected data.

It is particularly critical that any modules with which the user is to interact be robust. Inadvertent wrong keystrokes by a user can crash a program or, even worse, result in a program performing its computations with incorrect data. Robustness may be so critical in some systems that you may have to improve on the interaction capabilities provided by your programming language. Consider, for instance, what your version of C++ will do when a user enters

1.l5 (first character is a lowercase L)

instead of

1.15

in response to **cin >> x** where **x** is a real number. The accidentally typed lowercase "l" can crash the **>>** operator offered by many versions of C++.

One way to avoid these problems is to write your own function to read a real number (as you were asked to in an exercise in Chapter 7). In this function, read the input a character at a time and convert the incoming stream of characters to its corresponding real value. Because you are reading characters instead of reals, nothing the user types can crash your function. If a character that is not expected as part of a real is read, your function can take corrective action and warn the user of the problem.

A paradigm known as a *finite state machine* is often used by software engineers to perform such robustness checks on user input. A finite state machine is best described by a diagram referred to as a *state-transition diagram*. A state-transition diagram for the problem of reading a real number entered in decimal form appears in Figure 13.7.

Interpret the circles in this diagram as the states of the machine. Hence the machine of Figure 13.7 can be in a **LEADING_SPACES** state, a **LEFT** state, a **RIGHT** state, a **DONE** state, or an **ERROR** state. In a particular state, the machine is expecting certain characters as valid input for that state.

◆ FIGURE 13.7

State-transition diagram for reading a real number in decimal form

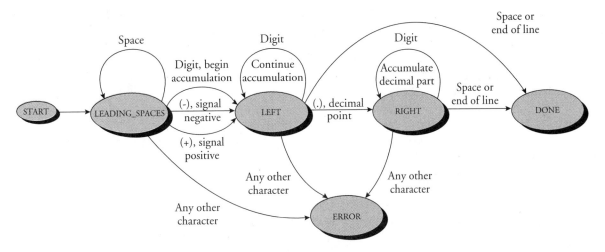

The arrows leading from the states are called *transitions*. Transitions indicate what the machine will do when it encounters a particular character in its current state. Each transition is labeled with one or more characters and, potentially, an action to take upon reading such a character. For instance, when the machine of Figure 13.7 is in the **LEADING_SPACES** state and it reads a space, it remains in the **LEADING_SPACES** state. Consistent with C++ syntax for entering a real number in decimal form, the machine must read a '+', '–', or digit before it can begin the accumulation of a real number value and switch to the **LEFT** state. Any other character read in the **LEADING_SPACES** state results in an error.

While in the **LEFT** state, the machine reads digits on a character-by-character basis. As each digit is read, its value must be added to a running total that will be returned from the function. The only valid transitions from the **LEFT** state occur when a space, end of line, or decimal point is encountered. In a similar fashion, the **RIGHT** state must read characters until the machine reaches the **DONE** or **ERROR** state. You should trace the action of the machine in Figure 13.7 on a variety of input sequences to convince yourself that it correctly handles all possibilities.

The following example illustrates that using C++'s enumerated type makes it relatively easy to translate a finite state machine into a C++ function.

EXAMPLE 13.7

Write a robust C++ function to read a real number employing the logic of the finite state machine in Figure 13.7.

The strategy of the function is to repeatedly read a character, which is then analyzed in a **switch** statement driven by the current state of the machine.

```
// Function: read_real
// Task: reads a real number in decimal form from current line of input
// characters. If current line of input characters does not constitute a valid
// real number, force user to retype the characters.
//
// Output: a real number

float read_real()
{

// This enumerated type captures the states of Figure 13.7

        enum possibilities {LEADING_SPACES, LEFT, RIGHT, ERROR, DONE};

        char ch;
        possibilities state;
        boolean negative;
        float value, multiplier;

        // Stay in the outer do loop until read a valid real
        // The inner loop embodies the logic of the finite state machine
           in Figure 13.7
        do
        {
                negative = FALSE;
                // Initially assume positive, toggle to signal negative
                multiplier = 0.1;
```

```
value = 0.0;
state = LEADING_SPACES;
do
{
        cin.get(ch);
        if (ch == '\n')
                // Have read an end of line
                state = DONE;
        switch (state)
        {
                case LEADING_SPACES:
                        if (('0' <= ch) && (ch <= '9'))
                        // Have read a digit
                        {
                                state = LEFT;
                                value = 10 * value
                                        + (ch - '0');
                        // convert
                        }
                        else if (ch == '-')
                        // Signal negative number
                        {
                                negative = TRUE;
                                state = LEFT;
                        }
                        else if (ch == '+')
                        // Leading positive sign
                                state = LEFT;
                        else if (ch != ' ')
                                state = ERROR;
                        break;
                case LEFT:
                        if (('0' <= ch) && (ch <= '9'))
                                // Have read a digit
                                        value = 10 * value
                                                + (ch - '0');
                        else if (ch == '.')
                        // Decimal point
                                state = RIGHT;
                        else if (ch == ' ')
                        // End of current number
                                state = DONE;
                        else
                                state = ERROR;
                        break;
                case RIGHT:
                        if (('0' <= ch) && (ch <= '9'))
                                // Have read a digit
                                {
                                        value = value
                                                + multiplier
                                                * (ch - '0');
                                        multiplier = multiplier * .1;
```

```
                                        }
                                        else if (ch == ' ')
                                        // End of current number
                                                state = DONE;
                                        else
                                                state = ERROR;
                                }
                        } while ((state != ERROR) && (state != DONE));
        // If there was bad input, force the user to reenter until get valid real
                if (state = ERROR)
                        cout << "Bad Number - Please reenter this number";
                if (negative)
                        value = - value;
        } while(state != DONE);
        return value;
}
```

To illustrate the use of the function **read_real**, consider the following driver program and the results of the sample run.

```
#include <iostream.h>
#include <iomanip.h>

int main()
(
        float number;

        cout << fixed << showpoint << setprecision(2);
        do
        {
                number = read_real();
                cout << setw(10) << number << endl;
        } while (number != 0.0);
        return 0;
}
```

A sample run is as follows:

```
45.61
        45.61
11.2
34.8
        11.20
        34.80
```
19.6 (Note that lowercase L typed instead of digit 1)
```
Bad Number - Please reenter this number
19.6
        19.60
0.0
        0.00
```

It is probably safe to say that no module of reasonable complexity can be guaranteed to be 100% robust. For each safeguard against invalid data, a user will no doubt find some way of inadvertently bypassing that safeguard. How robust an individual module must be is a reflection of how it fits into the overall modular structure of the system. It is not reasonable to expect every module in a system to guard itself against every potential kind of invalid data. Such a strategy would have the vast majority of modules more preoccupied with this issue than with their assigned responsibility within the system. A better strategy is to have a few modules whose only responsibility is to screen incoming data against invalid values. In this way we can assure that other modules will be called only when we have valid data to give them. The degree to which an individual module should be robust is thus intimately tied to the overall system design and should be stated as part of the specifications for that module.

White Box/Black Box Testing. One factor that can influence the design of test cases is the knowledge you have of the design and implementation of the module being tested. If you have detailed knowledge of the design and implementation, you can engage in *white box testing*. That is, the module represents a "white box" because you are aware of the internal logic and data structure implementations in the module. In white box testing, test cases can be partitioned into equivalence classes that specifically exercise each logical path through a module. In *black box testing,* the module is approached without knowledge of its internal structure. You know what the module is supposed to do, but not how it does it.

For instance, in Examples 13.2 and 13.4, we made the design decision to implement the list of students in the registrar's system with a one-key table keyed by student name. This decision allowed us to use fast retrievals in the specifications for the Find Student module. We'll work with this module again in the next example.

EXAMPLE 13.8

To design a complete set of test cases for function `find_student`, we use Table 13.1. The seven cases presented in the table exercise all logical paths through the binary search algorithm.

◇ **TABLE 13.1**

Test cases

Test Case	Number of Students	List	Target	Expected Results	Rationale
I	10	ALLEN BAKER DAVIS GREEN HUFF MILLER NOLAN PAYTON SMITH TAYLOR	Try each name in the Students list	Found TRUE. info_wanted contains associated record. Mid contains associated position	Can we find everything in the full list?

◇ **TABLE 13.1 (CONTINUED)**

Test cases

Test Case	Number of Students	List	Target	Expected Results	Rationale
II	10	Same as test case I	Try AARON, NATHAN, ZEBRA	Found FALSE.	Is Found correctly returned as FALSE for Target data items that precede all list elements, follow all list elements, and are interspersed in the middle of the list? This case tests the full list.
III	5	ALLEN DAVIS HUFF NOLAN SMITH	Same as test case I	Same as test case I	Can we find everything in a mid-sized list?
IV	5	Same as test case III	Same as test case II	Same as test case II	Same as test case II but for mid-sized list.
V	1	HUFF	HUFF	Same as test case I	Can we handle successful search in a one-element list?
VI	1	HUFF	Same as test case II	Same as test case II	Can we handle unsuccessful searches in a one-element list?
VII	0		HUFF	Same as test case II	Robustness check. What if we call on find_student with the empty list?

Note that, in Example 13.8, our test cases are sure to exercise the situation in which the table is completely full. This represents a boundary condition for the algorithm; we are aware of this condition because we are testing from a white box perspective. If we were testing from a black box perspective instead, it might not be possible to exercise all such boundary conditions.

System and Acceptance Testing. In practice, testing at the modular level tends to be white box testing since a well-designed module will be compact and focused. Hence it is relatively easy to explore the internal structure of a module and create test cases geared toward that internal structure. As modules merge into a full-fledged software system, the testing of the entire system takes on more of a black box perspective.

In *system testing*, you exercise the interfaces between modules instead of the logic of a particular module. System testing should not occur until each module has been individually tested by white box methods. In larger systems you may find it advantageous to test related subcollections of modules before jumping to a test of the entire system. This will allow you more easily to localize the location of any errors that are found.

Ultimately, the system is tested not only by technical people but by the end users who must work with the system on a regular basis. This final phase of *acceptance testing* carried out by end users is totally black box in nature. Typically end users neither want nor need detailed knowledge of *how* a system is implemented; instead, they have a very substantial interest in *what* the system does. Does it successfully meet the specifications that were described very early in the analysis phase of the project? Consequently, end users will test and ultimately accept or reject the system based on how it meets these specifications.

Debugging Errors Found During Testing. The main goal of all testing we have discussed is to find errors. Though at first glance this statement may seem counterproductive, remember that it is better for errors to be detected at the testing stage than when the software is in use (or when your instructor is assigning a grade). Given this negative premise of testing, you must also know how to debug your programs when testing achieves its goal of finding errors. If testing can be categorized as an art, debugging could facetiously be described as bordering on the occult.

The following general guidelines apply to the debugging of all programs:

1. Typing is no substitute for thinking. Don't be too quick to make changes in your source program. Instead, when an error occurs, take your test cases and trace them by hand through the logic currently present in your module. Here the advantage of modular testing becomes apparent. Such hand tracing is nearly impossible if you are working with an entire system; with merely one module it is quite manageable.

2. Make use of the various debugging tools provided with most compilers. These tools allow you to scatter tracer output (to display the value of key variables at various stages of an algorithm) and breakpoints (to halt program execution at a key step so that you can examine the values contained in variables) throughout your program in a conveniently interactive fashion. The time you spend learning how to use such tools will be repaid many times over.

3. Don't assume that, once you've repaired your program for the test case that generated the error, all previous tests cases will still work correctly. You now have a new program, and all of your carefully designed test cases need to be applied again.

4. Leave time to debug so you can avoid "bandage-type" corrections (often called patches). Debugging encourages alternatives that may actually improve the design of your program. There is nothing wrong with completely scrapping an approach that has been shown, by testing, to be ill-conceived. Indeed, to try to make such an approach work by installing repeated and intricate fixes can only lead to a system doomed to a very short life.

5. Keep your test cases in a file so that as you make future modifications you can use them again conveniently.

Maintenance

What follows acceptance testing of your system? Once your program has been thoroughly tested, it is ready to be released to the users who originally requested it. In theory, you are done; these users will live happily ever after using the program

A NOTE OF INTEREST

Software Reliability and Defense Systems

The issue of software testing takes on great importance as we begin to rely increasingly on the computer as an aid in the decision-making process.

In "Computer system reliability and nuclear war" [*Communications of the ACM*, Volume 30, No. 2 (February 1987): 112–131], Alan Borning of the University of Washington evaluated the problems of software testing for the Strategic Defense Initiative, popularly known as Star Wars:

> The SDI envisions a multilayer defense against nuclear ballistic missiles. The computer software to run such a defense would be the most complex ever built. A report by the Defensive Technologies Study Team, commissioned by the Department of Defense to study the feasibility of such a system, estimates a system with 6–10 million lines of code. Enemy missiles would first be attacked in their boost phase, requiring action within 90 seconds or so of a detected launch. This time interval is so short that the human role in the system could be minimal at best, with virtually no possibility of decision making by national leaders. Although pieces of the system could be tested and simulation tests performed, it would be impossible to test the entire system under actual battle conditions short of fighting a nuclear war. It has been the universal experience in large computer systems that there is no substitute for testing under actual conditions of use. The SDI is the most extreme example so far of an untestable system.

Such systems are somewhat unique in that (we hope) many of them will never actually be used. If they ever are used, it may be too late to engage in the repair of minor flaws that normally arise in the maintenance phase of the system life cycle. It is not an understatement to say that the future of the human race may be riding on the thoroughness with which the systems have been tested. Is there any testing strategy that can be convincing enough under these circumstances? The apparent success of American Patriot missiles in destroying Iraqi Scud missiles in the Persian Gulf War has refueled speculation about the role of computer-controlled defense systems. Of the 43 Scud missiles launched against coalition forces in Saudi Arabia and Kuwait, Patriot systems intercepted 29, while 11 others were allowed to land in the ocean or remote areas of the desert. However, mere numbers can be somewhat deceiving. In his article "Lessons from the Patriot missile software effort" [*IEEE Software*, Volume 8, No. 3 (May 1991): 105–108], Galen Gruman points out:

> In one case, an Iraqi missile intercepted by a Patriot system stationed in Israel was merely knocked off target. In several other cases, debris from the intercepted Scuds damaged homes and injured people. Tougher for any interceptor are missiles that fall apart in flight, since the Patriot at best will hit only one piece, which may not be the warhead. For example, of the Scuds launched against Saudi Arabia and Kuwait, seven (including some that were allowed to fall) broke up during flight and could not be targeted—including one missile whose debris fell on a military barracks near Dhahran, Saudi Arabia, killing 28 soldiers. The Scuds fell apart because they were apparently old and poorly maintained, but both the U.S. and Soviet Union have multiple-warhead missiles designed just to avoid total destruction by antimissile systems.

that you so painstakingly developed. In practice, unfortunately, it rarely works out this way. Instead, users begin to find flaws with your program. (Nobody is perfect!) These flaws typically are due to such factors as the following:

- Your misunderstanding the users' exact needs during the analysis phase
- Your system's slow performance when it encounters large volumes of user data
- User needs that have changed since you initially did your analysis
- Changes in computer hardware and operating system software.

When flaws like these arise, you must maintain your system. That is, you must make the necessary changes to correct the flaws. Here is where good program design and documentation pay off again. It is absolutely essential that you (or someone else assigned to *maintenance*) be able to understand your code after months or perhaps years away from it. Moreover, if your modules are functionally cohesive and minimally coupled, then you should be able to make the appropriate changes in them without causing problems in other modules of the system. That a program must be maintained is not an indication of poor design; it is rather a fact of the software life cycle. That a program can be easily maintained is actually an indication that it was soundly designed from its conception.

Obsolescence

As we saw in Chapter 1, despite all your best efforts, your program may become obsolete in time. At that point, the system life cycle must begin anew. You may then be asked to develop a new program to meet the changed needs of the user and to make use of any expanded software capabilities.

Dynamic Nature of the System Life Cycle

Let us recap the phases of the system life cycle: analysis, design, implementation (coding), testing and verification, maintenance, and obsolescence. Though we have discussed each as a separate entity, they are all interwoven into a dynamic, iterative process. The process is dynamic because the dividing lines between the phases are always changing. That is, as you are doing analysis, you are probably already beginning to consider many design and coding issues. The process is iterative in that, from one phase, you may frequently have to return to an earlier phase. For instance, though you may be designing your system, if a question arises about what the user wants, you will have to return temporarily to analysis before completing the design. Similarly, during implementation, you may find it necessary to alter certain design considerations. The fact that many people are usually involved in the system life cycle—users, analysts, designers, and programmers—also contributes to the volatile nature of systems development.

One way to deal with the dynamic nature of the software life cycle is to engage in a process of *iterative prototyping*. Using this method, analysts construct a simplified model of a system that performs just a few essential functions. Implementors then get this model up and running very quickly as a *prototype* of the entire system. Because the model and implementation are fairly simple at this point, mistakes and design flaws are easy to discover and correct. The system can then be extended and refined as a series of prototyes, which successively approximate the full functionality of the complete system. Object-oriented design, which we discuss more fully in Section 13.5, makes extensive use of iterative prototyping.

Perhaps one of the worst misconceptions about those of us who work in the computer field is that we deal with problems that have very rigid, well-defined solutions. We hope our discussion of the system life cycle has convinced you that nothing could be further from the truth. To truly contribute over the span of the entire life cycle, you must be skilled at communicating with people, thinking abstractly, and then following through on the details of a plan. The effective computer scientist must truly be a person for all seasons.

EXERCISES 13.3

1. Summarize what is involved in each of the phases of the system life cycle. If you were to specialize your career in one of these phases, which one would it be? Why? Provide your answer in essay form.

2. What is meant by the term *boundary conditions* for an algorithm?

3. What is a robust module? Should every module in a system be completely robust? Justify your answer in a written essay.

4. Consider the `compute_parking_fee` function discussed in this section (Example 13.5). Is it robust? What does it do if it does not receive a `'C'` or `'T'` for its `vehicle_category` parameter? Rewrite this module to make it more robust.

5. Employees at the University of Hard Knocks are paid by the following rules:

   - Employees who sign a contract for a total annual wage are paid 1/52 of that amount each week.

   - Hourly employees receive a paycheck based on the number of hours they work in a given week and their hourly rate. They are paid this hourly rate for each of the first 40 hours they work. After 40 hours, they are paid time-and-a-half for each additional hour of work. Moreover, work on a holiday is a special case for hourly employees. They get paid double-time for all holiday work.

   Write a function to compute the pay for an employee of the University of Hard Knocks and then dispatch the appropriate information to a check printing module. Completely test the function you write by integrating it with appropriate driver and stub modules and by designing a complete set of test data for the module.

6. Develop test data for the Add Student module of Example 13.3.

7. Design test data for function `read_real` of Example 13.7. Remember that robustness is a high priority for this module, so your test data should be designed with that in mind. If your test data detect any flaws in the algorithm, fix them.

8. Extend the finite state machine of Figure 13.7 to accept reals entered with C++'s "E" exponential notation. Then incorporate this extended finite state machine into the function `read_real` of Example 13.7. Finally, design test data for the extended function.

9. Extend the function `read_real` of Example 13.7 so that it rejects any number outside of a certain range (to be specified by additional parameters). Illustrate the use of your new function in a driver program.

10. Each type of computer has its own particular syntax for what it allows as a valid file name. Often such a file name may include an optional disk and directory specifier. Along the lines of Figure 13.7, develop a finite state machine to validate an input stream of characters intended to represent a file name on the computer system you use. Then translate your finite state machine into a robust function which returns in a string a file name entered by a user. Design test data for this function and create a driver program to test it.

11. This section has presented modular testing as the design of equivalence classes of test cases that exercise all the logical possibilities a module may encounter. You are working on a software system with a friend who claims that such comprehensive testing is impossible. As evidence, the friend cites a module she has written with 20 `if` statements in it. Your friend points out that there are approximately 2^{20} logical paths through this module, and that comprehensive modular testing is therefore impossible. In a written essay, refute your friend's claim. (*Hint:* Consider the cohesion of the module used as an example by your friend.)

13.4 Formal Verification (Optional)

The approach we have taken in Section 13.3 to ensure software reliability is to emphasize the construction of thorough and convincing test data as a means of verifying program/module correctness. However, this strategy of verification cannot be construed as a formal proof of the algorithm's correctness. We have attempted to show that an algorithm is correct by showing that it works for a comprehensive set of examples. But, from a mathematical perspective, a theorem cannot be proven by example. This is because there are infinitely many possibilities for such examples, hence making it impossible to test every one. Instead of testing, a formal approach to algorithm verification demands an airtight proof using the basic axioms and principles of logic.

Formal Algorithm Verification by the Method of Inductive Assertions

Some work has been done in this area of formal algorithm verification. We shall attempt to summarize one of the more frequently used techniques, known as the *method of inductive assertions*, by formally proving the correctness of the following algorithm. The algorithm is to compute N^M for N, a real, and M, a nonnegative integer. Our correctness proof will use the principle of mathematical induction. (This principle is covered extensively in most discrete mathematics texts; be sure to review it before proceeding if you are not familiar with it.)

```
float power(float n, int m)
{
    float r = 1.0;

    while (m > 0)
    {
        r = r * n;
        --m;
    }
    return r;
}
```

A formal proof of such an algorithm involves appropriately identifying the input assertions, output assertions, and loop invariants of the algorithm (see Chapter 5, Section 5.6, and Chapter 6, Section 6.5). All three of these are statements about the algorithm expressed in formal mathematical terms. The input assertions represent all necessary input conditions to the algorithm. For our example, the input assertions would be

$$N \in reals \qquad M \in integers \qquad M >= 0$$

The output assertions represent in formal terms the desired result. Here we would have $R = N^M$ as the lone output assertion for our algorithm.

Finally, we must identify the loop invariants of our algorithm. A *loop invariant* may be thought of as a special type of assertion that expresses a relationship between variables and remains constant through all iterations of a loop. Note that it is not the variables that remain fixed but rather the relationship between them. This is a key distinction to make. As we shall see, correctly identifying loop invariants is often the most crucial and difficult step in setting the stage for a proof (by induction) of an algorithm's correctness.

For the power algorithm under consideration, let R_k and M_k be the respective values of R and M after k times through the **while** loop. Both R and M change each time the loop is executed, while N remains fixed throughout the algorithm. The loop invariant relationship we wish to prove is then given by

$$R_k \times M_k$$

If we can prove this loop invariant, then it follows immediately that the algorithm is correct. Why? If the looping ends after j times through the loop, M_j will be zero because of the conditional test in the **while**. Hence, because of the loop invariant relationship, we will have

$$R_j \times N^{M_j} = N^M$$
$$\downarrow$$
$$R_j \times N^0 = N^M$$
$$\downarrow$$
$$R_j = N^M$$

Therefore, when the loop terminates after j iterations, R will contain the value N^M and thereby satisfy the output assertion. The entire problem of proving the algorithm's correctness has thus been reduced to achieving an inductive proof of the loop invariant relationship.

Inductive Proof

Now we will work through the inductive proof of

$$R_k \times N^{M_k} = N^M$$

Basis Step with k = 0. Before looping begins, $R_0 = 1$ and $M_0 = M$ since these are the values of the variable established by the input assertions. Hence the loop invariant relationship for $k = 0$ becomes

$$1 \times N^M = N^M$$

which is trivially true.

Inductive Step. By the standard inductive assumption, we assume

$$R_k \times N^{M_k} = N^M$$

and attempt to show

$$R_{k+1} \times N^{M_{k+1}} = N^M$$

In going from the kth pass through the **while** loop to the $(k + 1)$st pass through the loop we have

$$R_{k+1} = R_k \times N \qquad \text{and} \qquad M_{k+1} = M_{k-1}$$

Hence

$$R_{k+1} \times N^{M_{k+1}}$$
$$= (R_k \times N) \times N^{(M_k - 1)}$$
$$= R_k \times N^{M_k}$$
$$= N^M$$

by the inductive assumption.

The inductive step thus completes the formal proof of the algorithm's correctness. Note how the pivotal point in the entire proof was the determination of the loop invariant. This determination drives the rest of the proof. We can summarize the steps involved in the overall proof as follows:

1. Specification of input assertions
2. Specification of output assertions
3. Specification of loop invariants, from which the output assertions follow
4. Proof (via induction) of the loop invariants.

What Do Proofs Really Prove?

One of the valid criticisms of our proof is that it proves correct an algorithm that is obviously correct to start with. This criticism can often be made of formal correctness proofs as they presently stand. That is, the present state of the art in *formal verification* methods has not advanced to the point where they are of value in most realistically complex situations. Other criticisms of the method include the following:

1. The proof method assumes the correctness of the input and output assertions. If they are wrong, a proof of the program could be done but the program could still contain errors.
2. The proof method says nothing about how the program will act when exceptional conditions occur that deviate from the input assertions.
3. The proof method focuses only on the logic within an individual module. It verifies nothing with respect to how the modules of a system will interact.
4. The proof method relies on a completely accurate interpretation of the action dictated by a given algorithmic statement. This action is often called the *semantics* of the statement. If our interpretation of a statement's semantics does not match what actually happens when the program runs, the program may result in an error even though it has been proved correct.

A NOTE OF INTEREST

Program Verification: Is It Possible?

According to mathematical logician Jon Barwise, an article by University of Minnesota–Duluth, philosopher James Fetzer has touched off a debate that could be "just as exciting and just as acrimonious" as the debates about the nature of mathematics that raged in the early twentieth century. Fetzer's article, entitled "Program verification: The very idea" appears in the September 1988 issue of the *Communications of the ACM* (Volume 31, No. 8: 1048–1063). In it, Fetzer argues that computer programs, as "encodings of algorithms that can be compiled and executed by a machine," defy formal proofs of correctness in the sense discussed in Section 13.4 of this text. Arguing from the premise that "the function of a program is to satisfy the constraints imposed by an abstract machine for which there is an intended interpretation with respect to a physical system," Fetzer argues that "the behavior of that system cannot be subject to conclusive absolute verification but requires instead empirical inductive investigation to support inconclusive relative verifications."

To a degree, Fetzer's article can be viewed as an attack on much of the research being done in formally proving the correctness of programs. As such, it has been the subject of heated criticism from many computer scientists. For instance, one letter of response signed by 10 computer scientists from institutions including the University of Maryland, Cornell University, and Stanford University blasted the *Communications* for even publishing Fetzer's article:

However, by publishing the ill-informed, irresponsible, and dangerous article by Fetzer, the editors of *Communications* have abrogated their responsibility, to both the ACM membership and to the public at large, to engage in serious enquiry into techniques that may justify the practice of computer science as a socially responsible engineering endeavor. The article is ill-informed and irresponsible because it attacks a parody of both the intent and the practice of formal verification. It is dangerous because its pretentious and ponderous style may lead the uninformed to take it seriously [*Communications of the ACM*, Volume 32, No. 3 (March 1989): 287–288].

The war of letters and responses over Fetzer's article raged on in the April 1989 *Communications of the ACM*. At issue appears to be the role of abstract reasoning about algorithms in ensuring the correctness of software that runs on real-world machines. Like many philosophical questions, those raised by Fetzer will probably never be answered to the satisfaction of everyone involved in the debate. Nonetheless, as pointed out by Michael Evangelist, a senior researcher in software technology at MCC in Austin, Texas, "Fetzer has helped to draw the distinction better between reasoning about physical objects and about abstractions of those objects."

5. Practical machine limitations such as round-off and overflow are usually not considered in formal correctness proofs.

6. Proof techniques ignore the problem of unwanted side effects caused by an algorithm. Such side effects may result in an error in the overall system even though each module has been proved correct.

7. Proofs of nonnumerical algorithms such as searching and sorting are much more difficult than proofs of numerical algorithms. [These criticisms are set forth in more expanded form in Glenford Myer, *Software Reliability* (New York: Wiley & Sons, 1976), pp. 319–320.]

Formal correctness proofs must currently be considered as a technique that is mostly of theoretical importance. They simply are not sophisticated enough to find practical application in programs that solve realistically complex problems. However, a technique should not be rejected because it currently has little practical value. Many useful methods in computer science had their roots in pure theory. Perhaps the ultimate hope for the formal correctness methods we have discussed is that they can be automated. That is, in the future we may have software that receives input/output assertions as its input, generates the code to satisfy these assertions, and then proves the correctness of the code. Though it is obviously a long way from happening, such automatic program synthesis does not seem to be impossible in principle. (The potential of formal methods in algorithm verification is the feature topic in the September 1990 issues of *IEEE Computer* and *IEEE Software*.)

1. Use the method of inductive assertions to prove the correctness of the following algorithm:

```
// Function: difference
// Computes the difference of two integers
//
// Inputs: two integers
// Output: an integer representing the difference of
// the two input values

int difference (int x, int y)
{
        int result = x;
        int w = y;

        while (w > 0)
        {
                result--;
                w--;
        }
        return result;
}
```

2. Use the method of inductive assertions to prove the correctness of the following algorithm:

```
// Function: cube
// Computes the cube of an integer
//
// Inputs: an integer
// Output: an integer representing the cube of the input value

int cube(int x)
{
        int a, b, c, result;

        a = 1;
        b = 0;
        c = x;
        result = 0;
        while (c > 0)
        {
                result = result + a + b;
                b = b + 2 * a + 1;
                a = a + 3;
                c--;
        }
        return result;
}
```

3. Could an algorithm that has been proven correct by formal verification methods still produce a "wrong answer" when it is implemented in a particular programming language on a particular machine? Provide a written rationale for your answer.

13.5   Object-Oriented Design

In Chapters 7 and 8, we introduced object-oriented design as a way of building new data types. We saw that thinking of a new data type as a set of objects possessing encapsulated attributes and behavior and representing the new type as a C++ class is an excellent way to build a safe, maintainable, and reusable data type. Thus far in this text, however, we have not said anything about applying the principles of object-oriented design beyond the construction of individual data types. We will first discuss the use of object-oriented design to supplement the methods of software engineering introduced in this chapter. Then we will mention some methods that have been proposed to design entire systems along object-oriented lines.

The Place of Object-Oriented Design in the Software Life Cycle

Most of the currently existing software systems have not been designed with object-oriented methods. Many of them have been designed using the methods of analysis we have discussed so far in this chapter. Most systems have not been implemented in a purely object-oriented language, either; most are implemented in languages that support few, if any, object-oriented features. Even systems written in a hybrid language like C++ (with many object-oriented features) may consist of many modules that are not object oriented. For all of these reasons, it is important to consider how object-oriented design methods might be used in the context of more conventional methods such as the ones we have discussed so far.

The most obvious candidates for object-oriented design in a system are the modules that implement data structures. We first conceive these as abstract data types possessing attributes and behavior, which the servers or implementors provide to the clients or users. The benefits of designing or retooling existing ADTs along object-oriented lines are obvious: We gain flexibility in maintenance and reuse. For example, the one-key table class can be reused to implement a two-key table class, or it can be extended as a new subclass that supports traversal operations on its elements. As we saw in Chapter 12, good object-oriented design provides generic types that can be specialized for different applications, and it provides layered systems of types and abstract module interfaces throughout a system.

In the context of a conventional design, we might think of some of the modules in a data flow diagram or structure chart as consisting of classes or subsystems of classes. Each module is responsible for providing services to its clients; each module is responsible for properly using the servers on which it depends. In a hybrid language like C++, modules that are represented as classes can be coupled very nicely with parts of a system that are not strictly represented as classes, reflecting all of the specifications provided by data flow and structure charts. For example, the student table module that is at the center of the data flow diagram in Figure 13.2 is a class that provides attributes and behavior to the rest of the system. Supplementing a traditional structured design with object-oriented methods can reduce the amount of time spent in the implementation and testing phases, leaving more time for careful analysis and design.

Pure Object-Oriented Design

Recent research in software engineering has pointed to the desirability of designing entire software systems along object-oriented lines. According to this view, an entire system should consist of objects that interact as specified by their abstract attributes and behavior. The classes of objects in most systems of this kind fall into three major categories:

1. *Interface classes.* These classes are responsible for handling interaction between the system and its end users. A good example of this kind of class is the standard C++ **iostream** class for handling input and output of text. More sophisticated classes would be required for managing interactions among a mouse, windows, pull-down menus, and graphical icons. In the analysis and design phases, the end users are also considered to be objects with their own attributes and behavior. The end users are thus integrated into a model of the software system as clients of the interface classes.

2. *Entity classes.* These classes model real objects in a domain, such as bank accounts, personnel records, and lists of these. The classes that we have been using in applications that are not entirely object oriented are of this kind. Entity classes are also considered to be clients of the interface classes, insofar as the interface classes represent or display models of the entities to end users.

3. *Control classes.* These classes capture patterns of behavior that control the flow of data within an application. A good example is a menu-driven command interpreter. The input to the interpreter may come from an interface object that handles the display of a menu and the input of a command from an end user. The interpreter would then decode the command and dispatch a message to an entity object, such as a database, to perform some action. The entity object might then send a return message to the interpreter concerning the success of the action performed, so that the controller object could take the appropriate action.

Once analysts have decided which classes are necessary to model a system, an initial prototype can be constructed immediately from existing interface, entity, and control classes. This prototype is then iteratively extended and refined by adding new classes or derived classes to the system.

The design of large systems using object-oriented methods is a subject that you will explore in software engineering courses. In the rest of this text, we will use a combination of conventional and object-oriented analysis and design techniques that should prepare you for further work in software construction.

EXERCISES 13.5

1. Study the data flow diagram in Figure 13.2 and list which modules can be represented as classes, and which modules are simply operations.

2. Redesign the system depicted in Figure 13.2 so that it is entirely object oriented. Begin by classifying the modules into interface, entity, and control modules. This may require you to merge some of the modules that denote simple operations into one module denoting a class. As you go, be sure to base your classifications on the roles and responsibilities each module has to the others as client or server. At the end of the process, you should have a simplified diagram.

3. Define your interface and control modules from the previous exercise as C++ classes.

In this section, we complete an important part of the design of the registrar's system as begun in Example 13.2. In particular, we must develop the modules for representing the data structures used by the system. In object-oriented terms, these are the entity classes of the system. There are really just two kinds of entity in the system, a student and a table of students. We first specify the attributes and behavior of the student class, and then represent it as a C++ class definition. Then we do the same for the table class.

In the registrar's system, a student has five attributes, a name, total credits taken, total credits earned, total grade points, and a grade-point average. A name is a string of characters. Total credits taken and earned are integers. Total grade points and grade-point average are real numbers. The registrar must be able to create new student records with appropriately initialized attributes, be able to view these attributes, and be able to modify every attribute except for the student's name and grade-point average. The student object itself will be responsible for computing the grade-point average as a function of the other data in the record.

In addition, other clients of the student class, such as the table of students, must be able to compare two student objects by grade-point average (GPA), for purposes of ordering them for a traversal. All that the client needs to know in order to detect the ordering is whether or not two student's GPAs are in descending order. This operation is specified as a Boolean function. The complete behavior of the student class is specified in the following set of abstract operations:

Create operation

Preconditions: Receiver is a student in an unreliable state. **name** is the student's name. **gpa** is the student's grade point average.

Postcondition: Receiver is initialized with **name** and **gpa**.

get_name operation

Preconditions: Receiver is a student.

Postconditions: **name** returned.

get_gpa operation

Preconditions: Receiver is a student.

Postconditions: **gpa** is returned.

get_credits_earned operation

Preconditions: Receiver is a student.

Postconditions: **credits_earned** is returned.

get_credits_taken operation

Preconditions: Receiver is a student.

Postconditions: **credits_taken** is returned.

get_grade_points operation

Preconditions: Receiver is a student.

Postconditions: **grade_points** is returned.

set_credits_earned operation

Preconditions: Receiver is a student. **value** is the new total credits to be inserted.

Postconditions: **value** replaces **credits_earned** currently in the receiver.

set_credits_taken operation

Preconditions: Receiver is a student. **value** is the new total credits to be inserted.

Postconditions: **value** replaces **credits_taken** currently in the receiver.

set_grade_points operation

Preconditions: Receiver is a student. **value** is the new total credits to be inserted.

Postconditions: **value** replaces **grade_points** currently in the receiver.

Print operation

Preconditions: Receiver is a student.

> Postconditions: **name, credits_taken, credits_earned, grade_points,** and **gpa** have been printed on the terminal screen.
> **gpa_order operation**
> Preconditions: Receiver and **s** are students.
> Postconditions: Returns TRUE if receiver's **gpa >= s**'s **gpa**, or FALSE otherwise

The C++ class declaration module for **student** is

```
// Class declaration file: student.h

#ifndef STUDENT_H

#include "boolean.h"
#include "strlib.h"

// Declaration section

// We assume that types boolean and string are already defined.

class student
{
        public:
        // Class constructors

        student(string new_name, float new_gpa);
        student(const student &s);

        // Member functions

        string get_name();
        float get_gpa();
        int get_credits_taken();
        int get_credits_earned();
        float get_grade_points();
        void set_credits_taken(int value);
        void set_credits_earned(int value);
        void set_grade_points(float value);
        void print();
        boolean gpa_order(const student &s);
        student & operator = (const student &s);

        private:

        // Data members

        string name;
        float gpa, grade_points;
        int credits_earned, credits_taken;

};

#define STUDENT_H
#endif
```

The implementation module for the student class is left as an exercise.

Now we must decide how to define the list of students for the registar's system. We defined a one-key table class in Chapter 2 that supports keyed retrievals but no ordered traversals. We could start from scratch and make a new ADT to order for our application, but that would be wasting time and effort in reinventing a wheel that may already be available in our ADTs. By reusing one of them to solve our problem, we will illustrate an important point about object-oriented design.

We would like to use the fast, keyed retrieval operation of a one-key table, but also be able to traverse the data in the table in a specified order. We accomplish these two goals by extending the behavior of a one-key table as a new derived class. We call this derived class a *traversal table*. A traversal table has all of the attributes and behavior of a one-key table. In addition, it has a specialized traversal operation. This operation visits every data value in the table in the order specified by the client, and applies a client's operation to each data value. Thus, the traversal operation will expect two parameters:

1. A specification of the way in which the data values should be ordered for traversal
2. A specification of the operation to be applied during the traversal.

Both of these parameters will be operations. Here is a specification of the abstract traversal operation:

Traverse operation
Preconditions: Receiver is a traversal table. **compare**, which takes two data values as arguments, is the operation to be used to order the data values for traversal. **process**, which takes a single data value as an argument, is the operation to be applied to each data value during the traversal.
Postconditions: **process** has been applied to each data value in the receiver, according to the order specified by **compare**.

Note that a traversal table is just a one-key table that is traversable by some ordering mechanism within the data values. Storing, retrieving, and deleting data from this table still assume an ordering by a primary key value.

To represent a traversal table as a C++ class template, we define it as a derived class of the one-key table class template. The **traverse** operation must be specified as a member function declaration having two parameters of type *pointer to function*. We first present the declaration and then discuss it:

```
// Class declaration file: travtab.h

#ifndef TRAV_TAB_H

#include "onetable.h"

// Declaration section

template <class K, class E> class traversal_table :
     public one_key_table<K, E>
{
```

```
    public:

    // Class constructors

    traversal_table();
    traversal_table(const traversal_table<K, E> &table);

    // Member functions

    traversal_table& operator = (const traversal_table<K, E> &table);

    void traverse(boolean (*compare) (const E &item1, const E &item2),
            void (*process) (E &item));

    protected:

    // Data members

    int pointers[MAX_TABLE_SIZE];

    // Function members

    void prepare_to_traverse(boolean (*compare) (const E &item1,
            const E &item2));

};

#define TRAV_TAB_H
#endif
```

Note that the formal parameter list of the member function **traverse** has two parameters of type pointer to function. Be careful to enclose the ***<function name>** notation within parentheses so that C++ evaluates the operators in the right order. Note also that the base class is extended by adding a new data member, an array of integers. This array will be used to save the results of a pointer sort whenever the table is prepared for traversal.

The implementation of the **traverse** operation consists of two steps:

1. Call the protected member function **prepare_to_traverse** with the ordering function as a parameter. **prepare_to_traverse** performs a pointer sort on the table, leaving the pointers appropriately arranged in the protected data member **pointers.**
2. Loop through the data member for the table itself, using as index positions the pointers in the **pointers** data member, and apply the **process** function to the value at each position.

Here is the code for the top-level member function **traverse**:

```
template <class K, class E>
void traversal_table<K, E>::traverse(boolean (*compare) (const E &item1,
        const E &item2), void (*process) (E &item))
{
```

```
                              E value;

                              prepare_to_traverse(compare);
                              for (int i = 0; i < table_length; ++i)
                              {
                                      value = data[pointers[i]].get_value();
                                      process(value);
                              }
                      }
```

Note that the argument passed to **prepare_to_traverse** in this function is the name of the function, **compare**, to be used to order the data values for traversal. The implementation of **prepare_to_traverse** uses **compare** to perform a pointer sort:

```
template <class K, class E>
void traversal_table<K, E>::prepare_to_traverse(boolean (*compare)
    (const E &item1, const E &item2))
{
    int j, k, temp;
    boolean exchange_made;
    E value1, value2;

    // Initialize pointer array

    for (k = 0; k < table_length; ++k)
            pointers[k] = k;

    k = 0;
    exchange_made = TRUE;

    // Make up to n - 1 passes through array, exit early if no exchanges are made
    // on previous pass

    while ((k < table_length - 1) && exchange_made)
    {
        exchange_made = FALSE;
        ++k;
        for (j = 0; j < table_length - k; ++j)
        {
            value1 = data[pointers[j]].get_value();
            value2 = data[pointers[j + 1]].get_value();
            if (compare(value1, value2))
            {
                temp = pointers[j];        // Swap pointers
                pointers[j] = pointers[j + 1];
                pointers[j + 1] = temp;
                exchange_made = TRUE;
            }
        }
    }
}
```

A NOTE OF INTEREST

IBM and Apple = Pinstripes and T-Shirts

After signing the Treaty of Amiens in 1802, Napoleon said, "What a beautiful fix we are in now; peace has been declared." In July 1991, representatives of IBM and Apple announced an alliance that similarly shocked many industry analysts. IBM has long been positioned in the mainstream of the computer industry, gaining its reputation more from selling the reliability of its corporate image than from technological innovation. Apple, on the other hand, has based its claim to fame on bold new technologies developed by computer enthusiasts with a distinct bent toward "hacking." For instance, the window-based environment of the first Apple Macintosh in 1983 established a new and exciting mode of human–computer interaction. When IBM and Microsoft later "copied" the "look and feel" of the Mac environment to an IBM-compatible operating system, Apple promptly took them to court in a case whose effects on the software industry are still being debated.

Small wonder that eyebrows have been raised by the agreement between these two corporate antagonists. What are the underlying reasons for the move? According to joint press releases, the companies will cooperate on four fronts:

1. IBM will take steps to better integrate the Mac into IBM-based computer networks.
2. Apple will build future machines using IBM's RISC architecture chip technology.
3. The companies will work together on developing data standards for multimedia.
4. There will be a joint endeavor to produce a new, object-oriented operating system that will eventually be marketed for both IBM and Apple computers.

The last of these ventures is the one that seems to be generating the most excitement on an industry-wide basis. The two companies had been working individually on object-oriented operating systems. Apple had been calling their exploratory system Pink; IBM had called theirs Metaphor. It now appears that the Pink and Metaphor research groups will combine their efforts, with the long-range goal that users and third-party software developers will only have to deal with one common interface for a variety of different machines from the two companies. By taking advantage of the abstraction emphasized by the object-oriented approach, the details of the particular machine will be completely hidden.

It all sounds good in theory, but can researchers from two such historically different companies really define a common set of goals? If they can, will it destroy their own individual initiatives? Only time will tell.

RUNNING, DEBUGGING AND TESTING HINTS

1. When testing a large program, always test modules individually before testing the entire system.
2. When developing test cases, keep them in a file so that they can be used again easily after fixing errors.
3. The finite state machine paradigm is a systematic way of ensuring that users enter valid input to your program.
4. Be sure to design test data that exercise the boundary conditions of a module, which is is where an error is most likely to occur.

SUMMARY

Key Terms

acceptance testing	finite state machine	stub module
analysis	functionally cohesive	systems analyst
black box testing	iterative prototyping	system testing
boundary conditions	maintenance	test cases
coding phase	modular testing	test oracle
coupling	pointer to function	testing phase
data flow diagram	prototype	transitions
documentation	robust	traversal table
driver module	state-transition diagram	white box testing
equivalence classes		

Key Terms (Optional)

formal verification	loop invariant	method of inductive assertions

Key Concepts

◆ During the analysis phase of the software system life cycle you must determine the user's requirements. Typically, this involves considerable interaction between the systems analyst and end user. A data flow diagram is one example of a document that would be developed during this phase. Ultimately, the user's requirements must be described in a form suitable to pass on to the design phase.

◆ During the design phase, the user's requirements are examined, and the system that will ultimately meet these requirements begins to take shape. Software designers must turn out a blueprint of the eventual software system that can then be translated into program code. Typical of the documents produced during the design phase are modular structure charts, layout of data structures, and modular logic specifications.

◆ A good design is developed in a top-down fashion. Individual modules within the design should be functionally cohesive: They should focus on one particular task. Modules within the design should be minimally coupled; they should not transfer more information than necessary between themselves. This avoids the possibility of one module inadvertently affecting data being used by another.

◆ Testing and verification can consume up to 50% of the time spent in developing a software system. Each module should be tested as it is finished. Use drivers to feed inputs into the module and stubs to check the module's interactions with subordinate modules.

◆ System and acceptance testing follows modular testing.

◆ The maintenance phase of a system follows its release to users. During this phase, adjustments must be made to the system in response to bugs and changes in user requirements.

◆ Obsolescence is the sixth, and ultimately inevitable, phase of the software system life cycle.

Key Concepts (Optional)

◆ Formal algorithm verification by such methods as inductive assertions is of theoretical interest now and offers promise of more reliable software in the future.

1. Design a complete set of modular test cases for the system in the Focus on Program Design section. Be as thorough as possible in your testing; pay particular attention to robustness issues. Wherever your testing locates an error, modify the code to fix it. (An interesting class experiment for this program is to turn it into a contest. The student who finds and fixes the most errors wins.)

2. Invite the registrar of your university to your class to discuss the type of data processing operations in which the registrar's office is typically engaged. After this discussion (which should no doubt include time for questions), describe the data involved in the operations of your registrar's office in terms of abstract data types. Develop a data flow diagram to picture the way in which the registrar's office processes information.

3. Consider the following data declaration and function declaration.

```
enum kind_of_triangle {SCALENE, ISOSCELES, EQUILATERAL, IMPOSSIBLE};...

// Function: triangle_type
// Task: determines the type of triangle, given the lengths of the three sides
//
// Inputs: three integers representing the lengths of the three sides of a triangle
// Output:
//    EQUILATERAL, if all sides are equal
//    ISOSCELES, if two sides are equal
//    SCALENE, if all sides are different lengths
//    IMPOSSIBLE, if the integers do not constitute valid triangle sides

kind_of_triangle triangle_type (int side1, int side2, int side3);
```

For this problem, work with another student. Each of you should develop independently, first, a robust version of the function just described and, second, a complete set of test data (including robustness checks) for the function. Next, jointly develop a driver program and test your functions. Have your partner use his or her test data on the function you developed. Then use your test data on your partner's function. The winner is the one whose function fails for the fewer number of test cases.

4. In Exercise 8 of Section 13.2 you designed a system for the registrar at American Basket Weaving University. Implement and fully test that system.

5. In Exercise 10 of Section 13.3 you developed and tested a module to read strings that are valid file names on your particular computer system. Incorporate this module into a larger program that could be used to back up text files. The user should enter two file names: a source file and a destination file. Your program should then copy from the source to the destination. If your file name module does its job correctly, your program should never crash because it tries to access an "invalid file name."

6. In Chapter 8, you developed a program that allowed its user to enter rational numbers and then perform operations on them. Now make your program more user-friendly and robust by reading all rational numbers entered by the user in a module **read_rational**. The logic of this module should be driven by a finite state machine that filters out erroneous input. Submit a diagram of the finite state machine as part of the documentation accompanying your program.

7. In Chapter 8, you developed a program that allowed its user to enter complex numbers and then perform operations on them. Now make your program more user-friendly and robust by reading all complex numbers entered by the user in a mod-

ule `read_complex`. The logic of this module should be driven by a finite state machine that filters out erroneous input. Submit a diagram of the finite state machine as part of the documentation accompanying your program.

8. Assume that you would like to make some extra cash by writing a program to facilitate some activity for a particular business, organization, or school. Write a proposal that clearly explains what your program will do, how much it would cost, why the purchase of this program would be beneficial to the institution, and how soon you could complete this project. Be sure to limit your project so that it does not exceed your ability as a programmer.

9. Research the topic of formal methods in algorithm verification, using the September 1990 issues of *IEEE Computer* and *IEEE Software* as initial references. Then write a paper in which you discuss the role that formal algorithm verification may play in future software development. Your paper should address such issues as how formal verification can reduce the amount of time spent in testing software and how it can be used to ensure a degree of software reliability exceeding what can be achieved by testing alone. Be sure to respond to the criticisms of formal verification summarized in Section 13.4.

10. Interview a systems analyst at a local company or organization. Then, write a paper or prepare a presentation in which you describe the techniques used by that systems analyst to determine user needs and to document these user needs in written or diagrammatic form.

11. The September 1990 issue of *Communications of the ACM* was dedicated to the topic of object-oriented programming. Using the articles in this issue as a starting point, write a research paper in which you describe how software development will be affected by the object-oriented paradigm. Your paper should discuss such issues as building software libraries that are usable in a variety of contexts and building software systems that are easily extended when the need to do so arises.

CHAPTER 14 Linked Lists and Pointers

These are the ties which, though light as air, are strong as links of iron.
Edmund Burke
(1729–1797)

In the previous chapters we discovered that an array implementation (with binary search) of a one-key table requires $O(n)$ data interchanges for the add and delete operations. Attempting to maintain such an array-implemented list in order parallels the dynamics of waiting in a long line. When someone cuts into the middle of the line, there is a domino-like effect that forces everyone behind that person to move back. When someone in the middle of the line decides to leave the line, the reverse effect occurs; everyone behind the departed person is able to move ahead one slot. It is possible to draw an analogy between people waiting in a line and data items stored next to each other in computer memory. If the data items are arranged in some type of order and it becomes necessary to insert into or delete from the middle of the line, a considerable amount of data movement is involved. This data movement requires computer time and decreases program efficiency. The central motivation behind the linked list data structure is to eliminate the data movement associated with insertions into and deletions from the middle of the list. Of course, by now we might suspect that efficiency in eliminating such data movement can only come by trading off other efficiency factors. One of the crucial questions to ask yourself as we study linked lists is "What price are we paying to handle additions and deletions effectively?"

One way of conceptually picturing a linked list is to think of a game some parents use to make the opening of holiday gifts particularly exciting for their children. One feature of the game that helps to build children's anticipation ensures that minor gifts are opened first, gradually building up to the most substantial gift. (Recall from your own childhood experience the partial letdown that occurred when you opened a gift package containing a mere pair of socks after having already unwrapped something significantly more exciting such as a box of candy.) Thus, the premises of this gift-giving game are that gifts may be ranked according to their desirability and that the game is more fun when the most desirable gifts are opened last.

To achieve this end, parents will hide their child's wrapped gifts at various locations throughout the home. For instance, let us suppose a scenario in which parents have bought the following four gifts for their child, which are ranked and hidden as indicated:

Ranking	Gift	Hiding Place
Least desirable	Pair of socks	Under bed
↓	Box of candy	Kitchen drawer
	Video game	Basement cabinet
Most desirable	Bicycle	Garage

The parents will then tell the child *only* the location of the least desirable gift; here, for instance, they would give instructions to look under a bed for the first gift. Upon opening that gift, the child will find the uninspiring pair of socks *plus* a more intriguing note with the information that the child's next gift will be in a kitchen drawer. The pattern should now be obvious. From the box of candy, the child follows an informational pointer to a basement cabinet, where the video game is discovered along with a similar informational link to the garage as a location where something bigger and better may be found. Here the now-eager child will uncover a bike along with a final (and no doubt disappointing) note indicating that the end of the chain of gifts has been reached.

A conceptual picture of this chain of gifts is presented in Figure 14.1. This same conceptual picture applies to the *linked list* abstract data structure we are about to study. In this figure, the arrows connecting packages represent the informational note in each package that tells us the location of the next package. Conceptually, the form taken by this informational pointer is not important. However, it is crucial that we have a reliable *pointer* to the leading gift (often called a *head pointer*) and, thereafter, a reliable pointer in each package (often called a *node*) to the next package. Should any pointer be flawed, the remaining gifts on the chain become essentially inaccessible (much to the dismay of the child who wanted that bike so desperately).

◆ FIGURE 14.1
A linked chain of gifts

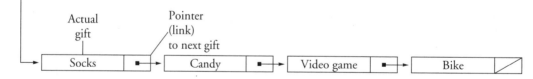

In addition to introducing us to much of the vernacular that comes with linked lists, this review of a simple childhood game can also give us a hint of the ease with which such a linked chain of nodes can handle additions and deletions. For instance, suppose that a sudden windfall allows the parents of the child in our example to buy a baseball glove in addition to the four gifts they had already purchased. Assuming that this new gift is ranked between the video game and the bicycle in desirability, consider what must be done to link it into the gift chain. We must do the following:

1. Find a place to hide it, for example, the attic.
2. Take the informational linking note from the video game package and put it in the baseball glove package. (Why?)

◆ **FIGURE 14.2**
Adding a baseball glove to
the chain of Figure 14.1

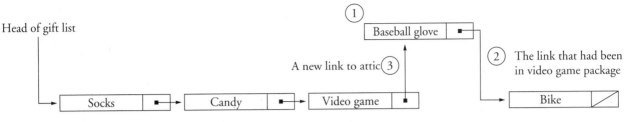

3. Insert a new informational pointer in the video game package, indicating the attic as the location of the next node. (Why?)

Figure 14.2 portrays such an addition with circled numbers corresponding to the three steps just described. The important aspect to note in this series of moves is that no gift that was already in place had to be moved to accommodate adding the new gift. From a conceptual perspective, this is why linked lists will be able to avoid the movement of data that was associated with an insertion into an array-implemented list.

Along the same lines, let us now suppose that our shameless parents devour all of their child's candy before the holiday arrives. Clearly they must remove this package from the chain to hide this disgusting behavior from their child. Using Figure 14.3, convince yourself that the following steps will accomplish this deletion:

1. Remove the now-empty candy package from the kitchen drawer.
2. Before throwing away the empty package, remove the linking note from it and put this note in the package containing the socks.
3. Dispose of the incriminating candy container and the linking note that originally was in the package with the socks.

◆ **FIGURE 14.3**
Removing candy from the
chain of Figure 14.2

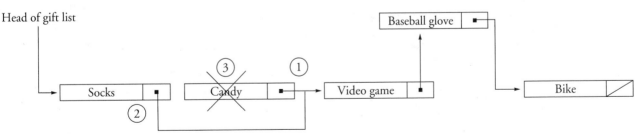

It is important to note again that no package remaining on the chain had to be physically moved to a new location—a situation much different from what happened when we removed a name from an array-implemented list in the last chapter.

Have we strayed too far from computer science in using such a nontechnical, elementary example to introduce our chapter on linked lists? Not at all! In fact, we've achieved two very important goals. First, if you understand all the details of the gift-giving game, then you essentially understand the important concepts involved in the linked list data structure. Second, this is just another illustration of the fact that computer techniques are often just formalizations in a logic machine of the way we, as human beings, have been doing things for many years. Consequently, you should never feel intimidated by such a computer technique; merely try to relate it to an analogous—and familiar—manual method. Doing this will help give substance to the more formal computer science method.

14.1 The Linked List as an Abstract Data Type

OBJECTIVES

- to formalize the notion of a linked list as an ADT
- to understand, at an abstract level, why a linked list allows additions and deletions of nodes with minimal data movement
- to realize, at an abstract level, the price paid in search efficiency for the efficiency gained in adding and deleting nodes
- to realize that, although a linked list may be viewed as an ADT, it is also a data structure that can be used to implement other ADTs, such as one-key tables

Recall from Chapter 12 that to specify an abstract data type (ADT) formally, we must describe the individual elements of the structure, the relationship(s) between these elements, and the logical operations to be performed on the structure.

A formalization for the intuitive notion of a linked list follows. This formalization uses the terminology *linear ordering*. By linear ordering, we mean any ordering of data in which there is an identifiable first element, second element, and so forth. For instance, a string could be viewed as a linear ordering of characters. Also, a one-key table has a linear ordering determined by key values. It is important to realize that linear ordering is a logical concept; it need not coincide with physical ordering of data.

Linked list: A linked list is a collection of elements called nodes. Each node contains a data portion and a pointer. The data portions in all nodes are of the same type. The pointer in a given node contains the location of the node that follows the given node in the linear ordering of the list. The entire list is referenced by a separate head pointer to the first node in the linear ordering. The head pointer is simply the location of this first node. It is not a linked list node and hence has no data associated with it. A special value designated as **NULL** is assigned to a pointer that references an empty linked list. The last node in the ordering contains a null pointer, indicating that there is no node following it. To facilitate movement through a linked list and access to nodes, a linked list also contains two special pointers, called **previous** and **current**. When the list is empty, these pointers each have the value **null**. When the list contains at least one node, **head** always points to the first node. Following an insertion operation, **current** points to the most recently inserted node. Following a removal operation, **current** points to the node after the most recently deleted node (or **NULL** if this was the last node in the list). Following a **next** operation, **current** points to the next node after the previous current one (or **NULL** if this was the last node in the list). **previous** either points to the node before the current node, or is **null** when the list is empty or when **current** points to the first node in the list. A linked list also has a **length** attribute, which records the current number of nodes in the list.

The operations that can be performed on a linked list are:

Create operation
Preconditions: Receiver is a linked list in an unpredictable state.
Postconditions: **head**, **previous**, and **current** are all set to **NULL**, and **length** is set to zero, so the list is considered empty.

Destroy operation
Preconditions: Receiver is a linked list.
Postconditions: Any existing nodes in the list are returned to the heap. **head**, **previous**, and **current** are all set to **NULL**, and **length** is set to zero, so the list is considered empty.

Empty operation

Preconditions: Receiver is a linked list

Postconditions: `empty` returns TRUE if receiver contains no nodes and FALSE otherwise.

At_end operation

Preconditions: Receiver is a linked list.

Postconditions: `at_end` returns TRUE if `current` points to the last node in the list and FALSE otherwise.

Length operation

Preconditions: Receiver is a linked list

Postconditions: `length` returns the number of nodes currently in the list.

Next operation

Preconditions: Receiver is a linked list.

Postconditions: If `current` is not `NULL`, `previous` is set to `current` and `current` is set to point to the next node or to `NULL` if there is no next node. Otherwise, no action.

First operation

Preconditions: Receiver is a linked list.

Postconditions: If `head` is not `NULL`, `current` is set to `head` and `previous` is set to `NULL`. Otherwise, no action.

Retrieve operation

Preconditions: Receiver is a linked list and `item` is a variable that will return the data in the current node.

Postconditions: If `current` is not `NULL`, the data in the node pointed to by `current` is returned in `item` and the operation returns TRUE. Otherwise, the operation returns FALSE and `item` is undefined.

Insert operation

Preconditions: Receiver is a linked list and `item` is the value to be inserted.

Postconditions: If there is enough memory for a new node, `item` is placed in a new node, the new node is inserted before the node that `current` points to, `current` is set to point to the new node, and `length` is incremented. If `current` originally pointed to `head`, `head` is also set to point to the new node.

Remove operation

Preconditions: Receiver is a linked list and `item` is a variable that will return the removed data.

Postconditions: If `current` is not `NULL`, then the current node is removed from the list, `previous` is set to `current`, `current` is set to the next node (or `NULL` if the removed node was the last one in the list), `item` is set to the removed node's data field, and `length` is decremented. If the removed node is the first node in the list, then `head` is set to the next node also. If `current` is `NULL`, no action. If the item is removed, the operation returns TRUE. Otherwise, the operation returns FALSE and item is undefined.

Traverse operation

Preconditions: Receiver is a linked list, `compare` is a function of two element arguments that specifies the desired ordering for the traversal. `process` is a function of one element argument to be applied to each element during the traversal.

Postconditions: `process` is applied to the data in each node in the list, in the order specified by `compare`.

◆ FIGURE 14.4

Actions of some linked list
operations

Figure 14.4 depicts the action of the **create, next, insert, first, last, retrieve, remove,** and **traverse** operations on a linked list of integers. Study this figure carefully and observe that every linked list will have three pointers associated with it. After the **create** operation, the pointers for the resulting empty list are **NULL**. For a list that is not empty, the pointer in the final node on the list is **NULL**. Note the distinction between a pointer that is **NULL** and a pointer that is undefined. The former reliably indicates a reference to an empty structure through a specific flagging value. The latter is completely unreliable in terms of what it references.

The figure also indicates that insertion into and deletion from a linked list require a pointer to the node to be acted on and a pointer to the node that precedes this node in the linear ordering of the list. For both of these operations, the pointer to the preceding node is necessary since the pointer within that node must be

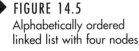

FIGURE 14.5
Alphabetically ordered
linked list with four nodes

altered as part of the operation. For example, in Figure 14.4, when we insert 46 after the node containing 19, the node containing 19 is altered by having its pointer reference the node containing 46 instead of the node containing 63. This alteration of the node containing 19 requires that we have a pointer (**previous**) that references it. In the event that the insertion or deletion occurs at the front of the list, the **previous** pointer is set to **NULL** to signal this special condition.

Finally, Figure 14.4 illustrates that the linear ordering of the linked list may not necessarily coincide with the natural ordering of data in the list. In this figure, the linear ordering of the list is not in correspondence with either ascending or descending order by integer value. What defines the linear ordering will vary from application to application.

One application we can immediately envision is to use a linked list as an implementation technique for the one-key table ADT. The linear ordering established by the links would mirror the order determined by the key fields in the nodes. For instance, Figure 14.5 depicts a linked list in which the links establish an alphabetical ordering according to key field.

The operations of adding a node and deleting a node from such a list may also be conveniently represented in such a schematic form. In fact, you will soon discover that the best way to conceive algorithms that manipulate linked lists is to draw what you want to happen via such logical pictures. Such a picture of a linked list is completely at the abstract level; it implies nothing about how the linked list will finally be implemented. Once you understand the concept from such a graphic representation, it is usually a straightforward matter to implement it.

For instance, we now wish to add a node containing PRIM to the list shown in Figure 14.5; all we need to do is to store PRIM in an available memory location outside of the list, such as the one pointed to by **p** in Figure 14.6. We then reset the pointer link of the node containing MARTHA to point to the node containing PRIM, and the pointer link of the node containing PRIM to point to the node containing SAM. This logically maintains the alphabetical order of the data in the nodes without physically moving any of the existing nodes.

Similarly, should you then wish to delete an existing node from the linked list, a graphic representation of the list can again indicate how the pointers should be altered to reflect such a change. For example, given the list of Figure 14.6, the diagram of Figure 14.7 pictorially outlines what must be done if we want to delete the node containing MARTHA. Notice in this figure that, as was the case for insertion, only pointers must be changed to delete a node. Again, no movement of data occurs.

The **destroy** operation is a special function used with classes that rely on dynamic memory, and is discussed in Section 14.3.

Efficiency Considerations for Linked Lists

These addition/deletion considerations may make a linked list an attractive alternative to an array implementation of a one-key table. The diagrams of Figures

◆ **FIGURE 14.6**

Insertion of node containing
PRIM into linked list of
Figure 14.5

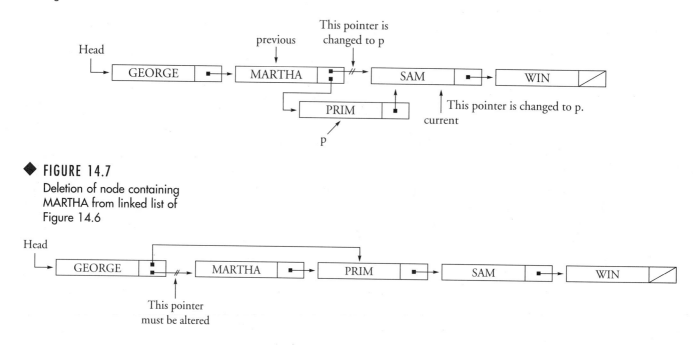

◆ **FIGURE 14.7**

Deletion of node containing
MARTHA from linked list of
Figure 14.6

14.6 and 14.7 indicate that insertions and removals merely require the exchange of two pointers. Since pointers are merely locations of other nodes, this means that we are usually manipulating mere integers or similarly simple data in doing such pointer operations. Hence, both additions and deletions would appear to be $O(1)$ operations in terms of data movement for linked lists. This compares very favorably to the massive movement of entire records that was forced by an addition or deletion on an array implementation of a list. In general, such insertion and removal operations will be $O(n)$ in terms of data movement in an array implementation of a list.

Despite this substantive advantage, you should proceed cautiously and not be too quick to adopt the linked list as a cure for all the ills involved with list-oriented systems. The experience you have already gained should make you suspicious that there has to be a trade-off involved to get this superior efficiency for insertion and removal operations. Here the price we pay is to give up random access to the nodes in the list. For example, to access the fourth node, we must follow the head pointer to the first node, the first node's pointer to the second, and so on, until we reach the fourth node. Hence, any operation that requires finding a particular node on the list will essentially have to invoke a sequential search algorithm.

The superb $O(\log_2 n)$ search efficiency that was possible with an array implementation of a list cannot be approached with a linked implementation of the same list because the binary search algorithm we used to achieve this efficiency requires random access into the list. Instead we must settle for the $O(n)$ efficiency of the sequential search. Note that this is even a deterring factor in insertion and removal operations because, typically, an appropriate spot in the list must be found before the addition or deletion can occur. Although the addition or deletion itself may require only $O(1)$ data movements, an $O(n)$ search must usually precede it. At best, if we order the data in the nodes randomly, all insertions could be at the beginning of the list, causing an $O(1)$ amount of work.

Despite this search inefficiency, linked lists can be used to tremendous advantage when implementing lists that are highly *volatile,* that is, lists that frequently undergo insertions and deletions. If the percentage of these operations is sufficiently high in relation to requests for finding and inspecting nodes, then the linked implementation will probably pay off.

Before proceeding, we should clarify one point regarding linked lists as an ADT. That is, although a linked list may be viewed from this abstract perspective, it also represents an implementation strategy for more general linear structures such as the one-key table ADT. In that sense, we can compare the linked list to the array implementation of a one-key table, which we have already studied, and to several other list implementation schemes, which we will present in future chapters.

Thus, a linked list is, from one perspective, an implementation strategy; from another, it's an abstract structure. This is entirely consistent with what we have said regarding the progression from abstraction to implementation that you go through as a designer of layered software systems. The linked list provides another implementation option for the representation of more general linear structures. But it remains an abstraction because we have not yet described how we shall implement a linked list. We turn our attention to these implementation considerations in the next section.

C++ Interface for the Linked List ADT

To develop an implementation of the linked list ADT, we provide a class declaration module. We will define a generic linked list class, parameterized for the type of data to be stored in the nodes:

```
// Class declaration file: linklist.h

#ifndef LINK_LIST_H

// Declaration section

#include "boolean.h"

template <class E> class linked_list
{

    public:

    // Class constructors

    linked_list();
    linked_list(const linked_list<E> &list);

    // Class destructor

    ~linked list();

    // Member functions
```

```
                 boolean empty();
                 boolean at_end();
                 int length();
                 void first();
                 void next();
                 boolean retrieve(E &item);
                 void insert(const E &item);
                 boolean remove(E &item);
                 void traverse(boolean (*compare) (const E &item1,
                        const E &item2), void (*process) (E &item));
                 linked_list<E>& operator = (const linked_list<E> &list);

                 // Protected data and member functions pertaining to
                 // the implementation would go here.

        };


        #define LINK_LIST_H
        #endif
```

EXERCISES 14.1

1. In what way is the data structure involved with the pointer sort in Chapters 11 and 12 not a linked list?

2. What are the advantages and the disadvantages of a linked list implementation of a one-key table compared to a physically ordered array implementation?

3. What are the advantages and disadvantages of a linked list implementation of a one-key table compared to an implementation that uses an unordered array with sequential search?

4. What are the advantages and the disadvantages of a linked list implementation of a one-key table when we use it to implement a two-key table?
   For Exercises 5 through 13, use *only* the C++ interface to the linked list ADT to write appropriate program segments.

5. Given that the element type is **int**, write a process function parameter for the traverse operation that will print the square root of each number in a linked list.

6. Given that the element type is **int**, write a process function parameter for the traverse operation that will print the value of each positive number in a linked list. Numbers in the list that are not positive should not be printed.

7. Given that the element type is **int**, write a loop that starts at the beginning of a linked list and returns the position of the first list node with the value zero in its data field. If no such node exists in the list, a zero should be returned.

8. Write a loop that applies a process function to each data value in a linked list, from the first to the last.

9. Write a function **sum** to sum the integers in a linked list of integers.

10. Write a function to remove all of the nodes in a linked list.

11. Write a function called **append** that takes two lists as parameters. The function should tack the contents of the second parameter onto the end of the first parameter. When the function returns, the first parameter should contain the contents of both lists, and the second parameter should be an empty list. Be sure that the operation handles the limiting cases of empty list parameters correctly (appending an empty list with a nonempty list should yield a list containing the data of the non-empty list).

12. Write a function called **merge** that receives two linked lists of integers arranged in ascending order. Your function should merge these two lists into a single list, also arranged in ascending order. The merged list should be returned as a third parameter.

13. Suppose you sort a list of input values by reading them in one at a time and inserting them into a linked list arranged in ascending order. Clearly, after you have read all of the input values you will have a sorted list. Let's call this algorithm the *linked list sort.* Analyze the time efficiency of this algorithm in terms of number of comparisons and number of data interchanges. Compare its efficiency to that of the other sort algorithms we have studied—insertion, bubble, selection, and radix sort.

14.2 Pointer Variables and Dynamic Memory Management in C++

Perhaps the biggest drawback of implementing linear data structures as arrays is the static nature of the memory storage associated with an array. Suppose, for example, we declare an array data of size 100. Then the storage in the array is static in the sense that it is allocated at the time the program is compiled, before it actually runs. Because of this, we are charged for 100 locations whether or not they are all used at run time. When we have only 50 objects to process in the array, 50% of the memory allocation is being wasted. Even more serious is the limitation that, if we have more than 100 objects to process, we must edit and recompile the program using a larger array size.

C++ pointer variables, on the other hand, are an example of a technique known as *dynamic memory management.* A feature that is not available in many older languages such as FORTRAN, COBOL, and BASIC, dynamic memory management is used by C++ to allow the programmer to claim only that amount of memory which is actually needed at that point during run time.

To understand dynamic memory management, we must first understand the configuration of memory when your program is loaded into it from an external file. As indicated in Figure 14.8,there are memory costs that must be paid in addition to the storage space required for the object code of your program. In particular, memory must have room to accommodate:

- Various operating system requirements
- A stack used by the operating system for function processing (to be explained in Chapter 15)
- The object code of your program; that is, the machine-language version of your program's instructions.

Notice that the three memory components listed generally will not consume all of the available computer memory. What remains is called the *heap.* Unless you have already used the dynamic memory allocation scheme of a language like C++, your programs have never been able to get at the heap and take advantage of it. With C++'s pointer variables, all this changes.

Working with Pointer Types and Variables

If we focus on a type definition for a moment, we see that a pointer type is defined in terms of a *base type.* The base type is the type of value pointed to by the pointer value. A pointer type to an integer could be defined as

```
typedef int *int_ptr_type;
```

◆ FIGURE 14.8

Computer memory configuration for typical program

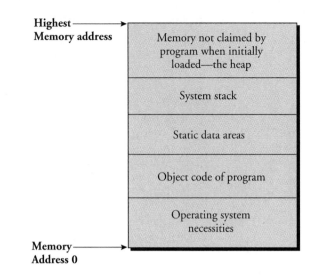

where **<base type name>** is the name of any C++ data type and **<pointer type name>** is any legitimate C++ identifier.

The declaration

```
int_ptr_type int_ptr;
```

declares **int_ptr** as a pointer variable. **int_ptr** cannot be assigned values of type **int**; **int_ptr** can only contain addresses of locations whose values are of type **int**. The code

```
typedef float *float_ptr_type;

float_ptr_type float_ptr;
```

defines a pointer type to a real number and declares a pointer variable that can hold the address of a real number.

The pointer variables **int_ptr** and **float_ptr** can also be declared without defining pointer types, as follows:

```
int *int_ptr;

float *float_ptr;
```

Initializing Pointer Variables

A null pointer is represented in C++ as the value 0. By convention, we use the symbolic constant **NULL** in this text to refer to the null pointer. You can define this constant with

```
const int NULL = 0;
```

or by including either the C++ library **stdlib.h** or the C++ library **stddef.h**:

```
#include <stdlib.h>
```

A pointer variable can be initialized in several ways:

1. Any pointer variable can be set to the **NULL** value. For example,

`ptr = NULL;`

will accomplish this.

2. Any pointer variable can be assigned the value of another pointer variable, as long as the two variables are of the same pointer type. Two pointer types are the same if they have the same base type. Thus, if **ptr1** and **ptr2** are variables of the same pointer type, the assignment

`ptr2 = ptr1;`

will copy the pointer value stored in **ptr1** into **ptr2**.

3. Any pointer variable can be initialized to point to a value of its base type. This is accomplished by using the operator **new**. For example,

`ptr = new int;`

has the effect of storing a pointer to an integer value in **ptr**. The state of the computer's memory can be depicted as

ptr   Location for
      integer value

Actually, **ptr** contains an address of a place where an integer value can be stored. We will see how to store an integer value in this place shortly. The general form for using **new** to initialize a pointer variable is

<pointer variable> = new <base type>;

where the pointer variable's type has the same base type as **<base type>**. When we use **new**, we essentially ask the system to allocate memory for storing a value of the pointer's base type. This memory is *dynamic,* because it was not reserved when the pointer variable was declared. In other words, **new** is a run-time request for memory. You are not charged for the memory requested until you ask for it, and you are not charged for an excess of memory that you may not even need for this particular run of the program.

After a call to **new** for a suitably declared pointer variable **ptr**, **ptr** is a memory address. As such, its actual value is of little concern to you. Suffice it to say that it is an address somewhere in the heap. How the heap manager was able to arrive at such an address involves a system-dependent process.

Verifying Memory Allocation

When the system processes a call to **new** from a program, it goes to the heap to allocate an area of the appropriate size for storing a new data value. The heap might be a large area of memory in most systems, but its size is finite. Therefore, after repeated calls to **new**, the memory available for dynamic allocation will be used up. To avoid errors, a program can check to see whether this is the case and take the appropriate action. When heap memory is still available, **new** returns a pointer to a chunk of this memory. If there is no more heap memory, **new** returns the **NULL** value. In programs that use a large amount of dynamic memory, the following kind of code is recommended:

```
        ptr = new base_type;
        if (ptr != NULL)
                process(ptr);
        else
                cout << "Error: no dynamic memory available." << endl;
```

where **process** indicates operations that access the area of memory pointed to by **ptr**. Alternatively, you might use the following code to halt program execution if the heap has no memory:

```
        ptr = new base_type;
        assert(ptr != NULL);
```

We will see shortly how to return unused dynamic memory from a program to the heap in order to mitigate this problem.

Defining Pointer Types and Declaring Pointer Variables

The previous definitions and declarations of pointer types and pointer variables are relatively uncomplicated; however, in actual practice, pointer types and variables are a bit more complex. For example, in the next section we will define a pointer to a data structure where one of the members in the data structure is a pointer to a data structure of the same type. These data structures are called *nodes,* and represent a very common use of pointers in programming. To define a node, we can use a C++ *structure definition.* An example is

```
struct node;                    // Empty structure definition introduces
                                // identifier for node.
typedef node *node_ptr;         // Type definition of type pointer to a node.

struct node                     // Completion of structure definition of a node type.
{
        int data;
        node_ptr next;
};


node_ptr ptr;                   // Declaration of a variable that can point
                                // to a node.
```

Notice that the completed structure definition specifies two *members* or pieces of data: an integer named **data** and a pointer to another node named **next**. You will frequently want each structure to point to another structure. Using a structure definition with one member for a pointer permits this. The use of a structure definition with pointers is so common in programming that we will specify its conventional form:

```
struct <node type name>;
typedef <node type name> *<node pointer type name>;
struct <node type name>
{
        <member declaration 1 for data stored in node>
        .
        .
        .
        <member declaration N for data stored in node>
        <node pointer type name> next;
};
```

Several things call for comment:

1. **struct** is a reserved word.
2. The components within the curly braces are called the *members* of the structure or node. They are similar to the data members of a class, except that they are treated as public here.
3. There may be several members of the node that contain the data stored there, such as names, phone numbers, and so forth. In this text, however, we will always store a single, perhaps complex, data object in a node.
4. There should be a member of the node that points to another node of the same type. Its name conventionally is **next**. In more complex structures, such as a *doubly linked list,* we would have a member called **previous** that points to the previous node in the list.
5. The structure definition ends with a semicolon (;) following the curly bracket (}).
6. A new type should always be defined to point to the node type. This is the purpose of the **typedef** immediately following the empty structure definition.

After a pointer to a node structure has been declared, it can be initialized. First, we use **new** to allocate dynamic memory for the structure:

```
ptr = new node;
```

Then we have to initialize the data and next members within the node. We use the *arrow operator,* **->**, for this with a node. This operation is also called a *dereference operation.* For example, we might input the integer value from the keyboard, and set the next pointer to **NULL** with an assignment:

```
cin >> ptr->data;
ptr->next = NULL;
```

Alternatively, we could use the *dereference operator,* *****, to accomplish the same things:

```
cin >> *ptr.data;
*ptr.next = NULL;
```

In this text, we will generally use the arrow operator to access the contents of nodes.

The state of the computer's memory after a node has been created and initialized is

Node pointer   Node

ptr   ptr->data ptr->next

The general form for using the **->** operator is

<pointer to a node>-><member name>

You should be careful to assign **NULL** to the **next** member when initializing structures of this sort. If you are forming a list of dynamic variables where each dynamic variable contains a pointer variable for pointing to the next one, you can use **NULL** as a way to know when you are at the end of a list.

`get_node`: A Useful Function

Because it is so important to initialize nodes properly and this is done so often in working with linked lists, we should design a function that makes this task simple and consistent. Whenever we need a new node for a linked list, we will call this function. The function takes as its parameter the data to be placed into the new node. It returns as its value a pointer to the new node. There are two postconditions that the caller of this function can count on:

1. The data sent to the function will be stored in the **data** member of the node.
2. The **next** member of the node will be set to **NULL**.

Assuming that the node should contain data of type **element**, our function would be called as follows:

```
ptr = get_node(data);
```

Assuming that it returns a pointer of type **node_ptr**, the function's declaration would be

```
// Function: get_node
// Gets a new node containing data
//
// Input: data to be stored in the node
// Output: a pointer to the node containing the data

node_ptr get_node(element data);
```

Assuming that **element** is the name of the type of data to be stored in the node, the function's implementation would be

```
node_ptr get_node(element data)
{
    node_ptr temp = new node;

    temp->data = data;
    temp->next = NULL;
    return temp;
}
```

As you can see, the **get_node** function hides a fair amount of low-level code that would have to be written every time a programmer needs a new node for a list. This is a good example of a function that can make programs more readable and safe.

For applications that use a large amount of dynamic memory, a "safer" **get_node** function would check the success of the **new** operation and halt execution if no more memory is available in the heap:

```
node_ptr get_node(element data)
{
    node_ptr temp = new node;

    assert(temp != NULL);
    temp->data = data;
    temp->next = NULL;
    return temp;
}
```

Some additional examples will serve to clarify the logic involving pointer variables.

EXAMPLE 14.1	Suppose we have a pointer type and two pointer variables, **p** and **q**, established by the following declarations:

```
struct node;
typedef node *node_ptr;

struct node
{
        int data;
        node_ptr next;
};

    node_ptr p, q;
```

and that a **get_node** function has been defined for nodes containing integer data. Describe the effect of the following sequence of instructions:

```
p = get_node(1);
```
{1}

p → [1 | ⧄]

```
q = get_node(2);
```
{2}

q → [2 | ⧄]

```
p->next = q;
```
{3}

p → [1 |] → [2 | ⧄]
                      ↑
                      q

```
p->data = 5;
```
{4}

p → [5 |] → [2 | ⧄]
                      ↑
                      q

```
p->next->data = 6;
```
{5}

p → [5 |] → [6 | ⧄]
                      ↑
                      q

```
p->next->next = get_node(7);
```
{6}

p → [5 |] → [6 |] → [7 | ⧄]
                  ↑
                  q

The easiest way to describe such code is to visualize its effect. Consequently, we provide an answer in the form of a series of snapshots, identified by the bracketed number that marks each line of code.

EXAMPLE 14.2	Given the declarations in the previous example, write the code that will create 10 nodes, containing integer values 1 through 10, and link them together in ascending order of data.

Obviously, we will need a loop that cycles through the specified range of integer values. On each pass through the loop, we get a new node with the current loop control value as data and link it into its proper place in the list. Our strategy for linking is to place each new node at the beginning of the list. Before we start the loop, we assume that the list (pointed to by **p**) contains one node whose data value is 10. Therefore, we must use a **for** loop that counts down from 9 to 1. We use **q** as a temporary pointer to each new node while we rearrange pointers to link it into the list:

```
p = get_node(10);
for (int i = 9; i <= 1; --i)
{
        q = get_node(i);
        q->next = p;
        p = q;
}
```

The effects of the three statements within the loop when **i** equals 9 are visualized below. Note the importance of the order in which the pointers are rearranged. We do not assign a new value to **p**, the head pointer to the entire list, until the next pointer of the new node has been aimed at the node currently at the beginning of the list.

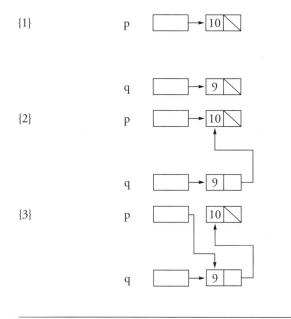

Clearly, programming with C++ pointer variables requires you to have an accurate mental image of the effects of each instruction. Faced with a bug, you must carefully draw linked list pictures and manually execute your code against those pictures until you find the instruction that is going awry.

Other Operations on Pointer Variables

When you use the operator **new** to initialize a pointer variable, you are asking for dynamic memory to hold a value. This memory should be used as needed, and then returned to the system for other use when not needed. To return a piece of dynamic memory to the system, you use the operator **delete**, as follows:

```
delete ptr;
```

The states of the computer's memory before and after this statement can be depicted as

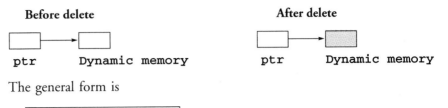

Before delete   **After delete**

ptr   Dynamic memory   ptr   Dynamic memory

The general form is

> delete <pointer variable>;

After you have returned a piece of dynamic memory to the system, you should not attempt to access a value in it with a pointer variable. It is possible to do so, but you will not be able to tell that you are now looking into deallocated space. Other parts of a program may now use this dynamic memory for their purposes. The pointer variable's value should be treated as unpredictable after a **delete**. The pointer should be reinitialized with either **NULL** or **new** before it can be used further.

Once they have been initialized, pointer variables can be compared for equality and inequality. For example, suppose pointer variables **p** and **q** have both been initialized to the **NULL** value. Then the comparison **(p == q)** will be TRUE, while the comparison **(p != q)** will be FALSE. The comparisons **(p == NULL)** and **(q == NULL)** will both be TRUE. Let's assume now that **q** is reset to point to an area of dynamic memory, with **q = new int**. Then the comparison **(p == q)** will be FALSE.

In general, you should remember that pointer variables contain the addresses of other areas of memory. Although C++ supports arithmetic and output operations for pointer variables, for our purposes, the only useful operations will be assignment, comparison, dereference, and return of dynamic memory to the system.

EXERCISES 14.2

Exercises 1 through 6 refer to the following data declarations:

```
struct node;
typedef node *node_ptr;

struct node
{
        int data;
        node_ptr next;
};

node_ptr a, b, c;
```

1. Specify which of the following statements are syntactically correct. For those that are wrong, explain why they are wrong.

   a. a = b;

   b. a = a->data;

   c. a = a->node_ptr;

   d. delete a;

   e. delete b->data;

   f. delete b;

2. Show how the schematic would be changed by each of the following:

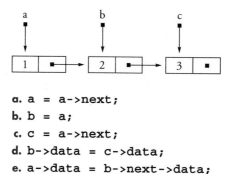

   a. a = a->next;
   b. b = a;
   c. c = a->next;
   d. b->data = c->data;
   e. a->data = b->next->data;
   f. c->next = a;

3. Write one statement to change

to

4. Consider the following list:

Write code to create a new linked list element with value 12 and insert it at the beginning of the list headed by **a**.

5. Consider the following list:

Write code to remove the element at the head of the list and then add this element at the end of the list.

6. Indicate the output for each of the following:
   a. a = new node;
     b = new node;
     a->data = 10;
     b->data = 20;
     b = a;
     a->data = 5;
     cout << a->data << " " << b->data << endl;
   b. c = new node;
     c->data = 100;
     b = new node;
     b->data = c->data % 8;
     a = new node;
     a->data = b->data + c->data;

```
            cout << a->data << " " << b->data << " " << c->data
                << endl;
        c. a = new node;
           b = new node;
           a->data = 10;
           a->next = b;
           a->next->data = 100;
           cout << a->data << " " << b->data << endl;
```

14.3 Implementing the Linked List ADT with C++ Pointer Variables

Now that we have covered the syntax and use of C++ pointer variables, we are ready to use them to provide an implementation for the linked list ADT. We begin by specifying the data members and protected utility functions in the linked list class definition module presented in Section 14.1:

```
// Class definition file: linklist.h

#ifndef LINK_LIST_H

// Declaration section

#include "boolean.h"

template <class E> class linked_list
{

    public:

    // Class constructors

    linked_list();
    linked_list(const linked_list<E> &list);

    // Class destructor

    ~linked_list();

    // Member functions

    boolean empty();
    boolean at_end();
    int length();
    void first();
    void next();
    boolean retrieve(E &item);
    void insert(const E &item);
    boolean remove(E &item);
    void traverse(boolean (*compare) (const E &item1,
        const E &item2), void (*process) (E &item));
    linked_list<E>& operator = (const linked_list<E> &list);

    protected:
```

```
// Data members

struct node;
typedef node *node_ptr;

struct node
{
    E data;
    node_ptr next;
};

int list_length;
node_ptr head, current, previous;

// Member functions

node_ptr get_node(E item);
```

```
};
```

```
#define LINK_LIST_H
#endif
```

Note that we define the new type names, **node** and **node_ptr**, which we discussed earlier. They are defined only for the use of the linked list class and its derived classes. Like the protected variable and function names, they are encapsulated within the class definition. The next few examples illustrate how the linked list operations are implemented by using the types **node** and **node_ptr**.

EXAMPLE 14.3

According to the abstract definition, creating a new linked list object requires setting the three pointers, **head**, **current**, and **previous**, to **NULL**, and setting **list_length** to zero:

```
template <class E>
linked_list<E>::linked_list()
{
    head = NULL;
    current = NULL;
    previous = NULL;
    list_length = 0;
}
```

Note that no new memory is allocated for nodes at this time, since the linked list should be empty. The state of a new linked list in the computer's memory is depicted as

list_length   0

head

previous

current

EXAMPLE 14.4

Three linked list operations, **empty**, **at_end**, and **length**, simply examine attributes of the list and return the appropriate information:

```
template <class E>
boolean linked_list<E>::empty()
{
     return list_length == 0;
}

template <class E>
int linked_list<E>::length()
{
     return list_length;
}

template <class E>
boolean linked_list<E>::at_end()
{
     return (current != NULL) && (current->next == NULL);
}
```

Note that the function **at_end** returns TRUE just when **current** points to a node and the **next** pointer of that node is **NULL** (this will be the last node in the list). The use of short-circuit evaluation in the Boolean expression in the **if** statement prevents the system from accessing a node's contents when **current** is NULL.

EXAMPLE 14.5

The linked list operation **next** should have the effect of moving both the **current** and **previous** pointers ahead in the list, if possible:

```
template <class E>
void linked_list<E>::next()
{
     if (current != NULL)
     {
          previous = current;
          current = current->next;
     }
}
```

The state of the computer's memory before and after this operation on a list containing two nodes is depicted as

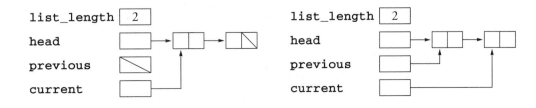

Note these two important things about this example:

1. We should always check to see whether a pointer really points to a node before attempting to access that node's contents with a dereference operation.
2. The order in which **previous** and **current** are reset is critical. If we moved **current** before moving **previous**, they would both point to the same node.

EXAMPLE 14.6

The abstract definition of the **insert** operation says that if there is enough memory for a new node, **item** is placed in a new node, the new node is inserted before the node that **current** points to, **current** is set to point to the new node, and **list_length** is incremented. If **current** originally pointed to **head**, **head** is also set to point to the new node. Because there are so many postconditions in this definition, we start with a pseudocode algorithm:

Get a new node with item as data
Set the next pointer of the new node to current
If current points to the first node (is equal to head)
        Set head to point to the new node
Else
        Set the next pointer of the previous node to point to the new node
Set current to point to the new node
Increment the length of the list

Because the new node will be placed before the node that **current** points to, the **next** pointer of the new node should first be aimed at this node. If **current** is **NULL** at this point, the node is being placed at the end of the list and the **next** pointer of the new node will remain **NULL**. Then we ask if we are inserting at the beginning of the list or somewhere else. If we are at the beginning, we redirect the **head** pointer to the new node. If we are somewhere else, then the **previous** pointer will point to the node after which our new node will be placed. Therefore, we aim the **next** pointer of the previous node at the new node. After we have considered these alternatives, we update the **current** pointer and the length of the list appropriately. The C++ code for this algorithm follows:

```
template <class E>
void linked_list<E>::insert(const E &item)
{
        node_ptr new_node = get_node(item);

        new_node->next = current;
        if (current == head)
                head = new_node;
        else
                previous->next = new_node;
        current = new_node;
        ++list_length;
}
```

The process of inserting a node in the middle of a linked list is depicted as follows:

Step 1: new_node = get_node(item);

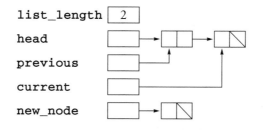

Step 2: new_node ->next = current;

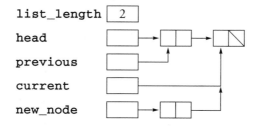

Step 3: previous->next = new_node;

Step 4: current = new_node;

Step 5: ++list_length;

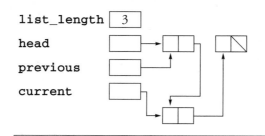

EXAMPLE 14.7

The abstract definition of the **remove** operation says that if **current** is not **NULL**, then the current node is removed from the list, **current** is set to the next node, **item** is set to the removed node's data field, and **list_length** is decremented. If the removed node is the first node in the list, then **head** is set to the next node also. If **current** is **NULL**, then there is no action. If the item is not removed, **item** is undefined.

Once again, the number of postconditions for the operation forces us to develop a pseudocode algorithm before coding in C++:

> If current is not NULL
>> Set item to the data in the current node
>> Set a temporary pointer to current
>> If current points to the first node
>>> Set head pointer to next pointer in current node
>> Else
>>> Set next pointer in previous node to next pointer in current node
>> Set current to next pointer in current node
>> Return removed node to system heap with temporary pointer
>> Decrement length of list
> Return TRUE
>
> Else
>> Return FALSE

The critical moves in this process are saving the data in the return parameter and keeping a temporary pointer to the node about to be removed. Recall that once a node has been returned to the system heap, we should not attempt to access its contents, either for the data or for the next pointer value. However, once the node is unlinked from the list, we need to locate it to return it to the heap. In general, a node should be returned to the heap only after its contents have been processed. Note also that we do not have to update the **previous** pointer, because the deleted node was located between the new current node and the previous node, if there was one. The C++ code is

```
template <class E>
boolean linked_list<E>::remove(E &item)
{
        node_ptr old_node = current;

        if (current != NULL)
        {
              item = current->data;
              if (current == head)
                    // Node at beginning of list
                    head = current->next;
              else
                    // Node in middle or at end of list
                    previous->next = current->next;
              current = current->next;
              delete old_node;
              --list_length;
              return TRUE;
        }
```

```
        else
            return FALSE;
}
```

The process of removing a node from the middle of a linked list is depicted as follows:

Step 1: old_node = current;

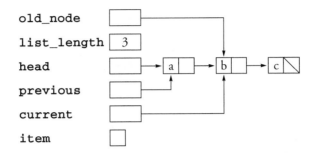

Step 2: item = current->data;

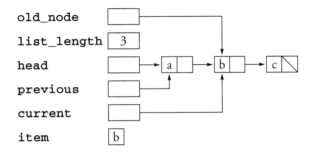

Step 3: previous->next = current->next;

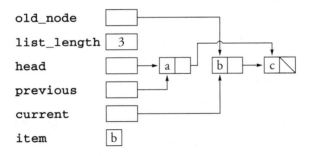

Step 4: current = current->next;

Step 5: delete old_node;

Step 6: --list_length;

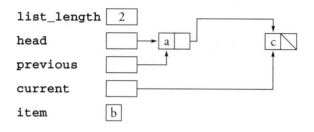

EXAMPLE 14.8   The implementation of the **get_node** function should closely resemble the one
we constructed in Section 14.2. The only complication is that **node_ptr** is not
globally defined, but rather is defined within the **linked_list** class. Therefore,
we prefix it with the class name so that the compiler can recognize it:

```
template <class E>
linked_list<E>::node_ptr linked_list<E>::get_node(const E &item)
{
        node_ptr temp = new node;

        assert(temp != NULL);
        temp->data = item;
        temp->next = NULL;
        return temp;
}
```

We consider the implementation of the **traverse** operation in Section 14.4.

The Copy Constructor for Linked Lists

The copy constructor for linked lists should create new nodes for the receiver
object and insert elements from the parameter object into them so that the order of
the elements in the two lists is the same. These requirements are accomplished by
iterating through the nodes of the parameter object and advancing the current
pointer of the receiver object after each insertion of a data element from the
parameter's current node:

```
template <class E>
linked_list<E>::linked_list(const linked_list<E> &list)
{
```

```
node_ptr probe = list.head;
node_ptr new_node, last;
list_length = 0;
head = NULL;
current = NULL;
previous = NULL;
while (probe != NULL)
{
        new_node = get_node (probe->data);
        if (head == NULL)
            head = new_node;
        else
            last->next = new_node;
        last = new_node;
        if (probe == list.previous)
            previous = last;
        else if (probe == list.current)
            current = last;
        probe = probe->next;
        ++list_length;
}
}
```

Note that the copy constructor copies the relative positions of the **current** and **previous** pointers of the parameter **list** to the receiver object.

Class Destructors and Memory Leakage

Consider the following function definition:

```
void leak_memory()
{
        linked_list<int> list;

        for (int i = 1; i < 10; ++i)
            list.insert(i);
}
```

This function appears to do nothing more than create a new linked list, store 10 integers in it, and return. However, because the implementation of the linked list class uses dynamic memory, an important side effect occurs: For each insertion operation that the client invokes, a piece of dynamic memory is obtained from the heap and used to insert a data element into the list. Thus, when this function returns, 10 pieces of dynamic memory have been taken from the heap and are no longer available for other clients. This phenomenon is called memory leakage, and is a common cause of errors in programs that use dynamic memory. If this function were called frequently enough, the computer would eventually run out of heap memory.

The best way to guard against memory leakage is to provide a class destructor for each class that uses dynamic memory. A class destructor declaration looks just like a default class constructor declaration, except that a tilde (~) precedes the declaration. The implementation of the destructor should contain code for returning any dynamic memory used by an instance to the heap. In the case of linked lists, the destructor would traverse the nodes and return each one to the heap with `delete`:

```
linked_list::~linked_list()
{
        node_ptr garbage;
        node_ptr probe = head;
        while (probe != NULL)
        {
                garbage = probe;
                probe = probe->next;
                delete garbage;
        }
        list_length = 0;
        head = NULL;
        current = NULL;
        previous = NULL;
}
```

If a destructor is defined for a class, the computer will automatically invoke it when the scope of a linked list variable or value parameter is exited. Thus, the function `leak_memory` returns after the computer has run the destructor function to deallocate the memory used for the `list` variable.

A NOTE OF INTEREST

Garbage Collection

Programs that make frequent use of dynamic memory can be error-prone. One kind of error that can occur is the failure to return pieces of dynamic memory to the heap when they are no longer needed. If this failure occurs often enough, the program will run out of memory, perhaps at a critical point in its task.

To avoid the problem of memory leakage, some programming languages have been designed so that the programmer does not have to worry about returning unused memory to the heap at all. The run-time system for these languages has a special module called a garbage collector that automatically recovers unused dynamic memory when it is needed.

Two such languages, Smalltalk and LISP, rely on dynamic memory for all of their data structures, so an automatic garbage collector is an essential part of their design. In Smalltalk, a pure object-oriented language, dynamic memory is used to create new objects. In LISP, which supports a linked list as a standard data structure, dynamic memory is used to add data elements to a list. When an application in either of these languages asks for a new piece of dynamic memory, the computer checks the heap to see whether the request can be satisfied. If not, the garbage collector is invoked, and all of the unused memory locations are returned to the heap. Then the request is granted, if enough dynamic memory is now available.

The garbage collection mechanism works roughly as follows. Every memory location is marked as either referenced by the application or not. A memory location is referenced if it is named by a variable or is part of a linked structure pointed to by such a variable. When memory is allocated for variables, it is marked as referenced. When memory becomes completely unlinked from any variable references in a program, it is marked as unreferenced. Thus, only unreferenced memory locations will be candidates for being returned to the heap.

Garbage collection in early versions of LISP and Smalltalk sometimes degraded the performance of a program. During a collection, an application would appear to pause for a moment while the mechanism did its work. This is one reason why Smalltalk and LISP applications have not received much play in industry, where efficiency in time-critical tasks is a priority. However, much research and devlopment has produced very efficient garbage collection algorithms, so that LISP and Smalltalk programs now perform as well as programs written in languages without any garbage collector.

1. Implement the **retrieve** operation for the linked list class.

2. Test the linked list class with a C++ driver program that inserts five integer input values into the list (in random order) and then prints the contents of the list.

3. Test the list processing functions that you wrote in Exercises 5 through 12 of Section 14.1.

4. In Exercise 12 of Section 14.1, you wrote a function that merges the sorted contents of two linked lists into a third list. This function uses new memory, in that new nodes are generated for the result list. Implement and add a more efficient merge function to the linked list interface that uses no new memory. The receiver should be the first list, and the parameter should be the second list. After the process is completed, the receiver should contain the merged list, and the parameter should be returned as an empty list.

5. In Exercise 11 of Section 14.1, you wrote a function that appends the contents of one linked list to the end of another linked list. This function uses new memory, in that the contents of the two input parameters are copied over into a result list. Implement and add a more efficient append function to the list interface that uses no new memory. The receiver should be the first list, and the parameter should be the second list. After the process is completed, the receiver should contain the contents of the two lists, and the parameter should be returned as an empty list. (*Hint:* An implementation requiring the fewest pointer rearrangements would aim the next pointer of the last node in the first list at the first node in the second list).

6. The **append** operation in the previous exercise still takes linear time to locate the last node in the first list. Maintaining a pointer to the last node in a linked list would allow the append operation to be performed in constant time. Add a new attribute to the linked list ADT called **last** (this will be a new data member in the C++ class definition module). Then update the **create, insert, remove**, and **append** operations so that **last** always points to the last node in a linked list, if there is one.

7. A **last** operation would take advantage of the **last** pointer to move the current pointer to the last node in a linked list in constant time. Discuss whether our current implementation of a linked list ADT would support this new operation.

14.4 Traversing a Linked List

In Chapter 13, we discussed the problem of traversing the data elements in a one-key table in an order specified by alternative key values within the data. We solved the problem by designing and implementing a derived class of the one-key table called a traversal table. This derived class supports a traversal operation that takes two functions as parameters. One function specifies the ordering principle for the traversal, and the other function specifies the operation to be applied to each data element during the traversal. The traversal process consists of two steps: First, order the table, and then, visit each data value according to the new ordering. By using a pointer sort with an extra array, we were able to perform the ordering and traversal steps without altering the ordering by the key values by which the table was originally set up.

Rather than reinventing the wheel to solve the problem of traversing a linked list, we fit the strategy developed in Chapter 13 into the new context of pointers and linked lists. The original strategy in Chapter 13 maintains an array of indices that specifies the desired ordering of elements in a data array. In the context of array processing, these indices are actually used as pointers to locate data. If we could think of a way of maintaining a list of pointers (not integers, but real pointers) in the new context of pointers and linked lists, then we could reuse our pointer sort algorithm to order a linked list for traversal.

If we choose an array of `node_ptr` for our list, we run into an immediate problem. What should be the maximum size of this array? There is no maximum size of a one-key table now that we are using a linked list to implement it. We are faced with the problem that motivated the use of linked lists to begin with: In many cases, either we will waste memory with this new array or we will not have enough memory.

We can solve this new problem by representing the list of pointers as a dynamic data structure. With this representation, there will be just enough memory to store the pointers for a given linked list, and no more. However, we will not have to go to the trouble of implementing this structure as another linked list.

Dynamic Arrays in C++

Many programming languages present the programmer with only two alternatives for representing linear data structures: arrays of fixed size or linked lists implemented with pointers. C++ provides a third alternative that represents a hybrid of arrays and dynamic data structures. We call it a *dynamic array*. In C++, a dynamic array starts out as a pointer variable. For example, the following data declarations would set up a new dynamic array of integers:

```
typedef int *int_array;

int_array ints = NULL;
```

Note that the variable `ints` is of type pointer to integer and has been initialized to the `NULL` pointer. Thus, we have created a new, empty dynamic array of integers requiring almost no memory.

When we wish to store data in a dynamic array, we must ask for new memory cells from the heap. The only constraint is that we must know how many cells to ask for. This integer value is passed as a parameter to the **new** operator, and a new block of cells is returned to represent the array. In our example, if we needed an array of 10 integers, we would write

```
ints = new int[10];
```

The integer value within the square brackets can be any C++ integer-valued expression. The important thing to note is that this value can be computed at run time, so we have the kind of dynamic memory that fits our application. For example, a linked list implementation might use the statement

```
pointers = new node_ptr[list_length];
```

to create a dynamic array capable of maintaining the results of a pointer sort of the data in the linked list.

A robust program will ask whether or not the **new** operation successfully allocated storage for a dynamic array by comparing the returned result to **NULL**:

```
pointers = new node_ptr [list_length];
if (pointers == NULL)
        <take corrective action>
else
        <process pointers>
```

This error checking is perhaps more important in the case of dynamic arrays than in the case of individual nodes in a linked list, because of the large chunks of memory requested.

When **new** is passed a parameter specifying the number of new cells desired, we receive a *contiguous block* of new cells from the heap. This means that the cells of dynamic memory map directly to consecutive physical memory locations in the heap. Therefore, C++ allows us to use standard array indexing to locate individual cells within this data area. For example, we might initialize the **ints** dynamic array with zeros in the following loop:

```
for (int i = 0; i < 10; ++i)
    ints[i] = 0;
```

When we are finished with the use of a dynamic array for a given problem, we can return its storage to the heap by invoking the **delete** operator. For example, the storage for the **ints** array could be recycled with

```
delete ints;
```

This will have the effect of returning the entire contiguous block of storage to the system heap.

The important thing to remember about a dynamic array in C++ is that it is declared like a pointer but processed like an array. In the case where the array contains pointers to the nodes in a linked list, we could traverse the list by iterating through the array:

```
for (int i = 0; i < list_length; ++i)
    process(pointers[i]->data);
```

The dynamic array appears to be the perfect data structure for solving the problem of modifying the traversal table class to work with linked lists. This is a good example of the way in which choosing the appropriate data structure can ease the solution of a problem.

Implementing the Traversal

The first step in realizing our new design is to add a data member for the dynamic array of pointers to the linked list class declaration module:

```
// Class declaration file: linklist.h

#ifndef LINK_LIST_H

// Declaration section

#include "boolean.h"

template <class E> class linked_list
{

    public:

    // Class constructors

    linked_list();
    linked_list(const linked_list<E> &list);
```

```
    // Class destructor

    ~linked_list();

    // Member functions

    boolean empty();
    boolean at_end();
    int length();
    void first();
    void next();
    boolean retrieve(E &item);
    void insert(const E &item);
    boolean remove(E &item);
    void traverse(boolean (*compare) (const E &item1,
            const E &item2), void (*process) (E &item));
    linked_list <E>& operator = (const linked_list<E> &list);

    protected:

    // Data members

    struct node;
    typedef node *node_ptr;

    struct node
    {
            int data;
            node_ptr next;
    };

    int list_length;
    node_ptr head, current, previous;
    node-_ptr *pointers:                     // New data member

    // Member functions

    node_ptr get_node(E item);
    void prepare_to_traverse(boolean (*compare)
            (const E &item1, const E &item2));

};

#define LINK_LIST_H
#endif
```

Note that we do not bother to define a new type name with **typedef** for our new data member. We simply specify the type of data pointed to, **node_ptr**, and use the * symbol to indicate that the data member **pointers** will be a pointer to a data value of type **node_ptr**. We do not define a separate type name to go with **pointers** because no values of this type will ever be passed as parameters or returned as the values of functions.

Let us now work through several examples to show how we use the dynamic array of pointers in our new implementation.

EXAMPLE 14.9

Recall that the design of the member function **traverse** in Chapter 13 consists of two steps: Prepare the array of indices by performing a pointer sort on the data array, and then traverse the data array using the indices in the pointers array. In the new version, we use a similar, top-down strategy. We assume that another member function, **prepare_to_traverse**, performs the first step. Then we accomplish the traversal of the linked list by looping through the pointers in the array. In addition to these two steps, the new implementation is responsible for allocating storage for the array before it is used, and deallocating the storage when its usage is finished:

```
template <class E>
void linked_list<E>::traverse(boolean (*compare) (const E &item1, const E &item2),
        void (*process) (E &item))
{

    if (list_length > 0)                        // Go ahead if list not empty
    {
        pointers = new node_ptr[list_length];   // Allocate new
                                                // dynamic array

        prepare_to_traverse(compare);           // Do pointer sort
        for (int i = 0; i < list_length; ++i)   // Traverse linked list
            process(pointers[i]->data);         // via pointers in array
        delete pointers;                        // Deallocate dynamic array

    }
}
```

A more robust version of this function would verify that storage has been allocated for the dynamic array before continuing with the processing.

EXAMPLE 14.10

The **prepare_to_traverse** operation was described in the Focus on Program Design section of Chapter 13. It essentially performs a pointer sort on the data array. In the new version, it performs a pointer sort on a linked list. We lift the pointer sort algorithm from Chapter 13, place it under a new function heading for traversing linked lists, and make some minor changes to the body of the function:

```
template <class E>
void linked_list<E>::prepare_to_traverse
        (boolean (*compare) (E item1, E item2))
{
        int j, k;
        boolean exchange_made;
        node_ptr probe, temp;

        // Initialize pointer array

        probe = head;
        for (k = 0; k < list_length; ++k)
```

```
            {
                    pointers[k] = probe;
                    probe = probe->next;
            }

        k = 0;
        exchange_made = TRUE;

        // Make up to n - 1 passes through array, exit early if no
        // exchanges are made on previous pass

        while ((k < list_length - 1) && exchange_made)
        {
            exchange_made = FALSE;
            ++k;
            for (j = 0; j < list_length - k; ++j)
                    if (compare(pointers[j]->data, pointers[j + 1]->data))
                    {
                            temp = pointers[j];        // Swap pointers
                            pointers[j] = pointers[j + 1];
                            pointers[j + 1] = temp;
                            exchange_made = TRUE;
                    }
        }
    }
```

The first change occurs in the initialization of the array. We initialize the array by setting a temporary pointer, **probe**, to point to the first node in the linked list. Then we iterate through the array and the list, storing pointers and advancing the **probe** pointer to the next node on each pass.

The second change occurs in the comparison step during the sort. We test two data values for ordering with the **compare** function, using the **->** operator. If **compare** returns TRUE, then the data are out of order and an exchange must be made.

EXERCISES 14.4

1. Perform a big-O analysis of the time and memory requirements of the traverse operation on linked lists.

2. Propose a reasonable solution to the problem of failure to allocate storage for the dynamic array used during a traverse operation. (*Hint:* You might inform the application about the success of the traversal.)

3. Write a compare function that, when passed as a parameter to traverse, would cause the nodes of a linked list to be visited in reverse order, from the last node to the first node.

14.5 Using a Linked List to Implement a One-Key Table

In Chapter 12, we analyzed the efficiency of an array-based implementation of a one-key table ADT. We discovered that the principal trade-off is that this implementation supports fast retrievals (with binary search) but slow insertions and removals. The latter operations require a linear number of copy operations, which can be very expensive for large data elements. When the data are particularly volatile, requiring frequent insertions or removals, it might be best to choose the trade-off associated with a linked list implementation. Here we would get linear search times but constant insertion and removal times (in the number of copies required). An additional factor in favor of a linked implementation has gone unnoticed until now. The array implementation of a one-key table forces an application to settle for a fixed upper bound on the number of data elements that can be inserted. This constraint may cause a program to waste memory or not have enough memory to solve a problem. A linked list implementation, which provides memory for a table on an as-needed basis, would use only enough physical memory to accommodate the logical size of the table, and no more.

Redefining the One-Key Table Class

We begin our new implementation of a one-key table by modifying the class declaration module from Chapter 12. We include the header file for the linked list class. The declarations of all of the public member functions (the interface to the class) remain the same. The only change in this module comes in the protected data members section. There we replace the array and the integer data members with a single data member that is a linked list:

```
// Class declaration file: onetable.h

#ifndef ONE_TABLE_H

#include "boolean.h"
#include "assoc.h"
#include "linklist.h"


// Declaration section

// Generic class for key type K and element type E.

template <class K, class E> class one_key_table
{

    public:

    // Class constructors

    one_key_table();
    one_key_table(const one_key_table &table);

    // Member functions

    int length();
    boolean empty();
    void store(const K &target, const E &item);
    boolean retrieve(const K &target, E &item);
    boolean remove(const K &target, E &item);
    one_key_table& operator = (const one_key_table &table);

    protected:
```

```
    // Data members

    linked_list<association<K, E>> list;

};


#define ONE_TABLE_H
#endif
```

Note that the type of data in each node in the underlying linked list will be **association**. This is specified by passing that type name to **linked_list** as a parameter when the data member for the list is declared. Also, the **table_length** data member is no longer needed, because the length of the table is just the length of the linked list.

Reimplementing the One-Key Table Class

Another benefit that we gain from representing a one-key table as a linked list rather than an array is that our implementation becomes more abstract. You will recall our discussion of the two-key table and the layering principle in Section 12.4. There we found that it is easier to work with high-level ADT operations than with low-level data structures like arrays that are built in to C++. The same ease of use occurs in the present case. We do not have to deal with array indices or with C++ pointer manipulations; instead we use high-level operations such as **first, next, insert**, and **remove**. A few examples will make this point clear.

EXAMPLE 14.11

The simplest member functions are those that examine attributes of the one-key table. **empty** and **length** return the answers to the same questions asked of the linked list:

```
template <class K, E>
boolean one_key_table<K, E>::empty()
{
        return list.empty();
}


template <class K, E>
int one_key_table<K, E>::length()
{
        return list.length();
}
```

EXAMPLE 14.12

For retrievals, a linked list operation must do a linear search for a data value stored by key value in the list. We begin by resetting the current pointer to the head of the list by invoking the **first** operation. Then there are two cases to consider:

1. The list is empty. Then we return FALSE.
2. The list has at least one node. Then we retrieve data from each node, compare the key in the data with the target key, and if the keys match, we return the data and TRUE. If we assume that the logical ordering of the

keys maps directly to the ordering of the nodes in the list, then we can stop an unsuccessful search when a node's key value is greater than the target or when we have just examined the last node in the list.

Since there are several cases to consider, we begin with a pseudocode algorithm:

Set success to FALSE
If list not empty
    Set done to FALSE
    Move current pointer to first position
    While not done do
        Retrieve data from the list
        If key associated with data equals target key
            Set item to data
            Set success to TRUE
            Set done to TRUE
        else if current pointer is at the end of the list or key > target
            Set done to TRUE
        else
            Move current pointer to the next node in the list

The C++ code is slightly more complex than the algorithm, because we must extract the key and the data from an association object:

```cpp
template <class K, E>
boolean one_key_table<K, E>::retrieve(K target, E &item)
{
    boolean done, success;
    K key;
    association<K, E> a;
    success = FALSE;
    if (! list.empty())                         // Are there nodes to examine?
    {
        done = FALSE;
        list.first();                           // Reset current pointer to
                                                // head of list

        while (! done)
        {
            list.retrieve(a);
            key = a.get_key();
            if (key == target)                  // Have we found a match?
            {
                item = a.get_value();
                success = TRUE;
                done = TRUE;
            }
            else if (list.at_end() || (key > target))    // Not in list?
                done = TRUE;
            else
                list.next();                    // Keep advancing
        }
    }
    return success;
}
```

EXAMPLE 14.13

To store a data value in a table, we create a new association with the key and item. Then if the list is empty, we just insert the new association into the list. Otherwise, we search for the first node in the list whose key is greater than or equal to the new item's key, and insert the node at that position. Once again, a pseudocode algorithm will clarify our strategy:

```
Create a new association with the key and item
If list is empty
        Insert the association into the list
else
        Set done to FALSE
        Move current pointer to first position
        While not done do
                Retrieve data from the list
                If key associated with data >= target key
                        Insert the association into the list
                        Set done to TRUE
                else if current pointer is at the end of the list
                        Move the current pointer to the next node in the list
                        Insert the association into the list
                        Set done to TRUE
                else
                        Move current pointer to the next node in the list
```

Note that there is a special case in the search loop where we must insert the new node after the last node in the list. In that case, we advance the current pointer beyond this node and perform the insertion, which has the effect of appending the new data to the end of the list. The C++ code is

```cpp
template <class K, E>
void one_key_table<K, E>::store(const K &target, const E &item)
    {
    association<K, E> new_data(target, item);
    association<K, E> data;
    K list_key;
    boolean done;

    if(list.empty)
        list.insert(new_data);                      // Insert as first node
    else
    {
        done = FALSE;
        list.first();                               // Reset current to head
        while (! done)                              // of list
        {
                list.retrieve(data);
                list_key = data.get_key();
                if (list_key >= key)                // Insert before a node?
                {
                        list.insert(new_data);
                        done = TRUE;
                }
```

```
        else if (list.at_end())              // Insert after last node?
        {
                list.next();
                list.insert(new_data);
                done = TRUE;
        }
        else
                list.next();                  // Advance the search
    }
  }
}
```

As you can see, we have a linear amount of work to do in searching for the position of the data to be inserted in the table, but the linked implementation gives us a constant amount of work to be done in moving data around in the table at that point.

A NOTE OF INTEREST

Computer Viruses

Many computer installations are now confronted with a threat akin to germ warfare, which could disable their largest machines. A computer "virus" attacks a computer system in essentially the same way a biological virus attacks the human body.

A computer virus is actually a small undetected program that, over time, infects other programs and eventually disables the entire system. A typical virus in a host program might contain the following instructions:

1. Temporarily suspend execution of host program.
2. Search the computer's memory for other likely un-infected programs.
3. If found, insert a copy of these instructions.
4. Return control of computer back to host program.

This virus would take less than a second to execute, would be virtually undetected, and could attack indefinitely. It can even spread to other computers, when an infected program is swapped or copied for another user.

Adding to the problem is the fact that the saboteur can add instructions to delay the signal for the virus to attack. As researcher Fred Cohen explains, in one company a disgruntled employee instructed the program to remain dormant until his personal password was removed from the system. Once the employee was fired, and his password removed, the virus shut down the entire system.

The Pentagon addresses this problem by isolating its top-secret computers. The military's most sensitive comput-ers are kept in electronically shielded rooms and, when necessary, connected with wire that runs through pipes filled with gas under pressure. The gas pressure would drop if someone attempted to penetrate the pipes to tap into the wires. Marvin Shaefer, chief scientist at the Pentagon computer security center, admits that computers without good access controls are vulnerable to virus attacks.

Computer scientists differ as to whether or not public dis-cussion of computer viruses should even be encouraged. Jerry Lobel, manager of computer security at Honeywell Interna-tional in Phoenix, expresses concern because "it only takes a halfway decent programmer about half a day of thinking to figure out how to do it. If you tell enough people about it there's going to be one crazy out there who's going to try."

Cohen disagrees, insisting that ignorance is always more dangerous than knowledge. "It's better to have somebody friendly do the experiments, tell you how bad it is, show you how it works, and help you counteract it, than to have somebody vicious come along and do it." If you wait, it might be too late.

If your curiosity is aroused, you can find more detailed accounts of the evolution of the computer virus problem in "Attack of the computer virus" by Lee Dembart (*Discover*, November 1984), "Is your computer infected?" by William D. Marbach (*Newsweek*, February 1, 1988), and *Computer Viruses, Worms, Data Diddlers, Killer Programs, and Other Threats to Your System* by John McAfee and Colin Haynes (New York: St. Martin's Press, 1989).

1. Use the new implementation of a one-key table to run the program in the Focus on Program Design section of Chapter 12. (Note that you won't have to change any code in the two-key table modules.)

2. Draw a diagram of the different layers of ADTs used in Exercise 1, and discuss the costs and benefits of the layering.

3. Add **merge** and **append** operations to the interface of the one-key table, and implement the operations. (Rely on the corresponding list operations developed in Exercises 14.3.)

4. The traversal table implementation must be updated to reflect the implementation of a one-key table as a linked list. Why can't the new implementation just invoke the traverse operation for linked lists? (Try it and see what happens.) Propose a new implementation of the traversal table, and discuss the maintenance issues that arise during this process.

FOCUS ON PROGRAM DESIGN

Although we can define the linked list as an ADT, a key theme of this chapter has been that the linked list is of great value when viewed as an implementation technique for other higher level ADTs and their logic. We have seen linked lists used to implement the one-key table and, indirectly, the traversal table and the two-key table ADTs.

Now, in this section, we will use the linked list to implement a very space-efficient version of the radix sort algorithm (see Section 11.4). Moreover, this will be one of those rare instances in which a space-efficient version is also more time efficient. To achieve this, we will specify that the sort algorithm receive a linked list of integers to be sorted, rather than an array. A top-level pseudocode description of radix sort is then given by

Set number_of_digits to the number of digits in largest number in the list
For each k from 1 to number_of_digits
    While the list to sort is not empty
        Transfer the first number in the sort list to the appropriate bin, keying on the kth digit
        (1 corresponding to ones digit, 2 to tens digit, and so forth).
    For each j from 0 to 9
        Append the numbers in jth bin to the list to sort

In our discussion of the radix sort in Section 11.4, we were somewhat shackled by approaches that employed static allocation of the bins used to classify numbers. For instance, we determined that sorting n numbers by this algorithm would require $11n$ storage locations—n for the numbers being sorted and an additional $10n$ locations for the bins associated with the 10 possible digits.

C++ pointer variables provide a new implementation strategy for the bins needed by radix sort. The dynamic allocation associated with these pointer variables will allow each bin to claim only the storage that it needs as the algorithm runs. We propose the following implementation for bins:

```
typedef linked_list bin_structure[9];
```

```
bin_structure bins;
```

We assume that the linked list class provides an **append** operation that uses constant time and memory (see Exercises 14.3). This assumption will enable us to

◆ FIGURE 14.9

Appending one bin to another

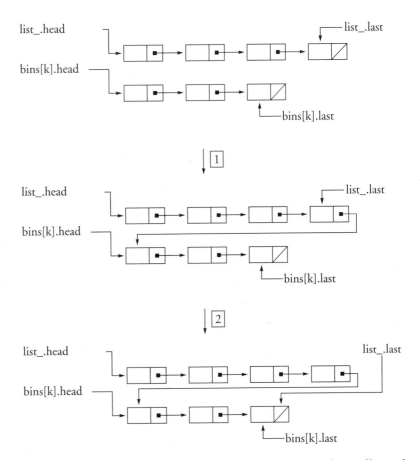

be particularly efficient during that phase of the algorithm that collects the bins associated with particular digits into a new master bin. Figure 14.9 depicts how this efficiency can be achieved. The process of appending bins from the bin structure to the **list_to_sort** requires rearrangement of two pointers in the linked list implementation for each bin.

Compare this to our implementation of bins by arrays in Section 11.4. There the process of appending a bin required physically moving each item in the bin to the array being sorted.

We can now refine our high-level pseudocode for this new version of radix sort. It will require the subordinate modules indicated in the structure chart shown in Figure 14.10. The specifications for each subordinate module are

Module: max_number_digits
Task: Make one pass through list to determine largest
Input: List of integers (assumed to be nonnegative)
Output: The number of digits in the largest integer in list

Module: digit
Task: Use modular arithmetic functions of C++
Inputs: Nonnegative integer number
        k representing a digit position in number,
        with k = 1 corresponding to ones digit, 2 to tens digit, and so on
Output: digit in position k of number

Module: transfer_list_to_bin
Inputs: List to sort
        A bin

◆ **FIGURE 14.10**
Structure chart for RadixSort

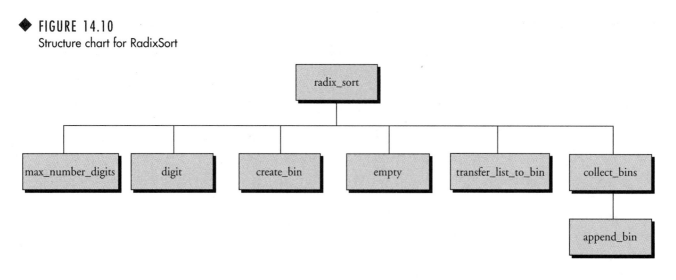

Outputs: First number in list to sort has been removed and added to bin
Module: collect_bins
Inputs: A bin_structure
           List to sort (empty when received)
Output: Sublists in bin_structure have been successively appended to sort list
           Order of appending runs from bin 0 to bin 9

These module specifications give rise to the following C++ function for the radix sort algorithm. We present only the top-level sort function; the subordinate modules are left for you to implement in the problems. You will also formally analyze the time and space efficiency of this new implementation of radix sort in the problems.

```
typedef linked_list<int> bin_structure[9];  // Global definition for
                                            // other modules.


void radix_sort(linked_list<int> &list)
{
        bin_structure bins;
        int data, number_of_digits, which_bin;
        boolean success;

        number_of_digits = max_number_digits (list);
        for (int k = 1; k <= number_of_digits; ++k)
        {
                for (int j = 0; j <= 9; ++j)
                        while (! list.empty())
                        {
                                list.first();
                                success = list.retrieve(data);
                                which_bin = digit(data, k);
                                transfer_list_to_bin(list, bins[which_bin]);
                        }
        }
        collect_bins(list, bins);
}
```

RUNNING, DEBUGGING AND TESTING HINTS

1. You must be very careful when programming with pointers; one misplaced pointer can "lose" an entire data structure. Consequently, modular testing is more important than ever. Test the reliability of each module before releasing it for use in a large program.

2. Be sure that you consider the boundary conditions when developing linked list algorithms. Are you sure that your logic covers the empty list, the first node on the list, the last node on the list? For instance, if your insertion algorithm works for all lists but the empty list, it might as well not work at all since you'll never be able to get any data on the list.

3. Never reference the contents of the memory pointed to by `ptr` when `ptr` is a `NULL` pointer. The following loop control structure

   ```
   while ((ptr->data != target) && (ptr != NULL))
   ```

   is asking for trouble. When `ptr` is `NULL`, the reference to `ptr->data` may cause a run-time error before the loop is exited. The positions of the two tests should be reversed to take advantage of short-circuit evaluation in C++.

4. Programming with pointers is programming with logical pictures of linked lists. Draw a picture of what you want to do with a pointer and then write the code to make it happen. When debugging, verify and trace your code by drawing pictures of what it does with your data. For instance, an assignment to a pointer in your code corresponds to aiming an arrow somewhere in your corresponding snapshot of the data structure.

SUMMARY

Key Terms

append	dynamic memory	linked list
arrow operator	management	list traversal
C++ pointer variables	dynamic data structure	merge
concatenation	head pointer	node
data movement	heap	pointer
dereference operation	linear ordering	structure definition
dynamic array	link	volatile list

Keywords

`delete new struct`

Key Concepts

◆ The linked list structure is especially convenient for implementing a variety of higher level list ADTs in situations where add and delete operations dominate search operations.

◆ The linked list allows insertions and removals to occur by mere pointer manipulation instead of large-scale data movement. The price paid for this gain is the inefficiency of a sequential search strategy.

◆ An overview of the advantages and disadvantages of a linked list versus an array implementation of a one-key table is given in the following table:

	Implementation of One-Key Table Using Array Maintained in Physical Order So That Binary Search May Be Used	Implementation of One-Key Table Using Linked List
Insert	$O(\log_2 n)$ comparisons to find location where insertion should occur. $O(n)$ data interchanges to rearrange list.	$O(n)$ comparisons to find location where insertion should occur. $O(1)$ pointer interchanges to rearrange list.
Retrieve	$O(\log_2 n)$ comparisons to find data item.	$O(n)$ comparisons to find data item.
Remove	$O(\log_2 n)$ comparisons to find data item to remove. $O(n)$ data interchanges to rearrange list.	$O(n)$ comparisons to find data item to delete. $O(1)$ pointer interchanges to rearrange list.
Other considerations	Size of list is bounded by physical size of array.	If C++ pointers are used to implement, size of list is bounded only by available space in heap.

PROGRAMMING PROBLEMS AND PROJECTS

1. Complete the development of a linked list radix sort (see the Focus on Program Design section) in stages.

   a. Write the necessary subordinate modules.

   b. Write a main program so that you can thoroughly test the algorithm.

   c. Design test data that are sure to exercise the various boundary conditions of the subordinate modules.

   d. Do a big-O analysis of the time and space requirements of this version of radix sort. If you also implemented an array version of radix sort in Chapter 11, profile both versions by counting the number of operations that each must perform (see the Focus on Program Design section in Chapter 11). Prepare a written report in which you compare the empirical performance of both versions.

2. Wing-and-a-Prayer Airlines maintains four scheduled flights per day, which they identify by the numbers 1, 2, 3, and 4. For each of these flights, they keep an alphabetized list of passengers. The database for the entire airline could hence be viewed as four linked lists. Write a program that sets up and maintains this database by handling commands of the following form:

   Command → Add

   Flight number → 3

   Passenger name → BROWN

   Command → Delete

   From flight number → 1

   Passenger name → JONES

   Command → List

   Flight number → 2

   (List alphabetically all passengers for the specified flight.)

   Use an appropriate string storage strategy for the passenger names.

3. In order to take care of their growing business, the Fly-by-Night Credit Card Company would like to update their customer data file. Write a program in a high-level language that sets up a doubly linked list that can support the following actions on a record:

a. Insert a record into the list in the correct place, sorted according to the social security number of the customer.

b. Update a record if the customer record exists.

c. Delete a record if the customer no longer wishes to patronize the company.

In the preceding data manipulation activities, the list should always remain in order sorted by the social security number.

4. As a struggling professional football team, the Bay Area Brawlers have a highly volatile player roster. Write a program that allows the team to maintain its roster as a linked list in alphabetical order by player last name. Other data items stored for each player are

Height

Weight

Age

University affiliation

As an added option, allow your program to access players in descending order of weight and age.

5. Develop a line-oriented text editor that assigns a number to each line of text and then maintains the lines in a linked list by line number order (similar to the fashion in which BASIC programs are maintained on many systems). Your program should be able to process the following commands:

I-line number 'text' (instruction to insert text at specified line number)

L-line1 -line2 (instruction to list line1 through line2)

D-line1 -line2 (instruction to delete line1 through line2)

If you feel really ambitious, incorporate into your program a string storage strategy that will allow the user to perform editing operations such as inserting and deleting characters within a given line.

6. Write a program that, given a file of text, will add to an index those words in the text that are marked by special delimiting brackets []. The words in the index will be printed after the text itself has been formatted and printed. Words in this index should be listed in alphabetical order with a page number reference for each page of text on which they are delimited by the special brackets. Note that this program would be part of a word processing system an author could use when developing a book with an index of terms.

7. Write a program that allows input of an arbitrary number of polynomials as coefficient and exponent pairs. Store each polynomial as a linked list of coefficient–exponent pairs arranged in descending order by exponent. Note that the coefficient–exponent pairs need not be input in descending order; it is the responsibility of your program to put them in that order. Your program should then be able to evaluate each of the polynomials for an arbitrary argument X and be able to output each of the polynomials in the appropriate descending exponent order. Be sure that your program works for all "unusual" polynomials such as the zero polynomial, polynomials of degree one, and constant polynomials.

8. Redo the Game of Life program that you developed for Problem 5 in Chapter 12, except now use linked lists to implement the two-dimensional table ADT.

9. Redo Problem 4 of Chapter 13, for the registrar of American Basket Weaving University, except now use linked lists to implement the ADTs that you designed for that program.

10. Consider the following problem, often referred to as the Josephus problem. Imagine that N people have decided to commit mass suicide by arranging themselves in a circle and killing the Mth person around the circle, with the size of the circle being reduced by one each time a person is killed. The problem is to find out which person is the last to die, or more generally, to find the order in which the people are executed. For example, if $N = 9$ and $M = 5$, then the people are killed in the order 5, 1, 7, 4, 3, 6, 9, 2, and 8. To solve the Josephus problem, write a program that inserts people 1 through N into a list and then appropriately deletes people from the list until only one is left.

11. Computers can store and do arithmetic only with integers of limited size. When integers surpass that limiting value, overflow occurs and the results will either be unreliable or cause your program to die with a run-time error. However, by altering the implementation of an integer, you can develop algorithms to do virtually limitless integer arithmetic. The basis of such an implementation is to store each digit of an integer in a list. That is, represent an integer as a list of digits. Then develop algorithms to do integer arithmetic operations on a digit-by-digit basis, taking carries, borrows, and so forth into account as you do when performing these operations by hand. After carefully considering which list implementation best suits the problem, develop functions to perform extended integer addition, subtraction, multiplication, and division (quotient and remainder). As one test case, add the following integers and print the sum:

$$5643127821$$
$$+\ 9276577159$$

12. By consulting reference manuals for your version of C++ and by writing a variety of experimental programs, attempt to discover the details of how your C++ compiler manages the allocation of memory in the heap. Prepare a written report in which you describe your findings.

13. Your friend offers the following criticism of linked lists: "The problem with linked lists is that they cannot be used with large databases stored in files since pointers represent locations in main memory." Explain the fallacy in your friend's criticism. Then, in a detailed statement, discuss how linked lists could be implemented for data stored in random access files.

CHAPTER **15** **Stacks and Queues**

Achilles: What would happen if you took some popping-tonic without having previously pushed yourself into a picture? Tortoise: I don't precisely know, Achilles, but I would be rather wary of horsing around with these strange pushing and popping liquids.
Douglas Hofstadter

The other line always moves faster.
Barbara Ettore

In the last chapter we introduced the linked list as a data structure designed to handle conveniently the insertion and deletion of entries in a linearly ordered list. In this chapter we study two special types of linearly ordered lists: the stack and the queue. These lists are special because of the restrictions imposed on the way in which entries may be inserted and removed. Both structures may be implemented by arrays or dynamically allocated linked lists.

The restriction placed on a stack is often described as *last-in/first-out* (*LIFO*). Consider, for example, the order in which a smart traveler will pack a suitcase. To minimize shuffling, the last item packed should be the first worn. Another familiar example of such a storage strategy is that of the pop-up mechanism used to store trays for a cafeteria line. The first trays loaded into the mechanism may well have a long wait before they escape to a passing diner.

A list of data items processed via a LIFO scheduling strategy is called a *stack*. As we shall see in this and later chapters, stacks are an extremely useful data structure. They find extensive applications in the processing of subroutine calls, the syntactical checking and translation of programming languages by compilers, and the powerful programming technique of recursion (see Chapter 16).

In contrast to the linear order of a stack, a *queue* is a *first-in/first-out* (*FIFO*) list. This latter name comes close to completely characterizing the restricted types of adds and deletes that can be performed on a queue. Insertions are limited to one end of the list, whereas deletions may occur only at the other end. The conceptual picture that emerges from the notion of a queue is that of a waiting line; for example, jobs waiting to be serviced by a computer, or cars forming a long line at a busy toll booth.

15.1 The Stack Abstract Data Type and its Implementation

The last-in/first-out nature of the stack implies that all additions and deletions occur at one designated end of the stack. That designated end is called the top, and the operations of adding to or deleting from the stack are referred to as *pushing* and *popping*, respectively. More formally, we define the stack ADT as follows.

Stack. A stack is a restricted list in which entries are added to and removed from one designated end called the top.

The operations to be performed on a stack are specified by the following preconditions and postconditions.

Create operation
Preconditions: Receiver is an arbitrary stack in an unpredictable state.
Postconditions: Receiver is initialized to the empty stack.
Empty operation
Preconditions: Receiver is a previously created stack.
Postconditions: Returns TRUE if receiver is empty, FALSE otherwise.
Push operation
Preconditions: Receiver is a previously created stack. `item` is a value to be added to the top of the stack. There is memory available to store the new item in the stack.
Postconditions: Receiver is returned with `item` added to the top of the stack.
Pop operation
Preconditions: Receiver is a previously created stack. The stack is not empty.
Postconditions: The stack has its top value removed, and this value is returned.
on_top operation
Preconditions: Receiver is a previously created stack. The stack is not empty.
Postconditions: Returns the value on the top of the stack. Unlike `pop`, the stack is left unchanged.

Figure 15.1 depicts the critical push and pop operations for the stack ADT. Conceptually, it is easiest to develop a mental image of the `push` and `pop` operations if you picture a stack as a vertical list with the first entry at the bottom and the last at the top. Then, as indicated in Figure 15.1, adding to the stack—that is, pushing—essentially makes this stack become taller, and removing from the stack—that is, popping—results in a shorter stack.

◆ FIGURE 15.1
Pushing onto and popping from the stack

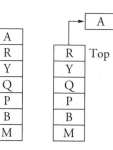

Stacks and Function Calls

Before we discuss methods of implementing a stack, we shall give some hint of their importance in the processing of function calls. Of key importance to the processing of functions in any language is that the return from a function must be to the instruction immediately following the call that originally transferred control to the function. For example, in the partial coding that follows:

```
int main()
{
      int q;
      .
      q = sub1(q);              // Call sub1
      cout << q;
      .
}

void sub3()
{
      .
      .
      .
}

void sub2(int q)
{
      .
      sub3();                   // Call Sub3
      p = p - q;
      .
}

void sub1(int b)
{
      .
      b = sub2(a);              // Call sub2
      a = a + b;
      .
}
```

the order of operations would be

1. Leave **main** and transfer to **sub1**.
2. Leave **sub1** and transfer to **sub2**.
3. Leave **sub2** and transfer to **sub3**.
4. Return from **sub3** to the instruction **p = p - q** in **sub2**.
5. Return from **sub2** to the instruction **a = a + b** in **sub1**.
6. Return from **sub1** to the instruction **cout << q** in **main**.
7. End of **main**.

Each time a call is made, the machine must remember where to return upon completion of that function.

A stack is precisely the structure capable of storing the data necessary to handle calls and returns in this sequence. The data for each call of a function is stored in a data structure called an *activation record*. This record contains space for

◆ FIGURE 15.2

Memory stack generated by
previous partial coding

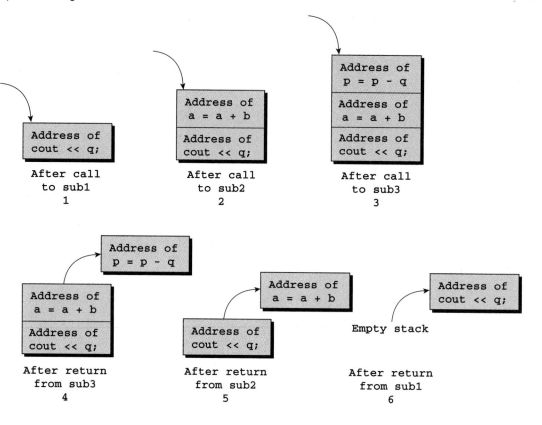

the return address (the address of the instruction following the call of the function)
and any values or addresses of actual parameters for that call of the function. Hence
the preceding partial coding would generate a stack that develops as illustrated in
Figure 15.2. (The numbers in the figure correspond to the order of operations just
shown on the preceding list.) Each time a call to a function is made, a return
address is placed in an activation record and this is pushed on top of the stack. Each
time a function is completed, the top record on the stack is popped to determine
the memory address to which the return operation should be made. The nature of
the leave–return sequence for functions makes it crucial that the first return address
accessed be the last one that was remembered by the computer. Because there is
only one point, the top, at which data may enter or exit a stack, it is the ideal data
structure to be used for this "last-stored, first-recalled" type of operation.

This description of the method by which a compiler actually implements
function calls is just one illustration of the utility of stacks. In Chapter 16, we'll
discuss a different type of function usage called recursion, and examine in detail the
role of the stack in handling such a recursive call.

C++ Interface for the Stack Abstract Data Type

The transition from defining a stack as an ADT to implementing this structure in
a computer language requires, as usual, an interface to the ADT's operations. A
C++ class declaration module for the stack ADT follows:

```
// Class declaration file: stack.h

#ifndef STACK_H

#include "boolean.h"
#include "element.h"

// We assume that constant MAX_STACK_SIZE
// is already defined in element.h

// Declaration section

template <class E> class stack
{

    public:

    // Class constructors

    stack();
    stack(const stack &s);

    // Member functions

    boolean empty();
    void push(const E &item);
    E pop();
    E on_top();
    stack<E>& operator = (const stack &s);

    // Protected data pertaining to
    // the implementation would go here.

};

#define STACK_H
#endif
```

We will discuss two implementations of the stack class in C++. The first uses an array and, consequently, limits the size to which a stack may grow. The second employs a linked list with pointer variables, thereby allowing the stack to become as large as the free space in the C++ heap.

Array Implementation of a Stack

Using an array to implement a stack is relatively straightforward. Because insertions and deletions occur at the same end of a stack, only one pointer will be needed. We call that pointer **top**. The array of elements will be called **data**, and its size is specified by the constant **MAX_STACK_SIZE**, defined in the application. Thus, the C++ protected data members for the stack class are

```
int top;
E data[MAX_STACK_SIZE];
```

In Figure 15.3, we trace it through the function example from Figure 15.2. As in Figure 15.2, the numbers below each array correspond to the operations performed in our previous sequence of function calls and returns. The empty stack is signaled

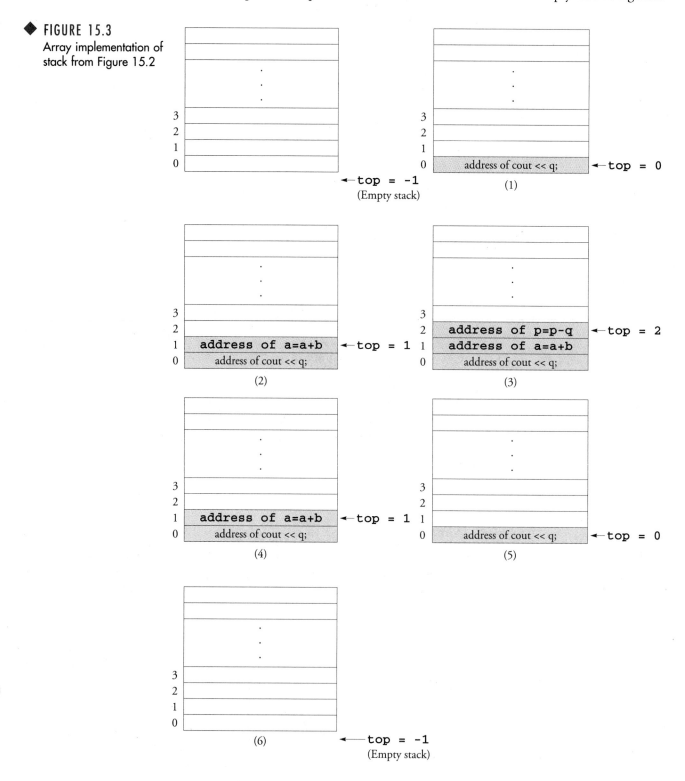

◆ FIGURE 15.3
Array implementation of stack from Figure 15.2

by the condition **top = -1**. If we think of **top** as pointing to the last entry pushed, then the two instructions

```
++top;
data[top] = item;
```

will push the contents of **item** onto the stack. Popping an entry from the stack into item requires

```
item = data[top];
--top;
```

Complete functions for the push and pop operations follow in Example 15.1.

EXAMPLE 15.1   Implement the **push** and **pop** operations for an array implementation of a stack.

```
template <class E>
void stack<E>::push(E item)
{
    assert(top < MAX_STACK_SIZE - 1);
    ++top;
    data[top] = item;
}

template <class E>
E stack<E>::pop()
{
    E item;

    assert(! empty());
    item = data[top];
    --top;
    return item;
}
```

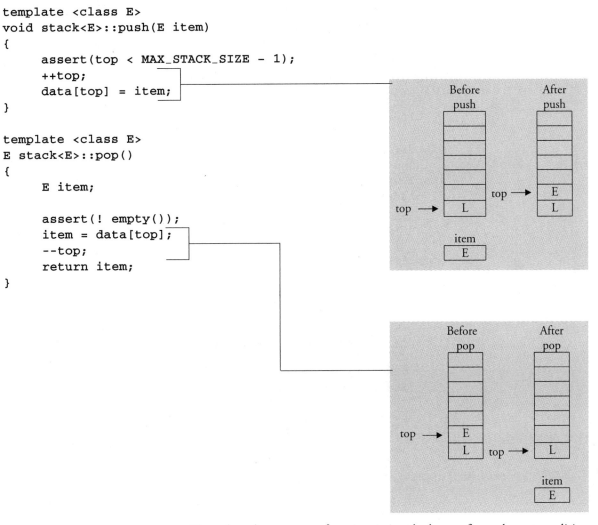

Note that the **assert** function is invoked to enforce the preconditions on each member function.

Linked List Implementation of a Stack

When we choose a linked list implementation of a stack, we are paying the price of a relatively small amount of memory space needed to maintain linking pointers for the dynamic allocation of stack space. A stack with the three integer entries 18, 40, and 31 would appear as follows:

We also have the benefit of reusing a class already developed. The easiest way to use the linked list class to implement a stack class is to make the stack class a derived class of the linked list class. The derived class adds functions for inserting, removing, and examining data at the beginning of a linked list. However, we must prevent clients of the stack class from using any of the operations on linked lists, such as **first** or **next**. Defining the mode of inheritance as **protected** rather than **public** will allow the stack class to inherit all of the public and protected operations from the linked list class, but prevent clients of the stack class from using them:

```
// Class declaration file: stack.h

#ifndef STACK_H

#include "boolean.h"
#include "linklist.h"

// Declaration section

template <class E> stack : protected linked_list<E>
{

    public:

    // Class constructors

    stack();
    stack(const stack<E> &s);

    // Class destructor

    ~stack();

    // Member functions

    boolean empty();
    void push(const E &item);
    E pop();
    E on_top();
    stack<E>& operator = (const stack<E> &s);
```

```
      };
```

```
#define STACK_H
#endif
```

Note that there are no data members in this definition. They are maintained in the parent class, `linked_list`. Note also that the module specifies a class destructor (~`stack()`). This kind of operation, introduced in Chapter 14, is used by the computer to return dynamic memory to the heap when objects using it go out of scope.

Functions to push and pop the stack now become nothing more than insertions to and deletions from the beginning of a linked list. As such, they use high-level linked list operations already developed in Chapter 14. You will write them as exercises at the end of this section.

EXAMPLE 15.2

To illustrate the use of stack operations in a program, let's consider a program that will check an arithmetic expression to make sure that parentheses are correctly matched (nested). Our program considers

(3 + 4 * (5 % 3))

to make sure that each left parenthesis is paired with a following right parenthesis in the expression.

A first-level pseudocode for this problem is

Get a character from the keyboard
While the character does not equal end of line
    If it is a '('
        push it onto the stack
    Else if it is a ')'
        Check for empty stack before popping previous '('
    Get a character from the keyboard
Check for empty stack

The growing and shrinking of the stack is illustrated in Figure 15.4. Assuming the existence of the basic stack operations, a program that examines an expression for correct use of parentheses is

```
// Program file: parens.cpp

#include <iostream.h>

#include "boolean.h"
#include "stack.h"

int main()
{
      stack<char> s;
      char symbol;

      cin.get(symbol);
      while (symbol != '\n')
      {
```

```
        if (symbol == '(')
            s.push(symbol);
        else if (symbol == ')')
            if (s.empty())
                cout << "The parentheses are not correct. " << endl;
            else
                symbol = s.pop();
        cin.get(symbol);
    }
    if (! s.empty())
        cout << "The parentheses are not correct. " << endl;
    return 0;
}
```

◆ FIGURE 15.4

Using a stack to check for balanced parentheses

*ɓ represents a blank space

This program will print an error message for an invalid expression and nothing for a valid expression. Several modifications of this short program are available and are suggested in the following exercises.

EXERCISES 15.1

1. Draw a picture of the stack of integers **s** after each one of the following operations is performed:

```
stack<int> s;
s.push(4);
s.push(10);
s.push(12);
item = s.pop();
s.push(3 * item);
item = s.on_top();
s.push (3 * item);
```

2. The **on_top** operation described in the definition of the stack as an abstract data type is actually unnecessary since it can be defined in terms of other stack operations. Provide such a definition of the **on_top** operation.

3. Write functions to implement each of the following operations for an array implementation of a stack. Be consistent with the operations already implemented in Example 15.1.

   a. **create** (do both the default constructor and the copy constructor)

   b. **empty**

   c. **on_top**

4. Write functions to implement each of the following stack operations for a linked list implementation of a stack.

   a. **create** (do both the default constructor and the copy constructor)

   b. **destroy**

   c. **empty**

   d. **push**

   e. **pop**

   f. **on_top**

5. Using the program for checking parentheses (Example 15.2), illustrate how the stack grows and shrinks when the following expression is examined:

   (5 / (3 – 2 * (4 + 3) – (8 / 2)))

6. Modify the program in Example 15.2 so that several expressions may be examined. Also provide more descriptive error messages.

7. Write a program that utilizes a stack to print a line of text in reverse order.

8. It is not necessary to use a stack to check expressions for matching parentheses. Write an algorithm that describes this task using a simple integer counter.

9. An alternative definition of the stack class in C++ does not derive the stack class from the linked list class. Instead, it maintains a linked list as a data member. Compare this implementation to the one that derives the stack class from the linked list class (*hint*: how will the copy constructor, the destructor, and the assignment operation be different?).

15.2 An Application of Stacks: Parsing and Evaluating Arithmetic Expressions

Often the logic of problems for which stacks are a suitable data structure involves the need to backtrack, to return to a previous state. For instance, consider the problem of finding your way out of a maze. One approach to take would be to probe a given path in the maze as deeply as possible. Upon finding a dead end, you would need to backtrack to previously visited maze locations in order to try other paths. Such backtracking would require recalling these previous locations in the reverse order from which you visited them.

Not many of us need to find our way out of a maze. However, the designers of compilers are faced with an analogous backtracking situation in the evaluation of arithmetic expressions. As you scan the expression

$$A + B / C + D$$

in left-to-right order, it is impossible to tell upon initially encountering the plus sign whether or not you should apply the indicated addition operation to A and the immediately following operand. Instead, you must probe further into the expression to determine whether an operation with a higher priority occurs. While you undertake this probing of the expression, you must stack previously encountered operation symbols until you are certain of the operands to which they can be applied.

Further compounding the backtracking problem just described are the many different ways of representing the same algebraic expression. For example, the assignment statements

$$Z = A * B / C + D;$$
$$Z = (A * B) / C + D;$$
$$Z = ((A * B) / C) + D;$$

should all result in the same order of arithmetic operations even though the expressions involved are written in distinctly different forms. The process of checking the syntax of such an expression and representing it in one unique form is called *parsing* the expression. One frequently used method of parsing relies heavily on stacks.

Infix, Postfix, and Prefix Notation

Conventional algebraic notation is often termed *infix* notation; the arithmetic operator appears between the two operands to which it is being applied. Infix notation may require parentheses to specify a desired order of operations. For example, in the expression $a/b + c$, the division will occur first. If we want the addition to occur first, the expression must be parenthesized as $a/(b + c)$.

Using *postfix* notation (also called reverse Polish notation after the nationality of its originator, the Polish logician Jan Lukasiewicz), the need for parentheses is eliminated because the operator is placed directly after the two operands to which it applies. Hence, $A / B + C$ would be written as $A B / C +$ in postfix form. This says:

1. Apply the division operator to A and B.
2. To that result, add C.

The infix expression $A / (B + C)$ would be written as $A B C + /$ in postfix notation. Reading this postfix expression from left to right, we are told to

1. Apply the addition operator to B and C.
2. Then divide that result into A.

Although relatively short expressions such as the preceding ones can be converted from infix to postfix via an intuitive process, a more systematic method is required for complicated expressions. We propose the following algorithm for humans (and will soon consider a different one for computers):

1. Completely parenthesize the infix expression to specify the order of all operations.
2. Move each operator to the space held by its corresponding right parenthesis.
3. Remove all parentheses.

Consider this three-step method as it applies to the following expression in which ^ is used to indicate exponentiation:

$$A \,/\, B \wedge C + D * E - A * C$$

Completely parenthesizing this expression yields

$$(((A \,/\, (B \wedge C)) + (D * E)) - (A * C))$$

Moving each operator to its corresponding right parenthesis, we obtain

$$(((A \,/\, (B \wedge C)\,) + (D * E)) - (A * C))$$

Removing all parentheses, we are left with

$$A \; B \; C \wedge \,/\, D \; E * + A \; C * -$$

Had we started out with

$$A \,/\, B \wedge C - (D * E - A * C)$$

our three-step procedure would have resulted in

$$((A \,/\, (B \wedge C)) - ((D * E) - (A * C)))$$

Removing the parentheses would then yield

$$A \; B \; C \wedge \,/\, D \; E * A \; C * - -$$

In a similar way, an expression can be converted into *prefix* form, in which an operator immediately precedes its two operands. The conversion algorithm for infix to prefix specifies that, after completely parenthesizing the infix expression according to order of priority, we move each operator to its corresponding left parenthesis. Applying the method to

$$A \,/\, B \wedge C + D * E - A * C$$

gives us

$$((A \,/\, (B \wedge C)) + ((D * E) - (A * C)))$$

and finally the prefix form

$$+ \,/\, A \wedge B \; C - * D \; E * A \; C$$

The importance of postfix and prefix notation in parsing arithmetic expressions is that these notations are completely free of parentheses. Consequently, an expression in postfix (or prefix) form is in unique form. In the design of compilers, this parsing of an expression into postfix form is crucial because having a unique form for an expression greatly simplifies its eventual evaluation. Thus, in handling an expression, a compiler must

1. Parse into postfix form.

2. Apply an evaluation algorithm to the postfix form.

We limit our discussion here to postfix notation. The techniques we cover are easily adaptable to the functionally equivalent prefix form.

Converting Infix Expressions to Postfix

First consider the problem of parsing an expression from infix to postfix form. Our three-step function is not easily adaptable to machine coding. Instead, we will use an algorithm that has the following as its essential data structures:

1. A stream of characters containing the infix expression and terminated by the special delimiter **#**

2. A stack named **op_stack**, which may contain
   a. Arithmetic operators: +, −, *, and /
   b. The left parenthesis, (. The right parenthesis,), is processed by the algorithm but never stored in the stack
   c. The special delimiter **#**

3. A string named **postfix** containing the final postfix expression.

To eliminate details that would only clutter the main logic of the algorithm, we will assume that the string representing the infix expression contains *tokens* (that is, incoming symbols) consisting only of the arithmetic operators +, −, *, and /; parentheses; the delimiting character **#**; and operands that each consist of a single uppercase alphabetic character. We will also assume that these tokens may be read from a line without any intervening spaces. Later, we will consider some of the complications introduced by tokens of varying size and type and by the exponentiation operator ^. Thus, for the present, the algorithm we discuss will convert infix expressions of the form

$$A * B + (C - D / E)$$

into their corresponding postfix notation.

The description of the algorithm is as follows:

1. Define a function **infix_priority**, which takes an operator, parenthesis, or **#** as its argument and returns an integer as

Character	*	/	+	−	(	)	#
Returned Value	2	2	1	1	3	0	0

This function reflects the relative position of an operator in the arithmetic hierarchy and is used with the function **stack_priority** (defined in step 2) to determine how long an operator waits in the stack before being appended to the postfix string.

2. Define another function `stack_priority`, which takes the same possibilities for an argument and returns an integer as

Character	*	/	+	–	(	)	#
Returned Value	2	2	1	1	0	Undefined	0

This function applies to operators in the operator stack as their priority in the arithmetic hierarchy is compared to that of incoming operators from the infix string. The result of this comparison determines whether or not an operator waits in the stack or is appended to the postfix string.

3. Initialize `op_stack` by pushing `#`.

4. Read the next character `ch` from the infix expression.

5. Test `ch` and

5.1 If `ch` is an operand, append it to the postfix string.

5.2 If `ch` is a right parenthesis, then pop entries from stack and append them to postfix until a left parenthesis is popped. Doing this ensures that operators within a parenthesized portion of an infix expression will be applied first, regardless of their priority in the usual arithmetic hierarchy. Discard both left and right parentheses.

5.3 If `ch` is a `#`, pop all entries that remain on the stack and append them to the `postfix string`.

5.4 Otherwise, pop from the stack and append to the postfix string operators whose `stack_priority` is greater than or equal to the `infix_priority` of `ch`. Stop this series of popping operations when you reach a stack element whose `stack_priority` is less than the `infix_priority` of `ch`. This comparison, keying on the priority of `ch` from the infix string and operators that have previously been pushed onto the operator stack, ensures that operators are applied in the right order in the resulting postfix string. After popping these operators, push `ch`.

6. Repeat steps 4 and 5 until `ch` is the delimiter `#`.

The key to the algorithm is the use of the stack to hold operators from the infix expression that appear to the left of another given operator even though that latter operator must be applied first. The defined functions `infix_priority` and `stack_priority` are used to specify this priority of operators and the associated pushing and popping operations. This entire process is best understood by carefully tracing through an example.

EXAMPLE 15.3

Parse the infix expression

$$A * B + (C - D / E) \text{ \#}$$

into its equivalent postfix form. Trace the contents of the operator stack and the postfix string as each character is read.

The solution to this problem is presented in Table 15.1. In this table, the parenthesized numbers in the Commentary column refer to subcases of step 5 in the preceding algorithm.

◇ **TABLE 15.1**
Parsing of infix expression
$A * B + (C - D/E)\#$

ch	op_stack	postfix	Commentary
	#		Push #
A			Read ch
		A	Append ch to postfix (5.1)
*			Read ch
	* #		Push ch (5.4)
B			Read ch
		AB	Append ch to postfix (5.1)
+			Read ch
	+ #	AB*	Pop *, append * to postfix, push ch (5.4)
(			Read ch
	(+ #		Push ch (5.4)
C			Read ch
		AB*C	Append ch to postfix (5.1)
−			Read ch
	− (+ #		Push ch (5.4)
D			Read ch
		AB*CD	Append ch to postfix (5.1)
/			Read ch
	/ − (+ #		Push ch (5.4)
E			Read ch
		AB*CDE	Append ch to postfix (5.1)
)			Read ch
	+ #	AB*CDE/−	Pop and append to postfix until (reached (5.2)
#			Read ch
		AB*CDE/− + #	Pop and append rest of stack to postfix (5.3)

The following C++ function implements our algorithm for converting infix expressions of the form we have specified. You should study and thoroughly understand this algorithm before moving on to this chapter's Focus on Program Design section. There, the infix-to-postfix algorithm will be the focal point for an entire program that works with expressions of a slightly more complicated form.

```cpp
void infix_to_postfix(string &postfix)
{
    char item, ch;
    stack<char> op_stack;
    op_stack.push('#');
    do
    {
        cin.get(ch);
        if (('A' <= ch) && (ch <= 'Z'))
            postfix.append_char(ch);
        else if (ch == ')')
        {
            item = op_stack.pop();
            while (item != '(')
            {
                postfix.append_char(item);
                item = op_stack.pop();
            }
        }
        else if (ch == '#')
        {
            while (! op_stack.empty())
            {
                item = op_stack.pop();
                postfix.append_char(item);
            }
        }
```

"A" < = ch AND ch < = "Z"

postfix   Q   Input ch

op_stack

In this case, transfer ch to postfix.

ch = ")"

)

postfix   Input ch

op_stack

In this case, pop stack until encounter matching left parenthesis.

ch = "#"

#

postfix   Input ch

op_stack

In this case, pop rest of stack to postfix.

```
else
{
    item = op_stack.pop();
    while (stack_priority(item) >= infix_priority(ch))
        {
            postfix.append_char(item);
            item = op_stack.pop();
        }
        op_stack.push(item);
        op_stack.push(ch);
    }
} while (ch != '#');
}
```

In this case, pop stack until encounter item of lower priority (+). Then push incoming ch.

Evaluating Postfix Expressions

Once an expression has been parsed and represented in postfix form, another stack plays an essential role in its final evaluation. To evaluate a postfix expression, we repeatedly read characters from the postfix expression. If the character read is an operand, push the value associated with it onto the stack. If it is an operator, pop two values from the stack, apply the operator to them, and push the result back onto the stack. After the last operand in the postfix expression has been processed, the value of the expression is the one entry on the stack. The technique is illustrated in the following example.

EXAMPLE 15.4

Consider the postfix expression from Example 15.3.

$A\,B*\,C\,D\,E/\,-\,+\,\#$

Let us suppose that the symbols A, B, C, D, and E had associated with them the following values:

Symbol	Value
A	5
B	3
C	6
D	8
E	2

The evaluation of the expression under this assignment of values proceeds as indicated in Figure 15.5.

◆ **FIGURE 15.5**
Evaluation of
AB∗CDE/−+#

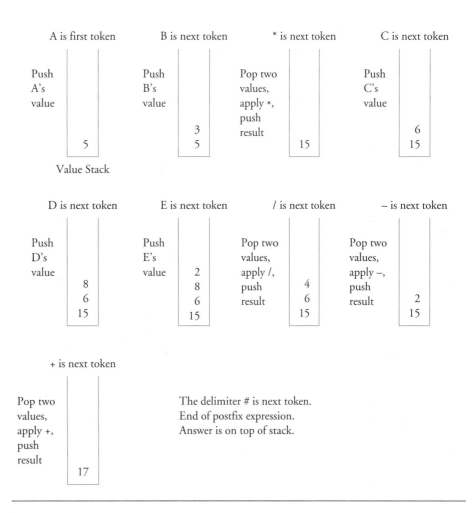

If we assume functions **value_of**, which will return the value associated with a particular symbol; **eval**, which will return the result of applying an operator to two values; and **next_token**, which will return the next token to be read from the postfix expression, the C++ function to evaluate a postfix expression is given by

```
// Assume a suitable implementation of the string ADT,
// augmented by a next_token operation.  next_token(s) is
// a function which returns successive characters from a
// string s.  That is, the first time it is called it returns the
// first character in s, then the second character in s, and so forth.

// Also we assume the existence of a function value_of which
// associates a character with its real value—similar to the
// fashion in which each variable in a program is associated with
// a value. Since our tokens are only single characters, an easy way
// of implementing value_of would be to use an array of reals
// indexed by the subrange 0 .. 25. In effect, this would create a
// mini, 26-location "memory." Finally, we assume the existence of
// an eval function which receives two real operands and the
// operator to apply to them. eval returns the result of applying
// that operator to the operands.
```

```
float evaluate(const string &postfix)
{
        char ch;
        float result, v1, v2;
        stack<float> value_stack;

        ch = next_token(postfix);
        while (ch != '#')
        {
                if (('A' <= ch) && (ch <= 'Z'))
                        value_stack.push(value_of(ch));
                else
                {
                    v2 = value_stack.pop();
                    v1 = value_stack.pop();
                    result = eval(v1, v2, ch);
                    value_stack.push(result);
                }
                ch = next_token(postfix);
        }
        return value_stack.on_top();
}
```

EXERCISES 15.2

1. What are the infix, postfix, and prefix forms of the following expression?:

   $A + B * (C - D) / (P - R)$

2. Trace the contents of the stack as the postfix form of the expression in Exercise 1 is evaluated. Assume the following assignment of values: $A = 6$, $B = 4$, $C = 3$, $D = 1$, $P = 12$, and $R = 11$.

3. Consider the expression with the infix notation

   $P + (Q - F) / Y$

   Using the algorithm discussed in this section to transform this into a postfix expression, trace the state of both the operator stack and postfix string as each character of the infix expression is processed. Conduct your trace following the style of Table 15.1.

4. Using the postfix expression you obtained in Exercise 3, trace the stack of real values that would develop as the postfix expression is evaluated. You should indicate the numeric values on the stack as each character in the postfix expression is processed. Assume the values $F = 4$, $P = 10$, $Q = 18$, and $Y = 2$.

5. Parse the infix expression

   $P * (Q / Y) + A - B + D * Y \#$

   using the following definitions of **infix_priority** and **stack_priority**:

Priority	*	/	+	−	(	)	#
Infix	2	2	4	4	5	0	0
Stack	1	1	3	3	0	Undefined	0

A NOTE OF INTEREST

Logic Programming and Backtracking

In the 1960s, J. Robinson, a mathematical logician, discovered an algorithm for automating the process of proving theorems in first-order predicate logic. This discovery made the discipline of logic programming possible. A logic program consists of a set of assertions. Some of these describe particular facts, such as "Ken is over 40 years old." Other assertions describe general facts or rules, such as "All people over 40 years old have gray hair." A program consisting of these two facts can be used to prove other facts, such as "Ken has gray hair." The proof can be executed on a computer after one enters the known facts, expressed in the syntax of a logic programming language, into a database and inputs a request for the proof of the unknown fact to the computer.

PROLOG is a logic programming language that provides a syntax for describing assertions and queries and an interpreter for user interaction and theorem proving. To return to our example, the known facts, expressed in the syntax of PROLOG, might be entered interactively at the `->` prompt into the database as follows:

```
-> assert(over_40(ken)).
OK
```

```
-> assert(gray_hair(X) :- over_40(X)).
OK
```

Queries for proofs of unknown facts might be entered as follows:

```
-> gray_hair(ken).
Yes
```

```
-> over_50(ken).
No
```

The PROLOG interpreter uses Robinson's algorithm to derive the unknown fact that Ken has gray hair from the fact that Ken is over 40 and the rule that if any individual is over 40, then it has gray hair. In our example, the algorithm starts with a goal of proving `gray_hair(ken)`. It finds a rule,

`gray_hair(X) :- over_40(X)`, whose consequent, `gray_hair(X)` matches the goal. The algorithm then tries to prove the rule's antecedent, `over_40(X)`, with `X = ken`. A fact that matches this goal, `over_40(ken)`, is found in the database, so the query or unknown fact, `gray_hair(ken)` has been proved.

Theorem proving is complicated by the fact that there may be rules that seem relevant but lead to dead ends. For example, suppose that the rules "All individuals with 4 children have gray hair" and "All individuals with weak backs have 4 children" are the other facts in the database. These rules might be expressed in PROLOG as follows:

1. `gray_hair(X) :-`
   `has_4_children(X)`
2. `has_4_children(X) :-`
   `has_weak_back(X)`

If the algorithm happens to try rule (1) before the one discussed earlier, it will not be able to prove that Ken has gray hair. It will try to prove that Ken as 4 children, and fail when it discovers no assertion that Ken has a weak back.

To solve this problem, the algorithm must backtrack, when a subgoal fails, to an earlier point in the process and try an alternative rule in the database. To support backtracking, the PROLOG interpreter maintains a stack of subgoals that are waiting to be proved. When a subgoal fails, the interpreter pops it off the stack and tries to prove the subgoal now at the top. In our example, the subgoals `has_weak_back(ken)` and `has_4_children(ken)` would both be popped off the stack, and the interpreter would then try our other rule for `gray_hair`. If the stack of subgoals becomes empty, then no proof of the given query can be found.

The use of a stack to implement the execution of a logic program is another example of the abstraction/implementation duality that we have emphasized throughout this book. At the abstract level, the logic programmer thinks in terms of first-order predicate logic, and does not worry about how the computer proves theorems. At the implementation level, a backtracking algorithm supported by stack operations handles the real work of finding proofs.

Trace this parsing operation following the style of Table 15.1.

6. Using the postfix string you obtained in Exercise 5, trace the stack of real numeric values that would develop as the postfix expression is evaluated. You should indicate the values on the stack as each character in the postfix expression is processed. Assume the values $A = 4$, $B = 3$, $D = 2$, $P = 1$, $Q = 4$, and $Y = 2$.

7. Write an implementation of the **append** operation that is suitable for use with postfix strings in this section's `infix_to_postfix` function.

8. Write implementations of the **next_token**, **value_of**, and **eval** operations that are suitable for this section's evaluate function.

9. Explain how the relationship between the stack priorities and infix priorities of **(**, **)**, *****, **/**, **+**, **−**, and **#** controls the parsing of the infix expression. Then explain how you would extend the definition of the stack and infix priority functions of this section to include an exponentiation operator **^**. The exponentiation operator should be right associative; that is, in an expression such as A **^** B **^** C, the exponentiations should occur in right-to-left order.

10. How would the functions **infix_priority** and **stack_priority** be extended to include the Boolean operators **<**, **>**, **<=**, **>=**, **==**, **!=**, **&&**, **||**, and **!**? Justify your choices of priority values for these Boolean operators.

15.3 The Queue Abstract Data Type: Its Use and Implementations

OBJECTIVES

• to understand the definition of the queue ADT

• to understand what is meant by a computer simulation

• to be able to use the queue ADT in a simulation program

• to examine three implementations of the queue ADT: array, circular array, and linked list

The stack ADT that we have studied in the first two sections of this chapter is a last-in/first-out list. The next type of restricted list that we will examine, the queue, is a first-in/first-out list. All additions to a queue occur at one end, which we will designate as the rear of the queue. Items that enter the queue at the rear must move up to the front of the queue before they can be removed. **enqueue** is the name of the operation that adds an item to the rear of a queue, and **dequeue** is the name of the operation that removes an item from the front of a queue.

The operations on a queue thus parallel the dynamics of a waiting line. The linear order underlying a queue is determined by the length of time an item has been in the queue. This concept is depicted in Figure 15.6. The analogy of a waiting line makes a queue the obvious ADT to use in many applications concerned with scheduling. Before we explore such applications, however, we must formally define a queue as an ADT.

Queue. A queue is merely a restricted form of a list. In particular, the restrictions on a queue are that all additions to the queue occur at one end, the rear, and all removals from the queue occur at the other end, the front. The effect of these restrictions is to ensure that the earlier an item enters a queue, the earlier it will leave the queue. That is, items are processed on a first-in/first-out basis.

The five basic operations on a queue are specified by the following preconditions and postconditions.

◆ FIGURE 15.6

Abstract data type queue as computer embodiment of waiting line

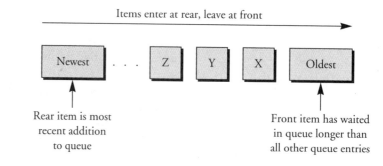

Items enter at rear, leave at front

| Newest | . . . | Z | Y | X | Oldest |

Rear item is most recent addition to queue

Front item has waited in queue longer than all other queue entries

Create operation
Preconditions: Receiver is an arbitrary queue in unknown state.
Postconditions: Receiver is initialized to the empty queue.

Empty operation
Preconditions: Receiver is a previously created queue.
Postconditions: Returns TRUE if queue is empty, FALSE otherwise.

Enqueue operation
Preconditions: Receiver is a previously created queue. `item` is a value to be added to the rear of the queue. There is memory available to store the new item in the queue.
Postconditions: `item` is added to the rear of the queue.

Dequeue operation
Preconditions: Receiver is a previously created queue. The queue is not empty.
Postconditions: Receiver has its front value removed, and `dequeue` returns this value.

at_front operation
Preconditions: Receiver is a previously created queue. The queue is not empty.
Postconditions: `at_front` returns the value at the front of the queue. Unlike `dequeue`, the queue is left unchanged.

EXAMPLE 15.5

To help conceptualize queue operations, consider the following sequence of actions on a queue of integers.

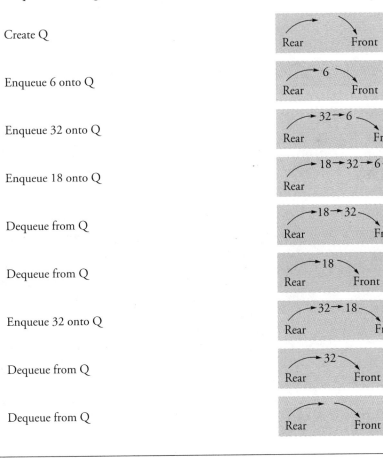

Create Q

Enqueue 6 onto Q

Enqueue 32 onto Q

Enqueue 18 onto Q

Dequeue from Q

Dequeue from Q

Enqueue 32 onto Q

Dequeue from Q

Dequeue from Q

Application of a Queue in Computer Simulation

Before discussing implementations of a queue, we will examine how this ADT can be used in an application known as computer *simulation*. To introduce the notion of a simulation, consider the following question.

> *The star car washing team at Octopus Car Wash requires precisely four minutes to wash a car. A car arrives on the average at Octopus every four minutes. In a typical 10-hour day at Octopus, how long does a car have to wait between its arrival and beginning its wash?*

It's tempting to answer this question by reasoning that the combination of four minutes to wash a car and four minutes between arrivals implies that no car should wait at all. However, such reasoning would not reflect the reality that cars arrive sporadically. Such sporadic arrival patterns are what can cause dreadful waiting lines.

That cars arrive, on the average, every four minutes really means that, in any given minute, there is a 25% chance that a car will arrive. We wish to reflect the notion of "chance" in a program that models the operation of Octopus Car Wash during a typical day. A computer simulation is a program that models a real-life event. To incorporate chance into simulations, a special function known as a *random number generator* is used.

A random number generator is a function that returns an unpredictable numerical value each time it is called. For our purposes, the value returned from a random number generator will be a real value greater than or equal to zero but less than 1. We will approach a random number generator as a "black box" function. That is, we will not worry about the internal logic of how such numbers are generated. Many versions of C++ supply a random number generator; if yours doesn't, you might use the one given by the **random_generator** class in Appendix 6. Our only concern in using a random number generator is that if we call on the function **random** in a loop such as the following

```
For each k from 1 to 100
        output random()
```

then we should see 100 values that obey statistical properties of randomness. Essentially these properties require that no pattern of values tends to recur and that values are evenly spread over the interval from 0 to 1. How will a random number generator be used to reflect the "reality" of cars arriving at Octopus Car Wash? We will view each iteration through a loop as one minute in the daily operation of Octopus. On each iteration, we will call on **random** to generate a random number. If it is less than or equal to 0.25 (corresponding to the 25% chance of an arrival), our program will interpret that as a car arriving during that minute. If the random number is greater than 0.25, the program decides that no car arrived during that minute.

When a car does arrive, it will be added to the waiting queue of cars. So that we may accumulate some statistical results, the car will be time-stamped with the time that it entered the queue. This time stamp will allow us to determine how long a car has been in the queue before it finally reaches the front. Conceptually, the queue at the core of this simulation is depicted in Figure 15.7. Pseudocode for the Octopus Car Wash simulation is

◆ **FIGURE 15.7**

Cars waiting at Octopus Car Wash, time-stamped with the minute of their arrival

Initialize statistical counters
Create the queue of time-stamped cars
For each minute in the day's operation
    Call on the random number generator to determine if a new car
        arrived
    If a new car arrived
        Time-stamp and enqueue in onto the queue of cars
    If no car is currently being washed and the queue of waiting cars is
        not empty
        Dequeue a car from the queue for washing
        Use the time stamp for the car just dequeued to
            determine
            how long it waited
        Add that wait time to the accumulating total wait time
        Record that we have just begun to wash a car
    If a car is being washed
        Reduce by one minute the time left before we are done washing it

To refine this pseudocode into a C++ main program, we must establish a formal C++ interface for the queue ADT.

C++ Interface for the Queue Abstract Data Type

```
// Class declaration file: queue.h

#ifndef QUEUE_H

#include "boolean.h"
#include "element.h"

// We assume that constant MAX_QUEUE_SIZE
// is already defined in element.h

// Declaration section

template <class E> class queue
{

    public:

    // Class constructors

    queue();
    queue(const queue<E> &q);

    // Member functions

    boolean empty();
    void enqueue(const E &item);
    E dequeue();
    E at_front();
    queue<E>& operator = (const queue<E> &q);

    // Protected data and member functions pertaining to
    // the implementation would go here.

};

#define QUEUE_H
#endif
```

EXAMPLE 15.6   Use the preceding C++ interface to write a main program for the Octopus Car Wash simulation. Assume the existence of a **random_generator** class.

```
// Program file: octopus.cpp
// A program to simulate the operation of the Octopus Car Wash over
// 10 hours (600 minutes) of operation.  The variables time_for_wash
// and prob_of_arrival represent the time it takes to run one car through
// Octopus's star car wash team and the probability that a car
// arrives for a wash in any given minute.  This program assumes the
// existence of a queue data type and a random number generator invoked
// by a call to the parameterless function random.
```

```cpp
#include <iostream.h>
#include <iomanip.h>

#include "boolean.h"
#include "queue.h"
#include "random.h"

random_generator generator;

float random();

int main()
{
        int time_for_wash,
        minute,
        time_entered_queue,
        cars_washed,
        total_queue_min,
        time_left_on_car;
        float prob_of_arrival;
        queue<int> car_queue;

        cout << "Enter time to wash one car: ";
        cin >> time_for_wash;
        cout << "Enter probability of arrival in any minute: ";
        cin >> prob_of_arrival;
        cars_washed = 0;
        total_queue_min = 0;
        time_left_on_car = 0;
        for (minute = 1; minute <= 600; ++minute)
        {
                if (random() < prob_of_arrival)
                        car_queue.enqueue(minute);
                if ((time_left_on_car == 0) && ! car_queue.empty())
                {
                        time_entered_queue = car_queue.dequeue();
                        total_queue_min = total_queue_min +
                                (minute - time_entered_queue);
                        ++cars_washed;
                        time_left_on_car = time_for_wash;
                }
                if (time_left_on_car != 0)
                        --time_left_on_car;
        }
        cout << setw(4) << cars_washed << " cars were washed" << endl;
        cout << "Average wait in queue " << setw(8) << setprecision(2)
                << float(total_queue_min) / cars_washed << endl;
        return 0;
}

float random()
{
        return generator.next_number(1,10)/10.0;
}
```

A sample run would appear as follows:

```
Enter time to wash one car 4
Enter probability of arrival in any minute 0.25
150 cars were washed
Average wait in queue 15.53
```

The sample run of the program in Example 15.6 provides an indication of how the sporadic arrival of cars can cause a backlog of work at Octopus Car Wash. One of the great values of simulation programs is that they allow cost-free experimentation with various scenarios to see if a situation might improve or worsen. For instance, the program we have written for Octopus could be used to explore how adding help to the car wash team (and correspondingly reducing the amount of time it takes to wash a car) could affect the build-up of cars waiting for service. You will get a chance to explore further the use of queues for computer simulations in the exercises and problems in the remainder of this chapter.

Another noteworthy point about Example 15.6 is that it works with a queue even though we have no idea of how the queue of cars is actually implemented. Of course, this should not be surprising; this is the value of designing programs and data structures from an ADT perspective. However, given the high-level logic in our example, we should now turn our attention to ways in which the scheduling queue might be implemented.

A NOTE OF INTEREST

Computer Simulations: Blessing or Curse?

The computer's ability to condense a large span of time (such as 600 minutes in Example 15.6) into the very short time frame required for a run of a simulation program is the blessing and the curse of computer simulations. It makes the computer a very valuable experimental tool. In addition to providing a much faster means of experimentation, simulation programs allow researchers and decisionmakers to set up initial conditions that would be far too risky if allowed in real life.

For example, consider the area of environmental studies. Here researchers can use simulation programs to create scenarios that would be far too time-consuming and dangerous if they were carried out in the environment. Researchers could use simulation software to see what might happen if pollution of a river were allowed to continue in an uncontrolled manner. If the results of the simulation indicate that all fish in the river would be gone within 10 years, nothing has really been lost. Moreover, some valuable information has been gained; decisionmakers in the environmental arena would know that some sort of pollution controls are necessary. Further experimentation with the simulation could be done to determine exactly what type and degree of controls should be imposed.

What can go wrong with decisions based on the result of computer simulation? Clearly, if the model on which the program is based is not an accurate reflection of the situation being simulated, results could be produced that would disastrously mislead decisionmakers. Additionally, we saw in Example 15.6, building the complex mathematical models used in simulation programs is a very sensitive process. Even models that seem to be relatively comprehensive can produce surprisingly inaccurate output. Hence, the real issue in using simulation results to support the decision-making process is the accuracy of the model on which the program is based. The authors of such a program must combine expertise in programming techniques with high levels of sophisticated knowledge in the relevant discipline(s). This is a situation in which computer science must truly become interdisciplinary.

The importance of simulation as an area of application within computer science is reflected in two issues of the *Communications of the ACM* that have been dedicated to this topic. The November 1985 issue (Volume 28, No. 11) reported on simulation models in such diverse areas as molecular genetics, aviation, and seismology. The October 1990 issue (Volume 33, No. 10) explored simulation in the context of parallel events, on-line scheduling, and semiconductor manufacturing.

Array Implementation of a Queue

From the definition of a queue, it is evident that two pointers will suffice to keep track of the data in a queue: one pointer to the front of the queue and one to the rear. This premise underlies all of the queue implementations we discuss in this section.

Let us consider computer jobs being scheduled in a batch processing environment, a good example of a queue in use. Suppose further that all job names are strings and that jobs are scheduled strictly in the order in which they arrive. Then an array and two pointers can be used to implement the scheduling queue. We will encapsulate the array and pointers in the class declaration module:

```cpp
// Class declaration file: queue.h

#ifndef QUEUE_H

#include "boolean.h"
#include "element.h"

// We assume that constant MAX_QUEUE_SIZE
// is already defined in element.h

template <class E> class queue
{

    public:

    // Class constructors

    queue();
    queue(const queue<E> &q);

    // Member functions

    boolean empty();
    void enqueue(const E &item);
    E dequeue();
    E at_front();
    queue<E>& operator = (const queue<E> &q);

    protected:

    // Data members

    int front, rear;
    E data[MAX_QUEUE_SIZE];

    // Member function

    boolean full();

};

#define QUEUE_H
#endif
```

If the **front** and **rear** pointers are initially set to 0 and –1, respectively, the state of the queue before any insertions or deletions appears as shown in Figure 15.8. Recalling that insertions may be made only at the rear of the queue, suppose that job NEWTON now arrives to be processed. The queue then changes to the state pictured in Figure 15.9. If job NEWTON is followed by PAYROLL, the queue's status must change to that of Figure 15.10, which shows that the addition of any item to the queue requires two steps:

```
++rear;
data[rear] = item;
```

If the system is now ready to process NEWTON, the front entry must be removed from the queue to an appropriate location designated by **item** in Figure 15.11. Here the instructions

```
item = data[front];
++front;
```

achieve the desired effect.

It should be clear that the conditions in Table 15.2 signal the associated boundary conditions for an array implementation of a queue.

The conditions allow us to develop our brief two-line sequences for adding to and removing from a queue into full-fledged functions. These in turn assume the existence of the Boolean-valued functions **empty** and **full** to check whether or not the **enqueue** and **dequeue** operations are possible. In the exercises, you will be asked to write the **create**, **empty**, and **full** operations.

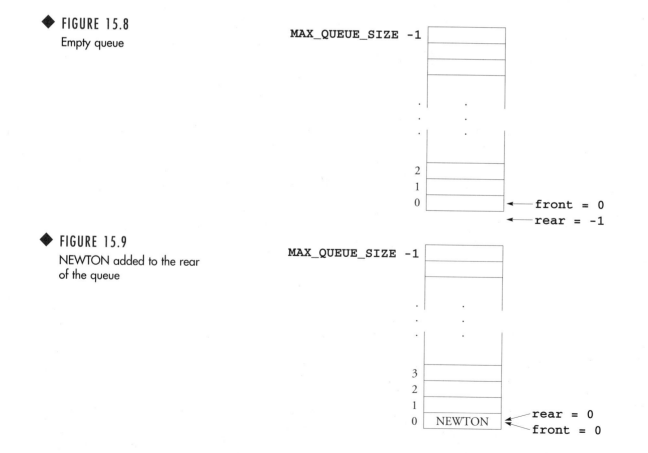

◆ FIGURE 15.8
Empty queue

◆ FIGURE 15.9
NEWTON added to the rear of the queue

◆ **FIGURE 15.10**
PAYROLL added after
NEWTON

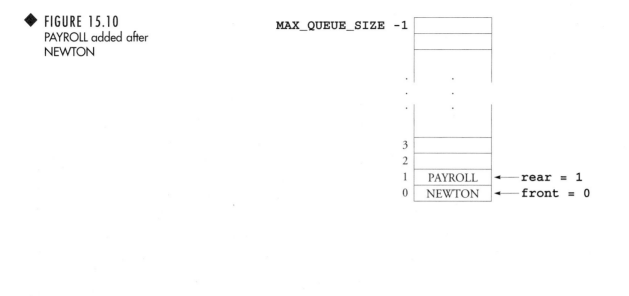

◆ **FIGURE 15.11**
NEWTON removed from the
queue

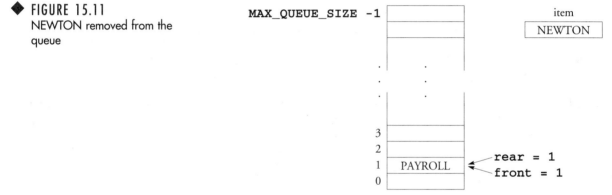

◇ **TABLE 15.2**
Boundary condition checks
for array implementation of
queue

Condition	Special Situation
`rear < front`	Empty queue
`front = rear`	One-entry queue
`rear = MAX_QUEUE_SIZE`	No more entries may be added to queue

EXAMPLE 15.7   Write the **enqueue** and **dequeue** operations for an array implementation of the
queue ADT.

```
void enqueue(E item)
{
        assert(! full());
        ++rear;
        data[rear] = item;
}

E dequeue()
```

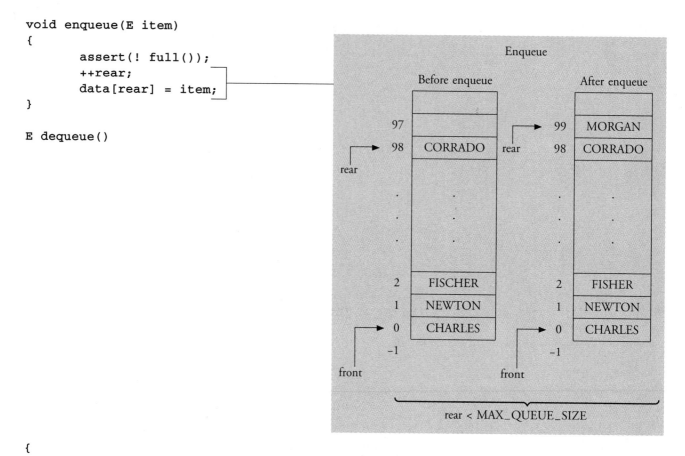

```
{
        E item;

        assert(! empty());
        item = data[front];
        ++front;
        return item;
}
```

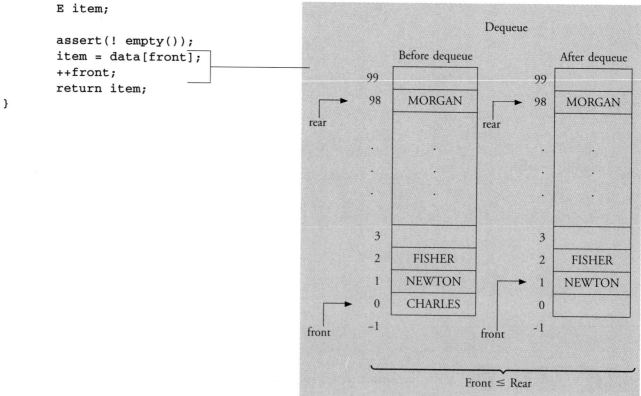

◆ FIGURE 15.12

A full queue

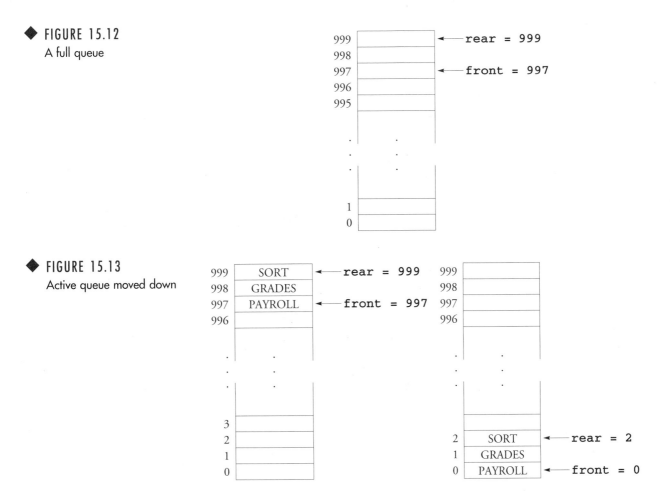

◆ FIGURE 15.13

Active queue moved down

As it now stands, our implementation of a queue as a scheduling structure for jobs in a batch environment functions effectively until **rear** matches **MAX_QUEUE_SIZE − 1**. Then a call to **enqueue** fails even though only a small percentage of slots in the array may actually contain data items currently in the queue structure. In fact, given the queue pictured in Figure 15.12, we should be able to use slots 0—996 again.

This is not necessarily undesirable. For example, it may be that the mode of operation in a given batch environment is to process 1000 jobs, then print a statistical report on these 1000 jobs, and finally clear the queue to start another group of 1000 jobs. In this case, the queue in Figure 15.12 is the ideal structure because data about jobs are not lost even after they have left the queue.

However, if the goal of a computer installation were to provide continuous scheduling of batch jobs, without interruption after 1000 jobs, then the queue of Figure 15.12 would not be effective. One strategy that could be employed to correct this situation is to move the active queue down the array upon reaching the condition **rear** equals **MAX_QUEUE_SIZE − 1**, as illustrated in Figure 15.13. If the queue contains a large number of items, however, this strategy would not be satisfactory because it would require moving all of the individual data items. We will discuss two other strategies that allow the queue to operate in a continuous and efficient fashion: a circular implementation and a linked list implementation.

Circular Implementation of a Queue

Circular implementation of a queue essentially allows the queue to wrap around upon reaching the end of the array. This transformation is illustrated by the addition of the item UPDATE to the queue in Figure 15.14. To handle the pointer arithmetic necessary for this implementation of a queue, we must make the front and rear pointers behave in a fashion analogous to an odometer in a car that has exceeded its mileage capacity. A convenient way of doing this is to use C++'s `%` operator. For instance, if we replace

```
++front;
```

in Example 15.7 with

```
front = front % MAX_QUEUE_SIZE;
```

and

```
++rear;
```

with

```
rear = rear % MAX_QUEUE_SIZE;
```

we will achieve the wraparound effect depicted in Figure 15.14. Unfortunately, it is clear from Figure 15.14 that **rear < front** will no longer suffice as a condition to signal an empty queue. To derive this condition, consider what remains after we remove an item from a queue that has only a single item in it. There are two possible situations, as illustrated in Figure 15.15. An inspection of both cases reveals that after the lone entry has been removed, the relationship

```
(rear % MAX_QUEUE_SIZE ) == front
```

holds between the pointers. There is a problem, however, with immediately adopting this as a check for an empty queue. This same relationship between pointers also exists when the queue is full.

◆ FIGURE 15.14

Queue wraps around when
UPDATE is added

◆ FIGURE 15.15
Removing from one-entry queue

Case 1: `front = rear < MAX_QUEUE_SIZE -1`

← front
rear

← front
← rear

Before removing
only entry

After removing
only entry

Case 2: `front = rear = MAX_QUEUE_SIZE -1`

← front
rear

← rear

← front

Before removing
only entry

After removing
only entry

◇ TABLE 15.3
Boundary condition checks
for circular queue with
encapsulated counter

Condition	Special Situation
Counter is 1	One-entry queue
Counter is 0	Empty queue
Counter is **MAX_QUEUE_SIZE**	Full queue

This apparent contradiction can be avoided easily if we add a counter to our encapsulation of the queue to keep track of the number of items currently in the queue. Then, as Table 15.3 indicates, tests for empty and full conditions need merely check this counter.

The actual implementation of queue operations using a circular array strategy is left for you to do in the exercises.

Linked List Implementation of a Queue

The linked list method allows a queue to be completely dynamic with size restrictions imposed only by the pool of available nodes. Essentially, the queue is represented as a linked list with an additional rear pointer to the last node in the list so that the list need not be traversed to find this node. We define a queue as a new derived class of linked list, and assume that the linked list class maintains a pointer to the last node as an attribute. Hence the linked list implementation of the queue containing PAYROLL, GRADES, and SORT would appear as in Figure 15.16. We will follow the convention that the front pointer for the queue points at the first node, while the rear pointer points at the last node. Hence we access the first actual item in the queue through the head pointer of the linked list, and the last actual item in the queue through the last pointer of the linked list.

The class declaration module for a queue as a derived class of linked list is

```
// Class declaration file: queue.h

#ifndef QUEUE_H

#include "boolean.h"

// Declaration section

template class <class E> queue : protected linked_list<E>
{

     public:

     // Class constructors

     queue();
     queue(const queue<E> &q);

     // Class destructor

     ~queue();

     // Member functions

     boolean empty();
     void enqueue(const E &item);
     E dequeue();
     E at_front();
     queue<E>& operator = (const queue<E> &q);

};

#define QUEUE_H
#endif
```

Note that the specifications of the data members for a queue disappear, in that they are inherited from the parent linked list class.

Appropriate functions for handling additions to and removals from the queue follow. Notice that from a calling module's perspective, it would make little difference whether these low-level functions used an array or a linked list to

◆ FIGURE 15.16
Queue with three data
nodes

implement the queue. For each implementation, we have bundled all the information involved with the queue into a single object of class queue. Hence the calling protocol for these modules is the same regardless of the implementation being used. Remember that is the essence of data abstraction: The details of how a data structure is actually implemented are hidden as deeply as possible in the overall program structure.

EXAMPLE 15.8

Code the **enqueue** and **dequeue** operations for a linked list implementation of a queue.

enqueue will insert data at the end of the linked list. Therefore, we move the **previous** pointer to the last node, set the **current** pointer to NULL, and call **insert** with the data:

```
template <class E>
void queue<E>::enqueue(E item)
{
     previous = last;
     current = NULL;
     insert(item);
}
```

dequeue will remove data from the beginning of the linked list. Therefore, we call **first** to position the pointers, and call **remove** to delete the data from the linked list:

```
template <class E>
E queue<E>::dequeue()
{
     E item;
     boolean success;

     assert(! empty());
     first();
     success = remove(item);
     return item;
}
```

Note that the second function implementation is more abstract and high level than the first, in that the second consists just of calls of public member functions, while the first accesses the underlying representation of the linked list. If this representation in the parent class were changed, we would have to update the first two lines of code in the **enqueue** function.

Priority Queues

So far we have used a batch scheduling application as an example of how a queue might be used in an operating system. Typically, such batch scheduling might also give higher priorities to certain types of jobs. For instance, at a university computer center, students in introductory computer science courses may receive the highest priority for their jobs to encourage a quick turnaround. Students in upper division courses may have the next highest priority, whereas jobs related to faculty research, which require a great deal of computation, get the lowest possible priority. These jobs could be classified as types A, B, and C, respectively. Any A job is serviced before any B or C job, regardless of the time it enters the service queue. Similarly, any B job is serviced before any C job. A data structure capable of representing such a queue requires just one *front pointer* but three *rear pointers,* one for each of the A, B, and C priorities.

A queue with eight jobs waiting to be serviced might appear as shown in Figure 15.17, which tells us that STATS, PRINT, and BANK are the A jobs awaiting service; COPY and CHECK, the B jobs; and UPDATE, AVERAGE, and TEST, the C jobs. If a new A job, PROB1, were to arrive for service, it would be inserted at the end of the A queue, between BANK and COPY. Because jobs can be serviced only by leaving the front of the queue, PROB1 would be processed before any of the B or C jobs.

Because insertions in such a *priority queue* need not occur at the absolute rear of the queue, it is clear that an array implementation may require moving a substantial amount of data when an item is inserted at the rear of one of the higher priority queues. To avoid this, you can use a linked list to great advantage when implementing a priority queue. Whenever an item arrives to be inserted into a given priority level, the rear pointer for that priority gives us an immediately accessible pointer to the node after which the item is to be inserted. This avoids a costly sequential search for the insertion point. If a dummy leader is included at the beginning of the list, the empty conditions for any given priority are as shown in Table 15.4. The specifics of writing a formal ADT definition of a priority queue

◆ **FIGURE 15.17**
Priority queue with eight jobs at three priority levels

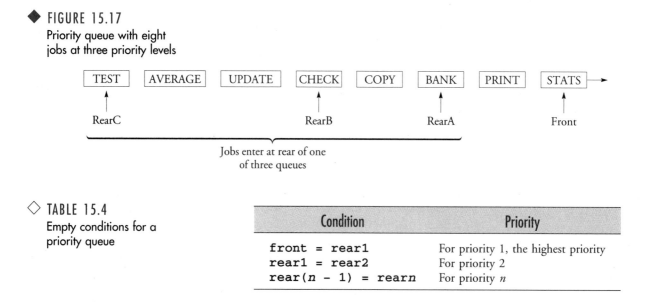

Jobs enter at rear of one
of three queues

◇ **TABLE 15.4**
Empty conditions for a priority queue

Condition	Priority
`front = rear1`	For priority 1, the highest priority
`rear1 = rear2`	For priority 2
`rear(n − 1) = rearn`	For priority n

and providing an implementation for it are included as exercises at the end of this section. In Chapter 17, we will see that priority queues may also be implemented using the special type of tree structure known as a heap (not to be confused with the heap maintained in C++ as described in chapter 14). Unlike the implementation we have just discussed, the heap will conveniently allow an unrestricted number of different priorities.

EXERCISES 15.3

1. Suppose you are given a queue that is known to contain only positive integers. Use only the fundamental queue operations to write a function

   ```
   void replace(queue<int> &q, int old_int, int new_int);
   ```

   which replaces all occurrences of the positive integer **old_int** in the queue with the positive integer **new_int**. Other than doing this, the queue is to remain unchanged. Avoid passing through the queue more than once.

2. Suppose that you are given a queue of real numbers. Using only the fundamental queue operations, write a function that returns the average value of an entry in the queue.

3. Augment the simulation program of Example 15.6 by
   a. Counting the number of minutes during the day when the Octopus Car Wash team is idle; that is, there are no cars in the queue waiting to be washed.
   b. Counting how many cars are left waiting in the queue at the end of the day.
   Make no assumptions about how the **car_queue** might be implemented.

4. Consider a circular array implementation of a queue in which the array is declared to have an index range 0..4. Trace the status of the array and the **front** and **rear** pointers after each of the following successive operations.

   ```
   enqueue SMITH
   enqueue JONES
   enqueue GREER
   dequeue
   enqueue CARSON
   dequeue
   enqueue BAKER
   enqueue CHARLES
   enqueue BENSON
   dequeue
   enqueue MILLER
   ```

5. Implement the **create** and **empty** operations for a (noncircular) array implementation of a queue. Be sure that your answers are consistent with the implementation of enqueue and dequeue in Example 15.7.

6. Provide data member declarations for a circular array implementation of a queue. Then use these declarations to implement each of the four basic queue operations.

7. Suppose that we adopt the following conventions for the **front** and **rear** pointers associated with a queue. **front** is to point at the next item to be removed from the queue. **rear** is to point at the first available location, that is, the next location to be filled. Following these conventions, implement all four queue operations for a noncircular array representation of the ADT.

8. Repeat Exercise 7 for a circular array representation.

9. In a queue used to schedule batch jobs on a computer system, it is often convenient to allow users to remove a job from the queue after submitting it. (They may, for example, realize that they accidentally submitted a job with an infinite loop.) Develop a function header for this removal operation. Be sure that you document it appropriately. Then implement it for a circular array representation of a queue.

10. Repeat Exercise 9 for a linked list representation of a queue.

11. Provide a formal ADT definition for the priority queue. Then implement the ADT under the assumption that possible priority values are drawn from a set that could be used to index an array. See if you can make your implementation of each operation $O(1)$ in its efficiency.

12. Discuss ways in which the Octopus Car Wash simulation of Example 15.6 does not reflect the way in which a car wash really operates. Then discuss ways in which the pseudocode logic behind this example should be modified to overcome these shortcomings.

A NOTE OF INTEREST

Operating Systems and Scheduling Resource Use in a Time-Sharing Environment

One of the primary problems facing designers of operating systems is the allocation and scheduling of resources that must be shared by a number of users. For instance, consider a simple time-sharing system that allows multiple users, each on a video terminal, and also has one shared printer. Suppose that the currently running process, called process A, makes a request to use the printer. Then, before this process completes its task on the printer, its allotted time (often called a time burst) expires, and it is replaced by process B as the currently running process. If process B requests the printer while it is running, we have a clear problem. If process B is granted the printer, its output will be interspersed with that from Process A, which did not complete its printing before its time burst expired. Obviously, we cannot let process B continue to run.

The solution developed by operating systems designers to honor both of these requests is to use multiple queues—one containing those processes that have cleared access to all resources they require to run, and one for processes that have requested a resource currently owned by another process. The former of these queues is often called the

ready queue; the latter is termed the blocked queue. Hence the solution to the scenario described in the first paragraph involves two steps.

1. Move process A from its currently running state to the ready queue when its time burst expires (because it has all the necessary resources to start running again).

2. Move process B to the blocked queue when it requests the printer already owned by process A. Here it would remain until process A is done with the printer, at which time the front entry in the blocked queue for the printer (B in this case) would be moved to the ready queue.

In practice, the addition and removal of processes to and from these queues is controlled by special flags called semaphores. For a thorough exposition on operating system queues and semaphores, see Abraham Silberschatz and Peter B. Galvin, *Operating System Concepts*, 4th ed. (Reading, Mass.: Addison-Wesley, 1994).

FOCUS ON PROGRAM DESIGN

The application of the parsing algorithm described in Section 15.2 is not limited to compilers. Many of the programs typically used by scientists, engineers, and mathematicians can be greatly enhanced by allowing the user to interactively enter an algebraic expression as opposed to embedding the expression inside the program. Consider, for instance, the situation described in the following memorandum from the head of the physics department at the University of Hard Knocks.

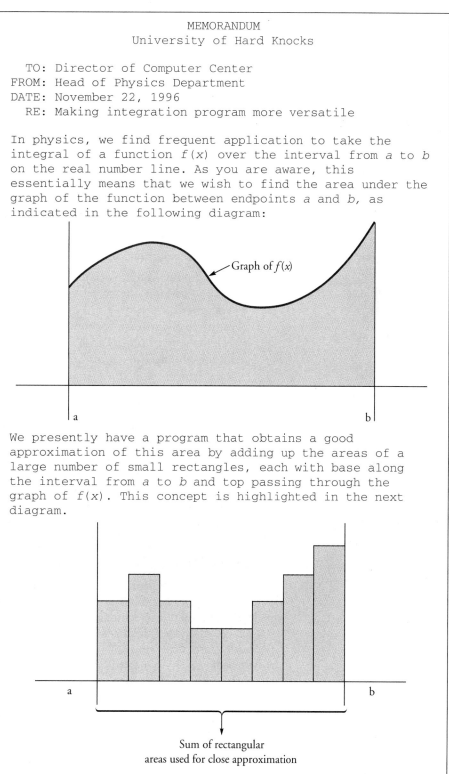

MEMORANDUM
University of Hard Knocks

```
  TO: Director of Computer Center
FROM: Head of Physics Department
DATE: November 22, 1996
  RE: Making integration program more versatile
```

In physics, we find frequent application to take the integral of a function $f(x)$ over the interval from a to b on the real number line. As you are aware, this essentially means that we wish to find the area under the graph of the function between endpoints a and b, as indicated in the following diagram:

Graph of $f(x)$

a   b

We presently have a program that obtains a good approximation of this area by adding up the areas of a large number of small rectangles, each with base along the interval from a to b and top passing through the graph of $f(x)$. This concept is highlighted in the next diagram.

a   b

Sum of rectangular
areas used for close approximation

> The user of our program can interactively enter the
> endpoints *a* and *b* and the number of rectangles. The
> result is a very good approximation when enough
> rectangles are used.
>
> Our problem is not with the accuracy of the approximation
> but with the fact that to change the function *f*(x), the
> user must edit the definition of the function in the
> source program and then recompile. Can you help us by
> writing a program which will allow the user to enter the
> function *f*(x) interactively? The functions we integrate
> in this fashion can be defined in terms of the standard
> arithmetic operations of addition, subtraction,
> multiplication, division, and exponentiation. Thanks in
> advance for your prompt assistance.

The physics department head has presented us with a substantial task in the preceding memorandum. Consider some of the subordinate problems with which we will be faced in writing this program:

- The evaluation of integrals; that is, areas under graphs of functions. Obtaining numerical answers to mathematical problems of this variety will serve to introduce us to a subject known as *numerical analysis*.
- The interactive *parsing* and evaluation of a function will give us an opportunity to adapt the algorithms introduced earlier.
- For the type of functions described in the memorandum, the problem of finding the next token in the expression can become complicated. Consider, for instance, a function defined by the expression

$$3.14 * X \wedge 3 + X \wedge 2$$

where $\wedge$ is used to denote exponentiation. Here, from a stream of incoming characters, we must be prepared to select a token that may be a real number, the variable X, or an arithmetic operator. The problem of recognizing tokens in an incoming stream of characters is called *lexical analysis*. To keep our situation relatively simple, we will assume that all tokens must be separated by a space and no other operations such as trigonometric functions may be used in defining the function f.

Modular Structure Chart for the Integral Evaluation System

With these comments in mind, we turn our attention toward designing a solution to the integration problem. Recall that the first step in this design process is to develop a modular structure chart reflecting the way in which we will partition the problem into subproblems (see Figure 15.18). Since both conversion from infix to postfix and the evaluation of a postfix expression require fundamental stack operations, we have located our stack processing modules at the deepest level of the structure chart. Here they will be accessible by both the parsing and evaluation algorithms.

Interestingly, our system will also make use of a queue. Because the tokens in the postfix expression are now more complicated objects than single characters, we need a data structure to append tokens to as they are processed by the infix-to-postfix algorithm. A queue emerges as a very nice ADT for this purpose. Hence the structure chart also indicates the presence of fundamental queue operations at a level accessible by both the parsing and evaluation algorithms.

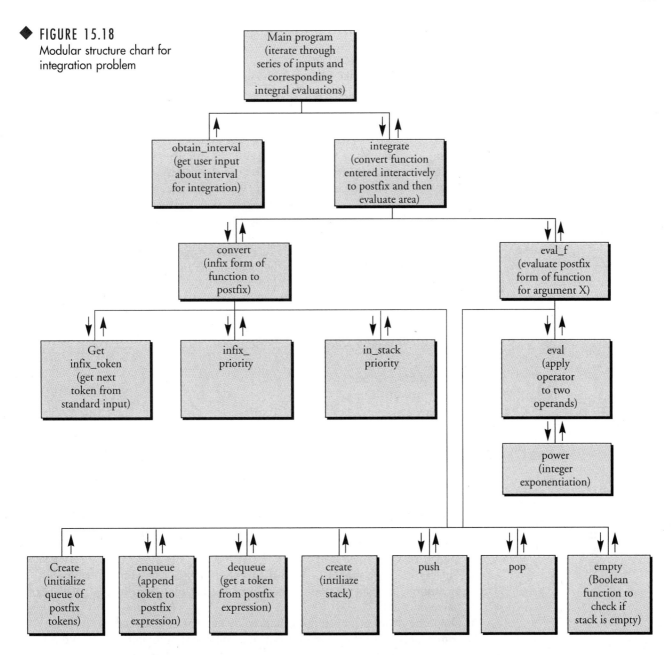

◆ **FIGURE 15.18**
Modular structure chart for
integration problem

Data Structures for the Integral Evaluation System

We will need a queue to store the postfix expression that is built as the infix
expression goes through our conversion algorithm. The data in this queue are more
complex than characters, however. This is because the tokens needed from the infix
string being entered by the user are not necessarily individual characters. Rather,
such tokens will fall into one of the three following categories:

1. *A real number:* If the token is a real number, the lexical analysis phase of our
   algorithm must convert it from the appropriate stream of digits and decimal
   point as typed by the user.
2. *The variable X:* The infix expression defines the function in terms of this general variable. When the function is evaluated, a particular value is then substi-
   tuted for *X*.

3. *An operator:* We broadly include **+**, **-**, *****, **/**, **^**, **( )**, and the special delimiter **#** in this category.

The problem with a token that may be either a real number or a character is that we essentially need a data type that can assume one of several identities, depending on the current token. In the abstract, we can think of each token as having two attributes: a *code* telling us which class of token it is (real number, operator, or variable) and a *value* that the particular token assumes (a particular real number, operator, or variable name). To represent this information, we place the code attribute in a new class called *token*. Because the codes are of the same type, the code attribute will be treated as the *fixed part* of a C++ structure. Because the values can be of different types (**float** or **char**), the value attribute will be treated as the *variant part* of a C++ structure. Structure variants can be represented in C++ as *unions*. A union allows several data members of different types to be declared in a structure, but only one of them may be used at any given time. The currently used member is identified by examining the value of the fixed part of the structure. The structure definition that we will use for tokens follows:

```
enum token_code {REAL_VALUE, VAR_X, OPERATOR};

struct token_record
{
    token_code code;
    union
    {
        float real_value;
        char operator;
        char var_x;
    };
};
```

The following points concerning variant parts or unions should now be made:

1. Each variant part or union should have associated with it a *tag member* in the fixed part of the structure.

2. The tag member should be an ordinal type, such as **int**, **char**, or an enumeration. This will allow examination of the tag member's value in a **switch** statement.

3. Only one member in a union can store a value at any given time.

4. Before storing a value in a member of a union, the programmer should set the corresponding tag member to the appropriate value. In our example, the tag member should be set to **REAL_VALUE** before storing a real number in the variant part, or to **OPERATOR** or to **VAR_X** before storing a character there.

5. Before using the value in a member of a union, the programmer should check to see that the corresponding tag member has the appropriate value. This is typically done with a **switch** statement. In our example, the programmer should use the value of the **real_value** member only if the tag member has the value **REAL_VALUE**.

6. Failure to adhere to the rules specified above can cause program errors. In our example, an attempt to access the **real_value** member of the variant part if the tag member contains the value **OPERATOR** may cause an error.

Variant parts or unions are defined by a form as follows:

```
union
{
      <type 1> <member 1>;
      <type 2> <member 2>;
      .
      .
      .
      <type n> <member n>;
};
```

union is a reserved word. The members of a union are indented for readability. The member names in a union lie in the same scope as the enclosing structure member names.

Here is the class declaration module for the token class:

```
// Class declaration file: token.h

#ifndef TOKEN_H

enum token_code {REAL_VALUE, VAR_X, OPERATOR};

// Declaration section

class token
{

        public:

        // Class constructors:

        token();
        token(token_code code);
        token(const token &t);

        // Member functions

        token_code code();
        float real_value();
        char op();
        char var_x();
        void set_code(token_code code);
        void set_real_value(float value);
        void set_op(char op);
        void set_var_x(char var_x);
        token& operator = (const token &t);

        protected:

        // Data members
```

```
                struct token_record
                {
                        token_code code;
                        union
                        {
                                float real_value;
                                char op;
                                char var_x;
                        };
                };

                token_record the_token;

        };
```

In processing any given token object, we first examine the code and then use the value appropriately. Moreover, we can use the token class as an element type in other data structures like stacks and queues. For example, the three kinds of token used in parsing can be created, pushed onto a stack of tokens, and then popped off and output:

```
token number(REAL_VALUE);
token operator(OPERATOR);
token variable(VAR_X);
stack<token> tokens;
token to_output;
number.set_real_value(3.14);
operator.set_operator('+');
variable.set_var_x('X');
tokens.push(number);
tokens.push(operator);
tokens.push(variable);

while (! tokens.empty())
{
        to_output = tokens.pop();
        switch (to_output.code())
        {
                case REAL_VALUE:    cout << to_output.real_value();
                                    break;
                case OPERATOR:      cout << to_output.operator();
                                    break;
                case VAR_X:         cout << to_output.var_x();
        }
        cout << endl;
}
```

Given this specification of a token type, an appropriate data structure for the postfix expression is a queue whose elements are of type **token**.

The final data structure needed by our program is a stack. Actually, two conceptual stacks are needed: one for operator symbols during the parsing phase and one for values during the evaluation phase. However, by making **token** the class of items in the stack, we can use just one stack structure for both of the conceptual stacks that are needed.

The module specifications for the integral evaluation problem posed by the head of the physics department follow.

1. **Module:** main program
   Task: Repeatedly call on modules to obtain input specifications and then evaluate integral.

2. **Module:** obtain_interval
   Task: Issue appropriate prompts and read user input. Terminate when $a >= b$.
   Outputs: Interval endpoints a and b, number_of_rectangles to use in approximating area

3. **Module:** integrate
   Task: Compute width of each rectangle as $(b - a)$/number_of_rectangles. Call on module convert to convert infix expression read from standard input to postfix notation. Initialize area to zero. Repeatedly evaluate f at the midpoint of the base of the current rectangle, multiply this by the width of the base, add resulting product to area accumulation.
   Inputs: Endpoints a and b, and number-of-rectangles for which area is to be accumulated
   Outputs: Approximation to area under graph of function entered interactively by user

4. **Module:** infix_to_postfix
   Task: Follow algorithm described in Section 15.2 of text.
   Outputs: Postfix queue of tokens, delimited by #, corresponding to what user enters from standard input

5. **Module:** get_infix_token {*Note:* This module is responsible for lexical analysis.}
   Task: Gets the next token from the standard input stream
   Inputs: Infix expression being read from standard input
   Outputs: from_infix, a token containing the next token read from standard input
   Logic: {*Note:* We assume all tokens separated by one space.}
   Initialize value field of from_infix to zero. {In case token is a real number.}
   Do
      Let ch be next character read from standard input
      switch ch
         1. case ' ' : We are done.
         2. case 'X' : Set from_infix to ch
         3. case '+', '−', '*', '/', '^', '(', ')', '#' : Set from_infix to ch
         4. case '.' : Set a Multiplier to 0.1 for future accumulation.
         5. case '0', '1', '2', .. '9':   if left of decimal
                                                Set value to 10 * value plus ch
                                          else
                                                Set value to value + multiplier*ch
      Divide multiplier by 10 for next iteration.
   While ch is not ' '

6. **Module:** infix_priority
   Task: See Section 15.2 of text.
   Inputs: t, a token
   Outputs: Infix priority rank of t

7. **Module:** in_stack_priority
   Task: See Section 15.2 of text.
   Inputs: *t*, a token
   Outputs: In-stack priority rank of *t*

8. **Module:** eval_f
   Task: See evaluation algorithm in Section 15.2 of text.
   Inputs: Postfix queue representation of function *f*, *x*, the real number at which *f* is to be evaluated
   Outputs: The real number *f*(*x*)

9. **Module:** eval
   Task: Select the appropriate C++ operation based on op.
   Inputs: v1, v2: the values of two operands and op: character containing operator +, −, *, /, ^
   Outputs: Numeric result of applying op to v1 and v2.

The complete C++ program for the integral evaluation system follows, with reference to the module specifications. Also included are graphic documentation and sample runs to give you a more detailed grasp of how the program functions in its interaction with a user.

```
// Program file: focus.cpp

// Program to compute area under curve of function entered
// interactively.  A stack is used to convert function
// expression to postfix notation (which is stored in a queue)
// and then to evaluate.
// Valid function expressions can contain the variable X,
// numeric constants, operators +, -, *, /, ^ (for
// exponentiation) and appropriate parentheses.

#include <iostream.h>
#include <iomanip.h>
#include <math.h>
#include <ctype.h>

#include "token.h"
#include "strlib.h"
#include "stack.h"
#include "queue.h"

const char END_TOKEN = '#';

void obtain_interval(float &a, float &b,
    int &number_of_rectangles);

void integrate(float a, float b, int number_of_rectangles,
    float &area);

void infix_to_postfix(queue<token> &postfix);

void get_infix_token(token &from_infix);
```

```
int infix_priority(token t);

int instack_priority(token t);

float eval_f(queue<token> postfix, float x);

float eval(float v1, float v2, char op);

boolean is_op(char ch);

int main()
{
    float a, b, area;
    int number_of_rectangles;

    obtain_interval(a, b, number_of_rectangles);
    cout << fixed << showpoint << setprecision(3);
    while (a < b)
    {
        integrate(a, b, number_of_rectangles, area);
        cout << "Approximation to area is " << setw(10)
            << area << endl;
        cout << endl;
        obtain_interval(a, b, number_of_rectangles);
    }
    return 0;
}
void obtain_interval(float &a, float &b,
    int &number_of_rectangles)
{

    cout << "Enter left and right endpoints "
        << "(left >= right to quit)--> ";
    cin >> a >> b;
    if (a < b)
    {
        cout << "Enter number of rectangles for "
            << "computing area--> ";
        cin >> number_of_rectangles;
    }
}

void integrate(float a, float b, int number_of_rectangles,
    float &area)
{
    stack<token> token_stack;
    queue<token> postfix;
    int count;
    float width, x;

    width = (b - a) / number_of_rectangles;
    count = 0;
```

```
    x = a;
    infix_to_postfix(postfix);

    while (count < number_of_rectangles)
    {
        area = area + eval_f(postfix, x + width / 2.0) * width;
        x = x + width;
        ++count;
    }
}

void infix_to_postfix(queue<token> &postfix)
{
    token bottom_stack(OPERATOR);
    token from_stack, from_infix;
    stack<token> token_stack;
    char ch;

    // Must push END_TOKEN to correspond with
    // algorithm in Section 14.2

    bottom_stack.set_op(END_TOKEN);
    token_stack.push(bottom_stack);
    cout << "Enter function with spaces between tokens, "
         << then <ENTER>";
    cin.get(ch);
    do
    {
        get_infix_token(from_infix);
        if ((from_infix.code() == REAL_VALUE)||
            (from_infix.code() == VAR_X))
            //We have an operand -- variable or number.
            postfix.enqueue (from_infix);
        else if (from_infix.op() == ')')
        {
            from_stack = token_stack.pop();
            while (from_stack.op() != '(')
            {
                postfix.enqueue (from_stack);
                from_stack = token_stack.pop();
            }
        }
        else if (from_infix.op() == END_TOKEN)
            while (! token_stack.empty())
            {
                from_stack = token_stack.pop();
                postfix.enqueue(from_stack);
            }
        else
    // We have one of arithmetic operators +, -, *, /, ^ or )
        {
            from_stack = token_stack.pop();
            while (instack_priority(from_stack) >=
```

```
                             infix_priority(from_infix))
                    {
                             postfix.enqueue(from_stack);
                             from_stack = token_stack.pop();
                    }
                    token_stack.push(from_stack);
                    token_stack.push(from_infix);
            }
        } while (! ((from_infix.code() !== OPERATOR) &&
            (from_infix.op() == END_TOKEN));
}
void get_infix_token(token &from_infix)
{
        const char SPACE = ' ';
        char ch = ' ';
        float multiplier = 0.1;
        boolean left_of_decimal = TRUE;
        int column = 0;

        do
        {
            ++column
            cin.get(ch);
            if (is_op(ch))
            {
                    from_infix.set_code(OPERATOR);
                    from_infix.set_op(ch);
            }
            else if (isdigit(ch))
            {
                    if (column == 1)
                    {
                            from_infix.set_code(REAL_VALUE);
                            from_infix.set_real_value(0);
                    }
                    if (left_of_decimal)
                    from_infix.set_real_value
                            (from_infix.real_value() * 10.0 + (ch - '0'));
                    else
                    {
                            from_infix.set_real_value
                                    (from_infix.real_value() * multiplier
                                            + (ch - '0'));
                            multiplier = multiplier / 10.0;
                    }
            }
            else if (ch == '.')
            {
                    left_of_decimal = FALSE;
                    multiplier = 0.1;
            }
            else if (ch == 'X')
            {
```

```
                    from_infix.set_code(VAR_X);
                    from_infix.set_var_x(ch);
            }
      } while ((ch != '\n') && (ch != SPACE) && (ch != END_TOKEN));
}

int infix_priority(token t)
{
      int priority = 0;

      switch (t.op())
      {
          case '^':            priority = 3;
                               break;
          case '*':
          case '/':            priority = 2;
                               break;
          case '+':
          case '-':            priority = 1;
                               break;
          case '(':            priority = 4;
                               break;
          case ')':
          case END_TOKEN:      priority = 0;
      }
      return priority;
}

int instack_priority(token t)
{
      int priority = 0;

      switch (t.op())
      {
          case '^':            priority = 3;
                               break;
          case '*':
          case '/':            priority = 2;
                               break;
          case '+':
          case '-':            priority = 1;
                               break;
          case '(':
          case END_TOKEN:      priority = 0;
      }
      return priority;
}

float eval_f(queue<token> postfix, float x)
{
      token result(REAL_VALUE);
      token t1, t2, t3;
      stack<token> token_stack;
```

```
    // Will push END_TOKEN
    t1 = postfix.dequeue();

    // Put token back into queue for next call to eval_f
    postfix.enqueue(t1);

    // We're done when encounter operator that is
    // END_TOKEN.

    while (! ((t1.code() == OPERATOR) && (t1.op() == END_TOKEN)))
    {
        if (t1.code() != OPERATOR)
            if (t1.code() == REAL_VALUE)
                token_stack.push(t1);
            else
            {
                t1.set_code(REAL_VALUE);
                t1.set_real_value(x);
                token_stack.push(t1);
            }
        else
        {
            t2 = token_stack.pop();
            t3 = token_stack.pop();
            result.set_real_value(eval(t3.real_value(),
                t2.real_value(),
                t1.op()));
            token_stack.push(result);
        }
        t1 = postfix.dequeue();
        postfix.enqueue(t1);
    }
    result = token_stack.pop();
    return result.real_value();
}

float eval(float v1, float v2, char op)
{
    float result = 1;

    switch (op)
    {
        case '+':   result = v1 + v2;
                    break;
        case '-':   result = v1 - v2;
                    break;
        case '*':   result = v1 * v2;
                    break;
        case '/':   result = v1 / v2;
                    break;
        case '^':   result = pow(v1, v2);
                    break;
    }
```

```
        return result;
}

boolean is_op(char ch)
{
        return (ch == '+') || (ch == '-') || (ch == '*')
               || (ch == '/') ||(ch == '^') || (ch == '(')
               || (ch == ')') || (ch == END_TOKEN);
}
```

Sample runs:

```
Enter left and right endpoints (left >= right to quit)-> 0 3
Enter number of rectangles for computing area-> 10
Enter function with spaces between tokens, then <ENTER>
3
Approximation to area is 9.000

Enter left and right endpoints (left >= right to quit)-> 0 3
Enter number of rectangles for computing area-> 10
Enter function with spaces between tokens, then <ENTER>
X ^ 2
Approximation to area is 8.978

Enter left and right endpoints (left >= right to quit)-> 0 3
Enter number of rectangles for computing area-> 100
Enter function with spaces between tokens, then <ENTER>
X ^ 2
Approximation to area is 9.000

Enter left and right endpoints (left >= right to quit)-> 0 1
Enter number of rectangles for computing area-> 100
Enter function with spaces between tokens, then <ENTER>
( X + 2 ) ^ 3 / ( X + 1 )
Approximation to area is 10.526

Enter left and right endpoints (left >= right to quit)-> 0 0
```

RUNNING, DEBUGGING
AND TESTING HINTS

1. In applications in which the size to which a stack or queue may grow is hard to predict, use a linked list to implement the ADT. That way, you can take advantage of C++'s dynamic memory management to avoid having to worry about a full data structure.

2. Many scientific and mathematical application programs can be enhanced by allowing users to enter function definitions at run time. This chapter's Focus on Program Design section provides an example of how such run-time definitions of a function can be done.

3. When debugging simulations, use a random number sequence that remains the same over different runs of the program. Without such a sequence, your program will behave differently on separate runs even though you provide it with identical inputs. This is because you are getting a different pattern of random numbers. Appendix 6 indicates how you can ensure a fixed sequence of random numbers from one run of the program to the next.

SUMMARY

Key Terms

activation record	numerical analysis	ready queue
blocked queue	parsing	rear pointer
first-in/first-out (FIFO)	pop	semaphores
fixed part	postfix	simulation
front pointer	prefix	stack
infix	priority queue	stack priority
infix priority	push	token
last-in/first-out (LIFO)	queue	union
lexical analysis	random number generator	variant part

Key Concepts

◆ Conceptually, a stack is simpler than a queue since all additions and deletions are limited to one end of the structure, the top. For this reason, a stack is also known as a last-in/first-out (LIFO) list. Like a queue, a stack may be implemented using either an array or a linked list.

◆ The simplicity of the stack as an abstract structure belies the importance of its application. Stacks play a crucial role in the parsing done by language compilers.

◆ Parsing, as we have studied it in this chapter, involves the conversion of an expression from infix to postfix notation. In infix notation, an algebraic operator is located between its two operands. In postfix notation, the operator follows its two operands.

◆ Expressions in postfix notation do not require parentheses to override the standard hierarchy of algebraic operations.

◆ Stacks process function calls when a program executes.

◆ A queue is a first-in/first-out (FIFO) data structure used in processing of data such as job scheduling in a large university computer environment. There are two basic pointers, front and rear, associated with this structure. New data items are added to the rear of the queue, and the data item that is about to be processed is removed from the front of the queue.

◆ The relative advantages and disadvantages of three implementations of queues—array, circular array, and linked list—are summarized in the following table:

Implementation	Advantages	Disadvantages
Array	A record of queue entries remains even after they have been removed.	Static allocation of storage limits overall queue size. Array locations cannot be reused once entries are removed from queue.
Circular array	Array locations can be reused once entries are removed from the queue.	Static allocation of storage limits overall queue size.
Linked list	With C++ pointer variables, the queue can grow dynamically to take full advantage of all space available in C++'s heap.	Could be less space efficient than array implementations since each node in queue must include a pointer field as well as data fields.

◆ Primary applications of queues are in the areas of operating systems and computer simulation of events.

PROGRAMMING PROBLEMS AND PROJECTS

1. Write a program that will parse infix expressions into prefix form.

2. Write a program to call for input of a decimal number and convert it to its binary equivalent using the method described in the following flowchart. Note that this method produces the binary digits for the given number in reverse order. Use a stack to get them printed in the correct order.

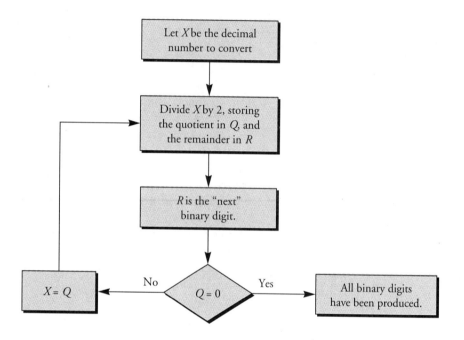

3. Programming Problem 2 for Chapter 14, you developed a passenger list processing system for the various flights of Wing-and-a-Prayer Airlines. Wing-and-a-Prayer management would now like you to extend this system so that it processes logical combinations of flight numbers. For example, the command

```
LIST 1 OR 2
```

should list all passengers whose name appears on the flight 1 list or the flight 2 list. Your program should also accept the logical operators **AND** and **NOT** and allow parenthesized logical expressions obeying the standard logical hierarchy

```
NOT
AND
OR
```

4. A tax form may be thought of as a sequence of items, each of which is either a number or defined by an arbitrary mathematical formula involving other items in the sequence. To assist them in their tax-planning strategy, top management at the Fly-by-Night credit card company desires a program that would allow them to enter interactively numbers or formulas associated with given lines of a tax form. Once all such lines have been defined, users of the program may redefine the number or formula associated with a particular line, and all other lines dependent on that one should be appropriately updated. Note that, since formulas may be entered interactively, your program will have to use a stack to evaluate them. You will in effect have written a small-scale spreadsheet program.

5. Write a program that will accept commands of the following form:

- ` INPUT <variable name> `
- ` <variable name> = infix expression involving variables names and arithmetic operators +, -, *, / `
- ` PRINT <variable name> `
- ` GO `

These commands are to be stored in an array of strings until the **GO** command is entered. Once the **GO** command is entered, your program should execute the previously stored commands. "Execute" here means the following:

- **For an INPUT command:** Send a question mark to the terminal and allow the user to enter a real number; this real number is then stored in the variable name.

- **For an assignment statement:** Parse the expression into postfix form and then evaluate it, storing the results in the variable name on the left of the equality sign.

- **For a PRINT instruction:** Write to the terminal the numerical contents of the specified variable name.

- To make things relatively easy you may assume a syntax that Allows variable names consisting of one uppercase alphabetical character.
- Allows only one variable name following the commands for **INPUT** or **PRINT**.
- Allows one blank space after the commands for **INPUT** and **PRINT** and no blank spaces anywhere else.

For an additional challenge, enable your program to handle successfully the exponentiation operator ^ within assignment statement expressions. The following example should illustrate the need for care in handling this exponentiation operator:

$3^{2^3} = 3^8$, not 9^3

6. This problem is an extension of Problem 5 for a "compiler" for a primitive programming language. Write a program that will accept commands of the following form:

- ` INPUT <variable name> `
- ` PRINT <variable name> `
- ` <variable name> = infix arithmetic expression involving variable names and arithmetic operators +, -, *, /, ^ `
- ` GOTO <line> ` $\begin{cases} \texttt{ALWAYS, or} \\ \\ \texttt{IF infix logical expression involving} \\ \quad \texttt{variable names and operators +, -,} \\ \quad \texttt{*, /, ^, \& (for AND),| (for OR),} \\ \quad \texttt{!(for NOT), <, >, =} \end{cases}$
- ` STOP `
- ` RUN `

These commands are to be stored in an array of strings until the **RUN** command is entered. Upon encountering the **RUN** command, your program should execute the previously stored commands. "Execute" here means the following:

- **For an INPUT command:** Send a question mark to the terminal and allow the user to enter a real number, which is stored in the variable name.
- **For a PRINT command:** Write to the terminal the numerical contents of the specified variable name.
- **For an assignment command:** Parse the expression into postfix form and then evaluate it. Store the result in the variable name on the left of the equality sign.
- **For a GOTO command:** Branch to the line number specified when the **AL-WAYS** condition follows the line number or when the infix expression that follows the **if** evaluates to true. Here "line number" refers to the relative position of the line in the sequence of lines that were entered prior to the **Run** command. The first line number in this sequence is "00".
- **For a STOP command:** Halt execution.

To make things relatively easy, you may assume a syntax that

- Specifies that one and only one blank space follows **INPUT**, **PRINT**, **GOTO**, and line number. No other blanks appear anywhere.
- Allows only one variable name to follow **INPUT** or **PRINT**.
- Only allows variable names consisting of one uppercase alphabetical character.
- Only allows line numbers consisting of two digits: 00 through 99.

The usual hierarchy for operators is assumed.

7. Modify the program in the Focus on Program Design section so that it also integrates expressions involving the functions sin, cos, tan, exp, and ln. Test your modified program by having it evaluate the following integrals:

   a. $\sin(X * 2) + \cos X / 2$ between 0 and 1
   b. $3 * (X + 4) \wedge 2 + \tan(X / 2)$ between 0 and 1
   c. $3 * (X + 4) \wedge 2 + \tan X / 2$ between 0 and 1
   d. $\exp \ln X \wedge 3$ between 1 and 3
   e. $\exp \ln (X \wedge 3)$ between 1 and 3

8. If you have access to a graphics library in your version of C++, write a program that allows a user to define interactively a function and then displays a graph of the function between two specified endpoints.

9. Develop a program to simulate the processing of batch jobs by a computer system. The scheduling of these jobs should be handled via a queue (or priority queue for more of a challenge). Examples of commands that your program should be able to process are

Command	Purpose
ADD	To add an entry to queue.
DELETE	To take an item out of the queue.
STATUS	To report on items currently in queue.

10. In Chapter 8 you developed a program to keep track of a bank's records. Now the bank has asked you to develop a program to simulate the arrival of customers in a waiting line at the bank. Factors to consider are the average time it takes to service one customer, the average number of customers that arrive in a given time period, and the number of service windows maintained by the bank. These factors should be provided as input to your program. Statistics such as the length of time the average customer has to spend in the waiting line could be very helpful in the bank's future planning.

11. Here is a problem typically encountered in text formatting applications.

Given a file of text, that text delimited by special bracketing symbols [and] is to be considered a footnote. Footnotes, when encountered, are not to be printed as normal text but are instead stored in a footnote queue. Then, when the special symbol # is encountered, all footnotes currently in the queue are printed and the queue should be returned to an empty state.

What you learn in solving this problem will allow you to make good use of string storage techniques discussed in earlier chapters.

12. To improve their services, the Fly-by-Night credit card company (Problem 3, Chapter 14) has decided to give incentives to their customers for prompt payment. Customers who pay their bills two weeks before the due date receive top priority and a 5% discount. Customers who pay their bills within one week of the due date receive next priority and a 1% discount. Third priority is given to customers who pay their bills on or within two days after the due date. The customers who pay their bills thereafter are assigned the lowest priority. Write a program to set up a priority queue to access customer records accordingly.

13. The Bay Area Brawlers professional football team (Problem 4, Chapter 14) has been so successful in recent weeks that the team management is considering the addition of several new ticket windows at the team's stadium. However, before investing a sizable amount of money in such an improvement, they would like to simulate the operation of ticket sales with a variety of ticket window configurations. Develop a computer program that allows input of such data as number of ticket windows, average number of fans arriving each hour as game time approaches, and average length of time to process a ticket sale. Output from your program should include statistics such as the average waiting-line length each hour as game time approaches and the amount of time the average fan had to wait in line before having his or her ticket request processed. Use queues to represent each of the waiting lines.

14. Consider the design for an implementation of the radix sort algorithm and its associated bin (sublist) structure that was discussed in Chapter 14's Focus on Program Design section. Note that queues could provide an alternative implementation for the bin structure needed by radix sort. What queue implementation would provide the most space-efficient bin structure for radix sort? Why? Develop a complete radix sort program that uses queues to implement the bins needed by the algorithm and then accesses these bins *only* through the defined ADT operations for a queue. Is this implementation of radix sort more or less time efficient than that described in Chapter 14's Focus on Program Design section? Justify your answer in a written memorandum.

15. As Director of Computer Operations for Wing-and-a-Prayer Airlines, you receive the following memorandum. Design and write a simulation program according to the specifications in the memorandum.

```
                    MEMORANDUM
               Wing-and-a-Prayer Airlines

   TO: Director of Computer Operations
 FROM: President, Wing-and-a-Prayer Airlines
 DATE: September 30, 1996
   RE: Wasted Fuel and Time

Wing-and-a-Prayer Airlines is becoming increasingly
concerned about the amount of fuel being wasted as its
planes wait to land at and take off from world-famous
O'Hair Airport. Could you please help us write a program
to simulate the operation of one day's activity at O'Hair
and report on the times spent waiting to land and take
off for each Wing-and-a-Prayer flight? Input data to the
program should include

 ■ Average number of Wing-and-a-Prayer arrivals each hour
 ■ Average number of other airline arrivals each hour
 ■ Average number of Wing-and-a-Prayer departures each
   hour
 ■ Average number of other airline departures each hour
 ■ Number of available runways
 ■ Average time a runway is in use for an arrival
 ■ Average time a runway is in use for a departure

By appropriately adjusting these parameters, we hope to
do some valuable ''what-if'' analyses regarding the time
spent waiting for a runway by our arrivals and
departures.
```

16. If an arithmetic expression is written in prefix notation, then there is no need to use parentheses to specify the order of operators. For this reason, some compilers translate infix expressions (such as 2 + 8) to prefix notation (+ 2 8) first and then evaluate the prefix string. Write a program that will read prefix expressions and then compute and display the value of the indicated arithmetic expression. Assume that the operands are single-digit positive integers separated by blanks. The operators can be +, −, *, and /, also separated by blanks and having their usual meanings of add, subtract, multiply, and divide.

17. Implement the following robustness enhancements for the program in this chapter's Focus on Program Design section.

    a. Make the **get_infix_token** module more robust by allowing the user to separate individual tokens with an arbitrary number of zero or more spaces.

    b. Make the **get_infix_token** module more robust by guarding against input of an invalid arithmetic operator.

    c. Make the **get_infix_token** module more robust by guarding against an invalid character in a stream of characters intended to be a real number. When such an invalid character is detected, allow the user to recover from the point of error rather than forcing the user to retype the entire line.

18. This chapter's Note of Interest on "Computer Simulations: Blessing or Curse?" cites two issues of the *Communications of the ACM* that have been dedicated to the topic of simulation. Using these two issues as a starting point, research and prepare a written report on computer simulation. Your report could discuss any or all of the following:

   a. Examples of disciplines and industries in which simulation has been used to great advantage.

   b. Limitations and inaccuracies that arise in modeling a system by computer simulation. Techniques that can be used to measure and monitor such inaccuracies.

   c. The reliance of many simulation programs on the effective generation of random numbers.

   d. The potential danger in relying on the results of simulation programs without examining the validity of their underlying models.

19. This chapter's Focus on Program Design section demonstrated how a computer program can be used to solve a mathematical problem in interactive fashion. In particular, the type of problem solved by this program is the evaluation of integrals. Explore other types of mathematical problems that can be solved interactively by software systems available at your school. (The *Mathematica* program from Wolfram Research is one example of such a system available at many universities.) Prepare a report on the results of your explorations. In keeping with the theme of this chapter's Focus on Program Design section, be sure that your report includes a discussion of the types of mathematical expressions that can be parsed and evaluated by such systems.

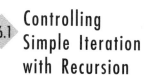 16 Recursion

It's deja vu all over again.

Lawrence Peter (Yogi) Berra

Research is the process of going up alleys to see if they are blind.

Marston Bates

In Chapter 6, we examined problems that are suited to iterative control by methods such as **while**, **do**, and **for** loops. Many of these problems can more easily be solved by designing functions that call themselves. In computer science this form of self-reference is called *recursion*. We are now ready to embark on a detailed study of recursive problem solving.

In this chapter, we first examine the essentials of recursive functions. Now that we are familiar with stack operations, we will also be able to explain how recursion is implemented. The "invisible" data structure underlying *recursive functions* is a stack used by the system to process the call-and-return pattern of functions in a program (Section 15.1). By examining the role of this system stack more closely, you will build confidence in your ability to express algorithms recursively. In time, you will use this technique without hesitation in your problem solving.

Then we will begin to use recursion to explore problems for which nonrecursive solutions would be exceedingly difficult to fathom. We hope that you will be amazed at the ease with which recursion handles such problems. We will demonstrate that recursion is a natural and elegant way to solve many complex problems. We will also begin to explore the price paid for this elegance: the compactness of a recursive solution to a complex problem is not necessarily an accurate statement of its time or space efficiency.

Finally, we will use recursion to develop a problem-solving methodology known as *trial-and-error*, or nondeterministic, *backtracking*. In theory this technique can solve a large variety of problems. Unfortunately, in practice, the technique is so computationally expensive that it can only be used to solve small instances of such problems in a reasonable amount of time.

16.1 Controlling Simple Iteration with Recursion

Any recursive algorithm must have a well-defined stopping state, or *termination condition*. Without careful logical control by means of such conditions, recursive functions can fall prey to looping in endless circles. To illustrate this, let us suppose that we have access to an output device known as a pen plotter. Such a device is equipped with a pen held by a mechanical hand that is under control of the computer.

- to examine the essentials of controlling simple iteration by recursion

- to be able to identify and distinguish tail-recursive algorithms

- to understand what is meant by the stack frame associated with a function or function call

- to understand the role of the system stack in processing calls made to a recursive function, particularly a function that is not tail recursive

- to be able to trace the contents of the system stack during execution of recursive functions with only one embedded recursive call

Typical functions to manipulate the pen could include

Function	Action
`line(n)`	Draw a line of length n in the current direction.
`right_turn(d)`	Alter current direction by rotating d degrees in clockwise direction.

Such functions are not unlike those found in the Logo programming language or the "turtle" graphics toolkits that accompany many popular C++ compilers. If you have access to such a compiler, you may wish to explore developing some recursive graphic figures.

If we assume that the pen is initially set to draw a line toward the north—the top of the plotting page—then the following sequence of instructions

```
line(10);
right_turn(90);
line(10);
right_turn(90);
line(10);
right_turn(90);
line(10);
```

will clearly draw a square with sides of length 10.

Let us now try to predict what will happen when the following recursive function draw is invoked by the initial call **draw(1)**.

```
void draw(int side)
{
        line(side);
        right_turn(90);
        draw(side + 3)        // Recursive call
};
```

The initial call **draw(1)** will result in a line of length 1 in a northerly direction. We then rotate the pen toward the east and, via a recursive call, generate a line of length 4. This is followed by a rotation to the south and a new invocation for a line of length 7. The emerging pattern should now be clear; the resulting right-angled spiral is shown in Figure 16.1.

Unfortunately, our spiral-producing function has tumbled into a vicious circle loop of self-reference. There is currently no way to turn off the *recursive calls* made to draw. Consider what happens, however, if we provide ourselves with a *recursive termination condition* (or recursive out) as in the following new version of **draw**:

```
void draw(int side)
{
    if (side <= 34)           // Recursive termination condition
    {
        line(side);
        right_turn(90);
        draw(side + 3)        // Recursive call
    }
}
```

Runaway recursive spiral

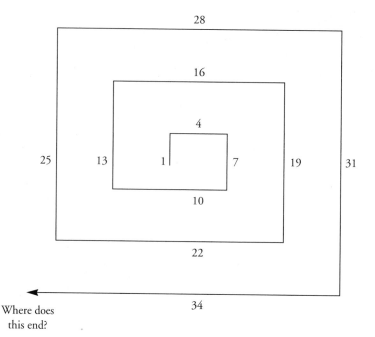

Where does
this end?

Now after drawing the line of length 34 in Figure 16.1, our **draw** function invokes itself once more, passing 37 for the parameter **side**. Since the recursive termination condition is now FALSE, no line of length 37 will be drawn. More importantly, no further recursive invocation of **draw** will be made. Hence, we return immediately from the call to **draw** with **side** being 37. Moreover, that return triggers returns (in reverse order) from all the previous invocations of **draw**, eventually ending up at the instruction following our initial call; that is, **draw(1)**.

The important point to stress here is that, to use recursion appropriately, we must use a recursive termination condition to avoid an infinite series of recursive calls. If we were to view each recursive call as a descent one level deeper into an algorithm's logic, we in effect must use a recursive termination condition to allow a corresponding ascent back to the level of the first call to the function. This concept is highlighted in Figure 16.2.

Linked Lists as Recursive Data Structures

In Section 16.1 we defined the linked list ADT. We can now reformulate that definition from a recursive perspective. The key to such a perspective is the realization that the pointer leading from each linked list node references another linked list. More formally:

Linked list: A linked list is a pointer that is either NULL (the recursive termination condition signaling an empty list) or references a node designated as the head node. The head node contains a data field and a pointer that satisfies the criteria for being a linked list.

Though an English composition teacher may find fault with our defining a linked list in terms of itself, our new definition is nonetheless completely free of ambiguity. For instance, to verify that the list in Figure 16.3 is a linked list, we note the following:

◆ FIGURE 16.2

Unwinding from descent
through recursive calls

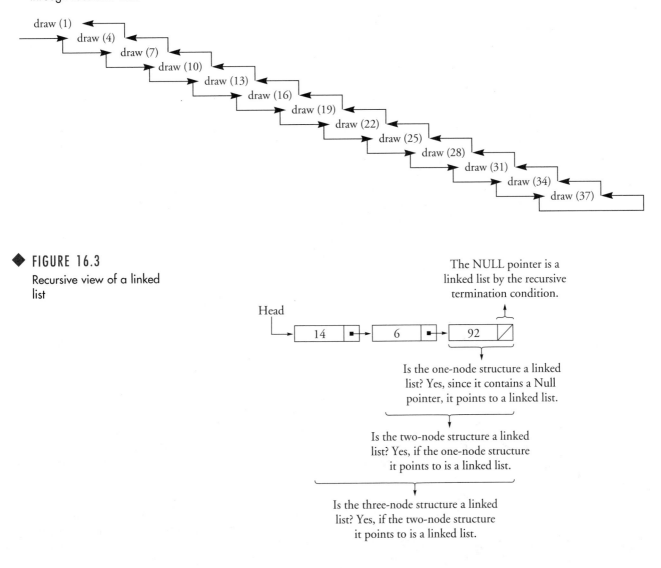

◆ FIGURE 16.3

Recursive view of a linked
list

1. The head node in the three-item structure contains a pointer to an embedded two-item structure, which we must verify as a linked list.
2. The head node in the two-item structure contains a pointer to an embedded one-item structure.
3. The head node in the one-node structure contains a NULL pointer.
4. By the recursive termination condition, a NULL pointer meets the criteria for being a linked list.
5. Hence the one-node structure in step 3 contains a pointer to a linked list and meets the criteria for being a linked list.
6. Similarly, we climb up the recursive ladder to verify that the two-node and, consequently, the three-node structures in steps 1 and 2 meet the criteria for being linked lists.

Not only does our recursive definition unambiguously specify the linked list ADT, but it also provides a natural way to implement linked list operations by recursive functions. Consider the following example.

EXAMPLE 16.1

A linked list is implemented by C++ pointer variables in the following declarations:

```
typedef struct node;
typedef node *linked_list;
struct node
{
    element data;
    linked_list next;
};
```

Develop a recursive implementation of the traverse operation.

The implementation literally flows from our recursive definition of the linked list structure. That is, if the list we are traversing is empty there is nothing to do; otherwise we must process the data in the head node and recursively traverse the linked list referenced by the **next** field in the head node. This logic is embodied in the following C++ function:

```
void traverse(linked_list list, void (*process (element &data))
{
    if (list != NULL)
    {
        process(list->data);
        traverse(list->next, process);
    }
}
```

A trace of the recursive function **traverse** for the list of Figure 16.3 is given in Figure 16.4. This trace shows that the function is initially called with a list pointer to the node containing 14. The data are processed, and the first recursive call then passes in a pointer to the node containing 6. The data item 6 is processed, and a pointer to the node containing 92 is recursively passed to the function. The node containing 92 is processed, and a NULL pointer is recursively passed to the function. Since the recursive termination condition (**list == NULL**) is now met, we unwind

◆ **FIGURE 16.4**
Trace of recursive function **traverse** on the linked list of Figure 16.3

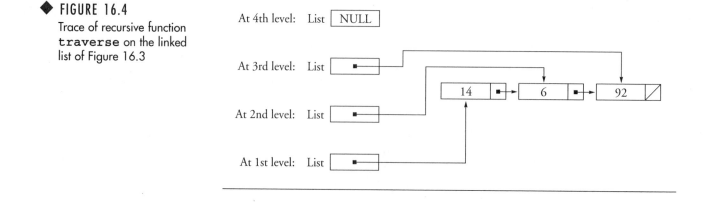

from the series of recursive calls. As we return to each prior recursive level, there is nothing left to do since the recursive call is the last operation at that level.

A recursive function is called *tail recursive* if only one recursive call appears in the function and that recursive call is the last operation performed at that procedural level. (That is, nothing else must be done after returning from a deeper recursive level.) The `traverse` function of Example 16.1 is clearly tail recursive. Typically, such a tail-recursive function can be easily recast in the form of a nonrecursive function using a `while` or `do` control structure. We have already seen how to do this for `traverse` in Chapter 14.

How Is Recursion Implemented?

As we begin to examine recursive algorithms that are not tail recursive, we will also need to understand in detail *how* a computer language implements recursion. Here again we encounter the abstraction/implementation duality we have emphasized throughout the book. Recursion is a powerful conceptual tool. But unless you understand details of how recursion is implemented, your use of it will be limited to an intuitive approach that often employs a trial-and-error strategy to reach a solution.

In Section 15.1, we indicated that the stack is an essential data structure in a compiler's implementation of function calls. The role of a system stack being manipulated by the function calls in your program becomes even more crucial as we use recursion. To illustrate this, let us consider a problem more computationally oriented than our previous graphics and linked list examples. N factorial, denoted N!, is defined by

$$N! = N \times (N-1) \times (N-2) \times \ldots \times 2 \times 1$$

That is, N! is the product of the first N integers. We note that an alternate way of defining N! is by means of using (N − 1)!

$$N! = \begin{array}{l} 1 \text{ if } N = 1 \text{ or } N = 0 \\ N * (N-1)! \text{ otherwise} \end{array}$$

Notice that this alternative definition is a *recursive definition* because it uses the notion of factorial to define factorial. Despite this circularity, we have a perfectly valid definition because of the recursive termination condition in the special definition of 1!.

To see how recursion works for factorial computation, think of the preceding definition as a series of clues that will eventually allow us to unravel the mystery of how to compute N!. That is, to compute N!, the recursive definition really tells us to

1. Remember what N is.
2. Go compute (N − 1)!.
3. Once we've computed (N − 1)!, multiply that by N to get our final answer.

Of course, when we use the definition to determine how to compute (N − 1)!, we find out that we must, in turn, compute (N − 2)!. Computing (N − 2)! will involve finding (N − 3)!. This downward spiral will eventually end with 1!, allowing us to begin the actual series of multiplications that will bring us to the appropriate answer. Figure 16.5 illustrates the logic of the recursive method for computing N factorial. In particular, if N were 4, the sequence of recursive invocations of the definition and resulting computations would be as shown in Figure 16.6.

The program in Example 16.2 calls a recursively defined `factorial` function. The associated run indicates the behavior of the program for an input of 4.

◆ FIGURE 16.5
Recursive computation of $N!$

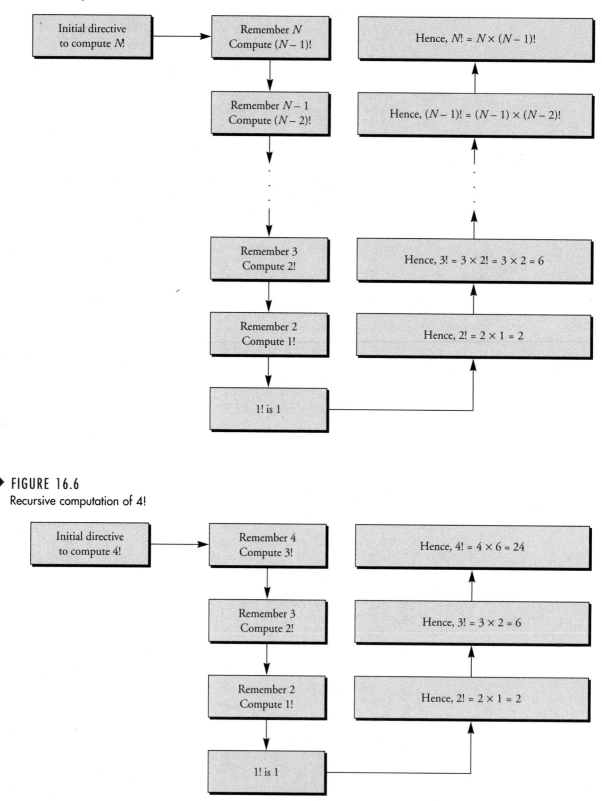

◆ FIGURE 16.6
Recursive computation of 4!

EXAMPLE 16.2

```cpp
// Program file: factor.cpp

#include <iostream.h>
#include <iomanip.h>

int indent = 0;

int factorial(int n);

int main()
{
    int m;

    cout << "ENTER NUMBER for FACTORIAL COMPUTATION-> ";
    cin >> m;
    cout << factorial(m) << endl;
    return 0;
}

int factorial(int n)
{
    int result;

    cout << setw(indent) << "" << "ENTERING FACTORIAL WITH N = " << n << endl;
    if ((n == 1) || (n == 0))
    {
        cout << setw(indent) << "" << "LEAVING FACTORIAL WITH N = " << n;
        cout << ", FACTORIAL(N) = " << 1 << endl;
        --indent;
        return 1;
    }
    else
    {
        ++indent;
        result = n * factorial(n - 1);
        cout << setw(indent) << "" << "LEAVING FACTORIAL WITH N = " << n;
        cout << ", FACTORIAL(N) = " << result << endl;
        --indent;
        return result;
    }
}
```

A sample run for the preceding code follows.

```
ENTER NUMBER for FACTORIAL COMPUTATION->4
  ENTERING FACTORIAL WITH N = 4
    ENTERING FACTORIAL WITH N = 3
      ENTERING FACTORIAL WITH N = 2
        ENTERING FACTORIAL WITH N = 1
        LEAVING FACTORIAL WITH N = 1, FACTORIAL(N) = 1
      LEAVING FACTORIAL WITH N = 2, FACTORIAL(N) = 2
```

```
LEAVING FACTORIAL WITH N = 3, FACTORIAL(N) = 6
LEAVING FACTORIAL WITH N = 4, FACTORIAL(N) = 24
24
```

The output statements used on entry to and exit from function **factorial** in Example 16.2 are not necessary but have been included to demonstrate the precise call and return sequence triggered by the initial call of **factorial(4)** in the main program. It is crucial to note that the output from output statements implies that we must in some sense have multiple copies of the variable N, one copy for each descent to a recursively deeper level. As we shall see, a stack keeps track of these multiple copies of N in the appropriate fashion.

It is also important to emphasize that function **factorial** would not be tail recursive even if the output statements were removed. This is because the recursive call to factorial is not the last operation performed by the algorithm. After a return from the call to factorial $(N - 1)$, we must multiply by N. It is this multiplication that is the final operation performed. The fact that we multiply by N after returning from a recursive call indicates that, for algorithms that are not tail recursive, we must have some means of preserving the values of parameters and local variables at each level of the recursive execution of the algorithm.

The comments // **Return Point 1** and // **Return Point 2** in Example 16.2 will allow us to trace the role played by a stack as this program is run. We have already alluded to the existence of a general system stack onto which return addresses are pushed each time a function or function call is made. Let us now explain it more fully. Each time a function or function call is made, an item called a *stack frame* or activation record will be pushed onto the system stack. The data in this stack frame consist of the return address and a copy of each local variable and parameter for the function. Figure 16.7 illustrates how stack frames are pushed and popped from the system stack when **factorial(4)** is invoked. Return addresses have been indicated by referring to the appropriate comments in the C++ code.

Although function **factorial** of Example 16.2 provides an illustration of an algorithm that is not tail recursive, you could still validly argue that the computation of $N!$ could be achieved more easily by a nonrecursive, iterative loop structure. To sense the real power and elegance of recursion, we must begin to explore algorithms that more subtly manipulate the stack frames hidden below the surface of recursive processing. These stack frames provide us with a "free" stack data structure; that is, a structure that we need not declare formally and that we control completely by the recursive calling pattern of our algorithm.

◆ FIGURE 16.7
Sequence of pushes and
pops in computing 4!

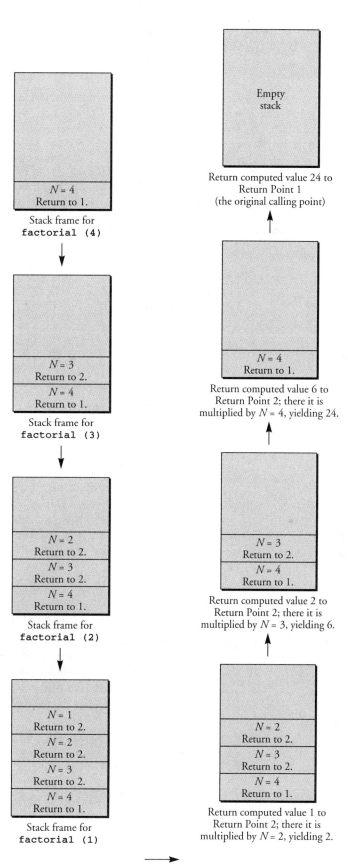

A NOTE OF INTEREST

Language Definition

The syntax of most computer languages can be recursively defined. This is of tremendous importance in the writing of compilers, most of which rely heavily on stacks and recursion to parse source programs.

A broader question than the definition and parsing of programming languages is the ability of the computer to process natural languages such as English. Researchers in the field of artificial intelligence are attempting to use more general recursive techniques to define the syntax of natural languages and, consequently, program the computer to cope with this more complex type of language. To date, their work has met with success only in highly restricted domains of natural language such as that used to express word problems in algebra or interact with databases in a structured query language. Despite these present limitations, research in language definition and the consequent processing of that language by a computer should be one of the most intensely explored fields within computer science in the future.

EXERCISES 16.1

1. Stand between two parallel mirrors and see how recursion works for you.

2. Consider the following pair of functions to compute $N!$

```
int factorial(int n)
{
    return fact_helper(n, 1);
}

int fact_helper(int n, int result)
{

    if ((n ==0) || (n == 1))
        return result;
    else
        return fact_helper(n - 1, n * result);
}
```

   Is `fact_helper` tail recursive? Will it work? Explain why or why not.

3. Each of the following functions offers a slight variation on the traverse function developed in Example 16.1. For each function, indicate what output would be produced if the function were called initially with the linked list of Figure 16.3 and the process function merely printed the data field of each node. If the function would crash with a run-time error for the data of Figure 16.3 or any other test case, explain why.

   a.
```
void traverse(linked_list list, void (*process) (element &data))
{
    if (list != NULL)
    {
        traverse(list->next, process);
        process(list->data);
    }
}
```

b.
```
void traverse(linked_list list, void (*process) (element &data))
{
     process(list->data);
     if (list->next != NULL)
          traverse(list->next, process);
}
```

c.
```
void traverse(linked_list list, void (*process) (element &data))
{
     if (list->next != NULL)
     {
          process(list->data);
          traverse(list->next, process);
     }
}
```

4. Which of the functions in Exercise 3 are tail recursive?

5. The following programs are intended to read a string character by character, put each character on the system stack, and then print the string of characters in reverse order. Which one(s) actually achieve the intent? Which one(s) don't? Why not? What will be the output of each program for input of 'MADAM'?

a.
```
// Print out a string in reverse order to check if palindrome
#include <iostream.h>
void reverse();
int main()
{
     reverse;
     return 0;
}
// Keep recursively stacking characters until end of string.
// Then print it out in reverse by unstacking.

void reverse()
{
     char ch;         // Here ch is locally declared
     cin.get(ch);
     if (ch != '\n')
     {
          reverse();
          cout.put(ch);
     }
     else
          cout.put('\n');
}
```

b.
```
// Print out a string in reverse order to check if palindrome
#include <iostream.h>
char ch;                   // Here ch is globally declared
void reverse();
int main()
{
     reverse;
     return 0;
}
```

```
// Keep recursively stacking characters until end of string.
// Then print it out in reverse by unstacking.

void reverse()
{
      cin.get(ch);
      if (ch != '\n')
      {
            reverse();
            cout.put(ch);
      }
      else
            cout.put('\n');
}
```

6. Given the declarations for the linked list structure in Example 16.1, write a recursive function to search the list for a particular item and return a pointer to the item in the list if it is found. If the item is not found in the list, a NULL pointer should be returned.

7. Suppose that **number_array** is declared as follows:

    typedef int number_array[100];

    Study the following function and determine what it computes. (*Hint:* Try to trace it for several small instances of the array and N values.)

```
int compute(number_array a, int n)
{
      if (n == 0)
            return a[n];
      else if (a[n] < compute(a, n - 1))
            return a[n];
      else
            return compute(a, n - 1);
}
```

8. Write a recursive function of two integer arguments M and N, both greater than or equal to zero. The function should return M^N.

9. Write a recursive function of two integer arguments M and N, $M > 1$ and $N > 0$. The function should return the integer log of N to the base M. This is defined to be the least integer L such that $M^{L+1} > N$. (*Hint:* Though your function only receives two arguments, embed within it an auxiliary function of three arguments—M, N, and L. Call on the auxiliary function initially with $L = 0$; the auxiliary function is then called recursively.)

10. Given the declaration of **number_array** in Exercise 7, write a function **product** that receives two arguments, one of type **number_array** and another argument **N** that indicates the logical size of **number_array**. Remember that the logical size of an array is the number of indices that store well-defined data items. Function **product** should return the product of the entries in the array from indices 1 through N.

11. Insert tracer output instructions at strategic points and use them to debug the following version of a function, which attempts to compute factorials recursively. After

you've debugged the function, write a statement in which you explain the behavior of the function as originally coded and also why the function did not work in this original form.

```
int factorial(int n)
{
        if ((n == 0) || (n == 1))
               return 1;
        else
        {
               --n;
               return n * factorial(n);
        }
}
```

16.2 Weaving More Complex Recursive Patterns

OBJECTIVES

- to recognize problems particularly suited to recursive solutions
- to be able to state the solutions to such problems as a simpler instance of the same problem
- to be able to trace the performance of a recursive algorithm using a run-time trace diagram
- to use an algorithm's run-time trace diagram to estimate the time and space efficiency of the algorithm
- to see how recursive algorithms that potentially involve more than one recursive call at each level may lead to an exponential time efficiency
- to develop an intuitive approach for developing recursive solutions to problems

The recursive algorithms we have examined so far share the property that, at each level of recursive execution of the algorithm, at most one recursive call will be made. The pattern of operations on the system stack for such algorithms is that a series of stack frames is pushed, a recursive termination condition is reached, and then all stack frames are successively popped until we return to the execution level of the main program. More complex recursive algorithms involve multiple recursive calls at each level of execution. Correspondingly, the pattern of operations on the system stack will not be a series of uninterrupted pushes followed by a series of uninterrupted pops. Instead, the system stack will initially grow a bit, then shrink, then grow again, then shrink, and so forth.

Towers of Hanoi Problem

An old legend has it that monks were given the painstaking task of moving a collection of n stone disks from one pillar, designated as pillar A, to another, designated as pillar C. Moreover, the relative ordering of the disks on pillar A had to be maintained as they were moved to pillar C. That is, as illustrated in Figure 16.8, the disks, all of different sizes, were to be stacked from largest to smallest, beginning from the bottom. Additionally, the monks were to observe the following rules in moving disks:

- Only one disk could be moved at a time.
- No larger disk could ever be placed on top of a smaller disk on any pillar.
- A third pillar B could be used as an intermediate to store one or more disks while they were being moved from their original source A to their destination C.

Consider the following recursive solution to this problem:

1. If $n = 1$, merely move the disk from A to C.
2. If $n = 2$, move the first disk from A to B. Then move the second disk from A to C. Then move the first disk from B to C.
3. If $n = 3$, call on the technique already established in step 2 to move the first two disks from A to B using C as intermediate. Then move the third

◆ FIGURE 16.8
Towers of Hanoi problem

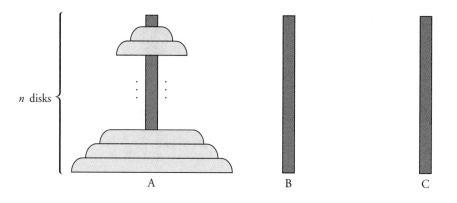

n disks

A   B   C

disk from A to C. Then use the technique in step 2 to move the first two disks from B to C using A as an intermediate

.
.
.

n. For general *n,* use the technique in the previous step to move $n - 1$ disks from A to B using C as an intermediate. Then move one disk from A to C. Then use the technique in the previous step to move $n - 1$ disks from B to C using A as an intermediate.

Notice that this technique for solving the Towers of Hanoi describes itself in terms of a simpler version of itself. That is, it describes how to solve the problem for n disks in terms of a solution for $n - 1$ disks. In general, any problem you hope to solve recursively must be approached in this fashion. This strategy is important enough to state as a principle.

Principle of recursive problem solving: When trying to solve a problem by recursion, always ask yourself "What could I do if I had a solution to a simpler version of the same problem?"

If you can see how to use the solution to a smaller version of the problem in solving the original problem, you have hurdled your toughest obstacle. All that remains is to determine the recursive termination conditions. This can be done by answering the question "Under what circumstances is this problem so simple that a solution is trivial?" Your answer to this question will define parameter values that trigger an immediate return from the recursive algorithm.

EXAMPLE 16.3

Implement a C++ solution to the Towers of Hanoi problem. Our earlier discussion has indicated that the problem for n disks can be defined in terms of $n - 1$ if we switch the roles played by certain pillars. This switching can be achieved by altering the order in which parameters are passed when recursive calls are made. When a value of 1 is passed in for n, we have reached the recursive termination condition. The comments // **Return Point 1** and // **Return Point 2** in the following C++ code will be used in a later trace of function **hanoi**.

```
void hanoi(int n, char source, char destination, char intermediate)
{
        if (n == 1)
                cout << "Move disk from " << source << " to " << destination;
        else
        {
                // In every recursive call hanoi works with n - 1


                hanoi(n - 1, source, intermediate, destination);    // Return Point 1
```

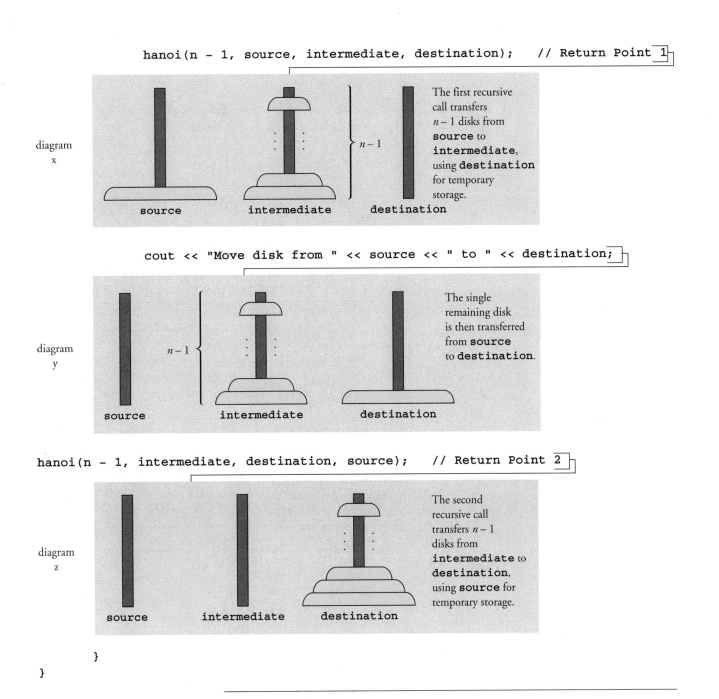

diagram x

The first recursive call transfers $n-1$ disks from **source** to **intermediate**, using **destination** for temporary storage.

```
                cout << "Move disk from " << source << " to " << destination;
```

diagram y

The single remaining disk is then transferred from **source** to **destination**.

```
                hanoi(n - 1, intermediate, destination, source);    // Return Point 2
```

diagram z

The second recursive call transfers $n-1$ disks from **intermediate** to **destination**, using **source** for temporary storage.

```
        }
}
```

Unlike previously studied recursive algorithms in which only one recursive call was made each time the function was invoked, function **hanoi** will reinvoke itself twice each time it is called with *n* > 1. The result is a more complicated algorithm that could not be implemented easily by using mere iterative control structures. Implicitly, through its recursive calls, function **hanoi** is weaving an intricate pattern of push and pop operations on the system stack.

EXAMPLE 16.4

To illustrate, we trace through the actions affecting the system stack when a call of the form

```
hanoi(3, 'A', 'C', 'B')
```

is initiated. The values in the return address portion of the stack are the documentary // **Return Point** labels in our **hanoi** function.

1. We enter **hanoi** with the following stack frame. **n** is not 1, so the condition in the **if** statement is FALSE.

2. We encounter **hanoi(n - 1, source, intermediate, destination)** with A, B, C as first, second, and third arguments. Because this represents a (recursive) function call, some stacking must be done.

3. We reenter **hanoi**. Notice that as we enter this time, the function's view of the parameters is **n** = 2, **source** = A, **destination** = B, and **intermediate** = C. Because **n** is not 1, the condition in the **if** statement is FALSE.

4. We encounter `hanoi(n - 1, source, intermediate, destination)`. Because this is a recursive call, stacking occurs.

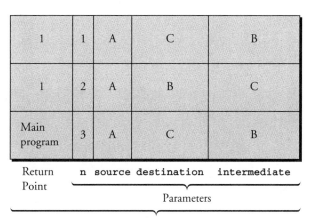

		n	source	destination	intermediate
1	1	A	C		B
1	2	A	B		C
Main program	3	A	C		B

Return Point — Parameters

Stack Frames

5. We reenter `hanoi` with **n** = 1, **source** = A, **destination** = C, and **intermediate** = B. Because **n** = 1, the condition in the **if** statement is TRUE.

6. Hence

`Move disk from A to C`

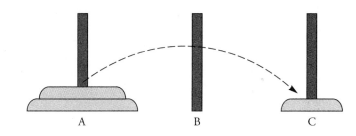

is printed and a return triggers a popping of a return address (1) and four parameters, leaving the system stack as follows:

		n	source	destination	intermediate
1	2	A	B		C
Main program	3	A	C		B

Return Point — Parameters

Stack Frames

7. Because the return address popped was 1

`Move disk from A to B`

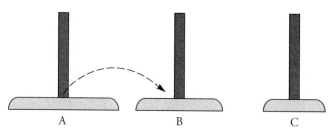

is printed and

`hanoi(n - 1, intermediate, destination, source)`

is encountered with **n** = 2, **source** = A, **destination** = B, and **intermediate** = C.

8. The call pushes a return address and four parameters onto the system stack.

Return Point	n	source	destination	intermediate
2	1	C	B	A
1	2	A	B	C
Main program	3	A	C	B

Parameters

Stack Frames

9. We reenter **hanoi**, this time with **n** = 1, **source** = C, **destination** = B, and **intermediate** = A.

10. Because **n** = 1, the **if** statement generates the output

`Move disk from C to B`

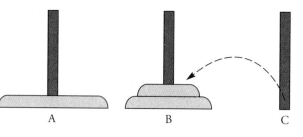

and a return.

11. The return pops a frame from the system stack and we return to the statement labeled by 2 with **n** = 2, **source** = A, **destination** = B, and **intermediate** = C.

12. But statement 2 triggers a return itself, so a stack frame is popped again and we return to the statement labeled 1 with **n** = 3, **source** = A, **destination** = C, and **intermediate** = B.

13. Statement 1 triggers the output

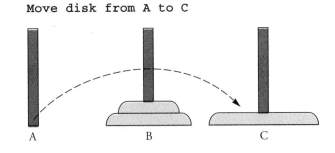

Move disk from A to C

and we are immediately at another call

```
hanoi(n - 1, intermediate, destination, source)
```

Hence the status of the system stack is changed to

2	2	B	C	A
Main program	3	A	C	B

Return Point	n	source	destination	intermediate

Parameters

Stack Frames

14. We reenter **hanoi** with **n** = 2, **source** = B, **destination** = C, and **intermediate** = A. Because **n** is not 1, another call is executed and more values are stacked.

1	1	B	A	C
2	2	B	C	A
Main program	3	A	C	B

Return Point	n	source	destination	intermediate

Parameters

Stack Frames

15. We reenter `hanoi`, with **n** = 1, **source** = B, **destination** = A, and **intermediate** = C. Because **n** = 1, we print

Move disk from B to A

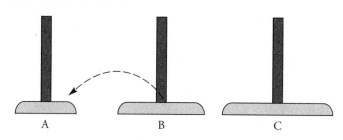

and return.

16. The return prompts the popping of the system stack. The return address popped is the statement labeled 1. Statement 1 causes output

Move disk from B to C

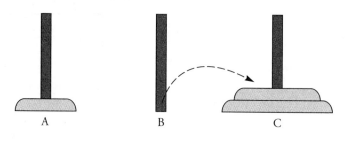

with the stack frames left at

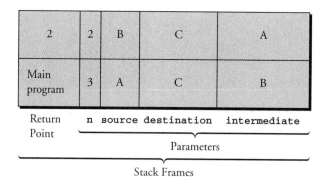

2	2	B	C	A
Main program	3	A	C	B

Return Point | n source destination | intermediate

Parameters

Stack Frames

17. The output from statement 1 is followed by a recursive call

`hanoi(n - 1, intermediate, destination, source)`

2	1	A	C	B
2	2	B	C	A
Main program	3	A	C	B
Return Point	n	source	destination	intermediate

Parameters

Stack Frames

Hence another frame is pushed onto the stack.

18. We reenter **hanoi** (for the last time), with **n** = 1, **source** = A, **destination** = C, and **intermediate** = B. Because **n** = 1, we output

Move disk from A to C

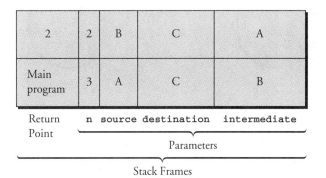

and return.

19. But now the return pops return address 2 from the stack, so return to statement 2 with the system stack given by

2	2	B	C	A
Main program	3	A	C	B
Return Point	n	source	destination	intermediate

Parameters

Stack Frames

20. Statement 2 is another return, so pop the stack again. The return address popped is 2, the same return point. But this time the return will transfer control back to the original calling location—and we are done!

As long-winded as this example is, it is essential that you understand it. Recursive functions are crucial to many of the algorithms used in computer science, and you can acquire the necessary familiarity with recursion only by convincing yourself that it really works. If you have some doubt or are not sure you understand, we recommend that you trace through the **hanoi** function with **n** = 4 (be prepared to go through a lot of paper).

Efficiency Analysis of the Recursive Towers of Hanoi Algorithm

An analysis of the time and space efficiency of a recursive algorithm is dependent on two factors. The first of these is the depth, that is, number of levels, to which recursive calls are made before reaching the recursive termination condition. Clearly, the greater the depth, the greater the number of stack frames that must be allocated and the less space efficient the algorithm becomes. It is also clear that recursive calls to a greater depth will consume more computer time and hence make the algorithm less time efficient. The second factor affecting efficiency analyses (particularly time efficiency) of recursive algorithms is the amount of resource (time or space) consumed at any given recursive level.

Figure 16.9 portrays this leveled view of a recursive algorithm as a hierarchy of the recursive calls that are (potentially) made as the algorithm executes. Such a

◆ **FIGURE 16.9**
Generalized hierarchy of calls by recursive algorithm

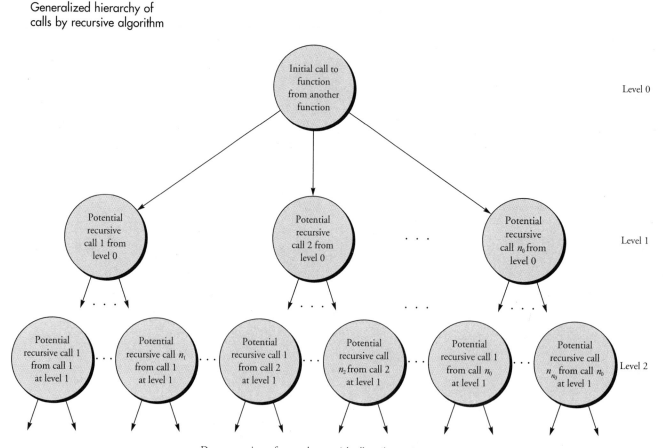

Descent continues from each potential call until recursive termination condition is reached.

Total time is sum of times spent processing at each level.

hierarchy can be used as a diagrammatic model of the run-time behavior of a recursive algorithm. Consequently, we will call the hierarchy associated with the execution of a particular recursive program a *run-time trace diagram* for that algorithm. Figure 16.10 presents a run-time trace diagram for the Towers of Hanoi algorithm with **n** = 4 disks.

A run-time trace diagram can often be used in analyzing the time and space efficiency of an algorithm. We will provide two general principles for carrying out such analyses and then illustrate them in the context of the Towers of Hanoi algorithm.

Space efficiency of a recursive algorithm: Because a stack frame must be allocated at each level of recursive execution, the space efficiency of a recursive algorithm will be proportional to the deepest level at which a recursive call is made for a particular set of values, that is, the deepest level in its run-time trace diagram.

Time efficiency of a recursive algorithm: Because processing time is associated with each recursive call, the time efficiency of a recursive algorithm will be proportional to the sum, over all levels, of the times spent processing at each level.

◆ **FIGURE 16.10**
Run-time trace of function Hanoi with *n* originally 4. (Numbers next to circles indicate order of recursive calls.)

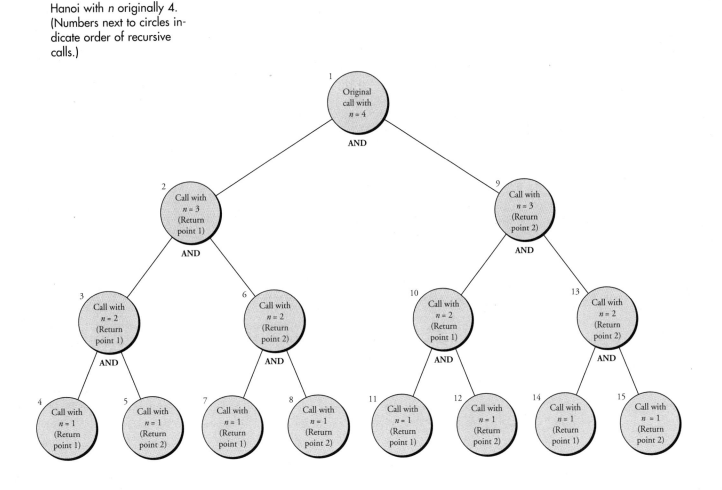

| EXAMPLE 16.5 | Use the run-time trace diagram of function **hanoi** to analyze the time and space efficiency of the algorithm. |

A graphic representation of this diagram for four disks is given in Figure 16.10. Note that the two calls descending from each call are linked by **AND**. This is to emphasize that, when **n** is not 1, both potential recursive calls in the function **hanoi** will be made. The fact that both potential calls are made has a rather dramatic effect on the time efficiency of the algorithm. In particular, calling **hanoi** initially with **n** = 4 results in a total of 15 calls in the run-time trace. The numbers outside the circles in Figure 16.10 indicate the order in which these 15 calls are made. Increasing **n** to 5 in this figure would add an additional level with 16 calls to the run-time trace. In general, adding one disk adds only one level to the run-time trace diagram but doubles (plus 1) the number of calls in the diagram. This implies that the space efficiency of hanoi relative to the system stack is $O(n)$, but, since every call in the run-time trace diagram will be made, the time efficiency is $O(2^n)$.

The analysis carried out in the preceding example demonstrates that the **hanoi** algorithm falls into the class of exponential algorithms as defined in Section 11.3. This is the first exponential algorithm we have encountered. Recall from our discussion of algorithm efficiency in Section 11.3 that such algorithms are impractical to run for even moderate values of **n**. We shall at this point complete the Hanoi legend by noting that, if the monks of Hanoi use the recursive algorithm that we have described here, the exponential efficiency of the algorithm insures that the world will exist for many more centuries.

Recursive Implementation of the Binary Search Algorithm

Do not let our solution to the Towers of Hanoi problem mislead you into thinking that every recursive algorithm having more than one recursive call will be exponential in its efficiency. Consider, for example, a recursive formulation of the binary search algorithm. Recall the interface to this algorithm that we developed in Section 11.5:

```
// Function: binary_search
// If data is found in list, return position of data, otherwise, return -1
//
// Inputs: A sorted list of data elements, the length of the list, and a
// target key
// Outputs: Function returns target's position if target is found in
// list, and -1 otherwise

int binary_search(list_type list, int n, key_type target);
```

The principle of recursive problem solving (stated in our discussion of the Hanoi problem) directs us to solve the binary search problem in terms of a simpler version of itself. Toward this end, we employ a perspective often used in recursive algorithms that act on an array: We view the algorithm as occurring between a certain subrange of array indices. For the binary search, that subrange is specified by **low ... high** where **low** is initially 0 and **high** is initially **n**. The "simpler version" of the binary search needed for a recursive statement of the algorithm is then a version that works on a smaller subrange of array indices. This subrange ultimately may become so small that it triggers the recursive termination condition for an unsuccessful search.

An intuitive recursive statement of the binary search logic then becomes:

If (recursive termination for unsuccessful search)
    Return –1 (and recursion terminated)
else
    Compute middle index between low and high
    If (target is found at middle index)
        Search is successful
        (and recursion terminated by returning middle index)
    Else if (target is less than data at middle index)
        Recursively call with same low and middle – 1 as high
    else
        Recursively call with middle + 1 as low and same high

According to this logic, the recursive calls result in a continual narrowing of the range to be searched until either the target is found or a recursive termination condition for an unsuccessful search is reached.

To determine what this unsuccessful recursive termination condition is, consider Figure 16.11. It portrays successive recursive calls on an array in which the target does not exist. The shaded regions of these array snapshots indicate the index subrange in which **target = 152** could possibly be found on successive recursive calls. Note that, on the fourth recursive call, no portion of the array is shaded; the condition **low = high** exists. This condition is therefore the recursive termination

◆ FIGURE 16.11
Unsuccessful search for array with 15 key values

Top-level call
low = 0
high = 14

First recursive call
low = 8
high = 14

Second recursive call
low = 8
high = 10

Third recursive call
low = 10
high = 10

Fourth recursive call
low = 10
high = 9

target = 152

check for an unsuccessful search. The following example presents the code for the recursive binary search in its entirety.

EXAMPLE 16.6 Developing a recursive version of the binary search requires that we use an auxiliary function to work with the index subrange **low ... high**. Using this auxiliary function will allow us to preserve the interface to function **binary_search.** This interface should not require its user to pass in an initial low value of 0. Instead, the user need only pass in the **n**, the number of objects in list. From there, the front-end portion of function **binary_search** need only call on its auxiliary function, passing in 0 for **low** and **n** for **high**.

```
int binary_search(list_type list, int n, key_type target)
{
return binary_search_aux(list, 0, n, target);
}

int binary_search_aux(list_type list, int low, int high, key_type target)

{

    int middle;

    if (low >= high)
        return -1;
    else
    {
        middle = (low + high) / 2;
        if (list[middle] == target)
            return middle;
        else if (list[middle] > target)
            return binary_search_aux(list, low, middle - 1, target);
        else
            return binary_search_aux(list, middle + 1, high, target);
    }
}
```

Efficiency Analysis of the Recursive Binary Search

As we did for the Towers of Hanoi problem, we will use a run-time trace diagram of potential recursive calls to analyze the efficiency of the recursive implementation of the binary search algorithm. This diagram appears in Figure 16.12. For the specific case of an array with 15 data items, the run-time trace stops at level 3, as indicated in Figure 16.13. The ORs that appear in these two figures are indicative of the fact that, at any given level, we will make, at most, one recursive call or the other, but not both. This is important and, as we have seen, different from the **AND** pattern of recursive calls in the Hanoi problem. It implies that the work done at any given level is simply the work done at one node along that level.

In the binary search, the work done at any node is $O(1)$ since we are merely comparing the **target** item to the data at the **mid** position. Hence the time efficiency of the recursive version of this algorithm will merely be proportional to the number of levels in the run-time trace for an array with **n** items. In Figures

◆ FIGURE 16.12

Run-time trace diagram of potential calls for recursive binary search algorithm

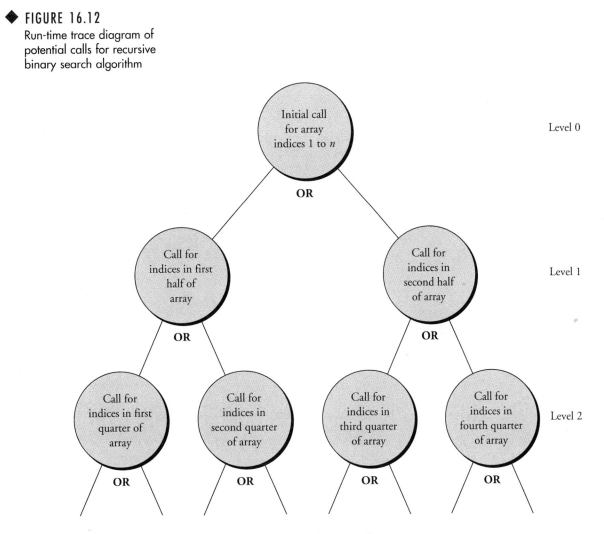

And so forth for eighths, sixteenths . . .

16.12 and 16.13, we can see that doubling the number of items in the array will merely add one level to the run-time trace diagram. That is, the number of levels in the diagram is $\log_2 n + 1$ (truncated). With the $O(1)$ work done at each level, we can thus conclude that the time efficiency of a recursive binary search is $O(\log_2 n)$. Similarly, since a stack frame will be allocated for each recursive level, the additional space requirements of the algorithm (beyond the array itself) are $O(\log_2 n)$. Note that our earlier nonrecursive implementation of the binary search algorithm did not carry with it this additional cost in space efficiency.

Recursive Computation of "N Choose K"

The preceding discussion of the binary search algorithm has honed our ability to use the run-time trace diagram to measure the efficiency of a recursive algorithm.

◆ **FIGURE 16.13**
Trace of Figure 16.12 for
specific case of array with
15 data items

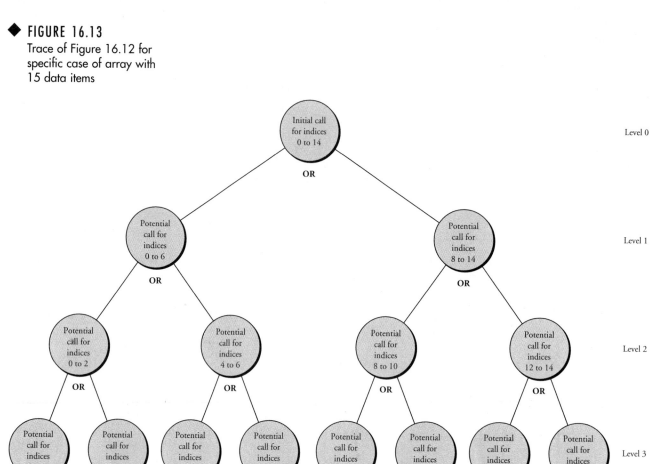

It did not, however, represent a solution to a problem that would be difficult to conceptualize without recursion. We close this section with an example in the latter category.

The phrase "N choose K" is often used in the combinatorics branch of mathematics to refer to the number of ways that we could choose K objects from among N different objects. For instance, "52 choose 13" represents the number of ways that you could be dealt a bridge hand (that is, 13 cards out of 52). We seek a recursive function to compute N choose K for arbitrary N and K, $K <= N$.

Our principle of recursive problem solving asks us to consider how we could use a solution to a simpler version of the same problem. For N choose K, a simpler version of the same problem could mean a solution for a smaller value of N or K. Let us designate our N objects as object #1, object #2, . . . , object #($N - 1$), object #N. Figure 16.14 indicates that we can partition selections of K objects from these N as those groups of K objects that come strictly from objects #1, #2, . . . , #$N - 1$ and those groups of K objects that include object #N in addition to $K - 1$ chosen among objects #1, #2, . . . , #$N - 1$. In other words,

A NOTE OF INTEREST

Recursion Need Not Be Expensive

We have seen that the use of recursion has two costs: extra time and extra memory are required to manage recursive function calls. These costs have led some to argue that recursion should never be used in programs. However, as Guy Steele has shown (in "Debunking the 'expensive procedure call' myth," *Proceedings of the National Conference of the ACM,* 1977), some systems can run recursive algorithms as if they were iterative ones, with no additional overhead. The key condition is to write a special kind of recursive function called a *tail-recursive function.* A function is tail recursive if no work is done in the function after a recursive call. For example, according to this criterion, the factorial function that we presented earlier is not tail recursive, because a multiplication is performed after each recursive call. We can convert this version of the factorial function to a tail-recursive version by performing the multiplication before each recursive call. To do this, we will need an additional parameter that passes the accumulated value of the factorial down on each recursive call. In the last call of the function, this value is returned as the result:

```
int fact_iter(int n, int result)
{
        if (n == 1)
                return result;
        else
                return fact_iter(n - 1,
                n * result);
}
```

Note that the multiplication is performed before the recursive call of the function, when its parameters are evaluated. When the function is initially called, the value of `result` should be 1:

```
int factorial(int n)
{
        return fact_iter(n, 1);
}
```

Steele showed that a smart compiler can translate tail-recursive code in a high-level language to a loop in machine language. The machine code treats the function parameters as variables associated with a loop, and generates an iterative process rather than a recursive one. Thus, there is no linear growth of function calls and extra stack memory is not required to run tail-recursive functions on these systems.

The catch is that a programmer must be able to convert a recursive function to a tail-recursive function and find a compiler that generates iterative machine code from tail-recursive functions. Unfortunately, some functions, like the one used to solve the Towers of Hanoi problem, are difficult or impossible to convert to tail-recursive versions, and the compiler optimizations are not part of the standard definitions of many languages, among them, C++. If you find that your C++ compiler supports this optimization, you should try converting some functions to tail-recursive versions and see if they run faster than the original versions.

◆ FIGURE 16.14

Formulating **choose (N, K)** in terms of **choose (N - 1, K)** and **choose (N - 1, K - 1)**

Any selection of $K-1$ objects from among these $N-1$ objects generates a selection of K objects by adding object #N to the $K-1$ selected.

Object #1	Object #2	Object #3	...	Object #$(N-2)$	Object #$(N-1)$	Object #N

Any selection of K objects from among these $N-1$ objects is also a selection of K objects from among object #1 ··· object #N.

```
choose(N, K) =

choose(N - 1, K)            Ways of selecting K objects from among the first N-1
+ choose (N - 1, K - 1)     Ways of selecting K - 1 objects from among the first
                            N - 1 and then including object #N
```

The preceding equation appears to be the recursive key we need to write our function. We need only develop recursive termination conditions to complete the puzzle. Note from the preceding equation that one of the terms being summed, **choose (N – 1, K)**, will recursively reduce N until it eventually equals K. But, in such a case, we are merely asking for the number of combinations of N objects selected N at a time—and there is trivially only one such combination. Hence, our first recursive termination condition is when $N = K$, for which we immediately return the value 1.

To develop the second recursive termination condition, we examine the second term, **choose(N – 1, K – 1)**, in the sum. Since both N and K will be reduced by this recursion, K will eventually reach 0. But the number of ways of choosing 0 objects from among N is again trivially 1. Consequently, the second recursive termination condition is when $K = 0$; this condition flags the immediate return of the value of 1.

EXAMPLE 16.7   Implement a recursive N choose K function based on the preceding discussion.

```
// Function: choose
// Computes N choose K, that is, the number of ways of selecting K objects from N
//
// Inputs: N, the number of objects being selected from
// and K, the number of objects being selected
// Outputs: The value of N choose K

int choose(int n, int k)
{
        if ((k == 0) || (n == k))
                return 1;
        else
                return choose(n - 1, k) + choose(n - 1, k - 1);
}
```

EXAMPLE 16.8   Trace the **choose(n, k)** function by developing the run-time trace diagram for choose(4, 2).

This diagram is provided in Figure 16.15. The numbers next to the circles indicate the order in which calls are made.

EXERCISES 16.2

1. Trace the stack frames that are pushed and popped from the system stack as the Towers of Hanoi algorithm executes for $n = 4$ disks.

2. Is the recursive binary search algorithm presented in this section tail recursive? Provide a written rationale for your response.

3. Construct run-time trace diagrams in the style of Example 16.8 for a variety of values of **n** and **k** in the function **choose(n, k)**. Judging from the run-time trace diagrams you construct, make conjectures about the time and space efficiency of this algorithm. Support these conjectures in a written statement.

4. Consider the following version of the function **binary_search_aux** from Example 16.6 to which a tracer output statement has been added. What output would

◆ FIGURE 16.15
Run-time trace diagram for
`choose(4, 2)`

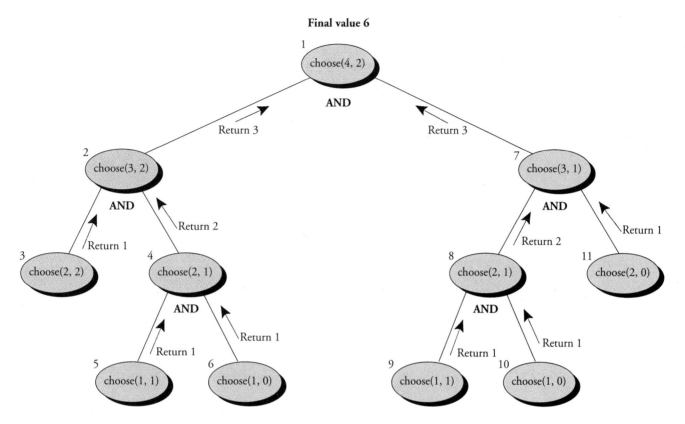

be produced from this tracer output if we were to call on function
binary_search from Example 16.6 with a list of 16 integers containing these
key values

12 34 67 89 113 125 169 180 191 201 225 237 256 270 299 304

and a **target** of 191?

```
int binary_search_aux(list_type list, int low, int high,
      key_type target)
{
      int middle;

      cout << low << " " << high << endl;              // Tracer output added here
      if (low > high)
            return -1;
      else
      {
            middle = (low + high) / 2;
            if (list[middle] == target)
                  return middle;
```

```
        else if (list[middle] < target)
                return binary_search_aux(list, low, middle - 1, target);
        else
                return binary_search_aux(list, middle + 1, high, target);
    }
}
```

5. Repeat Exercise 4 but this time with a **target** of 6.

6. We chose not to include **list** as a formal value parameter to the function **binary_search_aux** in Example 16.6. Analyze what would be the cost in space and time efficiency if **list** were to be included as a value parameter to this function.

7. Consider the following recursive function and associated top-level call. Comments of the form **// Return Point N** label possible return points from recursive calls. What would a stack frame for this function contain? Show by a series of stack "snapshots" how the stack would be manipulated for the calls indicated. Finally, provide the output that would be produced by these calls.

```cpp
#include <iostream.h>

int weird(int m, int n);

int main()
{
        cout << weird(1, 3) << endl;                        // Return Point 1
        return 0;
}

int weird(int m, int n)
{
        cout << m << "" << n << endl;
        if (m == 0)
                return n + 1;
        else if (n == 0)
                return weird(m - 1, 1);                     // Return Point 2
        else
                return weird(m - 1, weird(m, n - 1));   // Return Points 3 and 4
}
```

8. Function **hanoi** developed in this section specified the sequence of disk moves that would have to be performed to complete the Towers of Hanoi problem for n disks. Now write a recursive function that computes the exact number of disk moves needed to solve the Towers of Hanoi problem for n disks. (*Hint:* Express the number of individual moves necessary to transfer n disks in terms of the number of moves necessary to transfer $n - 1$ disks.)

9. Write a recursive function to determine the minimum entry in an array of n integers.

10. Write a recursive implementation of the insertion sort algorithm.

11. Suppose we have an amount of money M that is divisible evenly by 10 cents. Write a recursive function that computes the number of ways that M can be broken down into half dollars, quarters, and dimes.

12. In essay form, discuss some of the trade-offs in terms of time and space efficiency that are made when recursion is used.

13. Both a modular structure chart and a run-time trace diagram reflect a hierarchical pattern of how functions are called in a program. In a carefully written statement, explain the differences between these two diagrammatic techniques.

A NOTE OF INTEREST

Fractal Geometry and Recursive Patterns

Fractal geometry as a serious mathematical endeavor began with the pioneering work of Benoit Mandelbrot, a Fellow of the Thomas J. Watson Research Center, IBM Corporation. Fractal geometry is a theory of geometric forms so complex that they defy analysis and classification by traditional Euclidean means. Yet fractal shapes occur universally in the natural world. Mandelbrot has recognized them not only in coastlines, landscapes, lungs, and turbulent water flow but also in the chaotic fluctuation of prices on the Chicago commodity exchange.

The c-curve that appears on the cover of this book is an instance of a fractal shape. It represents a series of recursive patterns of increasing levels of complexity. When the level is zero, the c-curve is a simple line, specified by the endpoints <x1, y1> and <x2, y2>. A level N c-curve is composed of two level $N - 1$ c-curves connected at right angles. Thus, a level 1 c-curve is composed of two perpendicular lines, and a level 2 c-curve is three quarters of a square, which begins to resemble the letter C.

Our level 12 c-curve was generated on a graphics workstation by running a recursive function written in C++:

```cpp
void c_curve(int x1, int y1, int x2,
    int y2, int level)
{
    int xm, ym;

    if ( level == 0 )
        draw_line (x1, y1, x2, y2);
    else
    {
        xm = (x1 + x2 + y1 - y2)/2;
        ym = (x2 + y1 + y2 - x1)/2;
        c_curve(x1, y1, xm, ym,
            level - 1);
        c_curve(xm, ym, x2, y2,
            level - 1);
    }
}
```

16.3 Recursion, Trial-and-Error Backtracking, and Generalized Nested Loops

In the previous section, we have seen examples of recursive algorithms in which the number of recursive calls at each recursive level is (potentially) more than one. In this section we shall consider what happens when the number of recursive calls made on any given level is under the control of an iterative control structure such as a **for**, **while**, or **do** loop.

As an example of the class of problems we will study in this section, consider the notion of a permutation.

> **Permutation:** A permutation of the integers 1, 2, . . ., N is an ordered arrangement of these integers in which each integer appears exactly once.

For instance, two possible permutations of the integers 1, 2, 3, 4 are 3 2 1 4 and 2 4 3 1.

The Permutation Problem

We now pose the following problem: For input of N, devise a program that outputs all permutations of the integers 1, 2, . . . , N.

| EXAMPLE 16.9 | The following program solves this problem, but only for the special case where $N = 4$. |

```cpp
#include <iostream.h>

int main()
{
    for (int k1 = 1; k1 <= 4, k1++)
        for (int k2 = 1; k2 <= 4; k2++)
            if (k1 != k2)
                for (int k3 = 1; k3 <= 4; k3++)
                    if ((k2 != k3) && (k1 != k3))
                        for (int k4 = 1; k4 <= 4; k4++)
                            if ((k3 != k4) && (k2 != k4)
                                && (k1 != k4))
                                cout << setw(2) << k1 << " "
                                     << setw(2) << k2 << " "
                                     << setw(2) << k3 << " "
                                     << setw(2) << k4 << " "
                                     << endl;
    return 0;
}
```

The strategy of this program is to use a **for** loop to control a variable that runs through the four possibilities for each of the four permutation positions. Hence four loops emerge, nested within each other. When an inner loop generates a number that matches one at a previously generated position, the **if** statement is used to reject that number.

The program in Example 16.9 constitutes a simple and straightforward approach to the permutation problem. But it falls far short of solving the general problem as originally posed because it works only for the number 4, not for a general N to be input when the program runs. Note that the requirement that N be entered at run time is what causes the major complication. Certainly, the strategy of using nested loops would allow us to write one program that works for $N = 2$, another that works for $N = 3$, another for $N = 4$, and so on. However, in addition to having a ridiculous number of nested **for** loops for reasonably large N, the decision as to which permutations to generate would instead be made at the time the appropriate program is compiled and not when it runs. Computer scientists typically call this a *binding time problem*. Here we would prefer to bind a value to N when our program runs instead of when it compiles. Clearly, the later the binding time, the more versatile the program. To do this, we need some means of simulating arbitrarily deep nested loops when the program runs.

To see how we can use recursion to achieve such a simulation, consider the diagram of permutation possibilities in Figure 16.16. This diagram bears a resemblance to what we called a run-time trace of recursive calls in the preceding section. Interpret the diagram by viewing any given path from the node labeled Start down to the base level of the diagram as a potential candidate for a permutation of 1, 2, . . . , N. As we progress from one level to the next along a path, we encounter the next digit in this potential permutation.

◆ **FIGURE 16.16**

Candidates for permutations

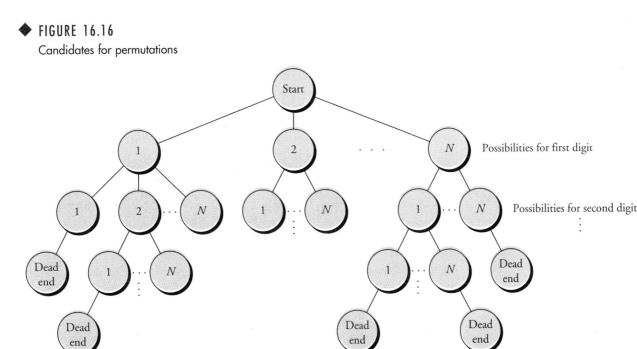

Conceptually we must use recursion to generate all the paths that appear in the figure. As soon as we generate a path with two equal numbers on it, we abandon that dead-end path and backtrack one level to continue the path along a potentially more fruitful route. If we ever complete one entire permutation along a path, we will output it, backtrack a level, and continue looking for more permutations that share the beginning of this path. At a given point in our search for a permutation, we need only store the current path. For this, a simple global array will do. Thus, the array `current_permutation` of Figure 16.17 will store in its *j*th subscript the number in the *j*th position of the permutation currently being generated. The limiting factor on the size of permutations generated by our program will be the dimension of this array.

A complete program to solve our permutation problem follows. The heart of the program is the recursive function `attempt`. This function receives three parameters:

Parameter	Explanation
`n`	The number of numbers to be permuted in the current run.
`level`	The level in the tree of Figure 16.16; that is, the position in `current_permutation` at which `attempt` is to attempt placement of a new value.
`possibility`	The new value to be placed at this level.

◆ **FIGURE 16.17**

Current exploration of permutations beginning with 2 1 4

current_permutation · · · max_permutation

1	2	3	4	5	· · ·	Size
2	1	4	Undefined	Undefined	· · ·	Undefined

attempt initially calls on a function **add_to_current_path** to actually place **possibility** at the appropriate level. Once this placement is made, there are three states in which the **current_permutation** array could be.

1. The placement of the value **possibility** at the designated level could have completed a successful permutation. In this case, call on a function to print the permutation and then remove **possibility** from **current_permutation** at the given **level** so that we may continue seeking additional permutations.

2. The placement of the value **possibility** at the designated level did not complete a permutation but does represent a valid beginning of length **level** for a potential permutation. For instance, this case would occur if **n**, **level**, and **possibility** were 6, 4, and 5, respectively, and we called **attempt** with **current_permutation** as pictured in Figure 16.17. The **current_permutation** array would be extended to contain 2 1 4 5. Here what we must do is to test the possible candidates for a value at the next position; that is, at depth **(level + 1)**. This is done by an iterative series of recursive calls to **attempt**, passing a variety of values for **possibility** at **(level + 1)**. This iterative series of recursive calls is what achieves the desired simulation of nested looping. After all of these deeper level possibilities (that is, those below the beginning of the current permutation in Figure 16.16) have been explored, we return and can remove **possibility** from **current_permutation** at position **level** since (recursively) all permutations with this beginning arrangement will have been generated.

3. The placement of the value **possibility** at **level** destroys the viability of the current path by adding a number that appeared earlier in the permutation. For instance, calling on **attempt** with **n** = 6, **level** = 4, and **possibility** = 1 would cause an invalid path for the state of **current_permutation** given in Figure 16.17. In this case we do nothing

◆ **FIGURE 16.18**
Modular structure chart for permutations program

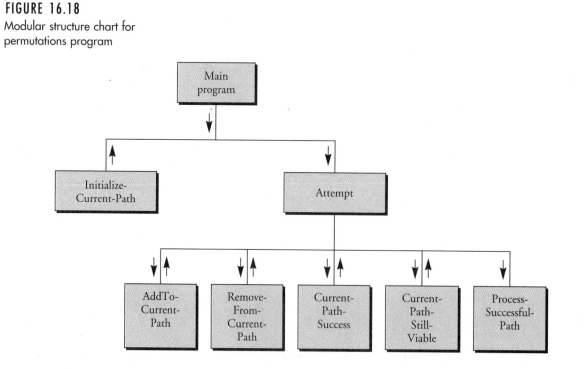

but retract from the placement of this invalid possibility before attempting to place other possible values.

You should carefully study how these three potential cases are handled in our recursive function attempt in the example program. The modular structure chart presented in Figure 16.18 indicates how **attempt** invokes other functions. In the Focus on Program Design section, we adapt the technique illustrated here to a broader class of problems.

```cpp
// Program file: permute.cpp

// Use recursion to find all permutations of 1,2, ..., N.

#include <iostream.h>
#include <iomanip.h>
#include <limits.h>

#include "boolean.h"

const int MAX_PERMUTATION_SIZE = 100;
const int UNDEFINED = INT_MAX;

int current_permutation[MAX_PERMUTATION_SIZE + 1];
// Function: initialize_current_path
// Initializes all indices in array to the UNDEFINED flag.
//
// Inputs: The current_permutation array in an unreliable state
// Outputs: The initialized array

void initialize_current_path();

// Function: attempt
// After locating possibility at specified level, check if we have a permutation.
// If so, print it. If not, check whether or not a permutation is still possible
// for this placement of possibility.  If so, attempt placement at deeper level
// by recursive call.
//
// Inputs: n, the number of numbers we are attempting to permute;
//         level, the current depth of the solution path as portrayed in
//         Figure 16.6
//         possibility, the number we wish to place at that level
// Outputs: Relative to this level, the array is returned unaltered.  However,
//         if permutation was found, contents of this array are printed.

void attempt(int n, int level, int possibility);

// Function: add_to_current_path
// Assign possibility to this level.
//
// Inputs: level, the current depth of the solution path
//         possibility, the number we wish to place at that level

void add_to_current_path(int level, int possibility);
```

```
// Function: remove_from_current_path
// Remove value at that level.
//
// Inputs:  the deepest level to which solution path has grown
// Outputs: Suitably altered array

void remove_from_current_path(int level);


// Function: current_path_success
// Check if contents of array through index level constitute a complete
// permutation of the first n numbers.
//
// Inputs:  The array, level, the depth to which the solution path has grown,
//               n, the number of numbers we are attempting to permute.
// Outputs: TRUE if permutation, FALSE otherwise.

boolean current_path_success(int n, int level);


// Function: current_path_still_viable
// Check if contents of array through index level constitute a viable
// beginning for the permutation of the first n numbers.
//
// Inputs:  The array, level, the depth to which the solution path has grown,
//               n, the number of numbers we are attempting to permute.
// Outputs: TRUE if viable, FALSE otherwise.
boolean current_path_still_viable(int level);


// Function: process_successful_path
// Write out first n indices of the array
//
// Inputs:  The array and n, the number of numbers we are attempting to permute.

void process_successful_path(int n);

int main()
{
       int n;
       initialize_current_path();
       cout << "Permutation  of integers from 1 to ? ";
       cin >> n;
       for (int k = 1; k <= n; ++k)
              attempt(n, 1, k);
       return 0;
}


void initialize_current_path()
{
       for (int k = 1; k < MAX_PERMUTATION_SIZE; ++k)
              current_permutation[k] = UNDEFINED;
}
void attempt(int n, int level, int possibility)
```

```
{
        add_to_current_path(level, possibility);
        if (current_path_success(n, level))
                process_successful_path(n);
        else if (current_path_still_viable(level))
                for (int k = 1; k <= n; ++k)
                        attempt(n, level + 1, k);
        remove_from_current_path(level);
}

void add_to_current_path(int level, int possibility)
{
        current_permutation[level] = possibility;
}

void remove_from_current_path(int level)
{
        current_permutation[level] = UNDEFINED;
}

boolean current_path_success(int n, int level)
{
        boolean success = TRUE;
        int k = 1;

        if (n > level)
                success = FALSE;
        else
                while ((k <= level - 1) && success)
                {
                        success = current_permutation[k] != current_permutation[level];
                        ++k;
                }
        return success;
}

boolean current_path_still_viable(int level)
{

        boolean viable = TRUE;
        int k = 1;

        while ((k <= level - 1) && viable)
                {
                        viable = current_permutation[k] != current_permutation[level];
                        ++k;
                }
        return viable;
}

void process_successful_path(int n)
{
```

```
for (int k = 1; k <= n; ++k)
      cout << setw(3) << current_permutation[k];
cout << endl;
}
```

You may have noticed that certain efficiency considerations have not been taken into account in writing the previous program. For example, the initialization of the `current_permutation` array actually is unnecessary in this particular implementation. Also, the call to `remove_from_current_path` could have been eliminated since the undefined flag that this function assigns is quickly replaced without ever being explicitly used. Finally, additional global data could be used to keep track of information that would eliminate the necessity of using loops in the `current_path_success` and `current_path_still_viable` functions. You will be asked to rewrite the program taking these economies into account in the exercises.

Our purpose in this section has not been to present the most compact version of a permutations program, but rather to illustrate how recursion can be used to simulate *generalized nested loops* whose nesting depth can be established at run time. Such generalized nested loops can then be used in situations where trial-and-error backtracking is an appropriate strategy in searching for a problem's solution. In this context, we have intended the permutations program to be illustrative of a general problem-solving approach rather than a solution to a particular problem.

Consider what we must abstract from the permutations program to view it as a general template for trial-and-error backtracking instead of a mere permutation printer. Figure 16.16 presents the problem of finding permutations as a problem in finding certain types of paths through a maze. We probe deeper and deeper along a given path (that is, add new numbers to the current permutation) until we reach a predefined goal or reach a dead end. As we take a new step along the current path, we must analyze the state in which it has placed us:

1. Have we reached a goal state?
2. Have we reached a state that, though not itself a goal, is still a viable start toward that goal?
3. Have we reached a dead end?

For each of the three cases we take appropriate action such as

1. Processing a goal state; for example, printing it out, tallying a counter, or setting a flag signaling that we are done.
2. Probing further along a viable path by recursively taking another step.
3. No action in the case of a dead end.

After taking the appropriate action, we then retract from the step that led us to the current state, possibly returning to a higher recursive level where we may find ourselves in the midst of a similar three-state analysis. The essence of this trial-and-error backtracking logic is illustrated in Figure 16.19. Upon reaching a dead end for path A, you must retrace steps $9 \rightarrow 8 \rightarrow 7 \rightarrow 6 \rightarrow 5$ before you can attempt new path B. The retracing of states that have been visited previously is conveniently done by unwinding from recursive calls.

In this chapter's Focus on Program Design section and the programming problems, you will see how this type of logic can be used to solve a wide variety of problems.

◆ **FIGURE 16.19**
Backtracking problem illustrated by maze solution

EXERCISES 16.3

1. Consider the permutations program discussed in Section 16.3. Suppose that $N = 3$ in a particular run of this program and that we printed out the contents of the **current_permutation** array each time the attempt function was invoked in this run. How many times would the array be printed? What would be the overall output?

2. Suppose you used the permutations function of this section to compute all permutations of 1, 2, 3, and 4. What would the complete run-time trace diagram of recursive function calls look like for such a run? Can you generalize from this diagram of function calls the efficiency of the permutations function? State your answer in big-O terms with respect to both stack size and number of stack operations. Provide justification for your answer in a written statement.

3. Rewrite the example program for permutations in a fashion that takes into account the efficiency considerations discussed in Section 16.3. These considerations are discussed in the paragraph that follows the program.

4. What is the output from the following program?:

```cpp
#include <iostream.h>

void y(int a, int b, int c);

int main()
{
        y(16, 1, 4);
        return 0;
}

void y(int a, int b, int c)
{
        int k;

        if (b <= c)
        {
                cout << a << endl;
                for (k = b; k <= c; ++k)
                        y(k, b + 1, c);
        }
}
```

5. What is the output from the following program?:

```cpp
#include <iostream.h>

void tough(int b, int c, int d);

int main()
{
        tough(1, 4, 12);
        return 0;
}

void tough(int b, int c, int d)
{
        int k;

        if (b <= c)
        {
                cout << d << endl;
                for (k = b; k <= c; ++k)
                        tough(b + 1, c, k);
        }
}
```

6. A car's odometer may be viewed as a physical implementation of a nested loop. Each loop cycles through the digits 0...9, with the one's digit cycling the fastest, then the ten's digit, and so forth. Write a function to simulate an *N*-digit odometer (*N* determined at run time) by creating a generalized nested loop structure that will run through, in sequence, all possible settings for the odometer.

FOCUS ON PROGRAM DESIGN

We have emphasized throughout this text that computer scientists must work at varying levels of abstraction. With this in mind, consider the program of the last section not merely as a permutation printer but rather as illustrative of a more abstract problem-solving technique. In fact, a careful examination of the function **attempt** in the permutations program will show that it is nearly independent of the particular problem of searching for permutations. That is, the algorithm behind **attempt** could be used in any analogous search for a solution in which there were *N* additional possibilities at the current level. We shall now indicate the power of this abstract approach to trial-and-error backtracking by sketching a solution to another problem that could be solved with the same methodology. You will then complete the solution in the programming problems.

The Eight Queens Problem

Consider what has come to be known as the Eight Queens problem. This problem has long intrigued chess fanatics. It requires determining the various ways in which eight queens could be configured on a chessboard so that none of them could capture any other queen. (The rules of chess allow a queen to move an arbitrary number of squares in a horizontal, vertical, or diagonal fashion.) Figure 16.20 illustrates one such configuration.

Applying backtracking logic to this problem we could attempt to find a path to a configuration by successively attempting to place a queen in each column of a

◆ FIGURE 16.20

One successful eight queens configuration

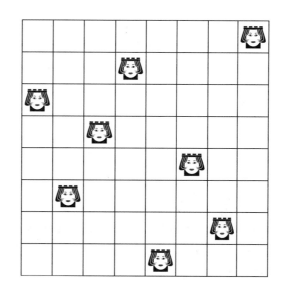

chessboard until we reach a dead end: a column in which the placement of queens in prior columns makes it impossible to place the queen being moved. This situation is pictured in Figure 16.21. Here, the sixth queen cannot be placed due to the placement of the first five queens.

When we reach such a dead end, we must backtrack one column (to column 5 in Figure 16.21), and attempt to find a new placement for the queen in that column. If placement in the previous column is impossible, we must backtrack yet another column to attempt the new placement. This backtracking through previous columns continues until we finally are able to reposition a queen. At that point, we can begin a new path by again attempting to position queens on a column-by-column basis until another dead end is reached or until a fully successful configuration is developed.

◆ FIGURE 16.21

Dead end in queen placement

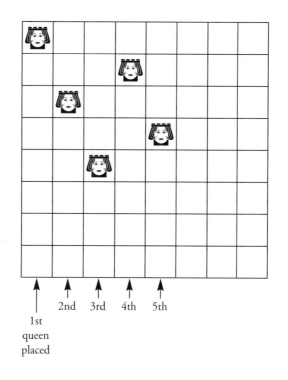

A NOTE OF INTEREST

Recursion, LISP, and the Practicality of Artificial Intelligence

Artificial intelligence, the science of implementing on computers the problem-solving methods used by human beings, is one of the most rapidly expanding fields within computer science. Research in this field includes enabling computers to play games of strategy, to understand natural languages, to prove theorems in logic and mathematics, and to mimic the reasoning of human experts in fields such as medical diagnosis. Only recently has artificial intelligence become a commercially viable area of application, capable of solving some real-life problems apart from the idealized setting of a pure research environment. More and more, we are seeing artificial intelligence systems that perform such practical functions as aiding business executives in their decision-making processes and providing a "near-English" user-interface language for database management software.

What has sparked the sudden emergence of artificial intelligence? Why wasn't it possible to produce commercially feasible programs in this field until recently? One of the primary answers to these questions is tied to the language in which most artificial intelligence programming is done. This language is called *LISP* (for LISt Processor). Interestingly, the control structures of LISP are based almost entirely on recursion. What a C++ programmer would view as normal iterative control structures (for example, `while`, `do`, and `for` loops) appear in various versions of LISP only as infrequently used, nonstandard extensions to the language.

One of the reasons that a recursively based language such as LISP is so ideally suited to this field is that most problem-solving methods in artificial intelligence involve searching for a particular goal state; that is, searching for a path leading to a complete problem solution. This is similar to the approaches we have taken in the permutation problem and the Eight Queens problem in this chapter.

The complexity of problems studied in artificial intelligence leads to run-time trace diagrams of enormous size. Interestingly, LISP has been available as a recursive language ideally suited to such problems for a long time. It is one of the oldest high-level programming languages, having been first developed by John McCarthy in the late 1950s.

Researchers who work in artificial intelligence have realized since LISP's introduction that its ability to process general data structures recursively was, on a theoretical basis, exactly what they needed. The problem through the years has been that, because of the very high overhead associated with recursion (and some other features built into LISP), computer hardware has not been fast enough to run LISP programs in practical applications. Thus, researchers were restricted not by LISP itself but rather by the ability of computer hardware to execute LISP programs in reasonable times. One of the major reasons for the recent emergence of artificial intelligence has been the increase in speed of computing hardware and the decrease in cost of this same hardware. This has made it possible for users to have dedicated computer resources capable of meeting the demands of LISP's recursive style. As hardware continues to improve, applications in LISP and artificial intelligence will become increasingly sophisticated.

If you are curious about LISP and the important role that it plays at some of the frontiers of research in programming languages, consult the September 1991 issue of the *Communications of the ACM* (Volume 34, no. 9). This entire issue was devoted to LISP and described its ability to adapt to many computing environments.

The key to a program that finds all possible configurations for the eight queens is a function that attempts to place a queen in a given square and, if successful, recursively calls itself to attempt the placement of another queen in the next column. Such a function in skeletal pseudocode form follows:

```
void try_queen (K, J)

// Place a queen in row K, column J.
// Analyze state reached by this placement.
// If appropriate, recurse to place queen in next column.

Actually put queen at position K, J
If this results in successful configuration
       Tally this configuration
Else if no queen in immediate danger
```

```
For each L from 1 to 8
            try_queen(L, J + 1)
Retract from position K, J
```

The similarities between this sketch of a solution to the Eight Queens problem and our complete solution to the permutation problem should convince you that, from an abstract perspective, both problems are really the same. We have intentionally left the Eight Queens problem unfinished. Still to be resolved are such issues as:

■ The initial call(s) to **try_queen**.
■ How to represent the chessboard.
■ How to check whether placing a queen at position **K, J** puts it in immediate danger. That is, how to determine whether there is currently another queen sharing the same row, column, or diagonal.

The resolution of these issues is left for your enjoyment in the programming problems at the end of the chapter. Additional problems given there further illustrate the far-reaching applicability of the trial-and-error backtracking method.

RUNNING, DEBUGGING AND TESTING HINTS

1. Recursion is an elegant and powerful tool. It combines iterative control with a built-in data structure, the system stack. To properly control that iteration, be sure that you provide an appropriate recursive termination condition for your algorithms.
2. Be sure that, when you invoke a function recursively, you are in some sense passing in a smaller, simpler version of the problem being solved. Otherwise, your algorithm will infinitely recur.
3. The use of tracer output can be valuable in debugging recursive algorithms. However, you must be careful not to insert so many tracer output statements that you become lost in the copious output they produce. Remember that recursive algorithms are often exponential in efficiency and, consequently, may be exponential in the amount of output produced by tracers also. You must be careful to insert tracer output statements judiciously. Where appropriate, use a Boolean constant that can be toggled to TRUE or FALSE to control whether or not the tracer output is produced.

SUMMARY

Key Terms

binding time problem
generalized nested loops
LISP
recursion
recursive call

recursive definition
recursive function
recursive termination
   condition
run-time trace diagram

stack frame
tail-recursion
termination condition
trial-and-error backtracking

Key Concepts

◆ Stacks process function calls when a program executes. Understanding the role of the stack in this application is essential to effective use of the programming technique known as recursion.
◆ A recursive function invokes itself with a simpler version of the same problem it was originally given. Ultimately there must be a recursive termination condition to break a series of recursive function calls.

◆ In tail recursion, no further processing occurs at any level of recursion after a return from a recursive call is made.

◆ A function's stack frame contains memory locations for all parameters and local variables and the machine address of the point to return to after the function completes execution at the current level.

◆ A run-time trace diagram can often be used to help analyze the efficiency of a recursive algorithm. If the diagram indicates that multiple recursive calls are made at each level, there is a good chance that the algorithm is in the class of exponential algorithms.

◆ Recursion can be used to solve a complex class of search problems by using a trial-and-error backtracking strategy. However, often such solutions can consume a tremendous amount of resources, particularly in terms of run-time efficiency.

◆ Do not be misled into thinking that recursion is necessarily the most efficient programming technique because the code that expresses it is often compact and lacking in any explicit loop control statements such as **while** or **do**. The very nature of a recursive call generates iteration without any need for **while** or **do**. The iteration control mechanism in recursion is the recursive termination condition that triggers a series of returns before another recursive call is made. Hence, from a time-efficiency perspective, a recursive algorithm's measure of effectiveness is closely tied to the number of times it must iterate its recursive call-and-return pattern. Moreover, with recursion, we pay a price in memory efficiency that is not present in other iterative control structures. This price is system stack space.

◆ The value of recursion lies in the way in which it enables us to express algorithms compactly and elegantly for a certain class of problems. Since we use recursion frequently throughout the rest of this text, you will learn to acquire a feel for the type of problems particularly suitable to this powerful technique. In the next chapter, we will see that recursion is an indispensable strategy for manipulating a data structure known as a tree. In later chapters, recursion will be explored as a means of sorting and searching.

PROGRAMMING PROBLEMS AND PROJECTS

1. Write a program to call for input of a decimal number and convert it to its binary equivalent using the method described in the following flowchart:

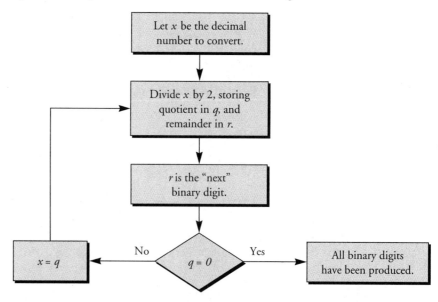

Note that this method produces the binary digits for the given number in reverse order. One strategy for printing the digits in the correct order would be to store them in an array as they are produced and then print the array. However, this strategy would have the drawbacks of allocating unnecessary storage for an array and then limiting the size of the binary number to the size of the array. Your program is not to employ this strategy. Rather call for input of the decimal number in your main program and then immediately transfer control to a function that in turn is called recursively, stacking the binary digits as they are produced. Once division by 2 yields 0, the succession of returns can be used to print the digits one by one as they are popped from this stack.

2. The Nth Fibonacci number is defined by

1 if N is 1.

1 if N is 2.

The sum of the previous two Fibonacci numbers otherwise.

Write a recursive function to compute the Nth Fibonacci number. Then, using a run-time trace diagram, analyze the efficiency of your function.

3. Euclid devised a clever algorithm for computing the greatest common divisor (GCD) of two integers. According to Euclid's algorithm,

$$GCD(M, N) = \begin{cases} GCD(N, M) \text{ if } N > M \\ M \text{ if } N = 0 \\ GCD(N, M \% N) \text{ if } N > 0 \end{cases}$$

Write a recursive function to compute GCDs via Euclid's method.

4. Suppose that you have N thousand dollars and can use it to buy a combination of Orange computers (which cost \$1000 each), HAL computers (which cost \$2000 each), or MAX computers (which cost \$4000 each). How many different combinations of Orange, HAL, and MAX computers could be bought with your N thousand dollars? Write a program that receives N as input and responds with the number of possible combinations.

Hint: If N were 100, then the number of combinations is

The number of combinations totaling \$100,000 and involving Orange and HAL computers only

PLUS

The number of combinations totaling \$96,000 and involving potentially all three brands

Think about this hint for a while and extend it to a recursive function that answers this question.

5. Ackermann's function is defined recursively for two nonnegative integers m and n as follows:

$$Ackermann(m,n) = \begin{cases} n + 1 \text{ if } m = 0 \\ Ackermann(m - 1, 1) \text{ if } n = 0 \\ Ackermann(m - 1, Ackermann(m,n - 1)) \text{ otherwise} \end{cases}$$

Write a recursive version of this function. Develop a run-time trace diagram for the function when $m = 2$ and $n = 3$. Attempt to deduce the big-O efficiency of the recursive version with respect to stack size and stack operations. Justify your answer in a written statement.

6. If you have access to an appropriate graphics device, write the functions `line` and `right_turn` described in Section 16.1. Then experiment by writing recursive functions that call on these functions (and others you may develop) to produce a variety of interesting figures.

7. Write a function that receives a set of N integers and then prints all subsets of this set.

8. Write a program that completes the solution of the Eight Queens problem as sketched in the Focus on Program Design section.

9. A K-permutation of the first N positive integers, $K <= N$, is a permutation of a K-element subset of $\{1, 2, \ldots, N\}$. Write a function to generate all possible K-permutations of the first N positive integers.

10. A continued fraction is a number of the form that follows (where each a_i is an integer):

$$a_1 + \cfrac{1}{a_2 + \cfrac{1}{a_3 + \cfrac{1}{a_4 + }}}$$

$$\frac{1}{a_n}$$

Though a continued fraction is composed of integers a_i, it has a real value. For example, consider the following continued fraction and its indicated real value.

$$1 + \cfrac{1}{2 + \cfrac{1}{6 + \cfrac{1}{5}}} = 1 + \cfrac{1}{2 + \cfrac{1}{\frac{31}{5}}} = 1 + \cfrac{1}{2 + \frac{5}{31}} = 1 + \cfrac{1}{\frac{67}{31}} = \frac{98}{67} = 1.46$$

Provide a type definition of your implementation of a continued fraction. Then, write a recursive function that receives a continued fraction and returns its associated real value.

11. There are five other teams in the same league as the Bay Area Brawlers (Problem 4, Chapter 14, and Problem 13, Chapter 15). Over a given five-week period, the Brawlers must play each of the other teams exactly once. Using recursion, write a program to determine the ways in which such a five-week schedule could be accomplished. For an added challenge, introduce more realistic scheduling considerations into this problem. For instance, have your program determine the ways in which a 15-game schedule could be constructed such that each of the six teams in the league plays each of the other teams exactly three times, but never consecutively.

12. Write a function that uses a random number generator to produce mazes. One way of viewing a maze is as a two-dimensional array of structures:

```
struct location
{
        boolean
        north_blocked,
        east_blocked,
        south_blocked,
        west_blocked;
};
```

At each square in the array, the Boolean attributes are set to indicate whether or not we can proceed in the indicated direction. After your maze-generating function is working, develop a function that uses trial-and-error backtracking to solve the maze.

13. A transportation network such as the following can be represented as a two-dimensional integer array with rows and columns indexed by the cities in the network. The number stored at position (**K**, **J**) of such an array represents the distance of the link between two cities. Zero indicates that two cities are not directly linked.

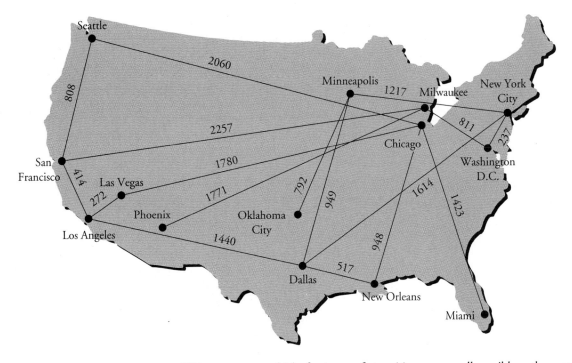

Write a program which, for input of two cities, outputs all possible paths connecting the two cities. Then modify the program so that it outputs only the shortest path linking the two cities. Use a trial-and-error backtracking strategy to do this. We will discuss a more efficient algorithm for solving this problem in the next chapter.

14. Another classic chess problem that can be solved by trial-and-error backtracking is known as the Knight's Tour. Given a chessboard with a knight initially placed at coordinates x_0, y_0 the problem is to specify a series of moves for the knight that will result in each board location being visited exactly once. From a given square on the chessboard, a knight may move to any of the eight numbered squares in the following diagram:

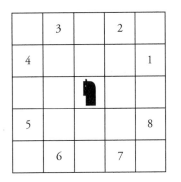

Write a program to find a valid Knight's Tour.

15. A famous theorem in mathematics states that four colors are enough to color any map in a fashion that allows each region on the map to be a different color from any of its adjacent neighbors. Write a program that initially allows input of a map. One way of doing this is to input each region followed by a list of its adjacent neighbors. This information can then be stored in a two-dimensional Boolean array with rows and columns indexed by region names. Store TRUE at row **K**, column **J**, if region **K** and region **J** are neighbors; otherwise store FALSE. Once your program has appropriately stored the information associated with the input map, it should use trial-and-error backtracking to find a pattern for coloring the map with four colors. Note that the Four-Color Theorem from mathematics guarantees that such a pattern can be found.

16. Write a program to find a solution to the following stable marriage problem (or indicate that no solution exists for the input data). According to this problem, we have N men and N women, each of whom has stated distinct preferences for their possible partners. The data regarding these preferences is the input for this problem. It can be stored in two two-dimensional arrays: one in which each woman has rated each of the men as 1st choice, 2nd choice, ..., Nth choice and another in which each man has similarly rated each of the women. Given this input, a solution to the stable marriage problem is to find N couples (marriages) such that

1. Each man is part of exactly one couple (marriage).
2. Each woman is part of exactly one couple (marriage).
3. There does not exist a man and a woman who are not married to each other but who would prefer each other to their current spouses.

If a pair as specified in requirement 3 does exist, then the assignment of N couples is said to be unstable and should be avoided. Note that the stable marriage problem is representative of many real-life problems in which assignments have to be made according to preferences.

17. Write a program to analyze football team scores by computing the point spread for any team A playing any team B. Your program should compute the point spreads as follows:

Level I analysis: Team A played B in past
Level II analysis: Average point spreads for situations such as

A played C—point spread 3
C played B—point spread 7

   Total point spread 10
Level III analysis: Average point spread for situations such as

A played C—point spread 3
C played D—point spread –14 (C lost)
D played B—point spread 7

   Total point spread –4
Level IV analysis: Average point spreads for situations such as

A played C—point spread 3
C played D—point spread –14
D played E—point spread 21
E played B—point spread 4

Total point spread 14

All level II point spreads are then averaged for a final level II point spread figure. Point spreads are similarly averaged for levels III and IV. Items that potentially need to be stacked (via recursion) in this program include

- Accumulated point spread at current position
- Number of scores reflected in the accumulated point spread at current position
- Current position; that is, team A playing team B
- Path to the current position; that is, teams played to get to the current position.

18. Write a solution to the Towers of Hanoi problem in which you use a nonrecursive iterative control structure and a stack. In effect, your stack will simulate the role played by the system stack in the recursive version of the algorithm. In a written statement, compare the time and space efficiency of your nonrecursive solution to the recursive solution presented in this chapter. Is your solution faster than the exponential recursive solution? If so, explain why it is. Otherwise, explain why it is still exponential in its run time.

19. If you have had a course in discrete mathematics, then you may be familiar with recurrence relations and methods for explicitly solving them. Use your knowledge of recurrence relations to analyze the time and space efficiencies of the Towers of Hanoi and recursive binary search algorithms. Your analysis should be presented as a precise mathematical argument, citing any results that you use but do not prove.

17 Binary Trees, General Trees, and Graphs

Except during the nine months before he draws his first breath, no man manages his affairs as well as a tree does.
George Bernard Shaw, 1856–1950

Human beings organize much of the world around them into *hierarchies*. For instance, an industrial body functions effectively only by defining a collection of client–server relationships among its participants. We have emphasized throughout the text that computer scientists design a software system by breaking it down into modules and defining hierarchical client–server relationships among those modules. In Chapter 16, we used hierarchical run-time trace diagrams to analyze the efficiency of recursive algorithms. To continue this discussion, we now introduce the idea of trees.

The familial parent-child relationship allows a natural breakdown of a family's history into a genealogical tree. In computer science, a *tree* is a data structure that represents such hierarchical relationships between data items.

To introduce some of the terminology of tree structures, consider the record of a student at a typical university. In addition to the usual statistical background information such as social security number, name, and address, a typical student record contains listings for a number of courses, exams and final grades in each course, overall grade-point average, and other data relating to the student's performance at the college. Figure 17.1 is a tree structure representing such a student record. As in genealogical trees, at the highest *level* (0) of a tree is its *root* (also called the *root node*). Here STUDENT is the root node. The nodes NAME, ADDRESS, SSN, COURSE, and GPA, which are directly connected to the root node, are the *child nodes* of the *parent node* STUDENT. The child nodes of a given parent constitute a set of *siblings*. Thus NAME, ADDRESS, SSN, COURSE, and GPA are siblings. In the hierarchy represented by a tree, the child nodes of a parent are one level lower than the parent node. Thus NAME, ADDRESS, SSN, COURSE, and GPA are at level 1 in Figure 17.1.

A link between a parent and its child is called a *branch* in a tree structure. Each node in a tree except the root must descend from a parent node via a branch. Thus LAST NAME, FIRST NAME, and MIDDLE NAME descend from the parent node NAME. The root of the tree is the *ancestor* of all the nodes in the tree.

◆ **FIGURE 17.1**
Tree structure representing a
student record

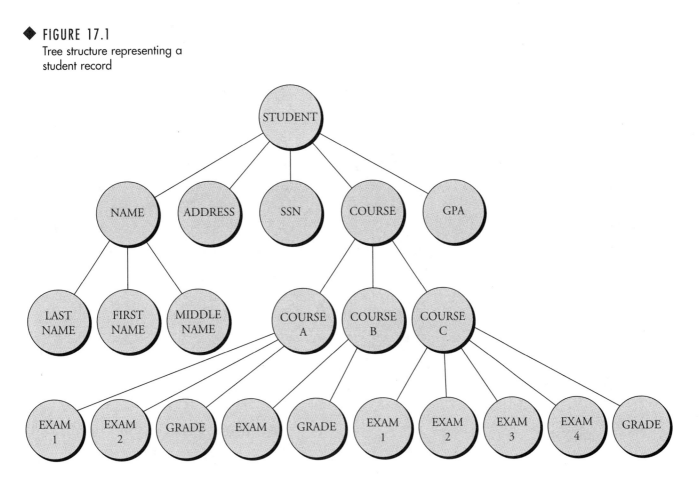

A node with no children is called a *leaf node.* In Figure 17.1, GPA is a leaf
node. LAST NAME, FIRST NAME, MIDDLE NAME, EXAM 1, and EXAM 2,
for instance, also are leaf nodes.

A *subtree* is a subset of a tree that is itself a tree; the tree in Figure 17.2 is a
subtree of the tree in Figure 17.1. This subtree has the root node NAME. Similarly,
the tree in Figure 17.3 is another subtree of the tree in Figure 17.1. Notice that the
tree in Figure 17.3 is a subtree of the tree in Figure 17.1 and the tree in Figure 17.4.

◆ **FIGURE 17.2**
Subtree of Figure 17.1

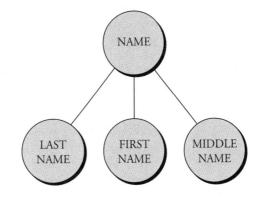

◆ **FIGURE 17.3**
Another subtree of Figure
17.1

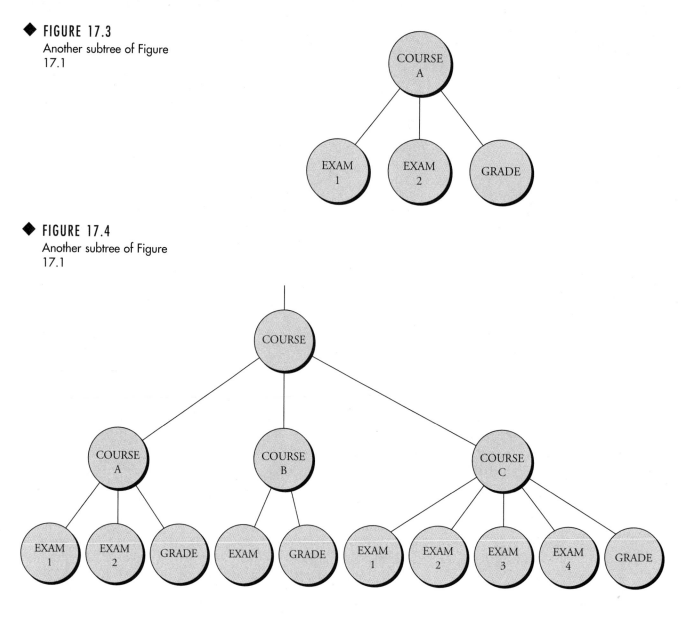

◆ **FIGURE 17.4**
Another subtree of Figure
17.1

17.1 **General Trees and Binary Trees as Abstract Data Types**

It is evident from the preceding discussion that a tree has the following interesting property: Any given node within a tree is itself the root node of a completely analogous tree structure. That is, a tree is composed of a collection of substructures, each of which also meets the criteria for being a tree. This sounds dangerously circular, and, to formally describe a tree in this fashion, we must be sure to give ourselves an escape from the recursion. This is done via the following definition of a tree as an abstract data type:

Tree: A general tree is a set of nodes that is either empty (the recursive termination condition), or has a designated node called the root from which descend zero or more subtrees. Each node is not an ancestor of itself, and each subtree itself satisfies the definition of a tree.

- to define partially the general tree ADT
- to define completely the binary tree ADT
- to understand conceptually the effect of each of the binary tree operations
- to become familiar with some examples of binary trees such as heaps, arithmetic expression trees, and binary search trees

We defer completing the definition of a general tree to Section 17.5, where we will more formally discuss the operations associated with this ADT.

Two points about this partial definition should be emphasized. First, the recursive fashion in which a tree is defined should provide a strong hint that most tree-processing algorithms will also be recursive. Second, most operations on the tree data structure are closely linked to the hierarchical relationship among nodes for that particular tree. This hierarchical relationship may vary greatly from tree to tree. To consider some examples of such relationships, which are found quite often in computer science applications, let us restrict our attention for the moment to an abstract data type called a *binary tree*.

Binary tree: A binary tree is a tree in which each node has exactly two subtrees. These two subtrees are designated as the left and right subtrees, respectively. Note that either or both of these subtrees could be empty.

We specify the following operations on a binary tree in terms of preconditions and postconditions.

Create operation
Preconditions: Receiver is a binary tree in an unpredictable state.
Postconditions: Receiver is initialized to the empty binary tree.

Empty operation
Preconditions: Receiver is a previously created binary tree.
Postconditions: Returns TRUE if the tree is empty, FALSE otherwise.

Insert operation
Preconditions: Receiver is a previously created binary tree based on a particular hierarchical property. `item` is a value to be inserted in the tree. There is memory available in the tree for the new item.
Postconditions: `item` is added to the tree in a way that maintains the tree's hierarchical property.

preorder_traverse operation
Preconditions: Receiver is a previously created binary tree, and `process` is an algorithmic process that can be applied to each node in the tree.
Postconditions: Each node of the tree is visited in the following order: root of the tree first, then recursively all nodes in left subtree, then recursively all nodes in right subtree. As each node is visited, `process` is applied to it.

inorder_traverse operation
Preconditions: Receiver is a previously created binary tree, and `process` is an algorithmic process that can be applied to each node in the tree.
Postconditions: Each node of the tree is visited in the following order: First visit recursively all nodes in left subtree of the tree, then visit the root of the tree, then recursively all nodes in right subtree. As each node is visited, `process` is applied to it.

postorder_traverse operation
Preconditions: Receiver is a previously created binary tree, and `process` is an algorithmic process that can be applied to each node in the tree.
Postconditions: Each node of the tree is visited in the following order: First visit recursively all nodes in left subtree of the tree, then visit recursively all nodes in right subtree, then visit the root of the tree. As each node is visited, `process` is applied to it.

Several remarks are in order concerning this definition. First, the three traversal procedures require some clarification. With a linked list, there is only one obvious traversal because there was only one node that could be reached from any given node. However, with a binary tree, at any node, some choices need to be made:

- Should we apply **process** to the data field of the root before proceeding to the left and right subtrees?
- Should we apply **process** to the nodes in the left subtree and right subtree before processing the data in the root?
- Should we apply **process** to all the nodes in one of the subtrees, then to the root, and finally to all the nodes in the other subtree?

The answers to these questions determine the type of traversal. Figure 17.5 demonstrates the different orders in which nodes are visited under the three traversals.

◆ **FIGURE 17.5**

Differences between preorder, inorder, and postorder traversals

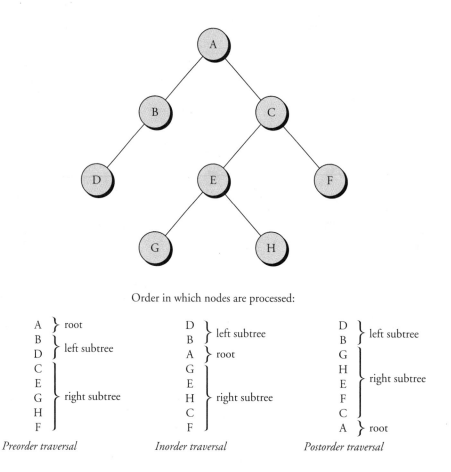

Order in which nodes are processed:

Preorder traversal	Inorder traversal	Postorder traversal
A } root	D } left subtree	D } left subtree
B } left subtree	B	B
D	A } root	G
C } right subtree	G	H
E	E	E } right subtree
G	H } right subtree	F
H	C	C
F	F	A } root

Second, the **insert** operation specified in our ADT definition for a binary tree provides a generic tree-building operation. That is, repeated applications of the **insert** operation on an initially empty binary tree typically lead to the construction of a binary tree. However, it is virtually impossible to define or implement the **insert** operation in a way that is general enough for all applications that will use a binary tree. Each instance of a binary tree is highly dependent on the hierarchical relationship between nodes that defines that particular binary tree. Therefore, we have linked our specification of the **insert** operation to the hierarchical relationship underlying a particular binary tree.

The following three examples provide illustrations of hierarchical relationships that can be used in defining binary trees. We will often use trees based on these hierarchical properties as examples in the remainder of the chapter. However, these three properties should by no means be considered exhaustive—virtually every application that uses a binary tree will have its own essential property. The point to be emphasized now is that the **insert** operation must, in its implementation, always be tailored to the property that defines a tree.

EXAMPLE 17.1

The tree of Figure 17.6 is a binary tree. Each node of this tree has two subtrees (null or non-null) designated as the left subtree and the right subtree. The particular hierarchical relationship underlying this tree is that the data in any given node of the tree are greater than or equal to the data in its left *and* right subtrees. A tree with this property is said to be a *heap* and to have the *heap property.* (This notion is not to be confused with the heap maintained by C++ for allocating space to pointer variables as described in Chapter 14.) We will discuss heaps in more detail in the next section. Also, they will prove particularly important in our discussion of more powerful sorting methods in Chapter 18. The programming problems at the end of this chapter also indicate how a heap may be used to implement the priority queue abstract data type introduced in Chapter 15. The heap property is one example of a hierarchical relationship that can underlie a tree and hence must be preserved when various operations are performed on the tree.

◆ **FIGURE 17.6**
Binary tree with the heap property

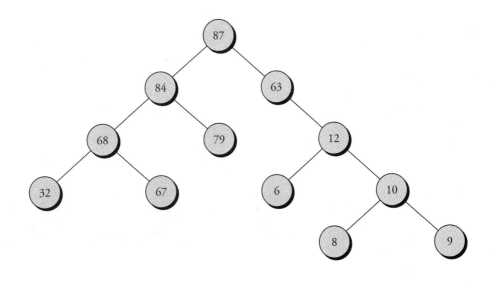

EXAMPLE 17.2

A second example of a hierarchical relationship underlying a binary tree structure is shown in Figure 17.7. This binary tree exhibits the property known as the *ordering property;* the data in each node of the tree are greater than all of the data in that node's left subtree and less than or equal to all the data in the right subtree. A binary tree with the ordering property is often called a *binary search tree.* We shall see the importance of trees possessing this property when we explore binary trees as a means of implementing a one-key table in Section 17.3.

◆ **FIGURE 17.7**
Binary search tree with the
ordering property

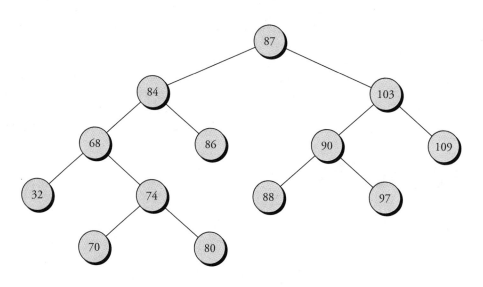

EXAMPLE 17.3

As a final example of a hierarchical relationship that can determine the arrangement of data in a binary tree, consider Figure 17.8, in which we have a binary tree representation of the infix algebraic expression

```
(A - B) + C * (E / F)
```

Take a moment to make particular note of Figure 17.8. Since we will be referring back to it frequently throughout this chapter, you may want to clip the page or mark it with a bookmark.

◆ **FIGURE 17.8**
Binary expression tree for
`(A - B) + C *`
`(E/F)`

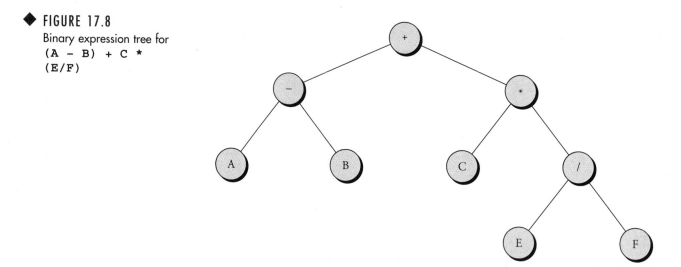

The hierarchical relationship of a parent to its children in this tree is that of algebraic operator to its two operands. Note that an operand may itself be an expression (that is, a subtree) which must be evaluated before the operator in the parent node can be applied. Note also that, if the order of evaluation in the expression changes as in

◆ FIGURE 17.9

Binary expression tree for
(A - B) + C * E/F

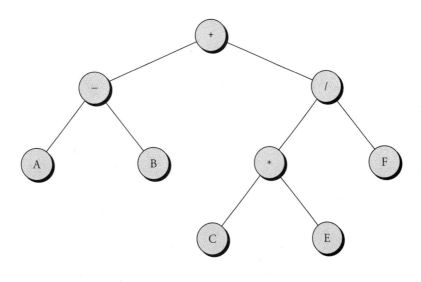

(A - B) + C * E / F

then the corresponding binary expression tree must also change as reflected in Figure 17.9.

Contemporary compilers make use of tree structures in obtaining forms of an arithmetic expression for efficient evaluation. As we've seen, there are basically three forms for an arithmetic expression such as that corresponding to Figure 17.8: infix, prefix, and postfix.

Expression	Form
(A - B) + C * (E / F)	infix
+ - A B * C / E F	prefix
A B - C E F / * +	postfix

All three of these forms are immediately available to us if we know exactly how the corresponding tree should be traversed. The *inorder traversal* of the binary tree for an arithmetic expression gives us the expression in unparenthesized infix form. The *preorder traversal* of the same tree leads us to the prefix form of the expression, whereas the *postorder traversal* of the tree yields the postfix form of the expression. We shall study procedures for these three traversals in Section 17.2, when we discuss a method of implementing a binary tree.

We close this section with a C++ interface for the binary tree ADT. In the sections that follow, we will analyze two implementations that adhere to this interface.

C++ Interface for the Binary Tree ADT

```
// Class declaration file: bintree.h

#ifndef BINARY_TREE_H

#include "boolean.h"
```

```
// Definition section

// We assume that type boolean is already defined

template <class E> class binary_tree
{

        public:

        // Class constructors

        binary_tree();
        binary_tree(const binary_tree<E> &bt);

        // Class destructor

        ~binary_tree();

        // Member functions

        boolean empty();
        void insert(const E &item);
        void preorder_traverse(void (*process) (E &item));
        void inorder_traverse(void (*process) (E &item));
        void postorder_traverse(void (*process) (E &item));
        binary_tree<E>& operator = (const binary_tree &bt);

        // Protected data and member functions pertaining to
        // the implementation would go here.

};

#define BINARY_TREE_H
#endif
```

EXERCISES 17.1

1. Draw a binary tree for the following expression:

   `A * B - (C + D) * (P / Q)`

2. Represent the following information as a binary tree:

   ```
   struct name
   {
           string first_name, last_name;
   };

   struct year
   {
           string first_sem, second_sem;
   };

   struct student
   ```

```
{
        name student_name;
        year year_of_study;
};
```

3. What, in an abstract sense, does a tree structure represent?

4. Indicate which of the following are binary search trees with the ordering property. Carefully explain what is wrong with those that are not.

a.

b.

c.

d.

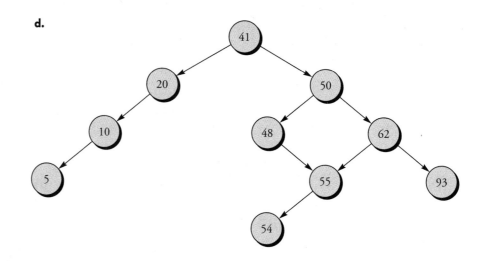

5. Indicate which of the following are binary trees with the heap property. Carefully explain what is wrong with those that are not.

c.

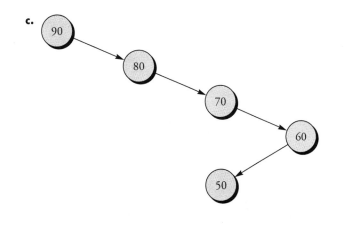

6. Given the following binary tree, indicate the order in which nodes would be processed for each of the preorder, postorder, and inorder traversals.

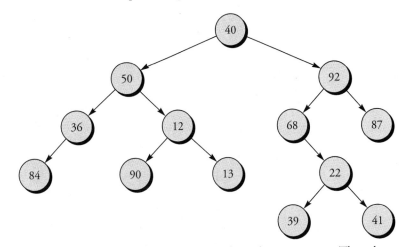

7. Construct some binary search trees with the ordering property. Then do some inorder traversals of these trees. What do you observe about the order in which nodes are processed? Be as specific as possible in stating your answer.

8. Given the following postorder and inorder traversals of a binary tree, draw the tree

Postorder: ABCDEFIKJGH
Inorder: CBAEDFHIGKJ

Attempt to deduce your answer in a systematic (and recursive) fashion, not by trial-and-error methods. After you have solved this problem, write a statement in which you describe the method you used to solve it and explain how this method could be applied to similar problems.

9. Draw binary expression trees corresponding to the algebraic expression whose:
   a. infix representation is `P / (Q + R) * X - Y`.
   b. postfix representation is `X Y Z P Q R * + /- *`.
   c. prefix representation is `+ * - M N P / R S`.

10. In a written statement, explain how the arrangement of data in a binary expression tree reflects the order of operations in the corresponding expression.

17.2 Linked Implementation of a Binary Tree

Consistent with the way in which we have studied other data structures, we now have a very good idea of *what* a tree is without any consideration of *how* we will implement it. We now explore this latter issue.

Two common methods are available for implementing binary trees. One method, known as *linked implementation,* uses dynamic allocation of nodes and pointers to these nodes. The other, which does not require the overhead of maintaining pointers, is called a *linear implementation* or *array inplementation.* In this section and the next, we focus on the linked implementation. We will see how this implementation is particularly well suited for binary search trees and binary expression trees.

Because each node in a binary tree may have two child nodes, a node in a linked implementation has two pointer members, one for each child, and one or more members for storing data. When a node has no children, the corresponding pointer members are NULL. Figure 17.10 is a linked representation of the binary expression tree of Figure 17.8. The left and right members are pointers to (that is, memory addresses of) the left child node and the right child node of the current node.

For the moment, let us give a detailed description of the linked representation of the binary tree of Figure 17.8. Once the concept is thoroughly understood, we will return to using C++ pointer variables for the actual implementation of binary trees. For example, we can implement the tree of Figure 17.10 as shown in Table 17.1 by building the left subtree for each node before considering the right subtree. The numbers on top of the cells in Figure 17.10 represent the addresses given in the left and right members.

In the linked representation, insertions and deletions involve no data movement except the rearrangement of pointers. Suppose we wish to modify the tree in Figure 17.8 to that in Figure 17.11. (This change might be needed due to some recent modification in the expression represented by Figure 17.8.) The insertion of the nodes containing – and P into the tree structure can be achieved easily by simply adding the nodes - and P in the next available spaces in the array and adjusting the corresponding pointers.

For the implementation of the tree shown in Figure 17.10, the effect of this insertion is given by Table 17.2. The adjusted pointers and data fields have been circled. Notice that the change in row 1 of the Right column and the additional rows 10 and 11 are all that is necessary. No data were moved.

◆ **FIGURE 17.10**

Linked representation of the binary expression tree of Figure 17.8

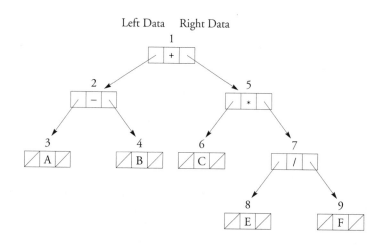

◇ TABLE 17.1
Implementation of Figure
17.10 using array of
records

Node	Data	Left	Right
1	+	2	5
2	–	3	4
3	A	NULL	NULL
4	B	NULL	NULL
5	*	6	7
6	C	NULL	NULL
7	/	8	9
8	E	NULL	NULL
9	F	NULL	NULL

◆ FIGURE 17.11
Desired modification of Figure 17.8

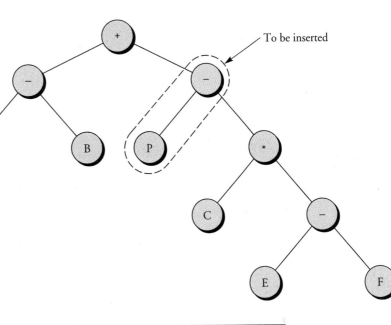

To be inserted

◇ TABLE 17.2
Modification of Table 17.1
by insertions into the tree of
Figure 17.8

Row	Data	Left	Right
1	+	2	10
2	–	3	4
3	A	NULL	NULL
4	B	NULL	NULL
5	*	6	7
6	C	NULL	NULL
7	/	8	9
8	E	NULL	NULL
9	F	NULL	NULL
10	–	11	5
11	P	NULL	NULL

Similarly, if we wish to shorten the tree in Figure 17.8 by deleting the nodes * and C, then all we must do is rearrange the pointers to obtain the altered tree, as shown in Figure 17.12. The effect of this deletion is given in Table 17.3. As before, the adjusted pointers and data fields have been circled.

A more formal statement of the algorithm underlying such insertions and deletions is dependent on the hierarchical property that forms the basis for the tree

◆ **FIGURE 17.12**
Another modification of Figure 17.8

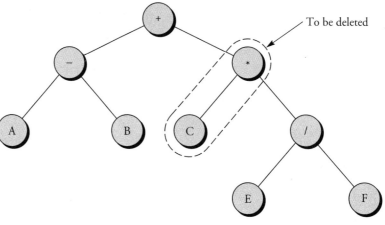

◇ **TABLE 17.3**
Modification of tree of Figure 17.8

Row	Data	Left	Right	Modified tree
1	+	2	7	
2	–	3	4	
3	A	NULL	NULL	
4	B	NULL	NULL	
5	*			Unused space after deletion of '*' and 'C'
6	C			
7	/	8	9	
8	E	NULL	NULL	
9	F	NULL	NULL	

structure. We will soon examine in detail insertion and deletion algorithms for binary search trees.

Now that we have explained the linked representation of a binary tree by using pointer values that can be explicitly traced, we will use the following general structure description with C++ pointer variables to implement this structure in the remainder of this and the next sections:

```
struct node;
typedef node *node_ptr;

struct node
{
        element data;
        node_ptr left;
        node_ptr right;
};
```

As we did for the pointer implementation of a linked list in Chapter 14, we embed this set of data definitions in the class definition for a binary tree, along with a data member for the root pointer:

```
// Class declaration file: bintree.h

#ifndef BINARY_TREE_H

#include "boolean.h"

// Declaration section

// We assume that type boolean is already defined

template <class E> class binary_tree
{

    public:

    // Class constructors

    binary_tree();
    binary_tree(const binary_tree<E> &bt);

    // Class destructor

    ~binary_tree();

    // Member functions

    boolean empty();
    void insert(const E &item);
    void preorder_traverse(void (*process) (E &item));
    void inorder_traverse(void (*process) (E &item));
    void postorder_traverse(void (*process) (E &item));
    binary_tree<E>& operator = (const binary_tree<E> &bt);

    protected:

    // Data members

    struct node;
    typedef node *node_ptr;
    struct node
    {
        E data;
        node_ptr left;
        node_ptr right;
    };

    node_ptr tree;
```

```
// Helper member functions would go here
};

#define BINARY_TREE_H
#endif
```

Note the comment about helper member functions. Because we will use recursion to implement many of the tree processing algorithms, we need a way of passing the tree data member as a parameter to each recursive function. Since this data member is protected, it cannot be a parameter of the public functions. Therefore, each of the operations in question will consist of a public function calling a protected helper function that carries out the recursive algorithm on the tree. We will need one such function for **insert** and for each of the traversal operations.

Recall that we also defined a utility function, **get_node**, in Chapter 14 to take care of the details of creating and initializing a new node for a linked list. We can write a similar function for binary trees as well:

```
template <class E>
binary_tree<E>::node_ptr binary_tree<E>::get_node(const E &data)
{
        node_ptr temp = new node;

        assert(temp != NULL);
        temp->data = data;
        temp->left = NULL;
        temp->right = NULL;
        return temp;

}
```

Note that **get_node** asks for new memory from the system heap and then checks for successful allocation before initializing the contents of a node. Now we have two pointers in a node to set to NULL. Therefore, if a pointer to a node is returned, the node is a leaf node.

EXAMPLE 17.4

Using the linked representation of a binary tree, implement the **insert** operation for a binary search tree with the ordering property. The **insert** operation passes the new element and the protected data member **tree** to a helper function, **insert_aux**:

```
template <class E>
void binary_tree<E>::insert(const E &data)
{
        insert_aux(tree, data);
}
```

The helper function **insert_aux** then performs the insertion:

```
template <class E>
void binary_tree<E>::insert_aux(node_ptr &tree, const E &data)
{
    if (tree == NULL)
        tree = get_node(data);
```

```
        else if (data < tree->data)
                insert_aux(tree->left, data);
        else
                insert_aux(tree->right, data);
}
```

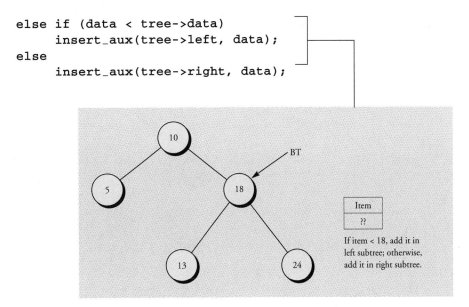

The **insert_aux** function of Example 17.4 implies that insertion of new nodes will always occur at the leaf nodes of a tree. As with insertion into a linked list, no data are moved; only pointers are manipulated. However, unlike the steps required by a linked list, we do not have to traverse the list sequentially to determine where the new node belongs. Instead, we use the *insertion rule*—if less than, go left; otherwise, go right—so that we traverse by subdividing the tree to determine the position for a new node. For example, if the **insert** function of Example 17.4 is successively fed numerical items in the following order:

```
16 8 -5 20 30 101 0 10 18
```

the binary search tree that results can be traced by the sequence in Figure 17.13. Note that the shape of the binary search tree is dependent on the order in which data items are given to the **insert** operation. This dependency of the shape of the tree on the order in which data arrive for insertion complicates any attempt to analyze the efficiency of the insert function in Example 17.4. We will provide a more detailed analysis of binary search trees with the ordering property in Section 17.3.

Implementing Traversal Operations on a Binary Tree

In Section 17.1 we described conceptually three different traversal operations on a binary tree: preorder, inorder, and postorder. In Example 17.3, we established correspondences between these three traversals and the prefix, infix, and postfix forms of the algebraic formula represented by a binary expression tree. However, it is important to reiterate that the three traversals apply broadly to all binary trees, regardless of the hierarchical relationship underlying their structure.

Recall from Section 17.1 the threefold dilemma facing us at each node we visit in a traversal of a binary tree:

1. Do we process the data contained in the node at which we are currently located?

◆ FIGURE 17.13
Growth of search tree when
data arrive in order 16 8 -5
20 30 101 0 10 18

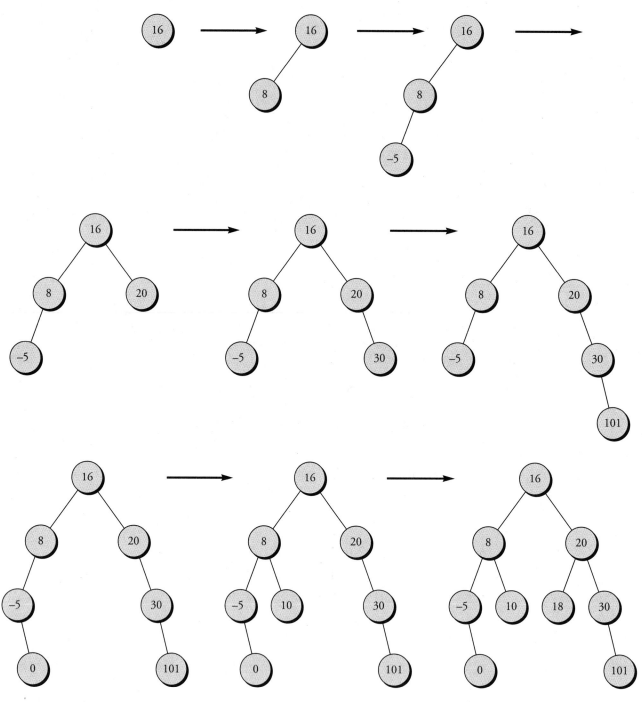

2. Do we remember the location of the current node (so that we can return to process it) and visit (and process) all nodes in its left subtree?

3. Do we remember the location of the current node (so that we can return to process it) and visit (and process) all nodes in its right subtree?

Each of the three choices represents a valid choice. The route chosen out of the three-way dilemma dictates the order in which the nodes are visited and processed.

Preorder Traversal of a Binary Tree

In a preorder traversal, the three options are combined in the following order:

1. First, process the root node.
2. Then, recursively visit all nodes in the left subtree.
3. Finally, recursively visit all nodes in the right subtree.

These three ordered steps are recursive. Once the root of the tree is processed, we go to the root of the left subtree, and then to the root of the left subtree of the left subtree, and so on until we can go no farther. Following these three steps, the preorder traversal of the tree of Figure 17.8 would process nodes in the order

```
+ - A B * C / E F
```

which is the prefix form of the expression

```
(A - B) + C * (E / F)
```

Hence we conclude that if to process a node means to print it, then a preorder traversal of a binary expression tree will output the prefix form of the expression.

The preorder traversal of an existing binary tree implemented via the linked representation can be accomplished recursively using the following pair of functions, where **preorder_aux** is the helper function for the public member function **preorder_traverse**:

```
template <class E>
void binary_tree<E>::preorder_traverse(void (* process) (E &item))
{
    preorder_aux(tree, process);
}


template <class E>
void binary_tree<E>::preorder_aux(node_ptr tree, void (* process) (E &item))
{
    if (tree != NULL)
    {
        process(tree->data);
        preorder_aux(tree->left, process);
        preorder_aux(tree->right, process);
    }
}
```

First, process root node.

Second, traverse left subtree.

Third, traverse right subtree.

Inorder Traversal of a Binary Tree

The inorder traversal of a binary tree proceeds as outlined in the following three ordered steps:

1. First, recursively visit all nodes in the left subtree.
2. Then, process the root node.
3. Finally, recursively visit all nodes in the right subtree.

By carefully following these steps for the tree of Figure 17.8 and assuming "process" means "print," we obtain the readily recognizable infix expression

```
A - B + C * E / F
```

Unless we add parentheses, this infix expression is not equivalent to the order of operations reflected in the tree of Figure 17.8. The fact that prefix and postfix notations do not require parentheses to avoid such ambiguities makes them distinctly superior to infix notation for evaluation purposes.

An implementation of the recursive algorithm for an inorder traversal is given in the following pair of functions for a linked representation of a binary tree:

```
template <class E>
void binary_tree<E>::inorder_traverse(void (* process) (E &item))
{
    inorder_aux(tree, process);
}


template <class E>
void binary_tree<E>::inorder_aux(node_ptr tree, void (* process) (E &item))
{
    if (tree != NULL)
    {
        inorder_aux(tree->left, process);
        process(tree->data);
        inorder_aux(tree->right, process);
    }
}
```

Second, process
root node.

First, traverse
left subtree.

Third, traverse
right subtree.

Postorder Traversal of a Binary Tree

The third standard traversal of a binary tree, the postorder traversal, entails an arrangement of options that postpones processing the root node until last.

1. First, recursively visit all nodes in the left subtree of the root node.
2. Then, recursively visit all nodes in the right subtree of the root node.
3. Finally, process the root node.

Applying these three steps to the binary expression tree of Figure 17.8 yields the postfix form of the underlying expression:

```
A B - C E F / * +
```

The actual implementation of the postorder traversal operation is completely analogous to the inorder and preorder operations. Consequently, we will leave it as an exercise.

Although we have illustrated the three traversal algorithms using binary expression trees, we emphasize that the traversals apply in general to *any* binary tree. Indeed, as we shall see in the next section, the inorder traversal when used in combination with a tree exhibiting the hierarchical ordering property of a binary search tree will neatly allow us to implement a one-key table using a binary tree.

Copying and Destroying a Binary Tree

Two of the binary tree class operations that require traversals are the copy constructor and the destructor. The copy constructor should copy all of the data elements in the original (parameter) tree to the new (receiver) tree. Not only should this operation preserve the ordering of the data in the new binary tree, but the structure of the nodes should be exactly the same as in the original tree. Thus, the root node of the new tree should contain the same data element as the root node of the original tree, and so on for each subtree. To guarantee both ordering and structure, we perform a preorder traversal of the original tree. When a node in the original tree is visited, its data element is inserted into the new tree with **insert**. Then the left and right subtrees are copied in the same manner. Unfortunately, we cannot use the **preorder_traverse** operation for copying the original tree, because the **process** function would have no access to the new tree. Therefore, a new helper function must be written that performs the preorder traversal directly. The code for the copy constructor and the helper function is

```
template <class E>
binary_tree<E>::binary_tree(const binary_tree<E> &bt)
{
// Pass the original tree's data member to the traversal function.
    copy_aux(bt.tree);
}


template <class E>
void binary_tree<E>::copy_aux(node_ptr tree)
{
    if (tree != NULL)
    {
// Copy from original to new (receiver) tree.
        insert(tree->data);
        copy_aux(tree->left);
        copy_aux(tree->right);
    }
}
```

Note that the identifier **tree** in the helper function refers to the data member of the original tree, not to the receiver tree's data member. The receiver tree's data member is accessed with the same identifier within the implementation of **insert**.

Recall from Chapter 14 that any class that uses dynamic memory in its implementation should have a class destructor operation. This function returns any memory used for nodes to the system heap. The class destructor is run automatically by the computer when a variable or parameter bound to an instance of the class goes out of scope. Given these requirements, we need a traversal algorithm that visits the leaf nodes of a tree first, deletes them from the tree, and then visits the leaf nodes at the next level up. Clearly, a preorder traversal will not work, because that would delete root nodes first. An inorder traversal would delete the left subtree before the root node, but the root node would be lost before we could visit the leaves of the right subtree. A postorder traversal would be just right because it would first delete the left subtree, and then the right subtree, before deleting a root node. The recursive process guarantees that the leaf nodes at any level in the tree are deleted first. Once again, we cannot use an established traversal operation, because of scope problems. So we present the code for the class destructor and a new helper operation that carries out a mass deletion in postorder:

```
template <class E>
binary_tree<E>::~binary_tree()
{
        destroy_aux(tree);
        tree = NULL;
}


template <class E>
void binary_tree<E>::destroy_aux(node_ptr tree)
{
        if (tree != NULL)
        {
                destroy_aux(tree->left);
                destroy_aux(tree->right);
                delete tree;          // Return leaf node to system heap.
        }
}
```

Note that the identifier **tree** refers in both of these functions to the receiver's data member. After **destroy_aux** has returned any nodes to the system heap, the top-level destructor operation sets the data member to NULL to indicate an empty binary tree.

EXERCISES 17.2

1. Using a preorder traversal of the tree you derived in Exercise 1 from Section 17.1, obtain the prefix form of the expression in that exercise.

2. Sketch the binary search tree that would result when the **insert** function of Example 17.4 is used for data that arrive in the following orders:
   a. 100 90 80 70 60 50 40 32 20 10
   b. 60 80 30 90 70 100 40 20 50 10
   c. 60 50 70 40 80 30 90 20 100 10

   Provide a brief written statement in which you describe how the shape of the binary search tree is related to the order in which data arrive for insertion into the tree.

3. Consider the following search trees with the ordering property. For each, specify an order of arrival of data items that would result in that particular tree if the insert function of Example 17.4 is used.

a.

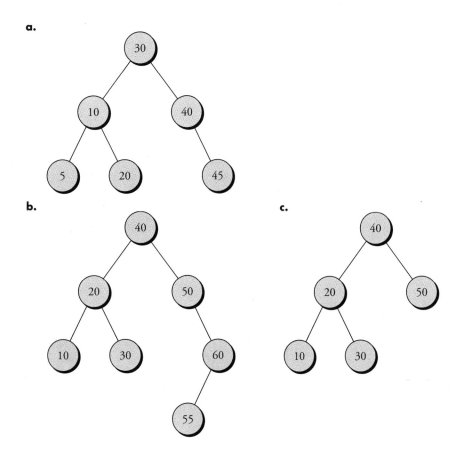

b.

c.

4. What is the output produced by the following function for the pictured tree?

```
void tree_walk(node_ptr tree)
{
    if (tree == NULL)
        cout << "OOPS" << endl;
    else
    {
        tree_walk(tree->right);
        tree_walk(tree->left);
        cout << tree->data << endl;
    }
}
```

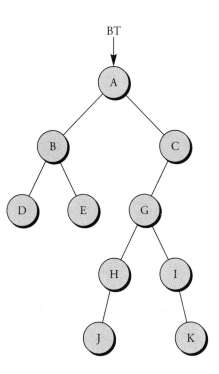

5. How does the output from Exercise 4 change if the statement

```
cout << tree->data << endl;
```

is moved ahead of the recursive calls to **tree_walk**?

6. How does the output from Exercise 4 change if the statement

```
cout << tree->data << endl;
```

is located between the recursive calls to **tree_walk**?

7. Repeat Exercises 4, 5, and 6 for the following tree:

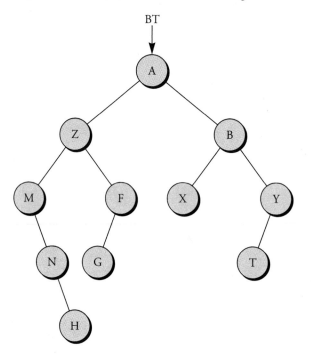

8. A *ternary tree* is a tree in which each node may have at most three children. A pointer/record structure for a linked implementation of such a tree could thus be given by the following declarations:

```
struct node;
typedef node *node_ptr;
struct node
{
     element data;
     node_ptr left;
     node_ptr middle;
     node_ptr right;
};
```

What would be the output produced by the following **tree_walk** function

```
void tree_walk(node_ptr tree)
{

      if (tree != NULL)
      {
          cout << tree->data << endl;
```

```
        tree_walk(tree->right);
        tree_walk(tree->middle);
        tree_walk(tree->left);
    }
}
```

if it were initially called with the root pointer to the tree in the following diagram?

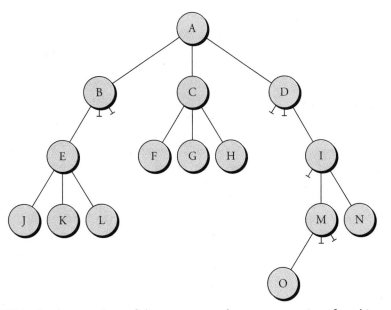

9. Write implementations of the **create** and **empty** operations for a binary search tree with the ordering property using the linked representation method.

10. Write an implementation of the postorder traversal operation for a linked representation of a binary tree.

11. Write a function that reads an algebraic expression in prefix notation and builds the binary tree corresponding to the expression (see Example 17.3). Assume that all tokens in the expression are individual characters.

12. Write a function that reads an algebraic expression in postfix notation and builds the binary tree corresponding to the expression (see Example 17.3). Assume that all tokens in the expression are individual characters.

13. Implement one of the traversal algorithms in a nonrecursive fashion by using a stack to keep track of pointers to nodes that must be visited when you finish processing the current subtree. Your stack will approximate the role played by the system stack in the recursive version of the algorithm.

14. Suppose that you have a binary tree representation of an algebraic expression consisting of the operators +, −, *, / and operands that are uppercase letters. Suppose also that you have a function value that, given an operand, will return the numeric value associated with that operand. Write a recursive function to evaluate the expression tree.

15. Write a function to solve the following puzzle. Assume that the element type is **char**. Your function receives two strings of the same length. The first represents the order in which the nodes of a tree would be visited by a preorder traversal. The second represents the order in which nodes from the same tree would be visited by an inorder traversal. Your function is to construct the tree from these two traversals.

16. Write a Boolean-valued function that receives two binary trees composed of the same type of data. The function should return TRUE if the two trees are identical,

that is, if they have precisely the same shape and have the same values in each node. Otherwise, it should return FALSE.

17. How could the inorder traversal of a binary tree be used to sort data logically? Provide your answer in the form of a precise written statement.

17.3 Binary Search Tree Implementation of a One-Key Table

The implementations we have considered for the one-key table have been found lacking in certain respects. The physically ordered array implementation of Chapter 12 allowed for the fast inspection of objects via the binary search algorithm but necessitated excessive data movement when objects were added to or deleted from the list. The linked list implementation suggested in Chapter 14 handled insertions and removals nicely but presented us with an undesirable $O(n)$ search efficiency due to the lack of random access.

In this section, we shall see that by implementing a one-key table using a binary tree with the ordering property, we can achieve efficiency in both searching and adding or deleting while at the same time keeping the list in order. Moreover, we do not have to pay too great a price in other trade-offs to achieve this best of both worlds. Indeed, binary trees with the ordering property are called binary search trees precisely because of their frequent application in efficiently implementing one-key tables.

A binary search tree is organized via the hierarchical ordering property discussed in Example 17.2 in Section 17.1. Recall that this ordering property stipulates the following:

For any given data item X in the tree, every node in the left subtree of X contains only items that are less than X with respect to a particular type of ordering. Every node in the right subtree of X contains only items that are greater than or equal to X with respect to the same ordering.

For instance, the tree of Figure 17.14 illustrates this property with respect to alphabetical ordering. You can quickly verify that an inorder traversal of this tree (in which the processing of each node consists merely of printing its contents) leads to the following alphabetized list:

ARPS	NATHAN
DIETZ	PERKINS
EGOFSKE	SELIGER
FAIRCHILD	TALBOT
GARTH	UNDERWOOD
HUSTON	VERKINS
KEITH	ZARDA
MAGILLICUDDY	

This allows us to reach the following important conclusion. That is, an inorder traversal of a binary search tree will visit nodes in ascending order. Hence such a tree may be viewed as an ordered table. The first table element is the first item visited by the inorder traversal. More generally, the nth element visited by the inorder traversal corresponds precisely to the nth element in the table. Given this view of a binary search tree as an implementation of a one-key table, let us now consider the operations of adding, deleting, and finding (retrieving) nodes in the table.

◆ FIGURE 17.14

Ordering property with respect to alphabetical ordering

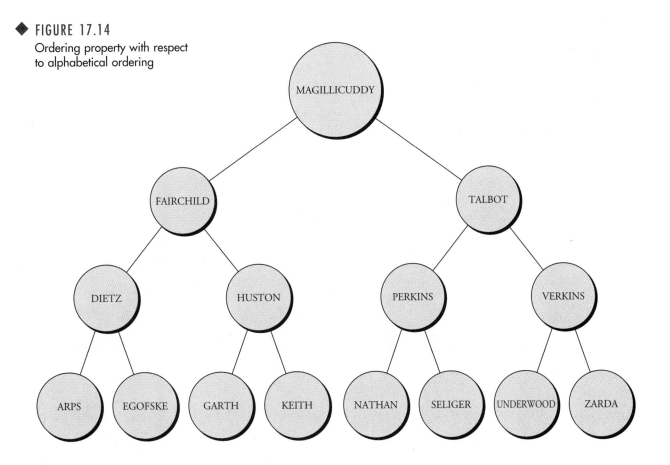

Adding Nodes to the Binary Search Tree Implementation of a One-Key Table

Insertion of a new key into such a tree is a fairly easy process that may well require significantly fewer comparisons than insertion into a linked list. The specifics of the insert operation were developed in Example 17.4. Consider, for example, the steps necessary to insert the key 'SEFTON' into the tree of Figure 17.14 in such a fashion as to maintain the ordering property. We must

1. Compare SEFTON to MAGILLICUDDY. Because SEFTON is greater than MAGILLICUDDY, follow the right child pointer to TALBOT.
2. Compare SEFTON to TALBOT. Because SEFTON is less than TALBOT, follow the left child pointer to PERKINS.
3. SEFTON is greater than PERKINS. Hence follow the right child pointer to SELIGER.
4. SELIGER is a leaf node, so SEFTON may be added as one of its children. The left child is chosen because SEFTON is less than SELIGER.

The resulting tree for the sample insertion is given in Figure 17.15.

Provided that the tree maintains a full shape, the number of nodes on a given branch will be at most

$$\log_2 n + 1$$

◆ FIGURE 17.15
Tree in Figure 17.14 with
the insertion SEFTON

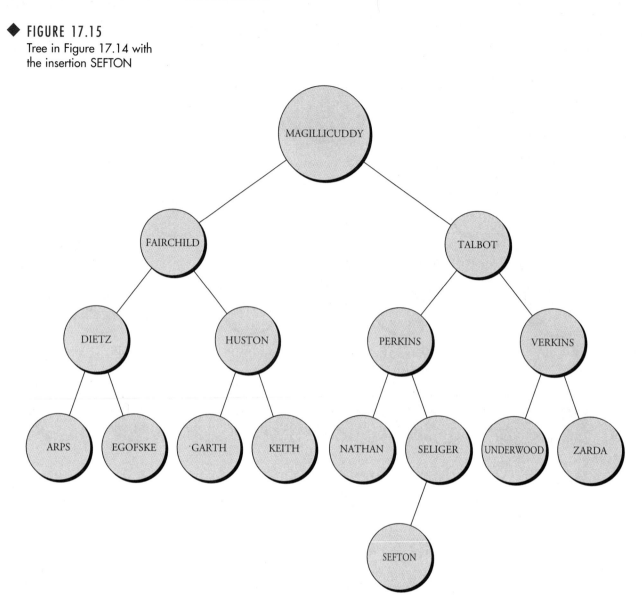

where *n* is the total number of nodes in the tree. By *full* we mean that all nodes
with fewer than two children must occur at level *m* or *m* – 1 where *m* is the deepest
level in the tree. In other words, all nodes above level *m* – 1 must have exactly two
children. Hence, adding ROBERTS to the tree of Figure 17.15 by the insertion
rule would destroy its fullness.

Given this definition of full, the ($\log_2 n$ + 1) figure for the maximum number
of nodes on a branch emerges immediately upon inspection or, more formally,
using a proof by mathematical induction. Our purpose here, however, is not to give
the details of such a proof but rather to emphasize that a binary search tree presents
an alternative to a linked list structure for the type of processing involved in
maintaining ordered lists. Moreover, it is a particularly attractive alternative when
the tree is full, because substantially fewer comparisons are needed to locate where
in the structure an insertion is to be made. For instance, if *n* is 1024, the linked list
may require as many as 1024 comparisons to make an insertion. Because $\log_2 1024$

is 10, the full binary search tree method will require at most 11 comparisons. This difference becomes even more dramatic as n gets larger. For an ordered list with 1,000,000 entries, a linked list may require that many comparisons, but the full binary search tree requires a mere 21 comparisons.

What happens when the tree is not full? We will comment on that situation at the end of this section, when we discuss the overall efficiency considerations for this implementation of a one-key table. Before that, however, consider the operations of finding and deleting data in a binary search tree.

Searching for Data in a Binary Search Tree Implementation of a One-Key Table

The insertion rule also dictates the search path followed through a binary search tree when we are attempting to find a given data item. Interestingly, if we trace the nodes visited on such a search path for a full tree, we will probe exactly the same items that we would in conducting a binary search on a physically ordered array containing the same data. For instance, if we are searching for SMITH in the tree of Figure 17.14, we will have to probe MAGILLICUDDY, TALBOT, and PERKINS. These are precisely the items that would be probed if the binary search algorithm were applied to the physically ordered list associated with Figure 17.14. Our analysis of such a tree has allowed us to conclude that, as long as the binary search tree remains full, the search efficiency for this method of implementing a one-key table matches that of the physically ordered array implementation. That is, the search efficiency is $O(\log_2 n)$.

Deleting Data in a Binary Search Tree Implementation of a One-Key Table

The deletion algorithm for a binary search tree is conceptually more complex than that for a linked list. Suppose, for instance, that we wish to remove TALBOT from the list represented by the tree of Figure 17.14. Two questions arise:

1. Can such a deletion be achieved merely by manipulating pointers?
2. If so, what does the resulting tree look like?

To answer these questions, begin by recalling that all that is necessary to represent a one-key table with a binary search tree is that, for each node in the tree

1. The left subtree must contain only items less than it.
2. The right subtree must contain only items greater than or equal to it.

With the preservation of this ordering property as the primary goal in processing a deletion, one acceptable way of restructuring the tree of Figure 17.14 after deleting TALBOT appears in Figure 17.16; essentially, SELIGER moves up to replace TALBOT in the tree. The choice of SELIGER to replace TALBOT is made because SELIGER represents the greatest data item in the left subtree of the node containing TALBOT. As long as we choose this greatest item in the left subtree to replace the item being deleted, we guarantee preservation of the crucial ordering property that enables the tree to represent the list accurately.

Given this general motivation for choosing a node to replace the one being deleted, let us now outline a case-by-case analysis of the deletion algorithm. Throughout this analysis, we assume that we have a pointer P to the item that we wish to delete. The pointer P may be one of the following:

◆ **FIGURE 17.16**
Restructuring the tree in Figure 17.14 after deleting TALBOT

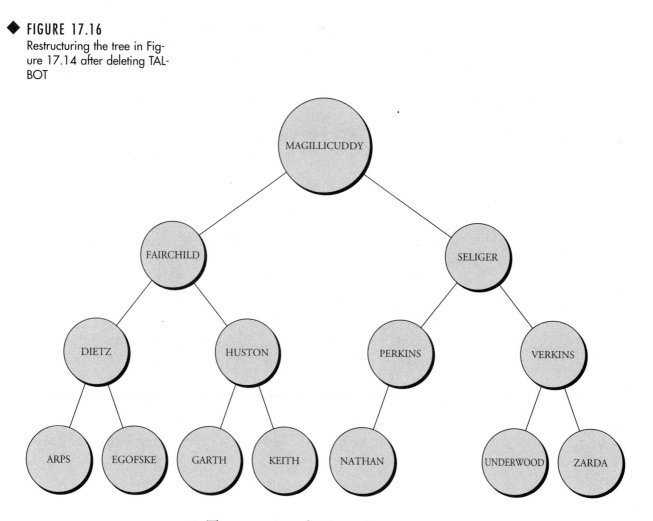

1. The root pointer for the entire tree.
2. The left child pointer of the parent of the node to be deleted.
3. The right child pointer of the parent of the node to be deleted.

Figure 17.17 highlights these three possibilities; the algorithm applies whether 1, 2, or 3 holds.

◆ **FIGURE 17.17**
Three possibilities for the pointer P

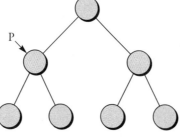

(1) Deleting the root   (2) Deleting a left child   (3) Deleting a right child

We now examine three cases of node deletion on a binary search tree:

1. The node to be deleted has no children.
2. The node to be deleted has a right child but no left child.
3. The node to be deleted has a left child.

Case 1. The node pointed to by P, that is, the node to be deleted, has no children. This is the easiest of all the cases. It can be compactly handled

```
X = P;
P = NULL;
delete X;
```

Case 2. The node pointed to by P, that is, the node to be deleted, has a right child but no left child. This case poses no more problems than case 1 and is described in Figure 17.18. The node to be deleted is merely replaced by its right child. The necessary C++ coding is

```
X = P;
P = X->right;
delete X;
```

◆ FIGURE 17.18
In case 2 the node pointed to by P has a right but no left child

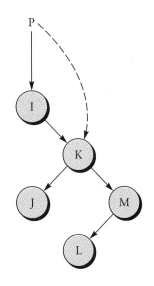

Case 3. The node pointed to by P, that is, the node to be deleted, has a left child. In Figure 17.19, node M is to be deleted, and it has left child K. In this case, because we have a non-null left subtree of the node to be deleted, our previous discussion indicates that we must find the greatest node in that left subtree. If the node pointed to by **P->left** (node K in the figure) has no right child, then the greatest node in the left subtree of P is **P->left** itself. Figure 17.19 pictorially describes this situation; the dotted lines indicate new pointer values.

The partial coding to achieve this pointer manipulation is given by:

```
X = P;
P = X->left;
P->right = X->right;
delete X;
```

If the node pointed to by **P->left** does have a right child, then to find the greatest node in the left subtree of P we must follow the right branch leading from

◆ **FIGURE 17.19**

Case 3 with `P->left`
(node K) having no right
children

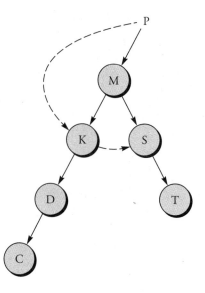

`P->left` as deeply as possible into the tree. In Figure 17.20, node R is the one
chosen to replace the deleted node. This figure gives the schematic representation,
with the pointer changes necessary to complete the deletion. The coding necessary
for this slightly more complicated version of case 3 is

```
X = P;
Q = X->left->right;
QParent = X->left;
```

◆ **FIGURE 17.20**
Case 3 with `P->left`
having a right child

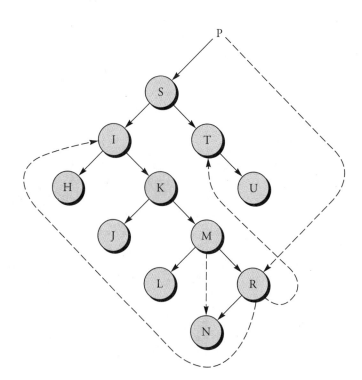

```
// Q will eventually point to node which will replace P.
// QParent will point to Q's parent.
// The following loop forces Q as deep as possible
// along the right branch from P->left.

while (Q->left != NULL)
{
        Q = Q->right;
        QParent = QParent->right;
}


// Having found node Q to replace P, adjust pointers
// to appropriately link it into the tree.

Q->right = X->right;
P = Q;
QParent->right = Q->left;
Q->left = X->left;
delete X;
```

Efficiency Considerations for Binary Search Tree Implementation of a One-Key Table

It is important to note that, in all three cases, the deletion of a node from the tree involved only pointer manipulation and no actual data movement. Hence, in a one-key table maintained with a binary search tree, we are able to process both insertions and deletions by the same pure pointer manipulation that makes linked lists so desirable. Moreover, the binary search tree approach apparently allows us to locate data for retrieval, insertion, or deletion much faster than a linked list representation would. However, there are aspects of the binary tree method that tarnish its performance in comparison to a linked list. These aspects are discussed next.

The binary search tree implementation requires more memory in two respects. First, each node has two pointers instead of the one required in a singly linked list. This proliferation of pointers is particularly wasteful because many of the pointers may be NULL. Second, we currently can traverse the tree in order only by using recursive techniques. Even in a language that allows recursion, a substantial amount of overhead is needed to maintain the stack used by recursive calls.

The $O(\log_2 n)$ efficiency of the binary search tree method is only an optimal, not a guaranteed, efficiency. It is contingent on the tree remaining nearly full. The tree remaining full is in turn contingent on the order in which the data are added and deleted. In the worst possible case, data entering the tree structure in the wrong order can cause the tree to degenerate into a glorified linked list with a corresponding $O(n)$ efficiency. (The exercises at the end of this section have you explore this relationship between the order in which data arrive for insertion and the resulting search efficiency of the binary search tree.)

Both of these drawbacks can be overcome. We can avoid the overhead associated with recursion if we use a technique (known as *threading*) that puts to good use the pointers that are otherwise wasted as NULL.

Moreover, by using a technique known as *height balancing,* the binary search tree can be maintained in a fashion that approaches fullness at all times, regardless of the order in which data arrive for entry. This nearly full form is enough to completely guarantee the $O(\log_2 n)$ search efficiency. Originally devised by G. M. Adelson-Velskii and Y. M. Landis, the height-balancing algorithm is sufficiently complex to be beyond the scope of this book. In-depth treatments of it and the threading technique cited above are given in *Data Structures in C++* by Ellis Horowitz and Sartaj Sahni (New York: Computer Science Press, 1990) and in *Introduction to Data Structures and Algorithm Analysis with C++* by George J. Pothering and Thomas L. Naps (St. Paul, Minn.: West Publishing, 1995).

Overall, the binary search tree implementation of a one-key table would seem to be the best of the three implementations we have studied for situations in which additions, deletions, and searches must all be processed efficiently. Even when steps are not taken to correct the two disadvantages we have cited, it offers the addition/deletion advantages of a linked list with a search efficiency that is bounded between $O(\log_2 n)$ and $O(n)$.

EXERCISES 17.3

1. Which of the following binary search trees are full?

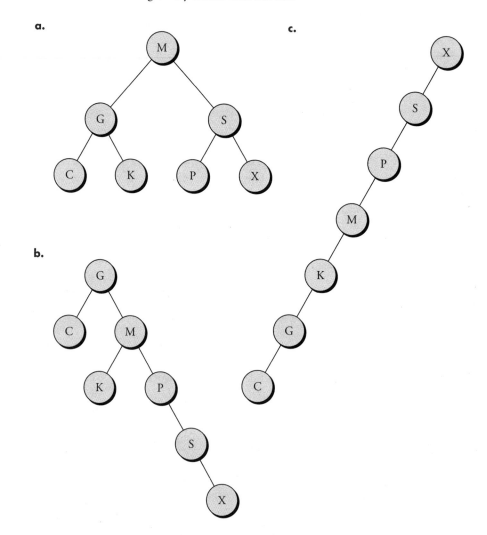

2. The key values 1 through 10 are to be inserted in a binary search tree. Specify orders of arrival for these values to create trees that correspond with each of the following shapes.

a.

b.   **c.**

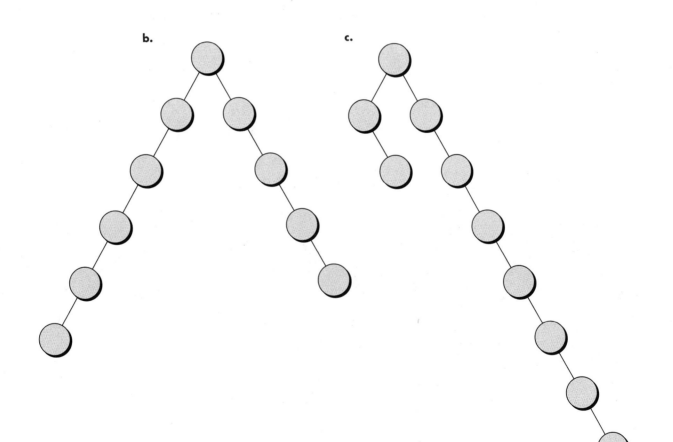

3. In an essay, discuss the relative merits of maintaining a one-key table by a binary search tree, a singly linked list, and a doubly linked list.

4. In an essay, discuss how the order in which data are entered into a binary search tree affects the fullness of the tree. Be sure to identify the best and worst possible cases. Analyze the efficiency of tree operations to add, delete, and find data for each of these cases.

5. The node containing 46 is to be deleted from each of the following binary search trees. Assuming the deletion algorithm described in this section is used, draw the tree after the deletion of 46.

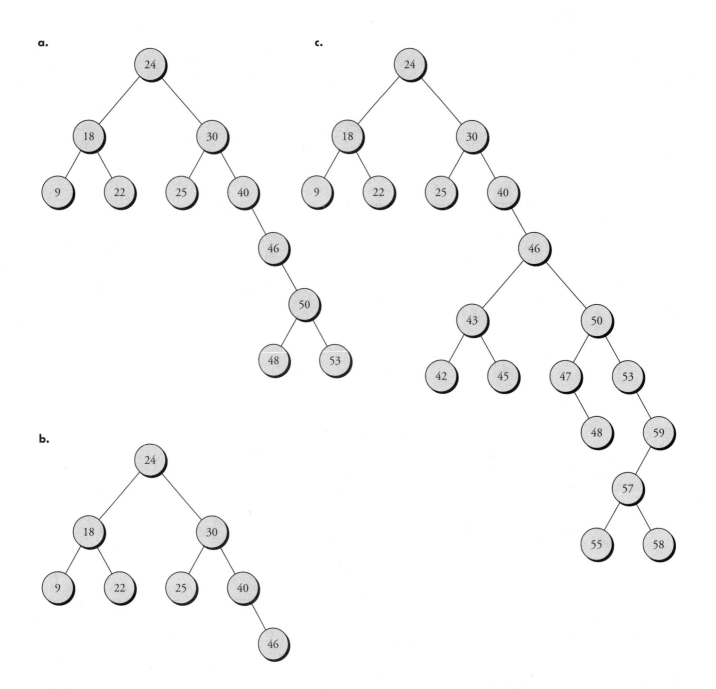

6. In Example 17.4 we provided an implementation of the **insert** operation for a binary search tree. What does the function in that example do when we try to insert a key value that already exists in the tree? Modify the function so that, when we try to insert such a key value, the tree is left unaltered.

7. The implementation of the **insert** operation for a binary search tree in Example 17.4 is recursive. Write a nonrecursive implementation of this operation.

8. Develop recursive and nonrecursive implementations of the algorithm to search for a particular data item in a binary search tree.

9. Develop a complete implementation of the algorithm to delete an item from a binary search tree. This will essentially require that you combine into one module the three cases discussed in this section. For an added challenge, try writing the function so that it handles deletion by using the "mirror image" of these three cases.

10. Look back to the definition of the one-key table ADT in Chapter 12. Provide a complete implementation of the table operations using a binary search tree as the underlying data structure. (*Hint:* You should provide comparison operations for the association class, so that associations can be the objects stored in binary trees.)

11. Suppose you are given a list of data in increasing order of keys. Develop a C++ algorithm that will load this list into an optimal binary search tree.

12. A binary search tree could itself be considered an ADT that is derived from the more generic binary tree ADT defined in Section 17.1. Write a complete definition and a C++ interface for the binary search tree as an ADT. Be sure that the set of operations you describe will allow your binary search tree ADT to be used as an implementation strategy for the one-key table ADT.

17.4 Linear Implementation of the Binary Tree Abstract Data Type

OBJECTIVES

- to become familiar with the linear implementation of the binary tree ADT

- to recognize the advantages and disadvantages of the linear implementation versus the linked implementation

- to see why the linear implementation is particularly well suited to representing a binary tree with the heap property

- to analyze the efficiency of the **insert** operation for a linear implementation of a binary tree with the heap property

The linear implementation of a binary tree uses a one-dimensional array of size $[2^{(d + 1)} - 1]$ where d is the depth of the tree, that is, the maximum level of any node in the tree. In the tree of Figure 17.8, the root + is at the level 0, the nodes – and * are at level 1, and so on. The deepest level in this tree is the level of E and F, level 3. Therefore, $d = 3$ and this tree will require an array of size $2^{(3+1)} - 1 = 15$.

Once the size of the array has been determined, the following method is used to represent the tree:

1. Store the root in the first location of the array.

2. If a node is in location n of the array, store its left child at location $2n$, and its right child at location $(2n + 1)$.

With the aid of this scheme, the tree of Figure 17.8 is stored in the array tree of size 15 shown in Figure 17.21. Locations **tree[7]** through **tree[12]** are not used.

An encapsulated definition of the binary tree ADT for this linear representation is given by:

```
protected:

// Protected data members

struct node                            // Either NULL or a node
{
    boolean null;
    E data;
};

node tree[MAX_TREE_NODES];             // Array of nodes
int number_nodes;                      // Number of nodes in tree
```

◆ FIGURE 17.21

Tree of Figure 17.8 stored in a linear representation using an array

BTData

0	+
1	−
2	*
3	A
4	B
5	C
6	/
7	NULL
8	NULL
9	NULL
10	NULL
11	NULL
12	NULL
13	E
14	F

Unused locations in the array

The **create** operation simply sets the **number_nodes** data member to zero and initializes the **null** member of all nodes in the array locations to TRUE. The **null** flags are necessary to detect whether or not a given tree node has children. A tree node at location n has a left subtree if and only if the node at location $2n$ contains a **null** flag of FALSE. A similar consideration applies to the right subtree of the tree node at location n.

Efficiency Considerations for the Linear Representation

The main advantages of this method lie in its simplicity and the fact that, given a child node, its parent node can be determined immediately. If a child node is at location n in the array, then its parent node is at location $n/2$.

In spite of its simplicity and ease of implementation, the linear representation method has all the costs that come with physically ordering items. Insertion or deletion of a node in a fashion that maintains the hierarchical relationships within the tree may cause considerable data movement up and down the array and hence use an excessive amount of processing time. Also, depending on the application, memory locations (such as locations 7 through 12 in Figure 17.21) may be wasted due to partially filled trees.

Using the Linear Implementation for a Heap

One type of binary tree for which the linear implementation of a binary tree proves to be ideal is the heap, as defined in Example 17.1. The data in a heap can be embedded in an array without ever wasting any locations. To prove this claim, we will show that, given a heap with $N - 1$ nodes embedded in an array with no gaps, we can add an Nth node and maintain the dense packing of data in the array.

To illustrate the algorithm for doing this, consider the heap with eight nodes pictured in Figure 17.22. The numbers outside the circular nodes in this figure indicate the array indices where data would be stored in the linear representation of a binary tree.

◆ **FIGURE 17.22**
A heap with eight nodes

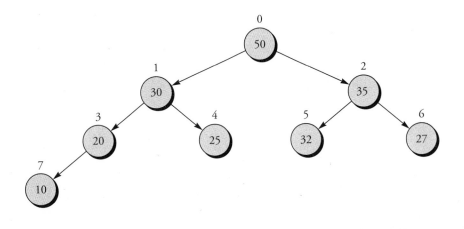

Now suppose we want to add 40 to the heap of Figure 17.22. We will begin by comparing 40 to the data in the least index, which does not yet have two children: 20 at index 3 in Figure 17.22. Figure 17.23 shows a series of data interchanges that "walk 40 up" a path until the tree is transformed into a heap. The algorithm to achieve this "walking up" is given in the following example.

◆ **FIGURE 17.23**
Transforming heap to accommodate insertion of 40 (numbers outside circles indicate array index positions)

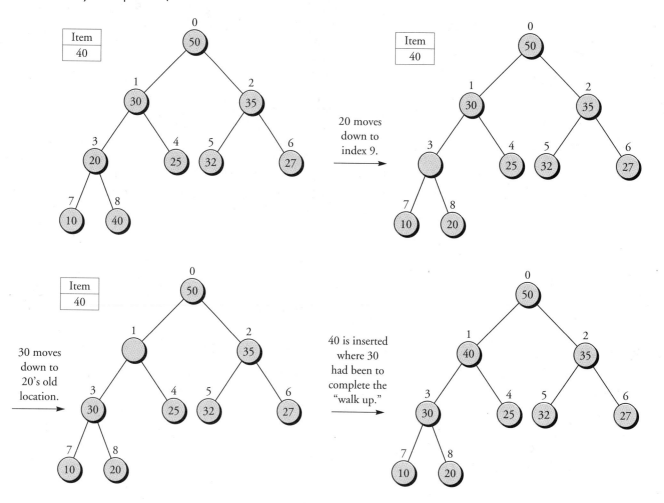

EXAMPLE 17.5 Implement the **insert** operation for a linear representation of a binary tree with the heap property.

```
template <class E>
void binary_tree<E>::insert(const E &item)
{
    int location, parent;

    assert(number_nodes < MAX_TREE_NODES);
    ++number_nodes;

    // Now walk the new item up the tree, starting at location
```

```
location = number_nodes;
parent = location / 2;
while ((parent >= 1) &&
      (tree[parent - 1].data < item))
{
      tree[location - 1] = tree[parent - 1];
      location = parent;
      parent = location / 2;
}
tree[location - 1].data = item;
tree[location - 1].null = FALSE;
}
```

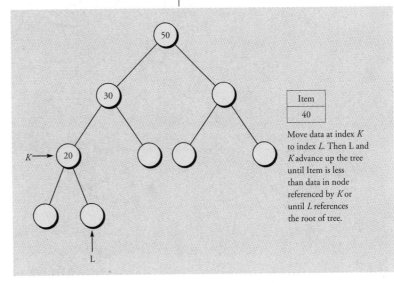

Item

40

Move data at index K to index L. Then L and K advance up the tree until Item is less than data in node referenced by K or until L references the root of tree.

Note that the logic of the algorithm is simplified if we pretend that the array representing the heap is indexed from 1 to **number_nodes,** rather than from 0 to **number_nodes** - 1. We map these logical indices to actual positions in the C++ array by subtracting one during each array reference.

Efficiency Analysis of `insert` for Linear Representation of Heap

Clearly the time efficiency of adding an item to the heap is directly proportional to the length of the path that the item must "walk up" as its appropriate position is determined. Because the linear representation of a heap leaves no unused gaps between values stored in the array, doubling the number of items in the heap will add only one level to the resulting binary tree. Thus, a heap with n nodes will have $\log_2 n$ levels using the linear representation. In other words, the length of the path that a new item will follow, and hence the efficiency of the **insert** operation, is $O(\log_2 n)$.

In the exercises at the end of this section, you will explore an algorithm to delete a node from a heap. That exploration will show how a heap could be used to implement the priority queue ADT defined in Chapter 15.

A NOTE OF INTEREST

Computer Security and Tree-Structured File Systems

One of the prime concerns in developing operating systems for multiuser computers is to ensure that a user cannot, in an unauthorized fashion, access system files or the files of other users. A convenient data structure to implement such a file directory system is a tree such as that pictured here:

every node in his or her subtree. That is, the user is viewed as the owner of every node in the subtree. To jump outside of this subtree of naturally owned files and directories requires that special permissions be given the user by other users or by the operating system itself. Hence the tree

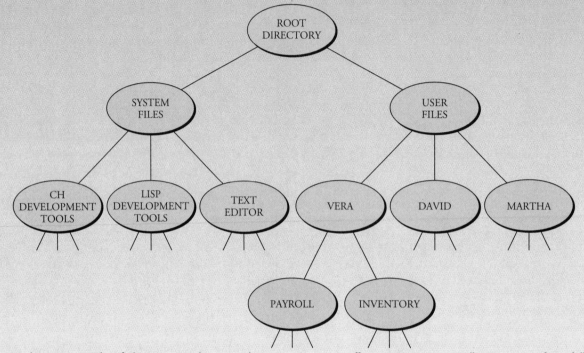

Each interior node of the tree can be viewed as a directory containing various system information about those files or subdirectories that are its descendants. Leaf nodes in the tree are the actual files. Hence, in the diagram, files can be broken down into system files and user files. System files consist of the C++ DEVELOPMENT TOOLS, the LISP DEVELOPMENT TOOLS, and the TEXT EDITOR. User directories are called VERA, DAVID, and MARTHA. One of the very convenient features of such a system is that it allows the user to extend this tree structure as deeply as desired. For instance, in the given tree directory structure, we see that user VERA has created subdirectories for files related to PAYROLL and INVENTORY. DAVID and MARTHA could have similarly partitioned subdirectories to organize their work.

In addition to offering users the convenience of being able to group their files into appropriate subdirectories, such a file system offers a very natural solution to the problem of file security. Since each individual user is, in effect, the root of a miniature subordinate file system within the overall system, a user is given, by default, free access to

structure offers convenience as well as a means of carefully monitoring the integrity of the file system.

AT&T's UNIX operating system, developed at Bell Laboratories in the early 1970s, was one of the first to use such a tree-structured directory system. The widespread popularity of UNIX today and the adoption of this scheme by a significant number of other operating systems is evidence of the attractive way in which it combines user convenience with system security. However, this is not to say that such systems are completely free of security problems. Once the security of such a system is slightly compromised, the tree structure lends itself to a cascade of far-reaching security breaks. Brian Reid's article "Reflections on Some Recent Widespread Computer Break-ins" in the February 1987 issue of *Communications of the ACM* (Volume 30, No. 2) provides an interesting account of how such security problems surfaced at Stanford University and spread to an entire network of computers. An entertaining narrative of another security incident is presented by Clifford Stoll in *The Cuckoo's Egg* (New York: Doubleday, 1989).

EXAMPLE 17.6

In this example, we illustrate how the postorder traversal algorithm may be implemented for a linear array implementation of a binary tree. The algorithm is slightly more difficult for this representation since the tree is the encapsulation of an array and a count of the number of nodes. Unlike the linked implementation, there is not an explicit root pointer for the tree; instead, the root of the entire tree is understood to be at index 0. The following function, **postorder_traverse**, compensates for this by acting as a mere "front-end" for a local auxiliary function, which is where the actual recursion takes place. Our front-end function **postorder_traverse** simply passes a root pointer value of 0 to the auxiliary function to start the recursion. We must also assume that a flagging null value of TRUE occupies array locations that are not currently storing data in the tree. This allows the auxiliary function to detect when the equivalent of a NULL pointer is passed. Finally, an offset of 1 is added to the values $2n$ and $2n + 1$ to obtain the locations of the left and right children, respectively, of a node in a C++ array where the first index position is zero.

```
template <class E>
void binary_tree<E>::postorder_traverse(void (*process) (E &item))
{
     if (number_nodes > 0)
          postorder_aux(1, process);
}


template <class E>
void binary_tree<E>::postorder_aux(int location,
     void (*process) (E &item))
{
     if (location < MAX_TREE_NODES)
          if (! tree[location].null)
          {
               postorder_aux(2 * location, process);
               postorder_aux(2 * location + 1, process);
               process(tree[location].data);
          }
}
```

Third, process
root node.

First, traverse
left subtree.

Second, traverse
right subtree.

EXERCISES 17.4

1. Suppose that items arrive for insertion into a heap in the following order:

10 20 30 40 50 60 70 80 90 100

Using the algorithm of Example 17.5, trace the contents of the tree array after each item is added to the heap.

2. Write implementations of the `create` and `empty` operations for a binary tree with the heap property using the linear array implementation. Be sure that your `create` operation is consistent with the postorder traversal algorithm of Example 17.6.

3. Write implementations of the preorder and inorder traversal operations for a linear array implementation of a binary tree.

4. Implement the following operation for a linear representation of a binary tree with the heap property.

```
void remove(E &item);
```

(*Hint:* When the root is removed, temporarily replace it with the tree node in the last active index of the array. Then develop an algorithm to walk this new root down a branch of the tree until the tree becomes a heap again.) In a written statement, indicate how the `insert` function of Example 17.5 and the `remove` function that you have written for this exercise could be used to implement a priority queue (Chapter 15) using a heap.

5. In a written statement discuss the relative advantages and disadvantages of the linear array implementation of a binary tree versus the linked implementation described in Section 17.2.

◆ 17.5 General Trees

OBJECTIVES

- to understand how a general tree may be implemented using a linked representation of a binary tree
- given the implementation of a general tree by a binary tree, to examine which traversal operations for the underlying binary tree make sense when it is interpreted as a general tree

We began this chapter with a discussion of the many ways in which hierarchical structures are used to organize information around us. We then quickly dictated that at most two children could be used, which focused all of our attention on the seemingly restricted case of the binary tree. What about all of those applications requiring a hierarchical relationship where a parent may have an unrestricted number of children? You may have become suspicious that we are avoiding such considerations because they are too difficult.

Fortunately, we have a much more educationally sound reason. That is, we may use a binary tree to implement a general tree. The nice implication of this rather surprising statement is that we will not have to spend a significant amount of time discussing general trees because we have unknowingly studied them in our thorough analysis of binary trees. Moreover, the formal operations on a general tree may be viewed as operations derived from those associated with a binary tree.

The real key to using a restricted type of tree such as a binary tree to implement a more general type of tree is to adjust our perspective. For example, consider the general genealogical tree of Figure 17.24. Here BILL is the first child of the JONES family, with KATY, MIKE, and TOM as BILL's siblings. Similarly, LARRY is the first child of MARY, with PAUL and PENNY as siblings. Now, in a linked representation of binary tree, we have two pointer fields associated with each node. We have called these pointer fields left and right because it suited our perspective at the time. However, we shall now switch that perspective in the following way. One of the pointer fields is to be viewed as a pointer to the leftmost child of a node in a general tree. The second pointer identifies the next sibling to the right of the node under consideration in the general tree. Since the children of a node taken in this context form an ordered set of nodes, we can regard the leftmost child of a node as first and the sibling to the right of this node as sibling. We will henceforth adopt this terminology for the two link fields involved with the

◆ FIGURE 17.24
Genealogical tree

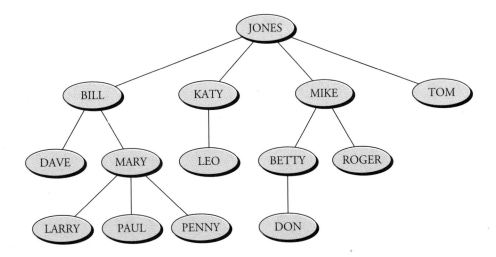

binary tree representation of a general tree. Figure 17.25 gives the binary representation of the general genealogical tree shown in Figure 17.24.

◆ FIGURE 17.25
Binary tree representation
of genealogical tree in
Figure 17.24

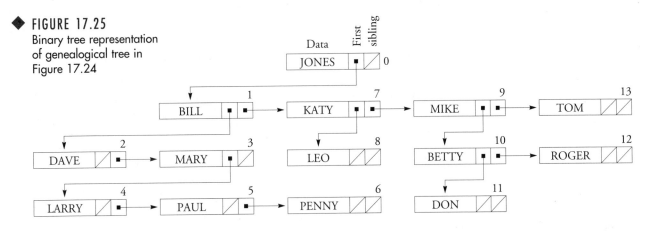

Note that we number the pointers in the tree of Figure 17.24. This numbering is reflected in Table 17.4. You should carefully check all first and sibling

◇ TABLE 17.4
Tree in Figure 17.24 stored
in array of records for data
and pointers

Location	Data	FirstChild	Sibling
0	JONES	1	0
1	BILL	2	7
2	DAVE	0	3
3	MARY	4	0
4	LARRY	0	5
5	PAUL	0	6
6	PENNY	0	0
7	KATY	9	9
8	LEO	0	0
9	MIKE	10	13
10	BETTY	11	12
11	DON	0	0
12	ROGER	0	0
13	TOM	0	0

values to convince yourself that the scheme used to fill this array was to store a node before any of its children, and then recursively store the leftmost child.

The representation in terms of C++ pointer variables (and the representation we shall henceforth use) requires the following type declarations:

```
protected:

// Protected data members

struct node;
typedef node *node_ptr;
struct node
{
        E data;
        node_ptr first;
        node_ptr sibling;
};

node_ptr tree;
```

Traversals of a General Tree Implemented Via a Binary Tree

Since this implementation scheme for a general tree is nothing more than a special interpretation of a binary tree, all of the traversals defined for a binary tree clearly exist for the general tree. A more relevant question than the mere existence of a traversal, however, is the significance of the order in which the nodes of a general tree are visited when its corresponding binary tree is traversed. Of particular interest in this regard are the preorder and postorder traversals.

You should verify that the preorder traversal algorithm for a binary tree applied to Figure 17.24 visits nodes in the following order:

```
JONES
    BILL
        DAVE
        MARY
            LARRY
            PAUL
            PENNY
    KATY
        LEO
    MIKE
        BETTY
            DON
        ROGER
TOM
```

The indentation here has been added to highlight the fact that the preorder traversal will recursively process a parent node, and then process the child nodes from left to right.

Relative to the general tree pictured in Figure 17.24, we see that the effect of the preorder traversal is to fix on a node at one level of the tree and then run through all of that node's children before progressing to the next node at the same level (the sibling). There is a hint here of a generalized nested loop situation which, as you will see, has some interesting applications in the programming problems at the end of this chapter.

The other traversal of interest in a binary tree representation of a general tree is the postorder traversal. In this regard, it should first be verified that the postorder traversal applied to Figure 17.24 (and its binary tree implementation in Figure 17.25) yields the following listing:

PENNY
PAUL
LARRY
MARY
DAVE
LEO
DON
ROGER
BETTY
TOM
MIKE
KATY
BILL
JONES

In general, the postorder traversal works its way up from the leaf nodes of a tree, ensuring that no given node is processed until all nodes in the subtree below it have been processed.

EXERCISES 17.5

1. How would you implement a preorder traversal to print nodes in a fashion that has children indented under their parents?

2. Consider the following abstract graphical representation of a general tree:

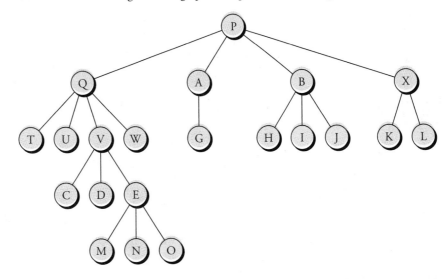

Provide a specific C++ record description for a node in this tree as you would represent it. (Do not make any assumption about maximum possible number of children.) Then draw a specific picture of how this tree would actually be stored using the record description you have chosen.

3. Given the tree from Exercise 2, in what order would nodes be visited by a preorder traversal? A postorder traversal?

4. For this exercise you are to assume a linked binary tree representation of a general tree. Write a function that meets the following specification:

```
// Function: add_child
// Insert a tree as the kth subtree of another tree.
// If the root node of the tree already has k or more subtrees, the new
// tree becomes the kth subtree and the former Kth subtree becomes
// the (K+1)st subtree.
// If the root node of the tree has fewer than K subtrees,
// then the new tree is inserted as the last subtree of the root node.

template <class E>
void general_tree<E>::add_child(node_ptr &gt, node_ptr st, int k)
```

5. Use the function you developed for Exercise 4 in another function to generate the following tree. Verify that you have generated the correct tree with a traversal function that outputs the tree in appropriate fashion.

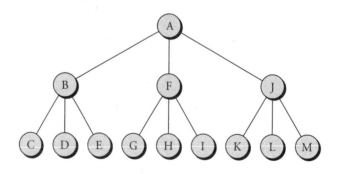

6. Is a binary tree a special case of a general tree? Provide a written rationale to justify your answer.

17.6 Graphs and Networks: Bidirectional Trees

The key defining characteristic of a tree is the hierarchical relationship between parent and child nodes. In a tree, this hierarchical relationship is a one-way relationship. That is, within the tree there is pointer information that allows us to descend from parent to child. However, there is generally no pointer information within the tree that allows us to ascend from a child node to its parent. In many information storage applications such a one-way relationship is not sufficient. Consider, for instance, the relationship between students and courses at a university. Each student is enrolled in several courses and could thus be viewed as a parent node with children consisting of the courses he or she is taking. Conversely, each course enrolls many students and could thus be viewed as a parent

- to understand the definition and operations for the graph ADT
- to understand the definition and operations for the network ADT
- to understand how a two-dimensional table may be used to implement the graph and network ADTs
- to realize why the two-dimensional table representation of a graph or network often results in a sparse matrix
- to understand traversal algorithms for graphs and networks
- to understand Dijkstra's algorithm for finding the shortest path between two nodes in a network

node with children consisting of the students enrolled in that particular course. The data structure that emerges from this type of bidirectional relationship is pictured in Figure 17.26.

In terms of an abstract data-type, the representation of such a bidirectional relationship between nodes is called a *graph*.

Graph: A graph consists of two sets. One set is a fixed set of objects called *nodes*. The other is a set of *edges,* the contents of which vary depending on the operations that have been performed on the graph. A node is a data element of the graph, and an edge is a direct connection between two nodes. A node may also be called a *vertex* of the graph. If an edge exists between two nodes, we say that the second node is adjacent to the first node.

The operations associated with the graph ADT are specified in terms of the following preconditions and postconditions:

Create operation

Preconditions: Receiver is graph in an unpredictable state.

Postconditions: Graph is initialized to a state with no edges. That is, no nodes are connected to any other nodes, including themselves.

add_edge operation

Preconditions: Receiver is an arbitrary graph that has been initialized by **create** and, potentially, affected by other operations. **node1** and **node2** are two nodes in the graph.

Postconditions: Receiver is returned with an edge from **node1** to **node2**. If an edge already existed from **node1** to **node2**, the graph is not affected.

remove_edge operation

Preconditions: Receiver is an arbitrary graph that has been initialized by **create** and, potentially, affected by other operations. **node1** and **node2** are two nodes in the graph.

Postconditions: If there is an edge from **node1** to **node2**, it is removed. Otherwise the graph is not affected.

Edge operation

Preconditions: Receiver is an arbitrary graph that has been initialized by **create** and, potentially, affected by other operations. **node1** and **node2** are two nodes in the graph.

Postconditions: **edge** returns TRUE if there is an edge from **node1** to **node2**, FALSE otherwise.

Traverse operation

Preconditions: Receiver is an arbitrary graph that has been initialized by **create** and, potentially, affected by other operations. **start** is a node at which the traversal is to start. **process** is an algorithmic process that can be applied to each graph node.

Postconditions: Receiver is returned with each node that can be reached from **start** affected by **process**. A given node can be reached from **start** if the given node is the start node or if there is a sequence of edges E_0, E_1, ..., E_n such that E_0 begins at the **start** node, the node at which E_i-1 ends is the node at which E_i begins, and n is the given node. In effect, the sequence of edges determines a path from **start** to the given node. The path is composed of edges between adjacent nodes. **process** is not applied to any node more than once.

◆ FIGURE 17.26

Bidirectional relationship between students and courses

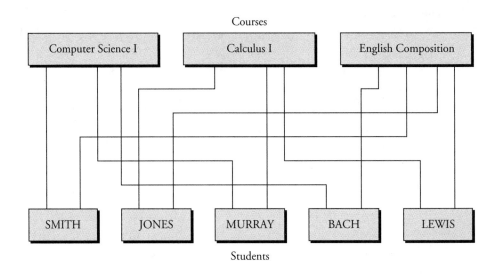

Notice that, as it relates to Figure 17.26, the formal definition of a graph does not rule out the possibility of an edge connecting two courses or connecting two students. It is merely the nature of this course–student relationship that makes the existence of such a course-to-course edge or student-to-student edge impractical. In other applications, such as the transportation network pictured in Figure 17.27, it may be entirely feasible for any node in the graph to have an edge connecting it to any other node.

To illustrate how a graph grows from an initial state with no edges, suppose that we start with a set of nodes labeled A, B, C, D. Figure 17.28 traces the effect

◆ FIGURE 17.27

Transportation network as graph in which edges represent flights between cities

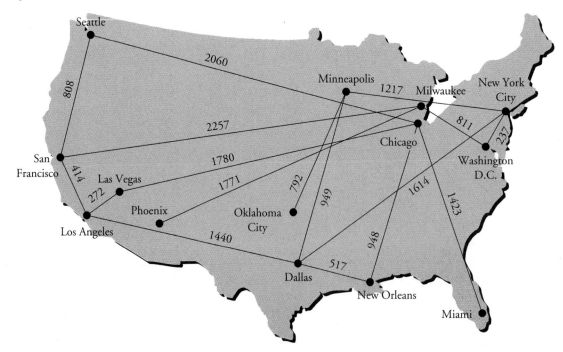

◆ FIGURE 17.28
Graph affected by sequence
of **add_edge** and
remove_edge operations

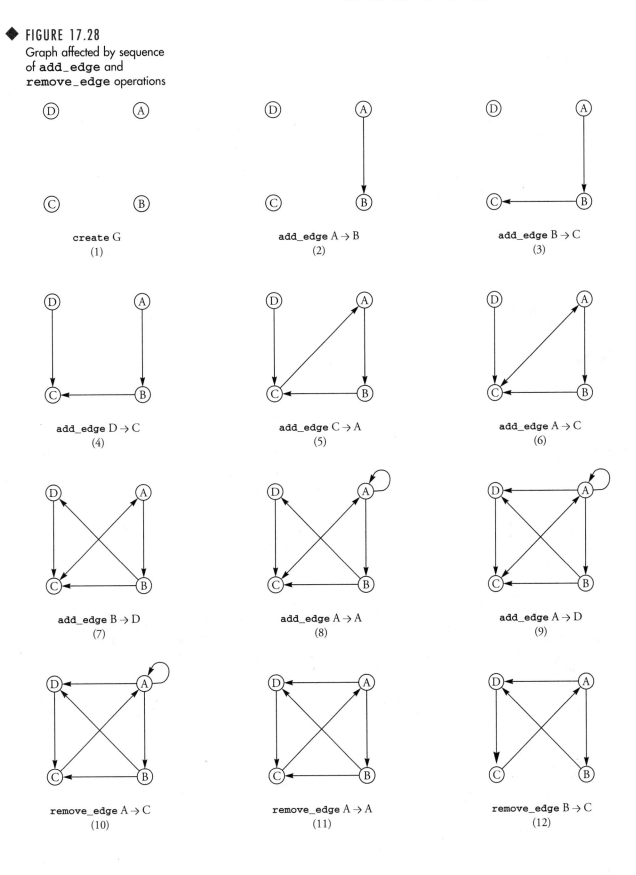

create G
(1)

add_edge $A \rightarrow B$
(2)

add_edge $B \rightarrow C$
(3)

add_edge $D \rightarrow C$
(4)

add_edge $C \rightarrow A$
(5)

add_edge $A \rightarrow C$
(6)

add_edge $B \rightarrow D$
(7)

add_edge $A \rightarrow A$
(8)

add_edge $A \rightarrow D$
(9)

remove_edge $A \rightarrow C$
(10)

remove_edge $A \rightarrow A$
(11)

remove_edge $B \rightarrow C$
(12)

of a sequence of `add_edge` and `remove_edge` operations on a graph with these nodes. Note from this figure that the concept of an edge carries with it the notion of a direction. That is, it is possible to have an edge from `node1` to `node2` in a graph G without there being a corresponding connection in the opposite direction. Figure 17.28, picture (8), also illustrates that it is possible to have an edge from a node to itself.

By convention, when we draw a graph without arrows on the edges, it is implicit that all edges run in both directions. Thus, in Figure 17.27, the line connecting San Francisco and Los Angeles implicitly represents two edges—the one from San Francisco to Los Angeles and the one from Los Angeles to San Francisco.

We will sometimes use the terminology *directional graph*, or *digraph*, to emphasize that a particular graph has some edges that exist only in one direction. Figure 17.29 illustrates a digraph. In a digraph, we use arrows on edges to specify the direction of an edge between nodes.

A NOTE OF INTEREST

Hypertext

Hypertext is a new technology that allows users to browse through any kind of information that can be stored electronically (text, images, sound, and video). Users experience hypertext associatively, as a set of one-key tables. Each entry in a table is a chunk of information presented to the user by some output device. Where the output device is a visual display, the keys for locating other entries in the tables are embedded as hotspots in the currently visible chunk of information. The user retrieves a desired entry by targeting a hotspot with a mouse or cursor device. This entry in turn may have other embedded keys. Each entry also has a hotspot for returning to the entry from which its key was triggered. More structured queries for entries can be executed by entering key terms into a search engine, which returns a list of all the entries that satisfy a query. Hypertext also has the feel of a graph, in that users can freely move back and forth in a nonlinear fashion among the entries or nodes.

As an example, one might begin with a query for Beethoven's Ninth Symphony. From the answer list one might then select a biography of the composer (text and images). After reading a couple of pages, one might next point at a hotspot referencing the last movement of the Ninth Symphony to listen to a few bars (sound). Returning to the biography, one might finally hit another hotspot to play a bit of *Immortal Beloved*, a film about Beethoven's life (video).

According to John B. Smith and Stephen F. Weiss (in "Hypertext," *Communications of the ACM* Volume 31, No. 7 (July 1988)), this unrestricted associativity among hypertext nodes parallels the flexibility of human memory. Smith and Weiss cite the following quotation from Vannevar Bush, a well-known electrical engineer who speculated as early as the 1940s about the way in which humans think:

The human mind . . . operates by association. With one item in its grasp, it snaps instantly to the next that is suggested by the association of thoughts, in accordance with some intricate web of trails carried by the cells of the brain.

Selection by association, rather than indexing may yet be mechanized. One cannot hope . . . to equal the speed and flexibility with which the mind follows an associative trail, but it should be possible to beat the mind decisively in regard to the permanence and clarity of the items resurrected from storage.

Early hypertext systems were implemented as a set of files residing on a single disk in the user's personal computer. With the growth of the INTERNET and networking technology, most hypertext systems are now distributed among many different physical sites. The World Wide Web, the most well known of these systems, supports public browsing by INTERNET users from thousands of sites around the world. The nodes of information in the Beethoven example mentioned earlier might each be located at different sites in different parts of the world, though from the user's perspective the information seems connected in a seamless way.

If the notion of electronic hypertext intrigues you, begin by consulting the *Communications of the ACM* issue cited above. More recently, *Communications of the ACM* Volume 33, No. 3 (March 1990), *Communications of the ACM* Volume 35, No. 1 (January 1992), and *Communications of the ACM* Volume 38, No. 8 (August 1995) have all been dedicated to this revolutionary and rapidly growing field.

◆ FIGURE 17.29
A four-node digraph

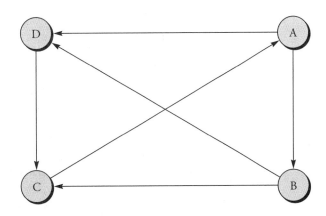

Before providing a C++ interface for the graph ADT, we should clarify a point of ambiguity in the definition of the traversal operation. In particular, this operation does not establish a unique order of visiting nodes that can be reached from the start node. The following examples illustrate two potential orders in which nodes can be visited starting at A in the graph of Figure 17.29.

EXAMPLE 17.7

Consider a traversal from start node A in the digraph of Figure 17.29 guided by the following strategy: a given path starting at A should be explored as deeply as possible before another path is probed. If we assume that B is the first node adjacent to A, then the traversal will proceed from A to B. If we then assume that C is the first node adjacent to B, the traversal will continue from B to C. From C, it is not possible to visit any nodes that have not already been visited. Hence, we will backtrack to B and, from there, continue the traversal to D since D is adjacent to B. Hence the overall order in which nodes would be visited by a traversal under the strategy and assumptions of this example is

    A, B, C, D

The strategy exemplified here is often called a *depth-first traversal* since a given path is probed as deeply as possible before we backtrack and explore another path.

EXAMPLE 17.8

Indicate the order in which nodes would be visited in a traversal starting at node A in the digraph of Figure 17.29 following a strategy that does not probe one path as deeply as possible but rather "fans out" to all nodes adjacent to a given node. Hence we would proceed from A to B and then to D, since both B and D are adjacent to A. Since all nodes adjacent to A have been exhausted, we would fan out from B, the first node we visited from A. This takes us to C by the edge B → A C, completing the traversal in the overall order

    A, B, D, C

The fan-out strategy exemplified here is often termed a *breadth-first traversal*.

Examples 17.7 and 17.8 just begin to scratch the surface of the variety of graph traversal strategies that exist. We shall soon examine the implementation of these traversal strategies more closely. At this time the point to emphasize is that the graph traversal operation is open to a variety of implementation techniques.

C++ Interface for the Graph ADT

Before we can develop graph algorithms in detail, we must provide a C++ interface for this ADT. This is done in the following class declaration module. The interface makes the assumption that the data in graph nodes are drawn from a range of values that can serve both as keys for tables and as values over which a **for** loop can iterate, such as **int, char,** or an enumerated type. Our reasons for making this assumption will become apparent when we discuss ways of implementing graphs.

```cpp
// Class declaration file: graph.h

#ifndef GRAPH_H

#include "boolean.h"

// Definition section

// We assume that type boolean is already defined

template <class Node> class graph
{

      public:

      // Class constructors

      graph();
      graph(const graph<Node> &g);

      // Member functions

      boolean add_edge(const Node &node1, const Node &node2);
      void remove_edge(const Node &node1, const Node &node2);
      boolean edge(const Node &node1, const Node& node2);
      void traverse(Node &start, void (*process) (Node &item));
      graph <Node>& operator = (const graph<Node> &g);

      // Protected data and member functions pertaining to
      // the implementation would go here.

};


#define GRAPH_H
#endif
```

The Network ADT

Graphs such as that shown in Figure 17.27 are somewhat special in that the edges have weights associated with them, here representing distances between nodes (cities). Such a graph is an example of the *network* abstract data type.

> **Network:** A network is a graph in which each edge has a positive numerical *weight*. The operations associated with the network ADT are the same as those for the graph ADT with the exceptions that the **add_edge** operation must now specify the weight of the edge being added and we must add an operation which, given two nodes, returns the weight of the edge that may exist between them.

These two new operations are specified by the following preconditions and postconditions.

---

add_edge operation

Preconditions: Receiver is an arbitrary network that has been initialized by create and, potentially, affected by other operations. **node1** and **node2** are two nodes in network. **weight** is a positive number representing the weight of an edge to be added from **node1** to **node2**.

Postconditions: Receiver has an edge of weight **weight** from **node1** to **node2**. If an edge already existed from **node1** to **node2**, the weight of that edge is now **weight**.

edge_weight operation

Preconditions: Receiver is an arbitrary network that has been initialized by **create** and, potentially, affected by other operations. **node1** and **node2** are two nodes in the network.

Postconditions: **edge_weight** returns zero if there is no edge from **node1** to **node2** and the numerical value of the edge if it exists.

Graphs and networks provide excellent examples of how a theoretical area of mathematics has found very relevant application in computer science. It is beyond the scope of this text to provide a comprehensive treatment of graphs and networks. Rather, our purpose in the rest of this section is to provide you with an overview of a data structure that you will no doubt encounter again as you continue your study of computer science. More in-depth treatments of graphs and networks can be found in numerous advanced texts on data structures such as *Data Structures in C++* by Ellis Horowitz and Sartaj Sahni (New York: Computer Science Press, 1990) and *Introduction to Data Structures and Algorithm Analysis with C++* by George J. Pothering and Thomas L. Naps (St. Paul, Minn.: West Publishing, 1995).

Implementation of Graphs and Networks

A graph may be conveniently implemented using a two-dimensional table of Boolean values. For instance, the information in Figure 17.26 is contained in Table 17.5, a two-dimensional table. In this table, the value TRUE indicates the presence of an edge between two nodes and the value FALSE indicates the absence of such an edge. In the case of a network, the two-dimensional table implementation still applies. Now, however, the data stored in the table is of a type compatible with edge weights. Such a two-dimensional table implementation of the transportation

◇ **TABLE 17.5**

Two-dimensional table implementation of graph from Figure 17.26

Course	SMITH	JONES	MURRAY	BACH	LEWIS
Computer Science	TRUE	FALSE	TRUE	TRUE	FALSE
Calculus I	FALSE	TRUE	TRUE	FALSE	TRUE
English Comp.	TRUE	TRUE	FALSE	TRUE	TRUE

network from Figure 17.27 is given in Table 17.6. Note that the data are mirrored across the diagonal of the table because all edges are bidirectional.

Table 17.6 illustrates a quality typically found in two-dimensional table implementations of large graphs and networks: the sparseness of nontrivial data. Hence, the methods we have discussed for implementing sparse tables actually provide alternative implementation strategies for graphs and networks. In fact, the pilot/flight database problem of Wing-and-a-Prayer Airlines, with which we introduced the two-key table ADT in Chapter 12, may now be viewed as a graph problem. This problem presented us with a bidirectional tree in which each pilot could have multiple flights as child nodes and, conversely, each flight could have multiple pilots as child nodes.

In the discussion of the two graph/network algorithms that follow, we do not tie ourselves to a particular implementation strategy for representing the underlying data structure. Rather, we discuss the algorithms in terms of the operations associated with the abstract data type involved and leave implementation considerations for the exercises at the end of this section and the programming problems at the end of the chapter.

◇ **TABLE 17.6**

Two-dimensional table implementation of network from Figure 17.27

	NY	Wash	Miam	Milw	Chi	NOrl	Mpls	OklC	Dals	LVeg	Phex	Stl	SFra	LA
NY		237		811			1217		1614					
Wash														
Miam				1423										
Milw	811										1771		2257	
Chi		1423				948				1780		2060		
NOrl					948				517					
Mpls	1217							792	949					
OklC						792								
Dals	1614				517	949								1440
LVeg					1780									272
Phex			1771											
Stl					2060									808
SFra			2257									808		414
LA										272			414	

Examples of Graph Algorithms: Depth-First and Breadth-First Traversals

In many practical applications of graphs, there is frequently a need to visit systematically all the nodes on a graph from a designated starting node. One such application occurs in a political campaign when the organizers of the campaign are interested in having their candidate visit all important political centers. The presence or absence of direct transportation routes (that is, edges) between such centers will determine the possible ways in which all the centers could be visited. At the moment, our only concern is the development of an algorithm that ensures that all possible nodes are visited. Such an algorithm will provide an implementation for the graph traversal operation. Later in the chapter we investigate how to determine the shortest possible distances from one node to all others.

Depth-First Traversal. This technique was illustrated in Example 17.7. The main logic of the depth-first algorithm is analogous to the preorder traversal of a tree. It is accomplished recursively as follows:

1. Designate the starting node as the search node and mark it as visited.
2. Find a node adjacent to the search node (that is, connected by an edge from the search node) that has not yet been visited. Designate this as the new search node (but remember the previous one) and mark it as visited.
3. Repeat step 2 using the new search node. If no nodes satisfying step 2 can be found, return to the previous search node and continue from there.
4. When a return to the previous search node in step 3 is impossible, the search from the originally chosen search node is complete.

This algorithm is called a depth-first traversal because the search continues progressively deeper into the graph in a recursive manner.

To illustrate this function more clearly, consider Figure 17.30; its table implementation is shown in Table 17.7. Suppose we have a function called `search_from`, which is invoked to begin a depth-first traversal from a given node on the graph. The steps followed by the algorithm are as follows:

1. We begin by marking node 1 visited and invoke `search_from(1)`.
2. Both nodes 2 and 3 are adjacent to node 1 according to the matrix implementation of the graph, but node 2 is encountered first on a left-to-right scan of the row for 1; so the search goes to node 2. We invoke `search_from(2)`, and node 2 is marked as visited.

◆ **FIGURE 17.30**
Graph to illustrate depth-first search

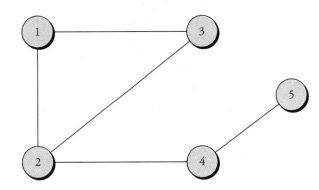

◇ **TABLE 17.7**
Table implementation of Figure 17.30

	1	2	3	4	5
1	FALSE	TRUE	TRUE	FALSE	FALSE
2	TRUE	FALSE	TRUE	TRUE	FALSE
3	TRUE	TRUE	FALSE	FALSE	FALSE
4	FALSE	TRUE	FALSE	FALSE	TRUE
5	FALSE	FALSE	FALSE	TRUE	FALSE

3. Since node 3 is the first unvisited node adjacent to node 2, the search now goes to node 3, `search_from(3)` is invoked, and node 3 is marked as visited.

4. Since there is no unvisited node adjacent to node 3, we say that this node has exhausted the search; the search goes back to its predecessor, that is, to node 2.

5. From node 2, we visit node 4.

6. From node 4, we proceed to node 5. All nodes have now been visited, and the depth-first traversal is complete.

Use Table 17.7 to verify these steps.

We note that the order in which nodes are visited in a depth-first traversal is not unique. This is because the order is dependent on the manner in which "adjacent" nodes are chosen. That is, given two unvisited nodes adjacent to another node, which one should be chosen to invoke the `search_from` function? In practice, this will usually be determined by the ordering of the data type used to implement the nodes in the graph.

EXAMPLE 17.9

Implement the depth-first traversal algorithm under the assumption that the node data type is a key value type.

As with our implementation of the postorder traversal operation for a binary tree in Example 17.6, we use an auxiliary function as the real recursive workhorse. The traverse function is itself merely a front-end, which appropriately sets the stage for the auxiliary function `search_from`.

We can now see the reason for the restriction placed on the node type in our C++ interface for the graph ADT. It must be a type capable of keying a table and controlling an iterative loop structure. Both of these properties are assumed in the code of Example 17.9.

Breadth-First Traversal. An alternate graph traversal to the depth-first strategy is the breadth-first traversal. Instead of proceeding as deeply as possible along one path from the current node in the graph, the breadth-first traversal examines all nodes adjacent to the current node before proceeding more deeply along any given path. Hence, for the graph of Figure 17.31, implemented by Table 17.8, a breadth-first traversal starting at node 1 would visit nodes in the order 1, 2, 3, 4, 5 (as opposed to the order 1, 2, 4, 5, 3 dictated by a depth-first traversal).

A breadth-first traversal of a graph involves the following steps:

1. Begin with the start node, and mark it as visited.

2. Proceed to the next node having an edge connection to the node in step 1. Mark it as visited.

◆ FIGURE 17.31
Graph to illustrate breadth-first traversal

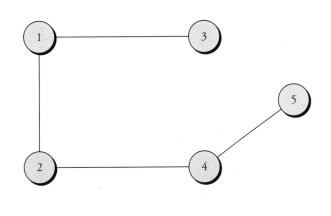

◇ TABLE 17.8
Table implementation of Figure 17.31

	1	2	3	4	5
1	FALSE	TRUE	TRUE	FALSE	FALSE
2	TRUE	FALSE	FALSE	TRUE	FALSE
3	TRUE	FALSE	FALSE	FALSE	FALSE
4	FALSE	TRUE	FALSE	FALSE	TRUE
5	FALSE	FALSE	FALSE	TRUE	FALSE

3. Come back to the node in step 1, descend along an edge toward an unvisited node, and mark the new node as visited.

4. Repeat step 3 until all nodes adjacent to the node in step 1 have been marked as visited.

5. Repeat steps 1 through 4 starting from the node visited in 2, then starting from the nodes visited in step 3 in the order visited. Keep this up as long as possible before starting a new scan.

You will be asked to explore this strategy in the programming problems at the end of the chapter.

Example of a Network Algorithm: Finding Shortest Paths

If the graph under consideration is a network in which edge weights represent distances, then an appropriate question is: From a given node called the **source**, what is the shortest distance to all other nodes in the network?

For instance, the network of Figure 17.32 could be thought of as showing airline routes between cities. An airline would be interested in finding the most economical route between any two given cities in the network. The numbers listed on the edges would, in this case, represent distances between cities. Thus, the airline wishes to find the shortest path that can be flown from node 3 in order to reach nodes 1, 2, 4, and 5.

Suppose we want to find the shortest path from node 1 to node 3. From Figure 17.32, we note that this path would be $1 \rightarrow 2 \rightarrow 3$, yielding a total weight of 800 + 410 = 1210. An algorithm to find such a path was discovered by E. W. Dijkstra. For convenience in discussing Dijkstra's algorithm, often called the shortest path algorithm, let us assume that the nodes in the network under consideration are numbered 1, 2, . . ., **number_of_nodes**. That is, the node type is the subrange of the integers given by 1 . . . **number_of_nodes**.

◆ **FIGURE 17.32**

Network with edge weights representing distances

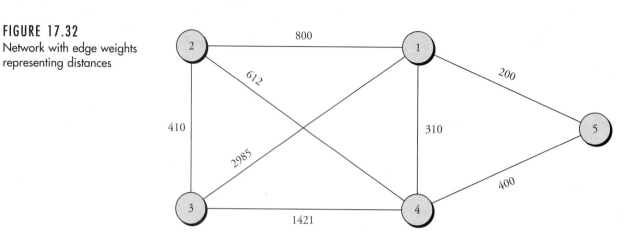

Given such a collection of nodes, Dijkstra's algorithm requires three arrays in addition to a suitable implementation of the network M. These three arrays are identified as follows:

```
int distance[MAX_DISTANCE_SIZE];
int path[MAX_PATH_SIZE];
boolean included[MAX_INCLUDED_SIZE];
```

Identifying one node as the source, the algorithm proceeds to find the shortest distance from source to all other nodes in the network. At the conclusion of the algorithm, the shortest distance from **source** to node **j** is stored in **distance[j]**, whereas **path[j]** contains the immediate predecessor of node **j** on the path determining this shortest distance. While the algorithm is in progress, **distance[j]** and **path[j]** are being continually updated until **included[j]** is switched from FALSE to TRUE. Once this switch occurs, it is known definitely that **distance[j]** contains the shortest distance from **source** to **j**. The algorithm progresses until all nodes have been so included. Hence it actually gives us the shortest distance from **source** to every other node in the network.

Given the source node in the network M, the algorithm may be divided into two phases: an initialization phase followed by an iteration phase, in which nodes are included one by one in the set of nodes for which the shortest distance from **source** is known definitely.

During the initialization phase, we must

1. Initialize included[source] to TRUE and included [j] to FALSE for all other j.
2. Initialize the distance array via the rule
   if j = source
       distance[j] = 0
   else if edge_weight(m, source, j) <>0
       distance[j] = edge_weight(m, source, j)
   else if j is not connected to source by a direct edge
   (that is, if edge_weight(m, source, j) = 0)
       distance[j] = Infinity
3. Initialize the path array via the rule
   if edge_weight (M, source, J) <> 0
       path[j] = source
   else
       path[j] = Undefined

Given this initialization, the iteration phase may be expressed in a generalized pseudocode form as follows:

Do

Find the node J that has the minimal distance among those nodes not yet included
Mark J as now included
For each R not yet included
    If there is an edge from J to R
        If distance[j] + edge_weight (M, J, R) < distance[R]
        distance[R] = distance[J] + edge_weight (M, J, R)
            path[R] = J
While all nodes are not included

The crucial part of the algorithm occurs within the innermost **if** of the **for** loop. Figure 17.33 provides a pictorial representation of the logic involved here. The nodes included with the circle represent those nodes already included prior to a given iteration of the **do** loop. Node J in Figure 17.33 represents the node found in the first step of the **do** loop; R represents another arbitrary node, which has not yet been included. The lines emanating from source represent the paths corresponding to the current entries in the distance array. For nodes within the circle—that is, those already included—these paths are guaranteed to be the shortest distance paths. If J is the node having the minimal entry in distance among those not yet **included**, we will add J to the circle of included nodes and then check to see if J's connections to other nodes in the network which are not yet **included** may result in a newly found shorter path to such nodes.

Referring to Figure 17.33 again, the sum of two sides of a triangle

```
distance [j] + edge_weight(m, j, r)
```

may in fact be shorter than the third side,

```
distance[r]
```

This geometric contradiction is possible because these are not true straight-sided triangles, but "triangles" whose sides may be very complicated paths through a network.

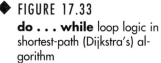

◆ FIGURE 17.33

do . . . while loop logic in shortest-path (Dijkstra's) algorithm

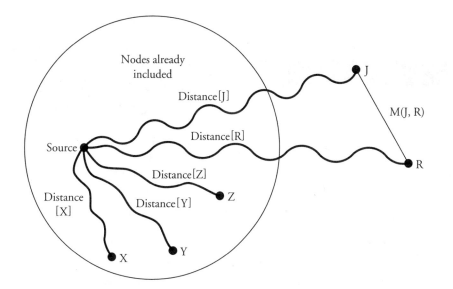

◆ FIGURE 17.34

Guaranteeing the minimality of distance to J once it is included

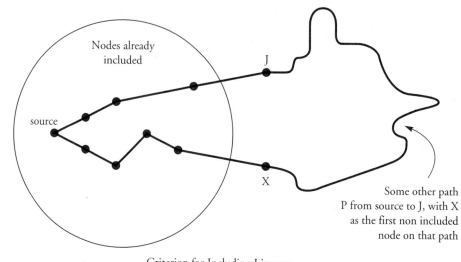

Criterion for Including J insures
Distance [J] ≤ Distance [X] ≤ Length of path P

It is also apparent from Figure 17.33 why Dijkstra's algorithm works. As the node J in this figure is found to have the minimal distance entry from among all those nodes not yet included, we may now include it among the nodes whose minimal distance from the source node is absolutely known. Why? Consider any other path P to J containing nodes that are not yet included at the time J is included. Let X be the first such nonincluded node on path P. Then clearly, as the first nonincluded node on the path P, X must be adjacent to an included node. However, as Figure 17.34 indicates, the criterion that dictated the choice of J as an included node ensures that

```
distance[J]   ≤ The total edge weight through node X on the path P
              ≤ Total edge weight of path P
```

This inequality demonstrates that, once J is included, there exists no other path P to J through a nonincluded node that can yield a shorter overall distance. Hence we have verified our claim that including a node guarantees our having found a path of shortest possible distance to that node.

EXAMPLE 17.10

To be sure you understand Dijkstra's algorithm before you attempt to implement it, trace it through on the network of Figure 17.32 with **source = 1**.
Initially, we would have

distance[2] = 800	path[2] = 1
distance[3] = 2985	path[3] = 1
distance[4] = 310	path[4] = 1
distance[5] = 200	path[5] = 1

in accordance with steps 2 and 3 of the initialization phase. According to the iteration phase of the algorithm, we would then, in order, perform these steps:

A NOTE OF INTEREST

Computer Networks—Their Use and Potential Abuse

It's a rare student who doesn't take advantage of electronic mail to stay in touch with friends at distant campuses. It could easily be argued that, more than any other single factor, interaction among distant users on the Internet has been responsible for making nearly everyone aware of the potential of computing. But the Internet is merely one part of the "Information Superhighway." According to Haruhisa Ishida and Lawrence H. Landweber in "Internetworking," *Communications of the ACM*, Volume 36, Number 3 (August 1993)

The National Information Infrastructure (NII) and the Electronic Superhighway are two of the titles used by the Clinton/Gore administration to describe plans for an enhanced communications environment. Video conferencing and telephony, entertainment, access to libraries and information repositions, and support for medical consultations are just some of the services to be available to homes, offices, and schools. All of this has been made possible by rapid advances in communications and networking technology over the last decade.

The potential for uses of information networks is unlimited. For example, Janet Murray provides details of how the K12 Network is finding growing use in elementary and secondary education in "K12 Network: Global Education Through Telecommunications," *Communications of the ACM*, Volume 36, Number 3 (August 1993). Some of the opportunities within the K12 Network include language exchanges with native speakers in French, German, Japanese, Spanish, and Russian; cooperative physics experiments, such as attempts of students in Oregon, California, Nova Scotia, and Maryland to replicate Eratosthenes' experiment in Alexandria to determine the size of the earth by measuring the length of a shadow cast by a stick; and the "MathMagic" problem challenge in which students post a variety of solutions to nontrivial problems.

For all of the wonders of networks, there is also a down side. As we begin to rely increasingly on networks, a variety of privacy-related problems arise. An excellent overview of these problems is presented in a series of four articles in the issue of *Communications of the ACM* cited earlier in this note.

1. Include node 5; no change in `distance` and `path` needed.

```
distance[2] = 800    path[2] = 1
distance[3] = 2985   path[3] = 1
distance[4] = 310    path[4] = 1
distance[5] = 200    path[5] = 1
```

2. Include node 4; update `distance` and `path` to

```
distance[2] = 800    path[2] = 1
distance[3] = 1731   path[3] = 4
distance[4] = 310    path[4] = 1
distance[5] = 200    path[5] = 1
```

(Note that it is shorter to go from node 1 to node 4 to node 3 than to follow the edge directly connecting node 1 to node 3.)

3. Include node 2; update `distance` and `path` to

```
distance[2] = 800    path[2] = 1
distance[3] = 1210   path[3] = 2
distance[4] = 310    path[4] = 1
distance[5] = 200    path[5] = 1
```

(Now we find that traveling from node 1 to node 2 to node 3 is even better than the path determined in step 2.)

4. Finally node 3 is included with (obviously) no changes made in `distance` or `path`.

EXERCISES 17.6

1. Indicate the order in which nodes would be visited if a depth-first traversal of the network in Figure 17.27 were initiated from SEATTLE. Use the adjacency relationships from Table 17.6.

2. Repeat Exercise 1 but initiate the traversal from MIAMI.

3. Repeat Exercise 1 for a breadth-first traversal.

4. Repeat Exercise 2 for a breadth-first traversal.

5. Trace the contents of the **distance, path,** and **included** arrays as Dijkstra's shortest path algorithm is applied to the transportation network of Figure 17.27. Use PHOENIX as the **source** node.

6. Repeat Exercise 5 with MILWAUKEE as the **source** node.

7. Using a two-dimensional table, write functions to implement each of the basic operations for the graph abstract data type. Then provide a big-O time efficiency analysis of each of the operations. How is this analysis affected by a particular sparse matrix technique that may be underlying the two-dimensional table? Be as specific as possible in stating your answer.

8. Using a two-dimensional table, write functions to implement each of the basic operations for the network abstract data type.

9. In a written statement, discuss the implications of eliminating the requirement that type **node** be a subrange of an ordinal type in the C++ interface for the graph ADT. Your statement should identify problems that this would cause and outline strategies for solving such problems.

FOCUS ON PROGRAM DESIGN

Throughout this text we have emphasized the importance of big-O algorithm analysis as a means of predicting beforehand the practicality of an algorithm in a given application. In this regard, big-O notation and analysis serve a vital purpose—the estimation of the time and space requirements of an algorithm in order of magnitude terms. However, when designing software systems in the very competitive and demanding real world, we often require a more detailed measurement of an algorithm's performance than that which can be achieved simply with a big-O analysis. One reason for this is the variety of complications that cannot be conveniently plugged into a big-O formula. Included among these complications are the following:

- The variety of hardware on which an algorithm must ultimately be executed. There will be vast differences in both the time and space limitations of such hardware. Moreover, the details of such limitations are often buried deep in system reference manuals and can be exceedingly hard to find.
- Discrepancies that frequently arise between a user's projection of his or her computer needs and the unforeseen demands that materialize once the software system is put into use. A good systems analyst can hold those discrepancies to a minimum but not totally eliminate them.
- The elements of chance and probability that are inherent in many algorithms.

An example of this final point is the order of arrivals for insertion into a binary search tree. We can guarantee that search efficiency in a binary search tree will be between $O(n)$ and $O(\log_2 n)$. We can specify best and worst cases. But what happens in between? When do we cross over from response times that are acceptable to those that are not? Real-life data are rarely best case or worst case. Hence the "in-between" question is often of vital importance. Yet it is also the one that a pure big-O analysis leaves relatively unanswered.

In this section, we present a program that can serve as a start toward further exploration of the questions just posed. The program reads a list of unordered integers from a file, creates a binary search tree containing those integers, and then prints the binary search tree using indentation to reflect the level at which various nodes occur in the tree. In its present form, the program will allow you to test hypotheses about the relationship of the order of arrivals for insertion into a binary search tree and the resulting shape of the tree. In the first programming problem, you will extend the exploratory capabilities of the program, making it a substantive experimental tool.

A modular structure chart for the program is given in Figure 17.35. The program essentially brings together tree processing modules that we have already discussed on an individual basis; therefore, we do not provide the module specifications here. Pseudocode for the main program is

Create the tree
While not end of file
        Get a number from the file
        Insert the number into the tree
Print the tree

One twist is needed in the preorder traversal algorithm. To achieve indentation reflecting the depth of a node in the tree, we must keep track of our current level as we recursively call and then return from function **preorder_traverse**. The ideal solution would be to declare a local counter in the function that would retain its value from one invocation of the function to the next. Unfortunately, this is impossible with local variables in C++.

We are left with two alternatives: Tag the level counter along as an additional reference parameter for the **preorder_traverse** function or use a global level counter. The former alternative will alter the procedural interface to the **preorder_traverse** operation and hence violate the ADT implementation rule (formulated in Chapter 12). Hence we choose the latter alternative—use of a global variable—as the lesser of two evils. You should be aware that the need to

◆ **FIGURE 17.35**
Modular structure chart for
testtree.cpp program

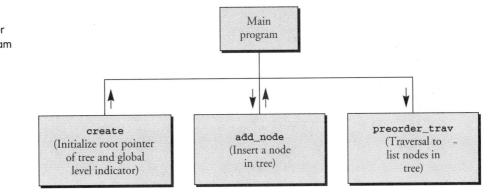

preserve the value of a variable between invocations of a function is one instance in which the use of a global variable in a function can be justified, provided that you carefully document its use.

Here is the change required in the implementation of the helper function `preorder_aux` for running the tests:

```
template <class E>
void binary_tree<E>::preorder_aux(node_ptr tree, void (*process) (E &item))
{
        if (tree != NULL)
        {
                process(tree->data);
                ++level;
// Increase before recursing
                preorder_aux(tree->left, process);
                preorder_aux(tree->right, process);
                --level;
// Decrease after recursing
        }
}
```

The complete program and a sample run follow. You will have the chance to explore the program more thoroughly in the end-of-chapter programming problems.

```
// Program file: testtree.cpp

// This program illustrates working with a binary tree.
// Input is an unordered list of integers from a file.
// Output is a character-based representation of the binary search
// tree that is constructed from the input integers.

#include <iostream.h>
#include <fstream.h>

int level = 0;                    // Global variable to maintain current level in tree.
                                  // Must be declared for access by tree module.

#include tree.h

const char SPACE = ' ';

void print(int &number);

int main()
{
    int number;
    ifstream input_file;
    binary_tree<int> tree;
```

```
        input_file.open("numbers");
        input_file >> number;
        while (! input_file.eof())
        {
               tree.insert(number);
               input_file >> number;
        }
        input_file.close();
        tree.preorder_traverse(print);
        return 0;
}

void print(int &number)
{
        if (level == 0)
               cout << setw(4) << number << endl;
        else
               cout << setw(level * 4) << SPACE << setw(4) << number << endl;
}
```

A sample run with the input file

| 34 | 23 | 78 | 90 | 12 | 20 | 50 | ■ |

results in the following output. Graphic lines have been added to highlight how the indentation reflects the tree structure.

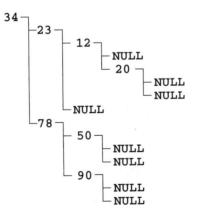

RUNNING, DEBUGGING AND TESTING HINTS

1. Trees are inherently recursive data structures, so learn to think recursively when devising algorithms that process trees.
2. When using the linear array representation of a binary tree, remember that all array locations must be initialized to a flagging Null value if the implementations of other operations are to work correctly.
3. The use of a preorder traversal to print a tree with indentation to reflect the depth of a node is a handy tracing tool to use when debugging a tree program that has gone awry. Keep such a function in your library, so it is readily available when the need arises. For more information, see this chapter's Focus on Program Design section.
4. When using a binary search tree to implement a one-key table, some experimentation may be necessary to determine the efficiency of this technique for the particular data of your application.

SUMMARY

Key Terms

ancestor
binary search tree
binary tree
binary implementation of a one-key table
binary tree implementation of general tree
branch
breadth-first traversal
child node
depth-first traversal
digraph
directional graph
edge
general tree

graph
heap
heap property
height balancing
hierarchy
inorder traversal
insertion rule
leaf node
level
linear implementation
linked implementation
network
ordering property

parent node
postorder traversal
preorder traversal
root
root node
siblings
subtree
ternary tree
threading
tree
tree traversal
vertex
weight

Key Concepts

◆ Trees are a data structure used to reflect a hierarchical relationship among data items. Indicative of this hierarchy is the parent–child terminology used to express the relationship between items on successive levels of the tree. Trees are by nature recursive structures, with each node of a tree being itself the root of a smaller, embedded subtree.

◆ Binary trees are trees in which each parent may have at most two child nodes. Although this seems like a major restriction, binary trees find a wide range of applications. Three such applications are the representation of algebraic expressions, one-key tables, and priority queues.

◆ Two ways of implementing a binary tree are the linear representation and the linked representation. The former method uses an array and requires no pointers but is prone to wasting a large number of array locations. The latter uses pointers and consequently is able to take advantage of C++'s dynamic memory allocation.

◆ There are three standard ways of traversing a binary tree: that is, three ways of visiting all nodes exactly once. These are the preorder, postorder, and inorder traversals.

◆ In a preorder traversal, the current root node is processed, followed recursively by the nodes in its left subtree and then its right subtree.

◆ In a postorder traversal, all nodes in the left subtree of the current root are recursively processed. Then all nodes in the right subtree are processed, and the root itself is processed last.

◆ In an inorder traversal, the nodes in the left subtree are processed first, followed by the root node, and finally the nodes in the right subtree of the root. The inorder traversal is critical in the binary tree implementation of a one-key table because the order in which it visits nodes corresponds precisely to the ordering of items as first, second, third, . . . , within the list represented by the tree.

◆ The binary search tree implementation of a one-key table is the third such table implementation we have studied. The other two were the array implementation (Chapter 12) and the linked list implementation (Chapter 14). The following table summarizes the relative advantages and disadvantages of the three methods.

Method	Search	Additions/Deletions	Other Comments
Physically ordered array	$O(\log_2 n)$ with binary search	Excessive data movement	Data must be physically ordered
Linked list	Requires sequential search, hence $O(n)$	Only pointer manipulation required	
Binary search tree	Bounded between $O(\log_2 n)$ and $O(n)$ though advanced methods can guarantee the former	Only pointer manipulation required	May necessitate the overhead associated with recursive traversals

◆ The binary tree may be used to implement the general tree structure. The preorder and postorder traversals emerge as the most important for this particular application.

◆ Graphs and networks are abstract data structures that are more complex than trees because they reflect bidirectional rather than hierarchical relationships. Depth-first and breadth-first traversals and finding the shortest path are examples of algorithms that manipulate graphs and networks.

PROGRAMMING PROBLEMS AND PROJECTS

1. Extend and experiment with the program from this chapter's Focus on Program Design section in the following ways:

   a. Use the program as it currently appears to acquire a feel for the relationship between the order of input data and the shape of the binary search tree that results.

   b. Instead of reading data from a file, randomly generate the data being inserted in the tree. Use the random number generator available in your version of C++ or, if none is available, the random number generator that appears in Appendix 6.

c. After a tree has been generated, add the capability to selectively delete nodes from the tree. Reprint the tree after deleting a node as verification that it has retained the critical ordering property.

d. Use the random generation capability from part b to build some very large trees. Instead of printing out these trees after they have been generated, compute the length of the average path that must be followed to find a node in the tree.

Do the results of your experiment indicate that, for random data, binary search trees yield a search efficiency that is $O(\log_2 n)$ or $O(n)$? Justify your conclusion with a written statement that is backed up by empirical data provided from your experimental runs.

e. Extend part d by computing the maximal path length in each randomly generated tree. What percentage of randomly generated trees has a maximal path length that is $O(n)$?

f. Depending on the availability of graphics functions in your version of C++, change the present character-based tree printout into a more appealing graphical representation.

2. Use a binary tree to implement the one-key table in the registrar's system from Example 13.1.

3. Modify the airline reservation system you developed for Wing-and-a-Prayer Airlines in Problem 2, Chapter 14, so that the alphabetized lists are maintained with binary trees instead of linked lists.

4. Write a program that sorts the records of the Fly-by-Night credit card company file (Problem 3, Chapter 14) in alphabetical order by the last name and then the first name of the customer. Use a binary tree and its inorder traversal to accomplish the sort.

5. Recall the roster maintenance system that you wrote for the Bay Area Brawlers in Problem 4 from Chapter 14. The system has been so successful that the league office would like to expand the system to include all the players in the league. Again the goal is to maintain the list of players in alphabetical order, allowing for frequent insertions and deletions as players are cut, picked up, and traded among teams. In addition to storing each player's height, weight, age, and university affiliation, the record for each player should be expanded to include team affiliation, years in league, and annual salary. Because the database for the entire league is many times larger than that for just one team, maintain this list as a binary search tree to increase efficiency.

6. Write a program that reads an expression in its prefix form and builds the binary tree corresponding to that expression. Then write functions to print the infix and postfix forms of the expression using inorder and postorder traversals of this tree. Then see if you can extend the program to evaluate the expression represented by the tree.

7. Given a file containing some arbitrary text, determine how many times each word appears in the file. Your program should print out in alphabetical order the words that appear in the file, with their frequency counts. For an added challenge, do not assume any maximum word length; this will enable you to combine trees with the string handling methods you have already learned.

8. Here is a problem you will encounter if you write statistical analysis software. Given an arbitrarily long list of unordered numbers with an arbitrary number of different values appearing in it, determine and print the marginal distribution for this list of numbers. That is, count how many times each different value appears in the list and then print each value along with its count (frequency). The final output should be arranged from smallest to largest value. This problem can be solved in elegant fashion using trees. An example of such output as produced by COSAP (Conversationally Oriented Statistical Analysis Package) of Lawrence University follows:

```
Command? Marginals Judge
                Pine County Criminal Cases
```

```
M A R G I N A L  F R E Q U E N C I E S
Variable Judge               JUDGE BEFORE WHOM CASE BROUGHT (2)
Value label                  Value       Absolute       Relative
                                         Frequency      Frequency


     ALLEN                      1            677           80.8%
     JONES                      2             88           10.5%
     KELLY                      3             26            3.1%
     MURCK                      5             47            5.6%
```

838 Valid 0 Missing 838 Total Observations

Here the data file contained 838 occurrences of the values 1, 2, 3, and 5. Each value was a code number assigned to a particular judge.

9. Many compilers offer the services of a cross-referencing program to aid in debugging. Such a program will list in alphabetical order all the identifiers that appear in a program and the various lines of the program that reference them. Write such a cross-reference for your favorite language using a binary tree to maintain the list of identifiers that are encountered.

10. A relatively easy game to implement with a binary tree is to have the computer try to guess an animal about which the user is thinking by asking the user a series of questions that can be answered by yes or no. A node in the binary tree to play this game could be viewed as

Yes/No pointers leading to

1. *Another question.*
2. *The name of the animal.*
3. *NULL.*

If NULL, have your program surrender and then ask the user for a new question that uniquely defines the animal being thought of. Then add this new question and animal to the growing binary tree database.

11. For this problem, you are to write a program that will differentiate expressions in the variable X. The input to this program will be a series of strings, each representing an infix expression to be differentiated. Each such expression is to be viewed as a stream of tokens. Valid tokens are integers, the variable X, the binary operators (+, −, *, /, ^), and parentheses. To make scanning for tokens easy, you may assume that each token is followed by exactly one space, with the exception of the final token, which is followed by the end-of-line character.

First your program will have to scan the infix expression, building up an appropriate binary tree representation of it. For this you should be able to borrow significantly on the work you did in parsing expressions in Chapter 15. The major difference here is that the end result of this parse is to be a binary tree instead of a postfix string.

Once the binary expression tree is built, traverse it, building up another binary expression tree, which represents the derivative of the original expression. The following differentiation rules should be used in this process:

Suppose C is a constant, and S and T are expressions in X:

```
Diff(C) = 0
Diff(X) = 1
Diff(S + T) = Diff(S) + Diff(T)
Diff(S - T) = Diff(S) - Diff(T)
Diff(S * T) = S * Diff(T) + T * Diff(S)
Diff(S / T) = ((T * Diff(S)) - (S * Diff(T))) / (T ^ 2)
Diff(S ^ C) = (C * S ^ (C - 1)) * Diff(S)    // the infamous chain rule
```

Finally, once the binary expression tree for the derivative has been built, print the expression. Print it in completely parenthesized infix notation to avoid ambiguity. Note that there are three distinct phases to this problem:

- Parsing of the original infix expression into a binary tree representation
- Building a binary tree representation of the derivative
- Printing the derivative in completely parenthesized infix notation.

For an added challenge on this problem, simplify the derivative before printing it. Simplify the expression for the derivative according to the following rules:

```
S + 0 = S
0 + S = S
S - 0 = S
S * 0 = 0
0 * S = 0
S * 1 = S
1 * S = S
0 / S = 0
S ^ 0 = 1
S ^ 1 = S
S - S = 0
0 / S = 0
S / S = 1
S / 0 = 'DIVISION BY ZERO'
0 / 0 = 'UNDEFINED'
```

12. Wing-and-a-Prayer Airlines (Problem 3) is expanding their record-keeping database. This database may now be pictured hierarchically as

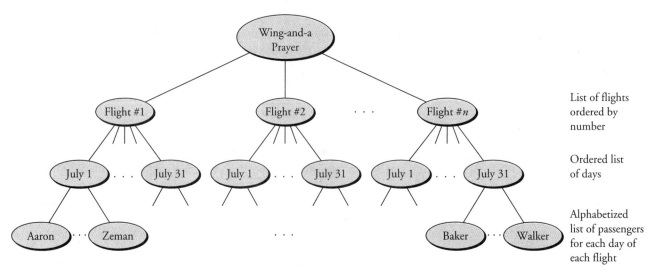

Write a program to maintain this database. Your program should process requests to add, delete, or list the following:

- Specified flight number
- Specified day of the month (for a given flight number)
- Specified passenger or all passengers (for a given flight number and day of the month).

13. Many statistical analysis packages support a "cross-tabulation" command designed to explore the relationship between statistical variables. A cross-tabulation between two variables produces a two-dimensional table containing a frequency count for each possible ordered pair of values of the two variables. However, these statistical packages typically allow this type of analysis to proceed even further than merely exploring two variables. For instance, in a legal-system database, we might be interested in cross-tabulating a defendant's age with the judge before whom the defendant stood trial. We may then wish to cross-tabulate this result with the sex of the defendant. Sex in this case is called the control variable. We would output one such cross-tabulation table for each possible value of sex. Note that this type of output is not limited to just one control variable. There may be an arbitrary number of control variables and tables to cycle through. Moreover, the variables have an arbitrary number of observations and are all in arbitrary order. Yet for each variable the list of possible values is always printed in smallest to largest order. The general tree structure that emerges for handling cross-tabulation is

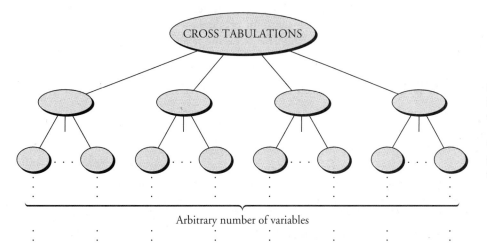

Final level of tree contains list of counters
for the innermost variable.

Write a program to handle the task of producing statistical cross-tabulations.

14. Write a program to print the nodes of a tree level by level; that is, all level 0 nodes, followed by all level 1 nodes, followed by all level 2 nodes, and so on. (*Hint:* This program will afford an excellent opportunity to practice using a queue in addition to a tree.)

15. Operating systems often use general trees as the data structure on which their file directory system is based. Leaf nodes in such a system represent actual files or empty directories. Interior nodes represent nonempty directories. For instance, consider the following situation:

A directory entry is specified by its pathname. A pathname consists of tree node names separated by slashes. Such a pathname is absolute if it starts at the root; that is, if it starts with a slash (/). It is relative to the current directory if it does not start with a slash.

In this assignment, you are to write a command processor that will allow a user to manipulate files within such a directory structure. The commands accepted by your processor will be in the form of numbers associated with particular operations and pathnames, as shown in the following table:

Number	Operation	Pathname
1	Change directory	Absolute pathname, relative pathname, or ". ." for parent
2	Make a new directory	Absolute or relative pathname
3	Make a new file	Absolute or relative pathname
4	Remove a file	Absolute or relative pathname
5	Remove a directory, but only if it is empty	Absolute or relative pathname
6	Remove a directory and, recursively, everything below it	Absolute or relative pathname
7	Print directory entries in alphabetical order	Absolute or relative pathname
8	Recursively print directory entries in alphabetical order	Absolute or relative pathname
9	Print current directory name	
10	Quit processing commands	

Since even intelligent tree-walking users can easily get lost, your command processor should be prepared to trap errors of the following variety:

- Specifying a nonexistent pathname
- Specifying a pathname that is a file when it should be a directory
- Specifying a pathname that is a directory when it should be a file.

Upon detecting such an error, have your command processor print an appropriate error message and then return to accept the next user command.

16. Trees have significant applications in the area of artificial intelligence and game playing. Consider, for instance, the game of FIFTEEN. In this game, two players take turns selecting digits between 1 and 9 with the goal of selecting a combination of digits that add up to 15. Once a digit is chosen, it may not be chosen again by either player. Rather than immediately considering a tree for the game of FIFTEEN, let us first consider a tree for the simpler game of SEVEN with digits chosen in the range 1 to 6. A tree that partially represents the states that may be reached in this game follows:

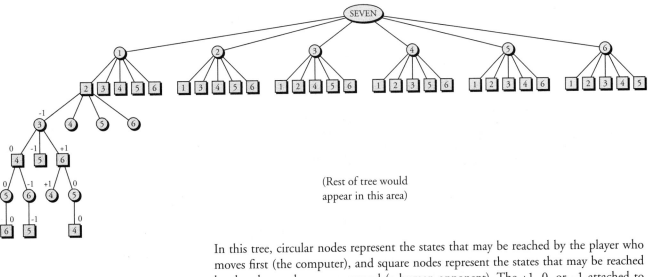

(Rest of tree would
appear in this area)

In this tree, circular nodes represent the states that may be reached by the player who moves first (the computer), and square nodes represent the states that may be reached by the player who moves second (a human opponent). The +1, 0, or –1 attached to each node represents weighting factors designed to help the computer choose the most advantageous move at any given stage of the game. The rules used to compute these weighting factors follow:

- If the node is a leaf node, its weight is determined by some static weighting function. In this case, the static weighting function used was to assign +1 to a leaf node representing a computer win, 0 to a leaf node representing a draw, and –1 to a leaf node representing a human win.
- If the node is a node in which the computer will move next (that is, a state occupied by the human opponent), then the weighting factor of the node is the maximum of the weighting factors of its children.
- If the node is a node in which the human opponent will move next, then the weighting factor of the node is the minimum of the weighting factors of its children.

In its turn, the computer should always choose to move to the node having the maximum possible weighting factor. The rationale behind this technique, called the minimax technique, is that the computer will move in such a way as to always maximize its chances of winning. The human opponent, if playing intelligently, will always move to a node having a minimum weighting factor. Thus in the partial game shown, the computer would choose 4 if the human had been naive enough to select the 6 node with the weighting factor of +1.

Write a program to build a weighted game tree for the game of FIFTEEN and then have the computer play against a human opponent. Note that this game is really the game of tic-tac-toe if one considers the following matrix:

4	9	2
3	5	7
8	1	6

All winning tic-tac-toe paths add up to 15.

Give some consideration as to the time and efficiency of your algorithm. Many games simply cannot be completely represented via a general tree because of space limitations. Consequently, a partial game tree is built in which the leaf nodes may not actually be the final moves made in the game. In such situations, the static weighting function applied to the leaf nodes in the game tree requires a bit more insight to develop.

17. Consider a priority queue (see Chapter 15, Section 15.3) in which each item is assigned a different priority. Discuss how a binary tree with the heap property could be used to maintain such a priority queue. Write functions for a heap implementation of the basic priority queue operations:

```
create
empty
insert(item, success)
remove(item, success)
```

Categorize the run-time efficiency of the **insert** and **remove** operations in big-O terms. Would a linear implementation or a linked implementation of the binary tree be most advantageous for this application? Explain why.

Finally, use your priority queue implementation to solve a problem such as Problem 12 in Chapter 15 or to simulate the servicing of priority-rated jobs on a time-sharing computing system.

18. Implement Dijkstra's shortest path algorithm using a suitable two-key table representation scheme to store the network data. Test your program with the transportation network pictured in Figure 17.27. Note that this same problem appeared in Chapter 16 as Problem 13. There you used a different algorithm for solving it. In a written statement, compare the efficiencies of the two algorithms.

19. A breadth-first traversal of a graph was discussed in Section 17.6. Implement this algorithm as a C++ function. (*Hint:* Use a queue.)

20. You are given a binary tree of integers implemented by a linked representation. Such a tree is said to be *weight balanced* if the sum of all the entries in the left subtree of the root equals the sum of all the entries in the right subtree of the root. Write a Boolean-valued function that receives a root pointer to such a tree and returns TRUE if the tree is weight balanced and FALSE otherwise. Then write a complete program to test your function. Finally, adjust your function so that it returns TRUE only when *every* subtree of the original tree is weight balanced.

21. Explore some additional graph and network algorithms in one of the advanced texts cited earlier in this chapter, such as Horowitz and Sahni, *Data Structures in C++* (New York: Computer Science Press, 1990) or Pothering and Naps, *Introduction to Data Structures and Algorithm Analysis with C++* (St. Paul, Minn.: West Publishing, 1995). Then prepare a written or oral report in which you explain the logic behind one of the algorithms you explore.

18 More Powerful Sorting Methods

Never mistake motion for action.
Ernest Hemingway,
1889–1961

In Chapter 11 we analyzed three simple sorting algorithms: bubble sort, insertion sort, and selection sort. We also discussed a technique, called a pointer sort, which can be combined with any of these three algorithms to minimize data movement when large records are being sorted by a particular key field. The essence of the pointer sort is to maintain an array of pointers that dictates the logical order of the records in an array of records. When the sorting algorithm dictates a swap, only the pointers must be interchanged, not the actual records.

With all three of our sorting algorithms, however, we ran into a barrier. This barrier was a run-time efficiency of $O(n^2)$ comparisons. Since the pointer sort technique reduces data movement but not the number of comparisons, this barrier exists whether or not we incorporate the pointer sort idea into the sorting algorithm. Our goal in this chapter is to study sorting algorithms that break the $O(n^2)$ comparisons barrier. These new algorithms will make use of what we have learned since Chapter 11. In particular, both recursion and a conceptual understanding of trees are essential prerequisites to analyzing these more powerful methods.

The general setup for the sort algorithms of this chapter is the same as the one we used in Chapter 11:

```
const int MAX_LIST_SIZE = 100;
typedef int element;
typedef element list_type[MAX_LIST_SIZE];
```

We wish to write a sort function that meets the following specifications:

```
// Function: sort
// Sorts a list of elements into ascending order
//
// Inputs: a list of elements in random order and its current length
// Output: the list of elements arranged in ascending order

void sort(list_type list, int n);
```

Although our algorithms for this chapter are presented in the context of sorting arrays in ascending order, they apply more generally to any list whose elements can be directly accessed (for example, one-key tables) and they can be easily modified to sort in descending order. Moreover, one of the methods we discuss (merge sort) actually does not require direct access into the list. Hence it could be applied to lists that are just sequentially accessible such as sequential files and linked lists.

18.1 The Shell Sort Algorithm

OBJECTIVES

- to understand the logic behind the shell sort algorithm
- to see the relationship between shell sort and insertion sort
- to develop a C++ function to perform shell sort
- to analyze the efficiency of the shell sort algorithm

The *shell sort,* named after its inventor D. L. Shell, incorporates the logic of the insertion sort to a certain extent. However, instead of sorting the entire array at once, it first divides the array into smaller, noncontiguous segments, which are then separately sorted using the insertion sort. The advantage of doing this is twofold. First, where a comparison dictates a swap of two data items in a segment, this swap within a noncontiguous segment of the array moves an item a greater distance within the overall array than the swap of adjacent array entries in the usual insertion sort. This means that one swap is more likely to place an element closer to its final location in the array when using shell sort than when using the simple insertion sort. For instance, a large-valued entry that appears near the front of the array will more quickly move to the tail end of the array because each swap moves it a greater distance in the array. The second advantage of dividing the array into segments is tied to the first; that is, because early passes tend to move elements closer to their final destination than early passes would in a straight insertion sort, the array becomes partially sorted quite fast. The fact that the array is likely to become partially sorted relatively early then allows the embedded insertion sort logic to make more frequent use of its check for an early exit from its inner loop. (Recall that this check is what makes the insertion sort particularly efficient for arrays that are partially sorted.) An example will help clarify this shell sort rationale.

EXAMPLE 18.1

Suppose we have an array containing the following integers:

80 93 60 12 42 30 68 85 10

We first divide this into three segments of three elements each.

```
80 12 68→ Segment 1
93 42 85→ Segment 2
60 30 10→ Segment 3
```

and sort each of the segments:

```
12 68 80
42 85 93
10 30 60
```

The original array, partially sorted, now appears as

Segment 1
Segment 2
Segment 3

We divide this partially sorted array as

| 12 10 85 80 60 | → Segment 1 |
| 42 68 30 93 | → Segment 2 |

These segments are then sorted and the array takes the form

Segment 1
Segment 2

Finally, this array is sorted as one segment; 12 and 30, and 93 and 85 are swapped to give us the sorted array

10 12 30 42 60 68 80 85 93

The key to the shell sort algorithm is that the whole array is first fragmented into K segments for some number K, where K is preferably a prime number. These K segments are given by

$a[0], a[K + 1], a[2 * K + 1], ..., a[2], a[K + 2], a[2 * K + 2], ...$

.
.
.

$a[K], a[2 * K], a[3 * K], ...$

Because each segment is sorted, the whole array is partially sorted after the first pass. For the next pass, the value of K is reduced, which increases the size of each segment, hence reducing the number of segments. Preferably, the next value of K is also chosen so that it is prime relative to its previous value, or *relatively prime*. (Two integers are said to be relatively prime to each other if they have no common factor greater than 1.) The process is repeated until $K = 1$, at which point the array is sorted. The insertion sort is applied to each segment, so each successive segment is partially sorted. Consequently, the later applications of the insertion sort become very efficient, dramatically increasing the overall efficiency of the shell sort.

To emphasize the fashion in which the shell sort algorithm relies on the logic of insertion sort, we present a `segmented_insertion_sort` function, which arranges each of k segments in an n-element array into ascending order. Compare this function with the function for insertion sort that was given in Chapter 11. You will see that `segmented_insertion_sort` moves an item from position j to position $j + k$. When $k = 1$, this is precisely the original insertion sort algorithm.

```
void segmented_insertion_sort(list_type list, int n, int k)
{
    int j;
    element item_to_insert;
    boolean still_looking;

    for (int i = k; i < n; ++i)
    {
        item_to_insert = list[i];
        j = i - k;
        still_looking = TRUE;
        while ((j >= 0) && still_looking)
            if (item_to_insert < list[j])
            {
                list[j + k] = list[j];
                j = j - k;
            }
            else
                still_looking = FALSE;
        list[j + k] = item_to_insert;
    }
}
```

With $n = 6$ and $k = 3$, the array is divided into three segments of two elements each.

```
80  93  60  12  42  30
```

80 12 --> Segment 1
93 42 --> Segment 2
60 30 --> Segment 3

Sort each of the segments:
```
12  80
42  93
30  60
```

Given the `segmented_insertion_sort` function, we now merely call on this with values of k that become successively smaller. Eventually, `segmented_insertion_sort` must be called with $K = 1$ to guarantee that the array, viewed as one segment, is completely sorted.

The function `shell_sort` that follows illustrates these successive calls to `segmented_insertion_sort` for values of k that are repeatedly halved.

```
void shell_sort(list_type list, int n)
{
    int k = n / 2;

    while (k > 0)
    {
        segmented_insertion_sort(list, n, k);
        k = k / 2;
    }
}
```

Efficiency of the Shell Sort

The shell sort is also called the *diminishing increment sort* because the value of k (the number of segments) continually decreases. The method is more efficient if the successive values of k are kept relatively prime to each other, thereby helping to ensure that a pair of values previously compared to each other are not compared again. D. E. Knuth has mathematically estimated that, with relatively prime values of k, the shell sort will execute in an average time proportional to $O[n(\log_2 n)^2]$ (see Donald E. Knuth, *Searching and Sorting*, Volume 3 of *The Art of Computer Programming* Menlo Park, Calif.: Addison-Wesley, 1973). However, the sort will work for any values of k, as long as the last value of k is 1. For instance, note that in the version of **shell_sort** we have given, the successive values of k will not often be relatively prime. When the values of k are not relatively prime, then the efficiency of the shell sort is of the order $O(n^r)$, where $1 < r < 2$. The particular value of r makes the sort less efficient than $O[n(\log_2 n)^2]$ for large values of n, but better than the $O(n^2)$ methods of Chapter 11.

The shell sort is most efficient on arrays that are nearly sorted. In fact, the first chosen value of k is large to ensure that the whole array is fragmented into small individual arrays, for which the insertion sort is highly effective. Each subsequent sort causes the entire array to be more nearly sorted, so that the efficiency of the insertion sort as applied to larger partially sorted arrays is increased. Trace through a few examples to convince yourself that the partially ordered status of the array for one value of k is not affected by subsequent partial sorts for a different value of k.

It is not known with what value of k the shell sort should start, but Knuth suggests a sequence of values such as 1, 3, 7, 15, . . . , for reverse values of k; that is, the $(j + \text{one})$th value is two times the jth value plus 1. Knuth suggests other possible values of k, but generally the initial guess at the first value of k is all that you need. The initial guess will depend on the size of the array and, to some extent, on the type of data being sorted.

EXERCISES 18.1

1. Consider the **shell_sort** function given in this section. Suppose we were to trace the contents of the array being sorted after each call to the function **segmented_insertion_sort**. What would we see as output if we called **shell_sort** with the following key array?

   60 12 90 30 64 8 6

2. Repeat Exercise 1 for a six-element array that initially contains

   1 8 2 7 3 6

3. Where did the shell sort get its name?

4. Why is the shell sort most efficient when the original data are in almost sorted order?

5. What advantage do the relatively prime values of the increments have over other values in a shell sort? Formulate your answer in a precise written statement that explains why relatively prime values are better.

6. What property must the sequence of diminishing increments in the shell sort have to ensure that the method will work?

7. Provide examples of best case and worst case data sets for the shell sort algorithm presented in this section. Justify your data sets by explaining why they generate best case and worst case performance.

8. In Chapter 11, **pointer_sort** used an index of pointers to sort data logically without rearranging it. Identify the sort algorithm that was behind the C++ **pointer_sort** function. Adapt the pointer sort function to the shell sort algorithm.

9. The version of shell sort presented in this section uses the following sequence of diminishing increments:

   $n/2$, $n/4$, . . ., 8, 4, 2, 1

Rewrite the shell sort so that the following sequence of diminishing increments is used:

$k, \ldots, 121, 40, 13, 4, 1$

Here k represents the largest member of this sequence, which is <= n where n is the logical size of the array being sorted.

18.2 The Quick Sort Algorithm

OBJECTIVES

- to understand the logic behind the Quick Sort algorithm
- to understand the role played by the partitioning subalgorithm in Quick Sort
- to develop a C++ function to perform Quick Sort
- to analyze the efficiency of the Quick Sort algorithm; in particular, to see the relationship between the efficiency of the QUICK SORT algorithm and the way in which the subordinate partitioning subalgorithm splits the array.

Even though the shell sort provides a significant advantage in run time over its $O(n^2)$ predecessors, its average efficiency of $O[n(\log_2 n)^2]$ may still not be good enough for large arrays. The next group of methods, including the *quick sort,* has an average execution time of $O(n \log_2 n)$, which is the best that can be achieved. Compared to $O[n(\log_2 n)^2]$ or $O(n^r)$ for $1 < r < 2$, an $O(n \log_2 n)$ sort is often a good choice as the main vehicle for large sorting jobs.

The essence of the quick sort algorithm, originally devised in 1961 by C. A. R. Hoare, is to rely on a subordinate algorithm to partition the array. The process of partitioning involves moving a data item, called the *pivot,* in the correct direction just enough for it to reach its final place in the array. The partitioning process, therefore, reduces unnecessary interchanges and potentially moves the pivot a great distance in the array without forcing it to be swapped into intermediate locations. Once the pivot item is chosen, moves are made so that data items to the left of the pivot are less than (or equal to) it, whereas those to the right are greater (or equal). The pivot item is thus in its correct position. The quick sort algorithm then recursively applies the partitioning process to the two parts of the array on either side of the pivot until the entire array is sorted.

In the next example, we illustrate the mechanics of this partitioning logic by applying it to an array of numbers.

EXAMPLE 18.2

Suppose the array contains integers initially arranged as

15 20 5 8 95 12 80 17 9 55

Table 18.1 shows a partitioning pass applied to this array. The following steps are involved:

1. Remove the first data item, 15, as the pivot, mark its position, and scan the array from right to left, comparing data item values with 15. When you find the first smaller value, remove it from its current position and put it in position `a[0]`. (This is shown in line 2.)

2. Scan line 2 from left to right beginning with position `a[1]`, comparing data item values with 15. When you find the first value greater than 15, extract it and store it in the position marked by parentheses in line 2. (This is shown in line 3.)

3. Begin the right-to-left scan of line 3 with position `a[7]` looking for a value smaller than 15. When you find it, extract it and store it in the position marked by the parentheses in line 3. (This is shown in line 4.)

◇ **TABLE 18.1**

Each call to `quick_sort` partitions an array segment. The asterisk (*) indicates the pivot value (here 15).

Line Number	a[0]	a[1]	a[2]	a[3]	a[4]	a[5]	a[6]	a[7]	a[8]	a[9]
										←
1	15*	20 →	5	8	95	12	80	17	9	55
2	9	20	5	8	95	12	80	17 ←	( )	55
3	9	( ) →	5	8	95	12	80	17	20	55
4	9	12	5	8	95 ←	( )	80	17	20	55
5	9	12	5	8	( )	95	80	17	20	55
6	9	12	5	8	15	95	80	17	20	55

4. Begin scanning line 4 from left to right at position `a[2]`. Find a value greater than 15, remove it, mark its position, and store it inside the parentheses in line 4. (This is shown in line 5.)

5. Now, when you attempt to scan line 5 from right to left beginning at position `a[4]`, you are immediately at a parenthesized position determined by the previous left-to-right scan. This is the location to put the pivot data item, 15. (This is shown in line 6.) At this stage, 15 is in its correct place relative to the final sorted array.

Notice that all values to the left of 15 are less than 15, and all values to the right of 15 are greater than 15. The method will still work if two values are the same. The process can now be applied recursively to the two segments of the array on the left and right of 15. Notice that these recursive calls eventually sort the entire array. The result of any one call to function `quick_sort` is merely to partition a segment of the array so that the pivotal item is positioned with everything to its left being less than or equal to it and everything to its right being greater than or equal.

The function `partition` that follows achieves one partitioning pass in the overall `quick_sort` algorithm as described in Example 18.2. The indices `lo` and `hi` represent the pointers that move from the left and right, respectively, until they meet at the appropriate location for the pivot. The pivotal value is initially chosen to be `a[lo]`. We will discuss later the possible implications of choosing a different pivot value. Note that it is crucial for `partition` to return in `pivot_point` the position where the pivotal value was finally inserted. This information will allow the `quick_sort` function that calls on `partition` to determine whether or not a recursive termination condition has been reached.

```
// Partition array between indices lo and hi.
// That is, using list[lo] as pivotal value, arrange
// entries between lo and hi indices so that all
```

```
// values to left of pivot are less than or equal
// to it and all values to right of pivot are
// greater than or equal to it.
//
// Input: array and lo and hi
// Output: Partitioned array, and pivot_point
// containing final location of pivot.

void partition(list_type list, int lo, int hi, int &pivot_point)
{
    element pivot = list[lo];

    while (lo < hi)
    {

        while ((pivot < list[hi]) && (lo < hi))
            --hi;
        if (hi != lo)
        {
            list[lo] = list[hi];
            ++lo;

        }
        while ((pivot > list[lo]) && (lo < hi))
            ++lo;
        if (hi != lo)
        {
            list[hi] = list[lo];
            --hi;
        }
    }
    list[hi] = pivot;
    pivot_point = hi;
}
```

pivot = 12

Right-to-left scan until smaller value found here

| 12 | 8 | 7 | 6 | 14 | 20 | 30 | 5 | 19 | 13 | 15 | hi = 7
| 0 | 1 | 2 | 3 | 4 | 5 | 6 | 7 | 8 | 9 | 10 |

pivot = 12

Left-to-right scan until larger value found here

| 5 | 8 | 7 | 6 | 14 | 20 | 30 | 5 | 19 | 13 | 15 | lo = 4
| 0 | 1 | 2 | 3 | 4 | 5 | 6 | 7 | 8 | 9 | 10 |

Right-to-left scan looking for smaller value on next iteration

| 5 | 8 | 7 | 6 | 14 | 20 | 30 | 14 | 19 | 13 | 15 | lo = hi
| 0 | 1 | 2 | 3 | 4 | 5 | 6 | 7 | 8 | 9 | 10 |

meeting point between lo and hi

| 5 | 8 | 7 | 6 | 12 | 20 | 30 | 14 | 19 | 13 | 15 | hi = lo = 4
| 0 | 1 | 2 | 3 | 4 | 5 | 6 | 7 | 8 | 9 | 10 | a[4] = pivot

Algorithm recursively called for this segment

And then for this segment

Given the previous **partition** function, **quick_sort** itself must call on **partition** and then use the returned value of **pivot_point** to decide whether or not recursive calls are necessary to perform more refined partitioning of the segments to the left and right of **pivot_point**. The recursive logic for this decision is given in the following function **quick_sort**:

```
void quick_sort(list_type list, int lower, int upper)
{
        int pivot_point;

        partition(list, lower, upper, pivot_point);
        if (lower < pivot_point)
            quick_sort(list, lower, pivot_point - 1);
        if (upper > pivot_point)
            quick_sort(list, pivot_point + 1, upper);
}
```

For instance, after the first call to **quick_sort** for a partitioning pass on the data in Table 18.1, we would then recursively call on **quick_sort** with **lower** = 1 and **upper** = 4. This would trigger deeper level recursive calls from which we would ultimately return, knowing that the segment of the array between indices 1 and 5 is now sorted. This return would be followed by a recursive call to **quick_sort** with **lower** = 6 and **upper** = 10.

The run-time trace diagram of recursive calls to **quick_sort** for the data of Table 18.1 is given in Figure 18.1. You should verify this call-return pattern by walking through the preceding function.

◆ FIGURE 18.1
Run-time trace diagram of (recursive) calls to **quick_sort** data in Table 18.1

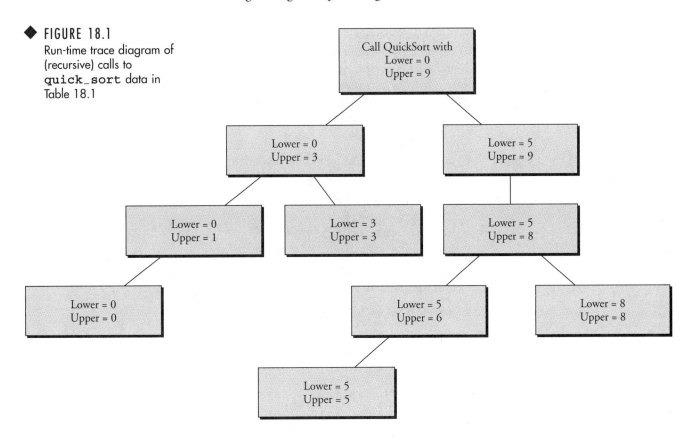

Efficiency of the Quick Sort

As mentioned earlier, the average run-time efficiency of the quick sort is $O(n \log_2 n)$, which is the best that has been achieved for a large array of size n. In the best case, it is quite easy to provide a rationale for this $O(n \log_2 n)$ figure. This best case occurs when each array segment recursively passed to **quick_sort** partitions at its midpoint; that is, the appropriate location for each pivotal value in the series of recursive calls is the midpoint of the segment being partitioned. In this case,

1 call to **quick_sort** (the first) is made with a segment of size n.
2 calls to **quick_sort** are made with segments of size $n/2$.
4 calls to **quick_sort** are made with segments of size $n/4$.
8 calls to **quick_sort** are made with segments of size $n/8$.

$\left.\phantom{\begin{matrix}1\\2\\3\\4\end{matrix}}\right\}$ Overall $\log_2 n$ levels

.
.
.

n calls to **quick_sort** are made with segments of size 1.

Since each call with a segment of size m requires $O(m)$ comparisons, it is clear that k calls with segments of size n/k will require $O(n)$ comparisons. Hence, the total number of comparisons resulting from the preceding sequence of calls will be $O(n \log_2 n)$.

If segments partition away from the midpoint, the efficiency of quick sort begins to deteriorate. In the worst case situation, when the array is already sorted, the efficiency of the quick sort may drop down to $O(n^2)$ due to the continuous right-to-left scan all the way to the last left boundary. In the exercises at the end of the section, you will explore how the worst case situation is affected by your choice of the pivotal element.

You may wonder how large a stack is needed to sort an array of size n. (Remember that this stack is implicitly created even when you use recursion.) Knuth has mathematically estimated that the size of the stack will generally not exceed $O(\log_2 n)$. However, in the worst case, it will be $O(n)$. (See D. E. Knuth's text, *Searching and Sorting*, cited in Section 18.1.)

EXERCISES 18.2

1. Consider the **quick_sort** function given in this section. Suppose we were to insert the following tracer output at the beginning of this function:

```
cout << lower << " " << upper << endl;
for (k = lower; k <= upper; ++k)
        cout << a[k];
cout << endl;
```

What would we see as output from these tracers if we were to call on **quick_sort** with the key array initially containing the following seven entries?:

60 12 90 30 64 8 6

2. Repeat Exercise 1 for a six-element array that initially contains

1 8 2 7 3 6

3. When is a bubble sort better than a quick sort? Explain your answer in a written statement.

A NOTE OF INTEREST

Privacy Issues Kill Lotus Database

The August 1989 issue of *Communications of the ACM* (Volume 32, No. 8) was dedicated to the role played by ethics in the education and career of a computer scientist. What are the social responsibilities that go along with state-of-the art capabilities to sort and search through gigabytes of information? A recent incident involving Lotus Development Corporation of Cambridge, Massachusetts, illustrated the importance of a social conscience in computing.

In late 1990, Lotus had planned the release of a product called MarketPlace. Designed for use on a personal computer equipped with CD-ROM storage, the so-called "household" version of MarketPlace supposedly contained information on 120 million Americans and 80 million households. This information included data on personal income, lifestyle, purchasing patterns, geographic location, and marital status. These data were compiled for Lotus by Equifax, the nation's largest credit reporting agency. Lotus foresaw a great demand for MarketPlace coming from a wide variety of large and small businesses. According to Michael W. Miller in the article "MarketPlace," which appeared in the November 13, 1990, issue of the *Wall Street Journal:*

> Advances in computers are making it easier to gather and piece together minutely detailed portraits of households, and marketers are gobbling these up to help choose targets for direct-mail and telephone campaigns.

One of the early Lotus press releases for MarketPlace began with the headline "We Found You . . . And Quite Frankly, It Really Wasn't That Hard."

What Lotus had not properly anticipated was the storm of protest that would arise from consumer advocacy groups and individual consumers concerning MarketPlace's apparent insensitivity to privacy issues. Miller's *Wall Street Journal* article described these concerns: "Privacy advocates' chief objection to MarketPlace was that it wouldn't be easy enough for consumers to delete their data, or correct any inaccuracies."

Lotus demonstrated its sensitivity to the ethical issues that had been raised by MarketPlace. In January 1991, James Manzi, Lotus's chairman, announced that Lotus was canceling the MarketPlace project. Manzi stated, "What drove our decision was the volume and tenor of the concerns that were being raised by consumers all over the U.S." Though Lotus may have exercised poor judgment in the original conception of MarketPlace, their decision to pull the plug after a sizable investment in the enterprise illustrates a high degree of social responsibility. Such ethical dilemmas are likely to play an increasing role in the careers of many computing professionals.

---

4. Under what circumstances would you not use a quick sort? Explain your answer in a written statement.

5. How does the choice of the pivotal value affect the efficiency of the quick sort algorithm? Suppose that the middle value or the last value in a segment to be partitioned was chosen as the pivotal value. How would this alter the nature of best case and worst case data sets? Give examples to illustrate your answer.

6. Develop run-time trace diagrams of function calls to **quick_sort** for a variety of test data sets (analogous to what was done in Figure 18.1). Use these diagrams to analyze the efficiency of **quick_sort.** What types of data sets yield $O(n \log_2 n)$ efficiency? What types yield $O(n^2)$ efficiency?

7. In Chapter 11, **pointer_sort** used an index of pointers to sort data logically without rearranging it. Adapt the pointer sort function to the quick sort algorithm.

8. Implement **quick_sort** in a nonrecursive fashion.

9. Implement a variation on the quick sort algorithm presented in this section, in which the pivot is chosen to be the median of the three values:

```
a[lo], a[(lo + hi) / 2], a[hi]
```

In a carefully written statement, explain why this variation should be more efficient than the version that chooses the pivot to be **a[lo]**.

18.3 The Heap Sort Algorithm

The *heap sort* is a sorting algorithm that is roughly equivalent to the quick sort; its average efficiency is $O(n \log_2 n)$ for an array of size n. The method, originally described by R. W. Floyd, has two phases. In the first phase, the array containing the n data items is viewed as equivalent to a full binary tree. That is, the array to be sorted is viewed as the linear representation of a full binary tree containing n items (see Chapter 17). (If you want to read Floyd's description of this method, see his article, entitled "Algorithm 245: Tree Sort 3" found in *Communications of the ACM* Volume 7, 1964: 701.) As an example, suppose we wish to sort the following array:

11 1 5 7 6 12 17 8 4 10 2

The tree now appears as shown in Figure 18.2.

The goal of phase 1 is to sort the data elements along each path from leaf node level to the root node. If we wish to sort in ascending order, then the numbers along any path from leaf node to root should be in increasing order. Eventually, after phase 1, the tree will be a heap as described in Chapter 17. That is, the data item at each node will be greater than or equal to both of its children. To achieve this, we take the following steps:

1. Process the node that is the parent of the rightmost node on the lowest level as follows: If its value is less than the value of its largest child, swap these values; otherwise do nothing.

2. Move left on the same level. Compare the value of the parent node with the values of the children. If the parent is smaller than the largest child, swap them.

3. When the left end of this level is reached, move up a level, and, beginning with the rightmost parent node, repeat step 2. Continue swapping the original parent with the larger of its children until it is larger than its children. In effect, the original parent is being walked down the tree in a fashion that ensures all numbers will be in increasing order along the path.

4. Repeat step 3 until the root node has been processed.

Figure 18.3 shows these steps applied to Figure 18.2.

Phase 2 of the heap sort finds the node with the largest value in the tree and cuts it from the tree. This is then repeated to find the second largest value, which is also removed from the tree. The process continues until only two nodes are left

◆ FIGURE 18.2
Full binary tree corresponding to array

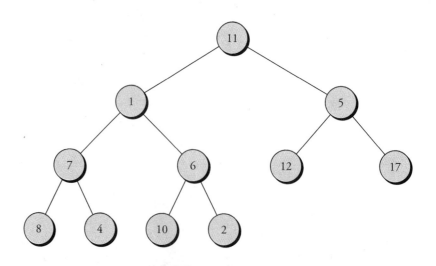

◆ **FIGURE 18.3**
Phase 1 of heap sort applied to the binary tree in Figure 18.2

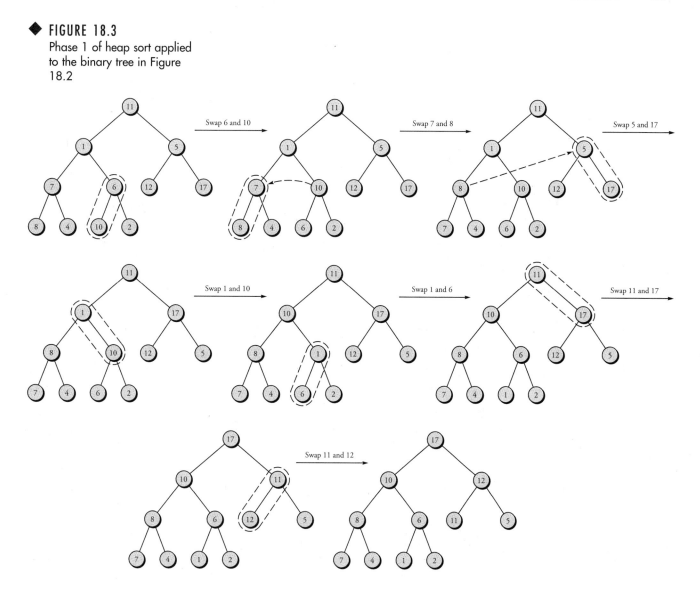

in the tree; they are then exchanged if necessary. The precise steps for phase 2 are as follows:

1. Swap the root node with the bottom rightmost child, and sever this new bottom rightmost child from the tree. This is the largest value.
2. Continue swapping the new root value with the larger of its children until it is not exceeded by either child. In effect, this new root value is now being walked down a path in the tree to ensure that all paths retain values arranged in ascending order from leaf node to root node. That is, the tree is being restored to a heap.
3. Repeat steps 1 and 2 until only one element is left.

Phase 2 of the heap sort begun in Figure 18.3 is shown in Figure 18.4 for the three highest values.

Both phase 1 and phase 2 use the same strategy of walking a parent down a path of the tree via a series of swaps with its children. The following function **walk_down**, isolates this crucial subordinate algorithm. In the linear representa-

◆ **FIGURE 18.4**
Phase 2 of heap sort for
three values

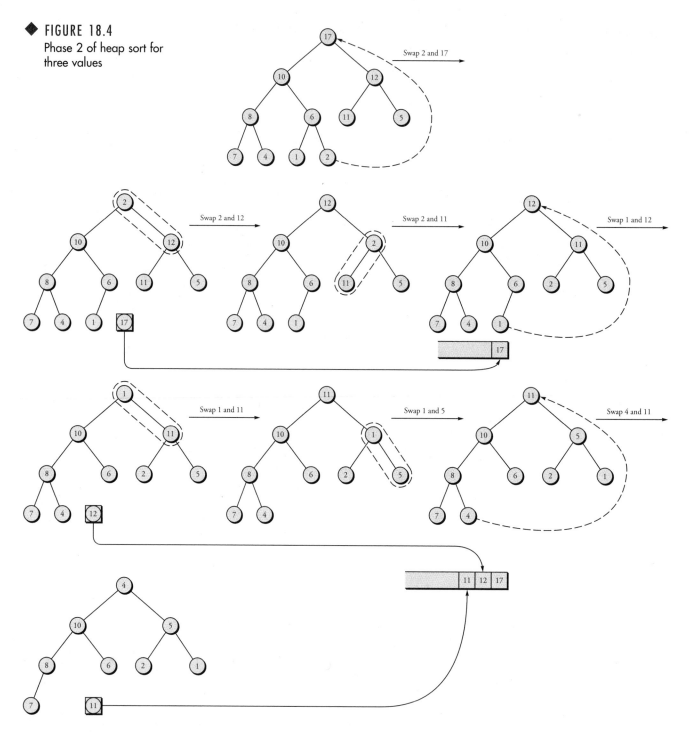

tion of a tree assumed by **walk_down**, the assignment statement $k = 2 * i$ will
make k reference the left child of the node indicated by i. That is, this statement
will allow us to descend a level deeper into the tree.

```
// Function: walk_down
// Repeatedly exchange this parent with child of
// greatest value until the original parent is
// greater than both of its children
//
```

```
// Inputs: Array to be viewed as full binary tree.
// n, the number of entires in the array.
// j, the index of a parent node within the tree.
// Outputs: Tree array, as altered by this task.

void walk_down(list_type list, int j, int n)
{
    int i, k;
    element ref;
    boolean found_spot = FALSE;

    i = j;
    ref = list[i];

    // list[i] will move along the appropriate path
    // in the tree

    k = 2 * i + 1;

    // Initially k references left child of list[i]

    while ((k < n) && ! found_spot)
    {
        if (k < n - 1)
            // Have k reference largest child
            if (list[k + 1] > list[k])
                ++k;
        if (list[k] > ref)
            // Child must move up
        {
            list[i] = list[k];
            i = k;
            k = 2 * i + 1;
        }
        else
            // Appropriate spot has been found
            found_spot = TRUE;
    }
    list[i] = ref;
}
```

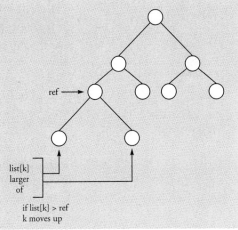

With the essential **walk_down** logic isolated in a separate function, phases 1 and 2 of **heap_sort** may now be developed easily. The loop for phase 1 repeatedly calls on **walk_down** to form the tree into a heap. Then a loop for phase 2 repeatedly swaps the root of the tree with the last child and calls on **walk_down** to allow this new root to find an appropriate position in the heap.

```
void heap_sort(list_type list, int n)
{
    int y;
    element temp;

    // First phase arranges the tree into a heap

    y = n / 2 - 1;    // y starts at last node to have child
    while (y >= 0)
    {
        walk_down(list, y, n);
        --y;
    }
```

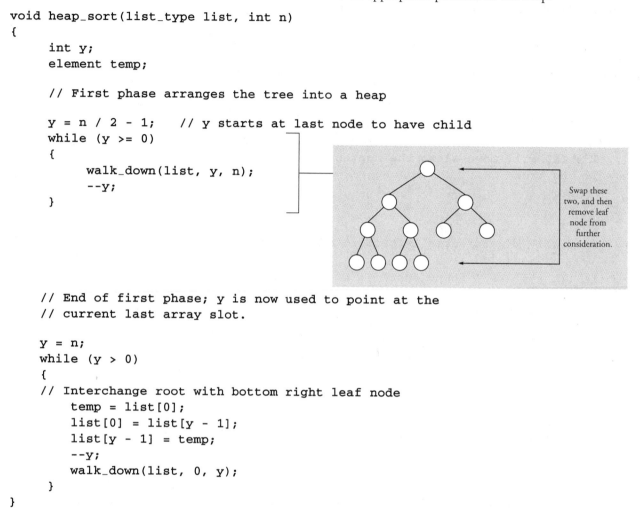

Swap these two, and then remove leaf node from further consideration.

```
    // End of first phase; y is now used to point at the
    // current last array slot.

    y = n;
    while (y > 0)
    {
    // Interchange root with bottom right leaf node
        temp = list[0];
        list[0] = list[y - 1];
        list[y - 1] = temp;
        --y;
        walk_down(list, 0, y);
    }
}
```

Efficiency of the Heap Sort

It is relatively easy to deduce that the heap sort requires $O(n \log_2 n)$ comparisons. To see this, note that the phase 1 loop in the preceding C++ function will execute $n/2$ times. Inside this loop we call **walk_down**, which in turn has a loop that will execute at most $\log_2 n$ times (because it merely follows a path down a full binary tree). Hence phase 1 requires at most

$$(n/2) * \log_2 n$$

iterations at its deepest level. Phase 2 may be similarly analyzed. The phase 2 loop iterates n times. Within each iteration, **walk_down** is called, again resulting in at most $\log_2 n$ operations. Thus, phase 2 requires at most $n * \log_2 n$ iterations at its deepest level. Overall, we get

$$1.5n * \log_2 n$$

as an upper bound for the number of iterations required by the combination of phases 1 and 2. Thus, both quick sort and heap sort yield $O(n \log_2 n)$ efficiencies. In *Searching and Sorting,* referenced in Sections 18.1 and 18.2, Knuth has shown that, on the average, quick sort will be slightly faster since its big-O constant of proportionality will be smaller than that for heap sort. However, heap sort offers the advantage of guaranteeing an $O(n \log_2 n)$ efficiency regardless of the data being sorted. As we have already noted for quick sort, worst case data can cause its performance to deteriorate to $O(n^2)$.

EXERCISES 18.3

1. Consider the **heap_sort** function given in this section. Note that **walk_down** is called at two points in the function: once in phase 1 and again in phase 2. Suppose that we were to trace the contents of the array being sorted after each call to **walk_down**. What would we see as output if we called **heap_sort** with an array that initially contained the following?:

   60 12 90 30 64 8 6

2. Repeat Exercise 1 for a six-element array that initially contains

   1 8 2 7 3 6

3. Where did the heap sort get its name?
4. What is a heap?
5. Is a heap sort always better than a quick sort? When is it? When isn't it? Explain your answer in a written essay.
6. What is the worst case and average case efficiency of the heap sort?
7. Give examples of arrays that generate the best and worst performances, respectively, for the heap sort algorithm. Explain why these arrays generate the best and worst performances.
8. In Chapter 11, **pointer_sort** used an index of pointers to sort data logically without rearranging it. Adapt the pointer sort function to the heap sort algorithm.

18.4 The Merge Sort Algorithm

OBJECTIVES

- to understand the logic behind the merge sort algorithm
- to understand merge sort's reliance on a sub-algorithm that merges two sorted lists
- to develop a C++ function to perform the merge sort
- to analyze the efficiency of the merge sort

The essential idea behind *merge sort* is to make repeated use of a function that merges two lists, each already in ascending order, into a third list, also arranged in ascending order. The merge function itself only requires sequential access to the lists. Its logic is similar to the method you would use if you were merging two sorted piles of index cards into a third pile. That is, start with the first card from each pile. Compare them to see which one comes first, transfer that one over to the third pile, and advance to the next card in that pile. Repeat the comparison, transfer, and advance operations until one of the piles runs out of cards. At that point, merely move what is left of the remaining pile over to the third merged pile.

This logic is reflected in the generalized merge function that follows. For reasons that will become apparent when we incorporate it into a full sorting function, this version of merge begins with the two sorted lists stored in one array. The first list runs from subscript **lower** to **middle** of array **source**. The second runs from subscript **middle + 1** to **upper** of the same array. The merged result of the two lists is stored in a second array **destination**.

```
// Function: merge
// Merge the two ordered segments of source into
// one list arranged in ascending order.
//
// Inputs: Array source arranged in ascending order
// between indices lower..middle and middle + 1..upper, respectively.
// Outputs: The complete ordered list in destination.

void merge(list_type source, list_type destination, int lower,
     int middle, int upper)
{
     int s1 = lower;
     int s2 = middle + 1;
     int d = lower;

     // Repeat comparison of current item from each list.

     do
     {
         if (source[s1] < source[s2])
         {
             destination[d] = source[s1];
             ++s1;
         }
         else
         {
             destination[d] = source[s2];
             ++s2;
         }
         ++d;
     } while ((s1 <= middle) && (s2 <= upper));

     // Move what is left of remaining list.

     if (s1 > middle)
         do
         {
             destination[d] = source[s2];
             ++s2;
             ++d;
         } while (s2 <= upper);
     else
         do
         {
             destination[d] = source[s1];
             ++s1;
             ++d;
         } while (s1 <= middle);
}
```

Clearly **merge** is an *O*(*n*) algorithm where *n* is the number of items in the two lists to be merged. A question remains: How can **merge** be used to actually sort an entire array? To answer this, we need another function called **order** that will take the values in indices **lower** through **upper** of an array source and arrange them in ascending order in subscripts **lower** through **upper** of another array called **destination**. Notice that **order** is itself almost a sorting function except that it produces a sorted list in a second array instead of actually transforming the array it originally receives. Our use of **order** will be to obtain two sorted half-length sequences from our original array.

Then we will use the **merge** function we have already developed to merge the two sorted half-length sequences back into the original array. Of course, this merely defers our original question of how to use **merge** to sort because now we are faced with the question of how **order** will be able to produce two sorted half-length sequences. Here is where recursion enters the picture. To produce a sorted half-length sequence, we use **order** to produce two sorted quarter-length sequences and apply **merge** to the results. Similarly, the quarter-length sequences are produced by calling on **order** to produce sorted eighth-length sequences and applying **merge** to the results. The recursive termination condition for this descent into shorter and shorter ordered sequences occurs when **order** receives a sequence of length 1.

Given the crucial **order** function, the **merge_sort** function itself is almost trivial. It need merely create a copy of the array to be sorted and then call on **order** to sort the elements of the copy into the original. Note that, because **order** continually calls on **merge** and **merge** cannot do its work within one array, the need to create a copy of the original array is unavoidable. Complete C++ versions of **merge_sort** and **order** follow:

```cpp
void merge_sort(list_type list, int n)
{
        list_type list_copy;

        for (int k = 0; k < n; ++k)                 // Make copy for call to order.
                list_copy[k] = list[k];
        order(list_copy, list, 0, n - 1);
}


// Function: order
// Transfer source in ascending order to destination,
// between indices lower...upper.
//
// Inputs: source and destination, two arrays that are
// initially identical between indices lower...upper.
// Outputs: destination arranged in order between lower and upper.

void order(list_type source, list_type destination, int lower, int upper)
{
        int middle;

        if (lower != upper)
        {
```

```
        middle = (lower + upper) / 2;
        order(destination, source, lower, middle);
        order(destination, source, middle + 1, upper);
        merge(source, destination, lower, middle, upper);
    }
}
```

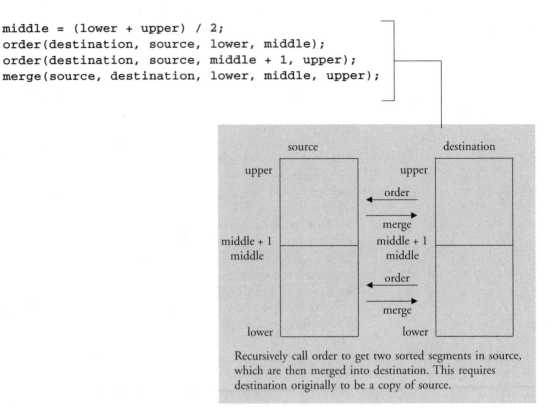

Recursively call order to get two sorted segments in source, which are then merged into destination. This requires destination originally to be a copy of source.

The run-time trace diagram of function calls in Figure 18.5 highlights the interaction between **order** and **merge** triggered by calling **merge_sort** with a sample array of size **n** = 11. The leaf nodes in this trace diagram represent the recursive termination condition reached when **lower = upper**.

Analysis of the Merge Sort

From a run-time trace of function calls such as that appearing in Figure 18.5, it is quite easy to deduce that merge sort requires $O(n \log_2 n)$ comparisons. The reasoning required for this deduction is as follows. All the merge operations across any given level of the trace diagram will require $O(n)$ comparisons. There are $O(\log_2 n)$ levels to the trace diagram. Hence, the overall efficiency is the product $O(n \log_2 n)$. Notice that, like the heap sort, the merge sort can guarantee this efficiency regardless of the original data. That is, there is no worst case that can cause its efficiency to deteriorate (as there is for quick sort).

The price paid for using merge sort is in the memory space it requires. Of course, there is the stack space associated with recursion. More important, however, is the need for a duplicate copy of the array being sorted. In applications where the original array barely fits in memory, this space requirement will make merge sort totally impractical.

As steep as the memory price is, there is an added benefit to merge sort that makes it the only possible choice for certain applications: Merge sort may be written in a way that necessitates only sequential access to the lists being manipulated. As we have presented it here, random access is required at only one point in the algorithm, namely, in the **merge** function to access the second list beginning at subscript (**middle + 1**) of **source**. The need for this could have

◆ FIGURE 18.5
Run-time trace of function
calls to **order** and
merge

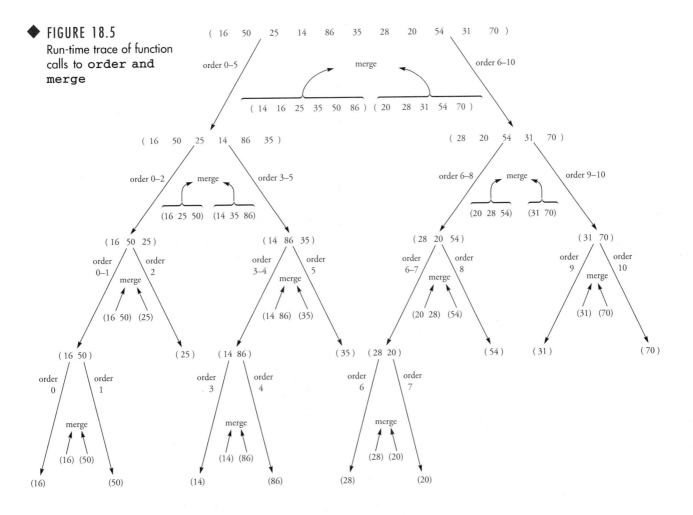

been eliminated by having **merge** work with two separate source arrays. That is, we would merge ordered arrays **source1** and **source2** into **destination.** This would be very costly with arrays since it would necessitate using three arrays to sort one array. However, it is less costly when the lists being manipulated are being implemented not by arrays but rather by dynamically allocated linked lists or sequential files. In both of these latter situations, the need to use sequential access would make the merge sort strategy the only appropriate sorting method. In the exercises at the end of the section and the programming problems at the end of the chapter, you will be asked to adapt **merge_sort** to such sequential implementations of a list. In particular, when the list exists in a file instead of main memory, the sorting method employed is said to be an *external sort* (as opposed to the *internal sorts* we have studied in this chapter).

EXERCISES 18.4

1. Consider the **merge_sort** function given in this section. Note that this function contains a subordinate function called **order.** Suppose that we were to insert the following tracer output at the beginning of the **order** function.

```
cout << lower << " " << upper << endl;
for (int k = lower; k < upper; ++k)
        cout << source[k] << " ";
cout << endl;
```

What would we see as output from these tracers if we were to call on **merge_sort** with an array that initially contained the following?:

60 12 90 30 64 8 6

2. Repeat Exercise 1 for a six-element array that initially contains

1 8 2 7 3 6

3. Implement **merge_sort** in a nonrecursive fashion.

4. In Chapter 11, **pointer_sort** used an index of pointers to sort data logically without rearranging it. Adapt the pointer sort function to the merge sort algorithm.

5. Identify and give an example of best case and worst case data sets for the merge sort algorithm. Explain why your data sets generate best and worst case performance.

6. A sorting method is said to be stable if two data items of matching value are guaranteed not to be rearranged with respect to each other as the algorithm progresses. For example, in the four-element array

60 42_1 80 42_2

a stable sorting method would guarantee a final ordering of

42_1 42_2 60 80

Classify each of the sorting algorithms studied in this chapter and in Chapter 11 as to their stability. (To see why stability may be important, consider Programming Problems 5 and 9 at the end of this chapter.)

7. You are to sort an array in a program in which the following considerations are to be taken into account. First, there is a large amount of data to be sorted. The amount of data to be sorted is so large that frequent $O(n^2)$ run times will prove unsatisfactory. The amount of data will also make it impossible for your program to use a large amount of overhead data (for example, stack space) to make the sort efficient in its run time. This is because the space required by the overhead data would potentially take up space needed by the array to be sorted. Second, you are told that the array to be sorted is often nearly in order to start with. For each of the seven sorting methods indicated, specify whether or not that method would be appropriate for this application and, in a brief statement, explain why your answer is correct.

a. bubble sort

b. insertion sort

c. selection sort

d. shell sort

e. quick sort

f. heap sort

g. merge sort

FOCUS ON PROGRAM DESIGN

We have stressed repeatedly that analysis of algorithms combines formal mathematical techniques with experimental methodology. Certainly, nowhere is this better illustrated than in the analysis of sorting algorithms. For instance, among the four algorithms studied in this chapter, only two—heap sort and merge sort—can be placed with certainty in the $O(n \log_2 n)$ category by purely mathematical analysis. The other two—shell sort and qick sort—are apparently much more dependent on the original arrangement of the data being sorted.

Public-Key Cryptography

The manner in which computers can sort through and in other ways manipulate information gives rise to concern over the security of electronic information. Cryptography is the science of encoding information to protect it from being viewed by unauthorized parties. Today, as an increasing amount of sensitive information is being transmitted in electronic and magnetic form, cryptography is becoming an increasingly important field.

A conventional encryption system works much like a mailbox with a combination lock. Anyone knowing the combination can open the box to leave a message or to read any of the messages in the box. In computerized information systems, the "combination" to the mailbox is a digital key; that is, a particular bit pattern that is applied to an electronic message to encode or decode it. In conventional systems, anyone knowing the digital key has access to the information in the electronic mailbox. Hence such systems are best suited to a small number of users and not to the networking of information among many computer installations that is possible with today's technology.

An interesting development in cryptography occurred in the early 1970s with the development of a theory for public-key encryption systems. Such systems work on two different digital keys: one for writing information into the electronic mailbox and the other to read encoded information that has been left in the mailbox. As a user of such an encryption system, you could freely give out the write key to your mailbox (the public key), allowing anyone to send you an encoded letter. However, you would keep the read key (the decoding key) secret so that only you would be able to make sense out of your mail.

The best known public-key encryption scheme is known as the RSA algorithm (after Rivest, Shamir, and Adleman, the mathematicians who developed it). This algorithm is based on the difficulty of factoring large numbers that are the product of two prime numbers. For instance, the number 51 = 3 × 17 would satisfy this criterion except that it is not nearly large enough.

In the RSA system, the product of the two prime factors would be linked to your public key. However, this public key would include only the product, not the prime factors that comprise the product. Your private key would include each of the individual prime factors. Why should such numbers be large? The answer to this question lies in the present limitations of the area of mathematics known as number theory. It turns out that, given the product of two such prime factors without being told the factors themselves, number theory provides no known way of factoring the number into its prime factors in a reasonable amount of time, even using the most advanced supercomputers. From a security perspective, this means that your code could not be broken by outside agencies, even if they were using a computer to assist them.

The role of public-key cryptography in electronic data systems will no doubt become increasingly important in the future. For an excellent discussion of the method and some of the social concerns arising from it, you may want to read the article "Encryption: Technology, Privacy, and National Security," by Tom Athanasiou in *Technology Review* (August/September 1986):57–66. A very readable description of the RSA and other encryption algorithms is presented in "Cloak and Dagger" by Rick Grehan in the June 1990 issue of *Byte* magazine (Volume 15, No. 6: 311–324).

In this section, we present components of a program whose structure facilitates experimentation with a sorting algorithm. In particular, our program will be useful in the exploration of the shell sort algorithm. However, the underlying structure of the program makes it easy to incorporate other sorting algorithms. All that must be altered is the function that implements the particular sorting algorithm being studied. This function must not only do the sorting, but also profile the algorithm in the sense described in Chapter 11. All the other modules in the program are geared toward construction of an environment in which you can experiment with the sorting algorithm. These modules remain the same regardless of which sorting algorithm is chosen.

Input to the program is the list of integers to be sorted. This input may be provided in one of three forms:

1. A randomly generated permutation of the integers from **1, 2, 3, . . . size - 1, size** where **size** is the logical size of the list being sorted.

Recall that a permutation is an arrangement of the integers in which no repetitions occur.

2. A list of integers entered interactively, allowing input of particular data sets for which you want to profile the sorting algorithm.

3. A list of integers read one per line from a text file.

This final form of input, coupled with the program's ability to save a particular data set in a text file format that can later be read, allows you to fine-tune the sorting algorithm for data sets that prove particularly interesting from an efficiency perspective. That is, if you encounter a randomly generated or interactively input data set for which the efficiency of the sort algorithm seems to deteriorate, you can save that data set in a text file. Then you can adjust the sort algorithm to allow for the characteristics of that data set and rerun the program, loading the saved data set to see if your adjustments made a substantial improvement. This mode of experimental use of the program is illustrated in the following sample runs:

First run:

```
        1 - Load a random array
        2 - Interactively load an array
        3 - Load array from previous round

        Enter 1, 2, or 3 —>1

        Enter the number of values —>10
        Do you want to see the array? (Y/N) —>y

ARRAY[0] =      1
ARRAY[1] =      3
ARRAY[2] =      2
ARRAY[3] =      4
ARRAY[4] =      5
ARRAY[5] =      8
ARRAY[6] =      6
ARRAY[7] =      9
ARRAY[8] =      7
ARRAY[9] =      10


Sort required 51 loop iteration(s).
Sort required 4 swap(s) of data.
Sort required 78 comparison(s).

Do you want to see the array after sorting? (Y/N) —>y

ARRAY[0]  = 1
ARRAY[1]  = 2
ARRAY[2]  = 3
ARRAY[3]  = 4
ARRAY[4]  = 5
ARRAY[5]  = 6
ARRAY[6]  = 7
ARRAY[7]  = 8
ARRAY[8]  = 9
ARRAY[9]  = 10
```

```
Save this list for another run? (Y/N) —>y
Name for save file —>test.dat
Another Shell Sort? (Y/N) —>n
```

Then fine-tune the program to improve efficiency, and run again.

Second run:

```
                1 - Load a random array
                2 - Interactively load an array
                3 - Load array from previous round

                Enter 1, 2, or 3 —>3

                Enter the name of the file —>test.dat
                Do you want to see the array? (Y/N) —>y
```

```
ARRAY[0] =      1
ARRAY[1] =      3
ARRAY[2] =      2
ARRAY[3] =      4
ARRAY[4] =      5
ARRAY[5] =      8
ARRAY[6] =      6
ARRAY[7] =      9
ARRAY[8] =      7
ARRAY[9] =      10
```

```
Sort required 42 loop iteration(s).
Sort required 4 swap(s) of data.
Sort required 61 comparisons(s).

Do you want to see the array after sorting? (Y/N) —>n
Save this list for another run? (Y/N) —>n
Another Shell Sort? (Y/N) —>n
```

Notice how the profiling output gives evidence of the improved efficiency of the second run.

The modular structure chart for our program is given in Figure 18.6. Modular specifications and a partial program listing follow. In the programming problems at the end of the chapter, you will be asked to complete the program and then use it in various forms of exploration with the shell sort. You will also be asked to incorporate the design of the program into a vehicle for exploring other sorting algorithms.

A first-level pseudocode development for the main program is

Initialize the random number generator (if necessary—see Appendix 6)
Do
                Initialize the global profiling counters.
                Load the array by user-chosen method. Also return a duplicate copy of the array for potential saving in a file.
                Print the array if user wants to see it.
                Apply shell sort to the array.
                Output the global profiling counters.
                Print the sorted array if the user wants to see it.

◆ FIGURE 18.6

Modular structure chart for
Shell experimentation program

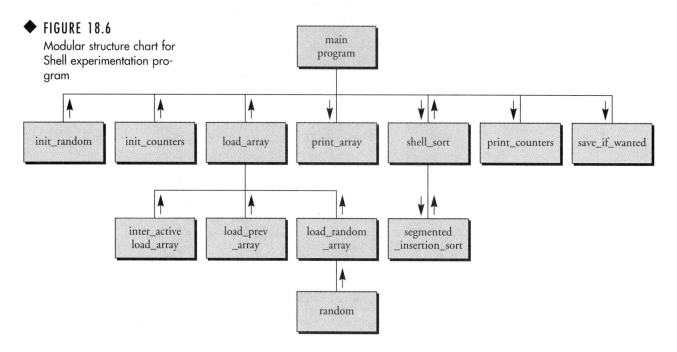

Save the copy of the original array if the user wants to.
Inquire if the user wants to shell sort another array.
While user indicates more sorts.

Modular specifications corresponding to the modular structure chart of Figure 18.6 are as follows:

Module: init_random
Task: Initialize the random number generator as described in Appendix 6. May be unnecessary if your version of C++ provides a random number generator.

Module: init_counters
Task: Obvious.
Inputs: Profiling counters as global variables—for number of comparisons, number of swaps, and number of loop iterations.
Outputs: Profiling counters set to zero.

Module: load_array
Task: Inquire about method for loading and then call on one of interactive-_load_array, load_prev_array, or load_random_array.
Outputs: The array to be sorted, a copy of that array for potential saving, number of values in array, integer indicating user choice for loading array: 1 for random permutation, 2 for interactive, 3 for file.

Module: interactive_load_array
Task: Inquire as to number of values. Then iterate through interactive input of that many values.
Outputs: Number of values in array, array to sort, and copy of that array for potential saving in file.

Module: load_prev_array
Task: Inquire as to name of file where array is stored. Then use while not eof loop to read data from file into array.

Outputs: Number of values in array, array to sort, and copy of that array for potential saving in file.

Module: random_load_array

Task: Inquire as to size of array. Generate a random permutation of the values 1, 2, . . ., size. There are several algorithms to do this. We leave it for you to discover one in the programming problems.

Outputs: Number of values in array, array to sort, and copy of that array for potential saving in file.

Module: random

Task: Use algorithm in Appendix 6 or random number generator provided with your version of C++.

Outputs: Randomly generated value.

Module: print_array

Task: Iterate through output of each array value.

Inputs: Array and its logical size.

Modules: shell_sort and segmented_insertion_sort

Task: See Section 18.1.

Inputs: Array of values and its logical size.

Outputs: Array sorted in ascending order.

Module: print_counters

Task: Print profiling counters to report on efficiency of algorithm for data set just sorted.

Inputs: Global profiling counters.

Module: save_if_wanted

Task: Inquire if user wants to save this list for further exploration. If user wants to save and list not originally loaded from file, write array to file in form compatible with load_prev_array module.

Inputs: Copy of original array, logical size of that array, integer indicating how user loaded array.

A partial program listing follows:

```
// Program file: focus.cpp

// This program allows the user to experiment with the shell_sort
// algorithm on a variety of different arrays of data.  The sort
// algorithm has been augmented to keep track of the number of
// swaps, comparisons, and loop iterations necessary to sort the
// current array. These can be used as a measure of comparison
// among various initial data arrays or among different sorting
// methods.  This method of measuring the amount of work required
// to sort the array is used because standard C++ has no built-in
// method of timing program execution.


// The data file created by the program when an array is saved is
// simply a text file with one element of the array per line of the
// file. Similarly, the program expects any file from which it is to
// read an array to have this format.


#include <iostream.h>
#include <fstream.h>
```

```
#include "strlib.h"
#include "random.h"
#include "boolean.h"

const int MAX_LIST_SIZE = 500;

typedef int element;
typedef element list_type[MAX_LIST_SIZE];

// File streams for loading and saving array contents to files.

ifstream input_file;
ofstream output_file;

// Global counters for measuring work required to sort data in array.

int num_iterations;
int num_swaps;
int num_comparisons;

// Function: save_if_wanted
// Write the array out to a file if the user indicates
// that he wants to save it for future runs.  The file
// handling may require modification on some systems.
//
// Inputs: Array to save, size of array, type of load performed.

void save_if_wanted(list_type list, int length, int choice_of_load);

// Function: load_array
// Determine which method the user wants to use to
// load the array of data and call the appropriate function.
//
// Outputs: Both arrays, the size of the arrays, and the
// user's selection of type of load to be performed.

void load_array(list_type list, list_type list_copy, int &length,
     int &choice_of_load);

// Function: load_prev_array
// Open the file containing the previous array the
// user desires to use, read the data into the
// array, and make a copy of the array.  The file
// handling may require modification on some systems.
//
// Outputs: Both arrays along with their size.

void load_prev_array(list_type list, list_type list_copy, int &length);

// Function: interactive_load_array
// Prompt user to input data for the array, read it in, and make a copy of it.
//
// Outputs: both arrays along with their size.
```

```
void interactive_load_array(list_type list, list_type list_copy, int &length);

// Function: load_random_array
// Fill the array with a randomly generated permutation of the integers
// between 1...length, and then make a copy of the array.
//
// Outputs: both arrays along with their size.

void load_random_array(list_type list, list_type list_copy, int &length);

// Function: print_array
// Print the contents of the specified range of the array to the terminal.
//
// Inputs: Array of data, low and high ends of the range of indices of the array
// to be printed.

void print_array(list_type list, int low, int high);

void init_counters();

void print_counters();

void shell_sort(list_type list, int n);

void segmented_insertion_sort(list_type list, int n, int k);

int main()
{
    list_type list, list_copy;      // Lists of data
    int length;                     // Logical size of list
    char query;                     // User's response
    int choice_of_load;             // User's choice for loading array
    random_generator generator;     // Set up random number generator

    do
    {
        init_counters();
        load_array(list, list_copy, length, choice_of_load);
        cout << "Do you want to see the array? (Y/N) -> ";
        cin >> query;
        if ((query == 'Y') || (query == 'y'))
                print_array(list, 0, length);
            shell_sort(list, length);
            print_counters();
            cout << "Do you want to see the array after sorting? (Y/N) -> ";
            cin >> query;
            if ((query == 'Y') || (query == 'y'))
                print_array(list, 0, length);
            save_if_wanted(list_copy, length, choice_of_load);
            cout << "Another Shell Sort? (Y/N) -> ";
            cin >> query;
    } while ((query == 'Y') || (query == 'y'));
    return 0;
}
```

```
void save_if_wanted(list_type list, int length, int choice_of_load)
{
}

void load_array(list_type list, list_type list_copy, int &length, int &choice_of_load)
{
        boolean valid;

        do
        {
                cout << endl << endl << endl;
                cout << " 1 - Load a random array" << endl;
                cout << " 2 - Interactively load an array" << endl;
                cout << " 3 - Load array from previous round" << endl;
                cout << endl;
                cout << " Enter 1, 2, or 3 -> ";
                cin >> choice_of_load;
                valid = (choice_of_load > 0) && (choice_of_load < 4);
                if (valid)
                        switch (choice_of_load)
                        {
                                case 1:     load_random_array(list, list_copy, length);
                                            break;
                                case 2:     interactive_load_array(list, list_copy,
                                            length); break;
                                case 3:     load_prev_array(list, list_copy, length);
                                            break;
                                default:    cout << choice_of_load << " is not a valid "
                                                 << "response - try again" << endl;
                        }
        } while (! valid);
}

void load_prev_array(list_type list, list_type list_copy, int &length)
{
}

void print_array(list_type list, int low, int high)
{
}

void init_counters()
{
        num_iterations = 0;
        num_swaps = 0;
        num_comparisons = 0;
}

void print_counters()
{
```

```
        cout << endl;
        cout << "Sort required " << num_iterations << " loop iteration(s)." << endl;
        cout << "Sort required " << num_swaps << " swap(s) of data." << endl;
        cout << "Sort required " << num_comparisons << " comparison(s)." << endl;
        cout << endl;
}

void shell_sort(list_type list, int n)
{
        int k = n / 2;

        ++num_comparisons;                                      // Efficiency stats
        while (k > 0)
        {
                ++num_iterations;                               // Efficiency stats
                segmented_insertion_sort(list, n, k);
                k = k / 2;
                ++num_comparisons;                              // Efficiency stats
        }
}

void segmented_insertion_sort(list_type list, int n, int k)
{
        int j;
        element item_to_insert;
        boolean still_looking;
        for (int i = k; i < n; ++i)
        {
                ++num_iterations;                               // Efficiency stats
                item_to_insert = list[i];
                j = i - k;
                still_looking = TRUE;
                ++num_comparisons;                              // Efficiency stats
                while ((j >= 0) && still_looking)
                {
                        ++num_iterations;                       // Efficiency stats
                        ++num_comparisons;
                        if (item_to_insert < list[j])
                        {
                                list[j + k] = list[j];
                                ++num_swaps;                    // Efficiency stats
                                j = j - k;
                        }
                        else
                                still_looking = FALSE;
                        ++num_comparisons;                      // Efficiency stats
                }
                list[j + k] = item_to_insert;
        }
}
```

RUNNING, DEBUGGING AND TESTING HINTS

1. To describe and understand the more complex sort algorithms, it is helpful to present them via subordinate algorithms and stepwise refinement. To this end, we have found it convenient initially to focus on subalgorithms (`segmented_insertion_sort` for `shell_sort`, `partition` for `quick_sort`, `walk_down` for `heap_sort`, and `merge` for `merge_sort`). Our method is illustrative of the stepwise refinement approach to problem solving: Break a complex problem down into smaller problems, solve these smaller problems, and then tie their solutions together to solve the original large problem.

2. Describing and understanding algorithms is a separate issue from their actual implementation in a specific programming language and on a real machine. One implication of this separation of algorithm description and algorithm implementation is the run-time cost associated with a function call. We must consider the hidden costs of making a function call and how deeply embedded the function call is in the iterative structure of the calling module.

3. Depending on the machine you are using, calling a function instead of directly inserting the code necessary may mean that your program spends more run-time handling the hidden cost of function calls than it does actually interchanging data items. If large data sets are being sorted and if run-time efficiency is of primary importance, then we should implement our algorithm without actually calling on a function.

4. Keep in mind the distinction between algorithm description and algorithm implementation when making decisions about whether or not to proceduralize a given sequence of instructions. What may be appropriately isolated as a trivial subalgorithm at the time when a designer is concerned with describing an algorithm may carry with it a steep price if implemented as a trivial function that is called on many times when the resulting program is put into use.

5. In making the decision whether to use functions or in-line code when implementing an algorithm, carefully weigh run-time considerations with respect to the clarity and readability of code. A useful rule of thumb is that only in exceptional circumstances should the code associated with a module exceed one printed page in length. This guideline allows in-line insertion of code for simple algorithmic units and assures that the overall software system does not become unwieldy.

SUMMARY

Key Terms

diminishing increment sort	merge sort	quick sort
external sort	partition	relatively prime
heap sort	pivot	shell sort
internal sort		

Key Concepts

◆ This chapter has added four sorting algorithms to those already presented in Chapter 11. This gives us a large variety of tools from which to choose when we need to perform a sorting job.

◆ The following comparison table summarizes the pros and cons of each sorting method we've covered.

Sorting Method	Chapter	Number of Comparisons in Terms of the Number of Data Items Being Sorted (n)	Space Requirement	Additional Comments
Binary tree	16	Between $O(n^2)$ and $O(n \log_2 n)$ depending on original data and whether tree height-balanced	Pointers for tree and possible stack space for recursive traversals	
Bubble	10	$O(n2)$	No additional overhead	Loop check allows early exit as soon as array is ordered.
Heap	17	$O(n \log_2 n)$	No additional overhead	
Insertion	10	$O(n^2)$	No additional overhead	Loop check allows early exit as soon as item is correctly placed.
Merge	17	$O(n \log_2 n)$	Requires duplicate array and stack space for recursion	Since only requires sequential access, can be used for linked lists and sequential files.
Pointer	10	Depends on method with which it is combined	Required list of pointers to maintain logical order	Can be combined with any method to substantially reduce size of data items being interchanged.
Quick	17	$O(n \log_2 n)$ on the average but $O(n^2)$ for worst cases	Stack space for recursion	
Radix	10, 13	$O(n)$	Space for bins	Though $O(n)$, large constant of proportionality. Not generalizable to all types of data, for example, real numbers.
Selection	10	$O(n^2)$	No additional overhead	
Shell	17	Between $O[n(\log_2 n)^2]$ and $O(n^{1.5})$ depending on increments used	No additional overhead	

PROGRAMMING PROBLEMS AND PROJECTS

1. Complete the partial program presented in this chapter's Focus on Program Design section. Then use the completed program to explore empirically the shell sort algorithm. In particular, experiment with different sequences of diminishing increments.

   Write a report on your exploration. In your report you should compare various sequences of diminishing increments and rate them as to their performance on a variety of data sets.

2. Modify the shell sort so that it employs bubble sort logic on segments instead of insertion sort. Incorporate this change into the program presented in this chapter's Focus on Program Design section. Compare the observed efficiency of this new version of shell sort with the original on a variety of data sets. Which performs better? Explain your answer in a carefully written statement.

3. Modify the program presented in this chapter's Focus on Program Design section so that it becomes an experimental tool for quick sort, heap sort, or merge sort. Then

use the modified program to conduct an experiment similar to the one you did for shell sort in Problem 1. For instance, for Quick Sort, you could experiment with the selection of a pivot element or try invoking insertion sort when the size of the array segment to be partitioned becomes sufficiently small. Whatever experimentation you choose to do, write a report on your exploration. In your report, draw conclusions about the efficiencies of various strategies. Support your conclusions with empirical data obtained from your exploratory runs.

4. Given a sequential file containing an unordered list of passengers and their flight numbers for Wing-and-a-Prayer Airlines (Problem 2, Chapter 14; Problems 3 and 12, Chapter 17), produce a listing arranged in flight-number order. Passengers on the same flight should be ordered by last name. The easy version of this program assumes that all information will fit in memory, allowing the use of an internal sort. For an added challenge, write the program using an external sort algorithm. (*Hint:* Adapt **merge_sort** along the lines discussed in the text.)

5. The Bay Area Brawlers professional football team (Problem 4, Chapter 14; Problem 5, Chapter 17) has stored the records of all the players who have played on the team during the history of the team. One player's record consists of

Name

Total points scored

Number of touchdowns

Number of field goals

Number of safeties

Number of extra points

Write a program that lists players in order from the highest scores in the team's history down to the lowest. Those players who have scored the same number of points should then be arranged in alphabetical order.

6. Take n randomly generated integers. Now apply a bubble sort, a shell sort, a quick sort, a heap sort, and a merge sort. Observe, compare, and plot their execution time for $n = 100$; $n = 1,000$; $n = 10,000$; $n = 100,000, \ldots$.

7. Put some hypothetical data in an external file and apply a modified merge sort to them.

8. Write a C++ program to complete the following steps:

- Artificially create a file with a large number of randomly chosen names.
- Read into an array all names that begin with A through some letter, say, G, chosen so that all the names will fit in the array.
- Sort this array with one of the sorting algorithms from this chapter and store this sorted array into another file.
- Now read into the array all those names from the file which begin with H through another appropriate letter.
- Sort the array and append it to the end of the new file.

Repeat this process until all names from the original file have been processed. The new file will be the sorted version of the original. Observe the execution time of your program. Analyze its efficiency in big-O terms.

9. Consider a list of records, each containing four fields:

Name

Month of birth

Day of birth

Year of birth

Write a program to sort this list in oldest-to-youngest order. People with the same birth date should be arranged alphabetically. One strategy you could employ would be to concatenate strategically the four fields into one, and then sort just that one field. Another strategy would be to sort the list four times, each time by a different field. (Think carefully about which field to sort first.) Which of the strategies would require that you choose a stable sorting algorithm? (See Exercise 7 in Section 18.4.)

10. Modify `merge_sort` so that it will sort a linked list instead of an array.

CHAPTER 19 More Powerful Search Methods

I do not search, I find.
Pablo Picasso

In earlier chapters, we analyzed three methods of searching for items within a list: sequential search, binary search, and binary search tree. The sequential search, though easy to implement and applicable to short lists, is limited in many practical situations by its $O(n)$ search efficiency. The binary search offers a much faster $O(\log_2 n)$ search efficiency but also has limitations. Foremost among these limitations are the need to maintain the list in physically contiguous order and the need to maintain a count of the number of records in the list. Both of these limitations are particularly restrictive for volatile lists; that is, lists in which insertions and deletions are frequently made. In Chapter 17, a binary search tree emerged as offering the best of both worlds. Insertions and deletions can be done on a binary search tree by merely manipulating pointers instead of moving data, and an $O(\log_2 n)$ search efficiency can be achieved if the tree remains close to full. Unfortunately, to guarantee that the tree remains nearly full and hence ensure the $O(\log_2 n)$ efficiency, a sophisticated technique known as height balancing (see Chapter 17) is required. The complications involved in implementing this technique frequently dictate that it not be used. Essentially, you must weigh the significant cost in development time to implement a height-balanced tree against the risk that the order in which data arrive for insertion may cause search efficiency to deteriorate from $O(\log_2 n)$ to $O(n)$. If data items arrive in a relatively random order, then taking that risk may well be the prudent choice.

The efficiency of all three of these techniques is dependent on the number of items in the list being searched. In this chapter, we shall study another alternative, called *hashing*. Its efficiency is measurable in terms of the amount of storage you are willing to waste. In this sense, hashing can achieve phenomenally fast search times regardless of how much data you have, provided that you can afford to keep a relatively large amount of unused list space available.

We shall also explore some of the special considerations that enter into searching for data stored in a disk file instead of main memory. These considerations lead to a variety of search schemes, all of which employ some variation of a data structure known as an *index*.

19.1 Density-Dependent Search Techniques

In an ideal data processing world, all identifying keys such as product codes, Social Security numbers, and so on, would start at 0 and follow in sequence thereafter. Then, in any given list, we would merely store the key and its associated data at the position that matched the key. The search efficiency for any key in such a list would be one access to the list, and all data processors could live happily ever after! Unfortunately, in the real world, users (not being concerned with the happiness of data processing personnel) desire keys that consist of more meaningful characters, such as names, addresses, region codes, and so on. For instance, it may be that in a given inventory-control application, product codes are numbered in sequence beginning with 10,000 instead of 0. A moment's reflection should indicate that this is still a highly desirable situation since, given a key, we need merely locate the key at position

```
key_value - 10000
```

in the list, and we still have a search efficiency of 1. What we have done here is to define what is known as a *key-to-address transformation,* or *hashing function.* The idea behind a hashing function is that it acts on a given key in such a way as to return the relative position in the list where we expect to find the key.

Most hashing functions are not as straightforward as the preceding one and present some additional complications that we can quickly illustrate. Suppose we use the following hashing function:

```
hash(key_value) = key_value % 4
```

Then the set of keys 3, 5, 8, and 10 will be scattered as illustrated here.

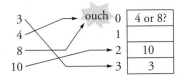

However, if we happen to have 3, 4, 8, and 10 as keys instead of 3, 5, 8, and 10, a problem arises: 4 and 8 hash to the same position. They are said to be *synonyms,* and the result is termed a *collision.* This situation, here a collision at position 0, is shown in the following illustration.

Clearly, one of the goals of the hashing functions we develop should be to reduce the number of collisions as much as possible.

The Construction of Hashing Functions

The business of developing hashing functions can be quite intriguing. The essential idea is to build a mathematical black box that will take a key value as input and issue as output the position in the list where that key value should be located. The position emitted should have a minimal probability of colliding with the position that would be produced for a different key. In addition, the black box we create must ensure that a given key will always produce the same position as output. You should begin to note a similarity between some of the properties possessed by a good hashing function and a good random number generator such as that used in our simulation case study in Chapter 15. Indeed, list access via a hashing function is sometimes called *randomized storage,* and the first type of hashing function we discuss makes direct use of a random number generator.

Method 1: Use of a Random Number Generator. Many high-level languages provide a random number generator to produce random sequences of real values between 0 and 1. If one is not provided, you may easily write one using a method such as that described in Appendix 6. (For readable discussions of other methods of random number generation, see Chapter 7 of *Numerical Recipes* by William H. Press, Brian P. Flannery, Saul A. Teukolsky, and William T. Vetterling, Cambridge, England: Cambridge University Press, 1986.) Typically, all of these methods rely on having a global seed to start the process of generating random numbers. Computations done on this seed produce the random number. At the same time, the computations alter the value of the seed so that the next time the random number generator is called, a different random number will almost surely be produced.

In typical applications of random number generation, you need merely initialize the seed to some arbitrary value to start the random sequence. Once the seed is supplied, the random sequence is completely determined. If you have access to a system function that returns the current time, day, month, and year, this can be called to initialize the seed in a fashion that ensures there is only a very small likelihood of generating the same random sequence twice.

How does all of this relate to hashing? For a hashing application, we must slightly alter the definition of our random number generator so that the seed is supplied as a value parameter. Then we supply the values of search keys as the seeds. The nature of the random number algorithm ensures that

- Each time the same key is passed to the function, the same random value will be returned.
- It is unlikely that two different keys will yield the same random value.

The random number between 0 and 1 that is correspondingly produced can then be appropriately multiplied, truncated, and shifted to produce a hash value within the range of valid positions.

Method 2: Folding. In situations where the key to be positioned is not a pure integer, some preliminary work may be required to translate it into a usable form. Take, for instance, the case of a Social Security number such as

387 - 58 - 1505

Viewed as one integer, this would cause overflow on many machines. By a method known as *shift folding,* this Social Security number would be viewed as three separate numbers to be added

387

58

+ 1505

producing the result 1950. This result could either be regarded as the hash position itself or, more likely, as a pure integer that now could be further acted on by method 1 or 4 to produce a final hash position in the desired range.

Another often-used folding technique is called *boundary folding*. The idea behind boundary folding is that, at the boundaries between the numbers making up the key under consideration, every other number is reversed before being added to the accumulated total. Applying this method to our Social Security number example, we would have

387

   85 (this number reversed)

+1505

yielding a result of 1977. Clearly, the two methods do not differ by much, and a choice between them must often be made on the basis of some experimentation to determine which will produce more scattered results for a given application.

Regardless of whether shift or boundary folding is used, one of the great advantages of the folding method is its ability to transform noninteger keys into an integer suitable for further hashing action. For keys such as names that contain alphabetic characters, the type of folding just illustrated may be done by translating characters into their ASCII (or other appropriate) codes.

Method 3: Digit or Character Extraction. In certain situations, a given key value may contain specific characters that are likely to bias any hash value arising from the key. The idea in *digit* or *character extraction* is to remove such digits or characters before using the result as a final hash value or passing it on to be further transformed by another method. For instance, a company may choose to identify the various products it manufactures by using a nine-character code that always contains either an A or B in the first position and either a 1 or 0 in the fourth position. The rest of the characters in the code tend to occur in less predictable fashion. Character extraction would remove the biased first and fourth characters, leaving a seven-character result to pass on to further processing.

Method 4: Division-Remainder Technique. All hashing presupposes a given range of positions that can be valid outputs of the hash function. In the remainder of this section, we assume the existence of a global constant `RECORD_SPACE,` which represents the upper limit of our hashing function. That is, the function should produce values between 0 and `RECORD_SPACE -1`. It should than be evident that

```
hash(key_value) = key_value % RECORD_SPACE
```

is a valid hashing function for integer `key_value`.

To begin examining criteria for choosing an appropriate `RECORD_SPACE`, let us load the keys 41, 58, 12, 92, 50, and 91 into a list with `RECORD_SPACE` = 15. Figure 19.1 shows the results. In this array, zeros are used to denote empty positions. However, if we keep `RECORD_SPACE` the same and try to load the keys 10, 20, 30, 40, 50, 60, and 70, we have many collisions, as shown in Figure 19.2.

Hence a different set of keys can cause disastrous results even though the list seemingly has plenty of room available. On the other hand, if we choose `RECORD_SPACE` to be 11, we have a list with considerably less room but no collisions. Figure 19.3 indicates the hashing positions when the same set of keys is acted on by 11 instead of by 15.

Although these examples of the *division-remainder technique* are far from conclusive, they suggest that choosing a prime number for `RECORD_SPACE` may produce a more desirable hashing function. The exercises at the end of this section

◆ FIGURE 19.1

Array with `RECORD_SPACE` = 15 loaded using a division-remainder hashing function

Position	Key
0	0
1	91
2	92
3	0
4	0
5	50
6	0
7	0
8	0
9	0
10	0
11	41
12	12
13	58
14	0

◆ FIGURE 19.2

Array from Figure 19.1, loaded differently, with several collisions

Position	Key			
0	30	← 60	(collision)	
1	0			
2	0			
3	0			
4	0			
5	20	← 50	(collision)	
6	0			
7	0			
8	0			
9	0			
10	10	← 40 ← 70	(collisions)	
11	0			
12	0			
13	0			
14	0			

have you explore this question more deeply. Apart from considerations of whether or not `RECORD_SPACE` should be prime, it is clear that the nature of a particular application may dictate against the choice of certain `RECORD_SPACE` values. For instance, in a situation where the rightmost digits of key values happen to follow certain recurring patterns, it would be unwise to choose a power of 10 for `RECORD_SPACE`. (Why?)

Despite such considerations, a hashing function usually cannot rule out the possibility of collisions; it can only make them less likely. You should quickly be able to imagine a key value that will produce a collision for the hashing function used in determining the list of Figure 19.3. Notice that, as the list becomes more full, the probability that collisions will occur increases. Hence, when using hashing as a search strategy, one must be willing to waste some positions in the list; otherwise search efficiency will drastically deteriorate. How much space to waste is an interesting question that we will soon discuss. Further, since hashing functions

◆ **FIGURE 19.3**

Array with same keys as
Figure 19.2, but with
`RECORD_SPACE = 11`:
no collision results

Position	Key
0	0
1	0
2	0
3	0
4	70
5	60
6	50
7	40
8	30
9	20
10	10

generally cannot eliminate collisions, we must be prepared to handle them when they occur.

Collision Processing

The essential problem in collision processing is to develop an algorithm that will position a key in a list when the position dictated by the hashing function itself is already occupied. Ideally, this algorithm should minimize the possibility of future collisions; that is, the problem key should be located at a position that is not likely to be the hashed position of a future key.

However, the nature of hashing makes this latter criterion difficult to meet with any degree of certainty, since a good hashing function does not allow prediction of where future keys are likely to be placed. We will discuss five methods of collision processing: linear, quadratic, rehashing, linked, and bucket. In all of the methods, it will be necessary to detect when a given list position is not occupied. To signify this, we use a global constant **EMPTY** to distinguish unoccupied positions. As you read, give some thought to the question of how deletions could be processed from a list accessed via one of these hashing methods. In particular, will the **EMPTY** flag suffice to denote positions that have never been occupied *and* positions previously occupied but now vacant? This question is explored in the exercises and in the programming problems at the end of this chapter.

Linear Collision Processing

The linear method of resolving collisions is the simplest to implement (and, unfortunately, the least efficient). *Linear collision processing* requires that, when a collision occurs, we proceed down the list in sequential order until a vacant position is found. The key causing the collision is then placed at this first vacant position. If we come to the physical end of our list in the attempt to place the problem key, we merely wrap around to the top of the list and continue looking for a vacant position. For instance, suppose we use a hashing function of

```
hash(key_value) = key_value % RECORD_SPACE
```

with **RECORD_SPACE** equal to 6. We then attempt to insert the keys 18, 31, 67, 36, 19, and 34. The sequence of lists in Figure 19.4 shows the results of these insertions. When a collision occurs at the third insert, it is processed by the linear method; 67 is thus loaded into position 5.

◆ FIGURE 19.4
Insertion with linear collision
processing

0	0
1	0
2	0
3	0
4	18
5	0
6	0

First
insert
hash(18) = 4

0	0
1	0
2	0
3	31
4	18
5	0
6	0

Second
insert
hash(31) = 3

0	0
1	0
2	0
3	31
4	18
5	67
6	0

Third
insert
hash(67) = 4

0	0
1	36
2	0
3	31
4	18
5	67
6	0

Fourth
insert
hash(36) = 1

0	0
1	36
2	0
3	31
4	18
5	67
6	19

Fifth
insert
hash(19) = 5

0	34
1	36
2	0
3	31
4	18
5	67
6	19

Sixth
insert
hash(34) = 6

EXAMPLE 19.1   Suppose that an array has been loaded with data using the linear collision processing strategy illustrated in Figure 19.4. Write a C++ algorithm to seek a target key in this array.

```
// Function: linear_hash
// Use linear hashing algorithm to search for target.
//
// Inputs: List of objects loaded by linear
// hashing method.
// target, the key of an object to be found.
// Outputs: If key matching target is found,
// return TRUE and the index at the key;
// otherwise; return FALSE.

boolean linear_hash(list_type list, key_type target,
    element &item)
{
    int k = hash(target);
    int j = k;
    boolean traversed = FALSE;
    boolean found = FALSE;

    while (! list[j].empty() && ! (found || traversed))
        if (target == list[j].get_key())
        {
            item = list[j].get_value();
            found = TRUE;
        }
        else
```

```
    {
        j = j % RECORD_SPACE;
        traversed = j == k;
    }
    return found;
}
```

0	419	target = 419
		hash(419) = RECORD_SPACE – 3
.	.	
.	.	
.	.	
RECORD_SPACE – 3	511	Repeated applications of
RECORD_SPACE – 2	312	**else** clause ensure eventual
RECORD_SPACE – 1	705	wraparound to first slot.

Several remarks are in order concerning the function in Example 19.1. First, note that the function as it stands would not handle list processing that requires deletions to be processed. In such a situation, an additional flagging value would be needed to indicate a list position that had once been occupied and is now vacant because of a deletion. Without this distinction, we would not know whether or not to exit the search loop upon encountering an empty slot. You will explore the problem of deletions from a list maintained by hashing in greater detail in the exercises and programming problems. Second, note that the linear method is not without its flaws. In particular, it is prone to a problem known as *clustering*. Clustering occurs when a collision processing strategy relocates keys that have a collision at the same initial hashing position to the same region (known as a cluster) within the storage space. This usually leads to further collisions with other relocated values until everything is resolved. With linear collision processing, the clustering problem is compounded because, as one cluster expands, it can run into another cluster, immediately creating a larger cluster. This one large cluster ultimately causes collision resolutions to be drawn out longer than they would otherwise be. Hence, linear hashing is more likely to result in the clustering phenomenon pictured in Figure 19.5 than the other methods we discuss.

Efficiency Considerations for Linear Hashing. A final point to note about the linear hashing method is its search efficiency. Knuth has shown that the average number of list accesses for a successful search using the linear method is

$$(1/2) * [1 + 1/(1 - D)]$$

where

```
D = (number of currently active records)/RECORD_SPACE
```

(See Donald E. Knuth, *Searching and Sorting,* Volume 3 of *The Art of Computer Programming,* Menlo Park, Calif.: Addison-Wesley, 1973.) An interesting fact about this search efficiency is that it is not solely dependent on the number of records in the list but rather on the density ratio of the number of records currently in the list

◆ FIGURE 19.5

Clustering due to biased
hashing function and linear
processing

Suppose keys 160, 204, 219, 119, 412, 390, and 263 are located with

hash(160) = 37
hash(204) = 37
hash(219) = 37
hash(119) = 38
hash(412) = 38
hash(390) = 38
hash(263) = 39

If a linear method were not used, these keys would not necessarily cluster in positions 37– 43.

divided by the total record space available. In other words, no matter how many records there are, a highly efficient result can be obtained if one is willing to waste enough vacant records. This is what is meant by a *density-dependent search technique.* In the case of searching for a key that cannot be found, Knuth's results indicate that the average search efficiency will be

$$(1/2) * [1 + 1/(1 - D)^2]$$

Table 19.1 illustrates the effectiveness of linear collision resolution by showing the computed efficiencies for a few strategic values of *D*.

Quadratic and Rehashing Methods of Collision Processing

Both the *quadratic* and *rehashing collision processing methods* attempt to correct the problem of clustering. They force the problem-causing key to immediately move a considerable distance from the initial collision. By the rehashing method, an entire sequence of hashing functions may be applied to a given key. If a collision results

◇ TABLE 19.1

Average search efficiency
for linear collision
processing

D	Efficiency for Successful Search (number of accesses)	Efficiency for Unsuccessful Search (number of accesses)
0.10	1.06	1.18
0.50	1.50	2.50
0.75	2.50	8.50
0.90	5.50	50.50

from the first hashing function, a second is applied, then a third, and so on, until the key can be successfully placed.

The quadratic method has the advantage of not requiring numerous hashing functions for its implementation. Suppose that a key value initially hashes to position k and a collision results. Then, on its first attempt to resolve the collision, the quadratic algorithm attempts to place the key at position

$$k + 1^2$$

Then, if a second attempt is necessary to resolve the collision, position

$$k + 2^2$$

is probed. In general, the rth attempt to resolve the collision probes position

$$k + r^2$$

(with wraparound taken into account). Figure 19.6 highlights this scattering pattern. At this point you should verify that, if the hashing function

```
hash(key_value) = key_value % RECORD_SPACE
```

is used with `RECORD_SPACE` equal to 7, the keys 17, 73, 32, and 80 will be located in positions 3, 4, 5, and 0 respectively.

Efficiency Considerations for the Quadratic and Rehashing Methods. Knuth's results (see *Searching and Sorting,* cited earlier in this section) demonstrate the effectiveness of the rehashing and quadratic methods versus the linear method. For the quadratic method, average search efficiencies improve to

$$1 - \log_e(1 - D) - (D/2)$$

FIGURE 19.6
Quadratic collision processing

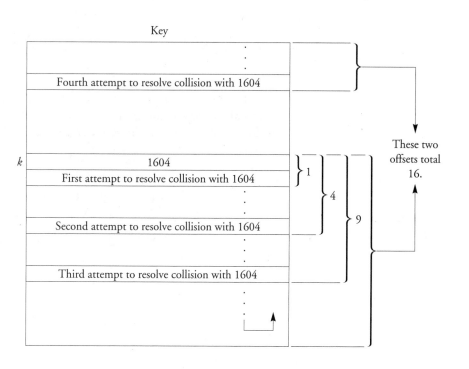

for the successful case and

$$1/(1 - D) - D - \log_e(1 - D)$$

for an unsuccessful search, where D is density ratio as defined earlier in this section and e is the base for the natural logarithm function.

Rehashing with a completely random sequence of rehashing locations for each key slightly improves the efficiencies of the quadratic method to

$$-(1/D) * \log_e(1 - D)$$

for the successful case and

$$1/(1 - D)$$

for an unsuccessful search. Compare the numbers presented in Table 19.2 for quadratic collision processing and (ideal) random rehashing to those in Table 19.1 for linear collision processing.

You may have surmised that the increased efficiency of the quadratic method entails at least some drawbacks. First, the computation of a position to be probed when a collision occurs is somewhat more obscure than it was with the linear method. We leave it for you to verify that the position for the rth probe after an initial unsuccessful hash to position k is given by

```
(k + r² - 1) % RECORD_SPACE
```

A more significant problem, however, is that the quadratic method seemingly offers no guarantee that we will try every position in the list before concluding that a given key cannot be inserted. With the linear method, as the list became relatively dense when keys and insertions were attempted, the only way that the insertion could fail would be for every position in the list to be occupied. The linear nature of the search, although inefficient, ensured that every position would be checked. However, with the quadratic method applied to the **RECORD_SPACE** of Figure 19.7, you can confirm that an initial hash to position 3 will lead to future probing of positions 3, 4, and 7 only; it will never check positions 0, 1, 2, 5, or 6.

A satisfactory answer to the question of what portion of a list will be probed by the quadratic algorithm was fortunately provided by Radke for values of **RECORD_SPACE** that are prime numbers which satisfy certain conditions. Radke's results and their application to the quadratic algorithm are explored in the exercises at the end of the section. (If you wish to read Radke's results, see C. E. Radke, "The

◇ TABLE 19.2

Average search efficiency for quadratic and rehashing collision processing

D	Efficiency for Successful Search (number of accesses)		Efficiency for Unsuccessful Search (number of accesses)	
	Quadratic	Rehashing	Quadratic	Rehashing
0.10	1.05	1.05	1.11	1.11
0.50	1.44	1.39	2.19	2.00
0.75	2.01	1.84	4.64	4.00
0.90	2.85	2.56	11.40	10.00

◆ FIGURE 19.7
Quadratic probing after
initial hash to 3

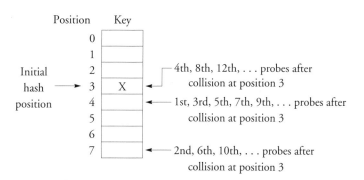

◆ FIGURE 19.7
Quadratic probing after
initial hash to 3

Use of Quadratic Residue Research," *Communications of the ACM,* Volume 13, No. 2 (February 1970):103–105.)

Linked Method of Collision Processing

The logic of *linked collision processing* completely eliminates the possibility that one collision begets another. It requires a storage area divided into two regions: a *prime hash area* and an *overflow area.* Each record requires a link field in addition to the `key` and `other_data` fields. The global constant `RECORD_SPACE` is applicable to the prime hash area only. This storage concept is illustrated in Figure 19.8.

Initially, the hashing translates function keys into the prime hashing area. If a collision occurs, the key is inserted into a linked list with its initial node in the prime area and all following nodes in the overflow area. Figure 19.9 shows how this method would load the keys 22, 31, 67, 36, 29, and 60 for a `RECORD_SPACE` equal to 7 and hashing function

```
hash(key_value) = key_value % RECORD_SPACE
```

◆ FIGURE 19.8
Storage allocation for linked
collision processing

◆ FIGURE 19.9

Loading keys with
`key_value % RECORD_SPACE`
and linked collision processing

Position	Key	Link
0	0	NULL
1	22	7 ▪
2	0	NULL
3	31	NULL
4	67	9 ▪
5	0	NULL
6	0	NULL
7	36	8 ▪
8	29	NULL
9	60	NULL
10	0	NULL
11	0	NULL
12	0	NULL
13	0	NULL
14	0	NULL
15	0	NULL
16	0	NULL

EXAMPLE 19.2

Suppose that an array has been loaded with data using the linked collision processing strategy illustrated in Figures 19.8 and 19.9. Write a C++ function to find a target key in this array.

We have made the **link** fields integer pointers to other array locations instead of C++ dynamic memory pointers to facilitate using the algorithm with a random access file. As written, the function assumes that all key locations in the prime area have had their corresponding key and link fields initialized to appropriate constant flags for **EMPTY** and **NULL**, respectively. The assumption is also made that no keys will be deleted.

```
// Function: linked_hash
// Use linked hashing algorithm to search for target.
//
// Inputs: List of objects loaded by linked hashing method.
// target, the value of a key to be found in list.
// Outputs: If record with key field matching target is found,
// return TRUE and object; otherwise, return False

boolean linked_hash(list_type list, key_type target element & item)
{
        int k = hash (target);
        boolean found = FALSE;

        do
        {
                if (target == list[k].get_key())
                {
                        item = list[k].get_value();
                        found = TRUE;
                }
        }
```

```
        else
            k = list[k].link();
    } while ((! found && (k != NULL)));
    return found;

}
```

Efficiency Considerations for Linked Hashing. Knuth's efficiency results for the linked hashing method depend on a density factor D, which is computed using the `RECORD_SPACE` in the prime hashing area only. Hence, unlike the other hashing methods we have discussed, the linked method allows a density factor greater than 1. For example, if the `RECORD_SPACE` for the primary hash area were 200 and the overflow area contained space for 300 additional records, then 400 active records would yield a density factor of 2. Given this variation, average search efficiencies for the successful and unsuccessful cases are $1 + D/2$ and D, respectively. Table 19.3 shows computations of this search efficiency for selected values of D, and should be compared to the corresponding results for the linear and quadratic methods, which were presented in Tables 19.1 and 19.2, respectively.

Bucket Hashing

In the bucket hashing strategy of collision processing, the hashing function transforms a given key to a physically contiguous region of locations within the list to be searched. This contiguous region is called a *bucket*. Thus, instead of hashing to the kth location, a key would hash to the kth bucket of locations. The number of locations contained in this bucket would depend on the bucket size. (We assume

◇ **TABLE 19.3**

Average search efficiencies
for the linked method

D	Efficiency for Successful Search (number of accesses)	Efficiency for Unsuccessful Search (number of accesses)
2	2	2
5	3.5	5
10	6	10
20	11	20

◆ FIGURE 19.10

Storage allocation for bucket
hashing

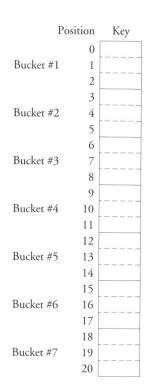

that all buckets in a given list are the same size.) Figure 19.10 illustrates this concept for a list with seven buckets and a bucket size of 3.

Having hashed to a bucket, the target must then be compared in sequential order to all of the keys in that bucket. On the surface, it would seem that this strategy could do no better than duplicate the efficiency of the linked hash method discussed earlier. Indeed, because a sequential search is conducted in both cases after the initial hash is made, the average number of list accesses for a successful or unsuccessful search cannot be improved by using buckets. Moreover, provisions for linking to some sort of overflow area must still be made in case a series of collisions consumes all of the space in a given bucket.

What then could be a possible advantage of using buckets? If the list to be searched resides entirely in main memory, there is no advantage. However, if the list resides in a disk file, the bucket method will allow us to take advantage of some of the physical characteristics of the storage medium itself. To see this, we must realize that a one-surface disk is divided into concentric *tracks* and pie-shaped *sectors* as indicated in Figure 19.11.

There are two ways in which the bucket hashing strategy may take advantage of the organization of the data on a disk. First, when records in a contiguous random access file are stored on a disk, they are generally located in relative record number order along one track, then along an adjacent track, and so on. The movement of the read/write head between tracks is generally the cause of the most significant delays in obtaining data from a disk. The farther the movement, the greater the delay. Hence, if our knowledge of the machine in question allows us to make a bucket coincide with a track on the disk, then hashing to the beginning of a bucket and proceeding from there using a sequential

◆ FIGURE 19.11
One-surface disk

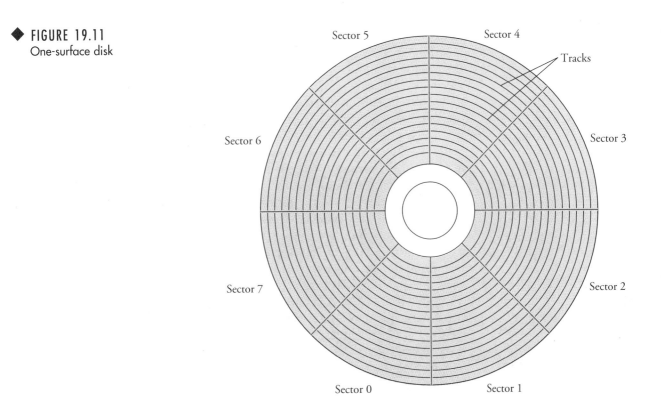

A NOTE OF INTEREST

Machine Translation

When the search algorithms discussed in this chapter were first discovered, they sparked a flurry of activity in an area known as machine translation. Programs in this area attempt to translate text from one natural language to another, for example, English to German. Early attempts at machine translation tended to view the process as essentially the searching of a large dictionary. Hence, to translate the English sentence

The sun is yellow

the program would simply find each of the words in a disk-based version of an English-to-German dictionary and arrive at the German sentence

Die Sonne ist gelb.

However, machine translation activity was soon slowed by the complexities of syntax (grammar) and semantics (meanings) in natural language. The translation of some sentences by these early systems produced some rather humorous results. According to computer folklore cited in the article "Computers Gain as Language Translators Even Though Perfect Not They Always" by William M. Bulkeley (*Wall Street Journal,* February 6, 1985, p. 25), the follow-

ing translations occurred in an early English-to-Russian system.

English Phrase	Russian Translation
The spirit is willing but the flesh is weak.	The vodka is good but the meat is rotten.
Out of sight, out of mind.	Invisible maniac.

Results such as these caused a government panel to declare, in 1966, that computerized translation would never be practical. Today, as linguists have more successfully formalized rules of syntax and semantics, machine translation is making somewhat of a comeback. In restricted domains, such as the translation of language specific to technology and business, products are being developed as time-saving aids to human translators.

Two issues of the *Communications of the ACM*—Volume 33, No. 5 (May 1990) and Volume 33, No. 8 (August 1990)—contain a variety of articles describing progress that has been made in processing natural languages. These articles provide an excellent starting point for you to explore this topic more thoroughly.

search within the bucket (that is, the track) will greatly reduce head movement. A linked hashing strategy, on the other hand, could cause considerable movement of the read/write head between tracks on the disk, thereby slowing program execution. This consideration is an excellent example of how one must examine more than just the number of list accesses when measuring the efficiency of a program involving disk files.

A second advantage of the bucket hashing algorithm when disk files are being searched is related to the way in which records are transferred between the disk and main memory. Frequently, programming languages create the illusion that each record accessed requires a separate disk access. However, records are frequently blocked, that is, positioned in contiguous regions on a track of the disk, so that a fixed number of them are brought into main memory when a record in that block is requested. This means that, if the record requested happens to be part of the block presently in main memory, a program statement that requests a record may not even require a disk access but only a different viewing window applied to the block already in main memory. Since main memory manipulations are orders of magnitude faster than the rate of data transfer to and from a disk, this means that positioning our buckets to coincide with a disk block will necessitate only one disk access each time an entire bucket is sequentially searched. Here again, the more scattered nature of a purely linked hashing algorithm would not allow this disk-oriented efficiency consideration to be taken into account.

EXERCISES 19.1

1. Assume a hashing function has the following characteristics:
   Keys 459 and 333 hash to 0.
   Key 632 hashes to 1.
   Key 1090 hashes to 2.
   Keys 1982, 379, 238, and 3411 hash to 9.
   Assume that insertions into a hashed file are performed in the order 1982, 3411, 333, 632, 1090, 459, 379, and 238.
   a. Indicate the position of the keys if the linear method is used to resolve collisions.

Record No.	Key
0	
1	
2	
3	
4	
5	
6	
7	
8	
9	
10	

b. Indicate the position of the keys if the quadratic method is used to resolve collisions.

Record No.   Key

0

1

2

3

4

5

6

7

8

9

10

c. Indicate the position of the keys and the contents of the link fields if the chaining (that is, linked) method is used to resolve collisions. Use zeros to represent NULL links and assume that the first record used in the overflow area is 11, then 12, then 13, and so on.

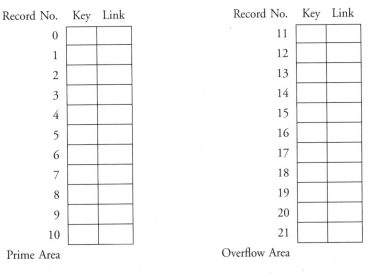

Record No.   Key   Link

0

1

2

3

4

5

6

7

8

9

10

Prime Area

Record No.   Key   Link

11

12

13

14

15

16

17

18

19

20

21

Overflow Area

2. Repeat Exercise 1 with the order of insertion of keys reversed.

3. We have covered binary search, linked lists, binary trees, and hashing as methods of implementing a one-key table ADT. Choose the method you would use to implement the data list involved for each of the following three real-world applications. In each case you should choose the most appropriate implementation technique. "Most appropriate" refers here to efficient handling of all of the required operations while not being too powerful; that is, not doing something that should be easy in an overly complicated way. Then provide a written rationale as to why yours would be the appropriate method.

a. The list to be maintained is the card catalog of a library. Frequent additions to and deletions from this catalog are made by the library. Additionally, users are frequently searching for the data associated with a given book's key. However, the library rarely prints out an ordered list of all its holdings. Hence ordering the list is not to be considered a high priority.

b. You are writing a program that maintains the lists of passengers on flights for an airline company. Passengers are frequently added to these lists. Moreover, quite often passengers cancel flight plans and must be removed from a list. You are also told that the airline frequently wants alphabetized listings of the passengers on a given flight and often needs to search for a particular passenger by name when inquiries are received from individuals.

c. You are writing a program to access a large customer database and build up counts for the numbers of customers from each of the 50 states plus the District of Columbia. To do this you will use a list of records consisting of the two-character state abbreviation and an integer representing the count of customers from that state. For each customer you read in from the database, you must find the customer's home state in your list and increase the corresponding count field. At the end, print out the counts in order alphabetized by the two-character state abbreviation.

4. Write functions to insert a key into a list to be searched by
   a. linear hashing
   b. quadratic hashing
   c. linked hashing
   d. bucket hashing

5. Write functions to search for a key via
   a. quadratic hashing
   b. bucket hashing

6. Devise strategies to delete keys from a list being maintained by each of the four hashing strategies in Exercise 4. Write C++ versions for each of these algorithms. Given your deletion strategy, describe in detail the modifications (if any) that must be made in the various search and insertion functions of Exercises 4 and 5.

7. In Section 19.1 we mentioned a result by Radke that answered the question of how many array slots would be probed by the quadratic hashing algorithm for certain values of **RECORD_SPACE**. In particular, Radke showed that if **RECORD_SPACE** is a prime number of the form $4m + 3$ for some integer m, then half of the array slots would be probed by the sequence of probes

$$k, k + 1^2, \ k + 2^2, \ k + 3^2, \ldots$$

where k is the original hash position. Radke also showed that the other half would be probed by the sequence

$$k - 1^2, \ k - 2^2, \ \mathrm{k} - 3^2, \ldots$$

Rewrite your insertion and search functions for the quadratic method in Exercises 4 and 5 to take into account Radke's result.

8. a. Given the arrival of integer keys in the order 67, 19, 4, 58, 38, 55, 86 and **RECORD_SPACE = 9** with

```
hash(key_value) = key_value % RECORD_SPACE
```

trace the insertion steps of linearly processing collisions.

Index   key_value

0	0
1	0
2	0
3	0
4	0
5	0
6	0
7	0
8	0

(0 indicates empty position)

b. Given the arrival of integer keys in the order 32, 62, 34, 77, 6, 46, 107 and
`RECORD_SPACE = 15` with

`hash(key_value) = key_value % RECORD_SPACE`

trace the insertion steps of quadratically processing collisions.

Index   key_Value

0	0
1	0
2	0
3	0
4	0
5	0
6	0
7	0
8	0
9	0
10	0
11	0
12	0
13	0
14	0

(0 indicates empty position)

c. Given the arrival of integer keys in the order 5, 3, 16, 27, 14, 25, 4 and
`RECORD_SPACE = 11` with initial hashing function

`hash1(key_value) = key_value % RECORD_SPACE`

trace the insertion steps of the rehashing collision processing method where the
secondary hashing function is

`hash2(key_value) = 5 * key_value % RECORD_SPACE`

Assume that if the secondary hashing function is not successful in locating a position for the key, then linear collision processing is used from the address indicated
by the secondary hashing function.

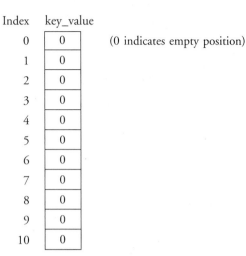

Index   key_value

0	0	(0 indicates empty position)
1	0	
2	0	
3	0	
4	0	
5	0	
6	0	
7	0	
8	0	
9	0	
10	0	

Comment on the effectiveness of rehashing with this particular secondary hashing function. Can you think of a better one? Explain why yours is better.

9. In a written statement explain how hashing could be used to search for keys that were not unique. For instance, you might have several people identified by the same name.

19.2 Two Abstract Data Types Revisited

We can analyze hashing from a pragmatic perspective by considering how it might be used to implement two ADTs introduced in Chapter 12: the one-key table and the two-key table. You will then be asked to carry out these implementations in the exercises and in the programming problems at the end of the chapter.

The One-Key Table ADT Implemented by Hashing

In this context, hashing emerges as yet another list maintenance strategy to be evaluated and compared to those strategies we have already discussed: array with binary search, linked list, and binary tree. Hence we must examine its performance with respect to the same **insert, retrieve, remove,** and **traverse** operations that were introduced in Chapter 12 and then used to evaluate these other one-key table implementation techniques. Assuming the existence of an appropriate hashing function to act on the key and a willingness to waste enough storage to allow for fast searching, hashing will clearly perform very well in all of these areas with the exception of ordering data. Here is where we have to pay a price for the scattered storage of records that are located via a hashing function.

Nonetheless, there are strategies that can be used to allow hashing and ordering of data to coexist. One such strategy would simply be to use a pointer sort algorithm (see Chapter 11) to sort the data logically when an ordered list is needed. This strategy has the drawback of not maintaining the list in order but actually performing a potentially costly sort algorithm each time an ordering is requested. Clearly, this strategy would not be wise if such an ordering were requested frequently and unpredictably.

In situations where requests for ordering would come frequently enough to make maintaining the list in order (as opposed to sorting) a necessity, we could follow a strategy that would combine the search speed of hashing with the ordered list advantages offered by a linked list implementation. This combination would have us use hashing to search for an individual record but would add link fields to each record so that a linked list for each desired ordering could be woven through the collection of hashed records. Implementing this combination of hashing and linked lists would entail the following considerations with respect to the one-key table operations:

- **insert**: In effect, the hashing/collision processing algorithm would provide us with an available node to store data. Each linked list involved would then have to be traversed to link the node into each ordering in the appropriate logical location.
- **retrieve**: There is no problem here because the hash algorithm should find the desired record quickly.
- **remove**: This is similar to the **retrieve** operation. Use hashing to find the record to be deleted, then adjust the link field appropriately. A doubly linked list could prove to be particularly valuable here. (Why?)
- **traverse**: There is no problem here because the linked lists constantly maintain the appropriate orderings.

The Two-Key Table ADT Implemented by Hashing

We have already suggested two implementation strategies for two-key tables.

1. In Section 12.4 we described a strategy that would simply create a list of the rows and columns corresponding to nontrivial values in the table. Thus, determining the value of the data at a conceptual row/column location is simply a matter of searching this list.
2. In Chapter 14, we described a strategy that would form a linked list of the nontrivial columns in each row. Here, determining the value of the data at a conceptual row/column location is reduced to the problem of sequentially searching a relatively small linked list.

At the time we explored these two strategies, the first one appeared to be less attractive. Because the data in the list of row/column coordinates corresponding to nontrivial values are likely to be volatile, physically ordering the data for a binary search would not be practical. Yet, without a binary search, requests to inspect the value at any given location are met with the $O(n)$ response time of a sequential search. Hashing allows us to search for a row/column coordinate in the list of the first strategy in a very efficient fashion, probably faster than the sequential search along the linked list representing a given row required by the second strategy. Moreover, since the order of the data in the list is not important for this application, the scattered nature of hashed storage does not present any obstacle at all.

The considerations we have discussed with respect to these two ADTs make it evident that hashing is a very attractive table implementation technique. It will be extremely efficient in regard to the **insert, retrieve,** and **remove** table operations if we are willing to pay the price of wasting enough storage to get a reasonably low density ratio. The only other drawback to hashing, in addition to this wasted storage, is the price that must be paid if various orderings of the data are frequently needed.

EXERCISES 19.2

1. Suppose that we combine hashing with a linked list in the fashion described in Section 19.2 so that all one-key table operations can be efficiently performed. Which of the variations on a linked list structure would be most effective in this context? Ex-

plain why in a carefully worded statement. (*Hint:* Think about the `retrieve` and `delete` operations.)

2. Give an example of an application where the hashing implementation of a two-dimensional table described in this section would be less efficient (overall) than the linked list implementation described in Chapter 14. Explain why in a carefully worded statement.

3. Provide implementations of all one-key table operations using the hashing strategy described in this section. Provide alternative implementations of the traverse operations: One should invoke a pointer sort and another should combine hashing with a linked list.

4. Provide implementations of all two-key table operations defined in Chapter 12 using the hashing strategy described in this section.

19.3 Indexed Search Techniques (Optional)

OBJECTIVES

- to understand the differences between searching in main memory and in random access disk storage

- to understand how an index may be used to advantage when searching for data in a random access file

- to study how the indexed sequential search methodology is implemented

- to discuss the efficiency of the indexed sequential search strategy

- to understand how the B-tree data structure may be used to implement an index for a random access file

- to discuss the efficiency of B-trees

- to understand how the trie data structure may be used to implement the index for a random access file keyed by strings of variable length

- to discuss the efficiency of tries

All of the search strategies we have studied up to this point could be applied to lists implemented in main memory or on a random access disk. However, with the exception of bucket hashing, none of the methods we have studied actually takes into account physical characteristics of disk storage in an attempt to enhance their efficiency. In practice, because retrieval of data from a disk file is orders of magnitude slower than retrieval from main memory, we often cannot afford to ignore these special characteristics of disk files if we want reasonable response time for our searching efforts. The indexing schemes that we are about to discuss in this section are primarily directed toward file-oriented applications and thus will take into account the operational properties of this storage medium. We encourage you to reread the discussion of bucket hashing at the end of Section 19.1 for a summary analysis of file storage considerations.

The idea behind the use of an index is analogous to the way in which we routinely use an address book to find a person whom we are seeking. That is, if we are looking for a person, we do not knock on the doors of numerous houses until we find the one where that person lives. Instead, we apply a search strategy to an address book. There we use the name of the person as a key to find a pointer—that is, an address—which swiftly leads us to where the person can be found. Only one actual "house access" must be made, although our search strategy may require numerous accesses into the address book index.

In a computer system, records (or more precisely blocks) could play the role of houses in the search scenario just described. Data records on disk are (when compared to main memory) terribly slow and awkward creatures to access. One of the reasons for this is that there is often so much data that must be moved from disk to main memory every time a record is accessed. Because of this, the conceptual picture for the general setup of an indexed search must be revised. The list of keys is no longer parallel to the actual data with which they are logically associated, rather it is parallel to a list of pointers, which will lead us to the actual data. The revised picture is presented in Figure 19.12.

The general strategy of an indexed search is to use the key to search the index efficiently, find the relative record position of the associated data, and from there make only one access into the actual data. Because the parallel lists of keys and relative record positions require much less storage than the data, frequently the entire index can be loaded and permanently held in main memory, necessitating only one disk access for each record being sought. For larger indices, it still remains

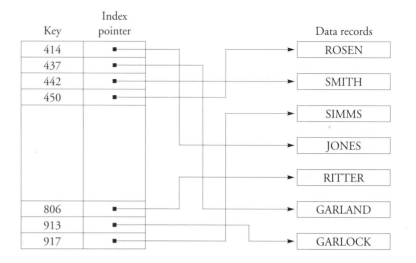

◆ **FIGURE 19.12**

General setup for an indexed search

true that large blocks of keys and associated pointers may be manipulated in main memory, thereby greatly enhancing search efficiency.

Indexed Sequential Search Technique

The *indexed sequential search* technique is also commonly recognized by the acronym *ISAM,* which stands for *indexed sequential access method.* Essentially it involves carefully weighing the disk-dependent factors of blocking and track size to build a partial index. The partial index, unlike some other index structures we will study, does not reduce to one the number of probes that must be made into the actual data.

To continue the analogy between searching for data and searching for a person, the indexed sequential strategy is somewhat like an address book that would lead us to the street on which a person lives but leave it to us to check each of the houses on that street. The ISAM method correspondingly leads us to an appropriate region (often a track or a cylinder containing multiple tracks within a disk pack) and then leaves it to us to search sequentially within that region.

As an example, let us suppose that we can conveniently fit the partial index, or directory, pictured in Figure 19.13 into main memory and that the organization of our disk file allows six records per track. This directory is formed by choosing the highest key value in each six-record track along with a pointer indicating where that track begins. Here our pointers are simply relative record numbers; in practice they could well be a more disk-dependent locator. The strategy to conduct an indexed sequential search follows:

1. Search the main memory directory for a key that is greater than or equal to the target.
2. Then follow the corresponding pointer out to the disk and there search sequentially until we find a match (success) or the key that the directory maintains as the high key within that particular region (failure).

For the data given in Figure 19.13, this technique would mean that the 36-record file would require no more than six main memory index accesses plus six disk accesses, all of which are located in the same track.

For larger files, it may be advantageous to have more than one level of these directory structures. Consider, for instance, the two-level directory structure for a

◆ FIGURE 19.13
One-level indexed sequential
file

FILE

Record No.	Key
0	14
1	20
2	33
3	60
4	70
5	89
6	94
7	110
8	114
9	120
10	204
11	211
12	212
13	390
14	414
15	491
16	499
17	500
18	509
19	519
20	580
21	591
22	603
23	611
24	620
25	640
26	650
27	700
28	712
29	734
30	748
31	784
32	800
33	823
34	846
35	903

DIRECTORY

	Key	Pointer
0	89	0
1	211	6
2	500	12
3	611	18
4	734	24
5	903	30

file with 216 records given in Figure 19.14. Here we might suppose that storage restrictions allow the entire primary directory to be kept in main memory, the secondary directory to be brought in from a disk file in blocks of six key–pointer pairs each, and the actual data records to be stored six per track. The primary directory divides the file into regions of 36 records each. The key in the primary directory represents the highest valued key in a given 36-record region, but the pointer leads us into the subdirectory instead of the actual file. So, we search the primary directory for a key greater than or equal to the target we are seeking. Once this is done, we follow the primary directory pointer into the secondary directory. Beginning at the position indicated by the primary directory's pointer, we again

◆ FIGURE 19.14
Two-level directory structure

SUBDIRECTORIES

	Key	Pointer
0	71	0
5	210	30
6		
11	603	66
12		
17	1240	102
18		
23	2044	138
24	2589	144
25	3300	150
26	4387	156
27	4923	162
28	5110	168
29	5310	174
30	5743	180
35	8412	210

PRIMARY
DIRECTORY

	Key	Pointer
0	210	1
1	603	6
2	1240	12
3	2044	18
4	5310	24
5	8412	30

FILE

Record No.	Key
0	40
143	2044
144	2060
145	2148
146	2249
147	2380
148	2461
149	2589
150	2744
151	2891
152	3011
153	3144
154	3281
155	3300
156	3410
157	4081
158	4099
159	4215
160	4361
161	4387
162	4712
163	4846
164	4847
165	4900
166	4911
167	4923
168	4924
169	4951
170	4983
171	5051
172	5060
173	5110
174	5240
175	5244
176	5286
177	5300
178	5301
179	5310
180	5390
215	8412

A NOTE OF INTEREST

Data Integrity, Concurrent Updates, and Deadlock

The problems of finding and allowing a user to access a particular record in a file are complicated somewhat in a system that allows several users to access that file simultaneously. To see why this is so, it is important to recall that when you actually manipulate a record or part of an index from a file, you really have a copy of that portion of the file in your main memory area. Now suppose that two users are not only accessing the same file simultaneously but also the same record in that file simultaneously. A scenario such as the following could emerge:

The solution used in many systems is that of a *record lock facility.* With such a facility, the user who has a file record in main memory for updating is considered the owner of that record to the exclusion of any other users accessing that record. That lock on the record exists until the user writes the (perhaps altered) record back to the disk file. Hence, in our scenario, User 2 would not have been able immediately to obtain the record for key XYZ. Instead, that user would sit idle in a wait state until the record became available.

Memory Area for User 1   Disk file   Memory Area for User 2
XYZ Record   XYZ Record

User 1 requests record associated with key XYZ.
User 2 requests record associated with key XYZ.
User 1 updates address field of that record.
User 2 updates inventory field of that record.
User 1 makes change in the file by writing that record to disk.
User 2 makes changes in the file by writing that record to disk.

What will be wrong with the new record that exists in the disk file? Clearly, the address change made by User 1 will have been destroyed when User 2's copy of the record is written back to the disk. We have what is known as a *data integrity* problem caused by the *concurrent updating* of the same record by two users. The situation can become much worse than merely losing an address change. Imagine the havoc created if one of the users deleted the record while the other was processing it or if the portion of the file being simultaneously updated by two users was not a data record but instead part of the file index.

The concurrent update problem must be avoided in any multiuser system if data integrity is to be ensured.

Although the record-locking approach guarantees data integrity, it is not without its own set of problems. For instance, consider the following scenario:

User 1 requests and gets record for key XYZ.
User 2 requests and gets record for key ABC.
To process record XYZ, User 1 needs data associated with record ABC.
Because record is owned by User 2, User 1 must wait in idle state.
To process record ABC, User 2 needs data associated with record XYZ.
Because record is owned by User 1, User 2 must wait in idle state.

Though data integrity has been maintained, we now have two users in an infinite wait state known as a *deadlock* or, more glamorously, *fatal embrace.* The avoidance and/or detection of deadlock situations in a multiuser environment is a nontrivial problem. If you are interested in exploring it more deeply, see Harvey M. Deitel's *An Introduction to Operating Systems,* 2nd ed. (Reading, Mass.: Addison-Wesley, 1990).

search for a key greater than or equal to the target. Notice that fetching one block of six key–pointer pairs from the subdirectory has necessitated one disk access in our hypothetical situation. In return for this single disk access, we are able to subdivide the 36-record region determined by the primary directory into six 6-record regions, each of which will lie entirely on one track by the time we get out to the actual disk file. Following the subdirectory's pointer to the file, we end up with a relatively short sequential search on the storage medium itself. In this example, the maximum number of disk accesses required to find any record would be seven, and six of those would be isolated on one track of the disk.

Efficiency Considerations for the Indexed Sequential Search. It should be clear from the preceding discussion that the search efficiency of the indexed sequential technique depends on a variety of factors. Included among them are the following:

- To what degree the directory structures are able to subdivide the actual file
- To what degree the directory structures are able to reside in main memory
- The relationship of data records to physical characteristics of the disk such as blocking factors, track size, cylinder size, and so on.

It should also be clear that the indexed sequential method may not be ideal for a highly volatile file. This is because, as implicitly indicated in Figures 19.13 and 19.14, the actual data records must be physically stored in increasing (or decreasing) key order. The requirement for physical ordering is obviously not conducive to frequent insertions and deletions. In practice, the solution to this problem is that each file subregion, which is ultimately the subject of a sequential search, is equipped with a pointer to an overflow area. Insertions are located in this overflow area and linked to the main sequential search area. As the overflow area builds up, the search efficiency tends to deteriorate. In some applications, this deterioration can be so severe that data processing personnel have been known to refer to the ISAM technique as the intrinsically slow access method.

The way to avoid deterioration is to reorganize the file periodically into a new file with no overflow. However, such reorganization cannot be done dynamically. It requires going through the file in key sequential order and copying it into a new one. Along the way, the indices must be rebuilt, of course. These types of maintenance problems involved with the ISAM structure have led to the development of several more dynamic indexing schemes.

Binary Search Tree Indexing

The concept of a binary search tree was covered in Chapter 16. The only twist added when the binary tree plays the role of an index is that each node of the tree contains a key and a pointer to the record associated with that key in some larger data aggregate. The advantages of using a binary search tree as an index structure include:

- A search efficiency potentially proportional to $\log_2 n$
- The ability to traverse the list indexed by the tree in key order
- Dynamic insertion and deletion capabilities.

These qualities make the binary search tree the ideal index structure for situations in which the entire tree can fit in main memory. However, if the data collection is so large that the tree index must itself be stored on disk, the efficiency of the structure is less than optimal. This is because each node of the index may lie in a disk block separate from the other nodes and hence require a separate disk access. Using an example of 50,000 keys, a search of a *binary tree index* could require 16 disk accesses. To solve this problem, we would like to cluster those nodes along a given search path into one, or at least relatively few, disk blocks. The *B-tree* index structure is a variation on the tree index that accomplishes this goal.

B-Tree Indexing

We begin this discussion of B-trees by reminding you that one index entry requires nothing more than a key and a pointer. Moreover, we have assumed that both the key and the pointer are integers, and we continue to operate under this assumption during our discussion of B-trees. We emphasize this point here because, in a B-tree, a given tree node will in fact contain many such key–pointer pairs. This is because a given B-tree node will in fact coincide with one disk block. The idea behind a B-tree is that we will somehow group key–pointer pairs that are related in the search algorithm into a few strategic B-tree nodes, that is, disk blocks. At this point, we make a formal definition; later, we'll clarify this definition via some examples.

B-tree of order *n*: A B-tree of order *n* is a structure with the following properties:

1. Every node in the B-tree has sufficient room to store $n - 1$ key–pointer pairs.
2. Additionally, every node has room for n pointers to other nodes in the B-tree (as distinguished from the pointers within key–pointer pairs, which point to the position of a key in the file).
3. Every node except the root must have at least $(n - 1) / 2$ key–pointer pairs stored in it.
4. All terminal nodes are on the same level.
5. If a nonterminal node has m key–pointer pairs stored in it, then it must contain $m + 1$ non-null pointers to other B-tree nodes.
6. For each B-tree node, we require that the key value in key–pointer pair KP_{i-1} be less than the key value in key–pointer pair KP_i, that all key–pointer pairs in the node pointed to by P_{i-1} contain keys that are less than the key in KP_i, and that all key–pointer pairs in the node pointed to by P_i contain key values that are greater than the key in KP_i.

According to property 5 of the definition, we can think of a B-tree node as a list

$$P_0, KP_1, P_1, KP_2, P_2, KP_3, \ldots, P_{m-1}, KP_m, P_m$$

where P_i represents the *i*th pointer to another B-tree node and KP_i represents the *i*th key–pointer pair. Note that a B-tree node will always contain one more pointer to another B-tree node than it does key–pointer pairs. With this picture in mind, the sixth and final property of our definition makes sense. Figure 19.15 illustrates how this rather involved definition applies to a B-tree node with three key–pointer pairs.

◆ FIGURE 19.15

Example of a B-tree node with three key–pointer pairs

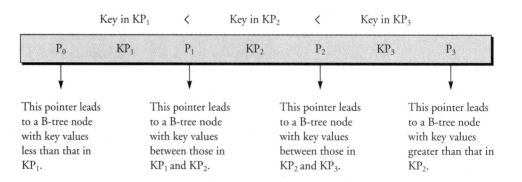

As a further illustration of this definition, a complete B-tree of order 6 serving as an index structure for the 36-record file of Figure 19.13 appears in Figure 19.16. (In this figure, the slash between numbers denotes a key–pointer pair; | denotes a null pointer.) Carefully verify that all six defining properties are satisfied.

◆ FIGURE 19.16
B-tree index of order 6 for file in Figure 19.13

The choice of order 6 for Figure 19.16 was made only for the purposes of making the figure fit on a page of text. In practice, the order chosen would be the maximum number of B-tree pointers and key–pointer pairs that we could fit into one disk block. That is, the choice should be made to force a disk block to coincide with a B-tree node. It is also worth noting that B-trees of order 3 have special application as a data structure apart from indexing considerations. This application is covered in the programming problems at the end of the chapter.

Efficiency Considerations for B-Tree Indexing. Let us now consider what is involved in searching a B-tree for a given key. Within the current node (starting at the root), we must search sequentially through the key values in the node until we come to a match, a key value that is greater than the one being sought, or the end of the key values in that particular node. If a match is not made within a particular B-tree node, we have a pointer to follow to an appropriate follow-up node. Again, you should verify this algorithm for several of the keys appearing at various levels of Figure 19.16. The sequential search on keys within a given node may at first seem unappealing. However, the important fact to remember here is that each B-tree node is a disk block that is loaded entirely into main memory. Hence, it may be possible to search sequentially on hundreds of keys within a node in the time it would take to load one new node from disk. Our main concern is to minimize disk accesses, and here we have achieved a worst case search for our 36-entry file in three disk accesses.

What in general is the search efficiency for a B-tree index? It should be clear from the nature of the structure that the maximum number of disk accesses for any particular key will simply be the number of levels in the tree. So the efficiency question really amounts to knowing the maximum number of levels that the six defining criteria would allow for a B-tree containing n key–pointer pairs. That is, this number would be the worst case search efficiency. To determine this number, we use the minimum number of nodes that must be present on any given level. Let l be the smallest integer greater than or equal to $k/2$ where k is the order of the B-tree in question. Then

> Level 0 contains at least 1 node.
> Level 1 contains at least 2 nodes.
> Level 2 contains at least $2l$ nodes.
> Level 3 contains at least $2l^2$ nodes.
> .
> .
> .
> Level m contains at least $2l^{m-1}$ nodes.

An argument based on Knuth's research (see *Searching and Sorting,* cited in Section 19.1) uses this progression to show that the maximum number of levels (and thus the worst case search efficiency) for n key–pointer pairs is

$$\log_k[(n + 1)/2]$$

Thus, a B-tree search has an $O(\log_k n)$ efficiency where n is the number of records and k is the order of the B-tree. Note that this can be considerably better than an $O(\log_2 n)$ search efficiency. As an example, the index for a file of 50,000 records, which would require on the order of 16 disk accesses using a binary tree structure, could be searched with 3 disk accesses using a B-tree of order 250. Note that, given typical block sizes for files, the choice of order 250 for this example is not at all unrealistic.

Unlike ISAM, the B-tree index can dynamically handle insertions and deletions without a resulting deterioration in search efficiency. We next discuss how B-tree insertions are handled; making deletions is left for an exercise. The essential idea behind a B-tree insertion is that we must first determine which bottom-level node should contain the key–pointer pair to be inserted. For instance, suppose that we want to insert the key 742 into the B-tree of Figure 19.16. By allowing this key to walk down the B-tree from the root to the bottom level, we could quickly determine that this key belongs in the node presently containing

```
712/28
734/29
748/30
784/31
```

Since, by the definition of a B-tree of order 6, this node is not presently full, no further disk accesses would be necessary to perform the insertion. We would merely need to determine the next available record space in the actual data file (36 in this case) and then add the key–pointer pair 742/36 to this terminal node, resulting in

```
712/28
734/29
742/36
748/30
784/31
```

A slightly more difficult situation arises when we find that the key–pointer pair we wish to add should be inserted into a bottom-level node that is already full. For instance, this would occur if we attempted to add the key 112 to the B-tree of Figure 19.16. We would load the actual data for this key into file position 37 (given the addition already made in the preceding paragraph) and then determine that the key–pointer pair 112/37 belongs in the bottom-level node

```
94/6
110/7
114/8
120/9
204/10
```

The stipulation that any B-tree node except the root have at least $(n - 1) / 2 = 2$ key–pointer pairs allows us to split this node, creating one new node with two key–pointer pairs and one with three key–pointer pairs. We also have to move one of the key–pointer pairs up to the parent of the present node. The resulting B-tree is given in Figure 19.17.

Although it does not happen in this particular example, note that it would be entirely possible that the movement of a key–pointer pair up to a parent node that is already full would necessitate a split of this parent node, using the same function. Indeed it is possible that key–pointer pairs could be passed all the way up to the root and cause a split of the root. This is in fact how a new level of the tree would be introduced. A split of the root would force the creation of a new root, which would only have one key–pointer pair and two pointers to other B-tree nodes. However, at the root level this is still a sufficient number of pointers to retain the B-tree structure. Because the insertion algorithm for a B-tree requires checking

◆ FIGURE 19.17
B-tree of Figure 19.16 after
insertion of 112/37 and
742/36

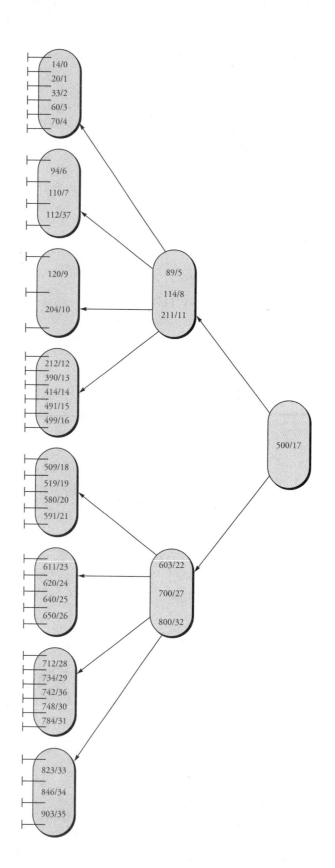

whether a given node is full and potentially moving back up to a parent node, it is convenient to allow space within a node to store both of the following:

- A count of the number of key–pointer pairs in the node
- A back pointer to the node's parent.

Trie Indexing

In all of the indexing applications we have discussed so far, the keys involved have been integers. In practice, however, we must be prepared to deal with keys of different types. Perhaps the worst case is that of keys that are variable-length character strings. *Trie indexing* has developed as a means of retrieving keys in this worst case. (The term itself is derived from the four middle letters of "retrieve," though it is usually pronounced "try.")

Let us suppose that the strings in the following list represent a set of keys. Each string may be thought of as a last name followed by initials and a delimiting $.

ADAMS BT$

COOPER CC$

COOPER PJ$

COWANS DC$

MAGUIRE WH$

MCGUIRE AL$

MEMINGER DD$

SEFTON SD$

SPAN KD$

SPAN LA$

SPANNER DW$

ZARDA JM$

ZARDA PW$

An individual node in a trie structure for these keys follows:

$ A B C D E F G H I J K L M N O P Q R S T U V W X Y Z

trie node

It is essentially a fixed-length array of 28 pointers: one for each letter of the alphabet, one for a blank, and one for the delimiter. Each pointer within one of these nodes can lead to one of two entities—either another node within the trie or the actual data record for a given key. Hence it may be convenient to embed a

Boolean flag in each pointer indicating the type of entity to which it is pointing. The trie structure for the preceding list of keys is given in Figure 19.18. In this figure, pointers to nodes labeled as data records lead us outside of the trie structure itself.

The logic behind a trie structure may best be seen by tracing through an example. This search algorithm involves examining the target key on a character-by-character basis. Let us begin by considering the easy case of finding the data record for ADAMS BT$. In this case, we look at A, the first character in the key, and follow the A pointer in the root node to its destination. From what we have previously said, we know that its destination will be either another node within the trie structure or an actual data record. If it were a node within the trie, it would be a node on the search path for all keys that begin with A. In this case, there is only one key in our list that begins with A, so the A pointer in the root node leads us directly to the actual data record for ADAMS BT$.

◆ FIGURE 19.18

Trie index structure

On the other hand, the search path to find the key COOPER CC$ in the trie is somewhat longer. We follow the C pointer from the root node down a level to a node shared by all keys starting with C. From there, the O pointer is followed to a trie node shared by all keys that start with CO. The process continues down level by level, following the O pointer to a trie node shared by all keys starting with COO, then the P pointer to a node for all keys starting with COOP, the E pointer to a node for all keys starting with COOPE, the R pointer to a node for all keys starting with COOPER, and the blank pointer to a node shared by all keys starting with COOPER followed by a blank. Notice that, as each character is read in, we must continue following these pointers from trie node to trie node (instead of from trie node to actual data record) until we finally reach a point where the next character to be read will uniquely define the key. At this point, the key in question need no longer share its pointer with other keys that match it on an initial substring. Hence the pointer may now lead to an actual data record. This is what happens in our example when we read in the next C to form the uniquely defined substring COOPER C.

Efficiency Considerations for Trie Indexing. The search efficiency for the trie index is quite easily determined. The worst case occurs when a key is not uniquely defined until its last character is read. In this case, we may have as many disk accesses as there are characters in the key before we finally locate the actual data record. You may have observed, however, that there is another efficiency consideration to take into account when using the trie method. This is the amount of wasted storage in the trie nodes. In our example using a short list of keys, only a small percentage of the available pointers are ever used. In practice, however, a trie would only be used for an extremely large file, such as the list represented by a phone book with names as keys. In such a situation, a much larger number of character combinations occurs and the resulting trie structure is correspondingly much less sparse.

A final point to consider relative to trie indexes is their ability to handle insertions and deletions dynamically. Here, we discuss insertions; deletions are left as an exercise. Insertions may be broken down into two cases. For both we must begin by reading the key to be inserted, character by character, and following the appropriate search path in the trie until

- we come to a trie node which has a vacant pointer in the character position corresponding to the current character of the insertion key.

or

- we come to an actual data record for a key different from the one that is being inserted.

The first case is illustrated by trying to insert the key COLLINS RT$ into the trie of Figure 19.18. We would follow the search path pointers until we came to the trie node shared by all keys starting with CO. At this point, the L pointer is null. The insertion is completed by merely aiming the presently null L pointer to a data record for the key COLLINS RT$. The second case is illustrated by trying to insert the key COOPER PA$ into the trie of Figure 19.18. Here, following the search path of the trie would eventually lead us to the data record for the key COOPER PJ$. The dynamic solution is to get a new trie node, aim the P pointer presently leading to the data record for COOPER PJ$ to this new trie node, and use the A and J pointers in the new trie node to lead us to data records for COOPER PA$

◆ FIGURE 19.19
Trie of Figure 19.18 after
inserting COLLINS RT$ and
COOPER PA$

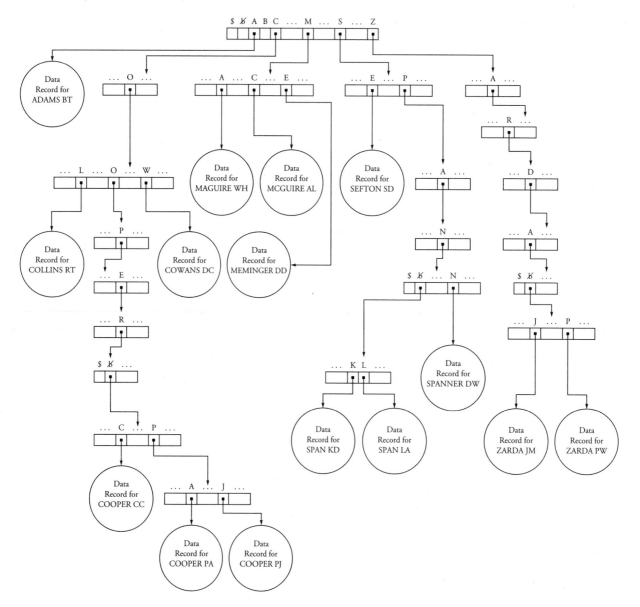

and COOPER PJ$, respectively. Both the COLLINS RT$ and COOPER PA$
insertions are shown with the resulting trie in Figure 19.19.

EXERCISES 19.3

1. **a.** Suppose that the records associated with keys 810, 430, 602, 946, 289, 106,
and 732 are stored in positions 0, 1, 2, 3, 4, 5, and 6 respectively of a file.
Draw a B-tree index of order 8 for this file.

   b. Suppose the key 538 then arrives for insertion in position 8. Redraw your B-tree
of order 8 after this insertion.

2. Suppose that the following strings arrive for insertion into a trie index:

CARTER
HERNANDEZ
HERMAN
HERMANSKI
HERSCHEL
HALL
CARSON
CARSWELL
CARSEN

    a. Draw the trie index.
    b. Draw the index after CARSWELL and HERMANSKI have been deleted.

3. Discuss the key deletion strategy for B-trees. Write a function to implement your strategy.

4. Discuss a key deletion strategy for trie indexes. Write a function to implement your strategy.

5. Carefully read your system reference material concerning the specifics of how disk file records are blocked. Then explain how this knowledge would influence your decisions in the construction of

    a. a B-tree index structure
    b. a trie index structure
    c. a bucket hashing structure
    d. an ISAM index structure

6. All of the search strategies we have discussed assume a key that is uniquely valued. That is, no two records have the same value for their key field. In practice, this will not always be the case. We may have duplicate keys. For instance, a list of personnel records may contain two records for different people with the same name. In a carefully worded statement, discuss how each of the search strategies we have covered would have to be modified to perform a duplicate key search. What effect would these modifications have on the performance of the algorithm?

7. Develop a function to search a list via ISAM. Initially assume just one directory. Then alter the function so that it would work with one subdirectory.

8. Devise functions to handle insertions into and deletions from a list maintained by the indexed sequential method. Do the strategies reflected by these functions require any modifications in your answers to Exercise 7? If so, explain the nature of these modifications.

9. Write the algorithm to insert a key into a B-tree.

10. Write an algorithm to insert a key and its data record into a trie.

FOCUS ON PROGRAM DESIGN

A theme of the Focus on Program Design section in the two previous chapters has been the development of programs that allow us to experiment with algorithms. Such programs are extremely useful for algorithms whose analysis defies purely mathematical techniques. Certainly the strategy of hashing, presented in Section 19.1, falls into this category of algorithms. The efficiency of hashing is dependent on a variety of factors: the randomness with which your hashing function scatters keys into the record space, the amount of space you are willing to sacrifice to empty storage locations, and the effectiveness of your collision-processing strategy in reducing clustering.

Because of hashing's dependency on these factors, an experimental tool for testing various hashing strategies can be very valuable in predicting how effective hashing will be for a particular application. In this section, we discuss the design of such an experimental program for situations in which we wish to study the effectiveness of hashing on keys that are strings.

As with the previous chapter's Focus on Program Design program, we want to choose between three forms of input for our experimentation:

1. A sequence of randomly generated string keys
2. A sequence of string keys that we enter interactively, so that we can enter specific data sets particularly relevant to our experimentation
3. A sequence of string keys read one per line from a file.

From last chapter's program, we will also borrow the facility to save a particularly interesting data set in a text file form that can later be read by the program. This will allow you to fine-tune the algorithm by altering the hashing function or selecting a different collision-processing method and then testing the new program with the same set of data. An example of such experimental runs with the program follows.

First Run: Hash Table with Record Space for 40, 30 Slots Filled with Random Strings.

```
How large is record space for hash table? 40
Choose method for loading hash table:

        1 - Load table with random strings
        2 - Interactively load the table
        3 - Load the table from a file

Enter 1, 2 or 3 → 1


Enter number of values in table → 30
Print the table? (Y/N) → y
NONEMPTY SLOTS OF THE TABLE:

        ARRAY[ 2] = \TUFqY]Y-tlLcTIxGRnPHUjikDzoxy
        ARRAY[ 3] = UVo{texGxxYSbwNMqI\UoGKR-YYdDe
        ARRAY[ 4] = Qrfh[oDFXECsJOdcotqoXaoD{paxhN
        ARRAY[ 5] = OTSK{onLIBZ^U'VfDwdKrmOhqbSjBx
        ARRAY[ 6] = MID\argowZc-Z[vMF[hZzBxkJiohi
        ARRAY[ 7] = Pr]Rncs{CXOREpjkyYRtmmFRaXHbWv
        ARRAY[10] = 'kgPl^[lJrmTsSfbw\JBXrVOVDTose
        ARRAY[14] = O'S'[SL^sVJn'Pdw'aJ^votElbqLFZ
        ARRAY[15] = J[lsvd{LwcRvQyiF{SPPKLDyrIIpGl
        ARRAY[16] = LkYsfFhnyvdKPnPe'Niiup{xXHMxGj
        ARRAY[18] = pKiWMJzLLNfho-jYGcPxJzVsDRDiqE
        ARRAY[19] = YC's^ZPOXZEnHe{BnbI'Xp'uEvOgr\
        ARRAY[20] = bT{bZGcKmhwGfdFxH]IOPrIbHQJ]oS
        ARRAY[21] = NILYPSQnhr-H'u{CuDnErrunYr[kif
        ARRAY[22] = \]kmBdbnLhSQBN{ncqjtwe\II\WFPe
        ARRAY[23] = fByLV{fqOhOLSfotfZYZReHYTn{Wp\
        ARRAY[24] = ^NSsPsYp\{kSKOUw[ISOWOjnzHbIVU
```

```
ARRAY[25] = eLWstIC'ZLPsUwHXgvhk\jzWpsHwlx
ARRAY[26] = IxV'GzjKFeq[IXptTukEjhdbuQ-wSQ
ARRAY[27] = HPyGpLkGZINJEh-pnVghemjPgZlJxx
ARRAY[28] = XPDHfZTwyCzkGCMokZNEv]dCllXN
ARRAY[29] = GvpO^bWgPubRY]\jEsI[OddGCRzM^]
ARRAY[30] = EZzxgV'ih'nLJ-nCLsdnqISzHvyMJl
ARRAY[31] = qwbs{HblUTCIwEzfox-nB^iHfRbPmu
ARRAY[32] = KWQcS[WdJSyZl]FeJbpl\HMVjiTCzs
ARRAY[35] = RUhjdEgb{x]d''NWPXx\OGjZaMcpOP
ARRAY[36] = ysb[z-gCgghfDskqOiqKRiFOPZ'bM^
ARRAY[37] = PngO'I\efYtwfJykbvnc-PWE'mqkiz
ARRAY[38] = KB]Uiq]kLxmylwUdXUTLMmlSOkh-cq
ARRAY[39] = iJtgsTbicsFueT]{uRqZdRKZGwdc\m
```

```
Average length for successful search 2.13
Average length for unsuccessful search 4.87


Save the input values for this table? (Y/N)→ y
Name for save file → test.dat
Another table? (Y/N) → n
```

Second Run: Now Adjust Hashing Function and/or Collision Processing, and Run Again

```
How large is record space for hash table? 40
Choose method for loading hash table:

        1 - Load table with random strings
        2 - Interactively load the table
        3 - Load the table from a file

Enter 1, 2 or 3 → 3

Enter the name of the file → test.dat
Print the table? (Y/N) → n
Average length for successful search 1.92
Average length for unsuccessful search 4.76

Save the input values for this table? (Y/N) → n
Another table? (Y/N) → n
```

Note the slight improvement in efficiency for the second run.

A modular structure chart for the program appears in Figure 19.20. Notice from the modular structure chart that a package of queue modules is used in the program. As a sequence of string keys is loaded into the hash table by the program, the keys are also placed on the queue. Then, after the hash table has been loaded, these keys are removed from the queue. As each key is removed from the queue, we search the hash table for it, accumulating a profiling counter as the search for the key is performed. The key is then returned to the tail of the queue. If the user chooses to save the sequence of string keys to a text file, we merely proceed through the queue, writing each key to the file as it is removed from the queue.

To accumulate the statistics for the average unsuccessful search, the program generates a fixed number of additional random keys—assuming that the probability

◆ FIGURE 19.20

Modular structure chart for
hashing experimentation
program

of any such key matching one already in the table is virtually zero. The program is
exercised by sending each of these randomly generated keys through the search
algorithm. A profiling accumulator for unsuccessful searches is maintained as these
keys are processed.

A first-level pseudocode development for the main program is given by:

Initialize the random number generator (see Appendix 6)
Create the queue used to store a copy of keys in order of generation
Initialize the value used to flag an empty slot
Do

    Initialize hash table to all empty slots
    Load the table of a specified logical record space with
        number of keys specified by user, also returning a queue
        containing the sequence of keys generated

If the user wants, print the hash table
Conduct searches: accumulate and print profiling counters
    for successful and unsuccessful searches
Save the sequence of keys from queue to a file if the user
    wants
Inquire if the user wants to load another table
While user indicates no more tables to load

Refinement of this pseudocode into C++ yields the following main program:

```
// Program file: focus.cpp

// This program allows users to experiment with hashing on
// an array implementation of a list of strings. A hashing
// function is provided, but users are encouraged to
// try their own hashing functions. The current implementation
// makes use of the linear collision processing strategy, but
// is written in such a way that other strategies can be substituted easily.

// The program is designed to create the list of strings
// in one of three ways: allow a user to interactively
// specify the contents of the list, generate a random list,
// or read a previously saved list in from a file. The
// program will also save the contents of the list for later
// reuse if desired.

// The data file created by the program when a table is saved is
// simply a text file with one element of the table per line of
// the file. Similarly, the program expects any file from which
// it is to read a table to have this format. Internally, the
// program uses a queue to store the incoming table elements
// in the order they arrive so that they can be saved to the
// file in that same order.

#include <iostream.h>
#include <fstream.h>

#include "strlib.h"
#include "queue.h"
#include "random.h"

const int MAX_HASH_TABLE_SIZE = 2000;

float average_search_length;          // Global statistic
random_generator generator;           // Random number generator

#include "hash.h"

int main()
{
    string empty_slot("");                  // String for empty hash table entry
    hash_table<string> table(empty_slot);      // Hash table
```

```cpp
queue<string> copies;             // Copies of keys generated
char query;                       // User's response
ifstream input_file;              // Input file stream
ofstream output_file;             // Output file stream

do
{
        load_table(table, choice_of_load, copies, input_file);
        cout << "Print the table? (Y/N) → ";
        cin >> query;
        if ((query == 'Y') || (query == 'y'))
                print_table(table, 1);
        conduct_search(table);
        save_if_wanted(copies, choice_of_load, output_file);
        cout << "Another table? (Y/N) → ";
        cin >> query;
} while ((query == 'Y') || (query == 'y'));
return 0;
}
```

Specifications for individual modules in the program follow. You will implement these specifications in the programming problems, thereby providing yourself with a means of exploring the effectiveness of a variety of hashing functions and collision-processing methods.

Module: load_table

Task: Determine logical size of record space in table and choice for loading. Dispatch to load_random_table, interactive_load_table, or load_table_from_file, respectively.

Inputs: table, an empty hash table, and copies, an empty queue.

Outputs: An integer indicating the user's choice for loading the hash table: 1 for randomly generated strings, 2 for interactively loaded strings, 3 for strings read from file. Table is returned loaded with strings generated by chosen method. Copies contains sequence of strings generated by chosen method.

Module: load_random_table

Task: Inquire as to number of strings to generate.
For each string,
Fill it with randomly generated characters.
Call on add_to_hash_table to load string into table.
Call on enqueue operation to add string to copies queue.

Outputs: Hash table loaded with randomly generated strings and a queue copies, which contains each of the strings in the order of their generation.

Module: interactive_load_table

Task: Inquire as to number of strings that will be entered.
For each string,
Allow user to enter it interactively.
Call on add_to_hash_table to load string into table.
Call on enqueue operation to add string to copies queue.

Outputs: Hash table loaded with strings entered interactively by user and a queue copies, which contains each of the strings in the order they were entered.

Module: load_table_from_file

Task: Inquire as to name of file to load.

> while not end of input file
>> Read string from file.
>> Call on add_to_hash_table to load string into table.
>> Call on enqueue operation to add string to copies queue.

Outputs: Hash table loaded with strings read from file and a queue copies, which contains each of the strings in the order they were read.

Module: conduct_search

Task: Perform empirical testing on hashing method for this particular data.

> For each queue in copies queue.
>> Dequeue that key.
>> Call on search_hash_table to find that key, accumulating a profiling count of number of probes into table that are required to find the key.
>> Enqueue that key back into copies queue.
> Report on average length for successful searches conducted in first step
> For a fixed number of unsuccessful searches
>> Randomly generate a key not in table.
>> Call on search_hash_table to attempt to find that key, accumulating a profiling count of the number of probes into table that are required to determine that the key cannot be located.
> Report profiling information for unsuccessful searches.

Inputs: Hash table. Copies queue containing string keys in order generated by load_table module.

Module: save_if_wanted

Task: Inquire if user wants to save this data set for further exploration. If user wants to save and data set was not originally loaded from file write copies queue to file in form compatible with load_table_from_file module.

Inputs: Copy queue containing keys in order originally generated.

Module: print_table

Task: Iterate through table from low to high, printing nonempty slots.

Inputs: Hash table. Low and high: indices of table between which nonempty table positions are to be printed.

RUNNING, DEBUGGING AND TESTING HINTS

1. When using hashing as a search strategy, provide yourself with a means of experimenting with your hashing function and collision-processing strategy. This will allow you to tailor your program to the particular kind of keys that are stored in the hash table.

2. Searching for data in a random access file involves different criteria than searching for data in main memory. Programs that search for data in random access files should minimize file accesses at the expense of main memory accesses. Indexed searches provide ways of doing this.

3. If a search program has to handle duplicate keys, that is, different records associated with the same key value, the search algorithm will have to be adjusted appropriately. Be sure you know and decide in advance whether this added complexity is necessary.

SUMMARY

Key Terms

boundary folding
buckets
clustering
collision
density-dependent search
   techniques
digit/character extraction
division-remainder technique
folding

hashing
hashing function
index
key-to-address transformation
linear collision processing
linked collision processing
overflow area
prime hash area

quadratic collision processing
randomized storage
rehashing collision processing
sectors
shift folding
synonyms
tracks

Key Terms (Optional)

binary tree index
B-tree
concurrent updating
data integrity

deadlock
fatal embrace
indexed sequential access
   method (ISAM)

indexed sequential search
record lock facility
trie indexing

Key Concepts

◆ The following table gives a concise synopsis of the search strategies that have been discussed in this and earlier chapters. Additional comments emphasize particular strengths or weaknesses of the strategy in terms of the one-key table operations we have considered throughout the text.

Method	Efficiency (n = number of records)	Other Components Regarding One-Key Table Operations
Binary	$O(\log_2 n)$	Data must be maintained in physical order, hence making insertions and deletions inefficient.
Binary tree index	$O(\log_2 n)$ index probes, 1 file probe	Guaranteeing this efficiency requires height balancing.
B-tree index order k	Worst case requires $1 + \log_k[(n+1)/2]$ disk accesses for index	Choose k so that index node coincides with disk block.
Indexed sequential	O(size of index) index probes, $O[n/$(size of index)] file probes	Index and file require physical ordering to maintain efficiency.
Linear hashing	Average successful: $(1/2) * [1 + 1/(1 - D)]$ Average unsuccessful: $(1/2) * [1 + 1/(1 - D)^2]$ where density $D = n/\mathbf{RECORD\_SPACE}$	Data not maintained in any order.
Linked hashing	Average successful: $1 + D/2$ Average unsuccessful: D (where $\mathbf{RECORD\_SPACE}$ used in computation of D is that in primary hash area)	Data not maintained in any order.
Quadratic hashing	Average successful: $1 - \log_e(1 - D) - (D/2)$ Average unsuccessful: $1/(1 - D) - D - \log_e(1 - D)$	Data not maintained in any order.
Rehashing	Average successful: $-(1/D) * \log_e(1 - D)$ Average unsuccessful: $1/(1 - D)$	Data not maintained in any order.
Sequential	$O(n)$	
Trie index	O(number of characters in target)	Specifically suited for character strings.

◆ In addition to hashing, other search strategies specifically oriented toward file structures include indexed sequential search, B-trees, and tries.

◆ As an implementation strategy for one-key tables, hashing fares very well in all of the operations except ordering. It thus represents a very viable addition to the list implementation strategies discussed in earlier chapters: array or random files with binary search, linked lists, and binary trees.

1. Complete the program designed in this chapter's Focus on Program Design section. Then use the program as a means of conducting experiments on hashing. In your experiments, you should try a variety of hashing functions and collision-processing strategies. You might also try to adjust the generation of random strings so that, although still random, the strings conform to rules for particular kinds of data. That is, if the data consist of names of the form

   `COOPER, J. C.`

   the random generation of characters could be modified based on the probabilities of certain letters being used and on the average length of last names. Write up a report in which you analyze each of the hashing functions and collision-processing strategies you use. Back up your analysis with empirical profiling data obtained from the `conduct_search` module of your program.

2. Implement the registrar's system described in Example 13.1 using hashing as a list maintenance technique. Be sure that you devise an appropriate strategy to output the ordered listings that the registrar must have.

3. Implement the Wing-and-a-Prayer flight/pilot database (Focus on Program Design, Chapter 12) using the implementation technique described in Section 19.2. For an added challenge, assume that the rows of the flight/pilot table are indexed by pilot name instead of pilot number. How could this complication be handled in a way that minimizes the memory needed to store the implementation of a two-key table?

4. A B-tree of order 3 is often called a 2–3 tree since each node has 2 or 3 children. Because of its low order, a 2–3 tree is not particularly applicable as a file index. However, if we store up to two actual data records in each node instead of up to two key–pointer pairs, then a 2–3 tree becomes an alternative to an ordered binary tree for implementing a list. Develop search, insertion, and deletion algorithms for such a 2–3 tree structure. Compare its performance characteristics with those of an ordered binary tree.

5. Implement the registrar's system of Problem 2 using a 2–3 tree representation of a list (see Problem 4.)

6. Wing-and-a-Prayer Airlines has the records of all its customers stored in the following form:
   ■ Last name
   ■ First name
   ■ Address
   ■ Arbitrarily long list of flights on which reservations have been booked.

   Using a trie index, write a search-and-retrieval program that will allow input of a customer's last name (and, if necessary, the first name and address to resolve conflicts created by matching last names) and then output all flights on which that customer has booked reservations.

7. SuperScout Inc. is a nationwide scouting service for college football talent to which the Bay Area Brawlers professional team subscribes. As the pool of college talent increases in size, SuperScout has found that its old record-keeping system has dete-

riorated considerably in its ability to quickly locate the scouting record associated with a given player in its file. Rewrite their scouting record system using a trie to look up the record location of the data associated with a given player's name.

8. Using a large collection of randomly generated keys, write a series of programs that will test various hashing functions you develop. In particular, your programs should report statistics on the number of collisions generated by each hashing function. This information could be valuable in guiding future decisions about which hashing functions and techniques are most effective for your particular system.

9. Consider a student data record that consists of

   - Student identification number
   - Student name
   - State of residence
   - Sex.

   Choose an index structure to process a file of such records. Then write a program to maintain such a file as a one-key table.

10. Suppose that data records for a phone book file consist of a key field containing both name and address, and a field containing the phone number for that key. Devise an appropriate index for such a file. Then write a program which calls for input of

    a. A complete key.
    b. If a complete key is not available, as much of the initial portion of a key as the inquirer is able to provide.

    In the case of part a, your program should output the phone number corresponding to the unique key. In the case of part b, have your program output all keys (and their phone numbers) that match the provided initial portion.

11. Consider the following problem faced in the development of a compiler. The source program contains many character-string symbols such as variable names, function names, and so on. Each of these character-string symbols has associated with it various attributes such as memory location, data type, and so on. However, it would be too time consuming and awkward for a compiler to actually manipulate character strings. Instead, each string should be identified with an integer that is viewed as being equivalent to the string for the purpose of compiler manipulation. In addition to serving as a compact equivalent form of a string symbol within the source program, this integer can also serve as a direct pointer into a table of attributes for that symbol. Devise such a transformation that associates a string with an integer, and which in turn serves as a pointer into a table of attributes. Test the structure(s) you develop by using them in a program that scans a source program written in a language such as C++. You will in effect have written the symbol table modules for a compiler.

12. Write a spelling checker program. Such a program must scan a file of text, looking up each word it finds in a dictionary of correctly spelled words. When a word cannot be found in the dictionary, the spelling checker should convey this fact to its user, giving the user the opportunity to take one of the following steps:

    a. Skip the word.
    b. Change the spelling of the word in the text file.
    c. Add the word to the dictionary so it will not be reported as incorrectly spelled in the future.

    Since the dictionary for such a program will be searched frequently and is likely to become quite large, an efficient search algorithm is an absolute necessity. One possibility in this regard is to use a trie index with pointers into a large string workspace instead of the pointers to data records described in Section 19.3. Test your program with a text file and dictionary large enough to handle all of the possibilities your algorithm and data structure may encounter.

13. If you solved one of the problems from Chapter 12 that involved maintaining a one-key table, redo that problem using hashing combined with linked lists as an implementation technique. When finished, write a report in which you empirically compare the performance of your two implementations.

14. If you solved one of the problems from Chapter 12 that involved maintaining a two-key table, redo that problem using hashing of row and column indices as an implementation technique. When finished, write a report in which you empirically compare the performance of your two implementations.

Appendixes

Appendix 1
Reserved Words

The following words have predefined meanings in C++ and cannot be changed. The words in bolface are discussed in the text. The other words are discussed in Stanley B. Lippman, *C++ Primer,* 2nd edition, Reading, MA: Addison-Wesley Publishing Company, 1993.

asm	continue	**float**	**new**	**signed**	try
auto	**default**	**for**	**operator**	sizeof	**typedef**
break	**delete**	**friend**	**private**	static	union
case	**do**	goto	**protected**	**struct**	**unsigned**
catch	**double**	**if**	**public**	**switch**	virtual
char	**else**	inline	register	template	**void**
class	**enum**	**int**	**return**	**this**	volatile
const	extern	**long**	**short**	throw	**while**

Appendix 2
Some Useful Library Functions

Some of the most commonly used library functions in the first course in computer science come from the libraries **math, ctype**, and **string**. Descriptions of the most important functions in each of these libraries is presented in the following three tables.

math

Function Declaration	Purpose
`double acos(double x);`	Returns arc cosine for x in range -1 to +1
`double asin(double x);`	Returns arc sine for x in range -1 to +1
`double atan(double x);`	Returns arc tangent of x
`double atan2(double y, double x);`	Returns arc tangent of y/x
`double ceil(double x);`	Rounds x up to next highest integer
`double cos(double x);`	Returns cosine of x
`double cosh(double x);`	Returns hyberbolic cosine of x
`double exp(double x);`	Returns e to the xth power
`double exp(double x);`	Returns absolute value of x
`double floor(double x);`	Rounds x down to next lowest integer
`double fmod(double x, double y);`	Returns remainder of x/y
`double ldexp(double x, double exp);`	Returns x times 2 to the power of exp
`double log(double x);`	Returns natural logarithm of x
`double log10(double x);`	Returns base 10 logarithm of x
`double pow(double x, double y);`	Returns x raised to power of y
`double sin(double x);`	Returns sine of x
`double sinh(double x);`	Returns hyberbolic sine of x
`double sqrt(double x);`	Returns square root of x
`double tan(double x);`	Returns tangent of x, in radians
`double tanh(double x);`	Returns hyperbolic tangent of x

`ctype`

Function Declaration	Purpose
`int isalnum(int ch);`	ch is letter or digit
`int isalpha(int ch);`	ch is letter
`int iscntrl(int ch);`	ch is control character
`int isdigit(int ch);`	ch is digit (0-9)
`int isgraph(int ch);`	ch is printable but not ' '
`int islower(int ch);`	ch is lowercase letter
`int isprint(int ch);`	ch is printable
`int ispunct(int ch);`	ch is printable but not ' ' or alpha
`int isspace(int ch);`	ch is a whitespace character
`int isupper(int ch);`	ch is uppercase letter
`int isxdigit(int ch);`	ch is hexadecimal digit
`int tolower(int ch);`	Returns lowercase of ch
`int toupper(int ch);`	Returns uppercase of ch

`string`

Function declaration	Purpose
`int *strcat(int *s1, const int *s2);`	Appends copy of s2 to end of s1
`int strcmp(const int *s1, const int *s2);`	Compares s1 and s2
`int *strcpy(int *s1, const int *s2);`	Copies s2 to s1, including '\0'
`int strlen(const int *s);`	Returns length of s, not including '\0'

Appendix 3
Syntax Diagrams

The following syntax diagrams correspond to the syntax forms used to describe the features of C++ discussed in the text. Two points of caution are in order. First, the diagrams in this appendix by no means represent an exhaustive description of C++. Second, many of the features discussed in this text have more than one syntactically correct construction (for example, **main** can be preceded by either **int** or **void**, but the C++ programming community prefers **int**). By confining your attention to preferred ways of using a small subset of features, we hope to place your focus on concepts rather than syntax. Students wanting to learn more features of C++ or other ways of expressing them are referred to Stanley B. Lippman, *C++ Primer,* 2nd edition, Reading, MA: Addison-Wesley Publishing Company, 1993.

The terms enclosed in ovals in the diagrams refer to program components that literally appear in programs, such as operator symbols and reserved words. The terms enclosed in boxes refer to program components that require further definition, either by another diagram or by reference to the text. The syntax of terms for which there are no diagrams, such as **identifier, number, string,** and **character**, should be familiar to anyone who has read this text.

Main program module

Preprocessor directive

Constant definition

Type definition

Simple type

Array type

Enumeration type

Pointer type

Struct type

List of members

Variable declaration

List of identifiers

Function declaration

Main program heading

Compound statement

Statement

Assignment statement

Function call statement

Input statement

Output statement

Return statement

If statement

Switch statement

For statement

While statement

Do statement

Increment statement

Decrement statement

Function implementation

Function heading

List of formal parameters

Parameter declaration

Expression

Relation

Simple expression

Term

Factor

Primary

Name

Function call

List of actual parameters

Logical operator

Adding operator

Comparison operator

Multiplying operator

Class declaration module

Class declaration heading

Class declaration

Access mode

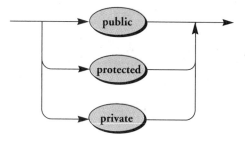

Appendix 4
The ASCII Character Set

The table included here shows the ordering of the ASCII character set. Note only printable characters are shown. Ordinals without character representations either do not have standard representation or are associated with unprintable control characters. The blank is denoted by " ♭ ".

The American Standard Code for Information Interchange (ASCII)

Left Digit(s)	Right Digit									
	0	1	2	3	4	5	6	7	8	9
3			♭	!	"	#	$	%	&	'
4	(	)	*	+	,	–	.	/	0	1
5	2	3	4	5	6	7	8	9	:	;
6	<	=	>	?	@	A	B	C	D	E
7	F	G	H	I	J	K	L	M	N	O
8	P	Q	R	S	T	U	V	W	X	Y
9	Z	[	\	]	^	—	`		a	b	c
10	d	e	f	g	h	i	j	k	l	m
11	n	o	p	q	r	s	t	u	v	w
12	x	y	z	{			}	~			

*Codes < 32 or > 126 are nonprintable.

Appendix 5
Some Useful Format Flags

The use of the manipulators **setw**, **setprecision**, **fixed**, and **showpoint** to format output was introduced in Section 2.3. Because the use of **fixed** and **showpoint** in C++ has not been standardized, the statement

```
cout << fixed << showpoint;
```

may not have the desired effect of displaying real numbers in fixed point format with trailing zeros in some implementations of C++. However, the following way of specifying the same kind of format is standard, though not as simple:

```
cout << setiosflags (ios::fixed | ios::showpoint);
```

The **setiosflags** manipulator takes a list of flags as a parameter. The general form for using **setiosflags** is

setiosflags(<flag$_1$> | <flag$_2$> | ... | <flag$_n$>)

setiosflags also works with output file streams, as in the following statement:

```
output_file << setiosflags(ios::fixed | ios::showpoint);
```

Some useful flags are listed in the following table:

Flag Name	Meaning
ios::showpoint	Display decimal point with trailing zeros
ios::fixed	Display real numbers in fixed point notation
ios::scientific	Display real numbers in floating point notation
ios::right	Display values right justified

Appendix 6
A Random Number Generator

Most programming languages currently in widespread use provide a function for generating random numbers. C++ provides a library function, **rand()**, that returns an integer between 0 and the compiler-dependent constant **RAND_MAX**, inclusive. Both the function and the constant are declared in the library header file **stdlib.h**. Unfortunately, the numbers generated by **rand** are not as random as we would like. The reason for this is that the number returned by **rand** depends on an initial value, called a *seed,* that is the same for each run of a program. Thus, the sequence of random numbers generated by a program that uses this method will be exactly the same on each run of the program.

To help solve this problem, another function, **srand(seed)**, also declared in **stdlib.h**, allows an application to specify the initial value used by **rand** at program start up. Using this method, two runs of a program that use different values for **seed** will thus receive different sequences of random numbers. The problem then becomes one of providing an arbitrary seed value. Rather than force a user to enter this value interactively, most applications obtain it by reading the current time from the computer's internal clock. The C++ function **clock()**, declared in the **time.h** library header file, returns the current time on the computer's clock. When converted to an integer, this value can serve as a fairly arbitrary seed for a random number generator in most programs.

To summarize the discussion so far, the following lines of code would display 10 random numbers between 0 and **RAND_MAX**, depending on the current time on the computer's clock at program start up:

```
#include <iostream.h>
#include <stdlib.h>
#include <time.h>

int  main()
{
    srand(int(clock));
    for (int i = 1;  i <= 10;  ++i)
        cout << rand() << endl;
    return 0;
}
```

Particular clients of a random number generator might desire a narrower or a wider range of numbers than **rand** provides. Ideally, a client would specify the range by passing integer values representing the lower and upper bounds of the desired range to a function. To see how we might use **rand** to implement this feature, first consider how to generate a number between 0 and an arbitrary upper bound, **high**, inclusive. For any two integers, a and b, $a \% b$ is between 0 and $b - 1$, inclusive. Thus, the expression **rand() % high + 1** would generate a random number between 0 and **high**, inclusive, where **high** is less than or equal to **RAND_MAX**. To place a lower bound other than 0 on the result, we can generate a random number between 0 and **high - low + 1**, and then add **low** to the result. Thus, the complete expression for computing a random number between a lower bound and an upper bound would be **rand() % (high - low + 1) + low**.

Now that we have settled the details of the system tools and arithmetic operations necessary for generating random numbers, we can specify a random number generator as a server or class in C++. The abstract operations are the following:

Create operation

Preconditions: Receiver is an arbitrary random number generator in an unpredictable state.

Postconditions: Receiver is seeded from the internal clock of the computer.

next_number operation

Preconditions: Receiver is a random number generator. **low** and **high** are integer values such that **low < high <= RAND_MAX**.

Postconditions: An integer representing a random number between **low** and **high**, inclusive, is returned.

Reset operation

Preconditions: Receiver is a random number generator.

Postconditions: The receiver is reinitialized with a new seed from the internal clock of the computer.

Note that we do not provide a **create** operation with a user-specified seed. This could easily be added. The class declaration and implementation modules follow:

```
// Class declaration file: random.h

#ifndef RANDOM_H

class  random_generator
{

    public:

    // Class constructor

    random_generator();

    // Member functions

    int next_number(int low, int high);
    void reset();

};
```

```
#define RANDOM_H
#endif

// Class implementation file: random.cpp

#include <stdlib.h>
#include <time.h>
#include <assert.h>
#include "random.h"

random_generator::random_generator()
{
     srand(int(clock()));
}

int random_generator::next_number(int low, int high)
{
     assert((low < high) && (high < RAND_MAX));
     return rand() % (high - low + 1) + low;
}

void random_generator::reset()
{
     srand(int(clock())));
}
```

The following short program uses an instance of the random generator class to
output 10 random numbers in the range from –50 to 50:

```
#include <iostream.h>
#include "random.h"

int main()
{
     random_generator numbers;

     for (int i = 1; i <= 10; ++i)
          cout << numbers.next_random(-50, 50) << endl;
     return 0;
}
```

Glossary

abstract data type (ADT)   A form of abstraction that arises from the use of defined types. An ADT consists of a class of objects, a defined set of properties of those objects, and a set of operations for processing the objects.

abstraction   The description of data structures at a conceptual level, apart from their implementation using a particular technique and language.

abstract syntax tree   *See* **parse tree.**

access adjustment   A method of changing the access mode of an inherited member from within a derived class. For example, a derived class may inherit all members from a base class in protected mode, and then make some members public by means of access adjustments. *See also* **access mode, base class, derived class,** and **inheritance.**

access mode   A symbol (**public, protected,** or **private**) that specifies the kind of access that clients have to a server's data members and member functions. *See also* **private member, protected member,** and **public member.**

accumulator   A variable used for the purpose of summing successive values of some other variable.

actual parameter   A variable or expression contained in a function call and passed to that function. *See also* **formal parameter.**

address   Often called address of a memory location, this is an integer value that the computer can use to reference a location. *See also* **value.**

ADT   *See* **abstract data type.**

ADT generality rule   An abstract data type should not be limited by the types of its components. Wherever possible, users should be able to specify the component types of a generic abstract data type.

ADT implementation rule   An implementation of an ADT must provide an interface that is entirely consistent with the operations specified in the ADT's definition.

ADT layering rule   Existing abstract data types should be used to implement new abstract data types, unless direct control over the underlying data structures and operations of the programming language is a critical factor. A well-designed implementation consists of layers of ADTs.

ADT use rule   An algorithm that uses an ADT should access variables of that abstract data type only through the operations provided in the ADT definition.

algorithm   A finite sequence of effective statements that, when applied to the problem, will solve it.

alias   A situation in which two or more identifiers in a program come to refer to the same memory location. An alias can become the cause of subtle side effects.

analysis phase   The first phase of the software system life cycle in which the systems analyst determines the user's needs and develops formal specifications describing the proposed system and its requirements.

ancestor   A tree node that is hierarchically related to another tree node at a lower level in the tree.

application software   Programs designed for a specific use.

argument   A value or expression passed in a function call.

arithmetic/logic unit (ALU)   The part of the central processing unit (CPU) that performs arithmetic operations and evaluates expressions.

array   A data structure whose elements are accessed by means of index positions.

array index   The relative position of the components of an array.

artificial intelligence (AI) The field of computer science in which the goal is to program the computer to mimic intelligent human behavior.

ASCII collating sequence The American Standard Code for Information Interchange ordering for a character set.

assembly language A computer language that allows words and symbols to be used in an unsophisticated manner to accomplish simple tasks.

assertion Special comments used with selection and repetition that state what you expect to happen and when certain conditions will hold.

assignment statement A method of putting values into memory locations.

association A data structure whose two parts are a key and a value.

association list A data structure consisting of a set of associations. *See also* **association.**

attribute A property that a computational object models, such as the balance in a bank account.

automatic program synthesis A process whereby one computer program can be given the specifications for another computer program, generate the code to satisfy those specifications, and then prove the correctness of that code.

Backus-Naur grammar A standard form for defining the formal syntax of a language.

base class The class from which a derived class inherits attributes and behavior. *See also* **derived class** and **inheritance.**

behavior The set of actions that a class of objects supports.

best case The arrangement of data items prior to the start of a sort function to finish in the least amount of time for that particular set of items. *See also* **worst case.**

big-O analysis A technique for estimating the time and space requirements of an algorithm in terms of order of magnitude.

big-O notation Saying that an algorithm is $O(f(n))$ indicates that the function $f(n)$ may be useful in characterizing how efficiently the algorithm performs for large n. For such n, we are assured that the operations required by the algorithm will be bounded by the product of a constant and $f(n)$.

bin sort *See* **radix sort.**

binary digit A digit, either 0 or 1, in the binary number system. Program instructions are stored in memory using a sequence of binary digits. Binary digits are called bits.

binary search The process of examining a middle value of a sorted array to see which half contains the value in question and halving until the value is located.

binary search tree A binary tree with the ordering property.

binary tree A tree such that each node can point to at most two children.

binary tree search A search algorithm driven by the hierarchical relationships of data items in a tree with the ordering property.

binding time The time at which a program variable is bound to a particular value. This can occur either at compile time or at run time.

bit *See* **binary digit.**

black box testing The method of testing a module whereby the tester is aware of only what the module is supposed to do, not the method of implementation or the internal logic. *See also* **white box testing.**

block The area of program text within a compound statement, containing statements and optional data declarations.

blocked queue In an operating system, the queue of processes that have requested a resource currently owned by another process.

Boolean expression An expression whose value is either true or false. *See also* **compound Boolean expression** and **simple Boolean expression.**

bottom-up testing Independent testing of modules.

boundary conditions Values that separate two logical possibilities. These are important cases to check when testing a module.

boundary folding A variation on shift folding: in boundary folding, the digits of every other numeric section are reversed before the addition is performed.

branch In a tree, a link between a parent and its child node.

breadth-first traversal A visiting of all nodes in a graph; it proceeds from each node by first visiting all nodes adjacent to that node.

B-tree An efficient, flexible index structure often used in database management systems.

bubble sort Rearranges elements of an array until they are in either ascending or descending order. Consecutive elements are compared to move (bubble) the elements to the top or bottom accordingly on each pass. *See also* **heap sort, insertion sort, merge sort, quick sort, radix sort, selection sort,** and **shell sort.**

bucket In bucket hashing, a contiguous region of storage locations.

bucket hashing Method of handling collisions whereby the hashing function sends the key to a bucket of locations rather than a single location. The key is then placed by performing a sequential search within the bucket.

bus A group of wires imprinted on a circuit board to facilitate communication between components of a computer.

byte   A sequence of bits used to encode a character in memory. *See also* **word.**

call   Any reference to a subprogram by an executable statement. Also referred to as invoke.

central processing unit (CPU)   A major hardware component that consists of the arithmetic/logic unit (ALU) and the control unit.

character set   The list of characters available for data and program statements. *See also* **collating sequence.**

child node   A node that descends from another node in a tree.

children   Nodes pointed to by a node in a tree.

circular linked list   A linked list whose last node points to the first or head node in the list.

class   A description of the attributes and behavior of a set of computational objects.

class constructor   A member function used to create and initialize an instance of a class.

class declaration module   An area of a program used to declare the data members and member functions of a class.

class destructor   A member function defined by the programmer and automatically used by the computer to return dynamic memory used by an object to the heap when the program exits the scope of the object. *See also* **dynamic memory.**

class implementation module   An area of a program used to implement the member functions of a class.

class template   A special kind of class definition that allows clients to specify the component types of objects of that class.

client   A computational object that receives a service from another computational object.

clustering   Occurs when a hashing function is biased toward the placement of keys in a given region of the storage space.

code (writing)   The process of writing executable statements that are part of a program to solve a problem.

cohesive subprogram   A subprogram designed to accomplish a single task.

collating sequence   The particular order sequence for a character set used by a machine. *See also* **ASCII collating sequence** and **EBCDIC collating sequence.**

collision   Condition in which more than one key hashes to the same position with a given hashing function.

column-major order   A means of traversing a two-dimensional array whereby all of the data in one column are accessed before the data in the next column. *See also* **row-major order.**

comment   A nonexecutable statement used to make a program more readable.

compatible type   Expressions that have the same base type. A parameter and its argument must be of compat-

ible type, and the operands of an assignment statement must be of compatible type.

compilation error   An error detected when the program is being compiled. *See also* **design error, logic error, run-time error,** and **syntax error.**

compiler   A computer program that automatically converts instructions in a high-level language to machine language.

compound Boolean expression   Refers to the complete expression when logical connectives and negation are used to generate Boolean values. *See also* **Boolean expression** and **simple Boolean expression.**

compound statement   Uses the symbols { and } to make several simple statements into a single compound statement.

conditional statement   *See* **selection statement.**

constant   A symbol whose value cannot be changed in the body of the program.

constant definition section   The section where program constants are defined for subsequent use.

constant parameter   A method of declaring a formal array parameter so that the value of an actual array parameter will not change in a function.

constant reference   A method of declaring a formal parameter so that the actual parameter is passed by reference but will not change in a function.

control structure   A structure that controls the flow of execution of program statements.

control unit   The part of the central processing unit that controls the operation of the rest of the computer.

copy constructor   A member function defined by the programmer and automatically used by the computer to copy the values of objects when they are passed by value to functions.

counter   A variable used to count the number of times some process is completed.

coupling   The amount of interaction between a pair of modules.

cubic algorithm   A polynomial algorithm in which the highest nonzero term is n^3.

data   The particular characters that are used to represent information in a form suitable for storage, processing, and communication.

data abstraction   The separation between the conceptual definition of a data structure and its eventual implementation.

data flow diagram   A graphic tool used by systems analysts to represent data flow and transformations as a conceptual process. Also referred to as a bubble diagram.

data member   A data object declared within a class declaration module.

data type   A formal description of the set of values that a variable can have.

data validation   The process of examining data prior to its use in a program.

deadlock   An infinite wait state in which two processes each own system resources the other needs and will not release until they have obtained the remaining resources they need. Also referred to as fatal embrace.

debugging   The process of eliminating errors or "bugs" from a program.

declaration sections   The sections used to declare (name) symbolic constants, data types, variables, and subprograms that are necessary to the program.

decrement   To decrease the value of a variable.

density   The number of storage locations used divided by the total number of storage locations available.

density-dependent search technique   A Search technique whose efficiency is determined solely by the density of the data.

depth-first traversal   A visiting of all nodes in a graph, proceeding from each node by probing as deeply as possible along one path leading from that node.

dereference   The operation by which a program uses a pointer to access the contents of dynamic memory. *See also* **dynamic memory** and **pointer variable.**

derived class   A class that inherits attributes and behavior from other classes. *See also* **base class** and **inheritance.**

design error   An error such that a program runs, but unexpected results are produced. Also referred to as a logic error. *See also* **compilation error, run-time error,** and **syntax error.**

design phase   The second phase of the software system life cycle. In this phase, a relatively detailed design plan is created from the formal specifications of the system produced in the analysis phase.

dictionary   A data structure consisting of a set of associations. *See also* **association.**

digit/character extraction   In creating a hashing function, the process of removing from a key those digits of characters that may bias the results of the function.

digraph   A graph having some edges that point in only one direction.

diminishing increment sort   A sort in which the number of segments in any one pass decreases with each successive pass. *See also* **shell sort.**

directional graph   *See* **digraph.**

divide-and-conquer algorithms   A class of algorithms that solves problems by repeatedly dividing them into simpler problems. *See also* **recursion.**

division-remainder technique   A hashing technique that ensures that the result will be a valid output. It uses the modulus operation to scale the value into the proper range.

dominant term   The highest power of n in a polynomial. For large n, the behavior of the entire polynomial will approach the behavior of a polynomial that contains only that term.

doubly linked list   A linked list in which each node has two pointers instead of one. One of these points to the previous node in the list and the other points to the next node in the list.

do . . . while loop   A post-test loop examining a Boolean expression after causing a statement to be executed. *See also* **for loop, loops,** and **while loop.**

dynamic memory   Memory allocated under program control from the heap and accessed by means of pointers. *See also* **heap** and **pointer variable.**

dynamic structure   A data structure that may expand or contract during execution of a program. *See also* **dynamic memory.**

EBCDIC collating sequence   The Extended Binary Coded Decimal Interchange Code ordering for a character set.

echo checking   A debugging technique in which values of variables and input data are displayed during program execution.

edge   A direct connection between two nodes in a graph.

effective statement   A clear, unambiguous instruction that can be carried out.

empty statement   A semicolon used to indicate that no action is to be taken. Also referred to as a null statement.

encapsulation   The process of hiding implementation details of a data structure.

end-of-file marker   A special marker inserted by the machine to indicate the end of the data file.

end-of-line character   A special character ('\0') used to indicate the end of a line of characters in a string or a file stream.

entrance-controlled loop   *See* **pretest loop.**

enumerated data type   A set of symbolic constants defined by the programmer.

equivalence classes   A partitioning of all the logical possibilities that can be checked when testing a module. All test cases within a single equivalence class are identical from the standpoint of the logic of the module.

error   *See* **compilation error, design error, logic error, run-time error,** and **syntax error.**

executable section   Contains the statements that cause the computer to do something.

executable statement   The basic unit of grammar in C++ consisting of valid identifiers, standard identifiers, reserved words, numbers, and/or characters, together with appropriate punctuation.

execute   To carry out the instructions of a program.

exit-controlled loop   *See* **post-test loop.**

expert system   A program able to reason as an expert in a limited domain.

exponential algorithm   An algorithm whose efficiency is dominated by a term of the form k^n.

exponential form   *See* **floating point.**

extended if statement   Nested selection where additional **if . . . else** statements are used in the else option. *See also* **nested if statement.**

factorial   The product of the first N positive integers (denoted as N!).

fatal embrace   *See* **deadlock.**

field width   The phrase used to describe the number of columns used for various output. *See also* **formatting.**

FIFO   *See* **queue.**

file stream   A data structure that consists of a sequence of components that are accessed by input or output operations.

finite state automata   Algorithms driven by a table indexed by the possible states that can exist and the possible categories of input symbols are called finite state algorithms. Machines running such algorithms are finite state automata.

first-in, first-out (FIFO)   *See* **queue.**

fixed-repetition loop   A loop used when it is known in advance the number of times a segment of code needs to be repeated.

fixed point   A method of writing decimal numbers where the decimal is placed where it belongs in the number. *See also* **floating point.**

floating point   A method for writing numbers in scientific notation to accommodate numbers that may have very large or very small values. *See also* **fixed point.**

folding   A method of hashing in cases where the key is not an integer value.. The nonnumeric characters are removed and the remaining digits are combined to produce an integer value.

for loop   A structured loop consisting of an initializer expression, a termination expression, an update expression, and a statement.

formal parameter   A name, declared and used in a function declaration, that is replaced by an actual parameter when the function is called.

formal verification   The use of logic to produce a proof of the correctness of an algorithm.

formatting   Designating the desired field width when printing integers, reals, and character strings. *See also* **field width.**

free store   *See* **heap.**

friend of a class   The process of making the data members of one class available to another class.

front pointer   The pointer to the front of a queue.

function   *See* **library function** and **user-defined function.**

function member   A function declared within a class declaration module.

functional abstraction   The process of considering only what a function is to do rather than details of the function.

generic abstract data type   An abstract data type whose component types are specified as parameters. For example, a generic stack ADT could be used to create stacks of integers as well as stacks of characters.

general list   A collection of data items that are related by their relative position in the collection.

general tree   A set of nodes that is either empty or has a designated node (called the root) from which descend zero or more subtrees.

generalized nested loops   Loops whose nesting depth is determined at run time using recursive logic.

global identifier   An identifier that can be used by the main program and all subprograms in a program.

global variable   *See* **global identifier.**

graph   A set of data elements called nodes and the paths between them called edges.

halting problem   A problem concerned with determining whether or not a given program will terminate or loop indefinitely when provided with a given set of input data.

hardware   The actual computing machine and its support devices.

has-a relation   The property of one class having an object of another class as a data member. *See also* **is-a relation.**

hashing   A density-dependent search technique whereby the key for a given data item is transformed using a function to produce the address where that item is stored in memory.

head pointer   A pointer to the first item in a list.

header file   A C++ file that provides data and function declarations in a library to client modules.

heap   An area of computer memory where storage for dynamic data is available.

heap   A binary tree with the heap property.

heap property   A binary tree has the heap property when the data at any given node are greater or equal to the data in its left and right subtrees.

heap sort   A sort in which the array is treated like an array implementation of a binary tree. The items are repeatedly manipulated to create a heap from which the root is removed and added to the sorted portion of the array. *See also* **bubble sort, insertion sort, merge sort, quick sort, radix sort, selection sort,** and **shell sort.**

height balancing   A technique for ensuring that an ordered binary tree remains as full as possible in form.

heuristics   Rules of thumb that cut down on the number of possible choices to examine. They often lead to quick solutions but do not guarantee a solution the way an algorithm does.

hierarchy   A relation between nodes whereby one is viewed as above or prior to another.

high-level language   Any programming language that uses words and symbols to make it relatively easy to read and write a program. *See also* **assembly language** and **machine language.**

identifiers   Words that must be created according to a well-defined set of rules but can have any meaning subject to these rules. *See also* **library identifiers.**

implementation file   A C++ file that provides the implementations of data and functions declared in a header file.

index   *See* **array index** or **loop index.**

indexed sequential access method (ISAM)   The most common method of indexed sequential search.

indexed sequential search   Use of a partial index based on disk-dependent factors to find the proper portion of the disk for sequential searching for a key.

index sort   Sorting an array by ordering the indices of the components rather than exchanging the components.

inductive assertion   A method of formally proving the correctness of an algorithm by using an inductive proof.

infinite loop   A loop in which the controlling condition is not changed in such a manner to allow the loop to terminate.

infix   Algebraic notation in which the operator appears between the two operands to which it will be applied.

infix priority   A function that ranks the algebraic operators in terms of their precedence.

information hiding   The process of suppressing the implementation details of a function or data structure so as to simplify its use in programming.

inheritance   The process by which a derived class can reuse attributes and behavior defined in a base class. *See also* **base class** and **derived class.**

inorder predecessor   The node preceding a given node in an inorder traversal.

inorder successor   The node following a given node in an inorder traversal.

inorder threads   Pointers to the inorder predecessor and successor of a node.

inorder traversal   A binary tree traversal in which a node's left subtree is visited first, then that node is processed, and finally the node's right subtree is visited.

input   Data obtained by a program during its execution.

input assertion   A precondition for a loop.

input device   A device that provides information to the computer. Typical devices are keyboards, disk drives,

card readers, and tape drives. *See also* **I/O device** and **output device.**

insertion rule   For binary trees, a rule whereby a new item is placed in the left subtree of an item greater than it or in the right subtree of an item less than it.

insertion sort   Sorts an array of elements that starts with an empty array and inserts elements one at a time in their proper order. *See also* **bubble sort, heap sort, merge sort, quick sort, radix sort, selection sort,** and **shell sort.**

instance   A computational object bearing the attributes and behavior specified by a class.

integer arithmetic operations   Operations allowed on data of type **int.** This includes the operations of addition, subtraction, multiplication, division, and modulus to produce integer answers.

interface   A formal statement of how communication occurs between subprograms, the main driver, and other subprograms.

invariant expression   An assertion that is true before the loop and after each iteration of the loop.

invoke   *See* **call.**

I/O device   Any device that allows information to be transmitted to or from a computer. *See also* **input device** and **output device.**

is-a relation   The property of one class being a derived class of another class. *See also* **has-a relation, derived class,** and **base class.**

iteration   *See* **loops.**

key   A field in a data structure that is used to access an element in that structure.

key-to-address transformation   A transformation in which the key of a data item maps to the address at which the data are stored.

keywords   Either reserved words or library identifiers.

last-in, first-out (LIFO)   *See* **stack.**

leaf   In a tree, a node that has no children.

level   All nodes in a tree with a path of the same length from the root node.

lexical analysis   The task of recognizing valid words or tokens in an input stream of characters.

l-value   A computational object capable of being the target of an assignment statement.

library constant   A constant with a standard meaning, such as **NULL** or **INT_MAX**, available in most versions of C++.

library function   A function available in most versions of C++. A list of useful C++ library functions is set forth in Appendix 2.

library identifiers   Words defined in standard C++ libraries. *See also* **identifiers.**

LIFO   *See* **stack.**

linear algorithm   A polynomial algorithm in which the highest nonzero term is n.

linear collision processing   Method of handling a collision in which the storage space is searched sequentially from the location of the collision for an available location where the new key can be placed.

linear ordering   Any ordering of data in which there is an identifiable first element, second element, and so forth.

linear representation (of binary tree)   An implementation of a binary tree in an array. For a given node stored at index position K, that node's left child is at position $2K$, and the right child is at position $2K + 1$.

linear search   *See* **sequential search.**

linked collision processing   Method of handling a collision in which the second key is stored in a linked list located in an overflow area.

linked list   A list of data items where each item is linked to the next one by means of a pointer.

linked representation   An implementation of a binary tree in which pointer fields are used to reference the right and left child of a node in the tree (as opposed to the linear representation of a binary tree).

LISP (LISt Processor)   A highly-recursive computer programming language used heavily in artificial intelligence (AI).

list traversal   The process of sequentially visiting each node in a list.

local identifier   An identifier that is restricted to use within a subblock of a program.

local variable   *See* **local identifier.**

logarithmic algorithm   An algorithm whose efficiency is dominated by a term of the form $\log n$.

logic error   *See* **design error.**

logical operator   Either logical connective (&, ||) or negation (!).

logical size   The number of data items actually available in a data structure at a given time. *See also* **physical size.**

logical order   An ordering of data items according to some defined criterion such as alphabetic, increasing numeric, and so forth. That logical order of the data may or may not be the physical order of the data as stored in the computer.

logically sorted   Data have been logically sorted when pointers to the data have been sorted, even though the data itself have not been touched. Hence, items that the sort places consecutively need not be physically adjacent.

$\log_2 n$ search algorithm   A search algorithm whose efficiency is dominated by a term of the form $\log_2 n$.

loop index   Variable used for control values in a loop.

loop invariant   An assertion that expresses a relationship between variables that remains constant throughout all iterations of the loop.

loop variant   An assertion whose truth changes between the first and final execution of the loop.

loop verification   The process of guaranteeing that a loop performs its intended task.

loops   Program statements that cause a process to be repeated. *See also* **for loop, do . . . while** loop, and **while loop.**

low-level language   *See* **assembly language.**

machine language   The language used directly by the computer in all its calculations and processing.

main block   The main part of a program.

main driver   The main program when subprograms are used to accomplish specific tasks. *See also* **executable section.**

main (primary) memory   Memory contained in the computer. *See also* **memory** and **secondary memory.**

main unit   A computer's main unit contains the central processing unit (CPU) and the main (primary) memory; it is hooked to an input device and an output device.

mainframe   Large computers typically used by major companies and universities. *See also* **microcomputer** and **minicomputer.**

maintenance phase   The fifth phase of the software system life cycle. In this phase, changes must be made in the original program either to fix errors discovered by the users of the program or to meet new user needs.

manifest interface   The property of a function such that, when the function is called, the reader of the code can tell clearly what information is being transmitted to it and what information is being returned from it.

mapping function   A function that transforms row-column array coordinates to the linear address of that array entry.

memory   The ordered sequence of storage cells that can be accessed by address. Instructions and variables of an executing program are temporarily held here. *See also* **main memory** and **secondary memory.**

memory location   A storage cell that can be accessed by address. *See also* **memory.**

merge   The process of combining lists. Typically refers to files or arrays.

merge sort   Sort in which the array is repeatedly split in half and then these pieces are merged together. *See also* **bubble sort, heap sort, insertion sort, quick sort, radix sort, selection sort,** and **shell sort.**

message   In object-oriented programming, a signal to perform an operation on an object.

message-passing   In object-oriented programming, one object's telling another object to perform an operation that is part of its encapsulation.

method of inductive assertions   Method of formally verifying the correctness of an algorithm by identifying the input assertions, output assertions, and loop invariants of the algorithm and constructing a verification proof by mathematical induction.

microcomputer A computer capable of fitting on a laptop or desktop, generally used by one person at a time. *See also* **mainframe** and **minicomputer.**

minicomputer A small version of a mainframe computer. It is usually used by several people at once. *See also* **mainframe** and **microcomputer.**

mixed-mode Expressions containing data of different types; the values of these expressions will be of either type, depending on the rules for evaluating them.

modular development The process of developing an algorithm using modules. *See also* **module.**

modularity The property possessed by a program that is written using modules.

module An independent unit that is part of a larger development. Can be a function or a class (set of functions and related data). *See also* **modular development.**

module specifications In the case of a function, a description of data received, information returned, and task performed by a module. In the case of a class, a description of the attributes and behavior.

modular structure chart A graphic tool used by software designers to display the hierarchical relationships among the modules of the software system.

modular testing A method of testing in which each module is tested immediately after it has been completed rather than when the entire system has been completed.

multilinked list A linked list in which each node has two or more link fields.

natural language A language by which humans normally communicate (such as English), as opposed to a formal programming language (such as C++).

negation The use of the logical operator ! to negate the Boolean value of an expression.

nested if statement A selection statement used within another selection statement. *See also* **extended if statement.**

nested loop A loop as one of the statements in the body of another loop.

nested selection Any combination of selection statements within selection statements. *See also* **selection statement.**

network A graph in which the edges have weight values associated with them.

node One data item in a linked list.

null character The special character ('\0') used to mark the end of a string in C++.

null statement *See* **empty statement.**

numerical analysis A field concerned with obtaining numerical answers to mathematical problems which involve much computation.

object code *See* **object program.**

object-oriented programming A programming paradigm in which a data object is viewed as the owner of operations, as opposed to procedural programming in which an operation is passed data objects as actual parameters. Object-oriented programming emphasizes the ADT approach and allows the users of an ADT to extend the operations of an ADT library in a convenient and efficient fashion.

object program The machine code version of the source program.

one-key table A set of values each of which is accessed by specifying a unique key value, where the key values are ordered.

opened for reading Positions an input stream pointer at the beginning of a file for the purpose of reading from the file.

opened for writing Positions an output stream pointer at the beginning of a file for the purpose of writing to the file.

opening a file Positions a pointer at the beginning of a file. *See also* **opened for reading** and **opened for writing.**

operating system A large program that allows the user to communicate with the hardware and performs various management tasks.

ordered collection A data structure that supports indexing for retrieval or change of data items, the detection of the logical size of the structure, and addition or removal of data items from the logical end of the structure.

order of magnitude Power of ten. Two numbers have the same order of magnitude if their representations in scientific notation have identical exponents to designate the power of ten.

ordering A means of arranging the elements in a list.

ordering property In a binary tree, the data in each node of the tree are greater than or equal to all of the data in that node's left subtree and less than or equal to all of the data in its right subtree.

ordinal data type A data type ordered in some association with the integers; each integer is the ordinal of its associated character.

output Information that is produced by a program.

output assertion A postcondition for a loop.

output device A device that allows you to see the results of a program. Typically it is a monitor or printer. *See also* **input device** and **I/O device.**

overflow In arithmetic operations, a value may be too large for the computer's memory location. A meaningless value may be assigned or an error message may result. *See also* **underflow.**

overloading The process of using the same operator symbol or identifier to refer to many different functions. *See also* **polymorphism.**

parallel arrays   Arrays of the same length but with different component data types.

parallel processing   The use of more than one processor to execute parts of a program concurrently. The effect is that these parts are completed in parallel rather than in sequence.

parameter   *See* **argument.**

parameter list   A list of parameters. An actual parameter list is contained in the function call. A formal parameter list is contained in the function declaration and heading.

parent   In a tree, the node that is pointing to its children.

parse tree   Tree representation of the syntactic structure of a source program produced by a compiler. Also referred to as abstract syntax tree.

parser   A program that checks the syntax of an expression and represents that expression in a unique form.

parser generator   A program that can take the input grammar for a language and produce the parser for that language.

parsing   The procedure of checking the syntax of an expression and representing it in one unique form.

partition   In quick sort, the process of moving the pivot to the location where it belongs in the sorted array and arranging the remaining data items to the left of the pivot if they are less than or equal to the pivot and to the right if they are greater than the pivot.

passed by reference   When the address of the actual parameter is passed to a subprogram.

passed by value   When a copy of the value of the actual parameter is passed to a subprogram.

path   A sequence of edges which connect two nodes in a graph or network.

peripheral memory   *See* **secondary memory** and **memory.**

permutation   An ordered arrangement of the first *n* positive integers in which each integer appears exactly once.

physical size   The number of memory units available for storing data items in a data structure. *See also* **logical size.**

pivot   Item used to direct the partitioning in quick sort.

pointer   A memory location containing the location of another data item.

pointer sort   A sort in which pointers to the data are manipulated rather than the data itself.

pointer variable   Frequently designated as `ptr`, a pointer variable is a variable that contains the address of a memory location. *See also* **address** and **dynamic memory.**

polymorphism   The property of one operator symbol or function identifier having many meanings. *See also* **overloading.**

polynomial algorithm   An algorithm whose efficiency can be expressed in terms of a polynomial.

postcondition   An assertion written after a segment of code.

postfix   Unambiguous algebraic notation in which the arithmetic operator appears after the two operands upon which it is to be applied.

postorder traversal   A binary tree traversal in which at any node, that node's left subtree is visited first, then that node's right subtree is visited, and finally that node is processed.

post-test loop   A loop where the control condition is tested after the loop is executed. `do . . . while` loop is a post-test loop. Also referred to as an exit-controlled loop.

precondition   An assertion written before a particular statement.

prefix   Unambiguous algebraic notation in which the arithmetic operator appears before the two operands upon which it is to be applied.

preorder traversal   A binary tree traversal in which at any node, that node is first processed, then that node's left subtree is visited, and finally that node's right subtree is visited.

pretest condition   A condition that controls whether the body of the loop is executed before going through the loop.

pretest loop   A loop where the control condition is tested before the loop is executed. A `while` loop is a pretest loop. Also referred to as an entrance-controlled loop.

primary memory   *See* **main memory** and **memory.**

prime hash area   In linked collision processing, the main storage area in which keys are placed if no collision occurs.

priority queue   A queue in which the entries on the queue are ranked into groups according to priority. Such a queue requires a rear pointer for each different possible priority value.

private member   A data member or member function that is accessible only within the scope of a class declaration.

profile an algorithm   A means of empirically measuring the execution of an algorithm by inserting counters to keep track of the number of times certain instructions are executed during a run of the program.

program   A set of instructions that tells the machine (the hardware) what to do.

program heading   The heading of the main block of any C++ program; it must contain the identifier `main`.

program proof   An analysis of a program that attempts to verify the correctness of program results.

program protection   A method of using selection statements to guard against unexpected results.

program walk-through   The process of carefully following, using pencil and paper, steps the computer uses to solve the problem given in a program. Also referred to as a trace.

programming language   Formal language that computer scientists use to give instructions to the computer.

prompt   A message or marker on the terminal screen that requests input data.

proportional   Term applied to two algebraic functions whose quotient is a constant.

protected member   A data member or member function that is accessible only within the scope of a class declaration or within the class declaration of a derived class.

protection   *See* **program protection.**

pseudocode   A stylized half-English, half-code language written in English but suggesting C++ code.

public member   A data member or member function that is accessible to any program component that uses the class.

quadratic algorithm   A polynomial algorithm in which the highest nonzero term is n^2.

quadratic collision processing   Method of handling a collision in which the storage space is searched in the k^2 place, for successive integer values of k starting at the location of the collision, until an available spot is found.

queue   A dynamic data structure where elements are entered at one end and removed from the other end. Referred to as a FIFO (first-in, first-out) structure.

quick sort   A relatively fast sorting technique that uses recursion. *See also* **bubble sort, heap sort, insertion sort, merge sort, radix sort, selection sort,** and **shell sort.**

r-value   A computational object capable of being assigned to a variable.

radix sort   Sorts integer data by repeatedly placing the items into bins and then collecting the bins, starting with the least significant digit for the first pass and finishing with the most significant digit. Also referred to as bin sort. *See also* **bubble sort, heap sort, insertion sort, merge sort, quick sort, selection sort,** and **shell sort.**

random access   Ability to access any elements in a list without first accessing all preceding elements.

random access file   A file whose components can be accessed using random access.

random number generator   A function that returns a number in a given range each time it is called. The numbers it returns are statistically random in that after repeated calls to the function, the sequence of numbers returned is evenly distributed over the interval yet each one is completely unpredictable.

randomized storage   A name given to list access via a hashing function.

range bound error   The situation that occurs when an attempt is made to use an array index value that is less than 0 or greater than or equal to the size of the array.

reading from a file   Retrieving data from a file.

ready queue   In an operating system, the queue of processes with cleared access to all the resources the processes require to run.

real arithmetic operations   Operations allowed on data of type `float`. This includes addition, subtraction, multiplication, and division.

rear pointer   The pointer to the rear of a queue.

receiver object   A computational object to which a request is sent for a service.

recursion   The process of a subprogram calling itself. A clearly defined stopping state must exist. Any recursive subprogram can be rewritten using iteration.

recursive step   A step in recursive process that solves a similar problem of smaller size and eventually leads to a termination of the process.

recursive subprogram   *See* **recursion.**

reference parameter   A formal parameter that requires the address of the actual parameter to be passed to a subprogram. The value of the actual parameter can be changed within the subprogram.

rehashing   Method of handling a collision in which a sequence of new hashing functions is applied to the key that caused the collision until an available location for that key is found.

rehashing collision processing   Resolving a collision by invoking a sequence of hashing functions on a key.

relational operator   An operator used for comparison of data items of the same type.

relative ordering   Ordering imposed on the entries in a list by their relative positions in that list.

relatively prime   Two numbers are relatively prime if and only if their only common factor is 1.

repetition   *See* **loops.**

reserved words   Words that have predefined meanings that cannot be changed. They are highlighted in text by capital boldface print; a list of C++ reserved words is given in Appendix 1.

return type   The type of value returned by a function.

robust   The state in which a program is protected against most possible crashes from bad data and unexpected values.

root   The first or top node in a tree.

row-major order   A means of traversing a two-dimensional array whereby all of the data in one row are accessed before the data in the next row. *See also* **column-major order.**

run-time error   Error detected when, after compilation is completed, an error message results instead of the correct output. *See also* **compilation error, design error, logic error,** and **syntax error.**

scope of identifier The largest block in which the identifier is available.

secondary memory An auxiliary device for memory, usually a disk or magnetic tape. *See also* **main memory** and **memory.**

sector A particular portion of a magnetic disk used at the machine language level in addressing information stored on the disk.

seed A global number used as the basis for generating random numbers in random number generating function.

selection sort A sorting algorithm that sorts the components of an array in either ascending or descending order. This process puts the smallest or largest element in the top position and repeats the process on the remaining array components. *See also* **bubble sort, heap sort, insertion sort, merge sort, quick sort, radix sort,** and **shell sort.**

selection statement A control statement that selects some particular logical path based on the value of an expression. Also referred to as a *conditional statement.*

self-documenting code Code that is written using descriptive identifiers.

semantics The semantics of an algorithmic statement is the action dictated by that statement.

semaphore In an operating system, special flags that regulate the addition and removal of processes to and from the blocked and ready queues.

sender A computational object that requests a service from another computational object.

sentinel value A special value that indicates the end of a set of data or of a process.

sequential access Requirement that elements of a list must be accessed according to the list's ordering so that before a particular element can be accessed, all preceding elements must be accessed first.

sequential access file A file whose components must be accessed using sequential access.

sequential algorithm *See* **straight-line algorithm.**

sequential search The process of searching a list by examining the first component and then examining successive components in the order in which they occur. Also referred to as linear search.

server A computational object that provides a service to another computational object.

shaker sort A variation on the bubble sort in which each pass through the data positions the (current) largest element in the (current) last array index *and* the (current) smallest element in the (current) first array index.

shell sort Sort that works by dividing the array into smaller, noncontiguous segments. These segments are separately sorted using the insertion sort algorithm. The number of these segments is repeatedly reduced on each successive pass until the entire array has been sorted. *See also* **bubble sort, heap sort, insertion sort, merge sort, quick sort, radix sort,** and **selection sort.**

shift folding A variation on folding in which each numeric part of the key is treated as a separate number, and these numbers are added to form an integer value. *See also* boundary folding.

short-circuit evaluation The process whereby a compound Boolean expression halts evaluation and returns the value of the first subexpression that evaluates to TRUE, in the case of ||, or FALSE, in the case of **&&.**

siblings The child nodes of a given node.

side effect A change in a variable, which is the result of some action taken in a program, usually from within a function.

sieve of Eratosthenes A technique devised by the Greek mathematician Eratosthenes for finding all prime numbers greater than 2 and less than or equal to a given number.

simple Boolean expression An expression where two numbers or variable values are compared using a single relational operator. *See also* **Boolean expression** and **compound Boolean expression.**

simulation A computer model of a real-life situation.

simulation of system stack Technique used to eliminate recursion by making a program explicitly perform the duties of the system stack.

software Programs that make the machine (the hardware) do something, such as word processing, database management, or games.

software engineering The process of developing and maintaining large software systems.

software reuse The process of building and maintaining software systems out of existing software components.

software system life cycle The process of development, maintenance, and demise of a software system. Phases include analysis, design, coding, testing/verification, maintenance, and obsolescence.

sort-merge The process of repeatedly subdividing a long list, sorting shorter lists, and then merging to obtain a single sorted list.

sorted collection A derived class of ordered collection, in which the data items are maintained in ascending or descending order. *See also* **ordered collection.**

source program A program written by a programmer. *See also* **system program.**

sparse table A table in which a high percentage of data storage locations will be of one uniform value.

stack A dynamic data structure where access can be made from only one end. Referred to as a LIFO (last-in, first-out) structure.

stack priority   Function to hierarchically rank algebraic operators in order of precedence.

standard simple types   Predefined data types such as `int`, `float`, and `char`.

state space   The space of all possible states which can be generated in the solution to a given problem.

state-transition diagram   A diagram used to model the logic of a finite state machine.

stepwise refinement   The process of repeatedly subdividing tasks into subtasks until each subtask is easily accomplished. *See also* **structured programming** and **top-down design.**

stopping state   The well-defined termination of a recursive process.

straight-line algorithm   Also called *sequential algorithm,* this algorithm consists of a sequence of simple tasks.

string   An abbreviated name for a string literal.

string literal   One or more characters, enclosed in double quotes, used as a constant in a program.

string data type   A data type that permits a sequence of characters. In C++, this can be implemented using an array of characters.

structure chart   A graphic method of indicating the relationship between modules when designing the solution to a problem.

structured design   A method of designing software by specifying modules and the flow of data among them.

structured programming   Programming that parallels a solution to a problem achieved by top-down design. *See also* **stepwise refinement** and **top-down design.**

stub programming   The process of using incomplete functions to test data transmission among them.

subblock   A block structure for a subprogram. *See also* **block.**

subprogram   A program within a program. Functions are subprograms.

subscript   *See* **array index** or **loop index.**

subtree   A subset of a tree that is itself a tree.

symbol table   A list of identifiers maintained by a compiler as it parses a source program.

synonyms   Two keys that hash to the same position and therefore cause a collision.

syntax   The formal rules governing construction of valid statements.

syntax diagramming   A method to formally describe the legal syntax of language structures; syntax diagrams are set forth in Appendix 3.

syntax error   An error in spelling, punctuation, or placement of certain key symbols in a program. *See also* **compilation error, design error, logic error,** and **run-time error.**

system software   The programs that allow users to write and execute other programs, including operating systems such as DOS.

system testing   Exercising the interfaces between modules instead of the logic of a particular module.

systems analyst   The person responsible for analyzing the needs of the users and then formally specifying the system and its requirements to meet those needs.

tail-recursive   The property that a recursive algorithm has of performing no work after each recursive step. *See also* **recursion.**

test cases   Collection of sets of test data that will exercise all the logical possibilities the module will encounter. Each test case has a corresponding expected result called the test oracle.

test oracle   The expected result for a particular test case when a module is being tested.

testing phase   The fourth phase of the software system life cycle. In this phase, the program code is thoroughly tested in an effort to discover errors both in the design of the program and in the code itself.

test program   A short program written to provide an answer to a specific question.

thread   A pointer contained in a tree node which leads to the predecessor or successor of the node relative to a specified traversal.

threaded tree   A tree in which threading is used.

threading   A technique of avoiding recursion in tree traversal algorithms whereby the pointers unused in tree formation are turned into pointers to the inorder predecessor and inorder successor of that node.

time/space trade-off   The maxim that an attempt to make a program more efficient in terms of time will only come as a result of a corresponding decrease in efficiency in terms of space, and vice versa.

token   A language symbol comprised of one or more characters in an incoming stream of characters. The basic unit in lexical analysis.

top-down design   A design methodology for solving a problem whereby you first state the problem and then proceed to subdivide the main task into major subtasks. Each subtask is then subdivided into smaller subtasks. This process is repeated until each remaining subtask is easily solved. *See also* **stepwise refinement** and **structured programming.**

trace   *See* **program walk-through.**

track   A particular portion of a magnetic disk used at the machine language level in addressing information stored on the disk.

tree   *See* **general tree.**

tree of recursive calls   *See* **run-time trace diagram.**

tree traversal A means of processing every node in the tree.

trial-and-error backtracking Recursion in which more recursive calls may be made after the first return operation occurs.

trie index A type of indexing used when the keys are variable-length character strings. Although taken from the word *retrieve*, trie is pronounced "try."

Turing machine A hypothetical computing machine which consists of input and output units, and infinite memory in the form of a sequentially organized tape to store characters from a finite alphabet, a finite collection of states in which the machine could exist in at any given time, and a control unit capable of checking and potentially modifying the contents of any memory cell.

two-dimensional array An array in which each element is accessed by a reference to a pair of indices.

two-key table A set of values each of which is accessed by two keys, where the set of primary keys is ordered and the set of secondary keys for each primary key is also ordered.

two-way merge The process of merging two sorted lists.

type *See* data type.

undecidable proposition A statement within an axiomatic system such that neither that statement nor its negation can be proven by reasoning within the system itself.

underflow If a value is too small to be represented by a computer, the value is automatically replaced by zero. *See also* **overflow.**

user-defined data type A new data type introduced and defined by the programmer.

user-defined function A new function introduced and defined by the programmer.

user-friendly A phrase used to describe an interactive program with clear, easy-to-follow messages for the user.

value Often called value of a memory location. Refers to the value of the contents of a memory location. *See also* **address.**

value parameter A formal parameter that is local to a subprogram. Values of these parameters are not returned to the calling program.

variable A memory location, referenced by an identifier, whose value can be changed during a program.

variable condition loop A repetition statement in which the loop control condition changes within the body of the loop.

variable declaration section The section of the declaration section where program variables are declared for subsequent use.

vertex A data object (or node) in a graph.

volatile list A list that undergoes frequent insertions and deletions.

weight The numeric value associated with an edge in a network.

while loop A pretest loop examining a Boolean expression before causing a statement to be executed.

white box testing The method of testing a module in which the tester is aware of the method of implementation and internal logic of that module. *See also* black box testing.

word A unit of memory consisting of one or more bytes. Words can be addressed.

worst case The arrangement of data items prior to the beginning of the sort procedure which causes that procedure to take the longest amount of time for that particular set of items. *See also* **best case.**

writing to a file The process of entering data to a file.

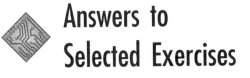

Answers to Selected Exercises

This section contains answers to selected exercises from the exercise sets at the end of each section. In general, answers to odd-numbered problems are given.

CHAPTER 2

Section 2.1

1. a and **c** are effective statements.
b is not effective because you cannot determine when to perform the action.
d is not effective because there is no smallest positive fraction.
e is not effective because you cannot determine in advance which stocks will increase in value.

3. a. 1. Select a topic
    2. Research the topic
    3. Outline the paper
    4. Refine the outline
    5. Write the rough draft
    6. Read and revise the rough draft
    7. Write the final paper
c. 1. Get a list of colleges
    2. Examine criteria (programs, distance, money, and so on)
    3. Screen to a manageable number
    4. Obtain further information
    5. Make a decision

5. a. First-level development:
    1. Get information for first employee
    2. Perform computations for first employee

3. Print results for first employee
4. ⎫
5. ⎬ Repeat for second employee
6. ⎭

Second-level development:
1. Get information for first employee
    1.1 get hourly wage
    1.2 get number of hours worked
2. Perform computations for first employee
    2.1 compute gross pay
    2.2 compute deductions
    2.3 compute net pay
3. Print results for first employee
    3.1 print input data
    3.2 print gross pay
    3.3 print deductions
    3.4 print net pay
4. ⎫
5. ⎬ Repeat for second employee
6. ⎭

Third-level development:
1. Get information for first employee
    1.1 get hourly wage
    1.2 get number of hours worked
2. Perform computations for first employee
    2.1 compute gross pay
    2.2 compute deductions
        2.2.1 federal withholding
        2.2.2 state withholding

        2.2.3 social security
        2.2.4 union dues
        2.2.5 compute total deductions
    2.3 compute net pay
        2.3.1 subtract total deductions from gross
3. Print results for first employee
    3.1 print input data
        3.1.1 print hours worked
        3.1.2 print hourly wage
    3.2 print gross pay
    3.3 print deductions
        3.3.1 print federal withholding
        3.3.2 print state withholding
        3.3.3 print social security
        3.3.4 print union dues
        3.3.5 print total deductions
    3.4 print net pay
4. ⎫
5. ⎬ Repeat for second employee
6. ⎭

7. There are several ways to solve this problem, one of which follows:
    1. Get the numbers as input
    2. Put them in order—small, large
    3. Check for a divisor
        3.1 if small is a divisor of large
            3.1.1 gcd is small
        else
            3.1.2 Decrease small until a common divisor is found

4. Print the results

   3.1.2 can be further refined as

   3.1.2 Decrease small until a common divisor is
found

      3.1.2.2 do

          if **gcd_candidate** is a common divisor

            gcd is **gcd_candidate**

          else

            Decrease **gcd_candidate**
by 1

          while a common divisor is not
found

Section 2.2

3. **a** is valid.

  b is a Pascal program heading.

  c is missing a return type and should omit parameters.

  d is missing a return type and should use lowercase letters.

5. a. `const char GENDER = 'F';`
   b. `const int AGE = 18;`
   c. `const float PI = 3.1416;`

Section 2.3

1. **a, d, e,** and **g** are valid.

  b has a decimal.

  c has a comma.

  f is probably larger than **INT_MAX.**

3. **a.** 1.73E2

  b. 7.43927E11

  c. −2.3E−8

  d. 1.4768E1

  e. −5.2E0

5. **a** and **d** are integers.

  b, c, and g are reals.

  e and **f** are string literals.

7. a. ```cout << setw(14) << "Score" <<
   endl << endl;
   cout << setw(13) << 86 << endl;
   cout << setw(13) << 82 << endl;
   cout << setw(13) << 79 << endl;```

CHAPTER 3

Section 3.1

1. **a.** 11   **f.** 63
   b. −49   **g.** −64
   c. 3   **h.** 108
   d. 24   **i.** 1
   e. 126   **j.** 7

3. **a** and **b, c, f, g,** and **j** are valid, type integer.

  e, h, and **i** are valid, type float.

  d is invalid.

5. Output will vary according to local implementation.

Section 3.2

1. **a, b, e, f,** and **h** are valid assignment statements.

  c is invalid. A real cannot be assigned to an integer variable.

  d is invalid. An operand cannot be on the left of an assignment statement.

  g is invalid. IQ/3 is a float.

3. **a.**

3		−5
A		B

  b.

26		31
A		B

  c.

−3		−5
A		B

  d.

9		9
A		B

5.
```
Gender      M
Age         23
Height      73 inches
Weight      186.5 lbs
```

7. column 11
```
*****************************
*                           *
*   Name      Age    Sex    *
*   ----      ---    ---    *
*   Jones      21     M     *
*                           *
*****************************
```

9.   column 10
```
        This reviews string formatting.
When a letterAis used,
        Oops! I forgot to format.
        When a letter A is used,
        it is a string of length one.
```

Section 3.3

1. **cin** is the name of the standard input stream. This stream is connected to the keyboard and allows data to be input from the user. **cout** is the name of the standard output stream. This stream is connected to the terminal screen, and allows data to be output to the user.

Section 3.6

7.
```
#include <iostream.h>

int main()
{
    for (int ascii_value = 'A'; ascii_value <= 'Z'; ++ascii_value)
            cout << char(ascii_value) << " " << ascii_value << endl;
    return 0;
}
```

CHAPTER 4

Section 4.2

1. **c** and **d** are valid.
   a has no types for the parameters.
   b has no return type.

Section 4.3

1. **a.** Both parameters should be declared as reference parameters rather than value parameters.
   b. width should be declared as a value parameter rather than a reference parameter.
   c. radius should be declared as a value parameter rather than a reference parameter.

Section 4.5

7. Identifiers for this program are represented schematically by the figure at right.

9. **10**
   20
   10

11. There are several syntax errors. **x1** is not visible in the main program block. **x** cannot be used as an actual parameter for function **sub1**, because **x** is a **float** and **sub1** expects an **int** as a parameter. **x** and **y** are not visible in the block of **sub1**.

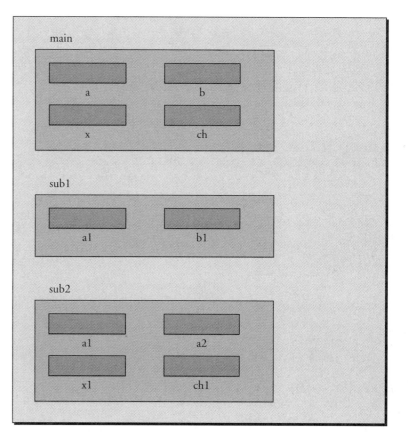

CHAPTER 5

Section 5.1

1. 1 1 0
   0

3. a and b are TRUE
c and d are FALSE

Section 5.2

1. a. 10   5
  b. No output
  c. 5   Since **b** has no value, the result will vary.
  d. 10   5
  e. 15   4
      15   4
  f. 10   5

3. a. has no error
  b. `3 < x < 10` cannot be evaluated. This should be `(3 < x) && (x < 10)`.
  c. The two statements following the condition should be enclosed in braces:

```
if (a > 0)
{
        count = count + 1;
        sum = sum + a;
}
```

5. Yes.

9.
```
{
    cin >> num1 >> num2 >> num3;
    total = total + num1 + num2 + num3;
    cout << num1 << " " << num2 << " " << num3 << endl;
    cout << total << endl;
}
```

11.
```
cin >> ch1 >> ch2 >>ch3;
if (ch1 <= ch2) && (ch2 <= ch3)
    cout << ch1 << ch2 << ch3 << endl;
```

Section 5.3

1. a. −14
  b. 5025
      175
  c. 105
      50

Section 5.4

1. a. 38.15   763.0
  b. −21.0   21.0
  c. 600.0   1200.0
  d. 3000.0   9000.0

3. a.
```
if (ch == 'M')
    if (sum > 1000)
            x = x + 1;
    else
            x = x + 2;
else if (ch == 'F')
    if (sum > 1000)
            x = x + 3;
    else
            x = x + 5;
```

```
b. cin >> num;
   if (num > 0)
        if (num <= 10000)
        {
             count = count + 1;
             sum = sum + num;
        }
        else
             cout << setw(27) << "Value out of range" << endl;
c. if (a > 0)
        if (b > 0)
             cout << setw(22) << "Both positive" << endl;
        else
             cout << setw(22) << "Some negative" << endl;
d. if (c < 0)
        if (a > 0)
             if (b > 0))
                   cout << setw(19) << "Option one" << endl;
             else
                   cout <<setw(19) << "Option two" << endl;
        else
             cout << setw(19) << "Option two" << endl;
   else
        cout<<setw(19)<<"Option one"<< endl;
```

7. 8   13   104
   a   b   c

Section 5.5

3. **a.** has a semicolon rather than a colon after third label and list of values as last label.
   b. has no colon after first label, a semicolon after third label, and a list of values as last label.
   c. has list of values as first label.
   d. reserved word **case** is missing from all labels.
   e. cases for 2 and 1 are missing statements.

CHAPTER 6

Section 6.2

1. a. *
        *
         *
          *
           *
            *
   b. 1 :   9
       2 :   8
       3 :   7
       4 :   6
       5 :   5
       6 :   4
       7 :   3
       8 :   2
       9 :   1
      10 :   0

c.   2
     3
     4
     5
     6
     7
     8
     9
    10
    11
    12
    13
    14
    15
    16
    17
    18
    19
    20

d.   1
     2
     3
     4
     5
     6
     7
     8
     9
    10
    11
    12
    13
    14
    15
    16
    17
    18
    19
    20
    21

3. a.
```
for (int j = 1; j <= 4; ++j)
    cout << " *" << endl;
```
b.
```
for (int j = 1; j <= 4; ++j)
        cout << setw(j + 3) << "***" << endl;
```
c.
```
cout << setw(6) << "*" << endl;
for (int j = 1; j <= 3; ++j)
        cout << setw(6 - j) << "*" setw(2 * j) << "*" << endl;
cout << "**** ****" << endl;
for (int j = 1; j <= 2; ++j)
        cout << setw(7) << "* *" << endl;
cout << setw(7) << "***" << endl;
```
d. This is a "look ahead" problem that can be solved by a loop within a loop. This idea is developed in Section 5.6.
```
for (int j = 5; j >= 1; --j)
{
        cout << setw(6 - j) << " ";               // Indent a line
        for (int k = 1; k <= 2 * j - 1; ++k)      // Print a line
                cout << "*";
        cout << endl;
}
```

5. a.
```
for (int j = 1; j <= 5; ++j)
    cout << setw(3) << j;
for (int j = 5; j >= 1; --j;
    cout << setw(3) << 6 - j;
```
b.
```
for (int j = 1; j <= 5; ++j)
        cout << setw(j) << '*' << endl
for (int j = 5; j >= 1; --j)
        cout << setw(6 - j) << '*' << endl;
```
7.
```
for (j = 2; j <= 10; ++j)
      cout << setw(j) <<j << endl;
```

Section 6.3

3. a.
```
1
2
3
4
5
6
7
8
9
10
```
b.
```
1    0
2    1
3    2
4    1
5    2
```
c. 54   50

d.
```
The partial sum is  1
The partial sum is  3
The partial sum is  6
The partial sum is 10
The partial sum is 15
The count is 5
```
e. 96.00   2.00

5. a.
```
while (num > 0)
{
    cout << setw(10) << num << endl
    num = num - .5;
}
```

Section 6.4

1. A pretest loop tests the Boolean expression before executing the loop. A post-test loop tests the Boolean expression after the loop has been executed.

3. a. This loop is infinite, because the value of **j** is never changed within the loop.

   b. This loop terminates.

   c. This loop is infinite, because the value of **a** will always be a power of 2, and thus never equal 20.

   d. This loop terminates.

Section 6.6

1. a.
```
for (int k = 1; k <= 5; ++k)
{
    cout << setw(k) << ' ';
    for (int j = k; j <= 5; ++j)
            cout << '*';
    cout << endl
}
```

   c.
```
for (int k = 1; k <= 7; ++k)
        if (k < 5)
        {
                for (int j = 1; j <= 3; ++j)
                        cout << '*';
                cout << endl;
        }
        else
        {
                for (int j = 1; j <= 5; ++j)
                        cout << '*';
                cout << endl;
        }
```

3.
```
4  5  6  7
4  5  6  7
4  5  6  7
4  5  6  7

5  6  7
5  6  7
5  6  7

6  7
6  7
```

Section 6.7

1. a. This is an infinite loop.

   b. The loop control variable, **k**, is unassigned once the **for** loop is exited. Thus, the attempt to use **k** in the expression **k % 3 = 0** may result in an error.

CHAPTER 7

Section 7.1

1. a, b, c, and **f** are FALSE.
3. a. i and ii are invalid on some implementation of C++.
iii, v, vi, and vii are all invalid.
b.
```
if (strcmp(a, b) < 0)
{
    strcpy(c, a);
    strcat(c, b);
}
else
{
    strcpy(c, b);
    strcat(c, a);
}
```

Section 7.2

1.
```
boolean string_less(string s1, string s2)
{
    return strcmp(s1, s2) < 0;
}

boolean string_greater(string s1, string s2)
}
    return strcmp(s1, s2) > 0;
}
```
3.
```
void make_lowercase(string s)
{
    int length = strlen(s);

    for (int i = 0; i < length; ++i)
            s[i] = tolower(s[i]);
}
```
5.
```
void remove_punctuation(string s)
{
    char ch = s[strlen(s) - 1];

    if ((ch == '.') || (ch == ',' || (ch == '?') || (ch == ':') || (ch == ';'))
            s[strlen(s) - 1] = '\0';
}
```
7.
```
void string_swap(string s1, string s2)
{
    string temp;

    strcpy(temp, s1);
    strcpy(s1, s2);
    strcpy(s2, temp);
}
```
9.
```
void append_char(string s, char ch)
{
    int length = strlen(s);

    if (length < MAX_STRING_SIZE)
    {
            s[length] =    ch;
```

```
            s[length + 1] = '\0';
        }
    }
```

Section 7.3

3. The reference to **data** in the string class implementation picks out the data member of the receiver string. The reference to **str.data** in the string class implementation picks out the data member of the parameter string.

CHAPTER 8

Section 8.2

1. The **account** class declaration is modified by including the header file for the **strlib** library, by adding a string parameter to the first two class constructors, and by adding a private data member **name**:

```
#include "strlib.h"
    .
    .
    .

    public:

    // Class constructors

    account(string initial_name);
    account(float initial_balance, string initial_name);
    account(const account &a);
    .
    .
    .

    private:

    // Data members

    float balance;
    string name;
};
```

The three constructors and the assignment operator are then updated in the implementation:

```
account::account(string initial_name)
{
    balance = 0.00;
    name = initial_name;
}

account::account(float initial_balance, string initial_name)
{
    balance = initial_balance;
    name = initial_name;
}

account::account(const account &a)
{
    balance = a.balance;
    name = a.name;
}
```

```
account& account::operator = (const account &a)
{
        balance = a.balance;
        name = a.name;
        return  *this;
}
```

3. We assume that a private data member **password** has been added to the class declaration, and that appropriate modifications have been made to the declarations of member functions **deposit**, **withdraw**, and **get_balance**. The implementations are updated as follows:

```
float account::deposit(float amount, string your_name, string your_password)
{

        if ((your_name == name) && (your_password == password))
        {
                balance = balance + amount;
                return balance;
        }
        else
                return 0;

}


float account::withdraw(float amount, string your_name, string your_password)
{
        if ((your_name == name) && (your_password == password))
                if (amount > balance)
                        return -1;
                else
                {
                        balance = balance - amount;
                        return balance;
                }
        else
                return 0;

}


float account::get_balance(string your_name, string your_password)
{
        if ((your_name == name) && (your_password == password))
                return balance;
        else
                return 0;

}
```

Section 8.3

3. Total number of operations = M times N.

5. The following implementations cover all of the possibilities. If the rational number is already in lowest terms, then the implementations can be simplified and made more efficient.

```
boolean rational::whole_number()
{
        return (denominator == 1) || (numerator % denominator == 0);
```

```
}

int rational::make_int()
{
        if (denominator == 1)
                return numerator;
        else
                return numerator / denominator;
}
```

Section 8.4

1. Define a password in the base class. Its access mode should be **protected**.

5. A derived class of the checking account class, with attributes and behavior for maintaining interest, would allow much of the software to be reused.

CHAPTER 9

Section 9.1

1. a. The first two input statements read the two data values from the file, and they are displayed by the first two output statements. The third input statement also reads the second data value, because the end of file has been reached. Thus, the third output statement displays the second data value also.

b. The first data value is read before the loop starts. It is output on the first pass through the loop, because the end-of-file condition is not yet true. Then the second data value is read at the bottom of the loop. The end-of-file condition is not yet true, so the loop is entered once more, where the second data value is output. At the bottom of the loop, the second data value is read once more, and the end-of-file condition becomes true, forcing an exit from the top of the loop.

c. Because the **>>** operator must be run three times before the end-of-file condition becomes true, three outputs will occur. Thus, the second data value in the file is output twice to the screen.

3. We use the **strlib** library for strings. Note that all input can be received as strings.

```
// Program file: person.cpp

#include <iostream.h>
#include <fstream.h>
#include <assert.h>
#include "strlib.h"

int main()
{
        string  string_var;
        ifstream in_file;

        in_file.open("myfile");
        assert(! in_file.fail());
        in_file >> string_var;
        cout << "Name:" << string_var << endl;
        in_file >> string_var;
        cout << "Address:" << string_var << endl;
        in_file >> string_var;
        cout << "Age:" << string_var << endl;
        in_file.close();
        assert(! in_file.fail());
        return 0;
    {
```

5. Note that the data for the person's name is received from a priming input, and also is received at the bottom of the loop.

```cpp
// Program file: persons.cpp

#include <iostream.h>
#include <fstream.h>
#include <assert.h>
#include "strlib.h"

int main()
{
        string string_var;
        ifstream in_file;

        in_file.open("myfile");
        assert(!  in_file.fail());
        in_file >> string_var;
        while (! in_file.eof())
        {
                cout << "Name:" << string_var << endl;
                in_file >> string_var;
                cout << "Address:" << string_var << endl;
                in_file >> string_var;
                cout << "Age:" << string_var << endl;
                in_file >> string_var;
        {
        in_file.close();
        assert(!  in_file.fail());
        return 0;
}
```

CHAPTER 10

Section 10.1

1. a. const int MAX_SCORES = 35;
   typedef int score_list[MAX_SCORES];
   score_list scores;
   b. const int MAX_PRICES = 20;
   typedef float price_list[MAX_PRICES];
   price_list prices;
   c. const int MAX_ANSWERS = 50;
   typedef boolean answer_list[MAX_ANSWERS];
   answer_list answers;
   d. const int MAX_GRADES = 4;
   typedef char grade_list[MAX_GRADES];
   grade_list grades;

3. a, b, d, e, f, h, and **I** are valid.

   c will run, but display the address of the array.

   g uses three indexes, but the array expects one.

   i attempts to input a value into the address of the array.

   j list[100] is a range error.

   k Type names cannot be indexed.

5. `waist_sizes`

34	0
36	1
32	2
30	3
33	4

7.
```
for (int i = 0; i < 10; ++i)
     list[i] = 0.0;
```

Section 10.2

1. a.

list

0	0
0	1
0	2
1	3
1	4

b. list   scores

4	0		1	0
5	1		1	1
6	2		2	2
7	3		2	3
8	4		2	4

c. **answers**

TRUE	0
FALSE	1
TRUE	2
FALSE	3
TRUE	4
FALSE	5
TRUE	6
FALSE	7
TRUE	8
FALSE	9

d. **initials**

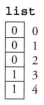

A	0
B	1
C	2
D	3
E	4
.	
.	
.	
S	20
T	19

3. The code counts the number of scores that are greater than 90.

5.
```
const int MAX_CHARS = 20;
typedef char name_type[MAX_CHARS];
name_type name;
int length = 0;
char ch;

cin >> ch;
while (ch != '\0')
{

     name[length] = ch;
     ++length;
     cin >> ch;

}
```

7.
```
for (int i = 0; i < 100; ++i)
     a[i] = 0;
```

9.
```
cout << "Test scores" << endl;
cout << "-----------" << endl;
for (int i = 0; i < 50; ++i)
     cout << setw(2) << i <<"." << setw(3) << test_scores[i] << endl;
```

Section 10.3

1. a is valid.

  b is invalid, because arrays are declared as reference parameters.

  c is valid.

  d is invalid, because arrays are declared as reference parameters.

  e is invalid, because a type name is ued to declare a parameter name.

  f is valid.

  g is invalid, because **name** has not been defined as a type.

  h is valid.

  i is invalid, because **name** has not been defined as a type.

  j is invalid, because arrays are declared as reference parameters.

3. a.
```
void input_scores(int scores[20]);
input_scores(scores);
```
  b.
```
int char_count(char name[50], char ch);
number = char_count(name, 'A');
```
  c.
```
void score_data(int scores[], int &length, int &count_90);
score_data(scores, length, count_90);
```

5.
```
void array_data(int data[MAX_ARRAY_SIZE], int &max, int &min, int &neg_values)
{
    max = INT_MIN;                    // Initial maximum value.
    min = INT_MAX;                    // Initial minimum value.
    neg_values = 0;                   // Initial count negative values.
    for (int i = 0; i < MAX_ARRAY_SIZE; ++i)
            if (data[i] > max)
                    max = data[i];
            if (data[i] < min)
                    min = data[i];
            if (data[i] < 0)
                    ++neg_values;
}
```

Section 10.4

1. First pass   Second pass

First pass		Second pass	
-20	0	-20	0
10	1	-2	1
0	2	0	2
10	3	10	3
8	4	8	4
30	5	30	5
-2	6	10	6

3. We use a new function, **find_maximum**, that locates the largest value in the unsorted portion of the array. On each pass, the largest remaining value will be placed at the end of the sorted portion of the array. Thus, at the end of the process, the array will be sorted from high to low.

```
void sort(int a[ ], int length)
{
        int min_index = 0;

        for (int j = 0; j < length - 1; ++j)
        {
                min_index = find_maximum(a, j, length);
                if (min_index != j)
                        swap(a[j], a[min_index]);
        }
}
```

```
5. void sort(int a[ ], int length, int &count)
   {
        int min_index = 0.
        count = 0;
        for (int j = 0; j < length - 1; ++j)
        {
                min_index = find_minimum(a, j, length);
                if (min_index != j)
                {
                        swap(a[j],  a[min_index]);
                        ++count;
                }
        }
   }
```

7. The sort of the test scores will have no effect on the order of the names. If the test scores are all the same, then there will be no change in the meaning of the table. Otherwise, the names will no longer always be correlated with their test scores.

Section 10.5

1. When **i = MAX_ARRAY_SIZE**, the program encounters a reference to **a[MAX_ARRAY_SIZE]**. This violates the precondition of the subscript operation for the safe array class, and the program will halt with a run-time error.

3. There are two limitations. First, a client might not want to be responsible for defining this constant, but would rather rely on the array class to provide a default maximum size. Second, a client might want to declare arrays with different maximum sizes for different applications. However, this implementation restricts a client to one maximum size for all arrays.

5. In general, there is no way of telling which cells in a safe array actually contain data intended for use by a program at any given time. This is especially true right after a safe array is declared, where the contents of all of the cells are unpredictable. In each of the examples, the run-time system might allow the operations to be performed, because the arrays at least contain "garbage" values. However, the meanings of the programs are impossible to determine by inspection, because:

   a has not initialized any cells in the array **a**.

   b has not initialized any cells in array **a** or **b**.

   c has not initialized any cells in the array **b**.

Section 10.6

1. The physical size of an array is the number of cells of memory allocated for storing data in it. The logical size of the array is the number of data values currently stored in it that have meaning for a program.

3. This proposal has two problems. First, the ordered collection requires an integer data member to maintain the current logical size of the data structure. Thus, there is no memory savings when compared with the use of the null character as a sentinel in an array. Second, the new implementation must replicate much of the code for string operations already available in the standard **string** library that was used for the array implementation. It is hard to find any benefits that outweigh these two costs of the proposal.

5. The member function takes a target element as a parameter and returns the index position if the element is found or –1 if the element is not found.

```
int ordered_collection::search(element e)
{
        index = 0;
        while ((index < c_length) && (e != a[index]))
                ++index;
        if (index == c_length)
                return -1;
        else
                return index;
}
```

7. The member function assumes that the client has opened the input stream before the operation and will close it following the operation. The declaration of the member function is

```
friend istream& operator >> (istream &is, ordered_collection &oc);
```

The implementation of the member function is

```
istream& operator >> (istream &is, ordered_collection &oc)
{
    element e;

    oc.c_length = 0;
    is >> e;
    while (! is.eof() && (oc.c_length < MAX_ARRAY_SIZE))
    {
        oc.add_last(e);
        is >> e;
    }
    if (! is.eof() && (oc.c_length == MAX_ARRAY_SIZE))
        cout << "Some elements could not be input into the collection."
            << endl;
    return is;
}
```

Section 10.7

1.
```
sorted_collection& sorted_collection::operator = (const sorted_collection &sc)
{
    for (int j = 0; j < sc.c_length; ++j)
        data[j] = sc.data[j];
    c_length = sc.c_length;
    return *this;
}
```

3. The subscript operator for ordered collections allows references to elements as l values or as r values. A sorted collection object should not allow references to elements as l values, because clients could then store elements that might violate the ordering of the elements in the collection.

5.
```
sorted_collection::sorted_collection(const ordered_collection &oc)
{
    c_length = oc.length();
    for (int i = 0; i < c_length; ++i)
        add(oc[i]);
}
```

Section 10.8

1.
```
const MAX_ROW_SIZE = 300;
const MAX_COL_SIZE = 400;

typedef boolean bitmap[MAX_ROW_SIZE] [MAX_COL_SIZE];
```

3.
```
boolean search(bitmap a, int target, int &row, int &col)
{
    boolean found = FALSE;

    row = 0;
    while (! found && (row < MAX_ROW_SIZE))        // Search rows.
    {
        col = 0;
        while (! found && (col < MAX_COL_SIZE)) // Search columns within a row.
            if (a[row] [col] == target)
                    found = TRUE;
                else
                    ++col;
```

```
                    if (! found)
                        ++row;
    }
    return found;
}
```

5. A safe bitmap class would behave in the same way as a safe array class, except that range checks would be performed on both the row and the column indexes on all references to data in the bitmap.

CHAPTER 11

Section 11.2

1. Insertion sort provides for a possible early exit from its inner loop. This early exit can potentially reduce the number of comparisons necessary, especially for data that are "almost" in order.

3. Selection sort does not provide for an early exit from either the outer or the inner loop; however, it does guarantee that only n data exchanges will be made—fewer than either insertion or selection sort can guarantee (both require n^2 data exchanges on average).

5.

	K=1	K=2	K=3	K=4	K=5	K=6
43	12	12	12	12	12	12
40	40	18	18	18	18	18
18	18	40	24	24	24	24
24	24	24	40	39	39	39
39	39	39	39	40	40	40
60	60	60	60	60	60	43
12	43	43	43	43	43	60

7. This sort algorithm resembles a bubble sort, but is different in that small array entries "bubble up" instead of having large array entries "bubble down" on each successive pass. That is, in the bubble sort we can guarantee that after the kth pass, the *largest k* array entries are in their rightful place; whereas, in this sort algorithm, we can guarantee that after the kth pass, the *smallest k* entries are in their rightful place.

Original	k=1	k=2	k=3	k=4	k=5	k=6
43	12	12	12	12	12	12
40	43	18	18	18	18	18
18	40	43	24	24	24	24
24	18	40	43	39	39	39
39	24	24	40	43	40	40
60	39	39	39	40	43	43
12	60	60	60	60	60	60

9. This sort algorithm resembles insertion sort in that it, too, positions the kth element in its rightful place among $k - 1$ entries already in order. The difference between the two sorts lies in the section of the array each has sorted with each successive iteration. In insertion sort, the *first k + 1* entries are in order after the kth pass; in this sort, the *last k* entries are in order after the kth pass.

Original	k=1	k=2	k=3	k=4	k=5	k=6
43	43	43	43	43	43	12
40	40	40	40	40	12	18
18	18	18	18	12	18	24
24	24	24	12	18	24	39
39	39	12	24	24	39	40
60	12	39	39	39	40	43
12	60	60	60	60	60	60

11. The integers

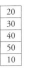

20
30
40
50
10

or any such arithmetically or alphabetically ordered data cause the bubble sort to make comparisons, but no data are interchanged until the 10 is "bubbled up" to the top. For the insertion sort, the inner loop is shut off after a single comparison, until the final 10 is reached. Then the 10 is inserted at the top.

13.
```
// Same inputs, outputs, and task as insertion sort.
// New logic: move element only after all comparisons
// per loop are finished.
void modified_insertion_sort(list_type list, int n)
{
    int i, j, k, remember;
    boolean done;

    for (k = 1; k < n; ++k)
    {
        j = k;
        remember = j;
        done = FALSE;
        while ((j >= 1) && ! done)
            if (list[remember].get_key() <
                list[j - 1].get_key())
                --j;
            else
                done = TRUE;
        if (j != remember)
        {
            for (k = remember; k >= j + 1; --k)
                list[k] = list[k - 1];
            list[j] = list[remember];
        }
    }
}
```

Section 11.3

1. **a.** Inner loop: $m - 6$ repetitions. Outer loop: n repetitions. For each outer loop repetition, the inner loop is traversed $m - 6$ times. Therefore, $(m - 6) \times n$ overall repetitions are performed. This is $O(n^2)$.
   b. The inner loop will be executed $\log_2 n$ times and the outer loop will be executed n times. Thus the loops are $O(n\log_2 n)$.
   c. The inner **do...while** is executed $n/2$ times for each execution of the outer loop. The outer **do...while** is executed n times. Thus there are $n \times (n/2)$ repetitions. Thus the loops are $O(n^2)$.

3. The efficiency of the algorithm in question is constant—32 operations—for all input. Remembering that in big-O analysis, we are concerned primarily with the order of magnitude of the algorithm's efficiency, we write this algorithm's efficiency as $O(1) * 32$. And recalling that constants bear no importance except in comparing algorithms with the same big-O, we drop the constant 32 to arrive at the big-O that most accurately characterizes the algorithm—$O(1)$.

5. **a.** The $n^3\log_2 n$ term dominates and this is $O(n^3\log_2 n)$.
   b. The 4^n exponential term will (eventually) dominate any polynomial terms. Thus this is $O(4^n)$.
   c. The 2^n exponential term will (eventually) dominate any polynomial terms. Thus this is $O(2^n)$.

7. For this small set of integers, the trace of the insertion sort is

20	20	20	20	10
30	30*	30	30	20
40	40	40*	40	30
50	50	50	50*	40
10	10	10	10	50

The inner loop of the insertion sort is "shut off" after one comparison for each value of K, until the "bottom" 10 is reached. At that point, four swaps are required to move it into the "top" position. For this almost ordered data, the insertion sort is $O(n)$.

9. Since n^2 dominates $n^2 + \log_2 n$, $O(n^2 + \log_2 n)$ is the same as $O(n^2)$. Hence, we have the following answers for a—d.
   a. You are both correct for any algorithm whose performance is dominated by a term such as n^k for $k \geq 2$ or a^n for any base $a > 1$.
   b. You are both wrong for any linear or logarithmic algorithm.
   c. No.
   d. No.

Section 11.4

1.

	K=1 J=1	K=1 J=2	K=1 J=3	K=1 J=4	K=1 J=5	K=1 J=6
1	2	2	2	2	2	2
2	1	3	3	3	3	3
3	3	1	4	4	4	4
4	4	4	1	5	5	5
5	5	5	5	1	6	6
6	6	6	6	6	1	7
7	7	7	7	7	7	1

K=2 J=1	K=2 J=2	K=2 J=3	K=2 J=4	K=2 J=5
3	3	3	3	3
2	2	2	2	2
4	4	5	5	5
5	5	4	6	6
6	6	6	4	7
7	7	7	7	4
1	1	1	1	1

K=3 J=1	K=3 J=2	K=3 J=3	K=3 J=4
3	3	3	3
2	5	5	5
5	2	2	2
6	6	6	7
7	7	7	6
4	4	4	4
1	1	1	1

K=4 J=1	K=4 J=2	K=4 J=3
3	3	3
5	5	5
2	2	7
7	7	2
6	6	6
4	4	4
1	1	1

K=5 J=1	K=5 J=2
3	3
5	7
7	5
2	2
6	6
4	4
1	1

K=6 J=1
7
3
5
2
6
4
1

3. Ten passes would be made through the outer **while** loop of the radix sort algorithm because the length of the longest data it em is ten characters. It is assumed that strings are padded with space beyond their last alphabetical character.

Pass 0:

List: CHOCOLATE VANILLA CARAMEL PEACH STRAWBERRY CHERRY

Pass 1:
Bins: Space: CHOCOLATE VANILLA CARAMEL PEACH CHERRY
  Y: STRAWBERRY
List: CHOCOLATE VANILLA CARAMEL PEACH CHERRY STRAWBERRY

Pass 2:
Bins: Space: VANILLA CARAMEL PEACH CHERRY
  E: CHOCOLATE
  R: STRAWBERRY
List: VANILLA CARAMEL PEACH CHERRY CHOCOLATE STRAWBERRY

Pass 3:
Bins: Space: VANILLA CARAMEL PEACH CHERRY
  R: STRAWBERRY
  T: CHOCOLATE
List: VANILLA CARAMEL PEACH CHERRY STRAWBERRY CHOCOLATE

Pass 4:
Bins: Space: PEACH CHERRY
  A: VANILLA CHOCOLATE
  E: STRAWBERRY
  L: CARAMEL
List: PEACH CHERRY VANILLA CHOCOLATE STRAWBERRY CARAMEL

Pass 5:
Bins: Space: PEACH
  B: STRAWBERRY
  E: CARAMEL
  L: VANILLA CHOCOLATE
  Y: CHERRY
List: PEACH STRAWBERRY CARAMEL VANILLA CHOCOLATE CHERRY

Pass 6:
Bins: H: PEACH
  L: VANILLA
  M: CARAMEL
  O: CHOCOLATE
  R: CHERRY
  W: STRAWBERRY
List: PEACH VANILLA CARAMEL CHOCOLATE CHERRY STRAWBERRY

Pass 7:
Bins: A: CARAMEL STRAWBERRY
  C: PEACH CHOCOLATE
  I: VANILLA
  R: CHERRY
List: CARAMEL STRAWBERRY PEACH CHOCOLATE VANILLA CHERRY

Pass 8:
Bins: A: PEACH
  E: CHERRY
  N: VANILLA
  O: CHOCOLATE
  R: CARAMEL STRAWBERRY
List: PEACH CHERRY VANILLA CHOCOLATE CARAMEL STRAWBERRY

Pass 9:
Bins: A: VANILLA CARAMEL
   E: PEACH
   H: CHERRY CHOCOLATE
   T: STRAWBERRY
List: VANILLA CARAMEL PEACH CHERRY CHOCOLATE STRAWBERRY

Pass 10:
Bins: C: CARAMEL CHERRY CHOCOLATE
   P: PEACH
   S: STRAWBERRY
   V: VANILLA
List: CARAMEL CHERRY CHOCOLATE PEACH STRAWBERRY VANILLA

5. An application in which the array of data items consumed all available memory would not have the space necessary to store the array of pointers.

7. Although the introduction of pointers into the bubble sort routine will not improve its $O(n^2)$ nature, there will most likely be an increase in run-time efficiency. This is because physical swapping of data is drastically reduced. If the data to be swapped were records with numerous fields of records themselves, many machine operations would be involved. But with pointers, only integers need be swapped, involving many fewer machine operations.

9. The pointer strategy would have the least effect on selection sort, because it guarantees a fewer number of data exchanges (only one per outer loop iteration) than either of the other sorts. Since the pointer sort affects the efficiency of data exchanges, and since fewer swaps are made with selection sort, less overall time is saved with selection sort than with the other two sorting algorithms; these sorting algorithms swap more often, and would therefore benefit more significantly from improved swapping efficiency.

11.
```
// Function: pointer_selection_sort
// Selection sort logic using pointers
//
// Inputs: a list of data values, a list of pointers,
//          and n, the logical size of the list
// Output: the list of pointers pointing to sorted data
void pointer_selection_sort(list_type  list,
   int_array pointers, int n)
{
   int min_position, temp;

   for (int k = 0; k < n - 2; ++k)
   {
       min_position = pointer[k];
       for (int j = k + 1; j < n - 1; ++j)
          if (list[pointer[j]].get_key( ) <
              list[min_position].get_key( ))
              min_position = pointer[j];
       temp = pointer[k];
       pointer[k] = pointer[min_position];
       pointer[mid_position] = temp;
   }
}
```

13.
```
// Function: digit
// Determine the kth digit of a number
//
// Inputs: integers number and k
// Output: the kth digit of number
int digit(int number, int k)
{
   int p = pow(10, k);
   int q = pow(10, k - 1);
   return (number - p * (number / p)) / q;
}
```

Section 11.5

1. Initial array with **low**, **high**, and **middle = (high + low) / 2**. **target** is 43. **found** is FALSE to begin.

```
Low             Mid             High
0   1   2   3   4   5   6   7   8   9
┌────┬────┬────┬────┬────┬────┬────┬────┬────┬────┐
│ 18 │ 40 │ 46 │ 50 │ 52 │ 58 │ 63 │ 70 │ 77 │ 90 │
└────┴────┴────┴────┴────┴────┴────┴────┴────┴────┘
```

```
Low Mid     High
0   1   2   3   4   5   6   7   8   9
┌────┬────┬────┬────┬────┬────┬────┬────┬────┬────┐
│ 18 │ 40 │ 46 │ 50 │ 52 │ 58 │ 63 │ 70 │ 77 │ 90 │
└────┴────┴────┴────┴────┴────┴────┴────┴────┴────┘
```

```
        Mid
        Low High
0   1   2   3   4   5   6   7   8   9
┌────┬────┬────┬────┬────┬────┬────┬────┬────┬────┐
│ 18 │ 40 │ 46 │ 50 │ 52 │ 58 │ 63 │ 70 │ 77 │ 90 │
└────┴────┴────┴────┴────┴────┴────┴────┴────┴────┘
```

Since 43 < 52, **high** points to 3.
Since 43 > 40, **low** points to 2.
Since 43 < 46, **high** points to 1 and the search ends with **found** = FALSE.

3. A symbol table is a list of the identifiers that have been declared in a program and which the compiler continually searches as the program is compiled. Since the sequential search is O(*n*), the continual searching of the symbol table uses up too much time to be practical.

5. 21 or fewer times.

7. This version of the binary search will work correctly provided the variable **n** never comes in as 0 (indicating an empty list). In this situation, **middle** will be computed to be 0, which will generate an array index out-of-range error.

11. Although still O(*n*) in its efficiency, the code for this version of the algorithm can reduce the number of comparisons by a factor of 2. This is because we need not test for the sentinel and the target data each time through the loop.

CHAPTER 12

Section 12.1

1. Characteristics of the software engineering approach to system development are
  - Analysis of the situation (interviews, observations, research, and so on).
  - Design of a solution (beginning with a completely abstract non-physical design).
  - Construction of a model (to anticipate various construction problems).
  - Construction of actual solution.
  - Maintenance.

3.

```
                        MEMORANDUM

    TO: Recalcitrant Team Member
  FROM: Dedicated Software Engineer
    RE: Tactful note defending software engineering
        principles

As a dedicated team member whose paycheck depends on
"getting it done" on time, I am as committed as you to
meeting the deadlines se t forth for this project. At
the same time, I do not care to fall prey to the
unreliable, inelegant methods of our predecessors in
this company, whose lack of planning often resulted in
software products with serious flaws—flaws that ended
up costing this company dearly. Let me offer two sound
reasons why delving into the details of Pascal code
without a conceptual model, as you have suggested,
would spell disaster. First, without a conceptual
model, our team would not be able to work as a team.
With potentially differing ideas of the system design,
individual members would inevitably waste time writing
pieces of the system that did not fit together.
Moreover, since team members would not have laid out
the system beforehand, they would not be cognizant of
what basic tasks are done frequently throughout the
system. Hence, many lines of redundant code would be
written, thus wasting time as well as space. Second,
what if the final system we've coded turned out not to
work? Flaws that we could have detected with a
conceptual model would not have been discovered until
the system was up and running. And by that time, all of
our hours of coding would have been wasted. In short,
if it is your interest to implement a reliable, working
system—and to do so on time—creating a conceptual
design simply cannot be avoided. Although it may seem
like a waste of time initially, it will more than pay
for itself in the end by ensuring that our final system
has the best design possible, and is reliable enough to
deserve the trust our company will need to place in it.
Our team will meet at 9:00 a.m. tomorrow morning to
begin carving out a conceptual design. We hope to see
you there.
```

Section 12.2

3. Because the keys are physically ordered in the array, we can do a binary search for the position where we should insert the new key. The search process will thus be logarithmic. However, the data movement required to make room for the new value in the array will still be linear, so the overall behavior of the algorithm will still be linear.

5. The answer to this problem is the same as the answer to Exercise 3.

7. The ordered and sorted collection ADTs allow data to be accessed by key values that are numeric index positions. However, data can be added to or removed from the beginning or end of an ordered collection, or can simply be added to a sorted collection, without specifying a key.

3. The class declaration module for a generic ordered collection class is

```cpp
// Class declaration file: ordercol.h

#ifndef ORDERCOL_H

// Definition section

// We assume that the constant MAX_ARRAY_SIZE has been
// defined by the application in element.h

#include "boolean.h"
#include "element.h"

// Generic class for element type E.

template <class E> ordered_collection
{

    public:

    // Class constructors

    ordered_collection();
    ordered_collection(const ordered_collection<E> &oc);

    // Member functions

    int length();
    E& operator [ ] (int index);
    ordered_collection<E>& operator =
        (const ordered_collection<E> &oc);
    boolean operator == (const ordered_collection<E> &oc);
    void add_last(E e);
    E remove_last();
    void add_first(E e);
    E remove_first();
    void remove(E e);

    protected:

    // Data members

    E data[MAX_ARRAY_SIZE];
    int c_length;

};

#define ORDERCOL_H
#endif
```

5. The `keys` member function returns a sorted collection of all of the keys currently used in the table:

```
template <class K, class E>
sorted_collection<K>  one_key_table<K, E>::keys()
{
    sorted_collection<K> the_keys;

    for (int j = 0; j < table_length; ++j)
        keys.add(data[i].get_key());
    return the_keys;
}
```

Section 12.4

3. The abstract specification of operations on a three-key table is

---

Create operation

Preconditions: Receiver is an arbitrary three-key table in an unpredictable state.

Postconditions: receiver is initialized to an empty table.

Empty operation

Precondition: Receiver is a three-key table.

Postcondition: If receiver contains no objects, the Boolean value TRUE is returned; otherwise, the Boolean value FALSE is returned.

Store operation

Preconditions: Receiver is a three-key table. `key1` is the key1 value. `key2` is the key2 value. `key3` is the key3 value. `item` is an object to be inserted in receiver. If `key1`, `key2`, and `key3` do not specify an item already in the table, there is memory available to store item.

Postconditions: If an object is already associated with `key1`, `key2`, and `key3` in the table, it is replaced by item. Otherwise, the table has item inserted and associated with the key1, key2, and key3 values.

Remove operation

Preconditions: Receiver is a two-key table. `key1`, `key2`, and `key3` are the key values associated with an object to be removed from the table.

Postconditions: If the object with the key values `key1`, `key2`, and `key3` can be found in the table, it is removed from the table, item contains the object associated with the key values `key1`, `key2`, and `key3`, and the operation returns TRUE. Otherwise, the operation returns FALSE, item's contents are undefined, and the table is left unchanged.

Retrieve operation

Preconditions: Receiver is a two-key table. `key1`, `key2`, and `key3` are the key values associated with an object to be found in the table.

Postconditions: If the pairing of `key1`, `key2`, and `key3` can be found in table, then item contains the object associated with key1, key2, and key3 and the operation returns TRUE. Otherwise, the operation returns FALSE, and item's contents are undefined. In either case, the table is left unchanged.

CHAPTER 13

Section 13.1

3. Here is one possible way to depict the flow of information:

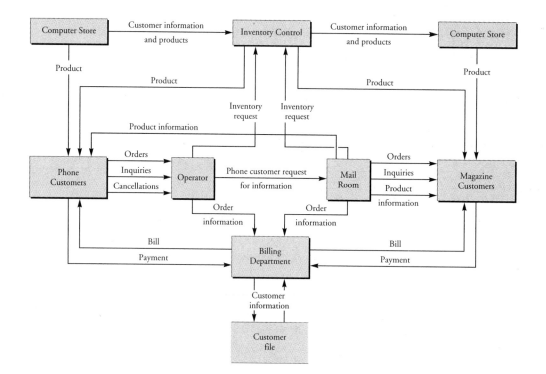

Section 13.2

1. A module that is functionally cohesive performs exactly one predefined task and does it without unexpected outcomes.

3. Since one of the modules performs two tasks, the system is not functionally cohesive. A better design would be

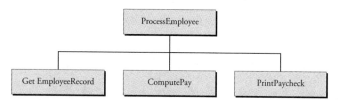

5. Using global variables is a poor strategy from a data coupling perspective because one function might corrupt the data needed by other functions.

7. Data flow diagrams and modular structure charts are similar in that both are used as devices to partition the system logically in to a set of subcomponents, each with a well-defined, specific task. The fundamental difference between these two modeling tools lies in the way in which each depicts the interaction among system subcomponents. Data flow diagrams present the system's subcomponents as a (more or less) linear sequence of modules through which system data flow and by which they are processed; modular structure charts present the system as a hierarchy depicting relationships among high-level (boss) and low-level (worker) modules. Thus, modular structure charts more accurately represent how the system will be designed in a computer language; they constitute the next logical refinement of the system in its evolution from abstraction to implementation.

Section 13.3

1. In the analysis phase, the system analyst, through interviews, inspections, observations, and so on reports what the user's needs are. In the design phase, the designer studies the analyst's report and designs a solution for the user. In the coding phase, the programmer codes the design provided by the design phase. In the testing phase, the system is checked for performance under varying conditions, especially boundary conditions in the data being used. In the maintenance phase, the system is modified and updated to meet changing user needs and/or to correct errors in the system.

3. A robust module is one that does not "bomb" when it receives invalid data. If every module in a system were completely robust, the system would most likely be too slow to be of practical use: too much time would be consumed by each module in checking to make certain that the data it received were valid.

7. Test data for **read_real** could be as follows. (Note that a space is indicated by "_".)

Val	Rationale	Expected Results
_00.000	a form of 0	valid
0.0	a form of 0	valid
–0.0	a form of 0	valid
+0	a form of 0	valid
5.356	"conventional" number	valid
0.002	"conventional" number	valid
_.05	nothing left of decimal	valid
0_5_.703	spaces between digits	invalid
56	no decimal	valid
75.	unguarded decimal	valid
.	decimal only	invalid
–7	– without decimal	valid
–.5	unguarded decimal	valid
+7	+ without decimal	valid
Hi.there	test a string	invalid
–.	test no digit case	invalid
+.	test no digit case	invalid
–_5.7	test space trailing sign	valid

Note that the current algorithm would accept "–.", ".", and "+." all of which would be invalid numbers.

11. Note that this finite state machine accepts digits only in the string before the '.'; in the extension, only letters and the underscore are acceptable (including the '_' immediately following the '.'). The associated function follows:

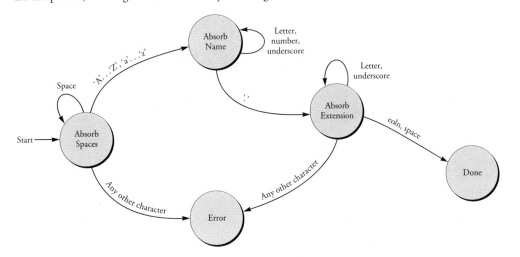

Section 13.4

3. It could. Proofs of correctness do not take into account the limitations of a particular machine. Factors such as rounding errors in arithmetic computation, faulty user input, and exceeding the overflow and underflow cutoffs for numeric storage can all cause a "proven" algorithm to fail.

CHAPTER 14

Section 14.1

1. The array involved in the pointer sort of Chapter 11 is not a linked list because its cells do not store links (to other array cells) that indicate the order in which the cells are to be traversed (the pointer array is always traversed sequentially). Instead, the pointers stored in the pointer array serve as indices to cells in a separate array (which contains the real data of interest).

3. With respect to search efficiency, both the linked list and unordered array implementations provide $O(n)$ access to list nodes; both require a sequential search. However, whereas both implementations require $O(n)$ comparisons to find a node, the linked list strategy requires only $O(1)$ data exchanges actually to delete the node. Compare this to the $O(n)$ exchanges needed by the array implementation. With respect to add efficiency, the linked list implementation strategy is at a disadvantage, requiring $O(n)$ operations to find a node's rightful place in the list, and $O(1)$ operations actually to insert it. The unordered array, on the other hand, provides $O(1)$ add efficiency, since nodes are always added to the end of the array. With respect to sort efficiency, the linked list is maintained in sequential order, so no sort is required to traverse it sequentially. In contrast, the unordered array requires an $O(n^2)$ pointer sort before it can be traversed sequentially. Here, the linked list strategy is at an advantage.

5.
```
void print_sqrt(int &x)
{
    cout << sqrt(x);
}
```

7.
```
int position_of_first_zero(linked_list<int> &list)
{
    int data, position;
    boolean found = FALSE;

    if (list.empty())
        return 0;
    else
    {
        list.first();
        position = 1;
        while (! found && (position <= list.length()))
        {
            list.retrieve(data);
            if (data == 0)
                found = TRUE;
            else
            {
                ++position;
                list.next();
            }
        }
        if (found)
            return position;
        else
            return 0;
    }
}
```

9.
```
int sum(linked_list<int> &list)
{
    int total, data;
    boolean found;
```

```
        total = 0;
        list.first();
        found = list.retrieve(data);
        while  (found)
        {
            total = total + data;
            list.next();
            found = list.retrieve(data);
        }
        return total;
    }
11. template <class E>
    void append(linked_list<E> &a,
        linked_list<E> &b)
    {
        int data;
        boolean found;

        a.first();
        while (! a.at_end())
            a.next();
        a.next();
        b.first();
        found = b.remove(data);
        while (found)
        {
            a.insert(data);
            a.next();
            found = b.remove(data);
        }
    }
```

Section 14.2

1. **a.**, **d.**, and **f.** are syntactically correct.

   b. Incorrect—cannot assign an integer to a pointer variable.

   c. Incorrect—cannot use a type name to refer to a member of a structure.

   e. Incorrect—cannot delete an integer.

3. `a->next->next = b;`

   effects the deletion of the second node.

5. `a->next->next->next->next = a;`
   `a = a->next;`
   `a->next->next->next->next = NULL;`

Section 14.4

1. The traverse operation uses a pointer sort, which is $O(n^2)$, to prepare the list of pointers for the traversal. The traversal itself is then $O(n)$. Thus, the overall efficiency of the operation is $O(n^2)$.

CHAPTER 15

Section 15.1

1.

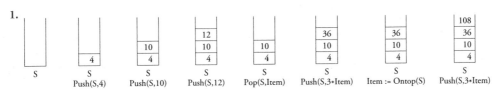

5. The stack would grow and shrink as follows:

9. Because the new stack declaration contains a linked list as a data member, the copy constructor, assignment operation, and destructor will be considerably simplified. Specifically, the copy constructor and the assignment operation merely use the assignment operator to copy the values of the data members from the parameter object to the receiver object. No destructor is in fact necessary, because the destructor for the linked list data member will be run automatically when a stack object goes out of scope. In short, using a linked list as a data member entirely relieves the implementer of the stack class of the need to access the implementation details of the linked list class.

Section 15.2

1. Infix: A+B*C–D/P–R
Postfix: ABCD–PR–/*+
Prefix: +A*B/–CD–PD

3.

Ch	OpStack	Postfix	Commentary
#			Push #
P			Read Ch
		P	Append Ch to Postfix
+			Read Ch
	+ #		Push Ch
(			Read Ch
	+ (#		Push Ch
Q			Read Ch
		PQ	Append Ch to Postfix
–			Read Ch
	– (+ #		Push Ch
F			Read Ch
		PQF	Append Ch
)		Read Ch	
	+ #	PQF–	Pop and Append
/			Read Ch
	/ + #		Push Ch
Y			Read Ch
		PQF–Y	Append Ch
#			Read Ch
		PQF–Y/+#	Pop and Append rest of stack

9. If operand 'A' has a stack priority that is greater than or equal to the infix priority of operand 'B,' then 'A' has equal or greater operator precedence; therefore, it is appended to the postfix string before B, and will be applied before B. Such precedence, however, can be overridden by parentheses, which force the operators between them to be unconditionally appended to the postfix string, regardless of their stack priority. In summary, the order in which operators are appended to the postfix string is dictated by stack priority relative to infix priority; equal or greater stack priority indicates either higher operator precedence (if the two operators being compared are different) or left-associativity, if the two operators being compared are the same. Hence, if we want to make the " operator right associative, we merely make its infix priority greater than its stack priority. Our infix and stack priority functions would then appear as follows:

Priority:	*	/	+	–	(	)	^	#
Infix	2	2	1	1	5	0	4	0
Stack	2	2	1	1	0	undefined	3	0

The adjusted infix and stack priorities reflect both the fact that exponentiation has the highest operator precedence, and the fact that all operators except exponentiation are left-associative.

Section 15.3

3. a. Introduce an integer variable **minutes_idle**, which is initialized to 0 before entering the **for** loop. We then add the following **ELSE** clause to the **IF ((time_left_on_car == 0) && car_queue.empty())** clause:

```
else if ((time_left_on_car == 0) && car_queue.empty())
      //This minute is idle
      ++minutes_idle;
```

b. To make this count, we merely dequeue the **car_queue** until it is empty after we have exited the **for** loop. In C++, this amounts to introducing an integer variable **cars_remaining**, which we initialize to zero before dequeuing begins:

```
int cars_remaining = 0;
```

Now we are prepared to execute a **while** loop:

```
while (! car_queue.empty())
{
      minute = car_queue.dequeue();
      ++cars_remaining;
}
```

CHAPTER 16

Section 16.1

3. a. 92
   6
   14
  b. 14
   6
   92

Note, however, that because this function neglects to test **list** for being NULL before referencing **list**, the program may behave mysteriously at run time.

  c. 14
   6

Note that because this function neglects to test **list** itself for being NULL before it references **list->next**, the program may behave mysteriously at run time when the empty list is passed in for **list**.

5. Program (a) will achieve the original intent presented. Its output is

MADAM

Program (b) will fail because it globally declares the characters being read so the recursive calls do not result in copies of the characters being pushed onto the system stack. Consequently, only the last character read is remembered and written when the recursion unwinds. Its output is

MMMMM

7. This function computes the smallest value in **number_array** within the subrange 1 . . *n*, where *n* is the value originally passed in.

Section 16.2

5. The output is as follows:

```
1 16
9 16
9 11
9 16
```

7. The stack frames for this function should contain three pieces of information: The current value of M, the current value of N, and the point in the program to which to return.

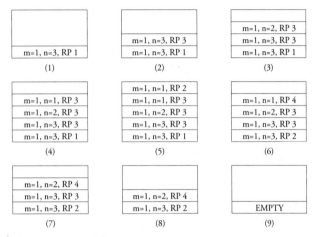

(1) m=1, n=3, RP 1

(2) m=1, n=3, RP 3 / m=1, n=3, RP 1

(3) m=1, n=2, RP 3 / m=1, n=3, RP 3 / m=1, n=3, RP 1

(4) m=1, n=1, RP 3 / m=1, n=2, RP 3 / m=1, n=3, RP 3 / m=1, n=3, RP 1

(5) m=1, n=1, RP 2 / m=1, n=1, RP 3 / m=1, n=2, RP 3 / m=1, n=3, RP 3 / m=1, n=3, RP 1

(6) m=1, n=1, RP 4 / m=1, n=2, RP 3 / m=1, n=3, RP 3 / m=1, n=3, RP 2

(7) m=1, n=2, RP 4 / m=1, n=3, RP 3 / m=1, n=3, RP 2

(8) m=1, n=2, RP 4 / m=1, n=3, RP 2

(9) EMPTY

The output is as follows:

```
1 3
1 2
1 1
1 0
0 1
0 2
0 3
0 4
5
```

11. *Hint:* Consider the number of ways that M can be broken down into quarters and dimes plus the number of ways that (M = 50 cents) can be broken down into half dollars, quarters, and dimes. The total of these two provide the answer in terms of quantities that are (recursively) easier to compute.

Section 16.3

5. The output is as follows:

```
12 1 2 3 4 3 3 4
 4 3 4 2 2 3 4 3
 3 4 4 3 4 3 2 3
 4 3 3 4 4 3 4 4
 2 3 4 3 3 4 4 3
 4
```

CHAPTER 17

Section 17.1

1.

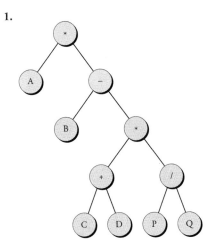

3. A tree is a hierarchically ordered data structure consisting of nodes and links to nodes. A tree is accessed by a node called the root.

5. a. and **c.** are binary trees with the heap property.

   b. is not, because the node containing 35 is a subtree of the node containing 19. Similar situation for the node containing 39.

9. a.   **c.**

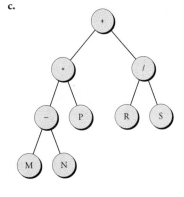

Section 17.2

17. As each node is visited during the traversal, its data contents are placed at the logical end of the structure (an array or file, perhaps) or device (output on a terminal screen, perhaps). At the end of the traversal, the data will appear in sorted order in the destination structure or on the destination device.

Section 17.3

1. a. is full.

   b. and **c.** are not full.

5. b. is full.

Section 17.4

1.

Item	1	2	3	4	5	6	7	8	9	10
10	10									

Item	1	2	3	4	5	6	7	8	9	10
20	20	10								

Item	1	2	3	4	5	6	7	8	9	10
30	30	10	20							

Item	1	2	3	4	5	6	7	8	9	10
40	40	30	20	10						

Item	1	2	3	4	5	6	7	8	9	10
50	50	40	20	10	30					

Item	1	2	3	4	5	6	7	8	9	10
60	60	40	50	10	30	20				

Item	1	2	3	4	5	6	7	8	9	10
70	70	40	60	10	30	20	50			

Item	1	2	3	4	5	6	7	8	9	10
80	80	70	60	40	30	20	50	10		

Item	1	2	3	4	5	6	7	8	9	10
90	90	80	60	70	30	20	50	10	40	

Item	1	2	3	4	5	6	7	8	9	10
100	100	90	60	70	80	20	50	10	40	30

Section 17.5

1. The indentation can be obtained by increasing the indentation before traversing the left (child) subtree and decreasing the indentation again before traversing the right (sibling) subtree.

3. Preorder traversal

```
P Q T U V C D E
M N O W A G B H
I J X K L
```

Section 17.6

1. The order of the nodes would be Seattle, Chicago, Miami, New Orleans, Dallas, New York, Washington, Milwaukee, Phoenix, San Francisco, Los Angeles, Las Vegas, Minneapolis, Oklahoma City.

3. One way the cities could be visited is as follows: Seattle, Chicago, San Francisco, Miami, New Orleans, Las Vegas, Milwaukee, Los Angeles, Dallas, Washington, Phoenix, Minneapolis, New York City, Oklahoma City.

9. Eliminating the requirement that **node** be a subrange of an ordinal type would mean that there would not be a convenient way to index the nodes in the graph, making the normal operations more difficult to perform. One strategy to overcome that problem would be to build an indexing scheme that would make use of a two-key table.

CHAPTER 18

Section 18.1

1.
```
60   12   90   20   64    8    6   8   12    6   20   64   90   60   6   12
 8   20   60   90   64    6    8  12   20   60   64   90
```

3. The shell sort is named after its inventor D. L. Shell.

5. Relatively prime values of the increments are better because they insure distinct increments that will not divide evenly into each other so that data that have been compared to each other are less likely to be compared again.

7. The best case for the shell sort algorithm presented in this section would be a data set with the data already in order: each segment would be in order and no data would be swapped. The worst case would be a data set arranged in descending order because every data element would be out of order and there would be a maximum number of data swaps.

Section 18.2

1. The output would be as follows:

```
1   7
60 12 90 30 64 8 6

  1  4
  6 12 8 30

  2 4
12 8 30

  2 2
  8

  4 4
30

  6 7
64 90

  7 7
90
```

3. The bubble sort is better than the quick sort when the data are already in order. The bubble sort can safely conclude that the data are in order after the first pass through the data; the quick sort must perform the entire sort even if the data are already in order.

5. The choice of the pivotal point will not change the overall efficiency of the quick sort; however, it does dramatically change the best and worst data sets.

9. All of the quick sort function would remain the same as in the book. One line in the partition function would change from

```
pivot := key[low];
```

to

```
// Assume that median gives the median of three values.
pivot := median(key[low], key[low + high] / 2,
    key[high]);
```

This variation should be more efficient because the pivot value is more likely to split the array being sorted more evenly. Quick sort is most efficient when the array is split at the midpoint.

Section 18.3

```
1. 60 12 90 30 64  8  6
   60 12 90 30 64  8  6
   60 64 90 30 12  8  6
    6 64 60 30 12  8 90
    8 30 60  6 12 64 90
   12 30  8  6 60 64 90
    6 12  8 30 60 64 90
    8  6 12 30 60 64 90
    6  8 12 30 60 64 90
```

3. The sort derives its name from the heap structure that it uses in sorting the data.

5. The heap sort is not always as efficient as the quick sort. On average, the quick sort is slightly better than the heap sort because its big-O constant of proportionality will be smaller. However, the heap sort handles data already sorted much faster than the quick sort.

Section 18.4

1. The output for **merge_sort** would be

```
 1   7
60 12 90 30 64 8 6

 1   4
60 12 90 30

 1   2
60 12

 1 1
60

 2   2
60 12

 2   2
60 12
```

and so on . . .

CHAPTER 19

Section 19.1

1. a. Record No.   Key

Record No.	Key
0	333
1	632
2	1090
3	459
4	379
5	238
6	
7	
8	
9	1982
10	3411

The keys would have the following positions.

c. With the chaining method, the keys and links would be

Record No.	Key	Link
0	333	13
1	632	0
2	1090	0
3		
4		
5		
6		
7		
8		
9	1982	12
10		

Record No.	Key	Link
11	3411	13
12	459	0
13	379	14
14	238	0
15		
16		
17		
18		
19		
20		
21		

3. a. The best method to implement the card catalog in this situation would be hashing. Hashing allows for very quick searches and is fairly good at handling additions and deletions. Since the library rarely prints out an ordered list of books, the time it takes to sort the list doesn't really matter.

c. The best method to implement the data base would be the binary search. The states are kept in order by two-letter code. All the program need do is access the record quickly, increment a field, and be able to print the list out in order. All these are handled very well by a binary search.

Section 19.2

1. As suggested in the text, the doubly linked list is the best choice for implementing linked lists with hashing. When the order of the list is disturbed during a change of a key field or during a deletion of an item in the list, the linked list must be rebuilt. If a doubly linked list is not used, the list would have to be traversed to find the predecessor node in the linked list. The doubly linked list makes rebuilding lists more efficient.

Section 19.3

1. a.

106/6
289/5
430/2
602/3
732/7
810/1
946/4

5. a. For the ISAM index, this knowledge will enable us to set the index so that the subsequent search on the disk will be more efficient.

c. The trie is constructed the same no matter what the disk structure may be.

Index

Credits

Photos

Notes Of Interest

Page 352: Computer Ethics: Viruses
From Philip J. Hilts, Science Lab, In the Washington Post National Weekly Edition, May 23-29, 1988. Reprinted by permission of The Washington Post.

Page 373: Monolithic Idea: Invention of the Integrated Circuit
Adapted from T. R. Reid, "The Chip," Science, February 1985, pp. 32-41.

Page 392: Too Few Women in the Computer Science Pipeline?
From Carol Wilson, Western Kentucky University, Bowling Green, Kentucky, 1991.

IMPORTANT: PLEASE READ BEFORE OPENING THIS PACKAGE
THIS PACKAGE IS NOT RETURNABLE IF SEAL IS BROKEN.

West Publishing Corporation
620 Opperman Drive
P.O. Box 64779
St. Paul, Minnesota 55164-0779

LIMITED USE LICENSE

Read the following terms and conditions carefully before opening this diskette package. Opening the diskette package indicates your agreement to the license terms. If you do not agree, promptly return the entire product and related documentation unused.

By accepting this license, you have the right to use this Software and the accompanying documentation, but you do not become the owner of these materials.

This copy of the Software is licensed to you for use only under the following conditions:

1. PERMITTED USES
You are granted a non-exclusive limited license to use the Software under the terms and conditions stated in this license. You may:
    a. Use the Software on a single computer.
    b. Make a single copy of the Software in machine-readable form solely for backup purposes in support of your use of the Software on a single machine. You must reproduce and include the copyright notice on any copy you make.
    c. Transfer this copy of the Software and the license to another user if the other user agrees to accept the terms and conditions of this license. If you transfer this copy of the Software, you must also transfer or destroy the backup copy you made. Transfer of this copy of the Software, and the license automatically terminates this license as to you.

2. PROHIBITED USES
You may not use, copy, modify, distribute or transfer the Software or any copy, in whole or in part, except as expressly permitted in this license.

3. TERM
This license is effective when you open the diskette package and remains in effect until terminated. You may terminate this license at any time by ceasing all use of the Software and destroying this copy and any copy you have made. It will also terminate automatically if you fail to comply with the terms of this license. Upon termination, you agree to cease all use of the Software and destroy all copies.

4. DISCLAIMER OF WARRANTY
Except as stated herein, the Software is licensed "as is" without warranty of any kind, express or implied, including warranties of merchantability or fitness for a particular purpose. You assume the entire risk as to the quality and performance of the Software. You are responsible for the selection of the Software to achieve your intended results and for the installation, use and results obtained from it. West Publishing Corporation does not warrant the performance of nor results that may be obtained with the Software. West Publishing Corporation does warrant that the diskette(s) upon which the Software is provided will be free from defects in materials and workmanship under normal use for a period of 30 days from the date of delivery to you as evidenced by a receipt.

Some states do not allow the exclusion of implied warranties so the above exclusion may not apply to you. This warranty gives you specific legal rights. You may also have other rights which vary from state to state.

5. LIMITATION OF LIABILITY
Your exclusive remedy for breach by West Publishing Corporation of its limited warranty shall be replacement of any defective diskette upon its return to West at the above address, together with a copy of the receipt, within the warranty period. If West Publishing Corporation is unable to provide you with a replacement diskette which is free of defects in material and workmanship, you may terminate this license by returning the Software, and the license fee paid hereunder will be refunded to you. In no event will West be liable for any lost profits or other damages including direct, indirect, incidental, special, consequential or any other type of damages arising out of the use or inability to use the Software even if West Publishing Corporation has been advised of the possibility of such damages.

6. GOVERNING LAW
This agreement will be governed by the laws of the State of Minnesota.

You acknowledge that you have read this license and agree to its terms and conditions. You also agree that this license is the entire and exclusive agreement between you and West and supersedes any prior understanding or agreement, oral or written, relating to the subject matter of this agreement.

West Publishing Corporation